PHILIP'S

STRE[...]S
Birmingham &
West Midlands

Birmingham, Coventry, Dudley, Sandwell, Solihull, Walsall, Wolverhampton

www.philips-maps.co.uk
First published in 1998 by Philip's
a division of Octopus Publishing Group Ltd
www.octopusbooks.co.uk
Endeavour House, 189 Shaftesbury Avenue
London WC2H 8JY
An Hachette UK Company
www.hachette.co.uk

Fourth colour edition 2011
First impression 2011
BWMDA

ISBN 978-1-84907-141-3 (pocket)

© Philip's 2011

Ordnance Survey®

This product includes mapping data licensed from Ordnance Survey® with the permission of the Controller of Her Majesty's Stationery Office. © Crown copyright 2011. All rights reserved. Licence number 100011710.

Contents

II	Mobile safety cameras
III	**Key to map symbols**
IV	**Key to map pages**
VI	**Route planning**
VIII	Major administrative and Postcode boundaries
1	**Street maps** at 2⅔ inches to 1 mile
163	**Street maps of Wolverhampton, Birmingham and Coventry centres** at 5⅓ inches to 1 mile
166	**Index** of towns, villages, streets, hospitals, industrial estates, railway stations, schools, shopping centres, universities and places of interest

Digital Data

The exceptionally high-quality mapping found in this atlas is available as digital data in TIFF format, which is easily convertible to other bitmapped (raster) image formats.

The index is also available in digital form as a standard database table. It contains all the details found in the printed index together with the National Grid reference and the map square in which each entry is named.

For further information and to discuss your requirements, please contact
philips@mapsinternational.co.uk

Mobile safety cameras

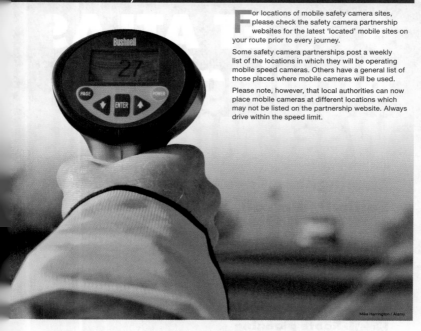

For locations of mobile safety camera sites, please check the safety camera partnership websites for the latest 'located' mobile sites on your route prior to every journey.

Some safety camera partnerships post a weekly list of the locations in which they will be operating mobile speed cameras. Others have a general list of those places where mobile cameras will be used.

Please note, however, that local authorities can now place mobile cameras at different locations which may not be listed on the partnership website. Always drive within the speed limit.

Mike Harrington / Alamy

Useful websites

West Midlands Casualty Reduction Scheme
www.wmsafetycameras.co.uk

Leicester, Leicestershire & Rutland Safety Camera Scheme
www.speedorsafety.com

Safety Cameras in Warwickshire
www.warwickshire.gov.uk

Staffordshire Safer Roads Partnership
www.staffssaferroads.co.uk

Safer Roads Partnership in West Mercia
www.srpwestmercia.org.uk

Further information
www.dvla.gov.uk

www.thinkroadsafety.gov.uk

www.dft.gov.uk

www.road-safe.org

Key to map symbols

Motorway with junction number (22)	
Primary route – dual/single carriageway	
A road – dual/single carriageway	
B road – dual/single carriageway	
Minor road – dual/single carriageway	
Other minor road – dual/single carriageway	
Road under construction	
Tunnel, covered road	
Speed cameras – single, multiple	
Rural track, private road or narrow road in urban area	
Gate or obstruction to traffic – may not apply at all times or to all vehicles	
Path, bridleway, byway open to all traffic, restricted byway	
Pedestrianised area	
BS22 Postcode boundaries	
County and unitary authority boundaries	
Railway with station	
Tunnel	
Railway under construction	
Metro station	
Private railway station	
Miniature railway	
Tramway, tramway under construction	
Tram stop, tram stop under construction	
Bus, coach station	

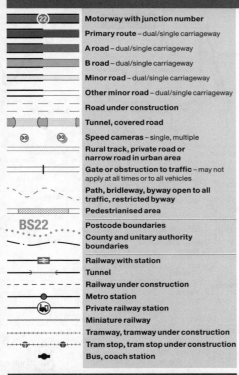

◆	Ambulance station
◆	Coastguard station
◆	Fire station
◆	Police station
✚	Accident and Emergency entrance to hospital
H	Hospital
+	Place of worship
i	Information centre – open all year
🛒	Shopping centre
P	Parking
P&R	Park and Ride
PO	Post Office
Ă	Camping site
⊕	Caravan site
ⴱ	Golf course
✕	Picnic site
Church	Non-Roman antiquity
ROMAN FORT	Roman antiquity
Univ	Important buildings, schools, colleges, universities and hospitals
	Built-up area
	Woods
River Medway	Water name
	River, weir
	Stream
	Canal, lock, tunnel
	Water
	Tidal water

112	Adjoining page indicators
58 ◀ 87	The small numbers around the edges of the maps identify the 1-kilometre National Grid lines
	The dark grey border on the inside edge of some pages indicates that the mapping does not continue onto the adjacent page

Abbreviations

Acad	Academy	Meml	Memorial
Allot Gdns	Allotments	Mon	Monument
Cemy	Cemetery	Mus	Museum
C Ctr	Civic centre	Obsy	Observatory
CH	Club house	Pal	Royal palace
Coll	College	PH	Public house
Crem	Crematorium	Recn Gd	Recreation ground
Ent	Enterprise		
Ex H	Exhibition hall	Resr	Reservoir
Ind Est	Industrial Estate	Ret Pk	Retail park
IRB Sta	Inshore rescue boat station	Sch	School
		Sh Ctr	Shopping centre
Inst	Institute	TH	Town hall / house
Ct	Law court	Trad Est	Trading estate
L Ctr	Leisure centre	Univ	University
LC	Level crossing	W Twr	Water tower
Liby	Library	Wks	Works
Mkt	Market	YH	Youth hostel

Enlarged maps only

	Railway or bus station building
	Place of interest
	Parkland

The map scale on the pages numbered in blue is 2⅔ inches to 1 mile
4.2 cm to 1 km • 1:23810

0	¼ mile	½ mile	¾ mile	1 mile
0	250m	500m	750m	1km

The map scale on the pages numbered in red is 5⅓ inches to 1 mile
8.4 cm to 1 km • 1:11900

0	220yds	440yds	660yds	½ mile
0	125m	250m	375m	500m

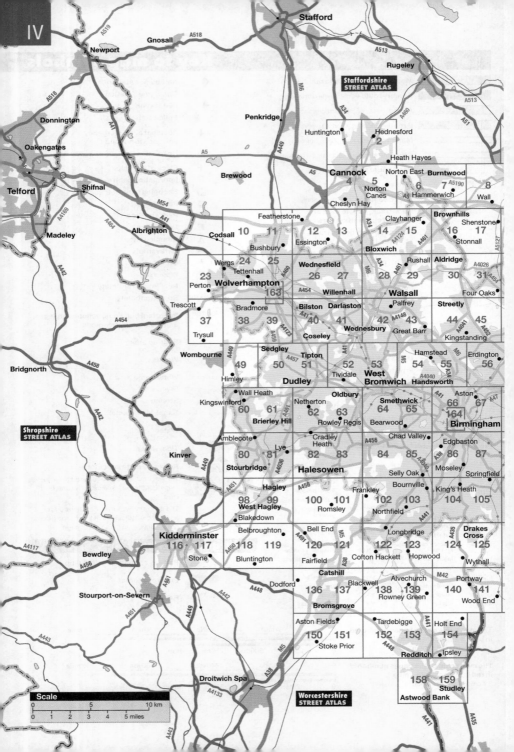

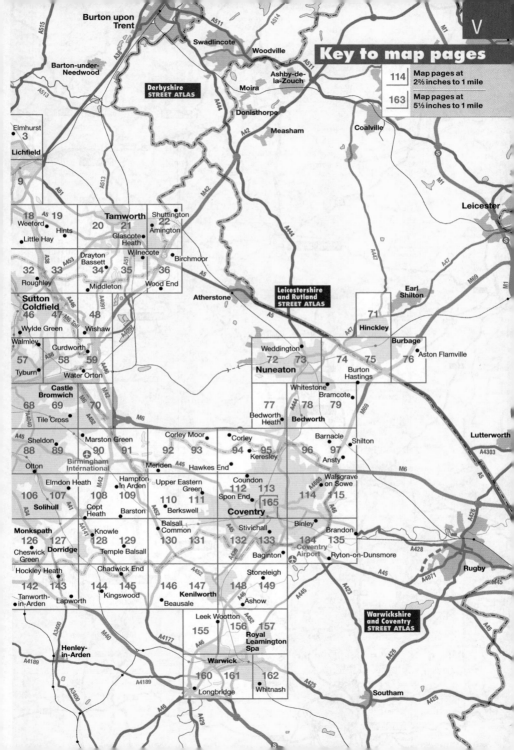

Key to map pages

114	Map pages at 2⅔ inches to 1 mile
163	Map pages at 5⅓ inches to 1 mile

Burton upon Trent

Swadlincote

Woodville

Barton-under-Needwood

Derbyshire STREET ATLAS

Ashby-de-la-Zouch

Moira

Donisthorpe

Measham

Coalville

Elmhurst **3**

Lichfield

9

Leicester

18 **19** Weeford Hints **20** **Tamworth** **21** Shuttington **22** Amington

Little Hay

Glascote Heath

Wilnecote

32 **33** Roughley

Drayton Bassett **34** **35** **36** Birchmoor

Middleton

Wood End

Sutton Coldfield **46** **47** **48** Wylde Green Wishaw

Atherstone

Leicestershire and Rutland STREET ATLAS

Earl Shilton

71

Walmley

Curdworth

57 **58** **59** Tyburn Water Orton

Hinckley

Burbage

Weddington

72 **73** **74** **75** **76** Aston Flamville

Nuneaton Burton Hastings

Castle Bromwich **68** **69** **70** Tile Cross

Whitestone

77 **78** **79** Bramcote

Bedworth Heath **Bedworth**

Lutterworth

Sheldon

88 **89** Olton

Marston Green **90** **91** **92** **93** **94** **95** Keresley **96** **97** Ansty

Corley Moor Corley

Barnacle Shilton

Birmingham International

Meriden Hawkes End

Elmdon Heath

106 **107** **108** **109** Copt **Solihull** Heath

Hampton In Arden

Upper Eastern Green **110** **111** Berkswell

Coundon **112** **113** Spon End **165**

Walsgrave on Sowe **114** **115**

Coventry

Barston

Balsall **Monkspath** Common **126** **127** **128** **129** **130** **131** **132** **133** Cheswick **Dorridge** Knowle Temple Balsall Green

Stivichall

Binley Brandon **134** **135**

Baginton Coventry Airport Ryton-on-Dunsmore

Rugby

Hockley Heath Chadwick End

142 **143** **144** **145** Tanworth- Lapworth Kingswood in-Arden Beausale

Stoneleigh

148 **149** Ashow

146 **147** **Kenilworth**

Leek Wootton

155 **156** **157** **Royal Leamington Spa**

Warwickshire and Coventry STREET ATLAS

Henley-in-Arden

Warwick

160 **161** **162** Longbridge Whitnash

Southam

Major administrative and Postcode boundaries

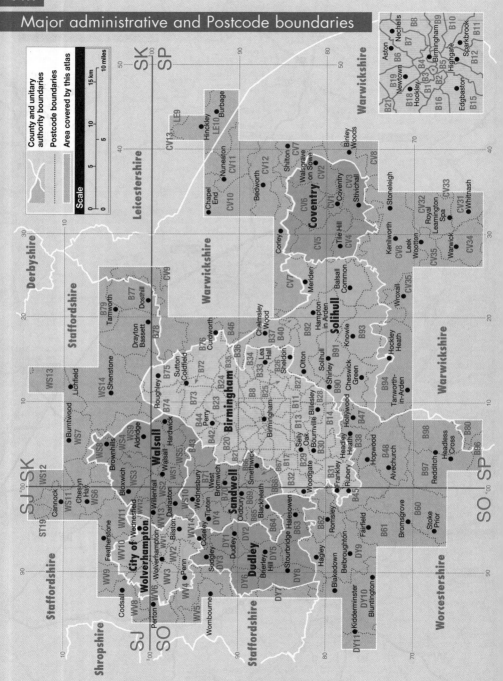

A34 Stafford **Staffordshire** STREET ATLAS

PEEL DR 1
COWLEY GN 2
BUCKTHORN CL 3

ST19

8

Dogintree
Estate

HUNTSMANS
RISE

Huntington
Belt

Cannock Chase
Tech Coll

7

WREKIN VIEW

13

Pear Tree
Farm

Huntington

Littleton
Leisure Park

Littleton
Bsns Pk

NIGHTINGALE

RAVEN CL

Littleton
Green
Com Sch

Oaklands
Farm

LIMEPIT LA

Common
Farm

6

Huntington
Ind Est

OAKLANDS

Westwood
Holdings

BILBERRY
BANK

PILLATON DR

WS12

COMFREY
CL

Blake
Valley
Tech Coll

**West
Chadsmoor**

Stadium

STRATFORD

5

NADEN
HO

CORNHILL

THE PINES PARK
HOME EST

WARDLE
PL

GLEN CL

12

Cavan's
Wood

COMMON WLK

ADDISON CL

WOODSIDE

Broomhill

Moorhill
Jun Sch

SHAKESPEARE GR 1
WILLIAM MORRIS GR 2
WORDSWORTH CL 3

CAVAN'S

Redhill
Prim
Sch

4

Shoal Hill

LONG
CROFT

JOHNSON RD

MASEFIELDS

BUNYAN PL

BOSWELL RD

BROOMHILL

THE
POPLARS

Chadsmoor

CAMELOT

KENILWORTH
DR

CEMETERY RD

Cemy

3

Shoal Hill Common
Nature Reserve

ANGLIA RD

MULBERRY
RD

FALLOW
FIELD

OLD FALLOW
AVE

OLD FALLOW RD

WALNUT CL

HEATH GAP RD

Shoal Hill
Farm

Oldfallow

TEDDESLEY
RD

CHETWYND AVE

LYSANDER
WAY

GRESHAM RD

COLUMBIAN
WAY

Blackfords

11

Cardinal Griffin RC
High Sch

CARDINAL WAY

FALCON
CT

BALTIC CL

HANOVER PL
GEORGIAN PL

Cannock Chase
High Sch

NEWHALL
GDNS

OAKHILL

BARNARD WAY

Hatherton
Hall

SHIREWOOD

WS11
CANNOCK

Sherbrook
Prim Sch

GRANGER

HENDERSFORD RD

PEBBLE MILL

2

KENSINGTON GDNS

MERLIN CL

BELGROVE

Cannock
Chase
Civic
Ctr

PENNINE
GR

CONEY LEA RD

Hollies
Bsns Pk

NEW PENKRIDGE RD

Chase
L Ctr

South
Staffordshire Coll
(Cannock
Campus)

KELVESTONE

WINDERMERE
CL

Mill Green
& Hawks Green
Valley Nature
Reserve

St Lukes
Prim Sch

HATHERTON RD

HATHERTON
HOLLOW

PARK RD

B5012

Liby

Clock
Twr

PENKRIDGE
CT

WOLVERHAMPTON
RD

KINGSTON ARC

HOLLIES AVE

1

WELLINGTON
DR

POPLAR LA

DORCHESTER

THE
WILLOWS

MAPLE
CRES

High Green Ct

QUEEN SQ

A5190

The Chase F

10

E1
1 WEAVING GDNS
2 KENILWORTH CT
3 BACKCROFTS
4 MARKET PL
5 The Forum
6 Cannock Sh Ctr

F2
1 MELBURY WAY
2 MELCHESTER WLK
3 STONEYFIELDS CL
4 MILLBROOK CL
5 EXONBURY WLK
6 STRATHMORE PL
7 HAWKESVILLE DR

F4
1 WOODFORD END
2 AVALON HO
3 HORTON CL
4 BETHANY MEWS

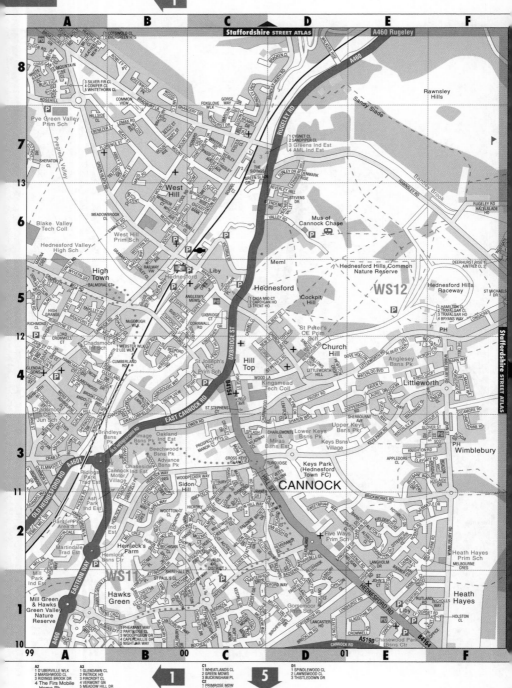

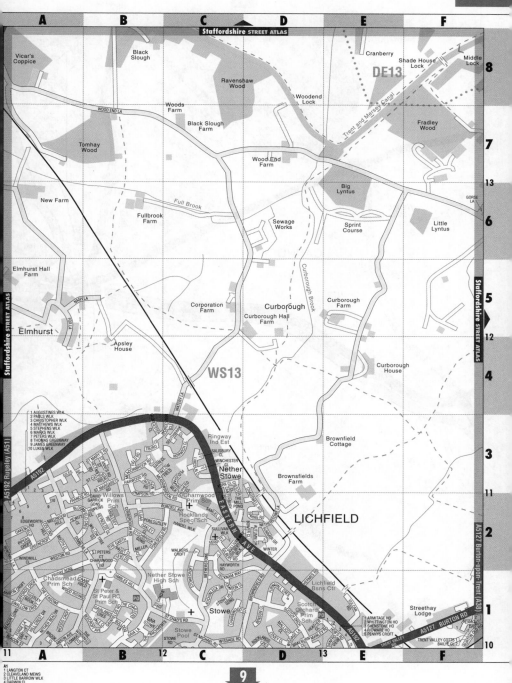

8

Vicar's Coppice

Black Slough

Cranberry

Shade House Lock

Middle Lock

DE13

Ravenshaw Wood

Woodend Lock

Woods Farm

WOOD END LA

Black Slough Farm

Fradley Wood

7

13

Tomhay Wood

Wood End Farm

Big Lyntus

GORSE LA

New Farm

Full Brook

Sewage Works

Sprint Course

Little Lyntus

6

Fullbrook Farm

Curborough Brook

Elmhurst Hall Farm

NASH LA

HOLT LA

Corporation Farm

Curborough

Curborough Farm

5

12

Elmhurst

Apsley House

Curborough Hall Farm

Curborough House

WS13

4

WATERY LA

1 AUGUSTINES WLK
2 PABLS WLK
3 CHRISTOPHER WLK
4 MATTHEWS WLK
5 STEPHENS WLK
6 MARKS WLK
7 PETERS WLK
8 THOMAS GREENWAY
9 JAMES GREENWAY
10 LUKES WLK

Brownfield Cottage

3

Ringway Ind Est

SALISBURY CL

WINCHESTER

Nether Stowe

Brownsfields Farm

A5192 Rugeley (A51)

A5192

St MARY'S RD

David Willows Prim Sch

Charnwood Prim Sch

Rocklands Speci Sch

LICHFIELD

11

EDGEWORTH

St PETERS CHARNWOOD

Nether Stowe High Sch

Lichfield Bsns Ctr

A5127 Burton-upon-Trent (A38)

2

Staffordshire STREET ATLAS

Staffordshire STREET ATLAS

WINDMILL LA

WALKERS CROFT

WINTER CL

Chadsmead Prim Sch

DIMBLES HILL

St Peter & St Paul RC Prim Sch

St CHAD'S RD

Stowe

Scotch Orchard Prim Sch

Lichfield Bsns Ctr

Streethay Lodge

1 ARMITAGE HO
2 WHITTINGTON HO
3 SHENSTONE HO
4 RIOWARE HO
5 PENNYS CROFT

BURTON RD

A5127

1

Stowe Pool

St MICHAEL RD

WISSAGE RD

TRENT VALLEY COTTS
BAILE CE 2

10

11   A   **B**   **12**   **C**   **D**   **13**   **E**   **F**

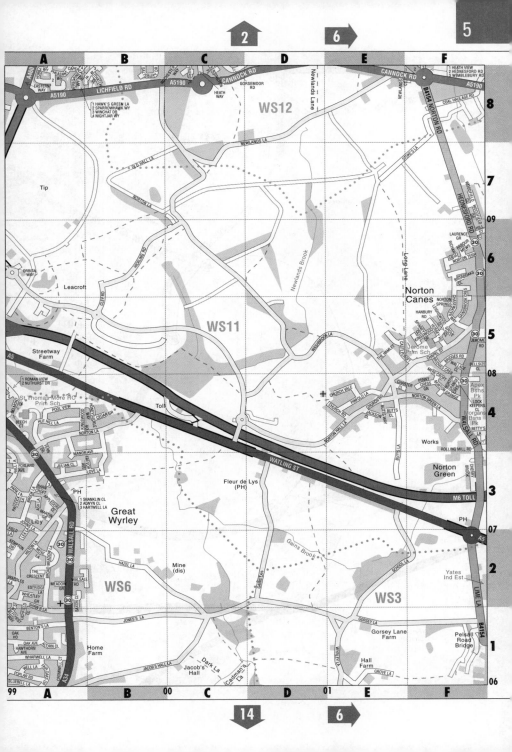

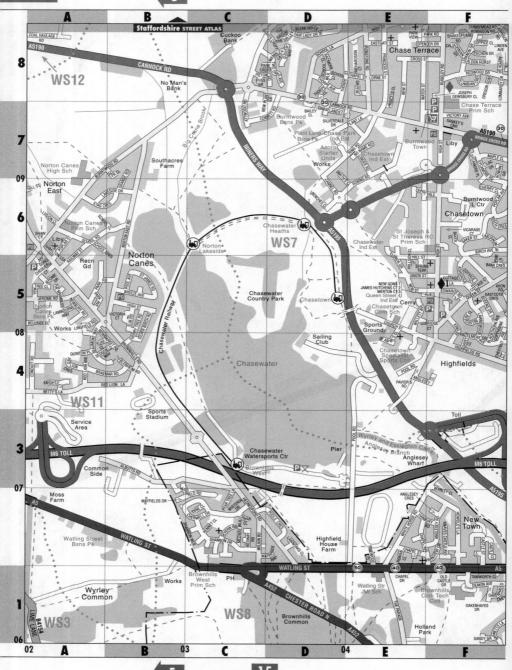

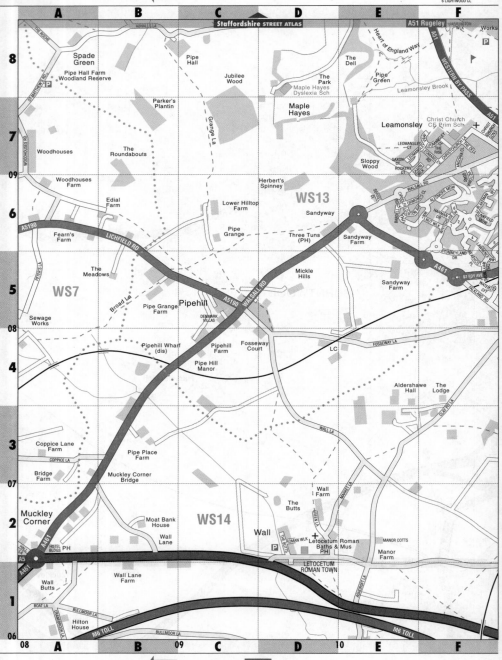

F6
1 BROADBENT CL
2 CATERBANCK WAY
3 COLLINS DR
4 MADDOCKE WLK
5 ALLINGTON AVE
6 LIGHTWOOD CL

A   B   C   D   E   F

Staffordshire STREET ATLAS

A51 Rugeley

8

Spade
Green

Pipe Hall Farm
Woodland Reserve

Pipe
Hall

Jubilee
Wood

The
Dell

Pipe
Green

The
Park
Maple Hayes
Dyslexia Sch

Heart of England Way

Leamonsley Brook

Works

WESTERN BY PASS

7

Parker's
Plantin

Grange La

Maple
Hayes

Leamonsley

Christ Church
CE Prim Sch

LEOMANSLEY
CT

SAXON
CT
ROOKERY
CT

The
RISE

09

Woodhouses

The
Roundabouts

Sloppy
Wood

WALSALL RD

6

Woodhouses
Farm

Edial
Farm

Herbert's
Spinney

Lower Hilltop
Farm

WS13

Sandyway

Fearn's
Farm

LICHFIELD RD

Pipe
Grange

Three Tuns
(PH)

Sandyway
Farm

A461

ST EDY AVE

5

WS7

The
Meadows

Broad La

Pipe Grange
Farm

Pipehill

A5190

WALSALL RD

Mickle
Hills

Sandyway
Farm

08

Sewage
Works

DENMARK
VILLAS

Pipehill Wharf
(dis)

Pipehill
Farm

Fosseway
Court

LC

FOSSEWAY LA

4

Pipe Hill
Manor

Aldershawe
Hall

The
Lodge

WALL LA

3

Coppice Lane
Farm

COPPICE LA

Pipe Place
Farm

07

Bridge
Farm

Muckley Corner
Bridge

Wall
Farm

2

Muckley
Corner

A461

HOTEL
BLDGS

Moat Bank
House

Wall
Lane

WS14

The
Butts

Wall

Letocetum Roman
Baths & Mus
PH

Manor
Farm

MANOR COTTS

A5

A461

Wall
Butts

Wall Lane
Farm

ROMAN WLK

LETOCETUM
ROMAN TOWN

1

BOAT LA

BULLMOOR LA

Hilton
House

M6 TOLL

BULLMOOR LA

M6 TOLL

06

08   A   B   09   C   D   10   E   F

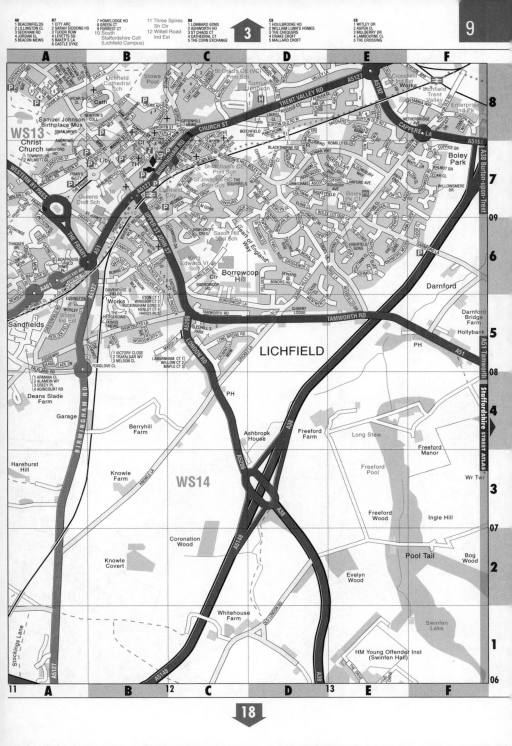

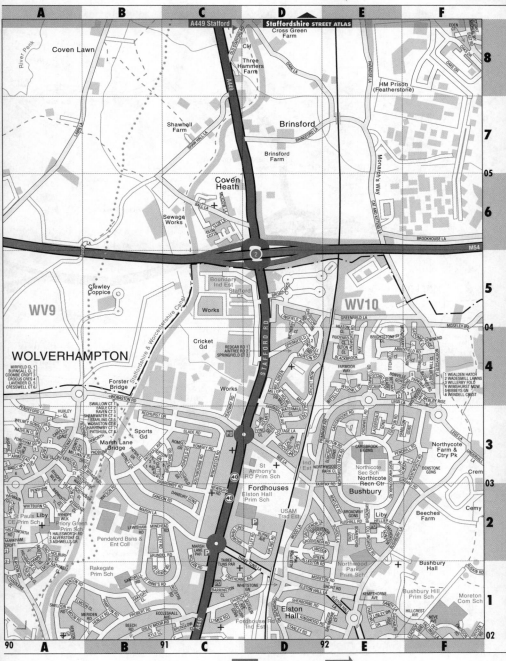

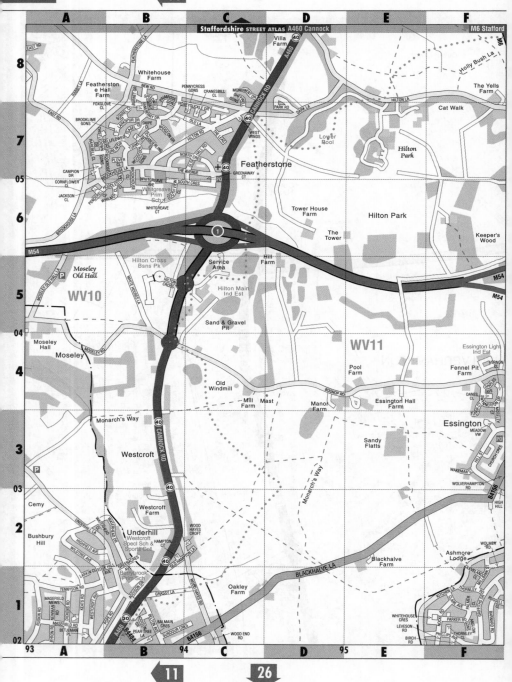

Staffordshire STREET ATLAS A460 Cannock

M6 Stafford

A B C D E F

8

Whitehouse Farm

Villa Farm

EAST RD

RAMBLA LA

Featherstone Hall Farm

NEW RD

PENNYCRESS GDNS

CRANESBILL CL

MONUMENT CL

PARK RD

DARK LA

HILTON LA

The Yells Farm

Cat Walk

7

FOXGLOVE CL

HONEYSUCKLE DR

OLD LA

HILTON RD

THE WEST

WEST WINDS

Lower Pool

Hilton Park

BROOKLIME GDNS

SNIPE

05

CAMPION DR

PLOVER

NORTH CRES

THE AVENUE

+ 40

GREENAWAY CT

Featherstone

CORNFLOWER CL

W.SOUTH CRES

6

JACKSON CL

Whitgreave Prim Sch

WHITGREAVE AVE

WHITGREAVE CT

Tower House Farm

Hilton Park

The Tower

Keeper's Wood

M54

Service Area

Hill Farm

5

Moseley Old Hall

Hilton Cross Bsns Pk

HILTON CROSS

WHITE HORSES LA

Hilton Main Ind Est

M54

M54

WV10

04

Sand & Gravel Pit

WV11

Essington Light Ind Est

Moseley Hall

MOSELEY RD

Moseley

VERNON CL

Pool Farm

Fennel Pit Farm

4

Old Windmill

BOGNOP RD

DANES CL

Monarch's Way

Mill Farm

Mast

Manor Farm

Essington Hall Farm

Essington

MEADOW VW

3

Westcroft

Sandy Flatts

WAKEMAN CL

CHURCH CRES

03

Cemy

CANNOCK RD

40

WOLVERHAMPTON RD

B4156

HIGH HILL

Bushbury Hill

Westcroft Farm

2

Underhill

Westcroft Specl Sch & Sports Coll

HAMPTON CL

WOOD HAYES CROFT

Ashmore Lodge

WOLMER RD

Blackhalve Farm

Berrybrook Prim Sch

40

OLD HAMPTON LA

BLACKHALVE LA

WHITEHOUSE CRES

THORNLEY

1

MASEFIELD MEWS

GRASSY LA

Oakley Farm

LEVESON RD

PARKER RD

BIRCH RD

PHILLIPS RD

THORNLEY

30

PEAR TREE

B4166

WOOD END RD

02

93 A B 94 C D 95 E F

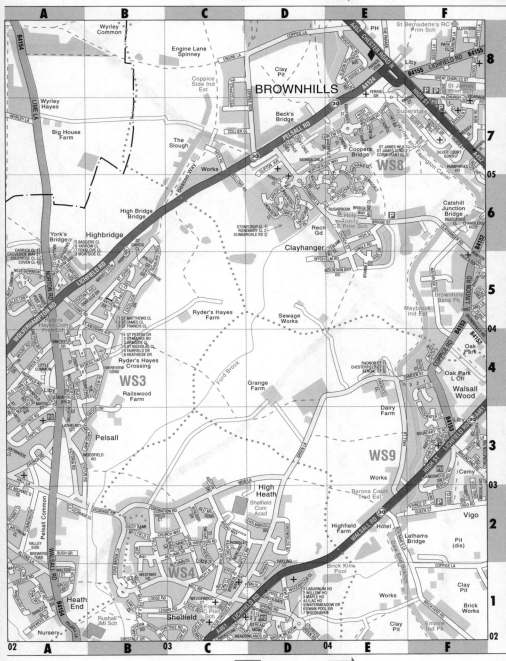

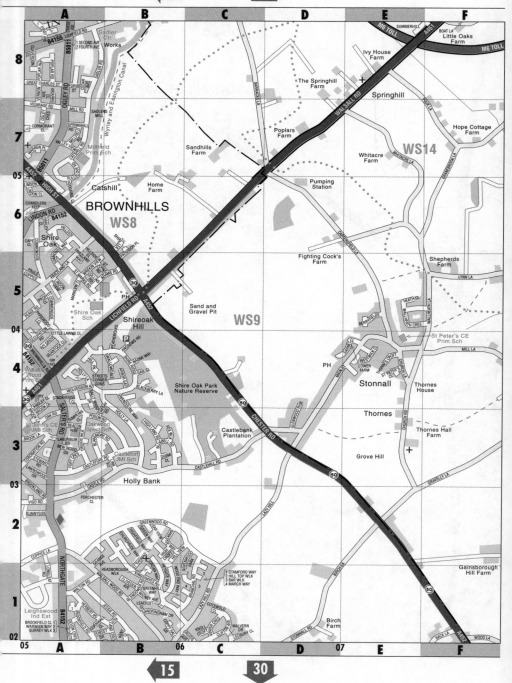

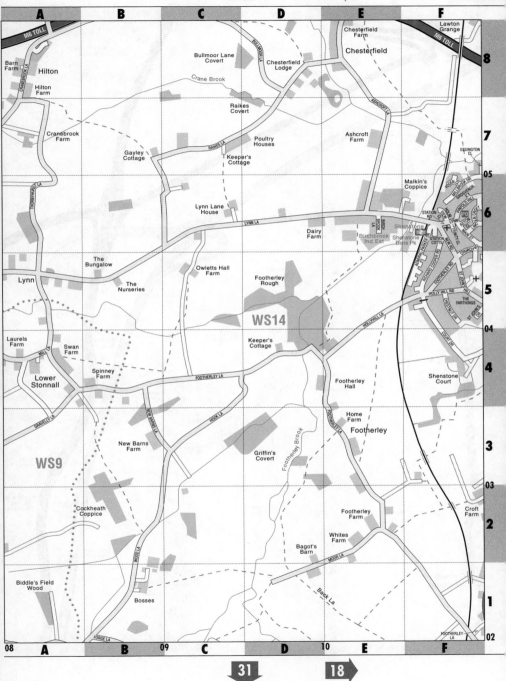

Barn Farm
Hilton
Hilton Farm
M6 TOLL
Cranebrook Farm
THORNYHURST LA
Lynn
Laurels Farm
Swan Farm
Lower Stonnall
GRAVELLY LA
MILL LA
Spinney Farm

WS9

Cockheath Coppice
New Barns Farm
Biddle's Field Wood
Bosses
FORGE LA
WOOD LA
NEW BARNS LA
HOOK LA

Crane Brook
Bullmoor Lane Covert
BULLMOOR LA
Chesterfield Lodge
Raikes Covert
RAIKES LA
Gayley Cottage
Keeper's Cottage
Poultry Houses
Lynn Lane House
LYNN LA
The Bungalow
The Nurseries
Owletts Hall Farm
Footherley Rough

WS14

Keeper's Cottage
FOOTHERLEY LA
Griffin's Covert
Footherley Brook
Bagot's Barn
Whites Farm
MOOR LA
Back La

Chesterfield Farm
Chesterfield
ASHCROFT LA
Ashcroft Farm
Dairy Farm
BIRCH BROOK LA
Birchbrook Ind Est
Shenstone Bsns Pk
Footherley Hall
HOLLYHILL LA
FOOTHERLEY LA
Home Farm
Footherley
Footherley Farm
Footherley Farm

Lawton Grange
M6 TOLL
ESSINGTON CL
Malkin's Coppice
HOZEN
GROSVENOR CT
MENNOCK DR
STATION RD
Shenstone
Shenstone Cotts
STATION FIELDS
ST JOHN'S
CHURCH RD
RICHARD COOPER RD
ADMIRAL PARKER DR
HOLLY HILL RD
THE FARTHINGS
CHESTNUT DR
ST JOHN'S DR
COURT DR
Shenstone Court
Croft Farm
FOOTHERLEY LA

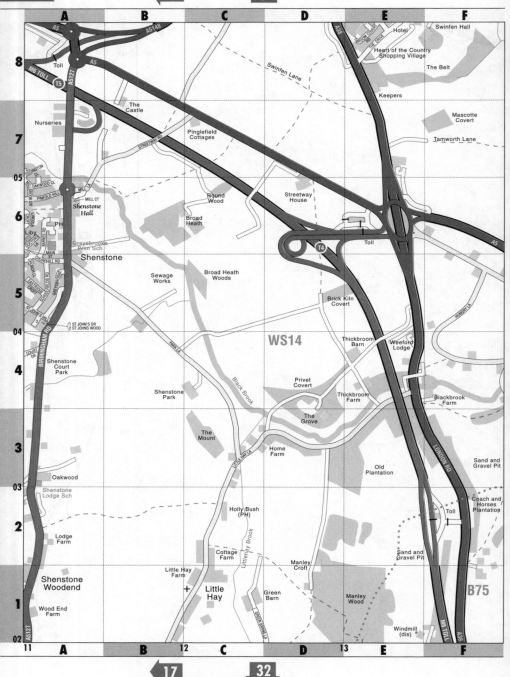

A51

Broadfields

8

Packington
Moor

Common
Barn

Moor
Covert

7

Tamworth Lane

KNOX'S GRAVE LA

Riding
School

A51 HOPWAS HILL

05

Buck's Head
Cottages

Sand and Gravel
Pit

6

WS14

Packington
Farm

PACKINGTON LA

Hare Park
Wood

50

The Devil's
Dressing
Room

5

Heart of England Way

Mast

Transmitting
Station

04

50

Weeford

B78

Hanging
Wood

4

Church
Wood

Buck's Head
Farm

Long
Island

Sand and Gravel
Pit

Common
Plantation

WATLING ST LA

Hints Lane
Farm

Bourne
House

The
Lodge

ROCK HILL

40

Black Brook

A5

3

Snake's
Hill

WATLING ST

40

Hints Hill

40

Hints

Manor
Farm

Rough
Leasow

Job's
Hill

Home
Farm

03

Bangley
Lodge

Ford

SCHOOL LA

Botley
House

2

Gorsey
Hill

ROOKERY LA

Rookery

HINTS LA

Resr

Baume Brook

Sand and
Gravel Pit

Crow's
Castle

B75

Rookery
Farm

White Owl
Farm

Roundhill
Wood

1

New
Plantation

BROCKHURST LA

02

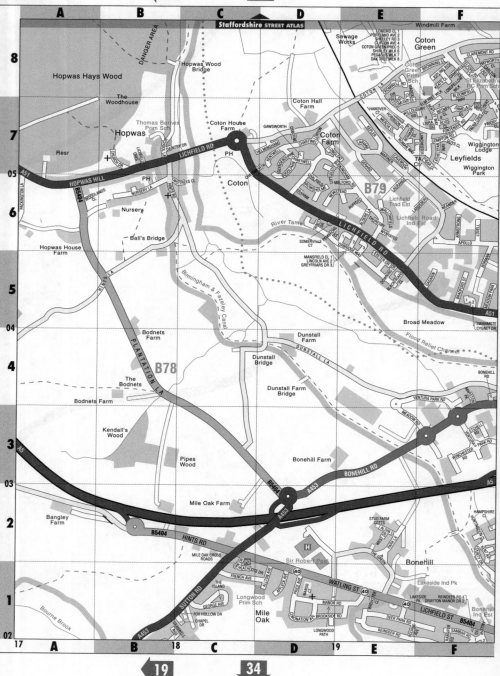

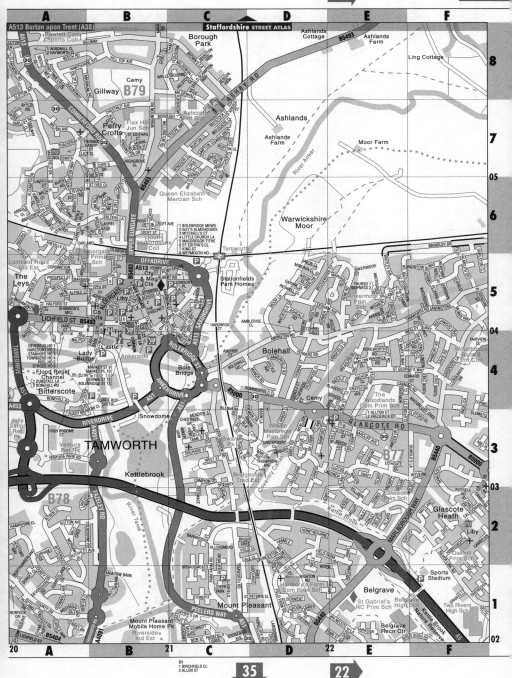

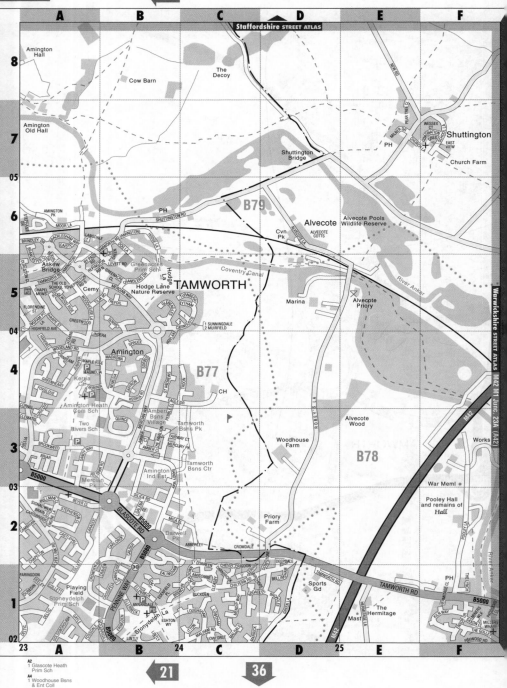

Staffordshire STREET ATLAS

Warwickshire STREET ATLAS M42 M1 Junc. 23A (A42)

A B C D E F

8 Amington Hall

Cow Barn

The Decoy

7 Amington Old Hall

Shuttington Bridge

WESSEX

PH Shuttington

EAST VIEW

Church Farm

05

6 AMINGTON PK

MOOR LA

PH

SHUTTINGTON RD

B79

Alvecote

Cvn Pk

ALVECOTE COTTS

Alvecote Pools Wildlife Reserve

Askew Bridge

Greenacres Prim Sch

Hodge Lane Nature Reserve

TAMWORTH

Coventry Canal

River Anker

5 Cemy

1 SUNNINGDALE
2 MUIRFIELD

Marina

Alvecote Priory

04

4 Amington

B77

CH

Alvecote Wood

Kerria

Amber Bsns Village

Tamworth Bsns Pk

Amington Heath Com Sch

Two Rivers Sch

QUINCE

Tamworth Bsns Ctr

MERCURY PK

Woodhouse Farm

ROBEY'S LA

B78

Works

03

B5000

Mercian Pk

Amington Ind Est

War Meml

Pooley Hall and remains of Hall

M42

2 PULLMAN CL

GLASCOTE RD

B5080

Darwell Pk

Priory Farm

POOLEY LA

ABBERLEY

CROMDALE

1 Playing Field

Stoneydelph Prim Sch

PENNINE WAY

Stonydelph La

DEEPDALE

BELLINGHAM

Sports Gd

TAMWORTH RD

PH

B5000

The Hermitage

Mast

River Anker

02

FARINGDON

A2
1 Glascote Heath Prim Sch
A4
1 Woodhouse Bsns & Ent Coll

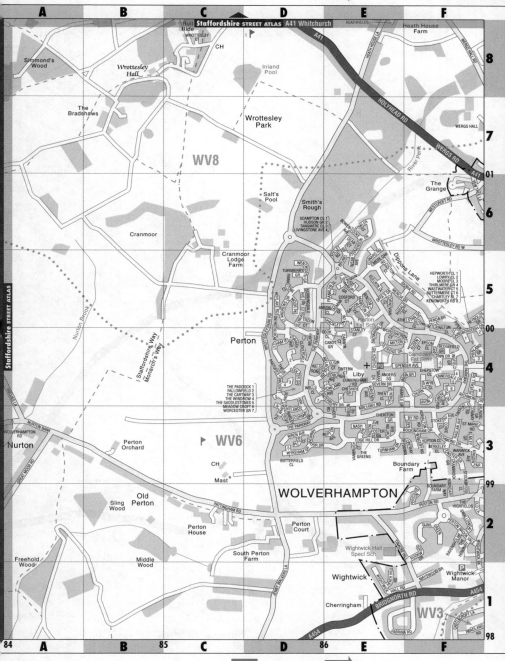

Staffordshire STREET ATLAS A41 Whitchurch

Bull
Ride
WROTTESLEY
CT
CH
HEATHFIELDS
Heath House
Farm
A41
HOLYHEAD RD

Simmond's
Wood

Wrottesley
Hall

Inland
Pool

WERGS HALL

WERGS RD

A41

The
Bradshaws

Wrottesley
Park

River Park

The
Grange

8

7

01

6

WV8

Salt's
Pool

Smith's
Rough

SCAMPTON CL 1
HUDSON GR 2
TANGMERE CL 3
LIVINGSTONE AVE 4

WESTCROFT RD

WROTTESLEY RD W

Cranmoor

Cranmoor
Lodge
Farm

Nurton Brook

Staffordshire STREET ATLAS

Staffordshire Way
Monarch's Way

Perton

Dippons Lane

HEPWORTH CL 1
LOWRY CL 2
MOORE CL 3
THIRLMERE GR 4
WASTWATER CT 5
BUTTERMERE CT 6
HARTLEY RD 7
KENILWORTH RD 8

Perton
Fst Sch

Sandown
Fst Sch

Liby

5

00

4

THE PADDOCK 1
FALLOWFIELD 2
THE CARTWAY 3
THE WINDROW 4
THE SADDLESTONES 5
MEADOW CROFT 6
WORCESTER GR 7

THE PARKWAY

Perton
Orchard

WV6

CH

Mast

BUTTERFIELD
CL

THE
GREENS

Boundary
Farm

BOUNDARY
FARM

WOLVERHAMPTON

Nurton

NURTON BANK

WOLVERHAMPTON
RD

GREAT MOOR RD

Old
Perton

Perton
House

Perton
Court

PATTINGHAM RD

PERTON RD

99

2

Sling
Wood

Middle
Wood

South Perton
Farm

Wightwick Hall
Specl Sch

Wightwick
Manor

Freehold
Wood

JENNY WALKERS LA

Wightwick

Cherringham

BRIDGNORTH RD

A454

WV3

A454

CASTLECROFT LA

SABRINA RD

HEADLAND
RD

1

98

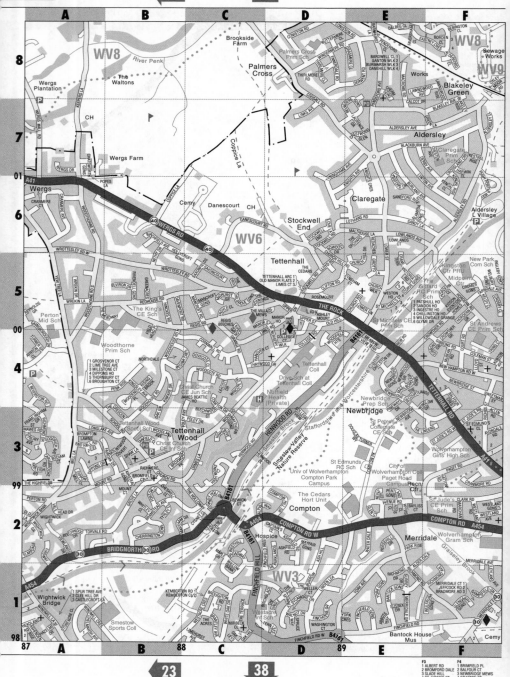

F3	F4
1 ALBERT RD	1 BRIMFIELD PL
2 BROMFORD DALE	2 BALFOUR CT
3 SLADE HILL	3 NEWBRIDGE MEWS
4 ST JUDE'S CT	4 GRAFTON CT
5 THE CEDARS	

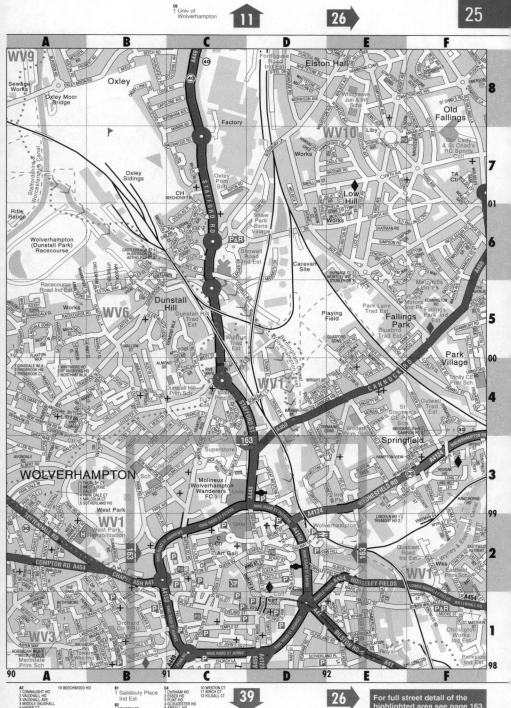

For full street detail of the
highlighted area see page 163.

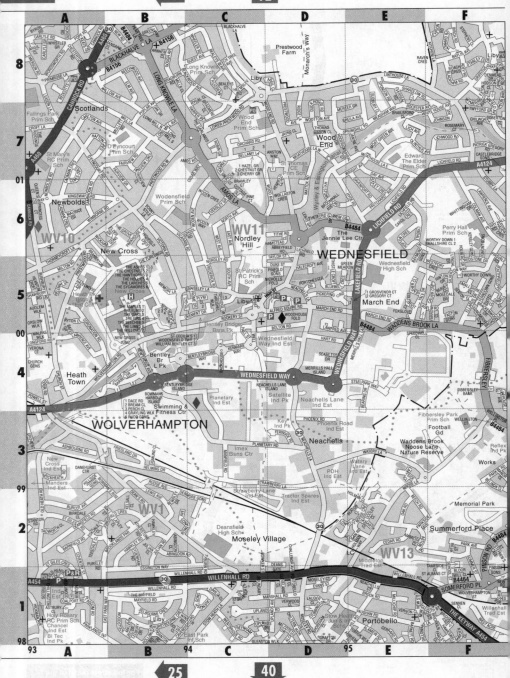

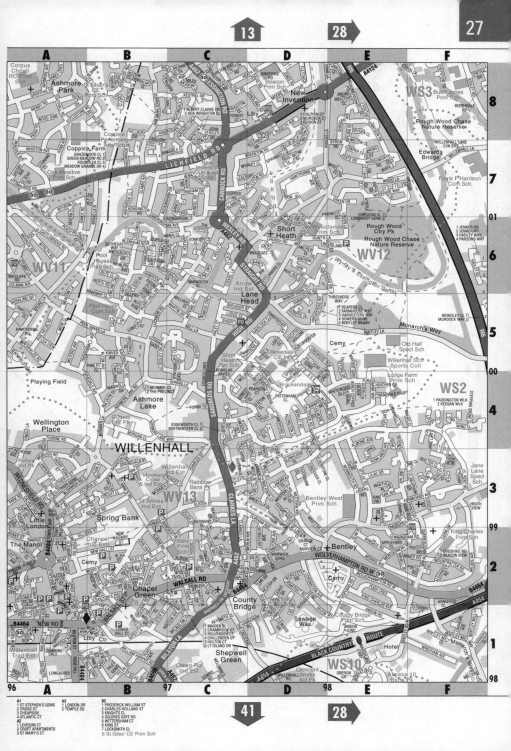

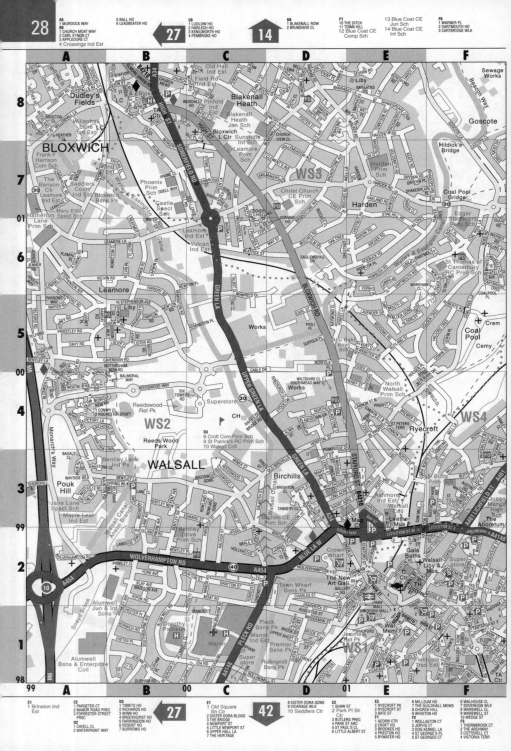

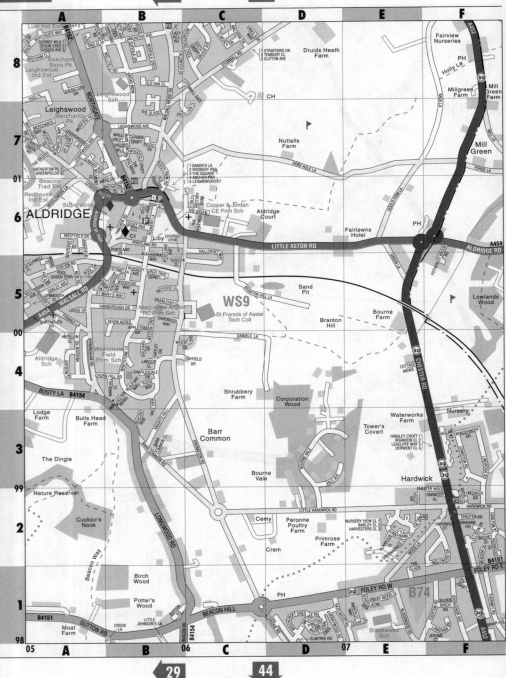

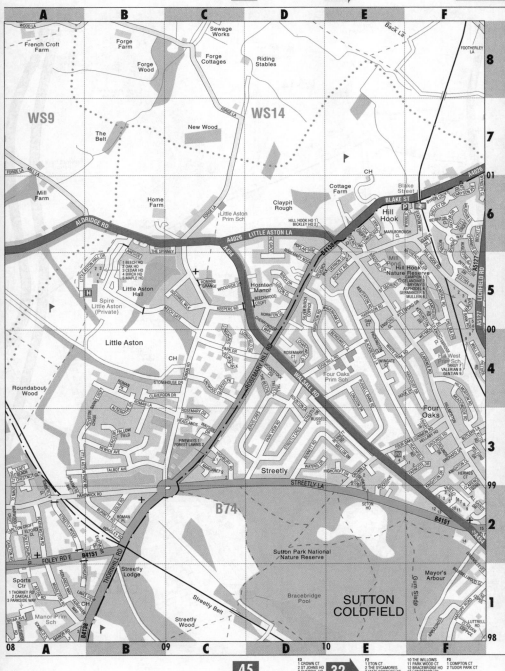

E3
1 CROWN CT
2 ST JOHNS HO
3 CHERRYL HO
4 AUSTIN CT
5 OAK PARK CT

F2
1 ETON CT
2 THE SYCAMORES
3 MARLBOROUGH CT
4 WINCHESTER CT
5 HARROW CT
6 DENSTON CT
7 OUNDLE CT
8 MALVERN CT
9 WREKIN CT
10 THE WILLOWS
11 PARK WOOD CT
12 BRACEBRIDGE HO
13 LONGMOOR HO
14 BURCOT CT
15 BELWELL LA
16 FOUR OAKS RD
17 PARK DR

F3
1 COMPTON CT
2 TUDOR PARK CT

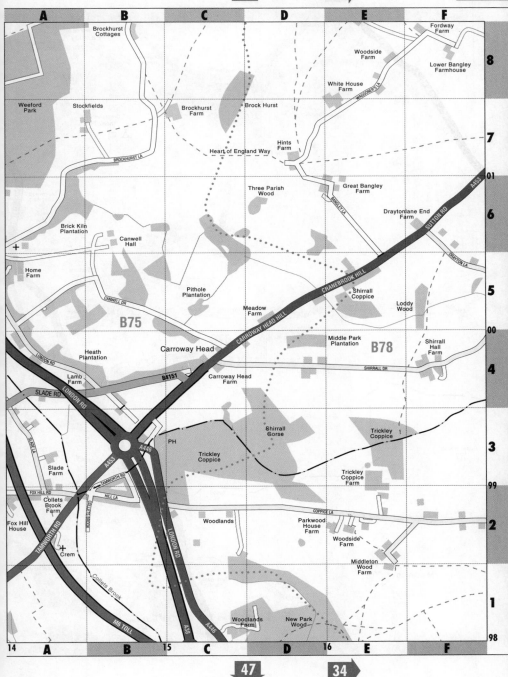

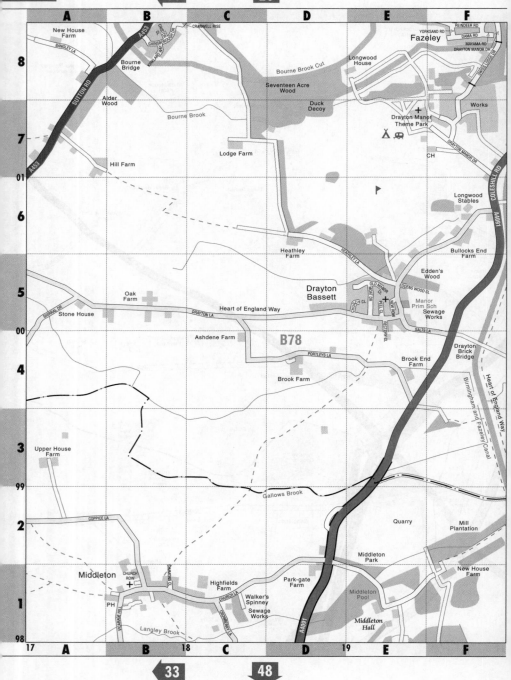

33
20

A B C D E F

8

New House
Farm

BANGLEY LA

Bourne
Bridge

CRANWELL RISE

Bourne Brook Cut

Longwood
House

Fazeley

YORKSAND RD
DAMA RD

REINDEER RD

MAYAMA RD
DRAYTON MANOR DR

WEST LODGE DR

Seventeen Acre
Wood

Alder
Wood

Bourne Brook

Duck
Decoy

Works

7

Drayton Manor
Theme Park

CH

Hill Farm

Lodge Farm

Longwood
Stables

01

6

Heathley
Farm

Bullocks End
Farm

Edden's
Wood

5

Oak
Farm

Stone House

DRAYTON LA

Heart of England Way

Drayton
Bassett

B78

OLD MANOR CL

GOAT DR

EDDENS WOOD CL

Manor
Prim Sch

Sewage
Works

Drayton
Brick
Bridge

00

Ashdene Farm

PORTLEYS LA

Brook End
Farm

SALIS LA

4

Brook Farm

3

Upper House
Farm

99

Gallows Brook

2

COPPICE LA

Quarry

Mill
Plantation

Middleton
Park

New House
Farm

1

Middleton

CHURCH ROW

Highfields
Farm

Walker's
Spinney

Park-gate
Farm

Middleton
Pool

Sewage
Works

Middleton
Hall

98

Langley Brook

17

A

B

18

C

D

19

E

F

33
48

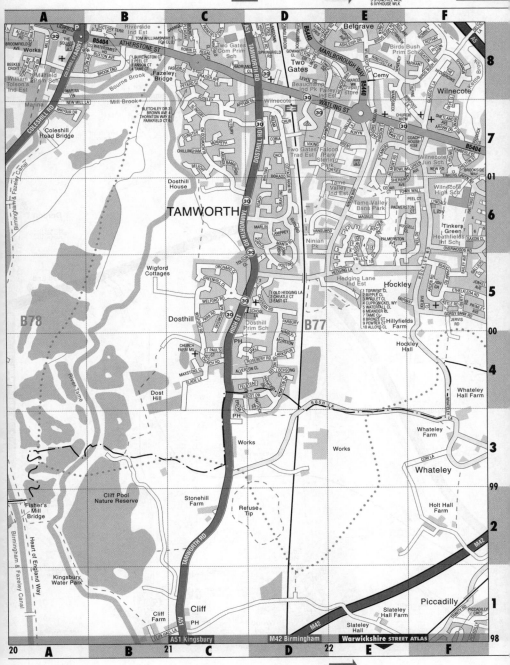

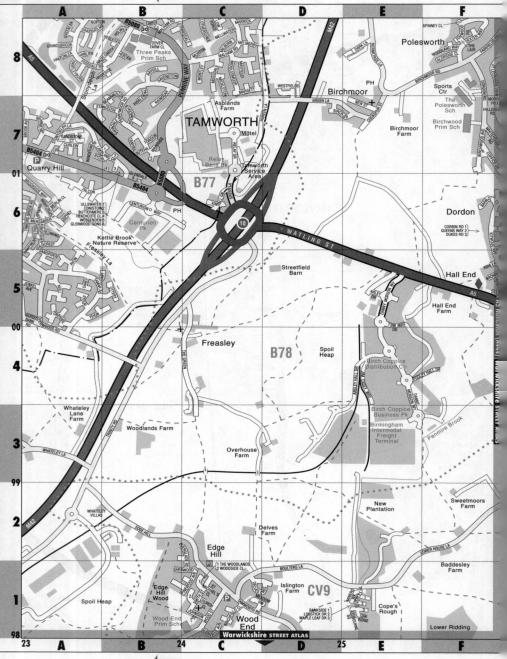

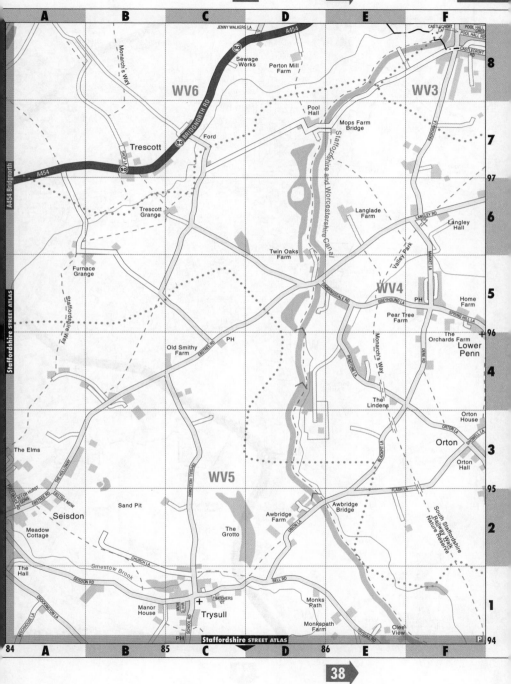

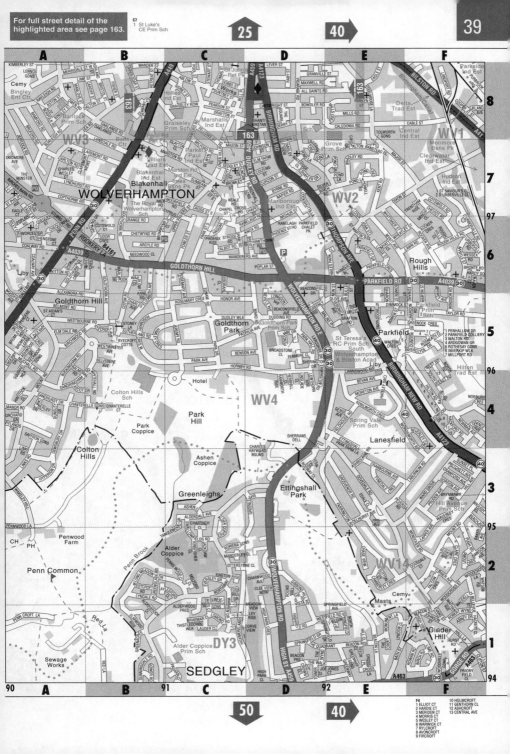

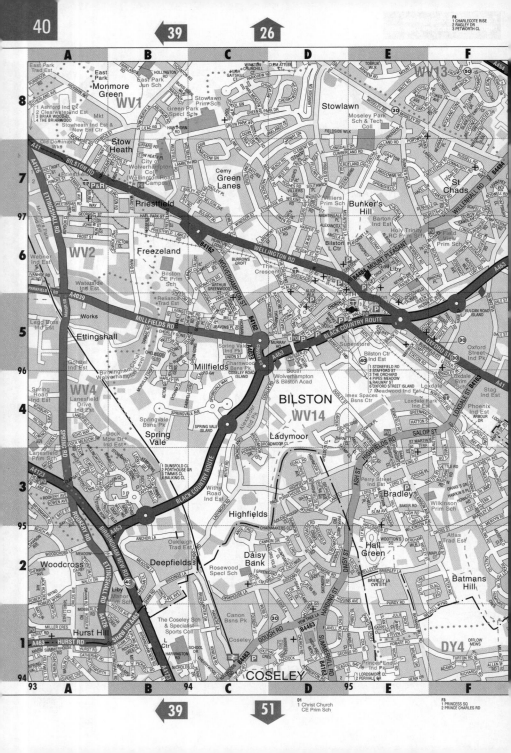

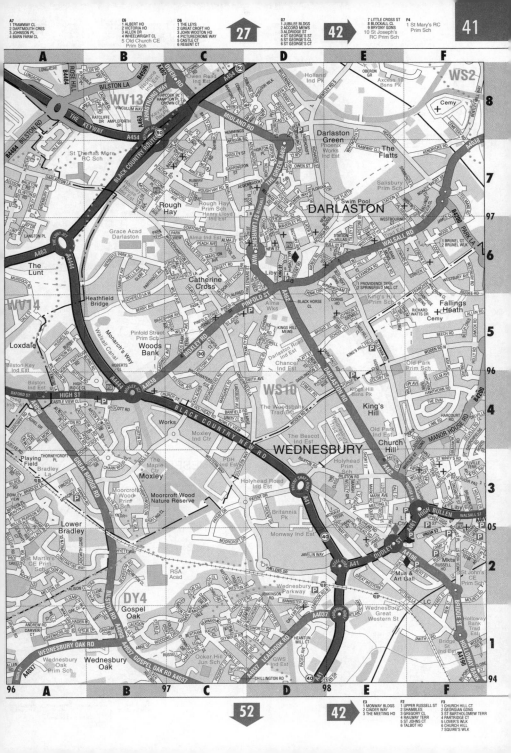

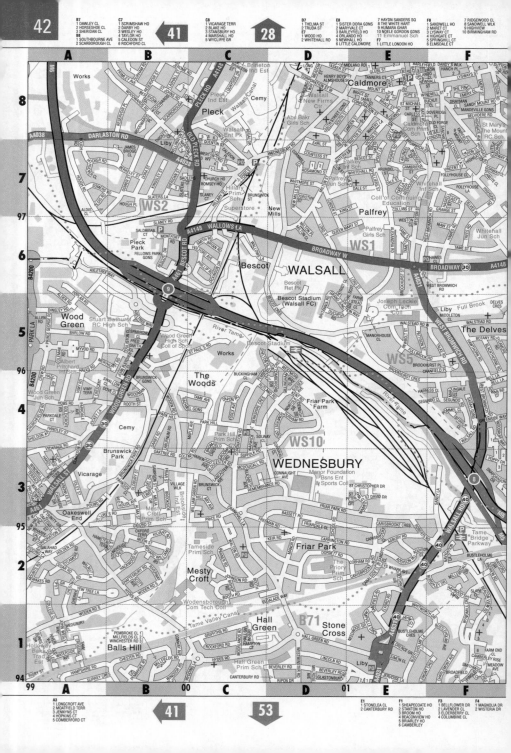

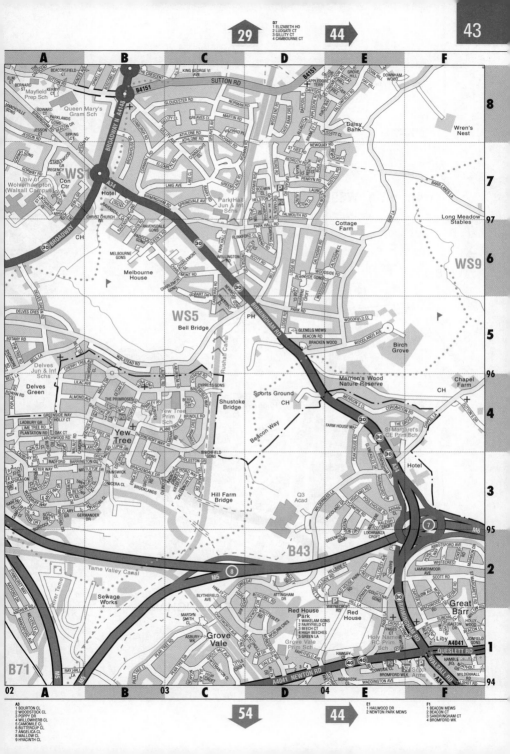

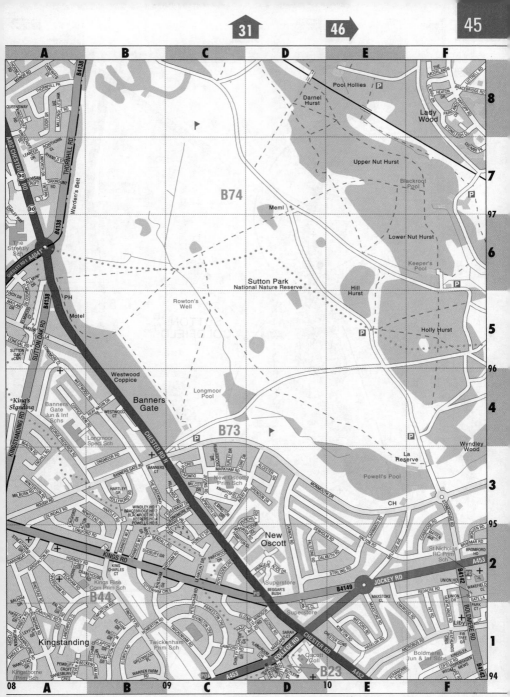

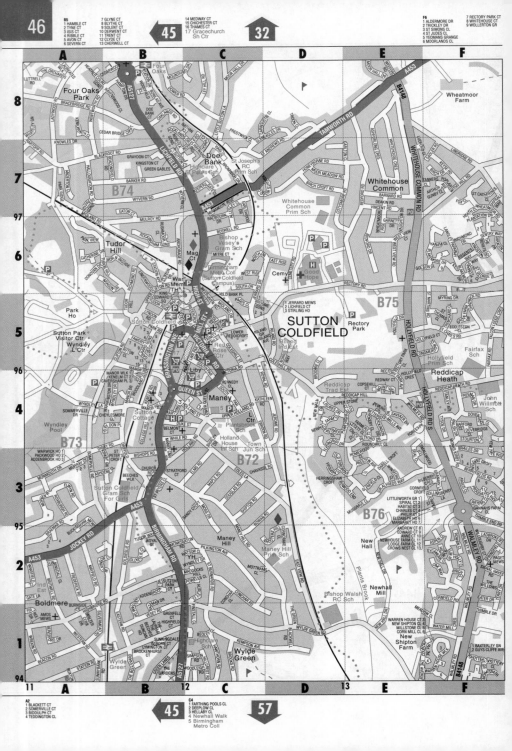

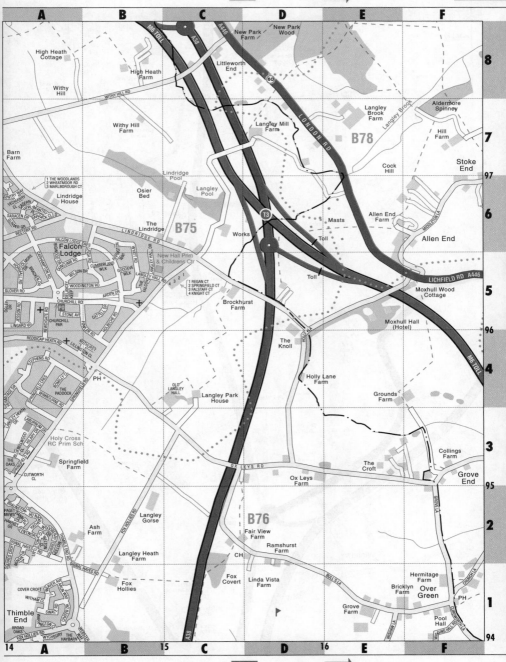

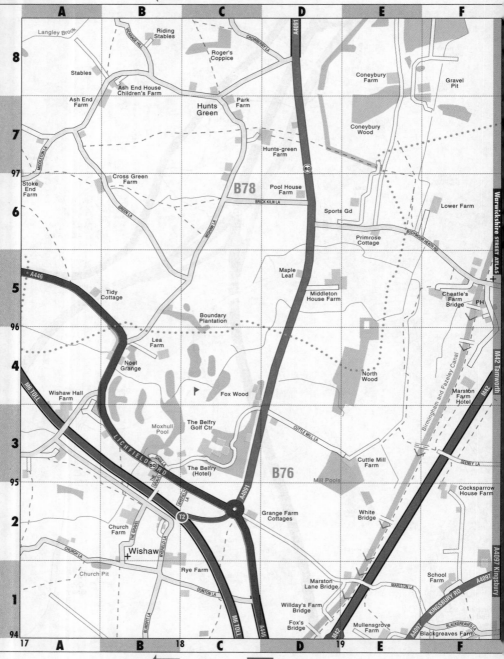

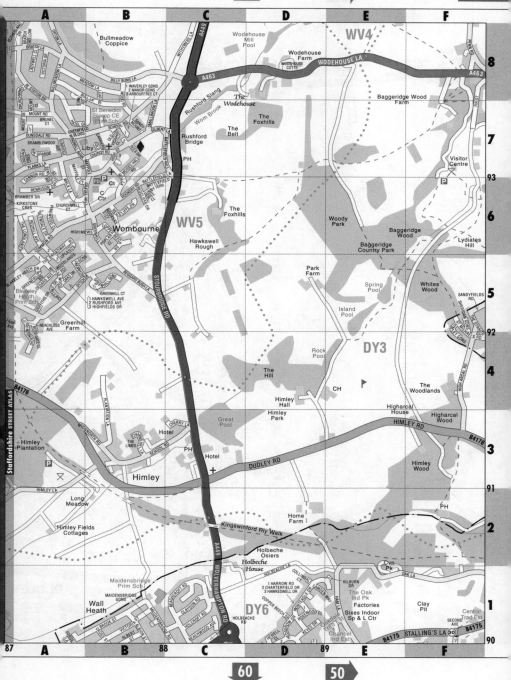

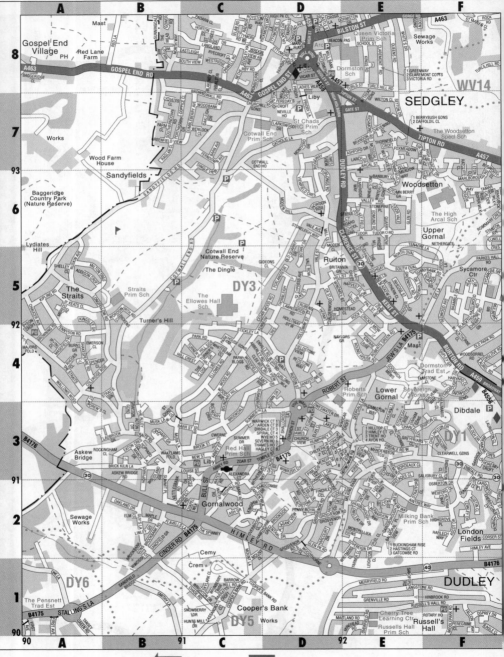

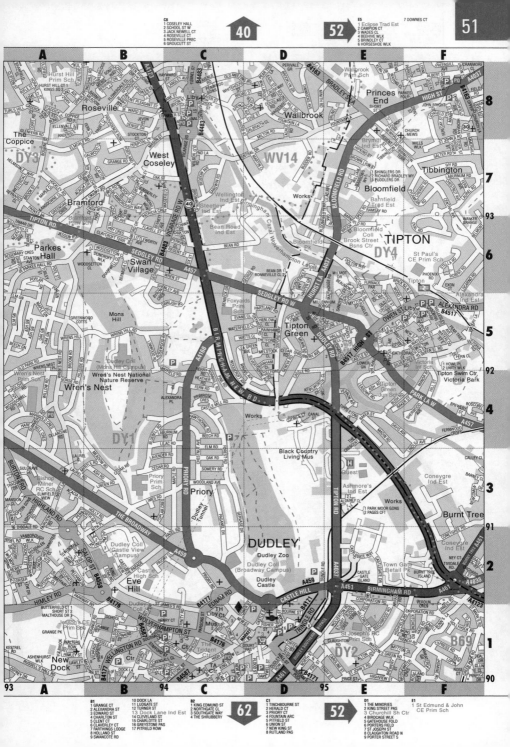

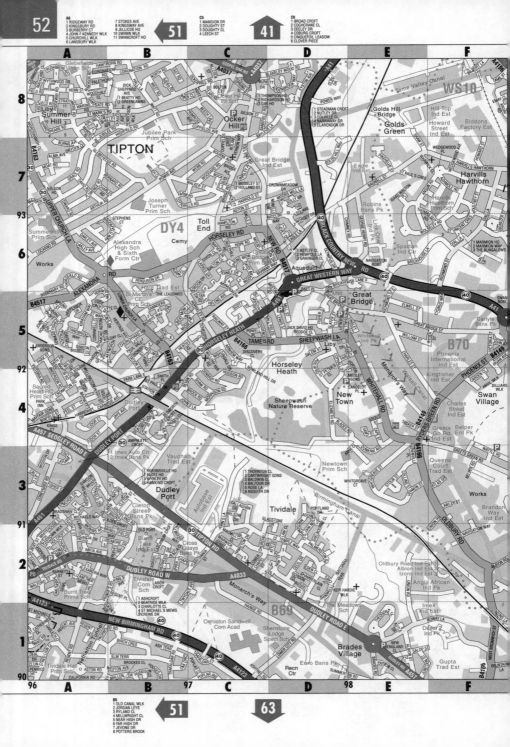

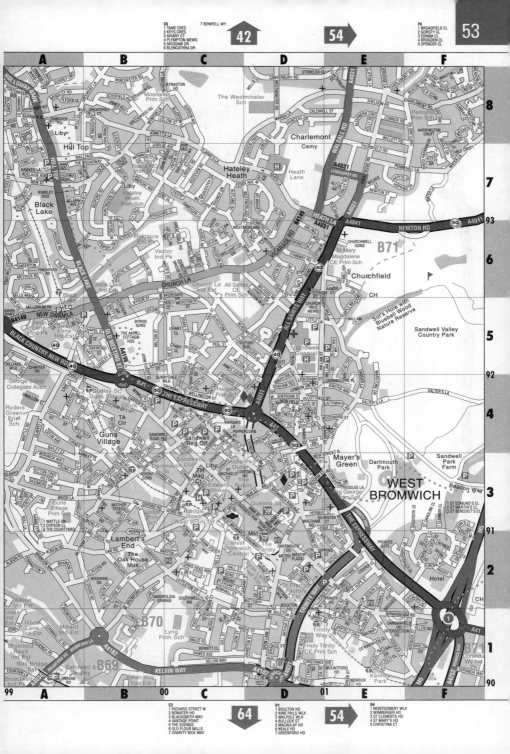

53
43

D8
1 BURRELTON WAY
2 GLENDENE DR
3 FAIRDENE WAY
4 GARSTON WAY

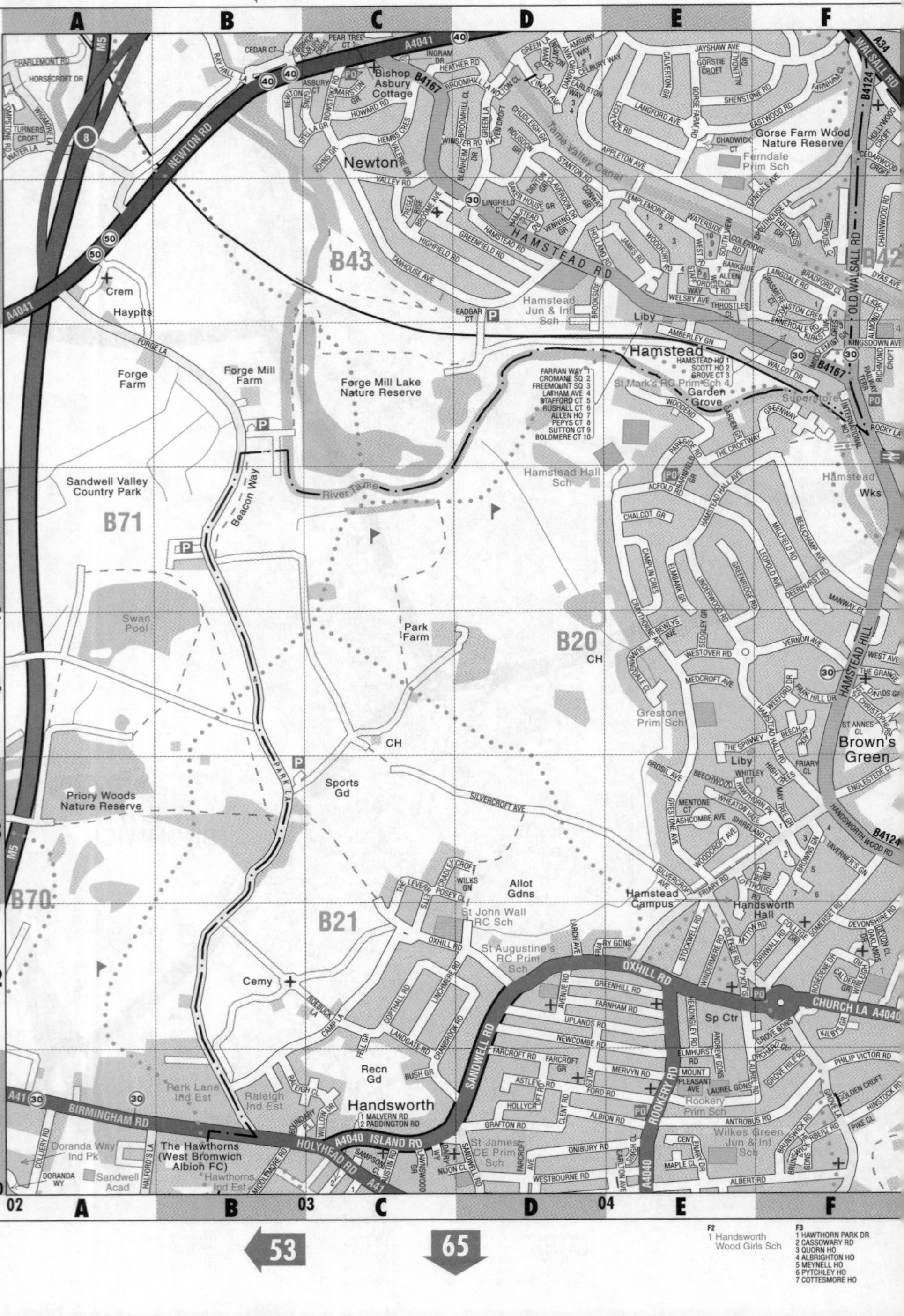

A	B	C	D	E	F

8

CHARLEMONT RD
HORSECROFT DR
TURNERS CROFT
WATER LA

CEDAR CT
PEAR TREE LA
A4041
40
Bishop
Asbury
Cottage
B4116
INGRAM RD
HEATHER RD

Gorse Farm Wood
Nature Reserve
CHADWICK CT
Ferndale
Prim Sch

NEWTON RD

Newton

Time Valley Coppice

HAMSTEAD RD

7

B43

Crem
Haypits

FORGE LA

30
50

93

A4041

Forge
Farm

Forge Mill
Farm

Forge Mill Lake
Nature Reserve

Hamstead
Jun & Inf
Sch

Liby

Hamstead

St Mark's RC Prim Sch

FARRAN WAY 1
CROMANE SQ 2
FREEMOUNT SQ 3
LARHAM AVE 4
STAFFORD CT 5
RUSHALL CT 6
ALLEN HO 7
PEPYS CT 8
SUTTON CT 9
BOLDMERE CT 10

Garden
Grove

Superstore

B4167

Hamstead
Wks

6

Beacon Way

Sandwell Valley
Country Park

B71

River Tame

Hamstead Hall
Sch

CHALCOT GR

5

P

Swan
Pool

Park
Farm

B20
CH

HAMSTEAD HILL

Grestone
Prim Sch

Brown's
Green

92

4

CH

Liby

3

Priory Woods
Nature Reserve

Sports
Gd

SILVERCROFT AVE

B4124

M5

B70

Allot
Gdns

B21

St John Wall
RC Sch

St Augustine's
RC Prim
Sch

Hamstead
Campus

Handsworth
Hall

91

2

Cemy

OXHILL RD

GREENHILL RD

Sp Ctr

CHURCH LA A4040

Rookery
Prim Sch

1

30

BIRMINGHAM RD

Park Lane
Ind Est

Raleigh
Ind Est

Recn
Gd

Handsworth
1 MALVERN RD
2 PADDINGTON RD

HOLYHEAD RD A4040 ISLAND RD

St James
CE Prim
Sch

Wilkes Green
Jun & Inf
Sch

SANDWELL RD

ROOKERY RD

A41

A4040

90

Doranda Way
Ind Pk

DORANDA WY

Sandwell
Acad

The Hawthorns
(West Bromwich
Albion FC)

Hawthorns
Ind Est

A	B	C	D	E	F

02 **03** **04**

53
65

F2
1 Handsworth
Wood Girls Sch

F3
1 HAWTHORN PARK DR
2 CASSOWARY RD
3 QUORN HO
4 ALBRIGHTON HO
5 MEYNELL HO
6 PYTCHLEY HO
7 COTTESMORE HO

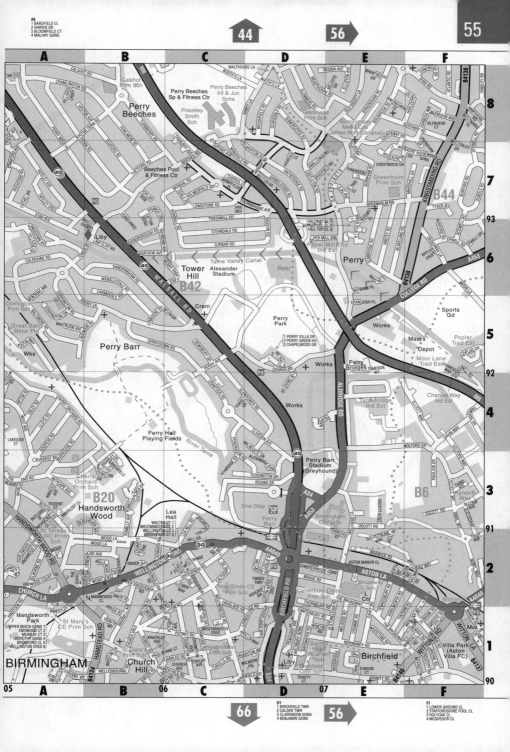

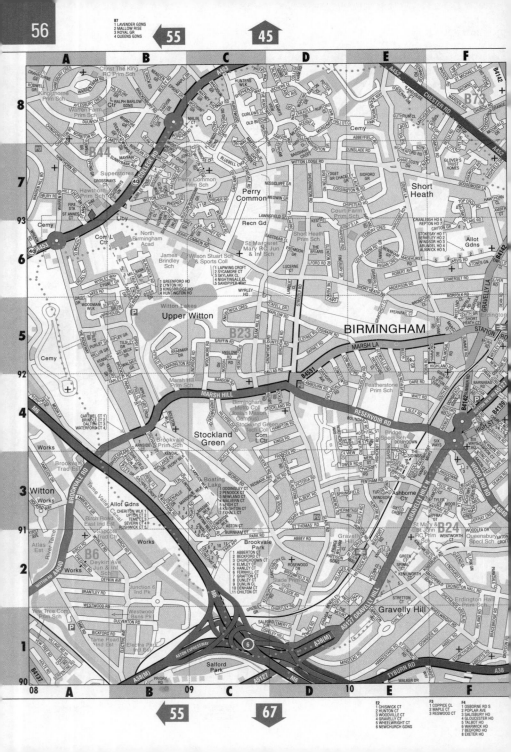

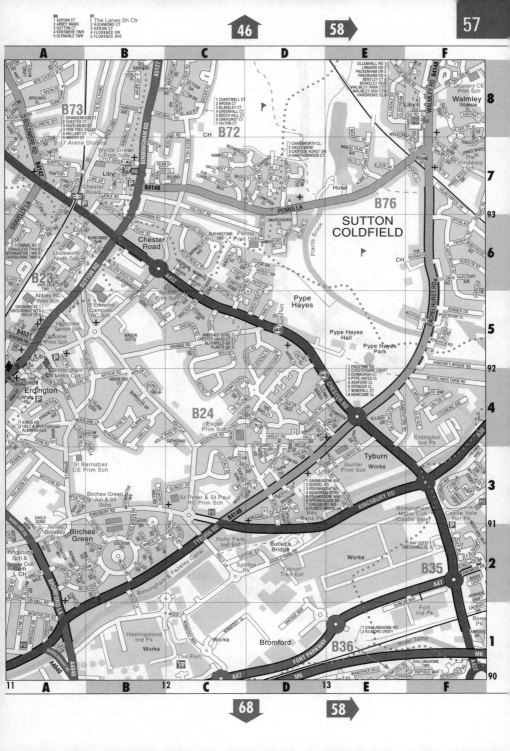

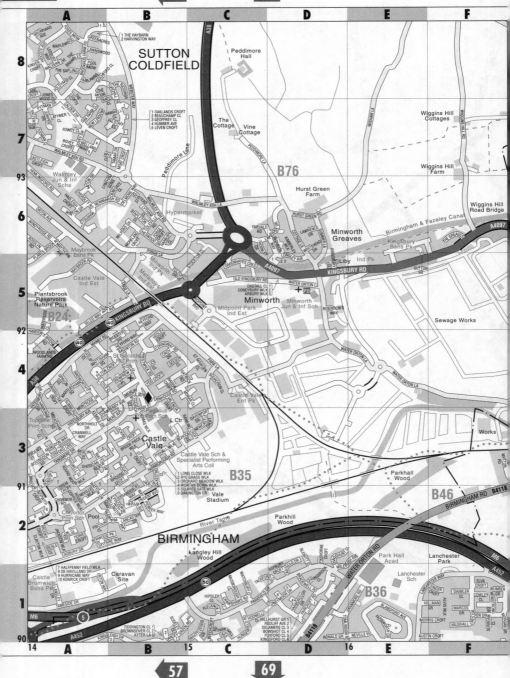

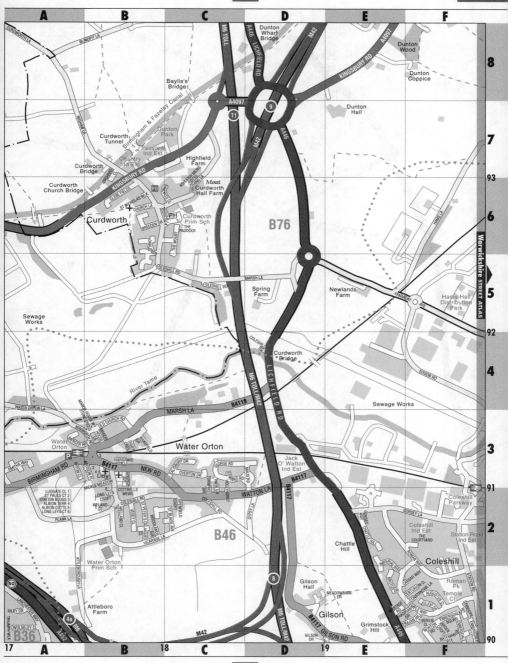

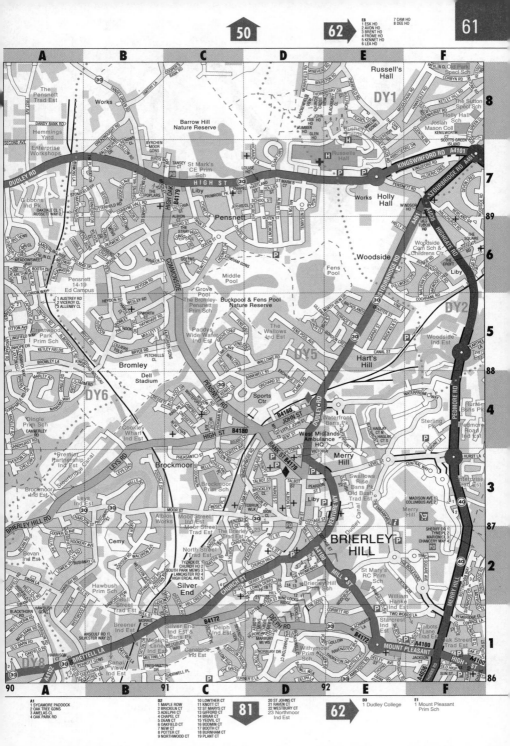

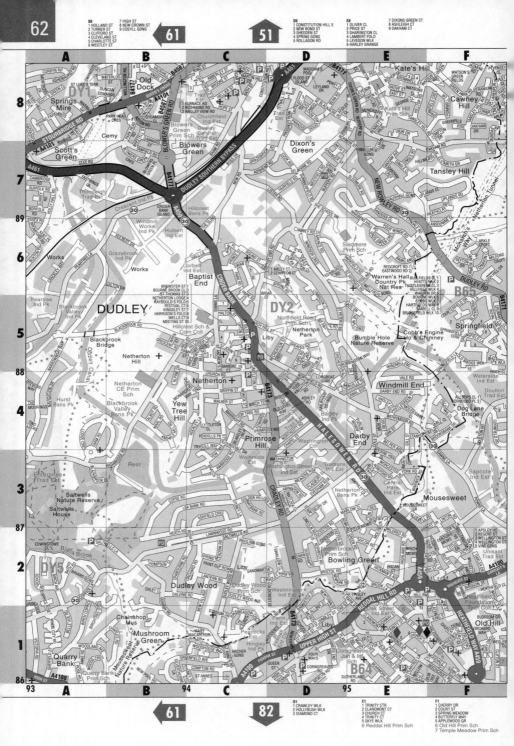

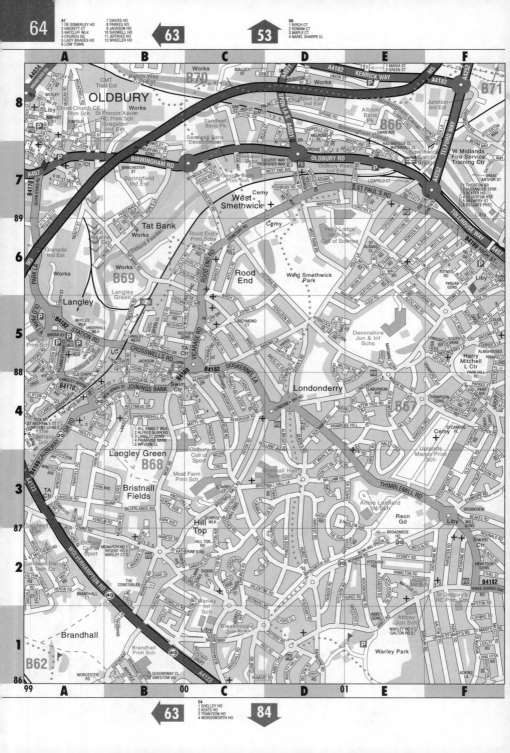

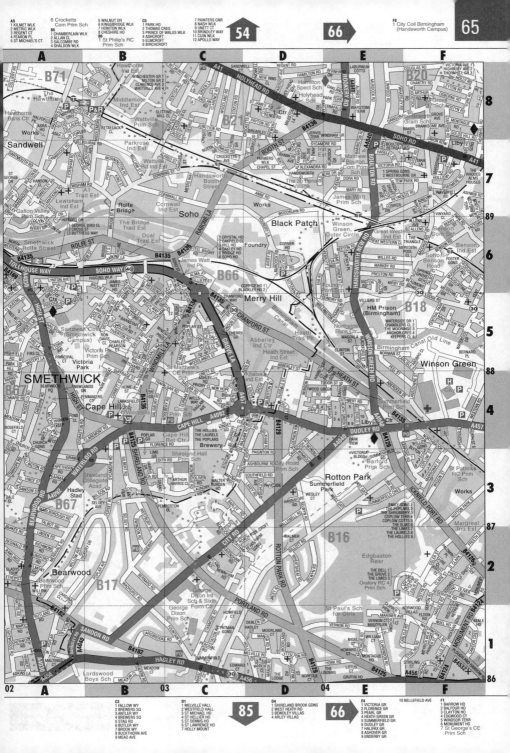

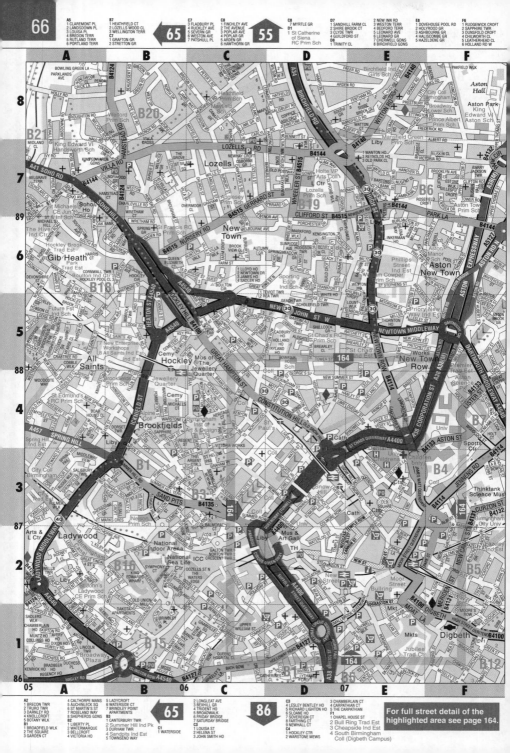

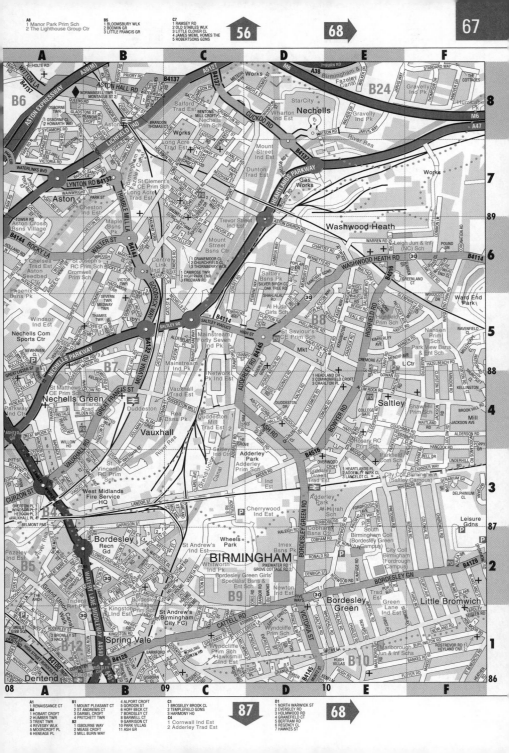

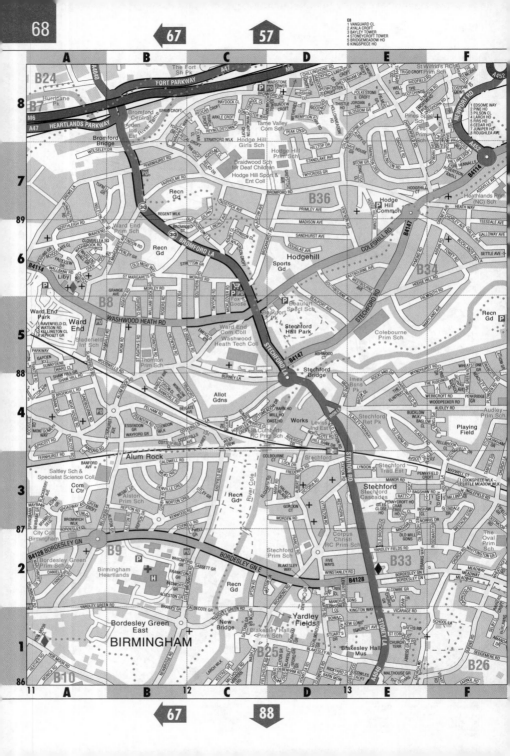

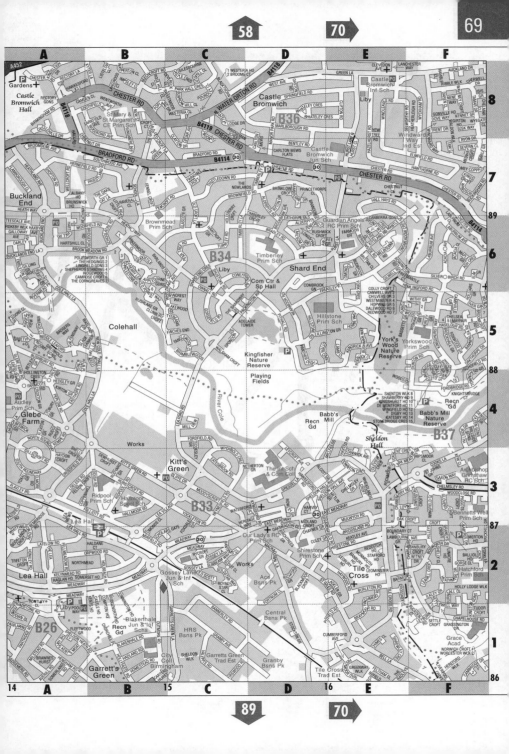

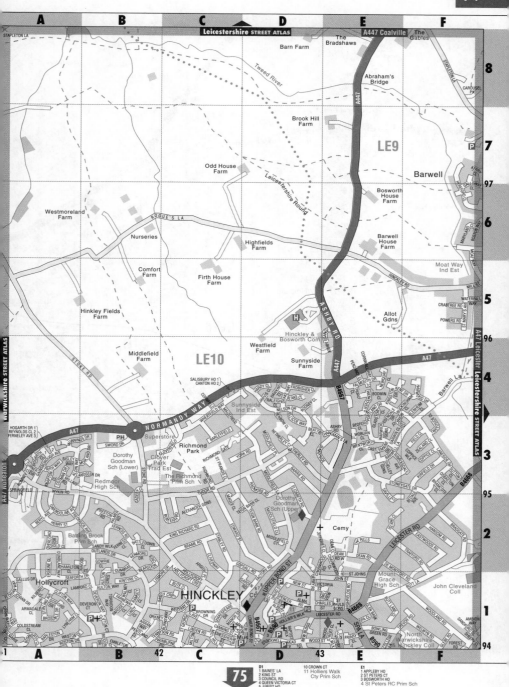

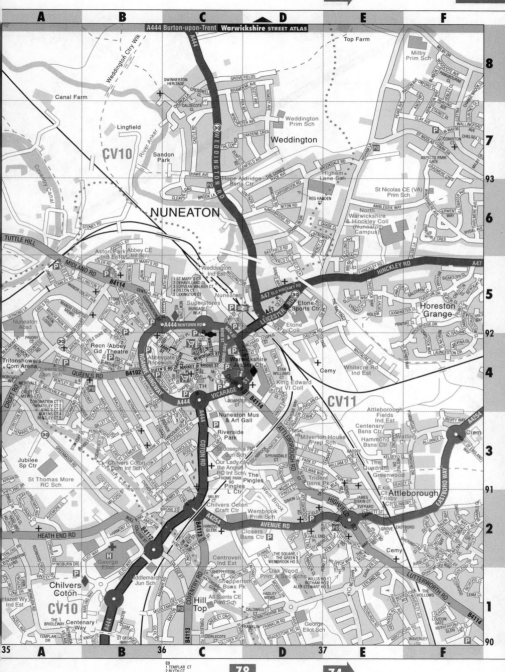

74

A B C D E F

A444 Burton-upon-Trent **Warwickshire** STREET ATLAS

Top Farm

Milby
Prim Sch

8

Canal Farm

SWINNERTON
HERITAGE

CRESSWELL

GROVE FIELDS

BRAMCOTE AVE

Weddington
Prim Sch

7

Lingfield

CV10

River Anker

Sandon
Park

CALDECOTE

OAKDENE CRES

Weddington

93

SHAWE AVE

Hope Aldridge
Bsns Ctr

Higham
Lane Sch

Etone CE
Prim Sch

St Nicolas CE (VA)
Prim Sch

6

NUNEATON

CARISBROOK RD

REG HADDEN

North
Warwickshire
& Hinckley Coll
Nuneaton
Campus

AMBLESIDE WAY

TUTTLE HILL

Aston Park Abbey CE
Ind Est

MIDLAND RD

B4114

ST MARY'S RD

Weddington
Ind Est

HINCKLEY RD

Hinckley Rd

A47

Horeston
Grange

5

CENTRAL AVE

1 ST MARY'S CT
2 DEHAVILLAND CL
3 EDYVEAN WALKER CL
4 DILLON CT
5 LEXINGTON CT

Nuneaton

A47 OLD HINCKLEY RD

LEICESTER RD

Etone
Sports Ctr

THE HASTINGS

92

Nuneaton
Acad

Superstores

BURGAGE
WLK

Etone
Coll

Recn
Gd

Abbey
Theatre

ABBEY

Warwickshire
Justice Ctr

Cemy

Whitacre Rd
Ind Est

4

Tritonshowers
Com Arena

QUEEN'S RD

B4102

ABBEYGATE
Ropewalk

MARKET

BRIDGE ST

STAN
WILLIAMS
CT

King Edward
VI Coll

CV11

Attleborough
Fields
Ind Est
Centenary
Bsns Ctr

LIBERTY WAY

A4254

Croft
Jun Sch

QUEENS RD

A444

VICARAGE ST

Milverton House
Prep Sch

Hammond
Bsns Ctr

Watling

Crem

CORONATION CT 1
WHATELEY CT 2
KINGS CT 3
QUEENS CT 4
BENTLEY CT 5

B4114

DEMPSTER
CT

Nuneaton Mus
& Art Gall

Riverside
Park

ATTLEBOROUGH RD

The
Quadrant

Greenwood
Ct

EASTBORO WAY

Attleborough

Jubilee
Sp Ctr

St Thomas More
RC Sch

COTON RD

St Joseph's RC
Jun Sch

Our Lady of
the Angels
RC Inf Sch

Springdale
Ind Est

PARK ST

Trident
Bsns Pk

91

HIGHFIELD RD

Frisby

HEATH END RD

B4112

BRIDGE ST

A444

A4254

AVENUE RD

Wembrook
Prim Sch

Closers
Bsns Ctr

Cemy

2

George
Eliot
Ind Est

Centrovell
Ind Est

COVENTRY RD

Chilvers
Coton

CV10

THE
BRIDLEWAY

Centenary
Way

B4113

Hill
Top

Shepperton
Bsns Pk

Oak Wood
Prim & Sec Schs

All Saints CE
Prim Sch

George
Eliot Sch

LUTTERWORTH RD

B4114

1

90

35 A 36 B C 37 D E F

78 74

1 TEMPLAR CT
2 BLYTH CT
3 DUGDALE HO
4 CHILVERS CT
5 ALDERSGATE
6 STONELEIGH GDNS
7 EDWARD CT
8 STONELEIGH CT
9 LYDGATE CT

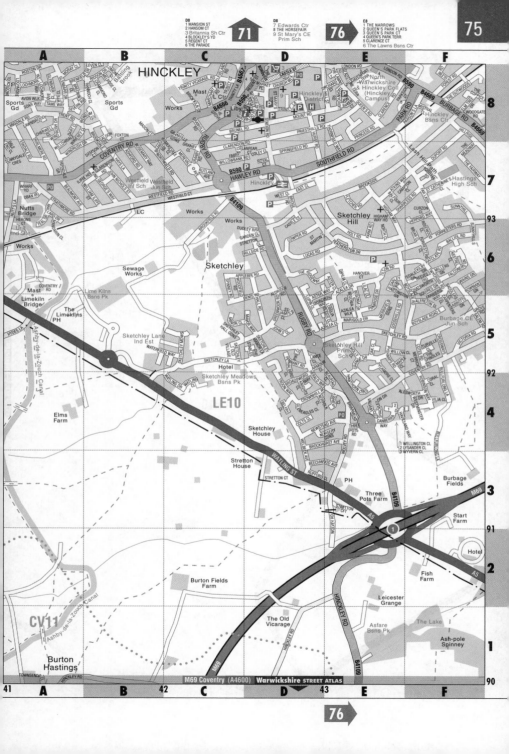

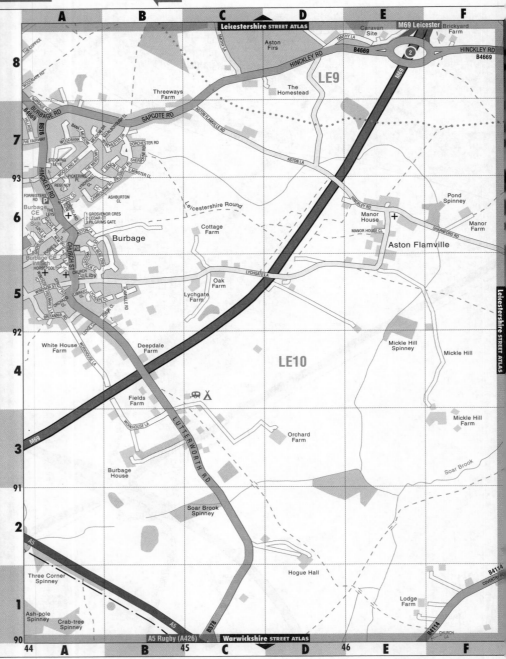

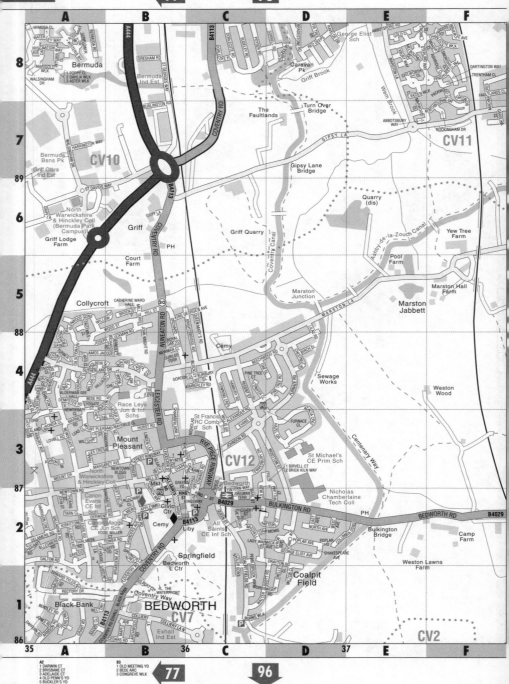

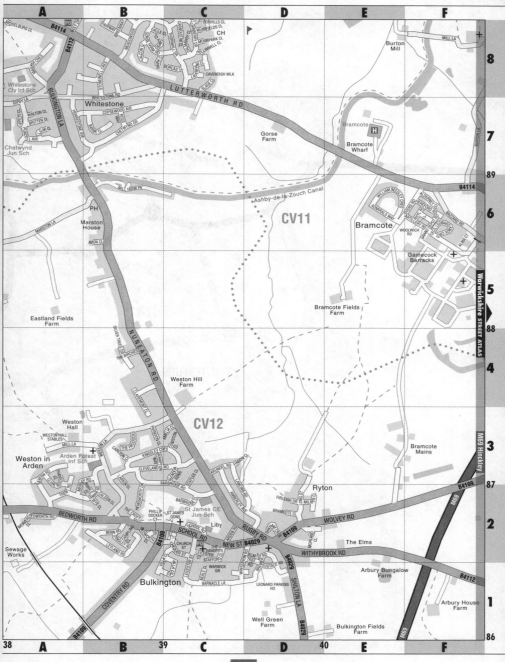

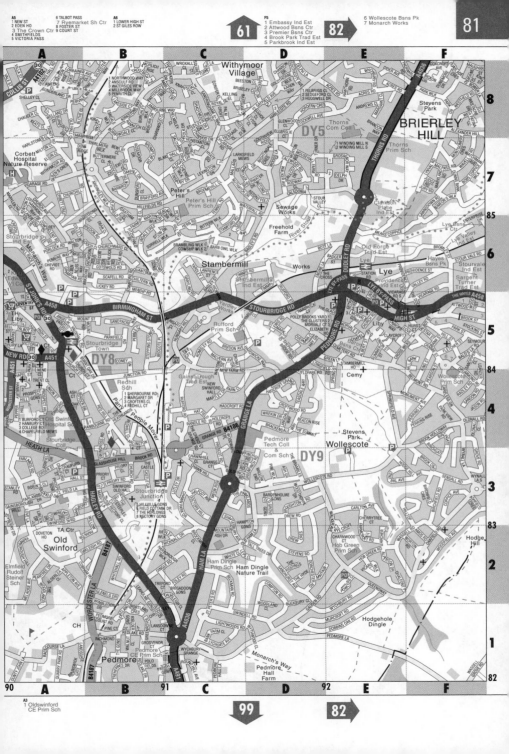

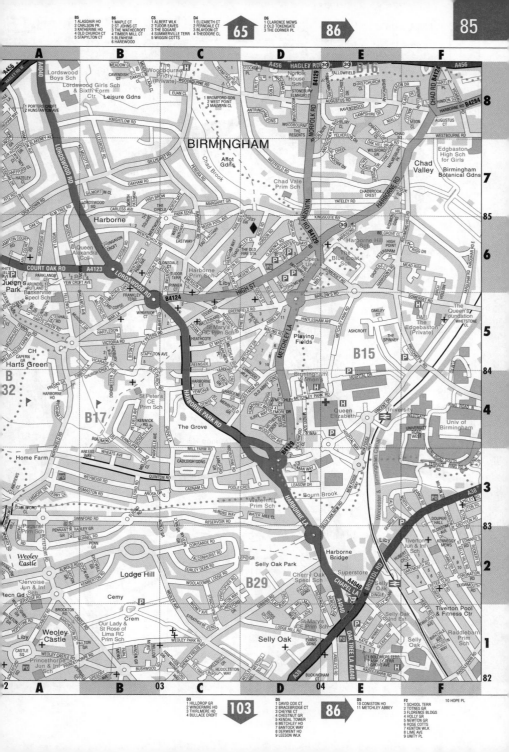

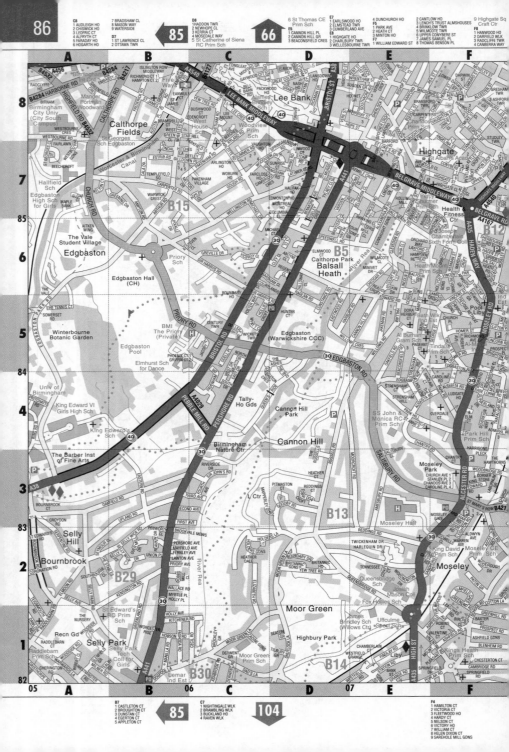

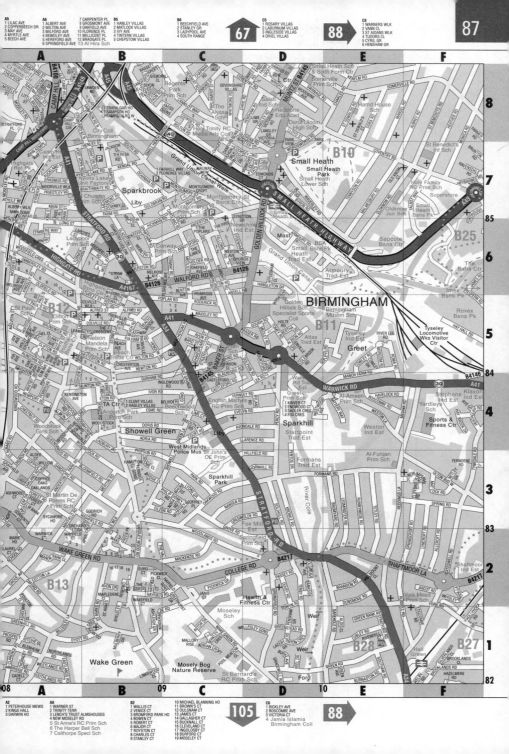

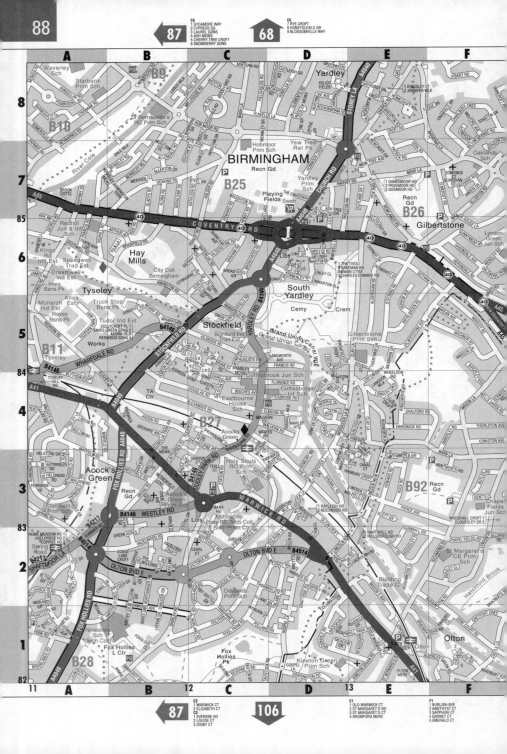

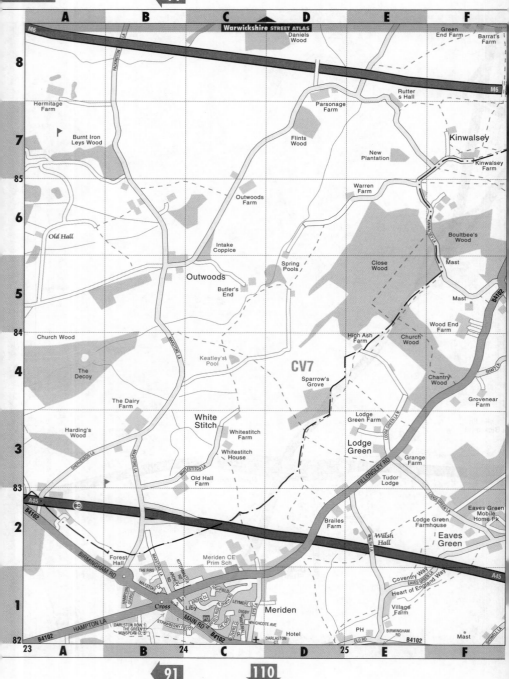

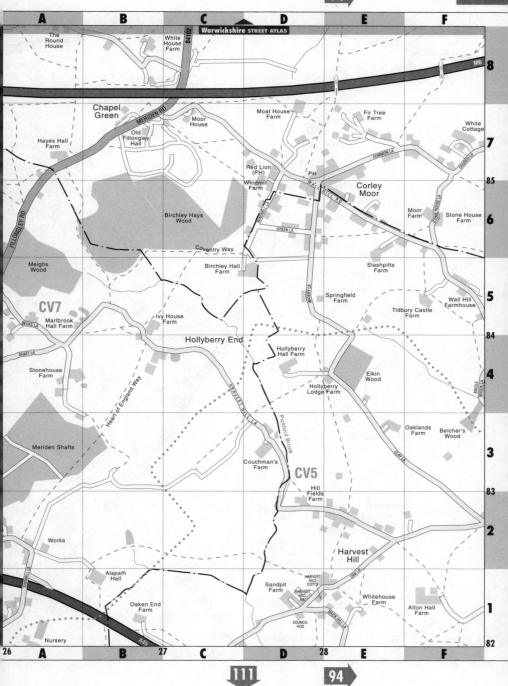

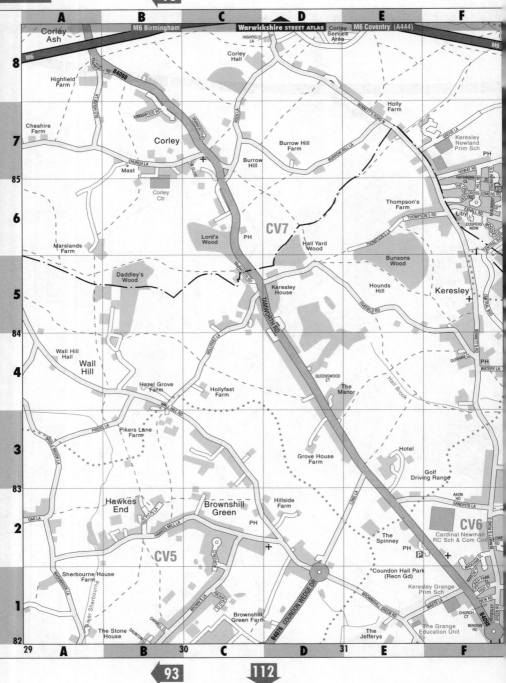

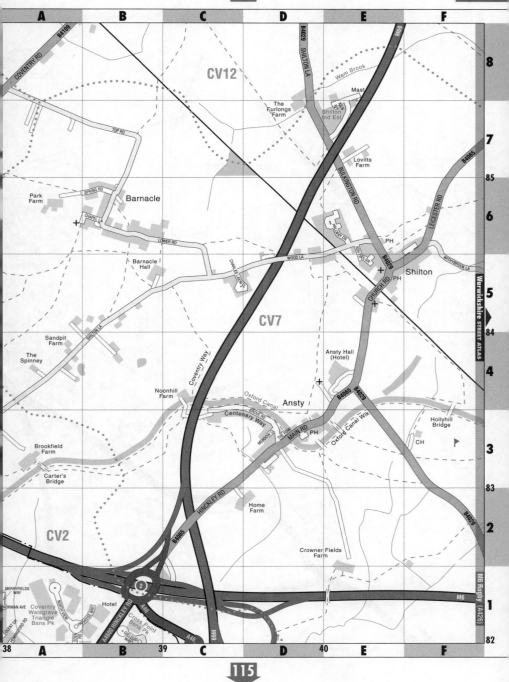

A   **B**   **C**   **D**   **E**   **F**

B4551

Dovehousefields Farm

Hunnington

Blue Bird Pk

Goodrest Farm

THE CLOSE

Breach Farm

RED HILL PK

Illeybrook Farm

Innage Farm   PH

Illey

Illey House Farm

Potters Farm

Lower Illey

Frankley Service Area

Warstohe Farm

8

81

7

Hollies Farm

Twiland Wood

Kettles Wood

Raven Hays Wood

6

Hunnington Farm

Horsepool Farm

Brookhouse Farm

Frankley Green La

Long Kettles Wood

5

Yew Tree Farm

PH

ST KENELM'S RD

Porch House Farm

Frankley On

B32

80

B62

Monarch's Way

LONGWOOD LA

Newbrook Farm

Romsley

St Kenelms CE Prim Sch

PH

Penny Fields

Yew Tree Farm

4

POPLAR LA

WINSTON RD

FORGE LA

Eli Wood

Dayhouse Wood

Long Saw Croft

Round Saw Croft

Yew Tree La

Frankley Hill Farm

Frankley Hill

POUND LA

FRANKLEY HILL LA

3

79

Romsley Manor Farm

Lower Hill Barn

EARLEY LA

Mast

PUTNEY LA

Newtown Farm

Sandhills Farm

NEWTOWN LA

B45

FABIAN CL

2

Romsley Hill

Mast

BISHOP CL 1
PRINCE CHARLES CL 2
PRINCESS ANNE DR 3
PRINCE EDWARD DR 4
FISHER CL 5

Holly Hill Methodist & CE Inf Sch

L Ctr

Frankley Comm High Sch

Liby

PD

Dayhouse Farm

DAYHOUSE LANE

OLD HOUSE LA

FORGE LANE

Gannow Green Farm

Gannow Green

Gannow Green La

Duck Pool Farm

North Worcestershire Path

Dayhouse Bank

PH

B4551

M5

CHAPMAN'S HILL

Waseley Hills Visitor Ctr

Waseley Hills Country Park

Heaside Jun Sch

BRYHER CL

NEW INNS LA

CROSS FARMS LA

RUBERY CT

78

1

A   **B**   97   **C**   **D**   98   **E**   **F**

F1
1 BROOKDALE CL
2 CHADDERSLEY CL
3 RUBERY LA S
4 HOLLY HILL
5 CALDY WLK

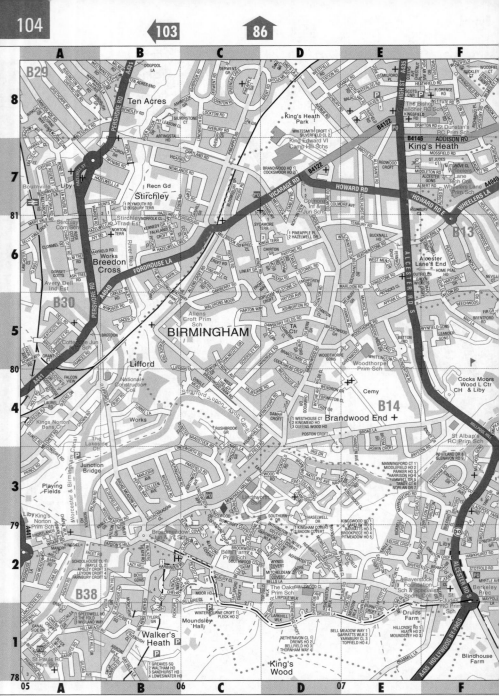

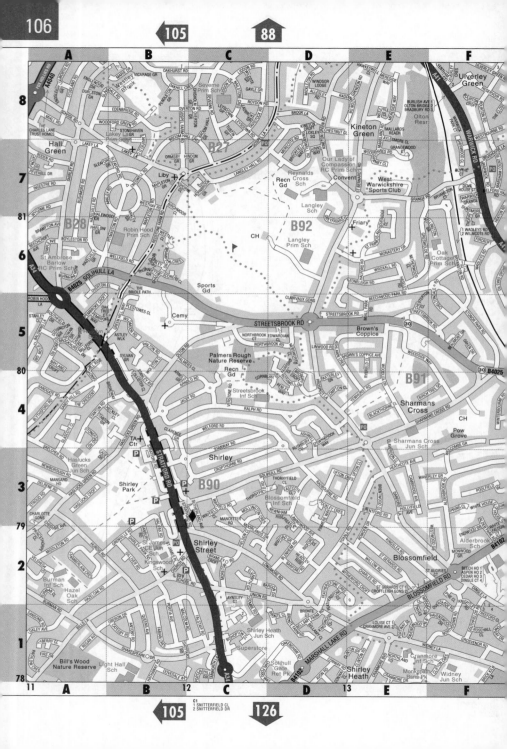

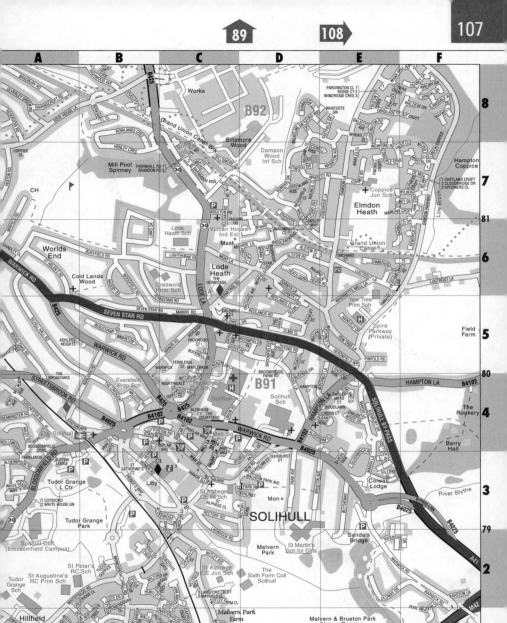

A1
1 BRADMORE CL
2 PINLEY WAY

B1
1 HABBERLEY CROFT
2 HAZELTON CL
3 ALDERTON CL
4 BRANTHILL CROFT
5 MAYTHORN GR
6 CRANFORD GR

C1
1 HILLFIELD HALL CT
2 MALTHOUSE MDW

C3
1 TOUCHWOOD SH CTR
2 CRESCENT ARC
3 LIBRARY SQ
4 MANOR WLK
5 WARWICK CT

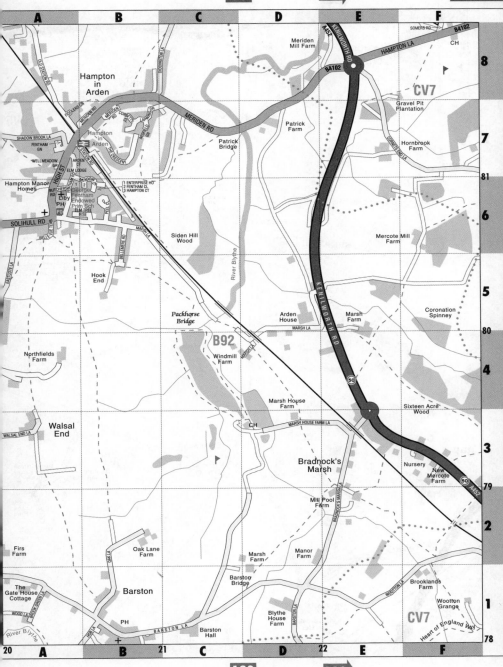

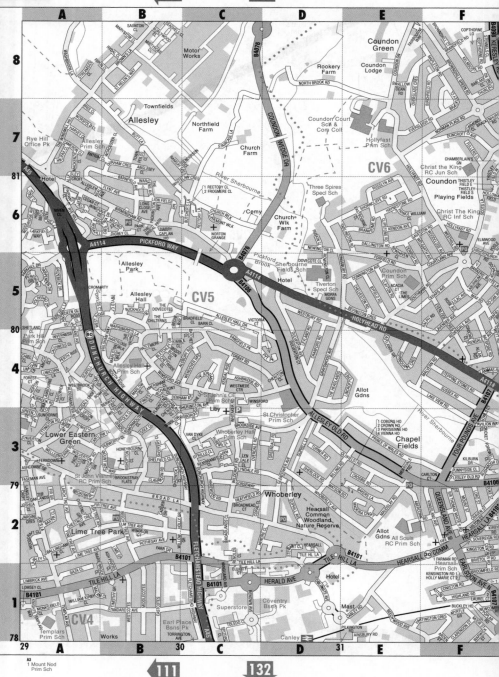

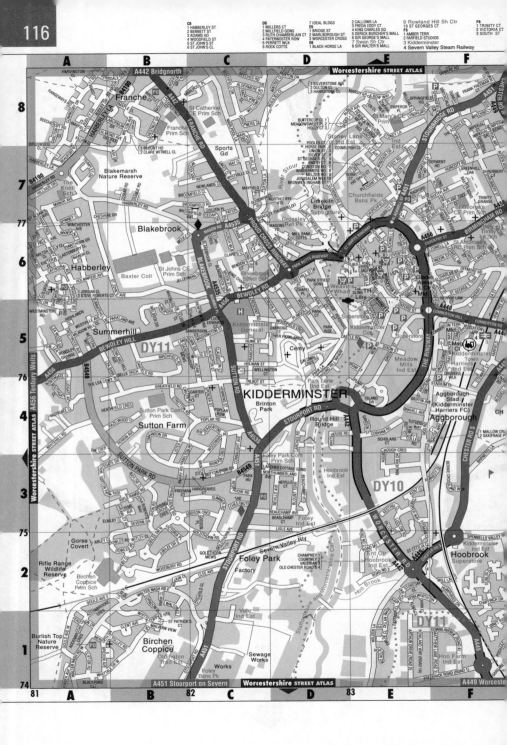

A5
1 THE HAWTHORNS
2 CHADDESLEY GDNS
3 SOMERLEYTON CT
4 COMBERTON MANS
5 COMBERTON CT

B6
1 MASEFIELD GDNS
2 GEORGE DANCE CL
3 KIPLING WLK
4 CHATTERTON WLK

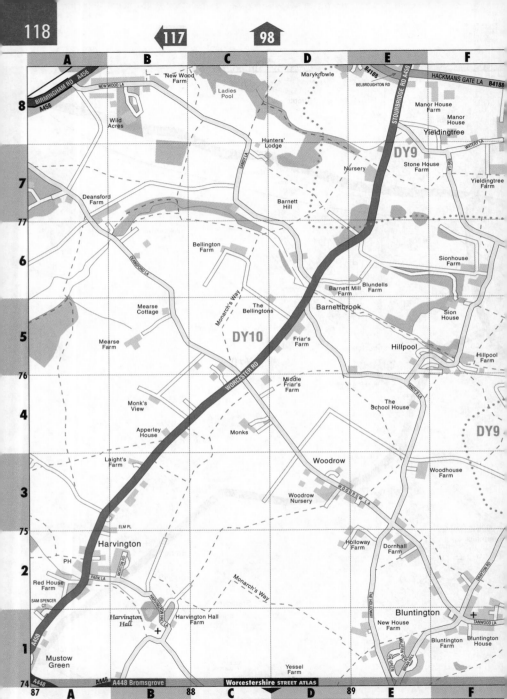

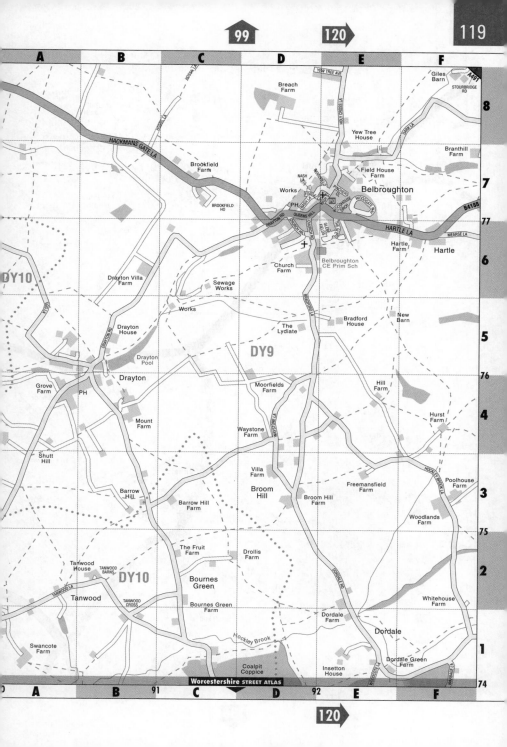

A6
1 HIMBLETON CROFT
2 SLIMBRIDGE CL
3 HIGHDOWN CRES
4 OLDERROW C
5 BELLINGTON CROFT
6 WESTGROVE AVE

B8
1 CHADBURY CROFT
2 LITTLEWOOD CL
3 HILLFIELD MEWS
4 MAYTHORN GR
5 GREYHURST CROFT
6 HUNNINGHAM GR

7 HILLFIELD RD
C8
1 CHIPSTONE CL
2 GLENFIELD CL
3 CHERRYWOOD CRES
4 LIBBARDS GATE
5 MERRINGTON CL

6 LITTLETON CROFT
7 THORNGROVE AVE

107

128

127

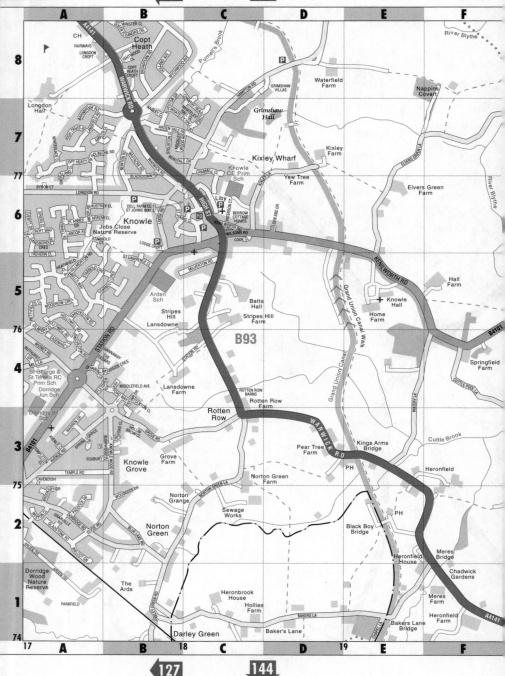

127
108

River Blythe

A4141

CH

FAIRWAYS
LONGDON
CROFT

Copt Heath

COPT HEATH CROFT

Grimshaw Villas

Waterfield Farm

Nappins Covert

Longdon Hall

Grimshaw Hall

Kixley Wharf

Kixley Farm

WARWICK RD

Knowle CE Prim Sch

Yew Tree Farm

Elvers Green Farm

River Blythe

BYRON CT

LONGDON RD

DELL FARM CL
ST JOHNS WAY

Knowle

Berrow Cottage Homes

Golden End La

Hall Farm

Jobs Close Nature Reserve

Knowle Hall

LODGE CROFT

Knowle Hall

Home Farm

KENILWORTH RD

B4101

ST LAWRENCE CL

MILVERTON RD

Arden Sch

Stripes Hill

Lansdowne

Batts Hall

Stripes Hill Farm

Grand Union Canal Walk

Grand Union Canal

B93

Springfield Farm

CUTTLE POOL LA

STATION RD

Lansdowne Farm

ROTTEN ROW BARNS

Rotten Row Farm

St George & St Teresa RC Prim Sch

Dorridge Jun Sch

Dorridge Inf Sch

WATERY LA

Rotten Row

WARWICK RD

Cuttle Brook

Kings Arms Bridge

Heronfield

B4101

TEMPLE RD

Knowle Grove

Grove Farm

Pear Tree Farm

PH

CAVENDISH CT

GRV GR

Norton Green Farm

PH

Heronfield House

Meres Bridge

Chadwick Gardens

Norton Green

Norton Grange

NORTON GREEN LA

Sewage Works

Black Boy Bridge

Dorridge Wood Nature Reserve

PARKFIELD

The Ards

Heronbrook House

Hollies Farm

BAKERS LA

Meres Farm

Heronfield Farm

A4141

Darley Green

Baker's Lane

Bakers Lane Bridge

127
144

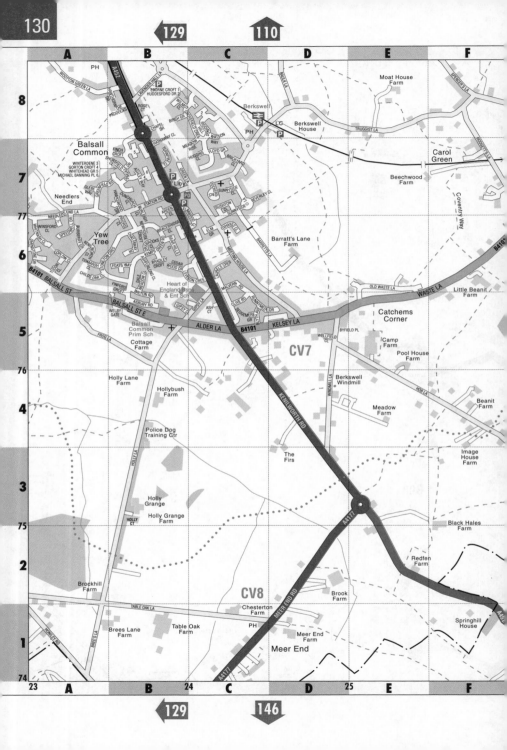

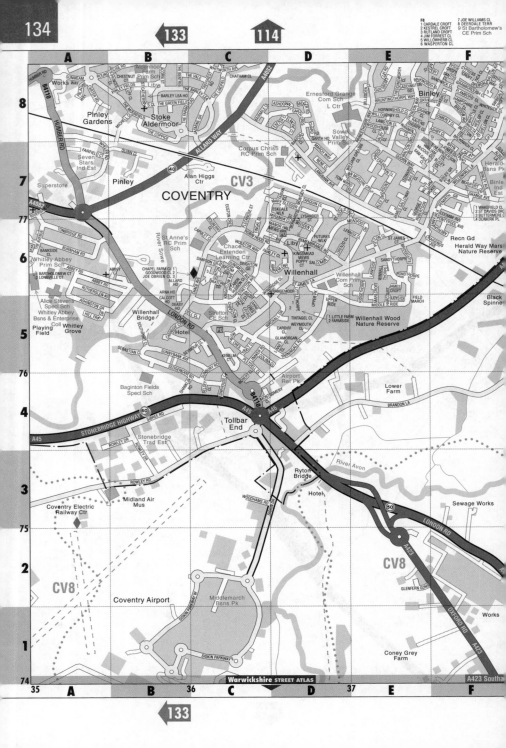

120

8

7

73

6

5

72

4

3

71

2

1

70

93 94 95

A B C D E F

Bournheath

Cottage
Farm

Yarnold Lane
Farm

Hilltop
Poultry Farm

Dodford

Holbourne
Wood

Valley
Farm

Hill
Farm

Sunnyhill
Coppice

Priory

PH

Worms Ash

Valley
Wood

The
Clock House

* Mast

Washingstocks
Farm

KEITH WINTER
CL

Monarch's Way

Forest
Farm

Dodford
Fst Sch

Crowfields
Farm

DODFORD
CT

Fockbury
Farm

Snakes
Lake

Fockbury Mill
Farm

Little
Dodford
Farm

B61

Perryfields

Sidemoor

Park
Farm

PH

Spout
House

Array
Fruit Farm

Sidemoor
Fst Sch

Battlefield
Farm

Park Gate

KIDDERMINSTER RD

Monsieurs
Hall

Red Cross

Red Cross
Farm

Warridge Lodge
Farm

Hotel

Monarch's Way

Sanders
Park

BROMSGROVE

Whitford
Farm

Bromsgrove
Sch

St John's CE
Mid Sch

Tickeridge
Farm

Cemy

Cemy

Millfields
Fst Sch

Bromsgrove Sch
(Senior Campus)

Bromsgrove Sch
(Prep Campus)

B60

150

Worcestershire STREET ATLAS A448 Kidderminster

A B C D E F

8
River Cole
The Poplars
Clowes Wood
Terry's Pool
THE MULTICHS
WOOD END LA
The Lakes
Terry's Green

Pound Close Farm
Forshaw Heath
Graves Coppice
Oaktree Farm Mobile Homes Pk
Yew Tree Farm
Forshaw Park Farm
White House Farm
Springbrook Farm
7
Checkley's Coppice
Woodside Pk Mobile Homes Pk
Glebe Farm
73
The Plantation
The Lyndons
Earlswood Trad Est
Small Lane Farm
Sewage Works
6
Rugby Football Ground
Spring Brook
M42

B48
Portway
Tyler's Grove
Windmill Naps
Ladbrookpark Coppice
B94
Poolhead Farm
5
Pool House Farm
72
Holly Farm
WHITEPITS LA
Cottage Farm
Little Ladbrooke Farm
Ladbrooke Hall
Ladbrooke Hall Farm
Wood End
B4101
4
Lion Wood
PENN LA
CH
PH

BROCKHILL LA
Brockhill Wood
High Park Farm
Rushbrook Farm
Rushbrook
Wood End
Hill Barn
3
BROAD LA
Gilbert's Green
71
Highpark Wood
Spring Brook
B98
Park Farm
2
Baylis Green
PH
Aspley Heath
Branson's Cross
BEOLEY LA
BROAD LA
Pinkfield Wood
BLIND LA
River Alne
1
Branson's Cross Farm
A435
Aspley Farm
Alderhanger Wood
B4101
70

8 A B 09 C D 10 E F

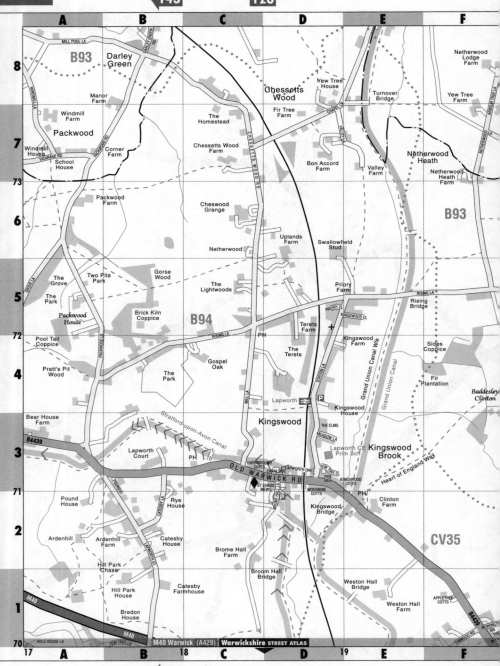

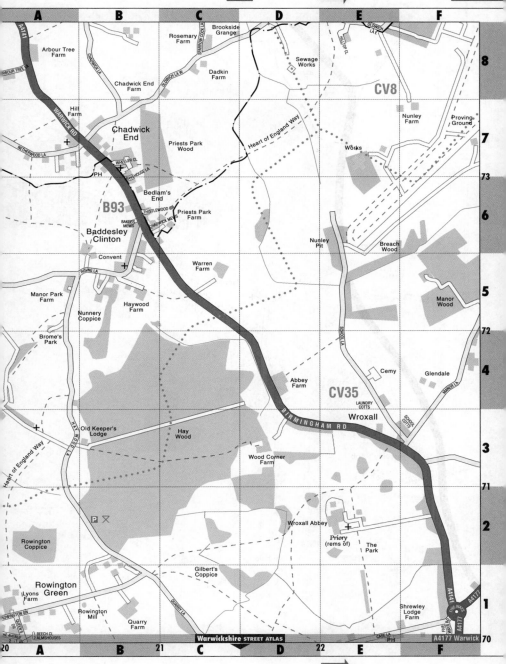

A   B   C   D   E   F

8

Arbour Tree Farm
Rosemary Farm
Brookside Grange
Sewage Works
OLDWICH LA E
HILLTOP PL
CV8

Chadwick End Farm
Dadkin Farm
Nunley Farm
Proving Ground

Hill Farm
7

Chadwick End
Priests Park Wood
Heart of England Way
Works

73

Bedlam's End
Priests Park Farm
Nunley Pit
Breach Wood
6

B93
Baddesley Clinton
BAKERS MEWS
THISTLEWOOD GR
CHADWICK MEWS

Convent
Warren Farm
Nunley Pit
Breach Wood

Manor Park Farm
Haywood Farm
Manor Wood
5

Nunnery Coppice
72

Brome's Park
SCHOOL LA
Cemy
Glendale
4

Abbey Farm
CV35
LAUNDRY COTTS

Old Keeper's Lodge
Hay Wood
BIRMINGHAM RD
Wroxall
SCHOOL COTTS
MANOR LA

Heart of England Way
3

Wood Corner Farm
71

P ✕
Wroxall Abbey
2

Rowington Coppice
Priory (rems of)
The Park

Gilbert's Coppice
A4177

Lyons Farm
Rowington Green
Shrewley Lodge Farm
1

Rowington Mill
Quarry Farm
BEECH CL
ALMSHOUSES
CASE LA
PH
A4177 Warwick
70

CV4

Westley
Bridge

Kingswood
House

Coventry Way

Crackley
Farm

Princes
Drive
Ind Est

Crackley
Cotts

Millburn
Grange

The
Dalehouse

Four
Winds

Crackley

Finham Brook

Ladyes
Hills

Crackley Hall
Sch

Kenilworth
Common
Nature Reserve

Common Lane
Ind Est

Dalehouse Lane
Ind Est

Centenary Way

Mill
End

THE CLOSE

Nature
Reserve

CH

Park Hill

South
Crest

Crew La

Park Hill
Jun Sch

PENRHYN
CL

Southcrest
Farm

Crewe
Gardens

KENILWORTH
CV8

St Nicholas
Com Prim Sch

Whitemoor

DENEMOOR

Crewe
Farm

Kenilworth Sch
& Sports Coll

Meadow Com
Sport Ctr

Woodside

B411

Bridge Works
Ind Est

Glasshouse
Wood

Thorns
Com Inf Sch

Grecian
Lodges

River Avon

Windy
Arbour

Stoneleigh
Abbey

Thornby Ave

Thickthorn
Mews

The
Grove

Thickthorn
Wood

Abbey
Farm

Oaklands
Ct

Leycester
Rd

Ashow

Grove Farm
House

Council La

Sunshine

Bullimore
Wood

River Avon

Wootton
Grange

Dial House
Farm

Bericote
Farm

CV32

E6
1 WAGGONERS CL
2 COUNTINGHOUSE WAY
3 KERRY HILL
4 MARTINGALE CL

F6
1 SUGARBROOK CT
2 Aston Fields Trad Est
3 Silver Birches Bsns Pk

151
138

151

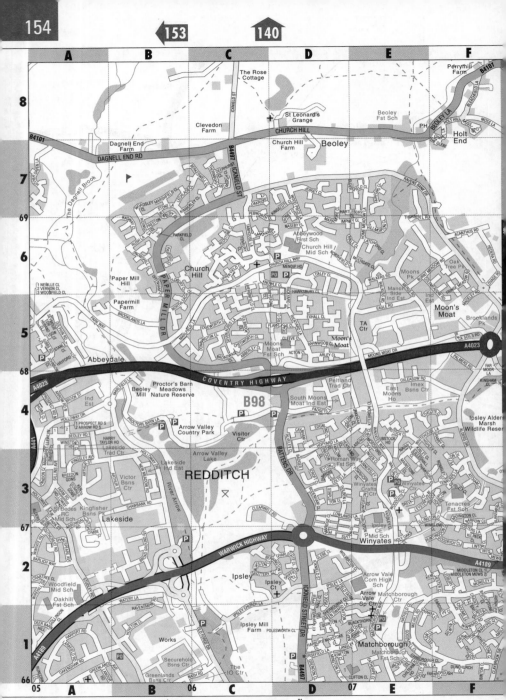

8

7

69

6

5

68

4

3

67

2

1

66

Warwickshire STREET ATLAS

Roundshill Farm

Abattoir

Camp Barn

Rouncil Farm

Woodcote Lodge

Little Woodcote

Bannerhill Farm

ROUNCIL LA

Goodrest Cottages

CV8

Leek Wootton

The Lunch

WALLER CL

Mast

Warwickshire (Police HQ)

WOODCOTE LA

QUARRY CL

MERRY FIELDS

WOODCOTE GR

PH

HOME FARM

Goodrest Farm

SPERRIN LA

Deer Park Farm

THE ELMS

Terrace Hill Wood

Stone Edge

THE HAYES

Larch Covert

DANGER AREA

CENTENARY WAY

Wootton Court

DANGER AREA

CH

Deer Park

Prospect Farm

CV35

Blacklow Hill

Gaveston's Cross

Wedgnock Old Park

Wedgnock Rifle Range

A46

Middle Woodloes

Blackbrake Plantation

Loes Farm

Woodloes Farm

WOODLOES LA

DWARRIS WLK

CV34

Woodloes Park

1 WEALE GR
2 SHELDON GR

Nursery

A429

WARWICK

WARWICK BY-PASS

Wedgnock Park Farm

CHANDERS RD

COVENTRY RD

Wedgnock Ind Est

Woodloes Prim Sch

Grand Union Canal Wlk

BIRMINGHAM RD

A4177

A46

Grand Union Canal

Ladbrook Park

155
148

D1
1 THE GRANGE MEWS
2 MILVERTON CRES
3 MILVERTON LODGE
4 MILVERTON CRES W
5 VODENA CT
6 GULISTAN CT
7 STUART CT
8 UPPER GROVE ST
9 GROVE ST

E1
1 MILVERTON CRES
2 GROSVENOR ST
3 LUNN POLY HO
4 POWERS CT
5 WATERLOO PL
6 CLARENCE TERR
7 CLARENCE HO
8 KILWORTH HO
9 THE CORNER HO

F1
1 BEAUCHAMP CT
2 GUY PL E
3 GUY PL
4 OXFORD PL
5 OXFORD ROW
6 WHITEHEADS CT
18 Royal Priors Sh Ctr

10 WINDSOR PL
11 BEDFORD ST
12 GUY PL W
13 GUY PL E
14 OXFORD PL
15 CHANDOS CT
16 OXFORD ROW
17 WHITEHEADS CT

19 ALVESTON PL
20 KENILWORTH ST
21 KIMMOND CT
22 GLADSTONE CT
F2
1 CLEVELAND CT
2 ARLINGTON CT
3 RIPLINGHAM
4 WHITE ROSE HO
5 ARLINGTON MEWS

6 WOOTTON CT
7 FININGS CT
8 PEMBROKE CT
9 BINSWOOD CT
10 ENGLAND HO
11 SAUNDERS HO
12 OAKFIELD HO
13 NORWOOD HO
14 BINSWOOD MANS
15 DORMER HO

153

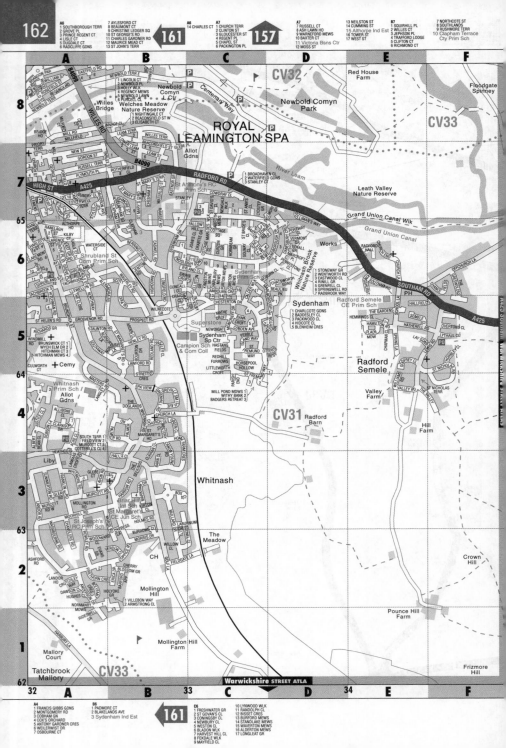

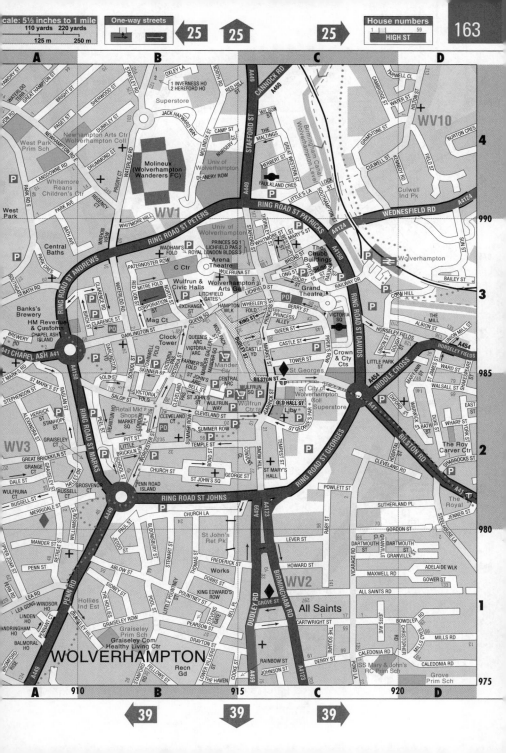

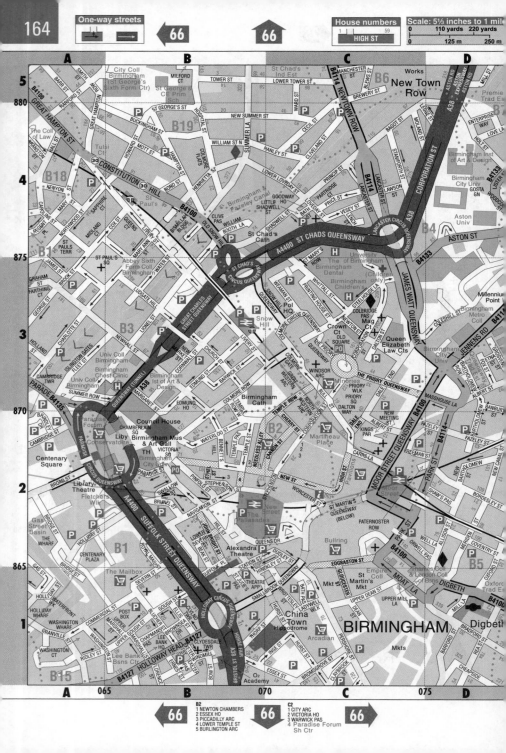

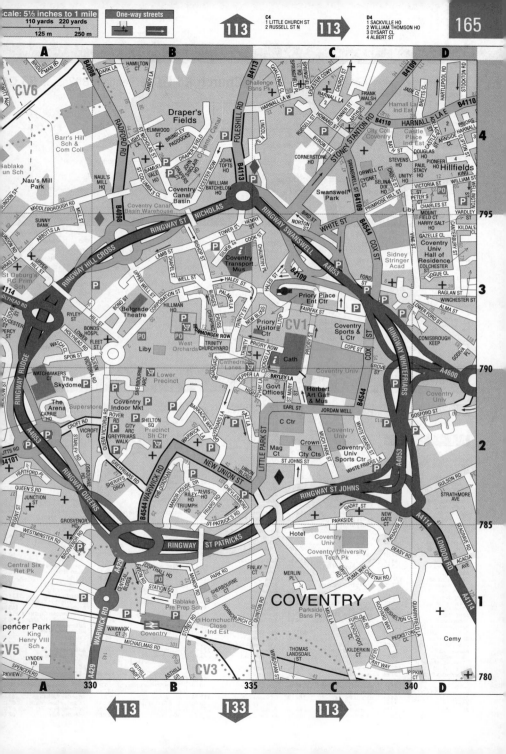

Index

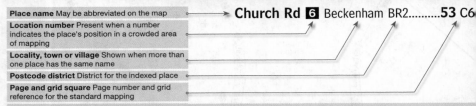

Place name May be abbreviated on the map

Location number Present when a number indicates the place's position in a crowded area of mapping

Locality, town or village Shown when more than one place has the same name

Postcode district District for the indexed place

Page and grid square Page number and grid reference for the standard mapping

Church Rd **6** Beckenham BR2........**53** C6

Cities, towns and villages are listed in CAPITAL LETTERS

Public and commercial buildings are highlighted in magenta   Places of interest are highlighted in blue with a star★

Abbreviations used in the index

Acad	Academy	Comm	Common	Gd	Ground	L	Leisure	Prom	Promenade
App	Approach	Cott	Cottage	Gdn	Garden	La	Lane	Rd	Road
Arc	Arcade	Cres	Crescent	Gn	Green	Liby	Library	Recn	Recreation
Ave	Avenue	Cswy	Causeway	Gr	Grove	Mdw	Meadow	Ret	Retail
Bglw	Bungalow	Ct	Court	H	Hall	Meml	Memorial	Sh	Shopping
Bldg	Building	Ctr	Centre	Ho	House	Mkt	Market	Sq	Square
Bsns, Bus	Business	Ctry	Country	Hospl	Hospital	Mus	Museum	St	Street
Bvd	Boulevard	Cty	County	HQ	Headquarters	Orch	Orchard	Sta	Station
Cath	Cathedral	Dr	Drive	Hts	Heights	Pal	Palace	Terr	Terrace
Cir	Circus	Dro	Drove	Ind	Industrial	Par	Parade	TH	Town Hall
Cl	Close	Ed	Education	Inst	Institute	Pas	Passage	Univ	University
Cnr	Corner	Emb	Embankment	Int	International	Pk	Park	Wk, Wlk	Walk
Coll	College	Est	Estate	Intc	Interchange	Pl	Place	Wr	Water
Com	Community	Ex	Exhibition	Junc	Junction	Prec	Precinct	Yd	Yard

Index of towns, villages, streets, hospitals, industrial estates, railway stations, schools, shopping centres, universities and places of interest

166 3b B−Add

3b Bsns Village The B21 . . **65** D7

A

A1 Trad Est B66. . . . . **65** A7
Aaron Ct B24 . . . . **56** F3
Abberley B77 . . . . **22** C2
Abberley Cl
 Halesowen B63 . . . . **82** F2
 Redditch B98 . . . . **154** C5
Abberley Ind Ctr B66 . . . . . **65** D5
Abberley Rd
 Birmingham B68 . . . . **84** B8
 Dudley DY3 . . . . **50** D4
Abberley St
 Dudley DY2 . . . . **62** C8
 Smethwick B66 . . . . **65** D5
Abberton Cl B63 . . . . **83** C3
Abberton Ct B83 . . . . **56** C2
Abberton Gr B90. . . . . **127** B7
Abberton Ho **4** B97. . . **153** A4
Abberton Way CV4. . . . . . **132** E3
Abbess Gr B25. . . . . **68** E1
Abbey CE Inf Sch CV11. . . **73** B5
Abbey Cl
 Bromsgrove B60 . . . . **137** C2
 West Bromwich B71 . . . . . **53** C5
Abbey Cres
 Halesowen B63 . . . . **82** D4
 Oldbury B68. . . . . **64** D1
Abbey Ct CV3 . . . . **134** B6
ABBEYDALE **153** F5
Abbeydale Cl CV3. . . . . . **114** F2
Abbeydale Rd B31 . . . . . . **103** A2
Abbey Dr WS3 . . . . **15** A5
Abbey End CV8 . . . . **147** F4
Abbeyfield Ho WV11 . . . . . **26** D5
Abbeyfield Rd
 Birmingham B23 . . . . **56** E8
 Wolverhampton WV10 . . **11** F4
ABBEY FIELDS **147** E5
Abbeyfields Dr B80 . . . . . **159** E6
Abbey Fields Swimming Pool
 CV8. . . . . **147** E5
Abbeygate Sh Ctr CV11. . . **73** C4
Abbey Gdns B67 . . . . **64** E1
Abbey Gn CV11 . . . . **73** B5
Abbey Hill CV8. . . . . **147** F5
Abbey Ind Est CV2 . . . . . **114** F5

Abbey Inf Sch B67 . . . . **64** E2
Abbey Jun Sch B67 . . . . . . **64** E1
Abbey Mans 2 B24 . . . . . **57** B6
Abbey Prim Sch WS3. . . . **13** E2
Abbey RC Prim Sch B23. . **57** A5
Abbey Rd
 Birmingham B67 . . . . **85** D5
 Birmingham, Gravelly Hill
 B23. . . . . **56** D2
 Coventry CV3. . . . . **134** A6
 Dudley, Gornalwood DY3 . . **50** C3
 Dudley, Netherton DY2 . . . **62** D6
 Halesowen B63 . . . . **82** C4
 Kidderminster DY11. . . . . **116** A6
 Redditch B97 . . . . **153** E4
 Smethwick B67 . . . . **64** E1
 Tamworth B77 . . . . **21** D3
Abbey Sixth Form Coll
 Birmingham B3. . . . . **164** A3
Abbey Sq WS3 . . . . **13** E2
Abbey St
 Birmingham B18 . . . . **66** A5
 Cannock WS12. . . . . **2** B7
 Dudley DY3 . . . . **50** C3
 Nuneaton CV11 . . . . **73** B5
Abbey Stadium Sports Ctr
 B97. . . . . **153** E6
Abbey Street N B18 . . . . . **66** A5
Abbey The CV8 . . . . **147** F5
Abbey Theatre CV11. . . . . **73** B4
Abbey Trad Ind Area
 B97. . . . . **153** E5
Abbey Way CV3 . . . . **133** F6
Abbeywood Fst Sch B98 **154** D6
Abbot Rd B63. . . . . **100** C8
Abbotsbury Cl CV2 . . . . . **115** A4
Abbotsbury Way CV11. . . . **78** E7
Abbots Cl
 Dorridge B93 . . . . **128** A7
 Walsall WS4. . . . . **29** C6
Abbotsfield Sch WS11. . . . . **1** E5
Abbotsford Ave B43. . . . . . **43** F2
Abbotsford Dr DY1. . . . . . . **61** E7
Abbotsford Rd
 Birmingham B11. . . . . **87** C6
 Lichfield WS14. . . . . **9** E7
 Nuneaton CV11 . . . . **73** E1
Abbotsford Sch CV8. . . . . **147** F6
Abbots Mews CV5. . . . . . . **61** D1
Abbots Rd B14. . . . . **104** E7
Abbots Way
 Birmingham B18 . . . . **66** B6
 Warwick CV34. . . . . **160** D6

Abbots Way continued
 Wolverhampton WV3 . . . . . **24** E1
Abbotts Gn LE10 . . . . **75** F5
Abbotts La CV1 . . . . **165** A3
Abbotts Pl WS3 . . . . **14** D1
Abbotts Rd B24. . . . . **56** F1
Abbotts St
 4 Royal Leamington Spa
 CV31. . . . . **161** F7
 Walsall WS3. . . . . **14** D2
Abbotts Wlk CV3. . . . . . . **135** C7
Abdon Ave B29 . . . . **103** C7
Abelia B77 . . . . **21** F3
Abercorn Rd CV5 . . . . **112** E2
Aberdeen Cl CV5 . . . . **112** A5
Aberdeen Rd CV11 . . . . . . **73** E1
Aberdeen St B18. . . . . **65** E4
Aberford Cl WV12 . . . . **27** D4
Abergavenny Wlk CV3. . . **134** F6
Abigails Cl B26 . . . . **89** B7
Abingdon Cl WV1 . . . . **26** B2
Abingdon Rd
 Birmingham B23 . . . . **56** B7
 Dudley DY2 . . . . **62** D3
 Walsall WS3. . . . . **13** F2
 Wolverhampton WV1. . . . . **26** B2
Abingdon Way
 Birmingham B35 . . . . **58** A3
 Nuneaton CV11 . . . . **73** F7
 Walsall WS3. . . . . **13** F2
Ablewell St WS1 . . . . **28** F1
Ablow St WV2 . . . . **163** B1
Abnalls La WS13 . . . . **8** B8
Abnalls Dr WV4 . . . . **39** F1
Abney Gr B44 . . . . **45** B2
Aboyne Cl B5 . . . . **86** D6
Abu Bakr Boys Sch WS2. . **28** E5
Abu Bakr Girls Sch WS1 . . **42** D8
Acacia Ave
 Birmingham B37 . . . . **69** F6
 Coventry CV1 . . . . **113** E1
 Walsall WS5. . . . . **43** A4
Acacia Cl
 Birmingham B37 . . . . **69** F6
 Dudley DY1 . . . . **51** A3
 Tipton B69. . . . . **52** B2
Acacia Cres CV8. . . . . **10** B4
Acacia Ct
 Coventry CV6. . . . . **112** C5
 Stourbridge DY8 . . . . **80** E6
Acacia Gr WS12. . . . . **2** F3

Acacia Rd
 Birmingham B30 . . . . **103** E8
 Nuneaton CV10 . . . . **72** E5
 Royal Leamington Spa
 CV32. . . . . **156** D1
Academy Dr CV34. . . . . . **160** B3
Acambus Rd B98 . . . . **154** F6
Accord Mews **2** WS10 . . . **41** D7
Ace Bsns Pk B33. . . . . **69** D2
Acfold Rd B20 . . . . **54** E5
Achal Cl CV6. . . . . **95** F2
Acheson Rd B28, B90 . . . . **105** F3
Achilles Cl WS6. . . . . **4** F1
Achilles Cl CV34 . . . . **161** F2
Achilles Rd CV6. . . . . **114** A7
Ackleton Gdns WV3 . . . . . . **38** F7
Ackleton Gr B29 . . . . **84** F1
ACOCK'S GREEN **88** B3
Acocks Green Prim Sch
 B27. . . . . **88** B3
Acocks Green Sta B27 . . . **88** C4
Acorn Cl
 Bedworth CV12 . . . . **95** C8
 Birmingham, Bournville
 B30. . . . . **103** E8
 Birmingham, Stockfield B27 **88** B5
 Cannock WS11. . . . . **2** C2
 Great Wyrley WS6 . . . . **5** A1
 Stoneleigh CV8 . . . . **149** B7
 West Bromwich B70 . . . . . **53** B2
Acorn Ct
 Birmingham B45 . . . . **122** D7
 Coventry CV2 . . . . **114** C2
 1 Royal Leamington Spa
 CV32. . . . . **157** A2
Acorn Ctr **1** WS1 . . . . **28** F1
Acorn Gdns B30 . . . . **104** A7
Acorn Gr
 Birmingham B1 . . . . **66** B3
 Stourbridge DY8 . . . . **60** E1
Acorn Rd
 Catshill B61. . . . . **137** B8
 Halesowen B62 . . . . **83** C8
 Wolverhampton WV11. . . . **13** A1
Acorn St
 Coventry CV3. . . . . **134** B8
 Willenhall WV13 . . . . **27** C2
Acorn Starter Units WS7 . . **6** D7
Acorns The B61. . . . . **137** A8
Acorn View WS7 . . . . **7** C6
Acre Cl CV31. . . . . **162** A4
Acre La B97 . . . . **152** E2
Acre Rise WV12. . . . . **27** B5

Acres Rd DY5. . . . . **81** E8
Acres The WV3 . . . . **24** C7
Acton Cl B98 . . . . **154** D5
Acton Dr DY3 . . . . **50** B3
Acton Gr
 Bilston WV14 . . . . **40** B4
 Birmingham B44 . . . . **45** A2
Acton Ho CV4. . . . . **111** F3
Adam Ct
 Cannock WS11. . . . . **1** D3
 Halesowen B63 . . . . **82** F4
Adam Rd **1** CV6 . . . . **113** F7
Adams Brook Dr B32. . . . . **84** B3
Adams Cl
 Smethwick B66 . . . . **64** D7
 Tipton DY4 . . . . **40** F1
Adams Ct DY10 . . . . **117** A4
Adams Hill B32 . . . . **84** B3
Adam's Hill DY9 . . . . **99** E4
Adams Ho **3** B47 . . . . . . **116** C6
Adamson Cl WS11 . . . . **1** B3
Adams Rd
 Brownhills WS8 . . . . **16** B5
 Wolverhampton WV3. . . . . **38** C6
Adams St
 Birmingham B7 . . . . **66** F5
 Walsall WS2. . . . . **28** C2
 West Bromwich B70 . . . . . **53** B3
Adam St DY11 . . . . **116** C2
Ada Rd
 Birmingham B25 . . . . **88** B4
 Smethwick B66 . . . . **65** B1
Ada Wrighton Cl WV12 . . . **27** C2
Adcock Dr CV8 . . . . **148** B5
Addenbrooke Cres DY11. **116** A1
Addenbrooke Dr B73. . . . . **46** B2
Addenbrooke Pl WS10 . . . **41** D2
Addenbrooke Rd
 Keresley CV7 . . . . **95** A6
 Smethwick B67 . . . . **64** F1
Addenbrooke St
 Darlaston WS10. . . . . **41** D2
 Walsall WS3. . . . . **28** C2
Addenbrook Ho
 3 Cradley Heath B64. . . **82** F8
 Sutton Coldfield B73 . . . . **146** B5
Addenbrook Way DY4. . . . **52** D2
Addenbrooke Gdns B8. . . . **67** D5
Adderley Park Cl B8 . . . . . **67** E4
Adderley Park Sta B8 . . . . **67** D5
Adderley Prim Sch B8 . . . **67** D4
Adderley Rd B8. . . . . **67** D4

Adderley Road S B8...... 67 C3
Adderley St
  Birmingham B9 .... 67 A1
  Coventry CV1............ 113 E4
Adderley Trad Est 2 B8 . . 67 C4
Addingham Cl 2 CV34 . . 155 E1
Addington Way B69...... 52 D3
Addison Cl
  Cannock WS11........... 1 E5
  Nuneaton CV10 .... 72 A5
  Wednesbury WS10 ...... 42 E2
Addison Croft DY3 ...... 50 A5
Addison Gr WV11 .... 12 B1
Addison Pl
  Bilston WV14........... 41 A7
  Water Orton B46........ 59 B3
Addison Rd
  Birmingham, King's Heath
   B14 .... 104 F7
  Birmingham, Nechells B7 . 67 C8
  Brierley Hill DY5 .... 61 B2
  Coventry CV6........... 113 A8
  Wednesbury WS10 ...... 42 E2
  Wolverhampton WV3..... 38 F8
Addison St WS10........ 41 F2
Adelaide Ave B70........ 53 A7
Adelaide Ct 3 CV12.... 78 A2
Adelaide Dr B12......... 2 F3
Adelaide Rd CV31, CV32 . 161 E8
Adelaide St
  Birmingham B12 .... 86 F8
  Brierley Hill DY5 .... 61 D3
  Coventry CV1........... 165 D4
  Redditch B97............153 D4
Adelaide Tower B34 ..... 69 C5
Adelaide Wlk WV2 ......163 D1
Adelphi Ct 8 DY5...... 61 D2
Adey Rd WV11 .... 26 F8
Adkins La B67 .... 65 A1
Admington Rd B33...... 89 C8
Admiral Gdns CV8 ...... 148 C6
Admiral Parker Dr WS14 . 17 F5
Admiral Pl B13 .... 86 F4
Admirals Way
  Bramcote CV11 .... 79 E6
  Rowley Regis B65 .... 63 B2
Admiral Wlk DY10...... 116 E8
Adonis Cl B79 .... 21 C7
Adrian Croft B13........ 87 C1
Adrian Ct 8 B24....... 57 B6
Adria Rd B11 .... 87 B4
Adshead Rd DY2........ 62 C7
Adstone Gr B31......... 103 A1
Advance Bsns Pk WS11.... 2 B3
Advanced Tech Unit
  CV4 .... 132 C6
Advent Gdns B70 .... 53 B3
Adwalton Rd WV6....... 23 F3
Aethelred Ct WV6....... 25 C6
Affleck Ave B78......... 20 D1
Agenoria Dr DY8........ 80 F5
AGGBOROUGH 116 C4
Aggborough Cres DY10. . 116 E3
Aggborough Stadium
  (Kidderminster Harriers
  FC) DY10............... 116 F4
Agincourt Rd
  Coventry CV3........... 133 E7
  Lichfield WS14.......... 9 A5
Agmore La B60.........138 B3
Agmore Rd B60.........138 B4
Aiden Ct WS13.......... 9 C7
Aimsbury Ct B26........ 89 C4
Ainsbury Rd CV5........132 E8
Ainsdale Cl
  Coventry CV6........... 96 B4
  Stourbridge DY8 .... 80 F2
Ainsdale Gdns
  Birmingham B24 .... 57 C5
  Halesowen B63 .... 82 D2
Ainsworth Rd
  5 Birmingham B31......103 D2
  Wolverhampton WV10.... 11 E4
Aintree Cl
  Bedworth CV12......... 78 B4
  Cannock WS12........... 2 F6
  Coventry CV6........... 113 E5
  Kidderminster DY11.....116 D8
  Upper Catshill B61......121 A1
Aintree Dr CV32........157 C3
Aintree Gr B34.......... 69 D6
Aintree Rd WV10....... 11 A6
Aintree Way DY1........ 50 F2
Aire Croft B31.......... 103 B1
Airfield Dr WS4, WS9 ... 29 E3
Airport Ret Pk CV3......134 D4
Airport Way B26........ 90 C3
Aitken Cl B78........... 21 A2
Aitken Wlk B15......... 86 A6
Ajax Cl WS6 .... 4 F1
Akon Ho CV6 .... 94 F2
Akrill Cl B70........... 53 B5
Akrill Cottage Hos The
  B70 .... 53 B5
Alameda Gdns WV6...... 24 E6
Al-ameen Prim Sch B11 . 87 E4
Alamein Rd WV13....... 26 E1
Alamein Way WV14 ..... 9 A5
Alan Bray Cl LE10....... 74 D7
Alandale Ave CV5.......111 E4
Alandale Ct CV12....... 95 C8
Alan Higgs Ctr CV3 ....134 C7
Alan Higgs Way CV4 ....131 C8
Alasdair Ho 1 B15..... 85 B5
Albany Cl DY10 ....117 B6
Albany Cres WV14 ...... 40 C6

Albany Ct
  1 Birmingham B62......84 A7
  Coventry CV1............113 A2
Albany Dr WS12.........2 E3
Albany Gdns B91........107 E4
Albany Gr
  Kingswinford DY6 ....60 E7
  Willenhall WV11 ....13 C1
Albany Ho B34...........69 A7
Albany Mews WS10 ...... 41 E6
Albany Rd
  Birmingham B17 ....85 C6
  Coventry CV5...........113 A1
Albany Terr CV32 ....156 E1
Albemarle Rd DY8 ......80 F2
Albermarle Rd DY6...... 61 A5
Albert Ave 1 B12...... 87 A6
Albert Bean Cl CV31.....162 A4
Albert Bradbeer Prim Sch
  B31 ....122 F7
Albert Cl B80...........159 E4
Albert Clarke Dr WV12 . . 27 C7
Albert Cres CV6........95 B3
Albert Davie Dr WS12 ... 2 E4
Albert Dr B63...........82 F2
Albert Fearn Gdns CV6 . . 95 F1
Albert Ho 1 WS10......41 C6
Albert Pritchard Inf Sch
  WS10 ....42 A5
Albert Rd
  Allesley CV5............111 A8
  Birmingham, Aston B6.... 66 F8
  Birmingham, Gravelly Hill B68, B84 C8
  Birmingham, Gravelly Hill
   B23 ....56 D3
  Birmingham, Handsworth
   B21 ....54 E1
  Birmingham, Harborne B17. 85 B5
  Birmingham, King's Heath
   B14 ....104 F7
  Birmingham, Stechford B33. 68 D3
  Bromsgrove B61 ....150 E8
  Fazeley B78 ....35 A8
  Halesowen B63 ....82 F3
  Hinckley LE10 ....71 D1
  Kidderminster DY10.....116 F6
  Tamworth B79 ....21 B5
  Wolverhampton WV6..... 25 A3
Albert Smith Pl B65.....63 A4
Albert St
  Birmingham B5 ....164 D3
  Brierley Hill DY5 ....61 D7
  Cannock, Broomhill WS11 . 1 E4
  Cannock WS12...........2 D5
  Coventry CV1...........113 E4
  4 Coventry CV1.......165 D4
  Kingswinford DY6 ......60 B8
  Nuneaton CV10 ....72 E3
  Oldbury B69............54 A8
  Redditch B97............153 E5
  Royal Leamington Spa
   CV32 ....156 C1
  Stourbridge DY8 ....80 F5
  Stourbridge, Lye DY9....81 E5
  Tipton DY4.............51 F8
  Walsall WS1............28 E2
  Warwick CV34...........160 D7
  Wednesbury WS10 ......41 F2
  West Bromwich B70 .....53 C1
Albion Par B66 ....60 B8
Albion Pl WS11 ....1 E4
Albion Rd
  Birmingham, Handsworth
   B21 ....54 E1
  Birmingham, Sparkhill B11. 87 D5
  Brownhills WS8 ....15 E8
  West Bromwich B70 .....53 A2
  West Bromwich, Sandwell
   B71...................65 B8
Albion Rdbt B70.........53 B4
Albion St
  Bilston WV14...........40 E6
  Birmingham B1 ....66 C3
  Brierley Hill DY5 ....61 D3
  Kenilworth CV8 ....148 A5
  Kingswinford DY6 ......60 B8
  Oldbury B69............52 E1
  Tamworth B79 ....21 C5
  Willenhall WV13 ....27 C2
  Wolverhampton WV1.....163 D3
Albion Terr B46.........59 B3
Albion Works DY5.......61 B3
Alborn Cres B38........122 D8
Albrighton Ho 4 B20.. 54 F3
Albrighton Rd B63......82 F3
Albrighton Wlk CV11.... 74 A2
Alburh Gram Sch B12.. 86 E5
Albury Rd B80...........159 E4
Albury Wlk B11.........87 A7
Albutts Rd WS11........6 B3
Alcester Dr
  Sutton Coldfield B73.... 45 D3
  Willenhall WV13 ....26 D1

Alcester Gdns B14 ...... 104 F7
Alcester Highway B98... 158 F8
Alcester Rd
  Birmingham B13 .... 86 F3
  Finstall B60 .... 137 F1
  Hollywood B47......... 124 F5
  Lickey End B60..........137 D5
  Portway B47, B48 ...... 140 F7
  Studley B80 .... 159 E3
  Tardebigge B60, B97 ... 152 B7
Alcester Road S
  Birmingham B47 .... 125 A8
  Birmingham, Billesley Common
   B14 .... 104 E6
  Birmingham, Highter's Heath
   B14 .... 104 F2
Alcester St
  Birmingham B12 .... 86 F8
  Redditch B98........... 153 E4
Alcombe Gr B33........ 68 E2
Alcott Cl B93 .... 127 F2
Alcott Gr B33.......... 69 E3
Alcott Hall Prim Sch B37. 70 B1
Alcott La B37........... 89 F8
Alcott Wood Nature
  Reserve* B37.......... 70 A1
Alcove The WS3 .... 14 D2
Aldbourgh La 4 B97... 153 B5
Aldbourne Rd CV1 ..... 113 C5
Aldbourne Way B38.... 123 E7
Aldbury Rd B14 .... 105 A3
Aldbury Rise CV5 ...... 112 C4
Aldeburgh Cl WS3 ..... 14 A3
Aldeford Dr DY5 .... 81 D8
Aldeney Cl DY1 .... 51 E3
Alden Hurst WS7....... 6 D8
Alder Ave DY10 .... 116 E8
Alderbrook Cl
  Redditch B97........... 153 B5
  Sedgley DY3............ 39 B1
Alderbrooke Dr CV11... 74 A1
Alderbrook Rd B91..... 106 F3
Alderbrook Sch B91 ... 106 F2
Alder Carr Cl B98 ...... 158 F8
Alder Cl
  Hollywood B47........ 125 B6
  Lichfield WS14.......... 9 F7
  Sutton Coldfield B76 ... 57 E7
Alder Coppice DY3 ..... 39 C2
Alder Coppice Prim Sch
  DY3 .... 39 C1
Alder Cres WS5 .... 43 B4
Alder Ct B13........... 87 A3
Alder Dale WV3 .... 24 E2
Alderdale Ave DY3 ..... 39 C3
Alderdale Cres B92 .... 107 E7
Alder Dr B37 .... 70 B1
Alderflat Pl B7........ 67 B7
Alderford Cl WV8 ...... 24 F8
Aldergate B79 .... 21 B5
Alder Gr B62 .... 83 E6
Alderham Cl B91 ...... 107 D4
Alderhithe Gr B74...... 31 B3
Alder Ho 2 CV34 ..... 161 D8
Alderlea Cl DY8 .... 81 A2
Alderley Cres WS3 ..... 28 E5
Alderley Rd B61 .... 150 D8
Alderman Gee Hall CV12. 78 A4
ALDERMAN'S GREEN.... 96 B3
Alderman's Green Ind Est
  CV2.................... 96 D2
Alderman's Green Prim Sch
  CV10................... 72 D2
Alder Mdw CV34 ...... 160 B3
Alder Meadow Cl CV6... 95 D4
Aldermere Rd DY11 .... 116 C8
Alderminster Cl B97 ... 158 E4
Alderminster Rd
  Coventry CV5.......... 112 A4
  Solihull B91 .... 107 C1
Aldermoor Farm Prim Sch
  CV3.................... 134 B8
Aldermoor La CV3 ..... 114 A1
Aldermore Dr 7 B75... 46 F6
Alderney Cl
  Bramcote CV11 .... 79 F6
  Coventry CV6.......... 95 B2
Alderney Gdns B38..... 103 D1
Alder Park Rd B91 ..... 106 F2
Alderpits Rd B34....... 69 D6
Alder Rd
  Birmingham B12 .... 87 A4
  Coventry CV6.......... 96 A2
  Kingswinford DY6 ...... 60 F5
  Wednesbury WS10 ..... 42 A5
Alders Cl B98 .... 154 A3
Alders Dr B98 .... 154 F4
Aldersea Dr B6 .... 66 F7
Aldersgate 8 B77 .... 73 C3
Alders Gr CV34 .... 160 D4
Aldershaw Rd B26 ..... 88 E6
Aldershaws B90 .... 126 A5
Alders La
  Nuneaton CV10 .... 72 A7
  Tamworth B79 .... 20 D6
ALDERSLEY............. 24 F7
Aldersley Ave WV6 .... 24 F7
Aldersley Cl WV6 ...... 24 F7
Aldersley High Sch WV8. 10 E1
Aldersley L Village WV6 . 24 F7
Aldersley Rd WV6....... 24 F6

Aldersmead Rd B31.... 103 C1
Alderson Rd B8........ 67 F4
Alders The
  Bedworth CV12 .... 77 E2
  Romsley B62........... 100 F4
Alderton Cl 3 B91 .... 107 B1
Alderton Dr WV3....... 38 E8
Alderton Mews 10 CV31. 162 C6
Alder Way
  Bromsgrove B60 .... 137 B2
  Sutton Coldfield B74 ... 44 E8
Alderwood Pl B91...... 107 C3
Alderwood Prec DY3 ... 39 C1
Alderwood Rise DY3 ... 50 D5
Aldgate Dr DY5 .... 81 C7
Aldgate Gr B19 .... 66 D5
Aldin Cl B78........... 20 E2
Aldington Cl B98....... 153 F1
Aldington Rd WS14 .... 71 A3
Aldis Cl
  Birmingham B28 .... 87 E1
  Walsall WS2............ 42 A7
Aldis Rd WS2 .... 42 A7
Aldrich Ave CV4 .... 111 E2
Aldridge Cl
  Birmingham B68 .... 84 C3
  Stourbridge DY8........ 81 A8
Aldridge Rd
  Aldridge, Little Aston B74,
   WS9 .... 31 B6
  Sutton Coldfield, Streetly
   B74 .... 44 E7
  Walsall WS4........... 29 C3
  Walsall WS5............ 30 A4
  1 Aldridge WS9...... 30 A1
Aldrin Way CV4 .... 131 E7
Aldwick Cl CV32 ...... 157 A4
Aldwych Cl WS9 .... 30 B8
Aldwyck Dr WV3 ...... 38 A8
Aldwyn Ave B13 .... 86 F2
Alesmore Mdw WS13.... 9 F6
Alesworth Dr LE10 .... 75 F4
Alexander Cl B61...... 121 A1
Alexander Ct 1 CV34 . 160 F7
Alexander Gdns
  Birmingham B42 .... 55 D3
  Hinckley LE10 .... 71 C2
Alexander Hill DY5 .... 81 F8
Alexander Ind Pk WV14 . 40 C4
Alexander Rd
  Bedworth CV12 .... 78 C3
  Birmingham B27 .... 88 C4
  Codsall WV8............ 10 C3
  Smethwick B67 .... 64 E2
Alexander Stad B42.... 55 C6
Alexander Terr B67 .... 64 F6
Alexandra Ave B21 .... 65 D7
Alexandra Cres B71 ... 53 E8
Alexandra Ct
  Dudley DY3............ 50 C3
  Kenilworth CV8 .... 148 A4
Alexandra High Sch & Sixth
  Form Ctr DY4........... 52 B6
Alexandra Hospl B98... 159 C6
Alexandra Ind Est DY4 . 51 F5
Alexandra Mews B79... 21 C5
Alexandra Pl
  Bilston WV14........... 40 D6
  Dudley DY1............ 51 C4
Alexandra Rd
  Birmingham, Handsworth
   B21 .... 65 D7
  Birmingham, Highgate B5.. 86 E7
  Birmingham, Stirchley B30. 104 A7
  Coventry CV1........... 113 F4
  Darlaston WS10........ 41 E6
  Halesowen B63 .... 82 F4
  Royal Leamington Spa
   CV31 .... 162 B6
  Tipton DY4............. 52 A6
  Walsall WS1............ 42 E6
  Wolverhampton WV4.... 39 A6
Alexandra St
  2 Dudley DY1......... 51 B1
  Nuneaton CV11 .... 73 B4
  Wolverhampton WV3....163 A3
Alexandra Terr CV6.... 95 E2
Alexandra Theatre* B5 . 164 B2
Alexandra Way
  Aldridge WS9.......... 30 B5
  Tipton B69............. 52 A2
Alex Grierson Cl CV3... 134 E7
Alex Stewart Ho CV11 . 73 E1
Alfall Rd CV2 .... 114 B5
Alfred Cl B60.......... 137 B2
Alfreda Ave B47....... 125 A8
Alfred Ct 8 B60 ..... 150 E2
Alfred Gunn Ho B68... 84 B5
Alfred Rd
  Birmingham, Handsworth
   B21 .... 65 E8
  Birmingham, Sparkhill B11. 87 B5
  Coventry CV1........... 113 F4
Alfred Squire Rd WV11. 26 D5
Alfred St
  Birmingham, Aston B6.... 67 B8

Add–All 167

Alfred St continued
  Birmingham, King's Heath
   B14 .... 104 F7
  Birmingham, Sparkbrook
   B12 .... 87 B5
  Darlaston WS10........ 41 C5
  Smethwick B66 .... 65 C7
  Tamworth B79 .... 21 A5
  Walsall WS3............ 14 B1
Alfreds Well B61....... 136 C6
Alfreton Cl LE10 .... 75 F5
Alfriston Rd CV3 ...... 133 C4
Alfryth Ct 3 B15..... 86 C8
Al-furqan Prim Sch B11.. 87 E3
Algate Cl CV6.......... 95 C3
Algernon Rd B16....... 65 D4
Alhambra Rd B60...... 137 C1
Al-hijrah Sch B9....... 67 E2
Al Hira Sch 13 B12.... 87 A6
Al Huda Girls Sch B8... 67 C5
Alice Arnold Ho 1 CV2. 96 B1
Alice Cl CV12 .... 77 F1
Alice St WV14 .... 40 D6
Alice Stevens Specl Sch
  CV3.................. 134 A6
Alice Wlk WV14........ 40 D6
Alison Cl DY4......... 41 A2
Alison Dr DY8.......... 80 E3
Alison Rd B62 .... 83 F3
Alison Sq CV6 .... 96 B4
Allan Cl
  2 Smethwick B66..... 65 B5
  7 Stourbridge DY8.... 80 F8
All Angels Wlk B68.... 64 B4
Allan Rd CV6.......... 112 F4
Allard B77............. 21 E2
Allard Ho CV3 .... 134 B6
Allard Way CV3 .... 134 C7
Allbut St B64 .... 62 D1
Allcock St
  Birmingham B9 .... 67 A1
  Tipton DY4............ 52 C8
Allcroft Rd B11........ 87 F2
Allenby Cl DY6........ 61 A5
Allen Cl
  Birmingham B43 .... 54 E7
  Studley B80........... 159 E3
Allendale Ave B80..... 159 E3
Allendale Cres B80.... 159 E3
Allendale Ct B80...... 159 E3
Allendale Gr B43...... 54 E8
Allendale Rd
  Birmingham B25 .... 88 B7
  Sutton Coldfield B76 ... 57 E8
Allen Dr
  3 Darlaston WS10.... 41 C6
  West Bromwich B70 ... 53 F1
ALLEN END 47 F6
Allen Ho B43 .... 54 E7
Allen Rd
  Tipton DY4............ 40 F1
  Wednesbury WS10 ..... 41 F5
  Wolverhampton WV6.... 25 A3
Allens Ave
  Birmingham B18 .... 65 F6
  West Bromwich B71 ... 53 A7
Allens Cl WV12 .... 27 B5
Allens Croft Prim Sch
  B14................... 104 C5
Allens Croft Rd B14.... 104 C6
Allens Farm Rd B31.... 102 E3
Allens La WS3 .... 14 F2
Allensmead B77 .... 21 C2
Allens Orch CV8 ...... 154 F2
Allens Rd B18......... 65 F6
Allen St 2 B77....... 21 C1
Allerdale Rd WS8 ..... 15 E6
Allerton Cl CV2 .... 114 E2
Allerton La B71........ 53 C8
Allerton Rd B25....... 88 B7
ALLESLEY............. 111 B7
Allesley Cl B74 .... 46 C7
Allesley Croft CV5..... 112 A6
Allesley Ct CV5........ 112 A6
Allesley Hall Dr CV5.... 112 C5
Allesley Hall Prim Sch
  CV5.................. 112 B4
Allesley Old Rd CV5... 112 D3
Allesley Prim Sch CV5.. 112 A7
Allesley Rd B92....... 106 D8
Alleston Rd WV10..... 11 D1
Alleston Wlk WV10.... 11 D2
Alleyne Gr B24........ 57 A2
Alleyne Rd B24........ 57 A2
Alley The DY3.......... 50 B3
Alliance Cl CV11...... 73 F3
Alliance Way CV2..... 114 A5
Allibone Cl CV31...... 162 A4
Allingham Gr 5 B43.. 8 F6
Allington Cl WS5...... 43 D8
Allison St B5.......... 164 D2
Allitt Gr CV8.......... 148 B5
Allman Rd B24........ 57 B4
Allmyn Dr B74........ 45 A6
Alloys Cl B77.......... 35 E5
Allport Mews WS11.... 1 E1
Allport Rd WS11...... 1 E1
Allport St WS11....... 1 E2
ALL SAINTS........... 66 A5
All Saints CE Inf Sch
  CV12.................. 78 C2

All Saints' CE Jun Sch
CV34 . . . . 156 A1
All Saints CE Prim Sch
Coventry CV1 . . . . 113 E1
Leek Wootton CV35 . . . . 156 A5
Nuneaton CV10 . . . . 73 C1
West Bromwich B71 . . . . 53 C6
All Saints Dr B74 . . . . 32 A2
All Saints Ind Est B18 . . . 66 A5
All Saints La CV1 . . . . . . 113 F3
All Saints Pl B61 . . . . . . 137 A4
All Saints Rd
Bedworth CV12 . . . . 77 F1
Birmingham, King's Heath
B14 . . . . 104 E7
Warwick CV34 . . . . 161 B8
Wolverhampton WV2 . . . 163 C1
All Saints' Rd
Birmingham, Hockley B18 . . 66 B5
Bromsgrove B61 . . . . . . 137 A3
Darlaston WS10 . . . . 41 E6
All Saints Sq CV12 . . . . . . 78 B3
All Saints' St B18 . . . . . . 66 A5
Alma Way B71 . . . . 53 D5
Allsops Cl B65 . . . . 62 A7
All Souls RC Prim Sch
CV5 . . . . 112 E2
Allton Ave B78 . . . . 20 D1
Allton Ct B77 . . . . 21 E3
Allwell Dr B14 . . . . 104 F2
Allwood Gdns B32 . . . . . . 84 A2
Allwood Ho B97 . . . . 153 C3
Alma Ave DY4 . . . . 52 A7
Alma Cres B7 . . . . 67 B4
Alma Ct CV11 . . . . 79 F6
Al-mahdi Inst B12 . . . . . 86 F5
Alma Ind Est WS10 . . . . . 41 C1
Alma Pl DY2 . . . . 51 C6
Alma Rd LE10 . . . . 71 D1
Alma St
Birmingham B19 . . . . 66 C6
Coventry CV1 . . . . 165 D3
Darlaston WS10 . . . . 41 C6
Halesowen B63 . . . . 82 C5
Smethwick B66 . . . . 65 C6
Walsall WS2 . . . . 28 D4
Wednesbury WS10 . . . . . 42 B3
Willenhall WV13 . . . . 27 B2
Wolverhampton WV10 . . 25 F2
Alma Way B19 . . . . 66 D7
Alma Wks WS10 . . . . 41 D5
Almond Ave
Kidderminster DY11 . . . . 116 B8
Nuneaton CV10 . . . . 72 C6
Royal Leamington Spa
CV32 . . . . 156 F3
Walsall, Yew Tree WS5 . . 43 A4
Willenhall WS2 . . . . 27 E4
Almond Cl
Birmingham B29 . . . . . . 103 A6
Cannock WS11 . . . . 2 C2
Walsall WS3 . . . . 14 F2
Almond Croft B42 . . . . . . 54 F7
Almond Gr
Warwick CV34 . . . . 156 A1
Wolverhampton WV6 . . . 25 C4
Almond Rd
Huntington WS12 . . . . . . 1 D8
Kingswinford DY6 . . . . . . 60 E8
Almond Tree Ave CV2 . . . 96 C2
Almshouses
Rowington Green CV35 . . 145 A1
Smethwick B67 . . . . 64 F5
Stoneleigh CV8 . . . . 149 C6
Warwick CV34 . . . . 160 E6
Alnwick Cl WS12 . . . . 2 E3
Alnwick Ho B23 . . . . 56 F6
Alnwick Rd WS3 . . . . 14 A4
Alperton Dr DY9 . . . . . . 81 E2
Alpha Bsns Pk CV2 . . . . . 96 D1
Alpha Cl B12 . . . . 86 E6
Alpha Ho CV2 . . . . 114 A4
Alpha Way WS6 . . . . 14 A8
Alpine Cl CV8 . . . . 148 A6
Alpine Ct CV8 . . . . 148 A6
Alpine Dr
Cannock WS12 . . . . 2 D4
Dudley DY2 . . . . 62 B4
Alpine Rise CV3 . . . . . . 133 A5
Alpine Way WV3 . . . . . . 24 C2
Alport Croft B9 . . . . 67 B2
Alspath La CV5 . . . . 111 F4
Alspath Rd CV7 . . . . 92 C1
Alston Cl
Cannock WS12 . . . . 2 E2
Solihull B91 . . . . 107 D6
Sutton Coldfield B74 . . . 32 A2
Alston Gr B9 . . . . 68 B2
Alston Ho B69 . . . . 63 D6
Alston Prim Sch B9 . . . . 68 B3
Alston Rd
Birmingham B9 . . . . 68 B1
Oldbury B69 . . . . 63 E7
Solihull B91 . . . . 107 D6
Alston St B16 . . . . 66 A2
Althorpe Dr B93 . . . . . . 127 E3
Althorpe Ho CV31 . . . . . 162 A6
Althorpe Ind Est 15
CV31 . . . . 162 A7
Althorpe St B15 . . . . . . 162 A7
Alton Ave WV12 . . . . 27 B5
Alton Cl
Coventry CV2 . . . . 96 D2
Redditch B97 . . . . 153 B1
Wolverhampton WV10 . . 11 E3

Alton Gr
Cannock WS11 . . . . 1 B1
Dudley DY2 . . . . 51 E1
West Bromwich B71 . . . . 53 E7
Alton Rd B29 . . . . 85 F3
Alum Cl CV6 . . . . 113 D8
Alum Dr B9 . . . . 68 A3
Alumhurst Ave B8 . . . . . . 68 B4
ALUM ROCK 68 B3
Alum Rock Rd B8 . . . . . . 68 B4
Alumwell Bsns & Enterprise
Coll WS2 . . . . 28 B1
Alumwell Cl WS2 . . . . . . 28 B1
Alumwell Jun & Inf Schs
WS2 . . . . 28 B2
Alum Well Rd WS2 . . . . . 28 B1
Alvaston Cl WS3 . . . . . . 14 C3
ALVECHURCH 139 B6
Alvechurch CE Mid Sch
B48 . . . . 139 B7
Alvechurch Highway
Lower Marlbrook B60 . . . 121 D2
Redditch B98, B97 . . . . 153 F3
Alvechurch Ho B60 . . . . . 137 B3
Alvechurch Rd
Birmingham B31 . . . . . . 123 B7
Halesowen B63 . . . . 82 F2
Alvechurch Sta B48 . . . . 139 A4
ALVECOTE 22 D6
Alvecote Cotts B79 . . . . 22 D6
Alvecote La B79 . . . . 22 D6
Alvecote Pools Wildlife
Reserve* B79 . . . . 22 E6
Alveley Cl B98 . . . . 154 D4
Alverley Cl DY6 . . . . 60 B8
Alverley Rd CV6 . . . . 113 C6
Alverstoke Cl WV9 . . . . . 11 A2
Alverstone Rd CV2 . . . . . 114 A4
Alverton Cl B77 . . . . 35 C4
Alverton Cl B98 . . . . 154 C2
Alveston Gr
Birmingham B9 . . . . 68 B2
Knowle B93 . . . . 128 B7
Alveston Pl 19 CV32 . . . 156 F1
Alveston Rd B47 . . . . 125 A7
Alvin Cl
Coventry CV3 . . . . 114 F1
Halesowen B62 . . . . 83 F8
Alvington Cl WV12 . . . . 27 D4
Alvis Cl B79 . . . . 20 F7
Alvis Ho CV1 . . . . 165 B2
Alvis Ret Pk CV5 . . . . . . 113 A3
Alvis Wlk B36 . . . . 58 B5
Alwen St DY8 . . . . 60 F2
Alwin Rd B65 . . . . 63 B2
Alwold Ct B29 . . . . 84 F2
Alwold Rd B29 . . . . 85 A2
Alwyn B77 . . . . 35 E7
Alwyn Cl WS6 . . . . 5 A3
Alwynne Freeman Ct CV7 . . 95 A6
Alwynn Wlk B23 . . . . 56 C3
Alyssa Sch The B10 . . . . 87 C8
Amal Way B6 . . . . 55 F3
Amanda Ave WV4 . . . . . . 38 A4
Amanda Dr B26 . . . . 68 F1
Ambassador Ct CV32 . . . 156 F3
Ambassador Rd B26 . . . . 90 C4
Ambell Cl B65 . . . . 62 F5
Amber Ct
Birmingham B23 . . . . 56 F7
Tamworth B77 . . . . 22 B3
Amber Dr B69 . . . . 64 A5
Ambergate Cl
8 Redditch B97 . . . . . . 153 B5
Walsall WS3 . . . . 14 C3
Ambergate Dr DY6 . . . . . 60 C8
Amber Gn WS11 . . . . 2 C2
Amberley Ave CV12 . . . . 79 C2
Amberley Gn B43 . . . . . . 54 E6
Amberley Gr B6 . . . . 56 A3
Amberley Ho CV8 . . . . . . 148 A3
Amberley Rd B92 . . . . . . 88 F4
Amberley Way B74 . . . . . 30 E1
Amber Terr 1 DY10 . . . 116 F5
Amber Way B62 . . . . 83 C6
Amberwood Cl WS2 . . . . 27 D3
Ambion Way LE10 . . . . . 71 F1
AMBLECOTE 80 F7
Amblecote Ave B44 . . . . 44 E2
Amblecote Prim Sch DY8 . . 80 F8
Amblecote Rd
Brierley Hill DY5 . . . . . . 81 D8
Kidderminster DY10 . . . . 117 B5
Ambler Gr CV2 . . . . 114 C3
Amblerise Cl B77 . . . . . . 21 D4
Ambleside
Birmingham B32 . . . . . . 84 C1
Coventry CV2 . . . . 96 E2
Ambleside Cl WV14 . . . . 40 E3
Ambleside Dr DY5 . . . . . . 81 C8
Ambleside Rd CV10 . . . . 78 A2
Ambleside Way
Bromsgrove B60 . . . . . . 137 B1
Kingswinford DY6 . . . . . . 60 D6
Nuneaton CV11 . . . . 73 E6
Ambrose Cl WV13 . . . . . 26 E2
Ambrose Cres DY6 . . . . . 60 D8
Ambury Way B43 . . . . . . 54 D8
Amelas Cl 8 DY5 . . . . . 61 A1
Amelia Cl CV12 . . . . 79 C3
Amersham Cl
Birmingham B32 . . . . . . 84 E5
Coventry CV5 . . . . 112 B4
Amesbury Rd B13 . . . . . . 86 E3

Ames Rd WS10 . . . . 41 C7
Amethyst Ct 2 B92 . . . . 88 F1
Amherst Ave B20 . . . . . . 55 A3
Amherst Rd CV8 . . . . 147 C6
Amhurst Bsns Ctr CV34 . . 160 B7
Amicombe B77 . . . . 22 C1
AMINGTON 22 B5
Amington Cl B75 . . . . 32 D3
Amington Hall B79 . . . . . 22 A8
Amington Heath Com Sch
B77 . . . . 22 A4
Amington Ind Est B77 . . . 22 B3
Amington Pk B77 . . . . . . 22 A6
Amington Rd
Birmingham B25 . . . . 88 B6
Solihull B90 . . . . 126 A8
Tamworth B77 . . . . 21 D4
Amiss Gdns B10 . . . . 87 C8
Amity Cl B66 . . . . 65 B5
Aml Ind Est WS12 . . . . . 2 C7
Amos Ave
Nuneaton CV10 . . . . 73 B2
Wolverhampton WV11 . . . 26 C7
Amos Jacques Rd CV12 . . 78 A4
Amos La WV11 . . . . 26 C6
Amos Mews B73 . . . . 46 A1
Amos Rd DY9 . . . . 81 F2
Amphlett Croft DY4 . . . . 52 B4
Amphlett Ct 2 B60 . . . . 137 A2
Amphletts Cl DY2 . . . . . 62 E3
Ampleforth Dr WV13 . . . 41 B8
Ampton Rd B15 . . . . 86 B7
Amroth Cl B45 . . . . 112 B6
Amroth Mews CV31 . . . . . 162 C6
Amwell Gr B14 . . . . 104 F3
Amy Cl CV6 . . . . 95 F4
Anchorage Rd
Birmingham B23 . . . . 56 D3
Sutton Coldfield B74 . . . 46 B6
Anchor Brook Ind Pk WS9 . . 29 F7
Anchor Cl
Birmingham B16 . . . . 65 E1
Wolverhampton WV14 . . . 40 B2
Anchor Cres B18 . . . . . . 65 F5
Anchor Ct B77 . . . . 21 C4
Anchor Dr DY4 . . . . 52 A3
Anchorfields DY10 . . . . 116 F6
Anchor Hill DY5 . . . . . . 61 C1
Anchor La
Bilston WV14 . . . . 40 B2
Wolverhampton WV14 . . . 40 B2
Anchor Rd
Aldridge WS9 . . . . 30 B6
Dudley WV14 . . . . 40 C2
Anchorway Rd CV3 . . . . . 133 B4
Anders B79 . . . . 21 A6
Andersleigh Dr WV14 . . . 58 B5
Anderson Cres B43 . . . . 43 E2
Anderson Dr CV31 . . . . . 162 A2
Anderson Gdns DY4 . . . . 52 A4
Anderson Rd
Birmingham B23 . . . . 56 E6
Smethwick B66 . . . . 65 A1
Tipton DY4 . . . . 52 A4
Anders Sq WV6 . . . . 23 E4
Anderton Cl B74 . . . . . . 46 A7
Anderton Park Prim Sch
B12 . . . . 87 A3
Anderton Park Rd B13 . . 87 A3
Anderton Rd
Bedworth CV12 . . . . 77 C1
Birmingham B11 . . . . 87 C6
Coventry CV6 . . . . 96 B4
Anderton St B1 . . . . 66 B3
Andover Cres 2 DY6 . . . 60 F4
Andover Pl WS11 . . . . . . 2 A4
Andover Rd B80 . . . . 66 F2
Andressy Mews B61 . . . . 137 A5
Andrew Cl WV12 . . . . 27 D6
Andrew Ct B76 . . . . 46 F3
Andrew Dr WV12 . . . . 27 D6
Andrew Gdns B21 . . . . . . 54 E1
Andrew Rd
Halesowen B63 . . . . 83 A3
Wednesbury DY4 . . . . . . 41 A1
West Bromwich B71 . . . . 42 F2
Andrews Cl
Bagington CV8 . . . . 133 F2
Brierley Hill DY5 . . . . . . 81 E8
Andrews Ho WS13 . . . . . 9 A7
Andrews Rd WS9 . . . . . . 16 B1
Andyfreight Bsns Pk DY9 . . 82 A6
Anerley Gr B44 . . . . 44 F4
Anerley Rd B44 . . . . 44 F4
Angela Ave
Coventry CV2 . . . . 96 E1
Rowley Regis B65 . . . . . . 63 D4
Angela Pl WV14 . . . . 40 D6
Angelica B77 . . . . 21 F4
Angelica Cl 7 WS5 . . . 43 A3
Angelina St B12 . . . . 86 F7
Angelo Ho B13 . . . . 105 D7
Angel Pas DY8 . . . . 81 A5
Angel St
Dudley DY1 . . . . 62 B8
Upper Bentley B97 . . . . 152 B1
Anglesey Ave B36 . . . . . 70 B6
Anglesey Bsns Pk WS12 . . 2 E4
Anglesey Cl
Allesley CV5 . . . . 112 B7
Burntwood WS7 . . . . 6 F4
Anglesey Cres
Brownhills WS8 . . . . 6 F2
Anglesey Mews WS12 . . . 2 C5
Anglesey Prim Sch B19 . . 66 C7

Anglesey Rd
Brownhills WS8 . . . . 6 F2
Lichfield WS13 . . . . 3 B2
Anglesey St
Birmingham B19 . . . . 66 C7
Cannock WS12 . . . . 2 B5
Angless Way CV8 . . . . . . 147 F3
Anglian Rd WS9 . . . . 29 C6
Anglia Rd WS11 . . . . 1 D3
Anglo African Ind Pk B69 . . 52 E2
Angorfa Cl WS13 . . . . 8 F7
Angus Cl
Coventry CV5 . . . . 112 A4
Kenilworth CV8 . . . . 148 C6
West Bromwich B71 . . . . 53 C6
Anita Ave DY4 . . . . 52 A2
Anita Croft B23 . . . . 56 E2
Ankadine Rd DY8 . . . . . . 81 B6
Anker Cl WS7 . . . . 6 F4
Ankerdine Ct B63 . . . . . 83 A3
Ankerdrive B79 . . . . 21 B4
Ankermoor Cl B34 . . . . . 69 B6
Ankermoor Ct B77 . . . . . 21 E5
Ankerside Sh Ctr B79 . . 21 B4
Anker View B77 . . . . 23 C3
Anley Way CV6 . . . . 113 C6
Annan Ave WV10 . . . . 25 F7
Annandale B77 . . . . 22 B1
Ann Cres WS11 . . . . 1 B6
Ann Croft B26 . . . . 89 D4
Anne Cl B70 . . . . 52 E3
Anne Cres CV3 . . . . 134 C5
Anne Ct B76 . . . . 46 F3
Anne Gr DY4 . . . . 41 B1
Anne Rd
Birmingham B66 . . . . 65 D7
Brierley Hill DY5 . . . . . . 62 A1
Wolverhampton WV4 . . . . 39 B6
Annie Lennard Inf Sch
B67 . . . . 64 E3
Ann Rd B47 . . . . 125 A3
Annscroft B38 . . . . 103 D2
Ann St WV13 . . . . 27 B3
Ansbro Cl B18 . . . . 65 F5
Anscuff Rd DY5 . . . . 61 B1
Ansell Dr CV6 . . . . 96 A5
Ansell Rd
Birmingham, Gravelly Hill
B24 . . . . 56 F1
Birmingham, Sparkbrook
B11 . . . . 87 C6
Ansell Way CV34 . . . . . . 160 D7
Ansley Cl B98 . . . . 154 F1
Ansley Comm CV10 . . . . 72 A7
Ansley Hall Dr B78 . . . . 36 E4
Ansley Rd CV10 . . . . 72 D7
Ansley Way B92 . . . . 107 D7
Anslow Gdns WV11 . . . . 12 F1
Anslow Rd B23 . . . . 56 C5
Anson Ave WS13 . . . . . . 3 A1
Anson Cl
Burntwood WS7 . . . . 7 C7
Great Wyrley WS6 . . . . . 4 F1
Perton WV6 . . . . 23 E5
Anson Ct B78 . . . . 35 B8
Anson Gr B27 . . . . 88 D2
Anson Junc WS2 . . . . 27 E1
Anson Rd
Great Wyrley WS6 . . . . . 4 F1
Walsall WS2 . . . . 27 E1
West Bromwich B70 . . . . 52 E7
Anson Way CV2 . . . . 114 F8
Anstey Croft B37 . . . . . . 70 A4
Anstey Ct B73 . . . . 57 A7
Anstey Gr B27 . . . . 88 B1
Anstey Rd B44 . . . . 55 E6
Anston Way WV11 . . . . . 26 D7
Anstree Cl WS6 . . . . 4 D1
Anstruther Rd B15 . . . . 85 E8
Ansty Dr WS12 . . . . 2 D1
Ansty Rd CV2 . . . . 114 E5
Antelope Gdns CV34 . . . 160 B8
Anthony Rd B8 . . . . 67 F4
Anthony Way CV2 . . . . . 114 C2
Antler Way 3 B16 . . . . 65 C3
Anton Dr B76 . . . . 58 A6
Antony Gardner Cres 5
CV31 . . . . 162 A4
Antony Rd B90 . . . . 106 B1
Antrim Cl CV5 . . . . 112 B7
Antringham Gdns B15 . . . 85 D8
Antrobus Rd
Birmingham B21 . . . . 54 E1
Sutton Coldfield B73 . . . 45 F1
Anvil Cres WV14 . . . . . . 40 C4
Anvil Dr B69 . . . . 52 E6
Anvil Wlk B70 . . . . 52 F4
Apex Bsns Pk WS11 . . . . 5 F4
Apex Rd WS8 . . . . 15 C7
Apley Rd DY8 . . . . 80 E7
Apollo B77 . . . . 20 F6
Apollo Cl WS11 . . . . 2 A5
Apollo Croft B24 . . . . . . 57 D3
Apollo Rd
Oldbury B68 . . . . 64 C6
Stourbridge DY9 . . . . . . 82 A5
Apollo Way
Birmingham B20 . . . . 55 D1
Royal Leamington Spa
CV34 . . . . 161 D5
12 Smethwick B66 . . . . 65 C5
Apperley Way B63 . . . . . 82 B7
Appian Cl
Birmingham B14 . . . . . . 104 E5
Tamworth B77 . . . . 35 D7

Appian Way B90 . . . . 126 D4
Applebee Rd LE10 . . . . . 75 D6
Applebees Mdw LE10 . . . 74 E6
Applebees Wlk LE10 . . . 74 F6
Appleby Cl B14 . . . . 104 D5
Appleby Gdns WV11 . . . . 13 C2
Appleby Gr B90 . . . . 127 B6
Appleby Ho 1 LE10 . . . 71 E1
Applecross B74 . . . . 31 F1
Applecross Cl CV4 . . . . 131 F6
Appledore Cl
Cannock WS12 . . . . 2 E3
Great Wyrley WS6 . . . . . 5 A3
Appledore Ct 8 WS3 . . 28 B8
Appledore Dr CV5 . . . . . 111 F5
Appledore Rd WS5 . . . . . 43 D8
Appledore Terr WS5 . . . 43 D8
Appledorne Gdns B34 . . . 69 B6
Applesham Cl B11 . . . . . 87 D6
Appleton Ave
Birmingham B43 . . . . 54 E8
Stourbridge DY8 . . . . . . 81 A2
Appleton Cl B30 . . . . . . 103 E8
Appleton Cres WV4 . . . . 39 A5
Appleton Ct 5 B15 . . . 86 B7
Appletree Cl
Birmingham B31 . . . . . . 102 F1
Catherine de B B91 . . . 108 B5
Apple Tree Cl
Birmingham B23 . . . . 56 B4
Kidderminster DY10 . . . 117 B7
Appletree Cotts CV35 . . 144 F1
Appletree Gr
Aldridge WS9 . . . . 30 B5
Wolverhampton WV6 . . . 25 C5
Appletree La B97 . . . . . 153 B5
Appletrees Cres B61 . . . 137 A6
Apple Wlk WS11 . . . . . . 2 C2
Applewood Gr 5 B64 . . 62 F1
Appleyard Cl
Bedworth CV12 . . . . 78 B2
Walsall WS2 . . . . 27 F2
Approach The CV31 . . . . 161 F6
April Croft B13 . . . . 87 B3
Apsley Cl B68 . . . . 84 A7
Apsley Croft B38 . . . . . . 104 B2
Apsley Gr
Birmingham B24 . . . . 57 A2
Dorridge B93 . . . . 127 F2
Apsley Ho B64 . . . . 62 F2
Apsley Rd B68 . . . . 84 A7
Aqueduct La B48 . . . . . . 138 F7
Aqueduct Rd B90 . . . . . . 105 E1
Aragon Dr
Royal Leamington Spa
CV34 . . . . 161 D6
Sutton Coldfield B73 . . . 46 B6
Aragon Ho Cv3 . . . . 133 C8
Arbor Cl B77 . . . . 21 D3
Arbor Ct B71 . . . . 53 E6
Arboretum Rd WS1 . . . . . 29 A3
Arboretum The CV4 . . . . 132 D3
Arbor Gate WS9 . . . . 16 B4
Arbor Way B37 . . . . 70 C1
Arbour Cl CV8 . . . . 148 B3
Arbour Dr WV14 . . . . 40 F4
Arbourfields Ct CV8 . . . 148 B8
Arbour Mews WS11 . . . . 5 F6
Arbourtree Ct WV5 . . . . 49 B7
Arbour Tree La B93 . . . . 144 F7
Arbury Ave
Bedworth CV12 . . . . 78 A3
Coventry CV6 . . . . 95 F2
Arbury Cl CV32 . . . . 157 A2
Arbury Ct CV10 . . . . 72 C3
Arbury Dr DY8 . . . . 60 D3
Arbury Garth CV10 . . . . 72 C3
Arbury Hall Barn & Gdns*
CV10 . . . . 77 D7
Arbury Hall Rd B90 . . . . 126 D8
Arbury Rd CV10 . . . . 72 D2
Arbury Wlk B76 . . . . 58 D5
Arcade WS1 . . . . 28 E1
Arcade The
Coventry CV3 . . . . 114 B2
Dudley DY3 . . . . 50 E5
Arcadian (Sh Ctr) B5 . . 164 C1
Arcal St DY3 . . . . 50 E7
Archbishop Grimshaw RC
Sch The B37 . . . . 69 F3
Archbishop Ilsley RC Tech
Coll & Sixth Form Ctr
B27 . . . . 88 C3
Archer Cl
Oldbury B68 . . . . 64 B4
Studley B80 . . . . 159 D4
Wednesbury WS10 . . . . . 41 E3
Archer Ct DY9 . . . . 81 E2
Archer Gdns B64 . . . . . . 62 C1
Archer Rd
Birmingham B14 . . . . . . 105 C4
Kenilworth CV8 . . . . 147 E3
Redditch B98 . . . . 153 E4
Walsall WS3 . . . . 14 E3
Archer Cl B23 . . . . 56 D8
Archer Terr B97 . . . . . . 153 C1
Archery Fields CV34 . . . 160 F6
Archery Rd
Meriden CV7 . . . . 92 B1
Royal Leamington Spa
CV31 . . . . 161 E8
Arches Ind Est CV5 . . . . 113 A3
Arch Hill St DY2 . . . . . . 62 C5
Archibald Rd B19 . . . . . . 66 C8
Arch Rd CV2 . . . . 114 E5
Arch The B5 . . . . 66 A2
Archway The 2 WS4 . . . 28 F3

Arcot Rd B28 . . . . 87 F2
Ardath Rd B38 . . . . 104 A2
Ardav Rd B70 . . . . 52 F8
Arden Bldgs B93 . . . . 127 F3
Arden Cl
  Balsall Common CV7 . . . . 130 B7
  Meriden CV7 . . . . 92 C1
  Stourbridge DY8 . . . . 80 E7
  Stourbridge, Wordsley DY8 . 60 C3
  Tamworth B77 . . . . 21 E5
  Warwick CV34 . . . . 156 A1
  Whitnash CV31 . . . . 162 B5
Ardencote Rd B13 . . . . . . 105 A6
Arden Croft
  Coleshill B46 . . . . 59 F1
  Solihull B92 . . . . 89 C4
Arden Ct
  Binley Woods CV3 . . . . . . 135 D6
  Dudley DY3 . . . . 50 D3
  Hampton-in-A B92 . . . . . 109 A7
  Sutton Coldfield B72 . . . . 57 C8
Ardendale B90 . . . . 126 C8
Arden Dr
  Birmingham B26 . . . . 88 F7
  Dorridge B93 . . . . 128 A1
  Sutton Coldfield, Falcon Lodge
    B75 . . . . 47 B5
  Sutton Coldfield, Wylde Green
    B73 . . . . 57 B8
Arden Forest Inf Sch
  CV12 . . . . 79 B3
Arden Gr
  Birmingham, Ladywood
    B16 . . . . 66 A1
  Birmingham, Lozells B19 . . 66 C8
  Oldbury B69 . . . . 64 A5
Arden Ind Est B8 . . . . 68 B8
Ardenleigh Way B24 . . . . . 57 A2
Arden Leys B94 . . . . 141 D2
Arden Meads B94 . . . . . . 143 C6
Arden Oak Rd B26 . . . . . . 89 D4
Arden Pl WV14 . . . . 41 B4
Arden Prim Sch B11 . . . . . 87 C5
Arden Rd
  Birmingham, Acock's Green
    B27 . . . . 88 A3
  Birmingham, Aston B6 . . . 66 D8
  Birmingham, Rubery B45 . 102 A1
  Birmingham, Saltley B8 . . 67 D3
  Bulkington CV12 . . . . 79 C2
  Dorridge B93 . . . . 127 F2
  Hollywood B47 . . . . 125 A6
  Kenilworth CV8 . . . . 148 B3
  Nuneaton CV11 . . . . 74 A1
  Smethwick B67 . . . . 65 A5
  Tamworth B77 . . . . 35 F5
Arden Sch B93 . . . . 128 B5
Arden St CV5 . . . . 132 F8
Arden Vale Rd B93 . . . . . . 128 B7
Arderne Dr B37 . . . . 70 A1
Ardgay Dr WS12 . . . . 1 F7
Ardgowan Gr WV4 . . . . . . 39 F5
Ardingley Wlk DY5 . . . . . . 81 B7
Ardley Cl DY2 . . . . 62 D8
Ardley Rd B14 . . . . 105 A5
Arena Park Sh Ctr CV6 . . . 95 F3
Arena Studios B27 . . . . . . 57 A7
Arena Theatre* WV1 . . . . 163 B3
Aretha Cl DY4 . . . . 61 A6
Argent Ctr The B1 . . . . . . 66 C3
Argil Cl
  Wednesfield WV11 . . . . . 26 D8
  Wolverhampton WV10 . . . 26 A8
Arguile Pl LE10 . . . . 71 C1
Argus Cl B76 . . . . 46 F3
Argyle Cl
  Stourbridge DY8 . . . . 60 E1
  Walsall WS4 . . . . 29 B3
Argyle Rd
  Walsall WS4 . . . . 29 B3
  Wolverhampton WV2 . . . . 39 B6
Argyle St
  Birmingham B7 . . . . 67 D8
  Tamworth B77 . . . . 21 E4
Argyll Cl WV12 . . . . 13 C1
Argyll Ho WV3 . . . . 25 C4
Argyll St CV2 . . . . 114 A3
Ariane B79 . . . . 20 E7
Arion Cl B77 . . . . 21 D5
Arkall Cl B79 . . . . 21 C7
Arkle B77 . . . . 35 D4
Arkle Croft
  Birmingham B36 . . . . 68 C8
  Rowley Regis B65 . . . . . . 62 F6
Arkle Dr CV2 . . . . 114 F7
Arklet Cl CV10 . . . . 72 C5
Arkley Gr B28 . . . . 106 B7
Arkley Rd B28 . . . . 106 B7
Arkwright Rd
  Birmingham B32 . . . . 84 C5
  Walsall WS2 . . . . 28 B5
Arlen Dr B43 . . . . 43 D1
Arlescote Cl CV35 . . . . . . 32 C2
Arlescote Rd B92 . . . . 89 C2
Arlesey Way B37 . . . . 85 B3
Arleston Way B90 . . . . . . 126 E8
Arley Cl
  Kidderminster DY11 . . . . 116 A2
  Oldbury B69 . . . . 63 D5
  Redditch B98 . . . . 154 D5
Arley Ct DY2 . . . . 62 C6
Arley Dr
  Stourbridge DY8 . . . . 80 E3
  Tamworth B78 . . . . 36 E5
Arley Gr WV4 . . . . 38 D5
Arley Mews CV32 . . . . . . 156 E1

Arley Rd
  Birmingham B29 . . . . 85 F3
  Birmingham, Saltley B8 . . 67 D6
  Solihull B91 . . . . 107 A4
Arley Villas B18 . . . . 65 D4
Arlidge Cl WV14 . . . . 40 D4
Arlidge Cres CV8 . . . . . . 148 C5
Arlington Ave CV32 . . . . . 156 F2
Arlington Cl DY6 . . . . 60 D8
Arlington Ct
  Royal Leamington Spa
    CV32 . . . . 156 F2
  Stourbridge DY8 . . . . 81 B4
Arlington Gr B14 . . . . . . 105 B2
Arlington Ho B15 . . . . 86 C7
Arlington Mews CV32 . . . 156 F2
Arlington Rd
  Birmingham B14 . . . . . . 105 B3
  West Bromwich B71 . . . . . 53 D6
Arlington Way CV11 . . . . . 73 F2
Arlon Ave CV10 . . . . 72 D7
Armada Cl
  Birmingham B23 . . . . 56 D1
  Lichfield WS14 . . . . 9 A5
Armadale Cl LE10 . . . . . . 71 A1
Armarna Dr CV5 . . . . 111 B8
Armfield St CV6 . . . . 114 A8
Armitage Ho WS13 . . . . . . 3 E1
Armorial Rd CV3 . . . . . . 133 B7
Armour Cl LE10 . . . . 75 D5
Armoury Rd B11 . . . . 87 D6
Armoury Trad Est B11 . . . 87 E6
Armscott Rd CV2 . . . . . . 114 C6
Armside Cl WS3 . . . . 15 B4
Armson Rd CV7 . . . . 78 A1
Armstead Rd WV9 . . . . . . 11 A3
Armstrong B79 . . . . 20 F6
Armstrong Ave CV3 . . . . . 114 B1
Armstrong Cl
  Stourbridge DY8 . . . . 81 B6
  Whitnash CV31 . . . . 162 A2
Armstrong Dr
  Birmingham B36 . . . . 58 F1
  Walsall WS2 . . . . 28 A4
  Wolverhampton WV6 . . . . 25 A5
Armstrong Way WV13 . . . 41 B8
Arna Ho CV3 . . . . 134 B6
Arncliffe Cl CV11 . . . . 74 A2
Arncliffe Way CV34 . . . . 155 F1
Arne Rd CV2 . . . . 115 A6
Arnhem Cl WV11 . . . . 26 B8
Arnhem Cnr CV3 . . . . 134 D6
Arnhem Rd WV13 . . . . . . 40 E8
Arnhem Way DY4 . . . . 52 C5
Arnold Ave CV3 . . . . 133 C5
Arnold Cl
  Tamworth B77 . . . . 21 A6
  Willenhall WS2 . . . . 27 F3
Arnold Gr
  Birmingham B30 . . . . . . 103 D4
  Solihull B90 . . . . 106 B4
Arnold Lodge Sch CV32 . . 156 F2
Arnold Rd B90 . . . . 106 C4
Arnotdale Dr WS12 . . . . . . 1 F7
Arnside Cl CV1 . . . . 165 D4
Arnside Ct B23 . . . . 56 B4
Arnwood Cl WS2 . . . . 27 F2
Arosa Dr B17 . . . . 85 B3
Arran Cl
  Birmingham B43 . . . . 43 E3
  Cannock WS11 . . . . 2 A3
Arran Dr B77 . . . . 35 F7
Arran Rd B34 . . . . 68 F6
Arran Way
  Birmingham B36 . . . . 70 B7
  Hinckley LE10 . . . . 71 B1
Arras Bvd CV35 . . . . 160 A7
Arras Rd DY2 . . . . 51 E2
Arrow Cl B93 . . . . 128 A6
Arrowdale Rd B98 . . . . . . 154 A3
Arrowfield Gn B38 . . . . . 123 D7
ARROWFIELD TOP 123 B1
Arrow Ho B68 . . . . 84 B8
Arrow Ind Est WV12 . . . . . 27 D6
Arrow Rd
  Nuneaton CV10 . . . . 72 F6
  Walsall WS3 . . . . 28 E6
Arrow Road N B98 . . . . . 154 A4
Arrow Road S B98 . . . . . 154 A4
Arrow Vale Com High Sch
  B98 . . . . 154 E2
Arrow Vale Sports Ctr
  B98 . . . . 154 E2
Arrow Valley Ctry Pk*
  B98 . . . . 154 C4
Arrow Wlk B38 . . . . 104 B1
Arsenal St B9 . . . . 67 C1
Artemis Dr CV34 . . . . . . 161 E5
Arter St B12 . . . . 86 F6
Arthingworth Cl CV3 . . . . 114 E1
Arthur Alford Ho CV12 . . . 77 D1
Arthur Dr (Road 2) DY11 . 116 E1
Arthur Greenwood Ct
  WV14 . . . . 40 C4
Arthur Gunby Cl B75 . . . . 46 F7
Arthur Harris Cl B66 . . . . 65 C3
Arthur Pl B1 . . . . 66 B3
Arthur Rd
  Birmingham, Edgbaston
    B15 . . . . 86 B7
  Birmingham, Erdington B24 57 B4
  Birmingham, Handsworth
    B21 . . . . 65 F8
  Birmingham, Hay Mills B25 88 B6
  Tipton DY4 . . . . 52 A7
Arthur St
  Bilston WV14 . . . . 40 D6

Arthur St continued
  Birmingham B10 . . . . 67 B1
  Cannock, Chadsmoor WS11 . 1 F4
  Cannock WS12 . . . . 2 E3
  Coventry CV1 . . . . 165 C4
  Kenilworth CV8 . . . . 148 A5
  Redditch B98 . . . . 154 B3
  West Bromwich B70 . . . . . 53 D1
  Wolverhampton WV2 . . . . 39 D7
Arthur Terry Sch The B74 . 32 A3
Arthur Terry Sports Ctr
  B74 . . . . 32 A3
Artillery Rd CV11 . . . . 79 F6
Artillery St B9 . . . . 67 C2
Artingstall Ho B30 . . . . . 104 B8
Arton Croft B24 . . . . 57 A2
Artrix Arts Ctr B60 . . . . . 137 B3
Arundel
  Birmingham B17 . . . . 85 A6
  Tamworth B77 . . . . 35 C7
Arundel Ave WS10 . . . . . . 41 F3
Arundel Cl CV34 . . . . . . 160 F8
Arundel Cres B92 . . . . 89 A1
Arundel Dr B69 . . . . 62 F8
Arundel Gr WV6 . . . . 23 F3
Arundel Ho B23 . . . . 56 F6
Arundel Pl B11 . . . . 87 A6
Arundel Rd
  Birmingham B14 . . . . . . 105 A1
  Bromsgrove B60 . . . . . . 137 B1
  Bulkington CV12 . . . . 79 C3
  Coventry CV3 . . . . 133 D6
  Stourbridge DY8 . . . . 60 C2
  Willenhall WV12 . . . . 27 C6
  Wolverhampton WV10 . . . 11 B2
Arundel St WS1 . . . . 42 E7
Arun Way B76 . . . . 47 A1
Asbury Ct B43 . . . . 54 C8
Asbury Rd
  Balsall Common CV7 . . . . 130 B5
  Wednesbury WS10 . . . . . 42 E2
Asbury Wlk B43 . . . . 43 C1
Ascot Cl
  Bedworth CV12 . . . . 78 B4
  Birmingham B16 . . . . 65 F2
  Coventry CV3 . . . . 134 C6
  Lichfield WS14 . . . . 9 E8
  Oldbury B69 . . . . 63 E6
Ascot Ct B29 . . . . 103 C7
Ascot Dr
  Cannock WS11 . . . . 4 C8
  Dudley DY1 . . . . 50 F2
  Tamworth B77 . . . . 35 D4
  Wolverhampton WV4 . . . . 39 A4
Ascote La B90 . . . . 126 A5
Ascot Gdns DY8 . . . . 60 D2
Ascot Rd B13 . . . . 86 F2
Ascot Ride CV32 . . . . 157 C3
Ascot Way B61 . . . . 121 B1
Ascot Wlk B69 . . . . 63 E6
Asfare Bsns Pk LE10 . . . . . 75 E1
Ash Ave B12 . . . . 87 A5
Ashborne Ctr B23 . . . . . . 56 E3
Ashborough Dr B91 . . . . . 127 C8
Ashbourne Cl WS11 . . . . . 2 A4
Ashbourne Gr B6 . . . . . . 66 E8
Ashbourne Rd
  Birmingham B16 . . . . 65 D3
  Walsall WS3 . . . . 14 C3
  Wolverhampton, Heath Town
    WV1 . . . . 26 A3
  Wolverhampton, Lanesfield
    WV4 . . . . 39 E3
Ashbourne Ridge B63 . . . 82 D5
Ashbourne Sq CV9 . . . . . . 36 E1
Ashbourne Way B90 . . . . 126 E8
Ash Bridge Ct B45 . . . . . 122 B6
Ashbrook Cres B91 . . . . . 127 C8
Ashbrook Dr B45 . . . . . . 122 B8
Ashbrook Gr B30 . . . . . . 104 C8
Ashbrook Rd B30 . . . . . . 104 C8
Ashburn Gr WV13 . . . . . . 27 C2
Ashburton Cl LE10 . . . . . . 76 A6
Ashburton Rd
  Birmingham B14 . . . . . . 104 D5
  Coventry CV2 . . . . 114 E8
Ashbury Covert B30 . . . . 104 C3
Ashby Cl
  Birmingham B8 . . . . 68 C6
  Coventry CV3 . . . . 134 F8
Ashby Ct
  Nuneaton CV11 . . . . 73 D3
  Solihull B91 . . . . 107 C1
Ashby Grange LE10 . . . . . 71 E5
Ashby Rd
  Hinckley LE9, LE10 . . . . . 71 E5
  Tamworth B79 . . . . 21 C8
Ash Cl WV8 . . . . 10 A3
Ashcombe Ave B20 . . . . . 54 F3
Ashcombe Dr CV4 . . . . . . 111 F3
Ashcombe Gdns B24 . . . . 57 D3
Ashcott Cl B38 . . . . 103 D2
Ash Cres
  Birmingham B37 . . . . 69 F6
  Kingswinford DY6 . . . . . . 60 E6
  Portway B47 . . . . 140 F8
Ashcroft
  Birmingham B15 . . . . 85 E5
  Smethwick B66 . . . . 65 C5
  Tipton DY4 . . . . 52 A2
  Wolverhampton WV4 . . . . 39 F4
Ashcroft Cl CV2 . . . . 115 A8
Ashcroft Gr B20 . . . . 55 D2
Ashcroft Inf Sch B79 . . . . 21 C7
Ashcroft La
  Lichfield WS14 . . . . 8 E1

Ashcroft La continued
  Shenstone WS14 . . . . 17 E7
Ashcroft Way CV2 . . . . . . 115 B8
Ash Ct
  Balsall Common CV7 . . . . 130 C5
  Oldbury B66 . . . . 64 C8
  Stourbridge DY8 . . . . 81 A4
Ashdale Cl
  Binley Woods CV3 . . . . . . 135 E2
  Huntington WS12 . . . . 1 C7
  Kingswinford DY6 . . . . . . 60 D8
Ashdale Dr B14 . . . . 105 A1
Ashdale Gr B26 . . . . 89 A8
Ashdale Rd B77 . . . . 21 D5
Ashdene Cl
  Kidderminster DY10 . . . . 117 C5
  Sutton Coldfield B73 . . . . 46 A3
Ashdene Gdns
  Kenilworth CV8 . . . . 148 B4
  Stourbridge DY8 . . . . 60 C2
Ashdown Cl
  Birmingham, Frankley
    B45 . . . . 102 A2
  Birmingham, Highgate B13 87 A1
  Coventry CV3 . . . . 134 D8
Ashdown Dr
  Nuneaton CV10 . . . . 72 F2
  Stourbridge DY8 . . . . 60 E3
Ashdown Gr WS2 . . . . 28 D4
Ash Dr
  Birmingham B31 . . . . . . 102 C1
  Hartshill CV10 . . . . 72 A8
  Kenilworth CV8 . . . . 148 A4
  Lower Marlbrook B61 . . . 121 B1
  West Bromwich B72 . . . . . 46 C2
Ashen Cl DY3 . . . . 39 C3
Ashenden Rise WV3 . . . . . 38 A8
Ash End House Children's
  Farm* B78 . . . . 48 B8
Ashenhurst Rd DY1 . . . . . 61 F8
Ashenhurst Wlk DY1 . . . . 51 A1
Ashe Rd CV10 . . . . 72 B3
Ashes Rd B69 . . . . 63 F3
Ashes The
  Birmingham B5 . . . . 86 D5
  Oldbury B69 . . . . 63 F3
  Wolverhampton WV11 . . . 26 B6
Ashfern Dr B76 . . . . 57 F7
Ashfield Ave
  Birmingham B14 . . . . 86 F1
  Coventry CV4 . . . . 111 D1
Ashfield Cl WS3 . . . . 28 F4
Ashfield Cres
  Dudley DY2 . . . . 62 C3
  Stourbridge DY9 . . . . 82 A3
Ashfield Ct B38 . . . . 103 E4
Ashfield Gdns B14 . . . . . . 86 F1
Ashfield Gr
  Halesowen B63 . . . . 82 E2
  Wolverhampton WV10 . . . 11 C3
Ashfield Ho B28 . . . . 105 E3
Ashfield Rd
  Bilston WV14 . . . . 41 A2
  Birmingham B14 . . . . 86 F1
  Kenilworth CV8 . . . . 148 B4
  Wolverhampton, Fordhouses
    WV10 . . . . 11 C3
  Wolverhampton WV10 . . . 24 D2
Ashford Cl B24 . . . . 57 D4
Ashford Dr
  Bedworth CV12 . . . . 78 A3
  Sedgley DY3 . . . . 50 E7
  Sutton Coldfield B76 . . . . 57 F5
Ashford Gdns CV31 . . . . . 161 F3
Ashford Ind Pk WV2 . . . . . 40 A7
Ashford La B94 . . . . 143 B7
Ashford Rd
  Hinckley LE10 . . . . 75 B7
  Whitnash CV31 . . . . 161 F2
Ashford St B12 . . . . 86 F8
Ashfurlong Cl CV7 . . . . . 130 B6
Ashfurlong Cres B75 . . . . 46 F7
Ash Gn DY1 . . . . 51 A5
Ash Gr
  Ash Green CV7 . . . . 95 C7
  Birmingham, Balsall Heath
    B12 . . . . 87 A5
  Birmingham, Bordesley
    B9 . . . . 67 B2
  Cannock WS11 . . . . 1 F4
  Dudley DY3 . . . . 50 C2
  Kidderminster DY11 . . . . 116 B7
  Lichfield WS14 . . . . 9 E8
  Stourbridge DY9 . . . . 81 D3
  Tamworth B79 . . . . 35 F5

Ashleigh Dr continued
  Nuneaton CV11 . . . . 73 F1
  Tamworth B77 . . . . 35 E8
Ashleigh Gr B13 . . . . 87 B1
Ashleigh Heights B91 . . . 107 A5
Ashleigh Ho B91 . . . . . . 107 C5
Ashleigh Mews Cotts B76 . 59 C6
Ashleigh Rd
  Oldbury B69 . . . . 63 C8
  Solihull B91 . . . . 107 B4
Ashley Cl
  Birmingham B15 . . . . 86 C7
  Kingswinford DY6 . . . . . . 60 C4
  Stourbridge DY8 . . . . 80 D2
Ashley Cres CV34 . . . . . . 161 B6
Ashley Ct B45 . . . . 122 A1
Ashley Gdns B8 . . . . 67 D4
Ashley Ho DY2 . . . . 62 D4
Ashley Mount WV6 . . . . . 24 D5
Ashley Rd
  Birmingham B23 . . . . 56 E3
  Smethwick B66 . . . . 65 C4
  Walsall WS3 . . . . 13 F1
  Willenhall WS3 . . . . 37 F8
  Wolverhampton WV4 . . . . 38 E5
Ashley St WV14 . . . . 41 A6
Ashley Way CV7 . . . . 130 B7
Ashmall WS7 . . . . 7 D4
Ashmead Dr B45 . . . . . . 122 C4
Ashmead Gr B24 . . . . 57 A2
Ashmead Rd WS7 . . . . 7 A8
Ashmead Rise B45 . . . . . 122 C4
Ashmeads B27 . . . . 88 C5
Ashmole Ave WS14 . . . . . . 7 E8
Ashmole Cl WS14 . . . . 9 E6
Ashmole Rd B70 . . . . 52 F7
Ashmore Ave WV11 . . . . . 13 A1
Ashmore Ind Est WS2 . . . 28 B3
Ashmore Lake Rd WV12 . . 27 B4
Ashmore Lake Way WV12 . 27 B4
ASHMORE LAKE 27 B4
Ashmore Rd
  Birmingham B30 . . . . . . 103 F5
  Coventry CV6 . . . . 113 B4
Ashmores Cl B97 . . . . . . 158 D5
Ashmore's Ind Est DY1 . . . 51 E3
Ashold Farm Rd B24 . . . . 57 D2
Asholme Cl B36 . . . . 68 C7
Ashorne Cl
  Birmingham B28 . . . . . . 106 B7
  Coventry CV2 . . . . 96 C2
  Redditch B98 . . . . 159 D8
Ashover Gr B18 . . . . 65 E4
Ashover Rd B44 . . . . 44 D3
ASHOW 148 E1
Ashow Cl CV8 . . . . 148 B4
Ash Park Ind Est WS11 . . . 2 B3
Ashperton Cl B98 . . . . . . 153 E1
Ash Priors Cl CV4 . . . . . . 112 B1
Ash Rd
  Birmingham B8 . . . . 67 D4
  Dudley DY1 . . . . 51 B3
  Tipton DY4 . . . . 51 E4
  Wednesbury WS10 . . . . . 41 F5
Ashridge Cl CV11 . . . . 78 F8
Ash St
  Bilston WV14 . . . . 40 E3
  Cradley Heath B64 . . . . . 62 F2
  Walsall WS3 . . . . 14 D1
  Wolverhampton WV3 . . . . 25 B1
Ashstead Cl B76 . . . . 58 B6
Ashted Cir B7 . . . . 67 A4
Ashted Wlk B7 . . . . 67 B4
Ash Terr B69 . . . . 52 B1
Ashton Cl B97 . . . . 153 B1
Ashton Croft
  Birmingham B16 . . . . 66 A2
  Solihull B91 . . . . 107 A1
Ashton Dr WS4 . . . . 15 C2
Ashton Park Dr DY5 . . . . . 61 C1
Ashton Rd B25 . . . . 88 C7
Ash Tree Ave CV4 . . . . . . 112 A2
Ashtree Cl DY5 . . . . 61 B1
Ashtree Ct WS11 . . . . 1 D4
Ash Tree Dr B26 . . . . 88 D7
Ashtree Gr WV14 . . . . 41 B3
Ash Tree Rd CV7 . . . . 97 E5
Ashtree Rd
  Birmingham B30 . . . . . . 104 A6
  Redditch B97 . . . . 153 B5
Ashurst Cl CV6 . . . . 96 B5
Ashurst Rd B76 . . . . 57 F7
Ash View WS12 . . . . 1 D8
Ashville Ave B34 . . . . 68 F7
Ashville Dr B63 . . . . 82 F5
Ashwater Dr B14 . . . . . . 104 D2
Ashway B11 . . . . 87 B5
Ash Way B23 . . . . 56 C7
Ashwell Dr B90 . . . . 106 D4
Ashwells Gr WV9 . . . . 11 A2
Ashwin Rd B21 . . . . 66 A7
Ash Wlk B76 . . . . 46 F2
Ashwood Ave
  Coventry CV6 . . . . 112 F5
  Stourbridge DY8 . . . . 60 D2
Ashwood Cl
  Oldbury B69 . . . . 63 F4
  Sutton Coldfield B74 . . . . 44 E8

Ashwood Ct
Birmingham B13 . . . . 87 A3
Birmingham, Stechford B34. 68 D5
Ashwood Dr B37. . . . . . . 70 D3
Ashwood Gr WV4 . . . . . . 39 A5
Ashwoodbay DY8 . . . . . . 60 F3
Ashwood Park Prim Sch
DY8. . . . . 60 D1
Ashwood Rd CV10. . . . . . 72 E5
Ashworth Ho
Cannock WS11. . . . . 2 A4
2 Lichfield WS13 . . . . . . 9 B8
Ashworth Rd B42 . . . . . . 44 B1
Askew Bridge Rd DY3 . . . 50 B3
Askew Cl DY3. . . . . 50 E5
Aspall Cl B97 . . . . 153 D3
Aspbury Croft B36 . . . . . 58 D1
Aspects Park Gate CV11 . . 73 F7
Aspen Cl
Birmingham B27 . . . . . . 88 B2
Coventry CV4. . . . . 111 D1
2 Lichfield WS13 . . . . . . 9 E8
Sutton Coldfield B76 . . . . 46 F2
Aspen Dr
Bedworth CV6 . . . . 96 C6
Birmingham B37 . . . . . . 90 C8
Aspen Gdns B20 . . . . 55 B1
Aspen Gr
Birmingham B9 . . . . 68 A3
Burntwood WS7. . . . . . . 6 F8
Hollywood B47. . . . . 125 B5
Willenhall WV12 . . . . . . 27 E7
Aspen Ho B91 . . . . 106 F2
Aspens Way B61 . . . . . . 137 A6
Aspen Way WV3 . . . . . . 25 A1
Asphodel B74. . . . . 31 F5
Asplen Ct CV8 . . . . 148 C4
ASPLEY HEATH 141 D2
Aspley Heath B94 . . . . . . 141 D2
Aspley Heath La B94 . . . . 141 D2
Asquith Dr
Cannock WS11. . . . . 2 C2
Oldbury B69. . . . . 52 D2
Asquith Rd B8 . . . . 68 B5
Asra Cl B66. . . . . 65 A8
Asra Ho B66. . . . . 65 A8
Astbury Ave B67 . . . . . . 64 F3
Astbury Cl
Walsall WS3. . . . . 14 A4
Wolverhampton WV1. . . . 26 A1
Astbury Ct 1 B68. . . . . . 84 B7
Aster Cl
Hinckley LE10 . . . . 75 E6
Nuneaton CV11 . . . . 74 A1
Aster Way
Hinckley LE10 . . . . 75 D6
Walsall WS5. . . . . 43 A3
Aster Wlk
Bedworth CV10 . . . . 78 A8
Wolverhampton WV9. . . . 11 A3
Asthill Croft CV3 . . . . . . 133 C8
Asthill Gr CV3 . . . . 133 C8
Astle Dr B69. . . . . 52 E1
Astle Park Outlet (Sh Ctr)
B70. . . . . 53 C3
Astley Ave
Coventry CV6. . . . . 95 E2
Halesowen B62 . . . . 83 F6
Astley Cl
Redditch B98 . . . . 159 A7
Royal Leamington Spa
CV32. . . . . 156 D2
Tipton DY4. . . . . 52 D6
Astley Cres B62. . . . . . . 83 F5
Astley La
Bedworth CV12 . . . . 77 C4
Nuneaton CV10 . . . . 72 B1
Astley Rd
Birmingham B21 . . . . . . 54 D1
Bromsgrove B60 . . . . . . 137 C1
Astley Wlk B90 . . . . 106 B5
ASTON. 67 A7
Aston Bridge B6. . . . . . . 66 F6
Aston Brook Gn B6 . . . . . 66 F5
Aston Brook St B6. . . . . . 66 F5
Aston Brook Street E B6 . 66 F5
Aston Bury B15 . . . . 85 D7
Aston Church Rd B7, B8 . . 67 D6
Aston Cl
Darlaston WV14. . . . . . . 41 A4
Shenstone WS14 . . . . . . 18 B6
Aston Cross Bsns Village
B6. . . . . 67 A6
Aston Ct B23 . . . . 56 C3
Aston Expressway B6 . . . 66 F6
Aston Expressway (Elevated
Rd) B6. . . . . 67 A8
ASTON FIELDS. 151 C8
Aston Fields Mid Sch
B60. . . . . 151 C8
Aston Fields Trad Est 2
B60. . . . . 150 F6
ASTON FLAMVILLE 76 E6
Aston Flamville Rd LE10. . 76 C7
Aston Hall* B6. . . . . 66 F8
Aston Hall Rd B6. . . . . . . 67 B8
Aston La
Aston Flamville LE10. . . . 76 D7
Birmingham B20 . . . . . . 55 E2
Hinckley LE10 . . . . 76 A6
Aston Manor Cl B20. . . . . 55 E2
Aston Manor Road Transport
Mus* B6. . . . . 55 F1
Aston Manor Sch B6. . . . . 66 F6
ASTON NEW TOWN 66 F6

Aston Park Ind Est CV11. . 73 B5
Aston Rd
Birmingham B6 . . . . 66 F5
Bromsgrove B60 . . . . . . 150 F6
Coventry CV5. . . . . 112 F1
Dudley DY2 . . . . 62 B8
Nuneaton CV11 . . . . 73 B5
Oldbury B69. . . . . 52 A1
Willenhall WV13 . . . . . . 26 E2
Aston Road N B6. . . . . . . 66 F6
Aston Science Pk B7. . . . 66 F4
Astons Cl DY5 . . . . 81 D7
Aston Seedbed Ctr B7 . . . 67 A6
Astons Fold DY5 . . . . 81 D7
Aston St
Birmingham B4 . . . . 164 D4
Tipton DY4. . . . . 52 A2
Wolverhampton WV3. . . . 39 A8
Aston Sta B6 . . . . 66 F8
Aston Tower Prim Sch B6 . 66 F7
Aston Univ B5 . . . . 164 D4
Astor Dr B13. . . . . 87 C1
Astoria Cl WV12 . . . . 13 D1
Astoria Gdns WV12. . . . . 13 D1
Astor Rd
Kingswinford DY6 . . . . . 60 F5
Sutton Coldfield B74 . . . . 31 A1
ASTWOOD BANK 158 F1
Astwood Bank Fst Sch
B96. . . . . 158 E2
Astwood La B96 . . . . 158 C2
Atcham Cl B98. . . . . 154 F3
Atcheson Cl B80 . . . . 159 E4
Athelney Ct WS3. . . . . . . 15 A3
Athelstan Gr WV6. . . . . . 23 F5
Athelstan Way B79. . . . . 20 F7
Athena Cl CV34. . . . . 161 E5
Athena Gdns CV6 . . . . . . 96 A1
Atherstone Cl
Redditch B98 . . . . 154 F1
Solihull B90 . . . . 105 E2
Atherstone Rd WV1 . . . . 26 B2
Atherstone St B77, B78 . . 35 B8
Atherston Pl CV4 . . . . . . 132 D6
Athlone Rd WS5 . . . . 43 C8
Athol Cl B32. . . . . 102 D8
Athole St B12. . . . . 87 A7
Atholl Cres CV10. . . . . . . 72 E2
Atholl Ct CV10 . . . . 72 E2
Athol Rd CV2 . . . . 115 A6
Atkinson Ct WV10. . . . . . 25 D6
Atkins Way LE10 . . . . . . 75 E7
Atlantic Ct 4 WV13 . . . . 27 A1
Atlantic Rd B44. . . . . 44 F1
Atlantic Way WV10. . . . . 41 E1
Atlas Croft WV10. . . . . . . 25 C6
Atlas Est
Birmingham, Tyseley B11. . 88 A5
Birmingham, Witton B6 . . . 56 A2
Atlas Gr B70. . . . . 52 F3
Atlas Trad Est
Birmingham B11 . . . . . . 87 D5
Coseley WV14 . . . . 40 F7
Attenborough Cl B19. . . . 66 E5
Attingham Dr
Birmingham B43 . . . . . . 43 D2
Cannock WS11. . . . . 2 B2
Attingham Dr DY3 . . . . . 51 B2
ATTLEBOROUGH 73 F2
Attleborough Fields Ind Est
CV11. . . . . 73 E3
Attleborough La B46. . . . 59 A1
Attleborough Rd CV11. . . 73 D3
Attlee Cl B69 . . . . 52 D2
Attlee Cres WV14 . . . . . . 40 E2
Attlee Gr WS11. . . . . 2 C2
Attlee Rd WS2 . . . . 27 E3
Attoxhall Rd CV2. . . . . . . 114 E4
Attwell Pk WV3 . . . . 38 D7
Attwell Rd DY4 . . . . 40 F1
Attwood Bsns Ctr 2 DY9. 81 F5
Attwood Cl B8 . . . . 67 E6
Attwood Cres CV2 . . . . . 114 C7
Attwood Gdns WV4 . . . . 39 E5
Attwood Rd WS7. . . . . . . 6 C7
Attwood St
Halesowen B63 . . . . 82 F5
Stourbridge DY9 . . . . . . 81 F5
Aubrey Rd
Birmingham B32 . . . . . . 84 E7
Birmingham, Small Heath
B10. . . . . 87 F8
Auchinleck Dr WS13 . . . . 3 C1
Auchinleck Sq 5 B15. . . . 66 B1
Auckland Dr B36. . . . . . . 70 B7
Auckland Ho B32 . . . . . . 84 F4
Auckland Rd
Birmingham B11 . . . . . . 87 A7
Kingswinford DY6 . . . . . 60 E4
Smethwick B67 . . . . 64 E5
Auden Ct WV6 . . . . 23 F4
Audleigh Ho 8 B15. . . . . 66 B1
Audlem Wlk WV10 . . . . . 26 A5
Audley Dr DY11 . . . . 116 A8
Audley Prim Sch B33. . . . 68 F4
Audley Rd B33. . . . . 68 F4
Audnam DY8 . . . . 60 F1
Augusta Pl CV32 . . . . . . 161 F8
Augusta Rd
Birmingham, Acock's Green
B27. . . . . 88 C5
Birmingham, Moseley B13. . 86 E4
Augusta Road E B13 . . . . 86 F4
Augusta St B18 . . . . 66 C4
Augustine Ave B80. . . . . 159 D4
Augustine Gr
Birmingham B18 . . . . . . 65 F6

Augustine Gr *continued*
Sutton Coldfield B74 . . . . 31 F5
Augustines Wlk WS13 . . . 3 A3
Augustus Cl B46 . . . . 59 F1
Augustus Cl B15 . . . . 85 F8
Augustus Rd
Birmingham B15 . . . . . . 85 E8
Coventry CV1. . . . . 113 F4
Augustus St WV2 . . . . . . 37 F1
Aulton Cres LE10. . . . . . . 71 B1
Aulton Rd B75 . . . . 32 E2
Aulton Way LE10. . . . . . . 71 B1
Ault St B70 . . . . 53 D1
Austcliff Cl B97 . . . . 158 D6
Austcliff Dr B91. . . . . . . 127 C8
Austen Cl CV32 . . . . 157 E5
Austen Pl B15 . . . . 86 B8
Austen Wlk B71. . . . . 53 D6
Austin Cl
Birmingham B27 . . . . . . 88 D4
Dudley DY1 . . . . 50 F2
Austin Cote La WS14 . . . . 9 F7
Austin Croft B36. . . . . . . 58 E1
Austin Ct 8 B74 . . . . 31 E3
Austin Dr CV6 . . . . 114 A7
Austin Ho WS4. . . . . 28 F3
Austin Rd
Birmingham B21 . . . . . . 54 C1
Bromsgrove B60 . . . . . . 150 E7
Austin Rise B81. . . . . 122 F7
Austin St WV6 . . . . 25 B4
Austin Way B42. . . . . 55 A5
Austrey Cl B93. . . . . 128 A6
Austrey Gr B29 . . . . 103 A8
Austrey Rd DY6. . . . . 61 A5
Austwick Cl CV34 . . . . . . 155 E1
Austy Cl B36. . . . . 68 E8
Autobase Ind Est B69 . . . 52 C3
Autumn Berry Gr DY3 . . . 50 E6
Autumn Cl WS4 . . . . 15 C1
Autumn Dr
Dudley DY3 . . . . 50 D4
Lichfield WS13. . . . . 3 D2
Walsall WS4. . . . . 15 C2
Autumn Gr B19 . . . . 66 C6
Auxerre Ave B98 . . . . . . 159 B8
Auxerre Ho B98. . . . . . . 159 B8
Avalon Cl B6 . . . . 56 A2
Avalon Ho 2 WS11 . . . . . 1 F4
Avalon Rd B60 . . . . 137 C2
Avebury Cl CV11 . . . . . . 73 F2
Avebury Gr B30. . . . . 104 C7
Avebury Rd B30. . . . . . . 104 C8
Ave Maria Cl B64 . . . . . . 62 E1
Avenbury Dr B91. . . . . . . 107 E4
Avenbury Dr B91. . . . . . . 154 F1
Avenue Albert B94. . . . . . 143 C7
Avenue Cl
Birmingham B7 . . . . 67 A6
Dorridge B93 . . . . 128 A3
Avenue Rd
Astwood Bank B96 . . . . . 158 E1
Birmingham, Aston B7, B6. . 67 A6
Birmingham, Erdington B23. 56 F4
Birmingham, Handsworth
B21. . . . . 54 D2
Birmingham, King's Heath
B14 . . . . 104 D8
Cannock WS12. . . . . 2 E2
Darlaston WS10. . . . . . . 41 D6
Dorridge B93 . . . . 128 A3
Dudley, Woodside DY1, DY2. 61 F6
Kenilworth CV8 . . . . 147 D6
Nuneaton CV11 . . . . 73 D2
Rowley Regis B65 . . . . . 63 D1
Royal Leamington Spa
CV31. . . . . 161 F7
Tipton DY14. . . . . 51 C8
Wolverhampton WV3 . . . 24 E2
Avenue The
Birmingham, Acock's Green
B27. . . . . 88 D3
Birmingham B45 . . . . . . 121 E7
2 Birmingham, Lozells B19 66 C8
Blackwell B60 . . . . 138 A6
Blakedown DY10 . . . . . . 98 B2
Coventry CV3. . . . . 134 A6
Featherstone WV10. . . . . 12 C7
Rownington Green CV35. 145 A1
Rowley Regis B65 . . . . . 63 A3
Sutton Coldfield B76 . . . . 46 F1
Averill Rd B26 . . . . 69 A1
Avern Cl DY4 . . . . 52 B6
Aversley Rd B38 . . . . . . 123 E8
Avery Croft B35. . . . . . . 57 F2
Avery Ct 6 CV34. . . . . . . 160 F7
Avery Dell Ind Est B30 . . 104 A6
Avery Dr B27 . . . . 88 C4
Avery Ho B46 . . . . 66 A1
Avery Myers Cl B68 . . . . 64 B5
Avery Rd
Smethwick B66 . . . . 65 B6
Sutton Coldfield B73 . . . . 45 C3
Aviary Ct 8 B71. . . . . . . 53 C6
Aviemore Cl CV10. . . . . . 73 A2
Aviemore Cres B43 . . . . 44 B4
Avill B77 . . . . 36 A5
Avill Gr DY11 . . . . 116 C7
Avington Cl DY3 . . . . 50 D7
Avion Cl WS1 . . . . 42 F7
Avion Cl WV6. . . . . 25 A4

Avocet Cl
Birmingham B33 . . . . . . 68 E3
Coventry CV2. . . . . 96 B3
Avocet Dr DY10 . . . . 117 A2
Avon B77. . . . . 36 A5
Avonbank Cl B97. . . . . . . 158 C6
Avon Bsns Pk WS11 . . . . 4 C7
Avon Cl
Brierley Hill DY5. . . . . . . 61 B7
Bromsgrove B60 . . . . . . 150 F6
Bulkington CV12 . . . . . . 79 B6
Perton WV6. . . . . 23 F4
Avon Cres WS3 . . . . 15 A1
Avoncroft 8 WV4. . . . . . 39 F4
Avoncroft Mus of Historic
Buildings* B60. . . . . . . 150 E5
Avoncroft Rd B60 . . . . . 150 D6
Avon Ct
Kenilworth CV8 . . . . 147 F5
5 Sutton Coldfield B73 . . 46 B5
Avondale Cl DY6. . . . . . . 60 E8
Avondale Rd
Birmingham B11 . . . . . . 87 D4
Brandon CV8 . . . . 135 F5
Coventry CV5. . . . . 133 A8
Royal Leamington Spa
CV32. . . . . 157 C4
Wolverhampton WV6. . . . 24 F3
Avon Dr
Birmingham, Castle Bromwich
B36. . . . . 69 F7
Birmingham, Moseley B13. . 87 D2
Willenhall WV13 . . . . . . 27 C2
Wythall B47. . . . . 124 E2
Avon Gr WS5 . . . . 43 A4
Avon Ho
8 Birmingham, Brandhall
B68. . . . . 84 B8
Birmingham, Lee Bank B15. 86 D8
Coventry CV4. . . . . 132 C6
Dudley, Dibdale DY3. . . . 50 E3
2 Dudley, Russell's Hall
DY1. . . . . 61 E8
Avonlea Rise CV32 . . . . . 156 D2
Avon Lodge CV11 . . . . . . 73 A5
Avon Rd
Burntwood WS7. . . . . . . 6 F5
Cannock WS11. . . . . 4 D8
Coventry CV4. . . . . 132 B6
Halesowen B63 . . . . 82 B5
Kenilworth CV8 . . . . 147 E3
Kidderminster DY11. . . . 116 B3
Solihull B90 . . . . 106 D1
Stourbridge DY8 . . . . . . 80 F3
Walsall WS3. . . . . 14 E1
Whitnash CV31 . . . . 162 A3
Avon St
Birmingham B11 . . . . . . 87 C5
Coventry CV2. . . . . 114 B5
Warwick CV34 . . . . 161 A7
Avon Wlk LE10. . . . . 75 B2
Avro Way B35 . . . . 58 B2
Awbridge Rd DY2 . . . . . . 62 C3
Awefields Cres B67 . . . . 64 E4
Awlmakers Gr WS3 . . . . 28 D7
Awson St CV6. . . . . 113 F6
Axcess 10 Bsns Pk WS10. 41 E8
Axholme Rd CV2 . . . . . . 114 E4
Axletree Way WS10 . . . . 42 B5
Axminster Cl CV11 . . . . . 73 F5
Ayala Croft 2 B36 . . . . . 68 E8
Aylesbury Cl B94. . . . . . . 143 C6
Aylesbury Cres B44 . . . . 56 A8
Aylesbury Rd B94 . . . . . 143 D7
Aylesdene Ct CV5 . . . . . 132 F8
Aylesford Cl DY3 . . . . . . 39 C2
Aylesford Ct 7 CV31. . . . 162 A6
Aylesford Dr
Birmingham B37 . . . . . . 90 A7
Sutton Coldfield B74 . . . . 31 E5
Aylesford Rd B21 . . . . . . 54 D1
Aylesford Sch & Language
Coll CV34. . . . . 160 C4
Aylesmore Cl
Birmingham B32 . . . . . . 84 C1
Solihull B92 . . . . 106 E8
Aynho Cl CV5 . . . . 112 A3
Aynsley Ct B90. . . . . 106 C2
Ayre Rd B24. . . . . 57 B4
Ayres Cl B34. . . . . 69 E6
Ayrshire Cl B36. . . . . 68 D8
Ayrton Cl WV6 . . . . 24 A4
Aysgarth Cl CV11 . . . . . . 73 A4
Azalea Cl
Codsall WV8. . . . . 10 B3
Hinckley LE10 . . . . 75 E5
Azalea Dr LE10. . . . . 75 E6
Azalea Gr B9 . . . . 67 F2
Azalea Wlk LE10 . . . . . . 75 E5
Aziz Isaac Cl B68. . . . . . 64 C6

B

Babbacombe Rd CV3. . . . 133 D5
Babb's Mill Nature Reserve*
B37. . . . . 69 F4
Bablake Cl CV6 . . . . 112 F8
Bablake Croft B92 . . . . . 89 A1
Bablake Jun Sch CV1 . . . 165 A4
Bablake Pre Prep Sch
CV1. . . . . 165 B1
Bablake Sch CV1. . . . . . . 113 B4

Babors Field WV14. . . . . . 40 A3
Babworth Cl WV9 . . . . . . 11 A2
Baccabox La B47 . . . . . . 124 E7
Bacchus Rd B18 . . . . 65 F6
Bache St B70 . . . . 53 D1
Bach Mill Dr B28. . . . . . . 105 D3
Backcester La WS13 . . . . 9 B8
Backcrofts 9 WS11. . . . . 1 E1
Backhouse La WV11. . . . . 26 C4
Back La
Aldridge WS9. . . . . 30 F8
Meriden CV7 . . . . 110 E5
Shenstone WS14 . . . . . . 17 E1
Solihull B90. . . . . 126 A5
Warwick CV34 . . . . 160 E6
Back Rd
Birmingham B38 . . . . . . 103 F2
Kingswinford DY6 . . . . . 60 D7
Back St CV11 . . . . 73 C5
BACON'S END. 70 B4
Badbury Cl B80 . . . . 159 D4
Badbury Gdns B80 . . . . . 159 D4
Baddesley Cl CV31. . . . . 162 C5
BADDESLEY CLINTON . . . 145 B6
Baddesley Clinton* B93. 144 F4
Baddesley Rd B92. . . . . . 88 E2
Bader Rd
Perton WV6. . . . . 23 E3
Walsall WS2. . . . . 27 F2
Bader Wlk B35. . . . . 57 F2
Badger Brook La B96 . . . 158 D1
Badger Cl
Cheswick Green B90 . . . 126 D4
Huntington WS12. . . . . . 1 D6
Redditch B98 . . . . 154 D3
Badger Ct WV10 . . . . . . 25 D4
Badger Dr WV10 . . . . . . 25 D4
Badger Rd CV3 . . . . 134 D8
Badgers Bank Rd B74 . . . 31 F5
Badgers Cl WS3 . . . . 15 A5
Badgers Croft B62 . . . . . 83 B7
Badgers Retreat CV31. . . 162 C4
Badger St
Dudley DY3 . . . . 50 E5
Stourbridge DY9 . . . . . . 81 E6
Badgers The B45 . . . . . . 122 A2
Badgers Way
Birmingham B34 . . . . . . 69 A5
Cannock WS12. . . . . 2 D1
Badger Way B60 . . . . . . 138 B5
Badminton Cl DY1 . . . . . 50 F3
Badon Covert B14. . . . . . 104 D2
Badsey Cl B31 . . . . 103 C4
Badsey Rd B69 . . . . 63 D5
Baggeridge Cl DY3. . . . . 50 A8
Baggeridge Ctry Pk (Nature
Reserve)* DY3 . . . . . . 49 E6
Baggott St WV2. . . . . 39 C7
BAGINTON. 133 F2
Baginton Cl B91 . . . . 107 B5
Baginton Fields Specl Sch
CV3 . . . . 134 B4
Baginton Rd
Birmingham B35 . . . . . . 58 B4
Coventry CV3. . . . . 133 C5
Bagley End DY4. . . . . 62 D4
Bagley's Rd DY5 . . . . 81 D6
Bagley St DY9 . . . . 81 C6
Bagnall Cl B25. . . . . 88 D6
Bagnall Rd WV14 . . . . . . 40 C5
Bagnall St
Walsall WS3. . . . . 28 C6
Wednesbury DY4 . . . . . . 41 C1
West Bromwich B70 . . . . 53 E2
West Bromwich, Harvills
Hawthorn B70. . . . . 52 E7
Bagnall Wlk DY5. . . . . . . 61 D1
Bagnall Rd B13 . . . . 104 F7
Bagot St B4. . . . . 164 C4
Bagot Way CV34 . . . . . . 161 E3
Bagridge Cl WV3 . . . . . . 38 B8
Bagridge Rd WV3. . . . . . 38 B8
Bagshaw Cl CV8 . . . . . . 135 A1
Bagshawe Croft B23 . . . 56 D7
Bagshaw Rd B33 . . . . . . 68 E3
Bague Wlk DY5 . . . . 61 C2
Bailey Ave B77. . . . . 35 F5
Bailey Cl
Burntwood WS7. . . . . . . 6 D8
Cannock WS11. . . . . 2 A4
Bailey Rd WV14 . . . . 40 B7
Baileys Ct B65 . . . . 63 B3
Bailey St
West Bromwich B70 . . . . 53 A4
Wolverhampton WV10. . . 163 D3
Bailye Cl WS13. . . . . 3 F1
Baines' La 1 LE10 . . . . . 71 D1
Bains Cl WS3 . . . . 9 A6
Baird Ho DY6 . . . . 60 F7
Bakehouse La B93 . . . . . 145 B6
Bakeman Ho B26 . . . . . . 88 D6
Baker Ave
Royal Leamington Spa
CV32. . . . . 161 F6
Wolverhampton WV14. . . 39 F2
Baker Cl WS13. . . . . 3 F1
Baker House Gr B43. . . . 54 D7
Baker Rd WV14 . . . . 40 E3
Bakers Ave
Coventry CV5. . . . . 112 E2
Dorridge B93 . . . . 128 D1
Sutton Coldfield B73, B74. . 45 A5
Baker's La
Aldridge WS9. . . . . 30 B6
Sutton Coldfield WS13 . . 9 B7
Bakers Mews B93. . . . . . 145 B6
Baker St
Bedworth CV6 . . . . 96 B6

Baker St *continued*
Birmingham, Handsworth
B21 .... 65 F8
Birmingham, Small Heath
B10 .... 67 D1
Birmingham, Sparkhill B11 . 87 C5
Burntwood WS7 .... 6 F4
Tipton DY4 .... 51 E4
West Bromwich B70 .. 53 B3
Bakers Way WS12 .... 2 B5
Bakers Wlk 1 B77 .... 35 F6
Bakewell Cl
Coventry CV3 .... 134 F8
Walsall WS3 .... 14 C3
Balaams Wood Dr B31 .. 102 B1
**Balaam's Wood Nature
Reserve★** B45 .... 102 A1
Balaclava Rd B14 ..... 104 C8
Balcaskie Cl B15 ...... 85 E7
Balden Rd B32 .... 84 F7
Baldmoor Lake Rd B23 .. 56 F6
Baird's La DY9 .... 81 F5
Baldwin Cl B69 .... 52 D2
Baldwin Croft CV6 .... 96 B1
Baldwin Gr WS11 ...... 2 C2
Baldwin Ho B19 .... 66 E6
Baldwin Rd
Birmingham B30 ...... 104 A3
Kidderminster DY10 .... 117 B7
Baldwins La B28 ...... 105 F4
Baldwin St
Bilston WV14 .... 40 F4
Smethwick B66 .... 65 B6
Balfour B79 .... 21 A4
Balfour Cl LE10 ...... 75 E7
Balfour Cres WV6 ..... 24 F4
Balfour Ct
Sutton Coldfield B74 .... 32 A3
2 Wolverhampton WV6 .. 24 F4
Balfour Dr B69 .... 52 D2
Balfour Ho 2 B16 .... 65 F1
Balfour Rd DY6 .... 60 E8
Balfour St B12 .... 86 E6
Balham Gr B44 .... 45 A2
Balholm B62 .... 83 D5
Balking Cl WV14 ...... 40 B3
Ballantine Rd CV6 ..... 113 B6
Ballarat Wlk DY8 ...... 80 F5
Ballard Cres DY2 ...... 62 D5
Ballard Rd DY2 .... 62 D5
Ballard Wlk B37 ...... 70 A6
Ball Fields CV4 .... 52 D5
Ball Ho 5 WS5 .... 24 F3
Ballingham Cl CV4 .... 112 A2
Balliol Bsns Pk WV9 ... 10 E3
Balliol Rd B77 .... 69 F2
Balliol Rd
Coventry CV2 .... 114 C4
Hinckley LE10 .... 75 F6
Ball La WV10 .... 11 C6
Ballot St B66 .... 65 B5
BALLS HILL 42 B1
Balls Hill WS1 .... 28 F2
Balls St WS1 .... 28 F2
Balmain Cres WV11 ... 12 B1
Balmoral Cl
Coventry CV2 .... 114 E6
Halesowen B62 .... 83 B7
Lichfield WS14 .... 9 D6
Tamworth B79 .... 21 B7
Walsall WS4 .... 29 D7
Balmoral Ct
Birmingham B1 .... 66 C3
Cannock WS11 .... 2 A5
Kidderminster DY10 .... 117 A5
Nuneaton CV10 ...... 72 E5
Balmoral Dr
Cannock WS12 .... 1 F7
Willenhall WV12 ...... 27 C7
Wombourne WV5 .... 38 A1
Balmoral Ho WV3 ..... 163 A1
Balmoral Rd
Birmingham B36 ..... 70 A7
Birmingham, Erdington B23 . 56 F5
Birmingham, Kitwell B32 . 102 B7
Stourbridge DY8 ...... 60 C2
Sutton Coldfield B74 .. 31 F5
Wolverhampton WV4 ... 39 A5
Balmoral View DY1 .... 50 F4
Balmoral Way
Rowley Regis B65 ..... 63 D4
Royal Leamington Spa
CV32 .... 157 C6
Walsall WS2 .... 28 B4
BALSALL COMMON ... 130 A7
Balsall Common Prim Sch
CV7 .... 130 B5
BALSALL HEATH 86 D6
Balsall Heath Rd B12 .... 86 E7
Balsall St B93, CV7 .... 129 D7
BALSALL STREET 129 E6
Balsall Street E CV7 .. 130 B5
Balthazar Cl CV34 .... 161 E4
Baltic Cl WS11 .... 1 E2
Baltimore Rd B42 ...... 55 A5
Balmoral Way B14 ... 105 C3
Balvenie Way DY1 .... 50 F4
Bamber Cl WV3 .... 38 E8
Bamburgh B77 .... 35 C7
Bamburgh Gr CV32 ... 156 E3
Bamford Cl WS3 ...... 14 C3
Bamford Ho WS3 ..... 14 C3
Bamford Rd
Walsall WS3 .... 14 C3
Wolverhampton WV3 ... 39 A8
Bamford St B77 .... 21 D3
Bampfylde Pl B42 ..... 55 C7
Bampton Ave 4 WS7 .. 7 A8

Bamville Rd B8 .... 68 A5
Banbrook Cl B92 ...... 107 D8
Banbury Cl DY3 .... 50 E6
Banbury Croft B37 .... 69 F2
Banbury Ho B33 ...... 69 E2
Banbury Rd
Cannock WS11 .... 4 C8
Warwick CV34 .... 161 A3
Banbury St B5 .... 66 F2
Bancroft B77 .... 21 F3
Bancroft Cl WV14 ..... 51 B7
Bandywood Cres B44 .. 44 F3
Bandywood Rd B44 .... 44 F3
Banebery Dr WV10 .... 12 B7
Banfield Ave WS10 .... 41 C7
Banfield Rd WS10 ..... 41 C4
Banford Ave B8 .... 68 A4
Banford Rd B8 .... 68 A4
Bangham Pit Rd B31 .. 102 E6
Bangley La
Drayton Bassett B78 ... 33 E6
Mile Oak B78 .... 34 A8
Bangor Ho B37 .... 70 B4
Bangor Rd B9 .... 67 D2
Bank Cres WS7 .... 6 F5
Bank Croft B31 .... 162 C5
Bankdale Rd B8 .... 68 B4
Bankes Rd B10 .... 67 F1
Bank Farm Cl DY9 ..... 81 C1
Bankfield Dr CV32 .... 156 C1
Bankfield Rd
Bilston WV14 .... 40 D5
Tipton DY4 .... 52 C8
Bank Ho B27 .... 88 C3
Banklands Rd DY2 .... 62 E6
Bank Rd
Dudley, Gornalwood DY3 ... 50 C2
Dudley, Netherton DY2 ... 62 D6
Banks Gn B97 .... 152 B2
BANK'S GREEN 152 A3
Bankside
Atherstone CV9 .... 36 E1
Birmingham, Great Barr B43 54 E7
Bankside Cl CV3 ...... 134 A6
Bankside Cres B74 .... 44 F7
Bankside Way WS9 ... 16 B2
Banks Rd CV6 .... 113 A5
Banks St WV13 .... 27 A2
Bank St
Bilston WV14 .... 40 E3
Birmingham B14 ...... 86 E1
Brierley Hill DY5 ...... 61 D3
Cannock WS12 .... 2 E1
Cradley Heath B64 .... 62 C1
Stourbridge DY9 ...... 81 F5
Tipton WV14 .... 51 C8
Walsall WS1 .... 28 F1
West Bromwich B71 ... 53 D6
Wolverhampton WV10 .. 25 E5
Bankwell St DY5 ...... 61 D4
Banky Mdw LE10 ...... 76 A7
Banner La
Coventry CV4 .... 111 D2
Solihull B92 .... 129 B8
Bannerhea Rd B37 .... 69 F5
Bannerley Rd B33 ..... 69 C1
Banners Ct B73 .... 45 B3
BANNERS GATE 45 B4
Banners Ct B73 .... 45 B4
Banners Gate Inf Sch B73 45 B4
Banners Gate Jun Sch
B73 .... 45 A4
Banners Gate Rd B73 .. 45 B3
Banners Gr B23 .... 57 A6
Banners La
Halesowen B63 ...... 82 D6
Redditch B97 .... 158 C5
Banners St B63 .... 82 D6
Banners Wlk B44 ..... 45 B2
Bannister Rd WS10 .... 41 D2
Bannister St B64 ...... 62 D2
Banquo App CV34 ..... 161 F3
Banstead Cl WV2 ..... 39 E7
Bantam Gr CV6 .... 95 A3
Bantams Cl B33 .... 69 C2
Bant Mill Rd B60 ..... 137 A1
Bantock Ave WV3 .... 38 F8
Bantock Cl WV3 ...... 38 E8
Bantock Gdns WV3 .... 24 E1
Bantock House Mus★
WV3 .... 24 F1
Bantock Prim Sch WV3 .. 39 A8
Bantock Rd CV4 ...... 111 E2
Bantocks The B70 .... 53 A4
Bantock Way 7 B17 .. 85 D5
Banton Cl B23 .... 56 D8
Bantry Cl B26 .... 89 C4
Baptist Cl CV2 .... 96 D5
BAPTIST END 62 C6
Baptist End Rd DY2 .... 62 C6
Baptist Wlk LE10 ..... 71 D1
Barbara Rd B28 ...... 105 E4
Barbara St B79 .... 21 A5
Barbel Dr WV10 .... 26 B4
**Barber Inst of Fine Arts
The★** B15 .... 86 A4
Barberry Ho B38 ..... 103 F1
Barbers La B91 .... 108 C6
Barbican Rise CV2 .... 114 E2
Barbourne Cl B91 .... 127 B7
Barbridge Cl CV12 .... 79 C2
Barbridge Rd CV12 .... 79 C3
Barchester Rd
Birmingham B29 ...... 85 A1
Dorridge B93 .... 128 A4

Barclay Ct WV3 .... 25 A2
Barclay Rd B67 .... 64 E1
Barcliff Ave B77 ...... 21 E3
Barcroft WV13 .... 27 C2
Barcroft Prim Sch WV13 .. 27 C2
Bardell Cl WS13 .... 8 E6
Bardenholme Gdns DY9 . 81 D3
Bardfield Cl 1 B42 .... 55 A8
Bardley Dr CV6 .... 113 C6
Bardon Dr B90 .... 106 D2
Bardsey Cl LE10 ...... 71 B1
Bard St B11 .... 87 C5
Bardwell Cl WV8 ...... 24 F8
Barford App CV31 ..... 162 B2
Barford Cl
Coventry CV3 .... 134 D8
Darlaston WS10 .... 41 C8
Redditch B98 .... 154 F1
Sutton Coldfield B76 ... 46 F4
Barford Cres 5 B38 .. 104 C2
Barford Ho B5 .... 86 E8
Barford Prim Sch B16 .. 65 E3
Barford Rd
Birmingham B16 ...... 65 F3
Kenilworth CV8 ...... 148 B3
Solihull B90 .... 106 D2
Barford St B5 .... 86 E8
Barham Cl B90 .... 127 A5
Barker Rd B74 .... 46 B7
Barker's Butts La CV6 . 113 A4
Barkers La B47 .... 125 A1
Barker St
Birmingham B19 ...... 66 B7
Oldbury B68 .... 64 C6
Bark Piece B32 .... 84 C3
Barlands Croft B34 .... 69 C6
Barle Gr B36 .... 70 A7
Barleston Dr LE10 ..... 71 A1
Barley Cl
Cannock WS12 .... 2 B5
Dudley DY3 .... 50 F7
Sutton Coldfield WS9 ... 30 E2
Wolverhampton WV8 ... 10 E1
Barley Croft
Perton WV6 .... 23 D3
Stoke Heath B60 ..... 150 E6
Barley Ct CV32 .... 156 F2
Barleyfield LE10 ...... 71 C3
Barleyfield Ho 3 WS1 . 42 E8
Barleyfield Rise DY6 ... 60 A8
Barleyfield Row WS1 ... 42 E8
Barley Lea Ho CV3 .... 134 B8
Barley Lea The CV3 ... 134 C8
Barley Mow La B61 ... 137 B8
Barley Rd B16 .... 65 C3
Barlich Way B98 ..... 154 A2
Barling Way CV10 .... 73 B1
Barlow Ave B77 ...... 21 D3
Barlow Cl
Birmingham B45 ...... 101 E2
Oldbury B68 .... 64 A3
Tamworth B77 .... 21 E4
Barlow Dr B70 .... 53 F1
Barlow Rd
Coventry CV2 .... 96 D2
Wednesbury WS10 .... 42 A5
Barlow's Rd B15 ...... 85 E5
Barmouth Cl WV12 .... 27 C6
Barnabas Rd B23 ..... 56 F4
Barnaby Sq WV10 .... 11 F4
Barnack Ave CV3 ..... 133 B5
Barnack Dr CV34 ..... 155 E1
BARNACLE 97 B6
Barnacle La CV12 ..... 79 C1
Barnard Cl
Birmingham B37 ..... 70 D1
Royal Leamington Spa
CV32 .... 157 C3
Barnard Pl WV2 .... 39 E6
Barnard Rd
Sutton Coldfield B75 .. 46 E7
Wolverhampton WV11 .. 12 F1
Barnard Way WS11 ..... 1 F2
Barn Ave DY3 .... 50 C7
Barnbridge B77 .... 21 C2
Barnbrook Rd B93 ... 128 A7
Barn Cl
Birmingham B30 ..... 104 B6
Coventry CV5 .... 112 C5
Cradley Heath B64 .... 82 E6
Dordon B78 .... 36 F6
Halesowen B63 ...... 82 E2
Lichfield WS13 .... 3 B3
Stoke Heath B60 ..... 150 E6
Whitnash CV31 ...... 162 B3
Barn Croft
Birmingham B32 ...... 84 E1
Burntwood WS7 .... 7 A4
Great Wyrley WS6 .... 5 A3
Barncroft Rd B69 ..... 63 A8
Barncroft St B70 ..... 53 A8
Barne Cl CV11 .... 79 B7
Barnes Cl B37 .... 69 E2
Barnes Hill B29 ...... 84 F2
Barnes Meadow Pl WV14 . 51 B8
Barnes Rd WS14 ...... 18 A6
Barnesville Cl B10 .... 88 A8
Barnet Rd B23 .... 56 C5
BARNETTBROOK 118 D5
Barnett Cl
Bilston WV14 .... 40 D4
Kingswinford DY6 ..... 60 D4
Barnett Gn DY6 ...... 60 D4
Barnett La DY6, DY8 .. 60 D4
Barnett Rd WV13 ..... 26 E1

Barnetts Cl DY10 ..... 117 B4
Barnetts Gr DY10 .... 117 A4
Barnetts La
Brownhills WS8 .... 6 F1
Kidderminster DY10 ... 117 A4
Barnett St
Stourbridge DY8 ..... 60 D3
Tipton B69 .... 52 A2
Tipton DY4 .... 52 A4
Barney Cl DY4 .... 51 F3
Barn Farm Cl 4 WV14 .. 41 A7
Barnfield Ave CV5 .... 112 B6
Barnfield Cl WS14 ..... 9 B6
Barnfield Dr B92 ..... 107 F6
Barnfield Gr B20 ...... 54 E5
Barnfield Rd
Bromsgrove B61 ..... 136 E1
Halesowen B62 .... 83 D7
Tipton DY4 .... 51 E6
Wolverhampton WV1 .... 26 A2
Barnfield Trad Est DY4 . 51 E7
Barnford Cl B10 ...... 67 C1
Barnford Cres B68 .... 64 A3
Barnfordhill Cl B68 .... 64 B4
Barn Gn WV3 .... 38 F7
Barn Ho B8 .... 68 D4
Barnhurst La WV8 .... 10 E2
Barn La
Birmingham, Handsworth
B21 .... 65 E7
Birmingham, King's Heath
B13 .... 105 A7
Solihull B92 .... 88 F3
Barn Leigh Dr CV4 ... 131 D6
Barn Mdw B25 .... 68 D1
Barnmoor Rise B91 ... 107 C7
Barn Owl Dr WS3 .... 14 F4
Barn Owl Ho WV10 ... 117 A2
Barn Owl Wlk DY5 .... 81 C6
Barnpark Covert 9 B14 . 104 C2
Barn Piece B32 .... 84 B1
Barnsbury Ave B72 .... 57 C6
Barns Croft WS9 ..... 15 F4
Barns Croft B74 ...... 31 B4
Barnsdale Cres B31 ... 102 E4
Barns La WS4 .... 29 D7
Barns Lane CV6 ...... 113 D8
Barnsley Hall Dr B60 .. 137 B6
Barnsley Hall Rd B61 .. 137 A6
Barnsley Rd
Birmingham B17 ...... 65 A1
Bromsgrove B61 ..... 137 B4
Barn St B5 .... 66 F2
Barnstaple Cl CV5 .... 111 F5
Barnstaple Rd B66 .... 65 B5
Barnswood Cl
Cannock WS11 .... 4 B8
Halesowen B63 ...... 82 C5
BARNT GREEN 138 A7
Barnt Green Rd B45 ... 122 C3
Barnt Green Sta B45 . 138 D8
Barn Way WS12 .... 2 F4
Barnwood Cl B98 ..... 154 D5
Barnwood Rd
Birmingham B32 ...... 84 F4
Wolverhampton WV8 ... 10 E1
Barons Bsns Ctr DY9 .. 81 E5
Barons Cl B17 .... 85 B6
Barons Court Trad Est
WS9 .... 15 E2
Barons Croft CV10 ... 72 C4
Baron's Croft CV3 .... 133 E7
Barons Ct B92 .... 89 C4
Baron's Field Rd CV3 .. 133 E8
Barpool Rd CV10 ..... 72 F4
Barrack Cl B75 .... 47 A6
Barrack La B63 .... 82 B6
Barracks Cl WS3 ..... 28 E8
Barracks La
Beausale CV35 .... 146 C2
Brownhills WS9, WS14 ... 16 C8
Walsall WS3 .... 28 E8
Barracks Pl WS3 ...... 28 E8
Barrack St
Birmingham B7 .... 67 A3
Warwick CV34 .... 160 E7
West Bromwich B70 ... 53 A8
Barracks Way CV1 ... 165 B2
Barra Croft B35 ...... 58 B4
Barrar Cl DY8 .... 80 E8
Barras Ct CV2 .... 114 A4
Barras Gn CV2 .... 114 A4
Barras La CV1 .... 113 B3
Barratts Croft DY5 ... 50 C1
Barratts Ho B14 ..... 104 E4
Barratts Rd B38 ..... 104 A1
Barr Beacon Language Coll
WS9 .... 44 B5
BARR COMMON 30 C3
Barr Common Rd WS9 .. 30 B3
Barr Common Rd WS9 .. 30 B3
Barr Rd CV3 .... 133 E8
Barrett Cl DY10 ...... 117 B6
Barrett Ct CV3 .... 130 C6
Barrett St B66 .... 65 C4
Barrhill Cl B43 .... 43 E2
Barrie Ave DY10 ..... 117 C7
Barrie Rd LE10 .... 71 D3
Barrington Cl
Walsall WS5 .... 43 A3
Wolverhampton WV10 .. 11 C1
Barrington Rd
Birmingham B45 ..... 121 E7
Solihull B92 .... 88 F2
Barr Lakes La
Aldridge WS9 .... 44 A7
Walsall WS5, WS9 ..... 43 F7
Barron Rd B31 .... 103 B3

Barrow Cl
Brownhills WS9 .... 15 F4
Coventry CV2 .... 115 B6
Redditch B98 .... 154 F3
Barrowfield Ct CV8 ... 147 F4
Barrowfield La CV8 ... 147 F4
BARROW HILL 61 C7
Barrow Hill Nature Reserve★
DY5 .... 61 C8
Barrow Hill Rd DY5 ... 50 C1
Barrow Ho 1 B16 ..... 65 F1
Barrow Rd CV8 ...... 147 F4
Barrows La B26 .... 89 A6
Barrows Rd B11 ...... 87 C6
Barrow Wlk B5 .... 86 E7
Barrs Cres B64 .... 82 F8
Barrs Rd B64 .... 82 E8
Barrs St B68 .... 64 A4
Barr St
Birmingham B19 ...... 66 C5
Dudley DY3 .... 50 C3
Barry Ho CV2 .... 96 D1
Barry Jackson Twr B6 .. 66 F7
Barry Rd WS5 .... 43 F4
Barsham Cl B5 .... 86 C6
Barsham Dr DY5 ...... 81 C8
BARSTON 109 B1
Barston Cl CV6 .... 96 A2
Barston La
Balsall Common CV7 .. 129 D8
Barston B92 .... 109 C1
Catherine de B B91 .... 108 B2
Eastcote B92 .... 108 D3
Solihull B91 .... 107 F2
Barston Rd B68 .... 84 B7
Bartestree Cl B98 .... 158 F1
Bartholomews La B61 ... 136 F5
Bartholomew Ct CV3 ... 134 A6
Bartholomew Row B5 .. 164 D3
Bartholomew St B5 ... 164 D2
Bartic Ave DY6 .... 60 F4
Bartleet Rd
Redditch B98 .... 159 E8
Smethwick B67 .... 64 D5
Bartlett Cl
Coventry CV6 .... 95 E2
3 Warwick CV34 .... 160 F7
Wednesbury DY4 ..... 41 B1
Bartley Cl B92 .... 88 F2
Bartley Dr B31 .... 102 E8
BARTLEY GREEN 102 D7
Bartley Green Com L Ctr
B32 .... 84 C1
**Bartley Green Tech & Sports
Coll** B32 .... 84 C1
Bartley Ho B32 ...... 102 D8
Bartley Mews B32 .... 102 E8
Bartley Woods B32 .... 84 B2
Barton Cres CV31 .... 162 C6
Barton Dr B93 .... 128 A6
Barton Ind Est WV14 .. 40 E6
Barton La DY6 .... 60 C8
Barton Lodge Rd B28 . 105 E4
Barton Rd
Bedworth CV12 .... 78 A4
Coventry CV6 .... 95 F2
Nuneaton CV10 ..... 73 C1
Wolverhampton WV4 ... 38 C6
Barton's Mdw CV2 ... 114 B6
Barton St B70 .... 53 C2
BARWELL 71 F7
Barwell Cl
Dorridge B93 .... 127 E4
Royal Leamington Spa
CV32 .... 156 F3
Barwell Cl 8 B6 ...... 67 B2
Barwell La LE10 ...... 71 E3
Barwell Rd B9 .... 67 B2
Barwick St B3 .... 164 C3
Bar Wlk WS9 .... 16 C1
Basant Cl CV34 ...... 161 A7
Bascote Cl B97 ...... 153 B1
Baseley Way CV6 .... 95 D4
Basford Brook Dr CV6 ... 95 F4
Basildon Wlk 3 CV2 . 115 A7
Basil Gr B31 .... 102 E4
Basil Rd B31 .... 102 E4
Basin La B77 .... 21 D3
Baskerville Specl Sch
B17 .... 85 A5
Baslow Cl
Birmingham B33 ...... 68 E4
Walsall WS3 .... 14 E3
Baslow Rd WS3 .... 14 E3
Basons La B68 .... 64 D5
Bassano Rd 1 B65 .... 63 C1
Bassenthwaite Ct DY6 .. 60 D6
Bassett Cl
Sutton Coldfield B76 .. 46 E4
Wolverhampton WV12 .. 27 D4
Wolverhampton WV4 ... 38 C6
Bassett Croft B10 .... 87 B8
Bassett Rd
Coventry CV6 .... 113 A5
Stourbridge B62 ...... 82 A4
Wednesbury WS10 .... 42 D3
Bassetts Gr DY7 ..... 69 E5
Bassett St WS2 ...... 28 C2

Bassnage Rd B63 . . . . . . 82 E2
Batchcroft
Bilston WV14 . . . . 40 D5
Darlaston WS10 . . . . 41 D8
Batchelor Cl DY8 . . . . . . 80 F8
BATCHLEY 153 B3
Batchley Fst Sch B97 . . 153 B4
Batchley Rd B97 . . . . . . 153 C4
Bateman Dr B73 . . . . . . 46 B1
Bateman Rd B46 . . . . . . 59 F1
Bateman's Acre S 🔢
CV6 . . . . 113 A4
BATEMAN'S GREEN . . . 124 F6
Batemans La B47 . . . . . 124 E5
Bates Cl B76 . . . . 58 B8
Bates Gr WV10 . . . . 26 A4
Bates Hill B97 . . . . 153 D4
Bates La B94 . . . . 141 F1
Bates Rd CV5 . . . . 132 E8
Bate St
🔢 Walsall WS2 . . . . 28 E3
Wolverhampton WV4 . . . 40 A3
Batham Rd DY10 . . . . . . 117 A8
Bath Ave WV1 . . . . 163 A3
Bath Cl 🔢 B29 . . . . 103 B7
Batheaston Cl B38 . . . . 123 D7
Bath Mdw B63 . . . . 82 E5
Bath Mews DY8 . . . . . . 80 F5
Bath Pas B5 . . . . 164 C1
Bath Pl 🔢 CV31 . . . . . . 161 F7
Bath Rd
Brierley Hill DY5 . . . . . . 62 A2
Cannock WS11 . . . . 1 E5
Nuneaton CV11 . . . . 73 C5
Stourbridge DY8 . . . . . . 80 F5
Tipton DY4 . . . . 52 A5
Walsall WS1 . . . . 42 E8
Wolverhampton WV1 . . . 163 A3
Bath Row B15 . . . . 66 C1
Bath St
Bilston WV14 . . . . 40 E5
Birmingham B4 . . . . . . 164 C4
Coventry CV1 . . . . 165 C4
Dudley DY2 . . . . 62 C8
Royal Leamington Spa
CV31 . . . . 161 F7
Sedgley DY3 . . . . 39 E1
Walsall WS1 . . . . 42 E8
Willenhall WV13 . . . . . . 27 B1
Wolverhampton WV1 . . . 163 D2
Bathurst Rd CV6 . . . . . 113 A6
Bath Walk Ind Est B12 . 86 E5
Bathway Rd CV3 . . . . . 133 A4
Bath Wlk B12 . . . . 86 E5
BATMANS HILL 40 F2
Batmans Hill Rd WV14,
DY4 . . . . 40 E1
Batsford Cl B98 . . . . . . 159 B5
Batsford Rd CV6 . . . . . 112 F4
Batson Rise DY5 . . . . . . 81 A8
Battalion Ct CV6 . . . . . . 95 A1
Battenhall Rd B17 . . . . . 85 A5
Battens Cl B98 . . . . . . 153 F3
Battens Dr B98 . . . . . . 154 D3
Battery Way B11 . . . . . . 87 E4
Battledown Cl LE10 . . . . 71 B2
Battlefield Hill WV5 . . . 49 B7
Battlefield La WV5 . . . . 49 B6
Battlefield Terr WV5 . . . 49 B6
Battling Brook Prim Sch
LE10 . . . . 71 B2
Baughan Ho B24 . . . . . . 57 D3
Baulk La CV7 . . . . 110 D1
Bavaro Gdns DY5 . . . . . 62 A2
Baverstock Foundation Sch
& Specialist Sports Coll
B14 . . . . 104 E2
Baverstock Rd B14 . . . 104 E2
Baxter Ave DY10 . . . . . 116 F7
Baxter Cl CV4 . . . . 112 A2
Baxter Coll DY11 . . . . . 116 B6
Baxter Ct
Birmingham B13 . . . . . . 86 F2
🔟 Royal Leamington Spa
CV31 . . . . 162 A7
Baxter Gdns DY10 . . . . 116 F7
Baxterley Gn
Solihull B91 . . . . 106 C4
Sutton Coldfield B76 . . . 46 F1
Baxter Rd DY5 . . . . 61 C2
Baxters Gn B90 . . . . . . 126 B8
Baxters Rd B90 . . . . . . 126 B8
Bay Ave WV14 . . . . 40 F4
Bayer St WV14 . . . . 51 C8
Bayford Ave
Birmingham, Coft Common
B31 . . . . 122 E6
Birmingham, Sheldon B26 . 89 C4
Bayley Cres WS10 . . . . . 41 C8
Bayley La CV1 . . . . 165 C2
Bayleys La DY4 . . . . 52 C8
Bayley Tower 🔢 B36 . . . 68 E8
Baylie Ct DY8 . . . . 80 F5
Baylie St DY8 . . . . 80 F4
Baylis Ave WV11 . . . . . . 26 F8
BAYLIS GREEN 141 A1
Bayliss Ave
Coventry CV6 . . . . 96 A4
Wolverhampton WV4 . . . 40 A3
Bayliss Cl
Bilston WV14 . . . . 40 C7
Birmingham B31 . . . . . 103 B5
Bayliss Ct WV3 . . . . 24 E2
Baynton Rd WV12 . . . . . 27 C8
Bayston Ave WV3 . . . . . 38 E8

Bayston Rd B14 . . . . . . 104 E3
Bayswater Rd
Birmingham B20 . . . . . . 55 D1
Dudley DY3 . . . . 50 D2
Bayton Rd CV7 . . . . 96 B7
Bayton Road Ind Est CV7 . 96 B8
Bayton Way CV7 . . . . . . 96 C7
Baytree Cl WS3 . . . . . . 14 A2
Bay Tree Cl
Birmingham B38 . . . . . 123 D8
Coventry CV2 . . . . 96 D1
Baytree Rd WS3 . . . . . . 14 A2
Baywell Cl B90 . . . . . . 127 A7
Bazzard Rd CV11 . . . . . . 79 F6
Beach Ave
Birmingham B12 . . . . . . 87 B5
Wolverhampton WV4,
WV14 . . . . 40 A2
Beach Brook Cl B11 . . . . 87 B5
Beachburn Way B20 . . . 55 B3
Beach Cl B31 . . . . 103 C1
Beachcroft Rd DY6 . . . . 49 C1
Beach Dr B63 . . . . 83 A5
Beach Rd
Bilston WV14 . . . . 40 D7
Birmingham B11 . . . . . . 87 B5
Beach St B63 . . . . 83 A5
Beach Trad Ctr B12 . . . . 87 B5
Beachwood Ave DY6 . . . 49 C1
Beacon Cl
Birmingham, Great Barr
B43 . . . . 43 F1
Birmingham, Rubery B45 . 122 A6
Smethwick B66 . . . . 65 A7
Beacon Ct
🔢 Birmingham B43 . . . . 43 F1
Sutton Coldfield B74 . . . 44 F8
Beacon Ctr for the Blind
WV4 . . . . 39 D4
Beacon Dr WS1 . . . . 43 A8
Beaconfields 🔢 WS13 . . . 9 A8
Beacon Gdns WS13 . . . . 3 A1
Beacon Hill
Aldridge WS9 . . . . 30 C1
Birmingham, Aston B6 . . . 66 E8
Birmingham B45 . . . . . 121 F5
Beacon Hts WS9 . . . . . . 44 B6
Beacon La
Birmingham B60, B45 . . 121 E4
Sedgley DY3 . . . . 39 E1
Beacon Mews
🔢 Birmingham B43 . . . . 43 F1
🔢 Lichfield WS13 . . . . . . 9 A8
Beacon Pas DY3 . . . . . . 39 D1
Beacon Prim Sch WV12 . 27 D8
Beacon Rd
Aldridge WS9 . . . . 30 B1
Birmingham, Pheasey WS9,
B43 . . . . 44 C6
Coventry CV6 . . . . 95 D3
Sutton Coldfield, Banners Gate
B44 . . . . 44 A3
Sutton Coldfield, Boldmere
B73 . . . . 46 A1
Walsall WS5 . . . . 43 D5
Willenhall WV12 . . . . . . 27 C8
Beacon Rise
Aldridge WS9 . . . . 30 B3
Sedgley DY3 . . . . 39 E1
Stourbridge DY9 . . . . . . 81 D4
Beaconsfield Ave DY9 . . 35 D5
Beaconsfield Cres 🔢 B12 . 86 E5
Beaconsfield Ct
Nuneaton CV11 . . . . 73 D5
Walsall WS1 . . . . 43 B8
Beaconsfield Dr WV4 . . . 39 D6
Beaconsfield Rd
Birmingham B12 . . . . . . 86 E5
Coventry CV2 . . . . 114 B2
Sutton Coldfield B74 . . . 46 B7
Beaconsfield St
Royal Leamington Spa
CV31 . . . . 162 B7
West Bromwich B71 . . . . 53 C5
Beaconsfield Street W
CV31 . . . . 162 B8
Beaconside Prim Sch
B45 . . . . 121 E6
Beacon St
Lichfield WS13 . . . . 9 A8
Walsall WS1 . . . . 29 A1
Wolverhampton WV14 . . . 39 F1
Beacon Trad Est WS9 . . . 30 A6
Beacon View
Birmingham B45 . . . . . 122 A6
Willenhall WS2 . . . . 27 F2
Beacon View Dr B74 . . . 44 F5
Beaconview Ho 🔢 B71 . . 42 F1
Beacon View Rd B71 . . . 42 F2
Beacon Way
Brownhills WS9 . . . . 16 A3
Cannock WS12 . . . . 2 F3
Beake Ave CV6 . . . . . . 113 B7
Beakes Rd B67 . . . . 64 F3
Beaks Farm Gdns B16 . . 65 D2
Beaks Hill Rd B38 . . . . 103 E2
Beak St B1 . . . . 164 B2
Beale Cl B35 . . . . 58 A2
Beale Ho B16 . . . . 65 F1
Beales St B6 . . . . 67 B8
Beale St DY8 . . . . 80 F5
Bealeys Ave WV11 . . . . 26 C8
Bealeys Cl WS3 . . . . . . 14 A3
Bealeys Fold WV11 . . . . 26 C8
Bealeys La WS3 . . . . . . 14 A2
Beamans Cl B92 . . . . . . 89 A3
Beaminster Rd B91 . . . 107 A4
Beamish Cl CV2 . . . . . . 115 A6

Bean Croft B32 . . . . 84 C2
Bean Dr DY4 . . . . 51 D5
Beanfield Ave CV3 . . . . 132 F4
Bean Rd
Dudley, Dixon's Green
DY2 . . . . 62 D8
Dudley, Swan Village DY4 . 51 C6
Bean Road Ind Est DY4 . 51 C6
Beardmore Rd B72 . . . . 57 C8
Bear Hill B48 . . . . 139 B5
Bear Hill Dr B48 . . . . . 139 B6
Bearing Dr WV11 . . . . . 26 E4
Bearley Croft B90 . . . . 126 C8
Bearmore Rd B64 . . . . . 62 E1
Bearnett Dr WV4 . . . . . 38 C2
Bearnett La WV4 . . . . . . 38 B2
Bearsden Cres LE10 . . . 71 B2
BEARWOOD 65 A2
Bearwood Ho B66 . . . . . 65 A2
Bearwood Prim Sch B66 . 65 A2
Bearwood Rd B66 . . . . . 65 A3
Beasley Gr B43 . . . . 44 B1
Beaton Cl WV13 . . . . . . 26 F3
Beaton Rd B74 . . . . 32 A3
Beatrice St WS3 . . . . . . 28 C6
Beatrice Wlk B69 . . . . . 52 A2
Beattie Cl LE10 . . . . 71 D3
Beatty Ho DY4 . . . . 52 B8
Beaty's Gdns CV32 . . . 157 A4
Beaubrook Gdns DY6 . . . 60 E3
Bede Rd
Bedworth CV12 . . . . 78 A4
Coventry CV6 . . . . 113 B6
Nuneaton CV10 . . . . 72 D3
Bedford Cl LE10 . . . . . . 71 E3
Bedford Dr B75 . . . . 46 E6
Bedford Ho
Birmingham B36 . . . . . . 70 B6
🔢 Birmingham, Erdington
B24 . . . . 56 F4
🔟 Wolverhampton WV3 . 25 C4
Bedford Pl
Cannock WS12 . . . . 2 B4
🔟 Royal Leamington Spa
CV32 . . . . 161 F8
Bedford Rd
Birmingham B12 . . . . . . 87 A8
Sutton Coldfield B75 . . . 46 E7
West Bromwich B71 . . . . 53 B7
Bedford St
Coventry CV1 . . . . 113 A2
Royal Leamington Spa
CV32 . . . . 161 F8
Tipton DY4 . . . . 52 B5
Wolverhampton WV1 . . . 40 B7
Bedlam La CV6 . . . . 95 E2
Bedlam Wood Rd B31 . . 102 C1
Bedlow Cl CV4 . . . . 112 A2
BEDWORTH 78 B1
Bedworth Cl CV12 . . . . . 79 B2
Bedworth Croft DY4 . . . 52 B4
Bedworth Gr B9 . . . . . . 68 B2
BEDWORTH HEATH 77 E1
Bedworth La CV12 . . . . . 77 D4
Bedworth L Ctr CV12 . . . 78 B1
Bedworth Rd
Bedworth Sta CV12 . . . . 78 C2
Bulkington CV12 . . . . . . 79 A2
Coventry CV6, CV7 . . . . . 96 A5
Bedworth's Sloughs Nature
Reserve★ CV12 . . . . . . 77 F3
Beebee Rd WS10 . . . . . . 41 F6
Beecham Bsns Pk WS9 . 30 A8
Beecham Cl WS9 . . . . . . 30 A8
Beech Ave
Birmingham B32 . . . . . . 84 D7
Birmingham, Chelmsley Wood
B37 . . . . 70 B1
🔢 Birmingham, Showell Green
B12 . . . . 87 A5
Halesowen B62 . . . . 83 C8
Tamworth B77 . . . . 21 E3
Beech Cl
Hartshill CV10 . . . . 72 A8
Rowington Green CV35 . 145 A1
Sedgley DY3 . . . . 39 E1
Sutton Coldfield B75 . . . 32 A4
Tamworth B79 . . . . 21 A8
Wolverhampton WV10 . . 25 B8
Beech Cliffe CV34 . . . . 160 F8
Beech Cres
Burntwood WS7 . . . . 6 F6
Tipton DY4 . . . . 52 C8
Wednesbury WS10 . . . . 41 F5
Beechcroft
Bedworth CV12 . . . . 77 F1
Birmingham B15 . . . . . . 86 A7
Beechcroft Ave B28 . . . 106 A6
Beechcroft Cres B74 . . . 30 D1
Beechcroft Ct B74 . . . . . 32 A1
Beechcroft Dr B61 . . . . 137 B4
Beechcroft Est B63 . . . . 82 C6
Beechcroft Pl WV10 . . . 25 C6
Beechcroft Rd
Birmingham B36 . . . . . . 69 B8
Cradley Heath B64 . . . . . 62 F1
Kidderminster DY11 . . . 116 A8
Beech Ct
Birmingham, Bournville
B30 . . . . 103 C4
Birmingham, Great Barr
B43 . . . . 43 D1
Birmingham, Longbridge
B45 . . . . 122 D7
Birmingham, Short Heath
B73 . . . . 56 F8
Cannock WS12 . . . . 2 B7
Great Wyrley WS6 . . . . . . 5 A4

Beckbury Ave WV4 . . . . . 38 C5
Beckbury Rd
Birmingham B29 . . . . . . 85 A1
Coventry CV2 . . . . 114 F6
Beck Cl B66 . . . . 65 A4
Beckenham Ave B44 . . . 45 B1
Beckensall Cl DY1 . . . . . 51 B1
Becket Cl B74 . . . . 31 F6
Beckett Cl B98 . . . . . . 153 F5
Beckett St WV14 . . . . . . 40 F6
Beckfield Cl
Birmingham B14 . . . . . 104 E2
Walsall WS4 . . . . 29 C8
Beckfoot Dr CV2 . . . . . . 96 F1
Beckford Croft B93 . . . 127 F3
Beckford Ct B23 . . . . . . 56 E2
Beckman Rd DY9 . . . . . . 81 C2
Beckminster Rd WV3 . . . 38 F7
Becks La CV7 . . . . 93 A5
Becks The B48 . . . . . . 139 A7
Beck The DY2 . . . . 62 E2
Beconsfield Cl B93 . . . . 127 F3
Bective Gr B42 . . . . 55 D7
Bedale Ave LE10 . . . . . . 71 F2
Bedcote Pl DY8 . . . . 81 B5
Beddoe Cl DY4 . . . . 52 D5
Beddow Ave WV14 . . . . 51 C7
Beddows Rd WS3 . . . . . 28 E5
Bede Arc 🔢 CV12 . . . . . 78 B3
Bede Rd
Bedworth CV12 . . . . 78 A4
Coventry CV6 . . . . 113 B6
Nuneaton CV10 . . . . 72 D3

Beech Ct continued
Oldbury B66 . . . . 64 C8
🔟 Royal Leamington Spa
CV34 . . . . 161 E2
Beechdale B68 . . . . 84 B7
Beechdale Ave B44 . . . . 44 E2
Beechdale Rd WS3 . . . . 27 F8
Beech Dene Gr B23 . . . . 56 E5
Beech Dr CV8 . . . . 148 B5
Beechen Gr WS7 . . . . 6 F8
Beecher Pl B63 . . . . 82 D5
Beecher Rd B63 . . . . . . 82 D5
Beecher Road E B63 . . . 82 D5
Beecher's Keep CV8 . . . 135 F5
Beecher St B63 . . . . 82 C5
Beeches Ave B27 . . . . . . 88 C4
Beeches Cl
Birmingham B45 . . . . . 121 D8
Kingswinford DY6 . . . . . 60 D5
Beeches Ct B45 . . . . . . 122 B7
Beeches Dr B24 . . . . 57 C5
Beeches Farm Dr B31 . . 123 A7
Beeches Mews DY9 . . . . 98 F4
Beeches Pl WS3 . . . . . . 28 D6
Beeches Pool & Fitness Ctr
B42 . . . . 55 C7
Beeches Rd
Birmingham B42 . . . . . . 55 C7
Kidderminster DY11 . . . 116 C8
Oldbury B68 . . . . 64 C3
Rowley Regis B65 . . . . . 63 C1
Walsall WS3 . . . . 28 D6
West Bromwich B70 . . . . 53 E3
Beeches Road Pas B70 . . 53 E2
Beeches The
Bedworth CV12 . . . . 77 E2
Birmingham B15 . . . . . . 86 C8
Sutton Coldfield B74 . . . 31 D4
Sutton Coldfield, Wylde Green
B73 . . . . 46 B1
Upton Warren B61 . . . . 150 A4
West Bromwich B70 . . . . 53 E2
Wolverhampton, Newbridge
WV1 . . . . 25 A3
Wolverhampton WV11 . . 26 B5
Beeches View Ave B63 . . 82 C4
Beeches Way B31 . . . . . 123 A7
Beeches Wlk B73 . . . . . . 46 B3
Beechey Cl B43 . . . . 44 D5
Beech Farm Croft B31 . 103 A3
Beechfield Ave 🔢 B11 . . 87 B6
Beechfield Cl B62 . . . . . 83 C8
Beechfield Dr DY11 . . . 116 C8
Beechfield Gr WV14 . . . 51 B7
Beechfield Rd
Birmingham B11 . . . . . . 87 B6
Smethwick B67 . . . . 64 F4
Beechfield Rise WS14 . . . 9 D8
Beech Gate B74 . . . . 31 C5
Beech Gdns WS14 . . . . . 9 C6
Beech Gdns B20 . . . . . . 54 F4
Beech Gn DY1 . . . . 51 A5
Beech Gr
Birmingham B14 . . . . . 105 A5
Huntington WS12 . . . . . . 1 D8
Warwick CV34 . . . . 156 B1
Beech Hill Ct B72 . . . . . 57 C8
Beech Hill Ho B32 . . . . 102 C8
Beech Hill Rd B72 . . . . . 57 C8
Beech Ho
Redditch B98 . . . . 158 F8
Solihull B91 . . . . 106 F2
Sutton Coldfield B74 . . . 31 B5
🔢 Warwick CV34 . . . . . 161 D8
Beechhouse La WV5 . . . 37 A1
Beech Hurst B38 . . . . . 123 E8
Beech Hurst Gdns WV5 . . 37 A2
BEECH LANES 84 E6
Beech Mews B64 . . . . . . 62 E2
Beechmore Rd B26 . . . . 89 A5
Beechmount Dr B23 . . . 57 A6
Beechnut Cl
Coventry CV4 . . . . 111 D2
Solihull B91 . . . . 107 D5
Beechnut La B91 . . . . . 107 E4
Beech Park Dr B45 . . . . 138 C8
Beech Pine CV WS12 . . . 2 A8
Beech Rd
Birmingham, Bournville
B30 . . . . 103 C6
Birmingham, Erdington B23 . 56 F8
Bromsgrove B61 . . . . . 136 F4
Coventry CV6 . . . . 113 B5
Dudley DY1 . . . . 51 C4
Hollywood B47 . . . . . . 125 B6
Kingswinford DY6 . . . . . 60 E5
Oldbury B69 . . . . 63 A8
Stourbridge DY8 . . . . . . 80 F3
Tamworth B79 . . . . 21 A8
Wednesbury WS10 . . . . 41 F5
Willenhall WV13 . . . . . . 26 E2
Wolverhampton WV10 . . 25 B8
Beech Tree Ave
Coventry CV4 . . . . 112 B2
Wolverhampton WV11 . . 26 C8
Beech Tree Cl
Kingswinford DY6 . . . . . 60 E8
Redditch B97 . . . . 153 B4
Beech Tree La WS11 . . . . 4 D8
Beech Tree Rd WS9 . . . . 15 F3
Beech Way B65 . . . . 65 B5
Beech Wlk B38 . . . . . . 123 F8
BEECHWOOD 131 A6
Beechwood B20 . . . . . . 54 E3
Beechwood Ave
Coventry CV5 . . . . 132 F8
Hinckley LE10 . . . . 75 D3
Wolverhampton WV11 . . 26 B8

Beechwood Bsns Pk WS11 2 B3
Beechwood Cl
Cheswick Green B90 126 D4
Walsall WS3 14 B3
Beechwood Cres B77 21 F5
Beechwood Croft
Kenilworth CV8 147 F2
Sutton Coldfield B74 31 D5
Beechwood Ct
1 Birmingham B30 104 C3
Coventry CV5 132 F8
Cradley Heath B64 83 A7
Wolverhampton WV6 24 C3
Beechwood Dr WV6 24 A2
BEECHWOOD GARDENS 132 E8
Beechwood Ho 10 WV3 25 A2
Beechwood Park Rd B91 106 E5
Beechwood Rd
Bedworth CV12 78 D4
Birmingham B67 84 F8
Birmingham, Great Barr B43 43 F2
Birmingham, King's Heath B14 104 F5
Dudley DY2 51 E1
Nuneaton CV10 72 D6
West Bromwich B70 53 B3
Beechwood Sch B11 87 C4
Beecroft Ave WS13 3 B1
Beecroft Ct WS11 1 E2
Beecroft Rd WS11 1 E1
Beehive Cl B61 121 A1
Beehive Hill CV8 147 E7
Beehive La B76 59 C6
Beehive Wlk 4 DY4 51 E5
Beekes Croft B78 35 A8
Bee La WV10 11 D3
Beeston Cl
Birmingham B6 67 A7
Brierley Hill DY5 81 D8
Coventry CV3 134 F8
Beeton Rd B18 65 E6
Beet St B65 63 C1
Beggars Bush B73 45 D2
Beggars Bush La WV5 49 B5
Begonia Cl LE10 75 E5
Begonia Dr LE10 75 E5
Beighton Cl B74 31 F6
Beilby Rd B30 104 B5
BELBROUGHTON 119 E7
Belbroughton CE Prim Sch DY9 119 E6
Belbroughton Cl B98 153 F2
Belbroughton Rd
Blakedown DY10 98 D1
Halesowen B63 82 F2
Holy Cross DY9 99 E2
Stourbridge DY8 80 E3
Belchers La B8, B9 68 A3
Beldray Rd WV14 40 E6
Belfont Trad Est B62 83 C4
Belfry Cl
Hinckley LE10 75 D4
Walsall WS3 14 A3
Belfry Dr DY8 80 E6
Belfry The WV6 23 D4
Belgrade Rd WV10 11 B1
Belgrade Theatre CV1 165 B3
BELGRAVE 21 E1
Belgrave Ct DY6 60 F4
Belgrave High Sch B77 21 E1
Belgrave Middleway B5, B12 86 E7
Belgrave Rd
Birmingham B12 86 F6
Coventry CV2 114 E4
Halesowen B62 83 D8
Tamworth B77 35 E8
Belgrave Sq CV2 114 E4
Belgrave Terr B21 66 A7
Belgrave Wlk WS2 28 B3
Belgravia Cl B5 86 E7
Belgravia Ct B37 70 A5
Belgrove Cl B15 85 E6
Belgrove Ho WS11 1 D1
Belinda Cl WV13 26 F3
Bellairs Ave CV12 77 E1
Bellamy Cl B90 106 D1
Bellamy Farm Rd B90 106 D1
Bellamy La WV11 26 C7
Bella Pais Cl WS9 44 B7
Bell Barn Rd B15 86 C8
Bellbrooke Cl CV6 96 B1
Bell Cl
Birmingham B36 70 B6
Birmingham, Bordesley Green B9 67 E3
Darlaston WS10 41 D7
Bellcroft 3 B16 66 B2
Bell Ct CV32 156 F2
Bell Dr
Ash Green CV7 95 E7
Birmingham B9 67 F3
Cannock WS12 2 C7
Walsall WS5 43 A5
Belle Cotts B94 143 D5
Bellefield Ave 10 B18 65 E4
Bellefield Rd B18 65 E4
Belle Isle DY5 61 C3
Bellemere Rd B92 109 B6
Bellencroft Gdns WV3 38 C7
BELL END 120 C7
Bell End B65 63 C3
Belle Orch DY11 116 B5
BELLE VALE 82 E5
Belle Vale B63 82 E5
Bellevue
Birmingham B5 86 D7
Dudley WV14 40 E2
Belle Vue
Nuneaton CV10 72 E3
Stourbridge DY8 60 D2
Belle Vue Ave B16 65 D4
Belle Vue Cl B61 121 C1
Belle Vue Ct DY8 60 D2
Belle Vue Dr B62 83 E6
Belle Vue Gdns B65 63 C3
Belle Vue Prim Sch DY8 60 C3
Bellevue Rd
Bilston WV14 41 A2
Birmingham B26 89 B7
Belle Vue Rd DY5 62 A1
Bellevue St WV14 39 F2
Belle Vue Terr B92 109 A6
Belle Wlk B13 87 B3
Bellfield
Birmingham B31 102 F4
Tamworth-In-A B94 142 A2
Bellfield Ho B14 104 D1
Bellfield Jun & Inf Schs B31 102 F4
Bellflower Cl WV10 12 A7
Bellflower Dr 1 WS5 42 F3
Bell Fold B68 64 C6
BELL GREEN
Coventry 114 B8
Hollywood 124 B5
Bell Green La B38 124 B5
Bell Green Rd CV6 114 A8
BELL HEATH 120 E8
Bell Heather Rd WS8 15 D6
Bell Heath Way B32 84 B2
Bell Hill 3 B31 103 A4
Bell Holloway B31 102 F5
Bellingham B77 22 D1
Bellington Croft 5 B90 127 A6
Bellis St B16 65 F1
Bell La
Birmingham, Kitt's Green B33 69 E1
Birmingham, Northfield B31 103 A4
Studley B80 159 E4
Walsall, Wallington Heath WS3 14 B1
Walsall, Yew Tree WS5 43 A5
Bellman Cl WS10 41 D7
Bell Mdw DY9 99 B8
Bell Mead B80 159 E4
Bell Meadow Way B14 104 E1
Bell Pl WV2 163 B1
Bell Rd
Dudley DY2 62 C5
Trysull WV5 37 D1
Walsall WS5 43 D6
Bells Farm Cl B14 104 C2
Bells Farm Prim Sch B14 104 C2
Bell Sh Ctr The B31 103 A4
Bellsize Cl WS11 5 F5
Bells La
Birmingham B14 104 D2
Stourbridge DY8 60 D2
Bells Moor Rd B70 53 A6
Bell St
Bilston WV14 40 C6
Brierley Hill, Barrow Hill DY5 61 D7
Brierley Hill, Silver End DY5 61 D2
Darlaston WS10 41 D7
Dudley WV14 40 C2
Stourbridge DY8 81 A5
Tipton DY4 51 E5
West Bromwich B70 53 D2
Wolverhampton WV1 163 B2
Bell Street S DY5 61 D2
Bell Tower Cl WS3 28 D8
Bell Tower Mews CV32 156 F3
Bellview Way CV6 96 B1
Bell Vue Rd B65 63 C2
Bellwood Rd B31 102 F4
Belmont Ave WS11 1 C2
Belmont Cl
Aldridge WS9 30 A7
Great Wyrley WS11 5 A4
Redditch B97 153 B1
Tipton DY4 51 F6
Belmont Covert B31 103 B6
Belmont Cres B31 103 B6
Belmont Ct
Royal Leamington Spa CV32 157 A4
Sutton Coldfield B72 46 B4
Belmont Dr CV32 157 A4
Belmont Gdns WV14 41 A4
Belmont Mews CV8 147 F4
Belmont Pas B4 67 A3
Belmont Rd
Birmingham, Handsworth B21 65 C8
Birmingham, Rubery B45 122 A6
Brierley Hill DY5 61 D6
Coventry CV6 114 A7
Smethwick B66 65 A2
Stourbridge DY9 81 F4
Tamworth B77 35 E7
Wolverhampton WV4 39 A5
Belmont Road E B21 65 C8
Belmont Row B4 67 A3
Belmont St WV14 41 A4
Belper DY1 51 B1
Belper Ent Pk B70 52 F4
Belper Rd
Walsall WS3 14 C3
West Bromwich B70 52 F3
Belper Row DY2 62 E4
Belsize B77 21 E2
Belstone Cl B14 104 D6
Belton Ave WV11 12 B1
Belton Cl B94 143 C5
Belton Gr B45 122 C8
Belt Rd WS12, WS11 2 A5
Belvedere Ave WV4 39 B5
Belvedere Cl
Burntwood WS7 6 F5
Kidderminster DY10 117 A5
Kingswinford DY6 60 F4
Tamworth B79 21 C7
Belvedere Dr B61 137 A4
Belvedere Gdns WV6 24 E7
Belvedere Rd
Birmingham B24 57 B2
Coventry CV5 133 A8
Belvide Gr B29 103 B8
Belvidere Gdns B11 87 C4
Belvidere Rd WS1 42 F8
Belvoir B77 35 C7
Belvoir Cl DY1 50 E2
Belvoir Rd B60 137 C1
Belwell Dr B74 32 A2
Belwell Gdns B74 32 A2
Belwell La B74 32 A2
Bembridge Cl WV12 27 B8
Bembridge Rd B33 69 A3
Benacre Dr B5 66 F2
Benbeck Gr DY4 51 C6
Benbow Cl LE10 71 D4
Benches Cl WS7 6 D6
Bencroft WV8 10 B4
Bendall Rd B44 45 B2
Benedictine Rd CV3 133 C8
Benedict Sq CV2 114 C8
Benedon Rd B26 89 B7
Bengrove Cl B98 159 A7
Benion Rd WS11 1 F5
Benjamin Gdns 4 B20 55 D1
Benmore Ave B5 86 D7
Bennett Ave DY1 51 B6
Bennett Ct CV8 135 F3
Bennett Dr CV34 161 C7
Bennett Rd B74 31 D3
Bennett's Hill
Birmingham B2 164 B2
Dudley DY2 62 E8
Bennetts Rd B8 67 D6
Bennett's Rd CV7 94 F4
Bennett's Road N CV7 94 E7
Bennett's Road S CV6 94 F2
Bennett St
Birmingham B19 66 D8
2 Kidderminster DY11 116 C6
Bennetts Well Prim Sch B37 69 F3
Ben Nevis Way DY8 81 A6
Bennick Trad Est WS11 4 E6
Bennitt Cl B70 53 C1
Benn Rd CV12 79 B2
Benson Ave WV4 39 D5
Benson Cl
Lichfield WS13 3 D1
Perton WV6 23 E5
Benson Com Sch B18 65 F6
Benson Ind Est B18 65 F6
Benson Rd
Birmingham, Highter's Heath B14 105 B1
Birmingham, Hockley B18 65 F6
Coventry CV6 95 A1
Benson View B79 21 C8
Bent Ave B32 84 D6
Benthall Rd CV6 95 F2
Bentham Ct B31 102 F5
BENTLEY 27 E2
Bentley Bridge Bsns Pk WV11 26 C5
Bentleybridge Island WV11 26 B4
Bentley Bridge L Pk WV11 26 B4
Bentleybridge Way WV11 26 C4
Bentley Cl
Redditch B97 153 D3
Royal Leamington Spa CV32 157 B3
Bentley Ct
Coventry CV6 95 C4
Nuneaton CV11 73 A4
Sutton Coldfield B76 57 F8
Bentley Dr WS2 28 B3
Bentley Drive Prim Sch WS2 28 B2
Bentley Farm Cl B93 127 E4
Bentley Gr B29 102 F8
BENTLEY HEATH 127 E5
Bentley Heath CE Prim Sch B93 127 F5
Bentley Heath Cotts B93 127 F5
Bentley La
Walsall, Birchills WS2 28 B3
Walsall, Leamore WS2 28 A5
Willenhall WV12 27 E5
Bentley Lane Ind Pk WS2 28 B3
Bentley Mill Cl WS2 27 F1
Bentley Mill La WS2 27 F1
Bentley Mill Way WS2 27 F1
Bentley New Dr WS2 28 B3
Bentley Pl WS2 28 B2
Bentley Rd
Bedworth CV7 78 A1
Birmingham B36 69 D7
Nuneaton CV11 73 A4
Wolverhampton WV10 11 E2
Bentley Road N WS2 27 E1
Bentley Road S
Darlaston WS10 41 E8
Bentley Road S *continued*
Walsall WS10 27 E1
Bentley Way B79 20 F7
Bentley West Prim Sch WS2 27 E3
Bentley Wharf WV12 27 D5
Bentmead Gr B38 104 A1
Benton Ave B11 87 C6
Benton Cl WV12 27 D4
Benton Cres WS3 14 D2
BENTON GREEN 110 E3
Benton Green La CV7 110 F2
Benton Rd B11 87 C6
Benton's Ct DY11 116 C6
Benton's La WS6 5 A1
Bentons Mill Croft B7 67 C8
Bentree The CV3 134 B8
Bent St DY5 61 D4
Ben Willetts Wlk 3 B65 63 C1
Benyon Ctr The WS2 28 A7
BEOLEY 154 D7
Beoley Cl B72 46 C1
Beoley Fst Sch B98 154 E8
Beoley Gr B45 122 A7
Beoley Hall B98 140 C1
Beoley La
Beoley B98 154 F8
Portway B98 141 B1
Beoley Road E B98 154 A4
Beoley Road W B98 153 F4
Berberry Cl B30 103 D6
Berchelai Ave B31 102 E6
Berenska Dr CV32 157 A2
Beresford Ave CV6 95 E1
Beresford Cres B70 53 B3
Beresford Dr B73 46 A1
Beresford Rd
Oldbury B69 64 C7
Walsall WS3 28 E8
Berets The B75 46 F6
Bericote Croft B27 88 D3
Bericote Rd CV32 156 E8
Berkeley Cl
Bromsgrove B60 151 B8
Nuneaton CV11 73 B3
Perton WV6 23 F3
Berkeley Dr DY6 60 C7
Berkeley Ho
Birmingham B23 56 F6
Sutton Coldfield B76 57 F8
Berkeley Mews B25 88 B7
Berkeley Prec B14 104 F2
Berkeley Rd
Birmingham B25 88 B7
Kenilworth CV8 147 E6
Solihull B90 105 F3
Berkeley Road E B25 88 B7
Berkeley Road N CV5 113 A1
Berkeley Road S CV5 133 A8
Berkeley St WS2 42 B7
Berkeswell Cl B98 154 C7
Berkett Rd CV6 95 B2
Berkley Cl WS2 27 F3
Berkley Cres B13 87 C1
Berkley Ct B1 66 C1
Berkley St B1 66 C1
Berkshire Cl
Nuneaton CV10 72 E3
West Bromwich B71 53 B7
Berkshire Cres WS10 42 C4
Berkshire The WS3 14 A3
BERKSWELL 110 D3
Berkswell CE Prim Sch CV7 110 C3
Berkswell Cl
Dudley DY1 50 E3
Solihull B91 107 B8
Sutton Coldfield B74 31 E4
Berkswell Hall CV7 110 C3
Berkswell Mus* CV7 110 C3
Berkswell Rd
Birmingham B24 57 B4
Coventry CV6 96 B2
Meriden CV7 110 C7
Berkswell Sta CV7 130 C8
Berkswell Windmill* CV7 130 D4
BERMUDA 78 A8
Bermuda Bsns Pk CV10 78 A7
Bermuda Cl DY1 51 B6
Bermuda Ind Est CV10 78 B8
Bermuda Rd CV10 73 A1
Bernard Pl B18 65 F5
Bernard Rd
Birmingham B17 65 B2
Oldbury B68 64 C2
Tipton DY4 52 B7
Bernard St
Walsall WS1 29 A1
West Bromwich B71 53 C4
Berners Cl CV4 111 E2
Berners St B19 66 D7
Bernhard Dr B21 65 E8
Bernie Crossland Wlk DY10 116 F3
Bernwall Cl DY8 80 F4
Berrandale Rd B36 57 F1
Berrington Cl B98 154 D2
Berrington Dr WV14 51 B8
Berrington Rd
Nuneaton CV10 72 D7
Royal Leamington Spa CV31 162 B6
Berrington Wlk B5 86 E7
Berrow Cottage Homes B93 128 C6
Berrow Dr B15 85 E7
Berrowside Rd B34 69 E6
Berrow View B61 150 D7
Berry Ave WS10 41 B5
Berrybrook Prim Sch WV10 12 B1
Berrybush Gdns DY3 50 E7
Berry Cl B19 66 D6
Berry Cres WS5 43 C4
Berry Dr
Aldridge WS9 29 E5
Barnt Green B45 122 A1
Smethwick B66 65 A6
Berryfield Rd B26 89 D6
Berryfields
Aldridge WS9 29 E5
Stonnall WS9 16 E5
Berryfields Rd B76 46 F3
Berry Hall La B91 108 B4
Berry Hill WS12 2 C4
Berrymound View B47 125 C7
Berry Rd
Birmingham B8 67 E5
Dudley DY1 51 C5
Berry St
Birmingham B18 65 F6
Coventry CV1 113 E4
Wolverhampton WV1 163 C3
Bertha Rd B11 87 D5
Bertie Rd CV8 148 A4
Bertie Terr CV32 156 E1
Bertram Cl DY4 41 C1
Bertram Rd
5 Birmingham B10 67 D1
Smethwick B67 64 E6
Berwick Cl
Coventry CV5 112 B4
Warwick CV34 155 E2
Berwick Dr WS11 4 B8
Berwick Gr
Birmingham, Frankley B31 102 D3
Birmingham, Pheasey B43 44 B4
Berwick Ho CV8 148 A3
Berwicks La B37 70 B1
Berwood Farm Rd B72 57 C6
Berwood Gdns B24 57 C6
Berwood Gr B92 89 B1
Berwood La B24 57 E3
Berwood Pk B35 58 A2
Berwood Rd B72 57 D6
Berwyn Ave CV6 95 A1
Berwyn Gr WS6 4 F3
Berwyn Way CV10 72 C4
Beryl Ave LE10 71 A2
Besant Gr B27 88 A1
Besbury Cl B93 127 E2
BESCOT 42 C6
Bescot Cres WS1 42 D5
Bescot Croft B42 55 B6
Bescot Dr WS2 42 B6
Bescot Ind Est The WS10 41 D4
Bescot Rd WS2 42 B6
Bescot Ret Pk WS1 42 D6
Bescot St WS1 42 E7
Bescot Stadium Sta WS1 42 D5
Bescot Stadium (Walsall FC) WS1 42 D5
Besford Gr
Birmingham B31 102 D3
Solihull B90 127 B6
Besom Way WS6 4 C2
Bessborough Rd B25 88 D8
Best Ave CV8 148 C7
Best Rd WV14 40 D7
Best St B64 62 F2
Beswick Gr B33 69 A4
Beta Gr B14 105 C4
Bethany Mews 4 WS11 1 F4
Bethesda Gdns B63 82 C7
Betjeman Ct DY10 117 B5
Betjeman Pl WV10 12 A1
Betley Gr B33 69 A5
Betony Cl WS5 43 A3
Betsham Cl B44 45 B1
Bettany Glade WV10 11 E4
Betteridge Dr B76 46 E4
Bettina Cl CV10 72 B5
Bettman Cl CV3 133 E6
Betton Rd B14 104 E5
Bett Rd B20 54 F3
Betty's La WS11 6 A4
Bevan Ave WV4 39 E4
Bevan Cl
Bilston WV14 40 F6
Walsall WS4 15 C1
Bevan Ct CV3 133 D7
Bevan Ind Est DY5 61 A2
Bevan Lee Rd WS11 1 D3
Bevan Rd
Brierley Hill DY5 61 A2
Tipton DY4 52 B4
Bevan Way B66 64 F7
Beverley Ave CV10 72 B4
Beverley Cl
Astwood Bank B96 158 E2
Balsall Common CV7 130 C7
Sutton Coldfield B72 57 D7
Beverley Court Rd B32 84 C6
Beverley Cres WV4 39 F4
Beverley Croft B23 56 D2
Beverley Ct 1 B62 84 A6
Beverley Dr DY6 60 C7
Beverley Gr B26 89 B5
Beverley Hill
Atherstone CV9 36 E1
Cannock WS12 2 D6

Beverley Rd
Birmingham B45 .... 122 A7
Royal Leamington Spa CV32 .... 156 D1
West Bromwich B71 .... 42 D1
Beverly Dr CV4 .... 132 D2
Beverston Rd
Perton WV6 .... 24 A4
Wednesbury DY4 .... 41 B2
Bevington Cres CV6 .... 112 E5
Bevington Rd B6 .... 66 F8
Bevin Rd WS2 .... 27 E3
Bevis Gr B44 .... 44 F3
Bewdley Ave [4] B12 .... 87 A6
Bewdley Dr WV1 .... 26 B2
Bewdley Grange DY11 .... 116 A5
Bewdley Hill DY11 .... 116 B5
Bewdley Rd
Birmingham B30 .... 104 B8
Kidderminster DY11 .... 116 C6
Bewdley Villas [3] B18 .... 65 D4
Bewell Ct B61 .... 136 F4
Bewell Gdns B61 .... 136 F4
Bewell Head B61 .... 136 F4
Bewick Croft CV2 .... 114 A5
Bewick Ct WV6 .... 24 C2
Bewlay Cl DY5 .... 81 B7
Bewley Rd WV12 .... 27 D4
Bewlys Ave B20 .... 54 E4
Bexfield Cl CV5 .... 112 A6
Bexhill Dr B77 .... 22 A5
Bexhill Gr [3] B15 .... 66 C1
Bexley Gr B71 .... 53 E7
Bexley Rd B44 .... 56 B8
Bexmore Dr WS13 .... 3 F1
Beyer Cl B77 .... 22 A2
Bhylls Acre Prim Sch WV3 .... 38 B7
Bhylls Cres WV3 .... 38 C7
Bhylls La WV3 .... 38 C7
Bibbey's Gn WV10 .... 11 F4
Bibsworth Ave B13 .... 105 D8
Bibury Rd B28 .... 105 E7
Bicester Sq B35 .... 58 B4
BICKENHILL 90 D1
Bickenhill Green Ct B92 .... 90 D1
Bickenhill La
Birmingham B37 .... 90 C6
Birmingham B40 .... 90 D4
Catherine de B B92 .... 108 C6
Bickenhill Park Rd B92 .... 88 E1
Bickenhill Parkway B37 .... 90 D6
Bickenhill Rd B37 .... 90 B7
Bickford Rd
Birmingham B6 .... 56 A1
Wolverhampton WV10 .... 25 F5
Bickington Rd B32 .... 84 D1
Bickley Ave
[1] Birmingham B11 .... 87 C6
Sutton Coldfield B74 .... 31 E5
Bickley Gr B26 .... 89 B5
Bickley Ho B74 .... 31 E5
Bickley Rd
Bilston WV14 .... 41 A7
Walsall WS4 .... 29 C7
Bicknell Croft B14 .... 104 E2
Bickon Dr DY5 .... 81 F8
Bickton Cl B24 .... 57 C5
Biddings La WV14 .... 40 B2
Biddles Hill B94 .... 141 C6
Biddlestone Pl WS10 .... 41 B7
Biddlestone Gr WS5 .... 43 C3
Biddulph Ct [3] B73 .... 46 A2
Bideford Dr B29 .... 85 C1
Bideford Rd
Coventry CV2 .... 114 C7
Smethwick B66 .... 65 B5
Bideford Way WS11 .... 4 B8
Bidford Cl B90 .... 106 D2
Bidford Rd B31 .... 102 E3
Bierton Rd B25 .... 88 C8
Bigbury Cl CV3 .... 133 E5
Biggin Cl
Birmingham B35 .... 58 A3
Perton WV6 .... 23 E5
Biggin Hall Cres CV3 .... 114 B2
Bigwood Dr
Birmingham B32 .... 84 D1
Sutton Coldfield B75 .... 47 A5
Bilberry Bank WS11 .... 1 E6
Bilberry Cres
Huntington WS12 .... 1 C5
Sutton Coldfield B76 .... 46 F3
Bilberry Dr B45 .... 122 A6
Bilberry Rd
Birmingham B14 .... 104 C6
Coventry CV2 .... 96 D2
Bilboe Rd WV14 .... 41 A3
BILBROOK 10 C4
Bilbrook CE Mid Sch WV8 .... 10 B3
Bilbrook Ct WV8 .... 10 B3
Bilbrook Gr
Birmingham B29 .... 84 F2
Codsall WV8 .... 10 B3
Bilbrook Rd WV8 .... 10 B4
Bilbrook Sta WV8 .... 10 A2
Bilbury Cl B97 .... 158 C6
Bilhay La B70 .... 53 A5
Bilhay St B70 .... 53 B5
Billau Rd WV14 .... 40 D2
Billesden Cl CV3 .... 134 E8
BILLESLEY 105 C6
BILLESLEY COMMON 105 A5
Billesley Indoor Tennis Ctr B13 .... 105 B7
Billesley La
Birmingham B13 .... 87 A1
Portway B48 .... 140 E6
Billesley Prim Sch B13 .... 105 C6
Billingham Cl B91 .... 127 B8
Billing Rd CV5 .... 112 D3
Billingsley Rd B26 .... 89 A8
Billinton Cl CV2 .... 114 E2
Bills La B90 .... 106 A1
Billsmore Gn B92 .... 107 C7
Bills St WS10 .... 41 E6
Bill's Wood Nature Reserve★ B90 .... 106 A1
Billy Buns La WV5 .... 49 B8
Billy La B45, B60 .... 138 A7
Billy Wright Cl WV4 .... 38 D6
Bilport La WS10 .... 52 F8
BILSTON 40 D4
Bilston Central Stop WV14 .... 40 E5
Bilston Centre Ind Est WV14 .... 40 E5
Bilston CE Prim Sch WV14 .... 40 B6
Bilston Craft Gall★ WV14 .... 40 E6
Bilston Ind Est WV14 .... 41 A4
Bilston Key Ind Est WV14 .... 41 A5
Bilston La WV13 .... 41 B8
Bilston L Ctr WV14 .... 40 D6
Bilston Rd
Darlaston WV13 .... 41 A8
Wednesbury, Church Hill WS10 .... 41 E3
Wednesbury, Gospel Oak DY4 .... 41 B2
Wolverhampton WV2 .... 39 F8
Bilston St
Darlaston WS10 .... 41 D6
Sedgley DY3 .... 50 E8
Willenhall WV13 .... 27 A1
Wolverhampton WV1 .... 163 C2
Bilton Grange Rd B26 .... 88 F8
Bilton Ind Est
Birmingham B38 .... 123 E8
Coventry CV3 .... 113 F1
Binbrook Rd WV12 .... 27 D4
Bincomb Ave B26 .... 89 B6
Binfield St DY4 .... 52 A4
Bingley Ave B8 .... 68 B4
Bingley Ent Ctr WV3 .... 39 A8
Bingley St WV3 .... 39 A8
BINLEY 134 E8
Binley Ave CV3 .... 134 F7
Binley Bsns Pk CV3 .... 115 A1
Binley Cl
Birmingham B26 .... 88 D6
Solihull B90 .... 126 A8
Binley Gr CV3 .... 134 F7
Binley Ind Est CV3 .... 135 A8
Binley Rd CV2, CV3 .... 114 D1
BINLEY WOODS 135 C7
Binley Woods Prim Sch CV3 .... 135 E7
Binns Cl CV4 .... 131 F8
Binstead Rd B44 .... 45 A2
Binswood Ave CV32 .... 156 F2
Binswood Cl CV2 .... 96 D2
Binswood Ct [9] CV32 .... 156 F2
Binswood Mans [14] CV32 .... 156 F2
Binswood Rd B62 .... 84 A7
Binswood St CV32 .... 156 E1
Binton Cl B98 .... 154 F1
Binton Croft B13 .... 104 F8
Binton Rd
Coventry CV2 .... 96 D2
Solihull B90 .... 105 F1
Birbeck Ho B36 .... 70 B6
Birbeck Pl DY5 .... 61 B6
BIRCH ACRE 140 D7
Birchall St B12 .... 66 F1
Birch Ave
Birmingham B31 .... 102 C1
Brierley Hill DY5 .... 62 A2
Brownhills WS8 .... 15 E8
Burntwood WS7 .... 6 F6
Cannock WS11 .... 4 C8
Birchbrook Ind Est WS14 .... 17 E6
Birch Brook La WS14 .... 17 E6
Birch Bsns Pk WS11 .... 4 F6
Birch Cl
Bedworth CV12 .... 78 D4
Birmingham B30 .... 103 E6
Coventry CV5 .... 111 F6
Sutton Coldfield B76 .... 46 F2
Birch Coppice DY5 .... 62 A1
Birch Coppice Bus Pk B78 .... 36 E3
Birch Coppice Distribution Ctr B78 .... 36 E4
Birch Coppice Gdns WV12 .... 27 E4
Birch Cres B69 .... 52 B1
Birchcroft [6] B66 .... 65 C5
Birch Croft
Aldridge WS9 .... 30 C8
Birmingham B37 .... 70 C1
Sutton Coldfield B24 .... 57 D5
Birch Croft Rd B75 .... 46 D7
Birch Ct
Birmingham B30 .... 103 E4
[1] Oldbury B66 .... 64 D8
Royal Leamington Spa CV34 .... 161 E2
Walsall WS4 .... 29 A4
[11] Wolverhampton WV3 .... 25 C4
Birchdale WV14 .... 40 D7
Birchdale Ave B23 .... 56 E3
Birchdale Rd B23 .... 56 D5
Birch Dr
Halesowen B62 .... 63 E1
Stourbridge DY8 .... 80 E6
Sutton Coldfield, Little Aston B74 .... 31 D5
Sutton Coldfield, Whitehouse Common B75 .... 46 F7
BIRCHEN COPPICE 116 B1
Birchen Coppice Prim Sch DY11 .... 116 B2
Birch End CV34 .... 161 B8
BIRCHENSALE 153 A5
Birchensale Farm [10] B97 .... 153 B5
Birchensale Mid Sch B97 .... 153 C4
Birchensale Rd B97 .... 153 C5
Birches Ave WV8 .... 10 C1
Birches Barn Ave WV3 .... 38 F7
Birches Barn Rd WV3 .... 38 F7
Birches Cl B13 .... 86 F1
Birches Fst Sch WV8 .... 10 B1
BIRCHES GREEN 57 A2
Birches Green Inf Sch B24 .... 57 B2
Birches Green Jun Sch B24 .... 57 B3
Birches Green Rd B24 .... 57 B2
Birches Ho B97 .... 153 B2
Birches La
Alvechurch B48 .... 138 F6
Kenilworth CV8 .... 148 B3
Birches Park Rd WV8 .... 10 A2
Birches Rd WV8 .... 10 B2
Birches Rise WV13 .... 26 F1
Birches The CV12 .... 79 B4
BIRCHFIELD 55 E1
Birchfield Ave WV6 .... 24 B6
Birchfield Cl
Halesowen B63 .... 82 E2
[1] Tamworth B77 .... 21 C1
Wood End CV9 .... 36 C1
Birchfield Com Sch B20 .... 55 D1
Birchfield Cres DY9 .... 81 F3
Birchfield Ct B97 .... 153 B2
Birchfield Gdns
[8] Birmingham B6 .... 66 D8
Walsall WS5 .... 43 C4
Birchfield Ind Girls Sch B6 .... 66 E8
Birchfield La
Oldbury, Round's Green B69 .... 63 F6
Oldbury, Whiteheath Gate B69 .... 63 E4
Birchfield Rd
Birmingham B20 .... 55 D2
Coventry CV6 .... 112 F8
Kidderminster DY11 .... 116 B5
Redditch B97 .... 153 B2
Stourbridge DY9 .... 81 F3
Birchfields Dr WS12 .... 2 D1
Birchfields Rd WV12 .... 27 A5
Birchfield Twr [1] B20 .... 55 D1
Birchfield Way WS5 .... 43 C4
Birchgate DY9 .... 81 F4
Birchglade WV3 .... 24 D1
Birch Gr
Balsall Common CV7 .... 130 B8
Birchmoor B78 .... 36 D7
Birmingham B68 .... 84 D7
Lichfield WS14 .... 9 D8
Birchgrave Cl CV6 .... 114 A7
Birch Ho
Redditch B98 .... 158 F8
Sutton Coldfield B74 .... 31 B5
Birch Hollow B15 .... 85 F6
BIRCHILLS 28 D3
Birchills CE Prim Sch WS2 .... 28 D2
Birchills St WS2 .... 28 D2
Birch La
Aldridge WS9 .... 16 D1
Birmingham B68 .... 84 D7
Walsall WS4 .... 15 C1
Birchley Ho
Oldbury B69 .... 63 D6
Redditch B97 .... 153 B1
Birchley Ind Est B69 .... 63 E5
Birchley Park Ave B69 .... 63 E6
Birchley Rise B92 .... 88 F4
Birch Meadow Cl CV34 .... 160 D7
BIRCHMOOR 36 E8
Birchmoor Cl B28 .... 106 B7
Birchmoor Rd B78 .... 36 F8
Birchover Rd WS2 .... 28 A4
Birch Rd
Birmingham, Rubery B45 .... 121 E6
Birmingham, Warley Woods B68 .... 84 D7
Birmingham, Witton B6 .... 56 A2
Sedgley DY3 .... 39 F1
Wednesfield WV11 .... 26 F8
Wolverhampton WV11 .... 12 F1
Birch Road E B6 .... 56 B2
Birch Road E Ind Est B6 .... 56 A3
Birch St
Oldbury B68 .... 64 C5
Tipton DY4 .... 51 F5
Walsall WS2 .... 28 D3
Wolverhampton WV1 .... 163 B3
Birch Terr DY2 .... 62 C4
Birchtree Gdns DY5 .... 62 A1
Birch Tree Gdns WS9 .... 30 B5
Birch Tree Gr B91 .... 106 F4
Birchtree Hollow WV12 .... 27 D5
Birchtree Rd CV10 .... 72 C6
Birchtrees B24 .... 57 D4
Birchtrees Croft B26 .... 88 D5
Birchtrees Dr B33 .... 69 D2
Birchway Cl CV32 .... 156 C1
Birch Wlk B68 .... 84 D8
Birchwood Ave B78 .... 36 F7
Birchwood Cl
Essington WV11 .... 13 A3
Kidderminster DY11 .... 116 A7
Birchwood Cres B12 .... 87 B4
Birchwood Prim Sch B78 .... 36 F7
Birchwood Rd
Binley Woods CV3 .... 135 C7
Birmingham B12 .... 87 A4
Lichfield WS14 .... 9 F7
Wolverhampton WV4 .... 39 A5
Birchwoods B32 .... 84 B2
Birchwood Wlk DY6 .... 60 E8
Birchy Cl B90 .... 125 F6
Birchy Leasowes La B90 .... 125 E5
Birdbrook Rd B44 .... 55 E8
Birdcage Wlk [4] DY2 .... 51 D1
Bird Cage Wlk B38 .... 103 F2
Bird End B71 .... 53 F8
Bird Grove Ct CV1 .... 113 D5
Birdhope B77 .... 22 C1
Birdie Cl B38 .... 103 D1
Birdlip Gr B32 .... 84 C6
Bird Rd CV34 .... 161 D4
Birds Bush Prim Sch B77 .... 35 E8
Birds Bush Rd B77 .... 35 F8
Birds Mdw DY5 .... 61 B7
Bird St
Coventry CV1 .... 165 C3
Dudley DY3 .... 50 C3
Lichfield WS13 .... 9 B7
Birdwell Croft B13 .... 104 F6
Birkdale Ave
Birmingham B29 .... 85 F1
Blackwell B60 .... 138 A5
Birkdale Cl
Coventry CV6 .... 95 B4
Nuneaton CV11 .... 74 A1
Stourbridge DY8 .... 80 F2
Wolverhampton WV1 .... 26 A2
Birkdale Dr B69 .... 63 A7
Birkdale Gr B29 .... 104 A8
Birkdale Rd WS3 .... 14 A3
Birkenshaw Rd B44 .... 55 E8
Birley Gr B63 .... 82 C1
Birlingham Ho B60 .... 137 B3
BIRMINGHAM 164 C1
Birmingham Botanical Gdns★ B15 .... 85 F7
Birmingham Bsns Pk B37 .... 90 E8
Birmingham Cath (St Philip's)★ B3 .... 164 B3
Birmingham Chest Clinic Hospl B2 .... 164 B3
Birmingham Children's Hospl B4 .... 164 C3
Birmingham Christian Coll B29 .... 103 D8
Birmingham City Univ (Birmingham Conservatoire) B2 .... 164 B2
Birmingham City Univ (City Ctr Campus at Millennium Point) B4 .... 66 F3
Birmingham City Univ (City North Campus) B42 .... 55 E3
Birmingham City Univ (City South Campus) B15 .... 86 A8
Birmingham City Univ (Gosta Green) B2 .... 164 D4
Birmingham Coll B3 .... 164 A3
Birmingham Conservatoire B1 .... 164 B2
Birmingham Dental Hospl The B4 .... 164 C4
Birmingham Great Pk B45 .... 122 B8
Birmingham Heartlands Hospl B9 .... 68 B2
Birmingham Hippodrome Theatre★ B5 .... 164 C1
Birmingham ICC★ B1 .... 66 C2
Birmingham Inst of Art & Design (Gosta Green) B4 .... 164 D4
Birmingham Inst of Art & Design (School of Art)
Birmingham B4 .... 164 B4
Birmingham B30 .... 103 E7
Birmingham Inst of Art & Design (School of Jewellery) B1 .... 66 C4
Birmingham Int Airport B40 .... 90 B4
Birmingham Int Coll B16 .... 86 A8
Birmingham Intermodal Freight Terminal B78 .... 36 E3
Birmingham Int Sta B40 .... 90 D4
Birmingham Metropolitan Coll (Castle Vale) B35 .... 57 F3
Birmingham Metropolitan Coll (Design Ctr) [5] B72 .... 46 C4
Birmingham Metropolitan Coll (Erdington) B24 .... 57 A4
Birmingham Metropolitan Coll (James Watt Campus) B44 .... 55 E7
Birmingham Metropolitan Coll (Josiah Mason Campus) B23 .... 56 C4
Birmingham Metropolitan Coll (Matthew Boulton Campus) B5 .... 164 D3
Birmingham Metropolitan Coll (Sutton Coldfield Campus) B74 .... 46 C6
Birmingham Mus & Art Gal★ B3 .... 164 B2
Birmingham Muslim Sch B11 .... 87 D5
Birmingham Nature Ctr★ B5 .... 86 C3
Birmingham New Rd
Dudley DY1, DY4, WV14 .... 51 C4
Wolverhampton WV4 .... 39 E4
Birmingham Rd
Aldridge WS9 .... 30 A4
Allesley CV5 .... 111 E7
Alvechurch B48 .... 139 B7
Birmingham, Buckland End B36 .... 69 A8
Birmingham, Rubery B45, B61 .... 121 D5
Blakedown DY10 .... 98 C2
Burton Green CV8 .... 131 A1
Coleshill B46 .... 70 E5
Dudley DY1 .... 51 E2
Hagley DY9 .... 99 D7
Halesowen B63 .... 83 B4
Hopwood B31, B48 .... 123 B4
Kenilworth CV8 .... 147 C8
Kidderminster DY10 .... 117 D7
Lichfield WS14 .... 9 A4
Lickey End B60, B61 .... 137 B6
Little Packington CV7 .... 91 E3
Lower Marlbrook B61 .... 121 B1
Oldbury B69 .... 64 B7
Redditch B97, B98 .... 153 E8
Rowley Regis B65 .... 63 C2
Shenstone WS14 .... 18 A4
Stoneleigh CV8 .... 149 B6
Studley B80, B98 .... 159 E7
Sutton Coldfield B72, B73 .... 46 B2
Walsall B43, WS1, WS5 .... 43 D5
Warwick CV34 .... 160 B8
Water Orton B46 .... 59 A3
West Bromwich B71 .... 54 A1
Wolverhampton WV2 .... 39 D7
Wroxall B93, CV35 .... 145 D3
Birmingham St
Darlaston WS10 .... 41 E6
Dudley DY2 .... 51 D1
Halesowen B63 .... 83 B3
Oldbury B69 .... 64 A7
Stourbridge DY8 .... 81 B5
Walsall WS1 .... 28 F1
Willenhall WV13 .... 27 C2
Birmingham Women's Hospl B15 .... 85 D4
Birnam B15 .... 86 A8
Birnham Cl DY4 .... 51 D5
Birstall Way B38 .... 123 C8
Birvell Ct CV12 .... 78 D3
Bisbrook Croft B91 .... 107 D6
Bisell Way DY5 .... 81 C6
Biset Ave DY10 .... 117 B5
Bishbury Cl B15 .... 85 E8
Bishop Asbury Cottage★ B43 .... 54 C8
Bishop Asbury Cres B43 .... 54 C8
Bishop Challoner RC Sch The B14 .... 104 F8
Bishop Cl
Birmingham B45 .... 101 E1
Cannock WS11 .... 1 D2
Dudley DY2 .... 62 E8
Bishopgate Bsns Pk CV1 .... 113 D5
BISHOPGATE GREEN 113 D5
Bishopgate Ind Est CV1 .... 113 D5
Bishop Hall Cres B60 .... 150 E7
Bishop Milner RC Sch DY1 .... 51 A3
Bishop Rd WS10 .... 42 C2
Bishops Cl B66 .... 65 C4
Bishop's Ct
Birmingham, Coleshill Heath B37 .... 90 E8
Birmingham, Northfield B31 .... 103 B3
Bishops Gate B31 .... 103 A2
Bishopsgate St B15 .... 66 B1
Bishops Mdw B75 .... 32 E3
Bishops Rd B73 .... 46 B3
Bishop St
Birmingham B5 .... 86 E8
Coventry CV1 .... 165 B3
Bishopstone Cl B98 .... 154 F2
Bishops Walk B64 .... 83 A6
Bishops Way B74 .... 31 F6
Bishops Wlk CV5 .... 133 B8
Bishopton Cl
Coventry CV5 .... 112 B3
Solihull B90 .... 106 C1
Bishopton Rd B67 .... 64 F1
Bishop Ullathorne RC Sch CV3 .... 132 F4
Bishop Vesey's Gram Sch B74 .... 46 C6
Bishop Walsh RC Sch B72 .... 46 D1
Bishop Wilson CE Prim Sch B37 .... 70 C3
Bishton Gr DY2 .... 62 D4
Bisley Gr B24 .... 57 B2
Bismillah Bldgs B19 .... 164 B4
Bissell Cl B28 .... 105 F6
Bissell Dr WS10 .... 42 B3
Bissell St
Birmingham B32 .... 84 A6
Birmingham, Highgate B5 .... 86 E8
Bissel St WV14 .... 40 F5

Bisset Cres 12 CV31 ... 162 C6
Bi Tec Ind Pk WV1 ... 26 A1
Biton Cl B17 ... 85 B5
Bittell Cl
Birmingham B31 ... 122 F7
Wolverhampton WV10 ... 11 E4
Bittell Ct B31 ... 122 F7
Bittell Farm Rd B48 ... 123 A2
Bittell La B45 ... 138 E8
Bittell Rd
Alvechurch B48 ... 139 A8
Barnt Green B45 ... 138 E8
Bitterne Dr WV6 ... 25 A4
Bittern Wlk DY5 ... 81 C6
Bittern Wood Rd DY10 ... 117 B3
BITTERSCOTE ... 21 A4
Bitterscote La B78 ... 21 A2
Blackacre Rd DY2 ... 62 D8
Black-a-Tree Ct CV10 ... 72 F5
Black-a-Tree Rd CV10 ... 72 E4
Blackbades Bvd CV34 ... 160 B4
BLACK BANK ... 78 A1
Black Bank CV7 ... 78 B1
Blackberry Ave
Birmingham B9 ... 68 A3
Hockley Heath B94 ... 143 C6
Lichfield WS14 ... 9 C7
Blackberry Cl DY1 ... 61 E8
Blackberry La
Brownhills WS9 ... 16 B4
Coventry, Neal's Green CV7. 95 C5
Coventry, Wyken Green CV2 ... 114 C6
Halesowen B63 ... 83 A2
Rowley Regis B65 ... 62 F5
Sutton Coldfield B74 ... 31 E4
Blackbird Croft B36 ... 70 A7
Blackbrook Cl DY2 ... 62 A3
Blackbrook Rd DY2 ... 62 B5
Blackbrook Valley Bsns Pk DY2 ... 62 B4
Blackbrook Valley Ind Pk DY2 ... 62 A5
Blackbrook Way WV10 ... 11 E4
Blackburn Ave WV6 ... 24 F7
Blackburne Rd B28 ... 105 F6
Blackburn Rd CV6 ... 95 F3
Blackbushe Cl B17 ... 84 F7
Blackcat Cl B37 ... 70 A3
Black Country Living Mus* DY1 ... 51 D3
Black Country New Rd
Darlaston WS10 ... 41 C4
Tipton B70, DY4 ... 52 D6
Black Country Route
Bilston WV14 ... 40 E5
Darlaston WV13, WS10 ... 41 B7
Walsall WS2, WS10 ... 27 E1
BLACKDOWN ... 156 F6
Blackdown B77 ... 22 C1
Blackdown Cl B45 ... 102 A2
Blackdown Hall CV32 ... 156 F6
Blackdown Rd B93 ... 128 B6
Blackett Ct 1 B73 ... 46 A2
Blackfirs La B37, B46 ... 90 D7
Blackford Cl
Halesowen B63 ... 82 D2
Kidderminster DY11 ... 116 A1
Blackford Rd
Birmingham B11 ... 87 C4
Solihull B90 ... 126 C8
BLACKFORDS ... 1 E2
Blackford St B18 ... 65 E5
Blackfriars Cl B79 ... 20 E5
Blackgreaves La B76 ... 48 F1
Blackhalve La WV11 ... 12 D1
Blackham Dr B73 ... 57 A7
Blackham Rd WV11 ... 26 F8
Black Haynes Rd B29 ... 103 A6
BLACKHEATH ... 63 B2
Blackheath Prim Sch B65 63 D2
Blackheath Trad Est B65 ... 63 E2
Black Horse Cl WS10 ... 41 D5
Blackhorse La DY5 ... 61 E1
Black Horse La 1 DY10 ... 116 E6
Black Horse Rd CV6, CV7 ... 96 B6
Black La CV32 ... 157 C2
BLACK LAKE ... 53 A7
Black Lake B70 ... 53 A6
Black Lake Ind Est B70 ... 53 B6
Black Lake La B60, B97 ... 152 A2
Black Lake Stop B70 ... 53 A6
Blackley Ho B66 ... 65 D6
Blacklow Rd CV34 ... 156 A1
Blackmoor Croft B33 ... 69 D2
Blackmore La B60 ... 137 A3
Black Pad CV6 ... 113 D8
BLACK PATCH ... 65 D6
Blackpit La WV4 ... 37 E3
Black Prince Ave CV3 ... 133 E6
Blackrock Rd B23 ... 56 B6
Blackroot Cl WS7 ... 7 D4
Blackroot Ho B73 ... 45 C2
Blackroot Rd B74 ... 46 B7
Blackshaw Dr CV2 ... 114 F6
Blacksmith Dr
Bromsgrove B60 ... 151 A7
7 Sutton Coldfield B75 ... 32 E3
Blacksmiths La B94 ... 143 C6
Blacksmith Way 3 B70 ... 53 C2
Black Soils Rd B98 ... 154 F5
Blackstitch La B97 ... 153 A1
Blackthorn Ave WS7 ... 6 F4
Blackthorn Cl
Birmingham B30 ... 103 C6
Coventry CV4 ... 132 D5
Blackthorn Ct B98 ... 154 E1
Blackthorne Cl
Dudley DY1 ... 50 F4
Solihull B91 ... 106 E4
Blackthorne Rd
Dudley DY1 ... 50 F5
Kenilworth CV8 ... 148 A3
Lichfield WS14 ... 9 D7
Smethwick B67 ... 64 D4
Walsall WS5 ... 42 F5
Blackthorn Gr CV11 ... 73 F2
Blackthorn Rd
Birmingham, Bournville B30 ... 103 D6
Birmingham, Castle Bromwich B36 ... 69 C8
Stourbridge DY8 ... 61 A1
Blackwatch Rd CV6 ... 113 C8
Blackwater Cl DY5 ... 61 A6
BLACKWELL ... 138 A5
Blackwell Fst Sch B60 ... 138 A6
Blackwell La 1 B97 ... 153 B5
Blackwell Rd
Barnt Green B45, B60 ... 138 B5
Coventry CV6 ... 113 E8
Sutton Coldfield B72 ... 46 D1
Blackwell St DY10 ... 116 E6
Blackwood Ave WV11 ... 26 C8
Blackwood Dr B74 ... 44 E8
Blackwood Rd
Bromsgrove B60 ... 137 B2
Sutton Coldfield B74 ... 30 E1
Tamworth B77 ... 35 C7
Blackwood Sch B74 ... 30 E1
Blades Rd B70 ... 52 D4
Bladon Cl CV11 ... 73 F8
Bladon Wlk 6 CV31 ... 162 C6
Blaenwern Dr B63 ... 82 B7
Blagdon Rd B63 ... 83 A6
Blair Dr CV12 ... 77 D1
Blair Gr B37 ... 70 D1
BLAKEBROOK ... 116 B6
Blakebrook DY11 ... 116 C6
Blakebrook Cl DY11 ... 116 C6
Blakebrook Gdns DY11 ... 116 C6
Blakebrook Specl Sch DY11 ... 116 C6
Blake Cl
Cannock WS11 ... 2 A5
Hinckley LE10 ... 71 D4
Nuneaton CV10 ... 72 A5
Blakedon Rd WS10 ... 41 E3
BLAKEDOWN ... 98 C2
Blakedown CE Prim Sch DY10 ... 98 C1
Blakedown Rd B63 ... 82 F1
Blakedown Sta DY10 ... 98 C2
Blakedown Way 4 B69 ... 63 E4
Blake Hall Cl DY5 ... 81 C7
Blake Ho 2 WS2 ... 42 C8
Blake La B9 ... 67 F2
Blakeland Rd B44 ... 55 E6
Blakelands Ave 2 CV31 ... 162 B6
Blakeland St B9 ... 67 F2
Blakeley Ave WV6 ... 24 F7
Blakeley Ct B72 ... 57 C8
BLAKELEY GREEN ... 24 F8
Blakeley Hall Gdns B69 ... 64 B7
Blakeley Hall Rd B69 ... 64 B7
Blakeley Heath Dr WV5 ... 49 A5
Blakeley Heath Prim Sch WV5 ... 49 A5
Blakeley Rise WV6 ... 24 F7
Blakeley Wood Rd DY4 ... 52 D8
Blakeman Way WS13 ... 8 F7
Blakemarsh Nature Reserve* DY11 ... 116 A7
Blakemere Ave B25 ... 88 E8
Blakemere Cl B98 ... 154 F3
Blakemore Cl B32 ... 84 F3
Blakemore Dr B75 ... 46 F6
Blakemore Rd
Brownhills WS9 ... 16 A3
West Bromwich B70 ... 53 A1
BLAKENALL HEATH ... 28 C8
Blakenall Heath WS3 ... 28 D8
Blakenall Heath Jun Sch WS3 ... 28 C8
Blakenall La WS3 ... 28 D8
Blakenall Row 1 WS3 ... 28 D8
Blakeney Ave
Birmingham B17 ... 85 A7
Stourbridge DY8 ... 80 D6
Blakeney Cl DY3 ... 50 C8
Blakenhale Jun & Inf Schs B33 ... 69 B1
Blakenhale Rd B33 ... 69 B1
BLAKENHALL ... 39 B7
Blakenhall Gdns WV2 ... 39 D7
Blakenhall Ind Est WV2 ... 39 B7
Blake Pl B9 ... 67 F2
Blake Rd B61 ... 137 B8
Blakes Field Dr B45 ... 122 A1
Blakesley Cl B76 ... 57 F5
Blakesley Gr B25 ... 68 D1
Blakesley Hall Mus* B25 ... 68 E1
Blakesley Hall Prim Sch B25 ... 68 D1
Blakesley Mews B25 ... 88 D8
Blakesley Rd B25 ... 68 D1
Blakesley Way B33 ... 68 D2
Blake St B74 ... 31 E6
Blake Street Sta B74 ... 31 F6
Blake Valley Tech Coll WS12 ... 1 F6
Blakewood Cl B34 ... 69 C5
Blanchfort Cl CV4 ... 111 F1
Blandford Ave B36 ... 58 E1
Blandford Dr
Coventry CV2 ... 114 F5
Stourbridge DY8 ... 60 E3
Blandford Gdns WS7 ... 7 C6
Blandford Rd
Birmingham B32 ... 84 F5
Royal Leamington Spa CV32 ... 156 C1
Blandford Way CV35 ... 160 A7
Blanefield WV8 ... 10 E2
Blanford Mere Prim Sch DY6 ... 60 E8
Blanning Ct B93 ... 127 E3
Blay Ave WS2 ... 28 B2
Blaydon Ave B75 ... 32 E2
Blaydon Ct 3 B17 ... 85 D4
Blaydon Rd WV9, WV10 ... 11 A1
Blaythorn Ave B92 ... 89 A3
Blaze Hill Rd DY6 ... 60 A8
Blaze La B96, B97 ... 158 A3
Blaze Pk DY6 ... 60 B8
Bleachfield La B98 ... 154 F8
Bleak Hill Rd B23 ... 56 C5
Bleak House Dr WS7 ... 6 D8
Bleakhouse Jun Sch B68 ... 64 C1
Bleakhouse Rd B68 ... 64 C1
Bleak St B67 ... 64 F6
Blencathra Dr 6 B71 ... 53 C6
Blenheim 5 B17 ... 85 B6
Blenheim Ave CV6 ... 95 C2
Blenheim Cl
Hinckley LE10 ... 71 F4
Nuneaton CV11 ... 73 F2
Tamworth B77 ... 21 C4
Walsall WS4 ... 29 D7
Blenheim Cres
Bromsgrove B60 ... 151 A8
Royal Leamington Spa CV31 ... 162 C5
Blenheim Ct
Birmingham B44 ... 55 F8
Solihull B91 ... 107 C4
Blenheim Dr
Birmingham B43 ... 54 D8
Darlaston WS10 ... 41 E5
Blenheim Rd
Birmingham B13 ... 86 F1
Burntwood WS7 ... 7 A8
Kingswinford DY6 ... 61 A6
Norton Canes WS11 ... 6 B4
Solihull B90 ... 106 D2
Willenhall WV12 ... 27 B6
Blenheim Way
Birmingham, Castle Vale B35 ... 58 B2
Birmingham, Old Oscott B44 55 F8
Dudley DY1 ... 50 E2
Blenheim Wlk CV6 ... 95 B4
Bletchley Dr
Coventry CV5 ... 112 B4
Tamworth B77 ... 35 C8
Bletchley Rd B24 ... 57 E4
Blewitt Cl B36 ... 58 D2
Blewitt St
Brierley Hill DY5 ... 61 C6
Cannock WS12 ... 2 B7
Blews St B6 ... 66 E5
Blick Rd CV34 ... 161 C4
Blind La
Berkswell CV7 ... 110 D4
Kenilworth CV8 ... 131 F1
Tanworth-In-A B94 ... 141 D1
Blindpit La B76 ... 59 B8
Bliss Cl CV4 ... 111 E3
Blithe Cl DY8 ... 81 A8
Blithfield Dr DY5 ... 81 B7
Blithfield Gr B24 ... 57 C5
Blithfield Pl WS11 ... 2 B1
Blithfield Rd WS8 ... 6 C2
Blockall WS10 ... 41 D7
Blockall Cl 8 WS10 ... 41 D7
Blockley Cl B97 ... 152 E2
Blockley Rd CV12 ... 78 C4
Blockley's Yd 4 LE10 ... 75 D8
Blondvil St CV3 ... 133 D7
BLOOMFIELD ... 51 E7
Bloomfield Coll DY4 ... 51 E6
Bloomfield Cres WS13 ... 3 B2
Bloomfield Ct 3 B42 ... 55 A8
Bloomfield Dr WV12 ... 13 D1
Bloomfield Pk DY4 ... 51 D6
Bloomfield Rd
Birmingham B13 ... 87 B3
Tipton DY4 ... 51 E7
Bloomfield Street N B63 ... 82 F5
Bloomfield Street W B63 ... 82 F4
Bloomfield Terr DY4 ... 51 E7
Bloomfield Way B79 ... 20 F8
Bloomsbury Gr B14 ... 104 C7
Bloomsbury St
Birmingham B7 ... 67 B5
Wolverhampton WV2 ... 163 B1
Bloomsbury Way WS14 ... 9 E7
Bloomsbury Wlk 1 B7 ... 67 B5
Bloor Mill Cl WV13 ... 26 F1
Blossom Ave B29 ... 85 F2
Blossom Dr B61 ... 137 A5
BLOSSOMFIELD ... 106 E2
Blossomfield Cl
Birmingham B38 ... 123 D8
Kingswinford DY6 ... 60 E8
Blossomfield Ct B38 ... 123 D8
Blossomfield Gdns B91 ... 107 A4
Blossomfield Inf Sch B90 ... 106 D3
Blossomfield Rd B91 ... 106 F2
Blossom Gr
Birmingham B36 ... 68 E8
Blossom Gr *continued*
Cradley Heath B64 ... 62 F1
Blossom Hill B24 ... 57 A4
Blossom Rd B24 ... 57 C4
Blossomville Way 9 B27 ... 88 C5
Blount Ho DY11 ... 116 B8
Blounts Rd B23 ... 56 D5
Blount Terr DY11 ... 116 D3
BLOWERS GREEN ... 62 C7
Blowers Green Cres DY2 ... 62 B7
Blowers Green Pl DY2 ... 62 B7
Blowers Green Prim Sch DY2 ... 62 B8
Blower's Green Rd DY2 ... 62 B8
Bloxcidge St B68 ... 64 B4
BLOXWICH ... 14 C1
Bloxwich Bsns Pk WS2 ... 28 A7
Bloxwich CE Prim Sch 11 WS3 ... 14 B1
Bloxwich Hospl WS3 ... 28 B8
Bloxwich La WS2 ... 28 A4
Bloxwich L Ctr WS3 ... 28 C8
Bloxwich North Sta WS3 ... 13 F2
Bloxwich Rd WS2, WS3 ... 28 D5
Bloxwich Road N WV12 ... 27 D6
Bloxwich Road S WV13 ... 27 A3
Bloxwich Sta WS3 ... 14 A1
Blucher St B1 ... 164 B1
Blue Ball La B63 ... 82 C7
Bluebell Cl
Cannock WS12 ... 2 B6
Nuneaton CV10 ... 72 A8
Stourbridge DY8 ... 60 C2
Bluebell Cres WV11 ... 26 D5
Bluebell Croft
Birmingham, Northfield B31 ... 102 F4
Birmingham, Perry Common B23 ... 56 C7
Bluebell Dr
Bedworth CV12 ... 77 E2
Birmingham B37 ... 70 E2
Bluebell La WS6 ... 5 A1
Bluebell Rd
Brownhills WS9 ... 16 B3
Cradley Heath B64 ... 62 E3
Dudley DY1 ... 51 B4
Bluebell Wlk CV4 ... 111 F1
Bluebellwood Cl
Sutton Coldfield B74 ... 31 F1
Sutton Coldfield B76 ... 47 A3
Bluebird Cl WS14 ... 9 D8
Blue Bird Pk B62 ... 101 B7
Bluebird Trad Est WV10 ... 25 E5
Blue Cedar Dr B74 ... 44 F6
Blue Cedars DY8 ... 80 C6
Blue Coat CE Comp Sch 12 WS1 ... 28 F1
Blue Coat CE Inf Sch 14 WS1 ... 28 F1
Blue Coat CE Jun Sch 13 WS1 ... 28 F1
Blue Coat Sch The B17 ... 85 E6
Blue Ice (Solihull Ice Rink) B92 ... 89 B3
Blue Lake Rd B93 ... 128 B2
Blue Lane E WS2 ... 28 E3
Blue Lane W WS2 ... 28 D2
Blue Rock Pl B69 ... 63 C7
Bluestone Wlk B65 ... 63 C6
Blundell Rd B11 ... 87 D5
Blundells The CV8 ... 148 A5
BLUNTINGTON ... 118 E1
Blyth Ave CV7 ... 130 C5
Blyth Cl CV12 ... 77 C1
Blyth Ct 2 CV11 ... 73 C3
Blythe Cl
Burntwood WS7 ... 7 D6
Redditch B97 ... 158 D7
Blythe Ct
Solihull B91 ... 106 F7
8 Sutton Coldfield B73 ... 46 B5
Blythefield Ave B43 ... 43 C2
Blythe Gate B90 ... 126 F3
Blythe Gr B44 ... 44 F3
Blythe Rd
7 Coleshill B46 ... 70 F7
Coventry CV1 ... 113 E4
Blythe St B77 ... 21 C4
Blythesway B48 ... 139 A6
Blythe Valley Pk B90 ... 126 F2
Blytheway B91 ... 107 E3
Blythewood Cl B91 ... 107 F1
Blythsford Rd B28 ... 106 A4
Blythswood Rd B11 ... 88 A4
Blyton Cl B16 ... 65 F3
BMI Edgbaston Hospl The (Private) B15 ... 85 F5
BMI Meridian Hospl the (Private) CV2 ... 115 A6
BMI Priory Hospl The B5 ... 86 C5
Boar Croft CV4 ... 111 F2
Board School Gdns DY3 ... 50 E6
Boar Hound Cl B18 ... 66 A4
Boathouse Field WS13 ... 9 A6
Boat La WS14 ... 7 F1
Boatman's La WS9 ... 15 A6
Bobbin Cl WS6 ... 4 F1
Bobbington Way DY2 ... 62 E5
Bobs Coppice Wlk DY5 ... 81 F7
Bockendon Rd CV4 ... 131 E5
Boddington Cl CV32 ... 157 E5
Bodenham Cl B98 ... 154 D3
Bodenham Rd
Birmingham, Brandhall B68. 84 B8
Birmingham, Frankley B31 102 E1
Boden Rd B28 ... 106 A7
Bodens La WS9 ... 44 B7
Bodiam Ct WV6 ... 24 A3
Bodicote Gr B75 ... 32 E3
Bodington Cl WS7 ... 7 E7
Bodington Rd B75 ... 32 B3
Bodmin Cl
Hinckley LE10 ... 71 E4
Walsall WS5 ... 43 D7
Bodmin Ct 16 DY5 ... 61 D2
Bodmin Gr 2 B7 ... 67 B5
Bodmin Rd
Coventry CV2 ... 114 F5
Dudley DY2 ... 62 D2
Bodmin Rise WS5 ... 43 D7
Bodnant Way CV8 ... 148 C6
Bodymoor Heath Rd B76 ... 48 E6
Bognop Rd WV11 ... 12 D4
Bohun St CV4 ... 111 F1
BOLDMERE ... 46 A1
Boldmere Cl B73 ... 57 A7
Boldmere Ct B43 ... 54 E7
Boldmere Dr B73 ... 57 A8
Boldmere Gdns B73 ... 57 A8
Boldmere Inf Sch B73 ... 45 F1
Boldmere Jun Sch B73 ... 45 F1
Boldmere Rd B73 ... 57 A8
Bolebridge Mews B79 ... 21 B5
Bolebridge St B79 ... 21 C4
BOLEHALL ... 21 D4
Bolehall Ho B77 ... 21 C4
Boley Cl WS14 ... 9 D7
Boley Cottage La WS14 ... 9 E7
Boley La WS14 ... 9 D7
Boleyn Cl
Cheslyn Hay WS6 ... 4 D2
Warwick CV34 ... 161 C6
Boleyn Rd B45 ... 101 E2
BOLEY PARK ... 9 F7
Boley Park Ctr WS14 ... 9 E7
Bolingbroke Dr CV34 ... 161 E3
Bolingbroke Rd CV3 ... 114 A1
Bolney Rd B32 ... 84 E4
Bolton Cl CV3 ... 133 E5
Bolton Ct DY4 ... 52 C8
Bolton Rd
Birmingham B10 ... 87 C8
Wednesfield WV11 ... 26 D5
Bolton St B9 ... 67 B2
Bolton Way WS3 ... 13 F3
Bolyfant Cres CV31 ... 162 A2
Bomers Field B45 ... 122 C7
Bond Dr B35 ... 58 A3
Bondfield Rd B13 ... 105 B6
Bond Gate CV11 ... 73 C4
Bonds Hospl CV1 ... 165 A3
Bond Sq B18 ... 66 A4
Bond St
Birmingham, Ladywood B19 ... 164 B4
Birmingham, Stirchley B30 104 A7
Coventry CV1 ... 165 B3
Dudley WV14 ... 51 A8
Nuneaton CV11 ... 73 C5
Rowley Regis B65 ... 63 E3
West Bromwich B70 ... 53 C2
Wolverhampton WV2 ... 163 B2
Bondway WS12 ... 1 F7
BONEHILL ... 20 E2
Bonehill Ind Est B78 ... 20 F1
Bonehill Rd B78 ... 20 E3
Bone Mill La WV1 ... 25 D4
Boney Hay Rd WS7 ... 7 B7
Bonfire Hill DY9 ... 120 E6
Bonham Gr B25 ... 68 D1
Boniface Rd 2 B16 ... 65 C3
Boningale Way B93 ... 127 E3
Bonington Dr CV12 ... 78 A4
Bonner Dr B76 ... 57 F5
Bonner Gr WS9 ... 29 F5
Bonneville Cl
Allesley CV5 ... 111 B8
Tipton DY4 ... 51 D6
Bonniksen Cl 7 CV31 ... 161 F5
Bonnington Way B43 ... 44 D4
Bonny Stile La WV11 ... 26 B6
Bonsall Rd B23 ... 57 A6
Bonville Gdns WV10 ... 11 E4
Booth Cl
Kingswinford DY6 ... 61 A6
Lichfield WS13 ... 3 A2
Walsall WS3 ... 28 D8
Booth Ct 17 DY5 ... 61 D2
Booth Ho WS4 ... 28 F3
Booth Rd WS10 ... 42 C2
Booths Farm Rd B42 ... 55 B8
Booths Fields CV6 ... 95 E2
Booth's La B42 ... 44 B1
Booth St
Birmingham B21 ... 65 D7
Cannock WS12 ... 2 B6
Darlaston WS10 ... 41 D8
Walsall WS3 ... 28 C8
Boot Piece La B97 ... 153 B5
Bordeaux Cl DY1 ... 50 E3
Borden Cl WV8 ... 24 F8
BORDESLEY
Birmingham ... 67 B2
Redditch ... 139 D1
Bordesley Abbey* B98 ... 153 F6
Bordesley Cir B10 ... 67 B1
Bordesley Cl B9 ... 68 A2
Bordesley Ct CV32 ... 157 A3
Bordesley Gn B9 ... 67 E2
BORDESLEY GREEN ... 67 E2
Bordesley Green E B9, B33 ... 68 C2

BORDESLEY GREEN EAST 68 B1
Bordesley Green Girls' Specialist Bsns & Ent Sch B9 .... 67 D2
Bordesley Green Prim Sch B9 .... 68 A2
Bordesley Green Rd B8 .. 67 D2
Bordesley Green Trad Est B9 .... 67 D3
Bordesley La B98 .... 153 E6
Bordesley Middleway B12 87 A8
Bordesley Park Rd B10 ... 67 B1
Bordesley St B5 .... 164 D2
Bordesley Sta B9 .... 67 A1
Bordesley Village Prim Sch B9 .... 67 B2
Bordsley Ct **7** B9 ..... 67 B2
Bore St WS13 .... 9 B7
Borman B79 .... 20 F5
Borneo St WS4 .... 28 F4
Borough Cres
  Oldbury B65 .... 63 E4
  Stourbridge DY8 ...... 80 E5
Borough Ct Bsns Ctr B63. 83 B4
BOROUGH PARK. 21 C8
Borough Rd B79 .... 21 C7
Borough The LE10 ...... 75 D8
Borough Way CV11. ..... 73 A4
Borrington Gdns DY10. . 117 B4
Borrington Rd DY10. .... 117 B5
BORROWCOP HILL. 9 C6
Borrowcop Ho WS14 ..... 9 C6
Borrowcop La WS14 ..... 9 C5
Borrowdale Cl
  Brierley Hill DY5 ...... 81 B8
  Coventry CV6 .... 113 A8
Borrowdale Dr CV32 ... 156 D2
Borrowdale Gr B31. .... 102 D3
Borrowdale Rd B31. .... 102 C3
Borrowell La CV8 ...... 147 E4
Borrowell Terr CV8 .... 147 E4
Borrow St WV13 .... 27 A3
Borwick Ave B70 .... 53 A3
Bosbury Terr B30 ...... 104 B7
Boscobel Ave DY4 .... 51 F4
Boscobel Cl DY1. .... 50 F3
Boscobel Cres WV1 ..... 25 C4
Boscobel Rd
  Birmingham B43 .... 43 D2
  Cheswick Green B90 .. 126 D5
  Walsall WS1. .... 43 B8
Boscombe Ave **2** B11. . 87 C6
Boscombe Rd B11 .... 87 E4
Bosmere Ct B31 .... 102 F3
Boss Dr DY2 .... 62 C7
Boss Gate Cl WV5 ...... 49 A5
Boston Cl B12 .... 2 E1
Boston Gr B44 .... 56 B8
Boston Pl CV6 .... 113 D8
Bosty La LE9 .... 71 F6
Bosty La WS9 .... 29 E5
Boswell Cl
  Darlaston WS10. .... 41 D5
  Wednesbury WS10 ..... 41 C7
Boswell Dr CV2 .... 115 A7
Boswell Gr CV34 .... 155 D1
Boswell Rd
  Bilston WV14 .... 40 F7
  Birmingham B44 .... 55 F6
  Cannock WS11. .... 1 D4
  Sutton Coldfield B74 ... 46 C6
Bosworth Cl
  Baginton CV8. .... 133 C2
  Dudley DY3 .... 51 A6
  Hinckley LE10 .... 71 A1
  Sedgley DY3. .... 50 F7
Bosworth Dr B37 .... 70 A2
Bosworth Ho **3** LE10. .. 71 E1
Bosworth Rd B26 .... 88 E4
Botany Dr DY3 .... 50 D6
Botany Rd WS5 .... 43 A5
Botany Wlk **5** B16. .... 66 A2
Botham Ho CV11. .... 73 E1
Botha Rd B9 .... 67 F2
Botoner Rd CV1. .... 113 F2
Botteley Rd B70 .... 53 A6
Bottetourt Rd B29 ..... 85 A2
Bottesville Rd B27 ..... 88 C2
Bott La
  Stourbridge DY9 .... 81 E6
  Walsall WS1. .... 28 F1
Bottle Cotts B17 .... 85 D4
Bott Rd CV5 .... 132 D8
Bottrill St CV11 .... 73 B5
Boughton Rd B25 .... 88 C7
Boulder Cl B77 .... 35 E6
Boulevard The
  Birmingham B5 .... 86 D4
  Brierley Hill DY5 ...... 61 F2
  Sutton Coldfield B73 ... 57 B8
Boultbee Rd B72. .... 57 C7
Boulters La CV9 .... 36 D1
Boulton Cir B19. .... 66 C6
Boulton Cl WS7. .... 7 C8
Boulton Ho **4** B70 ..... 53 D1
Boulton Ind Ctr B18. ... 66 B5
Boulton Rd
  Birmingham B21 .... 65 E7
  Smethwick B66 .... 65 D6
  Solihull B91 .... 107 C7
  West Bromwich B70 ... 53 D1
Boulton Retreat B21 ..... 65 E7
Boultons La B97 .... 158 D6
Boulton Sq B70 .... 53 D1

Boulton Wlk B23 .... 56 B4
Boundary Ave B65 .... 63 E2
Boundary Cl WV13 ...... 26 C1
Boundary Cres DY3 ..... 50 C3
Boundary Ct B37 .... 69 E2
Boundary Dr B13 .... 86 D2
Boundary Farm WV6 ... 23 F2
Boundary Hill DY3 ..... 50 C4
Boundary Ho B5 .... 86 C5
Boundary Ind Est WV10 .. 11 C5
Boundary La B90. ..... 126 A6
Boundary Pl B21. .... 54 B1
Boundary Rd
  Birmingham B23 .... 56 E4
  Brownhills WS9 .... 15 F3
  Sutton Coldfield B74 ... 44 F7
Boundary Way
  Wolverhampton, Penn WV4 .... 38 C5
  Wolverhampton, Tettenhall Wood WV6 .... 23 F2
Bourlay Cl B45. .... 101 E2
Bourn Ave B31. .... 102 C5
BOURNBROOK 86 A2
Bournbrook Ct B5 ...... 86 A3
Bournbrook Rd B29 .... 86 A2
Bourne Ave
  Fairfield B61 .... 120 F1
  Fazeley B78 .... 20 E1
  Halesowen B62 .... 83 F4
  Tipton DY4 .... 52 C7
Bournebrook Cl DY2 ... 62 C5
Bournebrook Cres B62... 84 A4
Bourne Cl
  Birmingham B13 ...... 105 D6
  Cannock WS12. .... 2 E2
  Solihull B91 .... 107 E6
Bourne Gn B32 .... 84 E6
Bourne Hill Cl DY2 ..... 62 E3
Bourne Rd
  Birmingham B6 .... 67 B7
  Coventry CV3. .... 114 C1
Bournes Cl B63 .... 82 E3
Bournes Cres B63 ...... 82 E4
BOURNES GREEN 119 C2
Bournes Hill B63. ...... 82 E4
Bourne St
  Dudley, Bramford DY3, WV14 .... 51 A7
  Dudley DY2, DY3 ...... 51 D1
Bourne Vale WS9 .... 30 D3
Bourne Way Gdns B29 .. 104 A8
Bourne Wlk B65 .... 62 F5
BOURNHEATH 136 D8
Bournheath Rd B61 ... 120 D2
Bourn Mill Dr B6. ...... 66 E6
BOURNVILLE 103 E7
Bournville Coll of FE
  B31. .... 103 E6
Bournville Coll of FE (The Construction Centre)
  B45. .... 122 D8
Bournville Coll of FE (The Hollymoor Centre) **1**
  B31. .... 102 C1
Bournville Inf Sch B30 . 103 E7
Bournville Jun Sch B30 . 103 E7
Bournville La B30 ..... 103 E6
Bournville Mews B30. .. 103 E7
Bournville Sch & Sixth Form Ctr B30 .... 103 C6
Bournville Sta B30. .... 104 A7
Bourton Cl **1** WS5 .... 43 A3
Bourton Croft B92 .... 106 F8
Bourton Dr CV31. ..... 162 B5
Bourton Rd B92. ...... 106 F8
Bovey Croft B76. .... 58 A7
Bovingdon Rd B35 ..... 58 A3
Bowater Ave B33 .... 68 D1
Bowater Ho
  Birmingham B19 ...... 66 D5
  2 West Bromwich B70. 53 C2
Bowater St B70 .... 53 C2
Bowbrook Ave B90. .... 127 A5
Bowcroft Gr B24 .... 57 C6
Bowden Rd B67. .... 64 E6
Bowden Way CV3 ...... 114 F1
Bowdler Rd WV2. ...... 163 D1
Bowen Ave WV4 .... 40 A3
Bowen-Cooke Ave WV6 . 23 E6
Bowen St **4** B13. ...... 87 B2
Bowen St WV4 .... 39 E5
Bower Cl WS13 .... 3 D2
Bowercourt Cl B91. .... 107 B2
Bower La DY5 .... 82 A8
Bowers Croft CV32. ... 157 A5
Bowes Dr WS11. .... 1 F4
Bowes Rd B45 .... 121 E7
Bowfell Cl CV5. .... 112 B4
Bowfell Way **7** B71. ... 53 C6
Bowlas Ave B74 .... 46 B8
BOWLING GREEN 62 E2
Bowling Green La
  Bedworth CV7, CV12 .. 95 E8
  Birmingham B20 .... 66 A8
Bowling Green Rd
  Birmingham B10 .... 67 C1
  Dudley DY2 .... 62 E2
  Hinckley LE10 .... 71 E1
  Stourbridge DY8 ...... 80 E5
Bowling Green St CV34. 160 D6

Bowls Ct CV5 .... 112 F3
Bowman Gn LE10 .... 75 F6
Bowman Rd B42 .... 44 B1
Bowmans Harbour Island
  WV10 .... 26 B4
Bowman's Rise WV1 ... 26 B3
Bowmore Rd B60 ..... 137 B1
Bowness Cl CV6 .... 113 A8
Bowness Gr WV11 ...... 13 B1
Bowness Rd B65. .... 63 D4
Bowood Cres B31. ..... 103 B2
Bowood Ct B97 .... 153 D4
Bowood Dr WV6 .... 24 D6
Bowood End B76 .... 46 E3
Bowshot Cl B36. .... 58 D1
Bow St
  Bilston WV14. .... 40 E6
  Birmingham B1 .... 164 B1
  Willenhall WV13 .... 27 A1
Bowstoke Rd B43 .... 54 C8
Bowyer Rd B8 .... 67 E4
Bowyer St B10. .... 67 A1
Box Cl CV31 .... 162 B3
Boxhill Cl B6. .... 66 F6
Boxhill The CV3 .... 114 B1
Boxnott Cl B97. .... 153 A2
Box Rd B37 .... 90 C8
Box St WS1. .... 28 F1
BOX TREES 125 E1
BOX Trees Rd B93, B94. 127 C1
Boyd Cl CV2 .... 115 A8
Boyden Cl WS11 .... 1 B1
Boydon Cl WV2 .... 40 A6
Boyleston Rd B28 ..... 106 A6
Boynton Rd B26 .... 89 B7
Boyslade Rd LE10 ...... 75 F6
Boyslade Road E LE10. . 75 F5
Boyton Gr B44. .... 44 F3
Brabazon Gr B35. ...... 57 F3
Brabham Cres B74 ..... 44 F6
Bracadale Ave B24 ...... 57 A4
Bracadale Cl CV3 ..... 115 A2
Bracebridge Cl CV7 ... 130 B6
Bracebridge Ct **2** B17 . . 85 D5
Bracebridge Ho
  Sutton Coldfield, New Oscott
  B73 .... 45 C2
  12 Sutton Coldfield, Streetly
  B74 .... 31 F2
Bracebridge Rd
  Birmingham B24 .... 56 F1
  Sutton Coldfield B74 ... 46 A8
Bracebridge St
  Birmingham B6 .... 66 E6
  Nuneaton CV11 .... 73 B3
Braceby Ave B13. ...... 105 C6
Braces La B60 .... 121 C1
Brace St WS1. .... 42 E8
Brackenbury Rd B44 ... 56 B8
Bracken Cl
  Burntwood WS7. .... 7 C7
  Cannock WS12. .... 2 D8
  Lichfield WS14. .... 9 E6
  Wolverhampton WV8. .. 10 E1
Bracken Croft **1** B37 . . 70 C3
Brackendale Dr
  Cannock WS10 .... 72 F3
  Walsall WS5. .... 43 B3
Brackendale Sh Ctr WV12 27 D4
Brackendale Way DY9... 81 D4
Bracken Dr B75. .... 47 A5
Brackenfield Rd
  Birmingham B44 .... 44 D3
  Halesowen B63 .... 82 E3
Brackenfield View DY1. . 61 D8
Bracken Gr B61. ...... 121 A1
Brackenhurst Rd CV6 ... 113 A7
Bracken Park Gdns DY8 . . 60 F2
Bracken Rd
  Birmingham B24 .... 57 C2
  Huntington WS12. .... 1 C5
Bracken Way
  Birmingham B38 ..... 123 D6
  Sutton Coldfield B74 ... 44 F8
Bracken Wood WS5 ..... 43 D5
Brackenwood Dr WV11. . 26 F5
Brackleham Way B77 .. 22 A6
Brackley Ave B20 ...... 55 C1
Brackley Cl CV6. ...... 112 F7
Brackleys Way B92 ..... 89 A2
Bracknell Wlk **1** CV2 . . 115 A7
Bradbeer Ho B16 .... 66 A1
Bradburne Way B7. ..... 67 A5
Bradburn Rd WV11. .... 26 B8
Bradbury Cl WS8. ...... 15 F5
Bradbury Ct WS12 .... 2 B7
Bradbury La WS12 .... 2 B8
Bradbury Rd B92. ..... 107 A8
Braddock Cl CV3. ..... 115 A1
Brade Dr CV2. .... 115 A8
Braden Rd WV4. .... 38 D4
Brades Cl B63 .... 82 B7
Brades Rd B69 .... 63 E8
Brades Rise B69 .... 63 E8
Bradestone Rd CV11. ... 73 D1
BRADES VILLAGE 52 E1
Bradewell Rd B36. ...... 58 D1
Bradfield Cl CV5. ..... 112 C5
Bradfield Ho B26 ...... 89 D6
Bradfield Rd B42. ...... 55 D7
Bradford Cl B43 .... 54 F7
Bradford Court Bsns Ctr B12 .... 87 A8
Bradford La
  Belbroughton DY9 .... 119 D5
  Walsall WS1. .... 28 E1

Bradford Mall WS1. ..... 28 E1
Bradford Pl WS1. .... 28 E1
Bradford Rd
  Birmingham B36 .... 69 B7
  Brownhills WS8 .... 15 E8
  Dudley DY2 .... 61 F6
Bradford St
  Birmingham B12, B5 ... 66 F1
  Cannock WS11. .... 2 A5
  Tamworth B79 .... 20 F5
  Walsall WS1. .... 28 E1
Bradgate Cl WV12. ..... 27 C6
Bradgate Dr B74 .... 31 E5
Bradgate Pl **1** B12 ..... 87 A6
Bradgate Rd LE10 ...... 71 C2
Brading Rd CV10. ...... 73 D6
Bradley Ave WV14 ...... 39 E4
BRADLEY. 40 E3
Bradley Croft CV7. .... 130 B6
Bradley La WV14. ...... 41 A3
Bradley Lane Stop WV14. 41 A3
Bradleymore Rd DY5. .. 61 D3
Bradley Rd
  Birmingham B34 .... 69 D6
  Stourbridge DY8 ...... 80 F6
  Wolverhampton WV2. .. 39 E7
Bradleys Cl B64. .... 82 E7
Bradley's La DY4, WV14 . 51 E8
Bradley St
  Bilston WV14. .... 40 F4
  Brierley Hill DY5 ...... 61 C7
  Tipton DY4 .... 51 F2
Bradley Thursfield Ct DY11 .... 116 C7
BRADMORE 38 E8
Bradmore Cl **1** B91. .. 107 A1
Bradmore Gr B29 ...... 103 A8
Bradmore Rd WV3 ...... 38 F8
Bradney Gn CV4 ...... 131 E7
Bradnick Pl CV4 ...... 111 F1
Bradnock Cl B13. ..... 105 C7
Bradnock's Marsh La B92 .... 109 E2
Bradshaw Ave
  Birmingham B38 ..... 103 D1
  Darlaston WS10. .... 41 C5
Bradshaw Cl
  7 Birmingham B15. .. 86 C8
  Tipton DY4 .... 52 A3
Bradshawe Cl B28 .... 105 D3
Bradstock Rd B30 ..... 104 C4
Bradwell Croft B75. .... 32 E3
Braeburn Cl WS13 .... 3 D1
Braemar Ave DY8 ...... 60 C1
Braemar Cl
  Coventry CV2. .... 114 E6
  Sedgley DY3. .... 39 C1
  Willenhall WV12 .... 27 B5
Braemar Dr B23 .... 56 B5
Braemar Gdns WS12 ..... 1 F7
Braemar Rd
  Coventry CV7 .... 95 F5
  Royal Leamington Spa CV32 .... 157 B4
  Solihull B92 .... 88 E1
  Sutton Coldfield B73 ... 46 A2
Braemar Way CV10. .... 73 A2
Braeside Croft B37 ..... 70 D2
Braeside Way WS3 ..... 14 F3
Bragg Rd B20. .... 55 D2
Braggs Farm La B90 .. 126 A4
Braham St B79 .... 20 D6
Braid Cl B38. .... 103 E1
Braidwood Sch for Deaf Children B36. .... 68 C7
Brailes Cl B92 .... 107 E7
Brailes Dr B76. .... 46 F3
Brailes Gr B9 .... 68 B1
Brailsford Cl WV11. .... 26 E8
Brailsford Dr B66 ...... 65 A5
Brain St B77 .... 36 A1
Braithwaite Dr DY6 ..... 60 D6
Braithwaite Rd B11 ..... 87 B7
Brake La DY8. .... 98 E6
Brakesmead CV31. .... 161 F5
Brake The DY8. .... 98 F6
Bramah Way DY4 .... 52 C6
Bramber B77 .... 21 D1
Bramber Dr WV5. .... 49 A7
Bramber Way DY8 ...... 80 F2
Bramble Cl
  Birmingham, Aston B6. .. 66 E7
  Birmingham, Shenley Fields
  B31. .... 102 F6
  Brownhills WS8. .... 15 E5
  3 Coleshill B46 ..... 70 F7
  Cradley Heath B64. .... 62 F4
  Nuneaton CV11 .... 73 F2
  Willenhall WV12 .... 27 C7
Bramble Dell B9. .... 68 A3
Bramble Dr
  Birmingham B26 .... 89 A6
  Cannock WS12. .... 2 C7
Bramble Gn DY1 .... 50 F5
Bramble Ho B98 ...... 158 F8
Bramble La WS7 .... 7 B8
Brambleside DY8 .... 60 F1
Bramble St CV1. ...... 113 E2
Brambles The
  Catshill B61 .... 137 A8
  Lichfield WS14 .... 9 D6
  Norton Canes WS11 ..... 6 A5
  Stourbridge DY9 ...... 81 D3
  Sutton Coldfield B76 ... 58 A8
Bramble Way B77 ...... 48 D4
Bramblewood B34 ...... 69 C5
Bramblewoods B34 ..... 69 C5

Brambling Rise DY10. . 117 B1
Brambling Wlk
  2 Birmingham B15. ... 86 C7
  Brierley Hill DY5 ...... 81 C6
BRAMCOTE 79 E6
Bramcote Cl
  Bulkington CV12 ...... 79 D2
  Hinckley LE10 .... 71 F3
Bramcote Dr B91 ...... 107 C7
Bramcote Hospl CV11. .. 79 E7
Bramcote Rd B32 ...... 84 C5
Bramcote Rise B75. .... 46 C7
Bramdean Wlk WV4 ..... 38 C6
Bramdene Ave CV10. .... 73 D8
Brame Rd LE10 .... 71 C2
Bramerton Cl WV11 ..... 26 A6
BRAMFORD 51 A7
Bramford Dr DY1 .... 51 B6
Bramford Prim Sch DY1 . 51 B6
Bramley Cl
  Birmingham B43 .... 44 D3
  Walsall WS5. .... 43 D8
Bramley Croft B90 .... 106 C2
Bramley Ct WV11 .... 26 C6
Bramley Dr
  Birmingham B20 .... 55 B3
  Hollywood B47. ...... 125 B6
Bramley Mews St B27. .. 88 C4
Bramley Rd
  Birmingham B27 .... 88 C5
  Walsall WS5. .... 43 B4
Brampton Ave B28 .... 106 A6
Brampton Cres B90 ... 106 B6
Brampton Dr WS12 ...... 2 E2
Brampton Way CV12 ... 79 B3
Bramshall Dr B93 .... 127 E3
Bramshaw Cl B14 ..... 104 F2
Bramshill Ct B15. ...... 86 B8
Bramstead Ave WV6 .... 24 B2
Bramston Cres CV4 ... 111 F1
Bramwell Dr WS6. .... 4 D1
Bramwell Gdns CV6 ..... 95 F5
Brancaster Cl B77 ...... 22 A5
Branchal Rd WS9 .... 16 C1
Branch Rd B38. .... 123 E8
Branden Rd B48 ...... 139 A5
Brandfield Rd CV6 .... 112 F8
Brandhall Ct B68. ...... 64 A2
Brandhall La B68 .... 64 B1
Brandhall Prim Sch B68. 64 B1
Brandhall Rd B68 ...... 64 B2
BRANDON 135 F5
Brandon Cl
  Dudley DY3. .... 50 E7
  Sutton Coldfield WS9. .. 30 F3
  West Bromwich B70 ... 53 A2
Brandon Ct
  Birmingham B31 ...... 103 B1
  Coventry CV3. .... 135 A7
Brandon Gr B31 .... 122 F7
Brandon La CV3, CV8 .. 135 C5
Brandon Marsh Wildlife Reserve* CV3 .... 135 A4
Brandon Par CV32 .... 162 A8
Brandon Pk WV3. .... 38 E7
Brandon Pl B34. .... 69 D7
Brandon Rd
  Birmingham B28 .... 87 E2
  Coventry CV3. .... 135 A8
  Halesowen B62 .... 63 E1
  Hinckley LE10 .... 75 B7
  Solihull B91 .... 107 C7
Brandon Thomas Ct B6. . 67 B8
Brandon Way
  Brierley Hill DY5 ...... 81 E8
  West Bromwich B70 ... 53 A2
Brandon Way Ind Est B70 52 F3
Brandon Wood Farm* CV8. .... 135 D5
Brandwood Cres B30. . 104 D3
BRANDWOOD END. 104 E4
Brandwood Gr B14. ... 104 D5
Brandwood Ho B14 ... 104 C4
Brandwood Park Rd B14 104 C4
Brandwood Rd B14 ... 104 D5
Branfield Cl WV14 ...... 51 A8
Branksome Ave B21. ... 65 F8
Branksome Rd CV6 .... 112 E6
Branscombe Cl B14 ... 104 D5
Bransdale Ave CV6. .... 95 D3
Bransdale Cl WV6. ..... 25 A5
Bransford Ave CV4. ... 132 D5
Bransford Rise B91 .... 108 B5
Bransford Twr B12. .... 86 F8
BRANSON'S CROSS. ... 141 C2
Branston St B18 .... 66 C4
Branstree Dr CV6. ...... 95 D2
Brantford Rd B25. ...... 88 C8
Branthill Croft **4** B91 . 107 B1
Brantley Ave WV3. ...... 24 C1
Brantley Rd B6. .... 56 A2
Branton Hill La WS9 .... 30 C5
Brantwood Ave WS7 ..... 7 A5
Brascote Rd LE10 ...... 74 F8
Brasshouse La B66. .... 65 A7
Brassie Cl B38 .... 103 D1
Brassington Ave B72, B73. 46 B5
Bratch Cl DY2. .... 62 C3
Bratch Common Rd WV5. 49 A8
Bratch La WV5. .... 49 A8
Brathay Cl CV3. .... 133 D6
Bratt St B70 .... 53 C4
Braunston Cl B76. ...... 47 A2
Brawnes Hurst B26 ..... 69 A1
Brayford Ave
  Brierley Hill DY5 ...... 81 B7
  Coventry CV3. .... 133 C6

Braymoor Rd B33 69 E1
Bray's La CV2 114 A3
Brays Rd B26 89 B6
Brays Sch B26 89 A6
Bray St WV13 27 B2
Braytoft Cl CV6 95 C2
Brazil St CV4 111 E2
Breaches La B98 159 D8
Bread and Meat Cl CV34 160 D6
Breadmarket St WS13 9 B8
Breakback Rd B61 150 D8
Bream B77 35 D7
Bream Cl
  Birmingham B37 70 C2
  Wolverhampton WV10 26 B4
Breamore Cres DY1 50 F3
Brean Ave B92 88 F5
Brearley Cl B19 66 E5
Brearley St
  Birmingham, Handsworth B21 65 D8
  Birmingham, Hockley B19 66 E5
Brechin Cl LE10 75 A8
Brecknell Rise DY10 116 F8
Brecknock Rd B71 53 A6
Brecon Ave B61 137 A5
Brecon Dr DY8 81 B6
Brecon Rd B20 66 B8
Brecon Twr 1 B16 66 A2
Bredon Ave
  Coventry CV3 134 F8
  Kidderminster DY11 116 A1
  Stourbridge DY9 81 C5
Bredon Croft B18 66 A5
Bredon Ct
  Halesowen B63 83 A3
  Sutton Coldfield B75 32 A4
Bredon Ho B98 159 B7
Bredon Rd
  Bromsgrove B61 150 D7
  Oldbury B69 63 D5
  Stourbridge DY8 81 B6
Bredon Terr 4 B18 66 A5
Bredon View B97 158 D8
Breech Cl B74 44 E7
Bree Cl CV5 112 A7
Breeden Dr B76 59 B6
BREEDON CROSS 104 B6
Breedon Ct B30 104 A5
Breedon Gdns B98 154 A3
Breedon Rd B30 104 A5
Breedon Way WS4 15 C1
Breener Ind Est DY5 61 B1
Breen Rydding Dr WV14 51 B8
Bree's La CV8 130 A1
Breeze Ave WS11 6 B5
Breeze The DY5 61 D3
Brelades Cl DY1 50 E3
Breme Lodge B60 151 A7
Brendon B77 22 B1
Brendon Way CV10 72 A3
Brenfield Dr LE10 75 A8
Brennand Cl B68 84 C8
Brennand Rd B68 84 B8
Brent B77 35 E7
Brentford Rd
  Birmingham B14 105 A5
  Solihull B91 106 E3
Brent Ho 3 DY1 61 E8
Brentmill Cl WV10 11 F4
Brentnall Dr B75 32 B3
Brenton Rd WV4 38 F3
Brent Rd B30 104 D8
Brentwood Ave CV3 133 C3
Brentwood Cl B91 106 E3
Brentwood Gdns CV3 133 C3
Brentwood Gr B44 55 E8
Brenwood Cl DY6 60 B7
Brereton Cl DY2 62 E8
Brereton Rd WV12 27 D7
Brese Ave CV34 155 F1
Bretby Cl B93 127 F5
Bretby Gr B23 57 A6
Bretford Rd CV2 96 C1
Bretshall Cl B90 126 F5
Brett Dr B32 102 C8
Brettell La
  Brierley Hill DY5, DY8 61 B1
  Stourbridge DY8 80 F8
Brettell St 5 DY1 62 B8
Bretton Gdns WV10 25 F6
Bretton Rd B27 88 D2
Bretts Cl CV1 165 D4
Bretts Hall Est CV10 72 A7
Brett St B71 53 B5
Brett Young Cl
  Halesowen B63 83 B3
  Kidderminster DY10 117 B5
Brevitt Rd WV2 39 D6
Brewer Rd CV12 79 D2
Brewers Cl CV3 115 A1
Brewers Dr WS3 15 A1
Brewer St WS2 28 E4
Brewers Terr WS3 15 A2
Brewery Rd WV1 163 A3
Brewery St
  Birmingham, Handsworth B21 65 D8
  Birmingham, New Town Row B6 164 C5
  Dudley DY2 51 E1
  Smethwick B67 64 F6
  Tipton DY4 51 F4
Brewins Way DY5 62 A4
Brewster Cl
  Coventry CV2 114 E2
  Fazeley B78 20 E1
Brewster St DY2 62 C5
Breydon Gr WV13 40 F8
Brian Rd B67 64 E6
Briar B77 22 A3
Briar Ave B74 31 A1
Briarbeck WS4 29 C8
Briar Cl
  Birmingham B24 57 A4
  Cannock WS12 2 A8
  Hinckley LE10 75 F6
  Lickey End B60 137 C6
  Royal Leamington Spa CV32 157 B2
Briar Coppice B90 126 D4
Briar Ct
  14 Brierley Hill DY5 61 D2
  Dudley DY2 62 C6
Briardene Ave CV12 78 B2
Briarfield Rd B11 88 A3
Briar Hill DY10 118 E1
Briar Hill Inf Sch CV31 162 B3
Briarley Ho 5 B71 42 F1
Briarmead LE10 75 E4
Briars Cl
  Brierley Hill DY5 61 C4
  Coventry CV2 114 C2
  Nuneaton CV11 73 E5
Briars The
  Aldridge WS9 30 A7
  Birmingham B23 56 D6
  West Hagley DY9 98 F4
Briar Way B38 124 A8
Briarwood Cl B90 126 D4
Briar Wood Cl WV2 40 A7
Briarwood The WV2 40 A7
Brickfield Rd B25 88 B6
Brickheath Rd WV1 26 A3
Brickhill Dr B37 70 A2
Brick Hill La CV5 111 E8
Brickhouse La
  Stoke Prior B60 150 C4
  West Bromwich B70 52 E6
Brickhouse Lane S DY4 52 E6
Brickhouse Prim Sch B65 63 A3
Brickhouse Rd B65 63 A4
Brickiln Ct 2 DY5 61 D2
Brickiln St WS8 15 F7
Brick Kiln La
  Birmingham B44 55 E6
  Dudley DY3 50 B3
  Middleton B78 48 D6
  Solihull B91 126 F8
  Wythall B47 124 F4
Brickkiln St WV13 26 F1
Brick Kiln St
  Brierley Hill, Hart's Hill DY5 61 E5
  Brierley Hill, Quarry Bank DY5 82 A8
  Hinckley LE10 75 C8
  Tipton DY4 51 F6
Brick Kiln Way CV12 78 D3
Brick St DY3 50 D8
Brickworks Rd WS12 2 E2
Brickyard Cl CV7 130 C7
Brickyard La B80 159 C4
Brickyard Rd
  Aldridge, Leighswood WS9 30 A7
  Aldridge, Leighswood WS9 30 A8
  Aldridge, Vigo WS9 15 F1
Bridal Path The CV5 112 B6
Briddsland Rd B33 69 E2
Bridgeacre Gdns CV3 114 F2
Bridge Ave
  Cheslyn Hay WS6 4 E4
  Tipton DY4 52 C7
Bridgeburn Rd B31 102 E8
Bridge Cl
  Birmingham B11 87 B3
  Brownhills WS8 15 E6
Bridgecote CV3 134 E6
Bridge Croft B12 86 E6
Bridge Cross Rd WS7 7 A7
Bridge Ct
  Cannock WS12 2 B5
  Stourbridge DY8 60 E2
BRIDGE END 160 F5
Bridge End CV34 160 F5
Bridgefield Wlk B65 62 F5
Bridgefoot Wlk WV8 10 F1
Bridgeford Rd B34 69 B6
Bridge Ho
  Royal Leamington Spa CV31 162 A8
  Smethwick B66 65 C6
Bridge Ind Est B91 107 C7
Bridgelands Way B20 55 D1
Bridgeman Croft B36 69 C8
Bridgeman Rd CV6 113 B4
Bridgeman St WS2 28 D1
Bridgemary Cl WV10 11 E4
Bridge Meadow Dr B93 127 F6
Bridgemeadow Ho 5 B36 68 E8
Bridgend Croft DY5 61 B6
Bridgenorth Ho B33 69 B2
Bridge Piece B31 103 B2
Bridge Rd
  Birmingham B8 67 E3
  Bromsgrove B60 151 A6
  Hinckley LE10 75 D7
  Tipton DY4 52 C7
  Walsall WS4 15 B1
Bridges Cres WS11 5 F5
Bridgeside Cl WS8 15 F6
Bridgeside Trad Est B77 21 C3
Bridge Specl Sch B23 56 E4
Bridges Rd WS11 5 F5
Bridge St
  Bilston WV14 40 E5
  Birmingham B1 164 A2
  Brownhills WS8 15 E6
  Cannock WS11 4 E5
  Coventry CV6 114 A7
  Halesowen B63 82 C7
  Kenilworth CV8 147 F5
  1 Kidderminster DY10 116 E5
  Nuneaton, Chilvers Coton CV11 73 C2
  Nuneaton CV11 73 C4
  Oldbury B69 64 A8
  Redditch B97 153 D4
  Stourbridge DY8 60 E1
  Tamworth B77 21 E5
  Tipton WV14 51 C8
  Walsall WS1 28 F2
  Warwick CV34 161 C8
  Wednesbury WS10 41 F1
  West Bromwich B70 53 B4
  Willenhall WV13 26 F1
  Wolverhampton WV10 25 E5
Bridge Street Ind Est WS10 41 F1
Bridge Street N B66 65 B7
Bridge Street S B66 65 B6
Bridge Street W B19 66 D5
Bridge The 3 WS1 28 E1
Bridge Trad Ctr The B64 82 D8
Bridge Trad Est The B66 65 B6
Bridge View
  Baginton CV8 133 D3
  3 Coleshill B46 70 F7
Bridgewater Ave B69 64 A4
Bridgewater Cres DY2 51 E1
Bridgewater Dr WV14 40 C2
Bridgewater St B77 21 D5
Bridge Way WS8 15 E6
Bridgnorth Gr WV12 27 B6
Bridgnorth Rd
  Himley DY3 49 B3
  Stourbridge DY7, DY8 80 C6
  Trescott WV6 37 C7
  Wolverhampton WV6 24 B2
BRIDGTOWN 4 E6
Bridgtown Bsns Ctr WS11 4 E6
Bridgtown Cty Prim Sch WS11 4 E6
Bridgwater Cl WS9 15 F3
Bridle Brook La CV5, CV7 94 A3
Bridle Gr B71 53 F7
Bridle La B74, WS9 44 E7
Bridle Mead B38 123 D8
Bridle Path The B90 106 B6
Bridle Rd DY8 80 D6
Bridleway The CV10 73 A1
Bridlewood B74 44 F8
Bridley Moor Rd B97 153 C5
Bridport Cl CV2 115 A4
Bridport Ho B31 102 E7
BRIERLEY HILL 61 E2
Brierley Hill Prim Sch DY5 61 D2
Brierley Hill Rd DY8 60 F2
Brierley La WV14 40 E2
Brierley Rd
  Bromsgrove B60 137 C1
  Coventry CV2 114 C8
Brierley Trad Est The DY5 61 C3
Brier Mill Rd B63 83 C3
Brier Specl Sch The DY6 60 F5
Briery Cl B64 82 F7
Briery Rd B63 82 E3
Brigadoon Gdns DY9 81 C2
Brigfield Cres B13 105 B5
Brigfield Rd B13 105 B5
Bright Cres B77 21 C2
Brightmere Rd CV6 113 B4
Brighton Cl WS2 28 D3
Brighton Mews 8 WV3 25 A2
Brighton Rd B12 87 A5
Brighton St CV2 113 F3
Bright Rd B68 64 B5
Bright St
  Coventry CV6 113 E6
  Darlaston WS10 41 D5
  Stourbridge DY8 80 D6
  Wolverhampton WV1 163 A4
Brightstone Cl WV10 11 F4
Brightstone Rd B45 102 B2
Brightwalton Rd CV3 133 D7
Brightwell Cres B93 127 E3
Brill Cl CV4 132 C5
Brimfield Pl 1 WV6 24 F4
Brimstone La B61 136 D7
Brindle Ave CV3 114 C2
Brindle Cl B26 88 E5
Brindle Ct B23 56 B3
Brindlefields Way DY4 52 B2
Brindle Rd WS5 43 C4
Brindley Ave WV11 13 A1
Brindley Cl
  1 Stourbridge DY8 60 E1
  Willenhall WS2 27 F5
Brindley Cres WS12 2 C8
Brindley Ct 5 DY4 51 E5
Brindley Dr
  Birmingham B1 164 A2
  Tamworth B77 21 F6
Brindley Heath Rd WS12 2 D8
Brindley Paddocks CV1 165 B4
Brindley Pl B1 66 B2
Brindley Point Apartments 7 B16 66 B2
Brindley Rd
  Bedworth CV7 96 B8
  Hinckley LE10 74 E8
Brindley Rd *continued*
  West Bromwich B71 53 A8
Brindleys Bsns Pk WS11 2 B3
Brindley Way 10 B66 65 C5
Brineton Gr B29 85 A1
Brineton Ind Est 1 WS2 28 C1
Brineton St WS2 28 C1
Bringewood Gr B32 102 B8
Brinklow Cl B98 159 D8
Brinklow Croft B34 69 D7
Brinklow Rd
  Birmingham B29 84 F2
  Coventry CV3 115 A2
Brinklow Twr 4 B12 86 F7
Brinley Way DY6 60 C6
BRINSFORD 11 D7
Brinsford La WV10 11 D7
Brinsford Rd WV10 11 C3
Brinsley Cl B91 107 B2
Brinsley Rd B26 89 B8
Brinton Cl DY11 116 C3
Brinton Cres DY11 116 C3
Brisbane Cl CV3 133 E6
Brisbane Ct 2 CV12 78 A2
Brisbane Rd B67 64 E5
Brisbane Way WS12 2 E3
Briscoe Rd CV6 95 D4
Briseley Cl DY5 81 D8
Bristam Cl B69 63 E6
BRISTNALL FIELDS 64 B3
Bristnall Hall Cres B68 64 C3
Bristnall Hall La B68 64 D3
Bristnall Hall Rd B68 64 C3
Bristnall Hall Tech Coll B68 64 D3
Bristol Cl WS11 2 B1
Bristol Ct 15 B29 103 C7
Bristol Rd
  Birmingham, Balsall Heath B5 86 C5
  Birmingham, Gravelly Hill B23 56 E3
  Coventry CV5 112 F2
  Dudley DY2 62 D2
Bristol Road S
  Birmingham B31 102 F2
  Birmingham, Bournville B29, B30, B31 103 C7
  Birmingham, Longbridge B31, B45 122 C8
Bristol St
  Birmingham B15 86 D8
  Wolverhampton WV3 39 B8
Briston Cl DY5 81 C8
Britannia Cl B98 153 F3
Britannia Gdns B65 63 C3
Britannia Gn DY3 50 E5
Britannia Mews B65 63 C3
Britannia Pk WS10 41 D3
Britannia Rd
  Bilston WV14 40 F3
  Hinckley LE10 76 A5
  Rowley Regis B65 63 C2
  Walsall WS1 42 D5
Britannia Sh Ctr 3 LE10 75 D8
Britannia St
  Coventry CV2 113 F3
  Oldbury B69 52 C2
Britannia Way WS13 9 F8
Britannic Gdns B13 86 D2
Britannic Ho B13 86 D2
Britford Cl B14 104 F3
Briton Rd CV2 114 A4
Brittain La CV34 161 C6
Brittan Cl B34 69 E6
Britten Cl CV11 79 A7
Britten St B97 153 D4
Britton Dr B72 57 C8
Britwell Rd B73 46 A2
Brixfield Way B90 126 B5
Brixham Cl CV11 73 F5
Brixham Dr CV2 114 C7
Brixham Rd B16 65 D4
Brixworth Cl CV3 134 E8
Broad Acres B31 102 E6
Broadbent Cl 1 WS13 8 F6
Broadcott Ind Est B64 83 A8
Broad Croft 1 DY4 52 C6
Broadfern Rd B93 128 B8
Broadfield Cl
  Kingswinford DY6 60 D5
  West Bromwich B71 42 F1
Broadfield House Glass Mus★ DY6 60 D5
Broadfields DY9 99 A6
Broadfields Rd B23 57 B7
Broadfield Wlk 1 B16 66 B1
Broadgate CV1 165 B3
BROAD GREEN 138 B1
Broad Ground Rd B98 154 B2
Broadhaven Cl CV31 162 C7
Broad Heath Cl B97 153 B5
Broad Heath Com Prim Sch CV6 113 E6
Broadheath Dr WS4 29 D8
Broadhidley Dr B32 84 B1
Broadhurst Gn WS12 2 A8
Broad La
  Birmingham B14 104 E4
  Burntwood WS7 8 B5
  Coventry CV5 111 D4
  Lichfield WS14 9 D6
  Tanworth-In-A B98 141 E3
  Walsall, Essington WS3 13 E4
  Walsall WS4 15 C2
  Wolverhampton WV3 38 E8
Broadlands WV10 11 D5
Broadlands Cl CV5 112 C2
Broadlands Dr DY5 61 E5
Broadlands Rise WS14 9 D7
Broad Lane Gdns WS3 14 A2
Broad Lane N WV12 27 B7
Broad Lanes WV14 40 C3
Broad Lane S WV11 27 A5
Broadlee B77 22 C1
Broad Mdw WS9 30 B8
Broadmead Ct CV5 112 C2
Broadmeadow DY6 60 E8
Broadmeadow Cl B30 104 B3
Broadmeadow Gn WV14 40 C7
Broadmeadow Ho B32 102 D8
Broadmeadow Inf Sch B30 104 B2
Broadmeadow Jun Sch B30 104 B2
Broad Meadow La
  Birmingham B30 104 B3
  Great Wyrley WS6 5 A2
Broadmeadows Cl WV12 27 E8
Broadmeadows Rd WV12 27 E8
Broadmede Ho B67 64 E2
Broadmere Rise CV5 112 A2
Broadmoor Ave B68 64 D2
Broadmoor Cl WV14 40 C4
Broadmoor Rd WV14 40 C3
Broad Oaks B76 47 A1
Broadoaks Cl WS11 5 F6
Broad Oaks Rd B91 107 A5
Broadoaks The B91 107 A4
Broad Park Rd CV2 114 D8
Broad Rd B27 88 B3
Broadsmeath B77 21 C1
Broad St
  Bilston WV14 40 D6
  Birmingham B15, B1 66 C2
  Brierley Hill DY5 61 C6
  Bromsgrove B61 136 F4
  Cannock WS11 4 E6
  Coventry CV6 113 E7
  Kidderminster DY10 116 E7
  Kingswinford DY6 60 D5
  Oldbury B69 64 A5
  Tipton WV14 51 C8
  Warwick CV34 160 F7
  Wolverhampton WV1 163 C3
Broadstone Ave
  Halesowen B63 82 B4
  Walsall WS3 28 D7
Broadstone Cl WV4 39 D5
Broadstone Rd B26 69 A1
Broad Street Jetty CV6 113 E7
Broadsword Way LE10 75 D4
Broadwalk 5 B1 66 C1
Broadwas Cl B98 154 C5
Broadwater CV5 133 A8
Broadwaters Ave WS10 41 C4
Broadwaters Dr
  Kidderminster DY10 117 A8
  West Hagley DY9 99 B4
Broadwaters Rd WS10 41 C4
Broadway
  Cannock WS12 1 F6
  Coventry CV5 113 A1
  Cubbington CV32 157 E5
  Oldbury B68 64 C1
  Solihull B90 106 B4
  Walsall WS5 43 A6
  Wolverhampton, Bushbury WV10 11 E2
  Wolverhampton WV3 24 C2
Broad Way WS4 15 C2
Broadway Ave
  Birmingham B9 68 A3
  Halesowen B63 83 A2
Broadway Com L Ctr The B20 55 E2
Broadway Croft
  Birmingham B26 89 A6
  Oldbury B68 64 C1
Broadway Gdns WV10 11 E2
Broadway Lower Sch B6 66 E8
Broadway Mans CV5 113 A1
Broadway N WS1 29 B2
Broadway Plaza B16 66 A1
Broadway Sch B20 55 E2
Broadway The
  Birmingham B20 55 E2
  Dudley DY1 51 B3
  Stourbridge DY8 80 D3
  West Bromwich B71 53 B7
  Wombourne WV5 49 A5
Broadway W WS1 42 D6
Broadwell Ct CV4 131 F6
Broadwell Ind Pk B69 53 A1
Broadwell Rd
  Oldbury B69 64 A8
  Solihull B92 89 A2
Broadwells Cres CV4 132 A5
Broadyates Gr B25 88 C6
Broadyates Rd B25 88 C6
Brobury Croft B91 106 D4
Brock Cl B45 102 A1
Brockenhurst Ct B73 46 B1
Brockenhurst Way CV6 96 B6
Brockeridge Cl WV12 13 C1
Brockfield Ho WV10 25 F4
Brockhall Gr B37 69 F5
Brockhill Dr B97 153 A5
Brockhill La
  Alvechurch B48 124 B2
  Beoley B98 140 F2
  Tardebigge B97 152 E8
Brockhurst Ave LE10 75 D4

Brockhurst Cres WS5 .... 42 E4
Brockhurst Dr
  Birmingham B28 ...... 106 A5
  Coventry CV4.......... 111 D2
  Wolverhampton WV6 .... 25 A4
Brockhurst Ho 4 WS2 .. 28 D3
Brockhurst La
  Solihull B90 .... 126 B5
  Weeford B75 .... 33 B7
Brockhurst Pl WS5...... 42 F5
Brockhurst Rd
  Birmingham B36 ...... 68 D6
  Sutton Coldfield B75 .... 32 D1
Brockhurst St WS1...... 42 E6
Brockley Cl DY5 .... 61 D3
Brockley Gr B13 .... 86 C1
Brockley Pl B7......... 67 C7
BROCKMOOR......... 61 C3
Brockmoor Cl DY9 ..... 61 C2
Brockmoor Ind Est DY5 .. 61 A3
Brockmoor Prim Sch DY5 61 C3
Brock Rd DY4.......... 52 C4
Brockton Rd B29....... 85 A1
Brockwell Dr B44 ...... 44 E4
Brockwell Rd B44...... 44 E4
Brockworth Rd B14 .... 104 C2
Brocton Cl
  Walsall WS3........... 28 A8
  Wolverhampton WV14.... 40 A3
Brodick Cl LE10........ 75 A8
Brodick Rd LE10 ...... 74 F8
Brodick Way CV10 ..... 72 F3
Brogden Cl 4 B71 ..... 53 F8
Brome Hall La B94 .... 144 D2
Bromfield Cl B6 .... 66 E7
Bromfield Cres WS10 ... 42 C4
Bromfield Ct WV6...... 24 B3
Bromfield Rd B97...... 153 D2
BROMFORD........... 57 D1
Bromford Central B8. ... 68 B8
Bromford Cl
  Birmingham, Erdington
    B23.................. 56 E5
  Birmingham, Handsworth
    B20................. 55 A2
Bromford Cres B24 .... 57 A2
Bromford Ct B8........ 68 B6
Bromford Dale 2 WV6.. 24 F3
Bromford Dell B31..... 103 C4
Bromford Gdns B15.... 85 C8
Bromford Hill B20 ..... 55 C3
Bromford Ho B73 ..... 45 F7
Bromford La
  Birmingham B8, B36 .... 68 C6
  West Bromwich B71 .... 53 B2
Bromford Mere 4 B92.. 88 E1
Bromford Park Ho 3 B13 87 B2
Bromford Rd
  Birmingham B36 ...... 68 D7
  Dudley DY2 .... 62 A6
  West Bromwich B69, B70 . 53 A1
Bromford Rise WV3.... 163 A1
Bromford Road Ind Est
  B70................... 53 A1
Bromford Wlk 4 B43 .. 43 F1
Bromhurst Way CV34.. 160 B4
Bromleigh Dr CV2...... 114 C2
Bromleigh Villas CV8. .. 133 F2
BROMLEY............ 61 B5
Bromley DY5 .... 61 B5
Bromley Cl
  Cannock WS12......... 2 C7
  Kenilworth CV8 .... 147 E6
Bromley Gdns CV8 .... 10 A4
Bromley Hills Prim Sch
  The DY5.............. 61 B5
Bromley Pl WV4 ...... 39 A5
Bromley St
  Birmingham B9 .... 67 A1
  Stourbridge DY9 ...... 81 F6
  Wolverhampton WV2.... 39 C7
Brompton Dr DY5...... 81 B7
Brompton Lawns WV6... 24 A3
Brompton Pool Rd B28.. 105 E3
Brompton Rd B44...... 44 D4
BROMSGROVE........ 136 E2
Bromsgrove Highway
  Bromsgrove B60 ...... 137 D1
  Redditch B97 .... 153 B2
  Tardebigge B60, B97 ... 152 C6
Bromsgrove Pre Prep Sch
  B60.................. 150 E5
Bromsgrove Rd
  Clent DY9............. 99 D4
  Dodford B61 .... 136 D6
  Halesowen B63 ...... 83 C4
  Mustow Green DY10 .. 117 F2
  Redditch B97 .... 153 B3
  Romsley B62 .... 101 A5
  Studley B80 .... 159 D2
Bromsgrove Ret Pk B60 137 A3
Bromsgrove Sch B61.. 136 F2
Bromsgrove Sch (Prep
  Campus) B60......... 136 F1
Bromsgrove Sch (Senior
  Campus) B61......... 136 F1
Bromsgrove St
  Birmingham B5 ...... 164 C1
  Halesowen B63 ...... 83 C4

Bromsgrove St continued
  Kidderminster DY10.... 116 E6
Bromsgrove Sta B60 .. 151 B7
Bromwall Rd B13 ...... 105 B6
Bromwich Cl CV3 ..... 134 F8
Bromwich Dr B75...... 46 C7
Bromwich La B9 ...... 99 B8
Bromwich Wlk B9 .... 68 A3
Bromwich Wood Nature
  Reserve★ B32 .... 102 B7
Bromwynd Cl WV2 .... 39 B6
Bromyard Ave B76.... 58 A8
Bromyard Rd B11..... 87 E3
Bronte Cl B90 .... 106 D1
Bronte Ct
  Solihull B90 .... 106 D1
  Tamworth B79 .... 21 A6
Bronte Dr
  Cannock WS11........ 2 C2
  Kidderminster DY10.... 117 C6
Bronte Farm Rd B90 .. 106 D1
Bronte Rd WV2 ...... 39 F6
Bronte Wlk CV2....... 114 D3
Bronwen Ingham Ct
  DY10................ 116 E7
Bronwen Rd WV14 .... 51 C7
Bronze Cl CV11....... 78 E8
Bronze Ct B77 .... 35 E6
Bronze View CV4 ..... 131 D7
Brook Ave B77........ 36 A7
Brookbank Ave B34 ... 69 D6
Brookbank Gdns DY3... 50 B2
Brookbank Rd DY3.... 50 B2
Brook Cl
  Birmingham B33 ..... 68 E4
  Brownhills WS9 ...... 16 A3
  Coventry CV1........ 113 E4
  Lichfield WS13........ 3 A1
  Solihull B90 .... 105 F1
Brook Cotts B25 ..... 88 A7
Brook Cres
  Kingswinford DY6 .... 60 C7
  Stourbridge DY9 ..... 81 F3
  West Hagley DY9 .... 99 B5
Brook Croft
  Birmingham, Lyndon Green
    B26................. 89 B7
  Birmingham, Marston Green
    B37................. 90 B7
Brook Ct B60 .... 137 B3
Brookdale
  Dudley DY3 .... 50 C3
  Hinckley LE10 .... 75 B7
  Kidderminster DY10.... 116 F8
Brookdale Cl B45..... 102 A1
Brookdale Dr WV4 .... 38 E6
Brookdale Rd CV10 ... 73 E7
Brook Dr B32......... 84 D1
Brooke Cl CV34 ..... 160 F5
Brooke Mews 6 CV34.. 160 F7
Brook End
  Burntwood WS7....... 7 A4
  Fazeley B78 .... 35 B8
Brookend Dr B45 .... 121 F7
Brooke Rd
  Cannock WS12......... 1 F6
  Kenilworth CV8 ...... 148 B4
Brookes Cl B69 ...... 52 B1
Brookes Ho 3 WS1 ... 28 F1
Brooke St DY2 .... 62 C8
Brook Farm Ind Est B94. 126 B2
Brook Farm Wlk B37 .. 70 D2
Brookfield Cl
  Aldridge WS9......... 16 A1
  Redditch B97 .... 158 D4
Brookfield Dr WS14 .... 4 E7
Brookfield Ho DY9 ... 119 C7
Brookfield Rd
  Aldridge WS9......... 16 A1
  Birmingham B18 ..... 66 A5
  Birmingham, Brandwood End
    B30................. 104 D3
  Codsall WV8.......... 10 B3
  Cubbington CV32.... 157 E5
  Hinckley LE10 .... 75 C6
BROOKFIELDS 66 B4
Brook Fields Cl B60 .. 121 C1
Brookfields Prim Sch B18 66 B4
Brookfields Rd B68 ... 64 C4
Brookfield Terr B18.... 66 A5
Brookfield Way
  Solihull B92 .... 106 D7
  Tipton DY4........... 52 B4
Brookford Ave CV6.... 95 A3
Brook Gr WV8 .... 10 B2
Brook Green La B92.. 109 A1
Brookhampton Cl B97... 158 E4
Brookhill Cl WV12 .... 13 D1
Brookhill Rd B8....... 68 A4
Brookhill Way WV12 .. 13 D1
Brook Holloway DY9 .. 81 F4
Brookhouse Cl WV10... 12 B6
Brookhouse La
  Featherstone WV10.... 12 B7
  Wolverhampton WV10.. 11 F6
Brookhouse Rd
  Blackwell B45 .... 137 F7
  Walsall WS5.......... 43 B7
Brookhurst Ct CV32 .. 156 D1
Brookhurst Prim Sch
  CV32................ 156 D1
Brookhus Farm Rd B76.. 58 A8
Brooking Cl B43 .... 44 D4
Brook La
  Birmingham B32 ..... 84 F5
  Birmingham, Billesley B13. 105 B7
  Brownhills WS9 ...... 15 F3
  Cradley Heath B64.... 62 E2

Brook La continued
  Great Wyrley WS6 ..... 5 A3
  Nuneaton CV10 .... 73 C6
  Solihull B92 .... 106 D8
Brookland Gr WS9 .... 15 F3
Brookland Rd
  Brownhills WS9 ...... 15 F3
  West Hagley DY9..... 99 A4
Brooklands
  Stourbridge DY8 ..... 60 F1
  Walsall WS5.......... 43 B3
Brooklands B66 ...... 54 F4
Brooklands Cl B28 .... 87 F1
Brooklands Dr B14.... 104 E5
Brooklands Ho B14 .. 161 D8
Brooklands Hospl B37 . 90 B8
Brooklands La B98.... 154 B5
Brooklands Par WV1 .. 26 B2
Brooklands Rd
  Birmingham B28 ..... 87 F1
  Cannock WS11........ 2 A4
Brooklands Way B37 .. 90 A8
Brooklea Gr B38 ..... 104 A1
Brooklime Gdns WV10 . 12 B7
Brooklyn Ave B6...... 66 F7
Brooklyn Gr
  Dudley WV14 .... 51 D8
  Kingswinford DY6 .... 60 B8
Brooklyn Rd
  Burntwood WS7....... 7 A4
  Cannock WS12........ 2 D1
  Coventry CV1........ 113 D6
Brookmans Ave B32... 84 D4
Brook Mdws WV8 ..... 10 B4
Brookmeadow Ct B28.. 105 D6
Brook Meadow Rd
  Birmingham B34 ..... 69 B6
  Walsall WS4.......... 29 D8
Brook Park Trad Est 4
  DY9.................. 81 F5
Brookpiece Ho B14 .. 104 E2
Brook Piece Wlk B35.. 58 B3
Brook Prim Sch DY8 ... 60 F1
Brook Rd
  Birmingham, Chad Valley
    B15................. 85 E7
  Birmingham, Rubery B45. 121 E7
  Bromsgrove B61 ..... 136 E1
  Cheslyn Hay WS6...... 4 E4
  Fairfield B61 .... 120 C2
  Oldbury B68.......... 64 A2
  Stourbridge DY8 ..... 81 B3
  Willenhall WV13 ..... 26 E1
Brooksbank Dr B64 ... 62 F4
Brooksby Gr B93..... 128 A2
Brooks Croft B35 .... 58 A2
Brookshaw Way CV2 .. 114 F8
Brookside
  Birmingham, Great Barr
    B43................. 54 D7
  Birmingham, Northfield
    B31................. 102 F5
  Cheswick Green B90... 126 D3
  Dudley DY3 .... 50 D2
  Hinckley LE10 .... 75 E7
  Wednesbury WS10 ... 42 A3
Brookside Ave
  Birmingham B13 ..... 105 B7
  Coventry CV5........ 112 C3
  Kenilworth CV8 ..... 147 E4
Brookside Cl
  Alvechurch B48 ..... 139 B6
  Birmingham B23 ..... 56 C7
  Halesowen B63 ...... 82 D3
Brookside Dr B61.... 136 F8
Brookside Ind Est WS10 . 42 B3
Brookside Rd B78..... 20 D1
Brookside Way
  Blakedown DY10 ..... 98 B2
  Kingswinford DY6 .... 60 C7
  Tamworth B77 .... 36 A6
Brooks Rd B72....... 57 C8
Brook St
  Bedworth CV12 ...... 78 B5
  Bilston WV14 .... 40 E5
  Birmingham B3 ...... 164 A3
  Brierley Hill DY5 .... 82 A8
  Dudley DY3 .... 51 F6
  Dudley, Gornalwood DY3.. 50 C3
  Kidderminster DY11.... 116 C6
  Kingswinford DY6 .... 49 B1
  Redditch B98 .... 154 A4
  Smethwick B66 ...... 65 B6
  Stourbridge, Amblecote DY8 60 F1
  Stourbridge, Lye DY9... 81 F5
  Tipton DY4........... 51 E6
  Walsall WS3.......... 28 D1
  Warwick CV34 .... 160 E6
  West Bromwich B70 .. 53 B3
Brookstray Flats CV5.. 112 B3
Brook Street Bsns Ctr
  DY4................. 51 E6
Brookthorpe Dr WV12.. 27 C4
Brook Vale WS11 ..... 4 F8
Brookvale Ave CV3... 114 E1
Brookvale Cl B61..... 137 B4
Brookvale Gr B92..... 88 D1
Brookvale Mews B29.. 85 F2
Brookvale Park Rd B23.. 56 B4
Brookvale Prim Sch B23 56 B3
Brookvale Rd
  Birmingham B23, B6... 56 A3
  Solihull B92 .... 88 D1
Brookvale Trad Est B6.. 56 A3
Brookview B67........ 64 F3

Brook View Cl B19 ..... 66 C6
Brook Way 7 B16 .... 65 C3
Brookweed B77........ 22 A3
Brookwillow Rd B63 .. 82 E1
Brookwood Ave B28 .. 105 D5
Brookwood Dr B45.... 138 C8
Broom Cl B60........ 137 B2
Broom Covert Rd WS14 . 18 E8
Broom Cres DY4 ..... 117 A6
Broomdene Ave B34 .. 69 A7
Broom Dr B14 .... 104 E4
BROOME............ 99 A2
Broome Ave B43 ..... 43 E7
Broome Cl 5 B63..... 83 A3
Broome Croft CV6 .... 95 B3
Broome Ct B36 ...... 69 C8
Broome Gdns B75..... 46 C5
Broomehill Cl DY5 .... 81 C7
Broome La DY9 ...... 99 B2
Broome Rd WV10 .... 25 E7
Broomfield B67....... 64 F5
Broomfield Ave B78 .. 35 A8
Broomfield Cl DY11 .. 116 C7
Broomfield Pl CV5 ... 113 A2
Broomfield Rd
  Birmingham B23 ..... 56 D2
  Coventry CV5........ 113 A1
  Kidderminster DY11.... 116 C7
  Wednesbury WS10 ... 42 C3
Broomfield Rise CV10 . 72 F2
Broomfields Ave B91.. 107 D5
Broomfields Cl B91... 107 D5
Broomfields Farm Rd
  B91................. 107 D5
Broomhall Av WV11... 26 D6
Broom Hall Cres B27.. 106 B8
Broom Hall Gr B27.... 106 C8
BROOMHILL.......... 1 E4
Broomhill Cl
  Birmingham B43 ..... 54 D8
  Cannock WS11........ 1 E4
Broomhill La B43 .... 54 D8
Broomhill Rd WV11... 13 B1
Broom Ho 3 B71..... 42 F1
Broomhurst B15 ..... 85 E8
Broomie Cl B75....... 46 D4
Broomie La B90 ..... 126 A6
Broomlea Cl B74..... 44 E8
Broom Rd
  Dudley DY1........... 51 A5
  Walsall WS5.......... 43 B3
Broom St B12........ 87 A8
Broombank CV8 ..... 148 B6
Broomy Cl B34....... 69 A5
Brosdale Dr LE10 .... 71 A1
Broseley Ave B31.... 123 B8
Broseley Brook Cl 1 B9. 67 C1
Brosil Ave B20 ...... 54 E3
Brotherton Ave B97 .. 152 F2
Brougham St B19 .... 66 B7
Brough Cl
  Birmingham B7 ...... 67 B6
  Wolverhampton WV4, WV9 39 F3
Broughton Cres B31 .. 122 D8
Broughton Ct
  2 Birmingham, Edgbaston
    B15................. 86 B7
  Birmingham, Pheasey B43.. 44 D4
  Perton WV6........... 24 A3
Broughton Rd
  Birmingham B20 ..... 66 A8
  Stourbridge DY9 ..... 81 D3
  Wolverhampton WV3.... 24 C1
Browett Rd CV6....... 95 B2
Brown Ave B77 ...... 35 C8
Brownfield Rd B34.... 69 C7
BROWNHILLS......... 16 B6
Brownhills Com Tech Coll
  WS8................. 6 F1
Brownhills Rd
  Brownhills WS8 ...... 16 A4
  Norton Canes WS11 ... 6 B4
Brownhills West Prim Sch
  WS8................ 6 C2
Brownhills West Sta★
  WS7................. 6 C3
Browning Ave CV34 .. 160 C5
Browning Cl
  Kidderminster DY10.... 117 B6
  Nuneaton CV10 ...... 72 A5
  Tamworth B79 .... 20 F8
  Willenhall WV12 ..... 27 E7
Browning Cres WV10... 11 C2
Browning Dr LE10.... 71 C1
Browning Gr WV6.... 23 E4
Browning Rd
  Burntwood WS7....... 7 C7
  Coventry CV2........ 114 C3
  Dudley DY3.......... 50 A4
Browning St B16...... 66 B2
Browning Twr B31.... 103 C3
Brownley Rd B90 .... 126 F7
Brown Lion St DY4.... 51 E7
Brownmead Prim Sch
  B34................. 69 B7
Brown Rd WS10...... 41 C7
Brown's Coppice Ave
  B91................. 106 E5
Browns Dr B73 ...... 56 F8
Brownsea Cl B45 .... 101 F1
Brownsea Dr B1..... 164 B1

Brownsfield Rd WS13 .... 3 D1
Browns Gn B20....... 54 F3
BROWN'S GREEN 54 F4
Brownshill Bsns Pk WS8.. 15 F5
Brownshill Ct CV6..... 112 F8
BROWNSHILL GREEN .. 94 C2
Brownshill Green Rd CV6. 94 E1
Brownshore La WV11 .. 13 A3
Browns La B93....... 127 E6
Brown's La
  Brownshill Green CV5.. 94 C1
  Dordon B78 .... 36 F5
  Tamworth B79 .... 21 C8
Brownsover Cl B36.... 58 B1
Brown St WV2........ 39 D7
Brownswall Rd DY3 ... 50 C7
Brownsholme B79 .... 20 D6
Broxell Cl CV34 ..... 155 C1
Broxwood Pk WV6 ... 24 B3
Bruce Rd
  Bedworth CV7 .... 95 F7
  Coventry CV6........ 113 B8
  Kidderminster DY10.... 117 B7
Brueton Ave
  Bromsgrove B60 .... 151 A8
  Solihull B91 .... 107 D3
Brueton Dr
  Birmingham B24 ..... 57 A3
  Redditch B98 .... 154 A3
Brueton Rd WV14 .... 41 A7
Bruford Rd WV3 ..... 39 A8
Brundard Cl 2 WS3... 28 D8
Brunel Cl
  Birmingham B12 ..... 87 A5
  Burntwood WS7....... 7 B8
  Coventry CV2........ 113 F3
  Tamworth B79 .... 21 B6
  Whitnash CV31 ..... 162 B2
Brunel Ct
  Darlaston WS10...... 41 F6
  Tipton WV14 .... 51 E8
  Wombourne WV5..... 49 A7
Brunel Dr WV4 ...... 40 E1
Brunel Gr WV6....... 23 E5
Brunel Rd
  Hinckley LE10 .... 75 C8
  Oldbury B69.......... 63 D6
Brunel St B1......... 164 B2
Brunel Way WV2 ..... 40 A7
Brunel Wlk WS10 .... 41 F6
Brunslow Cl
  Willenhall WV13 ..... 27 C1
  Wolverhampton WV10.. 11 C1
Brunswick Arc B1..... 66 B2
Brunswick Ct
  Wednesbury WS10 ... 42 C3
  Whitnash CV31 ..... 162 A5
Brunswick Gate DY8 .. 81 A1
Brunswick Gdns
  Birmingham B21...... 54 F1
  Wednesbury WS10 ... 42 B4
Brunswick Ho
  Birmingham, Buckland End
    B34................. 69 A7
  Birmingham, Marston Green
    B37................. 89 F8
Brunswick Park Rd WS10. 42 B3
Brunswick Rd
  Birmingham, Handsworth
    B21................. 54 F1
  Birmingham, Sparkbrook
    B12................. 87 A5
  Cannock WS11........ 1 E2
  Coventry CV1........ 113 B2
Brunswick St
  Birmingham B1 ...... 66 B2
  Royal Leamington Spa
    CV31............... 162 A5
  Walsall WS2.......... 42 C7
Brunswick Terr WS10 .. 41 F3
Bruntingthorpe Way
  CV3................. 134 E8
Brunton Cl CV3 ..... 115 B1
Brunton Rd B10....... 87 F7
Brushfield Rd B42 .... 55 D8
Brutus Dr B46 .... 59 E1
Bryan Ave WV4 ...... 38 D4
Bryan Budd Cl B65.... 63 B4
Bryan Rd WS2........ 42 C6
Bryanston Cl CV2 .... 115 A4
Bryanston Ct B91..... 106 F7
Bryanston Rd B91.... 106 F6
Bryans Way WS12..... 2 F4
Bryant Rd CV7 ...... 96 B2
Bryant St B18........ 65 E5
Bryce Rd DY5........ 61 B5
Bryher Wlk B65 ..... 101 E1
Brylan Croft B44..... 55 F6
Brymill Ind Est DY4 .. 51 E7
Brympton Rd CV3 .... 114 E2
Bryn Arden Rd B26... 88 E5
Bryndale Ave B14.... 104 C4
Bryn Jones Cl CV3 .. 134 F7
Brynmawr Rd WV14.. 40 A3
Bryn Rd DY4......... 113 F7
Brynside Cl B14..... 104 D2
Bryony Cl B29....... 85 A1
Bryony Croft B23 .... 56 B7
Bryony Gdns 9 WS10 . 41 D7
Bryony Rd B29 ...... 103 B7
Bsa Bsns Pk B11..... 87 D6
Bsns Ctr The B11 .... 87 F6
Bubbenhall Rd CV8 .. 132 D1
Buchanan Ave WS4... 29 A3
Buchanan Cl WS4 ... 29 A3
Buchanan Rd WS4 ... 29 A3
Buckbury Cl DY9..... 81 D2

Buckbury Croft B90 . . . . . **127** B6
Buckden B77 . . . . . **22** C1
Buckden Cl
Birmingham B37 . . . . . **69** F1
2 Warwick CV34 . . . . . **155** F1
Buckfast Cl
Bromsgrove B61 . . . . . **136** D1
Coventry CV3 . . . . . **133** E5
Buckhold Dr CV5 . . . . . **112** B5
Buckingham Cl
Hinckley LE10 . . . . . **71** F4
Nuneaton CV10 . . . . . **73** B1
Wednesbury WS10 . . . . . **42** D4
Buckingham Ct
Birmingham B29 . . . . . **85** D1
Birmingham, Griffin's Hill B29 . . . . . **103** D8
Buckingham Dr WV12 . . . . **27** B7
Buckingham Gdns WS14 . . . **9** B6
Buckingham Gr DY6 . . . . . **60** C7
Buckingham Mews B73 . . **46** A3
Buckingham Pl 3 WS12 . . . **2** C1
Buckingham Rd
Birmingham B36 . . . . . **69** F7
Rowley Regis B65 . . . . . **63** D4
Tamworth B79 . . . . . **20** E7
Wolverhampton WV4 . . . . . **39** A5
Buckingham Rise
Coventry CV5 . . . . . **112** B4
Dudley DY1 . . . . . **50** E2
Buckingham St B19 . . . . . **164** B4
Buckland Cl WS12 . . . . . **2** D1
BUCKLAND END **69** A7
Buckland End B34 . . . . . **69** A6
Buckland Ho 3 B15 . . . . . **86** C7
Buckland Rd CV6 . . . . . **95** B2
Bucklands End La B34 . . . . **68** F6
Buckle Cl WS1 . . . . . **42** E8
Buckler's Yd 5 CV12 . . . . . **78** A2
Buckley Ct B14 . . . . . **104** F8
Buckley Ho CV5 . . . . . **112** F1
Buckley Rd
Royal Leamington Spa CV32 . . . . . **157** C2
Wolverhampton WV4 . . . . . **38** D5
Buckleys Gn B48 . . . . . **139** A6
Buckleys The B48 . . . . . **139** A6
Bucklow Wlk B33 . . . . . **68** E4
Buckminster Dr B93 . . . . . **127** E4
Bucknall Cres B32 . . . . . **102** A8
Bucknall Ct 15 B13 . . . . . **87** B2
Bucknall Ho B14 . . . . . **104** E6
Bucknall Rd WV11 . . . . . **13** B1
Bucknell Cl B91 . . . . . **107** C5
BUCKPOOL **60** F2
Buckpool & Fens Pool Nature Reserve★ DY5 . . **61** C5
Buckridge Cl B38 . . . . . **123** D7
Buckridge La B90 . . . . . **126** A5
Bucks Hill CV10 . . . . . **72** C6
Buckthorn Ave 8 B16 . . . . . **65** C3
Buckthorn Cl WS12 . . . . . **1** F8
Buckton Cl B75 . . . . . **32** E2
Budbrooke Cl CV2 . . . . . **96** D2
Budbrooke Ind Est CV34 . **160** B7
Budbrooke Rd CV34 . . . . . **160** B7
Budbrook Gr B34 . . . . . **69** E6
Budden Rd WV14 . . . . . **51** D7
Bude Rd WS5 . . . . . **43** D7
Buffery Rd DY2 . . . . . **62** D7
Bufferys Cl B91 . . . . . **127** B8
Building Trade Ctr B92 . . . **88** E2
Buildwas Cl WS3 . . . . . **13** F2
Bulford Cl B14 . . . . . **104** F2
Bulger Rd WV14 . . . . . **40** C7
BULKINGTON **79** B1
Bulkington La CV11 . . . . . **79** A7
Bulkington Rd
Bedworth CV12 . . . . . **78** D2
Shilton CV7 . . . . . **97** E6
Bullace Croft 4 B15 . . . . . **85** D3
Bulldog La WS13 . . . . . **3** B1
Buller St WV4 . . . . . **39** E6
Bullfield Ave CV4 . . . . . **111** E1
Bullfields Cl B65 . . . . . **62** F5
Bullfinch Cl DY1 . . . . . **61** E8
Bullfurlong La LE10 . . . . . **75** F4
Bullimore Gr CV8 . . . . . **148** A2
Bullivents Cl B93 . . . . . **127** F5
Bull La
Darlaston WV14, WS10 . . . . **41** B3
West Bromwich B70 . . . . . **53** A3
Wombourne WV5 . . . . . **49** B7
Bullmeadow La WV5 . . . . . **49** A8
Bullmoor La WS14 . . . . . **8** A1
Bullock's Row WS1 . . . . . **28** F1
Bullock St
Birmingham B7 . . . . . **67** A5
4 West Bromwich B70 . . . . **53** D1
Bullows Rd WS8 . . . . . **15** C6
Bull Ring
4 Halesowen B63 . . . . . **83** B3
Kidderminster DY10 . . . . . **116** E6
Nuneaton CV10 . . . . . **73** B2
Sedgley DY3 . . . . . **50** D8
Willenhall WV13 . . . . . **27** A3
Bullring (Sh Ctr) B5 . . . . **164** C2
Bull Ring Trad Est 2 B12 . **66** F1
Bull's Head La CV3 . . . . . **114** B2
Bull's La B76 . . . . . **47** E1
Bull St
Birmingham B17 . . . . . **85** D5
Birmingham, Brookfields B4 . . . . . **164** C3
Brierley Hill DY5 . . . . . **61** B1
Darlaston WS10 . . . . . **41** E6
Dudley, Gornalwood DY3 . . . **50** C2
Dudley, Springs Mire DY1 . . **62** A8
Bull St *continued*
Nuneaton CV11 . . . . . **73** D2
West Bromwich B70 . . . . . **53** D3
Bull Street Trad Est DY5 . . **61** B2
Bulrush Cl WS8 . . . . . **15** E7
Bulwell Cl B6 . . . . . **67** A7
Bulwer Rd CV6 . . . . . **113** A6
Bulwick Cl CV3 . . . . . **115** B1
Bumble Hole La B61 . . . . . **136** E7
Bumble Hole Nature Reserve★ DY2 . . . . . **62** E5
Bunbury Gdns B30 . . . . . **103** D4
Bunbury Rd B30, B31 . . . . **103** C4
Bundle Hill B63 . . . . . **83** A4
Bungalows The B70 . . . . . **52** F6
BUNKER'S HILL **40** E7
Bunker's Hill La WV14 . . . . **40** E7
Bunneys Mdw LE10 . . . . . **74** E6
Bunn's La DY2 . . . . . **51** F1
Buntsford Dr B60 . . . . . **150** F6
Buntsford Gate Bsns Pk B60 . . . . . **150** F6
Buntsford Hill B60 . . . . . **150** F5
Buntsford Park Rd B60 . . **150** F6
Bunyan Pl WS11 . . . . . **1** E4
BURBAGE **76** B6
Burbage CE Inf Sch LE10 . **76** A5
Burbage CE Jun Sch LE10 **75** F6
Burbage Cl WV10 . . . . . **25** E6
Burbage Rd LE10 . . . . . **76** A7
Burbages La CV6 . . . . . **95** D4
Burberry Ct 3 DY4 . . . . . **52** A8
Burberry Gr CV7 . . . . . **130** A6
Burbidge Rd B9 . . . . . **67** E3
Burbury Cl
Bedworth CV12 . . . . . **78** C4
Royal Leamington Spa CV32 . . . . . **157** C2
Burbury Ct CV34 . . . . . **161** B8
Burbury St B19 . . . . . **66** C7
Burbury Street S B19 . . . . **66** C6
Burcher Gn DY10 . . . . . **117** B5
Burcombe Twr B23 . . . . . **57** B6
BURCOT **137** E4
Burcot Ave
Bromsgrove B60 . . . . . **137** B4
Wolverhampton WV1 . . . . . **26** A2
Burcot Ct 14 B74 . . . . . **31** F2
Burcote Rd B24 . . . . . **57** D3
Burcot Ho B60 . . . . . **137** B3
Burcot La B60 . . . . . **137** B3
Burdock Cl
Cannock WS11 . . . . . **2** B3
Walsall WS5 . . . . . **43** A3
Burdock Ho B38 . . . . . **103** F1
Burdock Rd B29 . . . . . **103** A6
Burdons Cl B34 . . . . . **69** A5
Bure Gr WV13 . . . . . **27** D1
Burfield Rd B63 . . . . . **82** C6
Burford Cl
Solihull B92 . . . . . **89** A3
Walsall WS5 . . . . . **43** A4
Burford Ct
18 Birmingham B13 . . . . . **87** B2
Stourbridge DY8 . . . . . **81** A4
Burford Mews 13 CV31 . . . **162** C6
Burford Park Rd B38 . . . . **123** E8
Burford Rd
Birmingham B44 . . . . . **55** F7
Hollywood B47 . . . . . **125** A6
Burgage Pl CV11 . . . . . **73** C4
Burgage Wlk CV11 . . . . . **73** C4
Burges CV1 . . . . . **165** B3
Burges Gr CV34 . . . . . **155** F1
Burgess Croft B92 . . . . . **107** F7
Burghley Cl CV11 . . . . . **73** F2
Burghley Dr
Kidderminster DY11 . . . . . **116** C5
West Bromwich B71 . . . . . **42** F2
Burghley Wlk DY5 . . . . . **81** B8
Burgh Way WS2 . . . . . **28** A4
Burgoyne St WS11 . . . . . **2** A5
Burhill Way B37 . . . . . **70** B5
Burke Ave B13 . . . . . **87** D1
Burkitt Dr DY4 . . . . . **52** C8
Burland Ave WV6 . . . . . **24** E6
Burleigh Cl
Balsall Common CV7 . . . . . **130** B7
Cannock WS12 . . . . . **2** A8
Willenhall WV12 . . . . . **27** B6
Burleigh Croft WS7 . . . . . **7** A4
Burleigh Rd
Hinckley LE10 . . . . . **71** C2
Wolverhampton WV3 . . . . . **39** A8
Burleigh St WS1 . . . . . **29** A1
Burleton Rd B33 . . . . . **69** E2
Burley Cl B90 . . . . . **105** F2
Burley Way B38 . . . . . **123** C8
Burlington Arc 5 B2 . . . . **164** B2
Burlington Ave B70 . . . . . **53** E1
Burlington Cl DY10 . . . . . **117** B4
Burlington Ct B78 . . . . . **35** B8
Burlington Rd
Birmingham B10 . . . . . **67** F1
Coventry CV2 . . . . . **113** F4
Nuneaton CV10 . . . . . **78** B7
West Bromwich B70 . . . . . **53** E1
Burlington St B6 . . . . . **66** E6
Burlish Ave 1 B92 . . . . . **88** F1
Burlish Top Nature Reserve★ DY11 . . . . . **116** A1
Burlywood Cl CV5 . . . . . **112** B8
Burman Cl
Leamington Spa CV32 . . . . **157** A4
Solihull B90 . . . . . **106** A2
Burman Dr B46 . . . . . **70** F5
Burman Inf Sch B90 . . . . . **106** A2
Burman Rd B90 . . . . . **106** A1
Burmarsh Wlk WV8 . . . . . **24** F8
Burmese Way B65 . . . . . **62** F6
Burnaby Cl CV10 . . . . . **72** B5
Burnaby Rd CV6 . . . . . **95** B1
Burnaston Cres B90 . . . . . **127** C6
Burnaston Rd B28 . . . . . **87** E1
Burnbank Gr B24 . . . . . **57** B4
Burn Cl B66 . . . . . **65** A4
Burncross Way WV10 . . . . **25** F6
Burnell Gdns WV3 . . . . . **38** E8
Burnel Rd B29 . . . . . **85** B2
Burnet Gr WV10 . . . . . **12** B8
Burnett Ho 12 B69 . . . . . **63** D5
Burnett Rd B74 . . . . . **31** B2
Burney La B8 . . . . . **68** C4
Burnfields Way WS9 . . . . . **30** A7
Burnham Ave
Birmingham B25 . . . . . **88** C6
Wolverhampton WV10 . . . . . **25** C8
Burnham Cl DY6 . . . . . **60** F4
Burnham Ct
Birmingham B23 . . . . . **56** C2
18 Brierley Hill DY5 . . . . . **61** D2
Burnham Gn WS11 . . . . . **4** B8
Burnham Mdw B28 . . . . . **106** A6
Burnham Rd
Birmingham B44 . . . . . **55** E7
Coventry CV3 . . . . . **134** A6
Burnham Rise CV11 . . . . . **74** A6
Burnhill Gr B29 . . . . . **103** A8
Burnlea Gr B31 . . . . . **103** C1
Burnsall Cl
Birmingham B37 . . . . . **69** F2
Wolverhampton WV9 . . . . . **11** A3
Burnsall Gr CV5 . . . . . **132** D8
Burnsall Rd CV5 . . . . . **132** D8
Burnsall Road Ind Est CV5 . . . . . **132** C8
Burns Ave
Tipton DY4 . . . . . **52** A7
Warwick CV34 . . . . . **160** C5
Wolverhampton WV10 . . . . . **11** D2
Burns Cl
Kidderminster DY10 . . . . . **117** B6
Lichfield WS14 . . . . . **9** B6
Redditch B97 . . . . . **158** C8
Stourbridge DY8 . . . . . **81** A8
Burns Dr WS7 . . . . . **7** C7
Burns Gr DY3 . . . . . **50** A4
Burnside CV3 . . . . . **115** A2
Burnside Ct B73 . . . . . **46** A1
Burnside Gdns WS5 . . . . . **43** D6
Burnside Way B31 . . . . . **122** F7
Burns Pl WS10 . . . . . **41** A5
Burns Rd
Coventry CV2 . . . . . **114** B3
Darlaston WS10 . . . . . **41** B5
Royal Leamington Spa CV32 . . . . . **157** B4
Tamworth B79 . . . . . **21** A6
Burns St WS11 . . . . . **2** A3
Burnsway LE10 . . . . . **71** C1
Burns Wlk CV12 . . . . . **78** C1
Burnthurst Cres B90 . . . . **127** A7
Burnt Meadow Rd B98 . . **154** F6
Burnt Oak Dr DY8 . . . . . **81** B5
BURNT TREE **51** F3
Burnt Tree DY4 . . . . . **51** F2
Burnt Tree Ind Est B69 . . . **52** B2
Burnt Tree Island DY1, DY4 . . . . . **51** F2
Burnt Tree Prim Sch B69 . **52** A2
BURNTWOOD **7** C5
Burntwood Bsns Pk WS7 . . **6** D7
BURNTWOOD GREEN **7** D6
Burntwood L Ctr WS7 . . . . . **6** F6
Burntwood Rd
Hammerwich WS7 . . . . . **7** D4
Norton Canes WS11 . . . . . **6** A7
Burntwood Town Sh Ctr WS7 . . . . . **6** F7
Burrelton Way 1 B43 . . . . **54** D8
Burrington Rd B32 . . . . . **102** A8
Burrowes St WS2 . . . . . **28** D3
Burrow Hill Cl B36 . . . . . **69** C8
Burrow Hill La CV7 . . . . . **94** D7
Burrows Cl CV31 . . . . . **162** B3
Burrows Croft WV14 . . . . . **40** C6
Burrows Ho 7 WS2 . . . . . **28** D3
Burrows Rd DY6 . . . . . **60** F4
Burrow The WV3 . . . . . **24** D1
Burrs Dr WS10 . . . . . **42** A1
Bursledon Wlk WV1 . . . . . **40** B8
Burslem Cl WS3 . . . . . **14** A3
Bursnips Rd WV11 . . . . . **13** C4
Burton Ave WS4 . . . . . **29** B8
Burton Cl
Brownshill Green CV5 . . . . **94** C2
Tamworth B79 . . . . . **21** C7
Burton Cres WV10 . . . . . **163** D4
Burton Farm Rd WS4 . . . . **29** B3
Burton Gr B64 . . . . . **82** E8
BURTON GREEN **131** C4
Burton Green CE Prim Sch CV8 . . . . . **131** B3
BURTON HASTINGS **75** A1
Burton La
Bramcote CV11 . . . . . **79** F7
Redditch B98 . . . . . **153** F3
Burton Old Rd WS13 . . . . . **3** F1
Burton Old Road E WS14 . . **9** E8
Burton Old Road W WS14 . **9** D8
Burton Rd
Dudley DY1 . . . . . **50** F4
Lichfield WS13 . . . . . **3** F1
Wolverhampton WV10 . . . . . **25** E3
Burton Wood Dr B20 . . . . **55** D2
Burwaye Cl WS13 . . . . . **9** A6
Buryfield Rd B91 . . . . . **107** B6
Bury Hill Rd B69 . . . . . **63** D8
Bury Ho CV4 . . . . . **111** F3
Bury Mound Ct B90 . . . . . **105** C2
Bury Rd CV31 . . . . . **161** F7
Busby Cl CV3 . . . . . **134** F7
Bush Ave B66 . . . . . **65** C5
Bushbery Ave CV4 . . . . . **111** F2
BUSHBURY **11** E2
Bushbury Croft B37 . . . . . **70** C3
Bushbury Hill Prim Sch WV10 . . . . . **11** F1
Bushbury La
Wolverhampton, Bushbury WV10 . . . . . **11** E2
Wolverhampton, Elston Hall WV10 . . . . . **25** D7
Bushbury Rd
Birmingham B33 . . . . . **69** A5
Wolverhampton WV10 . . . . . **26** A5
Bush Cl CV4 . . . . . **111** F3
Bush Ct CV2 . . . . . **114** B6
Bushell Dr B91 . . . . . **107** D4
Bushelton Cl CV1 . . . . . **165** C1
Bushey Cl B74 . . . . . **30** F2
Bushey Fields Hospl DY5 . **61** E8
Bushey Fields Rd DY1 . . . . **61** E7
Bushfield Ct WV14 . . . . . **40** F5
Bush Gr
Birmingham B21 . . . . . **54** C1
Walsall WS3 . . . . . **15** A2
Bushley Cl B98 . . . . . **159** A7
Bushley Croft B91 . . . . . **127** B8
Bushman Way B34 . . . . . **69** E5
Bushmore Rd B28 . . . . . **106** A7
Bush Rd
Dudley DY2 . . . . . **62** C2
Tipton DY4 . . . . . **51** E4
Bush St WS10 . . . . . **41** D7
Bushway Cl DY5 . . . . . **61** B2
Bushwood Ct B15 . . . . . **86** C8
Bushwood Dr B93 . . . . . **128** B3
Bushwood Rd B29 . . . . . **85** B1
Bushy End CV34 . . . . . **161** E4
Busill Jones Prim Sch WS3 . . . . . **27** F8
Bustleholme Ave B71 . . . . **42** F1
Bustleholme Cres B71 . . . . **42** E1
Bustleholme La B71 . . . . . **42** E1
Butchers La B63 . . . . . **82** C7
Butcher's La CV5 . . . . . **112** C6
Butchers Rd B92 . . . . . **109** A6
Butcroft Gdns WS10 . . . . . **41** E6
Bute Cl
Birmingham B45 . . . . . **101** E1
Hinckley LE10 . . . . . **71** C1
Willenhall WV12 . . . . . **27** B6
Butler Cl CV8 . . . . . **148** C7
Butler Rd B92 . . . . . **88** F3
Butlers Cl
Birmingham, Handsworth B20 . . . . . **55** A3
Birmingham, Perry Common B73 . . . . . **45** D1
Butlers Cres CV7 . . . . . **78** A1
Butlers End CV35 . . . . . **146** C2
Butler's Hill La B97 . . . . . **153** B5
Butlers La B74 . . . . . **32** A3
Butlers Lane Sta B74 . . . . **32** A3
Butlers Prec 3 WS1 . . . . . **28** E2
Butler's Rd B20 . . . . . **55** A3
Butler St
Astwood Bank B96 . . . . . **158** E1
West Bromwich B70 . . . . . **53** A4
Butler Way 6 B16 . . . . . **65** C3
Butlin Rd CV6 . . . . . **95** C4
Butlin St B7 . . . . . **67** C7
Buttercup Cl
Cannock WS12 . . . . . **1** C5
Kidderminster DY10 . . . . . **116** E8
6 Walsall WS5 . . . . . **43** A3
Buttercup Dr B60 . . . . . **137** C6
Buttercup Way CV12 . . . . . **77** D2
Butterfield Cl WV6 . . . . . **23** D3
Butterfield Ct DY1 . . . . . **51** A2
Butterfield Rd DY5 . . . . . **61** B7
Butterfly Way 4 B64 . . . . . **62** F1
Buttermere B77 . . . . . **36** B7
Buttermere Ave CV11 . . . . **74** A6
Buttermere Cl
Brierley Hill DY5 . . . . . **81** B7
Cannock WS11 . . . . . **2** A3
Coventry CV3 . . . . . **134** F7
Wolverhampton WV6 . . . . . **24** D8
Buttermere Ct WV6 . . . . . **23** F4
Buttermere Dr
Birmingham B32 . . . . . **84** F3
Essington WV11 . . . . . **13** A2
Buttermere Gr WV11 . . . . . **13** B1
Butter Wlk B38 . . . . . **123** C8
Butterworth Cl WV14 . . . . **40** A1
Butterworth Dr CV4 . . . . . **132** A6
Buttery Rd B67 . . . . . **64** E6
Butt La
Allesley CV5 . . . . . **112** B7
Hinckley LE10 . . . . . **71** F1
Butt Lane Cl LE10 . . . . . **71** E1
Button Dr B61 . . . . . **136** E2
Buttons Farm Rd WV4 . . . . **38** D3
Buttress Way B66 . . . . . **65** A6
Butts CV1 . . . . . **113** A2
Butts Cl WS11 . . . . . **5** E4
Butts La
Norton Canes WS11 . . . . . **5** E4
Stone DY10 . . . . . **117** D1
Tanworth-In-A B94 . . . . . **142** B2
Butts Prim Sch WS4 . . . . . **28** F3
Butts Rd
Coventry CV1 . . . . . **113** B2
Walsall WS4 . . . . . **28** F3
Wolverhampton WV4 . . . . . **38** F4
Butts St WS4 . . . . . **28** F3
Butts The
Lichfield WS14 . . . . . **8** D2
Walsall WS4 . . . . . **28** F3
Warwick CV34 . . . . . **160** E7
Butts Way WS11 . . . . . **5** E4
Buxton Ave B78 . . . . . **35** B8
Buxton Cl WS3 . . . . . **14** C3
Buxton Rd
Birmingham B23 . . . . . **56** B7
Dudley DY2 . . . . . **62** A6
Sutton Coldfield B73 . . . . . **57** A8
Walsall WS3 . . . . . **14** C3
Byfield Cl B33 . . . . . **69** E1
Byfield Pl CV7 . . . . . **130** D5
Byfield Rd CV6 . . . . . **112** E5
Byfleet Cl WV14 . . . . . **40** A3
Byford Cl B98 . . . . . **153** E2
Byford Ct CV10 . . . . . **72** F4
Byford St CV10 . . . . . **72** F4
Byford Way B37 . . . . . **90** B8
Byland B77 . . . . . **21** D3
Bylands Cl B61 . . . . . **136** E1
Byland Way WS3 . . . . . **13** F2
Bypass Link B91 . . . . . **107** F3
By Pass Rd B77 . . . . . **22** A5
Byrchen Moor Gdns DY5 . **61** B7
Byrne Rd WV2 . . . . . **39** D7
Byron Ave
Bedworth CV12 . . . . . **78** D2
Birmingham B23 . . . . . **56** B3
Lichfield WS14 . . . . . **9** B5
Warwick CV34 . . . . . **160** C4
Byron Cl
Birmingham B10 . . . . . **87** D7
Kidderminster DY10 . . . . . **117** B5
Byron Cres DY1 . . . . . **51** B6
Byron Croft
Dudley DY3 . . . . . **50** A5
Sutton Coldfield B74 . . . . . **31** F6
Byron Ct
Dorridge B93 . . . . . **128** A6
Sutton Coldfield B74 . . . . . **32** A5
Byron Gdns B71 . . . . . **53** B5
Byron Pl WS11 . . . . . **1** F5
Byron Rd
Birmingham B10 . . . . . **87** D7
Redditch B97 . . . . . **158** D8
Tamworth B79 . . . . . **21** A7
Willenhall WV12 . . . . . **27** E7
Wolverhampton WV10 . . . . . **12** A1
Byron St
Brierley Hill DY5 . . . . . **61** D7
Coventry CV1 . . . . . **165** C4
West Bromwich B71 . . . . . **53** B5
Byron Way B61 . . . . . **137** A8
Bywater Cl CV3 . . . . . **133** B5
Bywater Ho 5 WS1 . . . . . **28** F1
Byways WS3 . . . . . **14** C3

C

Caban Cl B31 . . . . . **102** E5
Cable Dr WS2 . . . . . **28** C5
Cable St WV2 . . . . . **39** F8
Cabot Gr WV6 . . . . . **23** E4
Cadbury Dr B35 . . . . . **58** A2
Cadbury Ho B19 . . . . . **66** D5
Cadbury Rd B13 . . . . . **87** B4
Cadbury Sixth Form Coll B38 . . . . . **103** F1
Cadbury Way B17 . . . . . **85** B5
Cadbury World★ B30 . . . . **103** F7
Cadden Dr CV4 . . . . . **112** B2
Caddick Cres B71 . . . . . **53** D7
Caddick Rd B42 . . . . . **44** B1
Caddick St WV14 . . . . . **51** A8
Cadeby Cl LE10 . . . . . **71** B3
Cadell Ct B13 . . . . . **87** A1
Cadet Dr B90 . . . . . **106** A3
Cadgwith Gdns WV14 . . . . **41** A2
Cadine Gdns B13 . . . . . **86** C1
Cadleigh Gdns B17 . . . . . **85** C3
Cadle Rd WV10 . . . . . **25** E7
Cadman Cl CV12 . . . . . **78** C3
Cadman Cres WV10 . . . . . **26** A7
Cadman's La WS6, WS3 . . . **14** D6
Cadnam Cl
Birmingham B17 . . . . . **85** C3
Darlaston WV13 . . . . . **41** B8
Cadogan Rd B77 . . . . . **35** D5
Caen Cl CV35 . . . . . **160** A7
Caernarfon Dr CV11 . . . . . **73** D3
Caernarvon Cl WV12 . . . . . **27** C7
Caernarvon Way DY1 . . . . . **50** E2
Caesar Rd CV8 . . . . . **147** E3
Caesar Way B46 . . . . . **59** E1
Cairndhu Dr DY10 . . . . . **117** B7
Cairn Dr WS2 . . . . . **27** F2
Cairns St WS2 . . . . . **28** C3
Caister B77 . . . . . **22** A6
Caister Dr WV13 . . . . . **40** F8
Caistor Cl B78 . . . . . **34** B8
Caithness Cl CV5 . . . . . **112** A4
Cakemore Rd B65 . . . . . **63** E2
Cala Dr B15 . . . . . **86** B7
Calcot Dr WV6 . . . . . **24** E7
Calcott Ho CV3 . . . . . **134** B5
Calcutt Way B90 . . . . . **126** A6
Caldecote Cl CV10 . . . . . **73** C8

Caldecote Gr B9 .... 68 C1
Caldecote Rd CV6 .... 113 C5
Caldeford Ave B90 .... 127 A7
Calder B77 .... 22 B2
Calder Ave WS1 .... 29 A2
Calder Cl
Bulkington CV12 .... 79 B2
Coventry CV3 .... 133 E7
Calder Dr B76 .... 58 A7
Calderfields Cl WS4 .... 29 A3
Calder Gr B20 .... 54 F2
Calder Rise DY3 .... 50 F6
Calder Twr 2 B20 .... 55 D1
Calder Wlk CV31 .... 162 C6
CALDMORE 42 E8
Caldmore Com Prim Sch
WS1 .... 42 E8
Caldmore Gn WS1 .... 42 E8
Caldmore Rd WS1 .... 42 E8
Caldon Cl LE10 .... 75 B8
Caldwall Cres DY11 .... 116 D5
Caldwell Ct
Nuneaton CV11 .... 73 D1
Solihull B91 .... 107 C5
Caldwell Gr B91 .... 107 C5
Caldwell Rd
Birmingham B9 .... 68 B3
Nuneaton CV11 .... 73 D1
Caldwell St B71 .... 53 D8
Caldy Wlk 5 B45 .... 101 F1
Cale Cl B77 .... 21 C2
Caledonia DY5 .... 81 D7
Caledonian B77 .... 21 F2
Caledonian Cl WS5 .... 43 C3
Caledonia Rd WV2 .... 163 D1
Caledonia St WV14 .... 40 E6
Caledon Pl WS2 .... 42 C7
Caledon St 5 WS2 .... 42 C7
Calewood Rd DY5 .... 81 D7
Calgary Cl CV3 .... 115 A2
Caliban Mews CV34 .... 161 E3
Calico Way CV6 .... 113 D7
CALIFORNIA 84 F2
California Ho B32 .... 84 E2
Californian Gr WS7 .... 6 F8
California Rd B69 .... 63 B8
California Way B32 .... 84 F3
Callaghan Dr B69 .... 52 C3
Callaghan Gr 3 WS11 .... 2 C2
Callcott Dr DY5 .... 81 D7
Callear Rd WS10 .... 41 D1
Callendar Cl CV11 .... 74 A7
Calley Cl DY4 .... 52 A3
Callis Wlk 2 B77 .... 35 F6
Callowbridge Rd B45 .... 121 F7
Callowbrook La B45 .... 121 F7
CALLOW HILL 158 A7
Callow Hill La B97 .... 158 B6
Callow Hill Rd B48 .... 139 A6
Callows La 2 DY10 .... 116 E6
Calmere Cl CV2 .... 114 F8
Calpurnia Ave CV34 .... 161 E2
Calshot Prim Sch B42 .... 55 B8
Calshot Rd B42 .... 55 A8
Calstock Rd WV12 .... 27 D4
Calthorpe Cl WS5 .... 43 E6
CALTHORPE FIELDS 86 B8
Calthorpe Mans 4 B15 .... 66 B1
Calthorpe Rd
Birmingham, Edgbaston
B15 .... 86 B8
Birmingham, Handsworth Wood
B20 .... 55 C2
Walsall WS5 .... 43 D6
Calthorpe Specl Sch 7
B12 .... 87 A8
Caludon Castle Sch CV2 .... 114 E4
Caludon Lodge CV2 .... 114 E5
Caludon Park Ave CV2 .... 114 E5
Caludon Rd CV2 .... 114 A4
Calver Cres WV11 .... 26 F5
Calver Gr B44 .... 44 D3
Calverley Rd B38 .... 123 D8
Calvert Cl CV3 .... 133 D6
Calverton Gr B43 .... 54 E8
Calves Croft WV13 .... 27 A3
Calvin Cl WV10 .... 11 D3
Calving Hill WS11 .... 1 E2
Camberley 6 B71 .... 42 F1
Camberley Cres WV4 .... 39 E2
Camberley Dr WV4 .... 39 A4
Camberley Gr B23 .... 56 E6
Camberley Rd DY6 .... 61 A4
Camberley Rise B71 .... 42 F1
Camberwell Terr CV31 .... 162 A7
Camborne Cl B6 .... 66 E7
Camborne Dr CV11 .... 73 F5
Camborne Rd WS5 .... 43 D7
Cambourne Ct 4 WS5 .... 43 D7
Cambourne Rd
Hinckley LE10 .... 76 A6
Rowley Regis B65 .... 63 C3
Cambrai Dr B28 .... 105 F8
Cambria Cl B90 .... 125 E7
Cambrian B77 .... 22 A2
Cambria St WS11 .... 1 D4
Cambridge Ave
Solihull B91 .... 106 E3
Sutton Coldfield B73 .... 57 B8
Cambridge Cl WS9 .... 30 B8
Cambridge Cres B15 .... 86 D7
Cambridge Dr
Birmingham B37 .... 69 F1
Nuneaton CV10 .... 72 E3
Cambridge Gdns CV32 .... 157 A1
Cambridge Rd
Birmingham B13 .... 86 F1
Dudley DY2 .... 62 A7
Smethwick B66 .... 65 A7
Cambridge St
Birmingham B1 .... 164 A2
Coventry CV1 .... 113 E5
Walsall WS1 .... 42 E7
West Bromwich B70 .... 53 B2
Wolverhampton WV10 .... 163 C4
Cambridge Twr B1 .... 164 A2
Cambridge Way B27 .... 88 D4
Camden Cl
Birmingham B36 .... 69 A8
Walsall WS5 .... 43 A4
Camden Dr
Birmingham B1 .... 66 C3
Tamworth B77 .... 21 E3
Camden St
Birmingham B18, B1 .... 66 B4
Brownhills WS9 .... 15 F4
Coventry CV2 .... 114 A4
Walsall WS1 .... 42 E8
Camden Way DY6 .... 49 D1
Camel Cl CV34 .... 161 C6
Camel Cotts DY9 .... 99 E2
Camellia Gdns
Stourbridge DY8 .... 60 E2
Wolverhampton WV9 .... 10 F3
Camellia Rd 1 CV2 .... 96 B2
Camelot Cl WS11 .... 1 F4
Camelot Gr CV8 .... 148 C5
Camelot Way B10 .... 87 C8
Cameo Dr DY8 .... 80 F8
Cameron Cl
Allesley CV5 .... 112 A7
Royal Leamington Spa
CV32 .... 157 A4
Cameron Rd WS4 .... 29 B3
Camford Gr B14 .... 104 F3
Cam Gdns DY5 .... 61 B6
Cam Ho 7 DY1 .... 61 E8
Camhouses B77 .... 22 B1
Camino Rd B32 .... 84 F3
Camomile Cl 5 WS5 .... 43 A3
Campbell Cl
Nuneaton CV10 .... 72 A4
Tamworth B79 .... 20 F8
Walsall WS4 .... 29 A3
Campbells Gn B26 .... 89 B4
Campbell St DY5 .... 61 C4
Campden Cl B97 .... 158 D6
Campden Gn B92 .... 89 A3
CAMP HILL 72 E5
Camp Hill
Birmingham B12 .... 87 A8
Stourbridge DY8 .... 60 E1
Camp Hill Cir B12 .... 87 A8
Camp Hill Dr CV10 .... 72 D7
Camp Hill Ind Est B12 .... 87 A7
Camp Hill Middleway B12 .... 87 A7
Camp Hill Prim Sch CV10 .... 72 E6
Camp Hill Rd CV10 .... 72 C7
Campian's Ave WS6 .... 4 D2
Campion B74 .... 31 F5
Campion Cl
3 Birmingham B38 .... 123 F8
Coventry CV3 .... 133 D6
Walsall WS5 .... 43 A3
Campion Ct 2 DY4 .... 51 E5
Campion Dr
Featherstone WV10 .... 12 A7
Tamworth B77 .... 21 C3
Campion Gdns B24 .... 57 C6
Campion Gn CV32 .... 157 A2
Campion Gr B63 .... 82 D3
Campion Ho
2 Birmingham B38 .... 123 E8
Wolverhampton WV10 .... 25 F4
Campion Rd CV32 .... 157 A2
Campion Sch & Com Coll
CV31 .... 162 C5
Campion Terr CV32 .... 157 A1
Campion Way
3 Bedworth CV12 .... 77 D2
Solihull B90 .... 126 A5
Camp La
Birmingham, Handsworth
B21 .... 54 C2
Birmingham, King's Norton
B38 .... 103 F3
Camplea Croft B37 .... 70 A2
Camplin Cres B20 .... 54 E5
Campling Cl CV12 .... 79 B2
Camp Rd B75 .... 32 D6
Campriano Dr CV34 .... 161 A8
Camp St
Birmingham B9 .... 67 C1
Wednesbury WS10 .... 41 F2
Wolverhampton WV1 .... 163 B4
Campton Cl LE10 .... 75 E7
Campville Cres B71 .... 42 E1
Campville Gr B37 .... 69 F5
Camp Wood Cl B30 .... 103 F8
Camrose Croft
Birmingham, Balsall Heath
B12 .... 86 F5
Birmingham, Castle Bromwich
B34 .... 69 B6
Camrose Gdns WV9 .... 11 A3
Camrose Twr B7 .... 67 B6
Camville CV3 .... 115 A2
Canal Ct B27 .... 88 E3
Canal La B24 .... 57 A1
Canal Rd CV6 .... 113 F8
Canalside
Bedworth CV6 .... 96 B6
Kingswood B94 .... 144 D3
Canal Side
Dudley DY2 .... 62 E4
Hopwood B48 .... 123 B2
Canalside Cl
Walsall WS3 .... 14 F1
Wednesbury WS10 .... 42 E2
Canal Side Dr B38 .... 104 A1
Canalside Ind Est DY5 .... 61 C1
Canal St
Brierley Hill DY5 .... 61 E5
Dudley DY1 .... 51 D4
Oldbury B69 .... 64 A7
Stourbridge DY8 .... 80 F6
Tipton WV14 .... 51 C8
Canal View Ind Est DY5 .... 61 B1
Canal Way LE10 .... 74 F7
Canary Gr B19 .... 66 C8
Canberra Ct 2 CV12 .... 77 F2
Canberra Gdns B34 .... 69 E6
Canberra Rd
Coventry CV2 .... 96 C4
Walsall WS5 .... 43 C6
Canberra Way
4 Birmingham B12 .... 86 F8
Hinckley LE10 .... 75 E4
Canford Cl
Birmingham B12 .... 86 F7
Coventry CV3 .... 133 C3
CANLEY 132 C7
Canley Ford CV4, CV5 .... 132 E7
Canley Ford Com Woodland
Nature Reserve★ CV4 .... 132 F6
CANLEY GARDENS 132 E8
Canley Rd CV5 .... 132 D8
Canley Sta CV5 .... 112 D1
Cannel Rd WS7 .... 6 D6
Cannes Ct CV4 .... 132 D6
Canning Cl WS5 .... 43 D6
Canning Gdns B18 .... 65 E4
Canning Rd
Tamworth B77 .... 21 F4
Walsall WS5 .... 43 D6
Canning St LE10 .... 71 C1
CANNOCK 1 D2
Cannock Chase High Sch
WS11 .... 1 E2
Cannock Chase Hospl
WS11 .... 1 E2
Cannock Chase Tech Coll
Cannock, Bridgtown WS11 .... 4 E7
Cannock WS12 .... 1 C8
Cannock Ind Ctr WS11 .... 4 D5
Cannock Motor Village
WS11 .... 2 B3
Cannock Rd
Burntwood, Chase Terrace
WS7 .... 6 D7
Burntwood, Gorstey Ley WS7 .... 7 B7
Cannock, Heath Hayes WS12 .... 5 C8
Cannock WS12, WS11 .... 2 A5
Featherstone WV10 .... 12 C7
Willenhall WV12 .... 27 C7
Cannock Sh Ctr 6 WS11 .... 1 E1
Cannocks La CV4 .... 132 D6
Cannock Sta WS11 .... 4 F8
Cannon Cl CV4 .... 132 F6
Cannon Dr WV14 .... 40 D2
CANNON HILL 86 D4
Cannon Hill Gr 2 B12 .... 86 E5
Cannon Hill Pl 1 B12 .... 86 E5
Cannon Hill Rd
Birmingham B12 .... 86 E5
Coventry CV4 .... 132 D5
Cannon Park Prim Sch
CV4 .... 132 D5
Cannon Park Rd CV4 .... 132 E5
Cannon Park Sh Ctr CV4 .... 132 C6
Cannon Rd WV5 .... 49 A7
Cannon St
Birmingham B2 .... 164 C2
Walsall WS2 .... 28 E4
Willenhall WV13 .... 27 B2
Cannon Street N WS2 .... 28 E4
Canon Bsns Pk WV14 .... 40 C1
Canon Dr CV7 .... 95 D6
Canon Evans CE Inf Sch
CV12 .... 78 A2
Canon Hudson Cl CV3 .... 134 C6
Canon Maggs CE Jun Sch
CV12 .... 78 B2
Canon Young Rd CV31 .... 162 B3
Canterbury Ave WV13 .... 27 D2
Canterbury Cl
Birmingham B23 .... 56 D2
Kenilworth CV8 .... 148 C3
Lichfield WS13 .... 3 C3
9 Rowley Regis B65 .... 63 E4
Studley B80 .... 159 C4
Tamworth B77 .... 21 D3
Walsall WS3 .... 15 A4
West Bromwich B71 .... 53 E8
Canterbury Cross Prim Sch
B20 .... 55 D1
Canterbury Dr
Birmingham B37 .... 90 A7
Burntwood WS7 .... 7 E7
Perton WV6 .... 23 E4
Canterbury Rd
Birmingham B20 .... 55 D1
Kidderminster DY11 .... 116 A6
West Bromwich B71 .... 53 D8
Wolverhampton WV4 .... 38 E5
Canterbury St CV1 .... 165 D3
Canterbury Twr 1 B1 .... 66 B3
Canterbury Way
Cannock WS12 .... 2 B1
Nuneaton CV11 .... 74 A8
Cantlow Cl CV5 .... 112 A3
Cantlow Ho 2 B12 .... 86 F7
Cantlow Rd B13 .... 105 A6
Canton Ho LE10 .... 71 C4
Canute Cl WS1 .... 42 F7
Canvey Cl B45 .... 101 E1
Canwell Ave B37 .... 69 F5
Canwell Dr B75 .... 33 B5
Canwell Gate B75 .... 32 E4
Canwell Gdns WV14 .... 40 C4
Capcroft Rd B13 .... 105 B6
Cape Cl WS8 .... 16 A6
CAPE HILL 65 B4
Cape Hill B66 .... 65 C4
Cape Hill Ret Ctr B66 .... 65 C4
Cape Ind Est CV34 .... 160 E7
Capener Rd B43 .... 44 A2
Cape Prim Sch B66 .... 65 C4
Capercaillie Dr WS11 .... 2 A1
Cape Rd CV34 .... 160 D8
Capern Gr B32 .... 84 F5
Cape St
Birmingham B18 .... 65 D4
West Bromwich B70 .... 52 E4
CAPE THE 160 D8
Capethorn Rd B66 .... 65 A3
Capilano Rd B23 .... 56 C7
Capmartin Rd CV6 .... 113 C7
Cappers La WS13, WS14 .... 9 F8
Capponfield Cl WV14 .... 40 B3
Capstone Ave
Birmingham B18 .... 66 A4
Wolverhampton WV10 .... 25 C8
Captain's Cl WV3 .... 24 D2
Captains Pool Rd DY10 .... 117 A1
Captain's Pool Rd DY10 .... 117 B2
Capulet Cl CV3 .... 134 C6
Capulet Dr CV34 .... 161 E3
Caradoc B77 .... 22 A2
Caradoc Cl CV2 .... 114 D7
Caradoc Hall CV2 .... 114 D7
Carcroft Rd B25 .... 88 D8
Cardale Croft 1 CV3 .... 134 F8
Cardale St B65 .... 63 D1
Carden Cl B70 .... 52 F4
Carder Cres WV14 .... 40 D4
Carder Dr DY5 .... 61 C2
Cardiff Cl CV3 .... 134 D5
Cardiff Gr B37 .... 70 A1
Cardiff St WV3 .... 39 B8
Cardigan Cl B71 .... 53 C7
Cardigan Dr WV12 .... 27 B6
Cardigan Ho WS12 .... 2 C5
Cardigan Pl WS12 .... 2 C5
Cardigan Rd CV12 .... 77 C1
Cardigan St B4 .... 66 F3
Cardinal Cl B17 .... 65 A2
Cardinal Cres B61 .... 136 D1
Cardinal Dr DY10 .... 117 B3
Cardinal Griffin RC High Sch
WS11 .... 1 D2
Cardinal Newman RC Sch &
Com Coll CV6 .... 94 F2
Cardinal Way WS11 .... 1 D2
Cardinal Wiseman RC Sch &
Language Coll CV2 .... 96 E1
Cardinal Wiseman RC Tech
Coll B44 .... 44 F2
Carding Cl CV5 .... 111 F4
Cardington Ave B42 .... 44 B1
Cardington Cl B98 .... 154 F3
Cardoness Pl DY1 .... 50 F2
Cardy Cl B97 .... 153 B4
Careless Gn DY9 .... 81 F4
Carey B77 .... 36 A5
Carey St CV6 .... 114 B8
Carfax WS11 .... 4 E8
Cargill Cl CV6 .... 95 F5
Carhampton Rd B75 .... 47 A5
Carillon Gdns B65 .... 63 C3
Carisbrooke B77 .... 22 A2
Carisbrooke Ave B37 .... 70 C2
Carisbrooke Cl WS10 .... 42 E2
Carisbrooke Cres WS10 .... 42 E3
Carisbrooke Dr B62 .... 83 D3
Carisbrooke Gdns WV10 .... 11 E3
Carisbrooke Rd
Birmingham B17 .... 65 B1
Perton WV6 .... 24 A3
Wednesbury WS10 .... 42 E2
Wolverhampton WV10 .... 11 E3
Carisbrook Rd CV10 .... 73 D6
Carlcroft B77 .... 22 B2
Carless Ave B17 .... 85 B7
Carless St WS1 .... 42 E8
Carl Eynon Ct 2 WS3 .... 28 B8
Carlisle Rd WS11 .... 4 B7
Carlisle St B18 .... 65 F5
Carlson Pk 2 B17 .... 85 B5
Carl St WS2 .... 28 D5
Carlton Ave
Bilston WV14 .... 40 F7
Birmingham B21 .... 54 E1
Stourbridge DY9 .... 81 E3
Sutton Coldfield B74 .... 31 A2
Wolverhampton WV11 .... 26 A7
Carlton Cl
Bulkington CV12 .... 79 B3
Cannock WS12 .... 2 D1
Dudley DY1 .... 51 C6
Kidderminster DY11 .... 116 A8
Redditch B97 .... 153 B1
Sutton Coldfield B75 .... 46 E7
Carlton Cres
Burntwood WS7 .... 7 A8
Tamworth B79 .... 20 F8
Carlton Croft B74 .... 31 A2
Carlton Ct CV5 .... 112 F2
Carlton Gdns CV5 .... 133 A8
Carlton Ho
8 Royal Leamington Spa
CV32 .... 161 F8
Sutton Coldfield B75 .... 32 B2
Carlton Mews B36 .... 69 D7
Carlton Mews Flats B36 .... 69 D7
Carlton Rd
Birmingham B9 .... 67 D1
Coventry CV6 .... 95 F1
Smethwick B66 .... 65 B8
Wolverhampton WV3 .... 39 A7
Carlyle Ave DY10 .... 117 B6
Carlyle Bsns Pk B70 .... 52 F5
Carlyle Gr WV10 .... 26 A8
Carlyle Rd
Birmingham, Edgbaston
B16 .... 65 E1
Birmingham, Lozells B19 .... 66 C8
Bromsgrove B60 .... 151 B8
Rowley Regis B65 .... 63 C2
Wolverhampton WV10 .... 26 A8
Carmel Cl WS12 .... 2 C5
Carmel Gr B32 .... 84 B1
Carmelite Rd CV1 .... 113 E2
Carmichael Cl WS14 .... 9 D7
Carmodale Ave B42 .... 55 B5
Carnation Way CV10 .... 78 A8
Carnbroe Ave CV3 .... 134 F7
Carnegie Ave DY4 .... 52 B4
Carnegie Cl CV3 .... 134 B5
Carnegie Dr WS10 .... 42 A3
Carnegie Rd B65 .... 63 B2
Carnford Rd B26 .... 89 B6
Carnforth Cl DY6 .... 60 B7
Carnforth Rd B60 .... 137 B1
Carnoustie B77 .... 22 C5
Carnoustie Cl
Bromsgrove B61 .... 150 D8
Nuneaton CV11 .... 79 C8
Sutton Coldfield B75 .... 46 C8
Walsall WS3 .... 14 A3
Carnwath Rd B73 .... 45 E2
Carol Ave B61 .... 136 D3
Carol Cres
Halesowen B63 .... 82 F5
Wednesfield WV11 .... 26 E6
Carol Gdns DY8 .... 80 F8
CAROL GREEN 130 F7
Caroline Cl CV11 .... 78 F7
Caroline Pl B13 .... 86 F3
Caroline Rd B13 .... 86 F4
Caroline St
Birmingham B3 .... 164 A4
Dudley DY2 .... 51 E1
West Bromwich B70 .... 53 B2
Carousel Pk LE9 .... 71 F8
Carpathian Ct 4 B18 .... 66 C4
Carpathian The 5 B18 .... 66 C4
Carpenter Glade B63 .... 82 D5
Carpenter Pl 7 B12 .... 87 A6
Carpenter Rd B15 .... 86 B7
Carpenters Cl LE10 .... 75 F5
Carpenters Ct B12 .... 86 F8
CARPENTER'S HILL 140 F1
Carpenter's Rd B19 .... 66 C7
Carpet Trades Way
DY11 .... 116 D7
Carrick Cl WS3 .... 15 A5
Carrie Ho CV1 .... 165 A2
Carriers Cl WS2 .... 27 F1
Carriers Fold WV5 .... 49 B7
Carrington Rd WS10 .... 42 D2
Carroll Wlk DY10 .... 117 C5
CARROWAY HEAD 33 C4
Carroway Head Hill B78 .... 33 D4
Carrs La B4 .... 164 C2
Carsal Cl CV7 .... 95 D5
Carshalton Gr WV2 .... 39 E7
Carshalton Rd B44 .... 45 A2
Cartbridge Cres WS3 .... 28 F6
Cartbridge La WS4 .... 29 A6
Cartbridge Lane S WS4 .... 29 A5
Cartbridge Wlk
3 Walsall WS3 .... 28 F6
Walsall WS3 .... 29 A6
Carter Ave
Codsall WV8 .... 10 B3
Kidderminster DY11 .... 116 B4
Carter Ct DY11 .... 116 C4
Carter Rd
Birmingham B43 .... 43 F2
Coventry CV3 .... 134 A8
Wolverhampton WV6 .... 25 B5
Carters Cl
Birmingham B37 .... 90 A7
Bromsgrove B61 .... 150 D7
Sutton Coldfield B76 .... 46 F3
Cartersfield La WS9 .... 16 E6
Carter's Gn B70 .... 53 B4
Carters Hurst B33 .... 69 B1
Carter's La
Birmingham B62 .... 84 A3
Halesowen B62 .... 83 F4
Carthorse La B97 .... 153 B5
Carthusian Rd CV3 .... 133 C7
Cartland Rd
Birmingham, Sparkbrook
B11 .... 87 C6
Birmingham, Stirchley B14,
B30 .... 104 C7
Cartmel Cl CV5 .... 112 A4
Cartmel Ct B23 .... 56 B4
Cartway The WV6 .... 23 D4
Cartwright Gdns B69 .... 52 C2
Cartwright Ho WS3 .... 14 B1
Cartwright Rd
Stoke Prior B60 .... 150 D2
Sutton Coldfield B75 .... 32 C3

Cartwright St WV2 ...... 163 C1
Carvell Cl CV5 ...... 94 B1
Carver Cl CV2 ...... 114 E2
Carver Ct
　Sutton Coldfield B24 ..... 57 C6
　Wednesbury DY4 .... 41 A1
Carver Gdns DY8 .... 80 E2
Carver St B1 .... 66 B4
Casa Mia Ct WS12 .... 2 C5
Cascade Ct CV3 .... 133 E6
Case La CV35 .... 145 E1
Casern View B75 .... 47 A6
Casewell Rd DY6 .... 60 C8
Casey Ave B23 .... 56 F8
Cash Joynson Ave WS10 .. 41 C8
Cashmore Ave CV31 .... 161 F5
Cashmore Rd
　Bedworth CV12 .... 77 E1
　Kenilworth CV8 .... 148 C4
Cash's Bsns Ctr CV1 .... 113 D5
Cash's La CV1 .... 113 D6
Casita Gr CV8 .... 148 C4
Caslon Cres DY8 .... 80 D4
Caslon Flats B63 .... 82 C4
Caslon Prim Sch B63 .... 82 C4
Caslon Rd B63 .... 82 C6
Caspian Way CV2 ...... 115 A8
Cassandra Cl
　Coventry CV4 .... 132 D3
　Dudley DY5 .... 50 C1
Cassandra Gr CV34 ..... 161 D4
Cassowary Rd 2 B20 ... 54 F3
Castello Dr B36 .... 58 D1
Castillo Ct B14 .... 105 A5
Castings The WV14 ..... 40 D2
Castlebridge Gdns WV11 .. 27 F2
Castlebridge Rd WV11 .. 27 A6
CASTLE BROMWICH 69 C8
Castle Bromwich Bsns Pk
　B35 .... 58 A1
Castle Bromwich Hall Gdns*
　B36 .... 69 A8
Castle Bromwich Inf Sch
　B36 .... 69 E8
Castle Bromwich Jun Sch
　B36 .... 69 E7
Castle Cl
　Brownhills WS8 .... 6 F2
　Coventry CV3 .... 133 D6
　Cradley Heath B64 ...... 63 B1
　Solihull B92 .... 89 B1
　Tamworth B77 .... 21 E4
　Warwick CV34 .... 160 E6
Castle Cres B36 .... 69 C8
CASTLECROFT 38 B8
Castlecroft WS11 .... 5 E5
Castle Croft B68 .... 84 D8
Castlecroft Ave WV3 ... 38 A8
Castlecroft Gdns WV3 ... 38 C8
Castlecroft Ho WV3 .... 38 A8
Castlecroft La WV6 .... 23 F1
Castlecroft Prim Sch
　WV3 .... 38 B8
Castlecroft Rd
　Bilston WV14 .... 40 F7
　Wolverhampton WV3 ... 38 B8
Castle Ct
　5 Darlaston WS10 ..... 41 D6
　Hinckley LE10 .... 75 D6
　Kenilworth CV8 .... 148 A6
Castleditch La B98 ...... 158 E7
Castle Dr
　Coleshill B46 .... 70 F5
　Willenhall WV12 .... 27 B5
Castle Dyke 8 WS13 .... 9 B7
Castle Farm Recn Ctr
　CV8 .... 147 E4
Castleford Gr B11 .... 87 C4
Castleford Rd B11 .... 87 C4
Castlefort JMI Sch WS9 .. 16 B3
Castlefort Rd WS9 ..... 16 A3
Castlegate Dr DY1 ..... 51 E2
Castle Gate Island DY2 .. 51 E2
Castlegate Mews 5
　CV34 .... 160 F7
Castlegate Way DY1 .... 51 E2
Castle Gn CV8 .... 147 D5
Castle Gr
　Kenilworth CV8 .... 147 E4
　Stourbridge DY8 ...... 81 B3
Castlehall B77 .... 22 A2
Castle High Sch DY1 ... 51 B2
Castle Hill
　Dudley DY1 .... 51 D2
　Kenilworth CV8 .... 147 E5
　Warwick CV34 .... 160 E6
Castlehill Rd WS9 ...... 16 C3
Castlehills Dr B36 ...... 69 A8
Castle Ho B33 .... 69 B2
Castle Mes B64 .... 83 B8
Castle La
　Solihull B92 .... 89 A2
　Warwick CV34 .... 160 E6
Castle Mews 6 CV34 ... 160 C6
Castle Mill B77 .... 21 C3
Castle Mill Rd DY1 ..... 51 C4
Castle Place Ind Est CV1. 51 C4
Castle Pool & Adventure Play
　Ctr The B35 .... 58 A2
Castle Rd
　Birmingham B29 .... 85 B1
　Birmingham, Kings Norton
　　B30 .... 103 F4
　Brownhills WS9 .... 16 A2
　Kenilworth CV8 .... 147 E5
　Kidderminster DY11 .... 116 E5

Castle Rd continued
　Nuneaton CV10 .... 73 C7
　Studley B80 .... 159 F4
　Tamworth B77 .... 35 F5
Castle Rd E DY4 .... 51 D4
Castlereagh Ct WV10 ... 25 C6
Castle Road E B68 ..... 84 D8
Castle Road W B68 ..... 84 C8
Castle Specl Sch WS3 ... 28 B7
Castle Sq B29 .... 85 A1
Castle St
　Astwood Bank B96 .... 158 E2
　Brownhills WS8 .... 6 F2
　Coventry CV1 .... 165 D4
　Darlaston WS10 .... 41 D6
　Dudley DY1 .... 51 D1
　Hinckley LE10 .... 75 D8
　Sedgley DY3 .... 50 D8
　Tipton DY4 .... 51 E5
　Warwick CV34 .... 160 E6
　West Bromwich B70 ... 53 A8
　Wolverhampton WV1 ... 163 C3
Castle The DY8 .... 81 B3
Castleton Ct 1 B15 .... 86 B7
Castleton Rd
　Birmingham B42 .... 55 D7
　Walsall WS3 .... 14 C3
Castleton St DY2 .... 62 C4
CASTLE VALE 58 B3
Castle Vale Com L Ctr
　B35 .... 58 A3
Castle Vale Ent Pk B76 .. 58 C4
Castle Vale Ind Est B76 .. 58 A5
Castle Vale Ret Pk B35 ... 57 F3
Castle Vale Sch & Specialist
　Performing Arts Coll
　B35 .... 58 B3
Castle View
　Dudley DY1 .... 51 B2
　Tamworth B77 .... 21 C3
Castle View Cl WS10 ... 41 A4
Castle View Rd WV14,
　WS10 .... 41 B4
Castle Wood Sch CV2 ... 96 D1
Castle Yd WV1 .... 163 C3
Caswell Rd
　Royal Leamington Spa
　　CV31 .... 162 B6
　Sedgley DY3 .... 50 C8
Catalpa Gr B74 .... 44 F6
Cat and Kittens La WV10 . 11 E6
CATCHEMS CORNER 130 E5
Caterbanck Way 2 WS13 .. 8 F6
Cater Dr B76 .... 46 D8
Caterham Dr DY6 ...... 60 F3
Catesby Dr DY6 .... 60 D8
Catesby Ho B37 .... 69 F4
Catesby La B94 .... 144 B2
Catesby Pk B38 .... 103 E3
Catesby Rd
　Coventry CV6 .... 113 B8
　Solihull B90 .... 106 B1
Cateswell Rd B11, B28 ... 87 F2
Cathcart Rd DY8 .... 80 E5
Cathedral Cl DY4 ...... 51 E5
Cathedral Ct 4 WS13 ... 9 B8
Cathedral Lanes Sh Ctr
　CV1 .... 165 B3
Cathedral Rise WS13 .... 9 A8
Cathel Dr B42 .... 55 A7
Catherine Cl B60 ...... 150 F8
Catherine Ct B24 ..... 57 C4
CATHERINE DE
　BARNES 108 B6
Catherine de Barnes La
　Bickenhill B92 .... 90 D1
　Catherine de B92 .... 108 C7
Catherine Dr B73 ..... 46 A6
Catherine Rd WV14 ... 40 A1
Catherine St
　Birmingham B6 .... 67 A7
　Coventry CV2 .... 113 F3
Catherine Ward Hall CV12 78 B5
Catherton Cl DY4 ..... 41 C1
Catholic La DY3 .... 50 D7
Catisfield Cres WV8 .... 10 F1
Catkins Cl B61 .... 121 B1
Cat La B34 .... 69 B7
Caton Gr B28 .... 106 A7
Cato St B7 .... 67 B5
Cato Street N B7 .... 67 C5
CATSHILL
　Bromsgrove 137 A8
　Brownhills 16 A6
Catshill Fst Sch B61 ... 137 A8
Catshill Mid Sch 1 B61. 136 F8
Catshill Rd WS8 .... 16 A7
Cattell Dr B75 .... 47 C6
Cattells Gr B7 .... 67 C6
Cattermole Gr B43 ..... 44 C3
Cattock Hurst Dr B72 ... 57 D7
Causeway B65 .... 63 C2
CAUSEWAY GREEN 63 F3
Causeway Green Prim Sch
　B68 .... 63 F3
Causeway Green Rd B68 . 64 A4
Causeway Rd WV14 ... 51 D8
Causeway The B25 ...... 88 D7
Causey Farm Rd B63 ... 100 C8
Cavalier Circus WV10 .. 11 E4
Cavalier Cl CV11 ...... 73 E2
Cavalier Dr B63 .... 83 A3
Cavandale Ave B44 ..... 44 E1

Cavans Cl CV3 .... 135 A8
Cavan's Cl WS11 .... 1 E4
Cavans Way CV3 ...... 135 A8
Cavans Wood Park Home Est
　WS12 .... 1 D5
Cavell Cl 1 WS2 .... 28 D2
Cavell Rd
　Burntwood WS7 .... 7 E8
　Dudley DY2 .... 51 F1
Cavendish B77 .... 20 E7
Cavendish Cl
　Birmingham B38 ...... 104 B1
　Kingswinford DY6 ..... 60 D4
　Lower Marlbrook B60 .. 121 C1
Cavendish Ct
　Birmingham B17 .... 85 B8
　Dorridge B93 .... 128 A3
Cavendish Dr
　Kidderminster DY10 ... 117 B7
　West Hagley DY9 ...... 98 F4
Cavendish Gdns
　Walsall WS2 .... 28 A4
　Wolverhampton WV1 ... 26 C1
Cavendish Rd
　Birmingham B16 .... 65 D4
　Coventry CV4 .... 111 E2
　Halesowen B62 .... 83 F4
　Walsall WS2 .... 28 B5
　Wolverhampton WV1 ... 26 C1
Cavendish Way WS9 .... 30 B5
Cavendish Wlk CV11 ... 79 C8
Caversham Cl CV11 .... 74 A7
Caversham Pl B73 ..... 46 B4
Caversham Rd B44 ..... 45 A2
Cawdon Gr B93 .... 127 F3
Cawdor Cres B16 ...... 65 F1
CAWNEY HILL 62 F8
Cawnpore Rd CV6 ...... 95 B2
Cawthorne Cl 1 CV11 .. 113 E4
Caxton Ct 4 WS11 ..... 4 E8
Caxton Gr B44 .... 45 C1
Caxton St WS11 .... 4 E8
Caynham Cl B98 ...... 154 D4
Caynham Rd B32 .... 102 B8
Cayton Gr B23 .... 56 F6
Cearl Ct B27 .... 88 C2
Cecil Ct CV31 .... 162 A8
Cecil Leonard Knox Cres
　CV11 .... 79 F6
Cecil Rd
　Birmingham, Gravelly Hill
　　B24 .... 56 F3
　Birmingham, Selly Park B13 86 C1
Cecil St
　Birmingham B19 ...... 164 C4
　Cannock WS11 .... 1 F4
　Stourbridge DY8 ...... 80 F5
　Walsall WS4 .... 28 F3
Cecily Rd CV3 .... 133 E7
Cedar Ave
　Birmingham B36 ...... 69 C8
　Brownhills WS8 .... 16 A8
　Willenhall WV14 ...... 51 B7
　Ryton-on-D CV8 ...... 135 B1
Cedar Bridge Croft B74 .. 46 B8
Cedar Cl
　Allesley CV5 .... 112 A6
　Birmingham, Brandhall B68. 84 C8
　Cannock WS12 .... 7 A6
　Lichfield WS14 .... 9 F7
　Royal Leamington Spa
　　CV32 .... 157 A4
　Stourbridge DY8 ...... 80 D2
　Walsall WS5 .... 43 B4
Cedar Cres DY11 ...... 116 C6
Cedar Ct
　Allesley CV5 .... 112 A6
　Birmingham B43 ...... 54 B8
　Hinckley LE10 .... 76 A6
　Tamworth B77 .... 35 E6
Cedar Dr
　Birmingham, Pype Hayes
　　B24 .... 57 C5
　Birmingham, West Heath
　　B31 .... 123 B7
　Bromsgrove B60 ...... 137 A1
　Kidderminster DY11 ... 116 C7
　Sutton Coldfield B74 .. 30 E1
　Tamworth B79 .... 21 A8
Cedar Gr
　Bilston WV14 .... 40 F7
　Codsall WV8 .... 10 B3
　Great Wyrley WS6 ..... 5 B4
　Warwick CV34 .... 156 A1
　West Hagley DY9 ...... 99 A6
　Wolverhampton WV3 .. 38 F7
Cedarhill Dr WS11 ...... 1 F3
Cedar Ho
　Birmingham B36 ...... 68 F8
　7 Royal Leamington Spa
　　CV32 .... 161 E8
　Solihull B91 .... 106 F1
　Sutton Coldfield B74 .. 31 B5
Cedarhurst
　Birmingham B32 ...... 85 A5
　Solihull B91 .... 107 C3
Cedar Park Rd
　Redditch B97 .... 153 D4
　Willenhall WV12 ...... 13 C1
Cedar Rd
　Birmingham B30 ...... 103 E6
　Burntwood WS7 .... 7 A7
　Dudley DY1 .... 51 B3
　Nuneaton CV10 .... 72 D6
　Redditch B97 .... 153 D4

Cedar Rd continued
　Tipton DY4 .... 51 D5
　Wednesbury WS10 ..... 42 A2
　Willenhall WV13 ...... 26 E2
Cedars Ave
　Birmingham B27 ...... 88 C4
　Coventry CV6 .... 112 F5
　Kingswinford DY6 ..... 60 D4
　Wednesbury WV5 ...... 49 A5
Cedars Bsns Ctr WS11 .. 4 C7
Cedars Hort Unit The
　WV3 .... 24 D2
Cedars Mews The 3
　CV32 .... 161 D8
Cedars Rd CV7 .... 78 B1
Cedars The
　Birmingham B25 ...... 68 E1
　Dorridge B93 .... 128 A4
　5 Wolverhampton, Newbridge
　　WV6 .... 24 F3
　Wolverhampton, Tettenhall
　　WV6 .... 24 D5
Cedar Terr B60 .... 137 A1
Cedar View B97 .... 153 C4
Cedar Way
　Birmingham B31 ...... 102 F1
　Wolverhampton WV11 .. 26 C7
Cedar Wlk 8 B37 .... 70 B2
Cedarwood B74 .... 46 B8
Cedarwood Croft B42 ... 54 F8
Cedar Wood Dr CV7 .... 130 B6
Cedar Wood Rd DY3 .... 50 D5
Cedric Cl CV3 .... 134 C5
Celandine
　Sutton Coldfield B74 .. 31 F5
　Tamworth B77 .... 21 C3
Celandine Cl DY6 ..... 60 C4
Celandine Rd
　Coventry CV2 .... 96 D2
　Dudley DY1 .... 51 A4
Celandine Way CV12 ... 77 E2
Celbury Way B43 ...... 54 D8
Celeste Rd B60 .... 137 C1
Celts B65 .... 63 C4
Celts Cl B65 .... 63 C4
Cemetery La B18 ...... 66 B5
Cemetery Rd
　Bilston WV14 .... 40 C6
　Cheslyn Hay WS6 ...... 4 C2
　Darlaston WS10 .... 41 F8
　Oldbury B68 .... 64 C6
　Redditch B97 .... 153 D3
　Smethwick B67 .... 64 F4
　Stourbridge DY9 ...... 81 E5
　Sutton Coldfield B75 .. 46 D6
　Willenhall WV13 ...... 27 A2
Cemetery St
　Bilston WV14 .... 40 C6
　Cheslyn Hay WS6 ...... 4 C2
　Stourbridge DY9 ...... 81 E3
　Tipton DY4 .... 51 F7
　13 Wolverhampton WV4 . 39 F4
Central Baths WV1 ..... 163 A3
Central Bldgs CV3 ..... 165 B1
Central Bsns Pk B33 ... 69 D1
Central Bvd
　Cheswick Green B90 ... 127 A3
　Coventry CV6, CV7 ..... 95 A5
Central City Ind Est CV6. 113 F5
Central Cl WS11 .... 14 A1
Central Dr
　Dudley, Gornalwood DY3. 50 D2
　Dudley, West Coseley
　　WV14 .... 51 D7
　Walsall WS3 .... 14 A1
Central Park Dr B18 .... 65 F5
Central Park Ind Est B9 . 67 E2
Central Rd B60 .... 137 A2
Central Six Ret Pk CV1 .. 165 A1
Central Sq B23 .... 57 A4
Central Trad Est
　Darlaston WS10 .... 41 E6
　Wolverhampton WV2 ... 39 F8
Central Way B5 .... 41 E6
Centre At7 CV6 .... 114 A7
Centre Ct B63 .... 83 B3
Centre La B63 .... 83 B3
Centre Link Ind Est B7 .. 67 B6
Centreway Ind Est CV11. 73 C2
Centurion Cl B46 ..... 59 F1
Centurion Pk B77 ...... 36 B6
Centurion Way B77 .... 36 B6
Century Ho B69 .... 63 D6
Century Ind Est B44 .... 44 E3
Century Mews B64 .... 62 F7
Century Pk B9 .... 90 C6
Century Rd B69 .... 64 A8
Century Twr B5 .... 86 C5

Century Way B63 ...... 82 D6
Chace Ave CV3 .... 134 C6
Chace Extended Learning Ctr
　CV3 .... 134 C6
Chaceley Cl CV2 ...... 115 A8
Chaceley Ct B97 .... 158 D8
Chaceley Gr B23 ...... 56 E7
Chacebrook Crest B15 .. 85 E7
Chadbury Croft 1 B91 . 127 B8
Chadbury Rd B63 ...... 83 C3
Chadcote Way B61 ..... 120 F1
Chaddersley Cl 2 B45 . 101 F1
Chaddesley Cl
　Oldbury B69 .... 63 D5
　Redditch B98 .... 153 F1
Chaddesley Dr DY9 .... 81 B1
Chaddesley Gdns 2
　DY10 .... 117 A5
Chaddesley Rd
　Birmingham B31 ...... 103 D2
　Halesowen B63 .... 83 C4
　Kidderminster DY10 ... 117 A5
Chadley Cl B91 .... 107 A6
Chad Rd
　Birmingham B15 ...... 85 F8
　Dudley DY1, WV14 ..... 51 B7
Chadsgrove Specl Sch 2
　B61 .... 136 F8
Chadshunt Cl B36 ...... 58 D2
Chadsmead Prim Sch
　WS13 .... 3 A1
CHADSMOOR 1 F4
Chadsmoor CE Jun Sch
　WS11 .... 2 A3
Chadsmoor Inf Sch WS11. 2 A4
Chadsmoor Terr B7 ..... 67 B6
Chad Sq B15 .... 85 E8
Chadstone Cl B90 ..... 127 B6
Chadswell Hts WS13 .... 3 D2
Chad Vale Prim Sch B15. 85 D7
CHAD VALLEY 85 F7
Chad Valley Cl B17 ..... 85 D6
Chadwell Dr B90 ...... 106 B4
Chadwell Gr DY1 ...... 120 F7
Chadwick Ave B45 .... 122 B6
Chadwick Cl
　Coventry CV5 .... 112 B3
　Wolverhampton WV4 .. 38 D6
Chadwick Ct B42 .... 54 E8
CHADWICK END 145 B7
Chadwick La
　Chadwick End B93 ..... 145 B8
　Temple Balsall B93 ... 129 B2
Chadwick Manor B93 .. 129 A1
Chadwick Mews
　Chadwick End B93 ..... 145 B6
　Redditch B98 .... 159 A7
Chadworth Ave B93 ... 127 E3
Chaffcombe Rd B26 .... 89 C7
Chaffinch Cl
　Cannock WS12 .... 2 B4
　Sedgley DY3 .... 39 C3
Chaffinch Dr
　Birmingham B36 ...... 70 B7
　Kidderminster DY10 ... 116 F2
Chaffinch Rd DY9 ...... 81 D3
Chainmakers Ct WV14 .. 40 D2
Chainshop Mus* DY2 ... 62 B1
Chain Wlk B19 .... 66 D7
Chalcot Dr WS12 .... 2 A7
Chalcot Gr B20 .... 54 E5
Chaldon Cl WV9 .... 11 A1
Chale Gr B14 .... 105 A3
Chalfield B79 .... 20 D6
Chalfont Ave WS11 .... 4 C7
Chalfont Cl
　Bedworth CV12 .... 78 A4
　Coventry CV5 .... 112 B4
Chalfont Ct WS11 ...... 4 C7
Chalfont Pl DY9 .... 81 E2
Chalford Rd B20 ...... 55 C1
Chalford Way B90 ..... 106 C1
Chalgrove Ave B38 .... 103 E1
Chalgrove Cres B91 .... 107 B1
Challenge Bsns Pk CV1. 113 D5
Challenge Cl CV1 ..... 165 C4
Challenor Ave WV13 ... 26 D1
Chaloner Cl CV2 ...... 96 C2
Chalybeate Cl B45 .... 101 F1
Chamberlain Cl
　Cubbington CV32 ...... 157 E5
　Oldbury B69 .... 52 D2
Chamberlain Cres B90 . 106 A2
Chamberlain Ct
　3 Birmingham, Hockley
　　B18 .... 66 C4
　Birmingham, King's Heath
　　B14 .... 86 E1
Chamberlaine St CV12 .. 78 B3
Chamberlain Health &
　Fitness Ctr B5 .... 86 F7
Chamberlain Ho B16 .... 66 A1
Chamberlain Rd B13 ... 105 B6
Chamberlain's Gn CV6 .. 112 F7
Chamberlain's La CV8 .. 38 E3
Chamberlain Sq B3 ... 164 B2
Chamberlain Wlk
　10 Coleshill B46 .... 70 F7
　1 Smethwick B66 ...... 65 B5
Champney B79 .... 20 D6
Chance Croft B68 ...... 84 B8
Chance Fields CV31 .... 162 F6
Chancel Ct B91 .... 107 C2

Chancel Ind Est
Darlaston WS10. . . . . 41 D5
Kingswinford DY6 . . . . 49 E1
Willenhall WV13 . . . . 27 B2
Wolverhampton WV1. . . . . 26 A1
Chancellors Cl CV4 . . . . . 132 D4
Chancellor's Cl B15 . . . . . . 85 E8
Chancel Way
Birmingham B6 . . . . 55 F5
Halesowen B62 . . . . 83 C6
Chancel Way Ind Est B6. . 55 F4
Chancery Ct CV10. . . . . . . 72 A7
Chancery Dr WS12 . . . . 2 C7
Chancery La CV10. . . . . . . 72 B7
Chancery Way DY5. . . . . . . 61 F2
Chanders Rd CV34 . . . . . 155 D1
Chandler Dr WV4 . . . . 38 D3
Chandler Ho B65. . . . . 63 D4
Chandlers CV31. . . . . 161 D7
Chandlers Cl
Birmingham B18 . . . . 65 F5
Redditch B97 . . . . 158 D7
Wolverhampton WV9. . . . 11 A1
Chandlers Dr B77 . . . . 22 B5
Chandlers Keep WS8 . . . . 16 A6
Chandlers Rd CV31. . . . . 162 A2
Chandley Wharf
Walsall CV34 . . . . 155 D1
 1 Walsall CV34 . . . . . . 160 D8
Chandos Ave B13 . . . . 86 F3
Chandos Ct 15 CV32. . . . 156 F1
Chandos Cross Sch B12. . 86 E8
Chandos St
Coventry CV2. . . . . 114 A3
Nuneaton CV11 . . . . 73 A4
Royal Leamington Spa
CV32. . . . . 156 F1
Change Brook Cl CV11 . . . 73 F8
Channel Way CV6 . . . . 96 B8
Channon Dr DY5. . . . . 81 D8
Chanston Ave B14 . . . . . 104 E4
Chanterelle Ct WV4 . . . . . . 39 B4
Chanterelle Gdns WV4 . . . 39 B4
Chantrey Cres
Bilston WV14 . . . . 40 F7
Birmingham B43 . . . . 44 D4
Chantries The CV1. . . . . . 113 E5
Chantry Ave WS3 . . . . 28 D8
Chantry Cl B47 . . . . 125 A7
Chantry Ct B13 . . . . 86 F3
Chantry Dr B62 . . . . 84 A6
Chantry Heath Cres B93. 128 C7
Chantry Ind Est B76. . . . . 59 B7
Chantry Rd
Birmingham, Handsworth
B21. . . . . 65 F8
Birmingham, Moseley B13. . 86 E4
Stourbridge DY7 . . . . 80 C7
Chantry The CV34 . . . . . . 156 A1
Chapel Ash WV3 . . . . 25 B2
Chapel Ash Island WV1. . 163 A3
Chapel Ave WS8 . . . . 6 E2
Chapel Cl B64 . . . . 83 B8
Chapel Ct
Astwood Bank B96 . . . . . 158 E1
Brierley Hill, Barrow Hill
DY5. . . . . 61 C7
 4 Brierley Hill, Silver End
DY5. . . . . 61 D2
 13 Royal Leamington Spa
CV32. . . . . 161 F8
Chapel Dr
Balsall Common CV7 . . . . 130 B8
Brownhills WS8 . . . . 6 E2
Mile Oak B78. . . . . 20 C1
Wythall B47 . . . . 124 F3
CHAPEL END. 72 B7
Chapel Farm Cl CV3. . . . 134 C6
Chapelfield Mews
Birmingham B45 . . . . . . 121 F6
Stourbridge DY8 . . . . 81 A4
Chapelfield Rd B45 . . . . . 122 A7
CHAPEL FIELDS 112 E3
Chapel Fields Jun Sch
B92. . . . . 88 F3
Chapel Fields Rd B92 . . . 88 F2
Chapel Gn WV13 . . . . 27 B2
CHAPEL GREEN
Coventry 93 B7
Willenhall. 27 B2
Chapel House La B63 . . . . 82 C6
Chapelhouse Rd B37 . . . . 69 F1
Chapel House St 1 B12. . 66 F1
Chapel La
Barnacle CV7. . . . . 97 B6
Beoley B98. . . . . 154 F8
Birmingham B29 . . . . 85 E2
Birmingham B47 . . . . . . 124 E3
Birmingham, Great Barr B43,
WS9 . . . . 44 A5
Kingswood B94 . . . . 144 D7
Lichfield WS14. . . . . 9 B6
Madeley Heath DY9. . . . . 120 D7
Romsley B62 . . . . 100 C6
Rowney Green B48 . . . . . 139 F4
Ryton-on-D CV8. . . . . . . 135 B2
Walsall B43 . . . . 43 F4
Wythall B47 . . . . 124 E2
Chapel Mews B77. . . . . . . 22 A5
Chapel Mill Apartments
B62. . . . . 83 C8
Chaplon B77 . . . . 22 A2
Chapel Pl DY11. . . . . 116 D6
Chapel Rd B96. . . . . 158 E1
Chapel Row 2 CV34 . . . . 160 E7

Chapel Sq WS6 . . . . 4 D3
Chapel St
Astwood Bank B96 . . . . . 158 E1
Bedworth CV12 . . . . 78 C3
Bilston WV14 . . . . 40 F4
Birmingham B5 . . . . 164 D3
Birmingham, Handsworth
B21. . . . . 65 D7
Brierley Hill, Barrow Hill
DY5. . . . . 61 C6
Brierley Hill, Quarry Bank
DY5. . . . . 61 F1
Brierley Hill, Silver End DY5 61 D2
Bromsgrove B60 . . . . 137 A2
Brownhills WS8 . . . . 6 E2
Burntwood WS7. . . . . 6 E8
Cannock WS12. . . . . 2 E1
Coventry CV1. . . . . 165 B3
Dudley DY2 . . . . 62 D4
Halesowen B63 . . . . 83 A3
Kidderminster DY11. . . . 116 D6
Kingswinford DY6 . . . . . . 60 B8
Norton Canes WS11 . . . . . 5 F5
Nuneaton CV11 . . . . 73 C4
Oldbury B69. . . . . 63 E7
Redditch B97 . . . . 153 D1
 5 Royal Leamington Spa
CV31. . . . . 162 A7
Stourbridge, Lye DY9. . . . 81 E5
Stourbridge, Wollaston DY8. 81 A4
Stourbridge, Wordsley DY8. 60 D3
Tipton DY4 . . . . 51 E5
Walsall, Blakenall Heath
WS3 . . . . 28 D8
Walsall WS3. . . . . 15 A3
Warwick CV34 . . . . 160 E7
Wednesbury WS10 . . . . . 41 E3
West Bromwich B70 . . . . 53 B5
West Hagley DY9. . . . . . . 99 A5
Wolverhampton WV2 . . . 39 D7
Chapel Street Prec 1
B60 . . . . 137 A2
Chapel View B67. . . . . 64 F4
Chapel Wlk
Birmingham B30 . . . . . . 104 A2
Bromsgrove B60 . . . . 137 A2
Dudley DY3 . . . . 50 C2
Chapelwood Gr B42. . . . . 55 D5
Chaplain Rd WS12 . . . . 2 E2
Chapman Cl CV31. . . . . . 162 E5
Chapman Ct CV34. . . . . . 161 C8
Chapman Rd B10 . . . . 87 C8
Chapman's Hill B62. . . . 101 E1
CHAPMAN'S HILL. 121 B8
Chapmans Pas B1. . . . . 164 B1
Chapter Ho B70. . . . . 53 A5
Chard Rd CV3. . . . . 134 D8
Charfield Cl B30 . . . . 103 D7
CHARFORD. 150 F7
Charford Fst Sch B60 . . . 150 F7
Charford Rd B60. . . . . . . 150 F8
Charingworth Rd B92 . . . 89 C3
Charity Bick Way 7 B70. 53 C2
Charity Rd CV7 . . . . 95 A7
Charlbury Ave B37. . . . . . 69 F2
Charlbury Cres B26 . . . . . 88 F8
Charlbury Mews CV31. . . 162 C6
Charlbury Twr 8 B5. . . . . 86 E8
Charlecote Cl B98 . . . . . 154 D2
Charlecote Croft B90. . . . 126 C8
Charlecote Dr
Birmingham B23 . . . . 56 E7
Dudley DY3 . . . . 50 E3
Charlecote Gdns
Royal Leamington Spa
CV31. . . . . 162 D5
Sutton Coldfield B73 . . . . 57 A8
Charlecote Rise 1 WV13. 40 F8
Charlecote Wlk CV11. . . . 78 F8
Charlecott Cl B13. . . . . . 105 D7
CHARLEMONT. 53 D8
Charlemont Ave B71 . . . . . 53 E8
Charlemont Cl WS5 . . . . . 43 C6
Charlemont Cres B71 . . . 42 E1
Charlemonte Cl WS12 . . . . 2 D3
Charlemont Gdns WS5 . . 43 C6
Charlemont Rd
Walsall WS5. . . . . 43 C6
West Bromwich B71 . . . . 53 F8
Charles Ave
Essington WV11. . . . . 12 F4
Rowley Regis B65 . . . . . . 63 C4
Wolverhampton WV4 . . . 39 B5
Charles Cl
Birmingham B8 . . . . 67 D4
Cheslyn Hay WS6. . . . . 4 D1
Charles Cres WS3. . . . . . . 15 A5
Charles Ct
 6 Birmingham B13. . . . . 87 B2
 14 Royal Leamington Spa
CV32. . . . . 162 A6
Sutton Coldfield B76 . . . . 46 F3
Warwick CV34 . . . . 160 C7
 1 Warwick, Emscote
CV34. . . . . 161 B8
Charlesdale Dr WS9. . . . . 30 B4
Charles Dr B7 . . . . 67 A5
Charles Eaton Rd CV12. . . 77 F3
Charles Edward Rd B26 . . 88 D6
Charles Foster St WS10 . . 41 C6
Charles Gardner Rd 6
CV31. . . . . 161 F6
Charles Hayward Bglws
WV4 . . . . 39 D3
Charles Henry St B12 . . . 86 F8
Charles Holland St 2
WV13 . . . . 27 B2

Charles Lakin Cl CV7 . . . . 97 C5
Charles Lane Trust Homes
The B28 . . . . 106 A8
Charles Pearson Ct B66. . 65 B5
Charles Rd
Birmingham, Aston B6. . . . 56 A1
Birmingham, Bordesley Green B9,
B10 . . . . 67 E1
Birmingham, Handsworth
B20 . . . . 55 C1
Brierley Hill DY5 . . . . 62 B1
Halesowen B63 . . . . 82 F4
Solihull B91 . . . . 106 E2
Stourbridge DY8 . . . . 80 E4
Tipton DY4 . . . . 52 A7
Charles St
Coventry CV1. . . . . 165 D4
Hinckley LE10 . . . . 71 E1
Kidderminster DY10. . . . 116 F6
Nuneaton CV11 . . . . 73 A5
Redditch B97 . . . . 153 C1
Smethwick B66 . . . . 65 C7
Walsall WS2. . . . . 28 D2
Warwick CV34 . . . . 161 A8
West Bromwich B70 . . . . 52 E5
Willenhall WV13 . . . . 27 B2
Charles Street Ind Est
B70. . . . . 52 F4
Charles Watson Ct 4
CV32 . . . . 157 A2
Charles Wesley Ct WV3 . . 39 A7
Charles Wlk B65 . . . . 63 C5
Charlesworth Ave B90. . . 127 B6
Charleville Rd B19 . . . . . . 66 B7
Charlewood Rd CV6. . . . . 95 B2
Charlock Gr WS11 . . . . 2 C3
Charlotte Cl
Nuneaton CV10 . . . . 72 C6
Tipton B69. . . . . 52 A2
Charlotte Gdns B90 . . . . 106 A3
Charlotte Rd
Birmingham, Edgbaston
B15. . . . . 86 C7
Birmingham, Stirchley B30 104 A6
Wednesbury WS10 . . . . . 41 C2
Charlotte St
Birmingham B3 . . . . 164 A3
Dudley DY2 . . . . 51 B1
 15 Dudley DY1. . . . . 51 B1
Royal Leamington Spa
CV31. . . . . 161 F6
Walsall WS1. . . . . 29 A2
Charlton Dr B64 . . . . 82 D7
Charlton Pl B8. . . . . 67 D5
Charlton Rd B44 . . . . 56 A8
Charlton St
Brierley Hill DY5 . . . . 61 A3
 4 Dudley DY1. . . . . 51 B1
Charminster Ave B25. . . . 88 D8
Charminster Dr CV3. . . . 133 D4
Charnwood Ave
Nuneaton CV10 . . . . 72 E2
Sedgley DY3 . . . . 39 D2
Charnwood Bsns Pk
WV14 . . . . 40 C5
Charnwood Cl
Birmingham B45 . . . . . . 102 B3
Birmingham DY5 . . . . 81 B8
Cannock WS12. . . . . 2 C3
Darlaston WV14 . . . . 41 B3
Hinckley LE10 . . . . 71 E2
Lichfield WS13. . . . . 3 C1
Charnwood Ct DY9. . . . . . 81 E2
Charnwood Ho WS13. . . . . 3 B8
Charnwood Prim Sch
WS13 . . . . 3 C2
Charnwood Rd
Birmingham B42 . . . . 54 F7
Hinckley LE10 . . . . 71 D2
Walsall WS5. . . . . 43 A4
Charnwood Way CV32 . . . 157 C2
Charter App CV34 . . . . . . 160 D5
Charter Ave CV4 . . . . 132 B7
Charter Cl WS11 . . . . 5 E4
Charter Cres B64 . . . . 83 B8
Charterfield Dr
Cannock WS12. . . . . 2 C1
Charterfield Sh Ctr DY6. . 60 D8
Charter Ho CV4 . . . . 132 A7
Charterhouse Dr B91 . . . 107 C1
Charterhouse Rd CV1 . . . 113 E2
Charter Prim Sch CV4 . . . 132 A8
Charter Rd B6 . . . . 10 B1
Charters Ave WV8 . . . . . . 10 B1
Charter St DY5. . . . . 61 E5
Charters The WS13 . . . . . . 3 B1
Chartist Rd B8. . . . . 67 D6
Chartley Cl
Dorridge B93 . . . . 127 E3
Perton WV6 . . . . 23 F4
Chartley Rd
Birmingham B23 . . . . 56 D1
West Bromwich B71 . . . . 53 D6
Chartway The WS3. . . . . . 15 B4
Chartwell B79 . . . . 20 D7
Chartwell Cl
Dudley DY1 . . . . 51 B6
Nuneaton CV11 . . . . 73 F1
Chartwell Ct B72. . . . . . . 57 C8
Chartwell Dr
Cheswick Green B90 . . . . 126 D5
Sutton Coldfield B74 . . . . 31 D4
Wolverhampton WV10 . . . 11 E1
Chartwell Grange B64. . . 83 A7
Chase Acad WS11 . . . . 4 E8
Chase Ave WS6 . . . . 4 D1
Chase Cl CV11 . . . . 73 E6
Chase Ctr The WS11. . . . . . 1 E1

Chase Gr B24 . . . . 57 D6
Chase La CV8. . . . . 147 B7
Chaselands WS7 . . . . 6 D7
Chase L Ctr WS11. . . . . 1 D2
Chaseley Ave WS11 . . . . . . 1 C2
Chaseley Croft WS11. . . . . 1 C2
Chaseley Gdns WS7 . . . . . 7 C7
Chase Park Ind Est WS7. . 6 D7
Chase Rd
Brownhills WS8 . . . . 7 A1
Burntwood WS7. . . . . 7 B6
Dudley DY3, DY5 . . . . 50 C1
Walsall WS3. . . . . 28 A8
Chaseside Dr WS11 . . . . . . 2 B3
Chaseside Ind Est WS11. . 2 B3
CHASE TERRACE. 6 E8
Chase Terrace Prim Sch
WS7 . . . . 6 F7
Chase Terrace Tech Coll
WS7 . . . . 7 A7
Chase The
Sutton Coldfield B76 . . . . 57 D7
Wolverhampton WV6 . . . . 25 B6
CHASETOWN. 6 E5
Chasetown Com Sch WS7. . 6 E5
Chasetown Ind Est WS7 . . 6 D7
**Chasetown Specialist Sports
Coll** WS7 . . . . 6 E5
Chasetown Sta 7 WS7 . . . 6 D5
Chase Vale WS7 . . . . 6 D6
Chase View WV4. . . . . 39 E2
Chasewater* WS7. . . . . . . 6 C4
Chasewater Country Pk*
WS7 . . . . 6 C5
Chasewater Heaths Sta*
WS7. . . . . 6 D6
Chasewater Rly* WS11. . . 6 E6
Chasewater Way WS11 . . . 5 F5
Chase Wlk WS12. . . . . 1 C4
Chasewood Park Bsns Cntr
WS12 . . . . 2 E1
Chater Dr B76 . . . . 47 A1
Chaters Cl DY4 . . . . 51 E5
Chatham Cl CV3 . . . . 134 C8
Chatham Rd B31. . . . . . . 103 A3
Chatillon Cl CV34 . . . . . . 161 E3
Chatsworth B79 . . . . 20 C7
Chatsworth Ave B43 . . . . . 43 C1
Chatsworth Cl
Cheswick Green B90 . . . . 126 E5
Hinckley LE10 . . . . 75 F6
Sutton Coldfield B72 . . . . 57 D7
Willenhall WV12 . . . . 27 B5
Chatsworth Cres WS4 . . . 29 D7
Chatsworth Dr
Cannock WS11. . . . . 2 A4
Nuneaton CV11 . . . . 73 F2
Chatsworth Gdns
Royal Leamington Spa
CV31. . . . . 162 D6
Wolverhampton WV6 . . . . 24 A7
Chatsworth Gr CV8. . . . . 148 C5
Chatsworth Rd B62 . . . . . 83 A7
Chatsworth Rise CV3. . . . 133 C6
Chattaway Dr CV7. . . . . . 130 B6
Chattaway St B7. . . . . 67 C7
Chatterton Ave WS13 . . . . 3 E6
Chatterton Wlk 4 DY10 . . 117 B6
Chattle Hill B46. . . . . 59 E2
Chattock Ave B91 . . . . . . 107 E3
Chattock Cl B36 . . . . 68 E7
Chatwell Gr B29 . . . . 85 B2
Chatwin Pl WV14 . . . . 40 E3
Chatwin St B66 . . . . 64 F7
Chatwins Wharf DY4 . . . . 51 F5
Chaucer Ave
Dudley DY3 . . . . 50 A5
Tipton DY4 . . . . 52 B8
Willenhall WV12 . . . . 27 E8
Chaucer Cl
Birmingham B23 . . . . 56 B3
Dudley WV14 . . . . 51 D8
Lichfield WS14 . . . . 9 B6
Stourbridge DY8 . . . . 81 A8
Tamworth B79 . . . . 21 A6
Chaucer Cres DY10. . . . . 117 C5
Chaucer Dr CV10. . . . . 72 A4
Chaucer Gr B27. . . . . 88 B2
Chaucer Ho B63 . . . . 82 B5
Chaucer Rd
Bromsgrove B60 . . . . 151 B8
Walsall WS3. . . . . 28 E8
Chauntry Pl CV1 . . . . 165 C3
Chauson Gr B91. . . . . . . 127 A8
Chavasse Rd B72 . . . . 46 D3
Chawn Hill DY9. . . . . 81 C3
Chawn Hill Cl DY9 . . . . . . 81 C3
Chawn Park Dr DY9 . . . . . 81 C3
Chaynes Gr B33. . . . . 69 D2
Cheadle Cl CV2 . . . . 96 A4
Cheadle Dr B23. . . . . 56 D8
Cheam Cl CV6 . . . . 96 A1
Cheam Gdns WV6 . . . . . . 24 E8
Cheapside
Birmingham B5, B12 . . . . 164 D1
Birmingham, Stirchley B30 104 A6
Willenhall WV13. . . . . 27 A1
Cheapside Ind Est 12 B66 F1
Cheatham St B7 . . . . 67 C6
Cheatle Ct B77. . . . . 35 D5
Checketts St WS2 . . . . . . 28 C2
Checkley Cl B90 . . . . 106 B4
Checkley Croft B76. . . . . . 57 F8
Cheddar Rd B12 . . . . 86 E6
Chedworth Cl
Birmingham B29 . . . . 103 B6
Redditch B98 . . . . 154 C5

Cheedon Cl B93 . . . . 127 E2
Cheetah Rd CV1 . . . . 165 C1
Chelford Cres DY6 . . . . . . 61 A3
Chells Gr B13. . . . . 105 B5
Chelmar Cl B36 . . . . 69 F8
Chelmar Dr DY5 . . . . 61 A6
Chelmarsh CV6 . . . . 113 C6
Chelmarsh Ave WV3 . . . . . 38 B8
Chelmarsh Cl B98. . . . . . 154 C7
Chelmorton Rd B42. . . . . . 55 D7
Chelmscote Rd B92 . . . . . 88 F1
Chelmsley Wood Sh Ctr
B37. . . . . 70 B2
Chelmsley Ave B46. . . . . . 70 F6
Chelmsley Circ B37 . . . . . 70 B3
Chelmsley La B37 . . . . . . 69 E3
Chelmsley La B37. . . . . . . 90 A8
Chelmsley Rd B37 . . . . . . 70 C2
CHELMSLEY WOOD. 70 C1
Chelmsley Wood Ind Est
B37. . . . . 70 B4
Chelney Wlk CV3 . . . . 115 A1
Chelsea Cl
Birmingham B32 . . . . 84 F4
Nuneaton CV11 . . . . 73 F7
Chelsea Ct 6 B29. . . . . . 103 B7
Chelsea Trad Est B7 . . . . . 67 A6
Chelsea Way DY6 . . . . 60 C6
Chelsey Rd CV2. . . . . 114 E8
Chelston Dr WV6 . . . . 24 E4
Chelston Rd B31. . . . . . . 102 E2
Cheltenham Ave B61. . . . 121 B1
Cheltenham Cl
Bedworth CV12 . . . . 78 B4
Wolverhampton WV6. . . . 25 B5
Cheltenham Croft CV2 . . 114 F7
Cheltenham Dr
Kingswinford DY6 . . . . . . 60 B6
Wolverhampton WV10 . . . 11 B5
Cheniltone Cl 8 B90 . . . . 126 C8
Cheltondale Rd B91. . . . . 106 F6
Chelveston Cres B91. . . . 107 B1
Chelveston Rd CV6. . . . . 112 E5
Chelwood Gdns WV14 . . . 40 E5
Chelwood Gr CV2 . . . . 96 F5
Chelworth Rd B38 . . . . . . 104 B2
Chem Rd WV14 . . . . 40 C5
Chenet Way WS11 . . . . 1 E2
Chenies Cl CV5 . . . . 112 B3
Cheniston Rd WV12 . . . . . 27 C7
Chepstow Cl
Coventry CV3 . . . . 134 C5
Perton WV6. . . . . 23 F4
Chepstow Dr B61 . . . . . . 121 B1
Chepstow Gr B45 . . . . . . 122 B6
Chepstow Rd
Walsall WS3. . . . . 13 F1
Wolverhampton WV10 . . . 11 D5
Chepstow Villas 5 B12 . . 87 B5
Chepstow Way WS3. . . . . 13 F1
Chequerfield Dr WV4 . . . . 39 A6
Chequers Ave WV5. . . . . . 38 A1
Chequers Ct WS11 . . . . 6 A5
Chequer St
Bulkington CV12 . . . . 79 C2
Wolverhampton WV3 . . . . 39 A6
Chequers The 3 WS11. . . 9 C5
Cherhill Covert 2 B14. . 104 C2
Cherington Cl B98 . . . . . 154 F1
Cherington Rd B29. . . . . 104 A8
Cheriton Cl CV5. . . . . 112 D4
Cheriton Gr WV6. . . . . 23 E3
Cheriton Wlk B23 . . . . 56 B3
Cherrington Cl B31. . . . . 102 F7
Cherrington Dr WS6 . . . . . . 4 F4
Cherrington Gdns
Stourbridge DY9 . . . . 99 C7
Wolverhampton WV6. . . . 24 B2
Cherry Bank WS12 . . . . 2 C6
Cherry Blossom Gr CV31 162 B2
Cherry Brook WS11 . . . . . . 5 F3
Cherrybrook Way CV2. . . . 96 C1
Cherry Cl
Burntwood WS7 . . . . 6 F6
Coventry CV6 . . . . 95 D2
Cherry Cres
Birmingham B24 . . . . 56 F3
Bromsgrove B61 . . . . 136 E2
Cherrydale Ct DY1 . . . . . . 50 F2
Cherry Dr
 1 Cradley Heath B64 . . . . 62 F1
Coventry Gn DY1. . . . . . . 50 F4
Cherry Gr
Barnt Green B45 . . . . 138 C8
Smethwick B66 . . . . 65 C5
Stourbridge DY8 . . . . 80 E4
Wolverhampton WV11 . . . 26 C7
Cherry Hill Ave B45 . . . . . 138 C8
Cherry Hill Rd B45 . . . . . 138 C8
Cherry Hill Wlk DY1. . . . . 62 A8
Cherry La
Himley DY3 . . . . 49 C3
Sutton Coldfield B73 . . . . 57 A7
Wednesbury WS10 . . . . . 42 A2
Cherry Lea B34 . . . . 69 B6
Cherryl Ho 3 B74. . . . . . . 31 E3
Cherry Oak Specl Sch
B29. . . . . 85 D2
Cherry Orch
Cradley Heath B64 . . . . . . 62 F1
Kenilworth CV8 . . . . 148 A5
Kidderminster DY10. . . . 116 F6

Cherry Orch *continued*
Lichfield WS14 . . . . 9 C7
Cherry Orchard Ave B63. . 82 F6
Cherry Orchard Cres B63. 82 F6
Cherry Orchard Dr B61. . 136 E3
Cherry Orchard Prim Sch
B20 . . . . 55 A3
Cherry Orchard Rd B20. . 55 A4
Cherry Pit La B98 . . . . . . 141 A1
Cherry Rd DY4 . . . . 51 F7
Cherry St
  Birmingham B2 . . . . . . 164 C2
  Halesowen B63 . . . . 82 F5
  Stourbridge DY8 . . . . . . 80 E4
  Tamworth B79 . . . . 21 B5
  Warwick CV34 . . . . 160 F7
  Wolverhampton WV3 . . . 25 B1
Cherry Tree Ave
  Nuneaton CV10 . . . . 72 E6
  Walsall WS5. . . . . 43 A5
Cherry Tree Croft B827 . . 88 C5
Cherrytree Ct DY9 . . . . . . 81 E3
Cherry Tree Gdns WV8 . . 10 B3
Cherry Tree La
  Codsall WV8. . . . . 10 B3
  Halesowen B63 . . . . 82 D1
Cherry Tree Learning Ctr
  DY1. . . . . 50 E1
Cherry Tree Rd
  Huntington WS12 . . . . . . 1 D8
  Kingswinford DY6 . . . . . 60 E8
  Norton Canes WS11 . . . . 6 B5
Cherry Tree Wlk
  Redditch B97 . . . . 153 B4
  Tamworth B79 . . . . 21 A8
Cherry Way CV8 . . . . 148 A5
Cherry Wlk B47 . . . . 125 B5
Cherrywood Cl WV14. . . . 40 C1
Cherrywood Cres ⊠
  B91 . . . . 127 C8
Cherrywood Ct B92 . . . . . 89 A2
Cherrywood Gn WV14. . . 40 D8
Cherrywood Gr CV5. . . . 111 F5
Cherrywood Ind Est B9. . 67 D3
Cherrywood Rd
  Birmingham B9 . . . . 67 E2
  Sutton Coldfield B74 . . . 30 D1
Cherrywood Way B74 . . . 31 D4
Chervil Cl B42 . . . . 55 C7
Chervil Rise WV10 . . . . . 25 F3
Cherwell B77 . . . . 21 D1
Cherwell Cl LE10. . . . . . . 75 A8
Cherwell Ct B73. . . . . 46 B5
Cherwell Dr
  Birmingham B36 . . . . . . 69 F8
  Brownhills WS8 . . . . 6 C2
Cherwell Gdns ⊡ B6. . . . 66 D8
Chesford Cres
  Coventry CV6. . . . . 96 B2
  Warwick CV34 . . . . 156 B1
Chesham St B12 . . . . 162 F7
Cheshire Ave B90. . . . . . 106 A2
Cheshire Cl
  Burntwood WS7 . . . . 7 F8
  Stourbridge DY8 . . . . . . 80 D8
Cheshire Gr
  Kidderminster DY11. . . 116 A7
  Perton WV6 . . . . 23 E4
Cheshire Ho ⊡ B66. . . . . 65 B5
Cheshire Rd
  Birmingham B6 . . . . 56 A2
  Smethwick B67 . . . . 65 A4
  Willenhall WS2. . . . . 27 F2
Chesholme Rd CV6. . . . . 95 B2
Cheshunt Ho B37 . . . . . . 70 B2
Chesils The CV3 . . . . 133 D6
Cheslyn Dr WS6 . . . . 4 D2
Cheslyn Gr B14 . . . . 105 A3
CHESLYN HAY 4 C3
Cheslyn Hay Prim Sch
  WS6 . . . . 4 C3
Cheslyn Hay Sport & Com
  High Sch WS6. . . . . 4 C3
Chessetts Gr B13 . . . . . . 105 A6
CHESSETTS WOOD 144 D8
Chessetts Wood Rd B94. 144 C7
Chessher St LE10 . . . . . . 71 C1
Chester Ave WV6 . . . . . . 24 F7
Chester Cl
  Birmingham B37 . . . . . . 70 A2
  Cannock WS11. . . . . 2 B1
  Lichfield WS13. . . . . 3 C3
  Willenhall WV13 . . . . . . 27 D2
Chester Ct
  ⊡ Birmingham, Chelmsley
    Wood B37. . . . . 70 D2
  ⊡ Birmingham, Weoley Castle
    B29 . . . . 103 B7
Chester Dr B74 . . . . 30 F2
CHESTERFIELD 17 E8
Chesterfield Cl B31 . . . . 103 B2
Chesterfield Ct
  Birmingham B38 . . . . . . 103 E4
  Brownhills WS9 . . . . 16 A4
Chesterfield Rd WS14. . . 9 A5
Chestergate Croft B24 . . 57 D4
Chester Gdns B31 . . . . . . 45 E1
Chester Hayes Ct B24 . . 57 C5
Chester Pl WS2 . . . . 28 B1
Chester Rd
  Aldridge B74 . . . . 30 E4
  Birmingham, Castle Bromwich
    B36 . . . . 69 E7
  Birmingham, Chelmsley Wood
    B37. . . . . 90 F8
  Cradley Heath B64. . . . . 82 C8

Chester Rd *continued*
  Dudley DY2 . . . . 62 D2
  Hampton-in-A B46, B92, CV7 91 B5
  Stonnall WS9 . . . . 16 D3
  Sutton Coldfield B23, B24, B35,
    B73. . . . . 57 E4
  West Bromwich B71 . . . . 42 B1
Chester Rise B68 . . . . . . 84 B8
CHESTER ROAD 57 B6
Chester Road N
  Brownhills WS8 . . . . 6 D1
  Kidderminster DY11. . . 117 A7
  Sutton Coldfield B73 . . . 45 B4
Chester Road S DY10. . . 116 F4
Chester Road Sta B73. . . 57 A7
Chester St
  Birmingham B6 . . . . 67 A6
  Coventry CV1. . . . . 113 B3
  Wolverhampton WV6. . . 25 B4
Chesterton Cl
  Redditch B97 . . . . 158 D4
  Solihull B91 . . . . 106 E5
Chesterton Ct B13 . . . . . 86 F1
Chesterton Dr
  Nuneaton CV10 . . . . 72 A5
  Royal Leamington Spa
    CV31. . . . . 162 C5
Chesterton Rd
  Birmingham B12 . . . . . . 87 B5
  Coventry CV6. . . . . 113 A7
  Wolverhampton WV10. . 26 A8
Chesterton Way B79 . . . 21 A7
Chesterwood B47. . . . . . 125 A6
Chester Wood WS9 . . . . 30 F2
Chesterwood Gdns B20. 55 D2
Chesterwood Rd B13. . . 104 F6
Chestnut Ave
  Dudley DY1 . . . . 51 C3
  Kenilworth CV8 . . . . . . 147 F3
  Tamworth B79 . . . . 21 B7
  Tipton DY4. . . . . 51 F7
Chestnut Cl
  Birmingham B27 . . . . . . 88 C4
  Cannock WS11. . . . . 2 C2
  Solihull B92 . . . . 106 D8
  Stourbridge DY8 . . . . . . 80 D3
  Sutton Coldfield B74 . . . 31 A3
Chestnut Cres CV10 . . . . 72 E6
Chestnut Ct
  Birmingham B36 . . . . . . 69 E7
  Burntwood WS7 . . . . 6 F4
  Coventry CV3. . . . . 134 B8
  Kidderminster DY11. . . 116 B8
  Royal Leamington Spa
    CV34. . . . . 161 E2
Chestnut Dr
  Birmingham, Buckland End
    B36. . . . . 69 B7
  Birmingham, Erdington B24 57 C4
  Birmingham, Rednal B45. 122 D4
  Cheslyn Hay WS6. . . . . . . 4 D3
  Great Wyrley WS6 . . . . . . 4 F3
  Nuneaton CV11 . . . . 73 E3
  Shenstone WS14 . . . . . . 17 F5
  Walsall WS4. . . . . 29 B8
  West Hagley DY9 . . . . . . 98 F4
  Wombourne WV5. . . . . . 49 A5
Chestnut Gr
  ⊡ Birmingham B17. . . . 85 D5
  Coventry CV4. . . . . 112 A2
  Kidderminster DY11. . . 116 B8
  Kingswinford DY6 . . . . . 60 F6
  Tamworth B77 . . . . 21 C3
  Wolverhampton WV11. . 26 C7
Chestnut Pl
  Birmingham B14 . . . . . . 104 E8
  Walsall WS3. . . . . 28 D6
Chestnut Rd
  Astwood Bank B96 . . . . 158 E1
  Bedworth CV12 . . . . 78 D4
  Birmingham, Brandhall B68. 84 C7
  Birmingham, Showell Green
    B13. . . . . 87 A4
  Bromsgrove B61 . . . . . . 136 F4
  Walsall WS3. . . . . 28 E6
  Wednesbury WS10 . . . . 42 A2
Chestnuts Ave B36 . . . . . 69 B7
Chestnut Sq CV32. . . . . . 157 B2
Chestnuts The
  Bedworth CV12 . . . . 77 E2
  Kidderminster DY11. . . 116 C3
  Wolverhampton WV10. . 26 A8
Chestnut Tree Ave CV4. 112 A2
Chestnut Way WV3. . . . . 38 D8
Chestnut Wlk ⊡ B37 . . . 70 D2
Cheston Rd WW14 . . . . . 40 B5
Cheston Ind Est B7 . . . . 67 B7
Cheston Rd B7. . . . . 67 B6
Cheswell Cl WV6. . . . . . . 24 B2
Cheswick Cl
  Coventry CV6. . . . . 114 A7
  Willenhall WV13 . . . . . . 40 F8
CHESWICK GREEN 126 E4
Cheswick Green Prim Sch
  B90. . . . . 126 E4
Cheswick Way B90. . . . . 126 D4
Cheswood Dr B76. . . . . . 58 B6
Chetland Croft B92 . . . . 107 F7
Chettle Rd WV14. . . . . . . 40 F3
Chetton Ave CV6 . . . . . . 113 C6
Chetton Gn WV10 . . . . . . 11 B3
Chetwode Cl CV5. . . . . . 112 B4
Chetwood Cl WV6. . . . . . 25 A5
Chetwynd Cl WS2. . . . . . 27 D3
Chetwynd Dr CV11 . . . . . 79 B7
Chetwynd Gdns WS11. . . 1 D3
Chetwynd Jun Sch CV11. 79 A7

Chetwynd Rd
  Birmingham B8 . . . . 68 B5
  Wolverhampton WV2. . . 39 B6
Cheveley Ave B45. . . . . . 122 B7
Chevening Cl DY3. . . . . . 50 E7
Cheval Ave CV6 . . . . 113 B6
Cheveral Rd CV12. . . . . . 78 A3
Cheverel Pl CV1 . . . . 73 B2
Cheverel St CV1. . . . . . . 73 B3
Cheveridge Cl B91. . . . . 107 A2
Cheverton Rd B31 . . . . . 102 E4
Cheviot B77 . . . . 22 C1
Cheviot Cl CV10. . . . . . . 72 B3
Cheviot Ct B75. . . . . 32 A4
Cheviot Rd
  Stourbridge DY8 . . . . . . 81 A6
  Wolverhampton WV2. . . 39 F7
Cheviot Rise
  Cannock WS12. . . . . 2 C5
  Royal Leamington Spa
    CV32. . . . . 157 C3
Cheviot The CV4 . . . . 132 D6
Cheviot Way B63. . . . . . . 82 C7
CHEYLESMORE. 133 E7
Cheylesmore Cl CV1 . . . 165 B2
Cheylesmore Ct B73 . . . 46 B4
Cheyne Cl B17 . . . . 85 D5
Cheyne Gdns B28 . . . . . 105 E3
Cheyne Pl B17 . . . . 85 D5
Cheyne Wlk DY5. . . . . . . 81 C7
Cheyney Cl WV6. . . . . . . 25 A5
Chichester Ave DY2. . . . 62 D5
Chichester Cl CV11. . . . . 74 A7
Chichester Ct ⊡ B73. . . . 46 B5
Chichester Dr
  Birmingham B32 . . . . . . 84 A5
  Cannock WS12. . . . . 2 C1
Chichester Gr B37 . . . . . 70 B1
Chideock Hill CV3 . . . . . 133 A6
Chiel Cl CV5. . . . . 111 F4
Chigwell Cl B35. . . . . 58 A3
Chilcote Cl B28 . . . . 105 F4
Chilcote Prim Sch B28 . 105 F4
Childs Ave WV14 . . . . . . 40 A2
Childs Oak Cl CV7. . . . . 130 A6
Chilgrove Gdns WV6 . . . 24 C5
Chilham Dr B37 . . . . 70 C2
Chillaton Rd CV6. . . . . . . 95 B2
Chillenden Ct WV13 . . . . 27 C2
Chillingham B37. . . . . . . 35 C7
Chillingham Rd B36. . . . 68 D8
Chillinghome Twr B36 . . 57 F1
Chillington Cl WS6. . . . . . 4 F1
Chillington Dr
  Codsall WV8. . . . . 10 A4
  Dudley DY1 . . . . 50 F3
Chillington Fields WV1 . . 26 A1
Chillington Ho WV6 . . . . 24 E5
Chillington Pl WV14. . . . 40 C5
Chillington Rd DY4. . . . . 41 C1
Chillington St WV1. . . . . 25 F1
Chillington Wlk B65. . . . 63 D3
Chillington Works Ind Est
  WV1 . . . . 25 F1
Chiltern Cl
  Cheslyn Hay WS6. . . . . . . 4 D1
  Dudley DY3 . . . . 50 D3
  Halesowen B63 . . . . 82 D1
Chiltern Ct
  ⊡ Coventry CV6 . . . . . 113 A5
  Sutton Coldfield B75 . . . 32 A4
  Chiltern Dr WV13 . . . . . 26 D1
Chiltern Ho
  Coventry CV5. . . . . 111 D4
  Redditch B98. . . . . 154 E1
  Chiltern Leys ⊡ CV6 . . . 113 A4
Chiltern Rd
  Stourbridge DY8 . . . . . . 81 B6
  Tamworth B77 . . . . 22 C1
Chilterns The
  Coventry CV5. . . . . 112 B4
  Oldbury B69. . . . . 63 E5
Chilton Ct B23. . . . . 56 C2
Chilton Rd B14 . . . . 105 D4
CHILVERS COTON 73 A1
Chilvers Coton Com Inf Sch
  CV11. . . . . 73 C2
Chilvers Coton Craft Ctr
  CV11. . . . . 73 C2
Chilvers Ct ⊡ CV11 . . . . 73 C3
Chilvers Gr B37 . . . . 69 F5
Chilwell Cl B91 . . . . 107 B1
Chilwell Croft B19 . . . . . 66 E6
Chilworth Ave WV11 . . . 26 F7
Chilworth Cl
  ⊡ Birmingham B6. . . . . 66 F6
  Nuneaton CV11 . . . . 78 E8
Chimes Cl B33. . . . . 69 E1
Chimney Rd DY4 . . . . 52 D6
CHINA TOWN 164 C1
Chines The CV10. . . . . . . 73 D7
Chingford Cl CV8. . . . . . . 60 C4
Chingford Rd
  Birmingham B44 . . . . . . 56 A8
  Coventry CV6. . . . . 96 A4
Chinley Gr B44 . . . . 45 C1
Chinn Brook Ho B14 . . . 105 B4
Chinn Brook Rd B13 . . . 105 B4
Chip Cl B38. . . . . 103 D2
Chipperfield Rd B36. . . . 68 E8
Chipstead Rd B23 . . . . . 56 E6
Chipstone Cl B91 . . . . . . 107 C1
Chirbury Gr B31 . . . . . . 103 B1
Chirton Cl CV10 . . . . 116 E2
Chirton Gr B14 . . . . 104 D4
Chiseldon Croft B14. . . . 105 A3
Chisholm Gr B27 . . . . . . 106 C8
Chiswell Rd B18. . . . . . . 65 E4

Chiswick Ct ⊡ B23. . . . . 56 E2
Chiswick Ho ⊡ B15. . . . . 86 C8
Chiswick Wlk B37. . . . . . 70 E2
Chivenor Ho B35. . . . . . . 58 A2
Chivenor Prim Sch B35 . 58 A2
Chivington Cl B90. . . . . . 127 B6
Chopin Cl WS11. . . . . 2 B2
Chorley Ave B34 . . . . 68 F6
Chorley Gdns WV14 . . . . 40 B5
Chorley Way CV6 . . . . . . 113 C6
CHRIST CHURCH 9 A8
Christ Church CE Inf Sch
  WV6. . . . . 24 B3
Christ Church CE Jun Sch
  WV6. . . . . 24 C4
Christ Church CE Prim Sch
  Birmingham B11 . . . . . . 87 B7
  ⊡ Dudley WV14 . . . . . . 40 D1
  Lichfield WS13. . . . . 8 F7
  Oldbury B69. . . . . 64 A8
  Walsall WS3. . . . . 28 D7
Christchurch Cl
  Birmingham B15 . . . . . . 85 E8
  Nuneaton CV10 . . . . 72 F1
Christ Church Gdns WS13 .8 F7
Christ Church Gr WS1. . . 43 A7
Christchurch La WS13. . . 8 F7
Christchurch Rd CV6. . . 113 A5
Christina Ct ⊡ B71 . . . . . 53 D4
Christine Cl DY4 . . . . 41 C2
Christine Ledger Sq ⊡
  CV31 . . . . 162 A6
Christopher Cadbury
  Wetland Reserve The ★
    B61. . . . . 150 B3
Christopher Hooke Ho
  CV6 . . . . 113 E8
Christopher Rd
  Birmingham B29 . . . . . . 85 C2
  Halesowen B62 . . . . 83 E3
  Wolverhampton WV2. . . 163 D1
Christopher Wlk WS13 . . 3 A3
Christ the King RC Inf Sch
  CV6 . . . . 112 F6
Christ the King RC Jun Sch
  CV6. . . . . 112 F7
Christ The King RC Prim Sch
  B44. . . . . 44 E6
Chub B77. . . . . 35 D7
Chubb Bldgs The ★ WV1. 163 B3
Chubb St WV1 . . . . 163 C3
Chuckery Prim Sch WS1. 29 A1
Chuckery Rd WS1. . . . . . 29 A1
CHUCKERY THE 29 A1
Chudleigh Gr B43. . . . . . 54 D8
Chudleigh Rd
  Birmingham B23 . . . . . . 56 E4
  Coventry CV2. . . . . 114 E7
Churchacre B23 . . . . 56 C8
Church Ave
  Birmingham, Handsworth
    B20 . . . . 55 C1
  Birmingham, Moseley B13. 86 F3
  Clent DY9. . . . . 99 F3
  Stourbridge DY8 . . . . . . 81 A7
  Water Orton B46. . . . . . . 59 B3
CHURCHBRIDGE. 4 F4
Churchbridge B69 . . . . . 63 F6
Churchbridge Pk WS11. . 4 E5
Church Cl
  Birmingham B37 . . . . . . 70 A6
  Drayton Bassett B78. . . . 34 E5
  Hartshill CV10 . . . . 72 B8
  Hinckley LE10 . . . . 76 A6
  Kyton-on-D CV8 . . . . . . 135 B2
  Shenstone WS14 . . . . . . 18 A5
  Whitnash CV31. . . . . . . 162 B4
  Wood End CV9 . . . . 36 C1
  Wythall B47. . . . . 124 F3
Church Cres WV11 . . . . . 12 F3
Church Croft
  Birmingham B17 . . . . . . 85 B4
  Halesowen B63 . . . . 83 A4
Church Cross View DY1 . 61 D8
Church Ct
  Astwood Bank B96 . . . . 158 E2
  Coventry CV6. . . . . 94 F1
  ⊡ Cradley Heath B64. . . 62 C1
  Stourbridge DY8 . . . . . . 81 A5
  Walsall WS1. . . . . 28 F1
Churchdale Cl CV10. . . . 72 C4
Churchdale Rd B44 . . . . 44 D3
Church Down Cl B97. . . 158 D6
Churchdown Ct B23. . . . 56 C2
Church Dr
  Birmingham B30 . . . . . . 104 B7
  Hopwas B78 . . . . 20 B7
  Kenilworth CV8 . . . . . . 147 F5
CHURCH END 114 C4
Church End CV31 . . . . . . 162 E6
Church Farm Barn & Cotts
  DY10 . . . . 99 B8
Church Farm Mews B77. 35 C4
CHURCHFIELD 53 E6
Churchfield Ave DY4 . . . 51 F8
Churchfield Cl B7. . . . . . 67 C6
Churchfield Ind Est DY2. 62 C8
Churchfield Rd WV10 . . 25 B8
Churchfields
  Birmingham B43 . . . . . . 44 D4
  Bromsgrove B61 . . . . . . 136 F3
  Kidderminster DY10. . . 116 F7
Churchfields Bsns Pk
  DY10. . . . . 116 E7
Churchfields Rd
  Bromsgrove B61 . . . . . . 136 F3

Churchfields Rd *continued*
  Wednesbury WS10 . . . . 42 A4
Churchfield St DY2. . . . . 62 C8
Church Gdns
  Smethwick B67 . . . . 65 A4
  Wolverhampton WV10. . 26 A4
Church Gn
  Bilston WV14 . . . . 40 D8
  Birmingham B20 . . . . . . 55 A2
Church Gr B13. . . . . 105 C5
Church Green E B98 . . . 153 E4
Church Green W B97. . . 153 E4
CHURCH HILL
  Birmingham. 55 B1
  Redditch 154 C6
  Wednesbury 41 E4
Church Hill
  Belbroughton DY9 . . . . 119 D6
  Beoley B98. . . . . 154 D8
  Birmingham, Northfield
    B31. . . . . 103 B3
  Brierley Hill DY5 . . . . . . 61 D2
  Cannock WS12. . . . . 2 D4
  Cubbington CV32. . . . . 157 E5
  Frankley B32 . . . . 102 B6
  Royal Leamington Spa
    CV32 . . . . 161 E8
  ⊡ Walsall WS1 . . . . 28 F1
  ⊡ Wednesbury WS10 . . 41 F3
  Wolverhampton WV4. . . 38 E4
Church Hill Cl B91 . . . . . 107 C2
Church Hill Ct ⊡ WS10. . 41 F3
Church Hill Dr WV6. . . . . 24 E5
Church Hill Mid Sch
  B98 . . . . 154 D6
Church Hill Rd
  Birmingham B20 . . . . . . 55 C1
  Solihull B91 . . . . 107 C3
  Wolverhampton WV6. . . 24 D5
Church Hill St B67 . . . . . 64 F6
Church Hill Way B98. . . 154 D6
Church Ho
  Brierley Hill DY5 . . . . . . 61 C2
  Walsall WS2. . . . . 42 C7
CHURCHILL. 98 C3
Churchill Ave
  Coventry CV6. . . . . 113 E8
  Kenilworth CV8 . . . . . . 148 A6
Churchill Cl B69 . . . . 52 C1
Churchill Dr
  Rowley Regis B65 . . . . . 63 B2
  Stourbridge DY8 . . . . . . 81 A7
Churchill Gdns DY3. . . . 50 C7
Churchill Ho ⊡ CV32. . . 161 F8
Churchill La DY10. . . . . . 98 B3
Churchill Par B75. . . . . . 47 A5
Churchill Pl B33 . . . . 69 B1
Churchill Rd
  Birmingham B9 . . . . 67 F3
  Halesowen B63 . . . . 82 F2
  Shenstone WS14 . . . . . . 18 A5
  Sutton Coldfield, Falcon Lodge
    B75 . . . . 47 A5
  Sutton Coldfield, New Oscott
    B73. . . . . 45 C3
  Upper Catshill B61. . . . 121 A1
  Walsall WS2. . . . . 27 E3
  Churchill Sch Ctr ⊡ DY2. 51 D1
Churchill Wlk ⊡ WS2. . . 42 A8
Church La
  Ash Green CV7 . . . . 95 E7
  Aston Flanville LE10 . . . 76 F1
  Berkswell CV7 . . . . 110 C3
  Bickenhill B92 . . . . 90 E2
  Birmingham, Aston B6. . 67 A8
  Birmingham, Handsworth
    B20. . . . . 55 A2
  Birmingham, Kitt's Green
    B33 . . . . 69 A3
  Bromsgrove B61 . . . . . . 136 F2
  Corley CV7 . . . . 94 B7
  Coventry, Middle Stoke
    CV2 . . . . 114 B3
  Coventry, Upper Eastern Green
    CV5. . . . . 111 C5
  Cubbington CV32. . . . . 157 E5
  Curdworth B76 . . . . 59 B6
  Halesowen B63 . . . . 83 B4
  Hammerwich WS7 . . . . . 7 D3
  Lapworth B94 . . . . 143 E3
  Leek Wootton CV35 . . . 155 F6
  Meriden CV7 . . . . 110 E8
  Middleton B78. . . . . 34 C1
  Nuneaton CV10 . . . . 73 C7
  Radford Semele CV31. . 162 E6
  Royal Leamington Spa
    CV32 . . . . 157 A3
  Shuttington B79 . . . . . . 22 E7
  Stoneleigh CV8 . . . . . . 149 C6
  Stonnall WS9 . . . . 16 E4
  Tamworth B79 . . . . 21 B5
  Trysull WV5 . . . . 37 B7
  West Bromwich B71 . . . 53 C6
  Whitnash CV31 . . . . . . 162 B4
  Wishaw B76. . . . . 48 A2
  Wolverhampton WV2. . . 163 D2
  Church Lane Ind Est B71. 53 C6
Church Mews
  Tipton DY4. . . . . 51 E8
  Walsall WS3. . . . . 28 E8
Church Moat Way ⊡ WS3. 28 B8
Church of the Ascension CE
  Prim Sch B96. . . . . 60 C8
Churchover Cl B76. . . . . 57 D6
Church Park Cl CV6 . . . . 94 F1

Church Pl
Birmingham B12 . . . . **86** F5
Walsall WS3. . . . . **28** D8
Church Rd
Astwood Bank B96 . . . . . . **158** E2
Baginton CV8. . . . . **133** F2
Belbroughton DY9 . . . . **119** D6
Birmingham, Aston B6. . . . . . **67** B7
Birmingham, Edgbaston B15 **86** A7
Birmingham, Erdington B24. **57** A4
Birmingham, Moseley B13. . **87** A3
Birmingham, Northfield B31. . . . . **103** A4
Birmingham, Perry Barr B42. . . . . **55** D5
Birmingham, Sheldon B26 . . **89** C6
Birmingham, South Yardley B25. . . . . **88** E8
Birmingham, Stechford B33. **68** F2
Bromsgrove B61 . . . . **136** F2
Brownhills WS8 . . . . **15** F7
Burntwood WS7. . . . . **7** D7
Catshill B61 . . . . **136** F8
Coseley, Daisy Bank WV14 . **40** D1
Dodford B61 . . . . **136** A7
Dudley, Netherton DY2 . . . . **62** C4
Halesowen B63 . . . . **82** C7
Hartshill CV10 . . . . **72** B8
Huntington WS11. . . . . **1** A2
Norton Canes WS11 . . . . **5** E4
Nuneaton, Stockingford CV10 . . . . **72** C3
Perton WV6 . . . . **23** E4
Redditch, St George's B97. **153** E4
Redditch, Webheath B97 . . **152** F2
Rowley Regis B65 . . . . **63** C3
Ryton-on-D CV8 . . . . **135** B2
Shenstone WS14 . . . . **17** F5
Shilton CV7 . . . . **97** E5
Smethwick B67 . . . . **65** A4
Solihull B90 . . . . **106** B2
Stonnall WS9 . . . . **16** E3
Stourbridge DY8 . . . . **60** E2
Stourbridge, Lye DY9. . . . . . **81** E5
Stourbridge, Old Swinford DY8 . . . . **81** B3
Sutton Coldfield B73 . . . . . . **56** F8
Sutton Coldfield, Maney B72, B73 . . . . **46** B3
Tamworth B77 . . . . **35** C4
Walsall WS3. . . . . **15** A3
Willenhall WV12 . . . . **27** D6
Wolverhampton, Oxbarn WV3 . . . . **38** F7
Wolverhampton, Oxley WV10 . . . . **11** C1
Wolverhampton, Tettenhall Wood WV6 . . . . **24** B3
Wolverhampton, Tettenhall WV6 . . . . **24** E5
Wombourne WV5. . . . . **49** B7
Church Row B78. . . . . **34** B1
Church Row Cotts DY9 . . . **99** F3
Churchside Way WS9 . . . . **16** B2
Church Sq 4 B69. . . . . **64** A7
Church St
Bilston WV14. . . . . **40** D5
Birmingham B3 . . . . **164** B3
Birmingham B35 . . . . **58** B4
Birmingham, Lozells B19. . . **66** C7
Brierley Hill, Barrow Hill DY5. . . . . **61** D7
Brierley Hill, Quarry Bank DY5. . . . . **61** F1
Brierley Hill, Silver End DY5 **61** C2
Bromsgrove B61 . . . . **136** F2
Brownhills WS8 . . . . **15** E6
Bulkington CV12 . . . . **79** C2
Burntwood WS7. . . . . **6** E5
Cannock, Bridgtown WS11 . . **4** D6
Cannock, Chadsmoor WS11. . **2** A4
Cannock WS11. . . . . **1** E1
Coventry CV1. . . . . **165** C4
Cradley Heath B64. . . . . **62** E1
Darlaston, Woods Bank WS10 . . . . **41** C4
Darlaston WS10. . . . . **41** D6
Dudley, Gornalwood DY3. . . **50** D3
Dudley, Kate's Hill DY2 . . . . **62** C8
Halesowen B62 . . . . **63** D1
Hinckley LE10 . . . . **76** A5
Kidderminster DY10. . . . . . **116** E6
Lichfield WS13, WS14 . . . . . . **9** C8
Nuneaton CV11 . . . . **73** C4
Oldbury B69. . . . . **64** A8
Royal Leamington Spa CV31. . . . . **162** A7
Stourbridge DY8 . . . . **81** A5
Studley B80 . . . . **159** E3
Tamworth B79. . . . . **21** B5
Tipton DY4 . . . . **52** A2
Walsall, Blakenall Green WS3 . . . . **28** B8
Walsall WS1. . . . . **28** F1
Warwick CV34 . . . . **160** E6
Wednesfield WV11 . . . . **26** C5
West Bromwich B70 . . . . **53** C4
West Hagley DY9. . . . . **99** A5
Willenhall WV13 . . . . **27** B2
Wolverhampton, Heath Town WV10 . . . . **26** A4
Wolverhampton WV2. . . . . **163** B2
Churchstone Cl B61. . . . . **136** F8
Church Terr
Cubbington CV32. . . . . **157** E5
Church Terr *continued*
1 Royal Leamington Spa CV31. . . . . **162** A7
Sutton Coldfield B75 . . . . . . **32** C3
Church Vale
Birmingham B20 . . . . **55** B1
Norton Canes WS11 . . . . **5** E4
West Bromwich B71 . . . . **53** D5
Church Vale Mews B71. . . . **53** D5
Church View
Aldridge WS9. . . . . **30** B6
Birmingham B11 . . . . **87** C6
Brownhills WS9 . . . . **15** F3
Dudley DY3 . . . . **50** D3
Tamworth B77 . . . . **35** F7
Wythall B47 . . . . **124** E2
Church View Cl WS3 . . . . . **28** D8
Church View Dr B64 . . . . . **62** F1
Churchward Cl DY8 . . . . . . **81** B6
Churchward Gr WV5 . . . . . **49** A8
Church Way
Bedworth CV12 . . . . **78** B2
Walsall WS4. . . . . **15** C2
Churchwell Ct
Halesowen B63 . . . . **83** B2
Wombourne WV5. . . . . **49** A6
Churchwell Gdns B71 . . . . **53** E6
Church Wlk
Allesley CV5. . . . . **112** C6
Birmingham B8 . . . . **68** A6
Hinckley LE10 . . . . **75** D8
Kidderminster DY11. . . . . . . **116** C6
Rowley Regis B65 . . . . **63** C4
1 Royal Leamington Spa CV31. . . . . **161** F7
Wolverhampton, Oxbarn WV3 . . . . **38** F7
Wolverhampton, Tettenhall WV6 . . . . **24** E5
Churchyard Rd DY4 . . . . . . **52** B5
Churnet Gr WV6 . . . . **23** F4
Churn Hill Rd WS9 . . . . . . **30** B4
Churns Hill La DY3 . . . . . . **49** B3
Churston Cl WS3. . . . . **14** A3
Chylds Ct CV5 . . . . **112** A5
Cicero App CV34. . . . . . . **161** E2
Cider Ave DY5 . . . . **81** E8
Cinder Bank DY2. . . . . **62** C6
Cinder Bank Island DY2 . . **62** B7
CINDER HILL. **39** F1
Cinder Rd
Burntwood WS7. . . . . **6** E7
Dudley DY3 . . . . **50** B2
Cinder Way 2 WS10 . . . . . **41** E3
Cinquefoil Leasow 5 DY4 . . . . **52** C6
Circle The
Birmingham B17 . . . . **85** C6
Nuneaton CV10 . . . . **72** F4
Circuit Cl WV13. . . . . **27** B3
Circular Rd B27. . . . . **88** C2
Circus Ave B37 . . . . **70** C2
Cirencester Cl B60. . . . . . **137** B2
City Arc
1 Birmingham B2. . . . . . . **164** C2
Coventry CV1. . . . . **165** B2
1 Lichfield WS13 . . . . **9** B7
City Coll Birmingham (Bordesley Green Campus) B9. . . . . **68** A2
City Coll Birmingham (City Academy Aston) B6. . . . . . **66** E8
City Coll Birmingham (City Academy Golden Hillock) B10. . . . . **87** D7
City Coll Birmingham (City Academy Saltley) B8. . . . **67** E3
City Coll Birmingham (City Technology Campus) B25. . . . . **88** B6
City Coll Birmingham (Fordrough Campus) B9. . . . . **67** E2
City Coll Birmingham (Handsworth Campus) 1 B21. . . . . **65** F8
City Coll Birmingham (Muath Ctr) B11. . . . . **87** A7
City Coll Birmingham (North West Skills Campus) B18. . . . . **66** A3
City Coll Birmingham (St George's Sixth Form Ctr) B19. . . . . **164** B5
City Coll Coventry CV1 . . **165** C3
City Est B64 . . . . **82** D8
City Hospl B18. . . . . **65** F4
City of Wolverhampton Coll (Metro One Campus) WV1 . . . . **163** C2
City of Wolverhampton Coll (Paget Road Campus) WV6 . . . . **24** E3
City of Wolverhampton Coll (Wellington Road Campus) WV14 . . . . **40** B7
City Rd
Birmingham B16 . . . . **65** C2
Oldbury B69. . . . . **63** C8
City Road Prim Sch B16. . **65** D3
City Trad Est B16. . . . . **66** A3
City View
Birmingham, Saltley B8 . . . . **67** D4
Birmingham, Stockland Green B23. . . . . **56** D3
Civic Cl B1 . . . . **66** C2
Cladsworth Ho 1 B97. . . . **153** A4
Claerwen Gr B31. . . . . **102** E5
Claines Cres DY10 . . . . . . **117** B5
Claines Rd
Birmingham B31 . . . . **103** C4
Halesowen B63 . . . . **82** D5
Claire Ct B26 . . . . **89** C7
Clairvaux Gdns B91 . . . . . **106** D5
Clancey Way B63 . . . . **82** E6
Clandon Cl B14 . . . . **104** C2
Clanfield Ave WV11 . . . . . . **26** F7
Clapgate Gdns WV14 . . . . . **40** A3
Clapgate La B32 . . . . **84** C2
Clapham Sq CV31. . . . . . . **162** B7
Clapham St CV31. . . . . . . **162** B6
Clapham Terr CV31 . . . . . **162** B7
Clapham Terrace Cty Prim Sch 10 CV31. . . . . **162** B7
Clapton Gr B44 . . . . **45** B1
Clarage Ho B62. . . . . **83** D8
Clara St CV2. . . . . **114** A2
Clare Ave WV11. . . . . **12** F1
Clare Cl CV32. . . . . **157** C2
Clare Cres WV14. . . . . **39** F2
Clare Ct B90. . . . . **105** D2
Clare Dr B15. . . . . **85** F8
CLAREGATE **24** E6
Claregate Prim Sch WV6 . **24** F7
Clarel Ave B8. . . . . **67** C3
Claremont Cl CV12. . . . . . . **79** B4
Claremont Cotts DY3. . . . . **50** E8
Claremont Ct 2 B64 . . . . . **62** E1
Claremont Mews WV3. . . . . **39** A7
Claremont Pl 1 B18 . . . . . **66** A5
Claremont Rd
Birmingham, Hockley B18 . . **66** B6
Birmingham, Sparkbrook B11. . . . . **87** B7
Royal Leamington Spa CV31. . . . . **161** F6
Sedgley DY3. . . . . **50** E8
Smethwick B66 . . . . **65** B4
Tamworth B79 . . . . **21** A8
Wolverhampton WV3. . . . . . **39** B7
Claremont St
Bilston WV14. . . . . **40** C6
Cradley Heath B64. . . . . **62** E1
Claremont Way B63. . . . . . **83** A3
Claremont Wlk CV5 . . . . . **112** C6
Clarence Ave B21. . . . . **65** C8
Clarence Ct
5 Hinckley LE10. . . . . **75** E8
Oldbury B68. . . . . **64** C2
Clarence Gdns B74. . . . . . . **31** F3
Clarence Gr B90 . . . . **106** B4
Clarence Ho 7 CV32. . . . . **156** F1
Clarence Mews 1 B17 . . . **85** D6
Clarence Rd
Bilston WV14. . . . . **40** F7
Birmingham B17 . . . . **85** D6
Birmingham, Gravelly Hill B23. . . . . **56** D3
Birmingham, Handsworth B21. . . . . **65** C8
Birmingham, King's Heath B13. . . . . **87** A1
Birmingham, Sparkhill B11 . **87** D4
Dudley DY2 . . . . **62** D6
Hinckley LE10 . . . . **75** E8
Sutton Coldfield B74 . . . . . . **31** F4
Wolverhampton WV1. . . . . **163** B3
Clarence St
5 Coventry CV1 . . . . **113** E4
Dudley DY3 . . . . **50** E5
Kidderminster DY10. . . . . . **116** F6
Nuneaton CV11 . . . . **73** A4
Royal Leamington Spa CV31. . . . . **162** A6
Wolverhampton WV1. . . . . **163** B3
Clarence Terr 6 CV32. . . . **156** F1
Clarenden Pl B17 . . . . **85** C5
Clarendon Ave CV32 . . . . **156** F1
Clarendon Cl B97 . . . . . . **153** B5
Clarendon Cres CV32. . . . **156** E1
Clarendon Dr DY4. . . . . **52** D8
Clarendon Gdns 3 B20 . . . **55** D1
Clarendon Ho LE10. . . . . . . **75** B7
Clarendon Pl
Birmingham B62 . . . . **84** A6
Royal Leamington Spa CV32. . . . . **156** E1
Walsall WS3. . . . . **14** F3
Clarendon Rd
Birmingham B16 . . . . **65** E1
Hinckley LE10 . . . . **75** C7
Kenilworth CV8 . . . . **148** A3
Smethwick B67 . . . . **64** F4
Sutton Coldfield B75 . . . . . . **32** C3
Walsall WS4. . . . . **15** C2
Clarendon Sq CV32 . . . . . **156** F1
Clarendon St
Coventry CV5. . . . . **112** F1
Royal Leamington Spa CV32. . . . . **157** A1
Walsall WS3. . . . . **14** B1
Wolverhampton WV3. . . . . . **25** A2
Clare Rd
Walsall WS3. . . . . **29** A6
Wolverhampton WV10. . . . . . **25** E7
Clare's Ct DY11 . . . . **116** C6
Clarewell Ave B91 . . . . . . **127** B8
Clare Witnell Cl DY11 . . . **116** B8
Clarion Way WS11 . . . . **1** E5
Clarke Ho WS3 . . . . **14** B1
Clarke's Ave CV8. . . . . . . **148** A3
Clarkes Gr DY4 . . . . **52** C6
Clarkes Ind Est B73 . . . . . . **46** A2
Clarkes La WV13 . . . . **27** C3
Clarke's La B71. . . . . **53** C7
Clarke St 1 B97 . . . . **153** E3
Clark Rd WV3. . . . . **24** F2
Clarks La B90. . . . . **126** A6
Clarksland Gr B37 . . . . **90** A8
Clarkson Cl CV11 . . . . **73** D4
Clarkson Dr CV31 . . . . . . **162** A4
Clarkson Place Ind Est DY5. . . . . **81** E7
Clarkson Rd WS10 . . . . **42** A3
Clark St
Birmingham B16 . . . . **65** F2
Coventry CV6. . . . . **96** A1
Stourbridge DY8 . . . . **80** E4
Clarry Dr B74 . . . . **45** F8
Clary Gr WS5 . . . . **43** A3
Clatterbach La DY9 . . . . . **100** A4
Claughton Ct DY11. . . . . . **116** C5
Claughton Rd DY2 . . . . **51** D1
Claughton Road N 8 DY2 **51** D1
Claughton St DY11. . . . . . **116** C5
Clausen Cl B43 . . . . **44** E4
Clavedon Cl B31 . . . . **102** E7
Claverdon Cl
Brownhills WS8 . . . . **16** A8
Redditch B97 . . . . **158** D4
Solihull B91. . . . . **106** E3
Claverdon Dr
Birmingham B43 . . . . **54** D7
Sutton Coldfield B74 . . . . . . **31** B4
Claverdon Gdns B27 . . . . . **88** B5
Claverdon Ho
Birmingham B13 . . . . **105** A7
Warwick CV34 . . . . **161** B8
Claverdon Rd CV5. . . . . . . **112** B3
Claverley Ct 6 DY1 . . . . . . **51** B1
Claverley Dr WV4 . . . . **38** D5
Clay Ave CV11 . . . . **73** F7
Claybrook Dr B98. . . . . . . **159** F7
Claybrook St B5 . . . . **164** C1
Claycroft Pl DY9 . . . . **81** E5
Claycroft Terr DY1 . . . . **51** B6
Claydon Gr 3 B14 . . . . . . **105** A3
Claydon Rd DY6. . . . . **49** C1
Clay Dr B32. . . . . **84** A5
Claygate Rd WS12 . . . . **2** E3
CLAYHANGER **15** D6
Clayhanger La WS8 . . . . . . **15** D6
Clayhanger Rd WS8 . . . . . . **15** F6
Clay La
Birmingham B26 . . . . **88** E5
Coventry CV2. . . . . **114** A4
Harvest Hill CV5 . . . . **93** E3
Oldbury B69. . . . . **64** A4
Claymore B77 . . . . **35** E7
Claypit Cl B70 . . . . **53** A3
Claypit La
Fairfield B61 . . . . **120** E1
West Bromwich B70 . . . . **53** A4
Clay Pit La
Lichfield WS14. . . . . **8** F3
Solihull B90. . . . . **126** A5
Claypitts Bvd CV34 . . . . . **160** B3
Clayton Cl WV2. . . . . **39** C7
Clayton Dr
Birmingham B36 . . . . **69** C7
Bromsgrove B60 . . . . **151** B7
Clayton Gdns B45. . . . . . . **122** A2
Clayton Ho 3 B16 . . . . **65** F1
Clayton Rd
Birmingham B8 . . . . **67** D5
Coventry CV6. . . . . **112** E5
Dudley WV14 . . . . **51** B7
Clayton Wlk B35 . . . . **58** A2
Clear View DY6 . . . . **60** B6
Clearwater Ind Est WV2 . . **40** A7
Clearwell Gdns DY1 . . . . . **50** F3
Clearwell Rd B98 . . . . **154** C3
Cleasby B77 . . . . **22** C1
Cleaveland Mews 2 WS13 **3** A1
Cleaver Gdns CV10. . . . . . . **73** C6
Clee Ave DY11 . . . . **116** C2
Clee Hill Dr WV3. . . . . **24** A1
Clee Hill Rd DY3 . . . . **50** D4
Clee Rd
Birmingham B31 . . . . **123** A8
Dudley DY2 . . . . **62** A7
Oldbury B68. . . . . **64** C4
Stourbridge DY8 . . . . **81** A6
Cleeton St WS12 . . . . **2** D1
Cleeve B77 . . . . **21** D3
Cleeve Cl B98. . . . . **154** D5
Cleeve Dr B74 . . . . **31** F6
Cleeve Ho B24. . . . . **57** A2
Cleeve Rd
Birmingham B14 . . . . **105** C4
Walsall WS3. . . . . **13** F3
Cleeves Ave CV34 . . . . . . **161** D6
Cleeve Way WS3. . . . . **13** F3
Clee View Mdw DY3. . . . . . **39** D2
Clegg Rd WS7 . . . . **7** E7
Clematis B77 . . . . **21** F3
Clematis Dr WV9. . . . . **10** F3
Clem Attlee Ct WV13 . . . . **40** D8
Clemens St CV31. . . . . **162** A7
Clement Ho CV8 . . . . **148** A5
Clement Pl WV14 . . . . **40** D7
Clement Rd
Bilston WV14. . . . . **40** D7
Halesowen B62 . . . . **63** D1
Clements Cl
Kenilworth CV8 . . . . **148** A5
Oldbury B69. . . . . **63** F4
Clements Rd B25 . . . . **88** D8
Clements St CV2. . . . . **114** A3
Clement St
Birmingham B1 . . . . **66** B3
Nuneaton CV11 . . . . **73** B3
Walsall WS2. . . . . **28** D1
Clennon Rise CV2 . . . . . . **114** D8
Clensmore St DY10. . . . . . **116** D7
CLENT **99** F3
Clent Ave
Kidderminster DY11. . . . . . **116** B1
Redditch B97 . . . . **158** D7
Clent Cott DY9. . . . . **99** F3
Clent Ct 5 DY1 . . . . **51** B1
Clent Dr
Hagley DY9 . . . . **99** D6
Nuneaton CV10 . . . . **72** B3
Clent Hill Dr B65. . . . . **63** A5
Clent Hills Ctry Pk* DY9. . . . . **100** A4
Clent Ho B63 . . . . **83** A2
Clent Parochial Prim Sch DY9. . . . . **99** F2
Clent Rd
Birmingham B45 . . . . **121** E8
Birmingham, Handsworth B21. . . . . **54** D1
Oldbury B68. . . . . **64** C1
Stourbridge DY8 . . . . **81** A6
Clent View B66 . . . . **65** B3
Clent View Rd
Birmingham B32 . . . . **84** A1
Halesowen B63 . . . . **82** C5
Stourbridge DY8 . . . . **80** C2
Clent Villas B12. . . . . **87** B4
Clent Way B32. . . . . **102** A8
Cleobury Cl B97 . . . . **153** B5
Cleobury La B94 . . . . **126** A3
Cleopatra Gr CV34 . . . . . **161** E4
Cleton St DY4. . . . . **52** B3
Cleton Street Bsns Pk DY4. . . . . **52** B3
Clevedon Ave B36. . . . . **69** E8
Clevedon Rd B12 . . . . **86** E6
Cleveland Cl
Willenhall WV13 . . . . **26** D1
Wolverhampton WV11. . . . . . **12** F1
Cleveland Ct
16 Birmingham B13. . . . . . . **87** B2
1 Royal Leamington Spa CV32. . . . . **156** F2
Wolverhampton WV2. . . . . **163** B2
Cleveland Dr
Barnt Green B45 . . . . **122** A2
Cannock WS11. . . . . **2** B4
Cleveland Pas WV1 . . . . . **163** B2
Cleveland Rd
Bulkington CV12 . . . . **79** B3
Coventry CV2. . . . . **114** A4
Hinckley LE10 . . . . **75** C8
Wolverhampton WV2. . . . . **163** C2
Cleveland St
14 Dudley, New Dock DY1. . **51** B1
4 Dudley, Old Dock DY1. . . **62** B8
Stourbridge DY8 . . . . **80** E4
Wolverhampton WV1. . . . . **163** B2
Cleveland Twr B1. . . . . . . **164** B1
Cleveley Dr CV10. . . . . **72** D7
Cleves Cres WS6. . . . . **4** D1
Cleves Dr B45 . . . . **121** E7
Cleves Rd B45 . . . . **121** E8
Clewley Dr WV9 . . . . **11** B3
Clewley Gr B32 . . . . **84** B5
Clews Cl WS1. . . . . **42** E7
Clewshaw La B38 . . . . **124** C4
Clews Rd B98. . . . . **158** F7
Cley Cl B5. . . . . **86** D6
Cley Rd WS11. . . . . **5** B5
Clifden Gr CV8. . . . . **148** C6
CLIFF **35** C1
Cliff Dr DY4 . . . . **52** D8
Cliffe Ct CV32. . . . . **156** D1
Cliffe Dr B33 . . . . **69** C3
Cliffe Rd CV32 . . . . **156** D1
Cliffe Way CV34. . . . . **161** A8
Cliff Hall La B78 . . . . **35** C1
CLIFF HILL. **160** F8
Clifford Bridge Prim Sch CV3. . . . . **115** A3
Clifford Bridge Rd CV3 . . **114** F4
Clifford Cl B77. . . . . **21** F3
Clifford Rd
Bentley Heath B93. . . . . . . **127** F4
Birmingham B11 . . . . **87** F3
Smethwick B67 . . . . **64** F1
West Bromwich B70 . . . . **53** B2
Clifford St
Birmingham B19 . . . . **66** D7
3 Dudley DY1. . . . . **62** B8
Tamworth B77 . . . . **21** E3
Wolverhampton WV6. . . . . . . **25** A3
Clifford Wlk B19. . . . . **66** D7
Cliff Pool Nature Reserve* B78. . . . . **35** B2
Cliff Rock Rd B45 . . . . . . **122** B7
Clift Cl WV12 . . . . **27** C6
Clifton Ave
Aldridge WS9. . . . . **16** C1
Brownhills WS8 . . . . **15** D7
Cannock WS11. . . . . **4** C7
Tamworth B79. . . . . **21** A7
Clifton Cl
Birmingham B6 . . . . **66** F7
Oldbury B69. . . . . **64** A4
Redditch B98. . . . . **159** E8
Clifton Cres B91 . . . . **106** F1
Clifton Ct
Hinckley LE10 . . . . **71** B1
5 Royal Leamington Spa CV31. . . . . **162** B7
Clifton Dr B73 . . . . **46** B6
Clifton Gdns WV8. . . . . **10** C3
Clifton Gn B28. . . . . **106** A5
Clifton La B71 . . . . **53** E8
Clifton Prim Sch B12. . . . . **87** A5

Clifton Rd
Birmingham, Aston B6 66 F7
Birmingham, Balsall Heath B12 87 A5
Birmingham, Castle Bromwich B36 69 E8
Halesowen B62 83 E8
Kidderminster DY11 116 A1
Nuneaton CV10 72 F4
Smethwick B67 64 F4
Sutton Coldfield B73 46 B5
Wolverhampton WV6 24 D5
Clifton Road Ind Est B12 86 F5
Clifton St
Coventry CV1 165 D4
Cradley Heath B64 62 F1
Dudley WV14 51 A8
Sedgley WV14 39 F1
Stourbridge DY8 80 F4
Wolverhampton WV3 25 B2
Clifton Terr B23 56 F4
Clifton Way LE10 71 A1
Clinic Dr
Nuneaton CV11 73 C3
Stourbridge DY9 81 E5
Clinton Ave
Hampton Magna CV35 160 A7
Kenilworth CV8 147 D6
Clinton Cres WS7 7 B8
Clinton Gr B90 106 E1
Clinton La CV8 147 D6
Clinton Prim Sch CV8 147 E3
Clinton Rd
Bilston WV14 41 A7
Coleshill B46 70 F6
Coventry CV6 95 F2
Solihull B90 106 E1
Clinton St
Birmingham B18 65 E5
2 Royal Leamington Spa CV31 162 A7
Clipper View B16 65 E1
Clipstone Rd CV6 112 E6
Clipston Rd B8 67 F4
Clissold Cl B12 86 E7
Clissold Pas B18 66 A4
Clissold St B18 66 A4
Clive Cl B75 32 D2
Cliveden Ave
Aldridge WS9 16 B1
Birmingham B42 55 D4
Cliveden Coppice B74 31 F1
Cliveden Wlk CV11 78 E8
Clivedon Way B62 83 B7
Cliveland St B19 164 C4
Clive Pas B4 164 B4
Clive Rd
Balsall Common CV7 130 C5
Birmingham B32 84 D7
Bromsgrove B60 151 B8
Burntwood WS7 7 A7
Redditch B97 153 D5
Clive St B71 53 C5
Clivesway LE10 71 C2
Clockfields Dr DY5 61 A1
Clock La B92 90 D2
Clockmill Ave WS3 14 E3
Clockmill Pl WS3 14 F3
Clockmill Rd WS3 14 E3
Clock Tower View DY8 60 E3
Clodeshall Rd B8 67 E4
Cloister Croft CV2 114 F6
Cloister Crofts CV32 156 F3
Cloister Dr B62 83 D3
Cloisters The
Royal Leamington Spa CV32 156 F3
Studley B80 159 D4
Walsall WS4 28 F3
Cloister Way CV32 156 F3
Clonmel Rd B30 104 A6
Clopton Cres B37 70 C4
Clopton Rd B33 89 C8
Closers Bsns Ctr CV11 73 D2
Close The
Birmingham B17 84 F7
Birmingham, Griffin's Hill B29 103 D8
Brandon CV8 135 F5
Dudley DY3 50 C4
Halesowen B63 82 D6
Hollywood B47 125 A5
Hunnington B62 101 A7
Kenilworth CV8 148 A6
Lichfield WS13 9 B8
Solihull B92 106 F8
Wednesbury WS10 41 E3
Whitnash CV31 162 A5
Clothier Gdns WV13 27 A3
Clothier St WV13 27 A3
Cloudbridge Dr B92 107 F7
Cloud Gn CV4 132 D5
Cloudsley Gr B92 88 F3
Clovelly Gdns CV2 114 C5
Clovelly Rd CV2 114 B5
Clovelly Way CV11 73 E5
Clover Ave B37 70 D2
Clover Ct B38 103 D2
Cloverdale
Perton WV6 23 D4
Stoke Prior B60 150 C3
Cloverdale Cl CV6 95 B4
Clover Dr B32 84 D2
Cloverfield LE10 71 C3
Clover Hill WS5 43 E8
Clover La DY6 60 B7
Clover Lea Sq B8 68 A6
Clover Ley WV10 25 F3
Clover Mdws WS12 2 C1
Clover Park Trad Est LE10 71 B3
Clover Piece 6 DY4 52 C6
Clover Rd B29 103 A7
Clover Ridge WS6 4 C3
Clover Way CV12 77 D2
Cloweswood La B94 141 F8
Club Cotts WV10 11 C6
Club La WV10 11 C6
Club Row DY3 50 E5
Club View B38 103 D2
Clunbury Croft B34 69 B5
Clunbury Rd B31 123 A8
Clun Cl B69 52 A1
Clunes Ave CV11 73 E6
Clun Rd B31 102 F6
Clusters The DY9 81 E5
Clyde Ave B62 83 E8
Clyde Ct 12 B73 46 B5
Clyde Mews DY5 61 B6
Clyde Rd
Bulkington CV12 79 A2
Dorridge B93 128 A2
Clydesdale B26 89 B5
Clydesdale Rd
Birmingham B32 84 B6
Brownhills WS8 15 E6
Clydesdale Twr B1 164 B1
Clyde St
Birmingham B12 67 A1
Cradley Heath B64 62 E1
Clyde Twr 3 B19 66 D7
CMT Trad Est B69 64 A8
Coach Cotts B45 138 D8
Coach House Mews 2 CV34 160 F7
Coach House Rise B77 35 F7
Coalash La B60 151 C2
Coalbourne Gdns B63 82 C5
Coalbourn La DY8 80 F7
Coalbourn Way DY5 61 A3
Coal Haulage Rd WS12 5 F8
Coalheath La WS4 29 C8
Coalmeadow Cl WS3 13 F3
COALPIT FIELD 78 D1
Coalpit Fields Rd CV12 78 C1
COAL POOL 28 F5
Coal Pool La WS3 28 F5
Coalpool Pl WS3 28 F6
Coalport Rd WV1 26 A1
Coalway Ave
Birmingham B26 89 C4
Wolverhampton WV3 39 A6
Coalway Gdns WV3 38 D7
Coalway Rd
Walsall WS3 28 A8
Wolverhampton WV3 38 E6
Coates Rd DY10 117 B7
Coat of Arms Bridge Rd CV3 133 A6
Coatsgate Wlk WV8 10 F1
Cobb Cl CV2 113 F4
Cobbett Rd WS7 6 D7
Cobbles The B72 57 C7
Cobble Wlk B18 66 A5
Cobbs Engine Ho & Chy* B65 62 E5
Cobbs Rd CV8 147 D6
Cobbs Wlk B65 62 F5
Cobden Ave CV31 162 C5
Cobden Cl
Cannock WS12 2 C7
Darlaston WS10 41 F6
Tipton DY4 51 F8
Cobden Gdns B12 86 E6
Cobden St
Coventry CV6 113 E5
Darlaston WS10 41 F6
Kidderminster DY11 116 D5
Stourbridge DY8 80 E5
Walsall WS1 42 D7
Cobham Bsns Ctr B9 67 D2
Cobham Cl
Birmingham B35 57 F3
Bromsgrove B60 150 F7
Cobham Court Mews DY9 99 D6
Cobham Gn 3 CV31 162 A4
Cobham Rd
Birmingham B9 67 D2
Halesowen B63 83 B4
Kidderminster DY10 116 E4
Stourbridge DY8 81 B2
Wednesbury WS10 42 E2
Cobia B77 35 D7
Cob La B30 103 C6
COBLEY HILL 138 E4
Cobley Hill B48 138 E4
Cobnall Rd B61 121 A2
Cobs Field B30 103 C6
Coburg Croft 4 DY4 52 C6
Coburg Ho CV5 112 E3
Coburn Dr B75 32 D2
Cochrane Cl
Stourbridge DY9 99 C8
2 Tipton DY4 52 C6
Cochrane Rd DY2 61 F5
Cockermouth Cl CV32 156 D2
Cock Hill La B45 121 F8
Cocksheds La B62 83 C8
COCKSHUT HILL 89 A8
Cockshut Hill B26 89 A8
Cockshut Hill Sports & Fitness Ctr B26 89 A8
Cockshut Hill Tech Coll B26 89 A8
Cockshutt La B61 136 D7
Cockshutts La WV2 39 D7
Cocksmead Croft B14 104 D5
Cocksmoor Ho B14 104 D7
Cocks Moors Wood L Ctr (& Liby) B14 104 F4
Cocksparrow La WS12, WS19 1 B5
Cocksparrow St CV34 160 D7
Cockspur St B78 36 E7
Cockthorpe Cl B17 84 F7
Cocton Cl WV6 23 E5
CODSALL 10 A3
Codsall Com High Sch WV8 10 A4
Codsall Coppice Nature Reserve* B64 82 E8
Codsall L Ctr WV8 10 A4
Codsall Mid Sch WV8 10 A3
Codsall Rd
Codsall WV8 10 C1
Cradley Heath B64 82 E8
Wolverhampton WV6 24 D7
Cofield Rd B73 45 F1
COFT COMMON 122 F6
Cofton Church La B45 122 D3
Cofton Cl B97 153 B5
Cofton Ct B45 122 D7
Cofton Gr B31 122 E6
Cofton Lake Rd B45 122 C3
Cofton Prim Sch B31 123 A6
Cofton Rd B31 123 B7
Cokeland Pl B64 82 D8
Colaton Cl WV10 25 E4
Colbourne Ct B33 68 D3
Colbourne Gr CV32 156 D2
Colbourne Rd
Tamworth B78 21 A2
Tipton DY4 52 A4
Colbrook B77 21 D1
Coldbath Rd B13 105 B8
Coldfield Dr B98 158 E7
Coldridge Cl WV8 10 F1
Coldstream Cl LE10 71 A1
Coldstream Dr DY8 60 E3
Coldstream Rd B76 57 E8
Cole Bank Rd B28 105 E8
Colebourne Prim Sch B33 68 E5
Colebourne Rd B13 105 D6
Colebridge Cres B46 70 F8
Colebridge Mews B46 70 F8
Colebrook Cl CV3 114 F2
Colebrook Croft B90 105 F2
Colebrook Rd
Birmingham B11 87 D5
Solihull B90 105 F2
Coleby Cl CV4 131 D7
COLE END 70 E8
Coleford Cl
Redditch B97 153 A2
Stourbridge DY8 60 C2
Coleford Dr B37 70 A2
Cole Gn B90 105 F2
COLEHALL 69 B5
Cole Hall La B34 69 A5
Colehill B79 21 B5
Colehurst Croft B90 126 F6
Coleman Rd WS10 42 A5
Coleman St
Coventry CV4 111 F3
Wolverhampton WV6 24 F4
Colemeadow Rd
Birmingham B13 105 B6
Coleshill B46 70 F7
Redditch B98 154 F6
Colenso Rd B16 65 D4
Coleraine Rd B42 55 A6
Coleridge Cl
Redditch B97 158 C8
Tamworth B79 21 A6
Walsall WS3 15 A5
Willenhall WV12 27 E7
Coleridge Dr WV6 23 E4
Coleridge Pas B4 164 C3
Coleridge Rd
Birmingham B43 54 E7
Coventry CV2 114 C3
Coleridge Rise DY3 50 A4
Colesbourne Ave B14 104 C2
Colesbourne Rd B92 89 B3
Coles Cres B71 53 B7
Colesden Wlk WV4 38 C6
COLESHILL 70 F6
Coleshill CE Prim Sch B46 70 F6
Coleshill Cl B97 158 C5
COLESHILL HEATH 90 C8
Coleshill Heath Prim Sch B37 70 C1
Coleshill Heath Rd
Birmingham B37 90 C7
Coleshill B37, B46 70 E2
Coleshill Ind Est B46 59 F2
Coleshill Parkway Sta B46 59 F2
Coleshill Rd
Birmingham, Hodgehill B34, B36 68 E6
Birmingham, Marston Green B37 90 B8
Curdworth B76 59 C5
Fazeley B78 35 A7
Hartshill CV10 72 A7
Sutton Coldfield B75 46 D5
Water Orton B46 59 B2
Coleshill St
Birmingham B5 164 D3
Fazeley B78 35 A8
Sutton Coldfield B72 46 C5
Coleside Ave B13 105 D7
Coles La
Sutton Coldfield B72 46 C3
West Bromwich B71 53 B7
Cole St DY2 62 E4
Cole Valley Rd B28 105 D6
Coleview Cres B33 69 E3
Coleville Rd B76 58 B6
Coley Cl LE10 75 D7
Coleys La B31 103 A2
Colgreave Ave B13 87 D2
Colina Cl CV3 134 C5
Colindale Rd B44 45 A3
Colinwood Cl WS6 4 F1
Colledge Rd CV6 95 D1
Colleen Ave B30 104 B3
College Cl WS10 42 A1
College Ct WV6 24 D4
College Dr
Birmingham B20 54 F2
Royal Leamington Spa CV32 156 F2
College Farm Dr B73 45 D1
College Gate B8 67 E4
College High Sch Com L Ctr The B44 56 B6
College Hill B73 46 B4
College La
Balsall Common CV8 129 E1
Hinckley LE10 71 E1
Tamworth B79 21 B5
College of Continuing Ed WS1 42 E7
College of Law The B18 164 A4
College Rd
Birmingham, Alum Rock B8 67 E4
Birmingham B32 84 A6
Birmingham, Handsworth B20 54 E2
Birmingham, Moseley B13 87 C2
Birmingham, Perry Common B44 56 B7
Bromsgrove B60 137 A2
Kidderminster DY10 116 E4
Stourbridge DY8 81 A4
Wolverhampton WV6 24 D4
College St
Birmingham B18 66 A4
Nuneaton CV10 73 C1
College View WV6 24 D3
College Wlk
Birmingham B29 103 D8
Bromsgrove B60 137 A2
Kidderminster DY10 116 E4
Collet Rd WV6 23 E5
Collets Brook B75 33 A2
Collett B77 22 A1
Collett Cl DY8 81 A6
Colletts Gr B37 69 F4
Collett Wlk 2 CV1 113 B3
Colley Ave WV10 25 F7
Colley Gate B63 82 C6
Colley La B63 82 C6
Colley Lane Prim Sch B63 82 C6
Colley Orch B63 82 C6
Colley St B70 53 D4
Collier Cl
Cheslyn Hay WS6 4 D2
Walsall WS8 15 C7
Colliers Cl WV12 27 B6
Colliers Fold DY5 61 B5
Colliers Way WS12 1 C6
Colliery Dr WS3 13 F3
Colliery La CV7 78 B1
Colliery Lane N CV7 78 B1
Colliery Rd
Smethwick B71 65 A8
West Bromwich B71 54 A1
Wolverhampton WV1 25 F2
Collindale Ct DY6 49 D1
Collingbourne Ave B36 68 E8
Collingdon Ave B26 89 C6
Collings Ho B16 66 A1
Collingtree Ct B92 88 D2
Colling Wlk B37 70 A5
Collingwood Dr B43 44 D3
Collingwood Ho B43 44 D3
Collingwood Rd
Birmingham, Brandwood End B30 104 D3
Coventry CV5 113 A2
Wolverhampton WV10 11 E2
Collins Cl B32 84 A5
Collins Dr 3 WS13 8 F6
Collins Gr CV4 132 D5
Collins Hill WS13 3 A2
Collinson Cl B98 154 A1
Collins Rd
Brownhills WS8 16 A5
Royal Leamington Spa CV34 161 D5
Wednesbury WS10 42 C3
Collins St
Walsall WS1 42 E7
West Bromwich B70 52 E3
Collis Cl B60 150 E7
Collis St DY8 80 F8
Collister Cl B90 106 B4
COLLYCROFT 78 A5
Colly Croft B37 69 F5
Collycroft Pl B27 88 B5
Colman Ave WV11 26 F6
Colman Cres B68 64 C2
Colman Hill B63 82 D5
Colman Hill Ave B63 82 D6
Colmers Com L Ctr B45 122 B8
Colmers Farm Inf Sch B45 122 B8
Colmers Farm Jun Sch B45 122 B8
Colmers Sch & Sports Coll B45 122 B8
Colmers Wlk B31 102 D1
Colmore Ave B14 104 D7
Colmore Circus Queensway B4 164 C3
Colmore Cres B13 87 B1
Colmore Dr B75 47 A5
Colmore Flats B19 164 B4
Colmore Gate B2 164 C3
Colmore Inf Sch B14 104 D7
Colmore Jun Sch B14 104 D7
Colmore Rd B14 104 D7
Colmore Row B3 164 B3
Coln Cl B31 102 F6
Colonial Ind Pk B64 82 D7
Colonial Rd B9 67 F2
Colshaw Rd DY8 80 E4
Colston Rd B24 57 B2
Colt Cl B74 44 E7
Coltham Rd WV12 27 D7
Coltishall Cl B35 57 F2
Coltman Cl WS14 9 D7
COLTON HILLS 39 B3
Colton Hills Sch WV4 39 B4
Colts Cl LE10 75 D4
Coltsfoot Cl WV11 26 E5
Coltsfoot View WS6 4 E2
Colts La B98 154 D3
Columbia Cl B5 86 D7
Columbia Gdns CV12 78 E2
Columbian Cres WS7 6 F8
Columbian Dr WS11 1 F3
Columbian Way WS11 1 F3
Columbine Cl 4 WS5 42 F3
Columbine Way CV12 77 E1
Columbus Ave DY5 61 F3
Colville Cl DY4 52 D8
Colville Rd B12 87 B5
Colville Wlk B12 87 B5
Colwall Rd DY3 50 D4
Colwall Wlk B27 88 D4
Colworth Rd B31 102 F4
Colyere Cl CV7 95 A6
Colyns Gr B33 68 F5
Combe Fields Rd CV3 115 F4
Comber Croft B13 105 D8
Comber Dr DY5 61 B6
Comberford Ct 5 WS10 42 A3
Comberford Dr WS10 42 D4
Comberford Rd B79 21 A7
COMBERTON 117 B5
Comberton Ave DY10 117 B5
Comberton Cl CV3 115 A2
Comberton Ct 5 DY10 117 A5
Comberton Gdns DY10 117 B5
Comberton Hill DY10 116 F5
Comberton Mans 4 DY10 117 A5
Comberton Park Rd DY10 117 B4
Comberton Pl DY10 116 F5
Comberton Prim Sch DY10 117 B4
Comberton Rd
Birmingham B26 89 B8
Kidderminster DY10 117 B4
Comberton Terr DY10 116 F5
Combine Cl B75 32 D4
Combrook Gn B34 69 D6
Comet Rd B26 90 C4
Comfrey Cl WS12 1 C5
Commainge Cl CV34 160 D7
Commercial Rd
Walsall WS2 28 A7
Wolverhampton WV1 25 E1
Commercial St B1 164 A1
Commissary Rd B26 90 A3
Commonfield Croft B8 67 D5
Common La
Birmingham, Sheldon B26 89 B6
Birmingham, Washwood Heath B8 67 F6
Cannock WS11 2 A3
Corley Moor CV7 93 E7
Kenilworth CV8 148 B7
Tamworth B79 21 B4
Common Lane Ind Est CV8 148 C7
Common Rd WV5 49 A6
Commonside
Brierley Hill DY5 61 C6
Brownhills WS8 16 A6
Walsall WS3 15 A2
Common View WS12 2 B7
Common Way CV2 114 A6
Common Wlk WS12 1 C5
Communication Row B15 66 C1
Compass Ct 4 CV1 113 B3
Compass Way B60 151 A7
COMPTON 24 D2
Compton Cl
Redditch B98 153 E2
Royal Leamington Spa CV32 157 C2
Solihull B91 106 D4
Compton Croft B37 70 D1
Compton Ct
Coventry CV6 95 D2
Dudley DY2 62 C6
1 Sutton Coldfield B74 31 F3

Compton Ct continued
7 Wolverhampton WV3 . . 25 A2
Compton Dr
Dudley DY2 . . . . 62 F8
Kingswinford DY6 . . . . . . 60 D5
Sutton Coldfield B74 . . . . 44 E7
Compton Gr
Halesowen B63 . . . . 82 C4
Kingswinford DY6 . . . . . . 60 D5
Compton Grange B64 . . . 82 C8
Compton Hill Dr WV3 . . . 24 D2
Compton Ho B33 . . . . 69 B2
Compton Pk WV6 . . . . . . 24 E5
Compton Rd
Birmingham B24 . . . . 56 E1
Coventry CV6 . . . . 95 D2
Cradley Heath B64 . . . . . 62 C1
Halesowen B62 . . . . 83 F5
Stourbridge DY9 . . . . 81 D2
Tamworth B79 . . . . 20 F7
Wolverhampton WV3 . . . 24 F2
Compton Road W WV3 . . 24 D2
Comrie Cl CV2 . . . . 114 F6
Comsey Rd B43 . . . . 44 B3
Comwall Cl WS3 . . . . 28 C7
Comyn St CV32 . . . . 157 B1
Conchar Cl B72 . . . . 46 C2
Conchar Rd B72 . . . . 46 C2
Concorde Dr B35 . . . . 57 F2
Concorde Rd B26 . . . . . . 90 C4
Condor Gr WS12 . . . . 2 C1
Condover Cl WS2 . . . . . . 27 D3
Condover Rd B31 . . . . . . 123 B8
Conduit Rd WS11 . . . . 6 A4
Conduit St WS13 . . . . 9 B8
Coneybury Wlk B76 . . . . 58 D5
Coneyford Rd B34 . . . . . 69 C6
Coney Gn DY8 . . . . 81 B5
Coney Green Dr B31 . . . 122 F8
Coneygree Rd DY4 . . . . . 52 A3
Coneygre Ind Est DY4 . . 51 F2
Congleton Cl
Coventry CV6 . . . . 95 E2
Redditch B97 . . . . 153 B5
Congreave CC CV34 . . . 155 F2
Congreve Wlk 9 CV12 . . 78 B3
Conifer Cl
Bedworth CV12 . . . . 78 C4
Brierley Hill DY5 . . . . 81 C8
Cannock WS12 . . . . 2 A8
Conifer Ct B13 . . . . 86 E2
Conifer Gr
Birmingham, Handsworth
B21 . . . . 65 E7
Birmingham, Northfield
B31 . . . . 103 B3
Conifer Gr
Bromsgrove B61 . . . . . . 136 F3
9 Royal Leamington Spa
CV31 . . . . 161 F5
Conifer Paddock
Coventry CV3 . . . . 114 E1
Halesowen B62 . . . . 83 E8
Conifer Rd B74 . . . . 44 E8
Conifers The CV8 . . . . . 148 B3
Coningsby Cl 3 CV31 . . 162 C6
Coningsby Dr DY11 . . . . 116 A8
Conington Gr B17 . . . . . . 85 A5
Conisbrough Keep CV1 . 165 C4
Coniston B77 . . . . 36 B7
Coniston Ave B92 . . . . . . 88 F4
Coniston Cl
Birmingham B28 . . . . . . 105 F7
Bromsgrove B60 . . . . . . 137 B1
Bulkington CV12 . . . . 79 C3
Coniston Cres B43 . . . . . 54 F7
Coniston Ct
Nuneaton CV11 . . . . 73 F7
2 Royal Leamington Spa
CV32 . . . . 156 D1
Coniston Dr
Coventry CV5 . . . . 111 D4
Kingswinford DY6 . . . . . . 60 B7
Coniston Grange CV8 . . 147 F5
Coniston Ho
8 Birmingham B17 . . . . . 85 D5
Kidderminster DY10 . . . . 116 E7
7 Oldbury B69 . . . . 63 D5
Coniston Rd
Birmingham B23 . . . . 56 D4
Coventry CV5 . . . . 112 F1
Royal Leamington Spa
CV32 . . . . 156 D1
Sutton Coldfield B74 . . . . 30 F3
Wolverhampton WV6 . . . 24 D8
Coniston Way
Cannock WS11 . . . . 1 E1
Nuneaton CV11 . . . . 73 F7
Connaught Ave
Kidderminster DY11 . . . . 116 C4
Wednesbury WS10 . . . . . 42 C3
Connaught Cl WS5 . . . . . 43 C7
Connaught Dr WV5 . . . . . 38 A1
Connaught Gdns B5. . . . . 86 E6
Connaught Ho 1 WV3 . . 25 A2
Connaught Rd
Bilston WV14 . . . . 40 F7
Bromsgrove B60 . . . . . . 137 C1
Wolverhampton WV1. . . . 25 A2
Connops Way DY9 . . . . . 81 F5
Connor Rd B71 . . . . 53 E8
Conolly Dr B45 . . . . 102 B1
Conrad Cl B11 . . . . 87 B6
Conrad Rd CV6 . . . . 113 A7
Consort Cres DY5 . . . . . . 61 C6

Consort Dr WS10 . . . . . . 41 C8
Consort Pl B79 . . . . 21 C5
Consort Rd B30 . . . . 104 A3
Constable Cl
Bedworth CV12 . . . . 78 A5
Birmingham B43 . . . . 44 D3
Constables The B68 . . . . 64 B2
Constance Ave B70 . . . . . 53 D1
Constance Cl CV12 . . . . . 95 F8
Constance Rd B5 . . . . 86 D5
Constantine La B46 . . . . . 59 F1
Constantine Way WV14 . . 41 A2
Constitution Hill
Birmingham B19 . . . . . . 164 B4
1 Dudley DY2 . . . . 62 D8
Constitution Hill E DY2 . . 62 D8
Consul Ho 6 LE10 . . . . . 71 D1
Convent Cl
Cannock WS11 . . . . 4 D8
Kenilworth CV8 . . . . 148 A7
Wolverhampton WV1. . . . 163 C2
Conway Ave
Birmingham B32 . . . . 84 B6
Coventry CV4 . . . . 131 D8
Oldbury B68 . . . . 64 B2
West Bromwich B71 . . . . 42 B1
Conway Cl
Dudley DY1 . . . . 51 C6
Kingswinford DY6 . . . . . . 60 F4
Solihull B90 . . . . 106 D1
Conway Cres WV12 . . . . 27 C7
Conway Dr B65 . . . . 63 B2
Conway Gr B43 . . . . 54 D7
Conway Ho WS3 . . . . 28 D6
Conway Prim Sch B11. . . 87 C6
Conway Rd
Birmingham B37 . . . . 70 B3
Birmingham, Sparkbrook
B11. . . . . 87 C6
Bromsgrove B60 . . . . . . 136 F1
Cannock WS11 . . . . 4 B8
Perton WV6 . . . . 23 F3
Royal Leamington Spa
CV32. . . . . 161 D8
Solihull B90 . . . . 106 D1
Conwy Cl
Nuneaton CV11 . . . . 73 D3
Walsall WS2 . . . . 28 A4
Conybere St B12 . . . . 86 F7
Conyworth Cl B27 . . . . . . 88 D4
Cook Ave DY2 . . . . 62 D7
Cook Cl
Knowle B93 . . . . 128 C6
Perton WV6 . . . . 23 E4
Cooke Cl
Coventry CV6 . . . . 96 A4
Warwick CV34 . . . . 155 F2
Cookes Croft B31 . . . . . 103 B2
Cookesley Cl B43 . . . . . . 44 D4
Cooke St WV2 . . . . 163 B1
Cookley Cl B63 . . . . 82 F2
Cookley Way B69 . . . . . . 63 E5
Cookley Wharf Ind Est
DY5. . . . . 61 B4
Cooknell Dr DY8 . . . . 60 E2
Cook Rd WS3 . . . . 14 D2
Cooksey La B44 . . . . 44 F4
Cooksey Rd B10 . . . . 87 C8
Cooks La B37 . . . . 70 A4
Cookspiece Wlk B33 . . . . 68 F3
Cook St
Birmingham B7 . . . . 67 C7
Coventry CV1 . . . . 165 B3
Darlaston WS10 . . . . 41 F6
Coombe Ave CV3 . . . . . 134 F7
Coombe Croft WV9 . . . . . 11 A3
Coombe Ct CV3 . . . . 115 A2
Coombe Ctry Pk* CV3 . . 115 E3
Coombe Dr
Binley Woods CV3 . . . . . 135 E7
Nuneaton CV10 . . . . 72 B4
Coombe Hill B64 . . . . 83 B8
Coombe Park Rd CV3 . . 114 F2
Coombe Pk B74. . . . . 45 F7
Coombe Rd
Birmingham B20 . . . . 55 E1
Solihull B90 . . . . 106 C2
Coombes La B33 . . . . . . 122 F7
Coombes Rd B62 . . . . . . 83 B7
Coombe St CV3 . . . . 114 B2
COOMBESWOOD 83 C7
Coombs Rd B62 . . . . 83 B7
Coombswood Way B65 . . 83 B8
Co-operative St CV2 . . . . 96 B3
Cooper Ave DY5 . . . . 61 A2
Cooper Cl
Bromsgrove B60 . . . . . . 150 E6
West Bromwich B70 . . . . 53 E2
Cooper & Jordan CE Prim
Sch WS9 . . . . 30 C6
COOPER'S BANK 50 C1
Cooper's Bank Rd DY5 . . 50 C1
Coopers Hill B48. . . . . . 138 E6
Cooper's La B62 . . . . 83 B7
Coopers Mdw CV7 . . . . . 94 F6
Coopers Rd B20 . . . . 55 A4
Cooper St
Nuneaton CV11 . . . . 73 D4
West Bromwich B70 . . . . 53 D3
Wolverhampton WV2 . . . 39 F8
Cope Arnolds Cl CV6 . . . 95 F4
Copeley Hill B23 . . . . 56 D1
Copenhagen Mews B73 . . 45 F1
Copes Cres WV10 . . . . . . 26 A7
Cope's Dr B79 . . . . 21 B7
Cope St
Birmingham B18 . . . . 66 A3
Coventry CV1 . . . . 165 C3

Cope St continued
Darlaston WS10. . . . . 41 E6
Walsall WS3. . . . . 28 C6
Cophall St DY4 . . . . 52 D5
Cophams Cl B92 . . . . 89 C2
Copland Pl CV4 . . . . 111 E1
Coplow Cl CV7 . . . . 130 A6
Coplow Cotts B16 . . . . . . 65 F3
Coplow St B16 . . . . 65 F3
Coplow Terr B16 . . . . 65 F3
Copnor Gr B26 . . . . 88 E6
Copperas St CV2 . . . . 96 B2
Copperbeech Cl B32 . . . . 84 F5
Copper Beech Cl CV6 . . . 95 E1
Copperbeech Dr 2 B12 . . 87 A5
Copper Beech Dr
Kingswinford DY6 . . . . . . 49 D1
Wombourne WV5 . . . . . . 49 B6
Copper Beech Gdns B20. . 55 A2
Copper Beech Rd CV10 . . 72 D6
Copperfield Rd CV2 . . . . 114 B3
Copperfields WS14 . . . . . . 9 D7
Copperkins Rd WS12 . . . . 2 E4
Coppice Ash Croft B19 . . 66 D8
Coppice Ave DY9 . . . . . . 81 F3
Coppice Cl
Birmingham B45 . . . . . . 121 F7
1 Birmingham, Erdington
B24. . . . . 56 F3
Brierley Hill DY5 . . . . 61 F1
Burntwood WS7. . . . . 6 F8
Cheslyn Hay WS6. . . . . . . 4 D4
Cheswick Green B90 . . . 126 C4
Hinckley LE10 . . . . 71 F3
Redditch B97 . . . . 153 C3
Sedgley DY3 . . . . 50 C7
Solihull B92 . . . . 107 A7
Wolverhampton WV11 . . . 13 A1
Coppice Cres WS8 . . . . . 15 D7
Coppice Ct WS11 . . . . 4 B7
Coppice Dr
Birmingham B27 . . . . 88 B2
Polesworth B78 . . . . 34 B3
Coppice Farm Way WV11 . 13 B1
Coppice Gate B47 . . . . . 125 A7
Coppice Gr WS14 . . . . 9 F7
Coppice Ho
Birmingham, Acock's Green
B27 . . . . 88 A2
Birmingham, Handsworth
B66. . . . . 65 D6
Willenhall WV12 . . . . 27 C7
Coppice Hollow B32 . . . . 84 B1
Coppice Hts DY11 . . . . . 116 B1
Coppice Jun Sch B92 . . . 107 E7
Coppice La
Aldridge WS9 . . . . 15 F1
Brierley Hill DY5 . . . . 62 A2
Brownhills WS8 . . . . 15 D8
Cheslyn Hay WS6. . . . . . . 4 D4
Middleton B78 . . . . 33 D2
Muckley Corner WS7, WS14 . 8 A3
Willenhall WV12 . . . . 27 C6
Coppice Oaks B13 . . . . . . 87 A3
Coppice Performing Arts Sch
WV11 . . . . 26 A8
Coppice Prim Sch B75 . . 32 B1
Coppice Prim Sch The
B47. . . . . 125 A6
Coppice Rd
Birmingham B13 . . . . 87 A3
Brownhills WS8 . . . . 15 F4
Cradley Heath B64. . . . . . 82 E7
Dudley WV14 . . . . 51 A8
Solihull B92 . . . . 107 E7
Whitnash CV31 . . . . 162 B2
Coppice Rise DY5 . . . . . . 62 A2
Coppice Side WS8 . . . . . 15 D8
Coppice Side Ind Est
WS8 . . . . 15 C8
Coppice St
Dudley DY1 . . . . 51 D4
Tipton DY4 . . . . 51 E5
West Bromwich B70 . . . . 53 A4
COPPICE THE 51 A7
Coppice The
Birmingham, Frankley
B31. . . . . 102 C2
Birmingham, Handsworth Wood
B20 . . . . 55 A2
Cannock WS12 . . . . 2 E1
Coventry CV3 . . . . 134 B8
Hinckley LE10 . . . . 75 F8
Coppy Nook La WS7 . . . . . 7 C5
Coppy Hall Gr WS9 . . . . . 16 B1
Copse Cl
Birmingham B31 . . . . . . 103 A2
Coppice Cres WS3 . . . . . 15 A4
Copse Dr CV5 . . . . 111 B8
Copshill Ct B75 . . . . 46 E4
Copse Rd DY2 . . . . 62 F4
Copse The
Bedworth CV7 . . . . 96 A4
Birmingham B13 . . . . 87 B2

Copse The continued
Sutton Coldfield B74 . . . . 31 F1
Copsewood Ave CV11 . . . 79 B7
Copsewood Prim Sch
CV3. . . . . 133 C6
Copsewood Sch CV6 . . . . 95 B3
Copsewood Terr CV3. . . 114 C2
Copson Cl B70 . . . . 53 A3
Copstone Dr B93 . . . . . . 127 F3
Copston Gr B29 . . . . 103 B8
Copthall Ho CV1 . . . . . . 165 B1
Copthall Rd B21 . . . . 54 C2
COPT HEATH 108 A1
Copt Heath Croft B93 . . 128 B8
Copt Heath Dr B93 . . . . 128 A7
Copthorne Ave WS7 . . . . . 6 F4
Copthorne Lo CV6 . . . . . 112 F8
Copthorne Rd
Birmingham B44 . . . . 44 E3
Coventry CV6 . . . . 112 F8
Wolverhampton WV3 . . . 39 A7
Copt Oak Cl CV4 . . . . . . 131 C6
Copyholt La
Stoke Prior B60 . . . . . . 151 D3
Upper Bentley B60, B97 . 152 A3
Coral Cl
Coventry CV5 . . . . 112 C2
Hinckley LE10 . . . . 75 F4
Coralin Cl B37 . . . . 70 C6
Corbet Rd CV6 . . . . 113 C7
Corbett Cl B60. . . . . 151 B8
Corbett Cres DY8 . . . . . . 81 A7
Corbett Dr B60 . . . . 150 C1
Corbett Ho 8 DY8 . . . . . 80 F8
Corbett Rd DY9 . . . . 80 F7
Corbett Hospl Nature
Reserve* DY8 . . . . 81 A7
Corbett Ind Est DY2 . . . . 62 C6
Corbett Rd
Brierley Hill DY5 . . . . 61 E1
Hollywood B47. . . . . 125 A7
Kidderminster DY11 . . . . 116 A8
Corbetts Cl B92 . . . . 109 B7
Corbett St B66. . . . . 65 B4
Corbin Rd B78 . . . . 36 F6
Corbison Ct CV34 . . . . . 155 D1
Corbizum Ave B80 . . . . . 159 D4
Corbridge Ave B44 . . . . . 44 F1
Corbridge Rd B73 . . . . . . 45 F2
Corbyn Rd
Birmingham B9 . . . . 68 B3
Dudley DY1 . . . . 61 F8
Corbyns Cl DY5 . . . . 61 B7
Corbyns Hall La DY5 . . . . 61 B7
Corbyns Hall Rd DY5 . . . 61 B7
Cordelia Gr CV34 . . . . . 161 D4
Cordley St B70. . . . . 53 B4
Corfe Cl
Birmingham B32 . . . . 84 F5
Coventry CV2 . . . . 114 F5
Perton WV6 . . . . 23 F3
Corfe Dr B69 . . . . 63 A8
Corfe Rd WV14 . . . . 51 A8
Corfton Dr WV6 . . . . 24 C3
Coriander Cl
Birmingham B45 . . . . . . 102 B2
Stoke Prior B60 . . . . . . 150 C1
Corinne Cl B45 . . . . 122 A6
Corinne Croft B37 . . . . . . 70 A4
Corinthian Pl CV2 . . . . . 114 D6
Coriolanus Sq CV34 . . . 161 F3
Corisande Rd B29 . . . . . . 85 C2
Corley Ave B31 . . . . 103 B3
Corley Cl B90 . . . . 105 E1
Corley Ctr CV7 . . . . 94 B6
Corley View CV7 . . . . 95 C6
Cormorant Cl WS8 . . . . . 15 F7
Cormorant Gr DY10 . . . . 117 B3
Cornbow Sh Ctr The B63 . 83 B3
Cornbrook Rd B29 . . . . . 102 F7
Cornbury Gr B91 . . . . . . 106 D4
Corncrake Cl B72 . . . . . . 46 D2
Corncrake Dr B36. . . . . . . 70 A7
Corncrake Rd DY1, DY3 . . 50 E7
Corndon Cl DY11. . . . . . 116 B2
Cornel B77 . . . . 21 F4
Cornel Cl B37 . . . . 90 C8
Cornelius St CV3 . . . . . . 133 D8
Corner Ho B66. . . . . 65 D6
Corner Ho 9 CV32. . . . . 156 F1
Corner La B97 . . . . 152 E2
Corner Pl The 3 B25 . . . . 85 D5
Cornerstone B13 . . . . 86 F3
Cornerstone Ho CV1 . . . 165 C4
Cornerway B38 . . . . 123 F7
CORNETS END 110 B6
Cornets End La CV7 . . . 109 E7
Cornet's End La CV7 . . . 110 A6
Corn Exchange The 5
WS13. . . . . 9 B8
Cornfield
Hinckley LE10 . . . . 71 C4
Wolverhampton WV8 . . . 10 F2
Cornfield Ave B60 . . . . . 150 D6
Cornfield Croft
Birmingham B37 . . . . 70 D3
Sutton Coldfield B76 . . . . 46 F3
Cornfield Dr WS14 . . . . . . 9 F7
Cornfield Pl B65 . . . . 62 F4
Cornfield Rd
Birmingham B31 . . . . . . 103 B4
Rowley Regis B65 . . . . . . 62 F4
Sutton Coldfield B76 . . . . 46 F2
Cornfield The CV3 . . . . . 114 C1

Cornflower Cl WV10 . . . . 12 A7
Cornflower Cres DY2. . . . 62 F8
Cornflower Rd WS8 . . . . . 15 D6
Corngreaves Jun & Inf Sch
B64. . . . . 62 D1
Corngreaves Rd B64 . . . . 82 E7
Corngreaves The B34 . . . 69 B6
Corngreaves Trad Est
B64. . . . . 82 D7
Corngreaves Wlk B64 . . . 82 E7
Cornhampton Cl 7 B97 . 153 B5
Cornhill WS11 . . . . 1 E5
Corn Hill
Walsall WS5. . . . . 43 E8
Wolverhampton WV10 . . 163 D3
Cornhill Gr
Birmingham B30 . . . . . . 104 C7
Kenilworth CV8 . . . . 148 C5
Cornish Cres CV10 . . . . . 73 A2
Corn Mdws CV12. . . . . . . 78 C2
Cornmill Cl WS1 . . . . 42 D7
Corn Mill Cl
Birmingham B32 . . . . 84 E1
Sutton Coldfield B76 . . . . 46 F1
Cornmill Gdns B60. . . . . 138 A5
Cornmill Gr WV6. . . . . . . 23 D3
Corns Ho WS10 . . . . 41 E6
Cornovian Cl WV6 . . . . . 23 E5
Cornwall Cl
Aldridge WS9. . . . . 16 A1
Kingswinford DY6 . . . . . . 60 D8
3 Warwick CV34 . . . . . . 160 F8
Wednesbury WS10 . . . . . 42 D3
Cornwall Gate WV12 . . . 27 B5
Cornwall Ho CV32. . . . . . 156 D1
Cornwall Ind Est
1 Birmingham B8. . . . . . . 67 C4
Smethwick B66 . . . . 65 C7
Cornwallis Rd B70 . . . . . 53 A1
Cornwall Pl
Royal Leamington Spa
CV32. . . . . 156 D1
Walsall WS2. . . . . 27 E3
Cornwall Rd
Birmingham, Handsworth
B20. . . . . 54 F2
Birmingham, Rubery B45. 101 E1
Cannock WS12. . . . . 2 B5
Coventry CV1 . . . . 113 E1
Smethwick B66 . . . . 65 C7
Stourbridge DY8 . . . . . . 80 D5
Walsall WS5. . . . . 43 B7
Wolverhampton WV6 . . . 24 C4
Cornwall St B83 . . . . 164 B3
Cornwall Twr B18. . . . . . . 66 B5
Cornwall Way LE10. . . . . 71 E4
Cornwell Cl
Redditch B98 . . . . 159 B5
Tipton DY4 . . . . 52 A5
Cornwood La B90 . . . . . 126 A5
Cornyx La B91 . . . . 107 D6
Coronation Ave
Mile Oak B78 . . . . 20 D1
Willenhall WV13 . . . . 27 D2
Coronation Cres B79 . . . . 22 F7
Coronation Ct CV11 . . . . 73 B4
Coronation Rd
Bilston WV14 . . . . 40 C6
Birmingham B29 . . . . 85 F2
Birmingham, Great Barr B43 43 E4
Birmingham, Washwood Heath
B8 . . . . 67 F6
Brownhills WS9 . . . . 16 A3
Coventry CV1 . . . . 113 F4
Tipton DY4 . . . . 52 B8
Walsall WS4. . . . . 15 B2
Wednesbury WS10 . . . . . 42 C4
Wolverhampton WV10 . . . 26 A5
Coronation St B79 . . . . . 21 A5
Coronation Terr B60 . . . 151 B7
Coronation Way DY10 . . 117 B5
Coronel Ave CV6. . . . . . . 95 E4
Corporation Rd DY2. . . . . 51 F1
Corporation St
Birmingham B2 . . . . 164 C3
Birmingham, New Town Row
B4. . . . . 164 D4
Coventry CV1 . . . . 165 B3
Kidderminster DY10 . . . . 116 E5
Nuneaton CV11 . . . . 73 B5
Walsall WS1. . . . . 42 E3
Wolverhampton WV1 . . . 25 B1
Corporation Street W
WS1. . . . . 42 D8
Corpus Christi RC Prim Sch
Birmingham B33 . . . . 68 D2
Coventry CV3. . . . . 134 D7
Wednesfield WV11 . . . . . 27 A8
Correen B77. . . . . 22 C1
Corrie Croft
Birmingham, Bartley Green
B32. . . . . 102 B7
Birmingham, Lyndon Green
B26. . . . . 89 B7
Corrie Roy Cotts B78. . . . 21 A4
Corrin Gr DY6 . . . . 60 C8
Corron Hill B63 . . . . 83 B4
Corser St
Dudley DY1 . . . . 51 A2
Stourbridge DY8 . . . . . . 81 A3
Wolverhampton WV1. . . . 25 F1
Corsican Cl
Burntwood WS7. . . . . 7 A8

Corsican Cl *continued*
  Willenhall WV12 .... 27 E7
Corsican Dr WS12......... 2 A8
Corston Mews CV31.. 162 C6
Cort Dr WS7............ 7 B8
Corunna Rd CV34 .... 160 C7
Corvedale Rd B29... 103 A6
Corve Gdns WV6...... 24 E5
Corve View DY3....... 39 C1
Corville Gdns B26... 89 C4
Corville Rd B62...... 83 F6
Corwen Croft B31.. 102 E6
Cory Croft DY4........ 52 A5
COSELEY 40 C1
Coseley Hall [1] WV14 .. 51 C8
Coseley L Ctr WV14 .... 40 B1
Coseley Rd WV14 ..... 40 C4
Coseley Road Island
  WV14................ 40 C4
Coseley Sch & Specialist
  Sports Coll The WV14 .. 40 B1
Coseley Sta WV14..... 40 C1
Cosford Cl
  Redditch B98.......154 F1
  Royal Leamington Spa
  CV32................157 B3
Cosford Cres B35.... 58 A3
Cosford Ct WV6....... 23 E5
Cosford Dr DY2....... 62 E5
Cosgrove Wlk WV8.. 10 F1
Cossington Rd B23.. 56 E7
Costard Ave CV34 ... 161 E3
Costers La B98 ......154 F2
Costock Cl B37........ 90 B8
Cosyll Gdns [9] DY1 .. 62 B8
Coten End CV34...... 160 E7
Coten End Prim Sch [14]
  CV34................ 160 F7
Cotes Rd LE10 .... 75 F5
Cotford Rd B14 ..... 105 A2
Cotheridge Cl B90 .. 127 C6
Cot La DY6, DY8 ...... 60 C5
Cotleigh Gr B43..... 44 D3
Cotman Cl
  Bedworth CV12 ...... 78 A4
  Birmingham B43 ..... 44 C3
Cotman Dr LE10 ..... 71 A3
COTON................ 20 C6
Coton Gr B90........ 105 E2
COTON GREEN 20 F8
Coton Green Prec B79 .. 20 F7
Coton Green Prim Sch
  B79................. 20 F8
Coton La
  Birmingham B23 ..... 56 F4
  Tamworth B79 .... 20 E8
Coton Rd
  Nuneaton CV11 ...... 73 C3
  Wolverhampton WV4 .. 39 B5
Cotsbale Rd WV4 ..... 38 E3
Cotsford B91 .... 107 A3
Cotswold Ave WS6.... 4 F3
Cotswold Cl
  Aldridge WS9........ 16 C1
  Birmingham B45 .... 102 B2
  Walsall WS3......... 2 A8
  Kidderminster DY11.. 116 C2
  Oldbury B69........ 63 E5
Cotswold Cres CV10.. 72 B3
Cotswold Croft B63 .. 82 C1
Cotswold Ct
  Sutton Coldfield B75 .. 32 A4
  Wolverhampton WV3.. 39 B6
Cotswold Dr CV3.... 133 C3
Cotswold Gr WV12 ... 13 B1
Cotswold Rd
  Cannock WS12........ 2 A8
  Stourbridge DY8 ..... 81 B6
  Wolverhampton WV2.. 39 F7
Cotswold Way B61.. 137 A5
Cottage Cl
  Burntwood WS7.......6 F5
  Cannock WS12........ 2 C8
  Nuneaton CV11 ...... 73 D4
  Royal Leamington Spa
  CV31................162 C6
  Wolverhampton WV11 .. 26 C6
Cottage Ct WS7......6 F5
Cottage Dr B60 .... 121 D1
Cottage Farm La B60.. 121 F6
Cottage Farm Lodge CV6.. 95 A1
Cottage Farm Rd
  Coventry CV6........ 95 A2
  Tamworth B77 .... 35 D7
Cottage Gdns B45... 121 F6
Cottage La
  Burntwood WS7.......6 F5
  Lower Marlbrook B60 .. 121 C1
  Minworth B76....... 58 D6
  Wolverhampton WV10.. 11 D3
Cottage Mews WV9 .. 30 E4
Cottage Sq CV31.... 162 C6
Cottage St
  Brierley Hill DY5 ..... 61 D3
  Kingswinford DY6 .... 60 D7
Cottage Terr
  Birmingham B24 ..... 67 F8
  Cradley Heath B63.. 82 E6
Cottage View WV8 ... 10 B4
Cottage Wlk
  [4] Tamworth B77 .... 35 F6
  West Bromwich B70 .. 53 D2
Cotterell Ct [3] WS4 .. 28 F3
COTTERIDGE......... 103 E5
Cotteridge Jun & Inf Sch
  B30................. 104 A5
Cotteridge Rd B30 .. 104 A4
Cotterills Ave B8..... 68 C4

Cotterill's Cl CV31 .... 162 B3
Cotterills La B8........ 68 C4
Cotterills Rd DY4 ..... 52 B7
Cottesbrook Cl CV3 .. 114 E1
Cottesbrook Inf Sch B27.. 88 D4
Cottesbrook Jun Sch B27.. 88 C4
Cottesbrook Rd B27.. 88 D4
Cottesfield Cl B8..... 68 B4
Cottesmore Cl B71... 53 F8
Cottesmore Ho [7] B20.. 54 F3
Cottle Cl WS2........ 27 F3
Cotton Dr CV8 ...... 148 C6
Cotton La B13........ 87 A2
Cotton Pool Rd B61.. 136 E2
Cotton Way CV4 .... 113 D7
Cottrells Cl B14...... 105 C4
Cottrells Mews B46 .. 59 B2
Cottrell St B71........ 53 D4
Cottsmeadow Dr B8.. 68 C4
Cotwall End Dr DY3.. 50 C7
Cotwall End Nature
  Reserve * 50 C5
Cotwall End Prim Sch
  DY3................. 50 D7
Cotwall End Rd DY3.. 50 C5
Cotysmore Rd B75.... 46 D7
Couchman Rd B8..... 67 E4
Coughton Dr CV31.. 162 D5
Coulter Gr WV6 ...... 23 D4
Coulter La WS7........7 E8
Council Cres WV12... 27 C4
Council Hos CV5..... 112 A6
Council House Birmingham *
  B3................. 164 B2
Council Rd [3] LE10.. 71 D1
COUNDON............ 112 B6
Coundon Court Sch & Com
  Coll CV6........... 112 E7
Coundon Gn CV6..... 112 E8
COUNDON GREEN ... 112 E8
Coundon Prim Sch CV6.. 112 E5
Coundon Rd CV1..... 113 B3
Coundon Wedge Dr CV5,
  CV6................ 112 D7
Counterfield Dr B65.. 62 F5
Countess Dr WS4 .... 29 D7
Countess Rd CV11... 73 A4
Countess's Croft The
  CV3................ 133 D7
Countess St WS1..... 42 D7
Countinghouse Way [2]
  B60................ 150 E6
Country Pk View B76.. 46 F1
COUNTY BRIDGE.... 27 C2
County Bridge Prim Sch
  WS2................ 27 E1
County Cl
  Birmingham B32 ..... 84 D3
  Birmingham, Stirchley B30.. 104 C6
County Dr B78....... 21 A2
County La DY8....... 98 D8
County Park Ave B62.. 83 D3
Courtaulds Way CV6.. 113 D6
Court Cres WV6..... 111 E7
Court Dr WS14....... 17 F4
Courtenay Gdns B43.. 43 E2
Courtenay Rd B44.... 55 E8
Court Farm Prim Sch B23.. 56 E6
Court Farm Rd B23... 56 E6
Court Farm Way B29.. 102 F7
Courthouse Croft CV8.. 148 C4
Courthouse Green Prim Sch
  CV6................ 114 A8
Court La B23........ 56 E7
Courtland Ave CV6... 112 F5
Courtland Rd DY6.... 60 E8
Courtlands Cl B5..... 86 C6
Courtlands The WV6.. 24 E4
Court Leet CV3 ..... 135 D7
Court Leet Rd CV3 .. 133 E7
Courtney CV10....... 116 E2
Courtney Cl CV11.... 73 F7
Court Oak Rd B17.... 85 A6
Court of Lady Katherine
  Leveson The B93... 129 B5
Court Par WS9....... 30 B6
Court Pas DY1....... 51 C1
Court Rd
  Birmingham, Balsall Heath
  B12................ 86 E5
  Birmingham, Sparkhill B11.. 87 C4
  Wolverhampton WV4.. 24 F4
  Woodcross WV4 .... 40 A3
Court St
  [2] Cradley Heath B64.. 62 F1
  Royal Leamington Spa
  CV31................162 A7
  [3] Stourbridge DY8.. 81 A5
Court Way WS2....... 28 E2
Courtway Ave B14... 105 B1
Courtyard The
  Coleshill B46........ 59 F2
  Solihull B91 .... 107 C4
  Stoke Prior B60 .... 150 D7
  Warwick CV34 ...... 160 F5
  West Bromwich B70.. 53 A3
Cousins St WV2...... 39 D7
Coveley Gr B18...... 66 A5
Coven Cl WS3........ 15 A5
Coven Gr B29........ 85 B2
COVEN HEATH....... 11 A6
COVEN LAWN......... 11 A8
Coven St WV10...... 27 E3
COVENTRY 165 C1
Coventry Airport CV8.. 134 B2

Coventry Blue Coat CE Sch
  CV1................ 113 F1
Coventry Bsns Pk CV5.. 112 D1
Coventry Canal Basin
  Warehouse CV1.... 165 B4
Coventry Cath * CV1.. 165 C3
Coventry Electric Railway
  Ctr * CV6........... 134 A3
Coventry Highway B98 .. 154 C4
Coventry Muslim Sch
  CV6................ 113 E8
Coventry Rd
  Aston Flamville LE10... 76 F1
  Baginton CV8....... 133 F2
  Barnacle CV7, CV12.... 97 A8
  Bedworth CV12 ...... 78 B2
  Bedworth, Hawkesbury CV2.. 96 E6
  Berkswell CV7 ...... 110 E3
  Bickenhill B26, B92.... 90 C6
  Birmingham B10, B25, B26.. 88 C6
  Bulkington CV12 ..... 79 B1
  Coventry CV3....... 115 F3
  Cubbington CV32.... 157 E7
  Hampton-in-A B92.... 91 B3
  Hinckley LE10 .... 75 B7
  Hinckley, Sketchley Hill LE10.. 75 F5
  Kenilworth CV8 .... 148 A7
  Nuneaton CV10 ..... 78 C7
  Stonleigh CV8, CV3.. 149 C7
  Warwick CV34 ..... 160 F8
Coventry Road Exhall CV7.. 96 A8
Coventry Sp & L Ctr CV1.. 165 C2
Coventry Sta CV1 .. 165 B1
Coventry Transport Mus *
  CV1................ 165 B3
Coventry Univ CV1.. 165 C2
Coventry University Tech Pk
  CV1................ 165 B3
Coventry Walsgrave Triangle
  Bsns Pk CV2........ 97 A1
Cove Pl CV2........ 114 C7
Cover Croft B76 ..... 47 A1
Coverdale Rd B92... 89 A4
Covers The B80.... 159 E6
Covert La B30 ...... 80 D2
Covert The WV8 ..... 10 E1
Covey Cl WS13....... 3 E2
Cowdray Cl CV31.... 162 C7
Cowdrey Ct DY4..... 81 A6
Cow La B78........ 35 F3
Cowles Croft B25.... 68 E1
Cowley Cl B36....... 68 F8
Cowley Ct B36....... 58 F1
Cowley Dr
  Birmingham B27 ..... 88 D4
  Dudley DY1......... 50 F2
Cowley Gn WS12..... 1 C8
Cowley Gr B11....... 87 E5
Cowley Rd
  Birmingham B11 ..... 87 E5
  Coventry CV2........ 114 B4
Cowper Cl
  Warwick CV34 ..... 155 E1
  Willenhall WV12 ..... 27 E7
Cowper Rd LE10 ..... 75 D6
Cowper Wlk DY10... 117 C6
Cowslip Cl
  [1] Birmingham, Hawkesley
  B38................ 123 F8
  Birmingham, Selly Oak
  B29................ 103 A7
  Cannock WS12....... 1 C6
Cowslip Wlk CV5..... 81 C6
Coxcroft Ave DY5.... 81 F8
Coxmoor Cl WS3..... 13 F3
Cox Rd WV14 .... 40 E1
Cox's Cl CV10....... 73 B3
Cox's La B64........ 62 F2
Cox's Orch [4] CV31.. 162 A4
Cox St
  Birmingham B3 .... 164 B4
  Coventry CV1....... 165 C3
Coxwell Ave WV10... 25 C5
Coxwell Gdns B16.... 65 F2
Coyne Cl DY4....... 51 D5
Coyne Rd B70....... 53 B2
Cozens Cl CV12 ..... 78 A4
Crabbe St DY9...... 81 F5
CRABBS CROSS.... 158 E6
Crabbs Cross La B97.. 158 E5
Crab La
  Cannock WS11........ 2 A3
  Willenhall WV12 ..... 13 D1
Crabmill Cl
  Birmingham B38 ... 123 E7
  Knowle B93........ 128 C7
Crabmill La
  Birmingham B38 ... 124 D8
  Coventry CV5....... 113 F7
Crabourne Rd DY2... 62 B2
Crabtree Cl
  Birmingham B31 ... 103 C2
  Redditch B98....... 154 A2
  West Bromwich B71.. 53 F8
  West Hagley DY9 .... 99 B6
Crabtree Ct B61 .... 136 E3
Crabtree Dr
  Birmingham B37 ..... 69 F2
  Bromsgrove B61 ... 136 F3
Crabtree Gr CV31... 162 C6
Crab Tree Ho B13.... 68 E3

Crabtree La B61 .... 136 E3
Crabtree Rd
  Barwell LE9 .... 71 F5
  Birmingham B18 ..... 66 A5
  Walsall WS1......... 29 A2
CRACKLEY 148 B7
Crackley Cotts CV8.. 148 B8
Crackley Cres CV8 .. 148 B8
Crackley Hall Sch CV8 .. 148 B7
Crackley La
  Coventry CV8....... 131 F3
  Kenilworth CV8 .... 148 A7
Crackley Way DY2 ... 62 A6
Crackley Wood Nature
  Reserve * CV8..... 132 A1
Craddock Cl CV10.... 72 C7
Craddock Dr CV10 ... 72 C7
Craddock Rd B67.... 64 E6
Craddock St WV6.... 25 B4
CRADLEY 82 D6
Cradley Cc Prim Sch B63.. 82 C7
Cradley Cl B98 .... 154 F2
Cradley Croft B21.... 54 B3
Cradley Fields B63.. 82 D5
Cradley Forge DY5... 82 A8
Cradley Heath Factory Ctr
  B64................ 82 B8
CRADLEY HEATH.... 82 D8
Cradley Heath Sta B64.. 82 B8
Cradley Park Rd DY2.. 62 D2
Cradley Rd
  Cradley Heath B64... 82 C8
  Dudley DY2......... 62 D3
Craddock Rd B8 .... 67 E5
Craig Cl CV21........ 162 B6
Craig Croft B37..... 70 D2
Craigends Ave CV3.. 134 E6
Crail Gr B43........ 44 B4
Crakston Cl CV2 .... 114 E2
Cramlington Rd B42.. 55 A8
Crammond Cl LE10... 75 B8
Cramore Cl DY4..... 52 A8
Crampers Field CV6.. 113 A5
Cramp Hill WS10..... 41 D6
Cranborne Chase CV2.. 115 A5
Cranbourne Ave WV4.. 39 E3
Cranbourne Cl B45.. 102 B2
Cranbourne Gr B44... 56 A8
Cranbourne Pl B71... 53 D4
Cranbourne Rd
  Birmingham B44 ..... 45 A1
  Stourbridge DY8 ..... 81 B4
Cranbrook Ct WV13... 27 D2
Cranbrook Gr WV6... 23 F3
Cranbrook Rd B21.... 54 C2
Cranby St B8........ 67 C5
Craneberry Rd B37... 69 E3
Cranebrook Hill B78.. 33 E5
Cranebrook La WS14.. 16 F7
Crane Cl CV34 ..... 155 D3
Crane Ct WS1........ 29 A3
Crane Dr WS7....... 7 A8
Crane Field WS13..... 3 B1
Cranehouse Rd B44.. 45 A2
Cranemoor Cl B7.... 67 C6
Crane Rd WV14 ..... 40 F3
Craner's Rd CV1.... 113 F4
Cranesbill Cl WV10.. 12 C7
Cranesbill Rd B29... 103 A6
Cranes Park Rd B26.. 89 C5
Crane St DY11...... 116 C6
Crane Terr WV6 ..... 24 E5
Cranfield Gr B26.... 88 F8
Cranfield Pl WS5.... 42 F4
Cranfield Rd WS7....7 A7
Cranford Gr [6] B91.. 107 B1
Cranford Pl WS11....1 F1
Cranford Rd
  Coventry CV5........ 112 D4
  Wolverhampton WV3.. 38 D8
Cranford St B66..... 65 C5
Cranford Way B66... 65 C5
Cranham Cl B97 ... 153 B1
Cranham Dr DY6.... 60 E5
Cranhill Cl B92...... 89 B1
Crankhall La WS10... 42 C3
Cranleigh Cl
  Aldridge WS9........ 30 B5
  Willenhall WV12 ..... 13 C1
Cranleigh Ho B23... 56 F6
Cranleigh Pl B44.... 55 E5
Cranleigh Way WS14... 9 E7
Cranmer Ave WV12... 27 D7
Cranmer Cl WS6..... 4 D1
Cranmer Dr WV6 .... 24 A6
Cranmere Ct WV6... 24 A6
Cranmer Gr
  Royal Leamington Spa
  CV34................161 D3
  Sutton Coldfield B74... 31 F6
Cranmoor Cres B63.. 83 A5
Cranmore Ave
  Birmingham B21 ..... 65 D7
  Solihull B90 .... 126 E8
Cranmore Bvd B90.. 126 D8
Cranmore Cl DY4.... 52 A8
Cranmore Dr B90... 106 E1
Cranmore Inf Sch B91.. 106 E1
Cransley Gr B91.... 107 A1
Crantock Cl WV11... 13 C1
Crantock Rd B42.... 55 C4
Crantock Way CV11.. 73 F4
Cranwell Gr B24.... 57 D3
Cranwell Rise B35... 20 C1
Cranwell Way B35... 58 A3

Crathie Cl CV2...... 114 F6
Crathorne Ave WV10.. 11 C1
Craufurd Ct DY8 ..... 81 A3
Craufurd St DY8 ..... 81 A3
Craven B77.......... 22 B1
Craven Ave CV3..... 135 D7
Craven Ct CV3..... 114 F2
Craven St
  Coventry CV5....... 112 F2
  Wolverhampton WV2.. 39 F6
Crawford Ave
  Darlaston WS10..... 41 C7
  Smethwick B67..... 64 F4
  Wolverhampton WV4.. 39 F3
Crawford Cl CV32 .. 157 B5
Crawford Rd
  Sutton Coldfield B76 .. 57 F8
  Wolverhampton WV3.. 25 A2
Crawford St B8...... 67 C5
Crawley Wlk [3] B64.. 62 D1
Crawshaws Rd B36.. 58 C1
Crayford Rd B44..... 45 A1
Craythorne Ave B20.. 54 E4
Crecy Cl B76........ 46 E4
Crecy Pl WS14..... 9 A5
Crecy Rd CV3....... 133 E7
Credenda Rd B70.... 53 A1
Crediton Cl
  Coventry CV3....... 133 C5
  Nuneaton CV11 ...... 73 F5
Creed Way B70...... 53 B4
Cregoe St B15...... 66 D8
Cremore Ave B8 .... 67 E5
Cremorne Rd B75... 32 B2
Cremorne Wlk B75... 32 B2
Crendon Cl B80.... 159 E5
Crendon Rd B65.... 63 A6
Crescent Arc [2] B91.. 107 C3
Crescent Ave
  Birmingham B18 ..... 66 B6
  Brierley Hill DY5 ..... 61 C1
  Coventry CV3....... 114 C2
Crescent Grange Rd The
  DY9................. 81 C4
Crescent Ho B97 ... 153 D2
Crescent Ind Pk The WS14.. 40 D6
Crescent Rd
  Darlaston WS10..... 41 D6
  Dudley DY2......... 62 B5
  Kidderminster DY11.. 116 C5
  Willenhall WV13 ..... 27 C2
Crescent Stop The WS14.. 40 D6
Crescent The
  Bilston WV14 .... 40 D6
  Birmingham, Coleshill Heath
  B37................. 90 E8
  Birmingham, Great Barr
  B43................. 44 A1
  Birmingham, Handsworth B21.. 66 B6
  Birmingham, Sparkbrook
  B12................. 87 B5
  Bromsgrove B60 ... 136 F1
  Cradley Heath B64... 83 A7
  Dudley DY1......... 51 E4
  Great Wyrley WS6 ....5 A2
  Hampton-in-A B92.. 109 B7
  Keresley CV7....... 94 F6
  Rowley Regis B65... 63 C2
  Solihull, Lode Heath B91.. 107 B4
  Solihull, Shirley B90.. 106 A4
  Walsall WS11........ 43 A8
  Wednesbury WS10 ... 42 A6
  West Hagley DY9 .... 98 F5
  Wolverhampton WV6.. 24 B3
Crescent Twr B1..... 66 C2
Crescent Works Ind Pk
  WS10............... 27 D1
Cressage Ave B31... 103 A1
Cressage Rd CV2.... 115 A6
Cressett Ave DY5.... 61 C4
Cressett La DY5..... 61 C4
Cressida Cl CV34... 161 F3
Cressington Dr B74.. 32 A1
Cresswell Cl CV10... 73 D8
Cresswell Cres WS3.. 13 F2
Cresswell Ct WV11... 11 A3
Cresswell Gr B24.... 57 D4
Cresswell Ho CV6... 113 B7
Crest The
  Birmingham B31 .... 123 C8
  Royal Leamington Spa
  CV32................157 D3
Crest View
  Birmingham B14 ... 105 B4
  Sutton Coldfield B74... 44 F8
Crestwood B77...... 22 A5
Crestwood Ave DY11.. 116 A6
Crestwood Dr B44... 55 E7
Crestwood Glen WV6.. 24 E7
Crestwood Park Prim Sch
  DY6................. 61 A5
Crestwood Sch The DY6.. 60 F5
Creswell Rd B28.... 106 B7
Creswick Gr B45.... 122 C7
Crewe Dr DY4....... 52 A2
Crew La CV8......... 148 E6
Crew Rd WS10...... 42 A4
Creynolds Cl B90... 126 D3
Creynolds La B90... 126 E4
Cricket Cl
  Coventry CV5....... 112 F1
  Walsall WS5......... 43 B7
Cricketers Mdw B64.. 82 F7
Cricket La WS14..... 9 C5

Cricket Mdw
Dudley DY3 ... 50 E5
Wolverhampton WV10 ... 11 D4
Crick La B20 ... 66 A8
Cricklewood Dr B62 ... 83 D3
Crigdon B77 ... 22 C1
Crimmond Rise B63 ... 82 E5
Crimscote Cl B90 ... 126 F6
Cringlebrook B77 ... 21 D1
Cripps Rd WS2 ... 27 E3
Crocketts Ave B21 ... 65 D7
Crocketts Com Prim Sch 6 B66 ... 65 A5
Crockett's La B66 ... 65 A6
Crocketts Rd B21 ... 65 D8
Crockett St DY1 ... 51 A2
Crockford Dr B75 ... 32 B3
Crockford Rd B71 ... 42 C1
Crockington La WV5 ... 37 A1
Crocus Cres WV9 ... 11 A3
Croft Apartments 2 WV13 ... 27 A2
Croft Ave B79 ... 21 B6
Croft Cl
Birmingham B25 ... 88 E8
Redditch B98 ... 154 D3
Warwick CV34 ... 161 C7
Croft Com Prim Sch 8 WS2 ... 28 D3
Croft Cres WS8 ... 15 D7
Croft Ct B36 ... 69 B8
Croftdown Rd B17 ... 85 A7
Croft Down Rd B92 ... 89 D4
Crofters Cl DY8 ... 81 B4
Crofters Ct B15 ... 85 E6
Crofters La B75 ... 32 E3
Crofters Wlk WV8 ... 10 E1
Croft Fields CV12 ... 78 B2
Croft Ho 2 WS1 ... 28 F1
Croft Ind Est B37 ... 70 D2
Croft Jun Sch CV10 ... 72 F3
Croft La WV10 ... 26 A7
Croftleigh Gdns B91 ... 106 E2
Croft Mews CV10 ... 73 A4
Croft Par WS9 ... 30 B6
Croft Pool CV12 ... 77 F2
Croft Rd
Bedworth CV12 ... 77 F2
Birmingham B26 ... 88 E8
Coventry CV1 ... 165 A2
Leek Wootton CV35 ... 156 A7
Nuneaton CV10 ... 72 F3
Crofts La B96 ... 158 B2
Croft St
Tamworth B79 ... 21 B6
Walsall WS2 ... 28 D3
Willenhall WV13 ... 27 A2
Crofts The B76 ... 58 A8
Croft The
Birmingham B31 ... 103 B2
Blakedown DY10 ... 98 C2
Bulkington CV12 ... 79 B2
Cheslyn Hay WS6 ... 4 E2
Coventry CV6 ... 95 F4
Dudley DY2 ... 61 F6
Kidderminster DY11 ... 116 A4
Meriden CV7 ... 92 C1
Sedgley DY3 ... 39 E1
Walsall WS5 ... 43 E8
Croftway The B20 ... 54 E6
Croftwood Rd DY9 ... 81 D4
Cromane Sq B43 ... 54 E7
Cromarty Cl CV5 ... 112 A5
Cromdale B77 ... 22 C1
Cromdale Cl CV10 ... 72 A3
Cromdale Dr B63 ... 82 D3
Crome Rd B43 ... 44 D3
Cromer Gdns WV6 ... 24 F5
Cromer Rd
Birmingham B12 ... 86 F5
Royal Leamington Spa CV32 ... 157 B2
Cromes Wood CV4 ... 111 D1
Crompton Ave B20 ... 55 C1
Crompton Cl WS2 ... 28 A5
Crompton Ct
Codsall WV8 ... 10 B4
Warwick CV34 ... 160 D6
Crompton Rd
Birmingham, Handsworth B20 ... 55 C1
Birmingham, Nechells B7 ... 67 C8
Birmingham, Rubery B45 ... 101 D1
Tipton DY4 ... 52 A4
Crompton St CV34 ... 160 D6
Cromwell Cl
Rowley Regis B65 ... 63 A5
Willenhall WS2 ... 27 E4
Cromwell Ct WS6 ... 5 A1
Cromwell Dr DY2 ... 62 F8
Cromwell La
Birmingham B31 ... 102 E8
Coventry CV4, CV8 ... 131 C6
Cromwell Prim Sch B7 ... 67 B6
Cromwell Rd
Cannock WS12 ... 2 E1
Tamworth B79 ... 20 E8
Wolverhampton WV10 ... 11 E4
Cromwells Mdw WS14 ... 9 C5
Cromwell St
Birmingham B7 ... 67 B5
Coventry CV6 ... 113 F6
Dudley DY2 ... 62 E8
West Bromwich B71 ... 53 C4
Crondal Pl B15 ... 86 B7
Crondal Rd CV7 ... 96 B7
Cronehills Linkway B70 ... 53 D3
Cronehills St B70 ... 53 D4
Crookham Cl B17 ... 84 F7
Crookhay La B71 ... 53 B8
Crook La
Aldridge WS9 ... 30 B1
Birmingham WS9 ... 44 A7
Crooks La B80 ... 159 D3
Croome Cl
Birmingham B11 ... 87 B3
Coventry CV6 ... 112 F4
Redditch B98 ... 154 F1
Cropredy Rd B31 ... 123 B8
Cropthorne Cl B98 ... 159 B7
Cropthorne Dr B47 ... 125 B7
Cropthorne Ho B60 ... 137 B3
Cropthorne Rd B90 ... 106 C3
Crosbie Rd
Birmingham B17 ... 85 B6
Coventry CV5 ... 112 E3
Crosby Cl
Birmingham B1 ... 66 B3
Wolverhampton WV6 ... 24 F5
Cross Cheaping CV1 ... 165 B3
Cross Cl B64 ... 62 F2
Cross Farm Rd B17 ... 85 D4
Cross Farms La B45 ... 101 F1
Crossfell B77 ... 22 B1
Crossfield Ind Est WS13 ... 9 E8
Crossfield Rd
Birmingham B33 ... 69 A3
Lichfield WS13 ... 9 E8
Cross Fields Rd 4 CV34 ... 160 F8
Crossfield Way WV14 ... 40 E5
Crossgate Rd
Dudley DY2 ... 61 F6
Redditch B98 ... 159 C7
Cross Ho WV2 ... 39 C7
Crossings Ind Est 4 WS3 ... 28 B8
Crossings The 5 WS14 ... 9 E8
Crosskey Cl B33 ... 69 E2
Cross Keys WS13 ... 9 B8
Cross Keys Island WS12 ... 2 C3
Cross La
Birmingham B43 ... 43 E1
Cubbington CV32 ... 157 E4
Lichfield WS14 ... 9 D6
Sedgley DY3 ... 39 E1
Crossland Cres WV6 ... 24 F7
Crossland Row LE10 ... 76 A6
Crossley Ct CV6 ... 113 F7
Crossley Ret Pk DY11 ... 116 D6
Crossley St DY2 ... 62 D4
Crossley Wlk B60 ... 150 E7
Cross Pl DY3 ... 39 E1
Cross Point Bsns Pk CV2 ... 115 B8
Cross Quays Bsns Pk B69 ... 52 B2
Cross Rd
Coventry CV6 ... 113 F8
Keresley CV7 ... 94 F6
4 Royal Leamington Spa CV32 ... 156 D1
Cross Road Ind Est CV6 ... 113 F7
Cross St
Bilston WV14 ... 40 F2
Birmingham B21 ... 65 C8
Burntwood WS7 ... 6 E8
Cannock, Bridgtown WS11 ... 4 E5
Cannock WS12 ... 2 E1
Cheslyn Hay WS6 ... 4 D2
Coventry CV1 ... 165 C4
Dudley DY1 ... 51 C1
Halesowen B63 ... 83 A3
Kingswinford DY6 ... 60 D6
Kingswinford, Wall Heath DY6 ... 60 B8
Nuneaton CV10 ... 72 D3
Oldbury B68 ... 64 A4
4 Rowley Regis B65 ... 63 C1
Royal Leamington Spa CV32 ... 157 A1
Smethwick B66 ... 65 A6
Stourbridge DY8 ... 80 E5
4 Stourbridge, Wordsley DY6 ... 60 D3
Tamworth B79 ... 21 B5
Tamworth, Kettlebrook B77 ... 21 C3
Walsall WS3 ... 15 A1
11 Warwick CV34 ... 160 F7
Wednesbury WS10 ... 41 E3
2 Willenhall WV13 ... 27 A1
Wolverhampton WV1 ... 25 F1
Cross Street N WV1 ... 25 D4
Cross Street S WV2 ... 39 C7
Cross The
Kingswinford DY6 ... 60 D6
Stourbridge DY9 ... 81 E6
Crossway La B44 ... 55 F6
Crossway Rd CV3 ... 133 B4
Crossways LE10 ... 75 F5
Crossways Ct B44 ... 56 B7
Crossways Gn B44 ... 56 B7
Crosswells Rd B68 ... 64 B5
Cross Wlk B69 ... 63 C8
Cross Wlks DY9 ... 81 E5
Crowberry Cl WS8 ... 15 D6
Crowberry La B78 ... 48 C8
Crowden Dr CV32 ... 157 A4
Crowden Rd B77 ... 22 A1
Crowesbridge Mews WV14 ... 51 B8
Crowhill Rd CV11 ... 74 A1
Crowhurst Rd B31 ... 122 E7
Crowland Ave WV6 ... 23 E4
Crowle Dr DY9 ... 81 C5
Crowmere Rd CV2 ... 114 F7
Crown Cl
Bromsgrove B61 ... 136 F2
Rowley Regis B65 ... 63 D4
Sedgley DY3 ... 39 D1
Crown Ct
Darlaston WS10 ... 41 C8
10 Hinckley LE10 ... 71 D1
1 Sutton Coldfield B74 ... 31 E3
Crown Gn CV6 ... 95 E2
Crownhill Mdw B61 ... 136 F7
Crownhill Rd LE10 ... 75 D4
Crown Ho CV5 ... 112 E3
Crown La
Iverley DY8 ... 98 C7
Kidderminster DY10 ... 116 E6
Stourbridge DY8 ... 80 F5
Sutton Coldfield B74 ... 31 E3
Crown Mdw
Alvechurch B48 ... 139 A7
Birmingham B48 ... 139 A6
Crownmeadow Dr DY4 ... 52 D7
Crown Meadow Fst Sch B48 ... 139 B7
Crownoakes Dr DY8 ... 60 E2
Crown Rd
Birmingham, Bordesley Green B9 ... 67 D2
Birmingham, King's Norton B30 ... 104 A4
Crown (Sh Ctr) The 3 DY8 ... 81 A5
Crown St WV1 ... 25 D4
Crown Terr CV31 ... 161 F7
Crown Way CV32 ... 157 B3
Crown Wharf Sh Pk WS2 ... 28 D2
Crown Wlk DY4 ... 52 A2
Crows Nest Cl B76 ... 46 F3
Crowther Gdns B63 ... 82 C7
Crowther Gr WV6 ... 24 F4
Crowther Rd
Birmingham B23 ... 56 D5
Wolverhampton WV6 ... 24 F5
Crowther St
Kidderminster DY11 ... 116 C6
Wolverhampton WV10 ... 25 E4
Croxall Way B66 ... 65 B5
Croxdene Ave WS3 ... 14 A1
Croxhall St CV12 ... 78 C3
Croxley Dr WS12 ... 2 C3
Croxley Gdns WV13 ... 40 F8
Croxstalls Ave WS3 ... 28 A8
Croxstalls Cl WS3 ... 14 A1
Croxstalls Pl WS3 ... 28 A8
Croxstalls Rd WS3 ... 28 A8
Croxton Gr B33 ... 69 A4
Croyde Ave B42 ... 55 A8
Croydon Cl CV3 ... 133 E6
Croydon Ct 20 B29 ... 103 C7
Croydon Rd
Birmingham B29 ... 85 F3
Birmingham, Erdington B24 ... 57 A2
Croy Dr B35 ... 58 B4
Crucible The WV14 ... 40 D2
Crummock Cl CV6 ... 95 D3
Crumpfields La B97 ... 152 F1
Crump Ho WS1 ... 28 F1
Crusader Cl B69 ... 63 E5
Crutchley Ave B78 ... 21 A2
Crutchley Way CV31 ... 162 A2
Crychan Cl B45 ... 102 B2
Cryersoak Cl B90 ... 127 B7
Cryfield Grange Rd CV4, CV8 ... 132 C2
Cryfield Hts CV4 ... 132 D2
Cryfield Village CV4 ... 132 B4
Crystal Ave DY8 ... 60 F1
Crystal Dr B66 ... 64 C8
Crystal Ho B66 ... 65 C6
Crystal L Ctr DY8 ... 80 F5
CTC Kingshurst Acad B37 ... 70 A4
CUBBINGTON ... 157 D6
Cubbington CE Prim Sch CV32 ... 157 F5
Cubbington Rd
Coventry CV6 ... 96 A2
Royal Leamington Spa CV32 ... 157 B3
Cubley Rd B28 ... 87 E1
Cuckoo Cl
Birmingham B33 ... 68 F4
Cannock WS11 ... 2 C2
Cuckoo La CV1 ... 165 C3
Cuckoo Rd B7 ... 67 D8
Cuckoo's Nook & the Dingle Nature Reserve* WS9 ... 30 A2
Cuin Rd B66 ... 65 C5
Cuin Wlk 11 B66 ... 65 C5
Culey Gr B33 ... 69 D2
Culey Wlk B37 ... 70 D2
Culford Dr B32 ... 102 C8
Culham Cl B27 ... 88 D2
Cullwick St WV1 ... 40 A8
Culmington Rd B31 ... 122 F8
Culmore Cl WV12 ... 27 D4
Culmore Rd B62 ... 63 E1
Culpepper Cl CV10 ... 72 E4
Culverhouse Dr DY5 ... 61 A1
Culverley Cres B93 ... 127 F6
Culvert Way B66 ... 64 D7
Culwell Ind Pk WV10 ... 163 D4
Culwell St WV10 ... 163 C4
Culwell Trad Est WV10 ... 25 F4
Culworth Cl CV31 ... 161 F5
Culworth Ct
Coventry CV6 ... 113 E7
Whitnash CV31 ... 162 A5
Culworth Row CV6 ... 113 E8
Cumberford Ave B33 ... 69 E1
Cumberland Ave 3 B5 ... 86 E7
Cumberland Cl DY6 ... 60 E4
Cumberland Cres
Burntwood WS7 ... 7 A8
Royal Leamington Spa CV32 ... 157 C3
Cumberland Dr
Nuneaton CV10 ... 72 E3
Tamworth B78 ... 21 A1
Cumberland Ho 7 WV3 ... 25 C4
Cumberland Rd
Bilston WV14 ... 40 D7
Birmingham B68 ... 84 B7
Cannock WS11 ... 2 A4
West Bromwich B71 ... 53 D7
Willenhall WV13 ... 27 D2
Cumberland St B1 ... 66 B2
Cumberland Wlk B75 ... 47 B5
Cumbernauld Wlk 7 CV2 ... 115 A7
Cumbrae Dr LE10 ... 71 B2
Cumbria Cl CV1 ... 113 A3
Cumbrian Croft B63 ... 82 D2
Cumbria Way B8 ... 67 D6
Cumming St 14 CV31 ... 162 A7
Cundall Cl CV31 ... 162 B6
Cunnery The CV8 ... 149 A3
Cunningham Rd
Perton WV6 ... 23 E4
Walsall WS2 ... 27 E2
Cupfields Ave DY4 ... 52 C8
Cupfields Cres DY4 ... 52 C7
Cupronickle Way B77 ... 35 E6
Curbar Rd B42 ... 55 C6
CURBOROUGH ... 3 D5
Curborough Rd WS13 ... 3 B2
Curdale Rd B32 ... 102 B8
CURDWORTH ... 59 B6
Curdworth La B76 ... 59 A8
Curdworth Prim Sch B76 ... 59 C6
Cur La B97 ... 152 D3
Curlew B77 ... 36 A7
Curlew Cl
Kidderminster DY10 ... 117 B2
Lichfield WS14 ... 9 E7
Curlew Dr WS8 ... 15 E7
Curlew Hill WS11 ... 2 A3
Curlews Cl B23 ... 56 C8
Curlieu Cl CV35 ... 160 A7
Curral Rd B65 ... 63 C3
Curran Cl CV31 ... 162 B4
Curriers Cl CV4 ... 131 D7
Curslow La DY10 ... 117 F1
Curtin Dr WS10 ... 41 B4
Curtis Cl
Finstall B60 ... 151 F8
Smethwick B66 ... 65 C4
Curtis Rd CV2 ... 114 D6
Curzon Ave CV6 ... 113 E8
Curzon Cl LE10 ... 75 F7
Curzon Gr CV31 ... 162 C6
Curzon St
Birmingham B4 ... 67 A3
Wolverhampton WV2 ... 39 D7
Cuthbert Rd B18 ... 65 E4
Cutlers Rough Cl B31 ... 102 F5
Cutler St B66 ... 65 B6
Cutsdean Cl B31 ... 102 F6
Cutshill Cl B36 ... 69 C8
Cut Throat La B94 ... 142 D7
Cutting The WS4 ... 28 F4
Cuttle Mill La B76 ... 48 D3
Cuttle Pool La B93 ... 128 F4
Cutworth Cl B76 ... 47 A3
Cwerne Ct DY3 ... 50 C3
Cygnet Cl
Alvechurch B48 ... 139 A7
Cannock WS12 ... 2 C7
Wolverhampton WV6 ... 24 C2
Cygnet Ct
Coventry CV1 ... 165 C4
Kidderminster DY10 ... 117 A1
Cygnet Dr
Brownhills WS8 ... 15 E7
Tamworth B79 ... 20 F5
Cygnet Gr B23 ... 56 B6
Cygnet La DY5 ... 61 C7
Cygnet Rd B70 ... 53 A5
Cygnus Way B70 ... 52 F5
Cymbeline Way CV34 ... 161 E4
Cypress Ave DY3 ... 50 D5
Cypress Croft CV3 ... 134 F8
Cypress Ct DY10 ... 117 A4
Cypress Gdns
Kingswinford DY6 ... 60 D4
Sutton Coldfield B74 ... 46 A7
Walsall WS5 ... 43 C4
Cypress Gr B31 ... 102 E1
Cypress La CV31 ... 162 B3
Cypress Rd
Dudley DY2 ... 51 F1
Walsall WS5 ... 43 C4
Cypress Sq 2 B27 ... 88 C5
Cypress Way
Birmingham B31 ... 122 F8
Nuneaton CV10 ... 72 D6
Cyprus Ave B96 ... 158 D2
Cyprus Cl B29 ... 103 A7
Cyprus St
Oldbury B69 ... 64 A8
Wolverhampton WV2 ... 39 C6
Cyril Gr 5 B10 ... 87 C8
Cyril Rd B10 ... 87 D8

D

Dace B77 ... 35 D7
Dacer Cl B30 ... 104 B5
Dace Rd WV10 ... 26 B4
Dadford View DY5 ... 61 B2
Dad's La B13 ... 86 C1
Daffern Rd CV7 ... 78 A1
Daffodil Cl DY3 ... 50 E7
Daffodil Dr CV12 ... 77 D2
Daffodil Pl WS5 ... 43 D8
Daffodil Rd WS5 ... 43 D8
Daffodil Way B31 ... 122 E8
Dagger La B71 ... 53 E4
Dagnall Rd B27 ... 88 D3
Dagnell End Rd B98 ... 154 B7
DAGTAIL END ... 158 E3
Dagtail La B97 ... 158 D3
Dahlia Cl
Hinckley LE10 ... 75 E6
Wolverhampton WV1 ... 26 C1
Dahlia Wlk CV10 ... 78 A8
Daimler Cl B36 ... 58 F1
Daimler Rd
Birmingham B14 ... 105 D3
Coventry CV6 ... 113 C5
Dainton Gr B32 ... 84 C1
Daintree Croft CV3 ... 133 C7
Daintry Dr B78 ... 20 B7
Dairy Cl DY4 ... 52 B5
Dairy Ct B68 ... 84 D7
Dairy La B97 ... 153 A5
Dairy Way B21 ... 54 C1
DAISY BANK ... 40 C2
Daisy Bank WS12 ... 1 F8
Daisy Bank Cl WS3 ... 15 B2
Daisy Bank Cres WS5 ... 43 D8
Daisy Croft CV12 ... 77 D2
Daisy Dr B23 ... 56 A5
Daisy Farm Rd B14 ... 105 B3
Daisy Mdw DY4 ... 52 C6
Daisy Rd B16 ... 65 F2
Daisy St
Dudley WV14 ... 40 D2
Wolverhampton WV6 ... 25 A4
Daisy Wlk WV9 ... 11 A3
Dakota Apartments B16 ... 66 B1
Dalbeg Cl WV8 ... 24 E8
Dalbury Rd B28 ... 105 E5
Dalby Cl CV3 ... 134 E8
Dalby Rd WS3 ... 28 F6
Dale Cl
Birmingham B43 ... 43 D1
Catshill B61 ... 136 F7
Smethwick B66 ... 65 A3
Tipton DY4 ... 52 D5
Warwick CV34 ... 161 A8
Dalecote Ave B92 ... 107 E8
Dale Ct WV1 ... 25 A3
Dale Dr WS7 ... 7 B7
Dale End
Birmingham B4 ... 164 C3
Darlaston WS10 ... 41 D6
Nuneaton CV10 ... 72 E5
Dale End Cl LE10 ... 75 A7
Dale Hill B60 ... 137 F6
Dalehouse Flats CV8 ... 148 B6
Dalehouse La CV8 ... 148 D7
Dalehouse Lane Ind Est CV8 ... 148 C6
Dale Meadow Cl CV7 ... 130 B6
Dale Rd
Birmingham B29 ... 85 E3
Halesowen B62 ... 83 F8
Redditch B98 ... 153 F5
Stourbridge DY8 ... 80 F2
Dales Cl WV6 ... 25 B6
Dalesman Cl DY6 ... 60 B7
Dale St
Bilston WV14 ... 41 A5
Royal Leamington Spa CV32 ... 161 E8
Smethwick B66 ... 65 A3
Walsall WS1 ... 42 E7
Wednesbury WS10 ... 41 E3
Wolverhampton WV3 ... 163 A2
Daleswood Pk B62 ... 100 F2
Dale Terr B69 ... 63 C8
Daleview Rd B14 ... 105 C4
Daleway Rd CV3 ... 133 B4
Dale Wlk B25 ... 88 B7
Dalewood Croft B26 ... 88 F6
Dalewood Rd B37 ... 69 F5
Daley Cl B1 ... 66 B3
Daley Rd WV14 ... 40 F2
Dalkeith Rd B73 ... 45 E2
Dalkeith St WS2 ... 28 C3
Dallas Rd B23 ... 56 D5
Dallimore Cl B92 ... 89 A3
Dallington Rd CV6 ... 112 E6
Dalloway Cl B5 ... 86 D6
Dalmahoy Cl CV11 ... 79 C8
Dalmeny Rd CV4 ... 131 D7
Dalston Cl DY2 ... 62 D6
Dalston Rd B27 ... 88 C4
Dalton Ct B23 ... 56 B3
Dalton Gdns CV2 ... 114 F4
Dalton Rd
Bedworth CV12 ... 78 A2
Coventry CV5 ... 113 B1
Walsall WS2 ... 28 A3
Dalton St
Birmingham B4 ... 164 C3
Wolverhampton WV3 ... 39 B8
Dalton Way B4 ... 164 C3
Dalvine Rd DY2 ... 62 B2
Dalwood Cl WV14 ... 51 B7

Dalwood Way CV6 ...... 96 B4
Damar Croft B14 ...... 104 D4
Dama Rd B78 .... 34 F8
Dame Agnes Gr CV6 .... 114 B8
Dame Elizabeth Cadbury
  Tech Coll B30 .... 103 D7
Dame Ellen Pinsent Sch
  B13 .... 105 A7
Damien Cl B67 .... 64 F5
Dam Mill Cl WV8 ...... 10 C1
Damson Cl
  Redditch B97 ...... 158 C6
  Wednesfield WV12 .... 27 A6
Damson Cl LE10 .... 75 B7
Damson La B91, B92 ... 107 C7
Damson Parkway B91,
  B92 .... 107 F7
Damson Wharf DY4 ..... 52 A3
Damson Wood Inf Sch
  B92 .... 107 D7
Dam St WS13 .... 9 B8
Danbury Cl B76 .... 47 A2
Danbury Gdns WV10 .... 11 C2
Danbury Rd B90 .... 106 B2
Danby Gr B24 .... 57 B2
Dando Rd DY2 .... 62 B8
Dandy Bank Rd DY6 .... 61 A8
Dandy's Wlk WS1 ...... 42 F8
Dane Gr B13 .... 104 D8
Danehill Wlk WV8 ..... 24 F8
Danehurst Ctr WV1 .... 26 A3
Danelagh Cl B79 ...... 20 F7
Dane Rd CV2 .... 114 B4
Danesbury Cres
  Birmingham B44 .... 56 A8
  Royal Leamington Spa
  CV31 .... 162 D6
Danes Cl WV11 .... 12 F4
Danescourt Rd WV6 .... 24 C6
Danesmoor Ho B26 .... 88 F7
Daneswood Dr WS9 .... 15 F3
Daneswood Rd CV3 .... 135 E7
Dane Terr B65 .... 63 C5
Daneways Cl B74 ...... 45 A8
Danford Cl DY8 .... 81 A4
Danford Gdns B10 .... 87 C8
Danford La B91 .... 106 E3
Danford Rd B47 .... 124 F6
Danford Way B43 ...... 54 D8
Dangerfield Ho B70 ... 53 E1
Dangerfield La WS10 .. 41 C4
Daniel Ave CV10 ...... 72 C3
Daniels La WS9 .... 30 C4
Daniels Rd B9 .... 68 A2
Danilo Rd WS11 .... 1 D1
Danks St DY4 .... 52 A2
Danny Morson Way B78 . 36 E4
Danzey Cl B98 .... 159 B5
Danzey Gr B14 .... 104 C3
Danzey Green La B94 .. 142 B1
Danzey Green Rd B36 .. 58 B1
Daphne Cl CV2 .... 96 C3
Darby Cl WV14 .... 40 A2
DARBY END 62 E4
Darby Ho 2 WS2 ...... 42 C7
Darby Rd
  Oldbury B68 .... 64 C5
  Wednesbury WS10 .... 42 B4
DARBY'S HILL 63 B8
Darbys Hill Rd B69 .. 63 B7
Darby St B65 .... 63 C1
Darbys Way DY4 .... 52 B5
Darell Croft B76 .... 46 E3
Daren Cl B36 .... 69 F8
Dare Rd B23 .... 56 E4
Darfield Wlk 2 B12 .. 86 F8
Darges La WV4 .... 4 F4
Darkhouse La WV14 ... 40 C2
Dark La
  Astwood Bank B96 .. 158 D1
  Bedworth CV12 ..... 77 D1
  Belbroughton DY9 .. 119 F8
  Birchmoor B78 ..... 36 E8
  Brinsford WV10 .... 11 D8
  Coventry CV1 ...... 165 B4
  Featherstone WV10 .. 12 D7
  Hollywood B38, B47 . 124 E7
  Romsley B62 .... 100 F4
  Stoke Heath B60 ... 150 D6
DARLASTON 41 E7
Darlaston Ct CV7 .... 92 D1
DARLASTON GREEN 41 E8
Darlaston La WV14 ... 41 A7
Darlaston Rd
  Walsall WS2 .... 42 A8
  Wednesbury WS10 .... 41 E4
Darlaston Road Ind Est
  WS10 .... 41 D5
Darlaston Swimming Pool
  WS10 .... 41 E7
Darley Ave B34 .... 68 F6
Darleydale Ave B44 .. 44 E1
Darley Dr WV6 .... 25 B5
DARLEY GREEN 144 B8
Darley Green Rd B93 . 128 B1
Darley Ho B69 .... 63 D6
Darley Mead Ct B91 .. 107 E4
Darley Rd LE10 .... 75 E6
Darley Way B74 .... 45 A7
Darlington St
  Darlaston WS10 .... 41 D5
  Wolverhampton WV1 .. 163 B3
Darlington Yd WV1 ... 163 B3
Darlston Row CV7 .... 92 B1
Darnbrook B77 .... 22 C1
Darnel Croft 3 B10 .. 67 B1
Darnel Hurst Rd B75 . 32 D3

DARNFORD 9 F6
Darnford Cl
  Birmingham B28 .... 106 A5
  Coventry CV2 ...... 114 F7
  Sutton Coldfield B72 . 57 D7
Darnford La WS14 .... 9 F6
Darnford Moors WS14 . 9 E6
Darnford View WS13 .. 3 E1
Darnick Rd B73 .... 45 D2
Darnley Rd B16 .... 66 A2
Darrach Cl CV2 .... 96 E1
Darris Rd B29 .... 104 A8
Dart B77 .... 36 A5
Dart Cl LE10 .... 75 A8
Dartford Rd WS3 ...... 13 F1
Dartington Way CV11 . 78 F8
Dartmoor Cl B45 ..... 102 A2
Dartmouth Ave
  Cannock WS11 ...... 4 C8
  Stourbridge DY8 ... 60 D3
  Walsall WS3 .... 28 E6
  Willenhall WV13 ... 27 A2
Dartmouth Cir B6 .... 66 F5
Dartmouth Cres 2 WV14 . 41 A7
Dartmouth Dr WS9 .... 30 A5
Dartmouth Ho 2 WS3 . 28 F6
Dartmouth Middleway B7 . 66 F4
Dartmouth Pl WS3 .... 28 F6
Dartmouth Rd
  Birmingham B29 .... 85 F2
  Cannock WS11 ...... 1 D1
  Coventry CV2 ...... 114 C5
  Smethwick B66 ..... 64 F8
Dartmouth Sq B70 .... 53 D2
Dartmouth St
  West Bromwich B70 . 53 B3
  Wolverhampton WV2 . 163 C1
Dartmouth Street Stop
  B70 .... 53 B3
Dart St B9 .... 67 B1
Darul Uloom High Sch
  B10 .... 87 D8
Darvel Rd WV12 .... 27 D4
Darwall St WS1 .... 28 E2
Darwell Pk B77 .... 22 B2
Darwin Cl
  Burntwood WS7 ..... 7 B7
  Cannock WS12 ...... 2 E2
  Coventry CV2 ...... 115 A6
  Hinckley LE10 ..... 71 E3
  Lichfield WS13 .... 3 A8
Darwin Ct
  Bedworth CV12 ..... 78 A2
  Perton WV6 .... 23 E4
Darwin Ho
  8 Birmingham, Chelmsley
  Wood B37 .... 70 C1
  8 Birmingham, Showell Green
  B13 .... 87 A2
  Kingswinford DY6 .. 60 F7
Darwin Pl WS2 .... 28 B6
Darwin St B12 .... 86 F8
Dassett Gr B9 .... 68 C2
Dassett Rd B93 .... 127 F4
Datchet Cl CV5 .... 112 C4
Datteln Rd WS11 ...... 2 A4
D'aubeny Rd CV4 ...... 132 C8
Dauntsey Covert B14 . 104 D2
Davena Dr B29 .... 84 E2
Davena Gr WV14 .... 40 D3
Davenham Rd B60 ..... 137 C1
Davenport Dr
  Birmingham B35 .... 58 C3
  Bromsgrove B60 .... 137 B1
Davenport Lodge Sch
  CV5 .... 133 B8
Davenport Rd
  Coventry CV5 ...... 133 B8
  Wednesfield WV11 .. 26 E6
  Wolverhampton WV6 . 24 B5
Davenport Terr LE10 . 75 E8
Daventry Gr B32 ..... 84 D6
Daventry Rd CV3 ..... 133 D7
Davey Cl WS7 .... 6 F4
Davey Rd
  Birmingham B20 .... 55 E1
  West Bromwich B70 . 53 A5
David Cox Ct 1 B17 .. 85 D5
David Garrick Gdns WS13 . 3 B2
David Harman Dr B71 . 53 F7
David Peacock Cl DY4 . 52 A5
David Rd
  Bedworth CV7 ...... 95 F8
  Birmingham B20 .... 55 B2
  Coventry CV1 ...... 113 F2
  Tipton DY4 .... 52 A7
Davids Cl B97 .... 153 D2
Davidson Ave CV31 ... 162 A7
Davids The B31 .... 103 C5
Davies Ave WV14 ..... 40 D3
Davies Ho
  7 Oldbury B69 ..... 64 A7
  Walsall WS3 .... 14 B1
Davies Rd CV7 .... 95 F7
Davies Rd B29 .... 51 E4
Davis Cl CV32 .... 156 D2
Davis Gr B25 .... 88 D6
Davison Rd B67 ...... 64 F5
Davis Rd
  Tamworth B77 ...... 21 F4
  Willenhall WV12 ... 27 D8
Davy Rd WS2 .... 28 A5
Dawberry Cl B14 ..... 104 D5
Dawberry Fields Rd B14 . 104 D5
Dawberry Rd B14 ..... 104 C6

DAW END 29 C5
Daw End La WS4 .... 29 C6
Daw End La WS4 .... 29 C6
Dawes Ave B70 .... 53 C1
Dawes Cl CV2 .... 114 A3
Dawes La WS8 .... 7 A1
Dawley Brook Prim Sch
  DY6 .... 60 C7
Dawley Brook Rd DY6 . 60 D7
Dawley Cl WS2 .... 42 B6
Dawley Cres B37 ..... 70 B1
Dawley Rd DY6 .... 60 C6
Dawley Trad Est DY6 . 60 D8
Dawlish Wlk CV2 ..... 115 A7
Dawlish Cl CV11 ..... 73 E5
Dawlish Dr CV3 ...... 133 D5
Dawlish Rd
  Birmingham B29 .... 85 F2
  Dudley DY1 .... 51 C5
  Smethwick B66 ..... 65 B5
Daw Mill Dr B78 ..... 36 E5
Dawn Dr DY4 .... 41 C1
Dawn Rd B75 .... 32 A4
Dawn Rd B11 .... 102 E6
Dawson Ave WV14 ..... 39 F2
Dawson Cl CV31 ...... 162 A2
Dawson Ct B24 .... 56 F4
Dawson Rd
  Birmingham B21 .... 65 F8
  Bromsgrove B61 .... 136 E2
  Coventry CV3 ...... 114 A1
Dawson Sq W14 .... 40 C5
Dawson St
  Smethwick B66 ..... 65 A3
  Walsall WS3 .... 28 D8
Day Ave WV1 .... 26 E7
Daybrook Cl B97 ..... 153 B5
Day Ho DY4 .... 52 C8
DAYHOUSE BANK 101 A1
Dayhouse Bank B62 .. 101 B1
Daylesford Inf Sch B92 . 89 A3
Daylesford Rd B92 .. 89 A3
Days Cl CV1 .... 113 E3
Day's La CV1 .... 113 F3
Day St WS2 .... 28 E3
Daytona Dr CV5 ...... 111 B8
Deacon St CV11 ...... 73 C3
Deakin Ave WS8 ...... 6 F1
Deakin Rd
  Birmingham B24 .... 57 A3
  Sutton Coldfield B75 . 46 E7
Deakins Rd B25 ...... 88 B7
Deal Ave WS7 .... 7 A8
Deal Dr B69 .... 52 A1
Deal Gr B31 .... 103 A3
Deanbrook Cl B90 ... 127 A6
Dean Cl
  Birmingham B44 .... 56 B8
  Hinckley LE10 ..... 71 E2
  Stourbridge DY8 ... 81 B6
  Sutton Coldfield B72 . 57 B7
Dean Ct
  5 Brierley Hill DY5 . 61 D2
  Perton WV6 .... 23 E4
Deanery CE Prim Sch B76 . 57 F8
Deanery Row WV1 .... 163 B4
Dean Rd
  Birmingham B23 .... 56 F5
  Brierley Hill DY5 .. 61 B5
  Hinckley LE10 ..... 71 E2
  Walsall WS4 .... 29 C7
Dean Road W LE10 .... 71 E2
Deans Cl B98 .... 154 D5
Deans Croft WS14 .... 9 C8
Deanscroft Dr B60 .. 137 C1
Deansfield High Sch WV1 . 26 C2
Deansfield Rd WV1 .. 26 A2
Dansford La DY10 ... 118 B6
Deans Gate WV13 .... 26 C2
Deans Pl WS3 .... 28 F6
Dean's Rd WV1 .... 26 C2
Deans Slade Dr WS14 . 9 A5
Dean St
  Birmingham B5 ..... 164 C1
  Coventry CV2 ...... 114 A3
  Sedgley DY3 .... 50 D8
Deanston Croft CV2 . 96 F1
Deansway
  Bromsgrove B61 .... 136 E2
  Walsall CV35 ...... 155 E4
  Warwick CV34 ...... 155 E1
Deans Way CV7 .... 95 D6
Deansway The DY10 .. 117 A7
Deansway The DY10 .. 117 A7
Dearman Rd B11 ..... 87 B7
Dearmont Rd B31 .... 122 E7
Dearne Ct DY3 .... 51 A6
Deasy Ho CV3 .... 134 B5
Deasy Rd CV1 .... 165 C1
Deavall Way WS11 .... 2 B2
Debden Cl B93 .... 127 E2
Debenham Cres B25 .. 68 D1
Debenham Rd B25 .... 68 D1
Deblen Dr B16 .... 65 D1
Deborah Cl WV4 ...... 39 C6
Deedmore Rd CV2 .... 96 D1
Deegan Cl CV2 .... 114 A5
De Gr
  Birmingham B38 .... 123 E8
  Cannock WS11 ...... 4 D8
Dee Ho 3 DY1 .... 61 A8
Deelands Rd B45 .... 121 F8
Deeley B77 .... 22 A1
Deeley Cl
  Birmingham B15 .... 86 C7
  Cradley Heath B64 . 82 E7
Deeley Dr 3 DY4 .... 52 C6
Deeley Pl WS3 .... 28 B8

Deeley St
  Brierley Hill DY5 .. 61 E1
  Walsall WS3 .... 28 B8
Deepdale B77 .... 22 D2
Deepdale Ave B26 ... 89 A4
Deepdale La DY3 ..... 50 E3
DEEPFIELDS 40 B2
Deeplow Cl 2 B72 ... 46 C4
Deepmoor Rd B33 .... 68 F3
Deepmore Ave WS2 ... 28 B2
Deepwood Cl WS4 .... 29 B8
Deepwood Gr B32 .... 102 B8
Deer Barn Hill B98 . 154 A1
Deer Cl
  Huntington WS12 ... 1 C6
  Norton Canes WS11 . 6 B7
  Walsall WS3 .... 14 C1
Dee Rd WS3 .... 14 E1
Deerdale Terr 3 CV3 . 134 F8
Deerdale Way CV3 ... 134 F8
Deerfold Cres WS7 .. 7 B7
Deerham Cl B23 ..... 56 D7
Deerhill B77 .... 22 D2
Deerhurst Cl B98 ... 154 C7
Deerhurst Ct B91 ... 107 D4
Deerhurst Rd
  Birmingham B20 .... 54 F5
  Coventry CV6 ...... 95 B2
Deerhurst Rise WS12 . 2 C6
Deer Leap The CV8 .. 148 B6
Deerpark Dr CV34 ... 160 E8
Deer Park Rd B78 ... 20 E1
Deer Park Way B91 .. 107 C1
Deers Cl CV3 .... 134 D6
Deer Wlk WV8 .... 10 E3
Dee Wlk B36 .... 70 A7
Defford Ave WS4 .... 15 C1
Defford Cl B97 ...... 152 E1
Defford Dr B68 ..... 64 B4
Dehavilland Cl CV11 . 73 B5
De Havilland Dr B35 . 58 A2
De Havilland Way WS10 . 41 A7
Deighton Gr CV3 .... 134 C6
Deighton Rd WS5 ... 43 B4
De-La-Bere Cres LE10 . 76 A6
Delage Cl CV6 .... 96 B4
Delamere Cl B36 .... 58 D1
Delamere Dr WS5 ... 43 C3
Delamere Rd
  Bedworth CV12 ..... 77 F2
  Birmingham B28 .... 105 F7
  Willenhall WV12 ... 27 C7
Delamere Way CV32 .. 157 C4
Delancey Keep B75 .. 47 A5
Delaware Rd CV3 .... 133 D8
Delf Ho CV2 .... 96 D1
Delhi Ave CV6 .... 95 D1
Delhurst Ave WV4 ... 39 E3
Delhurst Rd B44 .... 44 D1
Delingpole Wlk 6 B64 . 82 E8
Delius St CV4 .... 111 E1
Delius St B7 .... 67 A6
Dell Cl CV3 .... 134 C5
Dell Farm Cl B93 ... 128 B6
Dellow Gr B48 .... 139 A5
Dellows Cl B38 ..... 123 D7
Dell Rd
  Birmingham B30 .... 104 A5
  Brierley Hill DY5 .. 61 B5
Dells Farm B47 ..... 124 F6
Dell Stadium DY5 ... 61 B4
Dell The
  Birmingham, Edgbaston
  B16 .... 65 F2
  Birmingham, Shenley Fields
  B31 .... 102 D6
  Cannock WS12 ...... 2 F4
  Lichfield WS13 .... 8 F7
  Solihull B92 ...... 89 A1
  Stourbridge DY8 ... 80 E6
  Tamworth B79 ...... 21 B6
Delly Ct CV8 .... 80 B1
Delmore Way B76 .... 58 B6
Delph Dr DY5 .... 81 E7
Delphinium Cl B9 .. 67 F3
Delph La DY5 .... 81 D8
Delphi Cl CV34 ..... 161 E4
Delph Rd DY5 .... 61 C3
Delrene Rd B28, B90 . 105 F3
Delta Trad Est WV2 . 39 F8
Delta Way WS11 ..... 4 D7
Deltic B77 .... 22 A1
Deltic La B77 .... 35 F8
Delves Cres
  Walsall WS5 .... 43 A5
  Wood End DY5 ...... 61 A8
Delves Green Rd WS5 . 43 A5
Delves Jun Sch WS5 . 43 A5
DELVES THE 42 F5
Delves Rd WS5 .... 43 A7
Delville Cl WS10 .... 41 F3
Delville Rd WS10 ... 41 F3
Delville Terr WS10 . 41 F3
De Marnham Cl B70 .. 53 E1
De Montfort Ho B37 . 69 F5
De Montfort Rd
  Hinckley LE10 ..... 71 E1
  Kenilworth CV8 .... 147 E6
De Montfort Way CV4 . 132 D5
De Moram Gr B92 .... 107 F7
Dempster Ct CV11 ... 73 C4
Dempster Rd CV12 .. 78 A4
Demuth Way B69 .... 63 E8
Denaby Gr B14 ...... 105 D4
Denbigh Cl DY1 ..... 50 F2
Denbigh Cres B71 ... 53 B6
Denbigh Ct 3 B29 .. 103 C7
Denbigh Dr
  Wednesbury WS10 .... 42 D4
  West Bromwich B71 . 53 B6
Denbigh Rd
  Coventry CV6 ...... 112 C5
  Tipton DY4 .... 52 C4
Denbigh St B9 .... 67 D2
Denbury Cl WS12 .... 2 D1
Denby Bldgs 17 CV32 . 161 F8
Denby Cl
  Royal Leamington Spa
  CV32 .... 157 C3
Denby Croft B90 ... 127 B6
Dencer Cl B45 ...... 122 A8
Dencer Dr CV8 ...... 148 C4
Dencil Cl B63 .... 82 D5
Dene Ave DY6 .... 60 B6
Dene Court Rd B92 .. 88 F1
Dene Croft WS3 ..... 14 A1
Denegate Cl B76 .... 58 B6
Dene Hollow B13 ... 105 C4
Denehurst Cl B45 .. 122 A1
Denehurst Way CV10 . 72 F3
Denemoor Ct CV8 ... 148 B5
Dene Rd
  Lower Penn WV4 .... 37 F4
  Stourbridge DY8 ... 80 F3
Denewood Ave B20 .. 55 B2
Denewood Way CV8 .. 148 C6
Denford Gr B14 .... 104 D5
Dengate Dr CV7 ..... 130 B7
Denham Ave CV5 .... 112 C4
Denham Ct B23 ...... 56 C2
Denham Gdns WV3 .. 38 B8
Denham Rd B27 ...... 88 C5
Denholme Gr B14 ... 105 A3
Denholm Rd B73 .... 45 D2
Denise Dr
  Birmingham B17 .... 85 C4
  Birmingham, Kingshurst B37 . 69 F4
  Dudley WV14 .... 51 B8
Denis Rd LE10 .... 75 D5
Denleigh Rd DY6 .... 60 F4
Denmark Cl WV6 ..... 25 A4
Denmark Rise WS12 .. 2 D7
Denmark Villas WS13 . 8 C5
Denmead Dr WV11 ... 26 F8
Denmore Gdns WV1 .. 26 D7
Dennett Cl CV34 ... 155 F2
Dennfield Dr WS6 ... 4 C2
Dennis B77 .... 21 E2
Dennis Hall 9 DY8 . 80 F8
Dennis Hall Rd DY8 . 81 A8
Dennis Rd
  Birmingham B12 .... 87 B4
  Coventry CV2 ...... 114 B6
Dennis St DY8 .... 80 F8
Denshaw Croft CV2 . 115 A8
Denshaw Rd B14 .... 104 D6
Denston Ct 6 B74 .. 31 F2
Denstone Gdns WV10 . 11 F3
Denton Ct CV8 ...... 147 D6
Denton Croft B93 .. 127 D3
Denton Gr
  Birmingham, Great Barr
  B43 .... 54 D7
  Birmingham, Stechford B33 . 68 D2
Derby St DY8 .... 80 F8
Dent St B79 .... 21 C5
Denver Rd B14 ...... 105 A2
Denville Cl WV14 ... 40 E7
Denville Cres B9 ... 68 B3
Denville Rd CV32 .. 157 A3
Derby Ave WV6 ...... 24 F7
Derby Dr B37 .... 70 B2
Derby Rd LE10 ...... 71 D1
Derby St
  Birmingham B9 ..... 67 A2
  Walsall WS2 .... 28 E4
Dereham Cl B8 ...... 67 C4
Dereham Ct CV32 ... 157 A2
Dereham Wlk WV14 .. 40 E2
Dereton Cl DY1 ..... 50 E2
Derick Burcher's Mall 5
  DY10 .... 116 E6
Dering Cl CV2 .... 114 D8
Deronda Cl CV12 ... 78 A3
Derron Ave B26 .... 88 C5
Derry Cl B17 .... 85 A3
Derrydown Cl B23 .. 56 E3
Derrydown Rd B42 .. 55 B5
Derry St
  Brierley Hill DY5 .. 61 D2
  Wolverhampton WV2 . 163 C1
Dersingham Dr CV6 .. 96 B2
Derwent B77 .... 21 D1
Derwent Cl
  Brierley Hill DY5 .. 61 B6
  Coventry CV5 ...... 111 E4
  Royal Leamington Spa
  CV32 .... 156 D1
  Sutton Coldfield WS9 . 30 F3
  Willenhall WV13 ... 27 C2
Derwent Ct 10 B73 . 46 B5
Derwent Gr
  Birmingham B13 .... 86 C1
  Burntwood WS7 ..... 7 D6
Derwent Ho
  8 Birmingham B17 .. 85 D5
  Kidderminster DY10 . 116 F7

Derwent Ho continued
 5 Oldbury B69 . . . . 63 D5
Derwent Rd
 Bedworth CV12 . . . . 78 A2
 Birmingham B30 . . . . . . 104 C8
 Coventry CV6 . . . . 95 A2
 Wolverhampton WV6 . . . . 24 E8
Derwent Way
 Bromsgrove B60 . . . . . . 137 B1
 Nuneaton CV11 . . . . 73 F6
Desdemona Ave CV34 . . 161 E4
Desford Ave B42 . . . . . . 55 C7
Design CI B60 . . . . 151 A7
De Somerley Rd 1 B69 . 64 A7
Despard Rd CV5 . . . . . . 111 D4
Dettonford Rd B32 . . . . 102 B8
Devereux CI
 Birmingham B36 . . . . . . 69 C8
 Coventry CV1 . . . . 111 C1
Devereux Ho B79 . . . . . 21 A4
Devereux Rd
 Sutton Coldfield B75 . . . . 32 C1
 West Bromwich B70 . . . . 53 E1
Deveron Ct LE10 . . . . . . 71 B1
Deveron Way LE10 . . . . 71 B1
Devey Dr DY4 . . . . 52 C8
Devine Croft DY4 . . . . . 52 A5
Devitts CI B90 . . . . 126 F7
Devon CI
 Birmingham B20 . . . . . . 54 F2
 Nuneaton CV10 . . . . 72 F3
Devon Ct
 3 Birmingham B29. . . . 103 B7
 Cannock WS11. . . . . 4 C8
Devon Gr CV2 . . . . 114 B6
Devon Ho 4 DY8 . . . . . 80 F8
Devonport CI 3 B97 . . 153 B5
Devon Rd
 Birmingham B45 . . . . . . 101 F1
 Cannock WS11. . . . . 4 F8
 Smethwick B67 . . . . 84 E7
 Stourbridge DY8 . . . . . . 80 E7
 Wednesbury WS10 . . . . . 42 C4
 Willenhall WV13 . . . . . . 27 D1
 Wolverhampton WV1. . . 163 A4
Devonshire Ct B18. . . . . 65 F6
Devonshire Ct B74. . . . . 32 A2
Devonshire Dr
 Tamworth B78 . . . . 21 A1
 West Bromwich B71 . . . . 53 E3
Devonshire Inf Sch B67 . 64 E5
Devonshire Jun Sch B67 . 64 E5
Devonshire Rd
 Birmingham B20 . . . . . . 54 F2
 Smethwick B67 . . . . 64 E6
Devonshire St B18 . . . . 66 A6
Devonshire Villas B10. . 87 D8
Devon St B7. . . . . 67 C5
Devon Way B31. . . . . . 122 E8
Devoran CI
 Bedworth CV7 . . . . 96 B8
 Wolverhampton WV6 . . . 25 B4
Dewberry Dr WS5. . . . . 43 A3
Dewberry Rd 3 DY8 . . 60 F1
Dewhurst Croft B33. . . . 69 B3
Dewis Ho 4 CV2. . . . . . 96 B1
Dewsbury Ave CV3 . . . 133 B5
Dewsbury CI
 Astwood Bank B96 . . . . 158 E1
 Stourbridge DY8 . . . . . . 60 E3
Dewsbury Dr
 Burntwood WS7. . . . . . . 7 C6
 Wolverhampton WV4. . . . 39 A4
Dewsbury Gr B42 . . . . . 55 C5
Dexter Ho B67 . . . . 64 F6
Dexter Way B78. . . . . . . 36 F8
Dey Croft CV34 . . . . . . 160 B4
Deykin Ave B6. . . . . 56 B2
Deykin Avenue Jun & Inf Sch
 B6. . . . . 56 A2
Deykin Rd WS13 . . . . . . 9 A6
D'Eyncourt Prim Sch
 WV11 . . . . 26 B7
D'Eyncourt Rd WV10 . . 26 A7
Dial CI B14 . . . . 104 E2
Dial House La CV5 . . . . 111 F4
Dial La
 Stourbridge DY8 . . . . . . 80 E8
 West Bromwich B70 . . . . 52 F6
Diamond Ct 3 B64 . . . . 62 D1
Diamond Gr WS11 . . . . . 1 A2
Diamond Park Dr 3 DY8 . 60 E1
Diana CI WS9. . . . . 16 B3
Diana Dr CV2 . . . . 114 B2
Diane CI DY4 . . . . 41 B2
Dibble CI WV12 . . . . . . 27 D5
Dibble Rd B67 . . . . 64 F6
DIBDALE 50 F3
Dibdale Ct DY3 . . . . . . 50 D3
Dibdale Rd DY3 . . . . . . 50 E3
Dibdale Road W DY1. . . 50 E3
Dibdale St DY1 . . . . 51 A2
Dice Pleck B31 . . . . . . 103 C2
Dickens CI
 Dudley DY3 . . . . 50 A5
 Nuneaton CV10 . . . . . . 72 A4
DICKENS HEATH 126 A6
Dickens Heath Prim Sch
 B90. . . . . 126 A6
Dickens Heath Rd B90 . 126 A5

Dickens Rd
 Coventry CV6. . . . . 113 A8
 Dudley WV14. . . . . 40 D2
 Wolverhampton WV10. . . 12 A1
Dickinson Ave WV10 . . . 25 F8
Dickinson Dr
 Sutton Coldfield B76 . . . . 46 E4
 Walsall WS2. . . . . 42 C6
Dickinson Rd WV5 . . . . . 49 A4
Dickins Rd CV34 . . . . . 156 B1
Dick Sheppard Ave DY4 . 52 B8
Didcot CI B97. . . . . 158 C5
Diddington Ave B28. . . . 106 A5
Diddington La B92, CV7 . . 91 C1
Didgley Gr B37 . . . . 70 A5
Didsbury Rd CV7. . . . . . 78 A1
DIGBETH 164 D1
Digbeth
 Birmingham B5 . . . . . . 164 D1
 Walsall WS1. . . . . 28 E1
Digby CI CV5 . . . . 112 B6
Digby Cres B46 . . . . 59 B3
Digby Ct 8 B27 . . . . 88 C3
Digby Dr B37 . . . . 90 B6
Digby Ho B37 . . . . 69 F4
Digby PI CV7 . . . . 92 C1
Digby Rd
 Coleshill B46 . . . . 70 F6
 Kingswinford DY6 . . . . . 60 D8
 Sutton Coldfield B73 . . . . 46 B4
Dilcock Way CV4. . . . . . 131 F7
Dilke Rd WS9. . . . . 29 F5
Dillam CI CV6. . . . . 96 A4
Dilliars Wlk B70 . . . . . . 53 A5
Dillington Ho 8 B37 . . . 70 B2
Dillon Ct CV11. . . . . 73 B5
Dillotford Ave CV3 . . . . 133 D6
Dilloways La WV13. . . . . 40 F8
Dilwyn CI B98 . . . . 154 F1
Dimbles Hill WS13 . . . . . 3 B1
Dimbles La WS13 . . . . . . 3 A2
Dimmingsdale Bank B32 . 84 C4
Dimmingsdale Rd WV4. . 37 E5
Dimminsdale WV13 . . . . 27 A1
Dimmocks Ave WV14. . . 51 D8
Dimmock St WV4 . . . . . . 39 E5
Dimsdale Gr B31. . . . . . 102 E3
Dimsdale Rd B31 . . . . . 102 D3
Dinedor CI B98 . . . . . . 154 D3
Dingle Ave B64 . . . . 82 E8
Dingle CI
 Birmingham B30 . . . . . . 103 D7
 Coventry CV6 . . . . 113 A6
 Dudley DY2 . . . . 62 F7
Dingle Com Sch DY6. . . 61 A4
Dingle Ct B91. . . . . 106 F1
Dingle Hollow B69 . . . . 63 D8
Dingle La
 Solihull B91 . . . . 106 F2
 Willenhall WV13 . . . . . . 27 A4
Dingle Mead B14 . . . . . 104 C4
Dingle Rd
 Brownhills WS8 . . . . 15 E6
 Dudley DY2 . . . . 62 E7
 Kingswinford DY6 . . . . . 61 A4
 Stourbridge DY9 . . . . . . 81 C2
Dingleside B98 . . . . 153 E2
Dingle St B69. . . . . 63 E8
Dingle The
 Birmingham B29 . . . . . . 85 E2
 Cheswick Green B90 . . . 126 D5
 Nuneaton CV10 . . . . 72 E6
 Oldbury B69. . . . . 63 D8
 Wolverhampton WV3 . . . 24 D1
Dingle View DY3. . . . . . 50 C7
Dingley Rd
 Bulkington CV12 . . . . . . 79 B2
 Wednesbury WS10 . . . . . 42 A5
Dinham Gdns DY1. . . . . 50 E3
Dinmore Ave B31 . . . . . 103 B4
Dinmore CI B98. . . . . . 154 D3
Dinsdale Wlk WV6 . . . . . 25 A5
Dippons Dr WV6. . . . . . 24 A3
Dippons Ho WV6. . . . . . 24 A3
Dippons Mill CI WV6. . . 24 A3
Direct 2 Ind Pk B69 . . . 52 F1
Dirtyfoot La WV4 . . . . . 38 A5
Discovery CI DY4 . . . . . 52 C5
Discovery Way CV3 . . . 135 B7
District City WS12 . . . . . 2 C2
Ditchford CI B97. . . . . . 158 D4
Ditch The 10 WS1 . . . . . 28 F1
Ditton Gr B31. . . . . 122 F6
Dixon CI
 Birmingham B35 . . . . . . 58 A2
 Redditch B97 . . . . 153 D5
 Tipton DY4 . . . . 52 C6
Dixon Ct DY10 . . . . 117 C8
Dixon Ho B16. . . . . 66 A1
Dixon Rd B10 . . . . 87 B8
DIXON'S GREEN 62 D7
Dixon's Green Ct 7 DY2 . 62 E8
Dixon's Green Rd DY2. . 62 E8
Dixon St
 Kidderminster DY10. . . . 116 E5
 Wolverhampton WV2. . . . 39 E7
Doal Trad Est B66. . . . . 65 B6
Dobbins Oak Rd DY9 . . . 81 E1
Dobbs Mill CI B29. . . . . 86 B2
Dobbs St WV2 . . . . 163 B1
Dobson La CV31. . . . . . 162 A4
Dockar Rd B31. . . . . . . 102 E2
Dockers CI CV7 . . . . . . 130 A5
Dock La 10 DY1 . . . . . . 51 B1
Dock Lane Ind Est 10 DY1 51 B1
Dock Meadow Dr DY4 . . 40 A4
Dock Meadow Drive Ind Est
 WV4 . . . . 40 B4

Dock Rd DY8 . . . . 60 F2
Dock The
 Catshill B61 . . . . 137 A8
 Stourbridge DY9 . . . . . . 81 F5
Doctors CI B94 . . . . . . 142 A2
Doctors Hill
 Bournheath B61. . . . . . 136 D8
 Stourbridge DY9 . . . . . . 81 C3
 Tamworth-In-A B94 . . . 142 A2
Doctors La
 Kingswinford DY6 . . . . . 60 A4
 Shenstone WS14 . . . . . . 18 A6
Doctor's Piece WV13. . . 27 B2
Dodd Ave CV34 . . . . . . 161 C7
Doddington Gr B32 . . . 102 B8
DODFORD 136 A7
Dodford CI B45 . . . . . . 121 F7
Dodford Ct B61 . . . . . . 136 C6
Dodford Fst Sch B61 . . 136 A5
Dodford Ho B60 . . . . . . 137 B3
Dodford Rd B61. . . . . . 120 D1
Dodgson CI CV6 . . . . . . 96 A4
Dodwells Bridge Ind Est
 LE10 . . . . 74 E8
Dodwells Rd LE10. . . . . 74 E8
DOE BANK. 46 C7
Doe Bank Ct B74. . . . . . 46 B8
Doe Bank La
 Birmingham B43, WS9. . 44 D5
 Coventry CV1. . . . . 113 A3
Doe Bank Rd DY4 . . . . . 41 C1
Dogberry CI CV3 . . . . . 134 C6
Dogberry Way CV34. . . 161 F2
Dogge Lane Croft B27. . 88 B2
Dogkennel La
 Halesowen B63 . . . . 83 B3
 Oldbury B68. . . . . 64 C5
Dog Kennel La
 Solihull B90 . . . . 126 D7
 3 Walsall WS1. . . . . . . 28 F2
Dog La
 Tamworth B77 . . . . 22 B6
 Weeford WS14. . . . . 19 A4
Doglands The CV31 . . . 162 B4
Dogpool La B30. . . . . . . 86 B1
Doidge Rd B23. . . . . . . 56 D3
Dolan Park Hosp (Private)
 B60 . . . . 137 B5
Dolben La B98. . . . . . . 154 D3
Dollery Dr B5. . . . . 86 C5
Dollis Gr B44. . . . . 44 F3
Dollman St B7 . . . . 67 B4
Dolman Rd B6. . . . . 66 B6
Dolobran Rd B11. . . . . . 87 B7
Dolomite Ave CV4. . . . . 112 D1
Dolphin CI WS3. . . . . . . 14 F1
Dolphin Ctr The B60 . . 137 A2
Dolphin La B27 . . . . 88 C1
Dolphin Rd
 Birmingham B11 . . . . . . 87 D5
 Redditch B98. . . . . 154 A5
Dolton Way DY4. . . . . . 51 E6
Domar Rd DY11. . . . . . 116 B7
Dominic Dr B30. . . . . . 103 D4
Donalbain CI CV34 . . . 161 F3
Doncaster CI CV2 . . . . 114 D7
Doncaster Way B36 . . . . 68 C8
Don CI B15 . . . . 85 D8
Donegal CI CV4. . . . . . 132 A7
Donegal Rd B74 . . . . . . 44 F8
Dongan Rd CV34 . . . . . 160 E7
Don Gr WS11 . . . . 4 C2
Donibristle Croft B35 . . 58 A4
Donnington Ave CV6 . . 112 E5
Donnington CI B98. . . . 154 C5
Donnington Ct B91. . . . 50 F3
Donnington Ho B33. . . . 69 B2
Donnithorne Ave CV10,
 CV11 . . . . 73 D1
Donovan Dr B73 . . . . . . 46 A6
Dooley CI WV13. . . . . . . 26 E2
Doone CI CV2. . . . . 114 E6
Dorado B77 . . . . 35 D7
Dora Herbert Ct B12 . . . 86 E5
Doran CI B63 . . . . 82 D1
Doranda Way B71. . . . . 53 F1
Doranda Way Ind Pk B71. 54 A1
Dora Rd
 Birmingham B10 . . . . . . 87 E8
 Birmingham, Handsworth
 B21. . . . . 65 E7
 West Bromwich B70 . . . . 53 C1
Dorcas CI CV11 . . . . . . 79 C8
Dorchester CI WV12. . . . 27 C8
Dorchester Dr B17 . . . . 85 B4
Dorchester Rd
 Hinckley LE10 . . . . 76 B7
 Kidderminster DY11. . . . 116 C6
 Solihull B91 . . . . 107 A4
 Stourbridge DY9 . . . . . . 81 D2
 Willenhall WV12 . . . . . . 13 C1
Dorchester Way
 Coventry CV2 . . . . 115 A4
 Nuneaton CV11 . . . . . . 74 A7
DORDALE. 119 E1
Dordale CI B31. . . . . . . 102 C1
Dordale Rd DY9 . . . . . . 119 E2
DORDON 22 E6
Dordon CI B90 . . . . . . 105 E1
Doreen Gr B24. . . . . . . 57 B2
Doris Rd
 Birmingham B11 . . . . . . 87 B4
 Birmingham, Bordesley Green
 B9. . . . . 67 D2

Doris Rd continued
 Coleshill B46 . . . . 70 F8
Dorlcote Rd B8 . . . . 68 A4
Dorlecote Ct CV10 . . . . 73 C1
Dorlecote PI CV10 . . . . 78 C8
Dorlecote Rd CV10. . . . 78 C8
Dormer Ave B77 . . . . . . 21 D5
Dormer Harris Ave CV4. 111 F1
Dormer Ho 16 CV32 . . . 156 F2
Dormer PI CV32. . . . . . 161 F8
Dormie CI B38 . . . . 103 D1
Dormington Rd B44. . . . 44 F3
Dormston CI
 Redditch B98 . . . . 153 F1
 Solihull B91 . . . . 127 C8
Dormston Dr
 Birmingham B29. . . . . . 84 F2
 Sedgley DY3 . . . . 50 E8
Dormston Sch DY3. . . . 50 E8
Dormston Trad Est DY1 . 50 F4
Dormy Dr B31 . . . . 123 A7
Dorncliffe Ave B33. . . . 69 D7
Dorney CI CV5 . . . . 132 E8
Dornie Dr B38 . . . . 103 F1
Dornton Rd B30 . . . . . . 104 C8
Dorothy Adams CI 3 B64. 82 E8
Dorothy Gardner Sch
 (Lower) LE10 . . . . 71 B3
Dorothy Goodman Sch
 (Upper) LE10 . . . . 71 D2
Dorothy Pattison Hospl
 WS2. . . . . 28 B1
Dorothy Powell Way CV2. 96 F1
Dorothy Rd
 Birmingham B11 . . . . . . 88 B5
 Smethwick B67 . . . . 65 A4
Dorothys Gate B91. . . . 107 C2
Dorothy St WS1. . . . . . . 42 D7
DORRIDGE 127 E3
Dorridge CI B97 . . . . . 153 B1
Dorridge Croft B93 . . . 127 E2
Dorridge Jun & Inf Schs
 B93. . . . . 128 A4
Dorridge Rd B93 . . . . . 128 A2
Dorridge Sta B93 . . . . . 127 F2
Dorridge Wood Nature
 Reserve * B93. . . . . . . 128 A1
Dorrington Gn B42. . . . 55 A5
Dorrington Prim Sch B42 55 A5
Dorrington Rd B42. . . . 55 A5
Dorset CI
 Birmingham B45 . . . . . 101 F2
 Nuneaton CV10 . . . . . . 72 F3
 Tamworth B78 . . . . 21 A1
Dorset Cotts B30. . . . . 104 A6
Dorset Ct 2 B29 . . . . . . 103 B7
Dorset Dr WS9. . . . . . . 16 B1
Dorset PI WS3 . . . . 28 C7
Dorset Rd
 Birmingham B8 . . . . 67 C6
 Cannock WS11. . . . . 2 E1
 Coventry CV1. . . . . 113 C5
 Smethwick B17 . . . . 65 B3
 Stourbridge DY8 . . . . . . 80 D8
Dorsett Rd
 Darlaston WS10. . . . . . . 41 C6
 Wednesbury WS10 . . . . . 42 D2
Dorset Road Terr WS10. 41 C6
Dorset Twr B18 . . . . . . 66 B4
Dorsheath Gdns B23 . . 56 F4
Dorsington Rd B27. . . . 88 D1
Dorstone Covert B14. . 104 C2
Dorville CI B38 . . . . . . 123 D8
DOSTHILL. 35 C5
Dosthill Prim Sch B77. . 35 D5
Dosthill Rd B77 . . . . . . 35 D7
Dotterel PI DY10 . . . . . 117 A1
Douay Rd B24 . . . . 57 B6
Double Row DY2 . . . . . 62 E4
Doughty CI 3 DY4 . . . . 52 C5
Doughty St B7 . . . . 66 F6
Douglas Ave
 Birmingham B36 . . . . . . 68 D6
 Oldbury B68. . . . . 64 D4
Douglas Davies CI WV12. 27 C4
Douglas Ho CV1 . . . . . . 165 D4
Douglas PI WV10 . . . . . 25 C6
Douglas Rd
 Birmingham B27 . . . . . . 88 C4
 Birmingham, Handsworth
 B21. . . . . 65 C7
 Dudley WV14 . . . . 51 D8
 Halesowen B62 . . . . 63 E1
 Hollywood B47. . . . . . . 125 A7
 Oldbury B68. . . . . 64 D4
 Sutton Coldfield B72 . . . . 46 C3
Douglass Rd DY2 . . . . . 62 D8
Douglas Turner Way WV3 24 E3
Doulton CI
 Cannock WS11. . . . . 1 B1
 Hinckley LE10 . . . . 76 B7
 Walsall WS9. . . . . 16 B3
Doulton Ct CV12. . . . . . 96 E1
Doulton PI B65. . . . . . . 63 B3
Doulton Rd B64, B65. . . 65 A6
Doulton Rd B64, B65. . . 62 F4
Doulton Trad Est B65. . . 62 F4
Douper Hall B29. . . . . . 83 F3
Dove Bridge CI B76. . . . 46 F4
Dove Ct
 Bedworth CV12. . . . . . . 77 E3
 4 Birmingham B29. . . . . 88 E8
 Burntwood WS7. . . . . . . 7 D6
 Hinckley LE10 . . . . 75 A8
 Kidderminster DY10. . . . 117 B2
 Walsall WS11. . . . . 29 A1
 Wednesbury WS10 . . . . . 42 B4
Dovecote CI
 Coventry CV6. . . . . 112 D5

Dovecote CI continued
 Solihull B91 . . . . 107 B8
 Tipton DY4 . . . . 52 C5
 Wolverhampton WV6. . . . 24 C4
Dovecote Rd B61 . . . . . 136 E1
Dovecotes Prim Sch WV8 10 F1
Dovecotes The
 Coventry CV5. . . . . 112 B5
 Sutton Coldfield B75 . . . . 32 B3
Dovedale WS11 . . . . 2 A5
Dovedale Ave
 Coventry CV6. . . . . 95 F2
 Solihull B90 . . . . 106 B1
 Walsall WS3. . . . . 15 B5
 Willenhall WV12 . . . . . . 27 B4
Dovedale Ct
 10 Birmingham B29. . . . 103 C7
 Wolverhampton WV4 . . . 39 C7
Dovedale Dr B28. . . . . 105 F5
Dovedale Rd
 Birmingham B23 . . . . . . 56 C7
 Kingswinford DY6 . . . . . 60 E8
 Wolverhampton WV4 . . . 39 E3
Dove Dr DY8 . . . . 81 A8
Dove Gdns B38 . . . . . . 104 B2
Dove Hollow
 Cannock WS12. . . . . 2 E4
 Great Wyrley WS6 . . . . . 4 F1
Dovehouse CI CV34 . . . 160 B3
Dove House Ct B91 . . . 106 F7
Dovehouse Fields WS14. . 9 B6
Dovehouse La B91. . . . 106 F7
Dove House La CV5 . . . 112 E7
Dovehouse Pool Rd 1 B6 66 E8
Dover CI B32 . . . . 102 A7
Dovercourt Rd B26. . . . 89 C5
Doverdale Ave DY10. . . 117 B3
Doverdale CI
 Halesowen B63 . . . . 82 E5
 Redditch B98 . . . . 159 B7
Dover Farm CI B77. . . . 36 B8
Dover Ho WS3. . . . . 28 C7
Dover Ridge DY8 . . . . . 81 A7
Doveridge CI B91 . . . . 106 E6
Doveridge PI WS1 . . . . 42 F8
Doveridge Rd B28 . . . . 105 E5
Doversley Rd B14 . . . . 104 C5
Dover St
 Bilston WV14 . . . . 40 D6
 Birmingham B18 . . . . . . 66 A6
 Coventry CV1. . . . . 165 A3
Dovestone B77 . . . . 22 D1
Doveton Ho DY8 . . . . . . 81 A3
Dove Way B36 . . . . 69 F8
Dovey Dr B76. . . . . 58 A7
Dovey Gr B65 . . . . 63 B2
Dovey Rd
 Birmingham B13 . . . . . . 87 D2
 Oldbury B69. . . . . 63 D8
Dowar Rd B45 . . . . 122 C7
Dowells Ct B13 . . . . 86 F2
Dowells Gdns DY9 . . . . 60 D3
Doweries The B45 . . . . 121 F8
Dower Rd B75. . . . . 32 B1
Dowler's Hill Cres B98 . 159 A8
Dowles CI B29 . . . . 103 B6
Dowles Rd DY11 . . . . . 116 B2
Dowley Croft CV3 . . . . 115 B1
Downcroft Ave B38 . . . 103 E2
Downdery Way CV6 . . . 114 A6
Downend CI WV10 . . . . 11 F4
Downes Ct 7 DY4 . . . . 51 E5
Downesway WS11. . . . . 1 C2
Downey CI B11 . . . . 87 B7
Downfield CI WS3. . . . . 14 A4
Downfield Dr DY3. . . . . 50 E6
Downham CI WS5. . . . . 29 E1
Downham PI WV3. . . . . 38 F8
Downham Wood WS5 . . 43 E8
Downie Rd WV8 . . . . . . 10 C3
Downing CI
 Dorridge B93. . . . . 128 A4
 6 Rowley Regis B65. . . 63 C1
 Wednesfield WV11 . . . . . 27 A7
Downing Cres CV12 . . . 78 C4
Downing Ct 2 B68. . . . 84 B7
Downing Ho B79 . . . . . 20 E5
Downing Rd B37. . . . . . 70 B1
Downing St
 Halesowen B63 . . . . 83 A5
 Smethwick B66 . . . . 65 C7
Downland CI B38 . . . . . 103 F1
Downsell Ho B97 . . . . . 153 A2
Downsfield Rd B26. . . . 89 B7
Downside Rd B24 . . . . . 56 E1
Downs Rd WV13 . . . . . . 41 C8
Downs The
 Sutton Coldfield WS9. . . . 30 E2
 Wolverhampton WV10. . . 25 C6
Dowty Ave CV12 . . . . . . 77 D1
Dowty Way WV9 . . . . . . 11 A3
Doyle Dr CV6. . . . . 95 F3
Dragoon Fields B60 . . . 151 B8
Drake CI WS3. . . . . 14 B1
Drake Croft
 Birmingham B37 . . . . . . 70 D4
 4 Lichfield WS13 . . . . . 9 C8
Drake Ct WS3. . . . . 14 B1
Drake Rd
 Birmingham B23 . . . . . . 56 C3
 Smethwick B66 . . . . 64 E7
 Walsall WS3. . . . . 14 C1
Drakes CI
 Redditch B97. . . . . 158 C4

Drakes Cl *continued*
Wythall B47 124 F4
DRAKES CROSS 125 A6
Drakes Cross Par B47 125 A5
Drake's Gn WV14 40 F3
Drakes Hill Cl DY8 80 C4
Drake St
Coventry CV6 113 D7
West Bromwich B71 53 C5
Drake Way LE10 71 D4
Drancy Ave WV12 27 D6
Draper Cl CV8 148 C4
Drapers Ct CV1 165 B4
Draper's Field CV1 165 B4
DRAPER'S FIELDS 165 B4
Drawbridge Rd B90 125 E8
Draycote Cl B92 107 D6
Draycott Ave B23 56 D4
Draycott Cl
[9] Redditch B97 153 B5
Wolverhampton WV4 38 C5
Draycott Cres B77 21 D1
Draycott Dr B31 102 E7
Draycott Rd
Coventry CV2 114 C7
Smethwick B66 64 E7
Drayman Cl WS1 42 F8
DRAYTON 119 B4
DRAYTON BASSETT 34 D5
Drayton Cl
Hartshill CV10 72 A8
Redditch B98 159 D8
Sutton Coldfield B75 32 B3
Drayton Cres CV5 111 D5
Drayton Ct
Bromsgrove B60 151 B8
Warwick CV34 155 E2
Drayton La B78 34 C5
Drayton Manor Dr
Drayton Bassett B78 34 F7
Fazeley B78 34 F8
Drayton Manor Theme Pk★
B78 34 E7
Drayton Rd
Bedworth CV12 78 D2
Belbroughton DY9 119 B5
Birmingham B14 104 F8
Smethwick B66 65 A1
Solihull B90 126 E8
Drayton St
Walsall WS2 28 C2
Wolverhampton WV2 163 B1
Drayton Way CV10 72 C7
Dreadnought Rd DY5 61 B8
Dreamwell Ind Est B11 88 A6
Dreel The B15 85 E7
Dreghorn Rd B36 68 F8
Drem Croft B35 58 A2
Dresden Cl WV4 40 A4
Drew Cres
Kenilworth CV8 148 A4
Stourbridge DY9 81 D2
Drew Rd DY9 81 D3
Drews Ho B14 104 D1
Drews Holloway B63 82 D5
Drews Holloway S B63 82 D5
Drews La B8 68 A7
Drews Meadow Cl [1]
B14 104 C2
Driffield Cl B98 154 D2
Driffold B73 46 B3
Driftwood Cl B38 123 D7
Drinkwater Ho [7] CV1 113 B2
Drive Fields WV4 38 B6
Drive Sch at Tettenhall Coll
WV6 24 D4
Drive The
Birmingham, Gravelly Hill
B23 56 E2
Birmingham, Handsworth
B20 55 B2
Brierley Hill DY5 61 C5
Coventry CV2 114 E3
Halesowen, Cradley B63 82 D5
Halesowen, Hasbury B63 83 A3
Hopwood B48 123 B3
Redditch B97 152 C7
Shenstone WS14 18 E8
Walsall, Pelsall WS3 14 E2
Walsall WS4 15 C1
Wolverhampton WV6 24 C5
Droicon Ind Est B65 63 C5
Dronfield Rd CV2 114 B3
Drovers Way B60 150 E6
Drovers Wlk DY10 116 F5
Droveway The WV9 10 F2
Droxford Wlk WV8 10 E1
Droylsdon Park Rd CV3 133 B3
Druid Park Rd WV12 13 C1
Druid Rd CV2 114 B3
Druids Ave
Aldridge WS9 30 C8
Rowley Regis B65 63 D4
Druids La B14 104 D1
Druid St LE10 71 D1
Druids Wlk WS9 16 A3
Drummond Cl
Coventry CV6 112 F7
Wolverhampton WV11 13 A2
Drummond Gr B43 44 C3
Drummond Rd
Birmingham B9 68 A2
Bromsgrove B60 151 B8
Stourbridge DY9 81 F4
Drummond St WV1 163 B4
Drummond Way B37 70 C2
Drury La
Solihull B91 107 C3
Drury La *continued*
Stourbridge DY8 81 A5
Drybrook Cl B38 123 E8
Drybrooks Cl CV7 130 B6
Dryden Cl
Kenilworth CV8 147 F3
Tipton DY4 52 A7
Willenhall WV12 27 E8
Dryden Gr B27 88 B2
Dryden Pl WS3 28 E7
Dryden Rd
Tamworth B79 21 A6
Walsall WS3 28 E7
Wolverhampton WV10 11 F1
Drylea Gr B36 68 F8
Dual Way WS12 1 D8
Dubarry Ave DY6 60 C7
Duchess Pl B16 66 A1
Duchess Rd
Birmingham B16 66 A1
Walsall WS1 42 D5
Duckham Ct CV6 113 A4
Duckhouse Rd WV11 26 D7
Duck La WV8 10 B3
Duddeston Dr B8 67 D4
Duddeston Manor Rd B7 67 A4
Duddeston Mill Rd B7, B8 67 C4
Duddeston Mill Trad Est
B8 67 C4
Duddeston Sta B7 67 B4
Dudding Rd WV4 39 D5
Dudhill Rd B65 63 A3
Dudhill Wlk B65 63 A3
DUDLEY 51 D2
Dudley Castle★ DY1 51 D2
Dudley Central Trad Est
DY2 62 C8
Dudley Cl B65 63 A5
Dudley Coll (Castle View
Campus) DY1 51 B2
Dudley Coll (International
Glass Ctr) [1] DY5 61 D3
Dudley Coll of Tech
(Broadway Campus)
DY1 51 C2
Dudley Coll of Tech (Mons
Hill Campus) DY1 51 B5
Dudley Coll (Wolverhampton
St Campus) DY1 51 B1
Dudley Cres WV11 26 E6
Dudley Gn CV32 157 B2
Dudley Gr [6] B18 65 E4
Dudley Innovation Ctr
DY6 60 F7
Dudley L Ctr DY1 51 B1
Dudley Museum & Art Gall★
DY1 51 C1
Dudley Park Rd B27 88 C3
DUDLEY PORT 52 B3
Dudley Port DY4 52 A3
Dudley Port Sta DY4 52 B4
Dudley Rd
Birmingham B18 65 E4
Brierley Hill DY5, DY6 61 D4
Dudley DY3 50 E6
Halesowen B63 83 B5
Himley DY3 49 D3
Kenilworth CV8 147 F2
Kingswinford DY6 60 F7
Kingswinford, Wall Heath
DY6 60 C8
Oldbury B69 63 F8
Rowley Regis B65 63 A5
Stourbridge DY9 81 E6
Tipton DY4 51 E5
Wolverhampton WV2 39 D7
Dudley Rise LE10 75 D6
Dudley Road E B69 52 D1
Dudley Road W B69 52 B2
Dudley Row DY2 51 D1
DUDLEY'S FIELDS 28 A8
Dudley Southern Bypass
DY2 62 C7
Dudley St
Bilston WV14 40 D4
Birmingham B5 164 C2
Coventry CV6 96 A1
Kidderminster DY10 116 E7
Sedgley DY3 50 D8
Walsall WS1 28 E1
Wednesbury WS10 41 E2
West Bromwich B70 53 A5
Wolverhampton WV1 163 B3
Dudley Street, Guns Village
Stop B70 53 B4
Dudley Terr CV8 149 B6
Dudley Wlk WV4 39 C5
DUDLEY WOOD 62 C2
Dudley Wood Ave DY2 62 C2
Dudley Wood Prim Sch
DY2 62 C2
Dudley Wood Rd DY2 62 C2
Dudley Zoo★ DY1 51 D2
Dudmaston Way DY1 50 E3
Dudnill Gr B32 102 A8
Duffield Cl WV8 10 F1
Dufton Rd B32 84 E4
Dugdale Cl WS12 2 F3
Dugdale Cres B75 32 C3
Dugdale Ct [5] CV31 162 A6
Dugdale Ho [3] CV11 73 C3
Dugdale Rd CV6 113 B6
Dugdale St
Nuneaton CV11 73 C4
Smethwick B18 65 D4
Duggins La CV4, CV7 131 B8
Duke Barn Field CV2 114 A5
Dukes Rd
Birmingham B30 104 A3
Dordon B78 36 F6
Duke St
Coventry CV5 112 F2
Dudley DY3 50 D5
Nuneaton CV11 73 B4
Rowley Regis B65 63 B2
Royal Leamington Spa
CV32 157 A1
Stourbridge DY8 81 A6
Sutton Coldfield B72 46 B4
Wednesfield WV11 26 D5
West Bromwich B70 53 B4
Wolverhampton, Springfield
WV1 163 D2
Wolverhampton WV3 39 A7
Dulais Cl B98 153 E1
Dulvern Gr B14 104 D5
Dulverton Ave CV5 112 D4
Dulverton Ct CV5 112 D4
Dulverton Rd B6 56 B1
Dulwich Gr B44 56 B8
Dulwich Rd B44 56 A8
Dumbleberry Ave DY3 50 C7
Dumblederry Ct WS9 29 F5
Dumblederry La WS9 29 F6
Dumble Pit La B47, B48 140 F7
Dumolo's La B77 21 F3
Dumphouse La B48 140 C3
Dunard Rd B90 105 F3
Dunbar Avenue Ind Est
CV6 113 D8
Dunbar Cl
Birmingham B32 84 D1
Kidderminster DY10 117 C6
Dunbar Gr B43 44 B4
Dunblane Dr CV32 157 C5
Dunblane Way LE10 71 A2
Duncalfe Dr B75 32 B3
Duncan Edwards Cl DY1 62 A8
Duncan Ho B73 46 B1
Duncan St WV2 39 C7
Dunchurch Cl
Balsall Common CV7 130 B7
Redditch B98 154 F1
Dunchurch Cres B73 45 C3
Dunchurch Dr B31 102 E7
Dunchurch Highway
CV5 112 A4
Dunchurch Ho [4] B5 86 E8
Dunclent Cres DY10 117 B5
Dunclent La DY10 117 E3
Duncombe Gn [12] B46 70 F7
Duncombe Gr B17 85 A7
Duncombe St DY8 80 D5
Duncroft Ave CV6 112 F7
Duncroft Rd B26 89 A8
Duncroft Wlk DY1 51 B6
Duncumb Rd B75 47 A5
Dundalk La WS6 4 D2
Dundas Ave DY2 62 F8
Dunedin B77 22 A1
Dunedin Dr B45 122 B1
Dunedin Ho B32 84 F4
Dunedin Rd B44 44 F3
Dunham Croft B93 127 D3
Dunhill Ave CV4 111 E3
Dunkirk Ave B70 52 E3
Dunkirk Pl CV3 134 F7
Dunkley St WV1 163 B4
Dunley Croft B90 126 F6
Dunley Ct B23 56 C2
Dunlin Cl
Birmingham B23 56 C2
Kingswinford DY6 61 A6
Dunlin Dr
Featherstone WV10 12 B7
Kidderminster DY10 116 F2
Dunlop Rd B97 158 D5
Dunlop Way B35 57 F2
Dunnerdale Rd WS8 15 D6
Dunnigan Rd B32 84 F3
Dunnose Cl CV6 113 E8
Dunns Bank DY5 81 F7
Dunns Cl CV11 73 D2
Dunoon Dr WV4 39 F5
Dunrose Cl CV2 114 E2
Dunsfold Cl WV14 40 A3
Dunsfold Croft [3] B6 66 F6
Dunsford Cl DY5 81 B7
Dunsford Rd B66 65 A2
Dunsink Rd B6 55 F1
Dunslade Cres DY5 81 F8
Dunslade Rd B23 56 E7
Dunsley Dr DY8 60 E3
Dunsley Gr WV4 39 A4
Dunsley Rd DY8 80 C4
Dunsmore Ave CV3 134 C6
Dunsmore Dr DY5 81 F8
Dunsmore Gr B91 106 F7
Dunsmore Rd B28 87 E2
Dunstall Ave WV6 25 C4
Dunstall Cl B97 153 B2
Dunstall Gr B29 102 F8
DUNSTALL HILL 25 C5
Dunstall Hill WV6 25 C5
Dunstall Hill Prim Sch
WV6 25 C4
Dunstall Hill Trad Est
WV6 25 C5
Dunstall La
Hopwas B78 20 D4
Wolverhampton WV6 25 B5
Dunstall Pk (Wolverhampton
Racecourse)★ WV6 25 A6
Dunstall Rd
Halesowen B63 82 D3
Dunstall Rd *continued*
Wolverhampton WV6 25 B4
Dunstan Croft B90 126 C8
Dunstan Ct [3] B15 86 B7
Dunster B77 35 C7
Dunster Cl B30 104 C4
Dunster Gr WV6 23 F3
Dunster Pl CV6 95 D3
Dunster Rd B37 70 D2
Dunston Cl
Great Wyrley WS6 13 E8
Kingswinford DY6 60 D7
Dunston Dr WS7 7 A8
Dunsville Dr CV2 114 F8
Dunton Cl B75 32 A4
Dunton Hall Rd B90 126 A8
Dunton La B76 48 C1
Dunton Pk B76 59 C7
Dunton Rd B37 69 F5
Dunton Trad Est B7 67 D7
Dunvegan Cl
Coventry CV3 115 A2
Kenilworth CV8 148 C4
Dunvegan Rd B24 57 A4
Duport Rd LE10 75 F7
Durant Cl B45 101 D1
Durban Rd B66 65 C4
Durbar Ave CV6 113 D8
D'Urberville Cl WV2 39 F6
D'Urberville Rd WV2 39 F6
D'Urberville Wlk [1] WS11 2 A2
Durham Ave WV13 27 D3
Durham Cl
Bromsgrove B61 136 E4
Keresley CV7 94 F4
Tamworth B78 21 A2
Durham Cres CV5 112 B7
Durham Croft B37 70 B2
Durham Dr B71 53 D7
Durham Ho [1] WV3 25 C4
Durham Pl WS2 28 B1
Durham Rd
Birmingham B11 87 B4
Dudley DY2 62 D2
Rowley Regis B65 63 E4
Stourbridge DY8 80 D8
Walsall WS2 42 B8
Wednesbury WS10 42 D4
Durham Twr [3] B1 66 B3
Durley Dean Rd B29 85 C2
Durley Dr B73 45 C3
Durley Rd B25 88 C6
Durlston Cl B77 21 F5
Durlston Gr B28 106 A8
Durnford Croft B14 104 E1
Dursley Cl
Solihull B92 107 B8
Willenhall WV12 27 D4
Dursley Dr WS11 1 B2
Dursley Rd WS7 7 A7
Dusthouse La B60 151 D7
Dutton Rd CV2 96 D3
Dutton's La B75 32 E4
Duxford Cl B97 158 B8
Duxford Rd B42 55 B7
Dwarris Wlk CV34 155 E2
Dwellings La B32 84 B5
Dyas Ave B42 55 A7
Dyas Rd
Birmingham B44 44 E1
Hollywood B47 125 A7
Dyce Cl B35 58 A4
Dyers La B94 142 D8
Dyers Rd CV11 79 F6
Dymoke St B12 86 F8
Dymond Rd CV6 95 D3
Dynes Wlk B67 65 A5
Dyott Rd B13 87 A1
Dysart Cl
Coventry CV1 113 E4
[3] Coventry CV1 165 D4
Dyson Cl WS2 27 F3
Dysons Gdns B8 67 E5
Dyson St CV4 111 E3

E

Eachelhurst Rd B24, B76 57 F5
Eachus Rd WV14 51 D8
EACHWAY 121 F6
Eachway B45 121 F6
Eachway Farm Cl B45 122 A6
Eachway La B45 122 A6
Eacott Cl CV6 95 A3
Eadgar Ct B43 54 D7
Eadie Mews B97 153 D1
Eadie St CV10 72 D4
Eagle Cl
Cheslyn Hay WS6 4 D2
Dudley DY1 50 F1
Nuneaton CV11 79 B8
Rowley Regis B65 63 A4
Eagle Croft B14 104 E2
Eagle Ct
Wolverhampton, Pendeford
WV10 11 B3
Wolverhampton WV3 39 A7
Eagle Dr B77 22 C4
Eagle Gdns B24 57 A2
Eagle Gr
Birmingham B36 70 A8
Cannock WS12 2 C1
Eagle Ho CV1 113 D5
Eagle Ind Est DY4 52 E7
Eagle La
Kenilworth CV8 147 F3
Tipton DY4 52 D6
Eagle Rd B98 154 E5
Eagle St
Coventry CV1 113 D5
Royal Leamington Spa
CV31 162 A6
Tipton DY4 52 C6
Wolverhampton, Penn Fields
WV3 39 A7
Wolverhampton WV2 39 E8
Eagle Street E CV1 113 D5
Eagle Trad Est B63 83 A4
Eagleworks Dr WS3 28 D6
Eales Yd [9] LE10 71 D1
Ealing Gr B44 45 A1
Ealingham B77 22 B1
Eanwulf Ct B15 86 C8
Eardisley Cl B98 154 F1
Earl Place Bsns Pk CV4 112 B1
Earlsbury Gdns B20 55 D1
Earls Cl B97 152 F2
Earls Court Rd B17 85 A6
Earl's Croft The CV3 133 D7
EARLSDON 113 A1
Earlsdon Ave CV5 133 A8
Earlsdon Avenue N CV5 112 F1
Earlsdon Avenue S CV5 133 A8
Earlsdon Ho CV5 133 A8
Earlsdon Prim Sch CV5 113 A1
Earlsdon St CV5 132 F8
Earls Ferry Gdns B32 102 B7
Earls High Sch B63 83 B4
Earls Mdw CV34 160 B2
Earlsmead Rd B21 65 C7
Earlsmere B94 126 B1
Earls Rd
Nuneaton CV11 73 A5
Walsall WS4 29 D7
Earls Rivers Ave CV34 161 D3
Earl St
Bedworth CV12 78 C2
Bilston WV14 40 D5
Coventry CV1 165 C2
Dudley WV14 51 D8
Kingswinford DY6 60 D4
Royal Leamington Spa
CV32 157 A1
Walsall WS1 42 D7
West Bromwich B70 53 B4
Earlston Way B43 54 D8
Earls Way B63 83 B4
Earl's Wlk CV3 135 D7
EARLSWOOD 126 B1
Earlswood Comm B94 142 A6
Earlswood Cres WV9 11 A3
Earlswood Ct B20 55 A2
Earlswood Dr B74 46 C7
Earlswood Ho [1] B5 86 E7
Earlswood Lakes Craft Ctr★
B94 125 F2
Earlswood Rd
Birmingham, Brandwood End
B30 104 D3
Dorridge B93 127 D2
Kingswinford DY6 60 E8
Earlswood Sta B94 125 D1
Earlswood Trad Est B94 141 C6
Easby Way
Birmingham B8 67 E5
Walsall WS3 13 F2
Easedale Cl
Coventry CV3 133 B6
Nuneaton CV11 74 A6
Easemore Rd B98 153 F5
Easenhall Cl B93 128 A4
Easenhall La B98 154 E1
Easmore Cl B14 104 D2
Eastacre WV13 27 A1
East Ave
Bedworth CV12 78 D2
Coventry CV2 114 A2
Oldbury B69 63 C7
Wolverhampton WV11 26 C6
Eastboro Ct CV11 73 E2
Eastboro Fields CV11 74 A4
Eastboro Way CV11 73 F2
Eastbourne Ave B34 68 E6
Eastbourne Cl CV6 112 E6
Eastbourne House Sch
B27 88 C4
Eastbourne St WS4 28 F3
Eastbrook Cl B76 46 D4
Eastbury Dr B92 89 A3
East Cannock Rd WS12 2 C4
East Car Park Rd B40 90 F4
East Cl LE10 75 D7
EASTCOTE 108 E3
Eastcote Cl B90 106 D3
Eastcote Cres WS7 7 A5
Eastcote La B92 108 F4
Eastcote Rd
Birmingham B27 88 A1
Wolverhampton WV10 25 F5
Eastcotes CV4 112 B1
East Croft Rd WV4 38 C5
Eastdean Cl B23 56 D6
East Dene CV32 157 B2
East Dr B5 86 C4
Eastern Ave
Brierley Hill DY5 61 B2
Lichfield WS13 3 C2
Eastern Green Jun Sch
CV5 111 D5
Eastern Green Rd CV5 111 F4
EASTERN HILL 158 F2
Eastern Hill B96 158 F2

Eastern Rd
Birmingham B29 . . . . 86 B3
Sutton Coldfield B73 . . . . . 46 B1
Eastern Way WS11 . . . . 2 A2
Eastern Croft B14 . . . . 104 E2
East Farm Croft B10 . . . 87 D8
Eastfield Cl WS9 . . . . 30 A6
Eastfield Dr B92 . . . . . . 107 E8
Eastfield Gr WV1 . . . . . . 25 F2
Eastfield Prim Sch WV1 . . 25 F2
Eastfield Rd
Birmingham B9 . . . . 68 C3
Nuneaton CV10 . . . . 73 D6
Royal Leamington Spa
CV32 . . . . 162 A8
Tipton DY4 . . . . 52 A8
Wolverhampton WV1 . . . . . 25 F2
Eastfield Retreat WV1 . . 25 F2
East Gate B16 . . . . 65 E3
Eastgate Ct WS14 . . . . 9 C6
Eastgate Ho 4 CV34 . . 160 E6
Eastgate Mews 3 CV34 . 160 E6
Eastgate St WS7 . . . . 6 E8
East Gn WV4 . . . . 38 D6
East Gr CV31 . . . . 162 A6
Eastham Rd B13 . . . . . . 105 C6
East Holme B9 . . . . 67 C2
Easthope Rd B33 . . . . 69 A4
Eastlake Cl B43 . . . . 44 D3
Eastlands Gr CV5 . . . . . . 112 E4
Eastlands Rd B13 . . . . . . 87 A1
Eastleigh DY3 . . . . 50 C8
Eastleigh Ave CV5 . . . . . 132 F7
Eastleigh Croft B76 . . . . 58 A7
Eastleigh Dr B62 . . . . . . 101 A4
Eastleigh Gr B25 . . . . 88 D8
Eastley Cres CV34 . . . . . 160 B8
East Meadway B33 . . . . . 69 E3
East Mews B44 . . . . 44 D2
East Moons Ho B98 . . . 154 E4
Eastmoor Cl B74 . . . . 31 B2
Eastney Cres WV8 . . . . . 24 F8
Eastnor Cl
Kidderminster DY10 . . . . 116 E2
Redditch B98 . . . . 153 E1
Eastnor Gr CV31 . . . . . . 162 B7
Easton Gdns WV11 . . . . . 26 F5
Easton Gr
Birmingham B27 . . . . 88 C1
Hollywood B47 . . . . 125 B7
East Park Jun SchWV1 . . 26 B1
East Park Jun SchWV1 . . 40 A8
East Park Trad EstWV1 . . 40 A8
East Park Way WV1 . . . . . 26 A1
East Pathway B17 . . . . . . 85 C6
East Rd
Bromsgrove B60 . . . . 137 A1
Featherstone WV10 . . . . . 12 A7
Tipton DY4 . . . . 52 B8
Wolverhampton WV4 . . . . 39 F4
Eastridge Croft WS14 . . . 18 A5
East Rise B75 . . . . 46 D6
East St
Brierley Hill DY5 . . . . 82 A8
Cannock WS11 . . . . 4 E6
Coventry CV1 . . . . 113 E3
Dudley, Gornalwood DY3 . . 50 D3
Dudley, Kate's Hill DY2 . . . 62 E8
Kidderminster DY10 . . . . 116 F6
Tamworth B77 . . . . 35 D5
Wolverhampton WV1 . . . 163 D2
East View
Shuttington B79 . . . . 22 F7
Tamworth B77 . . . . 21 E3
East View Rd B72 . . . . 46 D2
Eastville B31 . . . . 103 B3
Eastward Glen WV8 . . . . 10 C1
Eastway
Birmingham B17 . . . . 85 C6
Birmingham, Bickenhill B40 . 90 F3
East Way B92 . . . . 91 B3
Eastwood Ave WS7 . . . . . . 7 A8
Eastwood Cl CV31 . . . . 162 D6
Eastwood Ct B96 . . . . . . 158 E1
Eastwood Dr DY10 . . . . 117 B5
Eastwood Rd
Birmingham, Balsall Heath
B12 . . . . 86 D5
Birmingham, Great Barr B43 54 F8
Dudley DY2 . . . . 62 E6
Eastwoods Rd LE10 . . . . . 71 F2
Eatesbrook Rd B33 . . . . . 69 C3
Eathorpe Cl
Birmingham B34 . . . . 69 D6
Coventry CV2 . . . . 96 C1
Redditch B98 . . . . 154 E1
Eaton Ave B70 . . . . 53 A4
Eaton Cl CV32 . . . . 156 D2
Eaton Cres DY3 . . . . 50 B3
Eaton Ct
Royal Leamington Spa
CV32 . . . . 156 D1
Sutton Coldfield B74 . . . . 46 B7
Eaton Pl DY6 . . . . 60 E5
Eaton Rd CV1 . . . . 165 B1
Eaton Rise WV12 . . . . . . 27 B6
Eaton Wood B24 . . . . 57 D4
Eaton Wood Dr B26 . . . . 88 D5
Eaves Court Dr DY3 . . . . 39 C1
EAVES GREEN. 92 F2
Eaves Green Gdns B27 . . 88 B5
Eaves Green La CV7 . . . . 92 E1
**Eaves Green Mobile Home
Pk** CV7 . . . . 92 F2
Ebbw Vale Terr CV3 . . . . 133 D7

Ebenezer St
Cannock WS12 . . . . 2 A7
Tipton WV14 . . . . 51 C8
West Bromwich B70 . . . . . 52 F6
Ebley Rd B20 . . . . 55 A4
Ebmore Dr B14 . . . . 104 D2
Eborall Cl CV34 . . . . 155 E2
Ebourne Croft CV7 . . . . 130 C8
Ebourne Cl CV8 . . . . 148 A4
Ebrington Ave B92 . . . . . 89 B3
Ebrington Cl B14 . . . . . . 104 D4
Ebrington Rd B71 . . . . . . 53 D6
Ebro Cres CV3 . . . . 114 F1
Ebrook Rd B72 . . . . 46 C4
Ebstree Mdw WV5 . . . . . . 37 A2
Ebstree Rd WV5 . . . . 37 A2
Ebury Rd B30 . . . . 104 B4
Eccles Cl CV2 . . . . 114 C8
Eccleshall Ave WV10 . . . . 25 C8
Eccleston Cl B75 . . . . 46 F5
Ecclestone Rd WV11 . . . . 27 A8
Echells Cl B61 . . . . 136 D2
Echo Way WV4 . . . . 40 A4
Eckersall Rd B38 . . . . . . 103 E3
Eckington Cl B98 . . . . . . 159 B8
Eckington Wlk B38 . . . . 123 E7
Eclipse Ind Est 1 DY4 . . 51 E5
Edale Cl
Kingswinford DY6 . . . . 60 B7
Wolverhampton WV4 . . . . 39 E3
Edale Gn LE10 . . . . 75 F6
Edale Rd B42 . . . . 55 C7
Edale Way CV6 . . . . 114 A7
Eddens Wood Cl B78 . . . 34 E5
Eddie Miller Ct CV12 . . . . 78 B2
Eddish Rd B33 . . . . 69 B3
Eddy Rd DY10 . . . . 116 E7
Edelweiss Cl WS5 . . . . . . 43 B3
Edenbridge Rd B28 . . . . 106 B8
Edenbridge View DY1 . . . 50 E3
Eden Cl
Birmingham B31 . . . . 122 E8
Cannock WS12 . . . . 2 E2
Oldbury B69 . . . . 52 D2
Studley B80 . . . . 159 D3
Edencroft B15 . . . . 86 C8
Eden Croft CV8 . . . . 148 B3
Eden Ct
Featherstone WV10 . . . . . 11 F8
Nuneaton CV10 . . . . 72 C7
Royal Leamington Spa
CV32 . . . . 157 D3
Edendale Dr LE10 . . . . . . 71 E4
Edendale Rd B26 . . . . 89 B6
Edenfield Cl B97 . . . . . . 153 A5
Edenfield Pl B77 . . . . 22 B1
Eden Gdns
Rowley Regis B65 . . . . 63 B2
Sedgley DY3 . . . . 50 E8
Eden Gr
Birmingham B37 . . . . 70 D1
West Bromwich B71 . . . . . 53 D5
Edenhall Rd B32 . . . . 84 B6
Eden Ho 2 B98 . . . . 81 A5
Edenhurst Rd B31 . . . . . 122 F7
Eden Rd
Coventry CV2 . . . . 115 A8
Solihull B92 . . . . 89 D3
Edensor Cl WV10 . . . . 25 E4
Eden St CV6 . . . . 113 F7
Edgar Cl B79 . . . . 20 F7
Edgar Stammers Prim Sch
WS3 . . . . 28 E4
EDGBASTON. 86 A6
Edgbaston Cres B5 . . . . . 86 C4
Edgbaston High Sch for Girls
B15 . . . . 85 F7
Edgbaston Park Rd B15 . . 86 A5
Edgbaston Rd
Birmingham B12 . . . . 86 D5
Smethwick B66 . . . . 65 A4
Edgbaston Road E B12 . . 86 F5
Edgbaston St B5 . . . . 164 C2
**Edgbaston (Warwickshire
Cty Cricket Club)** B5 . . . 86 C8
Edgcombe Rd B28 . . . . . . 87 F1
Edgefield Rd CV2 . . . . . . 115 A8
EDGE HILL. 36 C2
Edge Hill CV9 . . . . 36 B2
Edge Hill Ave WV10 . . . . . 12 B1
Edgehill Dr CV34 . . . . . . 160 B3
Edge Hill Dr
Perton WV6 . . . . 23 E3
Sedgley DY3 . . . . 39 C2
Edgehill Pl CV4 . . . . 111 C1
Edgehill Rd B31 . . . . 103 B1
Edge Hill Rd B74 . . . . 31 E4
Edgemond Ave B24 . . . . . 57 F4
Edgemoor Dr WS12 . . . . . . 2 C1
Edge St WV14 . . . . 51 D8
Edgewood Cl 2 B64 . . . . 82 F8
Edgewood Dr B45 . . . . . 122 B1
Edgewood Rd
Birmingham, King's Norton
B38 . . . . 123 F7
Birmingham, Rednal B45 . 122 B6
Edgeworth Cl
Redditch B98 . . . . 154 C5
Willenhall WV12 . . . . 27 C4
Edgeworth Ho WS13 . . . . . 3 A2
Edgmond Cl B98 . . . . . . 154 D4
Edgware Rd B23 . . . . 56 D5
EDGWICK. 113 F8
Edgwick Com Prim Sch
CV6 . . . . 113 E8

Edgwick Park Ind Est
CV6 . . . . 113 F8
Edgwick Rd CV6 . . . . 113 F7
Edgwood Ct 4 B16 . . . . . 65 F1
EDIAL. 7 F6
Edinburgh Ave WS2 . . . . . 27 F3
Edinburgh Cl DY10 . . . . 116 E8
Edinburgh Cres
Royal Leamington Spa
CV31 . . . . 161 F6
Stourbridge DY8 . . . . 60 C1
Edinburgh Ct B24 . . . . . . 57 D4
Edinburgh Dr
Walsall WS4 . . . . 29 D7
Willenhall WV12 . . . . 27 B6
Edinburgh La WS2 . . . . . . 28 A4
Edinburgh Rd
Bilston WV14 . . . . 40 F3
Birmingham B68 . . . . 84 B8
Dudley DY2 . . . . 62 D6
Nuneaton CV10 . . . . 72 D6
Walsall WS5 . . . . 43 B4
Edinburgh Villas CV8 . . . 133 F2
Edingale Rd CV2 . . . . . . 114 F8
Edison Cl WS12 . . . . 2 C7
Edison Gr B32 . . . . 84 D5
Edison Rd
Curdworth B46, B76 . . . . . 59 F4
Walsall WS2 . . . . 28 B5
Edison Wlk WS2 . . . . 28 B5
Edith Rd B66 . . . . 65 C3
Edmondes Cl CV34 . . . . 155 F1
Edmonds Cl B33 . . . . 69 B2
Edmondscote Rd CV32 . 161 D8
Edmonds Ct
Birmingham, Gilbertstone
B26 . . . . 88 F7
Birmingham, Small Heath
B10 . . . . 87 D7
Edmonds Rd B68 . . . . 64 C2
Edmonton Ave B44 . . . . . 45 B1
Edmonton Cl WS11 . . . . . . 2 B2
Edmonton Ho B5 . . . . 86 D7
Edmoor Cl WV12 . . . . 27 C6
Edmund Ho B3 . . . . 164 B3
Edmund Rd
Birmingham B8 . . . . 67 D4
Coventry CV1 . . . . 113 D5
Dudley DY3 . . . . 50 E6
Edmund St B3 . . . . 164 B3
Ednall La B60 . . . . 136 F1
Ednam Cl 3 B71 . . . . 53 F8
Ednam Gr WV5 . . . . 38 A1
Ednam Rd
Dudley DY1 . . . . 51 C2
Wolverhampton WV4 . . . . 39 C5
Edsome Way B36 . . . . 68 F8
Edstone Cl B93 . . . . 127 F4
Edstone Mews B36 . . . . . 68 F8
Edward Ave WS9 . . . . 30 A7
Edward Bailey Cl CV3 . . . 134 E7
Edward Cl WV14 . . . . 40 E3
Edward Ct
Birmingham B16 . . . . 65 C1
7 Nuneaton CV11 . . . . . . 73 C3
Sutton Coldfield B76 . . . . 46 F3
Tamworth B77 . . . . 21 F2
Walsall WS1 . . . . 43 A8
Edward Fisher Dr DY4 . . . 52 A5
Edwardian Cl B90 . . . . . 106 D5
Edward Mews 5 CV34 . . 160 E7
Edward Rd
Bedworth CV12 . . . . 78 C3
Birmingham B68 . . . . 84 C8
Birmingham, Balsall Heath
B12 . . . . 86 E5
Birmingham, Highter's Heath
B14 . . . . 105 A1
Coventry CV6 . . . . 95 A3
Halesowen B63 . . . . 82 E6
Perton WV6 . . . . 23 E5
Smethwick B67 . . . . 65 A4
Tipton DY4 . . . . 52 A7
Water Orton B46 . . . . 59 C3
Edwards Cl DY5. . . . . 81 A7
Edwards Gr CV8 . . . . 148 C5
Edward Rd
Birmingham B24 . . . . 57 A4
Burntwood WS7 . . . . 6 F5
Dudley DY2 . . . . 62 C4
Sutton Coldfield B75 . . . . 32 D3
Edward St
Birmingham B1 . . . . 66 C3
Cannock WS11 . . . . 1 E4
Coventry CV6 . . . . 113 E5
Darlaston WS10 . . . . 41 E6
3 Dudley DY1 . . . . 51 B1
Hinckley LE10 . . . . 71 C2
Nuneaton CV11 . . . . 73 C3
Oldbury B68 . . . . 64 A4
Redditch B97 . . . . 153 D4
Royal Leamington Spa
CV32 . . . . 156 C1
Tamworth B79 . . . . 21 A5
Walsall WS2 . . . . 28 C3
Warwick CV34 . . . . 160 D7
West Bromwich B70 . . . . . 53 C3
Wolverhampton WV4 . . . . 39 B5
Edward Street Hospl B70. 53 C3
Edward The Elder Prim Sch
WV11 . . . . 26 E7
Edward Tyler Rd CV7 . . . 78 A1
Edwin Ave (Road 4)
DY10 . . . . 116 F1
Edwin Cres B60 . . . . 150 F7
Edwin Ct B60 . . . . 150 F7
Edwin Phillips Dr B71 . . . 53 B8

Edwin Rd B30 . . . . 104 B7
Edwinstowe Cl DY5 . . . . 62 A2
Edyth Rd CV2 . . . . 114 E4
Edyvean Walker Ct CV11 . 73 B5
Eel St B69 . . . . 63 F7
Effingham Rd B13 . . . . . 105 C7
Egbert Cl B6 . . . . 67 B8
Egelwin Cl WV6 . . . . 23 E5
Egerton Ct 4 B15 . . . . . . 86 B7
Egerton Rd
Birmingham B24 . . . . 57 E3
Sutton Coldfield B74 . . . . 30 F1
Wolverhampton WV10 . . . 11 E3
Egghill La B31, B45 . . . . 102 B3
Eggington Rd DY8 . . . . . . 60 D6
Egginton Rd B28 . . . . . . 105 E5
Egg La DY9, DY10 . . . . . . 119 A5
Eglamour Way CV34 . . . . 161 F3
Egmont Gdns WV11 . . . . 26 F5
Egret Ct DY10 . . . . 117 A1
Egret Wlk CV2 . . . . 96 B3
Eider Cl DY10 . . . . 117 B1
Eights Croft WS7 . . . . 6 D8
Eileen Gdns B37 . . . . 69 F4
Eileen Rd B11 . . . . 87 C3
Elan Cl
Dudley DY3 . . . . 50 D3
Royal Leamington Spa
CV32 . . . . 157 C3
Elan Rd
Birmingham B31 . . . . 102 C2
Sedgley DY3 . . . . 50 C8
Elbow St B64 . . . . 62 F2
Elbury Croft B93 . . . . . . 127 F5
Elcock Dr B42 . . . . 55 D5
Eldalade Way WS10 . . . . . 42 D2
Elderberry Cl
Stourbridge DY8 . . . . 80 C3
3 Walsall WS5 . . . . 42 F3
Elderberry Way CV2 . . . 114 B6
Elder Cl WS11 . . . . 2 C2
Elderfield Rd B30 . . . . . . 104 B3
Elder Gr WV11 . . . . 26 B6
Elder La WS7 . . . . 7 C7
Eldersfield Cl B98 . . . . . 154 E7
Eldersfield Gr B91 . . . . . 127 B7
Elderside Cl WS8 . . . . 15 F8
Elder Way B23 . . . . 56 E2
Eldon Cl WS1 . . . . 28 F1
Eldon Dr B76 . . . . 57 E7
Eldon Rd
Birmingham B32 . . . . 84 A3
Birmingham, Edgbaston B16 65 F2
Halesowen B62 . . . . 83 F3
Eldon St
Darlaston WS10 . . . . 41 D7
Walsall WS1 . . . . 28 F1
Eldorado Cl B80 . . . . 159 D4
Eld Rd CV6 . . . . 113 E7
Eldridge Cl WV9 . . . . 10 F2
Eleanor Rd WV14 . . . . 40 D6
Electra Park Ind Pk B6. . 56 B1
Electric Ave B6 . . . . 56 B1
Elford Cl
Birmingham B14 . . . . 104 E5
Sutton Coldfield B74 . . . . 31 A2
Elford Gr
Bilston WV14 . . . . 40 C4
Birmingham B37 . . . . 70 B1
Elford Rd
Birmingham B17, B29 . . . . 85 B3
West Bromwich B71 . . . . . 42 E2
Elgar Cl
Cannock WS11 . . . . 1 E5
Lichfield WS13 . . . . 3 B2
Nuneaton CV11 . . . . 79 A7
Redditch B97 . . . . 158 C8
Elgar Cres DY5 . . . . 61 D7
Elgar Ho B1 . . . . 86 A7
Elgar Mews 2 B60 . . . . . 136 F2
Elgar Rd CV6 . . . . 114 B8
Elgin Cl
Sedgley DY3 . . . . 39 E1
Stourbridge DY8 . . . . 81 A7
Elgin Gr B25 . . . . 88 C7
Elgin Rd WS3 . . . . 14 A4
Elias Cl WS14 . . . . 9 E6
Eliot Cl
Tamworth B79 . . . . 21 A7
Warwick CV34 . . . . 155 E2
Eliot Croft WV14 . . . . 40 D2
Eliot Ct B74 . . . . 44 F7
Eliot Way CV10 . . . . 73 B2
Eliot Wlk DY10 . . . . 117 C6
Elisabeth Ct
Royal Leamington Spa
CV31 . . . . 162 B8
Sutton Coldfield B74 . . . . 32 B3
Elizabeth Ave
Bilston WV14 . . . . 40 F3
Wednesbury WS10 . . . . . 42 C3
Wolverhampton WV4 . . . . 39 B5
Elizabeth Cres B68 . . . . . 64 D2
Elizabeth Ct
2 Birmingham, Acock's Green
B27 . . . . 88 C2
1 Birmingham B17 . . . . . 85 D4
6 Coventry CV6 . . . . 113 A4
Warwick CV34 . . . . 161 B6
Elizabeth Dr B79 . . . . 21 A6
Elizabeth Gr
Dudley DY2 . . . . 62 F7
Solihull B90 . . . . 106 C2
Elizabeth Ho
Stourbridge DY9 . . . . 81 E5
Sutton Coldfield B76 . . . . 46 F3

Elizabeth Ho continued
1 Walsall WS5 . . . . 43 D7
Elizabeth Mews B69 . . . . 52 A2
Elizabeth Prout Gdns B65 63 B1
Elizabeth Rd
Birmingham, Moseley B13. . 86 C2
Birmingham, New Oscott
B73 . . . . 45 D1
Birmingham, Stechford B33. 68 D3
Cannock WS11 . . . . 1 E6
Halesowen B63 . . . . 82 F3
Hinckley LE10 . . . . 71 D2
Royal Leamington Spa
CV31 . . . . 161 F6
Walsall WS5 . . . . 43 C7
West Bromwich B70 . . . . . 52 D4
Elizabeth Way
Coventry CV2 . . . . 114 F7
Kenilworth CV8 . . . . 147 E5
Redditch B97 . . . . 153 D5
Elizabeth Wlk DY4 . . . . . . 41 A2
Eliza Gdns B61 . . . . 121 B1
Elkington Croft B90 . . . . 127 A6
Elkington St
Birmingham B6 . . . . 66 E5
Coventry CV6 . . . . 113 F8
Elkstone Cl B92 . . . . 89 B3
Elkstone Covert B14 . . . 104 C2
Ellacombe Rd CV2 . . . . . 114 D8
Elland Gr B27 . . . . 88 D2
Ellards Dr WV11 . . . . 26 F5
Ellenbrook Cl 6 B97 . . . 153 B5
Ellenburg Cl CV4 . . . . . . 111 C3
Ellen St B18 . . . . 66 B4
Ellenvale Cl WV14 . . . . . . 51 A8
Ellerbeck B77 . . . . 22 B1
Ellerby Gr B24 . . . . 57 E4
Ellerdene Cl B98 . . . . . . 158 D8
Ellerman Gdns CV6 . . . . . 95 F3
Ellerside Gr B31 . . . . . . 102 F2
Ellerslie Cl DY5 . . . . 81 D8
Ellerslie Rd B13 . . . . 105 C7
Ellerton Rd B44 . . . . 45 B1
Ellerton Wlk WV10 . . . . . . 25 F5
Ellesboro' Rd B17 . . . . . . 85 B7
Ellesmere Rd
Bedworth CV12 . . . . 78 A2
Birmingham B8 . . . . 67 D4
Ellice Dr B36 . . . . 70 B7
Elliot Cl WV4 . . . . 39 F4
Elliot Gdns B45 . . . . 122 B5
Elliot Cl WS11 . . . . 1 F5
Elliott Ct CV5 . . . . 112 C1
Elliott Rd B29 . . . . 85 E1
Elliotts La WV8 . . . . 10 A3
Elliott's Rd DY4 . . . . 51 E5
Elliott Way
Birmingham B6 . . . . 55 F3
Birmingham B6 . . . . 55 F4
Ellis Ave DY5 . . . . 61 A2
Ellison St B70 . . . . 53 C1
Ellis Park Dr CV3 . . . . . . 115 B1
Ellis St B1 . . . . 164 B1
Elliston Ave B44 . . . . 55 E8
Elliston Gr CV31 . . . . 162 C6
Ellis Wlk WS11 . . . . 4 F8
Ellowes Hall Sch The DY3 50 C5
Ellowes Rd DY3 . . . . 50 C4
Ellsmore Mdw WS13 . . . . . 9 A6
Ellys Rd CV1 . . . . 113 C5
Elm Ave
Bilston WV14 . . . . 40 D6
Birmingham B12 . . . . 87 A5
Wednesbury WS10 . . . . . 41 F4
Wolverhampton WV11 . . . 26 B8
Elmay Rd B26 . . . . 89 A7
Elm Bank B13 . . . . 87 A3
Elm Bank Cl CV32 . . . . . 157 A4
Elmbank Gr B20 . . . . 54 E5
Elmbank Rd
Kenilworth CV8 . . . . 147 E6
Walsall WS5 . . . . 43 C4
Elmbridge Cl B63 . . . . . . 82 D5
Elmbridge Dr B90 . . . . . 127 B6
Elmbridge Rd B44 . . . . . . 55 E6
Elmbridge Way
7 Birmingham B31 . . . . 103 D2
Sedgley DY3 . . . . 50 E6
Elm Cl
Binley Woods CV3 . . . . . . 135 C7
Dudley DY3 . . . . 50 D2
Stourbridge DY8 . . . . 80 D2
Elm Croft 5 B66 . . . . 65 C5
Elm Croft Rd B32 . . . . 84 C7
Elmcroft Ave B32 . . . . 84 A1
Elmcroft Gdns WV10 . . . . 11 E3
Elmcroft Rd B26 . . . . 88 F7
Elm Ct
Allesley CV5 . . . . 111 B8
Birmingham B13 . . . . 86 F4
Oldbury B66 . . . . 64 C8
Redditch B97 . . . . 153 D4
Walsall WS1 . . . . 43 A8
Elmdale B62 . . . . 84 A7
Elmdale Cres B31 . . . . . . 102 E4
Elmdale Dr
Aldridge WS9 . . . . 30 C8
Kidderminster DY10 . . . . 117 C5
Elmdale Gr B31 . . . . 102 E4
Elmdale Rd WV14 . . . . 51 A8
Elm Dale Rd WV4 . . . . 39 A5
Elmdene Rd CV8 . . . . . . 148 B4
Elmdon Cl
Solihull B92 . . . . 89 D2
Wolverhampton WV10 . . . 11 A1
Elmdon Coppice B92 . . . 107 F7
Elmdon Ct B37 . . . . 90 A7

ELMDON HEATH 107 E7
Elmdon La
Birmingham B37 90 A6
Solihull B26 90 A3
Elmdon Manor Nature Reserve* B92 89 D1
Elmdon Park Rd B92 89 D2
Elmdon Rd
Birmingham, Acock's Green B27 88 D4
Birmingham, Marston Green B37 90 A7
Birmingham, Selly Park B29 86 A2
Wolverhampton WV10 11 A1
Elmdon Trad Est B37 90 C5
Elm Dr
Birmingham, Frankley B31 102 C1
Birmingham, Grove Vale B43 43 D1
Blakedown DY10 98 B2
Halesowen B62 63 E1
Elm Farm Ave B37 89 F7
Elm Farm Rd WV2 39 D7
Elmfield Ave B24 57 F4
Elmfield Cres B13 86 F2
Elmfield Rd
Birmingham B36 69 F7
Nuneaton CV10 73 C7
Elmfield Rudolf Steiner Sch DY8 81 A3
Elmfield View DY1 51 A3
Elm Gdns WS14 9 C7
Elm Gn DY1 51 A5
Elm Gr
Balsall Common CV7 130 C6
Birmingham B37 69 F6
Bromsgrove B61 137 A4
Codsall WV8 10 A3
Huntington WS12 1 D8
ELMHURST 3 A5
Elmhurst B15 85 D8
Elmhurst Ave B65 63 C3
Elmhurst Cl B97 158 D4
Elmhurst Dr
Burntwood WS7 7 A4
Kingswinford DY6 60 F4
Elmhurst Rd
Birmingham B21 54 E1
Coventry CV6 96 A4
Elmhurst Sch for Dance B5 86 B5
Elmley Cl
Dudley WV14 51 B7
Kidderminster DY11 116 B3
Elmley Ct B23 56 C2
Elmley Gr
Birmingham B30 104 B2
Perton WV6 23 F3
Elmley Ho 9 B97 153 A4
Elm Lodge B92 109 A7
Elmore Cl
Birmingham B37 70 A4
Coventry CV3 134 D8
Elmore Green Cl WS3 28 B8
Elmore Green Prim Sch 10 WS3 14 B1
Elmore Green Rd WS3 14 B1
Elmore Rd B33 69 A3
Elmore Row WS3 14 B1
Elm Pl DY10 118 B3
Elm Rd
Birmingham B15 85 F5
Birmingham, Bournville B30 103 F8
Dudley DY1 51 C4
Kidderminster DY10 117 A6
Kingswinford DY6 60 E6
Norton Canes WS11 6 B5
Redditch B97 153 D4
Royal Leamington Spa CV32 157 B3
Sutton Coldfield B76 46 F2
Walsall WS3 28 D6
Elms Cl
Birmingham B38 123 C8
Solihull B91 107 D5
Elmsdale WV6 24 A2
Elmsdale Ave CV6 95 F2
Elmsdale Ct 6 WS1 42 F8
Elms Dr WS11 1 C1
Elms Farm Prim Sch B33 89 D7
Elms Rd B72 46 C3
Elm St
Willenhall WV13 27 C2
Wolverhampton WV3 25 A1
Elmstead Ave B33 89 D7
Elmstead Cl WS5 29 E1
Elmstead Twr 2 B5 86 E7
Elmstead Wood WS5 29 E1
Elms The
Bedworth CV12 77 E2
Birmingham B16 65 F3
Kingswood B94 144 D3
Leek Wootton CV35 155 F6
Wolverhampton WV11 26 B5
Elmstone Cl
Dudley DY3 50 F4
Redditch B97 158 C5
Elm Terr B69 52 B1
Elm Tree Ave CV4 112 B2
Elm Tree Dr LE10 75 F8
Elm Tree Gr B63 82 D6
Elmtree Rd B74 30 D1
Elm Tree Rd
Birmingham B17 85 A7
Birmingham, Stirchley B30 104 A6
Bulkington CV12 79 D2
Elm Tree Rise B92 109 B6
Elm Tree Way B64 62 F1
Elm Tree Wlk B79 20 F8
Elm Way CV10 72 A8
Elmwood Ave
Coventry CV6 112 F5
Essington WV11 13 A3
Elmwood Cl
Balsall Common CV7 130 C7
Cannock WS11 2 A3
Elmwood Ct
Birmingham B5 86 D6
Coventry CV1 165 B4
Sutton Coldfield B74 45 A5
Elmwood Gdns B20 55 B2
Elmwood Gr B47 125 A6
Elmwood Rd
Birmingham B24 57 C2
Stourbridge DY8 60 C2
Sutton Coldfield B74 45 A5
Elmwood Rise DY3 39 B1
Elmwoods B32 84 B2
Elmwood Sch WS4 29 B6
Elphin Cl CV6 95 A4
Elphinstone End B24 57 C6
Elsma Rd B68 84 C8
ELSTON HALL 25 D8
Elston Hall La WV10 11 D1
Elston Hall Prim Sch WV10 11 D2
Elstree Rd B23 56 D5
Elswick Gr B44 56 B8
Elswick Rd B44 45 B1
Elsworth Gr B25 88 C6
Elsworth Rd 6 B31 103 D2
Eltham Gr B44 45 B1
Eltham Rd CV3 133 E7
Elton Cl
Royal Leamington Spa CV32 157 C2
Wolverhampton WV10 11 E4
Elton Croft B93 127 F4
Elton Gr B27 88 A2
Eltonia Croft B26 89 B6
Elunda Gr WS7 6 E5
Elva Croft B36 58 F1
Elvaston Way B90 125 F5
Elvers Green La B92, B93 128 E7
Elvetham Rd B15 86 C8
Elviron Dr WV6 24 B5
Elwell Cres DY1 50 F6
Elwells Cl WV14 40 A3
Elwell St
Wednesbury WS10 42 B3
West Bromwich B70 52 E5
Elwy Circ CV7 95 C6
Elwyn Rd B73 46 A3
Ely Cl
Birmingham B37 70 B2
Cannock WS11 2 B1
Coventry CV2 115 A6
Kidderminster DY11 116 A6
Rowley Regis B65 63 E4
Ely Cres B71 53 B7
Ely Gr B32 84 F4
Ely Pl WS2 28 B1
Ely Rd WS2 28 B1
Emay Cl B70 52 F8
Embankment The DY5 61 E3
Embassy Dr
Birmingham B15 86 B8
Oldbury B69 63 E8
Embassy Ind Est 1 DY9 81 F5
Embassy Rd B69 63 E8
Embassy Wlk CV2 114 D8
Emberton Way B77 21 F5
Embleton Cl LE10 71 B1
Embleton Gr B34 69 A6
Emerald Ct
Birmingham B8 68 C5
5 Solihull B92 88 F1
Emerald Way CV31 161 F5
Emerson Cl DY3 50 A4
Emerson Gr WV10 25 F8
Emerson Rd
Birmingham B17 85 C6
Coventry CV2 114 C3
Wolverhampton WV10 25 E8
Emery Cl
Birmingham B23 56 D1
Coventry CV2 114 E7
Walsall WS1 42 F8
Emery Ct DY10 116 E7
Emery St WS1 42 F8
Emily Gdns B16 65 F3
Emily Rd B26 88 D6
Emily Smith Ho 2 CV2 96 B1
Emily St
Birmingham B12 86 F7
West Bromwich B70 53 B2
Emmanuel Rd
Burntwood WS7 7 B7
Sutton Coldfield B73 57 B8
Emmanuel Sch 11 WS1 42 E8
Emmeline St B9 67 B1
Emmott Dr CV31 162 B5
Emperor Pl DY10 116 E8
Empire Cl WS9 29 F8
Empire Coll B5 164 C2
Empire Ind Pk WS9 15 F1
Empire Rd CV4 111 E2
Empress Way WS10 41 D8
EMSCOTE 161 B8
Emscote Dr B73 57 B7
Emscote Gn B91 106 E2
Emscote House Sch CV32 161 D8
Emscote Inf Sch CV34 161 B8
Emscote Rd
Birmingham B6 55 F1
Coventry CV3 114 C2
Warwick CV34 161 B8
Emsworth Cres WV9 11 A2
Emsworth Gr B14 104 D6
Ena Rd CV1 113 D5
Endemere Rd CV6 113 D7
Enderby Cl B93 127 F4
Enderby Dr WV4 39 A5
Enderby Gr 9 B18 65 E4
Enderley Cl WS3 14 B3
Enderley Dr WS3 14 B3
End Hall Rd WV6 24 A3
Endhill Rd B44 45 A3
Endicott Rd B6 55 F1
Endmoor Gr B23 56 D6
Endsleigh Gdns CV31 162 B6
Endsleigh Gr B28 106 A8
Endwood Court Rd B20 55 A2
Endwood Ct
Birmingham B11 87 D4
Birmingham, Handsworth Wood B20 55 A2
Endwood Dr
Solihull B91 106 F2
Sutton Coldfield B74 31 C4
ENFIELD 153 D5
Enfield Cl
Birmingham B23 56 F6
Bromsgrove B60 150 E7
Enfield Ind Est B97 153 D5
Enfield Rd
Birmingham B15 86 B8
Coventry CV2 114 B3
Redditch B97 158 D5
Rowley Regis B65 63 D3
Enford Cl B34 69 D6
Engadine Rd B60 137 C1
Engine La
Brierley Hill DY5 61 F4
Darlaston WS10 41 A4
Stourbridge DY9 81 D6
Tamworth B77 22 A2
Walsall WS8 15 C8
Engine St
Oldbury B69 64 B6
Smethwick B66 65 B6
England Cres CV31 161 E7
England Ho 10 CV32 156 F2
Englestede Cl B20 54 F3
Engleton Rd CV6 113 A6
Englewood Dr B28 106 A8
English Martyrs CE Prim Sch B11 87 C4
Ennerdale Cl
Brownhills WS8 15 E7
Royal Leamington Spa CV32 156 D2
Ennerdale Cres CV11 73 F6
Ennerdale Dr
Halesowen B63 82 D2
Perton WV6 23 F4
Ennerdale La CV2 114 F4
Ennerdale Rd
Birmingham B43 54 F6
Wolverhampton WV6 24 D8
Ennersdale Bglws B46 59 F1
Ennersdale Cl B46 59 F1
Ennersdale Rd B46 59 F1
Enright Cl CV32 156 E2
Ensall Dr DY8 60 E1
Ensbury Cl WV12 27 D4
Ensdale Row WV13 27 A1
Ensdon Gr B44 45 B1
Ensford Cl B74 31 E5
Ensign Bsns Ctr CV4 131 F6
Ensign Cl CV4 111 D1
Ensor Cl CV11 74 A6
Ensor Dr B78 22 F1
Ensor's Pool Nature Reserve* CV10 72 F1
Enstone Rd
Birmingham B23 57 A7
Dudley DY1 61 F8
Enterprise Dr
Stourbridge DY9 81 F6
Sutton Coldfield B74 44 E7
Enterprise Gr WS3 15 B5
Enterprise Ho B92 109 A6
Enterprise Ind Pk WS13 9 F8
Enterprise Trad Est DY5 61 F3
Enterprise Way B7 164 D4
Enterprise Workshops DY6 61 A7
Enville Cl
Birmingham B37 70 B1
Walsall WS3 14 A3
Enville Gr B11 87 D5
Enville Pl DY8 80 E5
Enville Rd
Dudley DY3 50 D4
Kingswinford DY6 60 B8
Wolverhampton WV4 38 C4
Enville St DY8 80 F5
Epperston Ct CV31 161 F7
Epping Cl
Birmingham B45 102 B2
Walsall WS3 28 F6
Epping Gr B44 56 A7
Epping Way CV32 157 C4
Epsom Cl
Bedworth CV12 78 B4
Lichfield WS14 9 D7
Perton WV6 23 F4
Redditch B97 158 C8
Tamworth B77 35 C4
Epsom Ct 16 B29 103 C7
Epsom Dr CV3 134 C6
Epsom Gr B44 56 B8
Epsom Rd
Royal Leamington Spa CV32 157 C4
Upper Catshill B61 121 A1
Epwell Gr B44 55 F6
Epwell Rd B44 55 F6
Epworth Ct DY5 61 B5
Erasmus Rd B11 87 A7
Erasmus Way WS13 9 A8
Ercall Cl B23 56 A6
ERDINGTON 57 A4
Erdington Hall Prim Sch B24 56 F1
Erdington Hall Rd B24 56 F2
Erdington Ind Pk B24 57 F4
Erdington L Ctr B24 57 A4
Erdington Rd WS9 30 C3
Erdington Sta B23 56 F5
Erica Ave CV12 77 F2
Erica Cl B29 103 A8
Erica Dr CV31 162 B2
Erica Rd WS5 43 B3
Eric Grey Cl CV2 114 A5
Eringden B77 22 B1
Erithway Rd CV3 133 B4
Ermington Cres B36 68 E7
Ermington Rd WV4 39 D4
Ernesford Grange Com Sch CV3 134 D8
Ernesford Grange L Ctr CV3 134 E8
Ernesford Grange Prim Sch CV3 114 E1
Ernest Clarke Cl WV12 27 C4
Ernest Ct B38 104 A1
Ernest Rd
Birmingham B12 87 B4
Dudley DY2 51 F1
Smethwick B67 64 E6
Ernest Richards Rd CV12 78 B4
Ernest St B1 164 B1
Ernsford Ave CV3 114 B1
Ernsford Cl B93 127 F2
Erskine Cl LE10 71 A2
Erskine St B7 67 B3
Erwood Cl B97 153 B2
Esher Dr CV3 133 E7
Esher Rd
Birmingham B44 44 F4
West Bromwich B71 53 D6
Eshton Way B77 22 B1
Eskdale Cl WV1 26 A2
Eskdale Rd LE10 75 A7
Eskdale Wlk
Brierley Hill DY5 81 B8
Coventry CV3 134 D7
Esk Ho 1 DY1 61 E8
Eskrett St WS12 2 C5
Esme Rd B11 87 B4
Esmond Cl B30 103 D5
Essendon Gr B8 68 B4
Essendon Rd B8 68 B4
Essendon Wlk B8 68 B4
Essex Ave
Kingswinford DY6 60 B5
Wednesbury WS10 42 C4
West Bromwich B71 53 D7
Essex Cl
Coventry CV5 112 B3
Kenilworth CV8 147 E2
Essex Ct
5 Birmingham B29 103 C7
Warwick CV34 160 E8
Essex Dr WS12 2 B4
Essex Gdns DY8 80 D7
Essex Ho
2 Birmingham B2 164 B2
2 Wolverhampton WV3 25 C4
Essex Rd
Dudley DY2 62 A6
Sutton Coldfield B75 32 D2
Essex St
Birmingham B5 164 C1
Walsall WS2 28 E5
ESSINGTON 12 F3
Essington Cl
Lichfield WS14 9 A5
Shenstone WS14 18 A7
Stourbridge DY8 60 E1
Essington Light Ind Est WV11 12 F4
Essington Rd WV12 13 B1
Essington St B16 66 B1
Essington Way WV1 26 B1
Este Rd B26 69 A1
Esterton Cl CV6 95 C2
Estone Cl B8 67 E4
Estone Wlk B6 66 F7
Estria Rd B15 86 B7
Estridge La WS6 5 A2
Etchell Rd B78 20 F3
Ethelfield Rd CV2 114 B3
Ethelfleda Rd B77 35 F5
Ethelfleda Terr WS10 41 F3
Ethel Rd B17 85 D5
Ethelred Cl B74 32 A3
Ethel St
Birmingham B2 164 B2
Oldbury B68 64 A4
Smethwick B67 64 F2
Etheridge Rd WV14 40 D7
Etna St B5 164 D3
Eton Cl DY3 50 F6
Eton Ct
Lichfield WS14 9 B6
1 Sutton Coldfield B74 31 F2
Eton Dr DY8 81 A3
Etone Coll CV11 73 D5
Etone Ct CV11 73 B5
Etone Sp Ctr CV11 73 D5
Eton Rd B12 87 B4
Eton Wlk DY9 99 A6
Etruria Way WV14 40 E7
Etta Gr B44 44 F4
Ettingley Cl B98 159 B5
ETTINGSHALL 40 A5
ETTINGSHALL PARK 39 D3
Ettingshall Park Farm La WV4 39 E4
Ettingshall Rd
Bilston WV14 40 A2
Wolverhampton WV2 40 A7
Ettington Cl B93 127 D2
Ettington Rd
Birmingham B6 66 E8
Coventry CV5 112 A3
Ettymore Cl DY3 50 D8
Ettymore Rd DY3 50 D8
Ettymore Road W DY3 50 C8
Etwall Rd B28 105 E6
Euan Cl B17 85 C8
Eunal Ct B97 158 E5
Euro Bsns Pk B69 52 D1
Euro Ct B13 87 B2
Europa Ave B70 53 F2
Europa Way
Lichfield WS13 9 F8
Royal Leamington Spa CV34 161 D5
European Bsns Pk B69 63 E7
Eustace Rd CV12 79 D1
Euston Cres CV3 134 C6
Euston Pl CV32 161 F8
Euston Sq 1 CV32 161 F8
Evans Cl
Bedworth CV12 78 C3
Dudley DY4 51 C5
Evans Croft B78 21 A1
Evans Gdns B29 85 D1
Evans Gr CV31 162 A2
Evans Pl WV14 40 E7
Evans St
Willenhall WV13 26 D1
Wolverhampton, Dunstall Hill WV6 25 B4
Wolverhampton WV4, WV14 39 F1
Eva Rd
Birmingham B18 65 D6
Oldbury B68 64 D3
Evason Ct B6 55 E1
EVE HILL 51 B2
Eve La DY1 50 F5
Evelyn Ave CV6 95 F2
Evelyn Croft B73 57 A8
Evelyn Rd B11 87 D4
Evenlode Cl
Redditch B98 153 F1
Solihull B92 89 B3
Evenlode Cres CV6 112 F5
Evenlode Gr WV13 27 D1
Evenlode Rd B92 89 B3
Everard Ct CV11 73 E2
Everdon Rd CV6 95 B2
Everene Ho 1 B27 88 C3
Everest Cl B66 64 F8
Everest Rd
Birmingham B20 55 A3
Willenhall WS2 27 F3
Everglade Rd CV9 36 C2
Evergreen Cl WV14 51 B8
Evergreen Hts WS12 2 A8
Evergreens The CV10 72 F6
Everitt Dr B93 128 A6
Eversfield Prep Sch B91 107 B4
Eversleigh Rd CV6 112 E7
Eversley Dale B24 57 A2
Eversley Gr
Sedgley DY3 39 C2
Wolverhampton WV11 26 C6
Eversley Rd 2 B9 67 D1
Evers St DY5 82 A8
Everton Rd B8 68 C4
Eves Croft B32 84 C1
Evesham Cres WS3 13 F3
Evesham Ct DY11 116 D5
Evesham Ho B60 137 B3
Evesham Rd B96, B97 158 E3
Evesham Rise DY2 62 D3
Evesham Sq 3 B97 153 E3
Evesham St B97 153 E3
Evesham Wlk
Coventry CV4 132 D5
2 Redditch B97 153 E4
Eveson Rd DY8 80 E2
Ewart Rd WS2 27 E3
Ewell Rd B24 57 B4
Ewhurst Ave B29 85 F1
Ewhurst Cl WV13 40 F8
Ewloe Cl DY10 116 E1
Exbury Cl WV9 10 F2
Exbury Way CV11 78 E8
Excel L Ctr CV4 132 A7
Excelsior Gr WS3 15 B5
Exchange Ind Est WS11 4 E5
Exchange St
Brierley Hill DY5 61 D4
Kidderminster DY10 116 E6
Wolverhampton WV1 163 B3
Exchange The WS3 14 B1
Exe Croft B31 123 B8

Exeter CI
Coventry CV3............134 D8
Kidderminster DY11....116 A6
Exeter Dr
Birmingham B37 ....89 F8
Tamworth B79 ....20 E5
Exeter Ho 8 B24 ....56 F4
Exeter Pas B1 ....164 B1
Exeter PI WS2 ....28 B1
Exeter Rd
Birmingham B29 ....85 F2
Cannock WS11..........4 B8
Dudley DY2 ....62 D2
Smethwick B66 ....65 B5
Exeter St B1............164 B1
Exford CI DY5...........81 B7
EXHALL 96 B7
Exhall Cedars Inf Sch CV7 96 A8
Exhall CI
Redditch B98...........154 D5
Solihull B91 ....106 E2
Exhall Ct B23 ....56 C2
Exhall Gn CV7 ....95 F7
Exhall Grange Sch & Science
Coll CV7...............95 C5
Exhall Ind Est CV7 ....78 B1
Exhall Rd CV7...........95 A6
Exham CI CV14.........155 E1
Exhibition Way B40 ....90 D4
Exis Ct CV11............73 E2
Exley B77...............21 D1
Exminster Rd CV3......133 E5
Exmoor CI B61.........137 A4
Exmoor Dr
Bromsgrove B61 ....137 A4
Royal Leamington Spa
CV32...............157 C4
Exmoor Gn WV11 ....26 C7
Exmouth CI CV2.......114 C7
Exonbury Wlk 5 WS11...1 F2
Exon Ct DY4............51 F6
Expressway The B70 ...53 C4
Exton CI
Ash Green CV7 ....95 C6
Wednesfield WV11 ......26 F8
Exton Way B8 ....67 D5
Eyffler CI CV34........160 D7
Eyland Gr WS1..........28 F2
Eymore CI B29.........103 B6
Eynsham Ct WV6.......24 E5
Eyre St B18.............66 A3
Eyston Ave DY4........52 D8
Eyton CI B98..........154 D3
Eyton Croft B12........86 F7
Ezekiel La WV12 ....27 C6

F

Fabian CI
Birmingham B45 ....102 A2
Coventry CV3..........134 D7
Fabian Cres B90 ......106 B1
Fabius CI LE10 ....75 C7
Facet Rd B38..........104 A2
Factory La B61 ....136 F1
Factory Rd
Birmingham B18 ....66 A6
Hinckley LE10 ....71 D1
Tipton DY4.............51 E6
Factory St WS10 ......41 C6
Fairbanks CI CV2.....115 A7
Fairbourne Ave
Birmingham B44 ....44 E2
Rowley Regis B65 .....63 E4
Fairbourne Gdns B97..158 C7
Fairbourne Twr B23....52 A4
Fairbourne Way CV6 ..112 E8
Fairburn Cres WS3....15 B5
Faircroft CV3 ....147 F3
Faircroft Ave B76.....57 F6
Faircroft Rd B36......31 C6
Fairdene Way 8 B43...54 D8
Fairey Ind Est B77 ....35 E8
Fairfax Ct 7 CV34 ....160 F7
Fairfax Rd
Birmingham B31 ......123 A8
Sutton Coldfield B75...46 F5
Wolverhampton WV10...11 E3
Fairfax Sk B75.........46 F5
Fairfax St CV1 ....165 C3
FAIRFIELD.............120 D3
Fairfield CI WS12 ......2 D1
Fairfield Ct CV3.......134 A7
Fairfield Dr
Halesowen B62 ....63 E1
Walsall WS3............15 B4
Fairfield Fst Sch B61..120 D3
Fairfield Gr B62........63 E1
Fairfield Ho B60 ......137 B3
Fairfield Mount WS1...42 F8
Fairfield Park Ind Est B62 63 E1
Fairfield Rd
Birmingham B14 ......104 E8
Dudley DY2.............62 D7
Fairfield B61...........120 D1
Halesowen B63 ....83 A2
Halesowen, Hurst Green
B62...............63 E1
Stourbridge DY8.......60 F2
Fairfield Rise
Meriden CV7 ....92 C1
Stourbridge DY8.......80 D5
Fairfields Hill B78......36 F8

Fairford CI
Redditch B98..........154 E7
Solihull B91 ....106 D5
Fairford Gdns
Burntwood WS7........7 C6
Stourbridge DY8.......60 E3
Fairford Rd B44........55 F6
Fairgreen Gdns DY5....61 C5
Fairgreen Way
Birmingham B29 ....85 F1
Sutton Coldfield B74...31 A1
Fairground Way WS1...42 D8
Fairhaven Croft B62...63 E1
Fairhaven Prim Sch DY8 .60 D3
Fairhills DY3...........50 D8
Fairhill Way B11.......87 C7
Fairholme Rd B36......68 B7
Fairhurst Dr CV32....156 E3
Fair Isle Dr CV10......72 F2
Fair Lady Dr WS7.......6 D8
Fairlands Pk CV4 .....132 E5
Fairlawn B15..........86 A7
Fairlawn CI
Royal Leamington Spa
CV32...............156 D1
Willenhall WV12 ....13 C1
Fairlawn Dr DY6.......60 D4
Fairlawns
Birmingham B26 ....69 A1
Sutton Coldfield B76...58 A8
Fairlawn Way WV12....13 C1
Fairlie Cres B38.......103 D1
Fairlight Dr B45.......122 A1
Fairmead Rise B38....103 E1
Fairmile CI CV3.......134 C8
Fairmile Rd B63 ......83 A6
Fairmont Rd B60......151 B8
Fairmount Dr 5 WS11...4 E8
Fairoak Dr
Bromsgrove B60 ......150 F6
Wolverhampton WV6...24 B3
Fair Oaks Dr WS6.....14 A8
Fairview Ave B42......55 B6
Fairview CI
Cheslyn Hay WS6......4 D2
Tamworth B77 ....21 F5
Wolverhampton WV11..26 B7
Fairview Cres
Kingswinford DY6 .....60 F6
Wolverhampton WV11..26 B7
Fairview Ct WS2.......27 D2
Fairview Gr WV11.....26 B7
Fairview Ind Est B76...59 B7
Fairview Mews 9 B46...70 F7
Fairview Rd
Dudley DY1............51 A3
Wolverhampton, Scotlands
WV11...............26 B7
Curdworth B46, B76...59 F5
Fairview Wlk CV6 .....95 E2
Fairway
Birmingham B31 ......102 E3
Cannock WS11.........4 D6
Nuneaton CV11 ....79 B8
Tamworth B77 ....35 F5
Walsall WS4............15 D1
Fairway Ave B69.......63 A8
Fairway Ct B77........22 B3
Fairway Dr B45.......121 F6
Fairway Gn WV14 .....40 D8
Fairway Prim Sch B38 .103 D1
Fairway Rd B68........63 F2
Fairway Rise CV8 ....148 C6
Fairways B93..........158 A8
Fairways Ave DY8......80 E2
Fairways CI
Coventry CV5..........112 A6
Stourbridge DY8.......80 E2
Fairways Dr B60 ......138 B5
Fairways The
Royal Leamington Spa
CV32...............156 D2
Sutton Coldfield B76...57 F6
Fairway The
Birmingham B38 ......103 D2
Hinckley LE10 ....75 F7
Fairyfield Ave B43 ....43 D1
Fairyfield Ct B43.......43 D1
Fakenham Croft B17...84 F7
Falcon B77.............36 A6
Falcon Ave CV3 ......134 F8
Falcon CI
Cannock WS11.........1 C2
Cheslyn Hay WS6.......4 C2
Kidderminster DY10...116 E2
Nuneaton CV11 ....79 B8
Falcon Cres WV14 .....39 F2
Falcondale Rd WV12...13 C1
Falconers Gn LE10 ....75 F6
Falconhurst Rd B29...85 C2
FALCON LODGE........47 A6
Falcon Lodge Cres B75..47 A6
Falcon Pk B77.........35 E7
Falcon PI B69..........63 C7
Falcon Rd B68........63 F2
Falcon Rise DY8.......80 B5
Falconry Ctr The* DY9..98 F3
Falcons The B75.......47 B5
Falcon View B30.......104 A4
Falcon Way DY1 ....50 F1
Falfield CI B65........63 D6
Falfield Gr B31 ....122 E2
Falkener Ho CV6......113 F7
Falkland CI CV4......131 D7
Falkland Croft B30...104 B6
Falkland Rd WS14......8 F5
Falkland Way B36.....70 B5

Falkwood Gr B93 .....127 F6
Fallindale Rd B26......89 B6
FALLINGS HEATH.......41 F5
Fallings Heath CI WS10...41 F7
FALLINGS PARK........25 E5
Fallings Park Ind Est
WV10................25 E5
Fallings Park Prim Sch
WV10................26 A8
Fallowfield
Birmingham B15 ....85 E8
Perton WV6.............23 D4
Wolverhampton WV8...10 E2
Fallow Field
Cannock WS11..........1 E3
Lichfield WS13..........3 C3
Sutton Coldfield B74...31 B3
Fallowfield Ave B28...105 F5
Fallowfield Rd
Halesowen B63 ....82 D3
Rowley Regis B65 .....63 A3
Solihull B92 ....89 D2
Walsall WS5............43 E8
Fallowfields CV6 ......95 C4
Fallow Hill CV31 ......162 C6
Fallow Rd B78.........20 F1
Fallows Ho B19........66 E5
Fallows Rd B11........66 C3
Fallow Wlk B32........84 A2
Falmouth CI CV11.....74 A5
Falmouth Dr
Hinckley LE10 ....71 E4
Tamworth B77 ....21 F5
Falmouth Rd
Birmingham B34 ....68 F6
Walsall WS5............43 D7
Falna Cres B79.........20 F7
Falstaff Ave B47......125 A6
Falstaff CI
Nuneaton CV11 ....74 A1
Sutton Coldfield B76...58 B7
Falstaff Ct B75.........47 C5
Falstaff Gr CV34 .....161 E3
Falstaff Ho B13.......105 D7
Falstaff Rd
Coventry CV4..........111 E1
Solihull B90 ....106 C1
Falstone Rd B73.......45 D2
Fanad Ho B23..........56 E3
Fancott Dr CV8 ....147 F6
Fancott Rd B31.......103 A5
Fancourt Ave WV4....38 D4
Fane Rd WV11 ....13 B2
Fanshawe Rd B27....88 C1
Faraday Ave
Birmingham B32 ....84 D5
Birmingham B46, B76...59 F5
Faraday Ct B32........84 D5
Faraday Ho 8 B15....86 C8
Faraday Rd
Hinckley LE10 ....74 E7
Walsall WS2............28 B6
Farber Rd CV2........115 A6
Farbrook Way WV12...27 B6
Farclose Ho B15......86 C7
Farcroft Ave
Birmingham B21 ......65 D8
Coventry CV5..........111 D4
Farcroft Gr B21........54 D1
Farcroft Rd B21........54 D1
Fardon Way B23.......56 D8
Fareham Cres WV4....38 C6
Farewell La WV7.......7 E6
Farfield
Kidderminster DY10...116 F5
Stoke Prior B60 ......150 F4
Farfield CI B31........103 B2
Farfield Studios 2 B70 .53 B2
Far Gosford St CV1...113 E2
Far High Dr 8 DY4.....52 B5
Far Highfield B76......46 E4
Far Hill CI B71.........53 F8
Farlands Dr DY8.......81 A3
Farlands Gr B43.......54 F7
Farlands Rd DY8.......81 A3
Far Lash LE10.........75 F7
Farleigh Dr WV3.......38 A8
Farleigh Rd WV6......24 A3
Farley La B62..........100 F1
Farley Rd B23.........56 B4
Farley Sh Ctr The B70...53 D2
Farley St
Royal Leamington Spa
CV31...............162 B7
Tipton DY4.............52 D5
Farlow CI
Coventry CV6..........114 A6
Redditch B98..........154 D3
Farlow Croft B37......99 F8
Farlow Rd B31.........103 C3
Farmacre B9............67 B2
Farman Rd CV5........113 A2
Farm Ave B68..........64 A3
Farmbridge CI WS2....27 D3
Farmbridge Rd WS2...27 D3
Farmbridge Way WS2...27 D3
Farmbrook Ave WV10...11 D3
Farm CI
Birmingham B33 ....68 F3
Cannock WS12..........2 C3
Codsall WV8............10 B2
Kidderminster DY11...116 B2
Sedgley DY3............50 B7
Solihull B92 ....89 C2

Farm CI continued
Tamworth B79 ....21 C7
Farmcote CI B97......158 D4
Farmcote Lodge CV2...96 B4
Farmcote Rd
Birmingham B33 ....69 A4
Coventry CV2..........96 B4
Farm Croft B19 ....66 C6
Farmcroft Rd DY9......81 E2
Farmdale Gr B45.......122 A6
Farm End CI B71.......42 F1
Farm Rd B10 ....88 A7
Farmers Ct B76........46 E4
Farmers Ct B63........82 F4
Farmer's Fold WV1...163 B3
Farmers Rd B60 ......150 E7
Farmers Wlk B21......65 D7
Farmer Ward Rd CV8...148 A3
Farmer Way DY4.......41 C1
Farm House La 6 B75...32 E3
Farmhouse Rd WV12...27 D5
Farmhouse Way
Solihull B90 ....127 B7
Willenhall WV12 ....27 D5
Farm House Way B43...43 E4
Farmoor Gr B34 ....69 E6
Far Moor La B98......154 F5
Farmoor Way WV10...11 E4
Farm Rd
Birmingham B11 ....87 B7
Brierley Hill DY5 ......61 E1
Dudley DY2.............62 A4
Hinckley LE10 ....75 E6
Kenilworth CV8 ......147 E2
Oldbury B68...........64 A3
Redditch B98..........154 A3
Rowley Regis B65 .....63 A4
Royal Leamington Spa
CV32...............157 B3
Smethwick B67 ....64 E3
Tipton DY4.............52 B7
Wolverhampton WV3...38 C8
Farmside CV3 ....134 D5
Farmside CI DY9......82 A3
Farmside Gn WV9.....10 F2
Farm St
Birmingham B19 ....66 C6
Walsall WS2............28 E4
West Bromwich B70...53 C1
Farmstead CI WS1....42 E5
Farmstead Rd B92...89 C2
Farmstead The CV3...134 B8
Farnborough CI B98...154 F1
Farnborough Ct B75...46 E4
Farnborough Dr B90...126 F6
Farnborough Rd B35...58 B3
Farnbury Croft B38...104 B2
Farncote Dr B74......31 F3
Farndale Ave
Coventry CV6..........95 D3
Wolverhampton WV6...24 F5
Farndale CI DY5.......81 B6
Farndon Ave B37......90 B7
Farndon CI CV12......79 B3
Farndon Rd B8.........67 F4
Farneway LE10 ....71 B1
Farnham CI B43.......54 E2
Farnham Rd B21......54 E2
Farnhurst Rd B36.....68 B7
Farnol Rd B26.........68 F1
Farnworth Gr B36.....58 E1
Farquhar Rd
Birmingham B15 ....85 F6
Birmingham, Moseley B13...86 F3
Farquhar Road E B15...85 F6
Farran Way B43........54 E7
Farr Dr CV4.............112 B2
Farren Rd
Birmingham B31 ......102 D1
Coventry CV2..........114 E5
Farrier CI
Bromsgrove B60 ......150 E6
Sutton Coldfield B76...57 F8
Farrier Rd B43........44 D3
Farriers Mill WS3......14 E4
Farriers The B26.......89 B5
Farriers Way
Hinckley LE10 ....75 F6
Nuneaton CV11 ....73 F2
Farrier Way DY6.......60 A7
Farringdon Ho 5 WS2...28 D3
Farringdon St WS2....28 D3
Farrington Rd
Birmingham B23 ....56 B5
Wolverhampton WV4...39 E3
Farrow Rd B44.........44 E3
Farthing Ct 8 B1......66 C3
Farthing La
Curdworth B76........59 C6
Redditch B97..........153 B5
Sutton Coldfield B72...46 B4
Farthing Pools CI 1 B72...62 A7
Farthings La DY2......62 A7
Farthings The
Birmingham B17 ....85 D6
Shenstone WS14......17 F5
Farthing Wlk CV4.....131 D6
Farvale Rd B76........58 C6
Far View WS9 ....16 B2
Far Wood Rd B31.....102 E8
Farzens Ave CV34....160 B3
Faseman Ave CV4....111 F3
Fashoda Rd B29.......86 B1
Fasson CI B77.........21 B3
Fastlea Rd B32........84 D1
Fastmoor Oval B33...69 E1
Fast Pits Rd B25.......88 C7

Fatherless Barn Cres B63 82 D5
Faulconbridge Ave CV5 .111 E4
Faulconbridge Way
CV34.................161 E3
Faulkland Cres WV1 .163 C4
Faulkner CI DY8 ....80 F4
Faulkner Rd B92......89 B1
Faulkners Farm Dr B23...56 B6
Faulknor Dr DY5.......61 B7
Faultlands CI CV11....78 F8
Faversham CI
Willenhall WS2.........27 D3
Wolverhampton WV8...24 E8
Fawdry CI B73.........46 B5
Fawdry St
Birmingham B9 ....67 A2
Smethwick B66 ....65 C5
Wolverhampton WV1...163 A4
Fawley CI
Coventry CV3..........134 C6
Willenhall WV13 ....26 F1
Fawley Gr B14........104 B5
Fawn CI WS12 ....1 C6
Faygate CI CV3 ....114 F3
FAZELEY 34 E8
Fazeley CI B91........107 D4
Fazeley Ind Est B5 ...67 A2
Fazeley Rd
Tamworth B78 ....21 A4
Tamworth, Fazeley B78...21 B2
Fazeley St B5..........66 F2
Fearings Cotts B97...158 D5
Fearon PI 4 B66.......65 A5
Featherbed La
Coventry CV4..........132 A5
Redditch B97..........158 C5
Feathern Dr LE10 .....75 E6
FEATHERSTONE........12 C7
Featherstone
Nuneaton CV10 ....73 C2
Solihull B90 ....106 D2
Featherstone Cres B90 .106 D2
Featherstone La WV10...12 B8
Featherstone Prim Sch
B23...................56 E4
Featherston Rd B14...104 E6
Featherston Rd B74...31 A2
Feckenham Ho B60 ...137 B3
Feckenham Rd
Astwood Bank B96 ...158 E2
Redditch, Headless Cross
B97................158 C8
Redditch, Hunt End B97...158 C4
Fecknam Way WS13...3 C1
Feilding CI CV2........115 A6
Feilding Way CV10....72 A5
Fein Bank CV4........111 C2
Felbrigg CI DY5........81 D8
Feldings The B24......57 C4
Feldon La B62..........83 E7
Felgate CI B90........127 A6
Fellbrook CI B33......68 F4
Fell Gr
Birmingham B21 ....54 C2
Royal Leamington Spa
CV32...............157 C3
Fellmeadow Rd B33...69 A2
Fellmeadow Way DY3...50 E7
Fellmore Gr CV31.....162 D7
Fellows Ave DY6 ......60 C8
Fellows La B17 ....85 A5
Fellows Park Gdns WS2...42 B6
Fellows Rd WV14 .....40 D7
Fellows St WV2........53 B3
Felspar Rd B77.........22 B3
Felstead CI B77........35 C4
Felsted Way B7........67 A4
Felstone Rd B44.......44 E1
Feltham CI B33........69 E1
Felton CI
Coventry CV2..........96 E1
Redditch B98..........154 E1
Felton Croft B33.......69 A3
Felton Gr B91..........107 C1
Fenbourne CI WS4....29 C8
Fenchurch CI WS2....28 D4
Fen CI DY10...........116 E8
Fencote Ave B37......90 B8
FEN END 129 E3
Fen End Rd CV8........129 E4
Fenmere CI WV4......39 D5
Fennel CI WS6.........4 D3
Fennel Croft B34......69 B7
Fennell Ho 10 CV1....113 B2
Fennel Rd DY5.........81 C7
Fennis CI B93.........127 F3
Fenn Rise
Stourbridge DY8.......60 D3
Willenhall WV12 ....27 B5
Fenn St B77...........21 E1
Fennwood La CV8.....147 B1
Fens Cres DY5.........61 C5
Fenside Ave CV3 .....133 D4
Fens Pool Ave DY5....61 D5
Fensway The B34.....69 A5
Fenter CI B13.........86 F5
Fentham CI B92.......109 B6
Fentham Ct B92......106 F8
Fentham Grn B92 ....109 A7
Fentham Rd
Birmingham, Aston B6...66 E8
Birmingham, Gravelly Hill
B23...................56 E3
Hampton-in-A B92...109 A6
Fenton Rd
Birmingham B27 ....88 B5
Hollywood B47........125 A4

Fenton St
Brierley Hill DY5 . . . . 61 D3
Smethwick B66 . . . . 64 E7
Fenton Way B27 . . . . 88 B5
Fenwick Cl
Coventry CV6. . . . . 95 E1
Redditch B97 . . . . 153 B1
Fereday Rd WS9 . . . . 16 B3
Fereday's Croft DY3. . . . . 50 D7
Fereday St DY4 . . . . 51 F8
Ferguson Dr
Kidderminster DY11. . . . 116 A1
Tipton DY4. . . . . 52 B6
Ferguson Rd B68 . . . . . . 64 D5
Ferguson St WV11 . . . . . 13 A1
Fern Ave DY4 . . . . 51 F7
Fernbank B63 . . . . 82 E2
Fernbank Cres WS5 . . . . . 43 C4
Fernbank Rd B8 . . . . 68 A4
Fern Cl
Coventry CV2. . . . . 96 C2
Dudley WV14. . . . . 51 B8
Walsall WS4. . . . . 15 D1
Ferncliffe Rd B17 . . . . . . 85 B4
Ferndale Ave B43 . . . . . . 54 F7
Ferndale Cl
Burntwood WS7 . . . . 7 B6
Nuneaton CV11. . . . . 73 E5
Upper Catshill B61. . . . . 121 A1
West Hagley DY9. . . . . . . 99 A5
Ferndale Cres
Birmingham B12 . . . . 87 A8
Kidderminster DY11. . . . 116 B8
Ferndale Ct 8 B17. . . . . . 85 D4
Ferndale Dr CV8 . . . . . . 148 A2
Ferndale Gr LE10 . . . . . . 75 A7
Ferndale Pk DY9 . . . . 99 C8
Ferndale Prim Sch B43 . . 54 E8
Ferndale Rd
Binley Woods CV3 . . . . . 135 D7
Birmingham B28 . . . . . . 105 F8
Essington WV11. . . . . . . 13 B3
Oldbury B68. . . . . 64 A2
Sutton Coldfield B74 . . . . 44 F8
Fern Dale Rd CV7 . . . . . 129 F6
Fern Dell Cl WS11. . . . . . . 1 C2
Ferndene Rd B11 . . . . . . 88 A3
Ferndown Ave DY3. . . . . 50 C7
Ferndown Cl
Birmingham B26 . . . . . . 69 A1
Coventry CV4. . . . . 112 A3
Walsall WS3. . . . . 14 B4
Ferndown Gdns WV11 . . 26 F5
Ferndown Rd B91 . . . . . 107 C5
Fern Dr WS6. . . . . 5 A4
Ferneley Ave LE10 . . . . . 71 A3
Ferness Cl LE10 . . . . 71 B2
Ferness Rd LE10. . . . . . . 71 B2
Ferney Hill Ave B97 . . . 153 C3
Fern Gr CV12 . . . . 77 E2
Fernhill Cl CV8 . . . . 147 E6
Fernhill Dr B23 . . . . 56 C2
Fernhill Dr CV32. . . . . . 157 B1
Fernhill Gr B44 . . . . 44 F3
Fernhill La CV7, CV8 . . . 129 F5
Fernhill Rd B92 . . . . 88 E2
Fernhurst Dr DY5 . . . . . . 61 B7
Fernhurst Rd B8 . . . . 68 A3
Fernleigh B60 . . . . 137 A1
Fernleigh Ave WS7. . . . . . 7 A8
Fernleigh Ct WV1. . . . . . 107 C5
Fernleigh Gdns DY8. . . . 60 C3
Fernleigh Rd WS4. . . . . . 29 B3
Fernley Ave B29 . . . . 86 B2
Fernley Rd B11 . . . . 87 C4
Fern Leys WV3. . . . . 24 D1
Fern Rd
Birmingham B24 . . . . 57 A4
Dudley DY1 . . . . 51 C4
Huntington WS12. . . . . . . 1 D5
Wolverhampton WV3 . . . 163 A1
Fernside Gdns B13. . . . . 87 B3
Fernside Rd WV13 . . . . . 26 D3
Fernwood Cl
Redditch B98 . . . . 159 B5
Sutton Coldfield B73 . . . . 45 E1
Fernwood Croft
Birmingham B14 . . . . . . 104 E6
Tipton DY4. . . . . 51 F4
Fernwood Rd B73. . . . . . 56 E8
Fernwoods B32. . . . . 84 B2
Ferrers Cl
Coventry CV4. . . . . 111 F2
Sutton Coldfield B75 . . . . 32 D2
Ferrers Rd B77 . . . . 22 A2
Ferrie Gr WS8 . . . . 15 E8
Ferris Gr B27 . . . . 88 A1
Festival Ave WS10 . . . . . 41 C4
Festival Ct
Cannock WS11. . . . . 1 E5
Dudley DY2 . . . . 62 C5
Lichfield WS13. . . . . 9 A7
Festival Mews WS12 . . . . 1 F6
Festival Way WV6. . . . . . 25 B5
Fetherston Cres CV8 . . . 135 B1
Fetherston Ct 4 LE11 . . 161 F6
Fetherston Grange B94 . 143 F5
Fernfall Ct B23. . . . . 56 E5
Fibbersley WV11, WV13 . 26 F4
Fibbersley Bank WV13 . . 26 F4
Fibbersley Park Prim Sch
WV13. . . . . 26 F3
Fiddlers Gn B92 . . . . . . 109 A7
Field Ave B31. . . . . 102 F5
Field Barn Rd CV35 . . . . 160 A7
Field Cl
Birmingham B26 . . . . 89 A6
Bromsgrove B60 . . . . . . 150 E6

Field Cl *continued*
Hinckley LE10 . . . . 71 F3
Kenilworth CV8 . . . . 148 B5
Stourbridge DY8 . . . . 61 A2
Tamworth B77 . . . . 21 C2
Walsall, Blakenall Heath
WS3. . . . . 28 C8
Walsall WS4. . . . . 15 B2
Warwick CV34. . . . . 161 B7
Field Cottage Dr DY8. . . 81 B3
Field Ct
Coventry CV2. . . . . 114 D7
Walsall WS4. . . . . 15 B2
Fieldfare WS7 . . . . 7 D5
Fieldfare Cl B60 . . . . 62 F4
Fieldfare Croft B36 . . . . . 70 A8
Fieldfare Ct DY10 . . . . . 117 A1
Fieldfare Rd DY9. . . . . . . 81 D4
Field Farm La B98 . . . . 154 D2
Field Farm Rd B77 . . . . . 21 D1
Fieldgate La
Kenilworth CV8 . . . . 147 F6
Whitnash CV31 . . . . 162 B2
Fieldgate Lawn CV8 . . . 147 F6
Fieldgate Trad Est WS1 . 28 F1
Field Head La B34 . . . . . 161 B6
Field Head Pl WV6 . . . . . 24 B4
Field House Cl B76 . . . . . 58 C4
Field Ho CV8 . . . . 147 F5
Fieldhouse La B62 . . . . 100 E4
Fieldhouse Rd
Birmingham B25 . . . . 88 C8
Burntwood WS7. . . . . 7 A7
Cannock WS12. . . . . 1 F7
Wolverhampton WV4 . . . 39 E4
Fielding La B91. . . . . . . 127 B8
Field La
Birmingham B32 . . . . . . 102 B8
Catherine de B B91. . . . 108 A5
Clent DY9 . . . . 99 D4
Great Wyrley WS6. . . . . . 4 F3
Stourbridge DY8 . . . . 81 A3
Walsall WS4. . . . . 15 B2
Field Maple Rd B74. . . . . 44 F6
Field March CV3 . . . . . . 134 E5
Field Mews DY2 . . . . 62 E2
Fieldon Cl B90. . . . . 106 C2
Field Rd
Dudley DY2 . . . . 51 E2
Lichfield WS13. . . . . 3 B3
Tipton DY4. . . . . 52 A8
Walsall WS3. . . . . 14 C1
Field Road Ind Est WS3 . 28 C8
Fields Ct CV34 . . . . 160 F8
Fieldside La CV3 . . . . . . 114 F3
Fieldside Wlk WV14 . . . . 40 D8
Field St
Bilston WV14. . . . . 40 E3
Cannock WS11. . . . . 1 F3
Wolverhampton WV13 . . 27 A2
Wolverhampton WV10 . . 163 D4
Fields The WV8 . . . . 10 B4
Fieldstone View DY3 . . . 50 D4
Field View CV31 . . . . . . 162 B3
Fieldview Cl WV14 . . . . . 40 E2
Field View Dr B65. . . . . . 63 F3
Field View Prim Sch
WV14 . . . . 40 F6
Field Way B94 . . . . 143 C6
Fieldways Cl B47 . . . . . 125 A7
Field Wlk WS9 . . . . 30 B7
Fiery Hill Dr B45. . . . . . 138 C8
Fiery Hill Rd B45. . . . . . 138 C8
Fife Rd CV5. . . . . 112 F2
Fife St CV11 . . . . 73 A4
Fifield Cl CV11. . . . . 73 D2
Fifield Gr B33. . . . . 68 F3
Fifth Ave
Birmingham B9 . . . . 67 F2
Wolverhampton WV10 . . 25 E7
Filey B77 . . . . 21 F6
Filey Cl WS11. . . . . 4 C8
Filey Rd WV10 . . . . 11 B2
Fillingham Cl B37 . . . . . 70 D1
Fillongley Rd CV7. . . . . . 92 E3
Filton Ave B77 . . . . 35 F8
Filton Croft B35. . . . . . . 58 A4
Fimbrell Cl DY5. . . . . 81 A8
Finbarr Cl CV6. . . . . 113 E5
Finbury Cl B92. . . . . 88 F1
Finchall Croft B92 . . . . . 107 E7
Fincham Cl WV9 . . . . 11 A3
Finch Cl
Coventry CV6. . . . . 95 C2
Rowley Regis B65. . . . . . 62 F4
Finch Croft CV7. . . . . . . 130 B7
Finchdene Gr WV3 . . . . . 24 D1
Finch Dr B74. . . . . 45 A5
Finches End B34. . . . . . . 69 C5
FINCHFIELD 38 D8
Finchfield Cl DY8 . . . . . . 80 C4
Finchfield Gdns WV3. . . . 24 E1
Finchfield Hill WV3 . . . . 24 C1
Finchfield La WV3 . . . . . 38 C8
Finchfield Rd WV3 . . . . . 24 E1
Finchfield Road W WV3 . 24 D1
Finchley Ave 6 B19. . . . . 66 C8
Finchley Cl DY3. . . . . 50 D2
Finchley Rd B44 . . . . 45 B1
Finchmead Rd B33. . . . . 69 E2
Finchpath Rd B70. . . . . . 53 A6
Finch Rd B19 . . . . 66 C8
Finchfield Rd B14 . . . . . . 86 E1
Findon Cl
Bulkington CV12 . . . . . . 79 C3
Redditch B97. . . . . 153 A5
Findon Rd B8. . . . . 68 B6

Findon St DY10. . . . . . . 116 F6
Finery Rd WS10. . . . . 41 D4
Finford Croft CV7 . . . . . 130 B6
Fingal Cl CV3 . . . . 134 C6
Finger Post Dr WS3 . . . . 15 A5
Fingest Cl CV5. . . . . 112 B4
FINHAM 133 C3
Finham Cres CV8 . . . . . 148 B6
Finham Flats CV8 . . . . . 148 B6
Finham Gr CV3 . . . . 133 C3
Finham Green Rd CV3 . 133 B3
Finham Park Sch CV3 . . 133 A4
Finham Prim Sch CV3 . . 133 B3
Finham Rd CV8 . . . . 148 B6
Finings Cl 7 CV32 . . . . 156 F2
Finlarigg Dr B15. . . . . . . 85 F6
Finlay Cl CV1 . . . . 165 C1
Finmere B28 . . . . 105 F8
Finmere Way B90. . . . . . 106 D3
Finnemore Cl CV3 . . . . . 133 B5
Finnemore Rd B9 . . . . . . 68 A2
Finney Well Cl WV14 . . . 40 B3
Finsbury Dr DY5 . . . . 81 C7
Finsbury Gr B23 . . . . 56 D6
FINSTALL 137 D1
Finstall Cl
Birmingham B7 . . . . 67 A4
Sutton Coldfield B72 . . . . 46 C1
Finstall Fst Sch B60. . . . 137 B1
Finstall Rd
Bromsgrove B60 . . . . . . 151 C8
Finstall B60 . . . . 137 D1
Finwood Cl B92. . . . . . . 107 E8
Finwood Rd CV35 . . . . . 144 F1
Fir Ave B12. . . . . 87 A5
Firbank Cl B30. . . . . 103 E7
Firbank Way WS3 . . . . . . 14 F2
Firbarn Cl B76 . . . . 46 D3
Firbeck Gr B44 . . . . 45 A1
Firbeck Rd B44 . . . . 45 A1
Fir Cl WS12. . . . . 1 D8
Fircroft
Birmingham B31 . . . . . . 102 F8
Darlaston WV14. . . . . 41 A3
Solihull B91 . . . . 106 F6
9 Wolverhampton WV4 . 39 F4
Fircroft Cl
3 Cannock WS11 . . . . . . 2 A3
Stoke Heath B60 . . . . . . 150 D6
Fircroft Coll B29 . . . . . . 103 D8
Firecrest Cl
Birmingham B23 . . . . . . 56 B7
Cannock WS11. . . . . 2 C2
Firecrest Way DY10 . . . . 117 B1
Firedrake Croft CV1. . . . 113 F2
Firenze Rd B60 . . . . 137 C1
Fire Sta B44 . . . . 56 A7
Fire Station Flats B30 . . 103 F4
Firethorn Cres CV31. . . . 162 A2
Fir Gr
Birmingham B14 . . . . . . 104 F5
Coventry CV4. . . . . 112 A2
Stourbridge DY8 . . . . 80 D6
Wolverhampton WV3 . . . 25 A1
Firhill Croft B14 . . . . . . 104 D2
Firleigh Dr CV12 . . . . 79 D2
Firmstone Ct DY8. . . . . . 80 E7
Firmstone St DY8 . . . . . . 80 E7
Firsbrook Cl WV6 . . . . . . 25 A5
Firsbrook Ho WV6 . . . . . 25 A5
Firsby Rd B32. . . . . 84 E5
Firs Cl
Lower Marlbrook B60 . . . 121 D1
Smethwick B67 . . . . 65 A5
Firs Cl The DY10 . . . . . . 117 A5
Firs Dr B90. . . . . 106 A1
Firs Farm Dr B36 . . . . . . 68 F7
Firs Ho B36. . . . . 68 F8
Firsholm Cl B73. . . . . 57 A7
Firs La B67 . . . . 65 A5
Firs Mobile Home Pk The
WS11. . . . . 2 A2
Firs Prim Sch B36 . . . . . 68 F8
Firs Rd DY6. . . . . 60 E6
Firs St DY2 . . . . 51 D1
Fir St DY3 . . . . 49 F7
First Ave
Birmingham, Bordesley Green
B9 . . . . 68 A3
Birmingham, Selly Oak B29. 86 B3
Birmingham, Tyburn B35 . . 58 A5
Birmingham, Witton B6 . . 55 F2
Brownhills WS8 . . . . 16 A8
Coventry CV3. . . . . 114 C1
Kingswinford DY6. . . . . . 50 A1
Wolverhampton WV10 . . 25 E6
First Exhibition Ave B40. 90 D4
Firs The
Bedworth CV12 . . . . 77 E2
Birmingham B11 . . . . 87 C6
Coventry CV5. . . . . 133 B8
Kidderminster DY10. . . . 117 A5
Meriden CV7 . . . . 92 B1
Wolverhampton WV11 . . 26 B5
First Meadow Piece B32 . 84 E4
Firsvale Rd WV11 . . . . . . 26 F5
Firsway WV6 . . . . 24 A2
Firswood Rd B33 . . . . . . 69 C1
Firth Dr
Birmingham B14 . . . . . . 105 B5
Halesowen B62 . . . . 83 E8
Firth Park Cres B62 . . . . 83 E8
Fir Tree Ave CV4. . . . . . 112 B2
Fir Tree Cl
Birmingham B44 . . . . 44 F1
Redditch B97. . . . . 153 D4
Tamworth B79 . . . . 20 E7

Fir Tree Dr
Dudley DY3 . . . . 50 E7
Walsall WS5. . . . . 43 B4
Fir Tree Gr
Nuneaton CV11. . . . . 78 D8
Sutton Coldfield B73 . . . . 45 F1
Firtree Rd B24. . . . . 57 B2
Fir Tree Rd WV3 . . . . 38 D8
Fisher Cl B45 . . . . 101 E2
Fisher Rd
Coventry CV6. . . . . 113 E8
Oldbury B69. . . . . 64 C7
Walsall WS3. . . . . 13 F2
Fisher's Ct CV34 . . . . . . 160 D4
Fisher Dr B90. . . . . 125 F5
Fisher St
Brierley Hill DY5 . . . . 61 B2
Cannock WS12. . . . . 1 F8
Dudley DY2 . . . . 51 D1
Tipton, Burnt Tree DY4. . . 52 A3
Tipton, Great Bridge DY4 . 52 D5
Willenhall WV13 . . . . 27 C2
Wolverhampton WV3 . . . 39 B8
Fish Hill B97. . . . . 153 E4
Fish House La B60 . . . . . 150 E4
Fishing Line Rd B97. . . . 153 E5
FISHLEY. 14 C4
Fishley Cl WS3. . . . . 14 C4
Fishley La WS3 . . . . 14 D5
Fishponds Rd CV8 . . . . . 147 E3
Fishpool Cl B36. . . . . 68 C8
Fishpool La CV7 . . . . 91 B5
Fistral Gdns WV3 . . . . . . 38 F7
Fitchet's Bank WS7 . . . . . 7 F6
Fithern Cl DY3 . . . . 50 E5
Fitters Mill Cl B5. . . . . . . 86 E6
Fitton Ave DY6. . . . . 61 A5
Fitton St CV11 . . . . 73 B3
Fitzgerald Pl DY5 . . . . . . 81 B6
Fitzguy Cl B70. . . . . 53 E1
Fitzmaurice Rd WV11 . . 27 A7
Fitz Roy Ave B17. . . . . . . 84 F7
Fitzroy Cl CV2 . . . . 115 B6
Fitzroy Rd B31. . . . . 102 D3
Fivefield Rd CV7 . . . . 94 E5
Five Fields Rd WV12 . . . 27 A5
Five Oaks Rd WV13. . . . . 40 E8
Fives Gr WS7 . . . . 6 C8
Five Ways
Birmingham B33 . . . . 68 D2
Birmingham, Bordesley Green
B9 . . . . 67 D2
Birmingham, Ladywood B16. 66 B1
Churchill DY10 . . . . 98 A5
Cradley Heath B64. . . . . . 82 C8
Dudley DY3 . . . . 50 D3
Wolverhampton, Dunstall Hill
WV3 . . . . 25 C4
Wolverhampton WV3 . . . 38 C7
Wroxall CV35. . . . . 145 C1
Five Ways Prim Sch WV12 . 2 D2
Five Ways Rd CV35 . . . . 145 F1
Five Ways Sta B15 . . . . . 86 B8
Flackwell Rd B23 . . . . . . 56 E7
Fladbury Cl
Dudley DY2 . . . . 62 D3
Redditch B98. . . . . 159 B8
Fladbury Cres B29 . . . . . 85 D1
Fladbury Gdns B20. . . . . 66 C8
Fladbury Pl 3 B19. . . . . . 66 C7
Flamboro' Cl CV3 . . . . . 134 F8
Flamborough Cl B34 . . . . 69 A7
Flamborough Way WV14 . 51 B7
Flamingo Gdns B23 . . . . 56 C7
Flamville Rd LE10 . . . . . . 76 B5
Flanders Cl B98 . . . . 154 D5
Flanders Dr DY6 . . . . 60 D8
Flash La WV4 . . . . 37 E2
Flash Rd B69. . . . . 64 A7
Flatlea B31. . . . . 102 F4
Flats La WS14 . . . . 19 A6
Flats The B61 . . . . 136 F3
Flatts The WS10 . . . . 41 E7
FLATTS THE 41 E7
Flaunden Cl CV5 . . . . . . 112 B4
Flavel Cres CV31 . . . . . . 161 F7
Flavell Ave WV14 . . . . . . 40 D1
Flavell Cl B32. . . . . 84 B1
Flavells La
Birmingham B25 . . . . 88 C8
Dudley DY3 . . . . 50 C3
Wolverhampton WV4 . . . 38 F4
Flavel Rd B60. . . . . 150 E7
Flax Cl B47 . . . . 125 A5
Flax Gdns B38 . . . . 123 F8
Flaxhall St WS2 . . . . 42 B8
Flax Hill Jun Sch B79 . . . 21 B7
Flaxley Cl B33 . . . . 68 D3
Flaxley Parkway B33 . . . 68 E4
Flaxley Rd B33 . . . . 68 E4
Flaxton Wlk WV6 . . . . . . 25 A5
Flecknoe Cl B36 . . . . 58 C1
Flecknose St CV3 . . . . . . 134 C6
Fledburgh Dr B76. . . . . . 46 D4
Fleet St
Birmingham B3 . . . . 164 A3
Coventry CV1. . . . . 165 B2
Fleetwood Cl B97 . . . . . 153 A2
Fleetwood Gr B26. . . . . . 69 A1
Fleetwood Ho 3 B13 . . . . 86 F4
Fleming Pl WS2. . . . . 28 A6
Fleming Rd
Birmingham B32 . . . . 84 D5
Redditch B97. . . . . 153 D4
Walsall WS2. . . . . 28 A6
Fletchamstead Highway
CV5 . . . . 132 D7

Fletchamstead Highway Ind
Est CV5 . . . . 132 D7
Fletcher Gr B93. . . . . . . 128 B4
Fletcher Rd
Hinckley LE10 . . . . 75 E7
Walsall WV12 . . . . 13 D1
Willenhall WV12 . . . . 27 D8
Fletchers Drift La CV10. . 72 A7
Fletcher's La WV13 . . . . . 27 C2
Fletcher St DY9. . . . . 81 F5
Fletchers Walk Sh Mall
B3. . . . . 164 B2
Fletcher Wlk CV3 . . . . . 133 C4
Fletchworth Gate CV5 . 132 D8
Fletchworth Gate Ind Est
CV4. . . . . 132 D8
Fletton Gr B14. . . . . 105 A3
Fleur de-lys Ct CV34 . . . 161 B8
Flinkford Cl WS5. . . . . . . 43 D6
Flint Cl WS14. . . . . 9 D7
Flint Cl DY10. . . . . 116 E2
Flint Green Rd B27 . . . . . 88 B3
Flintham Cl B92 . . . . 89 B8
Flint Ho 3 WV3 . . . . 25 C4
FLINT'S GREEN. 111 B5
Flintway The B33 . . . . . . 68 E4
Floodgate St B5 . . . . 66 F1
Flood St DY2 . . . . 51 D1
Flood Street Island DY2 . 62 D8
Flora Cl B79 . . . . 21 C7
Flora Rd B25 . . . . 88 B7
Florence Ave
Birmingham B11 . . . . 87 C5
5 Sutton Coldfield B73 . . 57 B7
Wolverhampton WV4 . . . 40 A4
Florence Bldgs 3 B29 . . 85 F2
Florence Cl CV12 . . . . . . 95 F8
Florence Dr 4 B73 . . . . . 57 B7
Florence Gr
2 Birmingham B18. . . . . 65 E4
West Bromwich B71 . . . . 42 E1
Florence Ho 10 B12. . . . . 87 A6
Florence Rd
Birmingham, Acock's Green
B27. . . . . 88 D4
Birmingham, Handsworth
B21. . . . . 65 D8
Birmingham, King's Heath
B14. . . . . 104 F8
Codsall WV8. . . . . 10 C3
Coventry CV3. . . . . 115 A2
Oldbury B69. . . . . 63 E7
Smethwick B66 . . . . 65 B4
Sutton Coldfield B73 . . . . 57 B7
Tipton DY4. . . . . 52 A7
West Bromwich B70 . . . . 53 A7
Florence St
Birmingham B1 . . . . 164 B1
Cannock WS12. . . . . 1 F8
Walsall WS1. . . . . 29 A1
Florence Villas B11 . . . . 87 C7
Florendine Prim Sch 1
B77. . . . . 21 F5
Florendine St B77 . . . . . . 21 F5
Florian Gr WV14 . . . . 41 E7
Florian Way LE10 . . . . . . 71 A1
Florida Way DY6 . . . . 61 A6
Florin Cl CV4 . . . . 131 E6
Flowerdale Cl WV14. . . . 51 B8
Flowerdale Dr CV2 . . . . 114 B6
Floyd Gr CV7 . . . . 130 C7
Floyds La WS4. . . . . 29 C6
Floyer Rd B10 . . . . 67 F1
Flude Rd CV7 . . . . 95 C6
Flyford Cl B98 . . . . 153 F1
Flyford Croft B29. . . . . . 84 F2
Flynt Ave CV5. . . . . 112 B6
Fockbury Mill La B61. . . 136 E5
Fockbury Rd B61. . . . . . 136 B5
Focus Pk B90. . . . . 106 B2
Foden Cl WS14 . . . . 17 F6
Foden Rd B42 . . . . 55 A7
Foel Gr B31 . . . . 102 C6
Foinavon Cl B65 . . . . 62 F6
Fold St WV1 . . . . 163 B2
Fold The
Birmingham B38 . . . . . . 104 A1
Darlaston WS10. . . . . 41 D6
Wolverhampton WV4 . . . 38 F4
Foldyard Cl B76. . . . . 58 A8
FOLESHILL 96 A2
Foleshill CE Prim Sch
CV6 . . . . 96 A2
Foleshill Rd CV1, CV6 . . 113 D6
Foleshill Sports & L Ctr
CV6. . . . . 113 E7
Foley Ave WV6. . . . . 24 C3
Foley Bsns Pk DY11 . . . 116 C3
Foley Church Cl B74 . . . 31 A2
Foley Cr B74. . . . . 30 F1
Foley Dr WV6. . . . . 24 C3
Foley Gdns B60. . . . . . . 150 E3
Foley Ind Est DY11 . . . . 116 C2
Foley Park Com Prim Sch
DY11. . . . . 116 D3
Foley Rd
Birmingham B8 . . . . 68 B5
Stourbridge DY9. . . . . . . 81 C2
Foley Road E B74 . . . . . . 31 A2
Foley Road W B74 . . . . . 30 E1
Foley St WS10 . . . . 41 F4
Foley Wood Cl B74. . . . . 30 E1
Foliot Fields B25. . . . . . . 88 C8
Folkes Rd DY9 . . . . 82 A6

Folkestone Croft B36 68 E8
Folkland Gn CV6 113 A7
Folliott Rd B33 69 B3
Follis Wlk CV4 131 D6
Follyhouse Cl WS1 42 F7
Follyhouse La WS1 42 F7
Folly The B97 158 D8
Fontenaye Rd B79 20 F7
Fontley Cl B26 69 A2
Fontmell Cl CV2 115 A4
Fontwell Rd WV10 11 D4
FOOTHERLEY 17 E3
Footherley La WS14 17 C4
Footherley Rd WS14 17 F5
FORDBRIDGE 70 A3
Fordbridge Cl B97 153 C1
Fordbridge Rd B37 70 A5
Ford Brook La WS3 15 B2
Ford Cotts CV33 157 F2
Forder Gr B14 105 A2
Forde Way Gdns B38 123 D7
Fordfield Rd B33 69 C4
Fordham Gr WV9 11 A3
Fordhouse La B30 104 B6
Fordhouse Rd
Bromsgrove B60 137 B1
Wolverhampton WV10 11 D1
Fordhouse Road Ind Est WV10 11 D1
FORDHOUSES 11 D2
Fordraught La B62 101 B1
Ford Rd B61 136 E1
Fordrift The B37 90 A6
Fordrough B25 87 F7
Fordrough Ave B9 67 E3
Fordrough La B9 67 E2
Fordrough The
Birmingham B31 103 C1
Hollywood B90 125 C7
Sutton Coldfield B74 32 A1
Fords Rd B90 125 E7
Ford St
Birmingham B18 66 B5
Coventry CV1 165 C3
Nuneaton CV10 72 E4
Smethwick B67 64 F6
Walsall WS2 42 C7
Fordwater Rd B74 44 F6
Fordwell Cl CV5 112 F3
Foredraft Cl B32 84 C2
Foredraft St B63 82 D5
Foredraught B80 159 E4
Foredrift Cl B98 153 E2
Foredrove La B92 107 E7
Foregate St B96 158 E1
Forelands Gr B61 150 D8
Foreland Way CV6 95 A3
Fore St B2 164 C2
Forest Ave WS3 28 D7
Forest Cl
Lickey End B60 137 B6
Smethwick B66 64 E7
Sutton Coldfield B74 44 E7
Forest Ct
Birmingham B13 87 A3
Coventry CV5 112 A4
Dorridge B93 127 F3
Willenhall WV12 27 C8
Forest Dale B45 122 B6
Forestdale Prim Sch B45 102 B2
Forest Dr
Birmingham B17 85 D6
Cradley Heath B64 62 F3
Forester's Rd CV3 133 E6
Forester Way DY10 116 E3
Forest Gate WV12 27 D8
Forest Glade WS6 4 F2
Forest Hill Rd B26 89 C5
Forest La WS2 28 D5
Forest Lawns B74 31 C3
Forest Oak Sch B36 70 A6
Forest Pk B76 46 E4
Forest Pl WS3 28 E6
Forest Rd
Birmingham B68 84 C7
Birmingham, Moseley B13 87 A3
Birmingham, South Yardley B25 88 C6
Dorridge B93 127 F3
Dudley DY1 51 C4
Hinckley LE10 75 F8
Forest View B97 158 E6
Forest Way
Great Wyrley WS6 5 A1
Hollywood B47 125 B6
Nuneaton CV10 72 E2
Forfar Wlk B38 103 D2
Forfield Pl CV31 162 A7
Forfield Rd CV6 112 E5
Forge Ave B60 151 B7
Forge Cl
Cannock WS11 4 F5
Hammerwich WS7 7 D5
Wolverhampton WV8 10 E1
Forge Croft B76 58 B6
Forge Dr B61 136 F3
Forge La
Aldridge, Leighswood WS9 30 A5
Aldridge, Mill Green WS9 30 F7
Belbroughton DY9 119 D7
Blakedown DY10 98 B1
Burntwood WS7 7 F6
Cradley Heath B64 82 B8
Forge La *continued*
Halesowen B62 83 C5
Kingswinford DY6 60 A8
Lichfield WS13 3 A1
Shenstone B74, WS14 31 C7
Sutton Coldfield B74 31 C6
Sutton Coldfield B76 58 B5
West Bromwich B71 54 A6
Forge Mill Farm★ B71 54 B6
Forge Mill Lake Nature Reserve★ B43 54 C6
Forge Mill Needle Mus★ B98 153 F6
Forge Mill Rd B98 153 F6
Forge Rd
Darlaston WS10 41 C6
Kenilworth CV8 148 A6
Stourbridge DY8 80 F6
Walsall WS3 14 F5
Willenhall WV12 27 C4
Forge St
Cannock WS12 2 C4
Wednesbury WS10 41 E4
Forge The B63 82 B8
Forge Trad Est B62 83 C5
Forge Way
Coventry CV6 95 C3
Oldbury B69 63 E6
Forhill Ho B38 123 F3
Forknell Ave CV2 114 C5
Formans Rd B11 87 E3
Formans Trad Est B11 87 D3
Formby Ave WV6 23 D4
Formby Way WS3 14 A3
Forrell Gr B31 123 B7
Forrest Ave
Cannock WS11 4 E8
Essington WV11 13 A4
Forrest Ct 9 WS13 9 B7
Forresters Cl LE10 75 F6
Forresters Rd LE10 75 F6
Forrester St WS2 28 C2
Forrester Street Prec 3 WS2 28 C2
Forrest Rd CV8 147 E4
Forryan Rd LE10 75 F7
FORSHAW HEATH 141 C7
Forshaw Heath La B94 141 A7
Forshaw Heath Rd B94 125 C1
Forster St
Birmingham B7 67 A3
Smethwick B67 64 E7
Forsythia Cl B31 102 F8
Forsythia Gr WV8 10 A3
Fort Cres WS9 16 A3
Forth Dr B37 70 B4
Forth Gr B38 123 E8
Forth Way B62 83 E8
Forties B77 35 E7
Fort Ind Pk B35 57 F1
Fortnum Cl B33 69 D2
Forton Cl WV6 24 B2
Fort Parkway B24, B35, B36 57 D1
Fort Sh Pk The B24 57 C1
Forward Cotts B48 138 F6
Forward Rd B26 90 A3
Fosberry Cl CV34 161 B8
Fosbrooke Rd B10 88 A8
Fossdale Rd B77 36 A8
Fosse Cl LE10 76 A5
Fosseway WS14 9 A5
Fosseway Dr B23 56 E8
Fosseway La WS13, WS14 8 E4
Fosseway Rd CV3 133 B4
Fossil Dr B45 122 A7
Foster Ave
Cannock WS12 1 F6
Studley B80 159 E3
Wolverhampton WV14 40 B1
Foster Gdns B18 65 F6
Foster Gn WV6 23 E3
Foster Pl DY8 80 E6
Foster Rd
Coventry CV6 113 B7
Wolverhampton WV10 25 E7
Foster St
Darlaston WS10 41 D7
8 Stourbridge DY8 81 A5
Walsall WS3 28 D8
Foster Street E DY8 81 A5
Foster Way B5 86 C5
Fotherley Brook Rd WS9 30 F5
Founder Cl CV4 131 F7
Foundry La
Smethwick B66 65 D6
Walsall WS3 14 E3
Foundry Prim Sch B18 65 E6
Foundry Rd
Birmingham B18 65 E5
Kingswinford DY6 60 C8
Foundry St
Dudley WV14 40 C1
Kingswinford DY6 60 C8
Tipton DY4 51 E8
Fountain Arc 4 DY1 51 C1
Fountain Cl B31 122 E6
Fountain La
Tipton DY4, WV14 51 E8
West Bromwich B69 53 A1
Fountain Rd B17 65 C1
Fountains Rd WS3 13 E2
Fountains Way WS3 13 E2
Four Acres B32 84 C4
FOUR ASHES 127 D3
Four Ashes Rd B93 127 E4
Four Crosses Rd WS4 15 C1
Four Dwellings Com L Ctr B32 84 B4
Four Dwellings High Sch B32 84 B5
Four Dwellings Prim Sch B32 84 C5
Fourlands Ave B72 57 D7
Fourlands Rd B31 102 E6
FOUR OAKS
Meriden 110 C6
Sutton Coldfield 31 F3
Four Oaks Cl B98 158 D8
Four Oaks Common Rd B74 31 F3
Four Oaks Ct B74 32 B1
Four Oaks Dr B61 121 B1
FOUR OAKS PARK 46 A8
Four Oaks Prim Sch B74 31 E4
Four Oaks Rd B74 32 A1
Four Oaks Sta B74 46 B8
Four Pounds Ave CV5 112 F3
Four Stones Cl B91 107 A1
Four Stones Gr B5 86 D6
Fourth Ave
Birmingham, Bordesley Green B9 67 F2
Birmingham, Selly Oak B29 86 C3
Brownhills WS8 7 A1
Wolverhampton WV10 25 E6
Four Winds Rd DY2 62 E6
Fowey Cl B76 58 A7
Fowey Rd B34 68 F6
Fowgay Dr B91 106 F1
Fowler Cl
Perton WV6 23 E6
Smethwick B66 65 A8
Fowler Rd
Coventry CV6 113 B4
Sutton Coldfield B75 47 B5
Fowler St
Birmingham B7 67 B6
Wolverhampton WV2 39 C6
Fowlmere Rd B42 55 B8
Fownhope Cl B98 154 E3
Fow Oak CV4 111 C2
Fox Ave
Nuneaton CV10 73 D7
Willenhall WV13 27 A2
Foxbury Dr B93 128 B3
Fox Cl
Sutton Coldfield B75 46 F7
Tamworth B77 35 C8
Foxcote Ave B21 65 E7
Foxcote Cl
Redditch B98 154 F4
Solihull B90 126 D8
Foxcote Dr B90 126 D8
Foxcote La B63, DY9 82 B4
Fox Covert DY8 80 E5
Fox Cres B11 87 D4
Foxcroft Cl WS7 7 B5
Foxdale Dr DY5 61 B3
Foxdale Gr B33 69 C3
Foxdale Wlk 8 CV31 162 C6
Foxes Cl B60 138 B5
Foxes Mdw
Birmingham B30 103 F4
Sutton Coldfield B76 58 A8
Foxes Rake WS11 1 E3
Foxes Ridge B64 82 E8
Foxes Way
Balsall Common CV7 130 B6
Warwick CV34 160 D4
Foxfield B31 102 F4
Foxfield Dr DY8 81 A3
Foxfields Way WS12 1 C7
Fox Foot Dr DY5 61 C4
FOXFORD 96 A5
Foxford Cl
Birmingham B36 58 D1
Sutton Coldfield B72 57 D7
Foxford Cres CV2 96 B4
Foxford L Ctr CV6 96 A5
Foxford Sch & Com Arts Coll CV6 96 A5
Foxglove B77 22 A4
Foxglove Cl
Bedworth CV12 77 E1
Birmingham B27 88 B1
Coventry CV6 95 C2
Featherstone WV10 12 B7
Lichfield WS14 9 A5
Walsall WS3 15 A5
Wednesfield WV11 26 E5
Foxglove Cres B37 69 E3
Foxglove Rd DY1 51 A4
Foxglove Way
Birmingham B21 65 D7
Lickey End B60 137 C6
Fox Glove Way B23 56 B7
Foxglove Wlk WS12 2 C7
Fox & Goose Sh Ctr B8 68 C5
Fox Gr B27 88 A2
Fox Green Cres B27 88 A2
Fox Hill B29 103 C8
Foxhill Barns B48 138 E5
Foxhill Cl WS12 2 D2
Fox Hill Cl B29 103 C8
Foxhill La B48 138 E5
Fox Hill Rd B75 32 F2
Foxhills Cl CV11 74 C1
Foxhill's Cl WS7 7 A5
Foxhills Pk DY2 62 C4
Foxhills Rd
Stourbridge DY8 60 D1
Wolverhampton WV4 38 C4
Foxholes La B97 158 A6
Foxholes The DY10 116 F8
Foxhollies Dr B63 82 E4
Fox Hollies L Ctr B27 88 B1
Fox Hollies Rd
Birmingham B27, B28 88 A1
Sutton Coldfield B76 47 B2
Fox Hollies Sch
Birmingham, Acock's Green B27 88 A1
Birmingham, Moseley B13 86 E2
Foxhollow B61 150 D8
Fox Hollow WV6 24 C2
Fox Hollow Cl B45 122 C7
Fox Hollow Dr B78 20 C1
Foxhope Cl B38 104 B2
Foxhunt Rd B63 82 E2
Fox La
Bromsgrove B61 150 E8
Lichfield WS13 3 A5
Foxland Ave
Birmingham B45 122 C7
Great Wyrley WS6 5 A3
Foxland Cl
Birmingham B37 70 D2
Cheswick Green B90 126 D4
Foxlands Ave WV4 38 D3
Foxlands Cres WV4 38 C3
Foxlands Dr
Dudley DY3 50 D5
Gospel End Village WV4 38 D3
Sutton Coldfield B72 57 D7
Foxlea Rd B63 82 D1
Foxley Dr B91 108 B5
FOXLYDIATE 152 F3
Foxlydiate Cres B97 153 A4
Foxlydiate La B97 152 F3
Foxlydiate Mews 3 B97 153 A4
Foxlydiate Wood Nature Reserve★ B97 153 A3
Foxmeadow Cl DY3 50 E7
Fox Mill Est B11 87 D3
Foxoak Ent Ctr B64 62 D1
Foxoak St B64 62 C1
Fox's La WV6 25 C4
Fox St
Birmingham B5 164 D3
Dudley DY1 51 C6
Foxtail Pl B61 137 B8
Foxtail Way WS12 2 E4
Foxton Ct LE10 75 B7
Foxton Man B74 32 A1
Foxton Rd
Birmingham B8 67 F4
Coventry CV3 114 E1
Foxwalks Ave B61 150 D8
Foxwell Gr B9 68 C3
Foxwell Rd B9 68 C3
Fox Wlk WS9 16 B3
Foxwood Ave B43 44 B2
Foxwood Dr CV3 135 D7
Foxwood Gr B37 69 F5
Foxwood Rd B78 36 F8
Foxyards Cl DY4 51 D5
Foxyards Prim Sch DY4 51 C5
Foxyards Rd DY4 51 D5
Foyle Rd B38 103 F1
Fozdar Cres WV14 40 B1
Fradley Cl B30 103 D4
Framefield Dr B91 107 F6
Framlingham Gr
Kenilworth CV8 148 C6
Perton WV6 24 A3
Frampton Cl
Birmingham, Bournville B30 103 D7
Birmingham, Chelmsley Wood B37 70 D3
Frampton Way B43 44 D5
Frampton Wlk CV2 114 F4
Frances Ave CV34 161 A7
Frances Cres CV12 78 A3
Frances Dr WS3 14 B2
Frances Havergal Cl 2 CV31 161 F6
Frances Rd
Baginton CV8 133 F3
Birmingham, King's Norton B30 104 A5
Birmingham, Lozells B19 66 C8
Birmingham, Stockland Green B23 56 D3
FRANCHE 116 B8
Franche Prim Sch DY11 116 B8
Franche Rd DY11 116 C8
Franchise Gdns WS10 41 F6
Franchise St
Birmingham B42 55 E2
Darlaston WS10 41 F6
Kidderminster DY11 116 C5
Franciscan Rd CV3 133 D8
Francis Cl
1 Kingswinford DY6 60 D8
Sutton Coldfield B74 44 F8
Francis Gibbs Gdns 1 CV31 162 A4
Francis Rd
Birmingham, Acock's Green B27 88 D5
Birmingham, Edgbaston B16 66 A1
Birmingham, South Yardley B25 88 A6
Birmingham, Stechford B33 68 D2
Bromsgrove B60 150 F7
Lichfield WS13 3 A2
Smethwick B67 64 D4
Stourbridge DY8 80 C5
Francis St
Birmingham B7 67 A4
Coventry CV6 113 E7
Francis St *continued*
West Bromwich B70 53 D1
Wolverhampton WV1 25 C4
Francis Ward Cl B71 53 A8
Francis Wlk B31 123 A7
Frankburn Rd B74 44 F8
Frank F Harrison Com Sch WS2 27 F7
Frank Fisher Way B70 53 C2
Frankfort St B19 66 D6
Frank Freeman Ct DY10 116 F8
Frankholmes Dr B90 127 A6
Frankland Rd CV6 96 A1
FRANKLEY
Birmingham 102 B2
Frankley Green 102 B5
Frankley Ave B62 83 F5
Frankley Beeches Rd B31 102 D3
Frankley Com High Sch B45 101 F1
Frankley Com L Ctr B45 101 F1
Frankley Gn B32 101 D5
FRANKLEY GREEN 102 A5
Frankley Green La B32 101 E5
FRANKLEY HILL 101 F3
Frankley Hill La B32 102 A4
Frankley Ind Pk B45 102 B1
Frankley La B31, B32 102 D6
Frankley Lodge Rd B31 102 D4
Frankley Rd B68 84 B8
Frankley Terr B17 85 B5
Franklin Ct CV11 73 D1
Franklin Dr WS7 7 B7
Franklin Gr CV4 111 E1
Franklin Rd
Birmingham B30 103 F5
Nuneaton CV11 73 D1
Whitnash CV31 162 A3
Franklins Gdns CV3 115 B1
Franklin St B18 65 E5
Franklin Way B30 103 F6
Franklyn Cl WV6 23 E5
Frankpledge Rd CV3 133 E7
Frank Rd B67 64 E6
Frank St
Birmingham B12 86 F7
Nuneaton CV11 73 B3
Franks Way B33 68 E2
Frank Tommey Cl 5 B65 63 C1
Frankton Ave CV3 133 C5
Frankton Cl
Redditch B98 159 E8
Solihull B92 89 B2
Frankton Gr B9 68 B2
Frank Walsh Ho CV1 165 C4
Frankwell Dr CV2 96 E1
Fraser Cl CV10 72 B6
Fraser Rd
Birmingham B11 87 D5
Coventry CV6 95 A1
Fraser St WV14 40 E6
Frayne Ave DY6 60 C7
FREASLEY 36 C4
Freasley Cl B90 106 D3
Freasley Rd B34 69 E6
Freda Eddy Ct 3 DY10 116 E6
Freda Rd B70 53 D1
Freda Rise B69 63 D8
Fredas Gr B17 85 A4
Frederick Ave LE10 71 B2
Frederick Bird Prim Sch CV2 113 F5
Frederick Ct B77 21 E3
Frederick Eary Ho B98 159 B7
Frederick Neal Ave CV5 111 D4
Frederick Rd
Birmingham, Aston B6 66 F8
Birmingham, Beech Lanes B68 84 D7
Birmingham, Edgbaston B15 86 B8
Birmingham, Gravelly Hill B23 56 E2
Birmingham, Selly Oak B29 85 D2
Birmingham, Sparkhill B11 87 C4
Birmingham, Stechford B33 68 D3
Sutton Coldfield B73 46 A2
Wolverhampton WV11 26 C5
Frederick Rd (Road 1) DY10 116 F1
Fredericks Cl DY8 80 E4
Frederick St
Birmingham B1 66 C4
Walsall WS2 28 D1
West Bromwich B70 53 C4
Wolverhampton WV2 163 B1
Frederick William St 1 WV13 27 B2
Fred Lee Gr CV3 133 D4
Fred Smith Cl WS10 42 B5
Freeburn Cswy CV4 132 C7
Freeford Gdns WS14 9 E6
Freehold St CV1 113 F4
Freeland Gr 3 DY6 60 F4
Freeman Cl CV10 72 D4
Freeman Ct DY11 116 B3
Freeman Dr B76 46 F4
Freeman Pl WV14 40 E8
Freeman Rd
Birmingham B7 67 B6
Wednesbury WS10 42 D3
Freemans Cl CV32 156 E2
Freeman's La LE10 76 A5
Freeman St
Birmingham B5 164 C2
Coventry CV6 113 F6
Wolverhampton WV10 25 F2
Freemantle Ct B37 69 F5

Freemantle Dr B34. . . . . . 69 E6
Freemantle Ho B24 . . . . . . 57 D3
Freemount Sq B43 . . . . . 54 E7
Freer Dr WS7 . . . . .7 E7
Freer Rd B6 . . . . 66 E8
Freers Mews CV34 . . . . . 160 B4
Freer St
  Nuneaton CV11 . . . . 73 E2
  Walsall WS1. . . . . 28 F2
Freesland Rise CV10 . . . . 72 B6
Freeth Rd WS8 . . . . 7 A1
Freeth St
  Birmingham B16 . . . . 65 F2
  Dudley B69 . . . . 63 F8
FREEZELAND 40 B6
Freezeland St WV14. . . . . 40 B6
Fremantle Dr WS12 . . . . . 2 F2
Fremont Dr DY1 . . . . 50 E3
French Ave B78. . . . . . . 20 C1
French Rd DY2 . . . . 51 F1
Frensham Cl
  Birmingham B37 . . . . 70 C2
  Cheslyn Hay WS6. . . . . . . 4 E4
Frensham Dr CV10 . . . . . 72 B5
Frensham Way B17 . . . . . 85 C6
Frenshaw Gr B44 . . . . . . 55 F7
Freshfield Cl CV5 . . . . . . 94 C1
Freshwater Dr DY5. . . . . 81 B8
Freshwater Gr ■ CV31. . 162 C6
Fretton Cl CV6. . . . . . . 113 F7
Freville Cl B79 . . . . 21 A5
Frevill Rd CV6 . . . . 114 B8
Friardale Cl WS10. . . . . . 42 D3
FRIAR PARK 42 D2
Friar Park Rd WS10 . . . . 42 D3
Friar's Alley WS13 . . . . . .9 B7
Friars Cl
  Binley Woods CV3 . . . . . 135 E7
  Stourbridge DY8 . . . . 60 C3
Friars Gate B90 . . . . . . 126 E7
Friars Gorse DY7. . . . . . 80 C8
Friars' Rd CV1 . . . . 165 B2
Friars St CV34 . . . . 160 D6
Friar St WS10. . . . . 42 B3
Friars Wlk
  Birmingham B37 . . . . 70 D2
  Tamworth B77 . . . . 21 C3
Friary Ave
  Lichfield WS13 . . . . 9 A6
  Solihull B90 . . . . 127 A6
Friary Cl
  Birmingham B20 . . . . 54 F3
  Hinckley LE10 . . . . 71 E1
Friary Cres WS4 . . . . . . 29 C6
Friary Dr B74 . . . . 31 F3
Friary Gdns
  Birmingham B21 . . . . 54 D2
  Lichfield WS13 . . . . 9 A7
Friary Rd
  Birmingham B20 . . . . 54 E3
  Lichfield WS13 . . . . 9 A7
Friary St CV11 . . . . 73 B5
Friary The WS13 . . . . . . 9 A7
Friday Acre WS13 . . . . . . 3 A2
Friday Bridge ⑥ B1. . . . 66 C1
Friday La B92. . . . . 108 D4
Friesland Dr WV1. . . . . . 26 B3
Friezeland Rd WS2. . . . . 28 B2
Friezland La WS8 . . . . . 16 A5
Friezland Way WS8 . . . . 16 A5
Frilsham Way CV5 . . . . . 112 B4
Fringe Green Cl B60 . . . 151 A7
Fringe Meadow Rd B98 . 154 F6
Frinton Gr B21. . . . . 65 C7
Frisby Ct CV1 . . . . 73 E2
Frisby Rd CV4 . . . . 111 E2
Friston Ave B16. . . . . . . 66 B1
Friswell Dr CV6. . . . . . . 113 F8
Friswell Ho ■ CV2. . . . . 114 D8
Frith Way LE10. . . . . . . 71 A3
Frobisher Cl
  Great Wyrley WS6. . . . . . .4 F1
  Hinckley LE10 . . . . 71 D4
Frobisher Rd CV3 . . . . . 133 C5
Frobisher Way B66. . . . . 64 D7
Frodesley Rd B26 . . . . . 89 B8
Froggatt Rd WV14 . . . . . 40 D7
Froggatts Ride B76. . . . . 46 F3
Frog La
  Balsall Common CV7 . . . . 130 A5
  Lichfield WS13. . . . . 9 B7
Frogmere Cl CV5 . . . . . 112 C6
Frogmill Rd B45 . . . . . . 102 B2
Frogmoor Ho B26. . . . . . 88 E7
Frogmore La CV8 . . . . . 129 F2
Frome Cl DY3. . . . . 50 D2
Frome Dr WV11. . . . . . . 26 C5
Frome Ho ◢ DY1 . . . . . . 61 E8
Frome Way B14. . . . . . . 104 D6
Front Cotts B48 . . . . . . 138 F6
Frost St WV2 . . . . 40 A6
Froxmere Cl B91. . . . . . 127 C8
Froyle Cl WV6 . . . . 24 C5
Froysell St WV13. . . . . . 27 B2
Fryer Ave CV32 . . . . . . 156 E3
Fryer Rd B31 . . . . 123 B7
Fryers Cl WS3 . . . . 28 A7
Fryers Rd WS2, WS3 . . . 28 A7
Fryer St WV1 . . . . 163 C3
Frythe Cl CV8. . . . . 148 C6
Fuchsia Cl ■ CV2. . . . . 96 B2
Fuchsia Dr WV9. . . . . . . 10 F3
Fugelmere Cl B17. . . . . . 84 F7
Fulbrook Cl B98 . . . . . . 154 C5
Fulbrook Gr B29 . . . . . . 102 F8
Fulbrook Rd
  Coventry CV2 . . . . 96 C2
  Dudley DY1 . . . . 51 A1

Fulfen Prim Sch WS7 . . . . 7 D7
Fulford Cl B47 . . . . 125 C5
Fulford Dr B76. . . . . 58 B5
Fulford Gr B26. . . . . 89 C6
Fulford Hall Rd B90, B94 125 D3
FULFORD HEATH 125 D2
Fulham Rd B11 . . . . 87 B5
Fullbrook Cl B90. . . . . . 127 A5
Fullbrook Rd WS5 . . . . . 42 E5
Fullelove Rd WS8 . . . . . 16 A7
Fullers Cl CV6 . . . . 112 F7
Fullers Cl WV8 . . . . 10 E1
Fullwood Cl CV2 . . . . . . 96 E2
Fullwood Cres DY1, DY2 . 61 F6
Fullwoods End WV14. . . . 40 C1
Fulmar Cres DY10. . . . . 117 B2
Fulmer Wlk B18 . . . . . . 66 A3
Fulton Cl B60. . . . . 137 B1
Fulwell Gr B44. . . . . 56 A8
Fulwell Mews B37 . . . . . 90 B8
Fulwood Ave B62 . . . . . 83 F8
Furber Pl DY6 . . . . 60 F6
Furlong Ct B63 . . . . 82 C6
Furlong La B63 . . . . 82 D6
Furlong Mdw B31. . . . . . 103 C2
Furlong Rd CV1 . . . . . . 165 C1
Furlongs Rd DY3. . . . . . 50 D6
Furlongs The
  Stourbridge DY8 . . . . 81 B3
  Wolverhampton WV11. . . . 26 B5
Furlong The WS10 . . . . . 41 E5
Furlong Wlk DY3. . . . . . 50 D4
Furnace Cl CV12 . . . . . . 78 D3
Furnace Hill B63. . . . . . 83 B5
Furnace La B63 . . . . . . 83 B5
Furnace Par DY4. . . . . . 51 E6
Furnace Rd
  Bedworth CV12 . . . . 78 D4
  Dudley DY2 . . . . 62 C8
Furness Cl B77 . . . . 21 D3
Furness Cl WS3. . . . . . . 13 F3
Furnivall Cres WS13. . . . 3 D1
Furr Marsh The CV34. . . 160 B4
Furrows The B60 . . . . . 150 D6
Furst St WS8 . . . . 16 A8
Furzebank Way WV12 . . . 27 E4
Furze Way WS5 . . . . . . 43 E8
Future Fst Independent Sch
  B18. . . . . 66 A5
Futures Wlk CV3. . . . . . 134 D6
Fylde Ho CV2 . . . . 114 D4
Fynford Rd CV6. . . . . . . 113 B5

G

Gable Croft WS14 . . . . . .9 F6
Gables The
  Kingswinford DY6 . . . . . . 60 B8
  Sutton Coldfield B24 . . . . 57 D4
  Wolverhampton WV11. . . . 13 A4
Gaddesby Rd B14 . . . . . 104 F8
Gadds Dr B65. . . . . 63 D4
Gadsby Ave WV11. . . . . . 27 A7
Gadsby St CV11. . . . . . . 73 E3
Gadsby St CV11 . . . . . . 73 E3
Gads Gn DY2 . . . . 62 E5
Gads Green Cres DY2 . . . 62 E6
Gadshill CV34. . . . . 161 E4
Gads La
  Dudley DY1 . . . . 51 C1
  West Bromwich B70 . . . . . 53 A3
Gadwall Croft B23 . . . . . 56 B3
Gaelic Rd WS11. . . . . . . 1 D4
Gagarin B79 . . . . 20 F5
Gaiafields Rd WS13 . . . . .3 B1
Gaia St WS13 . . . . .9 B8
Gaialands Cres WS13. . . .3 B1
Gaia Stowe WS13. . . . . .3 B1
Gail Cl WS9. . . . . 16 B4
Gailey Croft B44 . . . . . . 44 E3
Gail Pk WV3 . . . . 38 D7
Gainford Cl WV8. . . . . . 10 F1
Gainford Rd B44. . . . . . 45 C1
Gainford Rise CV3 . . . . 115 A3
Gainsborough Ave LE10 . 71 A3
Gainsborough Cres
  Birmingham B43 . . . . 44 D4
  Dorridge B93 . . . . 128 A6
Gainsborough Dr
  Bedworth CV12 . . . . 78 A4
  Mile Oak B78 . . . . 34 B8
  Perton WV6 . . . . 24 A4
  Royal Leamington Spa
    CV31. . . . . 162 D6
Gainsborough Hill DY8 . . 81 A3
Gainsborough Mews
  DY11 . . . . 116 B5
Gainsborough Pl DY1 . . . 50 E2
Gainsborough Rd B42. . . 55 B6
Gainsborough Trad Est
  DY9 . . . . 81 C4
Gainsbrook Cres WS11. . .5 F5
Gainsford Dr B62 . . . . . 83 B6
Gains La WS3, WS11 . . . 5 D2
Gairloch Rd WV11. . . . . 13 B1
Gaitskell Terr B69 . . . . . 52 D2
Gaitskell Way B66. . . . . 64 F7
Gala Baths WS1. . . . . . 28 E2
Galahad Way WS10 . . . . 42 A2
Galbraith Cl WV14 . . . . 51 D8
Galena Cl B77 . . . . 22 B2
Galena Way B6 . . . . . . 66 E6
Gale Wlk B65. . . . . 62 F5
Galey's Rd CV3 . . . . . . 133 D8
Gallagher Bsns Pk
  Coventry CV6 . . . . 95 E5
  Walsall CV34 . . . . 161 D3

Gallagher Ct 🆖 B13. . . . . 87 B2
Gallagher Rd CV12. . . . . 78 A2
Gallagher Ret Pk CV6 . . 113 F8
Gallery Sq WS1 . . . . . . 28 E2
Gallery The WV4 . . . . . . 39 A6
GALLEY COMMON 72 A5
Galley Common Nature
  Reserve ★ CV10. . . . . . 72 A4
Galliards The CV4. . . . . 132 D4
Galliers Cl B77. . . . . . . 35 F5
Galloway Ave B34. . . . . 68 F6
Galloway Cl LE9 . . . . . . 71 F7
Gallows Hill CV34. . . . . 161 B4
Gallus Dr LE10. . . . . . . 71 A1
Galmington Dr CV3 . . . . 133 B6
Galton Cl
  Sutton Coldfield B24 . . . . 57 F4
  Tipton DY4 . . . . 52 C6
Galton Dr
  Birmingham B43 . . . . 43 F1
  Tipton DY2 . . . . 62 B6
Galton Ho B67 . . . . 64 F1
Galton Rd B67 . . . . 64 F1
Galtons La DY9 . . . . . . 120 A7
Galton Twr B1 . . . . 66 C2
Galton Valley Prim Sch
  B66 . . . . 65 A7
Galway Rd WS7 . . . . . . .7 A7
Gamesfield Gn WV3. . . . 24 F1
Gammage St DY2 . . . . . 62 B8
Gamson Cl DY10 . . . . . 116 E4
Ganborough Cl B98 . . . 154 E1
Gandy Rd WV12. . . . . . 27 A7
Gannahs Farm Cl B76 . . 46 F3
Gannaway B93. . . . . . . 128 A4
GANNOW GREEN 101 C1
Gannow Green La B45. . 101 D1
Gannow Manor Cres
  B45 . . . . 101 E2
Gannow Manor Gdns
  B45 . . . . 101 F1
Gannow Rd B45. . . . . . 121 E7
Gannow Wlk B45 . . . . . 121 E7
Ganton Rd WS3. . . . . . 14 A3
Ganton Wlk WV8. . . . . . 24 F8
Garden Cl B77 . . . . 21 D5
Garden Cl
  Birmingham, Frankley
    B45. . . . . 102 A2
  Birmingham, Ward End B8. . 68 A5
  Hinckley LE10 . . . . 75 D6
  Knowle B93 . . . . 127 F6
Garden Cres WS3 . . . . . 14 F3
Garden Croft WS9 . . . . . 30 B7
Garden Ct
  ◾ Birmingham B16. . . . . . 66 B1
  Warwick, Emscote CV34 . 161 D8
  Warwick, Packmores CV34 160 E2
Garden Gr
  Bedworth CV12 . . . . 95 F8
  Birmingham B20 . . . . 54 E6
Gardenia Dr CV5 . . . . . 112 B6
Garden Rd LE10. . . . . . 71 D1
Garden St WS2 . . . . . . 28 E3
Gardens The
  Birmingham, Chester Road
    B73 . . . . 57 B8
  Birmingham, Stockland Green
    B23. . . . . 56 E3
  Kenilworth CV8 . . . . . . 148 A3
  Radford Semele CV31 . . 162 E5
  Sutton Coldfield B72 . . . . 46 B1
Garden Wlk
  Bilston WV14 . . . . 40 F6
  Dudley WV3 . . . . 50 C2
Gardner Ho ◨ CV1 . . . . 113 B2
Gardner Way CV8. . . . . 148 A2
Garfield Rd B26. . . . . . . 89 B8
Garganey Ct DY10. . . . . 116 F1
Garibaldi Terr B60 . . . . 137 A1
Garland Cres B62 . . . . . 83 E8
Garlands Croft CV7 . . . . 95 A6
Garland St B9 . . . . 67 C3
Garlands The WV11 . . . . 26 C7
Garland Way B31 . . . . . 103 C1
Garlick Dr CV8 . . . . . . 148 C6
Garman Cl B43 . . . . . . 43 E2
Garner Cl WV14. . . . . . 40 D3
Garnet Ave B43 . . . . . . 44 B3
Garnet Cl WS9 . . . . 16 E4
Garnet Ct ◢ B92. . . . . . 88 F1
Garnett Dr B75. . . . . . . 46 E6
Garnet St CV10. . . . . . . 72 B5
Garrard Gdns B73. . . . . 46 B5
Garrat St DY5. . . . . 61 E5
Garratt Cl B68 . . . . 64 C4
Garratt's La B65 . . . . . . 63 A2
Garratt St B71 . . . . 53 B5
Garrett Ho WS14 . . . . . 104 E1
Garret Cl DY6. . . . . 60 D8
GARRETT'S GREEN 69 B1
Garretts Green La B26,
  B33 . . . . 89 A8
Garretts Green Trad Est
  B33 . . . . 89 C1
Garrett St CV11 . . . . . . 73 E2
Garrick Cl
  Coventry CV5 . . . . 111 C4
  Dudley DY3 . . . . 50 F3
Garrick Rd
  Bromsgrove B60 . . . . . . 137 C1
  Cannock WS11 . . . . 1 D4
Garrick Rise WS7 . . . . . .7 B7
Garrick Way B71 . . . . . . 53 E8
Garrigill B77. . . . . 22 B1
Garrington Rd B60 . . . . 151 B7

Garrington St WS10. . . . . 41 C7
Garrison Ct ❾ B9. . . . . . 67 B2
Garrison La B9 . . . . 67 C2
Garrison St B9. . . . . . . 67 B3
Garston Way ◢ B43. . . . 54 D8
Garth Cres CV3 . . . . . . 134 D8
Garth Ho CV3. . . . . 134 D8
Garth The
  Birmingham B14 . . . . . . 105 D4
  Lichfield WS13. . . . . 3 B2
Garway Cl
  Redditch B98. . . . . 154 E1
  Royal Leamington Spa
    CV32. . . . . 156 F4
Garway Gr B25. . . . . . . 88 C6
Garwood Rd B26. . . . . . 68 F2
Gas Sq B61. . . . . 136 F1
Gas St
  Birmingham B1 . . . . 66 C2
  Royal Leamington Spa
    CV31. . . . . 161 F7
Gas Street Basin ★ B1. . 164 A2
Gatacre St DY3 . . . . . . 50 D3
Gatcombe Cl WV10. . . . 11 F4
Gatcombe Rd DY1 . . . . . 50 E2
Gatehouse CV31 . . . . . 161 D7
Gatehouse Fold ⑤ DY2. . 51 D1
Gatehouse La B60. . . . . 151 A7
Gate House La B60. . . . 151 A7
Gatehouse Trad Est WS8. . .7 B1
Gate La
  Dorridge B93, B94. . . . . 127 C3
  Sutton Coldfield B73 . . . . 45 F2
Gateley Rd B68 . . . . . . 84 D7
Gateside Rd CV6 . . . . . 95 E2
Gate St
  Birmingham B8 . . . . 67 D5
  Sedgley DY3. . . . . 50 E7
  Tipton DY4 . . . . 52 A2
Gateway The B26 . . . . . 89 F3
Gatis St WV6. . . . . 25 A5
Gatwick Rd B35. . . . . . . 58 B4
Gauden Rd DY9 . . . . . . 81 D2
Gaulby Wlk CV3. . . . . . 115 A1
Gaunts The B48. . . . . . 139 B6
Gaveston Cl ◨ CV34 . . . 160 F8
Gaveston Rd
  Coventry CV6 . . . . 112 F6
  Royal Leamington Spa
    CV32. . . . . 156 E1
Gavin Way B6 . . . . 55 F4
Gawne La B64 . . . . 62 F3
Gawsworth B79 . . . . . . 20 D7
Gaydon Cl
  Perton WV6 . . . . 23 E5
  Redditch B98. . . . . 153 F1
Gaydon Gr B29 . . . . . . 85 A2
Gaydon Pl B73 . . . . 46 B4
Gaydon Rd
  Aldridge WS9 . . . . 30 A4
  Solihull B92 . . . . 89 D3
Gayer St CV6 . . . . 96 A1
Gayfield Ave DY5 . . . . . 61 E1
Gay Hill La B38 . . . . . . 124 B8
Gayhurst Cl CV3 . . . . . 134 E8
Gayhurst Dr B25 . . . . . 88 E8
Gayle B77 . . . . 22 A1
Gayle Gr B27 . . . . 106 C8
Gayton Rd B71. . . . . . . 53 D6
Gaywood Croft B15 . . . . 86 C8
Gaza Cl CV4 . . . . 112 A1
Gazelle Cl CV1 . . . . . . 165 D3
Geach St B19 . . . . 66 D6
Geach Twr B19 . . . . . . 66 D5
Gedney Cl B90. . . . . . . 105 C3
Geeson Cl B35. . . . . . . 58 B4
Gee St B19 . . . . 66 D6
Gemini Dr WS11 . . . . . .4 F6
Gendle Ct B77. . . . . . . 21 D4
Geneva Rd DY4 . . . . . . 51 D5
Genge Ave WV4. . . . . . 39 E4
Genners App B31. . . . . 102 D8
Genners La B31. . . . . . 102 D7
Genthorn Cl ⑪ WV4. . . . 39 F4
Gentian B74 . . . . 31 F4
Gentian Cl B31 . . . . . . 102 F6
Geoffrey Cl
  Coventry CV2 . . . . 114 B5
  Sutton Coldfield B76 . . . . 58 B7
Geoffrey Pl B11. . . . . . . 87 C3
Geoffrey Rd
  Birmingham B11 . . . . 87 C3
  Solihull B90 . . . . 105 F3
George Arthur Rd B8. . . 67 D5
George Ave
  Mile Oak B78 . . . . 20 C1
  Rowley Regis B65 . . . . . . 63 D2
George Betts Prim Sch
  B66. . . . . 64 C7
George Bird Cl B66 . . . . 65 A6
George Cl DY2 . . . . 62 E8
George Dance Cl ②
  DY10 . . . . 117 B6
George Dixon Int Sch & Sixth
  Form Centre B17 . . . . . 65 C2
George Dixon Prim Sch
  B17. . . . . 65 C2
George Eliot Ave CV12 . . 78 D2
George Eliot Hospl CV10 . 73 B2
George Eliot Rd CV1 . . . 113 D5
George Eliot St CV11 . . . 73 D1
George Eliot St CV11 . . . 73 C2
George Fentham Endowed
  Prim Sch B92. . . . . . . 109 B6
George Frederick Rd B73. 45 A4
George Henry Rd ◢ B20. . 52 E6

George Hodgkinson Cl
  CV4 . . . . 111 F3
George La WS13 . . . . . . .9 C8
George Law Ct DY10 . . . 116 F5
George Marston Rd CV3. 114 E1
George Park Cl CV2. . . . 96 C1
George Poole Ho ⑤ CV1 113 B2
George Rd
  Alvechurch B48 . . . . . . 139 A5
  Birmingham B29 . . . . 85 E3
  Birmingham, Edgbaston B15 86 B8
  Birmingham, Great Barr B43 43 F2
  Birmingham, South Yardley
    B25 . . . . 88 A6
  Birmingham, Stockland Green
    B23 . . . . 56 C3
  Coseley, Daisy Bank WV14. 40 D1
  Halesowen B63 . . . . 82 F4
  Oldbury B68. . . . . 64 C2
  Solihull B91 . . . . 107 D3
  Sutton Coldfield B73 . . . . 45 D1
  Warwick CV34 . . . . 161 A8
  Water Orton B46. . . . . . . 59 C3
George Robertson Cl
  CV3. . . . . 134 E7
George Salter Collegiate
  Acad B71 . . . . 53 A4
George St
  Birmingham, Balsall Heath
    B12. . . . . 86 F5
  Birmingham, Brookfields
    B3. . . . . 164 A3
  Birmingham, Handsworth
    B21. . . . . 65 C8
  Birmingham, Lozells B19. . . 66 B7
  ◨ Bromsgrove B61. . . . . 136 F2
  Cannock WS12. . . . . 2 C4
  Coventry CV1. . . . . 113 E5
  Dudley DY1 . . . . 51 B6
  Hinckley LE10 . . . . 75 D8
  Kidderminster DY10. . . . . 116 F6
  Nuneaton CV11 . . . . 73 E2
  Royal Leamington Spa
    CV31. . . . . 162 A1
  Stourbridge DY8 . . . . 60 F1
  Stow Heath WV2 . . . . . . 40 A7
  Tamworth B79 . . . . 21 B4
  Walsall WS1. . . . . 28 E1
  West Bromwich B70 . . . . . 53 D2
  Willenhall WV13 . . . . 27 A4
  Wolverhampton WV2. . . . 163 C2
George Street Ringway
  CV12 . . . . 78 B3
George Street W B18. . . 66 A4
George Wlk ⑤ B97. . . . . 153 E3
Georgia Pl WS11 . . . . . .1 E2
Georgian Ave WV14. . . . 40 D3
Geraghty Ct DY4 . . . . . . 41 A2
Geraldine Rd B25 . . . . . 88 B7
Gerald Rd DY8 . . . . 80 E7
Geranium Gr B9 . . . . . . 67 F3
Geranium Rd DY2. . . . . 62 F8
Gerard B79 . . . . 20 E7
Gerard Ave CV4 . . . . . . 132 B8
Gerardsfield Rd B33 . . . 69 E2
Germander B74. . . . . . . 31 F5
Germander Dr WS5 . . . . 43 A3
Gerrard Cl B19 . . . . 66 D7
Gerrard Rd WV13 . . . . . 26 E1
Gerrard St
  Birmingham B19 . . . . 66 D7
  ◨ Warwick CV34 . . . . . . 160 E6
Gertrude Pl B18 . . . . . . 66 A5
Gervase Dr DY1 . . . . . . 51 C3
George Bird Cl B66 . . . . 61 F8
Gettings Cl WS7 . . . . . .7 F7
Gheluvelt Ave DY10. . . . 116 F7
GIBBET HILL 132 E2
Gibbet Hill Rd CV4 . . . . 132 B3
Gibbet La DY7 . . . . 80 B4
Gibbins Rd B29 . . . . . . 85 D2
Gibbon's La B63 . . . . . 137 A8
Gibbons Cl CV4 . . . . . . 111 F2
Gibbons Gr WV6 . . . . . 24 F4
Gibbons Hill Rd DY3 . . . 39 D2
Gibbons Ind Pk DY6. . . . 61 A7
Gibbons La DY5. . . . . . 61 A7
Gibbons Rd
  Sutton Coldfield B75 . . . . 32 B3
  Wolverhampton WV6. . . . 24 F4
Gibbs Cl CV2 . . . . 115 B6
Gibbs Hill Rd B31 . . . . . 123 C7
Gibb Sq B12 . . . . 67 A1
Gibbs Rd DY9 . . . . 82 A5
Gibbs St WV6. . . . . 25 A4
Gibb St B9 . . . . 66 F1
GIB HEATH 66 A6
Gibson Cres CV12. . . . . 78 A1
Gibson Dr
  Birmingham B20 . . . . 66 B8
  Smethwick B66 . . . . 65 A6
Gibson Rd
  Birmingham B20 . . . . 66 B8
  Perton WV6 . . . . 23 E3
Gideon Cl B25 . . . . 88 D6
Gideons Cl DY3 . . . . . . 50 D5
Gielgud Way CV2 . . . . . 115 B8
Giffard RC Prim Sch The
  WV6. . . . . 24 F5
Giffard Dr
  Bilston WV1. . . . . 40 B7

Giffard Rd *continued*
Wolverhampton WV10 11 F3
Giffard Way CV34 155 E1
Gifford Ct 13 DY5 61 D2
Giffords Croft WS13 3 A1
Gigg La B76 48 B3
Gig Mill Prim Sch DY8 80 E4
Gigmill Way DY8 80 E4
Gilbanks Rd DY8 80 D7
Gilberry Cl B93 128 A4
Gilbert Ave B69 63 B7
Gilbert Cl
Bedworth CV12 78 B2
3 Coventry CV1 113 E3
Wednesfield WV11 27 A7
Gilbert Ent Pk WV12 27 B4
Gilbert Horal Cl CV4 111 F1
Gilbert La WV5 49 B7
Gilbert Rd
Bromsgrove B60 150 E7
Lichfield WS13 3 C2
Smethwick B66 65 B3
Gilbert Scott Way DY10 116 F7
Gilberts Ct WS4 29 A4
GILBERT'S GREEN 141 E3
Gilbert St DY4 52 A2
GILBERTSTONE 88 F6
Gilbertstone Ave B26 88 E5
Gilbertstone Cl B98 153 E1
Gilbertstone Prim Sch B26 88 E5
Gilbert Wlk WS13 3 C2
Gilbeys Cl 5 DY8 60 E1
Gilby Rd B16 66 A1
Gilchrist Dr B15 85 E8
Gildas Ave B38 104 A1
Giles Cl
Birmingham B33 68 E3
Coventry CV6 95 C2
Solihull B92 107 F7
Giles Close Ho B33 68 E3
Giles Rd
Lichfield WS13 3 A3
Oldbury B68 64 B5
Gilfil Rd CV10 73 B1
Gilldown Pl B15 86 B7
Gillespie Croft B6 66 F7
Gillet Cl CV11 73 B3
Gillhurst Rd B17 85 C7
Gillians Wlk CV2 115 A8
Gilling Gr B34 69 A6
Gillingham Cl WS10 42 D4
Gillity Ave WS5 43 C8
Gillity Cl WS5 43 C8
Gillity Ct 3 WS5 43 D7
Gilliver Rd B90 106 B2
Gillman Cl B26 89 D4
Gillott Cl B91 107 E3
Gillott Rd B16 65 D2
Gillows Croft B90 127 A7
Gillscroft Rd B33 69 A3
Gill St
Dudley DY2 62 E4
West Bromwich B70 53 C1
GILLWAY 21 B8
Gillway B79 21 B8
Gilmorton Cl
Birmingham B17 85 B7
Solihull B91 107 C1
Gilpin Cl B8 68 C7
Gilpin Cres WS3 15 A4
Gilpins Croft WS6 4 D1
Gilquart Way CV1 165 C1
GILSON 59 D1
Gilson Dr B46 70 D8
Gilson Rd B46 70 E8
Gilson St DY4 52 C8
Gilson Way B37 70 A5
Gilwell Rd B34 69 E6
Gimble Wlk 2 B17 84 F7
Ginkgo Wlk 2 CV31 161 F5
Gipsy Cl CV7 130 B5
Gipsy La
Balsall Common CV7 130 C5
Birmingham B23 56 B5
Nuneaton CV10, CV11 78 D7
Willenhall WV13 27 B1
Girdlers Cl CV3 133 B5
Girtin Cl CV12 78 A4
Girton Ho B36 69 F8
Girton Rd WS11 4 F8
Girvan Gr CV32 157 C5
Gisborn Cl B10 87 B8
Gisburn Cl
5 Redditch B97 153 B5
Warwick CV34 155 F1
Givens Ho 9 CV1 113 B2
GK Davies Ind Est DY9 82 A6
Glades Arena L Ctr DY10 116 E6
Gladeside Cl WS4 29 D8
Glades The WS9 30 B7
Glade The
Birmingham B26 89 D4
Cannock WS11 1 C2
Coventry CV5 111 F3
Stourbridge DY9 81 E5
Sutton Coldfield B74 30 E1
Wolverhampton WV8 10 E1
Gladman Bsns Quarter WV9 10 F3
Gladstone Cl LE10 71 E4
Gladstone Ct 22 CV32 156 F1
Gladstone Dr
Oldbury B69 52 D3
Stourbridge DY8 80 D6
Gladstone Gr 3 DY6 60 D8
Gladstone Rd
Birmingham, Gravelly Hill B23 56 D3
Birmingham, South Yardley B26 88 D6
Birmingham, Sparkbrook B11 87 B6
Cannock WS12 2 E1
Dorridge B93 128 A2
Stourbridge DY8 80 D6
Gladstone St
Birmingham B6 67 B8
Darlaston WS10 41 E6
Walsall WS2 28 D4
West Bromwich B71 53 C5
Gladstone Terr LE10 75 E8
Gladys Rd
Birmingham B25 88 B7
Smethwick B67 64 F2
Gladys Terr B67 65 A2
Glaisdale Ave CV6 95 E3
Glaisdale Gdns WV6 25 A5
Glaisdale Rd B28 106 B8
Glaisedale Gr WV13 27 C2
Glaisher Dr WV10 25 C6
Glamis Rd WV12 27 B7
Glamorgan Cl CV3 134 D5
Glanville Dr B75 32 A4
Glasbury Croft B38 123 E7
Glascote Cl B90 106 A4
Glascote Ct B77 21 E4
Glascote Gr B34 69 C6
GLASCOTE HEATH 21 F2
Glascote Heath Prim Sch 1 B77 22 A2
Glascote La B77 35 F8
Glascote Rd
Tamworth B77 22 B2
Tamworth, Glascote Heath B77 21 E3
Glaslyn Ave B65 63 B2
Glasscroft Cotts WS7 7 F7
Glassford Dr WV6 24 E6
Glasshouse Coll DY8 80 F7
Glasshouse Hill DY8 81 B3
Glasshouse La
Hockley Heath B94 143 F6
Kenilworth CV8 148 D4
Glastonbury Cl DY11 116 A6
Glastonbury Cres WS3 13 E2
Glastonbury Rd
Birmingham B14 105 C5
West Bromwich B71 42 D1
Glastonbury Way WS3 13 E1
Glaston Dr B91 107 A1
Gleads Croft B62 84 A3
Gleaston Wlk WV1 26 C1
Gleave Rd
Birmingham B29 85 E1
Whitnash CV31 162 A3
Glebe Ave CV12 77 E1
Glebe Cl
Coventry CV4 132 A7
Redditch B98 154 D2
Glebe Cres CV8 148 A3
Glebe Ct CV31 162 A3
Glebe Dr B73 56 F8
GLEBE FARM 69 A4
Glebefarm Gr CV3 114 F3
Glebe Farm Rd B33 69 A5
Glebe Fields
Curdworth B76 59 B6
Stourbridge DY9 119 E6
Glebefields Prim Sch DY4 52 A8
Glebefields Rd DY4 52 A7
Glebe La
Nuneaton CV11 73 F6
Stourbridge DY8 80 E4
Glebeland Cl B16 66 B1
Glebe Pl
Darlaston WS10 41 B6
Royal Leamington Spa CV31 162 B7
Glebe Rd
Alvechurch B48 139 A7
Hinckley LE10 71 F1
Nuneaton CV11 73 D4
Solihull B91 107 D5
Willenhall WV13 40 F8
Glebe St WS1 42 E8
Glebe The
Belbroughton DY9 119 E6
Beoley B98 154 F7
Corley CV7 94 C7
Glebe Way CV7 130 A7
Gledhill Pk WS14 9 C5
Gleeson Dr CV34 155 E1
Glenavon Rd B14 105 A3
Glen Bank LE10 71 E1
Glenbarr Cl LE10 75 A8
Glenbarr Dr LE10 75 A8
Glen Cl
Cannock WS11 1 E5
Walsall WS4 29 A3
Glencoe Dr WS11 2 A4
Glencoe Rd
Birmingham B16 65 C4
Coventry CV3 114 B1
Glencroft Rd B92 89 D4
Glen Ct
Codsall WV8 10 A4
Wolverhampton WV6 24 E2
Glendale Ave CV8 148 A6
Glendale Cl
Halesowen B63 83 B4
Wolverhampton WV3 38 C8
Glendale Ct B77 36 B6
Glendale Dr
Birmingham B33 68 F3
Wombourne WV5 49 A6
Glendale Gdns WS11 2 A4
Glendale Inf Sch CV10 72 F2
Glendale Twr 5 B23 57 B6
Glendale Way CV4 111 C2
Glendawn Cl 1 WS11 2 A3
Glendene Cres B38 123 C7
Glendene Dr 2 B43 54 D8
Glendene Rd WS12 2 D6
Glen Devon Cl B45 102 A2
Glendon Gdns CV12 79 C3
Glendon Rd B23 56 D6
Glendon Way B93 127 E3
Glendower App CV34 161 E3
Glendower Ave CV5 112 D3
Glendower Rd
Aldridge WS9 16 B1
Birmingham B42 55 D4
Gleneagles B77 22 B5
Gleneagles Cl
Hinckley LE10 75 D4
Nuneaton CV11 74 C1
Gleneagles Dr
Birmingham B43 43 E3
Blackwell B60 138 A5
Oldbury B69 63 A7
Sutton Coldfield B75 46 D8
Gleneagles Rd
Birmingham B26 89 A8
Coventry CV2 114 E6
Perton WV6 23 D5
Walsall WS3 13 F3
Glenelg Dr DY8 81 B2
Glenelg Mews WS5 43 D5
Glenfern Gdns CV8 134 E2
Glenfern Rd WV14 51 A8
Glenfield
Tamworth B77 21 C1
Wolverhampton WV8 10 E2
Glenfield Ave CV10 73 D7
Glenfield Cl
Redditch B97 158 D6
2 Solihull B91 127 C8
Sutton Coldfield B76 46 E3
Glenfield Gr B29 86 A1
Glengarry Cl B32 102 B7
Glengarry Gdns WV3 24 F1
Glenhill Dr B38 124 A8
Glen Ho DY1 61 D8
Glenhurst Cl WS2 27 D3
Glenmead Prim Sch B44 55 D8
Glenmead Rd B44 55 D8
Glenmore Ave WS7 7 A6
Glenmore Cl WV3 38 E7
Glenmore Dr
Birmingham B38 103 D2
Coventry CV6 95 F5
Glenmount Ave CV6 95 F5
Glenn St CV6 95 D3
Glenpark Rd B8 67 F5
Glen Park Rd DY3 50 D2
Glen Rd
Dudley DY3 50 E6
Stourbridge DY8 80 F3
Glenridding Cl CV6 95 F5
Glen Rise B13 105 C6
Glenrosa Wlk CV4 132 A7
Glenroy Cl CV2 114 E6
Glenroyde B38 123 E7
Glen Side B32 84 D2
Glenside Ave B92 89 C3
Glen The B60 138 A5
Glenthorne Dr WS6 4 E3
Glenthorne Ho WS6 4 D2
Glenthorne Prim Sch WS6 4 E3
Glenthorne Rd B24 57 A2
Glentworth B76 47 A2
Glentworth Ave CV6 95 A2
Glentworth Gdns WV6 25 B5
Glenville Ave CV9 36 C1
Glenville Dr B23 56 E5
Glenwood Cl DY5 81 D8
Glenwood Dr B90 126 D4
Glenwood Gdns
Bedworth CV12 78 A5
Tamworth B77 36 B6
Glenwood Rd B38 123 D8
Glenwood Rise WS9 16 D3
Globe St WS10 41 F1
Gloster Dr CV8 147 F6
Gloucester Cl
Lichfield WS13 3 B3
Nuneaton CV11 74 A7
Redditch B97 153 D4
Gloucester Ho
4 Birmingham B24 56 F4
4 Wolverhampton WV3 25 C4
Gloucester Pl WV13 27 D2
Gloucester Rd
Dudley DY2 62 D2
Walsall WS5 43 C8
Wednesbury WS10 42 C3
Gloucester St
Birmingham B5 164 C1
Coventry CV1 113 B3
3 Royal Leamington Spa CV31 162 A7
Wolverhampton WV6 25 B4
Gloucester Way
Birmingham B37 70 A1
Cannock WS11 2 B1
Glover Cl
Birmingham B28 105 F6
Warwick CV34 160 B4
Glover Rd B75 47 A5
Glovers Cl CV7 92 C1
Glovers Croft B37 69 F3
Glovers Field Dr B7 67 C7
Glovers Rd B10 87 D8
Glover St
Birmingham B9 67 A2
Cannock WS12 2 F3
Coventry CV3 133 D8
Redditch B98 153 E3
West Bromwich B70 53 D1
Glover's Trust Homes B73 56 F7
Glyde Ct B27 88 B2
Glyme Dr WV6 24 E5
Glyn Ave WV14 41 B3
Glyndebourne B79 20 D7
Glyn Dr WV14 41 B3
Glyne Ct 7 B73 46 B5
Glyn Farm Rd B32 84 C6
Glynn Cres B63 82 B7
Glynne Ave DY6 60 D5
Glynne Prim Sch DY6 60 C4
Glyn Rd B32 84 D6
Glynside Ave B32 84 D6
Godfrey Cl CV31 162 E5
Godiva Pl CV1 165 D3
Godiva Trad Est CV6 113 F8
Godolphin B79 20 D7
Godrich Ho B13 87 B3
Godson Cres DY11 116 C3
Godson Pl DY11 116 C3
Goffs Cl B32 84 F3
Gofton B77 36 A8
Goggbridge La CV34 160 B3
Goldacre Cl CV31 161 F4
Goldborough Cl WV14 40 D3
Goldby Dr WS10 41 E4
Gold Cl
Hinckley LE10 71 A2
Nuneaton CV11 78 E8
Goldcrest B77 36 A6
Goldcrest Cl DY2 62 D2
Goldcrest Croft B36 70 A8
Goldcrest Dr DY10 117 B2
Golden Acres La CV3 134 F7
Goldencrest Dr B69 63 E8
Golden Croft B20 54 F1
Golden Cross La B61 121 B1
Goldencross Way DY5 61 B1
Golden End Dr B93 128 D6
Golden Hillock Rd
Birmingham B11 87 D6
Dudley DY2 62 C3
Golden Hillock Sch Specialist Sports Coll B11 87 D5
Goldfinch Cl B30 103 D8
Goldfinch Rd DY9 81 C3
Goldicroft Rd WS10 42 A4
Goldieslie Cl B73 46 B2
Goldieslie Rd B73 46 B2
Goldsborough B77 22 A1
GOLDS GREEN 52 E8
Golds Hill Gdns B21 65 F7
Golds Hill Rd B21 65 F8
Golds Hill Way DY4 52 D7
Goldsmith Ave CV34 160 C5
Goldsmith Pl B79 21 A7
Goldsmith Rd
Birmingham B14 104 F8
Walsall WS3 28 E7
Goldsmith Wlk DY10 117 C5
Goldstar Way B33 69 C2
Goldtel Ind Est WV4 40 A5
Goldthorn Ave WV4 39 B6
Goldthorn Cl CV5 111 D4
Goldthorn Cres WV4 39 A6
Goldthorne Ave
Birmingham B26 89 C4
Cannock WS11 1 F2
Goldthorne Cl B97 153 C1
Goldthorne Wlk DY5 81 D8
GOLDTHORN HILL 39 A5
Goldthorn Hill WV2, WV4 39 C6
Goldthorn Mews DY11 116 C2
GOLDTHORN PARK 39 C5
Goldthorn Park Prim Sch WV4 39 D5
Goldthorn Pl DY11 116 C2
Goldthorn Rd
Kidderminster DY11 116 C2
Wolverhampton WV2, WV3 39 B6
Golf Dr CV11 74 B1
Golf La
Bilston WV14 40 D7
Whitnash CV31 162 B2
Golson Cl B75 46 F6
Gomeldon Ave B14 104 F3
Gomer St WV13 27 A2
Gomer Street W WV13 27 A2
Gonville Ho B36 69 F8
Gooch Cl DY8 81 B6
Gooch St B5 86 E8
Gooch Street N B5 86 E8
Goodall Gr B43 44 E5
Goodall St WS1 28 F1
Goodby Rd B13 86 D3
Goode Ave B18 66 A5
Goode Cl
Oldbury B68 64 C4
Warwick CV34 160 C7
Goode Croft CV4 111 F2
Goodeve Wlk B75 47 B5
Goodfellow St CV32 156 C1
Good Hope Hospl B75 46 D6
Goodison Gdns B24 57 B5
Goodleigh Ave B45 122 E6
Goodman Cl B28 105 F6
Goodman St B1 66 B3
Goodman Way CV4 111 C1
Goodrest Ave B62 84 A5
Goodrest Croft B14 105 C4
Goodrest La B38 123 F6
Goodrich Ave WV6 24 A3
Goodrich Cl B98 154 F2
Goodrich Covert 10 B14 104 C2
Goodrich Mews DY3 50 E4
Goodrick Way B7 67 B6
Good Shepherd RC Prim Sch 2 CV6 95 F1
Goodway Ct 9 CV34 160 F7
Goodway Ho
Birmingham B4 164 C4
Kenilworth CV8 148 A5
5 Royal Leamington Spa CV32 161 D8
Goodway Rd
Birmingham B44 55 F8
Solihull B92 89 E4
Goodwin Cl DY11 116 C7
Goodwood Cl
Birmingham B36 68 D8
Coventry CV3 134 C6
Lichfield WS14 9 D7
Goodwood Dr B74 44 F7
Goodwood Rd B61 121 B1
Goodwyn Ave B68 84 C7
Goodyear Ave WV10 25 E7
Goodyear Rd B67 64 E2
GOODYERS END 95 D8
Goodyers End La CV12 95 D8
Goodyers End Prim Sch CV12 95 E8
Goosehill Cl B98 154 E1
Goosehills Rd LE10 75 E5
Goosemoor La B23 56 F7
Goostry Cl B77 21 D5
Goostry Rd B77 21 D5
Gopsall Rd LE10 71 D2
Gopsal St B4 67 A3
Gorcott La B90 126 A5
Gordon Ave
Birmingham B19 66 D7
West Bromwich B71 53 C8
Wolverhampton WV4 39 F3
Gordon Cl
Bedworth CV12 78 C4
Oldbury B69 52 D2
Gordon Cres DY5 61 E5
Gordon Ct B33 68 D3
Gordon Dr DY4 52 C6
Gordon Pl WV14 40 C5
Gordon Rd
Birmingham B17 85 D6
Birmingham, Lozells B19 66 C8
Gordon St
5 Birmingham B9 67 B2
Coventry CV1 113 B2
Darlaston WS10 41 E6
Royal Leamington Spa CV31 162 A7
Wolverhampton WV2 163 C2
Gorey Cl WV12 27 B8
Gorge Rd
Sedgley DY3 50 E8
Wolverhampton WV14, DY3 39 F1
Goring Rd CV2 114 A4
Gorleston Gr B14 105 B2
Gorleston Rd B14 105 B2
GORNALWOOD 50 C2
Gorsebrook Rd WV6 25 B5
Gorse Cl
Birmingham, Fordbridge B37 69 F2
Birmingham, Selly Oak B29 103 A8
Gorse Dr WS12 1 D5
Gorse Farm Rd
Birmingham B43 54 E8
Nuneaton CV11 79 B8
Gorse Farm Wood Nature Reserve★ B43 54 F8
Gorsefield Rd B34 69 C5
Gorse Green La DY9 120 C8
Gorse La WS14 9 E6
Gorse Meadow Dr B45 138 B8
Gorsemoor Prim Sch WS12 2 D1
Gorsemoor Rd WS12 2 D1
Gorsemoor Way WV11 13 B3
Gorse Rd
Dudley DY1 51 A4
Wednesfield WV11 27 A8
Gorseway
Burntwood WS7 7 B5
Coventry CV5 112 C3
Gorse Way WS12 2 C8
Gorsey La
Cannock WS11 1 C1
Coleshill B46 59 F2
Great Wyrley WS6 4 F1
Norton Canes WS3 5 E1
Wythall B47 125 A3
Gorsey Way
Aldridge WS9 29 E5
Coleshill B46 59 E2
Gorsly Piece B32 84 C4
Gorstey Lea WS7 7 C7
GORSTEY LEY 7 C7
Gorstie Croft B43 54 E8
Gorsty Ave DY5 61 C3
Gorsty Bank WS14 9 E8
Gorsty Cl 2 B71 53 F8
Gorsty Hill Rd B65 83 B8
Gorsy Bank Rd B77 35 F5
Gorsymead Gr B31 102 C2
Gorsy Rd B32 84 D5
Gorsy Way CV10 72 D5
Gorton Croft CV7 130 B7

Gorway Cl WS1 . . . . 42 F7
Gorway Gdns WS1 . . . . . . 43 A7
Gorway Rd WS1 . . . . 43 A7
GOSCOTE 28 F8
Goscote Cl
  Redditch B97 . . . . 153 A5
  Walsall WS3 . . . . 28 F7
Goscote Ind Est WS3 . . . . 14 E1
Goscote La WS3 . . . . 28 F8
Goscote Lodge Cres WS3. 29 A7
Goscote Pl WS3. . . . . 29 A7
Goscote Rd WS3 . . . . 15 A1
Gosford Dr LE10 . . . . 71 A1
GOSFORD GREEN. 113 F2
Gosford Ind Est CV1. . . . 113 F2
Gosford Park Prim Sch
  CV1. . . . . 113 F2
Gosford St
  Birmingham B12 . . . . . . 86 F6
  Coventry CV1. . . . . 165 D2
Gosford Wlk B92. . . . . 89 B1
Gosmoor Ho B26. . . . . 88 E7
Gospel End Rd DY3 . . . . . . 50 B8
Gospel End St DY3 . . . . . . 50 D8
GOSPEL END VILLAGE. . . 50 A8
Gospel Farm Rd B27 . . . . 106 B8
Gospel La B27 . . . . 106 C8
GOSPEL OAK. 41 B1
Gospel Oak Rd
  Coventry CV6. . . . . 95 B4
  Wednesbury DY4 . . . . . . 41 B1
Gosport Cl WV1. . . . . 40 B7
Gosport Rd CV6. . . . . 113 E8
Goss Croft B29 . . . . 85 D1
Gossett La CV8 . . . . 135 F7
Gossey La B33 . . . . 69 C2
Gossey Lane Jun & Inf Sch
  B33. . . . . 69 C2
Goss The DY5. . . . . 61 D1
Gosta Gn B4. . . . . 164 D4
Gotham Rd B26. . . . . 88 E6
Goths Cl B65 . . . . 63 C4
Gough Ave WV11 . . . . 26 B8
Gough Dr DY4 . . . . 52 C5
Gough Rd
  Birmingham, Edgbaston
    B15. . . . . 86 C7
  Birmingham, Sparkhill B11. 87 D5
  Dudley WV14 . . . . 40 C1
Gough St
  Birmingham B1 . . . . . . 164 B1
  Willenhall WV13 . . . . . . 27 C2
  Wolverhampton WV1. . . 163 C3
Gould Avenue E DY11. . . 116 A2
Gould Avenue W DY11. . . 116 A1
Gould Firm La WS9 . . . . . . 30 E6
Gould Rd CV35. . . . . 160 A7
Governor's Ct CV34 . . . . 160 D8
Gowan Cl B77 . . . . 35 D8
Gowan Rd B8. . . . . 67 E4
Gower Ave DY6 . . . . 60 F4
Gower Ho B62 . . . . 83 F6
Gower Rd
  Halesowen B62 . . . . 83 F6
  Sedgley DY3. . . . . 50 B8
Gower St
  Birmingham B19 . . . . . . 66 D7
  Walsall WS2. . . . . 42 B7
  Willenhall WV13 . . . . . . 27 A2
  Wolverhampton WV2. . . 163 D1
Gowland Dr WS11. . . . . 1 B1
Gowrie Cl LE10 . . . . 71 B2
Goya Cl WS11. . . . . 2 D2
Gozzard St WV14 . . . . 40 E5
Grace Acad
  Birmingham B37 . . . . . . 69 F1
  Coventry CV2. . . . . 96 F1
Grace Acad Darlaston
  WS10 . . . . 41 B6
Gracechurch Sh Ctr [17]
  B72. . . . . 46 B5
GRACE MARY ESTATE. . . 63 C8
Gracemere Cres B28. . . . 105 E3
Grace Moore Ct WS11. . . . 1 F4
Gracewell
  Allesley CV5. . . . . 111 A8
  Birmingham B11 . . . . . . 87 C7
  Oldbury B69. . . . . 63 C8
  Tipton DY4. . . . . 52 A7
Gracewell Homes B13. . . 105 D8
Gracewell Rd B13. . . . . . . 87 D1
Grafton Cl
  Kenilworth CV8 . . . . . . 148 A3
  Redditch B98 . . . . 159 B7
Grafton Cres B60 . . . . . . 150 E8
Grafton Ct
  Birmingham B23 . . . . . . 56 C2
  Coventry CV4. . . . . 132 B7
  Wolverhampton WV6 . . . 24 A1
Grafton Dr WV13. . . . . 26 D1
Grafton Gdns DY3. . . . . . . 50 B3
Grafton Gr [1] B19. . . . . . 66 C7
Grafton Ho
  Bromsgrove B60 . . . . . . 137 B3
  Wolverhampton WV4. . . 39 E5
Grafton La B41. . . . . 150 C7
Grafton Pl WV14 . . . . 40 E7
Grafton Rd
  Birmingham, Handsworth
    B21. . . . . 54 D1
  Birmingham, Sparkbrook
    B11. . . . . 87 B7
  Oldbury B68. . . . . 63 F2
  Solihull B90 . . . . 105 C2
  West Bromwich B71 . . . . 53 D4
Grafton St CV1. . . . . 113 F2

Graham Cl
  Coventry CV6. . . . . 96 B1
  Wednesbury DY4 . . . . . . 41 B1
Graham Cres B45 . . . . . . 122 A7
Graham Ho B74. . . . . 30 F2
Graham Rd
  Birmingham, Saltley B9 . . . 67 F3
  Birmingham, South Yardley
    B25. . . . . 88 C6
  Halesowen B62 . . . . 83 E8
  Kingswinford DY6, DY8 . . 60 D4
  West Bromwich B71 . . . . 53 D4
Graham St
  Birmingham, Hockley B1. . 66 C3
  Birmingham, Lozells B19. . 66 C7
  Nuneaton CV11 . . . . 73 C5
Grainger Cl DY4 . . . . 52 D6
Grainger Ct WS11. . . . . 1 D2
Grainger's La B64. . . . . . . 82 D8
Grainger St DY2 . . . . 62 D7
Graiseley Ct WV3 . . . . . . 163 B2
Graiseley Hill WV2 . . . . . 163 B1
Graiseley La WV11 . . . . . . 26 C5
Graiseley Prim Sch WV2. 163 B1
Graiseley Row WV2 . . . . . 163 B1
Graiseley St WV3 . . . . . . 163 A2
Graith Cl B28 . . . . 105 E3
Grammar School La B63. . 83 A4
Grampian Rd DY8 . . . . 81 A6
Granada Ind Est B69 . . . . 63 F6
Granary Cl
  Cannock WS12. . . . . 2 B5
  Kingswinford DY6 . . . . . 60 A8
Granary La B76 . . . . 46 F3
Granary Rd
  Stoke Heath B60 . . . . . 150 E6
  Wolverhampton WV8. . . 10 E1
Granary The WS9 . . . . 30 B6
Granborough Cl CV3 . . . . 134 F8
Granborough Ct CV32. . . 157 A3
Granbourne Rd WS2 . . . . 27 D4
Granby Ave B33 . . . . 69 C1
Granby Bsns Pk B33 . . . . . 69 D1
Granby Cl
  Hinckley LE10 . . . . 75 C7
  Redditch B98 . . . . 154 F4
  Solihull B92 . . . . 106 E7
Granby Rd
  Hinckley LE10 . . . . 75 C7
  Nuneaton CV10 . . . . 72 F6
Grandborough Dr B91. . . 107 A1
Grandison Cl CV6 . . . . . . 113 A8
Grand Depot Rd CV11 . . . . 79 F6
Grand Junction Way WS1. 42 D5
Grand Theatre* WV1. . . 163 C3
Grandys Croft B37 . . . . . . 69 F2
Granefield Ct [4] B9 . . . . 67 D1
Grange Ave
  Aldridge WS9. . . . . 16 A1
  Birmingham B8 . . . . 68 B6
  Burntwood WS7. . . . . 7 B7
  Coventry, Binley CV3 . . . 134 F7
  Kenilworth CV8 . . . . . . 147 E2
  Sutton Coldfield B75 . . . 32 C3
Grange Cl
  Nuneaton CV10 . . . . 72 C7
  Tamworth B77 . . . . 35 C8
  Warwick CV34 . . . . 161 C8
Grange Cres
  Birmingham B45 . . . . . . 121 F8
  Halesowen B63 . . . . 83 B3
  Walsall WS4. . . . . 29 B8
Grange Ct
  [1] Dudley DY1. . . . . 51 B1
  [1] Redditch B98 . . . . . . 153 F4
  Stourbridge DY9 . . . . . . 81 C3
  Willenhall WS2. . . . . 27 D2
  Wolverhampton WV3. . . 163 A2
Grange Education Unit The
  CV6. . . . . 94 E1
Grange Farm Dr B38 . . . . 123 D8
Grange Farm Prim Sch
  CV3. . . . . 133 B5
Grangefield Cl WV8 . . . . . 10 F1
Grange Hill B62. . . . . 83 C2
Grange Hill Rd B38. . . . . 103 E1
Grangehurst Prim Sch
  CV6. . . . . 96 B4
Grange La
  Alvechurch B48 . . . . 139 B3
  [1] Kingswinford DY6. . . . 60 F4
  Stourbridge DY9 . . . . . . 81 D4
  Sutton Coldfield B75 . . . 32 D3
Grange Mews The [1]
  CV32 . . . . 156 D1
Grangemouth Rd CV6 . . . 113 B7
Grange Pk CV31 . . . . 51 A1
Grange Rd
  Balsall Common CV7 . . . 129 F7
  Birmingham, Aston B6. . . 66 E8
  Birmingham, Bordesley Green
    B14. . . . . 104 E8
  Birmingham, Erdington B24. 57 C5
  Birmingham, King's Heath
    B14. . . . . 104 D8
  Burntwood WS7. . . . . 7 A5
  Coventry CV6. . . . . 96 B5
  Cradley Heath B64. . . . . 83 B8
  Dorridge B93 . . . . 127 F6
  Halesowen B63 . . . . 83 C3
  Hockley Heath B94 . . . . 143 E8

Grange Rd continued
  Kidderminster DY11. . . . 116 B7
  Norton Canes WS11. . . . . 6 B6
  [2] Redditch B98 . . . . . . 153 F4
  Royal Leamington Spa
    CV32. . . . . 157 B3
  Smethwick B66 . . . . 65 A3
  Solihull B91 . . . . 106 E7
  Stourbridge DY9 . . . . . . 81 C4
  West Bromwich B70 . . . . 53 B3
  Wolverhampton, Blakenall
    WV2 . . . . 39 B6
  Wolverhampton, Tettenhall Wood
    WV6 . . . . 24 C4
Grange Rise B38. . . . . . . 123 F7
Grangers La B98. . . . . . . 158 F5
Grange St
  Dudley DY1. . . . . 51 B1
  Walsall WS1. . . . . 42 F7
Grange The
  Birmingham B20 . . . . . . 54 F4
  Cubbington CV32. . . . . . 157 F5
  Halesowen B62 . . . . 83 F6
  Royal Leamington Spa
    CV32. . . . . 157 B1
  Warwick CV34 . . . . 161 C7
  Wombourne WV5. . . . . . 49 A7
Grange Wlk
  Birmingham B31 . . . . . . 123 C7
  Coventry CV6. . . . . 96 B5
Grangewood Ct
  Solihull B92 . . . . 106 E7
  Sutton Coldfield B73 . . . 57 A7
Granhill Cl B98 . . . . 159 A8
Granleigh Ct CV32 . . . . . 157 E5
Granoe Cl CV3 . . . . 134 E8
Granshaw Cl B38 . . . . . . 103 F1
Grant Cl
  Kingswinford DY6 . . . . . 60 D8
  West Bromwich B71 . . . . 53 C5
Grant Ct B30. . . . . 104 A5
Grantham Rd B11. . . . . . . 87 B6
Grantham St CV2 . . . . . . 113 F3
Grantley Cres DY6 . . . . . . 60 C7
Grantley Dr B37 . . . . 70 B3
Granton Cl B14. . . . . 104 D5
Granton Rd B14. . . . . 104 D5
Grantown Gr WS3. . . . . . . 14 A4
Grant Rd
  Bedworth CV7 . . . . 78 A1
  Coventry CV3. . . . . 114 B2
Grant St
  Birmingham B15 . . . . . . 86 D8
  Walsall WS3. . . . . 28 B8
Granville B77 . . . . 21 F1
Granville Cl
  Bromsgrove B60 . . . . . . 137 B1
  Wolverhampton WV2. . . 163 C1
Granville Ct CV10 . . . . 117 B6
Granville Dr DY6. . . . . 60 F5
Granville Gdns LE10. . . . . 75 C8
Granville Rd
  Cradley Heath B64. . . . . 83 B8
  Dorridge B93 . . . . 128 A2
  Hinckley LE10 . . . . 75 C8
Granville Sq B1. . . . . 66 C1
Granville St
  Birmingham B1 . . . . . . 164 A1
  Royal Leamington Spa
    CV32. . . . . 157 A2
  Wolverhampton WV13 . . 27 A3
  Wolverhampton WV2. . . 163 C1
Grapes Cl CV6 . . . . 113 B5
Grasdene Gr B17 . . . . 85 C4
Grasmere Ave
  Coventry CV3. . . . . 132 F6
  Perton WV6. . . . . 23 F4
  Sutton Coldfield B74. . . 31 A2
Grasmere Cl
  Birmingham B43 . . . . . . 54 F7
  Kidderminster DY10. . . . 116 E7
  Kingswinford DY6. . . . . . 60 B7
  Wolverhampton, Palmers Cross
    WV6 . . . . 24 E8
Grasmere Cres CV11 . . . . 73 F7
Grasmere Ho [5] B69 . . . . 63 D5
Grasmere Pl WS11 . . . . . . 1 E5
Grasmere Rd
  Bedworth CV12 . . . . 78 B2
  Birmingham B21 . . . . . . 65 F7
  Wolverhampton WV3. . . 24 E1
Grassholme B77 . . . . 36 A8
Grassington Ave CV34. . . 155 F1
Grassington Dr
  Birmingham B37 . . . . . . 69 F1
  Nuneaton CV11 . . . . 74 A2
Grassmere Ct WS6. . . . . . . 4 D3
Grassmere Dr DY8 . . . . . . 80 F3
Grassmoor Rd B38 . . . . . 103 E2
Grassy La WV10, WV11. . . 12 C6
Gratham Cl B77. . . . . 81 B7
Gratley Croft WS12. . . . . . 1 C4
Grattidge Rd B27 . . . . 88 D2
Gratton Ct CV3 . . . . 132 F6
Gravel Bank B32. . . . . 84 D2
Gravel Hill
  Coventry CV4. . . . . 111 F1
  Wombourne WV5. . . . . . 49 B6
Gravel La WS12. . . . . 1 C5
Gravelly Ct [4] B23 . . . . . 56 E2
GRAVELLY HILL 56 E1
Gravelly Hill B23. . . . . 56 E1
Gravelly Hill N B23 . . . . . . 56 F3
Gravelly Hill Sta B23 . . . . 56 E2
Gravelly Hill Ind Pk B24. . 57 A8
Gravelly La
  Birmingham B23 . . . . . . 56 F5

Gravelly La continued
  Stonnall WS9. . . . . 16 F3
Gravel Pit La B48 . . . . . . 139 E3
Gravel The B76 . . . . 48 B2
Gray Cl DY10 . . . . 117 B6
Graydon Ct B74. . . . . 46 B7
Grayfield Ave B13. . . . . . . 87 A3
Grayland Cl B27 . . . . 88 B2
Graylands The CV3. . . . . 133 C4
Graylands Dr DY6 . . . . 60 C8
Grayling B77 . . . . 35 D6
Grayling Cl WS10 . . . . 41 B3
Grayling Rd DY9 . . . . 81 C6
Grayling Wlk
  Birmingham B37 . . . . . . 70 C3
  Wolverhampton WV10. . . 26 B4
Gray Rd WS12 . . . . 1 F6
Grayshott Cl
  Birmingham B23 . . . . . . 56 E5
  Bromsgrove B61 . . . . . . 136 E3
Grays Rd B17. . . . . 85 D6
Gray St B9. . . . . 67 B2
Grayston Ave B77 . . . . 21 E4
Graywood Ave CV5. . . . . 112 D4
Graswood Rd B31. . . . . . 122 F7
Grazebrook Croft B32. . . 102 D8
Grazebrook Ind Pk DY2 . . 62 B6
Grazebrook Rd DY2. . . . . 62 C7
Grazewood Cl WV12. . . . . 27 B7
Grazier Ave B77 . . . . 35 C8
Grazing La B97 . . . . 152 F2
Greadier St WV12. . . . . . . 27 C5
Great Arthur St B66. . . . . 64 F7
Great Barn La B97 . . . . . . 153 B1
GREAT BARR. 43 F2
Great Barr Bsna Pk B42 . . 55 A5
Great Barr L Ctr B44 . . . . 44 D1
Great Barr Prim Sch B44 . 44 D1
Great Barr Sch B44. . . . . . 44 D1
Great Bricklin St WV3 . . . 25 B1
Great Brickkiln St WV3 . . 25 B1
GREAT BRIDGE 52 E6
Great Bridge DY4 . . . . 52 D5
Great Bridge Ind Est DY4. 52 C7
Great Bridge Prim Sch
  DY4. . . . . 52 C6
Great Bridge Rd WV14 . . . 41 B3
Great Bridge St B70. . . . . 52 E5
Great Brook St B7 . . . . . . 67 A4
Great Charles St WS8 . . . 15 F8
Great Charles Street
  Queensway B3 . . . . 164 B3
Great Colmore St B15. . . 86 D8
Great Cornbow [3] B63 . . 83 B3
Great Croft Ho [2] WS10 . . 41 D6
Great Farley Dr B31. . . . . 102 C1
Greatfield Rd DY11. . . . . 116 B4
Great Francis St B7. . . . . . 67 B4
Great Gable Rd B71. . . . . 53 C6
Great Hampton Row
  B19 . . . . 164 A4
Great Hampton St
  Birmingham B18 . . . . . . 164 A4
  Wolverhampton WV1. . . 25 B4
GREAT HEATH 113 E6
Greatheed Rd CV32 . . . . 156 E2
Great Hockings La B97 . . 152 E2
Great King St WV19. . . . . . 66 C5
Great King Street N B19. . 66 C6
Great Lister St B7. . . . . . . 67 A4
Great Mdw DY4. . . . . 52 B5
Greatmead B21 . . . . 21 C1
Great Moor Rd WV6. . . . . . 23 A3
Great Oaks B26. . . . . 89 B5
Greatorex Ct B71. . . . . 53 B8
Great Stone Rd B31. . . . . 103 A3
Great Tindal St B16 . . . . . 66 A2
Great Western Arc B2. . . 164 C3
Great Western Bsns Pk
  B18 . . . . 65 E6
Great Western Cl B18. . . . 65 E6
Great Western St B27. . . . 88 C4
Great Western Dr B64. . . 63 A1
Great Western St
  Wednesbury WS10 . . . . . 41 E2
  Wolverhampton WV1. . . 163 C4
  Wolverhampton WV4. . . 52 D6
Great Wood Rd B10. . . . . . 67 C1
GREAT WYRLEY. 5 B3
Great Wyrley Performing
  Arts High Sch WS6. . . . . 4 F4
Greaves Ave WS5 . . . . 43 C8
Greaves Cl
  Walsall WS5 . . . . 43 C8
  Warwick CV34 . . . . 161 C7
Greaves Cres WV12 . . . . . 27 C8
Greaves Rd DY2 . . . . 62 D5
Greaves Sq B38 . . . . 104 B1
Greaves The B76 . . . . 58 F6
Grebe Cl B23 . . . . 56 B3
Greenacre Cl B77. . . . . . . 35 B3
Greenacre Dr WV8. . . . . . 10 B2
Greenacre Rd DY4 . . . . . . 41 A1
Greenacres
  Birmingham B32 . . . . . . 84 E2
  Sedgley DY3. . . . . 39 B1
  Sutton Coldfield B76 . . . 58 A8
Green Acres B27. . . . . 88 B2
Greenacres Ave WV10. . . 12 B2
Greenacres Prim Sch B77 22 B5
Greenacres Rd B61 . . . . . 136 E3
Green Acres Rd B38. . . . . 123 D8
Greenaleigh Rd B14. . . . 105 D3
Green Ave B28. . . . . 87 E1
Greenaway Cl B43 . . . . . . 44 C3
Greenaway Ct WV10. . . . . 12 C7

Greenbank B45 . . . . 138 D8
Green Bank Ave B28 . . . . 87 E1
Greenbank Gdns DY8 . . . . 60 E2
Greenbank Rd CV7. . . . . . 129 F6
Green Barns La WS14 . . . 32 C8
Green Bower Dr B61 . . . . 137 A5
Greenbush Dr B63. . . . . . 83 A5
Green Cl
  Studley B80 . . . . 159 E3
  Whitnash CV31 . . . . 162 B4
  Wythall B47. . . . . 125 A3
Greencroft
  Bilston WV14. . . . . 40 D6
  Kingswinford DY6 . . . . . 60 D4
  Lichfield WS13. . . . . 3 A2
Green Croft B9 . . . . 68 A3
Green Ct
  Birmingham, Gravelly Hill
    B23 . . . . 56 E2
  Birmingham, Hall Green
    B28 . . . . 105 F8
  [8] Lichfield WS13 . . . . . . 9 B7
Greendale Cl B61. . . . . . . 137 B8
Greendale Rd CV5 . . . . . . 112 D3
Green Dr
  Birmingham B32 . . . . . . 84 C1
  Wolverhampton WV10. . . 25 C7
Greenend Rd B13 . . . . 86 F3
Greenfels Rise DY2 . . . . . 62 F8
Greenfield Ave
  Balsall Common CV7 . . . 130 A7
  Cradley Heath B64. . . . . 62 B1
  Lower Marlbrook B60 . . . 121 D1
  Stourbridge DY8 . . . . . . 80 F5
Greenfield Bldgs WV5. . . 49 A7
Greenfield Cotts B48. . . . 139 A5
Greenfield Cres B15. . . . . 86 B2
Greenfield Croft WV14 . . 40 D2
Greenfield Ho B26 . . . . . . 89 D6
Greenfield La WV10. . . . . 11 E5
Greenfield Prim Sch
  Stourbridge DY8 . . . . . . 80 F5
  Walsall WS4. . . . . 29 C8
Greenfield Rd
  Birmingham B17 . . . . . . 85 D5
  Birmingham, Newton B43 . 54 D7
  Smethwick B67 . . . . 64 E4
Greenfields
  Aldridge WS9. . . . . 30 B7
  Cannock WS11. . . . . 1 E2
  Redditch B98 . . . . 153 E2
Greenfields Rd
  Kingswinford DY6 . . . . . 60 E6
  Walsall WS4. . . . . 29 D2
  Wombourne WV5. . . . . . 49 A5
Green Field The CV3 . . . . 134 B8
Greenfield View DY3 . . . . 50 B7
Greenfinch Cl
  Birmingham B36 . . . . . . 70 A7
  Kidderminster DY10. . . . 117 B3
Greenfinch Rd
  Birmingham B36 . . . . . . 70 A7
  Stourbridge DY9 . . . . . . 81 D3
Greenford Cl B97. . . . . . . 153 B5
Greenford Ho
  Birmingham B23 . . . . . . 56 B6
  [7] West Bromwich B70. . 53 D1
Greenford Rd B14. . . . . . 105 C3
Green Gables
  Hollywood B47. . . . . . . 125 A7
  Sutton Coldfield B74 . . . 46 B7
Greenheart B77 . . . . 22 A4
Green Heath Rd WS12. . . . 2 A7
GREENHILL 117 A8
Greenhill
  Blackwell B60 . . . . 137 F4
  Lichfield WS13. . . . . 9 C8
  Wombourne WV5. . . . . . 49 B6
Greenhill Ave DY10 . . . . . 116 F7
Greenhill Cl
  Tamworth B77 . . . . 35 C5
  Willenhall WV12 . . . . . . 27 B6
Green Hill Cl B60 . . . . . . 137 D6
Greenhill Dr
  Halesowen B62 . . . . 83 E7
  Sutton Coldfield B72 . . . 57 C8
  Wombourne WV5. . . . . . 49 B5
Greenhill Gdns
  Birmingham B43 . . . . . . 43 E2
  Halesowen B62 . . . . 83 D7
  Wombourne WV5. . . . . . 49 B5
Greenhill Ind Est DY10 . . 117 A7
Greenhill Mews WS13. . . . 9 C8
Greenhill Oak DY10. . . . . 116 F7
Greenhill Rd
  Birmingham, Handsworth
    B21. . . . . 54 E2
  Birmingham, Moseley B13. 87 A1
  Dudley DY3 . . . . 50 E5
  Halesowen B62 . . . . 83 D7
  Sutton Coldfield B72 . . . 57 C8
  Whitnash CV31 . . . . 162 B4
Greenhill Way WS9 . . . . . 16 B5
Green Hill Way B90. . . . . 106 B5
Greenholm Rd B44. . . . . . 55 E7
Greenhough Rd WS13 . . . . 9 A8
Greenhurst Dr B45. . . . . 122 A1
Greening Dr B15. . . . . 86 B8
Green La
  Aldridge WS9. . . . . 30 E5
  Balsall Common CV7 . . . 130 B7
  Birchmoor B77, B78 . . . . 36 D7
  Birmingham B32 . . . . . . 84 C6

Green La *continued*
Birmingham, Bordesley Green B9 ... 67 E1
Birmingham, Castle Bromwich B36 ... 69 E8
Birmingham, Great Barr B43 ... 43 D1
Birmingham, Handsworth B21 ... 65 C8
Birmingham, Hawkesley B38 ... 123 E8
Birmingham, Newton B43 ... 54 D8
Brownhills WS8 ... 7 B2
Cannock WS11 ... 4 E6
Coleshill B46 ... 70 F5
Corley Moor CV7 ... 93 D6
Coventry CV3 ... 133 B4
Dudley DY3 ... 50 F5
Halesowen B62 ... 63 D1
Kingswinford DY6 ... 60 D7
Lichfield WS14 ... 8 D2
Middleton B78 ... 48 B6
Nuneaton CV10 ... 72 C7
Redditch B97 ... 158 A7
Solihull B90 ... 105 E1
Stourbridge DY9 ... 81 E5
Studley B80 ... 159 B5
Tamworth B77 ... 36 C6
Upper Catshill B61 ... 121 A1
Walsall, Birchills WS2, WS3 ... 28 C5
Walsall, High Heath WS4, WS9 ... 15 D3
Walsall, Pelsall WS3 ... 15 A4
Warwick CV34 ... 160 F8
Wolverhampton WV6 ... 24 F7
Greenland Ave
Birmingham B31 ... 103 A2
Coventry CV5 ... 111 F5
Greenland Cl DY6 ... 60 E8
Greenland Ct
Birmingham B8 ... 67 E6
Coventry CV5 ... 111 F5
Greenland Rd B29 ... 86 B1
Greenland Rise B92 ... 107 D7
Greenlands Ave B98 ... 154 A1
Greenlands Bsns Ctr B98 ... 154 B2
Greenlands Dr B98 ... 158 F8
Greenlands Rd B37 ... 70 C1
GREEN LANE
Coventry ... 133 B5
Redditch ... 159 C6
Green Lane Ind Est B9 ... 67 E1
GREEN LANES ... 40 C7
Green Lanes
Bilston WV14 ... 40 C7
Sutton Coldfield B73 ... 57 B8
Green Lane Venture Ctr WS11 ... 4 E6
Greenlawns DY4 ... 52 B8
Greenlea B77 ... 36 A8
Greenleaf Cl CV5 ... 112 A3
Greenleas Gdns B63 ... 83 C3
Green Leigh B23 ... 56 F8
GREENLEIGHS ... 39 C3
Greenleighs DY3 ... 39 D3
Greenly Rd WV4 ... 39 D5
Green Mdw
Stourbridge DY9 ... 99 B7
Wednesfield WV11 ... 26 E5
Green Mdws 2 WS12 ... 2 C1
Green Meadow Prim Sch B29 ... 102 F7
Green Meadow Rd
Birmingham B29 ... 103 A7
Willenhall WV12 ... 27 B7
Greenmoor Rd
Hinckley LE10 ... 75 D5
Nuneaton CV10 ... 73 A3
Greenoak Cres
Birmingham B30 ... 104 C8
Dudley WV14 ... 51 A7
Green Oak Rd WV8 ... 10 B2
Greenock Cres WV4 ... 39 F5
Greenodd Dr CV6 ... 95 F5
Green Park Ave WV14 ... 40 C8
Green Park Dr WV14 ... 40 C8
Green Park Rd
Birmingham B31 ... 102 E2
Bromsgrove B60 ... 137 B2
Dudley DY2 ... 62 F8
Green Park Specl Sch WV14 ... 40 B8
Green Rd
Birmingham B28 ... 87 E1
Dudley DY2 ... 62 D7
Greenridge Rd B20 ... 54 E5
Green Rock La WS3 ... 14 D1
Green Rock Prim Sch WS3 ... 14 E1
Greenroyde DY9 ... 81 B1
Greensand Dr WV14 ... 40 D2
Greenside
Birmingham B17 ... 85 C5
Cheswick Green B90 ... 126 D4
Stoke Prior B60 ... 150 C2
Greenside Cl CV11 ... 74 C1
Greenside Rd B24 ... 57 C5
Greenside Way WS5 ... 43 A4
Greensill Ave DY4 ... 51 F8
Greens Ind Est WS12 ... 2 C7
Green Slade Cres B60 ... 121 C1
Greenslade Croft B31 ... 103 A2
Green Slade Gr WS12 ... 2 C7
Greenslade Rd
Sedgley DY3 ... 39 B2
Solihull B90 ... 105 C2
Walsall WS5 ... 43 C7
Greensleeves B74 ... 31 F1
Greensleeves Cl CV6 ... 95 B2
Greens Rd CV6 ... 95 A1
Green St
Birmingham B12 ... 66 F1
Kidderminster DY10 ... 116 E5
Oldbury B69 ... 64 A7
Smethwick B67 ... 64 F5
Stourbridge DY8 ... 80 F5
Tipton WV14 ... 51 C8
Walsall WS2 ... 28 C3
West Bromwich B70 ... 64 E8
Greenstead Rd B13 ... 87 D1
Greens The WV6 ... 23 E3
Greensward Cl CV8 ... 148 B6
Green Sward La B98 ... 154 D1
Greensward The CV3 ... 115 A2
Greensway WV11 ... 26 B8
Greens Yd CV12 ... 78 C3
Green The
Aldridge WS9 ... 30 C6
Birmingham, Castle Bromwich B36 ... 69 B7
Birmingham, Erdington B23 ... 57 A4
Birmingham, Frankley B31 ... 102 C2
Birmingham, King's Norton B38 ... 103 F2
4 Birmingham, Quinton B32 ... 84 A6
Bluntington DY10 ... 118 E1
Cannock, Blackfords WS11 ... 1 D1
Darlaston WS10 ... 41 D7
Fazeley B78 ... 20 E2
Freasley B78 ... 36 C4
Meriden CV7 ... 92 B1
Nuneaton CV11 ... 73 E2
Oldbury B68 ... 64 B1
Solihull B91 ... 107 D5
Stoneleigh CV8 ... 149 C6
Stourbridge DY8 ... 60 D2
Sutton Coldfield B72 ... 46 D1
Tamworth B77 ... 22 B5
Tanworth-In-A B94 ... 142 A2
Walsall WS3 ... 14 B1
West Hagley DY9 ... 98 F4
Greenvale B31 ... 102 F5
Greenvale Ave B26 ... 89 D6
Greenway
Birmingham B20 ... 54 F6
Nuneaton CV11 ... 79 B8
Sedgley DY3 ... 39 E1
Warwick CV34 ... 155 E1
Green Way WS9 ... 16 B2
Greenway Ave 2 DY8 ... 60 E1
Greenway Dr B73 ... 45 C3
Greenway Gdns
Birmingham B38 ... 123 E7
Sedgley DY3 ... 39 E1
Greenway Rd WV14 ... 40 E4
Greenways
Birmingham B31 ... 102 F8
Coventry CV4 ... 111 C2
Halesowen B63 ... 82 C6
Stourbridge DY8 ... 60 C1
Greenway St B9 ... 67 C1
Greenways The CV32 ... 157 B3
Greenway The
Birmingham, Marston Green B37 ... 90 A6
Sutton Coldfield, New Oscott B73 ... 45 B3
West Hagley DY9 ... 98 F5
Greenway Wlk B33 ... 69 E1
Green Wickets B13 ... 104 E6
Green Wlk 4 B17 ... 84 F7
Greenwood B25 ... 88 D8
Greenwood Ave
Birmingham B27 ... 88 B1
Oldbury B68 ... 64 C5
Rowley Regis B65 ... 63 D3
Greenwood Cl B14 ... 104 E5
Greenwood Cotts DY1 ... 51 A5
Greenwood Ct CV11 ... 73 E3
Greenwood Ct CV32 ... 157 B1
Greenwood Dr WS14 ... 9 B6
Greenwood Pk
Aldridge WS9 ... 16 C2
Cannock WS12 ... 2 B8
Greenwood Pl B44 ... 45 B1
Greenwood Rd
Aldridge WS9 ... 16 B2
West Bromwich B71 ... 53 B8
Wolverhampton WV10 ... 25 C7
Greenwood Sq 5 B37 ... 70 B2
Greenwoods The DY8 ... 80 E5
Greenwood Way B37 ... 70 B2
GREET ... 87 E5
Greethurst Dr B13 ... 87 C2
Greet Prim Sch B11 ... 87 D4
Greets Green Ind Est B70 ... 52 F4
Greets Green Rd B70 ... 52 F3
Greetville Cl B34 ... 69 A5
Gregory Ave
Birmingham B29 ... 103 A8
Coventry CV3 ... 133 A6
Gregory Cl 3 WS10 ... 41 F2
Gregory Ct WV11 ... 26 E5
Gregory Dr DY1 ... 51 A2
Gregory Hood Rd CV3 ... 133 E4
Gregory Rd
Burntwood WS7 ... 7 E7
Stourbridge DY8 ... 80 D5
Gregston Ind Est B69 ... 64 B8
Greig Ct WS11 ... 2 C2
Grendon Cl
Coventry CV4 ... 111 C1
Redditch B98 ... 154 D1
Grendon Dr B73 ... 45 D3
Grendon Gdns WV3 ... 38 D6
Grendon Prim Sch B14 ... 105 A3
Grendon Rd
Birmingham B14 ... 105 A3
Solihull B92 ... 106 E8
Grenfell Cl CV31 ... 162 D6
Grenfell Ct B73 ... 46 B1
Grenfell Dr B15 ... 85 F8
Grenfell Rd WS3 ... 14 D3
Grenville Ave CV2 ... 114 B3
Grenville Cl WS2 ... 27 D3
Grenville Dr
Birmingham B23 ... 56 B3
Smethwick B66 ... 64 D8
Grenville Pl B70 ... 52 E3
Grenville Rd
Dudley DY1 ... 50 E1
Solihull B90 ... 106 B2
Gresham Ave CV32 ... 157 B2
Gresham Pl CV32 ... 157 B2
Gresham Rd
Birmingham B28 ... 105 F6
Cannock WS11 ... 1 F3
Nuneaton CV10 ... 78 B8
Oldbury B68 ... 64 C6
Gresham St CV2 ... 114 A2
Gresham Twr B12 ... 86 F8
Gresley B77 ... 21 F1
Gresley Cl B74 ... 32 A4
Gresley Gr B23 ... 56 C1
Gresley Rd CV2 ... 114 D7
Gresley Row WS13 ... 9 C8
Gressel La B33 ... 69 D3
Gressingham Gr CV6 ... 113 D7
Grestone Ave B20 ... 54 E3
Grestone Prim Sch B20 ... 54 E4
Greswold Cl CV4 ... 111 F1
Greswolde Dr B24 ... 57 B4
Greswolde Park Rd B27 ... 88 B4
Greswolde Rd
Birmingham B11 ... 87 D3
Solihull B91 ... 106 E6
Greswoldes The CV31 ... 162 F6
Greswold Gdns B34 ... 69 A5
Greswold Prim Sch B91 ... 107 C6
Greswold St B71 ... 53 B5
Gretna Rd CV3 ... 132 F4
Gretton Cres WS9 ... 29 E5
Gretton Rd
Aldridge WS9 ... 29 F5
Birmingham B23 ... 56 D7
Greville Dr B15 ... 86 C6
Greville Ho 13 CV34 ... 160 F7
Greville Rd
Kenilworth CV8 ... 147 F4
Warwick CV34 ... 156 B1
Greville Smith Ave CV31 ... 162 B4
Grevis Cl B13 ... 86 F4
Grevis Rd B25 ... 68 E1
Greycoat Rd CV6 ... 95 A2
Greyfort Cres B92 ... 88 F1
Greyfriars Cl
Dudley DY1 ... 50 E3
Solihull B92 ... 106 D6
Greyfriars Ct CV6 ... 113 A7
Greyfriars Dr
Bromsgrove B61 ... 136 D2
Tamworth B79 ... 20 E6
Greyfriars La CV1 ... 165 B2
Greyfriars Rd CV1 ... 165 B2
Greyfriars Wlk CV1 ... 165 B2
Greyhound La
Lower Penn WV4 ... 37 E5
Stourbridge DY8 ... 80 D2
Greyhurst Croft 5 B91 ... 127 B8
Grey Mill Cl B90 ... 126 F6
Greysbrooke WS14 ... 18 A5
Greysbrooke Prim Sch WS14 ... 18 A6
Grey's Rd B80 ... 159 E3
Greystoke Ave B36 ... 68 D7
Greystoke Dr DY6 ... 60 D6
Greystone Cl B98 ... 154 C5
Greystone Pas 16 DY1 ... 51 B1
Grey Tree Cres B93 ... 127 E3
Grice St B70 ... 64 D8
GRIFF ... 78 B6
Griff Clara Ind Est CV10 ... 78 A7
Griffen La B90 ... 126 A5
Griffin Ave DY10 ... 116 E4
Griffin Bsns Pk B37 ... 70 C3
Griffin Cl
Birmingham B31 ... 103 B6
Burntwood WS7 ... 6 E8
Griffin Ct B5 ... 86 C5
Griffin Gdns B17 ... 85 D4
Griffin Ho B16 ... 65 E1
Griffin Ind Est B65 ... 63 F3
Griffin Rd
Birmingham B23 ... 56 C5
Warwick CV34 ... 161 C7
Griffins Brook Cl B30 ... 103 D7
Griffins Brook La B30 ... 103 D6
GRIFFIN'S HILL ... 103 D8
Griffins La B90 ... 126 A5
Griffin St
Dudley DY2 ... 62 C4
West Bromwich B70 ... 53 D3
Wolverhampton WV1 ... 25 F1
Griffiths Dr
Wolverhampton WV11 ... 13 A1
Wombourne WV5 ... 49 A5
Griffiths Rd
Dudley DY1 ... 51 A6
Griffiths Rd *continued*
West Bromwich B71 ... 42 C1
Willenhall WV12 ... 27 D8
Griffiths St DY4 ... 51 E5
Griff La CV10 ... 78 A6
Grigg Gr B31 ... 102 E1
GRIMES HILL ... 125 B4
Grimley Cl B98 ... 153 F1
Grimley La B60 ... 151 E6
Grimley Rd 2 B31 ... 103 D2
Grimley Way WS11 ... 1 F4
Grimpits La B38 ... 124 A7
Grimshaw Rd B27 ... 88 A1
Grimshaw Villas B93 ... 128 D8
Grimston Cl CV3 ... 115 A2
Grimstone St WV10 ... 163 C4
Grindleford Rd B42 ... 55 D7
Grindley Ho 5 CV1 ... 113 B2
Grindsbrook B77 ... 36 A8
Gristhorpe Rd B29 ... 104 A8
Grizebeck Dr CV5 ... 112 A5
Grizedale Cl B45 ... 102 B2
Grocott Rd WS10 ... 41 B4
Grosmont Ave 8 B12 ... 87 A6
Grosvenor Ave
Birmingham B20 ... 55 C2
Kidderminster DY10 ... 117 A6
Sutton Coldfield B74 ... 30 F1
Grosvenor Cl
Lichfield WS14 ... 9 D6
Sutton Coldfield B75 ... 32 C1
Wolverhampton WV10 ... 11 D2
Grosvenor Cres
Hinckley LE10 ... 76 A6
Wolverhampton WV10 ... 11 D2
Grosvenor Ct
Birmingham, Handsworth B20 ... 55 C2
Dudley DY3 ... 50 D2
2 Royal Leamington Spa CV32 ... 156 F1
Shenstone WS14 ... 17 F6
Stourbridge DY9 ... 81 B1
Wednesfield WV11 ... 26 E5
Wolverhampton, Tettenhall Wood WV6 ... 24 A3
Wolverhampton WV3 ... 163 B2
Grosvenor Gdns B61 ... 137 B5
Grosvenor Ho
Birmingham, Erdington B23 ... 57 A5
Coventry CV1 ... 165 A2
Redditch B97 ... 153 E4
Grosvenor Pk WV4 ... 38 F5
Grosvenor Rd
Birmingham, Aston B6 ... 67 B8
Birmingham B17 ... 85 A6
Birmingham, Handsworth B20 ... 55 C2
Coventry CV1 ... 165 A1
Dudley DY3 ... 50 D2
Oldbury B68 ... 64 A3
Solihull B91 ... 106 F1
Whitnash CV31 ... 162 A5
Wolverhampton, Bushbury WV10 ... 11 D2
Wolverhampton WV4 ... 39 E3
Grosvenor Road S DY3 ... 50 D2
Grosvenor Sq B28 ... 105 F5
Grosvenor St
Birmingham B5 ... 164 D3
Wolverhampton WV10 ... 25 F3
Grosvenor Street W B16 ... 66 B1
Grosvenor Way DY5 ... 81 E7
Grotto La WV6 ... 24 E5
Groucutt St 6 WV14 ... 51 C8
Grounds Dr B74 ... 31 F3
Grounds Rd B74 ... 31 F3
Grouse Way WS11 ... 2 A1
Grout St B70 ... 52 E4
Grove Ave
Birmingham B27 ... 88 B3
Birmingham, Handsworth B21 ... 65 F8
Birmingham, Moseley B13 ... 87 A2
Halesowen B63 ... 82 F3
Solihull B91 ... 107 C5
Grove Cl WS11 ... 5 F5
Grove Cottage Rd B9 ... 67 D2
Grove Cres
Brierley Hill DY5 ... 61 C5
Walsall WS3 ... 14 F3
Grove Ct
Birmingham B43 ... 54 F6
Coventry CV5 ... 133 B8
Nuneaton CV11 ... 73 E2
GROVE END ... 47 F3
Grove Farm Dr B75 ... 46 F5
Grovefield Cres CV7 ... 130 C8
Grove Fields CV10 ... 73 D8
Grove Gdns
Birmingham B20 ... 54 F2
Bromsgrove B61 ... 137 A6
Grove Hill WS5 ... 29 E1
Grove Hill Rd B21 ... 54 F1
Grovehurst Pk CV8 ... 149 B2
Grove La
Birmingham B17 ... 85 C4
Birmingham, Handsworth B20 ... 54 F1
Keresley CV7 ... 94 F7
Lapworth B94 ... 143 F4
Norton Canes WS3 ... 5 E1
Smethwick B66 ... 65 C5
Wishaw B76 ... 47 F2
Wolverhampton WV6 ... 24 B2
Groveland Rd DY4 ... 52 B3
Grovelands Cres WV10 ... 11 D3
Grovelands Ind Est CV7 ... 96 A6
Groveley La B31, B45 ... 122 E5
Grove Mews B31 ... 123 B8
Grove Pk
Hinckley LE10 ... 76 A6
Kingswinford DY6 ... 60 C8
Grove Pl
Nuneaton CV10 ... 72 D3
2 Royal Leamington Spa CV31 ... 162 A6
Grove Prim Sch WV2 ... 163 D1
Grove Rd
Ansty CV7 ... 97 D3
Birmingham, King's Heath B14 ... 104 D6
Birmingham, Sparkhill B11 ... 87 C2
Dorridge B93 ... 128 B3
Hinckley LE10 ... 76 A6
Nuneaton CV10 ... 72 D3
Oldbury B68 ... 64 D1
Solihull B91 ... 107 C5
Stourbridge DY9 ... 81 F3
Grove Sch B21 ... 65 F8
Groveside Way WS3 ... 15 A5
Grove St
Coventry CV1 ... 165 C3
Dudley DY2 ... 62 E8
Redditch B98 ... 153 E4
Royal Leamington Spa CV32 ... 161 E8
Smethwick B66 ... 65 D4
Wolverhampton, Springfield WV10 ... 25 F3
Wolverhampton WV2 ... 163 C1
Grove Terr WS1 ... 28 F1
Grove The
Bedworth CV12 ... 78 C3
Birmingham, Edgbaston B16 ... 65 F2
Birmingham, Great Barr B43 ... 43 E4
Birmingham, Lozells B19 ... 66 B7
Birmingham, Rednal B45 ... 122 D4
Birmingham, Saltley B8 ... 67 C4
Birmingham, West Heath B31 ... 123 B8
Brierley Hill DY5 ... 61 C1
Burntwood WS7 ... 6 D8
Coleshill B46 ... 70 F4
Hampton-in-A B92 ... 91 A1
Hinckley LE10 ... 75 C8
Rowley Regis B65 ... 63 C2
Studley B80 ... 159 D3
Sutton Coldfield B74 ... 31 D6
Walsall WS5 ... 43 B3
Wolverhampton, New Cross WV11 ... 26 B6
Wolverhampton, Parkfield WV4 ... 39 E5
GROVE VALE ... 43 C1
Grove Vale Ave B43 ... 43 C1
Grove Vale Prim Sch B43 ... 43 D1
Grove Villas B64 ... 82 D7
Grove Way B74 ... 44 F7
Grovewood Dr 2 B38 ... 103 E1
Guardhouse Rd CV6 ... 113 B8
Guardian Angels RC Prim Sch B34 ... 69 E6
Guardian Ct
Birmingham, Frankley B31 ... 102 D3
Birmingham, Gilbertstone B26 ... 88 F7
4 Bromsgrove B60 ... 137 A2
Solihull B91 ... 107 D3
Guardian Ho B68 ... 84 C7
Guardians Way B31 ... 102 E8
Guernsey Dr B36 ... 70 B6
Guest Ave WV11 ... 26 C8
Guest Gr B19 ... 66 C6
Guest Hospl DY1 ... 51 E3
Guild Ave WS3 ... 28 D8
Guild Cl B16 ... 66 A2
Guild Cotts The CV34 ... 160 D6
Guild Croft B19 ... 66 D6
Guild Ct 4 B60 ... 136 F2
Guildford Cl DY11 ... 116 A6
Guildford Croft B37 ... 89 F8
Guildford Ct
12 Birmingham B29 ... 103 C7
Coventry CV6 ... 113 D7
Guildford Dr B19 ... 66 D6
Guildford St 4 B19 ... 66 D7
Guildhall Mews The 7 WS1 ... 28 F1
Guild Rd
Bromsgrove B60 ... 136 F1
Coventry CV6 ... 113 D7
Guillemard Ct B37 ... 70 B1
Guilsborough Rd CV3 ... 134 E8
Guinea Cres CV4 ... 131 E6
Guinness Cl B98 ... 158 D8
Guiting Cl B97 ... 153 B1
Guiting Rd B29 ... 103 A7
Gulistan Ct 6 CV32 ... 156 E1
Gulistan Rd CV32 ... 156 E1
Gullane Cl B38 ... 103 D1
Gullet The B78 ... 22 F1
Gullick Way WS7 ... 6 D8
Gulliman's Way CV31 ... 162 D7
Gullswood Cl B14 ... 104 D2
Gulson Rd CV1 ... 113 E2
Gumbleberrys Cl B8 ... 68 C4
Gun Barrel Ind Ctr B63 ... 82 F6
Gundry Cl CV31 ... 162 A7
Gun La CV2 ... 114 A5
Gunmakers Wlk B19 ... 66 D7
Gunner Gr B75 ... 47 A6
Gunner La B45 ... 121 D7
Gunners La B80 ... 159 E4

Gunnery Terr 3 CV32 . . 156 D1
Gunns Way B92 . . . . 106 D7
Guns La B70 . . . . 53 B4
Gunstock Cl B74 . . . . 44 E7
GUNSTONE 10 A6
GUNS VILLAGE 53 B4
Guns Village Prim Sch
  B70 . . . . 53 A3
Gunter Prim Sch B24 . . . . 57 E3
Gunter Rd B24 . . . . 57 E3
Gunton Ave CV3 . . . . 134 C6
Guphill Ave CV5 . . . . 112 D2
Guphill La CV5 . . . . 112 D3
Gupta Trad Est B69 . . . . . 52 F1
Gurnard B77 . . . . 35 D6
Gurnard Cl WV12 . . . . 13 B1
Gurney Cl CV4 . . . . 111 E3
Gurney Pl WV2 . . . . 28 A5
Gurney Rd WV2 . . . . 28 A5
Guthrie Cl B19 . . . . 66 D6
Guthrun Cl
  Birmingham B23 . . . . . . 56 E8
  Perton WV6 . . . . 23 F5
Gutteridge Ave CV6 . . . . . 95 A2
Gutter The DY9 . . . . 120 E7
Guy Ave WV10 . . . . 25 E6
Guy Place E 13 CV32 . . . 156 F1
Guy Place W 12 CV32 . . . 156 F1
Guy Rd CV8 . . . . 147 F2
Guy's Almshouses B79 . . 21 B5
Guys Cl B79 . . . . 20 F7
Guy's Cl CV34 . . . . 161 A8
GUY'S CLIFFE 156 A2
Guys Cliffe Ave B62 . . . . . 83 E7
Guy's Cliffe Ave CV32 . . 156 D2
Guy's Cliffe Rd CV32 . . . 161 E8
Guy's Cliffe Terr CV34. . 160 F7
Guy's Cross Park Rd
  CV34 . . . . 160 F8
Guy's La DY3 . . . . 56 F4
Guys Motors Ind Pk WV10 25 F5
Guy St
  Royal Leamington Spa
  CV32 . . . . 156 F1
  Warwick CV34 . . . . 160 F7
Guy's Wlk B63 . . . . 137 A5
Gwalia Gr B23 . . . . 56 F4
Gwendoline Ave LE10 . . . 71 A2
Gwendoline Way WS9 . . . 16 B4
GWS Ind Est WS10 . . . . . 41 D1
Gypsy La
  Kenilworth CV8 . . . . . . 147 F2
  Redditch B97 . . . . 152 C5
  Water Orton B46 . . . . . . 59 D2

H

HABBERLEY 116 A6
Habberley Croft 1 B91. . 107 B1
Habberley La DY11 . . . . . 116 A8
Habberley Rd
  Kidderminster DY11. . . . 116 B7
  Rowley Regis B65 . . . . . . 63 D2
Habberley St 1 DY11. . . . 116 C6
Habitat Ct B76 . . . . 46 F3
Hackett Cl WV14 . . . . 39 F1
Hackett Ct 2 B69 . . . . 64 D7
Hackett Dr B66 . . . . 64 D7
Hackett Rd B65 . . . . 63 E3
Hackett St B67 . . . . 52 C7
Hackford Rd WV4 . . . . 39 F4
HACKMAN'S GATE 98 F1
Hackmans Gate La DY9 . 119 F7
Hack St B9 . . . . 67 A1
Hackwood Ho 10 B69 . . . . 63 D5
Hackwood Rd WS10 . . . . . 42 B2
Hadcroft Grange DY9 . . . . 81 D4
Hadcroft Rd DY9 . . . . 81 C4
Haddock Rd WV14 . . . . . . 40 C7
Haddon Cres WV12 . . . . . . 27 C7
Haddon Croft B63 . . . . 82 C1
Haddon Rd
  Birmingham B42 . . . . . . 55 D6
  Royal Leamington Spa
  CV32 . . . . 157 B2
Haddon St CV6 . . . . 114 A8
Haddon Twr 1 B15 . . . . . . 86 D8
Haden Arch Ct B64 . . . . . . 83 A7
Haden Cl
  Cradley Heath B64 . . . . . 83 A7
  Stourbridge DY8 . . . . . . 60 D2
Haden Cres WV11 . . . . 26 F6
HADEN CROSS 83 A8
Haden Cross Dr B64 . . . . . 83 A7
Haden Ct 5 WV3 . . . . 25 A2
Hadendale B64 . . . . 83 A7
Haden Hill WV3 . . . . 25 A2
Haden Hill L Ctr B64 . . . . 82 F8
Haden Hill Rd B63 . . . . . . 83 B6
Haden Park Rd B64 . . . . . . 82 F7
Haden Rd
  Cradley Heath B64 . . . . . 62 E2
  Wednesbury DY4 . . . . . . 41 A1
Haden St B12 . . . . 86 F6
Haden Way B12 . . . . 86 F6
Haden Wlk B65 . . . . 63 C3
Hadfield Cl B24 . . . . 57 E3
Hadfield Croft B19 . . . . . . 66 C5
Hadfield Way B37 . . . . 70 A4
Hadland Rd B33 . . . . 69 B1
Hadleigh Croft B76 . . . . . . 58 A6
Hadleigh Rd CV3 . . . . 133 C6
Hadley Cl
  Dudley DY2 . . . . 62 E4
  Hollywood B47 . . . . 125 A5
Hadley Croft B66 . . . . 65 A7

Hadley Ct B16 . . . . 65 D1
Hadley Mews CV11 . . . . . . 73 D1
Hadley Pl WV14 . . . . 40 C7
Hadley Rd
  Bilston WV14 . . . . 40 C7
  Willenhall WS2 . . . . 27 F6
Hadley St B68 . . . . 64 A4
Hadley Stadium B66 . . . . . 65 A3
Hadley Way WS2 . . . . 28 A6
Hadlow Croft B33 . . . . 89 D7
Hadrian Cl CV32 . . . . 157 B4
Hadrian Dr B46 . . . . 59 F1
Hadrians Cl B77 . . . . 35 D8
Hadyn Gr B26 . . . . 89 B6
Hadzor Ho 3 B97 . . . . . . 153 A4
Hadzor Rd B68 . . . . 84 D8
Hafren Cl B45 . . . . 102 B2
Hafton Gr B9 . . . . 67 D1
Haggar St WV2 . . . . 39 C6
Haglay Court N DY5 . . . . . 61 E4
Haglay Court S DY5 . . . . . 61 E4
HAGLEY 99 C6
Hagley Cl DY9 . . . . 99 C6
Hagley Cswy DY9 . . . . . . 100 B8
Hagley Ct DY3 . . . . 50 D3
Hagley Grange DY9 . . . . . 99 B6
Hagley Hall * DY9 . . . . . . 99 C6
Hagley Hall Gdns DY9 . . . 99 C6
Hagley Hill DY9 . . . . 99 C6
Hagley Ho B60 . . . . 137 B3
Hagley Mews DY9 . . . . . . 99 C6
Hagley Park B45 . . . . 122 A6
Hagley Prim Sch DY9 . . . . 99 B5
Hagley RC High Sch B98 . 98 F6
Hagley Rd
  Birmingham B16 . . . . . . 65 C1
  Halesowen B63 . . . . 82 E2
  Stourbridge DY8 . . . . . . 81 B3
Hagley Road W B32, B68 . 84 D7
Hagley Rd 3 B63 . . . . 83 B3
Hagley Sta DY9 . . . . 99 A6
Hagley View Rd DY2 . . . . . 62 E5
Hagley Villas B12 . . . . 87 B4
Hagley Wood La DY9,
  B62 . . . . 100 B7
Haig Cl
  Cannock WS11 . . . . 2 A5
  Sutton Coldfield B75 . . . 46 C7
Haig Pl B13. . . . . 105 A7
Haig Rd DY2 . . . . 51 F1
Haig St B71 . . . . 53 C5
Hailes Park Cl WV2 . . . . . 39 E6
Hailsham Rd B23 . . . . 56 F5
Hailstone Cl B65 . . . . 63 A5
Hailwood Dr 1 B43 . . . . . . 43 E1
Haines Cl DY4 . . . . 52 B4
Haines St B70 . . . . 53 D2
Hainfield Dr B91 . . . . 107 E5
Hainge Rd B69. . . . . 52 C1
Hainult Cl DY8 . . . . 60 D4
Halas Ct B64 . . . . 82 F8
Halas Ind Est B62 . . . . . . 83 C5
Halberd Cl LE10 . . . . 75 D5
Halberton St B66 . . . . 65 D4
Haldane Cl B33 . . . . 69 B2
Haldon Gr B31 . . . . 122 E7
Halecroft Ave WV11 . . . . . 26 D5
Hale Gr B24 . . . . 57 B2
Halesbury Ct B63 . . . . 82 F2
Halesbury Specl Sch B32 . 83 E7
Hales Cres B67 . . . . 64 E4
Halescroft Sq B31 . . . . . . 102 E6
Hales Gdns B23 . . . . 56 C8
Hales La B67 . . . . 64 E4
Halesmere Way B63 . . . . . 83 C3
HALESOWEN 83 C3
Halesowen CE Prim Sch
  B63 . . . . 83 B4
Halesowen Coll B63 . . . . . 83 C4
Halesowen Coll (E-Business
  Ctr) B62 . . . . 83 C8
Halesowen Coll
  (Whittingham main
  campus) B63 . . . . 83 B5
Halesowen Ind Pk B62 . . . 83 B6
Halesowen L Ctr 11 B63 . 83 B3
Halesowen Rd
  Dudley DY2, B64 . . . . . . 62 D4
  Halesowen B62 . . . . 83 F6
  Lower Marlbrook B61 . . 121 C3
Halesowen St
  Oldbury B69. . . . . 63 F7
  8 Rowley Regis B65. . . . 63 C1
Hales Park Ind Est CV6 . . 95 E4
Hales Rd
  Halesowen B63 . . . . 83 A4
  Wednesbury WS10 . . . . . 42 A5
Hales St CV1 . . . . 165 C3
Hales Way B69 . . . . 63 F7
Halesworth Rd WV9 . . . . . 10 F2
Hale Trad Est DY4 . . . . . . 52 B6
Halewood Gr B28 . . . . . . 106 A7
Haley St WV12 . . . . 27 C5
Halfcot Ave DY9 . . . . 81 C3
Halford Cres WS3 . . . . 28 F5
Halford Gr B24 . . . . 57 E4
Halford La CV6 . . . . 95 A2
Halford Lodge CV6 . . . . . . 95 A2
Halford's La B66 . . . . 65 A8
Halfords Pk B66 . . . . 65 A7
Halford St B79 . . . . 21 A5
Halfpenny Field Wlk B35 . 58 A3
Halfshire La DY10 . . . . 119 B1
Halfway Cl B44 . . . . 55 F6
Halifax Cl CV5 . . . . 112 A7
Halifax Gr 7 B18 . . . . 65 E4

Halifax Ho B5. . . . . 86 D7
Halifax Rd B90. . . . . 106 B2
Haliscombe Gr 4 B6. . . . . 66 E8
Halkett Glade B33 . . . . 68 D3
Halladale B38 . . . . 103 F1
Hallam Cl B71 . . . . 53 E5
Hallam Cres WV10 . . . . . . 25 E6
Hallam Ct B71 . . . . 53 E5
Hallam Dr B71. . . . . 53 E5
Hallam Rd CV6. . . . . 95 B2
Hallams Cl CV8 . . . . 135 F5
Hallam St
  Birmingham B12 . . . . . . 86 E5
  West Bromwich B71 . . . . 53 D5
Hallbridge Cl WS3 . . . . . . 14 F2
Hallbridge Way B69. . . . . . 52 B2
Hall Brook Rd CV6 . . . . . . 95 A4
Hallchurch Rd DY2 . . . . . . 61 E6
Hall Cl CV8 . . . . 149 B6
Hall Cres B71 . . . . 53 C6
Hallcroft Cl B72 . . . . 57 C7
Hallcroft Way
  Aldridge WS9 . . . . 30 C5
  Dorridge B93 . . . . 128 A6
Hall Dale Cl B28 . . . . 105 F5
Hall Dr
  Baginton CV8. . . . . 133 E3
  Birmingham B37 . . . . . . 90 A7
  Hagley DY9 . . . . 99 D6
HALL END 36 F5
Hall End
  Nuneaton CV11 . . . . 73 D2
  Wednesbury WS10 . . . . . 41 F3
Hall End Pl CV11 . . . . 73 D2
Hallens Dr WS10. . . . . 41 D2
Hallet Dr WV3 . . . . 163 A2
Hallewell Rd B16 . . . . 65 D3
Hallfields Cl V31 . . . . 162 E5
Hallfield Sch B15 . . . . 86 A7
HALL FLAT 137 C7
Hall Gr WV14 . . . . 51 C8
HALL GREEN
  Bilston 40 E2
  Birmingham 106 A7
  Coventry 42 C1
  Wednesbury. 42 C1
Hall Green Ind Est B28 . 105 F7
Hall Green Jun Sch B28 . 105 F7
Hall Green Rd
  Birmingham B71, B42 . . 10 D1
  West Bromwich B71 . . . . 42 D1
Hallgreen St WV14 . . . . . . 40 E2
Hall Green Sta B28. . . . . . 87 F1
Hall Green Wharf B71 . . . . 42 C1
Hall Hays Rd B34 . . . . 69 E7
Hall La
  Brownhills WS9 . . . . 15 E3
  Coventry CV2 . . . . 114 F6
  Dudley DY2 . . . . 62 C6
  Great Wyrley WS6 . . . . . . 5 A3
  Hagley DY9 . . . . 99 D6
  Hammerwich WS7 . . . . . . 7 E4
  Muckley Corner WS7, WS14 . 7 F2
  Tipton DY4. . . . . 52 A6
  Walsall WS3 . . . . 14 F3
  Wolverhampton WV14 . . 39 F1
Hall Mdw
  Hagley DY9 . . . . 99 D7
  Wedges Mills WS11. . . . . 4 B6
Hallmoor Rd B33 . . . . 69 B3
Hallmoor Specl Sch B33 . 69 B3
Hallot Cl B23 . . . . 56 D8
Halloughton Rd B74 . . . . . 46 A7
Hallow Cl 3 B31. . . . . 103 D2
Hall Park St WV14 . . . . . . 40 B7
Hall Rd
  Birmingham, Castle Bromwich
  B36 . . . . 69 A8
  Birmingham, Handsworth
  B20 . . . . 66 A8
  Birmingham, Saltley B8. . 67 D4
  Hinckley LE10 . . . . 75 D5
  Royal Leamington Spa
  CV32 . . . . 156 F1
  Smethwick B67 . . . . 64 E4
Hall's Cl CV31 . . . . 162 B3
Hall St
  Bilston WV14 . . . . 40 E5
  Birmingham B18 . . . . . 164 A4
  Cradley Heath B64 . . . . . 62 F2
  Darlaston WS10. . . . . . . 41 E7
  Dudley DY2 . . . . 51 D1
  Oldbury B68 . . . . 64 B5
  Sedgley DY3 . . . . 50 D8
  Stourbridge DY8 . . . . . . 81 A3
  Tipton DY4 . . . . 52 A6
  Walsall WS2. . . . . 28 D3
  Wolverhampton WV11 . . 26 C5
Hall Street E WS10 . . . . . . 41 C7
Hall Street S B70 . . . . 53 D1
Hallswelle Gr B43 . . . . . . 44 E4
Hallway Dr CV7 . . . . 97 E6
Hall Wlk B46 . . . . 70 F4
Halsbury Gr B44 . . . . 56 B8
Halstead Gr B91 . . . . 127 A8
Halston Rd WS7 . . . . 7 B8
Halswelle Gr B43 . . . . 64 D8
Halton Rd B73 . . . . 45 E2
Halton St DY2 . . . . 62 C5
Hamar Way B37 . . . . 70 B1

Hamberley Ct B18 . . . . 65 D5
Hamble B77 . . . . 21 D2
Hamble Cl
  Birmingham B36 . . . . . . 69 F8
  Brierley Hill DY5 . . . . . . 61 A6
Hamble Ct 1 B73. . . . . 46 B5
Hambledon Cl WV9 . . . . . . 11 A2
Hamble Gr WV6. . . . . 23 E4
Hamble Rd
  Birmingham B42 . . . . . . 43 F1
  Wolverhampton WV4 . . . 38 C6
Hambleton Rd B63. . . . . . . 82 D2
Hambletts Rd B70. . . . . . . 53 A3
Hambrook Cl WV6 . . . . 25 A5
Hambury Dr B14 . . . . 104 D7
Hamd House Sch B10 . . . . 87 E8
Ham Dingle Prim Sch
  DY9 . . . . 81 C2
Hamelin St WV11 . . . . 1 E3
Hamilton Ave
  Birmingham B17 . . . . . . 85 A7
  Halesowen B62 . . . . 83 C3
  Stourbridge DY8 . . . . . . 80 D6
Hamilton Cl
  Bedworth CV12 . . . . 77 C1
  Cannock WS12 . . . . 2 F4
  Hinckley LE10 . . . . 71 A2
  Lickey End B60. . . . . . . 137 C6
  Sedgley DY3. . . . . 50 C8
  Stourbridge DY8 . . . . . . 60 C2
Hamilton Ct
  Birmingham B29 . . . . . 103 D8
  Oldbury B69. . . . . 52 C2
  Stourbridge DY8 . . . . . . 60 C2
  Studley B80 . . . . 159 D3
Hamilton Gdns WV10. . . . 11 F3
Hamilton Ho WS3 . . . . 14 C1
Hamilton Lea WS11 . . . . . . 6 A6
Hamilton Rd
  Birmingham B21 . . . . . . 65 D8
  Coventry CV2 . . . . 114 A3
  Kidderminster DY11 . . . 116 B3
  Radford Semele CV31 . . 162 E5
  Redditch B97 . . . . 153 B4
  Smethwick B67 . . . . 64 E2
  Tipton DY4 . . . . 52 C6
Hamilton Specl Sch B21 . 65 D8
Hamilton St
  Oldbury B68 . . . . 84 B8
  Walsall WS1 . . . . 14 D1
Hamilton Terr CV32 . . . . 161 F8
Ham La
  Kingswinford DY6 . . . . . 49 E1
  Stourbridge DY9 . . . . . . 81 C2
Hamlet Cl CV11 . . . . 74 B1
Hamlet Gdns B28 . . . . . . 105 F8
Hamlet Rd B28 . . . . 105 F8
Hamlet The
  Leek Wootton CV35 . . . . 156 A7
  Norton Canes WS11 . . . . . 5 E5
Hammer Bank DY5 . . . . . . 82 A8
Hammersley Cl B63 . . . . . 82 C7
Hammersley St CV12 . . . . 77 E1
HAMMERWICH 7 D4
Hammerwich La WS7 . . . . . 7 F3
Hammerwich Rd WS7 . . . . 7 D5
Hammond Ave WV10 . . . . . 25 E8
Hammond Bsns Ctr CV1 . 73 E3
Hammond Cl CV11 . . . . . . 73 E3
Hammond Dr B23 . . . . 56 F5
Hammond Rd CV2 . . . . . . 113 F4
Hammonds Terr CV8 . . . . 147 D5
Hammond Way DY4 . . . . . 81 A7
Hampden Cl 3 DY5 . . . . . . 82 A8
Hampden Retreat B12. . . . 86 E6
Hamps Cl WS7 . . . . 7 D7
Hampshire Cl
  Coventry CV3 . . . . 134 F8
  Tamworth B78 . . . . 20 F2
Hampshire Ct 1 B29. . . . . 103 B7
Hampshire Dr B15 . . . . . . 85 E8
Hampshire Rd B71 . . . . . . 42 A1
Hampson Cl B11 . . . . 87 B6
Hampstead Glade B63. . . . 83 C2
Hampton Ave
  Bromsgrove B60 . . . . . . 151 A8
  Nuneaton CV10 . . . . 72 B4
Hampton Cl
  Coventry CV6 . . . . 113 F6
  Redditch B98 . . . . 159 B7
  Sutton Coldfield B73 . . . 45 C2
  Tamworth B79 . . . . 21 C7
Hampton Court Rd B17. . . 85 A6
Hampton Ct
  Birmingham B15 . . . . . . 86 B8
  Hampton-in-Arden B92 . 109 B6
  Solihull B91 . . . . 107 D4
  Wednesbury B71 . . . . . . 42 C1
  Wolverhampton WV10 . . 12 B2
Hampton Dr B74 . . . . 46 B8
Hampton Gdns DY9 . . . . . 81 D3
Hampton Gr
  Walsall WS11 . . . . 4 E7
Hampton Gr or
  Royal Leamington Spa
  CV32 . . . . 157 B1
  Walsall WS3. . . . . 15 A4
Hampton Grange CV7 . . . . 92 B4
HAMPTON-IN-ARDEN. . . 109 B8
Hampton in Arden Sta
  B92 . . . . 109 B7

Gun–Han 201

Hampton La
  Birmingham B36 . . . . . . 69 F8
  Catherine de B B91. . . . 108 B5
  Meriden CV7 . . . . 109 E8
HAMPTON MAGNA 160 A6
Hampton Pl WS10 . . . . 41 C8
Hampton Rd
  Birmingham, Aston B6. . . 66 D8
  Birmingham, Stockland Green
  B23 . . . . 56 D4
  Coventry CV6. . . . . 113 F6
  Knowle B93 . . . . 128 C8
  Warwick CV34 . . . . 160 B5
  Wolverhampton WV10 . . 11 B1
Hampton St
  Birmingham B19 . . . . . 164 B4
  Cannock WS11. . . . . 4 D7
  Dudley, Netherton DY2 . . 62 C5
  Dudley WV14 . . . . 51 B8
  Warwick CV34 . . . . 160 D6
Hampton View WV10 . . . . 25 F3
Hampton Wlk WV1. . . . . . 163 B3
Hams Hall Distribution Pk
  B46. . . . . 59 F5
Hams La B76 . . . . 59 F6
Hams Rd B8 . . . . 67 D4
HAMSTEAD 54 E6
Hamstead Cl WV11 . . . . . . 26 D6
Hamstead Hall Ave B20 . . 66 B7
Hamstead Hall B10 . . . . . . 54 E5
Hamstead Hall Rd B20 . . . 54 E5
Hamstead Hall Sch B20 . . 54 E6
Hamstead Hill B20 . . . . . . 54 E5
Hamstead Ho B43 . . . . 54 F7
Hamstead Rd
  Birmingham, Hamstead
  B43 . . . . 54 D7
  Birmingham, Lozells B19,
  B20 . . . . 66 B7
Hamstead Sta B42 . . . . . . 54 F6
Hamstead Terr WS10. . . . . 42 A2
Hanam Cl B75 . . . . 46 F6
Hanbury Cl
  Bromsgrove B60 . . . . . . 151 A8
  Halesowen B63 . . . . 82 E2
Hanbury Cres WV4 . . . . . . 38 E6
Hanbury Croft B27. . . . . . . 88 E3
Hanbury Ct DY8. . . . . 81 A4
Hanbury Hill DY8 . . . . 81 A4
Hanbury Ho B97 . . . . 153 B4
Hanbury Rd
  Bedworth CV12 . . . . 78 C4
  Brownhills WS8 . . . . 6 F2
  Dorridge B93 . . . . 127 F4
  Norton Canes WS11 . . . . . 5 F5
  Stoke Heath B60 . . . . . 150 D4
  Tamworth B77 . . . . 21 F4
  West Bromwich B71 . . . . 53 A3
Hanbury's Farm Com Prim
  Sch B77 . . . . 21 D1
Hanch Pl WS1 . . . . 42 F8
Hancock Gn CV4 . . . . 131 F8
Hancock Rd B8 . . . . 67 F4
Hancox St B68 . . . . 64 B2
Handcross Gr CV3 . . . . . . 133 A5
Handel Ct WS11 . . . . 2 C2
Handel Wlk WS13 . . . . 3 C2
Handley Gr
  Birmingham B31 . . . . . . 102 C2
  Warwick CV34 . . . . 155 D1
Handley's Cl CV8. . . . . . . 135 A1
Handley St WS10. . . . . 42 A4
HANDSWORTH 54 C1
Handsworth, Booth Street
  Stop B21 . . . . 65 C1
Handsworth Cres CV5 . . . 111 E4
Handsworth Dr B43 . . . . . . 44 A3
Handsworth Gram Sch
  B21. . . . . 65 F8
Handsworth L Ctr B20. . . . 65 F8
Handsworth New Rd B18 . 65 E6
HANDSWORTH WOOD. . . 55 B3
Handsworth Wood Girls' Sch
  1 B20 . . . . 54 F2
Handsworth Wood Rd
  B20 . . . . 55 A2
Hanford Cl CV6 . . . . 113 E6
Hanford Close Ind Est
  CV6. . . . . 113 E6
Hanger Rd B26 . . . . 90 A3
Hanging La B31 . . . . 102 E2
Hangleton Dr B11. . . . . 87 D6
Hangman's La LE10 . . . . . 71 E3
Hanley Cl B63 . . . . 82 D3
Hanley St B23 . . . . 56 C2
Hanley St B19 . . . . 164 C4
Hanley Villas 1 B12 . . . . . 87 B5
Hanlith B77 . . . . 36 A8
Hannaford Way WS11 . . . . 5 F2
Hannafore Rd B16 . . . . 65 D3
Hannah Rd WV14 . . . . 41 A3
Hanney Hay Rd WS7, WS8 . 7 B3
Hannon Rd B14 . . . . 104 E5
Hanover Cl B6 . . . . 66 E7
Hanover Ct
  Hinckley LE10 . . . . 75 E6
  Redditch B97 . . . . 158 D8
  Tamworth B79 . . . . 20 E7
  Walsall WS2. . . . . 27 E1
  Wolverhampton WV6 . . . 24 C4
Hanover Dr B24. . . . . 67 F8
Hanover Gdns 5 CV32 . . 157 A1
Hanover Glebe CV11 . . . . 73 C2

Hanover Ho **6** DY8 . . . . . . 80 F8
Hanover Pl
  Bromsgrove B60 . . . . 136 F1
  Cannock WS11 . . . . 1 E2
Hanover Rd B65 . . . . 63 C4
Hanover St B61 . . . . 136 F1
Hans Cl CV2 . . . . 113 F4
Hansell Dr B93 . . . . 127 E2
Hansom Ct **2** LE10 . . . . . 75 D8
Hansom Rd
  Birmingham B32 . . . . 84 C5
  Hinckley LE10 . . . . 71 F2
Hanson Cl B66 . . . . 65 A7
Hanson Gr B92 . . . . 88 F5
Hanson Man B74 . . . . 32 A1
Hanson's Bridge Rd B24 . 57 F5
Hanson Way CV6 . . . . 96 A4
Hanwell Cl B76 . . . . 58 B7
Hanwood Cl
  Birmingham B12 . . . . 86 F8
  Coventry CV5 . . . . 111 D4
Hanwood Ho **8** B12 . . . . 86 F8
Hanworth Cl CV32 . . . . . 157 C2
Hanworth Rd CV34 . . . . . 160 D8
Harald Cl WV6 . . . . 23 E5
Harbeck Ave B44 . . . . 55 F8
Harberrow Cl DY9 . . . . 99 A6
Harbet Dr B40 . . . . 90 A2
Harbinger Rd B38 . . . . . . 104 B2
HARBORNE 85 B6
Harborne Ct B17 . . . . 85 C4
Harborne Hill Sch B15 . . 85 E6
Harborne Ho B17 . . . . 85 A4
Harborne La B17 . . . . 85 D3
Harborne Park Rd B17 . . 85 C4
Harborne Prim Sch B17 . 85 C6
Harborne Rd
  Birmingham, Chad Valley
   B15 . . . . 85 E7
  Birmingham, Warley Woods
   B68 . . . . 84 E8
Harborough Cotts B94 . . 144 D3
Harborough Ct B74 . . . . . 32 A2
Harborough Dr
  Aldridge WS9 . . . . 30 B5
  Birmingham B36 . . . . 58 D1
Harborough Rd CV6 . . . . . 95 B2
Harborough Wlk DY9 . . . . 81 B2
Harbourne Cl CV8 . . . . . . 148 A5
Harbours Cl B61 . . . . 150 D7
Harbours Hill DY9 . . . . . 120 E6
Harbury Cl
  Redditch B98 . . . . 154 D1
  Sutton Coldfield B76 . . . . 58 B6
Harbury La CV33, CV34 . 161 E2
Harbury Rd B12 . . . . 86 D5
Harby Cl B37 . . . . 90 B8
Harcourt CV3 . . . . 134 E5
Harcourt Dr
  Dudley DY3 . . . . 50 D2
  Sutton Coldfield B74 . . . . 31 F4
Harcourt Gdns CV11 . . . . 73 C3
Harcourt Ho B79 . . . . 21 A4
Harcourt Rd
  Birmingham B23 . . . . 56 E6
  Cradley Heath B64 . . . . . . 82 F8
  Wednesbury WS10 . . . . . . 41 F4
HARDEN 28 E7
Harden Cl WS3 . . . . 28 E7
Harden Ct B31 . . . . 102 E1
Harden Gr WS3 . . . . 28 E7
Harden Keep B66 . . . . 65 A4
Harden Manor Ct B63 . . . 83 C3
Harden Prim Sch WS3 . . . 28 E7
Harden Rd WS3 . . . . 28 E7
Harden Vale B63 . . . . 82 E5
Hardie Ct **2** WV4 . . . . . . 39 F4
Hardie Gn WS11 . . . . 1 F3
Harding St WV14 . . . . 40 D2
Hardon Rd WV4 . . . . 39 F5
Hardware St B70 . . . . 53 D4
HARDWICK 30 E3
Hardwick Cl CV5 . . . . 112 A4
Hardwick Ct
  Stourbridge DY9 . . . . 81 D5
  Sutton Coldfield B74 . . . . 30 F2
  Tamworth B79 . . . . 21 C5
Hardwick Dr B62 . . . . 83 A7
Hardwicke Way DY9 . . . . . 81 D5
Hardwick Field La CV34 . 160 B3
Hardwick La B80 . . . . 159 F4
Hardwick Rd
  Solihull B92 . . . . 88 E4
  Sutton Coldfield B74 . . . . 31 A2
Hardwike Wlk B14 . . . . . . 104 D2
Hardwyn Cl CV3 . . . . 115 A1
Hardy Ave DY10 . . . . 117 A6
Hardy Cl
  Hinckley LE10 . . . . 71 D4
  Nuneaton CV10 . . . . 72 A4
Hardy Ct **4** B13 . . . . 86 F4
Hardy Pl WV11 . . . . 9 B6
Hardy Rd
  Coventry CV6 . . . . 113 A8
  Walsall WS3 . . . . 28 E8
  Wednesbury WS10 . . . . . . 42 A3
Hardy Sq WV2 . . . . 39 F6
Hare and Hounds La
  CV10 . . . . 73 A2
Harebell B77 . . . . 22 A4
Harebell Cl
  Cannock WS12 . . . . 2 D2
  Featherstone WV10 . . . . . 12 A7
  Walsall WS5 . . . . 43 A3
Harebell Cres DY1 . . . . . . 51 A4

Harebell Gdns B38 . . . . . 123 F8
Harebell Wlk **1** B37 . . . 70 D2
Harefield Ho CV2 . . . . . . 114 B3
Harefield La CV12 . . . . . . 77 F8
Harefield Rd
  Coventry CV2 . . . . 114 B3
  Nuneaton CV11 . . . . 73 C4
Hare Gr B31 . . . . 102 D3
Haresfield B90 . . . . 126 A5
Haresfield Cl B97 . . . . . . 153 D3
Hares St WV14 . . . . 40 F5
Harewell Dr B75 . . . . 32 C1
Harewood **6** B17 . . . . . . 85 B6
Harewood Ave
  Birmingham B43 . . . . 43 C2
  Wednesbury WS10 . . . . . . 42 C3
Harewood Cl B28 . . . . 105 E5
Harewood Rd CV5 . . . . . . 112 C2
Harford St B18 . . . . 164 A5
Hargate La B71 . . . . 53 D4
Hargate Prim Sch B71 . . 53 C4
Harger Ct CV8 . . . . 147 F4
Harger Mews CV8 . . . . . . 147 F4
Hargrave Cl
  Coventry CV3 . . . . 115 A1
  Water Orton B46 . . . . 59 B3
Hargrave Rd B90 . . . . 105 D1
Hargreave Cl B76 . . . . 57 F8
Hargreaves Ct DY11 . . . . 116 C3
Hargreaves St WV1 . . . . . 40 A7
Harington Rd CV6 . . . . . . 113 A5
Harland Cl B61 . . . . 136 D3
Harland Rd B74 . . . . 32 A3
Harlech Cl
  Birmingham B32 . . . . . . 102 A7
  Kenilworth CV8 . . . . 148 C5
  Oldbury B69 . . . . 52 A1
Harlech Ho **2** WS3 . . . . 28 C6
Harlech Rd WV12 . . . . 27 C6
Harlech Twr B23 . . . . 57 A6
Harlech Way
  Dudley DY1 . . . . 50 F2
  Kidderminster DY10 . . . . 116 E2
Harlequin Dr B13 . . . . 86 E2
Harlestones Ho DY8 . . . . 80 F7
Harleston Rd B44 . . . . 55 F8
Harley Cl WS8 . . . . 16 A6
Harley Dr WV14 . . . . 40 B4
Harley Grange **6** DY2 . . 62 E8
Harley St CV2 . . . . 114 A3
Harlow Gr B28 . . . . 106 A6
Harlow Wlk **8** CV2 . . . . . 115 A7
Harlstones Cl DY8 . . . . . . 81 A8
Harlyn Cl WV14 . . . . 41 A2
Harman Dr WS13 . . . . 8 F6
Harman Rd B72 . . . . 57 B6
Harmar Cl CV34 . . . . 155 D1
Harmer Cl CV2 . . . . 115 A7
Harmer St B18 . . . . 66 A5
Harmon Rd DY8 . . . . 80 C5
Harmony Ct **6** B12 . . . . 73 B2
Harmony Ho **8** B12 . . . . 67 C1
Harnall Cl B90 . . . . 126 E7
Harnall La CV1 . . . . 165 C4
Harnall Lane E CV1 . . . . . 113 E4
Harnall Lane Ind Est
  CV1 . . . . 165 C4
Harnall Lane W CV1 . . . . 165 C4
Harnall Row CV1 . . . . 113 E2
Harness Cl WS5 . . . . 42 F4
Harold Evers Way DY10 . 116 F7
Harold Rd
  Birmingham B16 . . . . 65 F1
  Coventry CV2 . . . . 114 D2
  Smethwick B67 . . . . 64 E3
Harold St WV11 . . . . 73 C3
Harpenden Dr CV5 . . . . . 112 A5
Harper Ave WV11 . . . . 26 C7
Harper Rd
  Bilston WV14 . . . . 40 D6
  Coventry CV1 . . . . 113 E2
Harpers Rd
  Birmingham, Highter's Heath
   B14 . . . . 105 A1
  Birmingham, Northfield
   B31 . . . . 103 A2
Harper St WV13 . . . . 27 A2
Harport Rd B98 . . . . 154 A1
Harpur Cl WS4 . . . . 29 A4
Harpur Rd WS4 . . . . 29 A4
Harrier Rd B27 . . . . 88 D2
Harriers Gn DY10 . . . . . . 117 B8
Harriers Ind Est DY10 . . 116 F5
Harriet Cl DY5 . . . . 61 B5
Harringay Dr DY8 . . . . 80 E3
Harringay Rd B44 . . . . 45 A2
Harrington Croft B71 . . . 53 F7
Harrington Ct CV3 . . . . . 114 F2
Harrington Way CV10 . . . . 78 A7
Harrington Wlk WS13 . . . . 8 F8
Harringworth St V14 . . . . 39 E6
Harriott Dr CV34 . . . . . . 161 D4
Harris Bsns Pk B60 . . . . 150 E2
Harris Cl B98 . . . . 158 F8
Harris Ct B18 . . . . 66 A6
Harris Dr
  2 Birmingham B42 . . . . 55 A8
  Smethwick B66 . . . . 65 B3
Harrison Cl
  Cheslyn Hay WS6 . . . . 4 D1
  Walsall WS3 . . . . 14 C1
Harrison Cres CV12 . . . . . 78 A2
Harrison Ct DY8 . . . . 61 A1
Harrison Ho B14 . . . . 104 D1

Harrison Rd
  Birmingham B24 . . . . 56 F4
  Cannock WS11 . . . . 4 E7
  Redditch B97 . . . . 158 C8
  Stourbridge DY8 . . . . 61 A1
  Sutton Coldfield B74 . . . . 31 E5
  Walsall WS4 . . . . 15 C2
Harrison's Fold DY2 . . . . 62 C5
Harrisons Gn B15 . . . . 85 E6
Harrisons Pleck B13 . . . . 86 F3
Harrison's Rd B15 . . . . . . 85 E6
Harrison St WS3 . . . . 14 C1
Harrison Way CV31 . . . . . 161 F5
Harris Rd
  Coventry CV3 . . . . 114 B2
  Warwick CV34 . . . . 160 C8
Harrold Ave B65 . . . . 63 E3
Harrold Rd B65 . . . . 63 E3
Harrold St DY4 . . . . 52 C7
Harrold Terr B19 . . . . 66 C8
Harrop Way DY8 . . . . 80 E8
Harrowbrook Ind Est
  LE10 . . . . 74 E7
Harrowbrook Rd LE10 . . 74 E7
Harrowby Ct WV10 . . . . . . 11 B3
Harrowby Dr DY4 . . . . 52 A4
Harrowby Pl WV13 . . . . . . 27 D1
Harrowby Rd
  Darlaston WV14 . . . . 41 A4
  Wolverhampton WV10 . . . 11 C2
Harrow Cl
  Coventry CV6 . . . . 96 A4
  Stoke Heath B60 . . . . . . 150 E6
  West Hagley DY9 . . . . 99 A6
Harrow Ct **6** B74 . . . . . . 31 F2
Harrowfield Rd B33 . . . . . 68 E4
Harrow Rd
  Birmingham B29 . . . . 85 F3
  Kingswinford DY6 . . . . . . 49 D1
  Whitnash CV31 . . . . 162 B3
Harrow St WV1 . . . . 25 B4
Harry Caplan Ho CV5 . . . . 111 B3
Harry Edwards Ho **2**
  CV2 . . . . 114 D8
Harry Mitchell L Ctr B67 . 64 F5
Harry Perks St WV13 . . . . 27 A3
Harry Price Ho **6** B69 . . 63 D5
Harry Rose Rd CV2 . . . . . 114 E3
Harry Salt Ho CV1 . . . . . 165 D3
Harry Stanley Ho CV6 . . 114 A8
Harry Taylor Fst Sch The
  B97 . . . . 158 E6
Harry Taylor Ho B98 . . . . 154 A4
Harry Truslove Cl CV6 . . 113 A7
Harry Weston Rd CV3 . . 115 A1
Hart Dr B73 . . . . 57 A8
Hartfield Cres B27 . . . . . . 88 B2
Hartfields Way B65 . . . . . 62 F5
Hartford Cl B17 . . . . 85 A7
Hartford Rd B60 . . . . 137 B1
Hartill Rd WV4 . . . . 38 D3
Hartill St WV13 . . . . 41 B8
Hartington Cl B93 . . . . . . 127 E3
Hartington Cres CV5 . . . 112 F1
Hartington Gn LE10 . . . . . 75 E6
Hartington Rd B19 . . . . . . 66 D7
Hartland Ave
  Bilston WV14 . . . . 114 B5
  Coventry CV6 . . . . 95 D1
Hartland Rd
  Birmingham B31 . . . . . . 122 E6
  Tipton DY4 . . . . 51 D5
  West Bromwich B71 . . . . . 53 F8
Hartland St DY5 . . . . 61 D7
HARTLE 119 F6
Hartlebury Cl
  Cannock WS11 . . . . 2 C2
  Dorridge B93 . . . . 127 F3
  Redditch B98 . . . . 154 E7
Hartlebury Rd
  Halesowen B63 . . . . 82 F2
  Oldbury B69 . . . . 63 D5
Hartledon Rd B17 . . . . 85 B5
Hartle La DY9 . . . . 119 F6
Hartlepool Rd CV1 . . . . . 165 D4
Hartleyburn B77 . . . . 36 A8
Hartley Dr WS9 . . . . 30 B4
Hartley Gr B44 . . . . 45 B3
Hartley Pl B15 . . . . 85 F8
Hartley Rd B44 . . . . 45 B3
Hartley St WV3 . . . . 25 A2
Harton Way B14 . . . . 104 C5
Hartopp Rd
  Birmingham B8 . . . . 67 E4
  Sutton Coldfield B74 . . . . 45 F8
Hart Rd
  Birmingham B24 . . . . 57 A5
  Willenhall WV11 . . . . 26 D4
Hartridge Wlk CV5 . . . . . 112 B4
Hartsbourne Dr B62 . . . . 83 D4
Harts Cl B17 . . . . 85 D6
HARTS GREEN 85 A5
Harts Green Rd B17 . . . . . 85 A5
Haswell Rd B63 . . . . 82 D4
Hatcham Rd B44 . . . . 45 C2
Hatchford Ave B92 . . . . . . 89 C3
Hatchford Brook Prim Sch
  B92 . . . . 89 C3
Hatchford Ct B92 . . . . 89 C3
Hatchford Wlk B37 . . . . . . 70 B1
Hateley Dr WV4 . . . . 39 E4
Hateley Heath Prim Sch
  B71 . . . . 53 B7
Hatfield Cl
  Birmingham B23 . . . . 56 D8

Hartwell Cl
  5 B91 . . . . 107 B1

Hartwell La WS6 . . . . 5 A3
Hartwell Rd B24 . . . . 57 B2
Hartwood Cres WV3 . . . . . 38 F5
Harvard Cl DY1 . . . . 50 F4
Harvard Rd B92 . . . . 89 B4
Harvest Cl
  Birmingham B30 . . . . . . 104 B6
  Dudley DY3 . . . . 50 E5
  Stoke Heath B60 . . . . . . 150 E6
Harvesters Cl
  Coventry CV3 . . . . 115 A2
  Sutton Coldfield WS9 . . . . 30 E2
Harvesters Rd WV12 . . . . 27 D5
Harvesters Way WV12 . . . 27 D5
Harvesters Wlk WV8 . . . . 10 E1
Harvester Way CV6 . . . . . . 60 A8
Harvest Fields Way B75 . . 32 D4
Harvest Gdns B68 . . . . 64 A4
HARVEST HILL 93 E2
Harvest Hill Cl **7** B31 . 162 C6
Harvest Hill Cotts CV5 . . 93 D1
Harvest Hill La CV5, CV7 . . 93 C4
Harvest Hill Pk CV5 . . . . . 93 D1
Harvest Rd
  Rowley Regis B65 . . . . . . 63 A3
  Smethwick B67 . . . . 64 D3
Harvest Wlk B65 . . . . 63 A3
Harvey Cl CV5 . . . . 112 A7
Harvey Ct B33 . . . . 69 C3
Harvey Dr B75 . . . . 32 C2
Harvey Mews B30 . . . . . . 103 D7
Harvey Rd
  Birmingham B26 . . . . 88 D6
  Walsall WS2 . . . . 28 B5
Harveys Terr DY2 . . . . 62 D4
Harvey Works Ind Est B63 . 82 F6
HARVILLS HAWTHORN . . 52 F7
Harvills Hawthorn B70 . . 52 F7
Harvills Hawthorn Prim Sch
  B70 . . . . 52 F7
Harvine Wlk DY9 . . . . 80 E3
Harvington Cl
  Kidderminster DY11 . . . . 116 A8
  Redditch B97 . . . . 153 B5
Harvington Dr B90 . . . . . 127 B6
Harvington Hall* DY10 . . 118 B1
Harvington Hall La DY10 . 118 B1
Harvington Rd
  Birmingham, Brandhall
   B68 . . . . 84 A8
  Birmingham, Weoley Castle
   B29 . . . . 103 A8
  Bromsgrove B60 . . . . 151 A8
  Dudley WV14 . . . . 40 B1
  Halesowen B63 . . . . 82 F2
Harvington Wlk **6** B65 . . 63 C3
Harwell Cl WV6 . . . . 21 C7
Harwin Cl WV6 . . . . 24 F7
Harwood Dr
  Hinckley LE10 . . . . 71 F4
  Tamworth B77 . . . . 35 D4
Harwood Gr **1** B90 . . . 126 C8
Harwood Rd WS13 . . . . 3 B3
Harwood St B70 . . . . 53 C2
HASBURY 82 E3
Hasbury CE Prim Sch B63 . 82 F2
Hasbury Cl B63 . . . . 82 E2
Hasbury Rd B32 . . . . 102 B8
Haselbech Rd CV3 . . . . . 114 F1
Haselbury Cnr CV10 . . . . 72 F1
Haseley Cl
  Redditch B98 . . . . 154 E1
  Whitnash CV31 . . . . 162 B5
HASELEY KNOB 146 A3
Haseley Rd
  Birmingham B21 . . . . 65 E7
  Coventry CV2 . . . . 96 C1
  Solihull B91 . . . . 106 E6
Haselour Rd B37 . . . . 45 E1
Haseltine Rd B37 . . . . 69 F5
Haselwell Dr B30 . . . . . . 104 D3
Hasilwood Sq CV3 . . . . . 114 B2
Haslett Cl WS1 . . . . 42 F7
Haslucks Croft B90 . . . . 106 A3
Haslucks Green Jun Sch
  B90 . . . . 106 A3
Haslucks Green Rd
  Solihull, Major's Green
   B90 . . . . 125 E7
  Solihull, Shirley B90 . . . . 106 B4
Hassop Rd B42 . . . . 55 D7
Hastang Fields CV31 . . . 162 C5
Hastings Cl B77 . . . . 35 F6
Hastings Ct DY1 . . . . 50 E3
Hastings High Sch LE10 . 75 F7
Hastings Rd
  Birmingham B23 . . . . 56 B7
  Bromsgrove B60 . . . . 150 E7
  Coventry CV2 . . . . 114 A4
Hatcham Rd B44 . . . . 45 C2

Hatfield Cl **continued**
  Redditch B98 . . . . 154 E1
Hatfield Rd
  Birmingham B19 . . . . 66 D8
  Stourbridge DY9 . . . . 81 C4
Hathaway Cl
  Balsall Common CV7 . . . 130 B7
  Willenhall WV13 . . . . 40 F8
Hathaway Dr
  Nuneaton CV11 . . . . 74 A1
  Warwick CV34 . . . . 155 E2
Hathaway Mews DY8 . . . . 60 C3
Hathaway Rd
  Coventry CV4 . . . . 111 D1
  Solihull B90 . . . . 106 B1
  Sutton Coldfield B74 . . . . 32 A4
Hatherden Dr B76 . . . . 47 A2
Hatherell Rd CV31 . . . . . 162 E5
Hathersage Rd B42 . . . . . 55 D7
Hatherton Gdns WV10 . . . 11 E2
Hatherton Gr B29 . . . . 84 F1
Hatherton Hollow WS11 . . 1 C1
Hatherton Lane Prim Sch
  WS2 . . . . 28 A6
Hatherton Pl WS9 . . . . 30 A7
Hatherton Rd
  Bilston WV14 . . . . 40 F6
  Cannock WS11 . . . . 1 C1
  Walsall WS1 . . . . 28 E2
Hatherton St
  Cheslyn Hay WS6 . . . . 4 C2
  Walsall WS1, WS4 . . . . . . 28 E3
Hatters Ct CV12 . . . . 78 D2
Hattersley Dr B31 . . . . . . 88 A3
Hatton Cres WV10 . . . . . . 26 A7
Hatton Gdns B42 . . . . 55 B7
Hatton Rd
  Wolverhampton WV6 . . . . 24 F3
Hatton St WV14 . . . . 40 E4
Haughton Rd B20 . . . . 55 D1
Haunch Cl B13 . . . . 105 A5
Haunch La B13 . . . . 105 A5
Haunchwood Dr B76 . . . . 57 F7
Haunchwood Rd CV10 . . . 73 B2
Havacre La WV14 . . . . 40 C1
Havefield Ave WS14 . . . . . . 9 E7
Havelock Cl WV3 . . . . 38 F8
Havelock Rd
  Birmingham, Handsworth
   B20 . . . . 55 C1
  Birmingham, Saltley B8 . . 67 D5
  Birmingham, Sparkhill B11 . 87 E4
Haven Croft B43 . . . . 54 D8
Havendale Cl CV6 . . . . . . 113 B5
Haven Dr B27 . . . . 88 B3
Haven The
  Barnt Green B45 . . . . 138 A6
  Birmingham B14 . . . . . . 105 D4
  Stourbridge DY8 . . . . 60 D2
  Wolverhampton WV2 . . . 163 B3
Haverford Dr B45 . . . . . . 122 B6
Havergal Wlk B63 . . . . 82 B8
Haverhill Cl WS3 . . . . 14 A3
Hawbridge Cl B90 . . . . . . 127 B6
Hawbush Gdns DY5 . . . . . 61 A3
Hawbush Prim Sch DY5 . . 61 B2
Hawbush Rd
  Brierley Hill DY5 . . . . 61 A2
  Walsall WS3 . . . . 28 E6
Hawcroft Gr B34 . . . . 69 C6
Hawes Cl WS1 . . . . 42 F6
Hawes La B65 . . . . 63 B3
Hawes Rd WS1 . . . . 42 F6
Haweswater Dr DY6 . . . . . 60 D6
Hawfield Cl B69 . . . . 63 C2
Hawfield Gr B72 . . . . 57 C2
Hawfield Rd B69 . . . . 63 C2
Hawfinch B77 . . . . 36 A6
Hawfinch Rise DY10 . . . . 117 A2
Hawford Ave DY10 . . . . . 117 B6
Hawk Cl CV11 . . . . 79 B8
Hawker Dr B35 . . . . 57 F2
HAWKESBURY 96 C5
Hawkesbury La CV2 . . . . . 96 D5
Hawkesbury Rd B90 . . . . 105 F1
Hawkes Cl B30 . . . . 104 A1
Hawkes Dr CV34 . . . . 161 D6
HAWKES END 94 B2
Hawkesford Cl
  Birmingham B36 . . . . 69 A8
  Sutton Coldfield B74 . . . . 32 B3
Hawkesford Rd B33 . . . . . 69 D2
Hawkes La B70 . . . . 53 A2
HAWKESLEY 123 F1
Hawkesley Church Prim Sch
  B38 . . . . 123 E1
Hawkesley Cres B31 . . . . 103 A1
Hawkesley Dr B31 . . . . . . 122 E8
Hawkesley End B38 . . . . . 123 E1
Hawkesley Mill La B31 . . 102 F7
Hawkesley Rd DY1 . . . . . . 51 A8
Hawkesley Sq B38 . . . . . 123 E6
Hawkes Mill La CV5 . . . . . 94 B3
Hawkesmoor Dr
  Lichfield WS13 . . . . 3 B1
  Solihull B91 . . . . 106 E8
Hawkesmore Dr B29 . . . . 103 A3
Hawkeswell Cl B92 . . . . . 106 C1
Hawkeswell Dr **4** DY6 . . 60 D7
Hawkesworth Dr CV8 . . . 148 A4
Hawkesyard Rd B24 . . . . . 56 E8
Hawkhurst Rd B14 . . . . . 104 F1
Hawkinge Dr B35 . . . . 58 A4

Hawkins Cl
Birmingham B5 .... 86 E6
Hinckley LE10 .... 71 D4
Lichfield WS13 .... 3 B2
Hawkins Croft DY4 .... 52 A3
Hawkins Dr WS11 .... 4 C4
Hawkin's Pl WV14 .... 40 F3
Hawkins Rd CV1 .... 113 A2
Hawkins St B70 .... 53 A8
Hawkley Cl WV1 .... 26 B2
Hawkley Rd WV1 .... 26 B2
Hawkmoor Gdns B38....124 A8
Hawksbury Cl B98 ..... 154 D5
Hawkshaw Cl WS6 .... 4 D2
Hawksford Cres WV10...25 E7
HAWKS GREEN 2 B1
Hawks Green La WS11 ... 2 A1
Hawkshead Dr B93...... 127 F6
Hawkside B77 .... 36 B8
Hawkshill Ind Est B9 ... 67 C1
Hawksmoor Dr WV6..... 23 D3
Hawkstone Cl DY11 .... 116 D8
Hawkstone Ct WV6...... 23 D5
Hawkswell WV5 .... 49 A5
Hawkswell Dr WV13..... 40 F8
Hawkswood Dr
Balsall Common CV7 .... 130 B7
Darlaston WS10 .... 41 B3
Hawkswood Gr B14 ..... 105 B3
Hawksworth B77......... 21 F2
Hawksworth Cres B37...70 D3
Hawksworth Dr ■ CV1.. 113 B3
Hawkyard Cl WS11....... 2 A4
Hawley Cl WS4 .... 28 F4
Hawley Ct B43 .... 43 E1
Hawley Rd LE10 .... 75 D7
Hawnby Gr B76 .... 47 A2
HAWNE 83 A6
Hawne Cl B63 .... 82 E6
Hawne La B63 .... 82 F6
Havnelands The B63.... 82 F5
Hawskford Cres WV10...25 D7
Hawthorn Ave WS6 .... 5 A1
Hawthorn Brook Way B23 56 E8
Hawthorn Cl
Balsall Common CV7 .... 130 B8
Birmingham B29 .... 85 C1
Lichfield WS14 .... 9 D8
Hawthorn Coppice DY9... 99 A6
Hawthorn Cres LE10 .... 75 E4
Hawthorn Croft B68.... 84 D7
Hawthorn Ct CV4 ..... 111 E1
Hawthornden Ct B76... 57 D7
Hawthorn Dr
Balsall Common CV7 .... 130 B8
Birmingham B29 .... 85 C1
Hawthorne Ave ■ 21 B8
Hawthorne Cres WS7 ... 7 A6
Hawthorne Croft B30 .. 103 D5
Hawthorne Dr B47 .... 125 B6
Hawthorne Gr DY3...... 50 D2
Hawthorne Ho 25 F3
Hawthorne Rd
Birmingham B15 .... 85 E7
Birmingham, Castle Bromwich
B36 .... 69 F7
Birmingham, King's Norton
B30 .... 103 D5
Cannock WS12...........2 F3
Cheslyn Hay WS6....... 4 E4
Dudley DY1 .... 51 C4
Essington WV11 .... 13 A3
Halesowen B63 .... 82 E2
Huntington WS12....... 1 D8
Wednesfield WV11 ..... 27 A5
Willenhall WV12 .... 27 D7
Wolverhampton WV3.... 39 D6
Hawthorne Terr CV10 .. 72 F5
Hawthorn Gr
⑥ Birmingham B19.... 66 C8
Kidderminster DY11... 116 A6
Hawthorn La CV4 ..... 111 E1
Hawthorn Park Dr ■ B20 54 F3
Hawthorn Pk B20 ..... 54 E3
Hawthorn Pl WS12 .... 27 E3
Hawthorn Prim Sch B44.. 56 A7
Hawthorn Rd
Bilston WV1 .... 40 B8
Birmingham B44 .... 56 A7
Brierley Hill DY5 ..... 81 E8
Bromsgrove B61 ..... 137 B4
Redditch B97 .... 153 A4
Royal Leamington Spa
CV31 .... 161 F6
Sutton Coldfield, Streetly
B74 .... 31 A1
Sutton Coldfield, Wylde Green
B72 .... 46 C1
Tipton DY4 .... 52 A8
Walsall, Bescot WS5 ... 42 F5
Walsall, Shelfield WS4.. 29 B8
Walsall WS4 .... 15 B1
Wednesbury WS10 ..... 41 A8
Hawthorns Bsns Ctr B66.. 65 A8
Hawthorns Ind Est B21... 54 B1
Hawthorns Sta & Stop The
B66................... 65 A8
Hawthorns The
Birmingham, Showell Green
B13................. 105 A8
Birmingham, Warley Woods
B68................. 84 D7
■ Kidderminster DY10...117 A5
West Hagley DY9 .... 98 F4
Wolverhampton WV11...26 B6

**Hawthorns The (West
Bromwich Albion FC)**
B21................... 54 B1
Hawthorn Terr WS10 ... 41 F4
Hawthorn Way CV10 ... 72 A8
Haxby Ave B34.......... 69 A6
Haybarn The B76 .... 58 A8
Haybridge Ave DY8 ..... 98 F5
**Haybridge High Sch & Sixth
Form** DY8 .... 98 F6
Hay Brook Dr B11....... 87 F4
Hay Cl DY11 .... 116 C7
Haycock Pl WS10 .... 41 C8
Haycroft Ave B8 .... 67 E5
Haycroft Dr B74 .... 32 A4
Haydn Sanders Sq ❼
WS1.................. 42 E8
Haydock Cl
Birmingham B36 .... 68 C8
Coventry CV6........... 96 B4
Wolverhampton WV6.... 25 B5
Haydock Rd B61 ..... 121 B1
Haydon Cl B93......... 127 F2
Haydon Croft B33...... 69 A3
Haydon Way B49 ..... 159 F1
Haye House Gr B36 .... 68 E7
Hayes Bsns Pk DY9 .... 81 F6
Hayes Cres B68 .... 64 D5
Hayes Croft B38 ..... 123 F7
Hayes Dr B24 .... 57 D5
Hayes Gr B24 .... 57 D6
Hayes Green Rd CV12 .. 95 F8
Hayes La
Bedworth CV7 .... 96 A8
Stourbridge DY9 .... 82 A6
Hayes Mdw B72......... 57 D7
Hayes Rd
Hartshill CV10 .... 72 A8
Oldbury B68 .... 64 D5
Hayes St B70 .... 53 A4
Hayes The
Birmingham B31 ..... 123 C7
Leek Wootton CV35 ... 155 F5
Stourbridge DY9 .... 82 A5
Willenhall WV12 .... 27 D7
Hayes Trad Est The DY9.. 82 A6
Hayes View Dr WS6..... 4 E4
Hayes Way WS12....... 2 C1
Hayfield Ct B13 .... 87 B2
Hayfield Gdns B13 .... 87 C2
Hayfield Rd B13 .... 87 B2
Hayford Cl B98 .... 154 A5
Hay Gn DY9............ 81 D5
Hay Gr WS8 .... 15 F8
Hay Green Cl B30 .... 103 D6
Hay Green La B30..... 103 D6
Hay Hall Rd B11 .... 87 F5
**Hayhead Wood Nature
Reserve★** WS4........ 29 E2
Hay La
Coventry CV1......... 165 C2
Solihull B90 .... 127 A6
Hayle Ave CV34 ..... 155 F1
Hayle Cl
Birmingham B38 ..... 104 B2
Nuneaton CV11 .... 74 A5
Hayley Ct
Kingswinford DY6 .... 60 D6
Sutton Coldfield B24 .. 57 C6
HAYLEY GREEN 82 C1
Hayley Green Rd B32.. 102 B8
Hayley Park Rd B63 .. 100 C8
Hayling Cl B45........ 101 F1
Hayling Ct WS4 .... 15 D1
Hayling Gr WV2......... 39 B6
Hayloft Cl B60 .... 150 E6
Haylofts The B63 ..... 82 C1
Haymaker Way WS12... 2 A8
Haymarket The WV8 ... 10 E1
Haymoor WS14...........9 E7
Haynes Cl B61 .... 137 B8
Haynes La WS5 .... 43 B4
Haynestone Rd CV6.... 112 E6
Haypits Cl B71......... 53 E7
Hay Pk B5............. 86 D6
Hay Rd B25............ 88 A7
Hayrick Dr DY6 .... 60 B7
Hayseech B64 .... 83 A7
Hayseech Rd B63 ..... 83 A6
Hays Kent's Moat The
B26................... 69 A1
Hays La LE10 .... 75 B7
Hayton Gn CV4 ..... 131 F8
Hay Tree Rd B14 .... 104 D5
Haytor Rise CV2 ..... 114 C7
Haywain Cl WV9 .... 10 F2
Hayward Rd B75....... 46 C7
Haywards Cl
Birmingham B23 .... 56 E5
Walsall WS3............ 14 F3
Hayward's Gn CV6.... 113 A7
Hayward St WV14 ..... 51 B8
Haywharf Rd DY5 ..... 61 B5
Haywood Dr
Halesowen B62 .... 83 C8
Wolverhampton WV6... 24 B5
Hay Wood La B93, CV35 .. 145 A3
Haywood Rd B33...... 69 E3
Haywood's Farm B71... 42 F2
Hayworth Cl B79...... 20 F8
Hayworth Rd WS13..... 3 C2

Hazel Ave
Birmingham B73 .... 45 C1
Wednesbury WS10 ..... 42 A4
Hazelbank B38 .... 103 E2
Hazelbeach Rd B8 ..... 67 F5
Hazelbeech Rd B70 ... 53 B3
Hazel Cl
Hartshill CV10 .... 72 A8
Royal Leamington Spa
CV32 .... 157 A2
Hazel Croft
Birmingham, Chelmsley Wood
B37.................. 70 B1
Birmingham, Northfield
B31................. 103 A3
Hazeldene Gr ⑤ B36... 66 E8
Hazeldene Rd
Birmingham B33 .... 89 D7
Halesowen B63 .... 82 E2
Hazel Dr
Birmingham B29 ..... 103 A7
Hollywood B47....... 125 B5
Hazeley Cl B17 .... 85 A7
Hazelgarth B77 .... 36 B8
Hazel Gdns
Birmingham B27 .... 88 C5
Codsall WV8............ 10 A4
Hazel Gr
Bedworth CV12 .... 78 D3
Bilston WV14 .... 40 E7
Hockley Heath B94 ... 143 C6
Lichfield WS14 .... 9 C7
Stourbridge DY8 .... 80 C3
West Bromwich B70 ... 53 C1
Wolverhampton WV11.. 26 C7
Wombourne WV5....... 49 A7
Hazelhurst Rd
Birmingham, Castle Bromwich
B36.................. 69 E7
Birmingham, King's Heath
B14................. 104 E7
Hazel La WS6............5 B2
Hazell Way CV10 .... 73 A1
Hazell Way Ind Est CV10.. 73 A1
Hazelmead Ct B73 .... 57 A7
Hazelmere Dr
Burntwood WS7..........6 F4
Wolverhampton WV3... 24 A1
Hazelmere Rd B28 ... 105 F8
Hazeloak Rd B90...... 106 A2
Hazel Oak Sch B90.... 106 A2
Hazel Rd
Birmingham B45 ..... 121 F6
Coventry CV6........... 96 B1
Dudley DY1 .... 51 C2
Kingswinford DY6 .... 60 E5
Nuneaton CV10 .... 72 D5
Redditch B97 .... 153 C5
Wednesbury WS10 ..... 41 D1
Wolverhampton WV3... 38 E2
Hazelslade Ho WS12 ... 2 F6
Hazels The DY9 .... 98 F5
Hazelton Cl
Catshill B61 .... 137 C8
■ Solihull B91....... 107 B1
Hazelton Rd B61 ..... 121 C1
Hazeltree Croft B27 ... 88 B2
Hazeltree Gr B93 .... 127 E3
Hazelville Gr B28 .... 106 A6
Hazelville Rd B28 .... 106 A7
Hazelwell Cres B30 .. 104 B6
Hazelwell Dr B14 .... 104 D6
Hazelwell Fordrough
B30.................. 104 B6
Hazelwell La B30 .... 104 B7
Hazelwell Rd B30 .... 104 A6
Hazelwell St B30 .... 104 A7
Hazelwood Cl
Cheslyn Hay WS6......4 D2
Kidderminster DY11...116 B4
Hazelwood Dr WV11 ... 26 A5
Hazelwood Gr
Cannock WS11...........4 C8
Willenhall WV12 .... 27 D5
Hazelwood Rd
Birmingham B27 .... 88 B2
Dudley DY1 .... 50 F5
Sutton Coldfield B74 .. 30 D1
Hazlemere Cl CV5.... 112 B4
Hazlemere Dr B74 .... 32 B1
Hazlemere Gr WS11 .... 4 B8
Hazlitt Gr B30 .... 103 D4
Headborough Rd CV2 .. 114 A5
Headborough Wlk WS9.. 16 B1
Headingley Rd B21... 54 E2
Headington Ave CV6 .. 95 A2
Headland Dr B8 .... 67 D5
Headland Rd WV3..... 24 A1
Headlands The
Coventry CV5......... 112 D4
Sutton Coldfield B74 .. 31 C3
HEADLESS CROSS 158 D8
Headless Cross Dr B97.. 153 D1
Headley Croft B38 ... 123 D8
Headley Rd B97 ..... 158 D8
HEADLEY HEATH 124 C6
Headley Heath La B38.. 124 B6
Headley Rise B90 .... 106 E3
Headway Rd WV10 ..... 11 C3
Heale Cl B63 .... 82 A7
Healey B77 .... 21 E2
Healey Ct CV34 ..... 160 F7
Health Centre Rd CV4.. 132 C4
Heanor Croft B6 .... 67 B8
Heantun Croft WV10 .. 26 A5
Heantun Ct WV3 .... 38 E8
Heantun Ho WV3 ..... 163 B2
Heantun Lodge WV14.. 40 C6

Heantun Mill Ct WS10... 41 D1
Heantun Rise WV3 .... 25 C4
Heantun Row WV13 ... 63 B2
Hearsall Comm CV5... 112 F2
**Hearsall Common Woodland
Nature Reserve★** CV5 ..112 D2
Hearsall Ct CV4......... 112 D2
Hearsall La CV5......... 112 F2
Hearsall Prim Sch CV5.. 112 F2
Heartland Mews B65.... 63 B2
Heartlands Acad B7.... 67 B4
Heartlands Parkway B7 . 67 D7
Heartlands Pl B8 .... 67 E4
**Heart of England Bsns & Ent
Sch** CV7............... 130 C6
Heart of England Way
CV11 .... 73 F3
**Heart of the Country Sh
Village★** WS14........ 18 E8
Heath Acres WS10 ..... 41 C4
Heath Ave CV12......... 77 E1
Heathbank Dr WS12 .... 1 C6
Heath Bridge Cl WS4... 29 A8
Heathbrook Ave DY6 .. 60 B7
Heath Cl
Birmingham B30 ..... 103 D5
Bromsgrove B60 ..... 150 E6
Stonnall WS14 .... 16 E5
Sutton Coldfield B75 .. 46 F7
Tipton DY4 .... 52 B5
Heathcliff Rd
Birmingham B11 .... 87 F4
Dudley DY2 .... 62 F7
HEATHCOTE 161 D3
Heathcote Ave B91 ... 106 E3
Heathcote Ct B77 ..... 36 B7
Heathcote La CV6 .... 113 A7
Heathcote Rd B28 ... 105 F3
Heathcote Ind Est CV34. 161 D4
Heathcote La
Royal Leamington Spa
CV34 .... 161 D4
Warwick CV34 .... 161 A5
Heathcote Rd
Birmingham B30 ..... 104 A5
Whitnash CV31 ..... 162 A4
Heathcote St CV6 .... 113 A7
Heathcote Way CV34. 161 D4
Heathcot Pl WS13........ 8 F5
Heath Cres CV14 ..... 114 A6
Heath Croft B31 ..... 123 A7
Heath Croft Rd B75 ... 32 D1
Heath Ct ② B12 .... 86 F5
HEATH END
Bloxwich 15 A1
Nuneaton 72 E2
Heath End Rd
Madeley Heath DY9 .. 120 D7
Nuneaton CV10 .... 72 E2
Heather Ave WS5 ..... 43 B4
Heather Cl
Birmingham B36 .... 70 A8
Lichfield WS13.......... 3 D1
Nuneaton CV10 .... 73 F3
Walsall WS5 .... 28 A8
Wednesfield WV11 ..... 26 E5
Heather Court Gdns B74. 46 A8
Heather Croft B44 ..... 44 F1
Heather Ct B13 .... 86 D3
Heather Dale B13 ..... 86 C2
Heather Dr
Bedworth CV12 .... 77 E2
Birmingham B45 ..... 121 F6
Huntington WS12...... 1 D5
Heather Gr
Solihull B91 .... 107 E6
Willenhall WV12 .... 27 E4
Heather Ho B38....... 103 F1
Heatherleigh Rd B36... 69 F8
Heather Mews ② 2 A8
Heather Rd
Binley Woods CV3 .... 135 D7
Birmingham, Great Barr
B43 .... 54 D8
Birmingham, Small Heath
B10................. 87 F8
Cannock WS12...........2 A8
Coventry CV2........... 96 C2
Dudley DY1 .... 51 C4
Smethwick B67 .... 64 E6
Walsall WS3............ 28 A8
Heather Valley WS12 .. 2 D6
Heath Farm Rd
Codsall WV8............ 10 B2
Stourbridge DY8 .... 80 E3
Heathfield Ave B20 ... 66 B8
Heathfield Cl
Cradley Heath B64.... 62 F2
Dorridge B93 .... 128 A5
Heathfield Cres DY11.. 116 B4
Heathfield Ct B19 ..... 66 B7
Heathfield Dr WS3 .... 14 B2
**Heathfield Foundation
Technology Coll The**
B64.................. 62 F2
Heathfield Gdns
Stourbridge DY8 .... 80 F4
Wolverhampton WV11.. 27 A5
Heathfield La WS10 ... 41 C6
Heathfield Lane W WS10. 41 B6
Heathfield Prim Sch B19.. 66 C8
Heathfield Rd
Birmingham, King's Heath
B14................. 104 F8
Birmingham, Lozells B19... 66 C8
Coventry CV5......... 112 C2
Halesowen B63 .... 82 E3

Heathfield Rd continued
Redditch B97 .... 153 A1
Sutton Coldfield B74 .. 31 F3
Heathfields B48 .... 23 E8
Heathfields Inf Sch B77.. 35 F6
Heathfield Way B64 ... 62 F1
Heath Gap Rd WS11..... 1 F3
Heath Gdns B91 ..... 106 D6
Heath Gn DY1 .... 50 F5
Heath Gr WV8 .... 10 B3
HEATH GREEN 140 F3
Heathgreen Cl B37... 70 D3
Heath Green La B8 ... 67 E4
Heath Green Rd B18 .. 65 E4
Heath Green Way CV4. 131 F6
HEATH HAYES 2 F1
Heath Hayes Prim Sch
WS12..................2 F2
Heath Hill Rd WV6 .... 23 E1
Heath Ho B14 .... 104 F2
Heath House La WV8 .. 23 E8
Heath La
Kidderminster DY10...117 C1
Stourbridge DY8 .... 81 A4
West Bromwich B71 ... 53 D7
Heathland Ave B34..... 69 A7
Heathland Ct WS12 .... 2 D2
Heathlands Cl DY6 .... 60 E8
Heathlands Cres B73.. 45 F1
Heathlands Rd B31 .. 103 A1
Heathlands Prim (NC) Sch
B34.................. 68 F7
Heathlands Rd B73.... 45 F1
Heathlands The
② Rowley Regis B65... 63 C1
Stourbridge DY8 .... 81 B4
Heath Lane Hospl B71 . 53 D7
Heathleigh Rd B38... 123 C8
Heathley La B78 .... 34 E5
Heathmere Ave B25.... 88 D8
Heathmere Dr B37 .... 69 F2
Heath Mill La B9 .... 67 A1
Heath Mount Prim Sch
B12.................. 86 F6
Heath Park Bsns & Ent Coll
WV11 .... 26 A5
Heath Rd
Bedworth CV12 .... 77 F1
Birmingham B30 ..... 103 D5
Coventry CV4......... 114 A4
Darlaston WS10....... 41 E8
Dudley DY2 .... 62 C2
Hollywood B47....... 125 A7
Solihull B91 .... 107 D6
Willenhall WV12 .... 13 D1
Heath Rise B14 ..... 105 A1
Heath Road S B31 ... 103 B4
Heathside Dr
Birmingham B38 ..... 104 B2
Walsall WS3............ 15 A4
Heath St
Birmingham B18 .... 65 E4
Cannock WS12...........2 B7
Rowley Regis B65 .... 63 C1
Tamworth B79 .... 21 C5
Heath Street Ind Est B66. 65 D5
Heath Street S B18.... 65 E4
Heath Terr
Beausale CV35......... 146 C2
Royal Leamington Spa
CV32................. 156 E1
HEATH TOWN 26 A4
Heath Trad Pk B66 .... 65 D5
Heath View
Cannock WS12...........5 E8
Willenhall WS2 .... 27 F3
Heath Way
Birmingham B34 .... 69 B6
Heathway CV34......... 69 A2
Heathy Farm Cl B32.. 84 B1
Heathy Rise B32 ..... 84 A2
Heaton Cl WV10 .... 11 E5
Heaton Dr
Birmingham B15 .... 85 E8
Sutton Coldfield B73 ... 45 F8
Heaton Rd B91 .... 107 A7
Heaton St B18......... 66 B5
Hebden B77 .... 36 B8
Hebden Ave CV34 .... 155 F1
Hebden Gr
Birmingham B28 ..... 105 E3
Willenhall WV12 .... 13 B1
Hebden Way CV11 .... 74 A2
Heckley Rd CV7 .... 96 A7
Heddle Gr CV6 .... 114 B8
Heddon Pl B7 .... 67 A3
Hedera Cl WS5 .... 43 B3
Hedera Rd B98 .... 154 F6
Hedgefield Gr B63 .... 82 C4
Hedgefield Way CV43. 131 E8
Hedgerow Cl
Cannock WS12...........1 F7
Redditch B97 .... 158 F8
Hedgerow Dr DY6...... 49 D1
Hedgerows The
Lichfield WS14.......... 9 B5
Nuneaton CV10 .... 72 F6
Romsley B62 .... 100 F4
Tamworth B77 .... 35 F8
Hedgerow Wlk
Coventry CV6........... 95 B4
Wolverhampton WV8... 10 E1
Hedgetree Croft B37... 70 C2

Hedge Way CV10. . . . . 72 C7
Hedging La B77. . . . . 35 E5
Hedging Lane Ind Est B77 35 E5
Hedgings The B34 . . . . . . 69 B6
Hedgley Gr B33 . . . . 69 A4
Hedingham Gr B37. . . . 70 D2
Hedley Croft B35 . . . . . . 58 B4
HEDNESFORD. 2 D5
Hednesford Hills Common
  Nature Reserve* WS12. . . 2 E5
Hednesford Hills Raceway*
  WS12 . . . . .2 F5
Hednesford Rd
  Brownhills WS8 . . . . 6 C2
  Cannock, Blackfords WS11 . . 1 F2
  Cannock WS12. . . . . 2 E1
  Norton Canes WS11 . . . . . . 5 F6
Hednesford St WS11 . . . . . 1 E1
Hednesford StaWS12 . . . . . .2 E1
Hednesford Valley High Sch
  WS12 . . . . .2 A6
Heeley Rd B29. . . . . 85 F1
Heemstede La CV32. . . 157 A2
Heera Cl CV6 . . . . 113 D8
Hefford Dr B66 . . . . 65 A6
Helena Cl CV10 . . . . 72 F3
Helena St B21 . . . . 66 C4
Helen Dixon Ct B B13 . . 86 F4
Helenny Cl WV11 . . . . 26 A5
Helen St CV6 . . . . 113 F6
Hele Rd CV3 . . . . 133 D6
Helford Cl DY4 . . . . 51 D4
Heligan Pl WS12 . . . . 2 E2
Hellaby Cl B73 . . . . 46 C4
Hellaby Ho B73 . . . . 57 A7
Hellaby Ho B74 . . . . 31 F3
Hellidon Cl B Cl CV32 . . 157 A2
Hellier Ave DY4. . . . . 52 B4
Hellier Rd WV10 . . . . 11 E2
Hellier St DY2 . . . . 62 C8
Helming Dr WV1. . . . . 26 B3
Helmingham Rd P WV9 . 20 D7
Helmsdale Rd CV32. . . 157 B5
Helmsdale Way DY3. . . 51 A7
Helmsley Cl DY5 . . . . 81 C8
Helmsley Rd WV11. . . . . 26 C8
Helmswood Dr B37 . . . . 90 C8
Helston Cl
  Nuneaton CV11 . . . . 74 A5
  Stourbridge DY8 . . . . 60 C2
  Tamworth B79 . . . . 21 C8
  Walsall WS5. . . . . 43 D7
Helston Gr B11 . . . . 88 A3
Helston Rd WS5. . . . . 43 D7
Helvellyn Way B71 . . . . . 53 C6
Hembs Cres B43 . . . . 54 C8
Hemdale CV11 . . . . 74 A4
Hemdale Bsns Pk CV11 . 74 A4
Hemingford Rd CV2 . . . 115 A8
Hemingford Rd B98. . . . 159 E8
Hemingford Croft B37 . . 90 A7
Hemlingford Rd
  Birmingham B37 . . . . 69 F6
  Sutton Coldfield B76 . . . . 58 A6
Hemlock Bsns CtrWS11. . .2 B2
Hemlock Pk WS11 . . . . . . .2 B2
Hemlock Way WS11. . . . . .2 B3
Hemmings Cl
  Radford Semele CV31. . . 162 E5
  Stourbridge DY8 . . . . 80 F5
  Wolverhampton WV10. . . 25 E3
Hemmings St WV13. . . . 41 C8
Hemming St DY11. . . . . 116 C4
Hemmings Yard Dy6. . . . 61 A8
Hemplands Rd DY8. . . . 80 F5
Hempole La DY4 . . . . 52 D6
Hemsby Cl CV4 . . . . 132 A7
Hemsworth Dr CV12. . . . 79 B2
Hembury Dr B37. . . . . 70 C4
Henbury Rd B27 . . . . 88 D3
Henderson Cl
  Allesley CV5. . . . . 112 C7
  Lichfield WS14. . . . . 9 D7
Henderson Ct D B68. . . 84 B8
Henderson Way B65 . . . 63 C1
Henderson Wlk DY4. . . . 52 B8
Hendon Cl
  Dudley DY2 . . . . 50 D2
  Wolverhampton WV10. . . 25 E7
Hendon Rd B11. . . . . 87 B5
Hendre Cl CV5 . . . . 112 D2
Heneage Pl B D B7. . . . . . 67 A4
Heneage St B7. . . . . 67 A4
Heneage Street W B7 . . 66 F4
Henfield Cl WV11 . . . . . . 26 D7
Hengham Rd B26 . . . . . . 69 A1
Hen La CV6 . . . . 95 D3
Henley Cl
  Burntwood WS7. . . . . 7 B5
  Nuneaton CV11 . . . . 73 F8
  Sutton Coldfield B73 . . . . 57 B8
  Tamworth B79 . . . . 21 C6
  Tipton DY4. . . . . 52 D5
  Walsall WS3. . . . . 14 E1
Henley Coll Coventry
  CV2 . . . . 114 C8
Henley Cres B91. . . . . . . 107 B7
Henley Ct
  Coventry CV2 . . . . 114 D7
  Lichfield WS14. . . . . 9 B6
Henleydale D B90. . . . . 126 C8
Henley Dr B74 . . . . 32 A3
HENLEY GREEN 114 D8

Henley Green Prim Sch
  CV2 . . . . 114 D7
Henley Mill La CV2 . . . . 114 C7
Henley Park Ind Est CV2 114 E7
Henley Rd
  Coventry CV2. . . . . 114 D7
  Whitnash CV31 . . . . 162 B5
  Wolverhampton WV10. . . 11 B1
Henley St B11 . . . . 87 B7
Henley Wlk CV2 . . . . 114 D8
Henlow Cl DY4 . . . . 51 D5
Henlow Rd B14. . . . . 105 A2
Hennalls The B36. . . . . . 68 F7
Hennals Ave B97. . . . . . 152 F2
Henn Dr DY4 . . . . 40 E1
Henne Dr WV14. . . . . 40 C1
Henne St WV4 . . . . 52 A8
Henrietta St
  Birmingham B19 . . . . . . 164 B4
  Coventry CV6. . . . . 113 E5
Henry Boteler Rd CV4 . . 132 B7
Henry Boys' Almshouses
  WS11 . . . . 42 D8
Henry Ct DY1 . . . . 51 B1
Henry Lloyd Ind EstWS10 41 C7
Henry Rd B25. . . . . 88 C7
Henry St
  Coventry CV1. . . . . 165 B3
  Hinckley LE10 . . . . 71 A2
  Kenilworth CV8 . . . . 148 A5
  Nuneaton CV11 . . . . 73 C2
  Walsall WS2. . . . . 28 D1
Henry Tanday Ct D
  CV32 . . . . 156 E1
Henry Wlk B60. . . . . 150 E7
Hensborough B90. . . . . 126 A5
Hensel Dr WV3 . . . . 38 C8
Henshaw Gr
  G Birmingham, Small Heath
    B10. . . . . 87 C8
  Birmingham, Yardley B25. . 88 C7
Henshaw Rd B10. . . . . . . 87 D8
Henson Rd CV12. . . . . . . 77 F1
Henstead St B15 . . . . . . 86 D8
Hentland Cl B98 . . . . . . 154 D4
Henwood Cl WV6 . . . . . . 24 C3
Henwood La B91. . . . . . 108 B4
Henwood Rd WV6. . . . . . 24 D3
Henzel Croft DY5 . . . . . . 61 C3
Hepburn Cl WV9. . . . . . . 30 A4
Hepburn Edge B24. . . . . 57 B4
Hepworth Cl WV6. . . . . . 23 F4
Hepworth Rd CV3 . . . . . 115 B1
Herald Ave CV5. . . . . 112 D1
Herald Bsns Pk CV3. . . 134 F7
Herald Ct D B13 . . . . 51 C1
Herald Rd B26. . . . . 90 C4
Heralds Ct D CV34. . . . . 161 B8
Herald Way
  Coventry CV3. . . . . 135 A7
  Hinckley LE10 . . . . 71 D2
Herald Way Marsh Nature
  Reserve* CV3 . . . . 134 F6
Herbert Art Gall & Mus*
  CV1. . . . . 165 C2
Herbert Austin Dr B60. . 121 E1
Herbert Rd
  Aldridge WS9. . . . . 16 A1
  Birmingham, Handsworth
    B21. . . . . 54 F1
  Birmingham, Small Heath
    B10. . . . . 87 C8
  Smethwick B67 . . . . 65 A1
  Solihull B91. . . . . 107 B4
Herbert's La CV8. . . . . . . 148 A5
Herberts Park Rd WS10 . 41 B6
Herbert St
  Bilston WV14 . . . . 40 B6
  Nuneaton CV10 . . . . 72 E3
  Redditch B98. . . . . 153 E4
  West Bromwich B70 . . . . 53 D3
  Wolverhampton WV1. . . 163 C4
Herbhill Cl WV4. . . . . 39 D4
Hereford Ave D B12. . . . 87 A6
Hereford Cl
  Aldridge WS9. . . . . 30 A8
  Barwell LE9 . . . . 71 F6
  Birmingham B45. . . . . . . 102 A2
  Kidderminster DY11. . . . 116 A5
  Nuneaton CV10 . . . . 72 E4
Hereford Ho WV1. . . . . . 163 B4
Hereford Pl B71 . . . . 53 B7
Hereford Rd
  Birmingham B68. . . . . . . 84 B7
  Bramcote CV11 . . . . 79 E5
  Cannock WS12. . . . . 2 B4
  Dudley DY2 . . . . 62 E3
Hereford St WS2. . . . . . . 28 E4
Hereford Way B78 . . . . . 21 A2
Hereford Wlk B37. . . . . . 69 F1
Hereward Coll CV4. . . . 111 F1
Hereward Rise B62 . . . . 83 C5
Herford Way LE10. . . . . . 75 F6
Heritage Cl B68. . . . . 64 C4
Heritage Ct
  Birmingham B18 . . . . 66 C4
  Coventry CV4. . . . . 132 D3
  Kenilworth CV8 . . . . 148 B7
  Lichfield WS14. . . . . 9 D6
Heritage Dr CV6 . . . . 96 D6
Heritage The D WS1. . . 28 E1
Heritage Way
  Birmingham B33 . . . . 69 D3
  Tipton DY4. . . . . 52 B5
Hermes Cl CV34. . . . . . . 161 E5
Hermes Cres CV34. . . . . 114 E6
Hermes Ct CV34 . . . . 161 E5
Hermes Rd B74. . . . . 31 F3

Hermes Rd
  Birmingham B26 . . . . 90 C4
  Lichfield WS13. . . . . 3 D1
Hermione Cl CV34. . . . . 161 F3
Hermitage Cl B78. . . . . . 22 F1
Hermitage Dr B76 . . . . . 47 A4
Hermitage Rd
  Birmingham B15 . . . . 85 C8
  Birmingham, Gravelly Hill
    B23 . . . . 56 E3
  Coventry CV2. . . . . 114 D4
  Solihull B91. . . . . 107 C6
Hermitage The B91. . . . 107 C6
Hermitage Way CV8. . . . 148 A3
Hermit's Croft CV3 . . . . 133 D8
Hermit St DY3 . . . . 50 D5
Hernall Croft B26 . . . . . . 89 F8
Herne Cl B18. . . . . 66 A4
Hernefield Rd B34 . . . . . 69 A7
Hernehurst B32. . . . . 84 C6
Heronbank CV4 . . . . 111 C2
Heron Cl
  Alvechurch B48 . . . . 139 A7
  Brownhills WS8 . . . . 15 E7
  Cheswick Green B90. . . . 126 D4
Heron Ct B B73 . . . . 57 B7
Herondale CV12 . . . . .2 B4
Herondale Cres DY8 . . . 80 C4
Herondale Rd
  Birmingham B26 . . . . 88 F6
  Stourbridge DY8 . . . . 80 C4
Heronfield Cl B98. . . . . 154 C5
Heronfield Dr B31. . . . . 122 F6
Heronfield Way B91. . . . 107 E5
Heron Ho CV3 . . . . 114 B2
Heron Mill WS3. . . . . 14 E3
Heron Rd B68 . . . . 64 A2
Heronry The WV6. . . . . . 23 F2
Herons Ct LE10 . . . . 75 A7
Heronsville Ho DY4 . . . . 52 B3
Herons Way B29 . . . . 85 C3
Heronswood Dr DY5 . . . 61 D1
Heronswood Prim Sch
  DY10. . . . . 117 A2
Heronswood Rd
  Birmingham B45 . . . . . . 122 B6
  Kidderminster DY10. . . . 117 A2
Heronville Dr B70. . . . . . 53 A7
Heronville Rd B70 . . . . . 53 A6
Heron Way B45. . . . . 121 F7
Herrick Rd
  Birmingham B8 . . . . 67 E5
  Coventry CV2. . . . . 114 D3
Herrick St WV3. . . . . 163 A2
Herringshaw Croft B76. . 46 E3
Hertford Pl CV1. . . . . 165 A2
Hertford St B11. . . . . 87 A5
Hertford Way B93. . . . . . 128 B4
Hervey Gr B24. . . . . 57 D6
Hesket Ave B68 . . . . 64 C5
Hesketh Cres B23. . . . . . 56 C5
Hesketh Pl B37 . . . . 99 F8
Hesleden B77. . . . . 36 B8
Heslop Cl CV3 . . . . 134 F8
Hessian Cl WV14. . . . . . . 40 B2
Hestia Dr B29. . . . . 103 E8
Heston Ave B42. . . . . 55 B8
Hetton Cl D CV34. . . . . . 155 F1
Hever Ave B44. . . . . 45 A1
Hever Cl DY1 . . . . 50 E3
Hewell Ave B45 . . . . 150 F7
Hewell Cl
  Birmingham B31. . . . . . . 122 F7
  Kingswinford DY6 . . . . . . 49 D1
  Redditch B97. . . . . 152 C6
Hewell La
  Barnt Green B45 . . . . . . 138 D8
  Redditch B60, B97. . . . . 152 D6
Hewell Rd
  Barnt Green B45 . . . . . . 138 D8
  Redditch B97. . . . . 153 D4
Hewell Road Swimming Pool
  B97. . . . . 153 C5
Hewitson Gdns B67 . . . . 64 F2
Hewitt Ave CV6 . . . . 113 B4
Hewitt Cl WS13 . . . . .3 A2
Hewitt St WS10 . . . . 41 C5
Hewston Croft WS12. . . . .2 D4
Hexby Cl CV2 . . . . 115 A6
Hexham Way DY1. . . . . . 50 F2
Hexton Cl B90. . . . . 105 D2
Hexworthy Ave CV3 . . . 133 B5
Heybarnes Cir B10 . . . . . 87 F7
Heybarnes Rd B10 . . . . . 88 A8
Heybrook Cl CV2 . . . . . . 114 C2
Heycott Gr B38 . . . . 104 C2
Heycroft CV4 . . . . 132 D4
Heydon Rd
  Brierley Hill DY5 . . . . 61 B6
  Finstall B60. . . . . 137 D1
Heyford Cl CV2 . . . . 96 D3
Heyford Gr B91 . . . . 127 C8
Heyford Way B35 . . . . . . 58 B4
Heygate Way WS9 . . . . . 16 B1
Heyland Cnr B10. . . . . . . 67 F1
Heynesfield Rd B33 . . . . 69 C3
Heythrop Gr B13 . . . . . . 105 D8
Heyville Croft CV8 . . . . 148 C3
Heywood Cl CV6. . . . . . . 114 A7
Hibberd Ct CV8. . . . . . . 147 F4
Hickling Rd WS11. . . . . . . 5 C6
Hickman Ave WV1, WV2. 40 A8
Hickman Gdns B16. . . . . 65 F1
Hickman Rd
  Bilston WV14. . . . . 40 C5
  Birmingham B11. . . . . . . 87 B6
  Brierley Hill DY5 . . . . 61 C4

Hickman Rd continued
  Tipton DY4. . . . . 51 F8
Hickman's Ave B64 . . . . 62 E2
Hickmans Ct D B62. . . . 84 A6
Hickmans Green Cl
  CV34 . . . . 160 B3
Hickman St DY9 . . . . 81 C6
Hickmerelands La DY3 . . 39 C1
Hickory Cl CV2. . . . . 96 F1
Hickory Ct WS11. . . . . 2 C2
Hickory Dr B17 . . . . 65 A2
Hicks Cl CV34 . . . . 155 E2
Hidcote Ave B76. . . . . . . 58 A8
Hidcote Cl
  Nuneaton CV11 . . . . 78 F8
  Royal Leamington Spa
    CV31. . . . . 162 C5
Hidcote Gr
  Birmingham, Garret's Green
    B33 . . . . 89 C8
  Birmingham, Marston Green
    B37 . . . . 90 A7
Hidcote Rd CV8. . . . . . . 148 C6
Hidson Rd B23. . . . . 56 C5
Higgins Ave WV14 . . . . . 40 D2
Higgins La B32 . . . . 84 C5
Higgins Wlk B66. . . . . . . 65 B6
Higgs Field Cres B64. . . 63 B1
Higgs Rd WV11. . . . . 13 A1
Higham La CV11 . . . . 73 E7
Higham Lane Sch CV10. . 73 D6
Higham's Cl B65. . . . . . . 63 B3
Higham Way
  Hinckley LE10. . . . . 75 E7
  Wombourne WV5. . . . . . . 49 A5
High Arcal Dr DY2 . . . . . 50 F7
High Arcal Rd DY3 . . . . . 49 F4
High Arcal Sch The DY3 . 50 F6
High Ash Cl CV7 . . . . 95 F7
High Ave B64 . . . . 82 F8
High Bank WS11. . . . . 4 E8
High Beech CV5 . . . . 112 A6
High Beeches B43 . . . . . 43 D1
HIGHBRIDGE. 15 B6
Highbridge Rd
  Dudley DY2 . . . . 62 B3
  Sutton Coldfield B73 . . . . 46 A1
High Brink Rd B46. . . . . . 70 F7
Highbury Cl WV9 . . . . . . 11 A2
High Broome Ct B78 . . . 21 A3
High Brow B17 . . . . 85 B7
Highbury Ave
  Birmingham B21 . . . . 65 F8
  Rowley Regis B65 . . . . . . 63 D3
Highbury Cl B65 . . . . 63 D3
Highbury Ct B13 . . . . . . 104 E7
Highbury Gn CV10 . . . . . 72 C7
Highbury Rd
  Birmingham B14 . . . . . . 104 D8
  Dudley B68. . . . . 64 B5
  Smethwick B66 . . . . 64 D7
  Sutton Coldfield B74 . . . . 31 C3
Highclare St Paul's Sch
  B74. . . . . 46 C7
Highclare St B72. . . . . . . 46 C1
Highclare Senior Sch B23 57 A5
High Clere B64 . . . . 83 A7
Highcliffe Rd B77 . . . . . . 35 D8
Highcrest Cl B31. . . . . . 123 A7
Highcroft WS3. . . . . 15 B6
High Croft
  Aldridge WS9. . . . . 16 B2
  Birmingham B43 . . . . 43 C1
Highcroft Cl B92 . . . . 89 C2
Highcroft Cl CV32 . . . . . 156 C1
High Croft Cres WS9 . . . . 9 C7
Highcroft Dr B74 . . . . 31 E3
Highcroft Rd B23 . . . . . . 56 E4
Highdown Cres D B90 . . 127 A6
Highdown Rd CV31. . . . 162 A6
High Elms La B60. . . . . . 151 E1
High Ercal Ave DY5 . . . . 61 C2
High Farm Rd
  Halesowen, Hasbury B63 . . 82 F3
  Halesowen, Hurst Green
    B62. . . . . 83 F8
Highfield Cl
  Cannock WS11. . . . . 2 B5
  Sutton Coldfield B73 . . . . 46 B1
Highfield Ct
  Birmingham B73 . . . . 56 F7
Highfield Gdns WS14. . . . .9 E6
Highfield La
  Birmingham B32 . . . . 84 B4
  Clent DY9 . . . . 100 A3
  Corley CV7 . . . . 94 D8
  D Halesowen B63 . . . . . 83 A3
Highfield Mews B63. . . . 82 D6
Highfield Pl B14. . . . . . . 105 D5
Highfield Prim Sch B8 . . 67 E5

Highfield Rd
  Birmingham, Edgbaston
    B15 . . . . 86 A8
  Birmingham, Moseley B13. . 87 B3
  Birmingham, Newton B43 . 54 C7
  Birmingham, Saltley B8. . . 67 E5
  Birmingham, Yardley Wood B14,
    B28 . . . . 105 D5
  Bromsgrove B61. . . . . . . 150 E8
  Burntwood WS7. . . . . 7 C7
  Cannock WS12. . . . . 2 E1
  Coventry CV2. . . . . 113 F4
  Dudley DY2. . . . . 51 E1
  Halesowen B63 . . . . 82 D5
  Kidderminster DY10. . . . 117 A8
  Nuneaton CV11 . . . . 73 E2
  Redditch B97 . . . . 158 D8
  Rowley Regis B65 . . . . . . 63 B1
  Sedgley DY3 . . . . 39 D1
  Smethwick B67 . . . . 65 A5
  Stourbridge DY8 . . . . 61 A2
  Studley B80. . . . . 159 D4
  Tipton DY4. . . . . 52 B8
  Walsall WS5. . . . . 15 A4
Highfield Road N WS3. . . 14 F5
HIGHFIELDS
  Burntwood. 6 F4
  Coseley 40 C3
Highfields
  Bromsgrove B61. . . . . . . 136 C1
  Burntwood WS7. . . . . 7 B7
Highfields Ct WV4 . . . . . 38 D6
Highfields Dr
  Dudley WV14 . . . . 40 D3
  Wombourne WV5. . . . . . . 49 A5
Highfields Grange WS6 . . 4 D1
Highfields Pk WS6 . . . . . . 4 D1
Highfields Prim Sch
  Burntwood WS7. . . . . 7 C7
  D Cradley Heath B65 . . . 83 C8
Highfields Rd
  Burntwood WS7. . . . . 6 F4
  Dudley WV14 . . . . 40 D3
  Hinckley LE10 . . . . 71 E1
Highfields Science Specialist
  Sch WV4 . . . . 38 C5
Highfields The WV6. . . . . 24 A3
Highfield Terr
  Birmingham B18 . . . . 66 A5
  Royal Leamington Spa
    CV32. . . . . 156 D1
Highfield Way WS9 . . . . . 16 B2
HIGHGATE. 86 F7
Highgate
  Dudley DY3. . . . . 50 E5
  Sutton Coldfield B74 . . . . 31 A1
Highgate Ave
  Walsall WS1. . . . . 42 F8
  Wolverhampton WV4. . . . 38 D6
Highgate Bsns Ctr B12. . 87 B6
Highgate Cl
  Birmingham B12 . . . . 86 F7
  Kidderminster DY11. . . . 116 A4
  Walsall WS1. . . . . 42 F7
Highgate Ct D WS1. . . . 42 F8
Highgate Dr WS1. . . . . . . 42 F7
Highgate Ho D B5. . . . . . 86 E8
Highgate Middleway B12. 86 F7
Highgate Pl B12 . . . . 87 A7
Highgate Rd
  Birmingham B12 . . . . 87 A6
  Dudley DY1, DY2. . . . . . . 61 F6
  Walsall WS1. . . . . 42 F7
Highgate Ret Pk B11. . . . 87 A7
Highgate Sq B12. . . . . . . 86 F7
Highgate Square Craft Ctr*
  D B12. . . . . 86 F7
Highgate St
  Birmingham B12 . . . . 86 F7
  Cradley Heath B64. . . . . . 62 F2
High Gn WS11. . . . . 1 D1
High Grange WS11. . . . . . 2 A5
High Green Ct Sh Ctr
  WS11. . . . . 1 D1
Highgrove
  Coventry CV4. . . . . 131 F5
  Wolverhampton WV6. . . . 24 C3
Highgrove Cl
  Tamworth B79. . . . . 21 B7
  Willenhall WV12 . . . . 27 B7
Highgrove Pl DY1. . . . . . . 50 F2
High Haden Cres B64 . . . 83 A8
High Haden Rd B64 . . . . 83 A8
HIGH HEATH 15 C2
High Heath Cl B30 . . . . 103 D5
High Hill WV11 . . . . 13 A2
High Holborn DY3. . . . . . 50 D7
High House Dr B45. . . . . 121 F3
High House La B60. . . . . 152 A6
Highland Ho B62. . . . . . . 83 C8
Highland Mews WV14. . . 40 D1
Highland Rd
  Birmingham, Erdington
    B23 . . . . 56 F6
  Birmingham, Great Barr B43 43 E3
  Cannock WS12. . . . . 1 C4
  Coventry CV5. . . . . 112 F1
  Cradley Heath B64. . . . . . 62 E2
  Dudley DY1. . . . . 51 A3
  Kenilworth CV8 . . . . 148 C7
  Royal Leamington Spa
    CV32. . . . . 157 B4
High Land Rd WS9 . . . . . 16 B3
Highland Ridge B62. . . . 83 E5
Highlands Cl
  Kidderminster DY11. . . . 116 A5
  Warwick CV34. . . . . 161 A8
Highlands Ct B90 . . . . . 126 E8

Hig–Hoc 205

Highlands Rd
Solihull B90 .... 126 F8
Wolverhampton WV3 .... 38 D8
Highland Way B98 .... 159 A7
High Leasowes B63 .... 83 A4
Highley Cl
Kidderminster DY11 .... 116 B2
Redditch B98 .... 154 E4
Highley Dr CV6 .... 113 C6
High Mdws
Bromsgrove B60 .... 150 D7
Wolverhampton WV6 .... 24 C3
Wombourne WV5 .... 49 B6
High Meadow Inf Sch B46 70 F8
High Meadow Rd B38 .... 104 A2
Highmoor Cl
Dudley WV14 .... 40 D3
Willenhall WV12 .... 27 B7
Highmoor Rd B65 .... 63 B3
High More Dr B32 .... 102 C8
High Mount St WS12 .... 2 B6
High Oak DY5 .... 61 C7
Highover Dr B75 .... 32 A4
Highpark Ave DY8 .... 80 D5
High Park Cl
Coventry CV5 .... 111 F3
Sedgley DY3 .... 50 D8
Smethwick B66 .... 65 B5
High Park Cnr B7 .... 67 B6
High Park Cres DY3 .... 39 D1
High Park Rd B63 .... 82 C5
High Park St B7 .... 67 B6
High Point B15 .... 85 E6
High Rd WV12 .... 27 C5
High Ridge WS9 .... 29 F5
High Ridge Cl
Aldridge WS9 .... 29 E5
Darlaston WS10 .... 41 A4
High St Duchess Par B70 .. 53 D3
High St Princess Par B70 .. 53 D3
High St
Aldridge WS9 .... 30 B6
Astwood Bank B96 .... 158 E1
Bedworth CV12 .... 78 B2
Belbroughton DY9 .... 119 E7
Bilston WV14 .... 40 D5
Birmingham, Aston B6, B19 .. 66 E7
Birmingham B4 .... 164 C2
Birmingham, Castle Vale B35 .... 58 B4
Birmingham, Erdington B23 .. 56 F4
Birmingham, Harborne B17 .. 85 D6
Birmingham, King's Heath B14 .... 104 E8
Birmingham, Quinton B32 .. 84 A6
Birmingham, Saltley B8 .... 67 D5
Brierley Hill, Barrow Hill DY5 .... 61 C7
Brierley Hill, Brockmoor DY5 .... 61 C4
Brierley Hill, Quarry Bank DY5 .... 82 A8
Bromsgrove B61 .... 137 A2
Brownhills, Clayhanger WS8 15 E6
Brownhills, Vigo WS9 .... 15 F3
Brownhills WS8 .... 15 F8
Burntwood, Chasetown WS7 .. 6 F6
Cheslyn Hay WS6 .... 4 D2
Coleshill B46 .... 70 F7
Coventry CV1 .... 165 C2
Coventry, Keresley CV6 .... 94 F1
Cradley Heath B64 .... 62 D1
Cubbington CV32 .... 157 E5
Darlaston WS10 .... 41 A4
Dudley DY1 .... 51 C1
7 Dudley, Old Dock DY1 .. 62 B8
1 Halesowen B63 .... 83 B3
Hampton-in-A B92 .... 109 A7
Kenilworth CV8 .... 147 E5
Kidderminster DY10 .... 116 E6
Kingswinford DY6 .... 60 E6
Kingswinford, Wall Heath DY6 .... 60 C8
Knowle B93 .... 128 C6
Norton Canes WS11 .... 6 B5
Nuneaton CV11 .... 73 B4
Rowley Regis B65 .... 63 C1
Royal Leamington Spa CV31 .... 162 A7
Ryton-on-D CV8 .... 135 B1
Sedgley DY3 .... 50 D8
Smethwick B66 .... 65 A5
Solihull B91 .... 107 C3
Solihull, Shirley B90 .... 105 D2
Stourbridge, Amblecote DY8 80 F7
Stourbridge DY8 .... 81 A5
Stourbridge, Lye DY9 .... 81 E5
Stourbridge, Wollaston DY8 .. 80 E7
Stourbridge, Wordsley DY8 .. 60 E2
Studley B80 .... 159 E4
Sutton Coldfield B72 .... 46 C5
Tamworth B77 .... 35 C5
Tipton, Princes End DY4 .... 51 F8
Tipton, Tipton Green DY4 .... 51 E5
Walsall, Pelsall WS3 .... 15 A4
Walsall, Wallington Heath WS3 .... 14 B1
Walsall WS1 .... 28 E1
Warwick CV34 .... 160 E6
Wednesfield WV11 .... 26 D5
West Bromwich B70 .... 53 C3
Wolverhampton WV6 .... 24 D4
Wombourne WV5 .... 49 B7
High Street Bordesley B12 .... 67 A1
High Street Deritend B12 .. 66 F1
Highters Cl B14 .... 105 B2
HIGHTER'S HEATH 105 B2
Highter's Heath La B14 .. 105 A2
Highters Heath Prim Sch B14 .... 105 B3
Highters Rd B14 .... 105 A3
High Timbers B45 .... 101 F1
HIGH TOWN 2 A5
Hightown B63 .... 82 C6
Hightree Cl B32 .... 84 B1
High Trees B20 .... 54 F3
High Trees Cl B98 .... 158 E7
High Trees Ho B69 .... 63 F3
High Trees Rd B93 .... 128 A7
Highview 9 WS1 .... 42 F8
High View WV14 .... 39 F1
Highview Dr DY6 .... 60 F4
High View Dr CV7 .... 95 C7
High View Rd CV32 .... 157 C5
Highview St DY2 .... 51 E1
Highwaymans Croft CV4 132 D5
Highwood Ave B92 .... 89 A1
High Wood Cl DY6 .... 60 C6
Highwood Croft B38 .... 103 D1
Hiker Gr 3 B37 .... 70 D2
Hilary Cres DY1 .... 51 B6
Hilary Dr
Aldridge WS9 .... 30 A5
Sutton Coldfield B76 .... 47 A3
Wolverhampton WV3 .... 38 D7
Hilary Gr B31 .... 102 F4
Hilary Rd
Coventry CV4 .... 132 E6
Nuneaton CV10 .... 72 F5
Hilden Rd B7 .... 67 B4
Hilderic Cres DY1 .... 61 F7
Hilderstone Rd B25 .... 88 C6
Hildicks Cres WS3 .... 28 F7
Hildicks Pl WS3 .... 28 F7
Hilditch Way CV11 .... 73 E2
HILL 32 A4
Hillaire Cl B38 .... 104 C2
HILL AND CAKEMORE 83 D7
Hillaries Rd B23 .... 56 D2
Hillary Ave WS10 .... 42 C3
Hillary Crest DY3 .... 50 E5
Hillary Prim Sch WS2 .... 42 C7
Hillary St WS2 .... 42 C7
Hill Ave WV4 .... 39 F3
Hill Avenue Prim Sch WV4 .... 39 F3
Hillbank B69 .... 63 D8
Hill Bank DY9 .... 81 F5
Hill Bank Dr B33 .... 68 D4
Hill Bank Rd
Birmingham B38 .... 104 A2
Halesowen B63 .... 82 D6
Hillborough Rd B27 .... 88 D2
Hillbrook Gr B33 .... 68 F3
Hillbrow Cres B62 .... 83 F8
Hillbury Dr WV12 .... 27 B8
Hill Cl
Birmingham B31 .... 103 C1
Royal Leamington Spa CV32 .... 157 A3
Sedgley DY3 .... 39 E1
Hill Crest
Cubbington CV32 .... 157 E5
Dudley DY3 .... 50 C4
Hill Crest (Alexandra Hospl) B98 .... 159 C6
Hillcrest Ave
Birmingham B43 .... 43 E2
Halesowen B63 .... 82 B7
Wolverhampton WV10 .... 11 E1
Hill Crest Ave DY5 .... 61 C2
Hillcrest Bsns Pk DY2 .... 62 C7
Hillcrest Cl
Dudley DY2 .... 62 C5
Tamworth B79 .... 21 B6
Hill Crest Dr WS13 .... 3 A1
Hill Crest Gdns WV12 .... 27 D5
Hill Crest Gr B44 .... 56 A7
Hillcrest Ind Est B64 .... 82 D8
Hillcrest Pk B47 .... 140 F8
Hillcrest Rd
Birmingham B43 .... 43 E2
Dudley DY2 .... 51 E1
Nuneaton CV10 .... 72 E5
Polesworth B78 .... 36 F7
Romsley B62 .... 101 A4
Sutton Coldfield B72 .... 46 C1
Hill Crest Rd B13 .... 86 E2
Hillcrest Rise WS7 .... 7 B4
Hillcrest Sch & Com Coll DY2 .... 62 C5
Hillcrest Sch & Sixth Form Ctr B32 .... 84 E3
Hillcroft Ho B14 .... 104 F2
Hillcroft Rd DY6 .... 60 E7
Hill Croft Rd B14 .... 104 C6
Hillcross Wlk B36 .... 68 F8
Hilldene Rd DY6 .... 60 C4
Hilldrop Gr 1 B17 .... 85 D3
Hilleys Croft B37 .... 69 F2
Hill Farm Ave CV11 .... 74 B1
Hill Farm Prim Sch CV6 .... 113 B7
HILLFIELD 107 A1
Hillfield Hall Ct 1 B91 .. 107 C1
Hillfield Mews 3 B91 .... 127 B8
Hillfield Rd
Birmingham B11 .... 87 D3
7 Solihull B91 .... 127 B8
HILLFIELDS
Manchester 165 D4
Romiley 113 E4
Hillfields B67 .... 64 D3
Hillfields Ho 1 CV1 .... 113 E3
Hillfields Rd DY5 .... 81 B7
Hillfield Wlk B65 .... 62 F5
Hill Fray Dr CV3 .... 134 A5
Hill Gr B20 .... 55 C2
Hill Grove Cres DY10 .... 117 A4
Hillgrove Gdns DY10 .... 117 A4
Hillhampton Cl B92 .... 89 C1
Hill Ho B66 .... 65 C6
HILL HOOK 31 E6
Hill Hook Ho B74 .... 31 E5
Hill Hook Nature Reserve★ B74 .... 31 E5
Hill Hook Rd B74 .... 31 F5
Hill House La B33 .... 68 F3
Hillhurst Gr B36 .... 58 D1
Hillhurst Rd B73 .... 45 C3
Hilliard Cl CV12 .... 78 B4
Hilliards Croft B42 .... 55 A8
Hillingford Ave B43 .... 44 D3
Hill La
Alvechurch B47, B48 .... 124 D1
Birmingham B43 .... 43 E2
Bromsgrove B60 .... 136 F1
Clent DY9 .... 99 E4
Middleton B75 .... 33 B2
Hillman B77 .... 21 E2
Hillman Dr DY2 .... 62 E7
Hillman Gr B36 .... 58 F1
Hillman Ho CV1 .... 165 B3
Hillmeads Dr DY2 .... 62 F7
Hillmeads Rd B38 .... 104 A1
Hillmorton B74 .... 31 F3
Hillmorton Cl B98 .... 154 E6
Hillmorton Rd
Coventry CV2 .... 96 C1
Dorridge B93 .... 128 A5
Sutton Coldfield B74 .... 31 F4
Hillmount Cl B28 .... 87 E2
Hill Pas B64 .... 62 E2
Hill Pk WS9 .... 16 A4
Hill Pl WV11 .... 13 A1
HILLPOOL 118 E5
Hill Rd
Keresley CV7 .... 94 F6
Tipton B69 .... 52 A2
Willenhall WV13 .... 26 E1
Hillrise LE10 .... 75 F8
Hill Rise View B60 .... 137 C6
Hillsborough Ho B27 .... 88 E2
Hillside
Brownhills WS8 .... 16 A6
Hartshill CV10 .... 72 A8
Lichfield WS14 .... 9 D6
Redditch B98 .... 153 D2
Hill Side
Coventry CV2 .... 114 A6
Dudley DY3 .... 50 C4
Hillside Ave
Brierley Hill DY5 .... 82 A8
Cradley Heath B65 .... 83 B8
Halesowen B63 .... 82 D6
Hillside Cl
Birmingham B32 .... 102 A8
Brownhills WS8 .... 16 A6
Burntwood WS7 .... 6 E5
Cannock WS12 .... 2 A7
Kidderminster DY11 .... 116 A7
Hillside Cres WS3 .... 14 F3
Hillside Croft B92 .... 89 E4
Hillside Ct B43 .... 43 E2
Hillside Dr
Birmingham, Great Barr B42 .... 55 A6
Birmingham, Kingshurst B37 69 F4
Kidderminster DY11 .... 116 A7
Lickey End B61 .... 137 B6
Nuneaton CV10 .... 72 C7
Sutton Coldfield B74 .... 44 F7
Hillside Gdns
Birmingham B37 .... 69 F4
Wolverhampton WV1 .... 26 A3
Hillside N CV2 .... 114 A6
Hillside Rd
Birmingham, Gravelly Hill B23 .... 56 D2
Birmingham, Great Barr B43 .... 43 D2
Dudley DY1 .... 51 A5
Hinckley LE10 .... 75 D6
Sutton Coldfield B74 .... 32 A4
Hill St
Bedworth CV12 .... 78 B5
Bilston WV14 .... 40 E3
Birmingham B5 .... 164 B2
Brierley Hill, Quarry Bank DY5 .... 82 A8
Brierley Hill, Silver End DY5 61 D2
Burntwood WS7 .... 6 E5
Cannock WS12 .... 2 C3
Cheslyn Hay WS6 .... 4 C2
Coventry CV1 .... 165 B3
Darlaston WS10 .... 41 E6
Dudley, Netherton DY2 .... 62 C5
Dudley, Upper Gornal DY3 .. 50 D5
Essington WV11 .... 12 F3
Halesowen B63 .... 83 A3
Hinckley LE10 .... 75 E8
Kidderminster DY11 .... 116 D6
Norton Canes WS11 .... 5 F6
Nuneaton CV10 .... 72 D4
Royal Leamington Spa CV32 .... 157 A1
Smethwick B66 .... 65 A6
Stourbridge, Amblecote DY8 80 F8
Stourbridge DY8 .... 80 F4
Stourbridge, Lye DY9 .... 81 F5
Tipton DY4 .... 51 F4
Walsall WS1 .... 28 F1
Warwick CV34 .... 161 B8
Hillstone Gdns WV10 .... 25 F8
Hillstone Prim Sch B34 .. 69 D5
Hillstone Rd B34 .... 69 D5
Hill The B32 .... 84 E2
HILL TOP
Cannock 2 C4
Nuneaton 73 C1
Oldbury 64 C3
West Bromwich 53 A7
Hilltop DY9 .... 81 F3
Hill Top
Coventry CV1 .... 165 C3
Redditch B97 .... 152 F1
West Bromwich B70 .... 53 A7
Hill Top Ave
Halesowen B62 .... 83 E7
Tamworth B79 .... 21 B8
Hilltop Cl CV8 .... 145 E8
Hill Top Cl B44 .... 55 E6
Hilltop Ct DY3 .... 50 E3
Hilltop Dr B36 .... 68 D7
Hill Top Ind Est B70 .... 52 F8
Hilltop Rd DY2 .... 62 E8
Hill Top Rd
Birmingham B31 .... 102 F3
Oldbury B68 .... 64 C2
Hill Top Wlk WS9 .... 16 C1
Hill View WS9 .... 16 B2
Hillview Cl
Halesowen B63 .... 82 E6
Lickey End B60 .... 137 C6
Hillview Rd
Birmingham B45 .... 121 E8
Lickey End B60 .... 137 C6
Hill Village Rd B75 .... 32 A4
Hillville Gdns DY8 .... 81 B3
Hill West Prim Sch B74 .. 31 F4
HILL WOOD 32 C5
Hill Wood WS3 .... 14 F2
Hillwood Ave B90 .... 127 A6
Hillwood Cl DY6 .... 60 C4
Hillwood Common Rd B75 .... 32 B6
Hillwood Rd
Birmingham B31 .... 102 E7
Halesowen B62 .... 83 C7
Sutton Coldfield B75 .... 32 C5
HILL WOOTON 156 C6
Hill Wootton Rd CV32, CV35 .... 156 C6
Hillyfields Rd B23 .... 56 C4
Hilly Rd WV14 .... 40 E2
Hilmore Way B77 .... 35 E8
Hilsea Cl WV8 .... 10 F1
Hilston Ave
Halesowen B63 .... 82 F4
Wolverhampton WV4 .... 38 C4
HILTON 17 A8
Hilton Ave
Birmingham B28 .... 105 F4
Nuneaton CV10 .... 72 B6
Hilton Cl WS3 .... 14 A2
Hilton Cross WV10 .... 12 B5
Hilton Cross Bsns Pk WV10 .... 12 B5
Hilton Ct
Coventry CV5 .... 112 F2
Sutton Coldfield B72 .... 57 C8
Hilton Dr B72 .... 57 C8
Hilton La
Featherstone WV10, WV11 .... 12 E8
Great Wyrley, Warstone WV11 .... 13 B7
Great Wyrley WS6 .... 5 A2
Hilton Main Ind Est WV11 12 C5
Hilton Park Service Area WV11 .... 13 B7
Hilton Pl WV14 .... 40 F5
Hilton Rd
Burntwood WS7 .... 6 C8
Featherstone WV10 .... 12 C7
Oldbury B69 .... 63 C8
Willenhall WV12 .... 13 C1
Wolverhampton WV4 .... 39 F4
Hilton St
West Bromwich B70 .... 53 A3
Wolverhampton WV10 .... 163 D4
Hilton Trad Est WV4 .... 39 F4
Hilton Way WV12 .... 27 C8
Himbleton Cl B98 .... 153 F1
Himbleton Croft 1 B90 .. 127 A6
Himbleton Dr CV3 .... 115 A2
HIMLEY 49 B3
Himley Ave DY1 .... 50 F2
Himley Cl
Birmingham B43 .... 43 C2
Willenhall WV12 .... 27 B5
Himley Cres WV4 .... 39 B5
Himley Ct DY3 .... 50 E3
Himley Gdns DY3 .... 49 F4
Himley Gr B45 .... 122 B6
Himley Hall★ DY3 .... 49 D4
Himley Rd
2 Bedworth CV12 .... 77 D2
Dudley DY1, DY3 .... 50 C2
Himley Rise B90 .... 126 E4
Himley St DY1 .... 51 A1
Hinbrook Rd DY1 .... 50 E1
Hinchliffe Ave WV14 .... 40 B2
Hinchwick Ct B93 .... 127 F3
Hinckes Rd WV6 .... 24 B5
HINCKLEY 75 B8
Hinckley & Bosworth Com Hospl LE10 .... 71 D5
Hinckley Bsns Ctr LE10 .. 75 F8
Hinckley Bsns Pk LE10 .. 74 F8
Hinckley & District Hospl LE10 .... 75 D8
Hinckley & District Mus★ LE10 .... 71 D1
Hinckley L Ctr LE10 .... 75 C8
Hinckley Rd
Ansty CV2, CV7 .... 97 C2
Aston Flamville LE10 .... 76 E6
Barwell LE9 .... 71 E5
Burbage LE9 .... 76 D8
Burton Hastings CV11, LE10 75 D1
Coventry CV2 .... 115 A8
Hinckley LE10 .... 76 A6
Nuneaton CV11 .... 73 E5
Hinckley St B5 .... 164 C2
Hinckley Sta LE10 .... 75 D7
Hincks St WV2 .... 40 A7
Hind Cl CV34 .... 155 F2
Hindhead Rd B14 .... 105 C4
Hindlip Cl B63 .... 82 F2
Hindlow Cl B7 .... 67 B4
Hindon Gr B27 .... 106 C7
Hindon Sq B15 .... 85 F8
Hindon Wlk B32 .... 84 C2
Hingeston St B18 .... 66 B4
Hingley Croft WS9 .... 30 F3
Hingley Ind Pk B64 .... 62 C1
Hingley Rd DY9 .... 82 A6
Hingley St B64 .... 62 D1
Hinsford Cl DY6 .... 60 E8
Hinstock Cl WV4 .... 39 A4
Hinstock Rd B20 .... 54 F1
Hintlesham Ave B15 .... 85 D5
Hinton Ave B48 .... 139 A6
Hinton Fields B61 .... 136 E7
Hinton Gr WV11 .... 26 F5
Hintons Coppice B93 .... 127 E6
HINTS 19 D3
Hints Ct B78 .... 19 D2
Hints La
Hopwas B78 .... 20 B5
Weeford B78 .... 19 F4
Hints Rd
Hopwas B78 .... 20 B6
Mile Oak B78 .... 20 C2
Hipkins St DY4 .... 51 E7
Hiplands Rd B62 .... 83 F4
Hipsley Cl B36 .... 58 C1
Hipsmoor Cl B37 .... 69 F3
Hipswell Highway CV2 .. 114 D3
Hirdemonsway B90 .... 126 A5
Hiron Croft CV3 .... 133 C8
Hiron The CV3 .... 133 C8
Hiron Way CV34 .... 160 B7
Histons Hill WV8 .... 10 A3
Hitchcock Cl B67 .... 64 D5
Hitches La B15 .... 86 B7
Hitchman Ct CV31 .... 162 A5
Hitchman Rd CV31 .... 162 A5
Hither Green La B98 .... 153 F7
Hitherside B90 .... 126 B5
Hive Ind Ctr The B18 .... 66 A6
Hoarestone Ave CV11 .... 79 A7
Hoarstone DY8 .... 98 F5
Hobacre Cl B45 .... 122 A8
Hobart Croft 1 B7 .... 67 A4
Hobart Ct B74 .... 32 A3
Hobart Dr WS5 .... 43 C6
Hobart Rd
Cannock WS12 .... 2 E2
Tipton DY4 .... 40 E1
Hobbis Ho B38 .... 123 C7
HOBBLE END 14 B7
Hobble End La WS6 .... 14 B7
Hobby Way WS11 .... 5 A8
Hobden Hall Farm Ind Units B60 .... 150 B3
Hobgate Cl WV10 .... 25 F4
Hobgate Rd WV10 .... 25 F4
Hob Green Prim Sch DY9 .. 81 E2
Hob Green Rd DY9 .... 81 E2
Hobhouse Cl B43 .... 54 F7
Hob La
Balsall Common CV7 .... 130 E4
Burton Green CV8 .... 131 A3
Temple Balsall B92 .... 129 A8
Hobley St WV13 .... 27 C2
Hob Moor Cl B10 .... 68 A1
Hobmoor Croft B25 .... 88 D7
Hobmoor Prim Sch B25 .. 88 C7
Hob Moor Rd B10, B25 .. 88 C8
Hobnock Rd WV11 .... 13 B5
Hobs Hole La WS9 .... 30 D7
Hob's Mdw B92 .... 89 B2
Hob's Moat Rd B92 .... 89 B3
Hobson Cl B18 .... 66 A5
Hobson Rd B29 .... 86 B1
Hobs Rd WS10 .... 42 A4
Hob's Rd WS13 .... 3 E1
Hockett St CV3 .... 133 D8
Hocking Rd CV2 .... 114 E4
HOCKLEY
Birmingham 66 B5
Coventry 111 C4
Tamworth 35 E5
Hockley Brook Cl B18 .. 66 A5
Hockley Brook La DY9 .. 119 F3
Hockley Brook Trad Est B18 .... 66 A6
Hockley Cir B18 .... 66 B6
Hockley Cl B19 .... 66 D6
Hockley Ct B94 .... 143 C7
Hockley Ctr 1 B18 .... 66 C4
HOCKLEY HEATH 143 D6
Hockley Heath Prim Sch B94 .... 143 C6
Hockley Hill B18 .... 66 B5

Hockley La
Coventry CV5 111 C5
Dudley DY2 62 C4
Hockley Pool Cl B18 66 B5
Hockley Rd
Birmingham B23 56 D4
Dudley WV14 51 A7
Tamworth B77 35 F5
Hockley St B19 66 C5
Hodder Gr B71 53 F7
HODGEHILL 68 D6
Hodge Hill Ave DY9 81 F3
Hodge Hill Comm B36 68 E7
Hodge Hill Cotts DY10 117 C7
Hodgehill Ct B36 68 E7
Hodge Hill Girls Sch B36 68 C7
Hodge Hill Prim Sch B36 68 D7
Hodge Hill Rd B34 68 E6
Hodge Hill Sports & Ent Coll B36 68 C7
Hodge La B77 22 B6
Hodge Lane Nature Reserve★ B77 22 B5
Hodges Dr B69 63 B8
Hodgetts Cl B67 64 D3
Hodgetts Dr B63 100 C8
Hodgett's La
Balsall Common CV7 130 F7
Coventry CV7, CV8 131 A6
Hodgkins Cl WS8 16 A6
Hodgkiss Cl WS10 41 E4
Hodgson Twr B19 66 D6
Hodnell Cl B36 58 C1
Hodnet Cl
Bilston WV14 40 B5
Kenilworth CV8 148 B5
Hodnet Dr DY5 61 C6
Hodnet Gr B5 86 E8
Hodnet Pl WS11 2 B2
Hodson Ave WV13 27 C1
Hodson Cl WV11 26 F8
Hodson Way WS11 2 B2
Hoff Beck Ct 6 B9 67 B2
Hogarth Cl
Bedworth CV12 78 A4
Birmingham B43 44 D5
Hinckley LE10 71 A3
Willenhall WV13 26 E2
Hogarth Dr LE10 71 A3
Hogarth Ho 6 B15 86 C8
Hoggs La B31 102 E4
Holbeache La DY6 49 D1
Holbeache Rd DY6 60 C8
Holbeach Rd B33 69 B2
Holbeche Rd
Dorridge B93 128 A7
Sutton Coldfield B75 47 B5
Holbein Cl CV12 78 A4
Holberg Gr WV11 26 F5
Holborn Ave CV6 95 C2
Holborn Hill B6, B7 67 C7
Holbrook Gr B37 70 A1
Holbrook La CV6 95 D2
Holbrook Park Est CV6 113 D8
Holbrook Prim Sch CV6 95 E1
HOLBROOKS 95 C3
Holbrook Tower B36 68 D8
Holbrook Way CV6 95 D1
Holbury Cl WV9 11 A2
Holcombe Rd B11 88 A3
Holcroft Rd
Halesowen B63 82 C5
Kingswinford DY6 49 C1
Stourbridge DY9 81 C4
Holcroft St
Tipton DY4 52 A2
Wolverhampton WV2 40 A7
Holden Cl B23 56 E2
Holden Cres WS3 28 F5
Holden Croft DY4 52 A3
Holden Pl WS3 28 E5
Holden Rd
Wednesbury WS10 42 A2
Wolverhampton WV4 38 D3
Holdens The B28 105 E6
Holder Dr WS11 1 B2
Holder Rd
Birmingham, South Yardley B25 88 C7
Birmingham, Sparkbrook B11 87 C6
Holders Gdns B13 86 C2
Holders La B13 86 C2
Holdgate Rd B29 103 C7
Hole Farm Rd B31 103 C5
Hole Farm Way B38 123 F7
Hole House La B94 143 F1
Hole La B31 103 C5
Holford Ave WS2 42 C6
Holford Dr B42, B6 55 F4
Holford Way B6 55 F3
Holifast Rd B72 57 C7
Holioak Dr CV34 161 B6
Holland Ave
Knowle B93 128 B8
Oldbury B68 64 D4
Holland Ho B19 66 D5
Holland House Inf Sch B72 46 C4
Holland Ind Pk WS10 41 D8
Holland Rd
Bilston WV14 40 E7
Birmingham B43 54 D7
Coventry CV6 113 A6
Sutton Coldfield B72 46 C4
Holland Road W 6 B6 66 F6
Hollands Pl WS3 14 D1
Hollands Rd WS3 14 D1
Holland St
Birmingham B3 164 A3
1 Dudley DY1 62 B8
Sutton Coldfield B72 46 C4
Tipton DY4 52 C7
Holland's Way WS3 14 F4
Hollaway Ct B63 82 D5
Hollemeadow Ave WS3 28 D7
Holliars Gr B37 69 F5
Hollicombe Terr CV2 114 D8
Holliday Rd
Birmingham, Erdington B24 57 A4
Birmingham, Handsworth B21 65 F7
Holliday St B1 164 A2
Holliday Wharf B1 164 A1
Hollie Lucas Rd B13 104 F7
Holliers Walk Cty Prim Sch 11 LE10 71 D1
Hollier's Wlk LE10 71 D1
Hollies Ave WS11 1 F1
Hollies Bsns Pk WS11 1 F1
Hollies Croft B5 86 C5
Hollies Ct WS11 1 F1
Hollies Dr
Halesowen B62 83 E6
Wednesbury WS10 41 F3
Hollies Ind Est WV2 163 B1
Hollies La WV6 23 A4
Hollies Park Rd WS11 1 F1
Hollies Rd B69 63 B8
Hollies Rise B64 82 F8
Hollies St DY5 61 D7
Hollies The
Barnt Green B45 122 A1
Birmingham, Aston B6 67 B8
Birmingham, Winson Green B16 65 F3
Burntwood WS7 7 E8
Smethwick B66 65 C4
Walsall WS6 13 E8
Wolverhampton, New Cross WV11 26 B5
Wolverhampton WV2 163 B1
Hollin Brow Cl B93 128 B3
Hollingberry La B76 46 F3
Hollings Gr B91 127 B8
Hollington Cres B33 69 A4
Hollington Rd WV1 26 B1
Hollington Way B90 127 C7
Hollinwell Cl
Nuneaton CV11 79 C8
Walsall WS3 14 A3
Hollis La CV8 147 E8
Hollis Rd CV3 114 A2
Hollister Dr B32 84 F3
Holloway
Birmingham B31 102 E5
Tamworth B79 21 B4
Holloway Bank
Wednesbury WS10 41 F1
West Bromwich B70, B71 53 A8
Holloway Bank Trad Est WS10 41 F1
Holloway Circus Queensway B1 164 B1
Holloway Dr B98 154 B3
Holloway Field CV6 113 A6
Holloway Head B1 164 B1
Holloway La B98 153 F3
Holloway Pk B98 154 A3
Holloway St
Dudley DY3 50 D4
Wolverhampton WV1 40 A7
Holloway Street W DY3 50 D4
Holloway The
Alvechurch B48 139 D3
Bluntington DY10 118 E2
Seisdon WV5 37 A3
Stourbridge DY8 80 F7
Warwick CV34 160 D6
Wolverhampton WV6 24 C2
Hollow Cres CV6 113 B5
Hollow Croft B31 103 B3
Hollow Croft Rd WV12 27 B7
Hollowfields Cl B98 153 E1
Hollowmeadow Ho B36 68 D8
Hollows The CV11 73 F1
Hollow The B13 86 E4
Hollowtree La B60 138 A3
Holly Ave
Birmingham, Balsall Heath B12 87 A5
Birmingham, Selly Oak B29 86 B1
HOLLY BANK 16 B3
Holly Bank CV5 133 A8
Hollybank Ave WV11 13 A3
Hollybank Cl WS3 14 A2
Hollybank Gr B63 82 D1
Hollybank Rd B13 105 A6
Hollyberry Ave B91 127 A8
Hollyberry Cl 8 B63 83 A3
Hollyberry Croft B34 69 C6
HOLLYBERRY END 93 C4
Hollybrow B29 103 B7
Holly Bush Gr B32 84 D7
Hollybush La
Coventry CV6 96 A4
Stourbridge DY8 80 F7
Wolverhampton WV4 38 D4
Hollybush Wlk 2 B64 62 D1
Holly Cl
Hinckley LE10 75 E5
Sutton Coldfield B76 46 F2
Holly Cl *continued*
Tamworth B79 21 B7
Willenhall WV12 27 C6
Hollycot Gdns B12 86 F6
HOLLYCROFT 71 A1
Hollycroft LE10 71 C1
Hollycroft Cres LE10 71 C1
Hollycroft Gdns WV6 24 B6
Hollycroft Rd B21 54 D1
Holly Ct
Balsall Common CV7 130 B3
Birmingham B23 57 A5
Kidderminster DY10 116 D8
Walsall WS5 43 A4
Hollydale Rd
Birmingham B24 57 C3
Rowley Regis B65 63 D2
Holly Dell B38 104 B2
Holly Dr
Birmingham B27 88 B2
Hollywood B47 125 B7
Ryton-on-D CV8 135 B1
Holly Farm Bsns Pk CV8 146 B7
Hollyfaste Rd B33 69 B1
Hollyfast La CV7 94 C4
Hollyfast Prim Sch CV6 112 E7
Hollyfast Rd CV6 112 E6
Hollyfield Ave B91 106 E3
Hollyfield Cres B75 46 E4
Hollyfield Ct B75 46 E5
Hollyfield Dr
Barnt Green B45 122 A1
Sutton Coldfield B75 46 E5
Hollyfield Prim Sch B75 46 F5
Hollyfield Rd B75 46 E5
Hollyfield Road S B76 46 F4
Holly Gr
4 Birmingham B29 85 F2
Birmingham, Bournville B30 103 F8
Bromsgrove B61 136 F3
Coventry CV4 112 B2
Stourbridge DY8 80 F5
Wolverhampton WV3 38 F7
Holly Grange B66 64 D7
HOLLY HALL 61 E7
Holly Hall Rd DY2 62 A7
Holly Hall Sch DY1 61 F8
Hollyhedge Cl
Birmingham B31 102 D6
Walsall WS2 28 C2
Hollyhedge La WS2 28 C2
Hollyhedge Rd B71 53 E7
Holly Hill
4 Birmingham B45 101 F1
Great Wyrley WS6 13 E8
Hollyhill La WS14 17 E5
Holly Hill Meth & CE Inf Sch B45 101 F2
Holly Hill Rd
Birmingham B45 102 A2
Shenstone WS14 17 F5
Hollyhock Rd
Birmingham B27 88 A2
Dudley DY2 51 F1
HOLLYHURST 96 F8
Hollyhurst
Bedworth CV12 77 F1
Water Orton B46 59 C2
Hollyhurst Dr DY6 60 E3
Hollyhurst Gr
Birmingham B26 88 E6
Solihull B90 126 B8
Hollyhurst Rd B73 45 B3
Holly La
Aldridge WS9 30 F8
Balsall Common CV7 130 B3
Birmingham, Erdington B24 57 C4
Birmingham, Marston Green B37 89 F8
Brownhills WS9 16 A4
Great Wyrley WS6 13 F8
Huntington WS12 1 C7
Portway B48 140 F5
Smethwick B66 64 E6
Sutton Coldfield B74 32 A3
Wishaw B76 47 D4
Holly Lodge High Sch Coll of Science B67 64 D6
Holly Lodge Wlk B37 69 F2
Holly Marie Ct CV5 112 F1
Hollymoor Way B31 102 B1
Hollymount B62 84 A7
Holly Mount 7 B15 65 D1
Hollyoak Croft B31 123 B8
Hollyoake Cl B68 64 A2
Hollyoak Gr B91 107 A1
Hollyoak Rd B74 44 F6
Hollyoak St B71 53 D4
Hollyoak Way WS11 1 F1
Holly Park Dr B24 57 C4
Holly Park Ind Est B24 57 C2
Hollypiece Ho B27 88 A2
Holly Pl B29 86 B2
Holly Rd
Birmingham B68 84 C8
Birmingham, Edgbaston B16 65 D1
Birmingham, Handsworth B20 66 A8
Birmingham, King's Norton B30 104 A4
Bromsgrove B61 136 F4
Dudley DY1 51 A3
Rowley Regis B65 63 B1
Wednesbury WS10 41 F5
West Bromwich B71 53 E8
Holly St
Cannock WS12 1 F6
Holly St *continued*
Dudley DY1 61 E6
Royal Leamington Spa CV32 157 B1
Smethwick B67 64 F5
Hollystitches Rd CV10 72 E6
Holly View WV11 13 A3
Hollywell Rd
Birmingham B26 89 B6
Dorridge B93 128 A5
Hollywell St WV14 40 A1
Holly Wlk
Baginton CV8 133 E2
Nuneaton CV11 73 F2
Royal Leamington Spa CV32 157 A1
HOLLYWOOD 125 B8
Holly Wood B43 44 A1
Hollywood By-Pass
Birmingham B47 104 F1
Hollywood B38, B47 124 E6
Hollywood Croft B42 54 F8
Hollywood Gdns B47 125 A8
Hollywood La B47 125 B7
Hollywood Motor Pk B47 125 A8
Hollywood Nature Reserve★ B43 44 A1
Hollywood Prim Sch B14 105 A1
Hollyword Dr B47 125 A8
Holman Cl WV13 26 E2
Holman Rd WV13 26 E2
Holman St DY11 116 C5
Holman Way
Nuneaton CV11 73 D3
Willenhall WV13 26 E2
Holmbridge Gr WS4 15 D2
Holmcroft
Coventry CV2 114 F8
10 Wolverhampton WV4 39 F4
Holmcroft Rd DY10 117 A5
Holme Mill WV10 11 D4
Holmes Ct CV8 147 F5
Holmes Dr
Birmingham B45 121 F6
Coventry CV5 111 D5
Holmesfield Rd B42 55 C7
Holmes La B60 151 B1
Holmes Rd
Whitnash CV31 162 B3
Willenhall WV12 27 D6
Holmes The WV10 11 D3
Holme Way WS4 29 B7
Holmewood Cl CV8 148 B5
Holmewood Ct CV8 148 B5
Holmfield Rd CV2 114 B3
Holmsdale Rd CV6 113 E7
Holm View Cl WS14 17 F6
Holmwood Ave DY11 116 A6
Holmwood Dr B97 153 C3
Holmwood Ho B97 153 C3
Holmwood Rd 3 B10 67 D1
Holroyd Ho CV4 111 F2
Holston Cl WS12 2 F1
Holsworth Cl B77 21 D1
Holsworthy Cl CV11 73 E5
Holt & Bracebridge Almshouses B24 57 A4
Holt Cres WS11 2 B2
Holt Ct B7 66 F4
Holte Arts Coll B19 66 D7
Holte Com L Ctr B6 66 D7
Holte Dr B75 32 D2
HOLT END 154 F8
Holte Rd
Birmingham, Aston B6 56 A1
Birmingham, Sparkhill B11 87 D5
Holtes Wlk B6 67 B8
Holt Gdns B80 159 E2
Holt Hill B98 154 F8
Holt Ho B61 137 A3
Holt La B62 100 D4
Holton Ct WV13 27 C2
Holt Rd
Halesowen B62 63 E1
Hinckley LE10 75 E6
Studley B80 159 E2
Holtshill La WS1 28 F2
Holt St B7 164 D4
Holt The CV32 157 B3
Holwick B77 36 B8
HOLY CROSS 99 E2
Holy Cross Ct CV2 114 E4
Holy Cross Gn DY9 99 E2
Holy Cross La DY9 119 E8
Holy Cross RC Prim Sch B76 47 A3
Holy Family RC Prim Sch
Birmingham B10 87 F7
Coventry CV6 95 B3
Holyhead L Ctr B21 65 D8
Holyhead Prim Sch WS10 41 E3
Holyhead Rd
Birmingham B21 65 D8
Codsall WV8 23 E7
Coventry CV5 112 E5
Darlaston WS10 41 C4
Wednesbury WS10 41 E3
Holyhead Road Ind Est WS10 41 D3
Holyhead Sch B21 65 D8
Holyhead Way B21 65 D8
Holy Name RC Prim Sch B43 43 E1
Holyoak Cl
Bedworth CV12 77 F1
3 Birmingham B6 55 F1
Holyoakes Field Fst Sch B97 153 D4
Holyoakes La B97 152 C5
Holy Oaks Cl B98 154 E2
Holyoke Gr CV31 162 B2
Holyrood Ct CV10 72 D5
Holyrood Gr 2 B6 66 E8
Holy Rosary RC Prim Sch WV1 26 A1
Holy Souls RC Prim Sch B27 88 C3
Holy Trinity CE Prim Sch
Birmingham B20 55 C2
Brownhills WS8 15 E6
West Bromwich B70 53 D1
Holy Trinity Int Sch DY10 116 F6
Holy Trinity RC Media Arts Coll B10 87 C8
Holy Trinity RC Prim Sch WV14 40 E6
Holywell Cl CV4 111 D1
Holy Well Cl B16 66 A2
Holywell La B45 121 D6
Holywell Prim Sch B45 121 D7
Holywell Rise WS14 9 D6
Home Cl B28 105 F6
Homecroft Rd B26 88 E8
Homedene Rd B31 102 E7
Home Farm
Leek Wootton CV35 155 F6
Stoneleigh CV8 149 A3
Home Farm Cres CV31 162 B4
Homefield Rd WV8 10 C3
Homelands B42 55 B7
Homelands Park The WV10 11 C6
Homelea Rd B25 88 D8
Homelodge Ho 7 WS13 9 B7
Homemead Gr B45 121 F7
Home Meadow Ct B13 105 A5
Home Meadow Ho B27 88 A2
Home Meadow La B98 154 E6
Home Park Rd CV11 73 C3
Home Peal Ho B14 104 E6
Homer Cl CV34 161 E5
HOMER HILL 82 B6
Homer Hill Rd B63 82 C7
Homer Rd
Solihull B91 107 B3
Sutton Coldfield B75 32 D2
Homer St B12 86 F5
Homerton Rd B44 45 B1
Homestead Cl DY3 50 E5
Homestead Dr B75 32 C3
Homestead Rd B33 69 B1
Homeward Way CV3 115 A1
Homewood Cl B76 46 E3
Honesty Cl WS8 15 D6
Honeswode Cl B20 66 A8
Honeyborne Rd B75 46 D7
Honeybourne B77 21 D2
Honeybourne Cl
Coventry CV5 112 B3
3 Halesowen B63 83 A3
Honeybourne Rd
Birmingham B33 89 C8
Halesowen B63 83 C3
Honeybourne Way WV13 27 C2
Honeychurch Cl B98 153 F3
Honeycomb Way B31 102 E3
Honeyfield Rd CV1 113 D5
Honeysuckle Ave DY6 60 E7
Honeysuckle Cl B32 84 B5
Honeysuckle Dr
Coventry CV2 96 B2
Featherstone WV10 12 C7
Walsall WS5 43 A3
Honeysuckle Gr 8 B27 88 C5
Honeysuckle Way WS6 5 B4
Honeytree Cl DY6 60 F3
HONILEY 146 D5
Honiley Ct CV2 96 D1
Honiley Dr B73 45 C2
Honiley Rd
Birmingham B33 69 A2
Honiley CV8 146 B6
Meer End CV8 130 A1
Honiley Way CV2 96 D1
Honister Cl DY5 61 F1
Honiton Cl B31 102 E4
Honiton Cres B31 102 E4
Honiton Rd CV2 114 C5
Honiton Way WS9 29 F5
Honiton Wlk 7 B66 65 B5
Honnington Ct 2 B29 84 F1
Honor Ave WV4 39 C5
HOOBROOK 116 F2
Hoobrook Ent Ctr DY10 116 E2
Hoobrook Ind Est DY10 116 E2
Hood Gr B30 103 D4
Hood St CV1 113 E3
Hoo Farm Ind Est DY10 116 F1
Hook Dr B74 31 F4
Hook La WS14 17 C3
Hoopers La B96 158 E1
Hooper St B18 65 F4
Hoo Rd DY10 116 E4
Hoosen Cl B62 84 A6
Hope Aldridge Bsns Ctr CV10 73 C6
Hope Cl CV7 95 A7
Hopedale Cl CV2 114 E3
Hopedale Rd B32 84 C5
Hope Pl 10 B29 85 F2
Hope Rd DY4 52 C6
Hope St
Birmingham B5 86 E8

Hope St continued
Coventry CV1 . . . . 113 B2
Dudley DY2 . . . . 62 C8
Halesowen B62 . . . . 83 D8
Stourbridge DY8 . . . . 60 D3
Walsall WS1 . . . . 42 E8
West Bromwich B70 . . . . . . 53 E2
Hope Terr DY2 . . . . 62 C5
Hopgardens Ave B60 . . . . 137 B2
Hopkins Ct 4 WS10 . . . . 42 A3
Hopkins Dr B71 . . . . 53 E7
Hopkins Rd CV6 . . . . 113 A4
Hopkins Dr DY4 . . . . 52 A2
Hopleys Cl B77 . . . . 21 E4
Hopstone Gdns WV4 . . . 38 F4
Hopstone Rd B29 . . . . 85 A1
Hopton Cl
Coventry CV5 . . . . 112 A4
Perton WV6 . . . . 23 F3
Wednesbury DY4 . . . . 41 C2
Hopton Cres WV11 . . . . . . 26 E6
Hopton Crofts CV32 . . . 156 C2
Hopton Dr DY10 . . . . 116 E1
Hopton Gdns DY1 . . . . . . 51 A3
Hopton Gr B13 . . . . 105 C5
Hopton Mdw WS12 . . . . . . 2 C1
HOPWAS 20 B7
Hopwas Gr B37 . . . . 69 F5
Hopwas Hill B78 . . . . 20 A6
HOPWOOD 123 B3
Hopwood Cl B63 . . . . 83 A2
Hopwood Gr B31 . . . . 122 E6
Hopyard Cl DY3 . . . . 50 B3
Hopyard Gdns WV14 . . . 40 B3
Hopyard La
Dudley DY3 . . . . 50 B3
Redditch B98 . . . . 154 D4
Hopyard Rd WS10 . . . . 41 A5
Horace St WV14 . . . . 51 A8
Horatio Dr B13 . . . . 86 F4
Hordern Cl WV6 . . . . 24 F5
Hordern Cres DY5 . . . . . . 81 D8
Hordern Gr WV6 . . . . 24 F5
Hordern Rd WV6 . . . . 24 F5
HORESTON GRANGE 73 F5
Horeston Grange Sh Ctr
CV11 . . . . 74 A5
Hornbeam B77 . . . . 22 A4
Hornbeam Cl
Birmingham B29 . . . . 103 B7
Nuneaton CV10 . . . . 72 D6
Hornbeam Dr CV4 . . . . . . 111 D1
Hornbeam Gr CV31 . . . . 162 C6
Hornbeam Wlk WV3 . . . . 25 A1
Hornbrook Gr B92 . . . . . 106 C7
Hornby Gr B14 . . . . 105 C4
Hornby Rd WV4 . . . . 39 C5
Hornchurch Close Ind Est
CV1 . . . . 165 B1
Hornchurch Cl CV1 . . . . 165 B1
Horndean Cl CV6 . . . . 113 E8
Horner Way B62 . . . . 63 C1
Horne Way B34 . . . . 69 E5
Horning Dr WV14 . . . . 40 C3
Horninghold Cl CV3 . . . 134 E8
Hornsey Cl CV2 . . . . 114 E7
Hornsey Gr B44 . . . . 45 A2
Hornsey Rd B44 . . . . 45 A2
Hornton Cl B74 . . . . 31 D5
Horrell Rd
Birmingham B26 . . . . 89 B7
Solihull B90 . . . . 105 F2
Horsecroft Dr B71 . . . . . . 54 A8
Horse Fair
Birmingham B1 . . . . 164 B1
Kidderminster DY10 . . . . 116 F2
Horsefair The 8 LE10 . . . 75 D8
Horseley Cl B24 . . . . 24 E2
Horseley Croft B8 . . . . 68 C4
Horseley Fields WV1 . . . 163 D3
HORSELEY HEATH 52 D5
Horseley Heath DY4 . . . . 52 C5
Horseley Rd DY4 . . . . 52 C5
Horsepool LE10 . . . . 76 A5
Horsepool Hollow CV31 . 162 C5
Horseshoe Cl 3 WS12 . . . 2 B1
Horseshoe Dr WS12 . . . . . 2 F4
Horse Shoe Rd CV6 . . . . . 96 A4
Horse Shoes La B26 . . . . . 89 B5
Horseshoe The B68 . . . . . 64 C2
Horseshoe Wlk 6 DY4 . . 51 F5
Horsfall Rd B75 . . . . 47 A5
Horsford Rd CV3 . . . . 133 E6
Horsham Ave DY8 . . . . 60 C3
Horshoe Cres B43 . . . . . . 44 B3
Horsley Rd
Birmingham B43 . . . . 44 D4
Sutton Coldfield B74 . . . . . 31 B2
Horton Cl
Bedworth CV7 . . . . 95 F7
2 Cannock WS11 . . . . 1 F4
Darlaston WS10 . . . . 41 D7
Sedgley DY3 . . . . 50 C8
Horton Gr B90 . . . . 127 A5
Horton Pl WS10 . . . . 41 D7
Horton Sq B12 . . . . 86 E7
Horton St
Darlaston WS10 . . . . 41 D7
Tipton DY4 . . . . 52 D5
West Bromwich B70 . . . . . 53 C2
Hosiery St CV12 . . . . 78 C2
Hospital Dr B15 . . . . 85 E4
Hospital La
Bedworth CV12 . . . . 77 B1
Cheslyn Hay WS6 . . . . 4 B2
Dudley WV14 . . . . 51 B7

Hospital Rd WS7 . . . . 7 B5
Hospital St
Birmingham B19 . . . . 164 B4
Birmingham, Newtown B19 . 66 D6
Birmingham, Stockland Green
B23 . . . . 56 E4
West Bromwich B70 . . . . . 21 B5
Walsall WS2 . . . . 28 D4
Wolverhampton WV2 . . . 163 C2
Hospital Way B29 . . . . 85 E4
Hossil La
Belbroughton DY9 . . . . . 119 C8
Clent DY9 . . . . 99 D1
Hotchkiss Way CV3 . . . . 135 A7
Hotel Bldgs WS14 . . . . 8 A2
Hothersall Dr B73 . . . . 56 F8
Hothorpe Cl CV3 . . . . 114 F1
Hotspur Rd B44 . . . . 44 F1
Hough Pl WS2 . . . . 42 B7
Hough Rd
Birmingham B14 . . . . 104 D6
Walsall WS2 . . . . 42 A7
Houghton Ct B28 . . . . 105 D4
Houghton St
Oldbury B69 . . . . 63 F6
West Bromwich B70 . . . . . 64 D8
Hough Way WV11 . . . . 13 A3
Houlbrooke Ho 1 WS14 . . 9 C8
Houldey Rd B31 . . . . 103 A2
Houldsworth Cres CV6 . . 95 C4
Houliston Cl WS10 . . . . . . 42 B5
Houndsfield Cl B47 . . . . 125 C6
Houndsfield Farm B47 . . 125 B5
Houndsfield Gr B47 . . . . 125 C5
Houndsfield La B47 . . . . 125 C6
Housman Cl B60 . . . . 150 E8
Housman Ct B60 . . . . 137 A3
Housman Pk B60 . . . . 137 A2
Housman Wlk DY10 . . . . 117 C6
Houting B77 . . . . 35 D5
Houx The DY8 . . . . 80 E8
Hove Ave CV5 . . . . 111 E4
Hove Rd B27 . . . . 88 C1
Hoveton Cl B98 . . . . 154 B2
Howard Ave B61 . . . . 136 E3
Howard Cl CV5 . . . . 111 E4
Howard Cres WS12 . . . . 2 C7
Howard Ct B16 . . . . 65 F3
Howard Rd
Bilston WV14 . . . . 40 F3
Birmingham, Handsworth
B20 . . . . 55 B2
Birmingham, King's Heath
B14 . . . . 104 E7
Birmingham, Newton B43 . 54 C8
Birmingham, South Yardley
B25 . . . . 88 C7
Nuneaton CV10 . . . . 73 A3
Redditch B98 . . . . 159 F8
Solihull B92 . . . . 88 E3
Wednesfield WV11 . . . . . . 26 F8
Howard Road E B13 . . . . 104 F7
Howard St
Birmingham B19 . . . . 164 B4
Coventry CV1 . . . . 165 C4
Tipton DY4 . . . . 52 A8
West Bromwich B70 . . . . . 52 F7
Wolverhampton WV2 . . . 163 C1
Howard Street Ind Est
B70 . . . . 52 F8
Howard Wlk CV31 . . . . . . 161 D6
Howarth Way B6 . . . . 67 A7
Howat Rd CV7 . . . . 94 B3
Howcotte Gn CV4 . . . . . . 131 E8
Howden Pl B33 . . . . 69 A5
Howdle's La WS8 . . . . 6 F2
Howe Cres WV12 . . . . 27 C6
Howell Rd WV2 . . . . 39 E7
Howells Cl CV12 . . . . 77 D1
Howes Croft B35 . . . . 58 A2
Howes La CV3 . . . . 133 D3
Howes Prim Sch CV3 . . . 133 E5
Howe St B4 . . . . 66 F3
Howfield Ct B16 . . . . 65 C1
Howford Gr B7 . . . . 67 B4
Howland Cl WV9 . . . . 10 F2
Howlette Rd B44 . . . . 111 E2
Howley Ave B44 . . . . 44 E1
Howley Grange Prim Sch
B62 . . . . 83 F5
Howley Grange Rd B62 . . 84 A4
Howl Pl DY4 . . . . 51 F5
Howlette Rd B77 . . . . 22 B4
Hoylake Cl
Nuneaton CV11 . . . . 74 B1
Walsall WS3 . . . . 14 B4
Hoylake Dr B69 . . . . 63 A7
Hoylake Rd WV6 . . . . 23 D5
Hoyland Way B30 . . . . . . 103 E8
HRS Bsns Pk B33 . . . . . . 105 A7
Huband Cl B98 . . . . 154 A5
Hubert Croft B29 . . . . 85 F2
Hubert Rd B29 . . . . 85 F2
Hubert St B6 . . . . 66 F5
Hucker Cl WS2 . . . . 42 A7
Hucker Rd WS2 . . . . 42 A7
Huddesford Dr CV7 . . . . 130 C8
Huddisdon Cl 8 CV34 . . . 155 F1
Huddlestone Cl WV10 . . 12 B6
Huddleston Way B29 . . . . 85 C1
Huddocks View WS3 . . . . 14 F5
Hudson Ave B46 . . . . 70 F6
Hudson Cl WS11 . . . . 1 B2
Hudson Dr WS7 . . . . 7 C6
Hudson Gr WV6 . . . . 23 E5
Hudson Ind Est WV2 . . . 39 F7

Hudson Rd
Birmingham B20 . . . . 55 A4
Tipton DY4 . . . . 52 C4
Hudson's Dr B30 . . . . 104 A4
Hudson Vale CV4 . . . . 111 C2
Hudswell Dr DY5 . . . . 81 D8
Huggins Cl CV7 . . . . 130 C7
Hughes Ave WV3 . . . . 38 F8
Hughes Cl
Warwick CV34 . . . . 155 D2
Whitnash CV31 . . . . 162 A2
Hughes Pl WV14 . . . . 40 D7
Hughes Rd
Bilston WV14 . . . . 40 D7
Darlaston WS10 . . . . 41 A5
Hughes The CV34 . . . . . . 160 E6
Hugh Gaitskill Ct WV14 . . 40 C8
Hugh Porter Way WV6 . . 24 F6
Hugh Rd
Birmingham B10 . . . . 67 E1
Coventry CV3 . . . . 114 A2
Smethwick B67 . . . . 64 F5
Hugh Villas B10 . . . . 67 E1
Huins Cl B98 . . . . 154 A4
Hulbert Dr DY2 . . . . 62 B6
Hulbert Ind Est DY2 . . . . . 62 B6
Hulland Pl DY5 . . . . 61 C3
Hullbrook Rd B13 . . . . . . 105 C6
Hulme Cl CV3 . . . . 115 B1
Humara Ghar 9 WS1 . . . 42 E8
Humber Ave
Coventry CV1 . . . . 113 F1
Sutton Coldfield B76 . . . . . 58 A7
Humber Gdns B63 . . . . . . 82 C5
Humber Gr B36 . . . . 58 F1
Humber Ho DY1 . . . . 61 D8
Humber Rd
Coventry CV3 . . . . 134 A8
Wolverhampton WV3 . . . . 25 A1
Humberstone Rd
4 Coventry CV6 . . . . 113 A5
Sutton Coldfield B24 . . . . . 57 E4
Humber Twr 2 B7 . . . . 67 A4
Hume St
Kidderminster DY11 . . . . 116 C5
Smethwick B66 . . . . 65 B4
Humpage Rd B9 . . . . 67 E1
Humphrey Ave B60 . . . . 150 F7
Humphrey Burton's Rd
CV3 . . . . 133 D8
Humphrey-Davy Rd CV12 . 95 D4
Humphrey Middlemore Dr
B17 . . . . 85 D4
Humphrey St DY3 . . . . 50 D3
Humphries Cres WV14 . . 40 F2
Humphries Dr DY10 . . . . 116 F2
Humphries Ho WS8 . . . . . 15 F7
Humphries Rd WV10 . . . . 25 D6
Humphris St CV34 . . . . . 161 B8
Hundred Acre Rd B74 . . . 44 F7
Hungary Cl DY9 . . . . 125 C6
Hungary Hill DY9 . . . . 81 C5
Hungerfield Rd B36 . . . . . 58 C1
Hungerford Rd DY8 . . . . . 80 E2
Hungry La WS14 . . . . 18 F5
Hunningham Gr 6 B91 . . 127 B8
HUNNINGTON 101 B8
Hunnington Cl B32 . . . . . 84 A1
Hunnington Cres B63 . . . 83 B2
Hunscote Dr WV10 . . . . . 105 F1
Hunscote Ho B90 . . . . 105 F1
Hunslet Cl B32 . . . . 84 F4
Hunslet Rd
Birmingham B32 . . . . 84 F4
Burntwood WS7 . . . . 7 B8
Hunstanton Ave B17 . . . . 84 F8
Hunstanton Cl B17 . . . . . . 81 C7
HUNT END 158 C5
Hunt End Ind Est B97 . . 158 C5
Hunt End La B97 . . . . 158 C5
Hunter Ave WS7 . . . . 7 B7
Hunter Cl WS14 . . . . 9 B8
Hunter Cres WS3 . . . . 28 F7
Hunter Ct B5 . . . . 86 D5
Hunter Rd WS11 . . . . 4 E8
Hunters Cl
Bilston WV14 . . . . 41 A7
Coventry CV3 . . . . 115 A2
Hunters Ind Tech Coll
B60 . . . . 137 F6
Hunters Rd B19 . . . . 66 B7
Hunter's Ride DY7 . . . . . . 60 B2
Hunters Rise B63 . . . . 82 D1
Hunter St WV6 . . . . 25 A4
Hunters Vale B19 . . . . 66 C6
Hunters Wlk B23 . . . . 56 C8
Hunter Terr CV3 . . . . 132 D8
Huntingdon Cl
Redditch B98 . . . . 154 F2
Tamworth B78 . . . . 20 F7
Huntingdon Rd
Coventry CV3 . . . . 133 A8
West Bromwich B71 . . . . . 53 B7
Huntingdon Way CV10 . . 72 E3
HUNTINGTON 1 D7
Huntington Rd WV12 . . . . 27 D8
Huntington Terrace Rd
WS11 . . . . 1 F4
Huntingtree Prim Sch
B63 . . . . 82 E3
Huntingtree Rd B63 . . . . . 82 E3
Huntlands Rd B63 . . . . 82 F2
Huntley Dr B91 . . . . 107 B2
Huntly Rd B16 . . . . 66 A1
Hunton Ct 2 B23 . . . . 56 E2
Hunton Hill B23 . . . . 56 E2

Hunton Rd B23 . . . . 56 E3
Hunt Paddocks CV8 . . . . 147 E1
HUNTS GREEN 48 C7
Hunt's La WV12 . . . . 27 D6
Hunts Mill Dr WV14 . . . . . 40 D2
Huntsman Gate WS7 . . . . . 7 B8
Huntsmans Rise WS12 . . . 1 C8
Hunts Mill Dr DY5 . . . . 50 C1
Hunts Rd B30 . . . . 104 B7
Hunt Terr CV4 . . . . 132 B7
HURCOTT 117 C8
Hurcott Ct DY10 . . . . 117 A8
Hurcott La DY10 . . . . 117 C8
Hurcott Rd DY10 . . . . 117 B8
Hurcott Wood Nature
Reserve* DY10 . . . . 117 C8
Hurdis Rd B90 . . . . 106 A2
Hurdlow Ave B18 . . . . 66 B5
Hurlbutt Rd CV34 . . . . . . 161 C4
Hurley Cl
Royal Leamington Spa
CV32 . . . . 157 A2
Sutton Coldfield B72 . . . . . 46 C2
Walsall WS5 . . . . 43 D6
Hurley Gr B37 . . . . 69 F5
Hurlingham Rd B44 . . . . . 45 A1
Hurn Way CV6 . . . . 96 B4
Huron Cl WS11 . . . . 2 B2
Hurricane B24 . . . . 68 A8
Hurricane Way B35 . . . . . 58 A2
Hursey Dr DY4 . . . . 52 A6
Hurstbourne Cres WV1 . . 26 B1
Hurst Bsns Pk DY6 . . . . . . 62 A4
Hurst Cl B36 . . . . 69 E7
Hurstcroft Rd B33 . . . . . . 69 B3
Hurst Cl DY9 . . . . 81 F5
HURST GREEN 83 F8
Hurst Green Prim Sch
B62 . . . . 83 E8
Hurst Green Rd
Bentley Heath B93 . . . . . 127 F4
Halesowen B62 . . . . 83 F8
Minworth B76 . . . . 58 D6
HURST HILL 40 A1
Hurst Hill Ct WV14 . . . . . . 51 A8
Hurst Hill Prim Sch WV14 . 51 A8
Hurst La
Birmingham B34 . . . . 69 E6
Brierley Hill DY5 . . . . 61 F3
Tipton DY4 . . . . 51 D6
Hurst Lane N B36 . . . . 69 E7
Hurst Rd
Bedworth CV12 . . . . 78 B3
Coventry CV6 . . . . 96 A4
Dudley WV14 . . . . 40 A1
Hinckley LE10 . . . . 75 D8
Sedgley WV14 . . . . 39 F1
Smethwick B67 . . . . 64 D2
Hurst St B5 . . . . 164 C1
Hurst The
Birmingham B13 . . . . 105 D7
Hollywood B47 . . . . 125 A6
Hurstway The B23 . . . . . . 56 C8
Hurst Wlk CV6 . . . . 96 A4
Hurstwood Rd B23 . . . . . . 56 C8
Huskison Cl B69 . . . . 52 B1
Huskisson Ct WV10 . . . . . 25 C6
Huskisson Way B90 . . . . 127 B4
Hussey Rd
Brownhills WS8 . . . . 15 E8
Norton Canes WS11 . . . . . . 5 F5
Husum Way DY10 . . . . . . 117 C7
Hutchings La B90 . . . . . . 126 B5
Hutton Ave B8 . . . . 67 D5
Hutton Rd
Birmingham, Handsworth
B20 . . . . 55 C1
Birmingham, Saltley B8 . . 67 D5
Huxbey Dr B92 . . . . 107 F8
Huxley Cl WV9 . . . . 11 A3
Hyacinth Cl 3 WS5 . . . . . 43 A3
Hyacinth Way LE10 . . . . . 75 D5
Hyatt Sq DY5 . . . . 81 C7
Hyatts Wlk B65 . . . . 62 F5
Hyde Cl B60 . . . . 137 B2
Hyde Pl CV32 . . . . 161 E8
Hyde Rd
Coventry CV2 . . . . 114 E4
Kenilworth CV8 . . . . 148 A5
Wednesfield WV11 . . . . . . 26 E6
Hydes La LE10 . . . . 74 E4
Hydes Rd
Wednesbury WS10 . . . . . . 42 B2
West Bromwich B71 . . . . . 42 C1
Hydesville Tower Sch
WS1 . . . . 29 A2
Hyde The DY9 . . . . 81 D2
Hyett Way WV14 . . . . 41 B2
Hylda Rd B20 . . . . 55 B1
Hylstone Cres WV11 . . . . 26 C6
Hylton St B18 . . . . 66 C5
Hypericum Gdns CV2 . . 114 C4
Hyperion Dr WV4 . . . . 39 A3
Hyperion Rd
Stourbridge DY7 . . . . 80 C7
Sutton Coldfield B36 . . . . . 57 F1
Hyron Hall Rd B27 . . . . . . 88 C2
Hyssop Cl
Birmingham B7 . . . . 67 A5
Cannock WS11 . . . . 2 B3
Hytall Rd B90 . . . . 105 C2
Hythe Gr B25 . . . . 88 D8

I

Ibberton Rd B14 . . . . 105 B3
Ibex Cl CV3 . . . . 114 F1
Ibis Cl DY10 . . . . 117 B3
Ibis Gdns DY6 . . . . 61 A6
Ibstock Cl B98 . . . . 154 E4
Ibstock Dr DY8 . . . . 81 A4
Ibstock Ho B98 . . . . 154 E4
Ibstock Rd CV6 . . . . 96 A5
Icknield Cl B74 . . . . 31 A1
Icknield Port Rd B16 . . . . 65 F3
Icknield Sq B16 . . . . 66 A3
Icknield St
Alvechurch B38 . . . . 124 B3
Beoley B48, B98 . . . . 140 C2
Birmingham B18 . . . . 66 B4
Birmingham B38 . . . . 124 B3
Redditch, Church Hill B98 . 154 C7
Redditch, Ipsley B98 . . . . 154 D2
Rowney Green B48 . . . . . 140 B6
Icknield Street Dr B98 . . 159 D7
Ida Rd
Walsall WS2 . . . . 28 C1
West Bromwich B70 . . . . . 53 D1
Idbury Rd B44 . . . . 56 A7
Ideal Bldgs 7 DY11 . . . . 116 D6
Ideal Wks DY9 . . . . 82 A6
Iden Rd CV1 . . . . 113 E4
Idmiston Croft B14 . . . . . 104 F2
Idonia Rd WV6 . . . . 23 F5
Ilam Pk CV8 . . . . 148 C5
Ilex Ct CV34 . . . . 161 A7
Ilford Cl CV12 . . . . 78 A3
Ilford Ct CV3 . . . . 135 D7
Ilford Dr CV3 . . . . 133 B5
Ilford Rd B23 . . . . 56 D6
Ilfracombe Gr CV3 . . . . . 133 A5
Iliffe Ho B17 . . . . 75 B7
Iliffe Way B17 . . . . 85 D4
Ilkley Gr B37 . . . . 69 F2
ILLEY 101 E8
Illeybrook Sq B32 . . . . 84 D2
Illey Cl B31 . . . . 102 C1
Illey La
Birmingham B32 . . . . 102 A7
Halesowen B62 . . . . 101 E8
Illshaw WV9 . . . . 11 A3
ILLSHAW HEATH 126 E1
Illshaw Heath Rd B90,
B94 . . . . 126 D2
Ilmington Cl
Coventry CV3 . . . . 133 B5
Redditch B98 . . . . 154 D1
Ilmington Dr B73 . . . . 45 C3
Ilmington Rd B29 . . . . 84 F1
Ilminster Cl LE10 . . . . 76 B7
Ilsham Gr B31 . . . . 122 E6
Ilsley Rd B23 . . . . 56 E4
Image Bsns Pk WS11 . . . . . 2 B3
Imber Rd DY10 . . . . 117 A1
Imex Auto Ctr DY4 . . . . . . 52 A3
Imex Bsns Ctr
Redditch B98 . . . . 154 E4
Wolverhampton WV13 . . . 26 C3
Imex Bsns Pk
Birmingham B11 . . . . 88 A6
Birmingham, Bordesley Green
B9 . . . . 67 D2
Birmingham, Stechford B33 . 68 E4
Tipton DY4 . . . . 52 A3
Wolverhampton WV3 . . . . 39 C7
Imex Ho WV2 . . . . 39 B7
Imex Rd B69 . . . . 52 E1
Imex Spaces Bsns Ctr
WV14 . . . . 40 E4
Imogen Gdns CV34 . . . . . 161 E1
Imperial Ave DY10 . . . . . 116 F8
Imperial Ct DY10 . . . . 116 F8
Imperial Gdns DY10 . . . . 116 F8
Imperial Rd DY10 . . . . . . 116 F8
Imperial Rd B9 . . . . 67 E1
Imperial Rise B46 . . . . 59 E2
Impney Cl B98 . . . . 154 E6
Impsley Cl B36 . . . . 69 B8
Inca Cl CV3 . . . . 134 F8
Ince Rd WS10 . . . . 41 C7
Incestre Dr B43 . . . . 43 D1
Inchbrook Rd CV8 . . . . . 148 C7
Inchcape Ave B20 . . . . 55 A3
Inchford Ave CV34 . . . . . 155 E2
Inchford Cl CV11 . . . . 73 F1
Inchford Rd B92 . . . . 107 E7
Inchlaggan Rd WV10 . . . . 25 F6
Infantry Pl B75 . . . . 47 A6
Infield Ho B63 . . . . 82 D7
Ingatestone Dr DY8 . . . . . 60 C3
Inge St B5 . . . . 164 C1
Ingestre Cl
Cannock WS11 . . . . 2 B1
Walsall WS3 . . . . 13 F1
Ingestre Dr B43 . . . . 43 F1
Ingestre Ho WV6 . . . . 24 E5
Ingestre Rd
Birmingham B28 . . . . 106 A2
Wolverhampton WV10 . . . 11 C1
Ingeva Dr B45 . . . . 122 A1
Ingham Way B17 . . . . 85 A8
Ingle Ct LE10 . . . . 75 C8
Ingleby Gdns WV6 . . . . . . 25 A5
Ingle Ct CV31 . . . . 161 E7
Ingledew Cl WS2 . . . . 27 D3
Inglefield Rd B33 . . . . 68 F3

Inglemere Gr B29 .... 102 F7
Inglenook Dr B20 .... 55 B2
Ingleside Villas 3 B11 ... 87 C5
Ingleton Cl CV11 .... 74 A2
Ingleton Rd B8 .... 68 A7
Inglewood Ave WV3 .... 38 F8
Inglewood Cl
Kingswinford DY6 .... 60 D5
Royal Leamington Spa
CV32 .... 157 A3
Inglewood Gr B74 .... 30 F2
Inglewood Rd B11 .... 87 C5
Ingoldsby Ct 17 B13 .... 87 B2
Ingoldsby Rd B31 .... 103 C3
Ingot Cl WS2 .... 28 B6
Ingram Dr B43 .... 54 C8
Ingram Gr B27 .... 88 A2
Ingram Pit La B77 .... 22 A5
Ingram Pl WS3 .... 14 D1
Ingram Rd
Coventry CV5 .... 132 D8
Walsall WS3 .... 14 D1
Inhedge St DY3 .... 50 E5
Inhedge The DY1 .... 51 C1
Inkberrow Cl 1 B65 .... 63 E4
Inkberrow Rd B63 .... 82 F2
Inkerman Gr WV10 .... 25 F2
Inkerman Ho B19 .... 66 E6
Inkerman St
Birmingham B7 .... 67 B4
Wolverhampton WV10 .... 25 F3
INKFORD 124 F1
Inland Rd B24 .... 57 B2
Innage Cl CV31 .... 162 B8
Innage Rd B31 .... 103 B4
Innage The B47 .... 125 A5
Innisfree Cl B47 .... 125 C4
Innis Rd CV5 .... 132 E8
Innsworth Dr B35 .... 58 A4
Insetton Cl B98 .... 154 D4
Inshaw Cl B33 .... 68 E3
Institute Rd B14 .... 104 F8
Instone Rd
Coventry CV6 .... 95 A1
Halesowen B63 .... 83 A3
Instow Cl WV12 .... 27 B8
Insull Ave B14 .... 105 B1
Intended St B63 .... 82 C7
International Ho B43 .... 54 F6
Intersection Ho B70 .... 53 F1
Intown WS1 .... 28 F2
Intown Row WS1 .... 28 F2
Int Sch and Com Coll The
B33 .... 69 D3
Inveraray Cl CV8 .... 148 C4
Inverclyde Dr WV4 .... 39 F5
Inverclyde Rd B20 .... 55 A3
Inverkip Wlk WV4 .... 39 F5
Inverness Cl CV5 .... 112 A4
Inverness Ho WV1 .... 163 B4
Inverness Rd B31 .... 102 F3
Invicta Rd CV3 .... 134 F8
Inworth WV9 .... 11 B3
IO Ctr The B98 .... 154 C1
IPSLEY 154 C2
Ipsley Alders Marsh Wildlife
Reserve* B98 .... 154 F4
Ipsley CE Mid Sch B98 .... 154 E3
Ipsley Church La B98 .... 154 C1
Ipsley Gr B23 .... 56 A5
Ipsley La B98 .... 154 D2
Ipsley St B98 .... 153 E3
Ipstones Ave B33 .... 68 F4
Ipswich Cres B42 .... 55 B7
Ipswich Wlk B37 .... 70 B2
Ireland Green Rd B70 .... 53 B2
Ireton Cl CV4 .... 111 C1
Ireton Rd
Birmingham B20 .... 55 A4
Wolverhampton WV10 .... 11 E3
Iris Ave CV10 .... 78 A8
Iris Cl
Birmingham B29 .... 103 B8
Dudley DY2 .... 51 F1
Hinckley LE10 .... 75 E5
Tamworth B79 .... 21 C6
Iris Dr B14 .... 104 D3
Irnham Rd B74 .... 32 B1
Ironbridge Way CV6 .... 96 B6
Iron Bridge Wlk DY9 .... 99 B8
Iron La B33 .... 68 D4
Ironmonger Row CV1 .... 165 B3
Ironstone Rd WS7 .... 6 E8
Iron Way B60 .... 151 B7
Irvan Ave B70 .... 52 F5
Irvine Cl WS3 .... 28 B7
Irvine Rd WS3 .... 28 B7
Irving Cl DY3 .... 50 A4
Irving Rd
Coventry CV1 .... 113 E2
Solihull B92 .... 89 E3
Wednesbury DY4 .... 41 A1
Irving St B1 .... 66 D1
Irwell B77 .... 21 E2
Irwin Ave B45 .... 122 C7
Isaac Walton Pl B70 .... 52 E7
Isambard Dr CV6 .... 95 F5
Isbourne Way 1 B9 .... 67 B2
Isis Ct 3 B73 .... 46 B5
Isis Gr
Birmingham B36 .... 69 F8
Willenhall WV13 .... 27 C2
Isis Ho DY1 .... 61 D8
Islamic Prep Sch WV1 .... 25 C4
Island Cl LE10 .... 71 E2
Island Dr DY10 .... 116 E4
Island Project Sch The
CV7 .... 91 C2
Island Rd B21 .... 54 C1
Island The B78 .... 20 C1
Islington B63 .... 83 A4
Islington Gates B3 .... 164 A3
Islington Row B15 .... 66 B1
Islington Row Middleway
B15 .... 86 C8
Ismere Rd B24 .... 57 B2
Itchen Gr WV6 .... 23 E4
Ithon Gr B38 .... 123 E8
Ivanhoe Ave CV11 .... 73 E1
Ivanhoe Rd
Birmingham B43 .... 44 C3
Lichfield WS14 .... 9 B6
Wolverhampton WV2 .... 40 A6
Ivanhoe St DY2 .... 62 A7
Ivatt B77 .... 21 F2
Ivatt Cl WS4 .... 29 B7
IVERLEY 98 B7
Iverley La DY10, DY8 .... 98 C5
Iverley Rd B63 .... 83 C4
Iverley Wlk DY9 .... 81 C2
Ivor Rd
Birmingham B11 .... 87 B4
Coventry CV6 .... 95 F2
Redditch B97 .... 153 D2
Ivy Ave
Birmingham B12 .... 87 A5
3 Birmingham B12 .... 87 B5
Ivybridge Gr B42 .... 55 C3
Ivybridge Rd CV3 .... 133 D6
Ivy Cl WS11 .... 4 D8
Ivy Croft WV9 .... 10 F3
Ivydale Ave B26 .... 89 C5
Ivy Farm La CV4 .... 132 D6
Ivyfield Rd B23 .... 56 B5
Ivy Gdns WS11 .... 6 A5
Ivy Gr
Brownhills WS8 .... 16 A4
Nuneaton CV10 .... 72 D6
Ivy Ho WS9 .... 16 A4
Ivyhouse La WV14 .... 51 B8
Ivyhouse Rd B38 .... 123 C8
Ivy House Rd B69 .... 63 D6
Ivyhouse Wlk 6 B77 .... 35 F6
Ivy La
Birmingham B9 .... 67 A2
Romsley B62 .... 100 D5
Ivy Lodge Cl B37 .... 90 A7
Ivy Rd
Birmingham, Handsworth
B21 .... 66 A7
Birmingham, Stirchley B30 104 A6
Dudley DY1 .... 51 A4
Sutton Coldfield B73 .... 45 F1
Tipton DY4 .... 51 F7
Ivy Way B90 .... 126 A6
Ivywood Dr B93 .... 127 E5
Izod St B97 .... 153 D4
Izons Ind Est B70 .... 53 A1
Izons La B70 .... 53 A1
Izons Lane Ind Est B70 .... 53 A1
Izons Rd B70 .... 53 C3

J

Jacamar Ave B33 .... 68 F4
Jacey Rd
Birmingham B16 .... 65 D2
Solihull B90 .... 106 B4
Jack Cade Way CV34 .... 161 E4
Jack David Ho DY4 .... 52 D5
Jackdaw Cl DY3 .... 39 C2
Jackdaw Dr B36 .... 70 A8
Jacker's Rd CV2 .... 96 B4
Jackfield Cl B98 .... 154 E1
Jack Hayward Way WV1 .... 163 B4
Jack Holden Ave WV14 .... 40 A2
Jacklin Dr CV3 .... 133 C4
Jacknell Cl LE10 .... 74 D8
Jacknell Rd LE10 .... 74 D8
Jack Newell Ct 3 WV14 .... 51 C8
Jack O'Watton Bsns Pk
B46 .... 59 D3
Jackson Ave B8 .... 67 F4
Jackson Cl
Birmingham B11 .... 87 B7
Featherstone WV10 .... 12 A6
Keresley CV7 .... 95 A7
Norton Canes WS11 .... 5 E4
Oldbury B68 .... 64 B5
Wednesbury DY4 .... 41 B1
Jackson Ct
Brierley Hill DY5 .... 61 F1
Oldbury B69 .... 63 F4
Jackson Dr B67 .... 64 D5
Jackson Gr CV8 .... 148 C4
Jackson Ho 9 B69 .... 64 A7
Jackson Rd
Birmingham B8 .... 67 F4
Coventry CV6 .... 95 D1
Lichfield WS13 .... 3 B3
Jackson St
Oldbury B68 .... 64 B4
Stourbridge DY9 .... 81 E6
Wolverhampton WV6 .... 25 B4
Jackson Way B32 .... 84 A5
Jackson Wlk B35 .... 58 A2
Jackwood Gn CV12 .... 95 C8
Jacmar Cres B67 .... 64 E6
Jacob Dr CV4 .... 132 D6
Jacobean La B93 .... 108 B1
Jacob's Hall La WS6 .... 5 B1
Jacoby Pl B5 .... 86 C5
Jacombe Cl CV34 .... 160 B3
Jacox Cres CV8 .... 148 C5
Jacquard Cl CV3 .... 133 D4
Jacquard Ho 3 CV1 .... 113 E4
Jade Cl CV1 .... 165 D4
Jade Gr WS11 .... 2 C2
Jaffray Cres B24 .... 56 F3
Jaffray Ct B23 .... 56 E3
Jaffray Rd B24 .... 56 F3
Jaguar B77 .... 21 E2
Jakeman Cl B98 .... 154 E4
Jakeman Rd B12 .... 86 E5
James Beattie Ho WV6 .... 24 C4
James Bridge Cl WS2 .... 42 B7
James Brindley Sch
(Ardenleigh Centre)
B24 .... 57 A2
James Brindley Sch
(Dovedale Ctr) B23 .... 56 B6
James Brindley Sch
(Northfield Centre)
B31 .... 103 A5
James Brindley Sch
(Parkway Ctr) B15 .... 86 C8
James Brindley Sch (Willows
Ctr) B13 .... 86 E1
James Cl
Darlaston WS10 .... 41 F7
Smethwick B67 .... 65 A5
James Clift Ho 3 B69 .... 63 D5
Jamescroft CV3 .... 134 E6
James Ct
Birmingham, King's Norton
B38 .... 103 F2
13 Birmingham, Moseley
B13 .... 87 B2
Warwick CV34 .... 160 F7
James Dawson Dr CV5 .... 111 B8
James Dee Cl DY5 .... 62 A1
James Diskin Ct CV11 .... 73 E2
James Eaton Cl B71 .... 53 C5
James Galloway Cl CV3 .... 134 E7
James Green Rd CV4 .... 111 F2
James Greenway WS13 .... 3 A2
James Ho
Birmingham B19 .... 66 C6
Coventry CV2 .... 114 C8
James Hutchens Ct WS7 .... 6 F5
James Lloyd Trust Flats
B30 .... 103 C5
James Meml Homes The 4
B7 .... 67 C7
Jameson Rd B6 .... 67 C8
Jameson St WV6 .... 25 B4
James Rd
Birmingham, Great Barr
B43 .... 54 E7
Birmingham, Tyseley B11 .... 87 F6
Coleshill B46 .... 70 F8
Kidderminster DY10 .... 117 A8
James Samuel Pl 7 B12 .... 86 F7
James Scott Rd B63 .... 82 A6
James St
Bilston WV14 .... 40 E6
Birmingham B3 .... 164 A3
Cannock WS11 .... 1 F5
Nuneaton CV11 .... 73 A5
Willenhall WV13 .... 27 A3
James Turner St B18 .... 65 E6
James Watt Dr B19 .... 66 C8
James Watt Ho B66 .... 65 B6
James Watt Ind Pk B66 .... 65 C6
James Watt Prim Sch
B21 .... 65 E7
James Watt Queensway
B4 .... 164 C3
James Watt St B71 .... 53 B8
Jamia Islamia Birmingham
Coll 4 B11 .... 87 C6
Jane Lane Sch WS2 .... 27 F3
Jane Lane Specl Cl WS2 .... 27 F4
Janice Gr B14 .... 105 B4
Janie Ct B13 .... 87 C2
Janine Ave WV11 .... 26 E7
Jaques Cl B46 .... 59 B2
Jardine Cl DY8 .... 81 A6
Jardine Cres CV4 .... 111 F2
Jardine Rd B6 .... 55 F1
Jarvis Cl LE10 .... 71 D4
Jarvis Cres B69 .... 64 A4
Jarvis Rd B23 .... 56 F6
Jarvis Way B24 .... 67 E8
JAS Ind Pk B65 .... 63 E4
Jasmin Croft B14 .... 104 E3
Jasmine Cl WV9 .... 11 A3
Jasmine Gr
Bromsgrove B61 .... 136 F4
Codsall WV8 .... 10 B3
Coventry CV3 .... 134 C8
Royal Leamington Spa
CV32 .... 157 A2
Jasmine Rd
Dudley DY2 .... 51 F1
Tamworth B77 .... 22 A4
Jasmine Way
Bedworth CV12 .... 77 D2
Darlaston WS10 .... 41 D7
Jason Cl B77 .... 21 D5
Jason Rd DY9 .... 81 F4
Javelin Ave B35 .... 58 B2
Javelin Way WS10 .... 41 D2
Jayne Cl
Wednesfield WV11 .... 26 D7
West Bromwich B71 .... 42 E1
Jay Park Cres DY10 .... 117 B2
Jay Rd DY6 .... 60 D8
Jays Ave DY4 .... 52 B4
Jays Cres B48 .... 123 B1
Jayshaw Ave B43 .... 54 E8
Jeal Cl B47 .... 124 E2
Jean Dr DY4 .... 52 D6
Jeavons Pl WV14 .... 40 C5
Jedburgh Ave WV6 .... 23 E4
Jedburgh Gr CV3 .... 133 A4
Jeddo St WV2 .... 163 B1
Jeffcock Rd WV3 .... 39 A7
Jefferies Cl LE10 .... 71 E2
Jefferson Cl B71 .... 53 B8
Jefferson Way CV4 .... 111 C3
Jeffrey Ave WV4 .... 39 F5
Jeffrey Cl CV12 .... 95 D8
Jeffrey Rd B65 .... 63 E3
Jeffrey Woods Cross
CV1 .... 113 F4
Jeffries Ho 11 B69 .... 64 A7
Jeffs Ave WV2 .... 163 C1
Jeliff St CV4 .... 111 F2
Jelleyman Cl DY11 .... 116 C6
Jellicoe Ho 9 DY4 .... 52 A8
Jellicoe Way LE10 .... 71 D3
Jenkins Ave CV5 .... 111 F4
Jenkins Cl WV14 .... 40 C5
Jenkinson Rd WS10 .... 41 D1
Jenkins St B10 .... 87 C8
Jenks Ave WV10 .... 25 E8
Jennens Rd B4 .... 66 F3
Jenner Cl WS2 .... 28 A6
Jenner Ho WS2 .... 27 F6
Jenner Rd WS2 .... 28 A6
Jenner St
Coventry CV1 .... 165 C4
Wolverhampton WV2 .... 163 D2
Jennifer Wlk B25 .... 88 E8
Jennings St B64 .... 62 F2
Jenny Cl WV14 .... 40 E1
Jennyns Ct 3 WS10 .... 42 A3
Jenny Walkers La WV6 .... 23 D1
Jensen B77 .... 21 E2
Jenton Rd CV31 .... 162 B6
Jephcott Gr B8 .... 68 A4
Jephcott Ho 2 CV1 .... 113 E3
Jephcott Rd B8 .... 68 A4
Jephsen Gdns* 20 CV32 161 F8
Jephson Ct CV2 .... 96 C4
Jephson Dr B26 .... 88 F7
Jephson Pl 3 CV31 .... 162 B7
Jeremiah Rd WV10 .... 25 F3
Jeremy Gr B92 .... 89 B3
Jeremy Rd WV4 .... 39 C5
Jerome Ct B74 .... 30 F1
Jerome Dr WS11 .... 6 A5
Jerome Prim Sch WS11 .... 5 F5
Jerome Rd
Norton Canes WS11 .... 6 A5
Sutton Coldfield B72 .... 46 D4
Walsall WS2 .... 28 B1
Jerome Way WS7 .... 7 C7
Jerrard Dr B75 .... 46 C6
Jerrard Mews B75 .... 46 C5
Jerry's La
Birmingham B23 .... 56 E6
Weeford WS14 .... 19 B8
Jersey Cl B98 .... 154 D7
Jersey Croft B36 .... 70 B6
Jersey Rd B8 .... 67 D4
Jerusalem Wlk DY10 .... 116 E7
Jervis Cl DY5 .... 61 C7
Jervis Cres B74 .... 31 D3
Jervis Ct 2 WS1 .... 28 F2
Jervis Pk B74 .... 31 C4
Jervis Rd B77 .... 35 F5
Jervis Terr B21 .... 65 D8
Jervoise Dr B31 .... 103 B5
Jervoise Jun & Inf Sch
B29 .... 85 A1
Jervoise La B71 .... 42 E1
Jervoise Rd B29 .... 85 A2
Jervoise St B70 .... 53 A4
Jesmond Gr B24 .... 57 E4
Jesmond Rd CV1 .... 113 F4
Jessel Rd WS2 .... 28 C2
Jessie Rd WS9 .... 16 B1
Jesson Cl WS1 .... 43 A7
Jesson Ct WS1 .... 43 A8
Jesson Rd
Dudley DY3 .... 51 A6
Sutton Coldfield B75 .... 47 A5
Walsall WS1 .... 43 A8
Jesson's CE Prim Sch
DY1 .... 51 B1
Jesson St B70 .... 53 E2
Jessop Dr B77 .... 21 E5
Jevons Dr 7 DY4 .... 52 B5
Jevons Rd B73 .... 45 C3
Jevon St WV14 .... 51 B8
Jewellery Quarter Sta & Stop
B18 .... 66 B4
Jew's La DY3 .... 50 E4
Jiggins La B32 .... 84 D1
Jill Ave B43 .... 43 C1
Jillcot Rd B92 .... 89 B3
Jill La B96 .... 159 B2
Jim Casey Way B78 .... 36 E4
Jim Forrest Cl 4 CV3 .... 134 F8
Jinnah Cl B12 .... 86 F8
Jinnah Rd B98 .... 153 E2
Joanna Dr CV3 .... 133 C3
Joan of Arc Ho CV3 .... 133 E6
Joan's Cl CV31 .... 162 C6
Joan St WV2 .... 39 E6
Joan Ward St CV3 .... 133 D8
Jobs Close Nature Reserve*
B93 .... 128 B6
Job's La CV4 .... 112 A2
Jockey Field DY3 .... 50 E6
Jockey La WS10 .... 42 A4
Jockey Rd B73 .... 46 A2
Jodrell St CV11 .... 73 B6
Joe Jones Ct DY3 .... 39 D1
Joe OBrien Cl CV3 .... 134 C6
Joe Williams Cl 7 CV3 .... 134 F8
Joeys La WV8 .... 10 C3
John Atkinson Sports Ctr
CV34 .... 161 B6
John Black Day Hospl
B37 .... 90 C8
John Bosco Cl B71 .... 53 B7
John Bright Cl DY4 .... 51 F8
John Bright St B1 .... 164 B2
John Cleveland Coll LE10 71 F1
John Corbett Way B60 .... 150 C1
John Cullis Gdns CV32 .... 156 F3
Johndory B77 .... 35 D6
John F Kennedy Wlk 4
DY4 .... 52 A8
John Fletcher Cl WS10 .... 42 B4
John Grace St CV3 .... 133 D8
John Gulson Prim Sch
CV1 .... 113 D5
John Harper St WV13 .... 27 B2
John Haynes Ct CV7 .... 96 A7
John Ho DY1 .... 61 D8
John Howell Dr DY4 .... 52 A5
John Kempe Way B12 .... 87 A7
John Knight Rd CV12 .... 78 B5
John McGuire Cres CV3 .... 134 E7
John Nash Sq CV8 .... 147 F3
John Nichols St LE10 .... 75 B7
John of Gaunt Ho CV3 .... 133 E6
John O'Gaunt Rd CV8 .... 147 E3
John Padden Cl B65 .... 63 B1
John Rd B62 .... 83 F3
John Riley Dr WV12 .... 27 C8
John Rous Ave CV4 .... 132 B7
Johns Cl B80 .... 159 C4
John's Cl LE10 .... 75 D5
Johns Gr B43 .... 54 C8
John Shelton Dr CV6 .... 95 D4
John Shelton Prim Sch
CV6 .... 95 D4
John Sinclair Ho CV1 .... 165 B4
Johns La WS6 .... 5 A3
John's La
Oldbury B69 .... 52 C3
Tipton DY4 .... 52 B4
John Smith Ho 3 B1 .... 66 C3
Johnson Ave WV11 .... 26 F7
Johnson Cl
Birmingham, Sparkhill
B11 .... 87 C5
Birmingham, Ward End B8 .... 68 C6
Darlaston WS10 .... 41 D5
Lichfield WS13 .... 3 C1
Redditch B98 .... 154 A5
Johnson Dr B35 .... 57 F3
Johnson Pl 3 WV14 .... 41 A7
Johnson Rd
Bedworth CV12 .... 78 C3
Birmingham B23 .... 57 A6
Burntwood WS7 .... 6 F8
Cannock WS11 .... 1 D4
Coventry CV6 .... 114 A8
Darlaston WS10 .... 41 D5
Wednesbury WS10 .... 42 C2
Willenhall WV12 .... 27 D7
Johnsons Bridge Rd B71 .... 53 C6
Johnsons Gr B68 .... 84 D8
Johnson St
Birmingham B7 .... 67 C6
Wolverhampton, Cinder Hill
WV14 .... 39 F1
Wolverhampton WV2 .... 39 D7
Wood End CV9 .... 36 C1
John St
Bedworth CV12 .... 78 A2
Birmingham B19 .... 66 B7
Brierley Hill DY5 .... 61 D4
Cannock, Chadsmoor WS11 .... 2 A4
Cannock, Wimblebury WS12 .... 2 F3
Hinckley LE10 .... 71 E1
Nuneaton, Coton CV11 .... 73 C2
Nuneaton, Stockingford
CV10 .... 72 E3
Oldbury B69 .... 64 A7
Rowley Regis B65 .... 63 C1
Royal Leamington Spa
CV32 .... 161 F8
Stourbridge DY8 .... 60 F1
Tamworth B77 .... 21 E4
Walsall WS2 .... 28 E3
West Bromwich, Great Bridge
B70 .... 52 F5
West Bromwich, Guns Village
B70 .... 53 B4
Willenhall WV13 .... 27 A1
Wolverhampton WV2 .... 40 A6
Johnstone St B19 .... 66 D8
Johnston St B70 .... 53 D1
John Street N B71 .... 53 B5
John Tofts Ho CV1 .... 165 B4
John Wesley Way WS10 .... 42 A1
John Wigley Way CV6 .... 113 F8
John Willmott Sch B76 .... 46 F4
John Wooton Ho 3
WS10 .... 41 D6
Joiners Croft B92 .... 107 E8
Joinings Bank B68 .... 64 B4
Jolly Sailor Ret Pk B78 .... 21 A3
Jonathan Rd CV2 .... 114 F8
Jon Baker Ct LE10 .... 75 E8
Jonesfield Cres WV1 .... 26 B2
Jones Ho WS2 .... 28 D3
Jones La WS7 .... 7 F7
Jone's La WS6 .... 5 B1

Jones Rd
Bedworth CV7 . . . . .78 A1
Walsall WV12 . . . . .13 D1
Willenhall WV12 . . . . .27 D8
Wolverhampton WV10 . . . .25 C6
Jones Wood Cl B76 . . . . . .58 A7
Jonfield Gdns B43 . . . . . . .43 F1
Jonkel Ave B77 . . . . .36 A5
Jonquil Cl B23 . . . . .56 C7
Jordan Cl
Kenilworth CV8 . . . . .148 B2
Kidderminster DY11 . . . . .116 A6
4 Lichfield WS13 . . . . .9 A8
Smethwick B66 . . . . .65 B5
Sutton Coldfield B75 . . . . . .32 B1
Jordan Ho B36 . . . . .68 E8
Jordan Leys 2 DY4 . . . . .52 B5
Jordan Pl WV11 . . . . .40 E3
Jordan Rd B75 . . . . .32 C2
Jordans Cl B97 . . . . .158 D6
Jordans The CV5 . . . . . . .112 C4
Jordan Way WS9 . . . . .16 B1
Jordan Well CV1 . . . . .165 C2
Joseph Cash Prim Sch
CV6 . . . . .113 C7
Joseph Chamberlain Sixth
Form Coll B12 . . . . .86 F6
Joseph Creighton Cl
CV3 . . . . .134 E7
Joseph Dewsbury Cl WS7 . .6 F8
Joseph Latham Ho 3
CV2 . . . . .96 B1
Joseph Leckie Com Tech
Coll WS5 . . . . .42 E5
Joseph Luckman Rd CV12 .78 B4
Joseph Perkins Cl B96 . .158 E2
Joseph St B69 . . . . .63 F6
Joseph Turner Prim Sch
DY4 . . . . .52 B7
Joshua Cl CV4 . . . . .112 A2
Josiah Mason Coll
Birmingham B13 . . . . .86 E2
Dudley DY1 . . . . .61 F8
Josiah Rd B31 . . . . .102 D2
Jourdain Pk CV34 . . . . . . .161 E3
Jovian Dr LE10 . . . . .71 A1
Jowett's La B71 . . . . .21 F2
Jowett's La B71 . . . . .53 B8
Joyberry Dr DY8 . . . . .81 A3
Joyce Pool 5 CV34 . . . . .160 E7
Joynson St WS10 . . . . .41 E5
Jubilee Ave
Redditch B97 . . . . .158 D7
West Bromwich B71 . . . . . .53 B7
Jubilee Bldgs 1 WS1 . . . . .1 D7
Jubilee Bsns Pk DY9 . . . .82 A5
Jubilee Cl
Great Wyrley WS6 . . . . .4 F2
Stoke Prior B60 . . . . .150 C1
Walsall WS3 . . . . .28 E6
Jubilee Cres CV6 . . . . . . .113 B8
Jubilee Ct
Birmingham, Acock's Green
B27 . . . . .88 C1
Birmingham, Turves Green
B31 . . . . .103 B1
Jubilee Dr B20 . . . . .55 A1
Jubilee Drive N DY11 . . . .116 B2
Jubilee Drive S DY11 . . . .116 B2
Jubilee Gdns B23 . . . . .56 B7
Jubilee Ho B98 . . . . .152 E8
Jubilee Park Prim Sch
B79 . . . . .53 B8
Jubilee Rd
Birmingham B45 . . . . .101 E2
Darlaston WV14 . . . . .41 A4
Tipton DY4 . . . . .52 B8
Jubilee Sports Ctr CV10 . .73 A3
Jubilee St B71 . . . . .53 D8
Jubilee Terr
Bedworth CV12 . . . . .78 B4
Stoke Prior B60 . . . . .150 C1
Jubilee Trad Ctr B5 . . . . . .66 E1
Judd Cl CV12 . . . . .77 F3
Judds La CV6 . . . . .95 E4
Judge Cl B69 . . . . .64 A7
Judge Rd DY5 . . . . .81 F7
Juggins La B94 . . . . .141 B7
Julia Ave B24 . . . . .57 F4
Julia Gdns B71 . . . . .53 F8
Julian Cl
Catshill B61 . . . . .137 A8
Coventry CV2 . . . . .114 F8
Great Wyrley WS6 . . . . .5 A3
Wolverhampton WV1 . . . . .26 B2
Julian Rd WV1 . . . . .26 B2
Julie Croft WV14 . . . . .40 E1
Juliet Cl CV11 . . . . .74 A1
Juliet Dr CV34 . . . . .161 F3
Juliet Gr WV10 . . . . .25 E7
Juliet Rd B62 . . . . .83 F3
Julius Dr B46 . . . . .70 A2
Junction 2 Ind Est B69 . . .63 F5
Junction 6 Ind Pk B6 . . . . .56 B2
Junction Ind Est B66 . . . . .64 F8
Junction Rd
Birmingham B21 . . . . .65 C8
Bromsgrove B61 . . . . .136 E3
Stourbridge, Amblecote DY8 .60 E1
Stourbridge DY8 . . . . .81 B4
Wolverhampton WV2 . . . . .40 F7
Junction St
Coventry CV1 . . . . .165 A2
Dudley DY2 . . . . .62 B8
Oldbury B69 . . . . .52 E1
Walsall WS1 . . . . .42 E7
Junction Street S B69 . . . .64 A5
Junction The 1 DY8 . . . . .80 E8

June Cres B77 . . . . .21 E5
June Croft B26 . . . . .89 D5
Juniper B77 . . . . .22 A4
Juniper Cl
Bedworth CV12 . . . . .77 E2
Birmingham B27 . . . . .88 B5
Burntwood WS7 . . . . .7 A6
Sutton Coldfield B76 . . . . .46 F3
Juniper Ct DY10 . . . . .117 A4
Juniper Dr
Coventry CV5 . . . . .111 F5
Sutton Coldfield B76 . . . . . .58 A7
Walsall WS5 . . . . .43 B4
Juniper Ho B36 . . . . .68 F7
Juniper Rise B63 . . . . .82 C5
Juno Dr CV31 . . . . .161 F5
Jurist Ho 5 LE10 . . . . .71 D1
Jury Rd DY5 . . . . .81 F7
Jury St CV34 . . . . .160 E6
Justice Cl CV31 . . . . .162 A4
Jutland Rd B13 . . . . .105 B8

K

Kanzan Rd CV2 . . . . .96 B4
Kareen Gr CV3 . . . . .135 C7
Karen Cl CV10 . . . . .72 E7
Karen Way DY5 . . . . .81 D8
Karlingford Cl CV5 . . . . . .132 D8
KATE'S HILL 62 E8
Kate's Hill Prim Sch DY2 . .62 E8
Katherine Ho 3 B17 . . . . .85 B5
Katherine Rd B67 . . . . .64 F2
Kathleen Ave CV12 . . . . . . .77 E1
Kathleen Rd
Birmingham B25 . . . . .88 C7
Sutton Coldfield B72 . . . . . .46 C4
Katie Rd B29 . . . . .85 E1
Katmandu Rd B60 . . . . . .137 C1
Katrine Cl CV10 . . . . .72 E7
Katsura Cl B74 . . . . .44 F6
Kayne Cl B96 . . . . .60 C7
Keanscott Dr B68 . . . . .64 C4
Keasden Gr WV13 . . . . . . .27 C3
Keating Gdns B75 . . . . . . .32 A4
Keatley Ave B33 . . . . .69 E2
Keats Ave
Birmingham B10 . . . . .87 D7
Cannock WS11 . . . . .1 E5
Keats Cl
Dudley DY3 . . . . .50 A5
Nuneaton CV10 . . . . .72 A4
Stourbridge DY8 . . . . .81 A8
Sutton Coldfield B74 . . . . . .31 F6
Tamworth B79 . . . . .20 F8
Keats Gr
Birmingham B27 . . . . .88 B1
Wolverhampton WV10 . . . .26 A8
Keats Ho
2 Oldbury B68 . . . . .64 C4
Redditch B97 . . . . .158 C8
Keats Pl DY10 . . . . .117 B6
Keats Rd
Coventry CV2 . . . . .114 D2
Walsall WS3 . . . . .28 E7
Willenhall WV12 . . . . .27 E7
Wolverhampton WV10 . . . .12 A1
Keble Cl
Burntwood WS7 . . . . .7 C7
Cannock WS11 . . . . .4 E8
Keble Gr
Birmingham B26 . . . . .89 B6
Walsall WS1 . . . . .43 A7
Keble Ho B37 . . . . .70 A2
Keble Wlk B79 . . . . .21 A6
Kebull Gn CV4 . . . . .131 E8
Kedleston Cl WS3 . . . . . . .14 A3
Kedleston Ct B28 . . . . . . .105 F4
Kedleston Rd B28 . . . . . .105 F5
Keegan Wlk WS2 . . . . .27 F4
Keel Dr B13 . . . . .87 D1
Keele Cl B98 . . . . .154 E6
Keele Ho B37 . . . . .70 B4
Keeley St B9 . . . . .67 B2
Keeley Dr WV11 . . . . .1 B8
Keelinge St DY4 . . . . .52 B5
Keeling Rd CV8 . . . . .148 B5
Keenan Dr CV12 . . . . .77 D1
Keen St B66 . . . . .65 D5
Keepers
Birmingham B18 . . . . .65 F5
Brownhills WS9 . . . . .15 F3
Kingswinford DY6 . . . . .60 B8
Lichfield WS14 . . . . .9 E7
Keeper's Cl WS7 . . . . .7 A6
Keepers Gate Cl B74 . . . .46 C7
Keepers Ho B73 . . . . .45 C2
Keepers La, WV6, WV8 . . .23 A8
Keepers Rd B74 . . . . .31 C5
Keepers Wlk CV12 . . . . . . .77 D1
Keer Ct B9 . . . . .67 B2
Kegworth Cl CV6 . . . . .96 A4
Kegworth Rd B23 . . . . . . .56 C2
Keir Cl CV32 . . . . .157 A2
Keir Hardie Wlk B69 . . . .52 D7
Keir Pl DY8 . . . . .80 E8
Keir Rd WS10 . . . . .42 D2
Keith Rd CV32 . . . . .157 B4
Keith Winter Cl B61 . . . .136 F6
Kelby Cl B31 . . . . .102 E4
Kelby Rd B31 . . . . .102 F4
Kele Rd CV4 . . . . .132 A7
Kelfield Ave B17 . . . . .85 B4
Kelham Pl B92 . . . . .89 B1
Kelia Dr B67 . . . . .64 F6

Kellett Rd B7 . . . . .67 A4
Kelling Cl DY5 . . . . .81 C8
Kellington Cl B8 . . . . .67 F4
Kelmarsh Dr B91 . . . . . . .107 B1
Kelmscote Rd CV6 . . . . . .112 F8
Kelmscott Rd B17 . . . . . . .85 B7
Kelsall Cl WV1 . . . . .26 B2
Kelsall Croft B1 . . . . .66 B3
Kelsey Cl
Birmingham B7 . . . . .67 B4
Nuneaton CV11 . . . . .73 E3
Kelsey La CV7 . . . . .130 D5
Kelsey's Cl CV8 . . . . .135 F3
Kelso Gdns WV6 . . . . .23 D4
Kelsull Croft B37 . . . . .70 A2
Kelton Ct B15 . . . . .86 A7
Kelvedon Gr B91 . . . . . . .107 C4
Kelverdale Gr B14 . . . . . .104 C4
Kelverley Gr B71 . . . . .43 A1
Kelvestone Ho WS11 . . . . .1 D1
Kelvin Ave CV2 . . . . .114 B5
Kelvin Cl DY11 . . . . .116 A8
Kelvin Dr WS11 . . . . .2 A3
Kelvin Pl WS2 . . . . .28 B6
Kelvin Rd
Birmingham B31 . . . . .103 B1
Royal Leamington Spa
CV32 . . . . .157 C5
Walsall WS2 . . . . .28 B6
Kelvin Way B70 . . . . .53 C1
Kelvin Way Trad Est B70 . .53 B1
Kelway CV3 . . . . .115 A2
Kelway Ave B43 . . . . .44 B3
Kelwood Dr B63 . . . . .83 A5
Kelynmead Rd B33 . . . . . .69 A2
Kemberton Cl WV3 . . . . . .24 C1
Kemberton Rd
Birmingham B29 . . . . .85 B2
Wolverhampton WV3 . . . . .24 C1
Kemble Cl WV12 . . . . .27 D3
Kemble Croft B5 . . . . .86 E7
Kemble Dr B35 . . . . .58 A3
Kemelstowe Cres B63 . . .100 C8
Kemerton Ho B97 . . . . . . .153 B4
Kemerton Way B90 . . . . .126 F6
Kempe Cl CV34 . . . . .161 A7
Kempe Rd B33 . . . . .69 A4
Kempley Ave CV2 . . . . . . .114 C2
Kempsey Cl
Halesowen B63 . . . . .82 E4
Oldbury B69 . . . . .63 E4
Solihull B98 . . . . .159 B7
Kempsey Covert B38 . . . .123 E7
Kempsey Ho B32 . . . . . . .102 A8
Kempsford Cl B98 . . . . . .158 F6
KEMPS GREEN 143 A1
Kemps Green Rd
Balsall Common CV7 . . . . .130 B6
Kemps Green B94 . . . . . . .143 A1
Kempson Ave
Sutton Coldfield B72 . . . . . .46 C1
West Bromwich B71 . . . . . .53 B5
Kempson Rd B36 . . . . .68 F8
Kempsons Gr WV14 . . . . .40 B3
Kempthorne Ave WV10 . . .11 E1
Kempthorne Gdns WS3 . .14 A2
Kempthorne Rd WV14 . . .40 F6
Kempton Cres CV32 . . . .157 C4
Kempton Ct B61 . . . . .121 A1
Kempton Dr
Great Wyrley WS6 . . . . .4 F2
Walsall WS6 . . . . .35 D4
Walsall CV34 . . . . .161 C8
Kempton Park Rd B36 . . . .68 D8
Kempton Way DY8 . . . . . . .80 E3
Kemsey Dr WV14 . . . . .40 F3
Kemshead Ave B31 . . . . .122 E8
Kemsley Rd B14 . . . . .104 F2
Ken Cl WS11 . . . . .73 E2
Kenchester Cl B98 . . . . . .154 F2
Kendal Ave
Birmingham B45 . . . . .122 B7
Coleshill B46 . . . . .70 F7
Royal Leamington Spa
CV32 . . . . .156 C2
Kendal Cl
Bromsgrove B60 . . . . .137 B1
Nuneaton CV11 . . . . .74 A6
Wolverhampton WV6 . . . . .24 F6
Kendal Ct
14 Birmingham, Selly Oak
B29 . . . . .103 C7
Birmingham, Stockland Green
B23 . . . . .56 E3
Brownhills WS9 . . . . .15 F4
Cannock WS11 . . . . .4 B8
Kendal End Rd B45 . . . . .122 D1
Kendal End Rd B45 . . . . .122 D1
Kendall Ho 12 B69 . . . . . . .63 D5
Kendall Rise DY6 . . . . .60 F5
Kendall Rd B11 . . . . .87 B7
Kendal Rise
Coventry CV5 . . . . .112 C4
Oldbury B68 . . . . .64 B3
Kendal Rise Rd B45 . . . .122 B7
Kendal Tower 8 B17 . . . . .85 D5
Kendon Ave CV6 . . . . .112 E6
Kendrick Ave B34 . . . . . . .69 E5
Kendrick Cl
Coventry CV6 . . . . .96 A4
Solihull B92 . . . . .107 F6
Kendrick Pl WV14 . . . . . . .41 A4
Kendrick Rd
Darlaston WV14 . . . . .41 A4
Sutton Coldfield B76 . . . . . .57 F5

Kendrick Rd continued
Wolverhampton WV10 . . . .25 E6
Kendricks Rd WS10 . . . . .41 F7
Kendrick St WS10 . . . . . . .42 A3
Kenelm Ct
Coventry CV3 . . . . .134 C5
Romsley B62 . . . . .101 A4
Sutton Coldfield B73 . . . . . .46 B4
Kenelm Rd
Birmingham B10 . . . . .87 E8
Dudley WV14 . . . . .40 C1
Oldbury B68 . . . . .64 A3
Sutton Coldfield B73 . . . . . .46 B4
Kenilcourt CV8 . . . . .147 D6
KENILWORTH 148 D5
Kenilworth Castle * CV8 147 D5
Kenilworth Cl
Balsall Common CV7 . . . . .130 A6
Redditch B97 . . . . .158 D6
Stourbridge DY8 . . . . .60 D2
Sutton Coldfield B74 . . . . . .46 A8
Tipton DY4 . . . . .51 D4
**Kenilworth Comm Nature
Reserve** * CV8 . . . . .148 B7
Kenilworth Cres
Walsall WS2 . . . . .28 A4
Wolverhampton WV4 . . . . .39 E4
Kenilworth Ct
Birmingham B15 . . . . .85 F8
Birmingham, Gravelly Hill
B24 . . . . .56 E2
Coventry CV3 . . . . .133 C8
Dudley DY1 . . . . .61 F8
Kenilworth Dr
Cannock WS11 . . . . .1 D4
Kidderminster DY10 . . . . .116 E2
Nuneaton CV11 . . . . .73 B3
Kenilworth Hall Mews
CV8 . . . . .147 F5
Kenilworth Ho
Birmingham B13 . . . . .105 A6
3 Walsall WS3 . . . . .28 C6
Kenilworth Rd
Balsall Common CV7,
CV8 . . . . .130 D4
Birmingham, Birchfield B20 .55 E2
Birmingham, Warley Woods
B68 . . . . .84 D7
Blackdown CV32 . . . . .156 E5
Bradnock's Marsh B92 . . .109 E5
Coventry CV4 . . . . .132 E3
Kenilworth CV8 . . . . .148 C8
Knowle B93 . . . . .128 E5
Lichfield WS14 . . . . .9 E3
Meriden CV7 . . . . .91 D1
Perton WV6 . . . . .23 F4
Royal Leamington Spa
CV32 . . . . .157 C6
Tamworth B77 . . . . .21 E4
**Kenilworth Sch Castle Sixth
Form** CV8 . . . . .148 C5
Kenilworth Sch & Sports Coll
CV8 . . . . .148 C5
Kenilworth 20 CV32 . . . .156 F1
Kenley Gr B30 . . . . .104 B8
Kenley Way B91 . . . . .106 D4
Kenmare Way WV11 . . . . .26 C4
Kenmore Ave WS12 . . . . . .1 F7
Kenmure Rd B33 . . . . .89 C8
Kennan Ave CV31 . . . . . .161 F6
Kennedy Cl
Kidderminster DY10 . . . . .116 F3
Sutton Coldfield B72 . . . . . .46 C4
Tamworth B77 . . . . .21 C1
Kennedy Cres
Darlaston WS10 . . . . .41 C7
Dudley DY3 . . . . .50 D4
Kennedy Croft B26 . . . . . .89 A7
Kennedy Ct B30 . . . . .103 B8
Kennedy Gr B30 . . . . .104 B6
Kennedy Ho WV10 . . . . . .163 D4
Kennedy Sq 3 CV32 . . . .157 A1
Kennegay Mews B29 . . . . .85 F2
Kennerley Rd B25 . . . . . . .88 D6
Kennet Cl
Brownhills WS8 . . . . .6 C2
Coventry CV2 . . . . .114 C8
Kennet Gr B36 . . . . .69 F8
Kennett Dr B23 . . . . .56 B5
Kennet Ho 5 DY1 . . . . .61 E8
Kenneth Vincent Cl B97 .158 C8
Kennford Cl B65 . . . . .63 C6
Kennington Rd WV10 . . . .25 F5
Kenpas Highway CV3 . . .133 A5
Kenrick Croft B35 . . . . . . .57 F2
Kenrick Ho
Birmingham B16 . . . . .66 A1
West Bromwich B70 . . . . . .53 E1
Kenrick Park Stop B70 . . .53 E1
Kenrick Way B70 . . . . .64 E8
Kensington Ave B12 . . . . .87 A4
Kensington Ct
Coventry CV5 . . . . .113 A1
Nuneaton CV10 . . . . .72 C6
Kensington Dr
Sutton Coldfield B74 . . . . . .31 F5
Tamworth B79 . . . . .21 B7
Kensington Gdns
Cannock WS11 . . . . .1 C2
Stourbridge DY8 . . . . .60 C1
Kensington Pl
Birmingham B18 . . . . .67 E5
Cannock WS11 . . . . .5 C8
Kensington Rd
Birmingham B29 . . . . .86 B2

Kensington Rd continued
Coventry CV5 . . . . .113 A1
Willenhall WV12 . . . . .27 B7
Ken Somner Gdns B98 . .154 A3
Kenswick Dr B63 . . . . .83 A2
Kent Ave
Fazeley B78 . . . . .20 F2
Walsall WS2 . . . . .28 B3
Kent Cl
Aldridge WS9 . . . . .16 B1
Coventry CV3 . . . . .133 E6
Kidderminster DY10 . . . . .116 E3
Walsall WS2 . . . . .28 E5
West Bromwich B71 . . . . . .53 C7
Kent Ct CV11 . . . . .71 F4
Kenthurst Cl CV5 . . . . . . .111 C4
Kentish Rd B21 . . . . .65 C8
Kentmere Cl CV2 . . . . .96 E2
Kentmere Rd B60 . . . . . . .137 C1
Kentmere Twr 4 B23 . . . . .57 B6
Kenton Ave WV6 . . . . .24 F4
Kenton Wlk 7 B29 . . . . . . .85 F2
Kent Pl
Cannock WS12 . . . . .2 F1
Dudley DY2 . . . . .62 A6
Kent Rd
Birmingham B45 . . . . .101 F1
Halesowen B62 . . . . .83 F5
Stourbridge DY8 . . . . .80 D7
Wednesbury WS10 . . . . . . .42 D4
Willenhall WS2 . . . . .27 F3
Wolverhampton WV2 . . . . .39 E7
Kent's Cl B92 . . . . .88 F3
Kents Ho B33 . . . . .69 B2
Kent St
Birmingham B5 . . . . .66 E1
Dudley DY3 . . . . .50 E5
Walsall WS2 . . . . .28 E5
Kent Street N B18 . . . . . . .65 F5
Kent St S B18 . . . . .66 E1
Kentwell B79 . . . . .20 D7
Kenward Croft B17 . . . . . .84 F7
Kenward B77 . . . . .125 A7
Kenwick Rd B17 . . . . .84 B4
Kenwood Rd B9 . . . . .68 B3
Kenwyn Gn CV7 . . . . .96 B8
Kenyon Cl
Bromsgrove B60 . . . . .137 A1
Stourbridge DY8 . . . . .81 A7
Kenyon St B18 . . . . .164 A4
Kepler B79 . . . . .20 E7
Keppel St CV1 . . . . .113 E5
Kerby Rd B23 . . . . .56 D4
Kererwin Cl B64 . . . . .63 A1
KERESLEY 94 F5
Keresley Brook Rd CV6 . . .95 A2
Keresley Cl
Coventry CV5 . . . . .95 A2
Solihull B91 . . . . .107 C5
Keresley Gr B29 . . . . .84 F2
Keresley Grange Prim Sch
CV6 . . . . .94 F1
Keresley Green Rd CV6 . . .94 F1
Keresley Newland Prim Sch
CV7 . . . . .94 F7
KERESLEY NEWLANDS . . .95 B6
Keresley Newlands CV6 . .113 A8
Kernthorpe Rd B14 . . . . .104 D4
Kerr Dr DY4 . . . . .51 E8
Kerria Ct 3 B15 . . . . .86 D8
Kerria Ctr B77 . . . . .22 A4
Kerria Rd B77 . . . . .22 B4
Kerridge Cl WV9 . . . . .11 A2
Kerris Way CV3 . . . . .115 A1
Kerr La B90 . . . . .126 A6
Kerry Cl
Barwell LE9 . . . . .71 F7
Birmingham B31 . . . . .102 F6
Brierley Hill DY5 . . . . .61 C4
Kerry Croft Cl B97 . . . . . .158 E5
Kerry Ct WS1 . . . . .43 A8
Kerry Hill B30 . . . . .150 E6
Kerry's Ho 4 CV1 . . . . . . .113 B2
Kersley Gdns WV11 . . . . .26 E5
Kerswell Cl B97 . . . . .153 B5
Kerswell Dr B90 . . . . .127 A5
Kesterton Rd B74 . . . . . . .31 E5
Kesteven Cl B15 . . . . .86 B6
Kesteven Rd B71 . . . . .53 C7
Keston Rd B44 . . . . .44 F4
Kestrel B77 . . . . .38 A6
Kestrel Ave B25 . . . . .88 C8
Kestrel Cl
Birmingham, Castle Vale
B35 . . . . .58 B3
Birmingham, Short Heath
B23 . . . . .56 D6
Kidderminster DY10 . . . . .116 E6
Lichfield WS14 . . . . .9 F8
Kestrel Ct WS7 . . . . .7 F8
Kestrel Dr B74 . . . . .31 F5
Kestrel Gr
Birmingham B30 . . . . .103 D8
Cannock WS12 . . . . .2 C1
Willenhall WV12 . . . . .27 C8
Kestrel Rd
Dudley DY1 . . . . .51 A3
Halesowen B63 . . . . .82 B7
Oldbury B65 . . . . .63 A4
Kestrel View B60 . . . . . . .137 C7
Kestrel Way WS6 . . . . .4 C2
Keswick Cl CV11 . . . . .74 A6
Keswick Dr DY6 . . . . .60 D6

Keswick Gn CV32 . . . . . . 156 D1
Keswick Gr B74 . . . . 30 F2
Keswick Ho 14 B69 . . . . . . 63 D5
Keswick Rd B92 . . . . 89 A4
Keswick Wlk CV2 . . . . . . 114 E4
Ketley Croft B12 . . . . 86 F7
Ketley Fields DY6 . . . . 61 A5
Ketley Hill Rd DY1 . . . . . . 61 F8
Ketley Rd DY6 . . . . 60 F6
KETTLEBROOK 21 B3
Kettle Brook Nature
  Reserve★ B77 . . . . 36 A6
Kettlebrook Rd
  Solihull B90 . . . . 127 C6
  Tamworth B77 . . . . 21 C3
Kettlehouse Rd B44 . . . . . 44 F3
Kettlesbank Rd DY3 . . . . . 50 B2
Kettles Wood Dr B32 . . . . 84 C2
Kettlewell Cl CV34 . . . . . 155 E1
Kettlewell Way B37 . . . . . 69 F1
Ketton Gr B33 . . . . 89 D7
Keviliok St CV3 . . . . 133 D6
Kew Cl
  Birmingham B37 . . . . 69 F3
  Kenilworth CV8 . . . . 148 C5
Kew Dr DY1 . . . . 51 A2
Kew Gdns B33 . . . . 68 E1
Kew Ho CV4 . . . . 111 F3
Kewstoke Cl WV12 . . . . . . 13 B1
Kewstoke Croft B31 . . . . 102 E6
Kewstoke Rd WV12 . . . . . 13 C1
Key Bsns Pk B24 . . . . 57 D3
Keyes Dr DY6 . . . . 49 D1
Key Hill B18 . . . . 66 B5
Key Hill Dr B18 . . . . 66 B5
Key Ind Pk WV13 . . . . 26 D3
Keynell Covert B30 . . . . . 104 C2
Keynes Dr WV14 . . . . 40 E6
Keys Bsns Village WS12 . . . 2 D3
Keys Cl WS12 . . . . 2 C3
Keys Cres 2 B71 . . . . 53 C6
Keyse Rd B75 . . . . 46 F7
Keysmith Cl WV13 . . . . . . 27 C1
Keys Park Rd WS12 . . . . . . 2 E3
Keyte Cl CV4 . . . . 52 A5
Keyway Jct WV13 . . . . 41 B8
Keyway Ret Pk WV13 . . . . 41 B8
Keyway The WV13 . . . . . . 41 A8
Keyworth Cl DY4 . . . . 52 B5
Khalsa Ind Est B66 . . . . . 65 D4
Khyber Cl WS10 . . . . 41 C8
Kidd Croft DY4 . . . . 41 C2
KIDDERMINSTER 116 D4
Kidderminster Coll DY10 116 E5
Kidderminster General Hospl
  DY11 . . . . 116 F2
Kidderminster Ind Est
  DY10 . . . . 116 F2
Kidderminster Rd
  Bromsgrove B61 . . . . . . 136 C3
  Iverley DY9 . . . . 98 C7
  Kingswinford DY6 . . . . . . 60 B7
  West Hagley DY9 . . . . . . 99 B5
Kidderminster Road S
  DY9 . . . . 98 F3
Kidderminster Sta 3
  DY10 . . . . 116 F5
Kidderminster Sta★
  DY10 . . . . 116 F5
Kidson Eventide Homes
  WV6 . . . . 24 F5
Kielder Cl
  Cannock WS12 . . . . 2 E2
  Walsall WS5 . . . . 43 C3
Kielder Dr CV10 . . . . 72 E2
Kielder Gdns DY9 . . . . . . 81 B1
Kier's Bridge Cl DY4 . . . . 52 B3
Kilberry Cl LE10 . . . . 71 A1
Kilburn Dr
  Coventry CV5 . . . . 112 F3
  Kingswinford DY6 . . . . . . 49 E1
Kilburn Gr B44 . . . . 44 F3
Kilburn Pl DY2 . . . . 62 D6
Kilburn Rd B44 . . . . 44 F3
Kilby Ave B16 . . . . 66 A2
Kilby Ct CV31 . . . . 162 A6
Kilbye Cl B77 . . . . 35 F5
Kilby Gr CV31 . . . . 162 C5
Kilbys Gr B20 . . . . 54 F2
Kilcote Rd B90 . . . . 105 C2
Kildale Cl CV1 . . . . 165 D3
Kilderkin Ct CV1 . . . . . . 165 C1
Kildwick Way 5 CV34 . . . 155 E1
Kilmarie Cl LE10 . . . . 71 A1
Kilmet Wlk 1 B67 . . . . . . 65 A5
Kilmore Croft B36 . . . . . . 68 E8
Kilmorie Rd
  Birmingham B27 . . . . 88 C5
  Cannock WS11 . . . . 1 C2
Kiln Cl
  Nuneaton CV10 . . . . 72 E3
  Royal Leamington Spa
    CV32 . . . . 157 A1
  Studley B80 . . . . 159 C4
Kiln Croft B65 . . . . 63 A4
Kiln La
  Birmingham B11 . . . . 88 B6
  Solihull B90 . . . . 126 A5
Kilnsey Gr CV34 . . . . . . 155 E1
Kiln Way
  Coventry CV7 . . . . 97 E7
  Polesworth B78 . . . . 22 F1
Kilpeck Cl B98 . . . . 154 F2
Kilsall Ct 12 WV3 . . . . . . 25 C4

Kilsby Gr B91 . . . . 127 C8
Kilvert Rd WS10 . . . . 42 B2
Kilworth Ho 6 CV32 . . . . 156 F1
Kimberley B77 . . . . 35 F7
Kimberley Ave B8 . . . . . . 67 E5
Kimberley Cl
  Coventry CV5 . . . . 111 F4
  Redditch B98 . . . . 154 B7
  Sutton Coldfield B74 . . . . 31 A2
Kimberley Pl WV14 . . . . . 51 B7
Kimberley Rd
  Baginton CV8 . . . . 133 F2
  Bedworth CV12 . . . . 78 C4
  Smethwick B66 . . . . 65 A7
  Solihull B92 . . . . 89 A1
Kimberley St WV3 . . . . . . 25 A1
Kimberley Wlk B76 . . . . . 58 D6
Kimble Cl CV5 . . . . 112 B4
Kimble Gr B24 . . . . 57 D3
Kimbley Rise B71 . . . . . . 53 A7
Kimbolton Dr B60 . . . . . 138 A5
Kimmond Ct B120 . . . . . 156 F1
Kimpton Cl B14 . . . . 104 E2
Kimsan Croft B74 . . . . . . 45 A7
Kinchford Cl B91 . . . . . . 127 B8
Kineton Cl B98 . . . . 154 D1
Kineton Croft
  Birmingham B32 . . . . . . 102 D8
  Solihull B92 . . . . 106 D8
KINETON GREEN 106 E8
Kineton Green Prim Sch
  B92 . . . . 88 D1
Kineton Green Rd B92 . . . 106 D8
Kineton Ho B13 . . . . 105 A6
Kineton La B90, B94 . . . . 127 A1
Kineton Rd
  Birmingham B45 . . . . . . 121 E7
  Coventry CV2 . . . . 114 C6
  Kenilworth CV8 . . . . . . 148 C4
  Sutton Coldfield B73 . . . . 45 E1
Kineton Rise DY3 . . . . . . 39 C2
Kinfare Dr WV6 . . . . 24 B4
Kinfare Rise DY3 . . . . 50 A8
King Charles Ave WS2 . . . 27 E2
King Charles Cl DY11 . . . 116 C6
King Charles Ct B44 . . . . 45 B2
King Charles I High Sch
  DY10 . . . . 117 A5
King Charles Prim Sch
  WS2 . . . . 27 F2
King Charles Sq 4 DY10 116 E6
King Cup Dr WS12 . . . . . . 1 C6
King David Prim Sch B13 . . 86 F4
King Edmund St 1 DY1 . . 51 B2
King Edward Ave B61 . . . 136 F5
King Edward Rd
  Birmingham B13 . . . . 86 F3
  Bromsgrove B61 . . . . . . 136 F5
  Coventry CV1 . . . . 113 F4
  Nuneaton CV11 . . . . 73 D4
King Edwards Cl B20 . . . . 66 B8
King Edwards Gdns B20 . . 66 B7
King Edwards Rd B1 . . . . 66 B3
King Edward's Row WV2 163 B1
King Edward's Sq B73 . . . 46 B5
King Edward St WS10 . . . . 41 D6
King Edward Wharf B16 . . 66 B2
King Edward VI Aston Sch
  B6 . . . . 66 F8
King Edward VI Camp Hill
  Sch For Boys B14 . . . . . 104 D7
King Edward VI Camp Hill
  Sch For Girls B14 . . . . . 104 D7
King Edward VI Coll
  Nuneaton CV11 . . . . 73 D4
  Stourbridge DY8 . . . . . . 81 A6
King Edward VI Five Ways
  Sch B32 . . . . 102 C8
King Edward VI Girls High
  Sch B15 . . . . 86 A4
King Edward VI Handsworth
  Sch for Girls B21 . . . . . . 66 A7
King Edward VI L Ctr WS14 9 C6
King Edward VI Sch WS14 . 9 C6
King Edward VI Sixth Form
  Coll CV1 . . . . 113 D6
Kingfield Rd
  Coventry CV1, CV6 . . . . . 113 D7
  Solihull B90 . . . . 105 C2
Kingfisher B77 . . . . 36 A6
Kingfisher Ave CV10 . . . . 72 C5
Kingfisher Bsns Pk B98 . . 154 A3
Kingfisher Cl
  Birmingham B26 . . . . 89 A6
  Brownhills WS8 . . . . 15 E7
  Sedgley DY3 . . . . 39 C2
Kingfisher Ct
  Alvechurch B48 . . . . . . 139 A7
  Burntwood WS7 . . . . 7 F8
  Hinckley LE10 . . . . 74 F6
Kingfisher Dr
  Birmingham B36 . . . . 70 A8
  Cannock WS12 . . . . 2 C5
  Stourbridge DY8 . . . . . . 80 C4
Kingfisher Gr
  Kidderminster DY10 . . . . 117 B3
  Willenhall WV12 . . . . 27 C8
Kingfisher Ind Est B70 . . . 52 F8
Kingfisher Nature Reserve★
  B34 . . . . 69 C5
Kingfisher Rd B23 . . . . . . 56 C7
Kingfisher Sch The 1
  B98 . . . . 154 D1
Kingfisher Sh Ctr 2 B97 153 E3
Kingfisher Sq B97 . . . . . 153 D4
Kingfisher View B34 . . . . 69 A5
Kingfisher Way B30 . . . . 103 D8

Kingfisher Wlk B97 . . . . . 153 D4
King George Ave B61 . . . 136 F4
King George Cl B61 . . . . 136 F4
King George Cres WS4 . . . 29 B6
King George Pl WS4 . . . . 29 B6
King George's Ave
  Bedworth CV12 . . . . 78 B5
  Coventry CV6 . . . . 95 F2
King George's Way LE10 . . 75 B7
King George VI Ave WS5 . . 29 C1
King George V Prim Sch
  B70 . . . . 53 D3
Kingham Cl
  Dudley DY3 . . . . 50 C2
  Redditch B98 . . . . 154 F4
Kingham Covert B14 . . . . 104 D2
King Henry VIII Prep Sch
  CV3 . . . . 133 B8
King Henry VIII Sch CV3 . 165 A1
Kingland Dr CV32 . . . . . 156 C1
Kingsbridge Ho B23 . . . . . 56 B6
Kingsbridge Rd
  Birmingham B32 . . . . 84 D1
  Nuneaton CV10 . . . . 73 D6
Kingsbridge Wlk 6 B66 . . 65 B5
Kingsbrook Dr B91 . . . . . 127 B8
Kings Bsns Pk B44 . . . . . . 44 E3
Kingsbury Ave B24 . . . . . 57 D3
Kingsbury Bsns Pk B76 . . . 58 E6
Kingsbury Cl
  Minworth B76 . . . . 58 D5
  Walsall WS4 . . . . 29 B4
Kingsbury Com L Ctr & Liby
  B24 . . . . 57 A2
Kingsbury Rd
  Birmingham B35, B76, . . . 58 B5
  Birmingham, Birches Green
    B24 . . . . 57 B3
  Birmingham, Tyburn B24,
    B35 . . . . 57 B5
  Coventry CV6 . . . . 112 E5
  Curdworth B76 . . . . 59 B6
  Minworth B76 . . . . 58 D5
  Tipton DY4 . . . . 52 A8
Kingsbury Sch & Sports Coll
  B24 . . . . 57 A2
Kingsbury Water Park★
  B78 . . . . 35 A1
King's CE Sch The WV6 . . . 24 B5
Kingsclere Wlk WV4 . . . . 38 C6
Kingscliff Rd B10 . . . . 88 A8
Kingscote Cl B98 . . . . . . 154 D7
Kingscote Gr CV3 . . . . . . 133 A4
Kingscote Rd
  Birmingham B15 . . . . 85 E6
  Dorridge B93 . . . . 127 E2
Kings Croft
  Birmingham, Castle Bromwich
    B36 . . . . 69 F7
  Birmingham, Sheldon B26 . 89 A5
  Cannock WS12 . . . . 2 E4
Kingscroft Cl B74 . . . . . . 45 A8
Kingscroft Rd B74 . . . . . . 45 A8
Kings Ct
  Stourbridge DY8 . . . . 80 E5
  Sutton Coldfield B75 . . . . 32 B3
  Tipton DY4 . . . . 52 A4
King's Ct CV11 . . . . 73 B4
Kingsdene Ave DY6 . . . . . 60 C4
Kingsdown Ave B42 . . . . . 55 A6
Kingsdown Rd B31 . . . . . . 84 F1
Kingsfield Rd B14 . . . . . 104 E8
Kingsford Cl B36 . . . . 58 D1
Kingsford Ct B92 . . . . 89 B3
Kingsford Nouveau DY6 . . 61 A5
Kingsford Rd CV6 . . . . . . 113 C7
Kings Gdn B30 . . . . 103 E4
Kings Gdns CV12 . . . . 78 C2
Kings Gr CV2 . . . . 114 B3
Kings Green Ave B38 . . . 103 F2
Kingsgrath Rd B13 . . . . . . 87 A2
Kingshayes Rd WS9 . . . . . 16 B1
KING'S HEATH 104 F7
Kings Heath Boys Sch
  B13 . . . . 105 A6
Kings Heath Prim Sch
  B14 . . . . 86 F1
King's High Sch for Girls The
  4 CV34 . . . . 160 E7
KING'S HILL 41 E4
Kings Hill Cl WS10 . . . . . 41 E5
Kingshill Dr B38 . . . . . . 103 F2
King's Hill Field WS10 . . . 41 E5
King's Hill La CV3 . . . . . 133 B2
King's Hill Mews WS10 . . . 41 D5
Kings Hill Park Ind Est
  WS10 . . . . 41 E4
King's Hill Prim Sch
  WS10 . . . . 41 E5
King's Hill Rd WS14 . . . . . 9 C6
Kings Ho B24 . . . . 57 A4
Kingsholm Cl B38 . . . . . 115 B1
KINGSHURST 70 A5
Kingshurst CV31 . . . . . . 162 E6
Kingshurst Ho B37 . . . . . . 69 F5
Kingshurst Prim Sch B37 . 70 A6
Kingshurst Rd
  Birmingham B31 . . . . . . 103 A3
  Solihull B90 . . . . 105 F1
Kingshurst Way B37 . . . . 69 F5
Kingsland Ave CV5 . . . . . 112 F2
Kingsland Dr B93 . . . . . . 127 E4

Kingsland Prim Sch B44 . 44 F4
Kingsland Rd
  Birmingham B44 . . . . 44 F4
  Wolverhampton WV1 . . . . 25 B3
Kingslea B73 . . . . 45 F1
Kingslea Rd B91 . . . . . . 106 E2
Kingsleigh Croft B75 . . . . 32 B2
Kingsleigh Dr B36 . . . . . . 69 A8
Kingsleigh Rd B20 . . . . . . 55 B2
Kingsley Ave
  Cannock WS12 . . . . 2 C7
  Redditch B98 . . . . 154 A3
  Wolverhampton WV6 . . . . 24 B4
Kingsley Bank Way B26 . . 89 B7
Kingsley Cl B79 . . . . 21 A6
Kingsley Coll B98 . . . . . . 159 C6
Kingsley Cres CV12 . . . . . 79 B3
Kingsley Ct
  Binley Woods CV3 . . . . . 135 D6
  Birmingham B25 . . . . 88 E8
Kingsley Gr DY3 . . . . 50 A5
Kingsley Rd
  Birmingham, Balsall Heath
    B12 . . . . 87 A6
  Birmingham, King's Norton
    B30 . . . . 103 D4
  Kingswinford DY6 . . . . . . 60 C5
  Kingsley Coll B98 . . . . . 159 C6
Kingsley St
  Dudley DY2 . . . . 62 C5
  Walsall WS2 . . . . 42 B7
Kingsley Terr CV2 . . . . . 114 E8
Kingsley Wlk CV2 . . . . . 114 E8
Kingslow Ave WV4 . . . . . . 38 D6
Kingsmead Mews CV3 . . 134 D6
King's Mdw CV10 . . . . 72 A3
King's Mdw WV9 . . . . 99 E3
Kingsmead Tech Coll
  WS12 . . . . 2 C4
Kingsmere Cl B24 . . . . . . 56 F2
Kings Mews WS9 . . . . 9 B5
KING'S NORTON 103 E2
King's Norton Boys Sch
  B30 . . . . 103 E4
King's Norton Bsns Ctr
  B30 . . . . 104 A4
King's Norton Com L Ctr
  B38 . . . . 123 F8
King's Norton Girls Sch &
  Language Coll B30 . . . . 103 F5
Kings Norton High Sch
  B38 . . . . 123 F8
King's Norton Nature
  Reserve★ B38 . . . . . . 103 D3
King's Norton Prim Sch
  B30 . . . . 104 A2
King's Norton Sta B30 . . . 103 F4
Kingsoak Gdns DY9 . . . . . 62 E7
Kings Par B84 . . . . 164 C2
Kings Park Dr CV3 . . . . . 115 B1
Kingspiece Ho 6 B36 . . . . 68 E8
Kings Rd
  Birmingham, Stirchley
    B14 . . . . 104 C6
  Birmingham, Stockland Green
    B23 . . . . 56 D4
  Cradley Heath B64 . . . . . 62 F1
  Darlaston WS10 . . . . 41 D6
  Dudley DY2 . . . . 51 A8
  Dudley, The Coppice WV14 . 51 A8
  Halesowen B63 . . . . 83 A4
  2 Hinckley LE10 . . . . 71 D1
  Royal Leamington Spa
    CV32 . . . . 157 A1
  Smethwick B66 . . . . 65 B7
  Stourbridge DY8 . . . . . . 80 F8
  Stourbridge, Lye DY9 . . . . 81 F5
  Tamworth B79 . . . . 21 B5
  Walsall WS1 . . . . 42 D7
  Wednesbury WS10 . . . . . 41 E3
  6 Willenhall WV13 . . . . . 27 B2
  Wolverhampton WV1 . . . . 26 A3
KINGSTANDING 55 E6
Kingstanding L Ctr B44 . . 56 B8
Kingstanding Rd B44 . . . . 55 F7
Kingstanding Sh Ctr B44 . 44 F3
Kings Terr B14 . . . . 104 D6
Kingsthorne Prim Sch
  B44 . . . . 45 A1
Kingsthorpe Rd B14 . . . . 105 A3
Kingston Arc WS11 . . . . . . 1 E1
Kingston Cl B79 . . . . 21 C7
Kingston Ct
  17 Birmingham, Selly Oak
    B29 . . . . 103 C2
  Sutton Coldfield B74 . . . . 46 B7
  Tamworth Ctr PRU WV6 . . 24 F5
Kingston Dr LE10 . . . . 71 E4
Kingston Ho CV12 . . . . . . 95 C8

Kingston Ind Est B9 . . . . . 67 B1
Kingston Mews CV31 . . . 162 C6
Kingston Rd
  Birmingham B9 . . . . 67 B1
  Coventry CV5 . . . . 112 F2
  Sutton Coldfield B75 . . . . 46 F6
Kingston Row B1 . . . . 66 C2
Kingston Way DY6 . . . . . . 60 C7
King Street Pas
  Brierley Hill DY5 . . . . 82 A8
  2 Dudley DY2 . . . . 51 D1
Kingsway
  Birmingham B68 . . . . 84 B7
  Cannock WS11 . . . . 2 A4
  Coventry CV2 . . . . 114 A3
  Essington WV11 . . . . 13 A4
  Nuneaton CV11 . . . . 73 B4
  Royal Leamington Spa
    CV31 . . . . 161 F6
  Stourbridge DY8 . . . . . . 80 E8
  Wolverhampton WV10 . . . 26 A6
Kingsway Ave 8 DY4 . . . . 52 A8
Kingsway Com Prim Sch
  CV31 . . . . 161 F6
Kingsway Dr B38 . . . . . . 103 F2
Kingsway Ho CV12 . . . . . . 78 C2
Kingsway Rd WV10 . . . . . 26 A6
Kingswear Ave WV6 . . . . . 23 F3
Kingswinford Com Sch The
  DY6 . . . . 60 F6
Kingswinford Rd DY1 . . . . 61 F7
Kingswinford Sch The
  DY6 . . . . 60 D7
KINGSWOOD 144 D3
KING'S WOOD 104 D1
Kingswood Ave
  Cannock WS11 . . . . 4 C7
  Corley CV7 . . . . 94 B8
KINGSWOOD BROOK . . . 144 E3
Kingswood Cl
  Birmingham B30 . . . . . . 104 E3
  Coventry CV6 . . . . 95 D1
  Kingswood B94 . . . . 144 E5
  Solihull B90 . . . . 106 D1
Kingswood Cotts B94 . . . 144 D3
Kingswood Croft B7 . . . . . 67 C7
Kingswood Dr
  Birmingham B30 . . . . . . 104 C3
  Great Wyrley WS6 . . . . 5 A4
  Norton Canes WS11 . . . . . 5 F5
  Sutton Coldfield B74 . . . . 44 F5
Kingswood Gdns
  Nuneaton CV10 . . . . 72 B4
  Wolverhampton WV4 . . . . 38 F6
Kingswood Ho B14 . . . . . 104 E2
Kingswood Rd
  Birmingham, Coft Common
    B31 . . . . 122 F7
  Birmingham, Moseley B13 . 87 A4
  Kingswinford DY6 . . . . . . 60 C4
  Nuneaton CV10 . . . . 72 B4
  Kingswood Sch B90 . . . . 106 B2
Kington Cl WV12 . . . . 27 B8
Kington Gdns B37 . . . . . . 69 F2
Kington Way B33 . . . . 68 E1
King William St
  Coventry CV1 . . . . 113 E4
  Stourbridge DY8 . . . . . . 80 F8
Kiniths Cres B71 . . . . 53 E5
Kiniths Way
  Halesowen B62 . . . . 63 E1
  West Bromwich B71 . . . . . 53 E4
Kinlet Ave B31 . . . . 103 C2
Kinlet Cl
  Coventry CV6 . . . . 113 C7
  Redditch B98 . . . . 154 E3
  Wolverhampton WV3 . . . . 38 A8
Kinloch Dr DY1 . . . . 50 F3
Kinnerley St WS1 . . . . . . 29 A1
Kinnersley Cl B98 . . . . . 154 E3
Kinnersley Cres B69 . . . . 63 D5
Kinnerton Cres B29 . . . . . 84 F2
Kinross Ave WS12 . . . . 1 F7
Kinross Cl CV10 . . . . 72 F2
Kinross Rd CV32 . . . . . . 157 B4
Kinross Way LE10 . . . . . . 71 A1
Kinsall Gn B77 . . . . 36 C6
Kinsey Gr B14 . . . . 104 F4
Kinsey Rd B66 . . . . 65 C4
Kinsham Dr B91 . . . . 127 B8
Kintore Croft B32 . . . . . 102 B7
Kintyre Cl
  Birmingham B45 . . . . . . 101 E1
  Hinckley LE10 . . . . 71 B1
Kintyre The CV2 . . . . . . 115 B7
Kinver Ave
  Kidderminster DY11 . . . . 116 A1
  Willenhall WV12 . . . . 27 B5
Kinver Cl CV2 . . . . 96 E1
Kinver Cres WS9 . . . . 16 C1
Kinver Croft
  Birmingham B12 . . . . 86 E7
  Sutton Coldfield B76 . . . . 58 A8
Kinver Ct B11 . . . . 87 D4
Kinver Dr
  Hagley DY9 . . . . 99 C7
  Wolverhampton WV4 . . . . 38 C5
Kinver Rd B31 . . . . 103 D2
Kinver St DY6 . . . . 60 E1
KINWALSEY 92 F7
Kinwalsey La CV7 . . . . . . 92 F6
Kinwarton Cl B26 . . . . . . 88 D6
Kipling Ave
  Dudley WV14 . . . . 40 B1
  Warwick CV34 . . . . 160 C4
Kipling Cl
  Nuneaton CV10 . . . . 72 A5
  Tipton DY4 . . . . 52 A8

Kipling Rd
Birmingham B30 103 C4
Coventry CV6 113 A8
Dudley DY3 50 A5
Willenhall WV12 27 E8
Wolverhampton WV10 11 D2
Kipling Rise B79 20 F8
Kipling Wlk 3 DY10 117 B6
Kirby Ave CV34 155 F1
Kirby Cl
Bilston WV14 40 E3
Brandon CV8 135 F5
Coventry CV1 113 D6
Kirby Cnr CV4 132 B5
Kirby Corner Rd CV4 132 B6
Kirby Ct DY1 50 E3
Kirby Rd
Birmingham B18 65 E6
Coventry CV5 112 F2
Kirfield Dr LE10 71 F3
Kirkby Gn B73 46 B3
Kirkdale Ave CV6 95 D3
Kirkham Gdns DY5 61 C6
Kirkham Gr B33 68 F4
Kirkham Way DY4 52 A5
Kirkland Way B78 34 B8
Kirkpatrick Dr DY8 60 E4
Kirkside Gr WS8 15 F7
Kirkstall Cl WS3 13 F2
Kirkstall Cres WS3 13 F2
Kirkstone Cres
Birmingham B43 54 F6
Wombourne WV5 49 A6
Kirkstone Ct DY5 81 B8
Kirkstone Rd CV12 78 A2
Kirkstone Way DY5 81 B8
Kirkstone Wlk CV11 74 A6
Kirkwall Rd B32 84 D1
Kirkwood Ave B23 56 F7
Kirmond Wlk WV6 25 C5
Kirstead Gdns WV6 24 B3
Kirtley B77 21 E2
Kirton Cl
Coventry CV6 94 F1
Whitnash CV31 162 B3
Kirton Gr
Birmingham B33 69 A4
Solihull B91 107 A1
Wolverhampton WV6 24 C4
Kitchener Rd
Birmingham B29 86 B1
Coventry CV6 113 E8
Dudley DY2 51 F1
Kitchen La
Wednesfield WV11 26 F8
Wolverhampton WV11 12 F1
Kitebrook Cl
Redditch B98 154 E4
Solihull B90 127 A7
Kitegreen Cl B37 70 D4
Kite La B97 153 A5
Kites Cl CV34 155 E2
Kites Nest La CV35 146 C1
Kitsland Rd B34 69 E6
Kitswell Gdns B32 102 A8
Kittermaster Rd CV7 92 C1
Kittiwake Dr
Brierley Hill DY5 81 D7
Kidderminster DY10 117 B3
Kittoe Rd B74 32 A3
KITT'S GREEN 69 C3
Kitt's Green Rd B33 69 B3
KITWELL 102 A7
Kitwell La B32 102 A8
Kitwell Prim Sch B32 102 A7
Kitwood Ave B78 36 F6
Kitwood Dr B92 107 D7
Kixley La B93 128 C6
KIXLEY WHARF 128 C7
Klaxon Ind Est B11 87 F4
Klevedon Cl CV11 74 A1
Knapton Cl LE10 71 A3
Knaresdale Cl DY5 81 C8
Knaves Castle Ave WS8 6 F2
Knebley Cres CV10 73 C1
Knebworth Cl B44 55 E8
Knibbs The 1 CV34 160 E7
Knight Ave CV1 113 E1
Knightcote Dr
Royal Leamington Spa
CV32 161 E8
Solihull B91 127 B8
Knight Ct B75 47 C5
Knight Ho B13 105 D7
Knightley Cl CV32 157 E5
Knightley Rd B91 106 F2
Knightlow Ave CV3 134 C6
Knightlow Cl CV8 148 C3
Knightlow Rd B17 85 B8
Knighton Cl B74 31 F3
Knighton Ct B23 56 C2
Knighton Dr B74 31 F3
Knighton Rd
Birmingham B31 103 C4
Cannock WS12 2 E3
Dudley DY2 62 D4
Sutton Coldfield B74 31 D5
Knights Ave WV6 24 E6
Knightsbridge Ave CV12 78 C4
Knightsbridge Cl B74 31 F4
Knightsbridge Ct B37 69 F5
Knightsbridge La WV12 27 C6
Knightsbridge Rd B92 89 A1
Knights Cl
Birmingham B23 56 E2
Hinckley LE10 75 D4
3 Willenhall WV13 27 B2
Knights Cres WV6 24 E7
Knights Ct B37 90 E8
Knights Ct LE10 74 E8
Knights Ct
Norton Canes WS11 6 A4
Warwick CV34 160 D6
Knightsfield Cl B73 45 C3
Knightsford Cl B97 152 F2
Knights Hill WS9 30 B3
Knights Rd
Birmingham B11 88 A4
Nuneaton CV10 73 B1
Knights Templar Way
CV4 112 A1
Knightstone Ave B18 66 A4
Knights Wood Cl B75 46 D7
Knightwick Cres B23 56 C5
Knipersley Rd B73 57 A7
Knoll Cl WS7 7 A5
Knollcroft 4 B16 66 A2
Knoll Croft
Aldridge WS9 16 C1
Cheswick Green B90 126 D4
Coventry CV3 133 C6
Knoll Dr
Coventry CV3 133 C6
Warwick CV34 155 E1
Knoll Sch The DY11 116 A7
Knoll The
Birmingham B32 84 C1
Kingswinford DY6 60 E5
Knott Ct 11 DY5 61 D2
Knottesford Cl B80 159 C3
Knotting Way CV3 114 C1
Knottsall La B68 64 B3
Knotts Farm Rd DY6 61 A4
Knowesley Cl B60 137 B2
Knowlands Rd B90 127 A7
KNOWLE 128 B6
Knowle CE Prim Sch
B93 128 C6
Knowle Cl
Birmingham B45 122 D7
Redditch B98 154 C6
KNOWLE GROVE 128 B3
Knowle Hill CV8 148 C6
Knowle Hill Nature Reserve★
CV8 148 B6
Knowle Hill Rd DY2 62 B4
Knowle La WS14 9 B3
Knowle Rd
Birmingham B11 87 D3
Eastcote B92 108 E2
Rowley Regis B65 63 A4
Knowles Ave CV10 72 C4
Knowles Dr B74 46 A7
Knowles Rd WV1 25 F1
Knowles St WS10 42 A3
KNOWLE THE 63 A4
Knowle Wood Rd B93 128 B3
Knox Cres CV11 73 F8
Knox Rd WV2 39 D6
Knox's Grave La WS14,
B78 19 D7
Knoyle Ct 1 DY8 80 F6
Knutswood Cl B13 105 D7
Kohima Dr DY8 80 E5
Kossuth Rd WV14 40 A1
Kurtus B77 35 D6
Kwikform Bldg CV6 95 E4
Kyle Cl WV10 11 B1
Kyles Way B32 102 B7
Kynaston Cres WV8 10 B2
Kynaston Ho B71 53 C8
Kyngsford Rd B33 69 D3
Kynner Way CV3 135 B8
Kynoch Wks B6 55 F3
Kyotts Lake Rd B11 87 B7
Kyotts Lake Unit Factory
B11 87 B7
Kyrwicks La B11 87 A7
Kyter La B36 69 B8

L

Laburnham Ct WS14 9 C5
Laburnham Rd DY6 60 E6
Laburnum Ave
Birmingham B37 69 F6
Cannock WS11 4 E7
Coventry CV6 112 F5
Kenilworth CV8 148 A4
Smethwick B67 64 E4
Tamworth B79 21 B8
Laburnum Cl
Bedworth CV12 77 E2
Birmingham B37 69 F6
Cannock WS11 4 E7
Hollywood B47 125 A5
Redditch B98 153 E2
Stourbridge DY8 80 E7
Walsall WS3 15 A2
Laburnum Cotts B21 65 E8
Laburnum Croft B69 52 B2
Laburnum Dr
Sutton Coldfield B76 47 A3
Whitnash CV31 162 B3
Laburnum Gr
Birmingham B13 86 F3
Bromsgrove B61 136 F4
Burntwood WS7 6 F6
Kidderminster DY11 116 B8
Nuneaton CV10 72 D6
Warwick CV34 156 B1
Willenhall WS2 27 F3
Laburnum Ho WS4 15 D1
Laburnum Rd
Bilston WV1 40 B8
Laburnum Rd *continued*
Birmingham B30 103 F8
Brownhills WS9 16 A3
Dudley DY1 51 C4
Tipton DY4 51 F7
Walsall WS5 43 C4
Wednesbury WS10 42 B4
Wolverhampton WV4 39 F3
Laburnum St
Stourbridge DY8 80 E7
Wolverhampton WV3 25 B1
Laburnum Trees B47 124 F7
Laburnum Villas 2 B11 87 C5
Laburnum Way B31 103 A1
Laceby Gr B13 87 D1
Lacell Cl CV34 155 E1
Ladbroke Dr B76 46 F2
Ladbroke Gr B27 106 C8
Ladbroke Pk CV34 155 E1
Ladbrook Cl B98 158 E7
Ladbrook Gr DY3 50 B3
Ladbrook Rd
Coventry CV5 112 A4
Solihull B91 107 C2
Ladbury Gr WS5 43 A4
Ladbury Rd WS5 43 A3
Ladeler Gr B33 69 E2
Ladies Wlk DY3 50 D8
Lady Bank
Birmingham B32 102 B7
Tamworth B79 21 B4
Lady Bracknell Mews
B31 103 C4
Lady Brades Ho 5 B69 64 A7
Lady Byron La B93 127 F8
Ladycroft
5 Birmingham B16 66 B2
Cubbington CV32 157 E5
LADYES HILLS 148 A7
Ladyfields Way CV6 95 B4
Lady Grey Ave CV34 161 E3
Lady Grey's Wlk DY8 80 D5
Ladygrove Cl B98 159 A8
Lady Harriet's La B98 153 F4
Lady Katherine Leveson CE
Prim Sch B93 129 B5
Lady La
Coventry CV6 95 F4
Earlswood B90, B94 126 B3
Kenilworth CV8 147 F4
Lady Lane Mobile Home Pk
CV6 95 F4
Ladymead Dr CV6 95 B2
Lady Meadow Cl B78 21 A3
LADYMOOR 40 D4
Ladymoor Rd WV14 40 C3
Ladypool Ave 3 B11 87 B6
Ladypool Cl
Halesowen B62 83 C4
Walsall WS4 29 A5
Ladypool Rd B11, B12 87 A5
Ladypool Sch B11 87 B6
Ladysmith Rd B63 82 C6
Lady Warwick Ave CV12 78 D2
Ladywell Cl WV5 49 A8
Ladywell Wlk B5 164 C1
LADYWOOD 66 A2
LADY WOOD 45 F8
Ladywood Arts & L Ctr
B16 66 A2
Ladywood Cl DY5 61 F2
Ladywood Middleway
B16 66 A2
Ladywood Rd
Birmingham B16 66 A1
Sutton Coldfield B74 46 A8
Laertes Gr CV34 161 F2
Laggan Cl CV10 72 C5
Lagonda B77 21 E3
Lagoon Rd B77 35 E6
Lagrange B79 20 E6
Laing Ho 2 B69 63 D5
Lair The B78 36 F8
Lake Ave WS5 43 C7
Lake Cl WS5 43 C7
Lakedown Cl B14 104 E1
Lakefield B31 102 F4
Lakefield Cl B28 106 B7
Lakefield Rd WV11 26 E5
Lakehouse Ct B23 56 E8
Lakehouse Gr B38 103 D3
Lakehouse Rd B73 56 F8
Lakeland Dr B77 36 B7
Lakeland Ho CV34 161 A7
Lakenheath B79 21 C7
Laker Cl DY8 81 A7
Lakes Cl DY11 116 C7
LAKESIDE 154 B3
Lakeside
Bedworth CV12 78 A2
Redditch B97 152 D7
Sutton Coldfield B74 31 B5
Lakeside Cl WV13 26 E3
Lakeside Ct
Birmingham B20 55 A4
Brierley Hill DY5 81 B8
Lakeside Dr
Birmingham B23 56 B6
Norton Canes WS11 6 B6
Solihull B90 126 F7
Lakeside Ind Est B98 154 B3
Lakeside Ind Pk B78 20 F1
Lakeside Pk B78 20 F1
Lakeside Prim Sch B77 21 E2
Lakeside Rd B70 53 A6
Lakeside Trad Est B98 154 A4
Lakeside Wlk B23 56 C3
Lakes Rd B23 56 A6
Lakes Sta The B94 141 F8
Lake St DY3 50 D3
Lakeview Ave B78 21 A2
Lakeview Cl B43 44 B2
Lake View Cl B30 103 E5
Lake View Rd CV5 112 F4
Lakewood Dr B45 102 B1
Lakey La B28 106 B7
Lakey Lane Prim Sch
B28 106 B7
Lakin Ct CV34 160 F8
Lakin Ho CV34 160 F8
Lakin Rd CV34 160 F8
Lambah Cl WV14 40 F7
Lamb Cl B34 69 E5
Lambert Cl B23 56 D6
Lambert Ct
Kingswinford DY6 60 D8
Warwick CV34 160 D6
Lambert Dr WS7 7 A8
Lambert End B70 53 B3
Lambert Fold 4 DY2 62 E8
Lambert Rd WV10 25 F6
LAMBERT'S END 53 B2
Lambert St B70 53 B3
Lambeth Cl
Birmingham B37 70 B4
Coventry CV2 114 E7
Lambeth Rd
Bilston WV14 40 B7
Birmingham B44 44 E3
Lambourn Cl WS3 14 C2
Lambourn Cres CV31 162 C6
Lambourne Cl
Coventry CV5 112 A4
Great Wyrley WS6 4 F3
4 Lichfield WS14 9 E8
Lambourne Gr B37 69 E2
Lambourne Way
Brierley Hill DY5 81 B8
Norton Canes WS11 6 A5
Lambourn Rd
Birmingham B23 56 D4
Willenhall WV13 27 D1
Lambscote Cl B90 105 C2
Lamb St CV1 165 B3
Lamerton Cl CV2 114 C6
Lamford Cl LE10 71 B1
Lamintone Dr CV32 156 D2
Lammas Cl B92 89 C1
Lammas Croft CV31 162 A3
Lammas Ct CV34 160 D6
Lammas Ho 6 CV6 113 A4
Lammas Rd
Coventry CV6 112 F4
Stourbridge DY8 60 C3
Lammas Wlk CV34 160 D7
Lammermoor Ave B43 43 F2
Lamont Ave B32 84 F3
Lamorna Cl
Nuneaton CV11 73 F4
Wolverhampton WV3 38 B8
Lamprey B77 35 D6
Lanark Cl DY6 60 F5
Lanark Croft B35 57 F3
Lancaster Ave
Aldridge WS9 30 B8
Birmingham B45 122 A8
Wednesbury WS10 42 C3
Lancaster Circus Queensway
B4 164 C4
Lancaster Cl B30 104 A6
Lancaster Dr B35 58 B2
Lancaster Gdns WV4 38 E5
Lancaster Ho
Cannock WS12 2 D1
7 Rowley Regis B65 63 E4
5 Stourbridge DY8 80 F8
Lancaster Pl
Kenilworth CV8 147 E2
Walsall WS3 14 C2
Lancaster Rd
Brierley Hill DY5 61 C2
Hinckley LE10 75 D8
Lancaster Sch B36 58 E1
Lancaster St B4 164 C4
Lance Cl LE10 75 D5
Lancelot Cl B8 67 E3
Lancelot Ho DY10 117 C8
Lancelot Pl B70 52 E4
Lanchester Cl B79 20 E7
Lanchester Rd
Birmingham B38 104 A1
Coventry CV6 113 B6
Lanchester Way B36 58 F1
Lancia Cl CV6 96 B4
Lancing Rd CV12 79 C2
Lander Cl B45 122 A6
Landgate Rd B21 54 C2
Land La B37 90 A7
Land Oak Dr DY10 117 B7
Landor Ho CV31 162 A2
Landor Rd
Dorridge B93 128 A6
Redditch B98 154 A1
Warwick CV34 160 D8
Whitnash CV31 162 A3
Landor St B8 67 B3
Landport Rd WV2 39 F8
Landrail Wlk B36 70 A8
Landrake Rd DY6 61 A5
Landsberg B79 20 F6
Landsdown Pl 2 B18 66 A5
Landseer Dr LE10 71 B3
Landseer Gr B43 44 D4
Landsgate DY8 81 A1
Landswood Cl B44 45 A1
Landswood Rd B68 64 C4
LANDYWOOD 14 A8
Landywood Ent Pk WS6 13 F8
Landywood Gn WS6 4 E2
Landywood La WS6 4 E2
Landywood Prim Sch
WS6 13 F8
Landywood Sta WS6 4 F2
Lane Ave WS2 28 B3
Lane Cl WS2 28 B3
Lane Croft B76 58 A8
Lane Ct 8 WV3 25 C4
LANE GREEN 10 C3
Lane Green Ave WV8 10 C1
Lane Green Ct WV8 10 B3
Lane Green Fst Sch WV8 10 B4
Lane Green Rd WV8 10 C2
Lane Green Rd Masionettes
WV8 10 B3
Laneham Pl CV8 148 B8
LANE HEAD 27 D5
Lane Rd WV4 40 A3
LANESFIELD 39 E4
Lanesfield Dr WV4 40 A4
Lanesfield Drive Ind Est
WV4 40 A4
Lanesfield Prim Sch WV4 40 A4
Laneside CV3 134 E6
Laneside Ave B74 44 F7
Laneside Dr LE10 71 F3
Laneside Gdns WS2 28 B2
Lanes Sh Ctr The 1 B73 57 B7
Lane St WV14 40 D3
LANEY GREEN 4 A3
Lanfear Ct LE10 75 C7
Langbank Ave CV3 134 D7
Langbay Ct CV2 114 F6
Langcliffe Ave CV34 155 F1
Langcomb Rd B90 126 A8
Langdale Ave CV6 95 D3
Langdale Cl
Brownhills WS8 15 E6
Royal Leamington Spa
CV32 157 D3
Langdale Croft B21 65 E7
Langdale Ct B77 22 A6
Langdale Dr
Bilston WV14 40 D7
Cannock WS11 4 C7
Nuneaton CV11 74 A6
Langdale Gn WS11 4 C7
Langdale Rd
Birmingham B43 54 F7
Hinckley LE10 75 A8
Langdale Way DY9 81 D4
Langdon St B9 67 B2
Langdon Wlk B27 88 E4
Langfield Rd B93 128 A7
Langford Ave B43 54 E8
Langford Cl WS1 29 A1
Langford Croft B91 107 C2
Langford Gr B17 85 C3
Langham Cl B26 89 A7
Langham Gn B74 30 F1
Langholm Dr
Birmingham B44 45 D1
Cannock WS12 2 E2
Langland Dr DY3 50 C8
LANGLEY 64 A5
Langley Ave WV14 51 C8
Langley Cl
Brownhills WS9 16 A3
Redditch B98 154 D1
Langley Cres B68 64 B4
Langley Croft CV4 112 A2
Langley Dr B35 58 A1
Langley Gdns
Oldbury B68 64 B4
Wolverhampton WV3 38 D7
Langley Gr B10 87 D8
LANGLEY GREEN 64 B3
Langley Green Rd B69 64 A4
Langley Green Sta B69 64 B5
Langley Hall Dr B75 47 B5
Langley Hall Rd
Solihull B92 106 C7
Sutton Coldfield B75 47 B5
Langley Heath Dr B76 47 A3
Langley High St B69 64 A5
Langley Mede B68 64 B5
Langley Parkway B75 46 F6
Langley Prim Sch
Oldbury B69 64 A5
Solihull B92 106 D6
Langley Rd
Birmingham B10 87 D8
Oldbury B68 64 B4
Whitnash CV31 162 A4
Wolverhampton WV3, WV4 38 B7
Langley Rise B92 89 D3
Langley Sch B92 106 D7
Langley Specl Sch B75 42 B1
Langleys Rd B29 85 E1
Langley Swimming Ctr
B68 64 A$
Langley Wlk B37 70 D2
Langlodge Rd CV6 95 B2
Langmead Cl WS2 27 D3
Langnor Rd CV2 114 C6
Langsett Rd WV10 25 E4
Langstone Rd
Birmingham B14 105 B3
Dudley DY1 50 F1
Langton Cl
Birmingham B36 70 B6
Coventry CV3 134 E8

Langton Ct **1** WS13...... 3 A1
Langton Pl WV14 .... 41 A6
Langton Rd B8.......... 67 E4
Langtree Ave B91...... 107 B1
Langtree Cl WS12...... 2 D1
Langwood Cl CV4 ...... 132 B7
Langwood Ct B36...... 69 B8
Langworth Ave B27 .... 88 C5
Lannacombe Rd B31 ... 122 E6
Lansbury Ave WS10 .... 41 C4
Lansbury Cl CV2 ...... 114 E7
Lansbury Dr WS11 ...... 1 E4
Lansbury Gn B64....... 83 B8
Lansbury Rd B64....... 83 B8
Lansbury Wlk **6** DY4... 52 A8
Lansdale Ave B92..... 107 F8
Lansdowne Cir CV32 ... 157 A1
Lansdowne Cl
  Bedworth CV12 .... 78 A3
  Dudley, West Coseley WV14 51 A7
  Rowley Regis DY2 ..... 62 F6
Lansdowne Cres
  6 Royal Leamington Spa
  CV32................. 157 A1
  Studley B80 .... 159 D3
  Tamworth B77 .... 35 D8
Lansdowne Ct DY9...... 81 C1
Lansdowne Rd
  Bilston WV14 .... 40 E7
  Birmingham, Erdington B24. 56 F3
  Birmingham, Handsworth
  B21................. 66 A8
  Halesowen, Hasbury B63 . 82 D2
  Halesowen, Hurst Green
  B62................. 63 F1
  2 Royal Leamington Spa
  CV32................. 157 A1
  Studley B80 .... 159 D3
  Wolverhampton WV1.... 163 A4
Lansdowne St
  Birmingham B18 .... 65 F4
  Coventry CV2.......... 113 F3
  Royal Leamington Spa
  CV32................. 157 A1
Lansdown Gn DY11.... 116 C5
Lansdown Ho B15...... 86 D8
Lant Cl CV7........... 131 B7
Lantern Rd DY2........ 62 C2
Lanthorn Cl WS13....... 9 A7
Lanton Cl WS3......... 14 A2
Lapal La B62.......... 83 F3
Lapal La B62.......... 84 A2
Lapal Lane N B62...... 83 E3
Lapal Lane S B32, B62 . 83 F2
Lapal Prim Sch B62.... 83 F4
Lapley Cl WV1......... 26 B2
Lappath Ho B32....... 102 D8
Lapper Ave WV4....... 39 F2
Lapwing B77.......... 36 A6
Lapwing Cl
  Brownhills WS8....... 15 E7
  Cheslyn Hay WS6....... 4 C1
  Kidderminster DY10... 117 B1
Lapwing Croft B23..... 56 C7
Lapwing Dr B92....... 109 B7
Lapwood Ave DY6...... 61 A5
LAPWORTH............ 143 E3
Lapworth CE Prim Sch
  B94................. 144 D3
Lapworth Dr B91...... 158 F7
Lapworth Dr B73....... 45 C3
Lapworth Gr B12....... 86 F6
Lapworth Oaks B94.... 144 D3
Lapworth Rd CV2....... 96 C1
Lapworth St B94...... 144 B2
Lapworth Sta B94..... 144 D1
Lara Cl B17........... 85 B8
Lara Gr DY4.......... 52 A2
Larch Ave B21........ 54 D2
Larch Cl
  Lichfield WS14........ 9 E7
  Nuneaton CV10 .... 72 D6
Larch Croft
  Birmingham B37 .... 70 B2
  Tipton B69........... 52 B2
Larch Dr B31......... 102 C1
Larches Cottage Gdns
  DY11................ 116 C3
Larches La WV3........ 25 A2
Larches Rd DY11...... 116 D4
Larches St B11........ 87 B6
Larches The
  Bedworth CV7 .... 96 B8
  Wolverhampton WV11... 26 B5
Larchfield Cl B20...... 55 B3
Larch Gdns WV14...... 40 F4
Larch Gr
  Sedgley DY3.......... 50 E2
  Warwick CV34 .... 156 A1
Larch Ho
  Birmingham B36 ...... 68 F8
  Stourbridge DY8 ...... 80 C6
Larchmere Dr
  Birmingham B28 ..... 105 F8
  Birmingham B28 ..... 106 E3
  Essington WV11....... 13 B3
Larch Rd DY6......... 60 E7
Larch Tree Ave CV4 ... 112 A2
Larch Wlk B25........ 88 B8
Larchwood Cres B74.... 44 E8
Larchwood Dr WS11 ... 2 A4
Larchwood Gn WS5..... 43 B4
Larchwood Rd
  Bedworth CV7 .... 78 B1
  Walsall WS5.......... 43 A4

Larcombe Dr WV4 ...... 39 D5
Large Ave WS10 .... 41 C4
Lark Cl B14.......... 105 A2
Larkfield Ave B36...... 69 B8
Larkfield Rd B98..... 154 A1
Larkfield Way CV5 .... 112 A6
Lark Hall Inf Sch **2** B79.. 21 A8
Larkhill DY10........ 116 E7
Larkhill Rd DY8....... 80 C4
Larkhill Wlk B14..... 104 D1
Larkin Cl
  Bulkington CV12 ...... 79 B3
  Wolverhampton WV10... 12 A1
Larkin Gr CV2........ 114 F6
Lark Meadow Dr B37... 69 F3
Larksfield B66........ 65 B4
Larksfield Mews DY5.... 81 C7
Larks Mill WS3....... 14 E4
Larkspur B77......... 35 D4
Larkspur Ave WS7 ..... 7 A5
Larkspur Croft B36.... 68 D8
Larkspur Ct CV2
  Bedworth CV12 .... 95 C8
  Halesowen B62........ 83 F7
Larkspur Dr WV10 ..... 12 B7
Larkspur Gr **5** CV12 .... 77 D2
Larkspur Way WS8..... 15 D6
Larkswood Dr
  Sedgley DY3.......... 50 D7
  Wolverhampton WV4.... 38 C3
Larne Rd B26......... 89 A7
Lashbrooke Ho B45 ... 121 F7
Lassington Cl B98.... 154 E4
Latches Cl WS10 ...... 41 E6
Latchford Cl B98..... 154 E6
Latelow Rd B33....... 69 A2
Latham Ave B43....... 54 E7
Latham Cres DY4 ..... 52 A3
Latham Rd CV5....... 113 A2
Lath La B66.......... 64 D8
Lathom Gr B33........ 68 F5
Latimer Cl CV8....... 148 A7
Latimer Gdns B15..... 86 D7
Latimer Pl B18........ 65 E6
Latimer St WV13...... 27 B3
Latymer Cl B76........ 58 A7
Lauder Cl
  Sedgley DY3.......... 39 C1
  Willenhall WV13...... 26 D1
Lauderdale Ave CV6.... 95 D3
Lauderdale Cl WS8..... 15 E6
Lauderdale Gdns WV10.. 11 E3
Laughton Cl B31...... 123 B7
Launce Gr CV34...... 161 F2
Launceston Cl
  Tamworth B77 .... 21 D2
  Walsall WS5.......... 43 D7
Launceston Ct CV1..... 73 F4
Launceston Rd WS5.... 43 D7
Launde The B28...... 105 E3
Laundry Cotts CV35 .. 145 E4
Laundry Rd B66....... 65 C3
Laureates Wlk B74..... 46 A8
Laurel Ave B12........ 87 A5
Laurel Bank B79....... 21 B6
Laurel Bank Mews B60.. 137 F4
Laurel Cl
  Coventry CV2......... 96 E2
  Dudley DY1.......... 51 A3
  Lichfield WS14........ 9 D8
  Redditch B98........ 153 E2
Laurel Ct
  Birmingham B13 .... 87 A2
  Coventry CV5........ 112 F1
Laurel Dr
  Burntwood WS7........ 7 C7
  Cannock WS12........ 2 E4
  Hartshill CV10....... 72 A7
  Smethwick B66........ 65 A8
  Sutton Coldfield B74.. 44 E8
Laurel Gdns
  Barnt Green B45..... 138 E8
  Birmingham B21 ...... 54 E1
  3 Birmingham, Stockfield
  B27................. 88 C5
Laurel Gr
  Birmingham B30 ..... 103 E6
  Bromsgrove B61..... 136 F4
  Darlaston WV14....... 41 A4
  Wolverhampton WV4.... 38 E6
  Laurel La B63........ 83 B3
Laurel Rd
  Birmingham, Handsworth
  B21................. 54 F1
  Birmingham, King's Norton
  B30................ 104 A4
  Dudley DY1.......... 51 A3
  Tipton DY4.......... 51 F7
  Walsall WS5.......... 43 B4
Laurel Road Com Sports Ctr
  B21................. 54 E2
Laurels Cres CV7..... 130 C6
Laurels The
  Bedworth CV12 .... 77 E2
  Birmingham B68 ...... 84 B6
  Birmingham WV11..... 13 B3
  Birmingham, Sheldon B26.. 89 C5
  Coventry CV4........ 132 F6
  Portway B47......... 140 F8
  Smethwick B66........ 65 C4
  Sutton Coldfield B73.. 46 B1
Laurence Ct B31...... 103 B5
Laurence Gr
  Cannock WS11......... 5 F6
  Wolverhampton WV6.... 24 E7
Lauriston Cl DY1....... 50 F3

Lavender Ave CV6...... 112 F5
Lavender Cl
  Bedworth CV12 .... 77 E1
  2 Walsall WS5....... 42 F3
  Wolverhampton WV9.... 10 F3
Lavender Gdns **1** B23.. 56 B7
Lavender Gr
  Bilston WV14 .... 40 F6
  Walsall WS3.......... 28 E5
Lavender Hall La CV7 . 110 C2
Lavender Ho B38...... 123 F8
Lavender La DY8...... 80 D3
Lavender Rd
  Dudley DY1.......... 51 B3
  Tamworth B77 .... 21 F4
Lavendon Rd B42...... 55 B5
Lavenham Cl CV11..... 79 C8
Lavinia Rd B62........ 83 E3
Law Cl B69........... 52 D2
Law Cliff Rd B42...... 55 B6
Lawden Rd B10........ 87 B8
Lawford Ave WS14...... 9 E7
Lawford Cl
  Birmingham B7 .... 67 A3
  Coventry CV3........ 114 E1
Lawford Gr
  Birmingham B5 .... 86 E8
  Solihull B90........ 105 D2
Lawford Rd CV31..... 162 B5
Lawfred Ave WV11..... 26 D5
Lawley Cl
  Coventry CV4........ 112 A2
  Walsall WS4.......... 15 B1
Lawley Middleway B4.. 67 A3
Lawley Rd WV14....... 40 B6
Lawley St
  Dudley DY1.......... 51 A1
  West Bromwich B70 ... 52 F3
Lawley The B63....... 82 D1
Lawn Ave DY8........ 80 E4
Lawn La WV9.......... 11 A7
Lawnoaks Cl DY9...... 81 B2
Lawn Rd WV2.......... 39 F6
Lawns Bsns Ctr The **6**
  LE10................ 75 E8
Lawnsdale Cl B46...... 70 F7
Lawnsdown Rd DY5.... 81 F6
Lawnside Gn B47...... 52 C7
Lawnswood DY3 .... 50 D4
Lawnside Gn WV14.... 40 D8
Lawns The
  Bedworth CV12 .... 77 C2
  Hinckley LE10 .... 75 E8
  Portway B47......... 140 F7
LAWNS WOOD......... 60 B2
Lawnswood
  Hinckley LE10 .... 75 A8
  Stourbridge DY7 ...... 60 A2
  Sutton Coldfield B76 . 58 A8
Lawnswood Ave
  Burntwood WS7........ 6 F5
  Solihull B90........ 106 D3
  Stourbridge DY8 ..... 60 C3
  Wolverhampton, Parkfield
  WV4................. 39 E4
  Wolverhampton WV6... 24 E8
Lawnswood Dr
  Brownhills WS9....... 16 A3
  Stourbridge DY7 ...... 60 A2
Lawnswood Gr B21.... 54 C1
Lawnswood Rd
  Dudley DY3.......... 50 D5
  Stourbridge DY7 ...... 60 A2
Lawnswood Rise WV6... 24 F8
Lawnwood Rd DY2..... 62 C2
Lawrence Ave
  Wednesfield WV11 .... 26 F6
  Wolverhampton WV10 .. 26 A4
Lawrence Ct
  Birmingham B68...... 84 B8
  Tamworth B79 .... 21 A6
Lawrence Dr B76....... 58 D6
Lawrence Gdns CV8... 148 A6
Lawrence La B62...... 62 E1
Lawrence Rd CV7...... 96 A8
Lawrence Saunders Rd
  CV6................. 113 B5
Lawrence St
  Stourbridge DY9 ...... 81 C6
  Willenhall WV13...... 27 A3
Lawrence Way WS13.... 8 F5
Lawrence Wlk B43..... 44 D4
Lawson Cl WS9........ 30 B4
Lawson St B4......... 164 C4
Law St B71........... 53 C5
Lawton Ave B29....... 86 B2
Lawton Cl
  Hinckley LE10 .... 74 F8
  Rowley Regis B65..... 63 D6
Lawyers Wlk CV3...... 25 B1
Laxey Rd B16......... 65 D3
Laxford Cl B12........ 86 E6
Laxton Cl DY6........ 61 A5
Laxton Gr
  Birmingham B25 ...... 68 D1
  Solihull B91........ 107 C7
Lay Gdns CV31....... 162 E5
Lazy Hill
  Birmingham B38 ..... 104 B2
  Stonnall WS9......... 16 D2
Lazy Hill Rd WS9...... 16 C1
Lea Ave WS10......... 41 D1
Lea Bank Ave DY11... 116 B5
Lea Bank Rd DY2...... 62 C3
Leabon Gr B17........ 85 C5
Leabrook B26........ 88 F8
Leabrook Rd DY4, WS14.. 41 D1
Lea Village B33....... 69 B3

Leabrook Road N WS10 . 41 D2
Leach Green La B45... 122 B6
Leach Heath La B45... 122 A7
Leacliffe Way WS9..... 30 F3
Leacote Dr WV6...... 24 C4
Leacrest Rd CV6....... 95 A2
Leacroft WV12........ 27 C7
Leacroft Ave WV10.... 25 E8
Leacroft Cl WS9....... 16 B1
Leacroft Gr B71....... 53 B7
Leacroft La WS11...... 4 F5
Leacroft Rd DY6....... 60 E8
Lea Croft Rd B97..... 158 D5
Lea Cswy The DY11... 116 D4
Leadbeater Ho **6** WS3 . 28 B8
Leadbetter Dr B61.... 136 D2
Lea Dr B26.......... 89 A6
Lea End La B48...... 123 D3
Leaf Ct CV3......... 133 D4
Leafdown Cl WS12..... 2 D3
Leafenden Ave WS7.... 7 A6
Leafield Cl CV2...... 114 F8
Leafield Cres B33..... 69 A3
Leafield Gdns B62.... 83 D8
Leafield Rd B92....... 89 C1
Leaf La CV3......... 133 E5
Lea Ford Rd B33...... 69 C4
Leaford Way DY6...... 60 F5
Leafy Glade B74....... 31 A3
Leafy Rise DY3........ 50 D4
Lea Gdns WV3........ 163 A1
Leagh Cl CV8........ 148 B7
Lea Green Ave DY4.... 51 D5
Lea Green Dr B47.... 125 C4
Lea Green La B47.... 125 C5
LEA HALL............ 69 A2
Lea Hall Rd B33...... 69 A2
Lea Hall Sta B33..... 69 B2
Leahill Croft B37..... 69 F2
Lea Hill Rd B20...... 55 C2
Lea Ho **6** DY1....... 61 E8
Leaholme Gdns DY9.... 81 B2
Leahouse Gdns B68.... 64 A3
Leahouse Rd B68...... 64 A3
Lea House Rd B30.... 104 A7
Leahurst Cres B17..... 85 C4
Lea La WS6........... 5 A3
Lealholme Ct CV5.... 132 F8
Lea Manor Dr WV4.... 38 E4
Leam Cl CV11......... 73 F1
Leam Cres B92........ 89 B1
Leam Dr WS7.......... 7 D7
Lea Mews B33......... 69 A3
Leam Gn CV4........ 132 D5
Leamington Cl WS11.... 4 C7
Leamington Rd
  Birmingham B12 ...... 87 B5
  Coventry CV3........ 133 C6
  Kenilworth CV8 ..... 148 B2
  Ryton-on-D CV8...... 135 B1
  Leamington Spa Art Gallery
  & Mus* CV32........ 161 F8
Leamington Spa Sta
  CV31................ 161 F7
LEAMONSLEY.......... 8 E7
LEAMORE............. 28 B6
Leamore Cl WS2...... 28 A7
Leamore Ind Est WS2 . 28 C6
Leamore La WS2...... 28 B6
Leamore Prim Sch WS3 . 28 C7
Leamount Dr B44...... 45 C2
Leam Rd CV31....... 161 D7
Leam Side Ho **9** WS4.. 161 D8
Leam St CV31........ 162 B7
Leam Terr CV31...... 162 B8
Leam Valley Nature
  Reserve* CV31....... 162 E7
Leander Cl WS6........ 4 F1
Leander Gdns B14.... 104 F5
Leander Rd DY9...... 81 F4
Leander Dr B74....... 45 A7
Lea Park Rise B61.... 136 F5
Lea Rd
  Birmingham B11 ...... 87 D4
  Wolverhampton WV3... 39 B8
  Walsall WS1.......... 42 C4
  Wolverhampton WV6... 25 B4
Lear Gr CV34....... 161 E4
Lear Rd WV5.......... 49 B8
Leas Cl CV12......... 78 A3
Leason La WV10....... 26 A7
Leasow Dr B15........ 85 D3
Leasowe Rd
  Birmingham B45 ..... 121 F8
  Tipton DY4.......... 51 E4
Leasowe's Ave CV3.... 132 E7
Leasowes Com Coll B62.. 83 E6
Leasowes Ct B63..... 82 F3
Leasowes Dr
  Perton WV6.......... 23 D4
  Wolverhampton WV4... 38 D6
Leasowes La B62...... 83 D4
Leasowes Rd B14..... 104 E3
Leasowes Sports Ctr B62. 83 E6
Leasowes The CV3..... 52 C5
Leasowes The WS13.... 3 A1
Leasow The WV10..... 29 E5
Lea St DY10......... 116 F6
Lea The WV10........ 12 C7
Lea The
  Birmingham B33 ...... 69 A2
  Kidderminster DY11... 116 A5
Leatherhead Cl **5** B6.. 66 F6
Lea Vale Rd DY4...... 80 F3
Leaveden Gr B26...... 89 A5
Lea View
  Aldridge WS9........ 29 E5
  Wednesfield WV12 .... 27 A5

Leaward Cl CV10...... 72 E2
Lea Wlk
  Birmingham B45 ..... 121 F8
  Ryton-on-D CV8...... 135 B3
Lea Wood Gr DY11 ... 116 A5
Lea Yield Cl B30..... 104 A7
Lebanon Gr WS7....... 6 F8
Lechlade Cl B98..... 154 B3
Lechlade Rd B43...... 54 E8
Leckhampton Cl B897.. 158 E6
Leckie Rd WS2....... 28 E4
Ledbrook Rd CV32.... 157 E5
Ledbury Cl
  Aldridge WS9......... 16 C1
  Birmingham B16 ...... 66 A2
  Redditch B98....... 154 F2
Ledbury Dr WV1....... 26 B1
Ledbury Ho
  Birmingham B33 ...... 69 E2
  Redditch B97....... 153 B4
Ledbury Rd CV31..... 162 C6
Ledbury Way B76...... 58 A8
Ledsam Gr B32........ 84 F6
Ledsam St B16........ 66 A2
Ledwell B90......... 126 A5
LEE BANK............ 86 D8
Lee Bank Bsns Ctr B1.. 164 B3
Lee Bank Ho B1...... 164 B3
Lee Bank Middleway B15. 86 C6
Leebank Rd B63....... 82 E2
Leech St **4** DY4...... 52 C5
Lee Cl CV34......... 155 E2
Lee Cres B15......... 86 C8
Lee Ct WS9.......... 15 F3
Lee Cl CV34.......... 95 C2
Leedham Ave B77...... 21 D6
Lee Gdns B67......... 64 E5
LEEK WOOTTON...... 155 F7
Lee Meadow CV34 ... 160 B4
Leeming Cl CV4..... 132 C6
Lee Mount B15....... 86 C8
Lee Rd
  Cradley Heath B64.... 82 F8
  Hollywood B47....... 125 A7
  Royal Leamington Spa
  CV31................ 161 E6
Leeson Wlk **9** B17... 85 D5
Lees Rd WV14........ 40 F3
Lees St B70......... 53 A8
Lee St B70.......... 53 A8
Lees Terr WV14....... 40 F3
Lee The CV5......... 112 C4
Lee Wlk WS11......... 2 B4
Legg Bros Ind Est WV4.. 40 A5
Legge La
  Birmingham B1 ...... 66 C3
  Dudley WV14......... 40 D3
Legge St
  Birmingham B4 ...... 164 D4
  West Bromwich B70 .. 53 E3
  Wolverhampton WV2... 39 E6
Legion Cl WS11....... 2 A5
Legion Rd B45....... 121 E7
Legs La WV10......... 11 F3
Le Hanche Cl CV7..... 95 A7
Leicester Cl B67..... 64 E1
Leicester Cswy CV1 .. 113 D5
Leicester Ct CV12.... 79 C2
Leicester La
  Cubbington CV32.... 149 E1
  Royal Leamington Spa
  CV32................ 157 C6
Leicester Pl B71..... 53 C7
Leicester Rd
  Bedworth CV12 ...... 78 B4
  Hinckley LE10 ...... 71 F2
  Nuneaton CV11...... 73 D5
  Shilton CV7......... 97 F6
Leicester Row CV1 ... 165 B4
Leicester St
  Bedworth CV12 ...... 78 B3
  Bulkington CV12 .... 79 C2
  Royal Leamington Spa
  CV32................ 157 A1
  Walsall WS1......... 28 E2
  Wolverhampton WV6... 25 B4
Leigham Dr B17...... 85 A7
Leigh Ave
  Burntwood WS7....... 7 B7
  Coventry CV3....... 133 C3
Leigh CE Prim Sch CV4. 131 D8
Leigh Cl WS4........ 29 A4
Leigh Ct
  Birmingham B23 ..... 56 C2
  Walsall WS4......... 29 A3
Leigh Jun & Inf (NC) Sch
  B8................. 67 E6
Leigh Rd
  Birmingham B8 ...... 67 E6
  Sutton Coldfield B75.. 47 B5
  Walsall WS4......... 29 A4
Leighs Cl WS4........ 15 C1
Leighs Rd WS4....... 15 C1
Leigh St **4** CV1..... 113 E4
Leigh Ct
  Birmingham B23 ..... 56 C2
  Walsall WS4......... 29 A3
LEIGHSWOOD......... 30 A7
Leighswood Ave WS9 .. 30 B7
Leighswood Cl WS9... 55 F5
Leighswood Ct WS9... 30 B6
Leighswood Ind Est WS9. 30 B8
Leighswood Rd WS9... 30 A6
Leighswood Sch WS9 .. 30 B8
Leighton Cl
  Birmingham B43 ..... 44 C3
  Coventry CV4....... 132 D2
  Dudley DY1.......... 50 E2
  Royal Leamington Spa
  CV32................ 157 C4

Leighton Rd
Birmingham B13 .... 86 F2
Darlaston WV14 .... 41 A4
Wolverhampton WV4 .... 38 F6
Leisure Wlk 🔲 B77 .... 35 F6
Leith Gr B38 .... 123 E8
Leliant Gr B17 .... 85 A5
Lellow St B71 .... 53 C8
Lemar Ind Est B30 .... 86 B1
Le More B74 .... 32 A2
Lemox Rd B70 .... 53 A8
Lench Cl
Halesowen B62 .... 63 C1
Redditch B97 .... 153 A5
Lench's Cl B13 .... 87 A3
Lenchs Gn B5 .... 86 E7
Lench St B4 .... 164 C4
Lench's Trust Almshouses 🔲
B12 .... 87 A8
Lench's Trust Almshouses 🔲
B17 .... 85 D4
Len Davis Rd WV12 .... 27 B7
Lennox Cl CV3 .... 134 E6
Lennox Gdns WV3 .... 39 A8
Lennox Gr B73 .... 57 A7
Lennox St B19 .... 66 D6
Lenton Croft B26 .... 88 E4
Lenton's La CV2 .... 96 E4
Lenwade Rd B68 .... 84 D8
Leofric Ct 🔲 B15 .... 86 C8
Leofric St CV6 .... 113 A5
Leomansley Cl WS13 .... 8 E7
Leomansley Ct WS13 .... 8 E7
Leomansley Rd WS13 .... 8 F7
Leomansley View WS13 .... 8 E7
Leominster Ct B45 .... 121 F8
Leominster Ho B33 .... 69 E2
Leominster Rd B11 .... 87 E3
Leominster Wlk B45 .... 121 F8
Leona Ind Est B62 .... 83 C6
Leonard Ave 🔲 B19 .... 66 D8
Leonard Gr 🔲 B19 .... 66 D8
Leonard Parkins Ho CV12. 79 D2
Leonard Rd
Birmingham B19 .... 66 D8
Stourbridge DY8 .... 80 C5
Leontes Mdws CV34 .... 161 E3
Leopold Ave B20 .... 54 F5
Leopold Rd CV1 .... 113 F4
Leopold St B12 .... 86 F8
Lepid Gr B29 .... 85 D2
Lerryn Cl DY6 .... 60 F5
Lerwick Cl DY6 .... 60 F5
Lesingham Dr CV4 .... 111 E1
Lesley Bentley Ho 🔲 B1.. 66 C5
Lesley Dr DY6 .... 60 E4
Leslie Dr DY4 .... 41 B1
Leslie Rd
Birmingham, Edgbaston
B16 .... 65 F2
Birmingham, Handsworth
B20 .... 55 D2
Sutton Coldfield B74 .... 31 B2
Wolverhampton WV10 .... 25 F4
Leslie Rise B69 .... 63 C8
Lesscroft Cl WV9 .... 11 A3
Lester Gr WS9 .... 30 E2
Lester St WV14 .... 40 F5
Leswell Gr DY10 .... 116 F6
Leswell La DY10 .... 116 F6
Leswell St DY10 .... 116 F6
Letchlade Cl CV2 .... 114 C8
Letocetum Roman Baths &
Mus* WS14 .... 8 D2
Levante Gdns B33 .... 68 D2
Level Dr DY5 .... 61 C3
Leven Cl LE10 .... 75 B8
Leven Croft B76 .... 58 A7
Leven Dr WV11 .... 13 B1
Leven Rd B77 .... 35 D8
Leven Way CV2 .... 115 A8
Levenwick Way DY6 .... 61 A5
Leverretts The B21 .... 54 C3
Lever St WV2 .... 163 C1
Leverton Rise WV10 .... 25 C6
Leveson Ave WS6 .... 4 E2
Leveson Cl DY2 .... 62 E8
Leveson Cres CV7 .... 130 B6
Leveson Ct
🔲 Willenhall WV13 .... 27 A2
Wolverhampton WV6 .... 25 A4
Leveson Dr DY4 .... 51 E6
Leveson Rd
Wednesfield WV11 .... 26 F8
Wolverhampton WV11 .... 12 F1
Leveson St WV13 .... 27 A2
Leveson Wlk 🔲 DY2 .... 62 E8
Levett Rd B77 .... 22 B5
Levetts Fields WS14 .... 9 C7
Levetts Hollow WS12 .... 2 D3
Levetts Sq 🔲 WS13 .... 9 B7
Levington Cl WV6 .... 23 F5
Leviss Ind Est B33 .... 68 D4
Lewis Ave WV1 .... 26 B2
Lewis Cl
Lichfield WS14 .... 9 E7
Willenhall WV12 .... 27 D5
Lewis Gr WV11 .... 26 D6
Lewisham Ind Est B66.... 65 A7
Lewisham Rd
Smethwick B66 .... 65 A7
Wolverhampton WV10 .... 11 B2
Lewisham St WV13 .... 53 D4
Lewis Rd
Birmingham, Brandhall
B68 .... 84 B7
Birmingham, Stirchley B30 104 C7
Coventry CV1 .... 113 D5

Lewis Rd continued
Radford Semele CV31.... 162 F5
Stourbridge DY9 .... 81 D5
Lewis St
Bilston WV14 .... 40 E6
Tipton DY4 .... 52 D5
Walsall WS2 .... 28 D3
Lewkner Almshouses The
B48 .... 139 A5
Lewthorn Rise WV4 .... 39 D4
Lexington Ct CV11 .... 73 B5
Lexington Gn DY5 .... 81 C7
Leybourne Cres WV9 .... 10 F2
Leybourne Gr B25 .... 88 C6
Leybrook Rd B45 .... 122 B8
Leyburn Cl
Coventry CV6 .... 95 E2
Nuneaton CV11 .... 74 A2
🔲 Warwick CV34 .... 155 F1
Willenhall WS2 .... 27 D3
Leyburn Rd
Birmingham B16 .... 66 A1
Birmingham B37 .... 69 F1
Leycester Cl B31 .... 123 A7
Leycester Pl 🔲 CV34 .... 160 E6
Leycester Rd CV8 .... 148 A2
Leycroft Ave B33 .... 69 D3
Leyes La CV8 .... 148 C5
LEYFIELDS 20 F7
Leyfields WS13 .... 3 B2
Leyfields Cres CV34 .... 160 D4
LEY HILL 32 B1
Ley Hill Farm Rd B31.. 102 E5
Ley Hill Prim Sch B31.. 102 E5
Ley Hill Rd B75 .... 32 C1
Leyland Croft B13 ..... 105 D7
Leyland Ave WV3 .... 24 F1
Leyland Croft WS3 .... 14 F4
Leyland Way CV3 .... 135 A7
Leyland Rd
Bulkington CV12 .... 79 B2
Coventry CV5 .... 112 D4
Nuneaton CV11 .... 73 E1
Tamworth B77 .... 21 E3
Leylands Way CV34 .... 160 B4
Leyman Cl B14 .... 105 C4
Leymere Cl CV7 .... 92 C1
Ley Rise DY3 .... 39 C1
Leys Cl DY9 .... 81 C2
Leys Cres DY5 .... 61 B3
Leysdown Gr B27 ..... 106 C8
Leysdown Rd B27 ..... 106 C8
Leyside CV3 .... 134 E5
Leys Ind Est DY5 .... 61 A3
Leys La CV7 .... 92 C1
Leys Rd DY5 .... 61 B3
Leysters Cl B98 .... 154 E3
LEYS THE 21 A5
Leys The
Bedworth CV12 .... 78 B4
Birmingham B31 .... 103 B5
🔲 Darlaston WS10 .... 41 D6
Hinckley LE10 .... 75 B8
Leys Wood Croft B26... 89 B6
Leyton Cl DY5 .... 81 D8
Leyton Gr B44 .... 45 A1
Leyton Rd B21 .... 65 F8
Libbards Gate 🔲 B91.. 127 C8
Libbards Way B91 ..... 127 B8
Liberty Cl WS6 .... 4 D3
Liberty Pl 🔲 B16 .... 66 A3
Liberty Rd B77 .... 35 F5
Liberty Way CV11 .... 73 F3
Libra Cl B79 .... 20 F7
Library Cl LE10 .... 76 A5
Library Rd CV4 .... 132 B5
Library Sq 🔲 B91 ..... 107 C3
Library Theatre* 🔲 B1 .. 164 A2
Library Way 🔲 B45 ..... 121 F7
Lich Ave WV11 .... 26 E7
Lichen Cl WS12 .... 1 C6
Lichen Gdns B38 .... 123 D7
Lichen Gn CV4 .... 132 D5
LICHFIELD 9 D5
Lichfield Bsns Ctr WS13 3 D1
Lichfield Cath* WS13 .... 9 B8
Lichfield Cathedral Sch
WS13 .... 9 B8
Lichfield City Sta WS14.. 9 B7
Lichfield Cl
Nuneaton CV10 .... 74 A7
Walsall WS6 .... 5 A2
Lichfield Cres B78 .... 20 B7
Lichfield Ct
Solihull B90 .... 105 D2
Sutton Coldfield B75 .... 46 C5
Walsall WS4 .... 29 A4
Lichfield Gates WV1 .. 163 B3
Lichfield Pas WV1 .. 163 C3
Lichfield Rd
Birmingham B6 .... 67 B8
Brownhills, Shireoak Hill WS8,
WS9 .... 16 B5
Brownhills WS8, WS14 .. 16 A8
Burntwood WS7 .... 7 D6
Cannock WS11 .... 5 B8
Coventry CV3 .... 133 D8
Lichfield SW7, SW13.... 8 B6
Sutton Coldfield B74 .. 32 A3
Tamworth B78, B79 ..... 20 C6
Walsall, Highbridge WS4.. 28 C5
Walsall, New Invention WS3,
WS4,WS8, WS9 .... 13 E1
Walsall, Rushall WS4 ... 29 E6
Walsall, Shelfield WS4.. 15 C1

Lichfield Rd continued
Walsall, Wallington Heath
WS3 .... 14 C2
Water Orton B46, B76.... 59 D4
Wednesfield WV11 .... 26 E6
Willenhall WV12 .... 27 D8
Wishaw B76, B78.. .... 48 B3
Lichfield Road Ind Est
B79 .... 20 E6
Lichfield St
Bilston WV14 .... 40 E5
Fazeley B78 .... 20 F1
Tamworth B79 .... 21 A5
Tipton DY4 .... 51 E5
Walsall WS1 .... 28 F2
Wolverhampton WV1 .. 163 C3
Lichfield Trad Est B79.. 20 E6
Lichfield Trent Valley Sta
WS13 .... 9 F8
Lichwood Rd WV11 .... 26 F7
Lickey Coppice B45 .. 122 C4
LICKEY END 137 C6
Lickey End Fst Sch B60 137 C6
Lickey Gr DY11 .... 116 B2
Lickey Grange Dr B60.. 121 E1
Lickey Hills Country Pk &
Visitor Ctr* B45 ..... 122 B3
Lickey Hills Prim Sch
B45 .... 121 F3
Lickey Rd
Birmingham B45 ..... 122 C6
Stourbridge DY8 .... 81 B6
Lickey Rock B60 ..... 121 D1
Lickey Sq B45 .... 122 A2
Liddiard Ct DY8 .... 80 E6
Liddon Gr B27 .... 106 C8
Liddon Rd B27 .... 106 C8
LIFFORD 104 B5
Lifford Cl B14 .... 104 E4
Lifford La B30 .... 104 B4
Lifford Way CV3 .... 135 A7
Lifton Croft DY6 .... 60 F5
Lightfields Wlk B65.... 63 A5
Lighthorne Ave B16.... 66 A1
Lighthorne Rd B91 .. 107 C6
Lighthouse Group Ctr The 🔲
B6 .... 67 A8
Light La CV1 .... 165 B4
Lightning Way B31 .. 123 B7
Lightoak Cl B97 ..... 158 C6
Lightwood Cl
Knowle B93 .... 128 B8
🔲 Lichfield WS13 .... 8 F6
Lightwood Rd DY1 ..... 51 A3
Lightwoods Hill B67.... 84 E8
Lightwoods Prim Sch
B68 .... 84 D8
Lightwoods Rd
Smethwick B67 .... 65 A1
Stourbridge DY9 .... 81 C1
Lilac Ave
🔲 Birmingham, Balsall Heath
B12 .... 87 A5
Birmingham, Perry B44.... 55 C7
Cannock WS11 .... 4 D7
Coventry CV6 .... 112 F5
Sutton Coldfield B74 .. 44 E8
Tipton DY4 .... 51 E7
Walsall WS5 .... 43 A4
Lilac Cl
Hinckley LE10 .... 75 E6
Redditch B98 .... 153 E2
Lilac Gr
Burntwood WS7 .... 6 F7
Walsall WS4 .... 27 E3
Warwick CV34 .... 156 A1
Wednesbury WS10 .... 42 A2
Lilac Ho WS4 .... 15 D1
Lilac La WS6 .... 14 A8
Lilac Rd
Bedworth CV12 .... 78 D5
Bilston WV14 .... 40 B8
Dudley DY1 .... 51 C4
Tamworth B79 .... 21 A8
Willenhall WV12 .... 27 D8
Lilac Way CV4 .... 132 D5
Lilac Way B63 .... 83 F8
Lilian Gr WV14 .... 40 E1
Lilleburne Dr CV10 .. 72 B7
Lilleshall Cl B98 ..... 154 E3
Lilleshall Cres WV2 ... 39 D7
Lilleshall Rd B26 ..... 89 B7
Lilley Cl CV6 .... 95 C2
Lilley Green Rd B48 .. 140 D5
Lilley La B31 .... 123 B8
LILLINGTON 157 C3
Lillington Ave CV32 .. 156 F2
Lillington Cl
🔲 Lichfield WS13 .... 9 A8
Royal Leamington Spa
CV32 .... 157 A3
Sutton Coldfield B75 ... 47 A4
Lillington Gr B34 ..... 69 D5
Lillington Prim Sch
CV32 .... 157 B3
Lillington Rd
Coventry CV2 .... 96 C1
Royal Leamington Spa
CV32 .... 157 A3
Solihull B90 .... 126 B8
Lilycroft La B38 ..... 124 A7
Lily Green La B97 .. 153 A4
Lily Rd B26 .... 88 D7
Lily St B71 .... 53 C5
Limberlost Cl B20 ... 55 A3
Limbrick Ave CV4 .. 112 A1
Limbrick Cl B90 ..... 105 F2

Limbrick Wood Nature
Reserve* CV4 .... 111 F2
Limbrick Wood Prim Sch
CV4 .... 111 F3
Limbury Gr B92 ..... 107 F8
Lime Ave
🔲 Birmingham B29.. .... 85 F2
Royal Leamington Spa
CV32 .... 157 A4
Walsall WS2 .... 27 E3
Lime Cl
Great Wyrley WS6 .... 4 F4
Hollywood B47 ..... 125 A5
Tipton DY4 .... 51 E5
Walsall WS2 .... 27 E3
West Bromwich B70 .. 53 A4
Lime Ct
Birmingham B11 ..... 87 C4
Kidderminster DY10.. 117 A4
Lime Gr
Bilston WV14 .... 40 C7
Birmingham B25, B26 ... 88 D6
Birmingham, Balsall Heath
B12 .... 86 F5
Birmingham, Chemsley Wood
B37 .... 70 B1
Birmingham, Lozells B19.. 66 C8
Birmingham, Small Heath
B10 .... 87 D8
Bromsgrove B61 ..... 136 F4
Burntwood WS7 .... 7 C6
Coventry CV4 .... 112 B2
Kenilworth CV8 ..... 148 A4
Lichfield WS14 .... 9 D8
Nuneaton CV10 .... 72 E5
Smethwick B66 .... 65 B3
Smethwick B66 .... 65 B4
Sutton Coldfield B73 ... 57 B7
Walsall WS4 .... 29 C6
Whitnash CV31 ..... 162 A2
Wolverhampton WV3.... 24 D1
Lime Kiln 🔲 B38 ..... 123 D7
Limekiln La
Birmingham B14 ..... 105 A4
Earlswood B94 ..... 126 D1
Lime Kilns Bus Pk LE10 .. 75 B5
Lime La
Norton Canes WS3 .... 6 A1
Walsall WS3 .... 15 A7
Limepit La
Dudley DY1 .... 51 A3
Huntington WS11, WS12 .. 1 D6
Lime Rd
Huntington WS12.. .... 1 D8
Sedgley DY3 .... 39 F1
Wednesbury WS10 .... 41 F4
Limes Ave
Brierley Hill DY5 .... 61 C5
Rowley Regis B65 .... 63 C2
Limescroft CV34 .... 29 B7
Limes Ct WV6 .... 24 D5
Limes Rd
Dudley DY1 .... 51 B3
Wolverhampton WV6.... 24 A4
Lime St
Walsall WS1 .... 41 A8
Walsall WS1 .... 29 A1
Wolverhampton WV3 .. 39 B8
Limes The
Bedworth CV12 .... 77 E2
Birmingham, Gravelly Hill
B24 .... 56 F3
Birmingham, Ladywood B16 65 F3
Birmingham, Rotton Park
B16 .... 65 F3
Birmingham, Sparkbrook
B11 .... 87 C6
Coventry CV6 .... 112 E5
Himley DY3 .... 49 B3
Walsall WS5 .... 29 A2
Wolverhampton WV11.. 26 B5
Limes View DY3 .... 50 D7
Lime Tree Ave
Coventry CV4 .... 112 A2
Wolverhampton WV6.... 24 A3
Lime Tree Cres B97 .. 153 B4
Lime Tree Gdns WV8.. 10 B3
Lime Tree Gr B31 .. 103 C2
LIME TREE PARK 112 A2
Limetree Rd B34 ..... 30 D1
Lime Tree Rd
Birmingham, Acock's Green
B27 .... 88 C5
Birmingham, Saltley B8.. 67 F6
Codsall WV8.. .... 10 B4
Walsall WS5 .... 43 A4
Linacre Ho B37 .... 69 F2
Linaker Rd CV3 ..... 134 C5
Lincoln Ave
Nuneaton CV10 .... 72 B7
Tamworth B79 .... 20 E6
Willenhall WV13 .... 27 D2
Lincoln Cl
Birmingham B27 .... 88 E3
🔲 Lichfield WS13 .... 3 C3
Warwick CV34 ..... 155 E1
Lincoln Croft WS14 .. 17 F6
Lincoln Ct
🔲 Birmingham B29.. .. 103 C7
Royal Leamington Spa
CV32 .... 162 A8
Lincoln Dr WS11 .... 4 F8
Lincoln Gn WV10.. ... 11 D2
Lincoln Gr B37.. .... 70 A1
Lincoln Ho WV10.. ..... 25 F3
Lincoln Rd
Birmingham B27 .... 88 D2

Lincoln Rd continued
Bromsgrove B61 ..... 136 E4
Dudley DY2 .... 62 D2
Smethwick B67 .... 64 E2
Walsall WS1 .... 29 A1
West Bromwich B71 .. 42 D1
Lincoln Road N B27 .. 88 E3
Lincoln St
Birmingham B12 .... 86 E6
Coventry CV1 .... 165 C4
Wolverhampton WV10.. 25 E3
Lincroft Cres CV5 .. 112 E4
Lindale Ave B36 ..... 68 C6
Lindale Cres DY5 ..... 81 B6
Linden Ave
Birmingham B43 .... 54 D8
Burntwood WS7 .... 7 A8
Halesowen B62 .... 83 E7
Kidderminster DY10.. 117 A7
Oldbury B69 .... 63 D8
Linden Cl
Tamworth B77 .... 21 F4
Warwick CV34 ..... 155 D2
Willenhall WS2 .... 27 D2
Linden Ct B91 ..... 107 E4
Linden Dr DY8 .... 81 A3
Linden Gdns DY10.. 117 A6
Linden Glade B63.... 83 A4
Linden Gr CV10 .... 73 A1
Linden La WV12 .... 27 E6
Linden Lea
Bedworth CV12 .... 78 B3
Wolverhampton WV3.... 24 D1
Linden Rd
Birmingham B30 ..... 103 E7
Dudley DY1 .... 51 B3
Hinckley LE10 .... 71 C1
Smethwick B66 .... 65 A2
Linden Road Instruction Pool
B30 .... 103 F7
Lindens Dr B74 .... 44 F5
Lindens Prim Sch B74.... 44 F6
Lindens The
Birmingham B32 .... 84 E7
Birmingham, Edgbaston B16 65 D1
Wolverhampton WV6.... 24 E3
Linden View WS12 ... 2 B4
Lindenwood B73 .... 46 B6
Lindera B77 .... 22 B4
Lindfield The CV3 ... 134 C8
Lindford Way B38 ... 104 B2
Lindhurst Dr B94 ..... 143 C6
Lindisfarne B77 ..... 21 D3
Lindisfarne Dr CV8.. 148 C4
Lindley Ave DY4 .... 51 F4
Lindley Rd
Bedworth CV12 .... 77 D2
Coventry CV3 .... 114 B2
Lindon Cl WS8 .... 16 A6
Lindon Dr WS8 .... 15 F7
Lindon Rd WS8 .... 16 A6
Lindon View WS8 ..... 16 A1
Lindop Cl CV32 ..... 157 D5
Lindrick Cl WS3 .... 13 F3
Lindridge Dr B76 ..... 58 C6
Lindridge Rd
Birmingham B23 .... 56 C5
Solihull B90 .... 105 F1
Sutton Coldfield B75, B76.. 47 B6
Lindrosa Rd B74 .... 30 F3
Lindsay Rd B42 .... 44 B1
Lindsey Ave B31 ..... 103 C4
Lindsey Cres CV8 .. 148 A1
Lindsey Pl DY5 .... 61 C3
Lindsey Rd B71 .... 53 C7
Lindsworth App B30 .. 104 C3
Lindsworth Ct 🔲 B30 .. 104 C3
Lindsworth North Sch
B23 .... 57 A6
Lindsworth Rd B30.. 104 C3
Lineholt Cl B98 ..... 159 A6
Linehouse La
Catshill B60 .... 137 D8
Lower Marlbrook B60 .. 121 D1
Linen St CV34 ..... 160 D6
Linfield Gdns DY3 ... 39 C1
Linford Gr B25 .... 68 D1
Linford Wlk CV2 .... 96 F1
Linforth Dr B74 .... 45 A7
Lingard Cl B7 .... 67 B5
Lingard Ho B37 .... 57 F8
Lingard Rd B75 .... 47 A5
Lingen Cl B98 ..... 154 E3
Lingfield Ave
Birmingham B44 .... 44 F1
Wolverhampton WV10.. 11 D5
Lingfield Cl WS6 .... 4 F2
Lingfield Ct
Birmingham B43 .... 54 D7
Coventry CV6 .... 96 B4
Lingfield Dr WS6 .... 4 F2
Lingfield Gdns B34.... 69 B6
Lingfield Gr WV6 .... 23 E4
Lingfield Rd WS11 ..... 6 A5
Lingfield Way DY6 ... 61 A5
Lingfield Wlk B61 .. 121 E1
Lingham Cl B92 ..... 107 D7
Ling Ho WV10 .... 25 F3
Lingmoor Gr WS9 .... 30 A7
Ling Rd WS12 .... 1 C5
Lingwood Dr CV10 ... 72 F3

Linhope Dr DY6.........61 A5
Link One Ind Pk DY4 ...52 E6
Link Rd
 Birmingham B16 ......65 E3
 Brownhills WS9 ....16 B3
 Wombourne WV5.......49 A7
Links Ave WV6.........24 D7
Links Cres B68.........84 B8
Links Dr
 Birmingham B45 .....122 A5
 Solihull B91 ....107 B6
 Stourbridge DY8 .....80 E2
Links Rd
 Birmingham, Brandhall
 B68 ....84 B8
 Birmingham, Highter's Heath
 B14 ....105 A1
 Wolverhampton WV4...39 A3
Links Side Way WS9 ...30 C8
Links The DY10 ....117 A4
Links View
 Halesowen B62 ....83 D4
 Sutton Coldfield B74 ..31 B1
Linkswood Cl B13.......87 B1
Link The B27 ....88 A1
Linkway CV31.........161 E6
Linkway Ret Pk WS11 ...4 B6
Linkwood Ind Est DY8...80 F6
Linley Cl WS9.........29 E5
Linley Dr WV10 ....11 E1
Linley Gr
 Birmingham B14 .....104 C6
 Dudley DY3 ....50 B2
Linley Lodge Ind Est WS9. 29 E6
Linley Rd WS4 ....29 D7
Linley Wood Rd WS9 ..29 E5
Linnet Cl
 Birmingham B30 .....103 E8
 Coventry CV3.........134 D5
 Halesowen B62 ....83 B6
 Huntington WS12......1 D7
Linnet Gr
 Birmingham B23 ......56 B6
 Willenhall WV12 ......27 C8
Linnet Rise DY10......116 F1
Linpole Wlk B14 ......104 D2
Linsey Rd B92 ....89 C2
Linslade Cl WV4 ......39 D4
Linstock Way CV6......96 B4
Linthouse La WV11....26 E8
Linthouse Wlk ■ B77 ..35 F6
LINTHURST 138 A6
Linthurst Newtown B60. 138 B5
Linthurst Rd B45, B60...138 A7
Lintly B77 ....22 B1
Lint Mdw B47.........125 B7
Linton Ave B91 ....107 A1
Linton Cl
 Halesowen B63 ....82 D5
 Redditch B98 ....154 F2
Linton Croft WV14 ....40 D5
Linton Mews B98 .....154 F2
Linton Rd
 Birmingham, Acock's Green
 B11................88 A4
 Birmingham, Great Barr
 B43................44 C3
 Cradley Heath B64.....62 F3
 Wolverhampton WV4...38 E5
Linton Wlk B23 ....56 C3
Linwood Cl LE10 ......71 B2
Linwood Ct B15.......86 D7
Linwood Dr
 Cannock WS12.........1 F7
 Coventry CV2.........96 F1
Linwood Rd
 Birmingham B21 ......65 E8
 Dudley DY1 ....51 B5
 Solihull B91 ....106 D5
Lionel St B3 ....164 B3
Lion Fields Ave CV5....112 B6
Lion Ind Est WS9......30 A8
Lion Pas DY8 ....80 F5
Lion's Den WS7, WS14 ..7 E2
Lion Sq DY10 ....116 E6
Lion St
 Kidderminster DY10....116 E6
 Stourbridge DY8 .....80 F5
Liskeard Cl CV11......74 A5
Liskeard Rd WS5.......43 D7
Lisko Cl DY5..........81 A8
Lisle Ave DY11........116 D3
Lisle Ct ■ CV31.......162 A6
Lismore Cl B45 ....101 E1
Lismore Croft CV2.....115 B7
Lismore Dr
 Birmingham B17 ......85 A3
 Hinckley LE10 ....71 C1
Lissimore Dr DY4 .....52 B2
Lisson Gr B44.........44 F4
Listelow Cl B36 ....69 B8
Lister Cl
 Tipton DY4...........52 A4
 Walsall WS2..........28 B5
Lister St
 Dudley DY2 ....62 D7
 Kidderminster DY11....116 B4
 Walsall WS2..........28 B5
Lister St
 Birmingham B7 ....66 F4
 Nuneaton CV11........73 D3
 Willenhall WV13 ......27 E3
Listowel Rd B14.......104 D6
Lisures Dr B76.........46 D4

Little Acre B97..........158 D6
Little Albert St ■ WS2 ..28 E2
Little Ann St B5.........66 F2
LITTLE ASTON 31 B4
Little Aston Hall B74 ...31 B5
Little Aston Hall Dr B74 . 31 B5
Little Aston Hospl Spire
 (Private) B74 ....31 B5
Little Aston La B74.....31 D6
Little Aston Park Rd B74 . 31 A3
Little Aston Prim Sch B74 31 C6
Little Aston Rd WS9.....30 C5
Little Barrow Wlk ■ WS13 3 A1
Little Birches WV3 .....38 F8
Little Brch WV3........67 A2
LITTLE BLOXWICH 14 E3
Little Bloxwich CE VC Prim
 Sch WS3 ....14 D3
Little Brickiln St WV3 ..163 B2
Little Bromwich Rd B9 ..67 F2
Little Bromwich Rd B9 ..68 C2
Little Broom St B12 ....87 A8
Little Caldmore ■ WS1 ..42 E8
Little Church La B79 ....21 B5
Little Church St ■ CV1..165 C3
Little Clothier St WV13 ..27 A3
Little Clover Cl ■ B7....67 C7
Little Comm WS3 ......15 A4
Little Cornbow B63 ....83 B3
Littlecote B79 ....20 D7
Littlecote Croft ■ B14..105 A3
Littlecote Dr B23 ......56 F7
Little Cottage St DY5....61 D2
Little Croft B43 ....43 C1
Little Cross St ■ WS10..41 D7
Little Cryfield CV4 .....132 C2
Little Duke St CV11 ....73 B4
Little Edward St B9 .....67 A2
Little Farm CV3 ....134 D5
Little Field CV2 ....114 A5
Little Fields Way B69...63 F7
Little Forge Rd B98 ....159 C8
Little Francis Gr ■ B7...67 B5
Little Gorway WS1 .....42 F7
Little Green Lanes B73 . 57 B7
Little Hall Rd B7 ....67 B5
Little Hardwick Rd WS9 . 30 D2
Little Hay La WS14.....18 C1
LITTLE HEATH 95 F1
Little Heath Croft B34 ..69 B7
Little Heath Ind Est CV6 . 95 F1
Little Heath La B60 ....137 D6
Little Heath Prim Sch ■
 CV6 ....95 F1
Little Hill WS10 ....41 F3
Littlehill Cres B63......82 C7
Little Hill WV8 ....104 A1
Little Hill Way B32.....84 D2
Little Island Dr WV13...27 C2
Little Johnson's La
 Aldridge WS9.........30 B1
 Walsall WS9..........44 B8
Little John St DY5......61 D6
Little La
 West Bromwich B71 ...53 D5
 Willenhall WV12 ......27 B8
Little Lawns Cl WS9.....16 A4
Little Pitts Cl B24 .....57 D5
Little London Ho ■ WS1..42 F8
Little London Ho ■ WS1..103 C1
Littlemead Ave B31 ....103 A5
Little Meadow Croft B31 102 F4
Little Meadow Wlk B33...68 F3
Littlemead Rd B90 .....125 E8
Little Moor Hill B67 ....64 F5
Little Newport St ■ WS1. 28 E1
Little Oaks Dr DY7 .....60 A2
Little Oaks Rd B6 ......66 E8
Littleover Ave B28 ....105 F6
LITTLE PACKINGTON ...91 C6
Little Park St
 Coventry CV1 ....165 C2
 Wolverhampton WV1 ..163 C3
Little Pk St B24 ....57 B5
Little Potter St DY5 ....61 D2
Little Pountney St WV2 . 163 B1
Little Shadwell St B4 ..164 C4
Littleshaw Croft B47 ...125 C4
Littleshaw La B47......125 C4
Little's La WV1 ....163 C3
Little South St CV1.....113 E3
Little St DY2...........51 D1
Little Station St ■ WS2 . 28 E2
Little Sutton La B75.....46 C8
Little Sutton Prim Sch
 B75 ....32 D3
Little Sutton Rd B75 ...32 D2
Littlethorpe CV3 ....134 D6
Littleton Cl
 Kenilworth CV8 ....148 A7
 Sutton Coldfield B76 ..47 A2
Littleton Croft ■ B91...127 C8
Littleton Dr WS12......1 C7
Littleton Green Com Sch
 WS12 ....1 C6
Littleton Rd WV12 .....27 E7
Littleton Street E WS1 ..28 F3
Littleton Street W WS1 . 28 E2
LITTLEWOOD 4 E4
Littlewood Cl ■ B91....127 B8
Littlewood Gn B80.....159 D3
LITTLEWOOD GREEN...159 D2
Littlewood La WS6......4 E4

Littlewood Rd WS6......4 E4
Little Woods B97 ....158 E6
Little Wood St WV13 ...27 A2
LITTLEWORTH 2 E4
Littleworth Ave DY1....51 B6
Littleworth Croft CV31 . 162 C5
Littleworth Gr ■ B76...64 E7
Littleworth Rd WV12 ...2 E4
LITTLE WYRLEY 14 E8
Litton B77 ....22 C1
Liveridge Cl B93 ....127 F6
Liverpool Croft B37 ....89 F8
Liverpool St B9........67 A2
Livery St
 Birmingham B3 ....164 B3
 Royal Leamington Spa
 CV32................161 F8
Livingstone Ave WV6...23 E5
Livingstone Rd
 Bilston WV14.........40 B5
 Birmingham, Handsworth
 B20 ....55 D1
 Birmingham, King's Heath
 B14 ....104 E6
 Coventry CV6.........113 E7
 Walsall WS3..........14 E2
 West Bromwich B70 ...53 B1
Lizafield Ct B66........64 F7
Llewellyn Rd CV31 .....162 A6
Lloyd Cl CV11.........73 D2
Lloyd Cres CV2 ....114 E3
Lloyd Dr WV4 ....38 C2
Lloyd George Gr WS11 . 2 C2
Lloyd Hill WV4 ....38 C3
Lloyd Ho B19 ....66 C6
Lloyd Rd
 Birmingham B20 ......55 A4
 Wolverhampton WV6...24 D5
Lloyd Roberts Bldgs WV4. 38 F1
Lloyds Rd B62 ....83 C8
Lloyd St
 Birmingham B10 ......87 D8
 Cannock WS11........1 D1
 Dudley DY2 ....62 D8
 Wednesbury WS10 ....41 E3
 West Bromwich B70 ...53 A8
 Wolverhampton WV6...24 F4
Lloyd Way DY7.........80 A4
Loach Dr CV2..........96 B4
Lobelia Cl LE10 ....75 E5
Lobstick Dr CV9 ....36 E1
Locarno Rd DY4 ....52 A6
Lochalsh Gr WV11 .....13 B1
Lochmore Cl LE10......75 A8
Lochmore Cl LE10......75 A8
Lochmore Dr LE10.....75 A8
Lochmore Way LE10....75 A8
Lochranza Croft B43 ...43 E2
Lochsong Cl B77 ....35 D4
Loch St CV3...........114 C1
Lock Cl B97 ....153 A4
Lock Dr B33 ....68 D3
Locke Cl CV6 ....95 A1
Locket Cl WS2.........27 F4
Locketts Ct WS11 ......1 F5
Lockfield Cl CV8 ......60 F2
Lockhart Cl CV8.......148 A4
Lockhart Dr B75 ....32 C1
Lockheed Cl ■ CV31...161 F5
Lockhurst La CV6 ......113 D7
Locking Croft B35 .....58 B3
Lockington Croft B62 ..83 F6
Lock Keepers Cl WS11 ...5 F4
Lock Keepers Reach
 B48 ....138 F6
Lock La CV34 ....160 D8
Lockley Cl WV10 ......25 F4
Lockside WS9 ....29 F7
Lockside Cl DY5 ....61 D1
Locksmith Cl ■ WV13...27 B2
Lock St WV1...........163 C4
Locks The CV31.......161 D7
Locks View DY8........60 E1
Lockton Rd B30........104 C8
Lockwood Rd B31......102 F4
Lode Heath Sch B91 ...107 C6
Lode La B91...........107 C6
Loder Cl CV4 ....111 F3
Lodge Cl
 Halesowen B62 ....83 E3
 Hinckley LE10 ....76 A5
 Walsall WS5..........43 D6
Lodge Cres
 Dudley DY2 ....62 A4
 Warwick CV34 ....160 D4
 West Hagley DY9......99 B5
Lodge Croft B93 ....128 B6
Lodge Dr B26..........88 F8
Lodge Farm Cl B76.....46 F3
Lodge Farm Prim Sch
 WV12 ....27 D5
Lodgefield Rd B62 .....83 B7
Lodge Forge Trad Est
 B64.................82 C7
Lodge Gr WS9.........30 A5
LODGE GREEN 92 E3
Lodge Green La CV7....92 F2
Lodge Green Lane N CV7. 92 E2
LODGE HILL 85 B2
Lodge Hill Rd B29.....85 D1
Lodge La
 Cheslyn Hay WS11.....4 C5
 Kingswinford DY6 .....60 B8
LODGE PARK 153 F2
Lodgepool Cl B44......55 E6
Lodge Pool Dr B98.....153 F1
Lodge Prim Sch B70 ...53 B3

Lodge Rd
 Bilston WV14.........40 F4
 Birmingham B18 ......65 F5
 Coventry CV3.........114 B1
 Darlaston WS10.......41 D5
 Knowle B93 ....128 B6
 Redditch B98 ....153 E3
 Smethwick B67 ....64 E7
 Walsall, The Chuckery WS5. 43 D6
 Walsall WS4..........15 B1
 West Bromwich B70 ...53 C3
 Wolverhampton WV10 . 25 B8
Lodge Rd/West Bromwich
 TH Stop B70..........53 C3
Lodge St
 Oldbury B69..........64 A7
 Willenhall WV12 ......27 C5
Lodge The B15 ....65 D1
Lodge View WS6.......4 C3
Loeless Rd B33 ....69 A3
Lofthouse Cres B31....102 F3
Lofthouse Gr B31......102 F3
Lofthouse Rd B20......54 F3
Loft Theatre CV32......46 F7
Loftus Cl B29 ....102 F8
Loftus Ct WS7 ....7 A5
Logan Cl WV10 ....25 C6
Logan Rd CV2 ....113 E1
Lole Cl CV6...........96 A4
Lollard Croft CV3 ......133 D8
Lomaine Dr B30 ....103 E4
Lomas Dr B31 ....102 E3
Lomas St WV1.........25 C4
Lomax Cl WS13 ....3 A1
Lomax Rd WS12.......2 B7
Lombard Ave DY2......62 D3
Lombard Gdns ■ WS13 . 9 B8
Lombard St
 Birmingham B12 ......86 F8
 Lichfield WS13........9 B8
 West Bromwich B70 ...53 C3
Lombard Street W B70 . 53 C3
Lombardy Croft ■ B62..84 A6
Lombardy Gdns WV12...27 E7
Lombardy Gr WS7 .....6 F8
Lomita Cres B77 ....35 D8
Lomond Cl
 Birmingham B34 ......69 E6
 Hinckley LE10 ....75 B8
 Tamworth B79 ....20 F8
Lomond Rd DY3 ....39 C1
Lomond Way CV10.....72 C5
Lomsey Cl CV4 ....112 A1
Londonderry Gr B67 ...64 F5
Londonderry La B67....64 E4
Londonderry Rd B68...64 D4
London Dr ■ WV13 ....27 A3
LONDON FIELDS.......50 F2
London Hts DY1 ....51 A2
London La
 Bromsgrove B60 ......151 F7
 Tardebigge B60 ....152 A6
London Pl WV2 ....163 B2
London Rd
 Birmingham B20 ......55 E2
 Coventry, Cheylesmore
 CV3 ....133 E8
 Coventry, Willenhall CV3 . 134 B5
 Hinckley LE10 ....75 E8
 Lichfield WS14........9 C5
 Middleton B75, B78....47 D7
 Nuneaton CV8 ....135 B1
 Shenstone B75, WS14...32 F7
 Sutton Coldfield B75 ..33 A4
 Weeford WS14........18 F3
London St B66.........65 C5
Lones Rd B71 ....65 B8
Longacre WS10 ....41 A8
Long Acre
 Birmingham B7 ....67 C7
 Kidderminster DY10...116 F7
Longacre Ind Est B7 ...67 C7
Longacres
 Cannock WS12........2 F5
 Sutton Coldfield B74 ..31 C4
Longbank Rd B69 ......63 C8
Longboat La DY8.......60 E1
Longboat Quay DY2....62 D4
Longborough Cl B97 ...158 B6
Longbow Rd B29......102 F7
Longbridge La B31.....122 E8
Long Bridge Rd WS14 ..9 C5
Longbridge Sta B31....122 E8
Long Brook La CV7, CV8. 129 E5
Long Cl DY9...........99 A4
Long Close Ave CV5....112 B6
Long Close Wlk B35....58 A3
Long Compton Dr DY9..99 A6
Long Croft WS12.......1 C4
Longcroft ■ WS10.....42 A3
Longcroft Cl ■ B35....58 A3
Longcroft The
 Halesowen B63 ....83 D7
 Walsall WS4..........29 C7
Longdales Rd B38......123 E7
Longdon Ave WV4 .....39 D5
Longdon Cl B98........159 B7
Longdon Croft B93.....128 A8
Longdon Dr B74 ....31 E4
Longdon Rd B93 ......128 A6
Longfellow Ave CV34...160 C4
Longfellow Cl B97 .....158 C7
Longfellow Gn DY10 ...117 C6
Longfellow Pl WS11....1 E4

Longfellow Rd
 Birmingham B30 ......103 D...
 Coventry CV2.........114 C...
 Dudley DY3 ....50 B...
Longfellow Wlk B79....20 F...
Longfield Cl
 Birmingham B28 .....105 F...
 Tamworth B77 ....21 E...
Longfield Dr B74.......31 D...
Longfield Ho
 Coventry CV6.........114 A...
 Wolverhampton WV10 . 25 F...
Longfield Rd
 Birmingham B31 .....102 E...
 Royal Leamington Spa
 CV31................162 B...
 Stourbridge DY9 .....81 D...
LONGFORD ....95 F...
Longford Cl
 Birmingham B32 ......102 A...
 Dorridge B93.........128 B...
Longford Ct WS11 .....4 B...
Longford Gn WS11 .....4 C...
Longford Gr B44.......45 A...
Longford Ind Est WS11...4 D...
Longford Park Prim Sch
 CV6 ....96 A...
Longford Prim Sch WS11. 4 C...
Longford Rd
 Bedworth CV7 ....96 A...
 Birmingham B44 ......45 A...
 Cannock WS11........4 D...
 Coventry CV6.........96 A...
 Wolverhampton WV10 . 26 A...
Longford Sq CV6.......96 A...
Long Furrow WV8......10 E...
Long Green Cl B31.....103 A...
Longham Croft B32 ....84 F...
Longhurst Croft B31 ..123 B...
Long Hyde Rd B67 .....64 F...
Long Innage B63.......82 B...
Long Knowle La WV11 . 26 B...
Long Knowle Prim Sch
 WV11 ....26 C...
Long La
 Brownhills Green CV5,
 CV7 ....94 D...
 Great Wyrley WS6 ....13 E...
 Halesowen B62 ....83 E...
Longlake Ave WV6 .....24 B...
Longlands Cl B38 ......123 C...
Longlands Dr B77......21 F...
Longlands Rd B62......83 E...
Longlands The
 Barnt Green B45......138 D...
 Wombourne WV5......49 A...
Long Lane Trad Est B62 . 83 D...
Long Leasow B29......103 B...
Longleat
 Birmingham B43 ......43 C...
 Tamworth B79 ....20 D...
Longleat Dr ■ CV31...162 C...
Longleat Rd WS9 ......16 A...
Long Ley WV10 ....26 A...
Longley Ave B76.......58 D...
Long Leys Croft B46....59 B...
Long Leys Ct B46 .....59 B...
Longley Wlk B37......70 C...
Long Mdw B65.........63 C...
Longmeadow Cl B75 ...46 F...
Longmeadow Cres B34 . 69 E...
Long Meadow Dr
 Hinckley LE10 ....74 F...
 Sedgley DY3..........39 B...
Longmeadow Gr B31...85 B...
Longmeadow Rd WS5 . 43 E...
Long Meadow Rd B60 . 137 C...
Long Mill Ave WV11....26 B...
Long Mill N WS11 .....26 B...
Long Mill S WV11 .....26 B...
Longmoor Cl
 Redditch B97 ....153 B...
 Wednesfield WV11 ....26 F...
Longmoor Dr CV3......114 C...
Longmoor Ho ■ B74...31 F...
Longmoor Rd
 Halesowen B63 ....82 E...
 Sutton Coldfield B73 . 45 B...
Longmore Ave WS2....27 F...
Longmore Cl B73 ......45 A...
Longmore Ho B73 .....45 E...
Longmore Rd B90.....106 D...
Longmore St
 Birmingham B12 ......86 E...
 Wednesbury WS10 ....41 F...
Long Mynd B63 ....82 D...
Long Mynd Cl WV11 ...13 B...
Long Mynd Rd B31....102 F...
Long Nuke Rd B31.....102 E...
Long Saw Dr B31 ......102 D...
Longshaw Gr B34 .....69 D...
Long Shoot The CV11 . 74 C...
Long St
 Birmingham B11 ......87 A...
 Bulkington CV12 ......79 D...
 Walsall WS1..........28 D...
 Wolverhampton WV1 ..163 C...
Longstone Cl B90 .....127 B...
Longstone Rd B42 .....55 C...
Longville Ct CV3 ......133 D...
Longwill Prim Sch for Deaf
 Children B31 ....103 A...

Long Wood B30. . . . . . . 103 E5
Longwood Cl CV4. . . . . . 131 F6
Longwood La WS5, WS4 . . 29 E2
Longwood Path B78. . . . . 20 D1
Longwood Prim Sch B78 . 20 D1
Longwood Rd
 Aldridge WS9. . . . . 30 B2
 Birmingham B45 . . . . . . 122 A7
Longwood Rise WV12 . . . 27 D5
Lonicera Cl WS5. . . . . . . 43 B3
Lonscale Dr CV3 . . . . . . 133 B5
Lonsdale Cl
 Birmingham B33 . . . . . . 68 D2
 Willenhall WV12 . . . . . . 27 B5
Lonsdale Ct B17 . . . . . . 85 C6
Lonsdale Rd
 Bilston WV14. . . . . 40 F6
 Birmingham B17 . . . . . . 85 B6
 Royal Leamington Spa
  CV32. . . . . 157 B4
 Smethwick B66 . . . . 64 D7
 Walsall WS5. . . . . 43 C6
 Wolverhampton WV3 . . . 39 B7
Loom Cl WS6. . . . . 4 F1
Lord Austin Dr B60. . . . . 121 E1
Lord Cromwell Ct WS11. . 2 A5
Lord Leycester Hospl ✶
 CV34. . . . . 160 E6
Lord Lytton Ave CV2 . . . 114 D2
Lord's Dr WS2 . . . . 28 E3
Lords La B80 . . . . 159 E2
Lordsmore Cl WV14. . . . 40 D1
Lord St
 Bilston WV14. . . . . 40 E3
 Birmingham B7 . . . . 66 F5
 Coventry CV5. . . . . 112 F2
 Walsall WS1. . . . . 42 E6
 Wolverhampton WV3. . . . 25 B1
Lord Street W WV14 . . . . 40 E3
Lordswood Boys Sch B17. 65 A1
Lordswood Cl B97 . . . . . 152 F2
Lordswood Girls Sch & Sixth
 Form Ctr B17. . . . . 85 A8
Lordswood Rd B17 . . . . . 85 A7
Lordswood Sq B17. . . . . 85 B7
Lorenzo Cl CV3 . . . . 134 D6
Lorien Cl WV4 . . . . 38 C6
Lorimer Way B43 . . . . . . 44 D5
Loriners Gr WS1 . . . . . . 29 B1
Lorne Gr DY10. . . . . 117 A6
Lorne St
 Burntwood WS7. . . . . . . 6 E8
 Kidderminster DY10. . . . 117 A5
 Tipton DY4. . . . . 51 F8
Lorrainer Ave DY5 . . . . . 81 A8
Lorton B79 . . . . 20 D7
Lothersdale B77 . . . . . . 36 C8
Lothians Rd
 Walsall WS3. . . . . 15 A5
 Wolverhampton WV6. . . . 24 E6
Lottie Rd B29. . . . . 85 E1
Lotus B77 . . . . 21 E3
Lotus Croft B67. . . . . . . 64 F4
Lotus Ct B16. . . . . 65 E1
Lotus Dr
 Cannock WS11. . . . . 1 E5
 Cradley Heath B64. . . . . 62 F2
Lotus Way B65. . . . . 63 A4
Loudon Ave CV6 . . . . . . 113 A5
Loudon Gate CV11 . . . . . 73 F1
Loughshaw B77 . . . . 22 C1
Loughton Gr B63. . . . . . 82 F4
Louisa Pl [3] B18 . . . . . . 66 A5
Louisa St [1] B1 . . . . . . 66 C3
Louis Ct B67. . . . . 64 F5
Louise Croft B14. . . . . . 104 E2
Louise Ct
 [2] Birmingham B27. . . . 88 C3
 Solihull B91. . . . . 106 E1
Louise Ho DY5. . . . . 61 D7
Louise Lorne Rd B13. . . . 86 F4
Louise Rd B21. . . . . 65 F7
Lount St DY3. . . . . 50 C3
Lount Wlk B19. . . . . 66 E5
Lovage Rd B98. . . . . 154 F6
Lovatt Cl WV4. . . . . 41 C1
Lovatt Pl WS11 . . . . 1 E5
Loveday Dr CV32. . . . . . 156 E2
Loveday Ho B70 . . . . . . 53 D3
Loveday St B4 . . . . 164 C4
Love La
 Birmingham B7 . . . . 164 D4
 Great Wyrley WS6 . . . . . 5 B3
 Hinckley LE10 . . . . 76 A6
 Hollywood B47. . . . . . . 124 F7
 Stourbridge, Lye DY9 . . . 81 F5
 Stourbridge, Old Swinford
  DY8. . . . . 81 A3
 Walsall WS1. . . . . 42 E7
 Wolverhampton WV6. . . . 24 D6
Lovelace Ave B91. . . . . . 127 D8
Lovell B79 . . . . 20 F6
Lovell Cl
 Bedworth CV7 . . . . 96 A8
 Birmingham B29 . . . . . . 103 B6
Lovell Field Cl CV34. . . . 160 B3
Lovell Rd CV12. . . . . 78 A3
Love Lyne B97 . . . . 158 B5
Lover's Wlk WS10 . . . . . 41 F3
Lovett Ave B69 . . . . 63 D5
Lovetts Cl LE10 . . . . 74 F8
Lowans Hill Cotts B97 . . 153 C5
Lowans Hill View B97 . . . 153 C4
Low Ave B43. . . . . 43 F2
Lowbridge Cl WV12 . . . . 27 C5
Lowbrook La B90 . . . . . . 125 D4
Lowcroft Gdns WV10. . . . 25 E8
Lowden Croft B26. . . . . . 88 E4

Lowdham B77 . . . . 22 C1
Lowe Ave WS10. . . . . . . 41 C7
Lowe Dr
 Kingswinford DY6 . . . . . . 60 E4
 Sutton Coldfield B73 . . . . 45 C3
Lower Ave CV31. . . . . . . 161 F7
Lower Beeches Rd B31. . 102 C2
Lower Bentley La B60. . . 151 F1
Lower Bond St LE10. . . . 71 D1
LOWER BRADLEY. 41 A2
Lower Cape CV34. . . . . . 160 D8
Lower Chapel St B69. . . . 52 C2
Lower Church La DY4 . . . 52 B5
Lower City Rd B69 . . . . . 52 D1
LOWER CLENT 99 B2
Lower Common La B97. . 153 B2
Lowercroft Way B74 . . . . 31 E6
Lowe Rd CV6 . . . . 95 A2
Lower Dartmouth St B9 . 67 B2
Lower Darwin St B12. . . . 86 F8
Lower Derry St DY5. . . . . 61 D2
LOWER EASTERN
 GREEN 112 A3
Lower Eastern Green La
 CV5. . . . . 111 F4
Lower Essex St B5 . . . . . 66 E1
Lower Farm WS9 . . . . . . 16 E4
Lower Farm Prim Sch
 WS3 . . . . 14 C3
Lower Ford St CV1 . . . . . 165 D3
Lower Forster St WS1. . . 28 F2
Lower Gambolds La B60. 151 B6
Lower Gn
 Tipton DY4. . . . . 51 E5
 Wolverhampton WV6. . . . 24 E5
LOWER GORNAL. 50 E4
Lower Grinsty La B97 . . 158 A8
Lower Gungate DY 55 F1
Lower Ground B79 . . . . . 21 B5
Lower Hall La WS1. . . . . 28 E1
Lower Hall St WS1 . . . . . 27 B1
Lower High St
 Cradley Heath B64. . . . . 82 C8
 Stourbridge DY8 . . . . . . 80 F4
 Wednesbury WS10 . . . . . 41 F2
Lower Higley Cl B32 . . . . 84 E4
Lower Holyhead Rd CV1. 165 A3
Lower Horseley Fields
 WV1. . . . . 25 F2
Lower House La CV9 . . . . 36 B1
LOWER ILLEY 101 D7
Lower Keys Bsns Pk WS12 . 2 D3
Lower Ladies Hills CV8. . 148 A6
Lower Leam St CV31 . . . 162 B7
Lower Lichfield St WV13 . 27 B2
Lower Loveday St B19. . . 164 C4
LOWER MARLBROOK. . . . 121 C1
Lower Mill St DY11. . . . . 116 D6
Lower Moor B30. . . . . . . 103 E8
Lower North St WS4 . . . . 28 E3
Lower Par B72. . . . . 46 C5
Lowerpark B77 . . . . 21 C1
Lower Parklands WV11 . . 116 C5
LOWER PENN. 37 F4
Lower Prec Sh Ctr CV11. 165 B2
Lower Prestwood Rd
 WV11. . . . . 26 C7
Lower Queen St B72 . . . 46 C4
Lower Rd
 Barnacle CV7 . . . . 97 C6
 Cannock WS11. . . . . 2 C3
Lower Reddicroft B73. . . 46 C5
Lower Rushall St WS1. . . 28 F2
Lower Sandford St WS13 . 9 A7
Lower Severn St B1. . . . 164 B2
Lower Shepley La B60. . . 137 E6
Lower St WV6 . . . . 24 E5
Lowerstack Croft B37 . . . 69 F3
LOWER STOKE 114 A1
LOWER STONNALL 17 A4
Lower Temple St [2] B2. 164 B2
Lower Tower St B19 . . . 164 C5
Lower Trinity St B9 . . . . 67 A1
Lower Valley Rd DY5 . . . 61 A2
Lower Vauxhall WV1. . . . 25 A3
Lower Villiers St
 [1] Royal Leamington Spa
  CV32. . . . . 157 A1
 Wolverhampton WV2. . . . 39 C7
Lower Walsall St WV1. . . 25 F1
Lower White Rd B32 . . . . 84 D5
Lowes Ave CV34 . . . . . . 155 E1
Lowes Dr B77. . . . . 35 B8
Lowesmoor Rd B26 . . . . 89 C7
Lowe St
 Birmingham B12 . . . . 87 A8
 Wolverhampton WV6. . . . 25 B4
Loweswater Cl CV11. . . . 74 B4
Loweswater Dr DY3. . . . . 50 D3
Loweswater Ho B38. . . . 104 B1
Loweswater Rd CV3. . . . 114 E1
Lowfield Cl B62. . . . . . . 84 A3
Lowfield La B97 . . . . . . 153 B5
Lowfield Rd CV3. . . . . . 114 C1
Lowforce B77. . . . . 22 C1
LOW HILL 25 E7
Low Hill Cres WV10 . . . . 25 E8
Lowhill La B45. . . . . . . 122 D6
Lowland Cl B64. . . . . . . 62 F1
Lowland Rd WS12. . . . . . 1 C5
Lowndes Rd DY8. . . . . . . 80 E6
Lowrey Ct B68. . . . . 64 C3

Lowry Cl
 Bedworth CV12 . . . . 78 A4
 Perton WV6. . . . . 23 F4
 Smethwick B67 . . . . 64 F6
 Willenhall WV13 . . . . 26 E2
Low St WS6 . . . . 4 D3
Low Thatch B38 . . . . . . 123 E7
Lowther Ct [1] DY5 . . . . . 61 D2
Lowther St CV2 . . . . 113 F4
Low Town [6] B69. . . . . . 64 A7
Low Wood Rd B23 . . . . . 56 E5
LOXDALE 41 A5
Loxdale Park Ind Est
 WV14. . . . . 40 E4
Loxdale Prim Sch WV14 . 40 F4
Loxdale Sidings WV14. . . 40 F4
Loxdale St WV14 . . . . . . 40 F4
Loxdale Stop WV14 . . . . 40 F4
Loxley Ave
 Birmingham B14 . . . . . . 105 C3
 Solihull B90. . . . . 105 F1
Loxley Cl
 Birmingham B31 . . . . . . 102 E8
 Coventry CV2. . . . . 96 D2
 Redditch B98 . . . . 154 D6
Loxley Cr CV2. . . . . 96 D2
Loxley Rd
 Smethwick B67 . . . . 64 F1
 Sutton Coldfield B75 . . . . 32 D3
Loxley Sq B92 . . . . 106 D8
Loxley Way CV32. . . . . . 157 A2
Loxton Cl B74. . . . . 31 A5
Loynells Rd B45 . . . . . . 122 B7
Loyns Cl B37 . . . . 69 E3
LOZELLS 66 C7
Lozells Prim Sch B19 . . . 66 D7
Lozells Rd B19. . . . . 66 C7
Lozells St B19 . . . . 66 C7
Lozells Wood Cl [2] B19. 66 B7
Luanne Cl B64 . . . . 63 A1
Lucas Ct CV32 . . . . 161 D8
Lucas Ho CV32. . . . . . . 156 F2
Lucas Rd LE10 . . . . 75 D6
Luce Cl B35 . . . . 58 B4
Luce Rd WV10 . . . . 25 E6
Lucerne Cl CV2 . . . . 96 C3
Lucerne Ct B23 . . . . 56 D6
Lucian Cl CV2. . . . . 115 B7
Lucknow Rd WV12 . . . . . 27 B5
Lucy Edwards Ct DY11. . 116 C5
Luddington Rd B92 . . . . 107 E8
Ludford Cl B75 . . . . 46 E7
Ludford Rd
 Birmingham B32 . . . . . . 84 A1
 Nuneaton CV10 . . . . 72 C6
Ludgate B79. . . . . 21 A5
Ludgate Ave DY11. . . . . 116 A4
Ludgate Cl
 Oldbury B69. . . . . 63 B8
 Water Orton B46. . . . . . . 59 B3
Ludgate Ct [2] WS5. . . . . 43 D7
Ludgate Hill B3. . . . . . . 164 B3
Ludgate Ho B13. . . . . . . 86 F4
Ludgate St [11] DY1 . . . . 51 B1
Ludgate La B79 . . . . 21 A5
Ludlow Cl
 Birmingham B37 . . . . . . 70 C2
 Cannock WS11. . . . . 2 C2
 Willenhall WV12 . . . . 27 B6
Ludlow Ct B11 . . . . 87 B6
Ludlow Ho
 Birmingham B13 . . . . . . 105 A6
 [1] Walsall WS3 . . . . 28 C6
Ludlow La WS2 . . . . 28 A4
Ludlow Rd
 Birmingham B8 . . . . 67 F4
 Coventry CV5. . . . . 113 A2
 Kidderminster DY10. . . . . 116 E2
 Redditch B97 . . . . 153 E3
Ludlow Way DY20. . . . . . 50 E2
Ludmer Way B20. . . . . . . 55 C2
Ludstone Ave WV4 . . . . . 38 D5
Ludstone Rd B29 . . . . . . 84 F1
Ludworth Ave B37 . . . . . 90 B8
Luff Cl CV3 . . . . 134 B8
Lugtrout La
 Catherine de B B91 . . . . 108 A6
 Solihull B91 . . . . 107 F6
Lukes Cl B64. . . . . 62 C1
Lukes Wlk WS13 . . . . . . 3 A2
Lulworth Cl B63 . . . . 82 C6
Lulworth Pk CV8. . . . . . 148 C6
Lulworth Rd
 Birmingham B28 . . . . 88 A1
 Burntwood WS7 . . . . 7 A7
Lulworth Wlk WV4 . . . . . 38 C6
Lumley Gr B37 . . . . 70 D2
Lumley Rd WS1. . . . . 29 A4
Lumsden Cl CV2. . . . . . 114 F8
Lunar Cl CV4 . . . . 132 D5
Lundy Cl LE10. . . . . 71 B1
Lundy View B36. . . . . . . 70 B6
Lunn Ave CV8. . . . . 147 E3
Lunn Poly Ho [3] CV32 . 156 F1
Lunns Croft WS11. . . . . . 1 E2
Lunt Gr B32 . . . . 84 D5
Lunt Jct The WV14. . . . . 41 A6
Lunt Pl WV14 . . . . 41 A6
Lunt Rd WV14. . . . . 40 F6
LUNT THE 41 A6
Lunt The ✶ CV4. . . . . . . 133 E3
Lupin Cl LE10 . . . . 75 D5
Lupin Gr
 Birmingham B9 . . . . 67 F3
 Walsall WS5. . . . . 43 A4
Lupin Rd DY2. . . . . 51 F1
Lupton Ave CV3. . . . . . . 133 C7

Lupton Ct B60 . . . . 137 A1
Lusbridge Cl B63 . . . . . . 82 B4
Luscombe Rd CV2. . . . . 114 E8
Luther Way CV5. . . . . . . 111 F4
LUTLEY 82 C3
Lutley Ave B63. . . . . 82 E4
Lutley Cl WV3 . . . . 38 E7
Lutley Dr DY9. . . . . 81 C3
Lutley Gr B32. . . . . 84 B1
Lutley La B63. . . . . 82 C2
Lutley Mill Rd B63. . . . . 82 E4
Lutley Prim Sch B63 . . . 82 D1
Luton Rd B29. . . . . 85 F3
Lutterworth Rd
 Coventry CV2. . . . . 114 C5
 Hinckley LE10 . . . . 76 C3
 Nuneaton CV11 . . . . 79 C8
Luttrell Rd B74 . . . . 32 A1
Lutwyche Cl CV5 . . . . . . 111 B8
Lyall Gdns B45. . . . . . . 101 E1
Lyall Gr B27 . . . . 88 A2
Lychgate Ave
 Birmingham B33 . . . . 89 D7
 Stourbridge DY9 . . . . 81 C1
Lychgate Cl
 Hinckley LE10 . . . . 76 A5
 Tamworth B77 . . . . 21 E3
Lychgate La LE10 . . . . . 76 C5
Lydate Rd B62. . . . . 83 F8
Lydbrook Covert [5] B38. 123 E8
Lydbury Gr B33. . . . . . . 69 A4
Lyd Cl WV11. . . . . 26 B5
Lydd Croft B35. . . . . 58 B4
Lyddington Dr B62. . . . . 83 B7
Lyde Gn B63. . . . . 82 B7
Lydford Cl CV2. . . . . . . 114 C7
Lydford Gr B24 . . . . 57 A1
Lydford Rd WS3 . . . . . . 14 B3
Lydgate Ct
 Bedworth CV12 . . . . 78 A4
 [9] Nuneaton CV11 . . . . . 73 C3
Lydgate Rd
 Coventry CV6. . . . . 113 B5
 Kingswinford DY6 . . . . . . 60 F6
Lydgate Gr B23 . . . . 56 D7
Lydham Cl
 Bilston WV14. . . . . 40 B4
 Birmingham B44 . . . . 56 A6
Lydia Croft B74. . . . . . . 31 E6
Lydian Cl WV6 . . . . 25 B4
Lydiate Ash Rd B60 . . . . 121 C3
Lydiate Ave B31 . . . . . . 102 D1
Lydiates Cl DY3. . . . . . . 50 B7
Lydney Cl
 Redditch B98 . . . . 154 D7
 Willenhall WV12 . . . . 27 D4
Lydney Gr B31. . . . . . . 102 F3
Lydstep Gr CV31 . . . . . . 162 C7
LYE. 81 E6
Lye Ave B32 . . . . 84 A2
Lye Bsns Ctr DY9. . . . . . 81 F6
Lye By-Pass DY9. . . . . . 81 E6
Lye Close La B32. . . . . . 84 A2
Lyecroft Ave B37 . . . . . . 70 D2
Lye Cross Rd B69 . . . . . 63 B7
Lye Sta DY9 . . . . 81 E6
Lye Valley Ind Est DY9. . 81 F6
Lygon Cl B98 . . . . 154 A5
Lygon Gr B32. . . . . 84 D2
Lymedene Rd B42. . . . . . 55 B5
Lyme Green Rd B33 . . . . 68 F4
Lymer Rd WV10 . . . . 11 C1
Lymesy St CV3 . . . . 133 D7
Lymington Cl CV6. . . . . 113 D8
Lymington Ct B73. . . . . . 46 B1
Lymington Dr CV6 . . . . . 96 A1
Lymington Rd WV13 . . . . 27 D2
Lymore Croft CV2. . . . . 115 A8
Lymsey Croft DY8. . . . . . 60 C3
Lynbrook Cl
 Dudley DY2. . . . . 62 D5
 Hollywood B47. . . . . . . 125 A7
Lynbrook Rd CV5. . . . . 132 D8
Lynchgate Ct CV4 . . . . . 132 C6
Lynchgate Ho CV4 . . . . . 132 C6
Lynchgate Rd CV4 . . . . . 132 C6
Lynch The
 Nuneaton CV11 . . . . 73 D2
 Polesworth B78 . . . . 22 F1
Lyncourt Gr B32 . . . . . . 84 B6
Lyncroft Rd B11 . . . . . . 87 F2
Lyndale DY1 . . . . 35 F6
Lyndale Cl CV5 . . . . 112 C3
Lyndale Dr WV11. . . . . . 26 E6
Lyndale Rd
 Coventry CV5. . . . . 112 C3
 Dudley DY2 . . . . 62 E6
 Sedgley DY3 . . . . 39 B2
Lynden Cl B61. . . . . . . 136 E3
Lynden Ho CV5. . . . . . . 133 B8
Lyndenwood B97 . . . . . 153 A2
Lyndholm Rd DY10. . . . . 117 A6
Lyndhurst Cl
 Bedworth CV6. . . . . 96 B6
 Hinckley LE10 . . . . 76 A7
Lyndhurst Croft CV5 . . . 111 C4
Lyndhurst Dr
 Kidderminster DY10. . . . . 116 E8
 Stourbridge DY8 . . . . . . 60 F1
Lyndhurst Rd
 Birmingham B24 . . . . 56 F2
 Cannock WS12. . . . . 2 E1
 West Bromwich B71 . . . . 53 E7
 Wolverhampton WV3 . . . . 39 A7

Lyndon Cl
 Birmingham, Castle Bromwich
  B36. . . . . 69 C8
 Birmingham, Handsworth
  B20. . . . . 55 C2
 Halesowen B63 . . . . 82 F4
 Sedgley DY3. . . . . 39 E1
Lyndon Croft B37 . . . . . . 90 B7
Lyndon Ct CV32. . . . . . . 161 E8
LYNDON END 89 A5
Lyndon Gr
 Kingswinford DY6 . . . . . . 60 B8
 West Bromwich B71 . . . . 53 D4
LYNDON GREEN 89 A7
Lyndon Green Inf Sch
 B26. . . . . 89 A6
Lyndon Green Jun Sch
 B26. . . . . 89 A6
Lyndon Ho B31 . . . . 103 B3
Lyndon Rd
 Birmingham, Rubery B45. 121 E7
 Birmingham, Stechford B33. 68 E3
 Halesowen B62 . . . . 83 C3
 Solihull B92. . . . . 88 E3
 Sutton Coldfield B73 . . . . 46 B5
Lyndon Sch B92 . . . . . . 89 A3
Lyndworth Rd B30 . . . . . 104 C8
Lyneham Cl
 Hinckley LE10 . . . . 71 A1
 Tamworth B79 . . . . 21 C8
Lyneham Gdns B76 . . . . 58 B6
Lyneham Way B35 . . . . . 57 F3
Lyne Ho [1] CV2 . . . . . . 114 D8
Lynfield Cl B38 . . . . 123 F7
Lyng Cl CV5 . . . . 112 A4
Lyng Hall Sch CV2 . . . . . 114 C6
Lyng La B70 . . . . 53 C2
Lyng Prim Sch B70 . . . . 53 C1
Lynmouth Cl
 Aldridge WS9. . . . . 30 A5
 Nuneaton CV11 . . . . 73 E5
Lynmouth Rd CV2 . . . . . 114 E8
Lynton Ave
 Smethwick B66 . . . . 65 A6
 West Bromwich B71 . . . . 53 C7
 Wolverhampton WV6. . . . 24 E6
Lynton Cl CV34 . . . . 155 E1
Lynton Ho B23. . . . . 56 B6
Lynton Rd
 Birmingham B6 . . . . 67 B7
 Coventry CV6. . . . . 95 F1
Lynval Rd DY5 . . . . 81 F7
Lynwood Ave DY6. . . . . . 60 B7
Lynwood Cl
 Willenhall WV12 . . . . 27 E8
Lynwood Dr DY10. . . . . . 98 C2
Lynwood Way B45 . . . . . 122 A3
Lynwood Wlk
 Birmingham B17 . . . . 85 D4
 [10] Royal Leamington Spa
  CV32. . . . . 162 C6
Lyon Ct B72 . . . . 46 C5
Lyon Dr B77 . . . . 35 D8
Lyons Gr B11 . . . . 87 C3
Lysander Cl LE10. . . . . . 75 F4
Lysander Rd B45. . . . . . 102 A2
Lysander St CV3 . . . . . . 134 D6
Lysander Way
 Birmingham B35 . . . . 58 B2
 Cannock WS11. . . . . 1 E3
Lyster Cl CV34 . . . . 160 B8
Lysway Ct [8] WS1. . . . . 42 F8
Lysways St WS1 . . . . . . 42 F8
Lythall Cl CV31. . . . . . . 162 F5
Lythalls La CV6 . . . . 95 E1
Lythalls Lane Ind Est CV6. 95 E1
Lytham B77. . . . . 22 C5
Lytham Cl
 Stourbridge DY8 . . . . . . 80 F2
 Sutton Coldfield B76 . . . . 58 B6
Lytham Croft B15. . . . . . 86 D8
Lytham Gr WS3 . . . . 14 A4
Lytham Rd WV6. . . . . . . 23 D4
Lythwood Dr DY5 . . . . . . 61 A4
Lyttelton Pl DY9 . . . . . . 99 C6
Lyttelton Rd
 Birmingham, Edgbaston
  B16. . . . . 65 D1
 Birmingham, Stechford B33. 68 D5
 Stourbridge DY8 . . . . . . 80 D5
 Warwick CV34 . . . . 160 E8
Lyttleton Ave
 Bromsgrove B61 . . . . . . 150 E7
 Halesowen B62 . . . . 83 E7
Lyttleton Cl
 Coventry CV3. . . . . 115 A1
 Dudley DY2. . . . . 62 C4
Lyttleton Ho B63 . . . . . . 83 A2
Lyttleton St B70 . . . . . . 53 C2
Lytton Ave WV4 . . . . 38 E4
Lytton Gr B27. . . . . 88 B1
Lytton La B32. . . . . 84 F3

M

Maas Rd B31. . . . . 103 A4
Mabey Ave B98 . . . . 153 F5
MacAdam Cl WS7. . . . . . 7 B8
MacArthur Rd B64. . . . . . 82 C8
MacAulay Ho [5] B70 . . . 53 D1
MacAulay Rd CV2 . . . . . 114 D4

McBean Rd WV6 . . . . 24 F4
Macbeth App CV34 . . . . 161 D4
McCalla Ho WV3 . . . . 25 B1
McConnell Cl B60 . . . . . 151 B7
MacDonald Cl B69 . . . . . . 52 D2
MacDonald Rd CV2 . . . . 114 D3
MacDonald St B5 . . . . . . 86 E8
McDonnell Dr CV6, CV7 . . 95 F6
McDougall Rd WS10 . . . . 42 C3
Macefield Cl CV2 . . . . . . 96 D2
Mace St B64 . . . . 62 E1
McGeough Wlk WS11 . . . . 2 B5
McGhie St WS12 . . . . 2 B6
McGregor Cl B6 . . . . 55 F1
McGregor Cres B77 . . . . 21 F3
MacGregor Tithe B79 . . . 21 B5
Machin Rd B23 . . . . 56 F4
Mackadown La B33 . . . . . 69 D2
Mackay Rd WS3 . . . . 14 D2
McKean Rd
  Oldbury B69 . . . . 64 A8
  West Bromwich B70 . . . . 53 C1
Mcken Ct B70 . . . . 53 C1
Mackenzie Cl CV5 . . . . . 112 A7
Mackenzie Rd B11 . . . . . . 87 C3
Mackmillan Rd B65 . . . . . 63 C2
McLean Rd WV10 . . . . . . 11 C1
McMahon Rd CV12 . . . . . 95 E8
Macmillan Cl B69 . . . . . . 52 C2
Macrome Rd WV6 . . . . . . 24 E8
Madam's Hill Rd B90 . . . 126 E7
Maddocke Wlk [4] WS13 . . 8 F6
Maddocks Hill B72 . . . . . 46 C2
Madehurst Rd B23 . . . . . 56 E6
Madeira Ave WV8 . . . . . . 10 A2
Madeira Croft CV5 . . . . . 112 E2
Madeira Ct DY8 . . . . 60 F1
MADELEY HEATH 120 E7
Madeley Rd
  Birmingham B11 . . . . . . 87 C5
  Kingswinford DY6 . . . . . 61 A4
  Madeley Heath DY9 . . . 120 D6
  Redditch B98 . . . . 154 F5
Madinatul Uloom Al Islamiya
  Sch DY10 . . . . 117 A5
Madin Rd DY4 . . . . 51 E4
Madison Ave
  Birmingham B36 . . . . . . 68 D6
  Brierley Hill DY5 . . . . . . 61 F3
  Walsall WS2 . . . . 28 B2
Madison Cl CV4 . . . . 111 C3
Madley Cl B45 . . . . 121 E8
Madox Cl B79 . . . . 20 E8
Madresfield Dr B63 . . . . . 83 B2
Madrona B77 . . . . 22 B4
Maer Cl B65 . . . . 63 C3
Mafeking Rd B66 . . . . . . 65 A7
Mafeking Villas B62 . . . . 83 B7
Magdala St B18 . . . . 65 E5
Magdalen Cl DY1 . . . . . . 51 A2
Magdalen Ct B16 . . . . . . 65 E1
Magdalene Rd WS1 . . . . 43 A7
Magee Cl LE10 . . . . 71 C2
Magna Cl WS6 . . . . 4 E3
Magness Cres WV12 . . . . 27 C5
Magnet Wlk B23 . . . . 56 C3
Magnolia B77 . . . . 22 A4
Magnolia Cl
  Birmingham B29 . . . . . 103 A7
  Coventry CV3 . . . . 133 B5
Magnolia Dr [1] WS5 . . . . 42 F4
Magnolia Gr
  Codsall WV8 . . . . 10 B3
  Willenhall WV12 . . . . . . 27 B4
Magnolia Way [1] DY8 . . . 60 F1
Magnum Cl B74 . . . . 44 F7
Magnus B77 . . . . 35 A5
Magpie Cl DY2 . . . . 62 E3
Magpie Ho CV5 . . . . 111 D5
Magpie La CV7 . . . . 129 E6
Magpie Way DY10 . . . . . 117 B2
Maguire Ind Est CV4 . . . 131 F8
Magyar Cres CV11 . . . . . 79 A8
Maidavale Cres CV3 . . . . 133 C4
Maiden Cl WV13 . . . . 27 C2
Maidendale Rd DY6 . . . . 60 B7
Maidensbridge Dr DY6 . . 60 C8
Maidensbridge Gdns DY6 . 49 B1
Maidensbridge Prim Sch
  DY6 . . . . 49 B1
Maidensbridge Rd DY6 . . 49 B1
Maiden Way B60 . . . . . . 151 A6
Maidstone Dr
  Burntwood WS7 . . . . 7 D6
  Stourbridge DY8 . . . . . 60 E3
Maidstone Rd B20 . . . . . . 55 E1
Maidwell Dr B90 . . . . . . 126 E8
Mailbox (Sh Ctr) The B1 . 164 B1
Main Rd
  Ansty CV7 . . . . 97 D3
  Meriden CV7 . . . . 110 D8
  Tamworth B79 . . . . 21 B8
Main St
  Birmingham B11 . . . . . . 87 A7
  Brandon CV8 . . . . 135 F4
  Shenstone WS14 . . . . . 17 F6
  Solihull B90 . . . . 126 A5
  Stonnall WS9 . . . . 16 D4
Mainstone Cl B98 . . . . . 154 E3
Mainstream Forty Seven Ind
  Pk B7 . . . . 67 C5
Mainstream Way B7 . . . . 67 C5
Main Terr B11 . . . . 87 A7
Mainwaring Dr B75 . . . . . 32 E2
Maisemore Cl B98 . . . . . 154 D6

Maitland B77 . . . . 21 F2
Maitland Rd
  Birmingham B8 . . . . 67 F4
  Dudley DY1 . . . . 50 E1
Maizefield LE10 . . . . 71 C4
Majestic Way B65 . . . . . . 63 D4
Major Ct [6] B13 . . . . 87 B2
Majors Fold DY3 . . . . 50 A4
MAJOR'S GREEN 125 D8
Major St WV2 . . . . 39 E7
Majuba Rd B16 . . . . 65 C4
Makepeace Ave CV34 . . 155 F1
Malam Cl CV4 . . . . 112 A1
Malcolm Ave
  Birmingham B24 . . . . . . 57 C5
  Bromsgrove B61 . . . . . 136 E3
Malcolm Ct WV1 . . . . 25 A3
Malcolm Gr B45 . . . . . . 122 A7
Malcolm Rd B90 . . . . . . 106 B1
Malcolmson Cl B15 . . . . . 85 F8
Maldale B77 . . . . 22 C1
Malfield Ave B97 . . . . . . 152 F3
Malfield Dr B27 . . . . 88 E3
Malham Cl CV11 . . . . 74 A2
Malham Rd
  Tamworth B77 . . . . 36 C8
  Warwick CV34 . . . . 155 F1
Malhay Gdns [4] B42 . . . . 55 A8
Malin Ct B23 . . . . 56 B8
Malins Rd
  Birmingham B17 . . . . . . 85 D5
  Wolverhampton WV4 . . . 39 E5
Malins The CV34 . . . . . . 161 B6
Malins View Rd DY3 . . . . 50 D4
Malkit Cl WS2 . . . . 27 F4
Mallaby Cl B90 . . . . 126 A8
Mallard Ave
  Kidderminster DY10 . . . 117 B3
  Nuneaton CV10 . . . . . . 72 C6
Mallard Cl
  Birmingham B27 . . . . . . 88 C3
  Brierley Hill DY5 . . . . . . 81 C7
  Redditch B98 . . . . 153 F5
  Walsall WS3 . . . . 15 A5
Mallard Croft [5] WS13 . . . 9 C8
Mallard Dr
  Birmingham B23 . . . . . . 56 B3
  Hinckley LE10 . . . . 75 A7
  Oldbury B69 . . . . 63 F4
Mallard Rd B80 . . . . 159 F4
Mallards Reach B92 . . . . 106 E8
Mallender Dr B93 . . . . . 127 F6
Mallen Dr B69 . . . . 52 B1
Mallerin Croft CV10 . . . . 72 B5
Mallicot Cl WS13 . . . . 3 D1
Mallin Gdns DY1 . . . . 61 E8
Mallin St B66 . . . . 64 D7
Mallory Cres WS3 . . . . . . 14 D2
Mallory Dr
  Kidderminster DY11 . . . 116 D8
  Warwick CV34 . . . . 160 D7
Mallory Rd WV6 . . . . 23 E3
Mallory Rise B13 . . . . 87 C1
Mallory Way CV6 . . . . 95 E4
Mallow Cl [8] WS5 . . . . . . 43 A3
Mallow Cres DY10 . . . . . 116 F4
Mallow Croft CV12 . . . . . 77 E2
Mallow CV6 . . . . 25 E5
Mallow Dr B61 . . . . 136 F6
Mallow Rise [2] B23 . . . . . 56 B7
Mall Sh Ctr B72 . . . . 46 B5
Malmesbury Pk B15 . . . . 85 E7
Malmesbury Rd
  Birmingham B10 . . . . . . 87 E7
  Coventry CV6 . . . . 95 A3
Malpas Dr B32 . . . . 102 C8
Malpass Rd DY5 . . . . 81 F7
Malpas Wlk WV10 . . . . . . 26 A4
Malt Cl B17 . . . . 85 D6
Malthouse Croft B6 . . . . . 66 E8
Malthouse Dr DY1 . . . . . . 51 A2
Malthouse Gdns B19 . . . . 66 D7
Malthouse Gr B25 . . . . . . 68 E1
Malthouse La
  Birmingham B8 . . . . 67 E6
  Birmingham, Great Barr
    B42 . . . . 55 D8
  Earlswood B94 . . . . . . 141 E7
  Kenilworth CV8 . . . . . . 147 E6
  Wolverhampton WV6 . . . 24 E6
Malthouse Mdw [2] B91. . 107 C1
Malthouse Rd DY4 . . . . . 51 E5
Malthouse Row B37 . . . . . 90 A8
Malthouse The B1 . . . . . . 65 A1
Maltings The
  Aldridge WS9 . . . . 30 C6
  Nuneaton CV11 . . . . . . 73 B8
  Royal Leamington Spa
    CV32 . . . . 156 F2
  Solihull B94 . . . . 141 F8
  Studley B80 . . . . 159 D4
  Wolverhampton WV1 . . 163 C4
Malt Mill La B62 . . . . 83 D8
Malt Mill Lane Trad Est
  B62 . . . . 83 D8
Malton Ave B65 . . . . 63 D6
Malton Gr B13 . . . . 105 B7
Malvern Ave
  Nuneaton CV10 . . . . . . 72 B3
  Stourbridge DY9 . . . . . . 81 C5
Malvern & Brueton Park
  Nature Reserve * B91 . . 107 D1
Malvern Cl
  Birmingham B15 . . . . . . 85 C8
  West Bromwich B71 . . . . 53 D5
  Willenhall WV12 . . . . . . 27 B4
Malvern Cres DY2 . . . . . . 61 F6

Malvern Ct
  Birmingham, Stockfield
    B27 . . . . 88 C4
  Birmingham, Stockland Green
    B23 . . . . 56 C2
  [8] Sutton Coldfield B74 . 31 F2
  Wolverhampton WV10 . . 25 D8
Malvern Dr
  Aldridge WS9 . . . . 30 C8
  Kidderminster DY10 . . . 116 E3
  Sutton Coldfield B76 . . . 58 A8
  Wolverhampton WV11 . . 26 B1
Malvern Hill Rd B7 . . . . . 67 C7
Malvern Ho
  Coventry CV5 . . . . 111 D4
  [7] Halesowen B63 . . . . 83 A3
  Redditch B97 . . . . 153 C1
Malvern Park Ave B91 . . 107 D3
Malvern Rd
  Balsall Common CV7 . . 130 C6
  Barnt Green B45 . . . . . 122 A2
  Birmingham, Acock's Green
    B27 . . . . 88 C4
  Birmingham, Handsworth
    B21 . . . . 54 C1
  Bromsgrove B61 . . . . . 150 D7
  Coventry CV5 . . . . 112 F4
  Redditch B97 . . . . 153 D8
Malvern St B12 . . . . 87 A5
Malvern View
  Bluntington DY10 . . . . . 118 E1
  Kidderminster DY11 . . . 116 B6
Malvern View Rd DY3 . . . 50 D4
Mamble Rd DY8 . . . . 80 E5
Mammoth Dr WV10 . . . . . 25 D6
Manby Cl WV6 . . . . 25 A4
Manby Rd B35 . . . . 58 A4
Manby St DY4 . . . . 51 F8
Mancetter Rd
  Nuneaton CV10 . . . . . . 72 D7
  Solihull B90 . . . . 106 C3
Manchester St
  Birmingham B6 . . . . . . 164 C5
  Oldbury B69 . . . . 64 B7
Mancroft Cl DY6 . . . . 60 A6
Mancroft Gdns WV6 . . . . 24 C5
Mancroft Rd WV6 . . . . . . 24 C5
Mandale Rd WV10 . . . . . 25 F6
Mandarin Ave DY10 . . . . 117 B3
Mandarin Cl LE10 . . . . . . 75 A6
Mander Gallery WV1 . . . 163 B3
Mander Ctr CV34 . . . . . . 160 C4
Manderley Cl
  Coventry CV5 . . . . 111 C5
  Sedgley DY3 . . . . 39 C2
Mander Portman Woodward
  B15 . . . . 86 A8
Manders Cl B96 . . . . . . 158 D1
Mander (Sh Ctr) WV1 . . 163 B3
Manders Ind Est WV1 . . . 26 A3
Mander Sq WV1 . . . . . . 163 B3
Mander St WV3 . . . . 163 A1
Manderston Cl DY1 . . . . . 51 A2
Manderville Gdns WV6 . . 24 C5
Mandeville Gdns WS1 . . . 42 F8
Mandeville Way B61 . . . 136 F5
Mandrake Cl CV6 . . . . . . 95 D4
MANEY 46 C4
Maney Cnr B72 . . . . 46 B4
Maney Hill Prim Sch B72 . 46 D2
Maney Hill Rd B72 . . . . . 46 C2
Manfield Ave CV2 . . . . . 115 A7
Manfield Rd WV13 . . . . . 26 C3
Manhattan Way CV4 . . . 111 C3
Manifold Cl WS7 . . . . 7 D6
Manifoldia Grange B70 . . 53 B2
Manilla Rd B29 . . . . 86 B1
Manitoba Croft [2] B38 . . 123 F8
Manley Cl B70 . . . . 53 A3
Manley Rd WS13 . . . . 3 D1
Manlove St WV3 . . . . 39 A8
Manningford Ct B14 . . . 104 F3
Manningford Rd B14 . . . 104 E3
Manor Abbey Rd B62 . . . 83 E4
Manor Ave
  Cannock WS11 . . . . 1 D1
  Great Wyrley WS6 . . . . . 5 A4
  Kidderminster DY11 . . . 116 A7
Manor Avenue S DY11 . . 116 A6
Manor Cl
  Birmingham B16 . . . . . . 65 D1
  Codsall WV8 . . . . 10 B4
  Hinckley LE10 . . . . 75 C5
  Kidderminster DY11 . . . 116 A6
  Willenhall WV13 . . . . . . 26 F3
  Wolverhampton WV4 . . . 38 F4
Manor Cotts WS14 . . . . . . 8 E2
Manor Court Ave CV11 . . 73 B5
Manor Court Mews CV11 . 73 A5
Manor Court Rd
  Bromsgrove B60 . . . . . 150 F8
  Nuneaton CV11 . . . . . . 73 A5
Manor Ct
  [5] Birmingham, Hurst Green
    B62 . . . . 84 A7
  Birmingham, King's Norton
    B30 . . . . 104 A2
  Dorridge B93 . . . . 127 F2
  Dudley DY2 . . . . 62 C5
  Kenilworth CV8 . . . . . . 148 A6
  Mile Oak B78 . . . . 20 D1
  Royal Leamington Spa
    CV31 . . . . 161 F7
  Walsall WS2 . . . . 28 C1
Manor Dr
  Dudley DY3 . . . . 50 B3

Manor Dr continued
  Sutton Coldfield B73 . . . 46 B4
Manor Est CV8 . . . . 135 F3
Manor Farm Dr WV12 . . . 27 D5
Manor Farm Rd B11 . . . . 87 E4
Manor Flats DY3 . . . . 50 D8
Manorford Ave B71 . . . . . 43 A1
Manor Foundation Bsns Ent
  & Sports Coll WS10 . . . 42 D3
Manor Gdns
  Birmingham B33 . . . . . . 68 D2
  Wednesbury WS10 . . . . 41 F4
  Wombourne WV5 . . . . . 49 B7
Manor Hall Mews CV3 . . 134 D6
Manor Hill B73 . . . . 46 A4
Manor Ho WV6 . . . . 24 D5
Manor Hospl WS2 . . . . . . 28 C1
Manor Ho The CV31 . . . . 161 F7
MANOR HOUSE 96 C2
Manorhouse Cl WS1 . . . . 42 E5
Manor House Cl
  Aston Flamville LE10 . . . 76 E6
  Birmingham B29 . . . . . . 84 F1
Manor House Dr
  Birmingham B29 . . . . . 103 B7
  Coventry CV1 . . . . 165 B2
Manor House La
  Birmingham B96 . . . . . 158 E3
  Birmingham B26 . . . . . . 88 F6
  Water Orton B46 . . . . . . 59 B3
Manor House Pk WV8 . . . 10 B4
Manor House Rd WS10 . . 41 F4
Manor House Way B46 . . 59 B3
Manorial Rd B75 . . . . 32 E3
Manor Ind Est WS2 . . . . . 28 C1
Manor La
  Halesowen B62 . . . . 83 E4
  Honiley CV8, CV35 . . . . 146 A5
  Lower Marlbrook B61 . . 121 C4
  Stourbridge DY8 . . . . . . 80 D3
  Wroxall CV35 . . . . 145 F4
Manor Mews B80 . . . . . . 159 E4
Manor Park B13 . . . . 87 A2
Manor Park Gr B31 . . . . 102 C1
Manor Park Prim Sch
  [1] Birmingham B6 . . . . . 67 A8
  Coventry CV3 . . . . 133 D7
Manor Park Rd
  Birmingham B36 . . . . . . 69 D8
  Nuneaton CV11 . . . . . . 73 A5
Manor Pk DY6 . . . . 60 D6
Manor Pl LE10 . . . . 71 D1
Manor Prim Sch
  Drayton Bassett B78 . . . 34 E5
  Sutton Coldfield B74 . . . 31 A1
  Wolverhampton WV14 . . 40 B2
Manor Rd
  Birmingham, Birchfield B6. . 55 F1
  Birmingham, Edgbaston B16 65 D1
  Birmingham, Stechford B33 . 68 E3
  Coventry CV1 . . . . 165 B1
  Dorridge B93 . . . . 127 F3
  Ettingshall WV4 . . . . . . 40 A5
  Kenilworth CV8 . . . . . . 147 F6
  Mile Oak B78 . . . . 20 D1
  Royal Leamington Spa
    CV32 . . . . 157 B3
  Smethwick B67 . . . . 64 E4
  Solihull B91 . . . . 107 C5
  Stourbridge DY8 . . . . . . 60 E2
  Studley B80 . . . . 159 E4
  Sutton Coldfield B74 . . . 31 A1
  Sutton Coldfield, Streetly
    B74 . . . . 45 A8
  Tamworth B77 . . . . 21 D4
  Tipton DY4 . . . . 51 F4
  Upper Bentley B97 . . . . 152 B1
  Walsall WS2 . . . . 28 C2
  Wednesbury WS10 . . . . 42 D2
  Wolverhampton, Oxley
    WV10 . . . . 25 C7
  Wolverhampton WV4 . . . 38 F4
  Wythall B47 . . . . 125 A3
Manor Rise
  Burntwood WS7 . . . . 7 A5
  Lichfield WS14 . . . . 9 C7
Manor Road N B16 . . . . . 65 D1
Manor Road Prec [2] WS2 . 28 C2
Manor Side Ind Est B98 . 154 E6
Manor Sq B91 . . . . 107 C3
Manor St
  Hinckley LE10 . . . . 71 C1
  Wolverhampton WV6 . . . 24 E5
Manor Terr CV8 . . . . 148 A6
MANOR THE 47 A2
Manor View CV8 . . . . . . 135 F3
Manor Way
  Halesowen B62, B63 . . . 83 D3
  Hinckley LE10 . . . . 75 D5
  Manor Way Prim Sch B63 83 C3
Manor Wlk
  [4] Solihull B91 . . . . . . 107 C3
  Sutton Coldfield B73 . . . 46 B4
Mansard Cl
  Wolverhampton, Bradmore
    WV3 . . . . 38 F8
  Wolverhampton, Scotlands
    WV10 . . . . 26 B8
Mansard Ho B90 . . . . . . 106 A3
Manse Cl CV7 . . . . 78 A1
Manse Gdns B80 . . . . . . 159 E3
Mansell Cl B63 . . . . 82 E6
Mansell Rd
  Redditch B97 . . . . 158 D7
  Tipton DY4 . . . . 52 A8
Mansel Rd B10 . . . . 87 E8
Mansel St CV6 . . . . 113 E8

Mansfield Cl B79 . . . . 20 E6
Mansfield Green Com Sch
  B6 . . . . 66 E8
Mansfield Ho B37 . . . . . . 70 D3
Mansfield Rd
  Birmingham, Aston B6. . . 66 E8
  Birmingham, South Yardley
    B25 . . . . 88 C5
Mansion Cl DY1 . . . . 51 A3
Mansion Cres B67 . . . . . . 64 E4
Mansion Ct B62 . . . . 83 E7
Mansion Dr
  Hammerwich WS7 . . . . . . 7 D4
  Tipton DY4 . . . . 52 C5
Manston Cl [1] LE10 . . . . 75 D8
Manston Dr WV6 . . . . 23 C5
Manston Rd B64 . . . . 63 A1
Manston Dr WV6 . . . . 23 E5
Manston Rise B26 . . . . . . 89 B7
Manston View B79 . . . . . 21 C8
Manta Rd B77 . . . . 35 D6
Mantilla Dr CV3 . . . . 133 A5
Manton Croft B93 . . . . . 127 E3
Manton Ho B19 . . . . 66 E7
Manway Cl B20 . . . . 54 F4
Manwoods Cl B20 . . . . . . 55 B2
Maple Ave
  Bedworth CV7 . . . . 78 B1
  Wednesbury WS10 . . . . 42 C4
Mapleback Ct B91 . . . . . 107 C5
Maple Bank B15 . . . . 86 A7
Maplebeck Cl CV5 . . . . . 113 A3
Maple Bsns Pk B7 . . . . . . 67 B6
Maple Cl
  Birmingham B21 . . . . . . 54 E1
  Burntwood WS7 . . . . 6 F7
  Dudley WV14 . . . . 51 A7
  Hinckley LE10 . . . . 75 E5
  Kidderminster DY11 . . . 116 B8
  Stourbridge DY8 . . . . . . 80 D2
Maple Cres WS11 . . . . 1 C1
Maple Ct CV13 . . . . 104 F5
Maple Ct
  Bilston WV14 . . . . 40 F2
  [2] Birmingham, Erdington
    B24 . . . . 56 F3
  [1] Birmingham, Harborne
    B17 . . . . 85 B6
  Lichfield WS14 . . . . 9 C5
  [3] Oldbury B69 . . . . . . 64 D8
Maple Ctr The WS10 . . . . 41 B3
Mapledene B13 . . . . 87 B2
Mapledene Prim Sch B26 89 D6
Mapledene Rd B26 . . . . . 89 D6
Maple Dr
  Birmingham B44 . . . . . . 56 C8
  Dudley DY3 . . . . 50 B2
  Huntington WS12 . . . . . . 1 D8
  Walsall, Shelfield WS4 . . 29 B8
  Walsall, Yew Tree WS5 . . 43 B4
Maple Gn DY1 . . . . 51 A5
Maple Gr
  Birmingham, Aston B19 . . 66 D8
  Birmingham, Kingshurst B37 69 F6
  Kingswinford DY6 . . . . . 60 C6
  Lichfield WS14 . . . . 9 C7
  Warwick CV34 . . . . 156 A1
  Wolverhampton WV3 . . . 24 C2
Maple Hayes Dyslexia Sch
  WS13 . . . . 8 D8
Maple Ho
  Redditch, Greenlands
    B98 . . . . 158 F8
  Redditch, Webheath B97 153 B2
  Sutton Coldfield B74 . . . 31 B5
  Walsall WS4 . . . . 15 D1
Maple Leaf Dr
  Atherstone CV9 . . . . . . 36 E1
  Birmingham B37 . . . . . . 90 B8
Maple Leaf Ind Est WS22 . 28 A3
Maple Leaf Rd WS10 . . . . 41 C1
Maple Rd
  Birmingham B45 . . . . . 121 F6
  Birmingham, Selly Oak
    B30 . . . . 103 E8
  Dudley DY1 . . . . 51 C3
  Halesowen B62 . . . . 83 D8
  Nuneaton CV10 . . . . . . 72 E5
  Royal Leamington Spa
    CV31 . . . . 161 F6
  Sutton Coldfield B72 . . . 46 C3
  Walsall WS4 . . . . 14 F2
  Wolverhampton WV3 . . . 38 E8
Maple Rise
  Oldbury B68 . . . . 64 C2
  Tamworth B77 . . . . 22 A4
Maple Row [1] DY5 . . . . . 61 D2
Maple St WS3 . . . . 14 D2
Maples The
  Bedworth CV12 . . . . 77 E2
  Wolverhampton WV11 . . 26 B5
Mapleton Gr B28 . . . . . . 106 B7
Mapleton Rd
  Birmingham B28 . . . . . 106 B7
  Coventry CV6 . . . . 112 F8
Maple Tree La B63 . . . . . 82 C6
Maple Way B31 . . . . 102 F1
Maple Wlk
  [4] Birmingham B37 . . . . 70 B2
  Coventry CV5 . . . . 95 F5
Maplewood B76 . . . . 58 A8
Mapperley Cl CV2 . . . . . 115 A8
Mapperley Gdns B13 . . . . 86 C3
Mappleborough Cl B97 . . 153 B5
Mappleborough Rd B90 . 105 E1
Mapps Cl B63 . . . . 82 C6
Marans Croft B38 . . . . . 123 D7

Marble Alley B80 .... 159 E4
Marbury Cl B38 .... 103 D2
Marbury Dr WV14 .... 41 A6
Marbury Mews DY5 ...... 61 D1
Marchant Rd
  Bilston WV14 .... 40 D7
  Hinckley LE10 .... 75 C8
  Wolverhampton WV6 .... 24 F2
March Cl WS6 .... 4 D1
MARCH END 26 E5
March End Rd WV11 ..... 26 D5
Marchfont Cl CV11 ...... 74 A1
Marchmont Rd B9 .... 68 A2
Marchmount Rd B72 .... 57 C8
March Way
  Aldridge WS9 .... 16 C1
  Coventry CV3 .... 134 D7
Marchwood Cl B97 ...... 153 A5
Marcliff Cres B90 .... 105 C2
Marconi Pl WS12 .... 2 C7
Marcos Dr B36 .... 58 F1
Marcot Rd B92 .... 88 F5
Marcroft Pl CV31 .... 162 D6
Marden Cl WS13 .... 26 F1
Marden Gr B31 .... 123 A7
Marden Wlk B23 .... 56 C3
Mardol Cl CV2 .... 114 D7
Mardon Rd B26 .... 89 C5
Maree Gr WV11 .... 13 B1
Maree Wlk B77 .... 35 E8
Maret Ct [2] WS1 .... 42 F8
Marfield Cl B76 .... 58 A6
Margam Cres WS3 ...... 13 F2
Margam Terr WS3 ...... 13 F2
Margam Way WS3 ...... 13 F2
Margaret Ave
  Bedworth CV12 .... 78 B3
  Halesowen B63 .... 82 F4
Margaret Cl DY5 .... 81 E8
Margaret Dr
  Cannock WS11 .... 1 E6
  Stourbridge DY8 .... 81 B4
Margaret Gdns B67 ..... 64 E5
Margaret Gr B17 .... 85 C7
Margaret Ho B76 .... 46 F5
Margaret Llewellyn Davies Cl
  B98 .... 154 A3
Margaret Rd
  Birmingham, Harborne
    B17 .... 85 C5
  Birmingham, New Oscott
    B73 .... 45 D1
  Darlaston WS10 .... 41 C4
  Walsall WS2 .... 27 E3
Margaret St
  Birmingham B3 .... 164 B1
  West Bromwich B70 ..... 53 B2
Margaret Vale Dr WV14 . 41 C1
Margaret Vine Cl B62 ... 63 F1
Margeson Cl CV2 .... 114 E2
Margesson Dr B45 ...... 122 D1
Margetts Cl CV8 .... 147 F4
Margreal Ind Est B16 ... 65 F3
Marholm Cl CV4 .... 10 F2
Marian Croft B26 ...... 89 D5
Maria St B70 .... 64 E8
Marie Brock Cl CV4 .... 112 B1
Marie Dr B27 .... 106 B8
Marigold Cl WS11 .... 2 C3
Marigold Cres DY1 ..... 51 A4
Marigold Dr LE10 ...... 75 E5
Marigold Wlk CV10 ..... 72 B5
Marina Cl CV4 .... 131 E7
Marina Cres WS12 ..... 2 A5
Marina View B78 .... 35 A8
Marine Cres DY8 .... 60 E1
Marine Dr B44 .... 55 E6
Marine Gdns DY8 ...... 60 E1
Mariner B79 .... 20 E6
Mariner Ave B16 .... 65 E1
Marion Cl DY5 .... 61 F2
Marion Rd
  Coventry CV6 .... 113 D7
  Smethwick B67 .... 64 E5
Marion Way B28 .... 105 E7
Marish The CV34 ...... 160 E8
Maria Cl DY2 .... 62 E3
Marjoram Cl B38 .... 123 F8
Marjorie Ave B30 ...... 104 B3
Mark Antony Dr CV34 . 161 D4
Mark Ave WS10 .... 41 E3
Markby Rd B18 .... 65 E6
Mark Cl B98 .... 153 E2
Mark Ct WS1 .... 29 A3
Market Cnr
  [7] Royal Leamington Spa
    CV31 .... 161 F6
MARKET END 77 C2
Market End Cl CV12 .... 77 D2
Market Hall Mus* CV34 160 E6
Market Hall St WS11 .... 1 E1
Market La
  Lichfield WS14 .... 8 E2
  Lower Penn WV4 .... 37 F5

Market Pl continued
  Willenhall WV13 .... 27 A1
Market Sq
  Cradley Heath B64 ..... 82 C8
  Wolverhampton WV3 ... 163 B2
Market St
  Bromsgrove B61 .... 136 F2
  Cannock WS11 .... 2 C5
  Kidderminster DY10 .... 116 E5
  Kingswinford DY6 ..... 60 D6
  Lichfield WS13 .... 9 B8
  Oldbury B69 .... 64 A8
  Stourbridge DY8 .... 81 A5
  Tamworth B79 .... 21 B4
  Warwick CV34 .... 160 D6
Market Way
  Bilston WV14 .... 40 D5
  Hagley CV9 .... 99 C6
Market Wlk [4] B97 .... 153 E4
Markfield Rd B26 ...... 89 B8
Markham Cres B92 ..... 89 F1
Markham Dr
  Kingswinford DY6 ..... 60 E4
  Whitnash CV31 .... 162 B3
Markham Rd B73 ...... 45 C3
Mark Ho B13 .... 87 A2
Marklew Cl WS8 .... 16 A5
Markin Ave WV10 ...... 11 D1
Mark Rd WS10 .... 41 E3
Marksbury Cl CV3 ..... 134 C7
Marks Mews [7] CV34 .. 160 E6
Marks Wlk WS13 ...... 3 A2
Marlbank Rd DY8 ...... 61 A1
Marlborough Ave B60 .. 151 A8
Marlborough Cl
  Hinckley LE10 .... 76 B7
  Sutton Coldfield B74 ... 31 E6
Marlborough Ct
  Bromsgrove B60 ...... 151 B8
  Lichfield WS13 .... 9 B7
  [3] Sutton Coldfield B74 31 F2
  Sutton Coldfield, Falcon Lodge
    B75 .... 47 A6
Marlborough Dr
  Royal Leamington Spa
    CV31 .... 162 D5
  Stourbridge DY8 ...... 81 A3
Marlborough Gdns
  Stourbridge DY8 ...... 60 D2
  Wolverhampton WV6 .. 24 E4
Marlborough Gr B25 ... 68 D1
Marlborough Ind Est
  WV2 .... 39 D7
Marlborough Inf Sch B10. 67 E1
Marlborough Jun Sch
  B10 .... 67 E1
Marlborough Mews B80. 159 E4
Marlborough Rd
  Birmingham, Castle Bromwich
    B36 .... 69 D8
  Birmingham, Small Heath
    B10 .... 67 E1
  Coventry CV2 .... 114 A3
  Dudley DY3 .... 50 F6
  Nuneaton CV11 .... 73 B3
  Smethwick B66 .... 65 A3
Marlborough St
  [2] Kidderminster DY10 116 E5
  Walsall WS3 .... 28 C8
Marlborough Way B77 . 21 F2
Marlbrook Cl B92 ..... 89 C4
Marlbrook Dr WV4 .... 39 B6
Marlbrook Gdns B61 .. 121 B1
Marlbrook La B60 ..... 121 D2
Marlcliff Gr B13 ...... 105 A6
Marlcroft CV3 .... 134 D3
Marldon Rd B14 ...... 104 E6
Marlene Croft B37 .... 70 C1
Marler Rd CV4 .... 131 F7
Marley Hts B27 .... 88 D4
Marley Rd DY6 .... 61 A4
Marlfield La B98 ...... 154 B4
Margrove Ct B61 ..... 137 B8
Marlin B77 .... 35 C8
Marling Croft B92 .... 107 F7
Marlissa Dr CV6 ...... 95 E2
Marloes Wlk CV31 .... 162 C6
Marlow Cl
  Coventry CV5 .... 112 B4
  Dudley DY2 .... 62 E3
Marlowe Cl DY10 ..... 117 B6
Marlow Rd
  Birmingham B23 ...... 56 D5
  Tamworth B77 .... 21 D5
Marlow St
  Rowley Regis B65 ..... 63 B1
  Walsall WS2 .... 28 E3
Marlpit La
  Redditch B97 .... 153 C1
  Sutton Coldfield B75 .. 32 D3
Marlpit Rise [1] B75 .. 32 E3
Marlpool Ct DY11 .... 116 C8
Marlpool Dr
  Redditch B97 .... 153 C1
  Walsall WS3 .... 15 A1
Marlpool La DY11 .... 116 C8
Marlpool Pl DY11 .... 116 C8
Marl Rd DY2 .... 62 B4
Marlston Wlk CV5 .... 112 B8
Marl Top B38 .... 103 F2
Marlwood Cl CV6 .... 95 F4
Marmion Dr B43 ..... 43 F2
Marmion Gr DY1 ..... 62 A8
Marmion Ho B70 .... 52 F6

Marmion Pk B79 ...... 21 B6
Marmion St B79 ...... 21 B5
Marmion Way B70 .... 52 F6
Marne Cl CV34 .... 161 A8
Marnel Dr WV3 ...... 38 E7
Marner Cres CV6 ..... 113 B5
Marner Rd
  Bedworth CV12 .... 78 A3
  Nuneaton CV10 .... 73 B1
Marnhull Cl CV2 ..... 114 F4
Marquis Dr B62 ..... 83 A7
Marrick B77 .... 22 C1
Marriners La CV5 .... 112 B5
Marriott Rd
  Bedworth CV7 .... 77 D2
  Coventry CV6 .... 113 A4
  Dudley DY2 .... 62 C4
  Smethwick B66 ...... 64 D7
Marroway St B16 .... 65 F3
Marrowfat La B21 ... 65 F7
Mars Cl WV14 .... 40 A1
Marsdale Dr CV10 ... 72 E3
Marsden Cl B92 ..... 88 E1
Marsden Rd B98 .... 153 E3
Marsett B77 .... 36 C8
Marshall Cl WS9 .... 30 B4
Marshall Cres DY8 .. 60 F7
Marshall Gr B44 .... 55 F7
Marshall Ho [4] WS2 . 42 C8
Marshall Lake Rd B90. 106 D1
Marshall Rd
  Bedworth CV7 .... 95 F8
  Oldbury B68 .... 64 A7
  Willenhall WV13 ..... 26 D1
Marshalls Ind Est WV2 . 39 C7
Marshall St
  Birmingham B1 ...... 164 B1
  Smethwick B67 ...... 64 D7
  Tamworth B77 .... 21 A4
Marsham Cl CV34 .... 161 B8
Marsham Court Rd B91. 106 F7
Marsham Rd B14 .... 104 F3
Marshbrook Cl
  Coventry CV2 .... 96 E3
  Sutton Coldfield B24 . 57 E4
Marshbrook Rd B24 . 57 E4
Marsh Cres DY8 .... 60 E5
Marsh Ct DY9 ...... 99 D3
Marshdale Ave CV6 . 95 E3
Marsh End B38 ..... 124 A8
Marshfield B90 ..... 126 B5
Marshfield Cl B98 .. 154 B7
Marshfield Dr CV4 .. 132 D2
Marshfield Gdns B24. 56 F2
Marsh Gr DY10 ..... 116 E8
Marsh Hill B23 ..... 56 C4
Marsh Hill Prim Sch B23. 56 C4
Marsh Ho CV2 ...... 115 A7
Marsh House Farm La
  B92 .... 109 D3
Marsh La
  Birmingham B23 .... 56 E5
  Bradnock's Marsh B92. 109 D5
  Curdworth B76 ..... 59 D5
  Hampton-in-A B92 .. 109 B6
  Lichfield WS14 ..... 9 C5
  Solihull B91 .... 107 E3
  Water Orton B46 ... 59 C3
  West Bromwich B71 . 53 D8
  Wolverhampton WV10. 11 B2
Marshland Way WS2 . 27 E1
Marsh Lane Par WV10. 11 C2
Marshmont Way B23. 56 D8
Marsh St WS2 ...... 28 E2
Marsh The WS10 ... 41 E3
Marsh Way B61 .... 120 F1
Marshwood Cl [2] WS11. 1 A2
Marshwood Croft B62. 84 A3
Marsland Cl B17 .... 65 C1
Marsland Rd B92 ... 106 E8
Marston Ave WS10 . 41 C6
Marston Cl
  Royal Leamington Spa
    CV32 .... 157 B2
  Stourbridge DY8 .... 80 D4
Marston Croft B37 . 89 F7
Marston Dr B37 .... 70 A5
Marston Gn B43 ... 54 C2
MARSTON GREEN ... 90 A8
Marston Green Inf Sch
  B37 .... 90 A7
Marston Green Jun Sch
  B37 .... 89 F7
Marston Green Sta B37. 89 F7
Marston Ind Est WV2 . 39 C7
MARSTON JABBETT .. 78 E5
Marston La
  Bedworth CV12 .... 78 D5
  Nuneaton CV11 .... 78 E8
  Wishaw B76 .... 48 E1
Marston Pk B78 .... 20 C2
Marston Rd
  Birmingham B29 .... 102 F8
  Cannock WS12 ..... 1 F6
  Dudley DY1 .... 61 E8
  Sutton Coldfield B73 . 57 A7
  Wolverhampton WV2 . 39 C7
Marston St WV13 ... 27 C2
Marten Cl CV35 .... 160 A7
Martham Dr WV6 .. 24 B2
Martin Cl
  Birmingham B26 .... 88 D6
  Bromsgrove B61 .... 136 F5
  Coventry CV5 ...... 111 E4
  Dudley DY1 .... 51 D7
Martin Croft WS13 . 3 A1
Martindale WS11 ... 2 A2
Martindale Rd CV7 . 96 C8

Martindale Trad Est WS11 . 2 A2
Martindale Wlk DY5 ... 81 B6
Martin Dr WV12 ...... 27 C5
Martineau Pl (Sh Ctr)
  B2 .... 164 C2
Martineau Twr B19 ... 66 D5
Martingale Cl
  [4] Bromsgrove B60 ... 150 E6
  Walsall WS5 .... 42 F4
Martin Gr WS6 .... 5 A3
Martin Hill St DY2 .... 62 C8
Martinique Sq CV34 .. 160 D6
Martin Rd
  Bilston WV14 .... 40 F3
  Tipton DY4 .... 52 A4
  Walsall WS5 .... 43 C8
Martin Rise B37 ..... 89 F8
Martins Rd CV12 .... 77 E1
Martin St WV4 ...... 39 F5
Martlesham Sq B35 .. 58 A4
Martley Cl
  Coventry CV2 .... 115 A2
  Redditch B98 .... 159 B7
Martley Croft
  Birmingham B32 .... 84 E4
  Solihull B91 .... 127 B8
Martley Dr DY9 ..... 81 C4
Martley Rd
  Oldbury B69 .... 63 C5
  Walsall WS4 .... 15 C2
Marton Ave WS7 .... 7 A8
Marton Cl B7 .... 67 B6
Marton Rd B43 ..... 43 C1
Martyrs' Cl The CV3 . 133 D8
Marwood Cl CV11 .. 78 E7
Marwood Croft B74 . 31 A2
Mary Ann St
  Birmingham B3 ..... 164 B4
  Wolverhampton WV1. 163 D2
Mary Elliot Specl Sch
  WS2 .... 28 A7
Mary Herbert St CV3. 133 D7
Maryland Ave B34 .. 68 F5
Maryland Cl LE9 .... 71 F6
Maryland Dr B31 ... 103 B5
Maryland Rd DY5 .. 81 A7
Marylebone Cl DY8 . 81 A7
Mary Macarthur Dr B64. 62 C1
Mary Rd
  Birmingham, Handsworth
    B21 .... 65 E7
  Birmingham, Stechford B33. 68 D2
  Oldbury B69 .... 63 C8
  West Bromwich B70 . 53 D1
Mary Rose Cl WS6 .. 4 D1
Mary Slessor St CV3 . 134 D7
Mary St
  Birmingham, Balsall Heath
    B12 .... 86 E5
  Birmingham, Brookfields
    B3 .... 164 A4
  Cannock WS12 ..... 2 B7
  Walsall WS2 .... 28 D3
Marystow Cl CV5 ... 112 B8
Maryvale Ct
  Lichfield WS14 ..... 9 D7
  [7] Walsall WS2 ..... 42 E8
Maryvale Inst The B44. 44 E2
Maryvale RC Prim Sch
  B44 .... 44 E1
Mary Vale Rd B30 .. 103 F6
Marywell Cl B32 ... 102 B7
Masefield Ave
  Dudley DY1 .... 51 C7
  Warwick CV34 ..... 160 C4
Masefield Cl
  Bilston WV14 ...... 40 F7
  Lichfield WS14 .... 9 E7
Masefield Dr B79 .. 21 A7
Masefield Gdns [1] DY10. 117 B6
Masefield Ho B79 .. 1 E4
Masefield Mews WV10. 12 A1
Masefield Rd
  Dudley DY3 .... 50 A4
  Walsall WS3 .... 28 E7
  Wolverhampton WV10. 12 A1
Masefield Rise B62 . 83 D3
Masefield Sq B31 .. 103 C4
Masham Cl B33 .... 68 E3
Mashie Gdns B38 .. 103 D1
Maslen Pl B63 ..... 83 B3
Maslin Dr WV14 ... 40 A1
Mason Ave CV32 .. 157 C3
Mason Ct LE10 .... 75 B8
Mason La B94 ..... 125 C4
Masonleys Rd B31 . 102 D3
Mason Rd
  Birmingham B24 .. 57 A4
  Coventry CV6 ..... 95 F1
  Kidderminster DY11. 116 D6
  Redditch B97 ..... 158 D8
Mason St
  West Bromwich B70 . 51 B7
  Wolverhampton WV2. 39 C7
Masons View B24 .. 57 A2
Masons Way B92 .. 88 F1
Mason Way B15 ... 86 C8
Massbrook Gr WV10. 25 F6
Massbrook Rd WV10. 25 F6
Masser Rd CV6 .... 95 D4

Masshouse La
  Birmingham, Digbeth B5 . 164 D3
  Birmingham, King's Norton
    B38 .... 103 E1
Masters La B60 .... 63 E1
Masters Rd CV31 ... 162 A4
MATCHBOROUGH ... 154 E1
Matchborough Ctr B98. 154 E1
Matchborough Fst Sch
  B98 .... 154 E1
Matchborough Way B98. 154 E1
Matchlock Cl B74 .. 44 E7
Matfen Ave B73 ... 45 F2
Mathe Croft CV31 . 162 C5
Math Mdw B32 ... 84 F5
Matlock Cl
  Dudley DY2 .... 62 D3
  Walsall WS3 .... 14 C3
Matlock Dr WS11 .. 2 A4
Matlock Rd
  Birmingham B11 ... 87 F3
  Coventry CV1 ...... 113 D6
  Walsall WS3 .... 14 C3
Matlock Villas [2] B12. 87 B5
Matterson Rd CV6 . 113 A5
Matthew Boulton Com Prim
  Sch B21 .... 65 E7
Matthew La (Road 3)
  DY10 .... 116 F1
Matthews Cl B65 ... 63 B1
Matthews Wlk WS13 . 3 A2
Mattox Rd WV11 .. 26 D6
Matty Rd B68 ..... 64 C4
Maud Rd
  Water Orton B46 .. 59 D3
  West Bromwich B70 . 53 C1
Maudslay Rd CV5 .. 112 E2
Maughan St
  Brierley Hill DY5 .. 82 A8
  Dudley DY1 .... 51 B1
Maund Cl B60 .... 150 E7
Maureen Cl CV4 .. 111 C1
Maurice Gr WV10 . 26 A6
Maurice Mead Ct [2]
  CV31 .... 162 A6
Maurice Rd
  Birmingham B14 .. 104 E5
  Smethwick B67 ... 64 E2
Mavis Gdns B68 .. 84 B8
Mavis Rd
  Birmingham B31 .. 102 E5
  Cannock WS12 ... 2 B7
Mavor Dr CV12 .. 77 D1
Mawgan Dr WS14 . 9 D6
Mawnan Cl CV7 .. 96 B8
Maw St WS1 ..... 42 F6
Maxholm Rd B74 .. 44 E8
Max Rd
  Birmingham B32 .. 84 D5
  Coventry CV6 .... 112 F5
Maxstoke Cl
  Birmingham B32 .. 102 A7
  Meriden CV7 ..... 92 B4
  Redditch B98 .... 154 D1
  Sutton Coldfield B73 . 45 E2
  Tamworth B77 ... 35 C8
  Walsall WS3 ..... 14 A3
Maxstoke Croft B90. 126 C6
Maxstoke Gdns CV31. 161 E6
Maxstoke La
  Coventry CV7 .... 92 B4
  Meriden CV7 .... 92 B3
  White Stitch CV7 . 92 B3
Maxstoke Rd B73 . 45 E1
Maxstoke St B9 .. 67 B2
Maxted Rd B23 .. 56 C7
Maxwell Ave B20 . 55 B1
Maxwell Cl WS14 . 9 C7
Maxwell Ct B33 .. 68 F3
Maxwell Rd WV2 . 163 C1
Mayall Dr B75 ... 32 D4
Mayama Rd B78 .. 34 F8
Maybank B9 ..... 67 F3
Maybank Cl WS14 . 9 E8
Maybank Pl B44 .. 55 E6
Maybank Rd DY2 . 62 C3
Mayberry Cl B14 . 105 B2
Maybridge Dr B91. 127 B8
Maybrook Bsns Pk B76. 58 A6
Maybrook Ind Est WS8. 15 F5
Maybrook Rd
  Brownhills WS8 ... 15 F5
  Sutton Coldfield B76 . 58 A5
Maybush Gdns WV10. 11 C1
Maycock Rd CV6 .. 113 E7
Maycroft Cl WS12 . 1 F7
Maydene Croft B12. 86 F6
MAYER'S GREEN .. 53 E3
Mayfair
  Birmingham B37 .. 69 E5
  Stourbridge DY9 .. 81 E2
Mayfair Cl
  Birmingham B44 .. 56 B7
  Dudley DY1 .... 51 A2
Mayfair Dr
  Fazeley B78 ...... 35 A7
  Kingswinford DY6 . 60 C7
Mayfair Gdns
  Tipton DY4 .... 52 A4
  Wolverhampton WV3. 24 D2
May Farm Cl B47 . 125 A6
Mayfield B77 ..... 36 C8
Mayfield Ave B29 . 86 B2

Mayfield Cl
Bedworth CV12 . . . . 78 B3
Fairfield B61 . . . . 120 F1
Kidderminster DY11. . . . 116 A8
9 Royal Leamington Spa
CV31. . . . . 162 C6
Solihull B91 . . . . 107 C1
Mayfield Cres B65 . . . . . . 63 A3
Mayfield Ct
Birmingham B13 . . . . 87 A2
Kidderminster DY11. . . . 116 C7
Mayfield Dr CV8 . . . . . . 148 C4
Mayfield Prep Sch WS1 . . 43 A8
Mayfield Rd
Birmingham, Acock's Green
B11. . . . . 87 B1
Birmingham, Lozells B19. . 66 C8
Birmingham, Moseley B13. . 87 A3
Birmingham, Stirchley B30 104 A6
Coventry CV5 . . . . 113 A1
Dudley DY1 . . . . 51 C4
Halesowen B62 . . . . 63 F1
Halesowen, Hasbury B63 . . 82 E2
Nuneaton CV11 . . . . 73 E2
Sutton Coldfield, Boldmere
B73. . . . . 46 A2
Sutton Coldfield, Streetly
B74. . . . . 44 F8
Wolverhampton WV1 . . . . 26 B1
Mayfields B98 . . . . 153 E2
Mayfield Sch B19 . . . . . . 66 C8
Mayfield Dr W58 . . . . 6 B2
Mayfield The WV1 . . . . . . 26 B1
Mayflower Cl B19 . . . . . . 66 D6
Mayflower Dr
Brierley Hill DY5 . . . . . . 61 A7
Coventry CV2. . . . . 114 E2
Mayford Gr B13. . . . . . . 105 B6
Maygrove Rd DY6 . . . . . . 60 C7
Mayhurst Cl
Hollywood B47. . . . . . . 125 C6
Tipton DY4. . . . . 52 A8
Mayhurst Rd B47 . . . . . . 125 B6
May La
Birmingham B14 . . . . . . 104 F5
Hollywood B47. . . . . . . 125 A7
Mayland Dr B74. . . . . 45 A5
Mayland Rd B16 . . . . 65 C2
Maynard Ave
Bedworth CV12 . . . . 95 D8
Stourbridge DY8 . . . . 80 D3
Warwick CV34 . . . . 161 A2
Maynard Rd B16 . . . . 65 C3
Mayo Dr CV8 . . . . 148 A4
Mayor's Croft CV4 . . . . . 132 B7
Mayou Ct WS3 . . . . 15 A4
Maypole Cl B64 . . . . 82 B8
Maypole Cl WV5 . . . . 49 A6
Maypole Dr DY8 . . . . 80 E5
Maypole Fields B63 . . . . . 82 A8
Maypole Gr B14. . . . . . . 105 A2
Maypole Hill B63 . . . . . . 82 A7
Maypole La B14 . . . . 105 A2
Maypole Rd B68 . . . . 64 B1
Maypole St WV5 . . . . 49 B7
May St
Coventry CV6. . . . . 113 E8
Walsall WS3. . . . . 28 D6
Mayswood Dr WV6 . . . . . 23 F1
Mayswood Gr B32 . . . . . 84 D4
Mayswood Rd B92 . . . . . 89 C2
Maythorn Ave B76 . . . . . 58 A6
Maythorn Gdns
Codsall WV8. . . . . 10 A4
Wolverhampton WV6 . . . . 24 C3
Maythorn Gr 4 B91. . . . . 127 B8
Maytree Cl B37 . . . . 70 A2
May Tree Gr B20. . . . . . . 54 F3
May Trees B47. . . . . 124 F6
Maywell Dr B92. . . . . . . 107 F8
Maywood Cl DY6. . . . . . . 60 B6
Meaburn Cl B29 . . . . . . 103 A7
Mead Ave 9 B16 . . . . 65 C3
Mead Cl WS9 . . . . 30 B6
Mead Cres B9 . . . . 68 A3
Meadfoot Ave B14 . . . . . 104 F3
Meadfoot Dr DY6 . . . . . . 60 B7
Meadfoot Rd CV3 . . . . . 134 E6
Meadow Ave B71 . . . . . . 53 F8
Meadowbank B78 . . . . . . 21 B1
Meadowbank Dr B46. . . . . 59 D1
Meadowbank Grange WS4 . 4 E4
Meadowbrook Cl WS12. . . . 2 B6
Meadowbrook Gdns WV8. 10 B4
Meadowbrook Rd
Halesowen B63 . . . . 82 E3
Lichfield WS13. . . . . 3 B3
Meadow Brook Rd B31. . 102 F5
Meadow Cl
Ansty CV7 . . . . 97 D3
Birmingham B17 . . . . 65 B1
Hockley Heath B94 . . . . . 143 C6
Royal Leamington Spa
CV32. . . . . 157 C4
Solihull B90 . . . . 126 D8
Sutton Coldfield B74 . . . . 30 F2
Sutton Coldfield B73 . . . . 46 A4
Walsall WS4. . . . . 29 C8
Meadow Com Sports Ctr
CV8. . . . . 148 B5
Meadow Croft
Cannock WS12. . . . . 1 C4
Perton WV6 . . . . 23 D3
West Hagley DY9. . . . . . . 98 F4
Wythall B47. . . . . 125 A3

Meadowcroft Cl CV4 . . . . 131 F8
Meadow Ct
Birmingham B17 . . . . 65 B1
Nuneaton CV11 . . . . 73 B4
Meadow Dr
Hampton-in-A B92. . . . . 109 B7
Hinckley LE10 . . . . 76 A7
Meadowfield Rd B45 . . . 122 A6
Meadowfields Cl DY8 . . . 60 E2
Meadow Gate B31 . . . . . 102 E2
Meadow Gr
Great Wyrley WS6 . . . . 5 A2
Solihull B92 . . . . 88 D1
Meadow Grange Dr WV12 27 B7
Meadow Green Prim Sch
B47. . . . . 125 A3
Meadowhill Cl DY11. . . . 116 A5
Meadowhill Cres B98 . . . 153 F5
Meadow Hill Dr DY8 . . . . 60 E2
Meadow Hill Dr 5 WS11 . . 2 A3
Meadowhill Rd B98 . . . . 153 F5
Meadow Hill Rd B38 . . . 103 E2
Meadow Ho 5 CV1 . . . . . 113 B3
Meadow La
Alvechurch B48 . . . . 139 B6
Coven Heath WV10 . . . . . 11 C6
Kingswood B94 . . . . 144 D3
Wednesfield WV12 . . . . . . 27 A5
Wolverhampton WV14 . . . . 40 B2
Wombourne WV5. . . . . . . 49 B8
Meadowlands Dr WS4. . . . 15 D1
Meadow Lark Cl WS12 . . . . 2 B4
Meadow Mills Ind Est
DY10 . . . . 116 E5
Meadowpark Rd DY8. . . . . 80 D8
Meadow Pk B79 . . . . 20 F5
Meadow Pleck La B90. . . 126 A6
Meadow Rd
Aldridge WS9. . . . . 30 A4
Birmingham B32 . . . . 84 A6
Birmingham, Harborne B17. 65 B1
Catshill B61. . . . . 136 F8
Coventry CV6 . . . . 95 B4
Dudley DY1 . . . . 51 B3
Halesowen B62 . . . . 83 C8
Hartshill CV10 . . . . 72 A8
Oldbury B68. . . . . 64 B3
Smethwick B67 . . . . 65 A4
Tamworth B78 . . . . 20 E3
Warwick CV34 . . . . 161 A7
Wolverhampton WV3 . . . . 38 D8
Wythall B47 . . . . 125 A3
Meadow Rise
Balsall Common CV7 . . . . 130 C7
Birmingham B30 . . . . . . 103 D7
Meadows Fst Sch B61. . . 137 A3
Meadows Gr WB. 10 A4
Meadowside CV11 . . . . . . 79 B8
Meadowside Cl B43 . . . . . 43 E1
Meadowside Rd B74 . . . . 31 F3
Meadows Prim Sch The
B31. . . . . 102 B8
Meadows Sch The B69 . . . 52 E1
Meadow St
Coventry CV1. . . . . 165 A2
5 Cradley Heath B64. . . . 82 F8
Nuneaton CV11 . . . . 73 B5
Tamworth B77 . . . . 21 C3
1 Wolverhampton WV1 . . 25 B2
Meadows The
Aldridge WS9. . . . . 29 E5
Catshill B61. . . . . 136 F8
Hinckley LE10 . . . . 76 A7
Leek Wootton CV35 . . . . . 156 A7
Stourbridge DY9 . . . . 99 B7
Wedges Mills WS11. . . . . . . 4 B5
Meadowsweet Ave B38 . . 123 D7
Meadowsweet Pl DY10 . . 116 D8
Meadowsweet Way
Cannock WS12. . . . . 2 E4
Kingswinford DY6 . . . . . . 61 A6
Meadow Vale WV8 . . . . . 10 B2
Meadowvale Rd B60 . . . . 137 C6
Meadow View
Birmingham B13 . . . . . . 105 C8
Burntwood WS7. . . . . 7 D6
Sedgley DY3. . . . . 39 C1
Wolverhampton WV11 . . . . 12 F3
Wood End DY5 . . . . 61 E4
Meadow View Ct B80 . . . 159 E3
Meadow View JMI Sch
WS3. . . . . 44 D5
Meadow View Terr WV6. . . 24 E4
Meadow Way
Cannock WS12. . . . . 1 C4
Stourbridge DY8 . . . . 60 C2
Meadow Wlk
Birmingham B14 . . . . . . 104 E1
Cradley Heath B64. . . . . . 82 D8
Mead The DY3 . . . . 50 B8
Meadthorpe Rd B44. . . . . 55 D8
Meadvale Rd B45 . . . . . . 122 B6
Meadway
Birmingham B33 . . . . 69 B2
Coventry CV2. . . . . 114 B6
Meadway Cl WS12 . . . . . . 2 C3
Meadway N CV7 . . . . 96 B8
Meadway The
Hinckley LE10 . . . . 75 F7
Redditch B97 . . . . 153 C1
Wolverhampton WV6 . . . . 24 A5
Meakind Ind Est WV14 . . . 40 E5
Meakins Cl CV34 . . . . . . 160 B4
Meander CV7. . . . . 35 E5
Mears Cl B23 . . . . 56 D8

Mears Coppice DY5 . . . . . 81 E6
Mears Dr B33 . . . . 68 D4
Mearse Cl B48 . . . . 66 A5
Mearse La
Barnt Green B45 . . . . . . 122 A1
Madeley Heath DY9. . . . . 120 B6
Mease Ave WS7 . . . . 7 D6
Mease Croft 2 B9 . . . . . . 67 B2
Measham Gr B26 . . . . . . 88 E5
Measham Way WV11 . . . . 26 E7
Meaton Gr B32 . . . . 102 B8
Medcroft Ave B20. . . . . . . 54 E4
Medici Rd B60. . . . . 137 C2
Medina B77 . . . . 21 E1
Medina Cl WV10 . . . . 11 F4
Medina Rd
Birmingham B11 . . . . 87 E4
Coventry CV6. . . . . 95 E1
Medina Way DY6. . . . . . . 60 C6
Medland Ave CV3 . . . . . . 132 F5
Medley Gdns DY4 . . . . . . 52 E4
Medley Gr CV31 . . . . . . 161 F3
Medley Rd B11 . . . . 87 D5
Medlicott Rd B11. . . . . . . 87 C6
Medway B77. . . . . 21 E1
Medway Cl DY5. . . . . 61 A6
Medway Croft B36. . . . . . 69 F7
Medway Ct 4 B73 . . . . . . 46 B5
Medway Gr B38. . . . . . . 123 E8
Medway Rd WS8. . . . . 6 C2
Medway Twr B7 . . . . 67 B5
Medway Wlk WS8. . . . . . . 6 C2
Medwin Gr B23 . . . . 56 D7
Meerash La WS7 . . . . 7 C3
Meer End B38 . . . . 123 D7
Meer End Rd CV8 . . . . . . 130 D1
Meerhill Ave B90 . . . . . . 127 A6
Meeting Ho The 3 WS10. 41 E3
Meeting House La
Balsall Common CV7 . . . . 130 C6
Birmingham B31 . . . . . . 103 A4
Meeting La DY5. . . . . 61 B1
Meeting Lane Ind Est DY5 61 B1
Meeting St
Dudley DY2 . . . . 62 C5
Tipton DY4 . . . . 52 D5
Wednesbury WS10 . . . . . . 41 E3
Meg La WS7 . . . . 7 C8
Mehdi Rd B69 . . . . 63 E8
Meir Rd B98 . . . . 159 C8
Melbourne Ave
Birmingham, Newtown
B19 . . . . 66 C6
Birmingham, Selly Oak B66 . 65 B7
Bromsgrove B61 . . . . 136 E4
Melbourne Cl
Bromsgrove B61 . . . . 136 E3
Kingswinford DY6 . . . . . . 60 E4
Nuneaton CV11 . . . . 73 F6
West Bromwich B70 . . . . . 53 A7
Melbourne Cres WS12. . . . 2 F2
Melbourne Ct 3 CV12. . . . 77 F2
Melbourne Gdns WS5 . . . 43 B6
Melbourne Rd
Birmingham B34 . . . . 69 E6
Bromsgrove B61 . . . . 136 E3
Cannock WS12. . . . . 2 F2
Coventry CV5. . . . . 113 A2
Halesowen B63 . . . . 83 B5
Smethwick B66 . . . . 65 B7
Melbury Cl WV3 . . . . 25 A1
Melbury Gr B14. . . . . . . 104 E5
Melbury Way 1 WS11 . . . . 1 F2
Melchester Wlk 2 WS11 . . 1 F2
Melchett Rd B30. . . . . . . 104 A4
Melcote Gr B44. . . . . 55 E8
Meldon Dr WV14. . . . . . . 41 A2
Meldrum Rd CV10. . . . . . 72 D4
Melen St 3 B97 . . . . 153 D4
Melford B79 . . . . 20 E6
Melford Cl DY3 . . . . 39 C2
Melford Hall Rd B91 . . . . 106 F7
Melfort Cl
Coventry CV2. . . . . 114 F2
Nuneaton CV10 . . . . 72 C5
Melfort Gr B14. . . . . 105 A3
Melksham Sq B35. . . . . . . 58 A3
Mellis Gr B23. . . . . 56 A5
Mellish Ave B71 . . . . 53 E6
Mellish Ct WS4 . . . . 29 A3
Mellish Dr WS4 . . . . 29 B3
Mellish Rd WS4. . . . . 29 B3
Mellor Dr B74 . . . . 31 E3
Mellors Cl B17. . . . . 85 B3
Mellowdew Rd
Coventry CV2. . . . . 114 C4
Stourbridge DY8 . . . . 60 C3
Mellowship Rd CV5 . . . . 111 D5
Mell Sq B91 . . . . 107 C4
Mell Square Sh Ctr B91 . 107 C4
Mellwaters B77 . . . . 36 C8
Melmerby B77 . . . . 36 C8
Melplash Ave B91. . . . . . 107 A4
Melrose Ave
Bromsgrove CV12 . . . . . . 95 D8
Birmingham, Sparkbrook
B12 . . . . 87 A6
Birmingham, Sparkhill B11 . 87 C6
Stourbridge DY8 . . . . 81 A2
Sutton Coldfield B73 . . . . 45 E2
West Bromwich B71 . . . . . 42 D1
Melrose Cl
Birmingham B38 . . . . . . 103 F1
Hinckley LE10 . . . . 75 B8
Melrose Ct WS4 . . . . 29 B3
Melrose Dr
Cannock WS12. . . . . 1 F7

Melrose Dr continued
Perton WV6 . . . . 23 E4
Melrose Gr B19. . . . . 66 B7
Melrose Pl B66 . . . . 64 D8
Melrose Rd B20. . . . . 55 E1
Melstock Cl DY4 . . . . 51 D5
Melstock Rd B14. . . . . . . 104 D7
Melton Ave B92. . . . . 89 B4
Melton Dr B15. . . . . 86 B7
Melton Rd
Birmingham B14 . . . . . . 104 F8
Royal Leamington Spa
CV32. . . . . 157 B4
Melverley Gr B44 . . . . . . 55 F7
Melverton Ave WV10 . . . . 25 E8
Melville Cl CV7 . . . . 96 A8
Melville Hall 1 B16. . . . . 65 D1
Melville Rd
Birmingham B16 . . . . 65 D1
Coventry CV1. . . . . 113 A3
Coventry CV6. . . . . 95 B1
Melvina Rd B7 . . . . 67 B5
Melzer Ho DY10. . . . . . . 116 E7
Membury Rd B8 . . . . 67 D6
Memorial Cl WV13 . . . . . 27 A2
Memory La
Darlaston WS10 . . . . 41 D8
Wolverhampton WV11. . . . 26 B5
Menai Cl WV12 . . . . 27 C6
Menai Wlk B37 . . . . 70 B4
Mendip Ave B8 . . . . 67 E5
Mendip Cl
Bromsgrove B61 . . . . 137 A5
Dudley DY3 . . . . 50 D3
Wolverhampton WV2 . . . . 39 F7
Mendip Dr CV10 . . . . 72 B3
Mendip Ho B98 . . . . 154 D6
Mendip Rd
Birmingham B8 . . . . 67 E5
Halesowen B63 . . . . 82 D1
Smethwick B61 . . . . 81 B6
Mendip Way B77 . . . . 22 C1
Menin Cres B13. . . . . . . 105 B2
Menin Rd
Birmingham B13 . . . . . . 105 B8
Tipton DY4 . . . . 51 D5
Mentone Ct B20 . . . . 54 E3
Meon Gr
Birmingham B33 . . . . 89 B8
Perton WV6 . . . . 23 F4
Meon Rise DY9 . . . . 81 C3
Meon Way WV11 . . . . 26 F7
Meranti Cl WV12. . . . . . . 27 C8
Mercer Ave
Coventry CV2. . . . . 114 A5
Water Orton B46. . . . . . . 59 A3
Mercer Gr WV11. . . . . . . 26 D7
Mercers Mdw CV7 . . . . . . 95 A6
Merchants Ct 5 CV32. . . . 157 A1
Merchants Pk WS9. . . . . . 30 A7
Merchants Rd WV6 . . . . . 24 D4
Mercia Ave CV8. . . . . . . 147 F4
Mercia Bsns Village CV4. 131 F6
Mercia Cl
Bromsgrove B60 . . . . 150 F7
Tamworth B79 . . . . 20 E7
Mercia Dr
Birmingham B14 . . . . . . 104 D6
Perton WV6 . . . . 23 E5
Mercia Ho CV1. . . . . 165 B3
Mercian Ct WS14 . . . . 9 C7
Mercian Pk B77 . . . . 22 A3
Mercian Way B77 . . . . . . 22 B3
Mercia Way CV34 . . . . . . 161 B7
Mercot Cl B98 . . . . 159 A6
Mercury Pk B77 . . . . 22 B3
Mercury Rd WS11. . . . . . . 2 A5
Mere Ave B35 . . . . 58 B3
Mere Cl WV12 . . . . 27 A5
Merecote Rd B92 . . . . . . 106 D7
Mere Croft WS11 . . . . 2 A5
Meredith Gn DY11 . . . . . 116 A1
Meredith Pool Cl B18 . . . 65 F6
Meredith Rd
Coventry CV2. . . . . 114 A3
Dudley DY3 . . . . 50 A5
Wolverhampton WV11. . . . 26 C8
Meredith St B64 . . . . 82 D8
Mere Dr B75. . . . . 32 B2
Mere Gn B23 . . . . 32 C2
Mere Green Rd B75. . . . . . 32 C2
Mere Oak Rd WV6 . . . . . . 23 E5
Mere Pool Rd B75 . . . . . . 32 E2
Mere Rd
Birmingham B23 . . . . 56 D3
Stourbridge DY8 . . . . 80 E3
Mereside Way B92 . . . . . 106 E8
Mere St B23. . . . . 32 C5
Mere St B23 . . . . 32 B3
Merevale Ave
Hinckley LE10 . . . . 75 C7
Nuneaton CV11 . . . . 73 A4
Merevale Cl
Hinckley LE10 . . . . 75 C7
Redditch B98 . . . . 159 D8
Merevale Ct CV11. . . . . . 73 A4
Merevale Rd B92 . . . . 89 B2
Mere View WS4. . . . . 29 C8
Mereways B90. . . . . 126 A5
Merganser B77 . . . . 36 A6
Merganser Way B66. . . . . 65 B6
MERIDEN 92 D1
Meriden Ave DY8. . . . . . . 80 D6
Meriden Bsns Pk CV5 . . . 111 B8
Meriden CE Prim Sch
CV7 . . . . 92 C1

Meriden Cl
Birmingham B25 . . . . 88 B7
Cannock WS11. . . . . 4 B8
Stourbridge DY8. . . . . . . 80 D6
Meriden Cross * CV7 . . . . 92 B1
Meriden Dr B37 . . . . 70 A6
Meriden Hill CV7. . . . . . 110 E8
Meriden Park Homes
CV7 . . . . 110 C8
Meriden Rd
Berkswell CV7 . . . . 110 C4
Chapel Green CV7. . . . . . 93 B7
Hampton-in-A B92. . . . . 109 C7
Wolverhampton WV10 . . . . 25 A8
Meriden Rise B92 . . . . . . 89 D3
Meriden St
Birmingham B5 . . . . 164 D2
Coventry CV1. . . . . 113 B3
Meridian Pl B60 . . . . 137 A1
Merino Ave B31. . . . . . . 123 A8
Merlin Ave CV10 . . . . 72 B6
Merlin Cl
Birmingham B35 . . . . 58 A3
Dudley DY1 . . . . 61 F8
Tamworth B77 . . . . 36 A6
Merlin Ct WS7 . . . . 7 F8
Merlin Dr DY10 . . . . 117 B3
Merlin Gr B26 . . . . 89 B5
Merlin Pl CV1. . . . . 165 C1
Merlin Way B35. . . . . 58 B4
Merrick Cl B63 . . . . 82 D2
Merrick Ct LE10. . . . . 75 F5
Merrick Rd WV11 . . . . . . 27 A6
MERRIDALE. 24 E2
Merridale Ave WV3 . . . . . 24 F2
Merridale Cres WV3 . . . . 25 A2
Merridale Ct WV3. . . . . . . 24 F1
Merridale Gdns WV3 . . . . 25 A1
Merridale Gr WV3. . . . . . 24 E1
Merridale La WV3. . . . . . 25 A2
Merridale Prim Sch WV3. 25 A1
Merridale Rd WV3 . . . . . . 25 A1
Merridale St WV3. . . . . . . 25 B2
Merridale Street W WV3 . . 39 A8
Merriemont Dr B45 . . . . . 122 A1
Merrifield Gdns LE10. . . . 75 E5
Merrill Cl WS6. . . . . 4 E2
Merrill Gdns B60. . . . . . 121 D2
Merrills Hall Island WV11. 26 D4
Merrills Hall La WV11 . . . 26 C4
Merrington Cl 1 B91. . . . 127 C8
Merrion's Cl B43. . . . . . . 43 E4
Merrion's Wood Nature
Reserve * B43. . . . . 43 E4
Merrishaw Rd B31. . . . . . 123 A8
Merritt's Brook Cl B29 . . 103 A5
Merritt's Brook La B31 . . 102 E5
Merritts Hill B31 . . . . . . 102 E6
Merrivale Rd
Coventry CV5. . . . . 112 E3
Halesowen B62 . . . . 83 F8
Smethwick B66 . . . . 65 A2
Merryfield Cl B92 . . . . . . 107 D7
Merryfield Gr B17. . . . . . 85 C4
Merryfield Rd DY1 . . . . . . 50 E1
Merryfields Way CV2. . . . . 96 F1
MERRY HILL
Brierley Hill 61 E3
Smethwick 65 D5
Wolverhampton 38 D7
Merry Hill DY5. . . . . 61 F2
Merryhill Dr B18. . . . . . . 65 F6
Merryhills Ent Pk WV10 . . 25 F5
Merry Hill Sh Ctr DY5 . . . 61 F3
Merse Hurst Pl LE10. . . . . 74 E7
Merse Rd B98 . . . . 154 E6
Mersey Gr B38. . . . . 123 E8
Mersey Rd
Bulkington CV12 . . . . 79 A3
Walsall WS3. . . . . 14 E1
Merstal Dr B92 . . . . 107 F7
Merstone Cl
Bilston WV14 . . . . 40 C6
Birmingham B37. . . . . . . 90 C8
Merstowe Cl B27 . . . . 88 B3
Merton Cl
Kidderminster DY10. . . . . 117 B7
Oldbury B68. . . . . 64 B2
Merton Ct WS7 . . . . 6 F5
Merton Ho B37 . . . . 70 A4
Merton Rd B13 . . . . 87 B3
Merton Way WS2 . . . . . . 42 C7
Mervyn Pl WV14 . . . . 41 A3
Mervyn Rd
Bilston WV14 . . . . 41 A3
Birmingham B21 . . . . 54 E1
Meryhurst Rd WS10. . . . . 42 B5
Merynton Ave CV4 . . . . . 132 E5
Meschines St CV3. . . . . . 133 D6
Mesnes Gn WS14 . . . . 9 C7
Messenger La B70, B71. . 53 D3
Messenger Rd B66. . . . . . 65 B6
Mesty Croft Prim Sch
WS10. . . . . 42 B3
Metalloys Ind Est B76 . . . 58 B5
Metcalf Cl WS7 . . . . 7 C8
Metcalfe Cl WS12 . . . . 2 C6
Metchley Abbey 1 B17 . . 85 C5
Metchley Ct B17. . . . . 85 D4
Metchley Dr B17 . . . . 85 D5
Metchley Ho 6 B17 . . . . . 85 D5
Metchley La B17 . . . . 85 D4
Metchley Park Rd B15. . . 85 E4

Metchley Rise B17 . . . . 85 C5
Meteor Way B7 . . . . 67 C8
Metfield Cl B79 . . . . 21 C8
Metfield Croft
 Birmingham B17 . . . . 85 D4
 Kingswinford DY6 . . . . . . 60 F6
Metlin Gr B33. . . . . 69 E3
Metric Wlk ☑ B67 . . . . . . 65 A5
Metro Ct B70 . . . . 53 D2
Metro Way B66 . . . . 65 C7
Mews Rd CV32. . . . . 161 D8
Mews The
 Bedworth CV12 . . . . 78 B2
 Birmingham B27 . . . . 88 B3
 Cannock WS11. . . . . 1 D1
 Kenilworth CV8 . . . . 147 E3
 Rowley Regis B65 . . . . . . 63 B2
Mey Coppice B36 . . . . 69 F7
Meynell Ho B20 . . . . 54 F3
Meyrick Rd B70 . . . . 53 A6
Meyrick Wlk B35 . . . . 65 F1
Miall Rd B91 . . . . 106 E5
Miall Rd B28. . . . . 106 A8
Mica Cl B77 . . . . 22 D2
Michael Banning Pl CV7. 130 B7
Michael Banning Gdns
 B93 . . . . 127 E3
Michael Banning Ho ⑩
 B13 . . . . 87 B2
Michael Ct B5 . . . . 86 D6
Michael Dr B15 . . . . 86 D6
Michael Drayton Jun Sch
 CV10. . . . . 72 B8
Michaelmas Rd CV3. . . . . 165 B1
Michael Rd
 Darlaston WS10. . . . . 41 B7
 Smethwick B67 . . . . 64 E6
Michaelwood Cl B97 . . . . 152 F2
Michell Cl CV3. . . . . 134 B8
Michelle Cl B13. . . . . 105 A5
Michigan Cl WS11. . . . . . . 2 B2
Micklehill Dr B90 . . . . . . 126 B8
Mickle Mdw B46 . . . . 59 B3
Mickleover Rd B8. . . . . . . 68 C5
Mickleton B77 . . . . 36 C8
Mickleton Ave B33 . . . . . . 89 C8
Mickleton Cl B98 . . . . . . 158 E7
Mickleton Rd
 Coventry CV5. . . . . 133 A8
 Solihull B92 . . . . 106 D8
Mickley Ave WV10 . . . . . . 25 E5
Midacre WV13. . . . . 27 A1
Middelburg Cl CV11. . . . . 74 A1
MIDDLE 4 A4
Middle Acre Rd B32. . . . . . 84 E2
Middle Ave WV13 . . . . 40 E8
MIDDLE BICKENHILL. 91 A3
Middle Bickenhill La B92. 91 A4
Middleborough Rd CV1. 165 A4
Middlecotes CV4. . . . . . . 112 B1
Middle Cres WS3 . . . . 29 A7
Middle Cross WV1 . . . . . . 163 D3
Middle Dr B45 . . . . 122 D4
Middle Entry B79 . . . . 21 B4
Middlefield WV8. . . . . 10 E2
Middlefield Ave
 Dorridge B93 . . . . 128 B4
 Halesowen B62 . . . . 63 F1
Middlefield Cl
 Halesowen B62 . . . . 63 F1
 Hinckley LE10 . . . . 71 D2
Middlefield Ct LE10 . . . . . 71 D2
Middlefield Dr CV3. . . . . 115 B1
Middlefield Ho B14 . . . . . 104 F3
Middlefield La
 Hinckley LE10 . . . . 71 D3
 West Hagley DY9. . . . . . . 99 B6
Middlefield Pl LE10 . . . . . 71 D3
Middlefield Rd
 Bromsgrove B60 . . . . . . 151 B7
 Oldbury B69. . . . . 63 A8
Middle Field Rd B31 . . . . 103 D2
Middlefield Dr CV3. . . . . 115 A1
Middle Gdns WV13 . . . . . . 27 B2
Middlehill Rise B32 . . . . . 84 D3
Middle House Dr B60 . . . 121 D1
Middlehouse La B97. . . . 153 E6
Middle La
 Wolverhampton WV9. . . . 11 A5
 Wythall B38. . . . . 124 D5
Middle Leaford B34. . . . . . 69 A5
Middle Leasowe B32 . . . . . 84 D4
Middlemarch Bsns Pk
 CV3. . . . . 134 C2
Middlemarch Jun Sch
 CV10. . . . . 73 B1
Middlemarch Rd
 Coventry CV6. . . . . 113 C7
 Nuneaton CV10 . . . . 73 C1
Middle Mdw DY4. . . . . 52 B5
Middle Meadow Ave B32. . 84 C5
Middlemist Gr B43. . . . . . . 54 F6
Middlemore Bsns Pk WS9 29 E6
Middlemore Cl B80 . . . . . 159 D3
Middlemore La WS9 . . . . . 30 A6
Middlemore Lane W WS9. 29 E6
Middlemore Rd
 Birmingham B31 . . . . . . 103 B3
 Smethwick B66 . . . . 65 B8
Middle Park Cl B29 . . . . . 103 B8
Middle Park Dr B31. . . . . 103 B6
Middlepark Rd DY1. . . . . . 61 F8
Middle Park Rd B29. . . . . 103 C8
Middle Piece Dr B97 . . . . 153 B1
Middle Piece Way WV13. . 27 B2

Middle Rd
 Fairfield B61 . . . . 120 F4
 Upper Bentley B60. . . . . 152 A2
Middle Ride CV3. . . . . 134 E5
Middlesmoor B77 . . . . 36 C8
MIDDLE STOKE. 114 A3
MIDDLETON 34 A1
Middleton Cl
 Hammerwich WS7 . . . . 7 D4
 Redditch B98 . . . . 154 F2
 Walsall WS5. . . . . 42 F5
Middleton Gdns B30 . . . . 103 D4
Middleton Grange B31. . 103 C4
Middleton Hall B30 . . . . 103 E4
Middleton Hall ★ B78. . . . 34 E1
Middleton Hall Rd B30 . . 103 E4
Middleton La B78. . . . . . . 47 F6
Middleton Mews B98. . . . 154 F2
Middleton Rd
 Birmingham B14 . . . . . . 104 F7
 Bromsgrove B61 . . . . 136 F4
 Brownhills WS8 . . . . 7 A1
 Solihull B90 . . . . 106 A2
 Sutton Coldfield B74 . . . . 31 A1
Middleton Trad Est WV13. 26 E1
MIDDLETOWN 159 D1
Middletown B80 . . . . 159 D1
Middletown La B96, B80. 159 D1
Middletree Rd B63. . . . . . . 82 C7
Middle Vauxhall ☑ WV1. . 25 A2
Middleway Ave DY8. . . . . . 60 C3
Middleway Gn WV14 . . . . . 40 C8
Middleway Rd WV14 . . . . . 40 C8
Middleway View B18. . . . . 66 A3
Middlewood Cl B91. . . . . 107 D6
Midford Gr B15. . . . . 86 C8
Midgley Dr B74. . . . . 32 A2
Midhill Dr B65. . . . . 63 C6
Midhurst Dr WS12 . . . . 2 C7
Midhurst Gr WV6 . . . . 24 C5
Midhurst Rd B30. . . . . . . 104 B3
Midland Air Mus★ CV8. . 134 B3
Midland Cl B21 . . . . 66 A7
Midland Croft B33 . . . . . . 69 D3
Midland Ct B83 . . . . 164 A4
Midland Dr B72. . . . . 46 C5
Midland Oak Ind Est CV6. 95 E1
Midland Oak Trad Est
 CV6. . . . . 95 E2
Midland Rd
 Birmingham B30 . . . . . . 103 F5
 Coventry CV6. . . . . 113 E5
 Darlaston WS10. . . . . 41 C8
 Huntington WS12. . . . . 1 C5
 Nuneaton CV11 . . . . 73 A5
 Sutton Coldfield B74 . . . . 46 A6
 Walsall WS1. . . . . 28 E1
Midland St B9 . . . . 67 C3
Midpoint Bvd B76. . . . . . . 58 C5
Midpoint Ctr WV6. . . . . . . 24 F5
Midpoint Park Ind Est
 B76. . . . . 58 C5
Midvale Dr B14. . . . . 104 D2
Mikado Rd B60 . . . . 137 D1
Milbrook Gdns B13 . . . . . 105 B8
Milburn B77 . . . . 36 C8
Milburn Hill Rd CV4 . . . . 132 B6
Milburn Rd B44. . . . . 45 A3
Milby Ct CV11. . . . . 73 C2
Milby Dr CV11 . . . . 74 A7
Milcote Ct B98. . . . . 159 A7
Milcote Dr
 Sutton Coldfield B73 . . . . 45 C3
 Willenhall WV13 . . . . 26 D1
Milcote Rd
 Birmingham B29 . . . . . . 103 A8
 Smethwick B67 . . . . 64 F1
 Solihull B91 . . . . 107 B4
Milcote Way DY6 . . . . 60 B7
Mildenhall B79 . . . . 21 C8
Mildenhall Rd B42 . . . . . . 44 A1
Mildred Rd B64. . . . . 62 E2
Mildred Way B65. . . . . 63 C6
Milebrook Gr B32. . . . . . . 102 B8
Milebush Ave B36. . . . . . . 58 D1
Mile End B98 . . . . 142 A2
Mile Flat DY6. . . . . 60 A7
Mile La CV1 . . . . 165 C1
MILE OAK 20 D1
Mile Oak Cross Rds B78. . 20 C2
Miles Gr DY2. . . . . 62 F7
Miles Mdw CV6 . . . . 96 B1
Miles Meadow Cl WV12 . . 27 C7
Milestone Croft B63. . . . . 82 C5
Milestone Ct WV6. . . . . . . 24 A3
Milestone Dr DY9. . . . . . . 98 F4
Milestone Ho ☑ CV1. . . . 113 B2
Milestone La B21 . . . . 65 D8
Milestone Way WV12. . . . . 27 C8
Mile Tree La CV2. . . . . 96 F7
Milfoil Cl LE10 . . . . 74 F7
Milford Ave
 ☑ Birmingham B12. . . . . 87 A6
 Willenhall WV12 . . . . 27 A5
Milford Cl
 Allesley CV5. . . . . 112 B6
 Redditch B97 . . . . 158 C6
 Stourbridge DY8 . . . . 60 E3
Milford Copse B17. . . . . . . 85 B5
Milford Croft B65 . . . . 62 F6
Milford Ct
 Birmingham B19 . . . . . . 164 B5
 Royal Leamington Spa
  CV31. . . . . 162 A8
Milford Gr B90. . . . . 127 C7
Milford Pl B14. . . . . 104 E8

Milford Rd
 Birmingham B17 . . . . 85 B5
 Wolverhampton WV2 . . . . 39 C7
Milford St CV10. . . . . 73 B2
Milhill Rd B98 . . . . 154 E1
Milholme Gn B92 . . . . . . 107 D8
Milking Bank DY1. . . . . . . 50 E2
Milking Bank Prim Sch
 DY1. . . . . 50 E2
Milk St B5. . . . . 66 F1
Millais Cl CV12. . . . . 78 A4
Millais Rd LE10 . . . . 71 A3
Millard Ind Est B70 . . . . . 53 A1
Millard Rd WV14. . . . . 40 B1
Millbank CV34. . . . . 156 B1
Mill Bank DY3 . . . . 50 D8
Mill Bank Cotts DY11 . . . 116 D6
Millbank Gr B23 . . . . 56 B6
Mill Bank Mews CV8 . . . . 148 B6
Millbrook Cl ☑ WS11 . . . . 1 F1
Millbrook Ct B62. . . . . 83 A7
Millbrook Dr WS14. . . . . . 17 F6
Mill Brook Dr B31. . . . . . 122 E8
Millbrook Rd B14 . . . . . . 104 C6
Mill Brook Way B5 . . . . . . 81 B8
Mill Burn Way ☑ B9 . . . . . 67 B2
Mill Cl
 Blakedown DY10. . . . . . . 98 B2
 Bromsgrove B60 . . . . . . 150 F6
 Coventry CV2. . . . . 96 B3
 Dudley DY3. . . . . 50 D6
 ☑ Hollywood B47. . . . . . 125 A7
 Nuneaton CV11 . . . . 73 F1
 Wolston CV8 . . . . 135 F3
Mill Cres WS11 . . . . 2 B2
Mill Croft WV14. . . . . 40 E6
Millcroft Cl B32. . . . . 84 E2
Millcroft Rd B74 . . . . 45 A8
Mill Ct
 Birmingham B48 . . . . . . 139 C6
 Shenstone WS14 . . . . 18 A6
Milldale Cl DY10 . . . . 116 E8
Milldale Cres WV10 . . . . . 11 D3
Milldale Rd WV10 . . . . 11 D4
Mill Dr B66. . . . . 65 B5
MILL END 148 A6
Mill End CV8 . . . . 148 A6
Millennium Cl WS3 . . . . . 15 A4
Millennium Gdns B64 . . . 62 F2
Millennium Point B4. . . . 164 D4
Millennium Way
 Codsall WV8. . . . . 10 B4
 Wolston CV8 . . . . 135 F3
Miller Cl
 Bromsgrove B60 . . . . . . 150 E6
 Lichfield WS13 . . . . 3 B2
Miller Cres WV14 . . . . 40 A1
Millers Cl WS12. . . . . 27 F1
Millers Ct
 ☑ Kidderminster DY11. . 116 D6
 Solihull B90 . . . . 105 F2
Millersdale Dr B71. . . . . . . 42 F2
Millers Gn LE10 . . . . 75 F6
Millers Green Dr DY6. . . . 60 A8
Millers Rd CV34. . . . . 160 E8
Miller St B6 . . . . 66 E5
Millers Vale WS12 . . . . 2 D1
Millers Wharf B78 . . . . . . 22 F1
Millers Wlk WS3. . . . . 14 E3
Mill Farm Pk CV12 . . . . . . 79 B6
Mill Farm Rd B17 . . . . 85 C3
Millfield
 Birmingham B31 . . . . . . 103 A4
 Royal Leamington Spa
  CV31. . . . . 162 A8
Millfield Ave
 Walsall, Little Bloxwich
  WS3 . . . . 14 D3
 Walsall WS4. . . . . 15 B1
Millfield Gdns ☑ DY11. . 116 D6
Millfield Prim Sch
 Brownhills WS8 . . . . 16 A7
 Fazeley B78 . . . . 35 A8
Millfield Rd
 Birmingham B20 . . . . 54 F5
 Bromsgrove B61 . . . . 136 E1
 Brownhills WS8 . . . . 16 A7
MILLFIELDS 40 C5
Millfields B33. . . . . 69 E3
Millfields Cl B71. . . . . 42 B1
Millfields Fst Sch B61. . . 136 E1
Millfields Rd
 Bilston WV14, WV4 . . . . . 40 B5
 West Bromwich B71 . . . . . 42 B1
Millfield View B63 . . . . . . 82 E4
Millford Cl B28 . . . . 106 A5
Mill Gdns
 Birmingham B14 . . . . . . 105 D5
 Smethwick B67 . . . . 64 F3
Mill Gn WV10 . . . . 11 D4
Mill Gr WV8 . . . . 10 C3
MILL GREEN
 Aldridge. 30 F7
 Cannock. 4 F8
Mill Green & Hawks Green
 Valley Nature Reserve★
 WS11 . . . . 1 F1
Millhaven Ave B30 . . . . . 104 B6
Mill Hill
 Baginton CV8. . . . . 133 D3
 Smethwick B67 . . . . 64 F3
Mill Hill Rd LE10 . . . . 71 C1
Mill Ho B8. . . . . 68 D4
Mill House Cl CV32. . . . . 161 C8
Millhouse Ct CV6 . . . . . . 113 F7

Mill House Dr CV32 . . . . . 161 C8
Millhouse Rd B25 . . . . 88 C8
Mill House Terr CV32. . . . 161 C8
Millicent Cl WS12. . . . . 2 B6
Millicent Pl ☑ B12. . . . . . 87 A6
Millichip Rd WV13 . . . . . . 26 E1
Millington Rd
 Birmingham B36 . . . . 68 E7
 Tipton DY4. . . . . 40 F1
 Wolverhampton WV10 . . . 25 E6
Millisom's Wood Nature
 Reserve★ CV5. . . . . 111 A7
Millison Gr B90 . . . . 127 A7
Mill La
 Aldridge WS9. . . . . 31 A7
 Bentley Heath B93. . . . . 127 F4
 Birmingham B32 . . . . 84 B6
 Birmingham, Digbeth B5. 164 D1
 Birmingham, Northfield
  B31. . . . . 103 A2
 ☑ Birmingham B12. . . . . 87 A6
 Tamworth B79 . . . . 21 A7
 Warwick CV34 . . . . 160 C5
Milton Ave
 Bedworth CV12 . . . . 78 D1
 Bentley Heath B93. . . . . 127 F4
 Hinckley LE10 . . . . 71 C1
 Kidderminster DY11. . . . 116 A6
 Redditch B97 . . . . 158 C8
 Stourbridge DY8 . . . . 81 A7
 Walsall WS1. . . . . 42 D6
 Willenhall WV12 . . . . 27 E7
Milton Cres
 Birmingham B25 . . . . 88 D7
 Dudley DY3. . . . . 50 A5
Milton Ct WV6 . . . . 23 E4
Milton Dr DY9 . . . . 99 D7
Milton Gr
 Birmingham, Edgbaston
  B29 . . . . 85 F3
 Birmingham, Handsworth
  B21. . . . . 65 C8
 Milton Ho B63 . . . . 82 B5
Milton Pl WS1 . . . . 42 D6
Milton Rd
 Bentley Heath B93. . . . . 127 F4
 Cannock WS11. . . . . 1 E4
 Catshill B61 . . . . 137 A8
 Dudley WV14 . . . . 51 D8
 Smethwick B67 . . . . 64 E5
 Wolverhampton WV10. . . . 26 A5
Milton St
 Birmingham B19 . . . . 66 E6
 Brierley Hill DY5 . . . . 51 F1
 Coventry CV2. . . . . 114 A4
 Walsall WS1. . . . . 42 D7
 West Bromwich B71 . . . . . 53 B5
MILVERTON 156 D2
Milverton Cl
 Halesowen B63 . . . . 83 A6
 Sutton Coldfield B76 . . . . 57 F7
Milverton Cres CV32 . . . . 156 E1
Milverton Crescent W ☑
 CV32 . . . . 156 E1
Milverton Ct
 ☑ Birmingham B62. . . . . 84 A7
 Royal Leamington Spa
  CV32. . . . . 161 E8
Milverton Hill CV32 . . . . 161 E8
Milverton House Prep Sch
 CV11. . . . . 73 D3
Milverton Lodge ☑
 CV32. . . . . 156 E1
Milverton Prim Sch
 CV32. . . . . 156 E1
Milverton Rd
 Birmingham B23 . . . . 56 E4
 Coventry CV2. . . . . 96 D2
 Knowle B93 . . . . 128 C5
 Milverton Terr CV32. . . . 161 E8
Milward Sq ☑ B97 . . . . . 153 E3
Mimosa Cl
 Birmingham B29 . . . . . . 103 B7
 Nuneaton CV10 . . . . 78 A8
Mimosa Wlk DY6. . . . . 60 B8
Mincing La B65 . . . . 63 D3
Mindelsohn Way B15. . . . 85 D4
Minden Gr B29 . . . . 85 B1
Minehead Rd
 Dudley DY1 . . . . 61 D8
 Wolverhampton WV10. . . . 11 B2
Miner St WS2. . . . . 28 C3
Miners Way WS7. . . . . 6 C7
Minerva Cl
 Tamworth B77 . . . . 21 D5
 Willenhall WV12 . . . . 27 E4
Minerva La WS1 . . . . 25 E1
Minewood Cl WS3 . . . . . . 13 F3
Minith Rd WV14. . . . . 51 D8
Miniva Dr B76 . . . . 47 A2
Minivet Dr B12 . . . . 86 E6
Minley Ave B17 . . . . 84 F7
Minories Sh Ctr B4. . . . . 164 C3
Minories The ☑ DY2 . . . . 51 D1
Minors Hill WS14 . . . . 9 D6
Minstead Rd B24. . . . . 56 D1
Minster Cl
 Knowle B93 . . . . 128 B8
 Rowley Regis B65 . . . . . . 63 E3
Minster Ct B29 . . . . 102 A2
Minsterley Cl WV3 . . . . . . 38 E8
Minsterpool Wlk WS13 . . . 9 B8
Minster The WV3 . . . . 39 A7
Minster Wlk B61. . . . . . . 136 F8

Millward St continued
 West Bromwich B70 . . . . . 53 A3
Mill Wlk CV11. . . . . 73 C4
Mill Wlk The B31 . . . . . . 102 F1
Millwright Ct ☑ DY4 . . . . 52 B5
Milner Cl CV12. . . . . 79 D2
Milner Cres CV2 . . . . 96 E1
Milner Dr B79 . . . . 22 E7
Milner Rd B29 . . . . 86 A1
Milner Way B13. . . . . 105 D8
Milnes Walker Ct B44 . . . 44 E1
Milo Cres B78 . . . . 21 A2
Milrose Way CV4. . . . . . . 131 F8
Milsom Gr B34. . . . . 69 D6
Milstead Rd B26 . . . . 69 A1
Milston Cl B14. . . . . 104 E1

Mintern Rd B25 88 C8
Minton Cl WV1 26 A1
Minton Ho 3 B12 86 F5
Minton Mews B60 151 B8
Minton Rd
Birmingham B32 84 F4
Coventry CV2 96 E1
MINWORTH 58 C5
Minworth Cl B97 153 B2
MINWORTH GREAVES 58 D6
Minworth Ind Pk B76 58 B5
Minworth Jun & Inf Sch
B76 58 D5
Minworth Rd B46 59 A3
Miranda Cl
Birmingham B45 102 A2
Coventry CV3 134 D7
Miranda Dr CV34 161 E2
Miras Bsns Est WS12 2 D3
Mirbeck Cl WV3 24 C1
Mirfield Cl WV9 11 A3
Mirfield Rd
Birmingham B33 69 B2
Solihull B91 107 A6
Missing Oak Cl CV12 77 F3
Mission Cl B64 63 A1
Mission Dr DY4 52 A3
Mistletoe Dr WS5 43 B3
Mistral Cl LE10 75 F8
Mistyrose Cl CV5 112 B8
Mitcham Cl WS12 1 F7
Mitcham Gr B44 45 B1
Mitcheldean Cl B98 158 E7
Mitcheldean Covert B14 104 D2
Mitchell Ave
Coventry CV4 132 A7
Dudley WV14 40 B1
Mitchell Ho
Coventry CV4 132 A7
3 Warwick CV34 160 E7
Mitchell Rd CV12 78 C2
Mitchell's Ct B79 21 B5
Mitchel Rd DY6 60 F4
Mitford Dr B92 107 D7
Mitre Cl
Essington WV11 13 A3
Willenhall WV12 27 D7
Mitre Ct
Bromsgrove B61 137 A3
Sutton Coldfield B74 46 C6
Mitre Fold WV1 163 B3
Mitre Rd
Cheslyn Hay WS6 4 D2
Stourbridge DY9 81 E5
Mitten Ave B45 102 A1
Mitton Rd B20 54 E2
Moat Ave CV3 132 F5
Moat Coppice B62 84 A1
Moat Croft
Birmingham B37 70 A2
Sutton Coldfield B76 58 B7
Moat Dr
Birmingham B34 69 A6
Drayton Bassett B78 34 E5
Halesowen B62 63 F1
Moat Farm Dr
Bedworth CV12 95 C8
Birmingham B32 84 A1
Moat Farm Prim Sch B68 64 C3
Moat Farm Way WS3 15 A5
Moatfield Terr 2 WS10 42 A3
Moat Gn CV35 160 A1
Moat Green Ave WV11 26 E7
Moat Hall Prim Sch WS6 4 F3
Moat House La CV4 132 C7
Moathouse Lane E WV11 26 E7
Moathouse Lane W WV11 26 D7
Moat House Prim Sch
CV2 96 D1
Moat House Rd B8 68 A4
Moat La
Birmingham, Digbeth B5 164 C1
Birmingham, South Yardley
B26 88 E7
Great Wyrley WS6 5 A2
Solihull B91 107 C6
Moat Mdws B32 84 E4
Moatmead Wlk B36 68 E8
Moat Rd
Oldbury B68 64 B3
Tipton DY4 52 A7
Walsall WS2 28 C2
Moatside Cl WS3 15 A5
Moat St WV13 27 A2
Moat Way LE9 71 F6
Moat Way Ind Est LE9 71 F5
Moatway The B38 123 E7
Mobberley Rd WV14 40 A1
Mob La WS4 15 C3
Mockley Wood Rd B93 128 B7
Modbury Ave B32 84 D1
Modbury Cl CV3 133 D5
Moden Cl DY3 50 D6
Moden Hill DY3 50 D6
Mogul La B63 82 A7
Mohawk Bend CV4 111 C3
Moillett St B18 65 D4
Moilliett Ct B66 65 C6
Moira Cres B14 105 C4
Moises Hall Rd WV5 49 B7
Moland St B4 164 C4
Mole St B11 87 B6
Molesworth Ave CV3 114 A1
Molineux St WV1 163 B4
Molineux (Wolverhampton
Wanderers FC) WV1 163 B4
Mollington Cres B90 106 C3
Mollington Rd CV31 162 A3
Molyneux Rd DY2 62 E2
Momus Bvd CV2 114 C2
Monarch Dr DY4 52 C6
Monarch Ho B68 64 B2
Monarch Ind Est B11 88 A5
Monarch Way DY2 62 C4
Monarch Works 7 DY9 81 F5
Mona Rd B23 56 F5
Monastery Dr B91 106 E6
Monckton Rd B68 84 A7
Moncrieff Dr CV31 162 C5
Moncrieffe Cl DY2 62 E8
Moncrieffe St WS1 29 A1
Mondrian Rd B60 137 C1
Money La B61 121 A7
Monica Rd B10 87 F8
Monins Ave DY4 52 A2
Monk Cl DY4 52 B3
Monkgate Dr B71 53 C6
Monk Rd B8 68 B5
Monk's Croft The CV3 133 C7
Monks Dr B80 159 D4
Monkseaton Rd B72 46 B2
Monksfield Ave B43 43 D1
Monks Field Cl CV4 112 A1
Monkshood Mews B23 56 B7
Monkshood Retreat B38 123 F8
Monks Kirby Rd B76 46 F3
MONKS PARK 95 C1
MONKSPATH 127 B5
Monkspath
Solihull B90 127 A6
Sutton Coldfield B76 46 F1
Monks Path B97 152 F4
Monkspath Bsns Pk B90 126 F8
Monkspath Cl B90 126 D7
Monkspath Hall Rd B90,
B91 127 B7
Monkspath Prim Sch
B90 127 B6
MONKSPATH STREET 126 E6
Monks Rd
Binley Woods CV3 135 C7
Coventry CV1 113 F2
Monksway B38 104 B1
Monks Way
Tamworth B77 21 F5
Warwick CV34 160 D6
Monkswell Cl
Birmingham B10 87 D7
Brierley Hill DY5 61 D1
Monkswood Ave B31 103 C2
Monkswood Cres CV2 114 D8
Monkton Rd B29 85 A2
Monmer Cl WV13 27 B3
Monmer Close Ind Est
WV13 27 B3
Monmer Ct WV12 27 B5
Monmer La WV12, WV13 27 B4
Monmore Bsns Pk WV2 39 F7
MONMORE GREEN 40 A8
Monmore Park Ind Est
WV2 40 A6
Monmore Rd WV1 40 A7
Monmouth Cl
Coventry CV5 112 B3
Kenilworth CV8 147 F6
Monmouth Dr
Sutton Coldfield B73 45 D3
West Bromwich B71 53 B7
Monmouth Gdns CV10 72 E3
Monmouth Ho B33 69 E2
Monmouth Rd
Birmingham, Bartley Green
B32 102 D8
Birmingham, Warley Woods
B67 84 E8
Walsall WS2 27 E3
Monnington Ho CV8 148 B7
Monsal Ave WV10 25 E4
Monsaldale Cl WS8 15 D7
Monsal Rd B42 55 C7
Monsieurs Hall La B61 136 B3
Mons Rd DY2 51 F1
Montague Ho
Birmingham B16 65 E1
Warwick CV34 161 A8
Montague Rd
Birmingham, Birches Green
B24 57 A1
Birmingham, Edgbaston B16 65 E1
Birmingham, Handsworth
B21 65 F8
Smethwick B66 65 C3
Warwick CV34 161 A8
Montague St
Birmingham, Aston B6 67 B8
Birmingham, Bordesley B9 67 A2
Montalt Rd CV3 133 E7
Montana Ave B42 55 A5
Montana Wlk CV10 72 E3
Montano Dr WV10 25 E6
Monteagle Dr DY6 49 D1
Montford Gr DY3 50 D7
Montfort Rd
Coleshill B46 70 F5
Walsall WS2 42 B6
Montfort Wlk B32 84 A2
Montgomery Cl
Coventry CV3 134 C4
Upper Catshill B61 121 A1
Montgomery Cres DY5 81 F7
Montgomery Croft B11 87 C7
Montgomery Prim Sch
B11 87 C7
Montgomery Rd
Walsall WS2 27 E2
Whitnash CV31 161 F4
Montgomery St Bsns Ctr
B11 87 D7
Montgomery St B11 87 C7
Montgomery Way B8 68 A4
Montgomery Wlk 1 B71 53 D4
Monticello Way CV4 111 C3
Montjoy Cl CV3 134 D7
Montley B77 36 C8
Montpelier Ho CV8 147 F5
Montpelier Rd B24 57 A1
Montpellier Cl CV3 133 C6
Montpellier Gdns DY1 50 E2
Montpellier St B12 87 A6
Montreal Ho B5 86 D7
Montrose Ave CV32 157 B5
Montrose Cl WS11 1 F5
Montrose Dr
Birmingham B35 58 A4
Dudley DY1 62 A8
Nuneaton CV10 72 F3
Montsford Cl B93 127 F6
Monument Ave DY9 81 E4
Monument Dr WV10 12 C8
Monument Ho 6 B16 65 F1
Monument La
Birmingham B45 121 F4
Hagley DY9 99 D7
Sedgley DY3 39 E1
Monument Rd B16 65 F2
Monway Bldgs 1 WS10 41 E3
Monway Ind Est WS10 41 E3
Monway Terr WS10 41 E3
Monwood Gr B91 106 F2
Monyhull Hall Rd B30 104 C3
Moodyscroft Rd B33 69 C3
Moon's La WS6 4 D1
MOON'S MOAT 154 F5
Moons Moat Dr B98 154 E5
Moons Moat Fst Sch
B98 154 D5
Moons Pk B98 154 E6
Moorbrooke CV10 72 A7
Moor Cl WS7 7 B7
Moorcroft Cl
Nuneaton CV11 74 B1
Redditch B97 158 B6
Moorcroft Dr WS10 41 C2
Moorcroft Gdns B97 158 B6
Moorcroft Pl 5 B7 67 A4
Moorcroft Rd B13 86 E3
Moorcroft Wood Nature
Reserve* WS10 41 B3
Moorcroft Wood Prim Sch
WV14 41 B3
Moor Ct B24 56 F3
Moordown Ave B92 89 A2
Moore Cl
Coventry CV6 96 A5
Perton WV6 23 F4
Sutton Coldfield B74 31 F6
Warwick CV34 155 E2
Moore Cres B68 64 C3
Moorend Ave B37 70 B2
Moor End Ct B24 57 B4
Moor End La B24 57 B4
Moore Rd WV12 27 D8
Moore's Row B5 66 F1
Moore St
Cannock WS12 2 C7
Wolverhampton WV1 25 F1
Moore Wlk CV34 161 C7
Moorfield Ave B93 127 F6
Moorfield Dr
Bromsgrove B61 136 F3
Halesowen B63 83 A5
Sutton Coldfield B73 57 A8
Moorfield Rd
Birmingham B34 69 B6
Wolverhampton WV2 39 C7
Moorfields Cl WS9 30 A7
Moorfield The CV3 134 B8
Moorfoot Ave B63 82 C1
Moorgate B79 21 A5
Moorgate Cl B98 154 E6
Moorgate Prim Sch B79 21 A5
Moorgate Rd B60 151 A2
MOOR GREEN 86 D1
Moor Green La B13 86 D2
Moor Green Prim Sch
B13 86 C1
MOOR HALL 32 D1
Moor Hall Dr
Clent DY9 100 A1
Sutton Coldfield B75 32 D1
Moor Hall Prim Sch B75 32 D2
Moorhen Cl WS8 15 E7
Moorhill Inf Sch WS11 1 E5
Moorhill Jun Sch WS11 1 E4
Moorhill Rd CV31 162 A3
Moorhills Croft B90 126 B8
Moor Ho B14 104 C2
Moorings Bsns Pk The
CV6 96 A6
Moorings The
Birmingham B18 65 F5
Brierley Hill DY5 62 A4
Oldbury B69 63 E8
Royal Leamington Spa
CV31 161 D7
Wolverhampton WV9 10 F2
Moor La
Birmingham B6 56 A4
Rowley Regis B65 63 B3
Moor La continued
Shenstone WS14 17 E2
Tamworth B77 22 A6
Tamworth, Bolehall B77 21 D5
Moorland Ave WV10 25 C6
Moorland Ct B16 65 D1
Moorland Rd
Birmingham B16 65 D1
Cannock WS11 1 E5
Walsall WS3 28 A8
Moorlands Ave CV8 147 F3
Moorlands Cl 6 B75 46 F6
Moorlands Ct B65 63 D4
Moorlands Dr B90 106 C2
Moorlands Lodge CV8 147 F3
Moorlands Prim Sch B71 53 B8
Moorlands Rd B71 42 C1
Moorlands The B74 45 F8
Moor Lane Ind Est B6 55 F5
Moor Leasow B31 103 C2
Moor Meadow Rd B75 46 D7
Moorpark Cl CV11 79 C8
Moorpark Rd B31 103 A1
Moor Pk
Perton WV6 23 D5
Walsall WS3 14 B3
Moor Pool Ave B17 85 C6
Moor Rd CV10 72 A8
Moors Croft B32 84 B1
Moorside Gdns WS2 28 B3
Moorside Rd B14 105 D3
Moors La B31 102 E7
Moors Mill La DY4 52 D7
Moorsom St B6 66 E5
Moorsom Way B60 151 B7
Moor St
Brierley Hill DY5 61 C3
Coventry CV5 112 F1
Tamworth B79 21 A5
Wednesbury WS10 42 B2
West Bromwich B70 53 C2
Moors The B36 68 F8
Moor Street Ind Est DY5 61 C3
Moor Street Queensway
B5 164 C2
Moor Street S WV2 39 C7
Moor Street Sta B5 164 C2
Moor Street Trad Est DY5 61 C2
Moor The B76 58 A8
Moorville Wlk B11 87 A7
Moorwood Cres CV10 72 A8
Moorwood La CV10 72 A7
Morar Cl B35 58 C4
Moray Cl
Halesowen B62 83 E8
Hinckley LE10 75 A8
Morcom Rd B11 87 E5
Morcroft WV14 41 A3
Mordaunt Dr B75 32 E2
Morden Rd B33 68 D3
Mordern Mobile Home Pk
WV10 11 C6
Mordiford Cl B98 154 E4
Moreall Mdws CV4 132 D3
Morecroft Dr CV34 160 B4
Moreland Croft B76 58 B6
Moreland Pl B31 102 F1
Morelands The B31 103 B1
Morestead Ave B26 89 C5
Moreton Ave
Birmingham B43 44 C3
Wolverhampton WV4 39 E4
Moreton Cl
Birmingham, Queen's Park
B32 84 F5
Birmingham, Yardley B25 88 B7
Wednesbury DY4 41 B2
Moreton Com Sch WV10 11 F1
Moreton Rd
Solihull B90 106 C2
Wolverhampton WV10 11 D1
Moreton St
Birmingham B1 66 B4
Cannock WS11 1 F4
Morey St CV6 113 E7
Morfa Gdns CV6 112 D5
Morford Rd WS9 30 A7
Morgan Cl
1 Cradley Heath B64 82 E8
Oldbury B69 63 D8
Studley B80 159 F2
Willenhall WV12 27 B4
Morgan Ct B24 57 C6
Morgan Gr B36 58 F1
Morgan Rd B78 21 A2
Morgans Bsns Pk WS11 5 F4
Morgans Rd CV5 111 C4
Morgrove Ave B93 127 F6
Morillon Ct DY10 117 A1
Morjon Dr B43 43 F2
Morland Cl CV12 79 D2
Morland Dr LE10 71 B3
Morland Rd
Birmingham B43 44 C4
Coventry CV6 95 C2
Morley Gr WV6 25 C4
Morley Rd
Birmingham B8 68 B6
Burntwood WS7 7 B7
Morlich Rise DY5 81 B8
Morlings Dr WS7 7 B8
Morning Pines DY8 80 E4
Morningside
Coventry CV5 133 B8
Sutton Coldfield B73 46 B6
Mornington Rd B66 65 B7
Morpeth B77 35 C7
Morrell St CV32 156 F1
Morris Ave
Coventry CV2 114 D4
Walsall WS2 27 E2
Morris Cl B27 88 D4
Morris Croft B36 58 F1
Morris Ct
Brierley Hill DY5 61 B1
4 Wolverhampton WV4 39 F4
Morris Dr
Nuneaton CV11 73 D1
Whitnash CV31 162 B2
Morris Field Croft B28 105 E4
Morris Hill B78 36 F7
Morrison Ave WV10 25 D8
Morrison Rd DY4 52 C4
Morris Rd B8 68 C6
Morris St B70 53 C1
Morris Way B40 90 D5
Morris Wlk B60 150 E8
Morsefield La B98 154 D1
Morse Rd CV31 162 B3
Morston B77 35 D4
Mortimer Rd CV8 147 F2
Mortimers Cl B14 105 B1
Morton Cl CV6 95 A1
Morton Ho B97 153 A3
Morton La B97 158 B7
Morton Rd
Brierley Hill DY5 81 D7
Harvington DY10 118 B2
Morton St CV32 156 F1
Morvale Ct DY9 81 E5
Morvale Gdns DY9 81 E5
Morvale St DY9 81 E5
Morven Rd B73 46 A3
Morville Cl B93 127 D3
Morville Croft WV14 40 B5
Morville Rd DY2 62 E4
Morville St B16 66 B2
Mosborough Cres B19 66 C5
Mosedale Dr WV11 26 F5
Mosedale Way 4 B15 86 D8
MOSELEY 86 F2
Moseley Ave CV6 113 A4
Moseley Bog Nature
Reserve* B13 87 C1
Moseley CE Prim Sch B13 86 F2
Moseley Ct
19 Birmingham B13 87 B2
Essington WV11 12 F3
Willenhall WV13 26 D1
Moseley Dr B37 89 F8
Moseley Gate B13 86 F3
Moseley Hall Hospl B13 86 E3
Moseley Old Hall* WV10 12 A5
Moseley Old Hall La
WV10 12 A5
Moseley Park Sch & Tech
Coll WV14 40 E8
Moseley Prim Sch CV6 113 A4
Moseley Rd
Bilston WV14 40 E8
Birmingham B12 86 F6
Kenilworth CV8 148 B3
Willenhall WV14, WV13 26 D1
Wolverhampton WV10 12 A4
Moseley Road Swimming
Pool B12 86 F5
Moseley Sch B13 87 C2
Moseley Sch Health &
Fitness Ctr B13 87 D2
Moseley St
Birmingham B12 86 F8
Tipton DY4 52 C7
Wolverhampton WV6 25 C4
MOSELEY VILLAGE 26 C2
Mossbank Ave WS7 7 A6
Moss Cl
Aldridge WS9 30 A5
Walsall WS4 29 A3
Moss Cres WS12 1 C5
Mossdale B77 36 C8
Mossdale Cl CV6 113 B6
Mossdale Cres CV10 72 F2
Mossdale Way DY3 50 E7
Moss Dr B72 46 C3
Mossfield Rd B14 104 F7
Moss Gdns WV14 40 B3
Moss Gr
Birmingham B14 104 D6
Kenilworth CV8 148 B7
Kingswinford DY6 60 D7
Moss House Cl B15 66 B1
Moss La B98 154 F8
Moss Lane Cl B98 154 F8
Mossley Cl WS3 13 F1
Mossley La WS3 13 F2
Mossley Prim Sch WS3 13 F2
Mosspaul Cl CV32 156 D2
Moss Rd WS11 2 A3
Moss St
Cannock WS11 2 A4
12 Royal Leamington Spa
CV31 162 A7
Mossvale Cl B64 62 F1
Mossvale Gr B8 67 F5
Moss Way B74 44 F7
Mosswood St WS11 4 D7
Mostyn Cres B71 53 A7
Mostyn Rd
Birmingham, Edgbaston
B16 65 F2
Birmingham, Handsworth
B21 65 F8
Mostyn St WV1 25 B4
Mother Teresa Ho B70 53 B3
Mott Cl DY4 52 C8
Mottistone Cl CV3 133 D6

Mottram Cl B70...... 53 B2
Mottrams Cl B72...... 46 C2
Mott St B19 .... 164 B4
Moule Cl DY11........ 116 C6
Moundsley Gr B14 .... 105 A3
Moundsley Ho B14.... 104 F2
Mounds The B38....... 123 E8
Mountain Ash Dr DY9 .. 81 C2
Mountain Ash Rd WS8.. 15 E5
Mountain Pine Cl WS12 .. 2 A8
Mount Ave
  Brierley Hill DY5 ..... 61 C4
  Cannock WS12......... 2 B7
Mountbatten Ave CV8 .. 148 C3
Mountbatten Cl B70... 53 F2
Mountbatten Rd WS2 .. 27 F2
Mount Cl
  Birmingham B13 ...... 86 F4
  Cheslyn Hay WS6...... 4 E2
  Dudley DY3 .... 50 C2
  Wombourne WV5...... 49 A7
Mount Cl WV6 .... 24 B2
Mount Dr
  Bedworth CV12 .... 78 A3
  Wombourne WV5...... 49 A7
Mountfield Cl B14 .... 105 A2
Mount Field Ct CV1 ... 165 D4
Mountford Cl WS3 .... 63 C3
Mountford Cres WS9 .. 30 C8
Mountford Dr B75 .... 46 B8
Mountford Ho B70 .... 53 E1
Mountford La WV14 .. 40 D6
Mountford Rd B90 .... 105 D1
Mountford St B11..... 87 D5
Mount Gdns CV5 ..... 133 B8
Mount Grace High Sch
  LE10 .... 71 E1
Mountjoy Cres B92... 89 C3
Mount La
  Clent DY9............ 99 E4
  Dudley DY3 .... 50 C2
Mount Nod Prim Sch 🔢
  CV5 .... 112 A3
Mount Nod Way CV5 .. 112 B3
MOUNT PLEASANT
  Bedworth............. 78 B3
  Coventry 115 B8
  Tamworth............. 21 C1
Mount Pleasant
  Bilston WV14 .... 40 E6
  Birmingham, King's Heath
    B14................. 86 F1
  Birmingham, Small Heath
    B10 .... 67 B1
  Brierley Hill DY5 ..... 61 E1
  Cheslyn Hay WS6...... 4 E2
  Kingswinford DY6 .... 60 C4
  Redditch B97.........153 D2
  Tamworth B77 .... 21 C1
Mount Pleasant Ave B21 .. 54 E1
Mount Pleasant Cotts
  CV7 .... 115 A7
Mount Pleasant Ct 🔢 B10 .. 67 B1
Mount Pleasant Mobile
  Home Pk B77 .... 21 C1
Mount Pleasant Prim Sch 🔢
  DY5.................. 61 E1
Mount Pleasant Rd CV12 .. 78 A3
Mount Pleasant St
  Dudley WV14......... 51 B8
  West Bromwich B70 ... 53 C2
Mount Pleasant Terr
  CV10 .... 72 F6
Mount St WS1 ...... 28 E1
Mount Rd
  Birmingham B21 ..... 65 D7
  Burntwood WS7 .... 7 B6
  Fairfield B61 .... 120 E2
  Hinckley LE10 .... 75 D8
  Oldbury B69.......... 63 E8
  Rowley Regis B65 .... 63 E3
  Stourbridge, Stambermill
    DY8................. 81 B5
  Stourbridge, Wordsley DY8 .. 60 E2
  Walsall WS3........... 15 A4
  Willenhall WV13 ..... 40 E8
  Wolverhampton, Goldthorn Hill
    WV4 .... 39 A4
  Wolverhampton, Tettenhall Wood
    WV6 .... 24 A3
  Wolverhampton, Woodcross
    WV4 .... 39 F2
  Wombourne WV5...... 49 A7
Mount Nod Real Est WS7.. 7 B6
Mount Rd B60 .... 137 B1
Mount Side St WS12 .. 2 C7
Mounts Rd WS10...... 41 F2
Mount St
  Birmingham B7 ...... 67 C7
  Cannock WS12........ 2 B7
  Coventry CV5........ 112 F2
  Halesowen B63 ...... 83 A3
  Nuneaton CV11 .... 73 A4
  Redditch B98 .... 153 E3
  Stourbridge DY8 ..... 81 B5
  Tipton DY4........... 52 C6
  Walsall WS1.......... 42 E8
Mount Street Bsns Ctr B7 .. 67 C7
Mount Street Ind Est B7.. 67 D7
Mount Street Pas CV11.. 73 B4
Mounts Way B7........ 67 C7
Mount The
  Birmingham B23 ..... 56 D1
  Coventry CV3......... 114 A1
  Curdworth B76........ 59 D6
Mount Vernon Dr B61.. 137 A5
Mount View B75 ..... 46 E4

Mountwood Covert WV6 .. 24 B3
Mousehall Farm Rd DY5.. 81 D7
Mouse Hill WS3........ 14 F3
Mouse La DY11 .... 116 B8
MOUSESWEET 62 F3
Mousesweet Brook Nature
  Reserve* DY5........ 62 B1
Mousesweet Cl DY2.... 62 E4
Mousesweet La DY2.... 62 E3
Mowbray Cl B45 ..... 102 A2
Mowbray St
  Birmingham B5 ...... 86 E8
  Coventry CV2........ 113 F3
Mowe Croft B37 ...... 90 B7
Mows Hill Rd B94.... 143 A1
Moxhull Cl WV12...... 13 C1
Moxhull Dr B76....... 57 E7
Moxhull Gdns WV12... 13 C1
Moxhull Rd B37....... 70 A5
MOXLEY.............. 41 B3
Moxley Ind Ctr WS10 .. 41 C4
Moxley Act WS10...... 41 A4
Moxley Rd WS10...... 41 C5
Moyle Cres CV5 ...... 111 D4
Moyle Dr B63......... 82 B7
Moyses Croft B66 .... 65 A8
Mozart Ct WS11....... 2 C2
Muchall Rd WV4 ...... 39 A5
Much Park St CV1..... 165 C2
MUCKLEY CORNER 8 A2
MUCKLOW HILL....... 83 D6
Mucklow Hill B62..... 83 D5
Mucklow Hill Trad Est
  B62................. 83 A5
Muirfield B77......... 22 C5
Muirfield Cl WS3...... 14 A3
Muirfield Cres B69.... 63 B7
Muirfield Gdns B38 .. 103 D1
Muirfields Cl CV11.... 79 C8
Muirville Cl 🔢 DY8.... 60 D3
Mulberry Cl CV32.... 157 A2
Mulberry Ct CV8..... 147 F4
Mulberry Dr
  Birmingham B13 ..... 87 B1
  🔢 Lichfield WS13 .... 9 E8
  🔢 Warwick CV34.... 160 F8
Mulberry Gn DY1 .... 50 F5
Mulberry Pl WS3..... 13 F1
Mulberry Rd
  Birmingham B30 .... 103 C5
  Cannock WS11........ 1 E3
  Coventry CV6....... 114 A7
  Walsall WS3......... 14 D2
Mulberry Way CV10 .. 72 A8
Mulberry Wlk B74.... 44 E8
Muldoon Cl WS11..... 2 B4
Mullard Dr CV31.... 162 B3
Mull Cl B45.......... 101 E1
Mull Croft B36....... 70 B7
Mullein Cl B74........ 31 F5
Mullensgrove Rd B37 .. 70 A5
Mullett Rd WV11..... 26 B7
Mullett St DY5........ 61 B5
Mulliners Cl 🔢 B37 .. 70 D2
Mulliner St CV6...... 113 F5
Mullion Croft B38.... 103 E1
Mulroy Rd B74........ 46 B6
Mulwych Rd B33..... 69 F3
Munches La B62..... 120 C8
Munnings Dr LE10 ... 71 A3
Munro Cl DY10....... 117 C6
Munsley Cl B98..... 154 F2
Munslow Gr B31..... 122 F8
Muntz Cres B94..... 143 C6
Muntz Ho B16........ 66 A1
Muntz St B10......... 87 D8
Murcott Ct CV31.... 162 A3
Murcott Road E CV31.. 162 A3
Murcott Road W CV31.. 162 A3
Murcroft Rd DY9..... 81 E1
Murdoch Dr DY6..... 60 C7
Murdoch Rd WV14 ... 41 A6
Murdoch Gr B21..... 65 E7
Murdock Rd
  Birmingham B21..... 65 E8
  Smethwick B66...... 65 D6
Murdock Way 🔢 WS2.. 28 A5
Murray Ct
  Sutton Coldfield B73 .. 46 A3
Murrayfield Way WS3.. 115 B1
Murray Ho WV14..... 40 D5
Murray Rd CV6 ..... 113 A7
Murrell Cl B5........ 86 D7
Murton B77 .... 36 C8
Musborough Cl B36... 58 C1
Muscott Gr B17....... 85 B5
Muscovy Rd B23..... 56 C3
Musgrave Cl B76..... 46 E3
Musgrave Rd B18 .... 65 E5
MUSHROOM GREEN .. 62 B2
Mushroom Hall Rd B68.. 64 B5
Musketts Ct B97..... 153 B2
Musk La DY3.......... 50 B3
Musk Lane W DY3.... 50 B3
Mus of Cannock Chase*
  WS12............... 2 B5
Mus of the Jewellery
  Quarter* 🔢 B19 .... 66 C5
Musson Cl B37....... 90 B8
Mustow Green WS13.. 117 F1
Muswell Cl B91..... 107 D5
Muxloe Cl WS3 ...... 14 A3
Myatt Ave
  Aldridge WS9........ 29 F5
  Burntwood WS7 ...... 7 A7
  Wolverhampton WV2 .. 39 E6

Myatt Cl WV2......... 39 E6
Myatt Way WS9....... 29 F5
Myddleton St B18..... 66 A4
Myles Ct DY5......... 61 D4
Mylgrove CV3........ 133 D3
Mynors Cres B47..... 125 A6
Myring Dr B75........ 46 F5
Myrtle Ave
  🔢 Birmingham, Balsall Heath
    B12 .... 87 A5
  Birmingham, Highter's Heath
    B14................. 104 F2
  Redditch B98 .... 153 E2
Myrtle Cl WV12 ...... 27 E7
Myrtle Gr
  🔢 Birmingham B19... 66 C8
  Coventry CV5........ 112 F1
  Wolverhampton WV3 .. 38 E6
Myrtle Pl B29........ 86 B2
Myrtle Rd DY1 .... 51 B3
Myrtle St WV2 .... 39 F6
Myrtle Terr DY4...... 40 E1
Myton Cres CV34.... 161 C6
Myton Crofts CV31... 161 D7
Myton Dr B90........ 105 D1
Myton Gdns CV34.... 161 A6
Myton La CV34....... 161 C6
Myton Rd CV31, CV34.. 161 B6
Myton Sch CV34.... 161 B6
Mytton Gr DY4....... 51 E5
Mytton Rd
  Birmingham B30 .... 103 C5
  Water Orton B46..... 58 F3
Myvod Rd WS10...... 42 A5

N

Naden Ho WS12 ...... 1 C5
Naden Rd B19........ 66 B6
Nadin Rd B73........ 57 A8
Naesby Rd WV6...... 23 F3
Nafford Gr B14..... 104 F2
Nagersfield Rd DY5 .. 61 A2
Nailcote Ave CV4.... 131 C8
Nailcote La CV7..... 131 A7
Nailers Cl
  Birmingham B32 .... 83 F2
  Stoke Heath B60 .... 150 E6
Nailers Dr B97....... 158 F3
Nailers Dr WS7 ...... 7 D6
Nailers Fold WV14 ... 40 D2
Nailstone Cres B27 .. 106 C8
Nailsworth Rd
  Dorridge B93....... 127 D2
  Redditch B98 .... 153 F2
Nairn Cl
  Birmingham B28 .... 105 F5
  Nuneaton CV10 ...... 73 A2
Nairn Rd WS3 .... 14 A4
Nally Dr WV14 ...... 40 A2
Nanaimo Way DY6 ... 61 A4
Nansen Prim Sch B8.. 67 F5
Nansen Rd
  Birmingham B8 ..... 67 F5
  Birmingham, Sparkhill B11 .. 87 C3
Nantmel Gr B32..... 102 C8
Naomi Way WS9 ..... 16 B4
Napier B77 .... 21 E3
Napier Dr DY4...... 52 C6
Napier Rd
  Walsall WS2......... 28 A5
  Wolverhampton WV2 .. 39 D7
Napier St CV1 ...... 113 E3
Napton Cl B98..... 154 D1
Napton Dr CV32.... 157 A2
Napton Gn CV5 ..... 112 A3
Napton Gr B29....... 84 F2
Narberth Way CV2... 114 F8
Narcissus Gr 🔢 B38.. 123 D8
Nardino Gr DY4...... 52 D8
Narrowboat Cl CV6... 96 B6
Narrowboat Way DY5, DY2 .. 62 B4
Narrow Hall Mdw CV34.. 160 B4
Narrow La
  Brownhills WS8...... 15 F8
  Halesowen B62...... 83 E8
  Walsall WS2......... 42 B7
Narrows The 🔢 LE10.. 75 E8
Naseby Cl
  Coventry CV3....... 134 F8
  Redditch B98 ...... 154 D6
Naseby Dr B63....... 82 D2
Naseby Rd
  Birmingham B8 ..... 67 F5
  Solihull B91 .... 107 B6
Nash Ave WV6....... 23 E3
Nash Cl B65 .... 63 C1
Nash Croft B37 ...... 90 B8
Nash Ct DY10....... 117 C5
Nash Ho B15........ 86 D8
Nash La
  Belbroughton DY9 .. 119 D7
  Lichfield WS13...... 3 A5
  Stourbridge DY9 ... 119 D7
Nash Rd B24......... 68 B8
Nash Sq B42......... 55 D4
Nash Wlk 🔢 B66..... 65 C5
Nately Gr B29....... 85 C2
Nathan Ct B75....... 46 C4
Nathaniel Newton Inf Sch
  CV10............... 72 B8
National Construction Coll
  B30................. 104 B4
National Exhibition Ctr (NEC)
  The B40............. 90 E4

National Indoor Arena*
  B1.................. 66 B2
National Motorcycle Mus
  The* B92............ 91 A2
National Sea Life Ctr*
  B1.................. 66 B2
Naul's Mill Ho CV1 ... 165 B4
Naunton Cl B29...... 103 A7
Naunton Rd WS2..... 28 A3
Navenby Cl WS9..... 105 C3
Navigation Dr
  Birmingham B30 .... 104 D3
  Brierley Hill DY5 .... 62 A4
Navigation La B71 ... 42 F2
Navigation Rdbt DY4.. 52 E6
Navigation St
  Birmingham B2 ..... 164 B2
  Walsall WS2......... 28 D1
  Wolverhampton WV1 .. 25 E1
Navigation Way
  Birmingham B18 .... 65 F5
  Cannock WS11........ 2 A2
  Coventry CV6....... 114 A8
  West Bromwich B70 .. 52 F2
Navigators Rd B27 ... 88 D3
Nayland Croft B28 ... 106 A5
Naylor Cl DY11....... 116 B3
Naylors Gr DY3....... 50 E4
NEACHELLS........... 26 D3
Neachells La
  Wednesfield WV11 .. 26 D5
  Willenhall WV13 .... 26 D3
Neachells Lane Ind Est
  WV11............... 26 D4
Neachells Lane Island
  WV11............... 26 D4
Neachless Ave WV5 .. 49 A5
Neachley Gr B33..... 68 F4
Neal Ct CV2......... 115 A8
Neale Ave CV5...... 112 A6
Neale Ct CV12....... 79 C1
Neale Ho
  🔢 West Bromwich B70.. 53 D1
Neale St CV6........ 113 A8
NEAL'S GREEN 95 F3
Neander B79 .... 20 F6
Near High Dr 🔢 DY4.. 52 B5
Nearhill Rd B38..... 123 C8
Near Lands Cl B32 ... 84 B4
Nearmoor Rd B34.... 69 D6
Near Oak Ho B32.... 102 D8
Neasden Gr B44..... 56 B8
Neath Rd WS3 ...... 13 F2
Neath Way
  Dudley DY3 .... 51 A6
  Walsall WS3......... 13 F2
Nebsworth Cl B90... 106 D5
NECHELLS........... 67 D8
Nechells Com Sports Ctr
  B74................. 67 A5
Nechells Park Rd B7 . 67 C7
Nechells Parkway B7.. 67 A5
Nechells Pl B7....... 67 C5
Nechells Prim Sch B7.. 67 C8
Needham St B7...... 67 C7
Needhill Cl B93..... 127 F6
Needle Cl B80...... 159 E4
Needle Mill La B98.. 153 E6
Needlers End La CV7.. 130 A7
Needless Alley B2 ... 164 B2
Needwood Cl WV2 ... 39 B6
Needwood Dr WV14.. 51 B8
Needwood Gr B71 ... 42 E1
Needwood Ho B77... 88 D3
Neighbrook Cl B97.. 152 F2
Neilston St 🔢 CV31.. 162 A7
Nelson Ave
  Bilston WV14........ 40 C7
  Warwick CV34...... 161 A8
Nelson Cl WS14....... 9 B5
Nelson Cl 🔢 B13..... 86 F4
Nelson Dr
  Cannock WS12........ 2 F4
  Hinckley LE10 ...... 71 D4
Nelson Ho DY4....... 52 A7
Nelson La CV34..... 161 A8
Nelson Mandela Prim Sch
  B12................. 87 B5
Nelson Prim Sch B1 .. 66 B3
Nelson Rd
  Birmingham B6 ..... 55 F1
  Dudley DY1 .... 51 B1
Nelson St
  Birmingham B1 ..... 66 B3
  🔢 Coventry CV1 .... 113 E4
  Oldbury B69......... 64 B6
  West Bromwich B71 .. 53 C5
  Willenhall WV13 .... 27 B3
Nemesia B77 .... 22 A5
Nene Cl
  Coventry CV3....... 134 D7
  Stourbridge DY9 .... 81 A5
Nene Way B36........ 69 F8
Neptune Ind Est WV13.. 41 B8
Neptune St DY4...... 51 E5
Nesbit Gr B9 .... 68 B3
Nesfield Cl B38..... 103 C1
Nesfield Gr B92..... 109 B7
Nesscliffe Gr B23 ... 56 E7
Nest Comm WS3..... 14 F5
Nest Croft B30....... 104 A6
Nestor Ho B13....... 105 D7
Netheravon Cl B14.. 104 D1
Nether Beacon WS13.. 3 A1

Netherbridge Ave WS14 ....9 E7
Netherbrook Prim Sch
  DY2................. 62 D2
Netherby Rd DY3 .... 50 C8
Nethercote Gdns B90.. 105 E3
Netherdale Cl B72 .... 57 C7
Netherdale Rd B14.. 105 A1
Netherend Cl B63..... 82 A7
Netherend La B63..... 82 B7
Netherend Sq B63.... 82 A7
Netherfield B98...... 159 A8
Netherfield Gdns B27.. 88 B3
Nethergate WS7 ...... 6 E5
Netherhall Ave B43 .. 44 B1
Netherhouse Cl B44.. 44 E3
Nether La WS7....... 7 D8
Netherley Ct LE10 ... 71 D3
Netherley Rd LE10 .. 71 D3
Nethermill Rd 🔢 CV6.. 113 A5
Netherstone Gr 🔢 B74.. 31 F5
NETHER STOWE 3 C3
Netherstowe WS13... 3 C2
Nether Stowe High Sch
  WS13............... 3 B1
Netherstowe La WS13.. 3 D2
NETHERTON.......... 62 C4
Netherton Bsns Pk DY2 .. 62 E3
Netherton CE Prim Sch
  DY2................. 62 B4
Netherton Gr B33.... 69 C3
Netherwood Cl B91.. 106 E6
Netherwood La B93.. 145 A7
Netley Dr WV6 ...... 24 B5
Netley Gr B11........ 87 F3
Netley Ho B32....... 84 F5
Netley Rd WS3....... 13 E2
Netley Way WS3 .... 13 E2
Network Park Ind Est B7.. 67 C4
Nevada Way B37..... 70 C1
Neve Ave WV10...... 25 F8
Nevill Cl CV31...... 161 F6
Neville Ave
  Kidderminster DY11.. 116 D3
  Wolverhampton WV4.. 39 D5
Neville Cl B98 ...... 154 A5
Neville Ct
  Birmingham B13 .... 104 F6
  Kidderminster DY11.. 116 D3
  🔢 Warwick CV34.... 160 E6
Neville Gr CV34..... 155 F1
Neville Ho 🔢 DY3.... 50 D7
Neville Rd
  Birmingham, Castle Bromwich
    B36................. 58 E1
  Birmingham, Stockland Green
    B23................. 56 C3
  Solihull B90 .... 105 F1
Neville St B77....... 21 E3
Neville Wlk B35...... 58 A2
Nevin Gr B42........ 55 C5
Nevis Ct WV6....... 24 E2
Nevis Gr WV12...... 13 B1
Nevison Gr B43..... 44 B4
Newall Cl CV7...... 130 B6
Newark Croft B26... 89 B6
Newark Rd
  Dudley DY2 .... 62 D2
  Willenhall WV12 .... 27 C7
New Art Gall The* WS2 .. 28 E2
New Ash Dr CV5 .... 111 F5
Newbank Gr B9..... 68 A3
New Barns La WS14 .. 17 B3
New Bartholomew St
  B5................. 164 C2
New Birmingham Rd B69,
  DY2................. 52 B1
New Bldgs
  Coventry CV1....... 165 C3
  Darlaston WS10 ..... 41 E6
  Hinckley LE10 ...... 71 D1
Newbold Cl
  Bentley Heath B93.. 127 F5
  Coventry CV3....... 114 F1
  Lichfield WS13....... 9 A5
Newbold Comyn L Ctr
  CV32............... 162 B8
Newbold Comyn Pk*
  CV32............... 162 D8
Newbold Croft B7 ... 67 B7
Newbold Ct B63..... 83 B3
Newbold Lawn CV32 .. 162 A8
Newbold Pl CV32.... 162 A8
NEWBOLDS.......... 26 A6
Newbolds Rd WV10.. 26 A6
Newbold St CV32 ... 162 A8
Newbold Terr CV32 .. 162 A8
Newbold Terrace E CV32 .. 162 B8
Newbold Rd WV14.... 40 E6
Newbolt St WS5...... 42 E5
New Bond St
  Birmingham B9 ..... 67 B1
  🔢 Dudley DY2....... 51 B1
Newborough Gr B28, B90 .. 105 F3
Newborough Rd
  Birmingham B28 .... 105 F4
  Solihull B90 .... 106 A3
Newbourne Hill B48.. 139 E4
NEWBRIDGE.......... 24 E5
Newbridge Ave WV6 .. 24 E4
Newbridge Cres WV6.. 24 E4
Newbridge Dr WV6... 24 E4
Newbridge Gdns WV6.. 24 E4
Newbridge Mews 🔢 WV6 .. 24 E4
Newbridge Prep Sch WV6 .. 24 E4

Newbridge Rd
Birmingham B9 . . . . 68 B1
Kingswinford DY6 . . . . 60 C8
Newbridge St WV6 . . . . . . 24 F4
Newbrook Farm★ B32 . . 101 D4
New Brook St 图 CV32 . . 161 E8
Newburgh Cres CV34. . . 160 E8
Newburgh Prim Sch
CV34 . . . . 160 C4
Newburn Croft B32 . . . . 84 B5
Newbury Cl
Great Wyrley WS6 . . . . 4 F2
Halesowen B62 . . . . 83 D3
Lower Marlbrook B61 . . . 121 B1
图 Royal Leamington Spa
CV31 . . . . 162 C6
Newbury Ho 图 B69 . . . . 63 D5
Newbury La B69 . . . . 63 D6
Newbury Rd
Birmingham B19 . . . . 66 E7
Norton Canes WS11 . . . . . . 6 A5
Stourbridge DY8 . . . . 60 D1
Wolverhampton WV10 . . . 11 C2
Newbury Wlk B65 . . . . . . 63 C6
Newby Cl CV3 . . . . 133 E6
Newby Gr B37 . . . . 70 B5
New Canal St B5 . . . . . . 164 D2
Newcastle Croft B35 . . . 58 C3
New Century Pk CV3 . . . . 114 C2
New Century Way CV11. . 73 B4
Newchurch Gdns 图 B24 . 56 E2
New Church Rd B73. . . . . 57 A8
New Cole Hall La B33, B34 69 B5
New Coll B60 . . . . 137 B3
New College Cl WS1 . . . . 43 A7
Newcombe Rd
Birmingham B21 . . . . 54 D2
Coventry CV5. . . . . 113 A1
Newcome Ct B24 . . . . . . 57 D4
Newcomen Cl
Bedworth CV12 . . . . 95 D8
Burntwood WS7. . . . . 7 C8
Newcomen Ct WS4. . . . . . 29 B7
Newcomen Dr DY4. . . . . . 51 F3
Newcomen Rd CV12. . . . . 77 D1
New Coppice Ct B97 . . . 158 E6
Newcott Cl WV9 . . . . 10 F2
New Coventry Rd B26 . . . 89 A5
New Croft B19 . . . . 66 E7
Newcroft Gr B26. . . . . . . 88 E7
NEW CROSS 26 B6
New Cross Ave WV10. . . . 26 B4
New Cross Hospl WV11. . . 26 B5
New Cross Ind Est WV1 . . 26 A3
New Cross Junc WV10 . . . 26 B4
New Cross St
Darlaston WS10 . . . . 41 D5
Tipton DY4 . . . . 51 E5
New Crown St 图 DY1 . . . 62 B8
New Ct 图 DY5 . . . . 61 D2
Newdegate Cl CV12 . . . . . 78 A4
Newdegate Pl CV11 . . . . . 73 C4
Newdegate Rd CV12. . . . . 78 A3
Newdegate St CV11 . . . . . 73 C4
Newdigate CV31 . . . . . . 162 C5
Newdigate Prim Sch
CV12. . . . . 77 C1
Newdigate Rd
Coventry CV6. . . . . 113 F6
Sutton Coldfield B75 . . . . . 47 A5
NEW DOCK 51 A1
New Dudley Rd DY6. . . . . 60 C8
Newells Dr DY4. . . . . 52 D7
Newells Rd B26. . . . . 89 B8
New England B62. . . . . . . 83 E7
New England Cl B69 . . . . 52 E1
Newent Cl WV12 . . . . 27 D3
Newent Rd B31 . . . . 103 C4
New Ent Workshops B18 . 66 A5
Newey Ave CV12 . . . . 95 D8
Newey Cl B45. . . . . 122 A6
Newey Dr CV8 . . . . 148 A2
Newey Rd
Birmingham B28 . . . . . . 105 F6
Coventry CV2. . . . . 114 D4
Wednesfield WV11 . . . . . . 27 A8
Newey St DY1 . . . . 51 A2
New Farm Rd DY9. . . . . . 81 C4
Newfield Ave CV8 . . . . . . 148 B3
Newfield Cl
Solihull B91 . . . . 107 D6
Walsall WS2. . . . . 28 C5
Newfield Cres B63 . . . . . . 83 A5
Newfield Dr DY6 . . . . 60 E4
Newfield Gdns DY9 . . . . . 99 A4
Newfield La B63 . . . . 83 B5
Newfield Park Prim Sch
B63 . . . . 83 A5
Newfield Pl DY9 . . . . 99 A4
Newfield Rd
Coventry CV1 . . . . 113 C5
Oldbury B69. . . . . 63 F8
West Hagley DY9. . . . . 99 A4
New Forest Rd WS3. . . . . 28 F6
New Fosse Way B76. . . . . 58 B5
Newgale Wlk CV31. . . . . 162 C7
New Gas St B70. . . . . 53 A5
New Gate Ct CV1. . . . . . 165 C2
Newgate St WS7 . . . . 7 A5
New Gdns WS7 . . . . 6 F5
New Green Pk CV2. . . . . 114 D8
Newhall Cres WS11 . . . . . . 2 B3
Newhall Ct 图 B3 . . . . . . 66 C3

New Hall Dr
Sutton Coldfield, Maney
B75. . . . . 46 D4
Sutton Coldfield, Wylde Green
B76. . . . . 46 E2
Newhall Farm Cl B76. . . . 46 D4
Newhall Gdns WS11. . . . . . 1 F2
Newhall Hill B1. . . . . 66 C3
Newhall Ho 图 WS1 . . . . . 42 E8
Newhall Pl B1 . . . . 66 C3
New Hall Pl WS10. . . . . . 42 A3
New Hall Prim & Childrns
Ctr B75 . . . . 47 B5
Newhall Rd
Coventry CV2. . . . . 114 D7
Rowley Regis B65 . . . . 63 C3
Newhall St
Birmingham B3 . . . . 164 B3
Cannock WS11. . . . . 1 D1
Tipton DY4 . . . . 51 E8
Walsall WS1. . . . . 42 E8
West Bromwich B70 . . . . . 53 C2
New Hall St WV13. . . . . . 27 B2
Newhall Wlk (Sh Ctr) 图
B72. . . . . 46 C4
Newham Gn WV10 . . . . . . 72 C7
Newhampton Arts Ctr
Wolverhampton Coll
WV1 . . . . 163 B4
Newhampton Road E
WV1. . . . . 163 A4
New Hampton Road W
WV6. . . . . 24 F4
Newhaven Cl
Birmingham B7 . . . . 67 A5
Coventry CV6. . . . . 112 E6
Newhay Croft B19 . . . . . . 66 C7
New Heath Cl WV11 . . . . . 26 B5
New Henry St B68. . . . . . 64 B4
Newhome Way WS3. . . . . 28 D8
Newhope Cl 图 B15. . . . . . 86 D8
New Hope Rd B66. . . . . . . 65 C4
New Horse Rd WS6 . . . . . . 4 E3
Newhouse Croft CV7 . . . 130 B6
Newhouse Farm Cl B76 . . 46 F3
New House Farm Dr
B31 . . . . 103 C6
Newick Ave B74 . . . . 31 B3
Newick Gr B14. . . . . 104 C4
Newick St DY2 . . . . 62 C4
New Imperial Cres B11. . . 87 F3
Newington Cl CV6 . . . . . 112 D6
Newington Rd B37 . . . . . . 90 B8
New Inn Rd 图 B19. . . . . . 66 D8
New Inns Cl B21 . . . . 65 D8
New Inns La B45 . . . . . . 101 E1
NEW INVENTION 27 D8
New Invention Jun & Inf
Schs WV12 . . . . 27 C7
New John St
Birmingham B6 . . . . 66 E5
Halesowen B62 . . . . 83 C8
New John Street W B19 . . 66 D5
New King St 图 DY1 . . . . . 51 C1
Newland Cl
Redditch B98 . . . . 159 B7
Walsall WS4. . . . . 15 C2
Newland Ct B23 . . . . 56 C3
Newland Gdns B64. . . . . . 82 E7
Newland Gr DY2 . . . . 61 F7
Newland La CV7 . . . . 95 B7
Newland Rd
Birmingham B9 . . . . 67 F1
Coventry CV1. . . . . 113 D5
Royal Leamington Spa
CV32. . . . . 157 C3
Newlands Cl
Kidderminster DY11. . . . 116 C7
Stourbridge DY9 . . . . 99 C6
Willenhall WV13 . . . . 27 A1
Newlands Ct
Cannock WS12. . . . . 5 E8
Coventry CV3. . . . . 113 F2
Newlands Dr B62 . . . . 83 E7
Newlands Gn B66. . . . . . . 65 A4
Newlands La
Birmingham B37 . . . . 90 A6
Norton Canes WS12 . . . . . 5 D8
Newlands Rd
Bentley Heath B93. . . . . . 127 F4
Birmingham B30 . . . . 104 C2
Newlands The
Birmingham B34 . . . . 69 C7
Studley B80 . . . . 159 D3
New Landywood La WS6 . 13 E7
New Leasow B76. . . . . 58 A7
Newlyn Cl
Lichfield WS14. . . . . 9 D7
Nuneaton CV11 . . . . 73 F4
Newlyn Rd
Birmingham B31. . . . . . . 102 F3
Cradley Heath B64. . . . . . 82 D8
Newman Ave WV4 . . . . . . 39 F4
Newman Cl CV12. . . . . . . 78 B4
Newman College B32. 102 C8
Newman Coll of Higher Ed
B32. . . . . 102 C8
Newman Pl WV14. . . . . . . 40 F7
Newman Rd
Birmingham B24 . . . . 56 F4
Wednesbury DY4. . . . . 41 C6
Wolverhampton WV10. . . 12 A1
Newmans Cl B66. . . . . . . 65 C4
Newman Way B45 . . . . . 122 A6
Newmarket Cl
Coventry CV6. . . . . 96 B4
Wolverhampton WV6 . . . . 25 A5
Newmarket Rd WS11. . . . . 6 B4

New Market St B3 . . . . . 164 B3
Newmarket Way B36. . . . . 68 B7
Newmarsh Rd B76. . . . . . 58 A6
New Meadow Cl B31. . . . 103 B2
New Meadow Rd B98 . . . 154 B3
New Meeting St
Birmingham B4 . . . . 164 C2
Oldbury B69. . . . . 64 A8
New Mill La B78 . . . . 35 A7
New Mills St WS1. . . . . . . 42 D7
New Mill St DY2 . . . . 51 C1
Newmore Gdns WS5 . . . . 43 C5
New Moseley Rd B12. . . . . 87 A8
Newnham Gr B23 . . . . . . 56 E6
Newnham Ho B36. . . . . . . 70 B5
Newnham Rd
Birmingham B16 . . . . 65 C2
Coventry CV1. . . . . 113 F5
Royal Leamington Spa
CV32. . . . . 157 B3
Newnham Rise B90 . . . . 106 D3
NEW OSCOTT. 45 D2
New Oscott Prim Sch B73 45 C3
New Park Com Sch WV6 . 24 F5
New Penkridge Rd WS11 . 1 C1
New Plant La WS7 . . . . . . 6 C8
New Pool Rd B64 . . . . 82 B8
Newport B77. . . . . 21 F5
Newport Cl B97. . . . . 158 B6
Newport Rd
Birmingham, Balsall Heath
B12. . . . . 87 A4
Birmingham, Buckland End
B36. . . . . 68 F8
Coventry CV6. . . . . 95 D1
Newport St
图 Walsall WS1. . . . . 28 E1
Wolverhampton WV10 . . . 25 E4
Newquay Cl
Hinckley LE10 . . . . 71 E4
Nuneaton CV11 . . . . 73 F5
Walsall WS5. . . . . 43 E7
Newquay Rd WS5 . . . . . . 43 D7
New Railway St WV13 . . . 27 B2
New Rd
Aldridge WS9. . . . . 30 A5
Ash Green CV7 . . . . 95 B6
Astwood Bank B96 . . . . . 158 E1
Bedworth CV12 . . . . 77 A3
Birmingham B45 . . . . 121 F7
Bromsgrove B60 . . . . 137 A1
Bromsgrove, Sidemoor
B61. . . . . 136 E3
Brownhills WS8 . . . . 15 F7
Burntwood WS7. . . . . 7 B6
Coventry CV6. . . . . 94 F1
Dudley DY2 . . . . 62 C7
Fairfield B61 . . . . 120 E2
Halesowen B63 . . . . 83 B4
Hinckley LE10 . . . . 76 A6
Hollywood B47 . . . . 125 A8
Kidderminster DY10. . . . 116 E5
Shenstone WS14 . . . . 17 F6
Shuttington B79. . . . . 22 E8
Solihull B91 . . . . 107 D3
Stourbridge DY8 . . . . 81 A5
Studley B80 . . . . 159 E3
Tamworth B77 . . . . 35 F7
Tipton DY4 . . . . 52 D6
Water Orton B46. . . . . 59 B3
Willenhall WV13 . . . . 27 A1
Wolverhampton, Newbridge
WV6 . . . . 24 A1
Wolverhampton, Scotlands
WV10 . . . . 26 B8
New Row B78. . . . . 34 E5
New Rowley Rd DY2. . . . . 62 E7
New Shipton Cl B76. . . . . 46 F1
Newshire Ind Est B11 . . . 87 D6
Newsholme Cl 图 CV34 . 155 E1
New Spring St B18. . . . . . 66 A4
New Spring Street N B18 . 66 A4
New St
Bedworth CV12 . . . . 78 C2
Birchmoor B78. . . . . 36 E7
Birmingham B23 . . . . 57 A4
Birmingham, Castle Bromwich
B36. . . . . 69 E8
Birmingham, Digbeth B2. 164 C2
Birmingham, Erdington B23. 56 F5
Birmingham, Frankley B45 102 A1
Brierley Hill DY5 . . . . 82 A8
Bulkington CV12 . . . . 79 D2
Burntwood, Chase Terrace
WS7. . . . . 6 E8
Burntwood, Chasetown WS7. 6 E5
Cannock, Bridgtown WS11 . 4 E6
图 Cannock, Mill Green WS11 4 E8
Cannock WS12. . . . . 2 C4
Cubbington CV32 . . . . . . 157 E5
Darlaston WS10. . . . . 41 D6
Dudley, Lye End DY1. . . . . 51 D1
Dudley, Gornalwood DY3 . 50 C3
Essington WV11. . . . . 13 A3
Ettingshall WV2 . . . . 40 A6
Fazeley B78 . . . . 35 B8
Great Wyrley WS6 . . . . 5 A1
Hinckley LE10 . . . . 71 D1
Kenilworth CV8 . . . . 147 F6
Kingswinford DY6 . . . . . . 60 D8
Kingswinford, Wall Heath
DY6. . . . . 60 C8
Royal Leamington Spa
CV31. . . . . 162 A7
Stourbridge DY8 . . . . 80 E5
Stourbridge, Wordsley DY8 60 D2
Tamworth, Bolehall B77. . . 21 E4

New St continued
Tamworth, Mount Pleasant
B77 . . . . 21 C1
Tipton DY4 . . . . 51 F5
Walsall, Rushall WS4. . . . . 29 B7
Walsall, The Chuckery WS1 . 28 F1
Walsall, Wallington Heath
WS3 . . . . 14 B1
Walsall WS4. . . . . 15 D1
Warwick CV34 . . . . 160 E6
Wednesbury WS10 . . . . . 41 F1
West Bromwich, Hill Top
B70. . . . . 53 A7
West Bromwich, Mayer's Green
B70. . . . . 53 D3
Willenhall WV13 . . . . 26 E1
Wolverhampton, Merry Hill
WV3 . . . . 38 D7
Wolverhampton, Parkfield
WV4 . . . . 39 E6
Newstead B79 . . . . 20 D6
Newstead Ave LE10 . . . . . 75 D4
Newstead Cl CV11. . . . . . 73 F2
Newstead Rd B44. . . . . . . 45 B3
Newstead Way CV3 . . . . 115 B1
New Street N B71. . . . . . . 53 D3
New Street Sta B2. . . . . . 164 B2
New Summer St B19 . . . . 164 B4
New Swan La B70. . . . . . . 53 A5
New Swinford Hall DY9 . . 81 C4
NEWTON 54 C8
Newton Chambers 图
B2 . . . . 164 B2
Newton Cl
Birmingham B43 . . . . 43 C1
Coventry CV2. . . . . 114 F7
Redditch B98 . . . . 159 A6
Newton Gdns B43. . . . . . . 54 B8
Newton Gr 图 B29. . . . . . . 85 F2
Newton Ind Est B9. . . . . . 67 D3
Newton Manor Cl B43. . . 54 D8
Newton Park Mews 图
B43 . . . . 43 E1
Newton Pl
Birmingham B18 . . . . 66 A7
Walsall WS2. . . . . 28 B6
Newton Rd
Birmingham, Balsall Heath
B11. . . . . 87 B5
Birmingham, Newton B43 . 54 B8
Bromsgrove B60 . . . . 151 A7
Hinckley LE10 . . . . 74 E7
Knowle B93 . . . . 128 B7
Walsall WS2. . . . . 28 B5
West Bromwich B71 . . . . . 53 F6
Newton's Coll WS13. . . . . 9 B8
Newton Sq
Birmingham B43 . . . . 43 E1
Bromsgrove B60 . . . . 151 A7
Newton St
Birmingham B4 . . . . 164 C3
West Bromwich B71 . . . . . 53 E7
Newton Works B60 . . . . . 151 A6
NEWTOWN 14 B6
NEW TOWN
Birmingham 66 C6
Brownhills. 6 F2
Tipton. 52 D4
New Town
Brierley Hill DY5 . . . . 61 C4
Dudley DY2 . . . . 62 D1
Newtown B86. . . . . 66 C5
Newtown Dr B19. . . . . . . 66 C6
Newtown La
Cradley Heath B64. . . . . . 62 D1
Madeley Heath B62. . . . . 120 D8
Romsley B62 . . . . 101 D2
Newtown Middleway B6. 166 E5
Newtown Prim Sch B70 . . 52 D3
Newtown Rd
Bedworth CV12 . . . . 78 A2
Nuneaton CV11 . . . . 73 C5
NEW TOWN ROW. 164 C5
Newtown Row B6. . . . . . . 66 C5
Newtown Sh Ctr B19. . . . 66 C6
Newtown St B64. . . . . 62 D2
New Union St CV1 . . . . . 165 B2
New Village DY2 . . . . 62 D7
New Wharf Cotts B60 . . 152 B7
New Wlk 图 B97. . . . . . . 153 E4
New Wood Cl DY7. . . . . . . 80 C8
New Wood Dr B31. . . . . . 102 D1
New Wood Gr WS9. . . . . . 16 A3
New Wood La DY10 . . . . 118 B8
Ney Ct DY4 . . . . 51 F5
Niall Cl B15. . . . . 85 E8
Nibletts Hill B61. . . . . . . 136 B7
Nicholas Chamberlaine Tech
Coll CV12. . . . . 78 D3
Nicholas Cl CV12. . . . . . . 78 C3
Nicholas Rd B74. . . . . 44 E8
Nicholls Cl WV14 . . . . 40 B1
Nicholls Fold WV11 . . . . . 26 D5
Nicholls Rd WV11 . . . . . . 40 E1
Nicholls St
Coventry CV2. . . . . 113 F4
West Bromwich B70 . . . . . 53 E2
Nicholls Way WS12 . . . . . . 2 F1
Nichols Cl B92. . . . . 107 F1
Nicholson Cl CV34 . . . . . 155 F1
Nickson Rd CV4. . . . . 111 E1
Nigel Ave B31 . . . . 103 A5
Nigel Ct B16. . . . . 65 E1
Nigel Rd
Birmingham B8 . . . . 67 E6
Dudley DY1 . . . . 50 F3
Nightingale Ave B36. . . . . 70 A8

Nightingale Cl
Birmingham B23 . . . . 56 C7
Huntington WS12. . . . . 1 C7
Nightingale Cres
Brierley Hill DY5 . . . . 81 D7
Willenhall WV12 . . . . 27 C8
Nightingale Ct
Burntwood WS7. . . . . 7 F8
Royal Leamington Spa
CV31. . . . . 162 B8
Solihull B91 . . . . 107 C4
Nightingale Dr
Kidderminster DY10. . . . 117 B2
Tipton DY4 . . . . 52 C5
Nightingale La CV5 . . . . 132 E7
Nightingale Pl WV14 . . . . 40 D7
Nightingale Wlk
图 Birmingham B15. . . . . 86 C7
Burntwood WS7. . . . . 7 FE
Nightjar Gr B23. . . . . 56 C6
Nightjar Way WS11 . . . . . . 2 B3
Nighwood Dr B74. . . . . . . 44 F7
Nijon Cl B21. . . . . 54 D1
Nimbus B77 . . . . 35 D4
Nimmings Cl B31 . . . . . . 122 F6
Nimmings Rd B62. . . . . . . 63 D3
Nimmings Visitor Ctr★
B62. . . . . 100 B6
Nineacres Dr B37 . . . . . . 70 A3
Nine Days La B98. . . . . . 159 B6
Nine Elms La WV10 . . . . . 25 E4
Ninefoot La B77 . . . . 35 EB
Nine Leasows B66 . . . . . . 64 E7
Nine Locks Ridge DY5. . . 61 D2
Nine Pails Wlk 图 B70. . . 53 D1
Ninestiles Sch (Tech Coll)
B27 . . . . 88 B1
Nineveh Ave B21. . . . . . . 65 F7
Nineveh Rd B21. . . . . 65 F7
Ninfield Rd B27 . . . . 88 A4
Ninian Pk B77 . . . . 35 D6
Ninian Way B77. . . . . 35 E6
Ninian Way CV4 . . . . 1 C2
Nith Pl DY1. . . . . 51 B3
Niton Rd CV10 . . . . 73 D6
Niven Cl CV5 . . . . 112 A6
Noakes Ct WS10 . . . . 41 F7
Noble Cl CV34 . . . . 160 D5
Noble Way B6. . . . . 55 F2
Nocke Rd WV11 . . . . 12 F1
Nock St DY4 . . . . 52 C7
Noddy Park Rd WS9. . . . . 30 B7
Noddy Pk WS9. . . . . 30 B7
Node Hill B80. . . . . 159 D3
Node Hill Cl B80 . . . . . . 159 D3
Nod Rise CV5 . . . . 112 B3
Noel Ave B12. . . . . 87 A6
Noel Gr B97 . . . . 158 C8
Noele Gordon Gdns 回
WS1. . . . . 42 E8
Noel Rd B16. . . . . 65 F1
Nolan Cl CV6 . . . . 95 D4
Nolton Cl B43. . . . . 54 D8
No Name Rd WV7 . . . . 8 A5
Nonsuch Prim Sch B32. . 84 D2
Nooklands Croft B33. . . . 69 A2
Nook The
Brierley Hill DY5 . . . . 61 B5
Cheslyn Hay WS6. . . . . 4 C3
Nuneaton CV11 . . . . 73 E2
Noonan Cl B97. . . . . 153 B2
Noose Cres WV13 . . . . . . 26 E2
Noose La WV13 . . . . 26 E3
Nora Rd B11. . . . . 87 C3
Norbiton Rd B44 . . . . 56 A6
Norbreck Cl B43 . . . . 43 D3
Norbury Ave WS3. . . . . . . 15 A3
Norbury Cl B98 . . . . 154 B2
Norbury Cres WV4 . . . . . . 40 A4
Norbury Dr DY5. . . . . 61 D3
Norbury Gr B92. . . . . 89 A3
Norbury Rd
Bilston WV14 . . . . 40 F6
Birmingham B44 . . . . 44 F3
West Bromwich B70 . . . . . 53 A7
Wolverhampton WV10. . . 25 F6
Norcombe Gr B90. . . . . . 127 A5
Nordic Drift CV2 . . . . 115 A6
Nordley Rd WV11 . . . . 26 C5
Nordley Rd WV11 . . . . 26 C5
Norfolk Ave B71 . . . . 53 D7
Norfolk Cl
Birmingham B30 . . . . 104 B6
Hinckley LE10 . . . . 75 D4
Norfolk Cres
Aldridge WS9. . . . . 30 B8
Nuneaton CV10 . . . . 72 E4
Norfolk Ct
Birmingham B16 . . . . 65 D3
图 Birmingham, Selly Oak
B29. . . . . 103 C2
Norfolk Dr
Tamworth B78 . . . . 21 A1
Wednesbury WS10 . . . . . . 42 D4
Norfolk Gdns B75. . . . . . . 46 B7
Norfolk Gr WS6. . . . . 4 F1
Norfolk Ho
Birmingham, Short Heath
B23 . . . . 56 F5
Birmingham, Walker's Heath
B38. . . . . 123 E8
Norfolk House Sch B15 . . 85 D8
Norfolk New Rd WS2. . . . . 28 A4
Norfolk Pl WS2 . . . . 28 D5
Norfolk Rd
Birmingham, Brandhall
B68. . . . . 84 B2

Norfolk Rd continued
Birmingham, Chad Valley
B15.....................85 D8
Birmingham, Erdington B23. 56 F5
Birmingham, Frankley B45 101 F2
Dudley DY2 ....62 A7
Stourbridge DY8 ....80 D8
Sutton Coldfield B75 .....46 C7
Wolverhampton WV3 .....39 A8
Norfolk St
Coventry CV1.............113 B3
Royal Leamington Spa
CV32..................157 A1
Norfolk Twr B18 ....66 B5
Norgrave Rd B92 ....89 C2
Norlan Dr B14...........104 F3
Norland Rd B27 ....88 C1
Norley Gr B13 ....105 C7
Norman Ashman Coppice
CV3 ....135 C7
Norman Ave
Birmingham B32 ....84 E7
Coventry CV2.............96 F1
Nuneaton CV11 ....73 B4
Normanby Mdws CV31 . 162 A2
Norman CI B79 ....20 E7
Normandy CI CV35 ....160 A7
Normandy Rd B20 ....55 E1
Normandy Way LE10 .....71 C3
Norman Place Rd CV6.. 112 F7
Norman Rd
Birmingham B31 ....103 B3
Smethwick B67 ....64 E2
Walsall WS5..............43 D7
Normansell Twr B6 ....67 B8
Norman St
Birmingham B18 ....65 E5
Dudley DY2 ....62 E7
Normanton Ave B26......89 D5
Normanton Twr B23 ......57 A6
Normid Ct B13...........87 A4
Norrington Gr B31 ....102 C3
Norrington Rd B31.......102 D3
Norris Dr B33.............68 E3
Norris Rd B6 ....55 F1
Norris Way B75...........46 D5
Northampton St B18 .....66 C4
Northam Wlk WV6 ....25 B4
Northanger Rd B27 ....88 B2
North Ave
Bedworth CV12 ....78 D2
Birmingham B40 ....90 F5
Wolverhampton WV11....26 C6
North Birmingham Acad
B44....................56 B6
Northbourne Dr CV11.....78 F7
North Bromsgrove High Sch
B60....................137 B3
Northbrook Ct B90......106 C5
Northbrook Rd B90......106 D5
North Brook Rd CV6......112 D8
Northbrook St B16.......65 F4
North CI
Cubbington CV32.......157 E5
Hinckley LE10 ....75 E6
Northcliffe Hts DY11 ...116 C7
Northcote Rd B33........68 D4
Northcote St
7 Royal Leamington Spa
CV31..................162 B7
Walsall WS2.............28 D4
Northcott Rd
Bilston WV14............40 F4
Dudley DY2 ....62 D4
North Cres WV10 ....12 C7
Northcroft Way B23......56 B4
Northdale WV6 ....24 B4
Northdown Rd B91......106 F1
North Dr
Birmingham, Balsall Heath
B5.....................85 C4
Birmingham, Lozells B20.. 66 B8
Sutton Coldfield B75 ....46 C6
North East Worcestershire
Coll (Redditch Campus) ⬛
B98...................153 E4
Northey Rd CV6.........113 D8
NORTHFIELD.............103 B4
Northfield CI B98........154 D6
Northfield Gr WV3 ....38 C7
Northfield Manor Prim Sch
B29....................103 B7
Northfield Pool & Fitness Ctr
B31....................102 F3
Northfield Rd
Birmingham B17, B32 ....85 A3
Birmingham, King's Norton
B30...................103 E4
Coventry CV1............113 F2
Dudley DY2 ....62 D4
Hinckley LE10 ....75 C7
Northfield Road Prim Sch
DY2....................62 D5
Northfield Sh Ctr B31 ...103 A4
Northfield Sta B31.......103 A2
Northfields Way WS8 ...15 D7
Northfolk Terr CV4.......132 B7
Northgate
Aldridge WS9............30 A7
Cradley Heath B64.......82 D8
Warwick CV34...........160 E7
North Gate B17..........85 C7
Northgate CI
2 Dudley DY1..........51 B2
Kidderminster DY11.....116 A4
Northgate St CV34 .....160 E7

Northgate Way WS9.....30 A8
North Gn WV4 ....38 D6
North Holme B9 ....67 C2
Northicote Recn Ctr
WV10 ....11 E3
Northicote Sec Sch WV10 11 E3
Northland Rd B90........106 E1
Northlands Rd B13.......87 A1
Northleach Ave B14.....104 D2
Northleach CI B98 ......154 B5
North Leamington Com Sch
& Arts Coll CV32 ......156 F4
Northleigh Rd B8 ....68 A6
Northmead B33..........69 A2
Northmoor Ind Est ⬛
DY5....................61 D2
Northolt Dr B35..........58 A4
Northolt Gr B42..........43 F1
North Oval DY3 ....50 E5
Northover CI WV9.......11 A2
North Park Rd B23.......56 B3
North Pathway B17 .....85 B7
North Rd
Birmingham, Edgbaston
B29....................85 F3
Birmingham, Handsworth
B20....................55 E2
Birmingham, Harborne B17. 85 D6
Bromsgrove B60........137 A2
Tipton DY4..............52 B8
Wolverhampton, Dunstall Hill
WV1....................25 C4
Wolverhampton, Parkfield
WV4...................39 F5
North Roundhay B33.....69 A4
Northside Bsns Ctr B18 . 65 E5
Northside CI B98.........158 E7
Northside Dr B74........44 F8
North Solihull Sports Ctr
B37....................70 A3
North Springfield DY3.. 39 E1
North St
Brierley Hill DY5 ....61 C2
Cannock WS11 ....4 E6
Coventry CV2............114 B5
Dudley DY2 ....51 D1
Nuneaton CV10 ....72 F3
Smethwick B67 ....64 F5
Walsall WS2, WS4........28 E3
Wednesbury WS10 ......41 F3
Wolverhampton WV1.....163 B3
North Street Ind Est DY5 . 61 C2
Northumberland Ave
Kidderminster DY11.....116 D3
Nuneaton CV10 ....72 F3
Northumberland CI B78.. 21 A1
Northumberland Lodge
CV32..................156 F3
Northumberland Mews
CV32..................156 F3
Northumberland Pk
CV32..................156 F3
Northumberland Rd
Coventry CV1............113 A3
Royal Leamington Spa
CV32..................156 E2
Northumberland St B7.. 67 A3
Northvale CI CV8.......148 B6
North View CV2..........97 A1
North View Dr DY5.......61 E5
North Villiers St CV32 ...157 A1
North Walsall Prim Sch
WS2...................28 E4
North Warwickshire &
Hinckley Coll (Bedworth
Campus) CV12..........78 B3
North Warwickshire &
Hinckley Coll (Bermuda
Park Campus) CV10....78 A6
North Warwickshire &
Hinckley Coll (Hinckley
Campus) LE10 ....75 E8
North Warwickshire &
Hinckley Coll (Nuneaton
Campus) CV11..........73 E6
North Warwick St 1 B9.. 67 D1
Northway
Birmingham B40 ....90 F5
Sedgley DY3.............39 C2
Whitnash CV31 ....162 A5
North Western Arc B2.. 164 C3
North Western Rd B65 .. 63 A6
North Western Terr B18.. 65 F7
Northwick Cres B91.....107 B1
North Wlk B31...........103 C1
Northwood Ct B3 ....61 D2
Northwood Park CI WV10. 11 E3
Northwood Park Prim Sch
WV10 ....11 E3
Northwood Park Rd WV10 11 E3
Northwood St B3 ....164 B4
Northwood Way DY5.....81 B8
Northycote Farm & Cntry Pk*
WV10 ....11 F4
Northycote La WV10 ....11 F4
NORTON.................80 D2
NORTON CANES.........5 F6
Norton Canes Bsns Pk
WS11 ....6 A5
Norton Canes High Sch
WS11 ....6 A7
Norton Canes Prim Sch
WS11 ....6 A6
Norton CI
Birmingham B31 ....103 A3
Redditch B98 ....154 F2
Smethwick B66 ....65 C5
Tamworth B79 ....21 C7

Norton CI continued
Wolverhampton WV4......38 C3
Norton Cres
Bilston WV14............40 D1
Birmingham B9 ....68 B3
Dudley DY2 ....62 E3
Norton Dr
Warwick CV34...........155 E2
Wythall B47.............125 C4
NORTON EAST 6 A6
Norton East Rd WS11 ....6 B6
Norton Gate B38........103 F1
Norton Grange
Allesley CV5.............112 C6
Norton Canes WS11 .....5 F4
Norton Green La
Dordridge B93 ....128 C2
Norton Canes WS11 .....5 F4
Norton Hall La WS11 .....5 D4
Norton Hill Dr CV2 ......114 E6
Norton La
Burntwood WS7..........7 C6
Great Wyrley WS6 ....5 A4
Norton Canes WS12 .....5 A4
Tidbury Green B47, B90,
B94....................125 E3
Norton Lakeside Sta*
WS11 ....6 C6
Norton Mews B61.......137 A4
Norton Rd
Coleshill B46 ....70 F8
Kidderminster DY10.....117 B6
Norton Canes WS11, WS12.. 5 F8
Stourbridge DY8 ....80 E2
Walsall WS3.............15 A5
Norton Springs WS11 ....5 F5
Norton St
Birmingham B18 ....66 A6
Coventry CV1............165 C3
Norton Terr
Birmingham B30 ....104 B6
Norton Canes WS11 .....5 F6
Norton Twr B1...........66 C2
Norton View B14.........104 D7
Norton Wlk B23..........56 C3
Nortune CI B38 ....103 D2
Norwich CI
Lichfield WS13 ....3 C3
Nuneaton CV11 ....74 A8
Norwich Croft B37 ......69 F1
Norwich Dr
Birmingham B17 ....84 F8
Coventry CV3............133 B5
Norwich Rd
Dudley DY2 ....62 D2
Walsall WS2.............28 B1
Norwood Ave B64.......82 E7
Norwood CI LE10 ....71 E3
Norwood Gr
Birmingham B19 ....66 B7
Coventry CV6............92 E2
Norwood Ho
Birmingham B9 ....67 E2
Brierley Hill DY5 ....61 C3
Norwood Villas B16......65 F1
Nottingham Dr WV12.....27 C7
Nottingham New Rd WS2. 28 A5
Nottingham Way DY5 ....61 F2
Nova Croft CV5 ....111 C4
Nova Ct B43.............44 B1
Nova Lodge CV32 ....156 E3
Nova Scotia St B4......164 D3
Nowell St WS10..........41 E5
Nuffield Ho B36..........70 A8
Nuffield Rd
Coventry CV6............114 A7
Hinckley LE10 ....74 E7
Nugent Cl B6 ....66 E7
Nugent Gr B90..........126 D3
NUNEATON..............73 C6
Nuneaton Acad
Nuneaton CV10 ....72 D2
Nuneaton CV11 ....73 A5
Nuneaton Mus & Art Gall*
CV11...................73 C3
Nuneaton Rd
Bedworth CV12 ....78 B4
Bulkington CV12 ....79 B4
Nuneaton CV10 ....72 D8
Nuneaton Sta CV11 .....73 C5
Nunts La CV6.............95 B3
Nunts Park Ave CV6......95 B4
Nursery Ave
Aldridge WS9............30 B5
Birmingham B12 ....86 F5
Nursery CI
Birmingham B30 ....103 F5
Hinckley LE10 ....116 B8
West Hagley DY9.........99 A4
Nursery Dr B30 ....103 F5
Nursery Gdns
Hinckley LE10 ....75 E4
Solihull B90 ....125 E8
Stourbridge DY8 ....60 F1
Nursery Gr DY11 ....116 B8
Nursery La
Hopwas B78 ....20 B6
Sutton Coldfield B74 ....32 A2
Whitnash CV31 ....162 A5
Nursery Rd
Birmingham, Cotteridge
B30...................103 D5
Birmingham, Harborne B15. 85 B7
Birmingham, Lozells B19.. 66 C6
Walsall WS3.............28 B7

Nursery St WV1..........163 B4
Nursery The B29.........86 A1
Nursery View CI WS9....30 E2
Nursery Wlk WV6 ....24 D4
NURTON 23 A3
Nurton Bank WV6........23 A3
Nutbrook Ave CV4 .....111 E2
Nutbush Dr B31.........102 D6
Nutfield Wlk B32........84 F5
Nuthall La CV4...........104 F7
Nuthatch CI WS11........5 B8
Nuthatch Dr DY5........81 C7
NUTHURST.............143 C4
Nuthurst B75 ....47 B4
Nuthurst Dr WS11 ....4 F4
Nuthurst Gr
Birmingham B14 ....104 F2
Dorridge B93 ....128 A4
Nuthurst Grange Rd B94 143 C4
Nuthurst La B94 ....143 C5
Nuthurst Rd
Birmingham B31 ....122 F6
Kemps Green B94 ....143 A2
Nutley Dr DY4 ....52 D8
Nutmeg Gr WS1 ....29 A2
Nuttall Gr B21 ....65 C7
Nutt's La LE10 ....75 A7
Nymet B77 ....35 E8

0

O2 Acad* B1.............164 B1
Oakalls Ave B60 ....137 B2
Oak Apple Rd B61.......137 B8
Oak Ave
Birmingham B12 ....87 A5
Great Wyrley WS6 ....5 A1
Huntington WS12........1 D8
Walsall WS2.............27 E3
West Bromwich B70 .....53 B3
Oak Bank B18 ....66 A5
Oak Barn Rd B62........83 E8
Oak CI
Baginton CV8............133 F2
Bedworth CV12 ....78 C4
Birmingham B17 ....85 A6
Hinckley LE10 ....75 E5
Wednesbury DY4 ....41 A1
Oak Cottage Prim Sch
B91...................106 F6
Oak Cotts B14 ....105 C2
Oak Cres
Bilston B69..............52 B1
Walsall WS3.............28 D6
Oak Croft B37 ....69 E3
Oakcroft Rd B13 ....105 C7
Oak Ct
Coventry CV3............133 F7
Halesowen B63 ....82 F2
Oldbury B66.............64 C8
Sutton Coldfield B74 ....31 E5
Oak Dr B74..............31 A1
Oakdale CI
Brierley Hill DY5 ....61 A7
Oldbury B68.............64 A2
Oakdale Rd
Binley Woods CV3 ......135 C7
Birmingham B36 ....68 E2
Oldbury B68.............64 A2
Oakdale Trad Est DY6 ...49 E1
Oakdene CI WS6.........4 D2
Oakdene Cres CV10 .....73 D7
Oakdene Dr B45 ....138 C8
Oakdene Rd WS7 ....7 A6
Oakden Pl DY11.........116 C7
Oak Dr
Birmingham B23 ....56 C7
Hartshill CV10 ....72 A8
Mile Oak B78 ....20 C1
Oaken Dr
Solihull B91 ....106 F5
Willenhall WV12 ....27 E7
Oakenfield WS13 ....3 A2
Oaken Gdns WS7 ....7 A8
Oaken Grange WS6 .....4 F1
Oakenhayes Cres
Brownhills WS8 ....6 F1
Minworth B76 ....58 C5
Oakenhayes Dr WS8 .....6 F1
Oaken Pk WV8............10 A2
OAKENSHAW...........158 E6
Oakenshaw Rd
Redditch B98 ....154 A1
Solihull B90 ....106 D1
Oakeswell St WS10......42 A3
Oakeywell St DY2 ....54 E4
Oak Farm CI B76.........58 A7
Oak Farm Rd B30 ....103 C6
Oakfield Ave
9 Birmingham, Balsall Heath
B12....................87 A6
Birmingham, Sparkbrook
B11....................87 C6
Dudley DY1 ....51 B6
Kingswinford DY6 ....60 E5
Oakfield CI
Smethwick B66 ....65 C6
Stourbridge DY8 ....60 F1
Oakfield Ct 6 DY5 ......61 D2
Oakfield Dr
Birmingham B45 ....122 D4
Walsall WS3.............15 B5

Oakfield Ho
Coventry CV3...........115 A1
12 Royal Leamington Spa
CV32..................156 F2
Oakfield Rd
Birmingham, Balsall Heath
B12....................86 E5
Birmingham, Erdington B24. 56 F3
Birmingham, Selly Oak B29 . 86 B3
Codsall WV8.............10 C2
Coventry CV6............112 F5
Kidderminster DY11.....116 B5
Smethwick B66 ....65 C6
Stourbridge DY8 ....61 A1
Stourbridge, Wollescote
DY9....................81 F2
Oakfields Way B91......108 B5
Oakford Dr CV5..........111 C6
Oak Gn
Dudley DY1 ....51 A5
Wolverhampton WV6 ....24 B3
Oak Gr
Birmingham B31 ....102 C1
Kidderminster DY10.....117 A5
Oak Green Way B68.....64 A4
Oakhall Dr B93 ....127 F4
OAKHAM 63 A8
Oakham Ave DY2 ....62 E7
Oakham CI B98 ....159 A5
Oakham Cres
Bulkington CV12 ....79 D2
Dudley DY2 ....62 E7
Oakham Ct 9 DY2 ......62 E8
Oakham Dr DY2 ....62 E8
Oakham Prim Sch B69 .. 63 B7
Oakham Rd
Birmingham B17 ....85 B7
Dudley DY2 ....62 F7
Oldbury B69.............63 A7
Oakham Way B92 ....89 A1
Oak Hill WV3 ....24 C1
Oakhill Ave DY10........116 E4
Oakhill CI B17 ....85 B8
Oakhill Cres B27 ....106 B8
Oakhill Dr DY5..........81 B7
Oak Hill Dr B15 ....85 E7
Oakhill Fst Sch B98 ....154 A2
Oakhill Prim Sch B77 ...21 F2
Oakhill Rd WS11.........1 F2
Oak La
Great Wyrley WS6 ....5 A1
Sutton Coldfield B74 ....31 B5
7 Warwick CV34 ......161 D8
Oak House Mus The*
B70....................53 B2
Oakhurst WS14 ....9 C7
Oakhurst Dr B60.........137 A3
Oakhurst Rd
Birmingham B27 ....106 B8
Sutton Coldfield B72 ....57 C8
Oak Ind Pk The DY6 .....49 E1
Oakington Dr B35........58 A3
Oak La
Barston B92.............109 B2
Harvest Hill CV5 ....93 E1
Kingswinford DY6 ....50 A1
West Bromwich B70 .....53 B3
Oakland CI B77 ....107 E4
Oakland Dr B23..........21 A5
Oakland Gr B93 ....50 B2
Oakland Rd DY3.........137 B4
Oakland Ho B74 ....32 A4
Oakland Rd
Birmingham, Handsworth
B21....................65 E8
Birmingham, Moseley B13.. 87 A3
Walsall WS3.............28 E7
Oaklands
Birmingham B62 ....84 A4
Birmingham, Northfield
B31....................102 F4
Curdworth B76 ....59 B6
Oaklands Ave B17.......85 A5
Oaklands CI WS12........1 C6
Oaklands Croft B76 .....58 B7
Oaklands Ct
Bromsgrove B61........150 D6
Kidderminster DY10.....117 A7
Oaklands Dr B20.........54 F2
Oaklands Gn WV14......40 D8
Oaklands Ind Est WS12... 2 B3
Oaklands Prim Sch The
B27....................88 C2
Oaklands Rd
Sutton Coldfield B74 ....46 B8
Wolverhampton WV3 ....39 B8
Oaklands Sch B26 ....88 F7
Oaklands The
Birmingham B37 ....90 A7
Coventry CV4............112 A2
Halesowen B62 ....83 F6
Kidderminster DY10.....117 A7
Oaklands Way
Birmingham B31 ....102 C1
Walsall WS3.............15 B3
Oaklea Dr B64...........62 F2
Oakleaf CI B32..........84 C2
Oak Leasow B32.........84 B4
Oakleigh B31...........103 C2
Oakleigh Ct 8 WV3 .....25 B2

Oakleigh Dr
Codsall WV8. . . . . 10 A3
Sedgley DY3. . . . . 50 C7
Oakleigh Rd DY8. . . . . 81 B2
Oakleighs DY8. . . . . 60 C1
Oakleigh Trad Est WV14 . . . 40 B2
Oakleigh Wlk DY6. . . . . 60 E8
Oakley CV8 . . . . 129 F1
Oakley Ave
Aldridge WS9. . . . . 30 A5
Tipton DY4. . . . . 52 A6
Oakley Cl WS13 . . . . 3 B2
Oakley Ct
Bedworth CV12 . . . . 77 D1
Birmingham B15 . . . . 85 E5
Oakley Gr WV4 . . . . 38 D5
Oakley Ho
Bromsgrove B60 . . . . 137 A1
Smethwick B66 . . . . 65 C6
Oakley Rd
Birmingham, Sparkbrook
B10. 87 C7
Birmingham, Stirchley B30 104 B5
Wolverhampton WV4 . . . . . . 38 D5
Oak Leys WV3 . . . . 24 C1
Oakley Wood Dr B91. . . . . . 107 E4
Oakley Wood Rd CV33. . . . 161 F1
Oakly Rd B97 . . . . 153 D3
Oakmeadow Ave B24. . . . . . . 57 D3
Oakmeadow Cl
Birmingham, Acock's Green B26,
B27. . . . . 88 D4
Birmingham, Tile Cross B33 69 D3
Oak Meadow Prim Sch
WV11 . . . . 27 A7
Oakmeadow Way B24 . . . . . . 57 D3
Oakmoor Pl WV9. . . . . 30 F2
Oakmoor Rd CV6. . . . . 96 A4
Oakmount Cl WS3 . . . . 14 F3
Oakmount Rd B24. . . . . 45 A7
Oak Park Ct
Stourbridge DY8 . . . . 60 F1
🖪 Sutton Coldfield B74 . . . . 31 E3
Oak Park L Ctr WS9 . . . . 15 F4
Oak Park Rd DY8. . . . . 60 F1
Oak Rd
Birmingham B68 . . . . 84 C7
Brownhills WS9. . . . . 16 A3
Catshill B61 . . . . 137 B8
Dudley DY1. . . . . 51 C3
Tipton DY4. . . . . 51 E6
Walsall, Pelsall Wood WS3 . 14 F5
Walsall WS4. . . . . 15 C1
West Bromwich B70 . . . . 53 B2
Willenhall WV13 . . . . 26 E2
Oak Ridge CV9. . . . . 36 E1
Oakridge Cl
Redditch B98 . . . . 154 C2
Willenhall WV12 . . . . 27 C4
Oakridge Dr
Cheslyn Hay WS6. . . . . 4 E2
Willenhall WV12 . . . . 27 C4
Oakridge Rd
Birmingham B31 . . . . 103 D2
Royal Leamington Spa
CV32. . . . . 157 C4
Oak Rise B46. . . . . 70 F5
Oakroyd Cres CV10. . . . . 72 D7
Oaks Cres WV3 . . . . 25 A1
Oaks Dr
Cannock WS11. . . . . 1 C1
Featherstone WV10. . . . . 11 F8
Wolverhampton WV3. . . . . . . 25 B2
Wombourne WV5. . . . . 49 A5
Oakslade Dr B92. . . . . 107 E8
Oaks Pl CV6. . . . . 96 A3
Oaks Prec CV8. . . . . 147 E3
Oaks Prim Sch The B14 . 104 D2
Oaks Rd CV8. . . . . 147 E2
Oak St
Brierley Hill DY5 . . . . 61 F1
Cradley Heath B64. . . . . 62 B1
Dudley, Darby End DY2 . . . . 62 E4
Dudley, West Coseley DY1,
WV14 . . . . 51 B7
Kingswinford DY6 . . . . 60 D6
Wolverhampton WV3. . . . . . . 25 A1
Oaks The
Bedworth CV12 . . . . 77 F2
Birmingham B34 . . . . 69 B7
Birmingham, Hawkesley
B38. . . . . 123 F7
Portway B47 . . . . 140 F8
Redditch B98 . . . . 158 F7
Royal Leamington Spa
CV32. . . . . 161 D8
Smethwick B67 . . . . 64 F5
Sutton Coldfield B76 . . . . . . 47 A3
Walsall WS3. . . . . 14 A1
Wolverhampton, Merridale
WV3 . . . . 25 A2
Wolverhampton WV11. . . . . . 26 B5
Oak Street Trad Est B62 D1
Oak Street Trad Est DY5 . 61 F1
Oakthorpe Dr B37. . . . . 69 F5
Oakthorpe Gdns B69. . . . . . . 52 A2
Oak Tree Ave
Coventry CV4. . . . . 133 A6
Redditch B97 . . . . 153 B4
Oaktree Cl B48 . . . . 139 A7
Oak Tree Cl
Bentley Heath B93. . . . . 127 E4
Royal Leamington Spa
CV32. . . . . 157 A2
Oak Tree Cres B62. . . . . 83 F6

Oak Tree Ct
Birmingham B28 . . . . 106 A5
Royal Leamington Spa
CV32. . . . . 157 A2
Oaktree Farm Mobile Homes
Pk B94. . . . . 141 B7
Oak Tree Gdns
Birmingham B28 . . . . 105 E3
🖪 Stourbridge DY8. . . . . 61 A1
Oak Tree Ho B30. . . . . 103 E7
Oak Tree La
Birmingham B29 . . . . 85 E1
Hollywood B47. . . . . 125 B6
Sambourne B96. . . . . 159 B2
Oak Tree Pk B98 . . . . 154 F6
Oaktree Rd WS10 . . . . 42 B3
Oak Tree Rd
Birmingham B8 . . . . 67 D6
Coventry CV3. . . . . 135 A7
Oak Trees B47. . . . . 125 A7
Oak Tree Wlk B79. . . . . 20 F7
Oak Turn Dr B38. . . . . 123 D8
Oak View WS2. . . . . 27 E3
Oak Way
Coventry CV4. . . . . 111 D2
Sutton Coldfield B76 . . . . . . 46 F2
Oak Wlk The B31 . . . . 103 A1
Oakwood & Blacklow
Spinney Nature Reserve★
CV34. . . . . 156 A1
Oakwood Cl
Brownhills WS9 . . . . 15 E4
Essington WV11. . . . . 13 B3
Hollywood B47. . . . . 18 A6
Oakwood Cres DY2. . . . . 61 F6
Oakwood Croft B91 . . . . 107 C1
Oakwood Ct B63. . . . . 83 A4
Oakwood Dr
Birmingham B14 . . . . 104 D4
Sutton Coldfield B74 . . . . . . 44 E8
Oakwood Gr CV34. . . . . 156 A1
Oak Wood Prim & Sec Sch
CV11. . . . . 73 D1
Oakwood Rd
Birmingham B11 . . . . 87 C3
Hollywood B47. . . . . 125 A6
Smethwick B67 . . . . 64 F4
Sutton Coldfield B73 . . . . . . 45 E1
Walsall WS3. . . . . 28 E7
Oakwoods WS11. . . . . 4 D8
Oakwood Specl Sch WS9. 16 A3
Oakworth Cl CV2. . . . . 115 A7
Oasis The DY9 . . . . 98 F5
Oast Ho B8 . . . . 68 D4
Oasthouse Cl
Kingswinford DY6 . . . . 60 A7
Stoke Heath B60 . . . . 150 D6
Oaston Rd
Birmingham B36 . . . . 69 D8
Nuneaton CV11. . . . . 73 D4
Oatfield Cl WS7. . . . . 7 A4
Oatlands Cl CV4. . . . . 95 C4
Oatlands Way WV6. . . . . 23 D3
Oatlands Wlk 🖪 B14. . . . . . 104 C2
Oatmill Cl WS10 . . . . 41 E5
Oban Dr CV10. . . . . 73 A2
Oban Rd
Coventry CV6. . . . . 95 F5
Hinckley LE10 . . . . 75 A7
Solihull B92 . . . . 88 F1
Oberon Cl
Birmingham B45 . . . . 102 A2
Nuneaton CV11. . . . . 74 A1
Royal Leamington Spa
CV34. . . . . 161 E4
Oberon Dr B90. . . . . 106 B1
Oberon Gr WS10 . . . . 27 E1
Occupation Rd
Brownhills WS9 . . . . 16 A4
Coventry CV2. . . . . 114 C3
Occupation St DY1. . . . . 51 A2
Ocean Dr WS10 . . . . 41 E1
Ockam Croft B31 . . . . 103 C2
OCKER HILL 52 C8
Ocker Hill Inf Sch DY4 . . 52 C8
Ocker Hill Jun Sch DY4 . 41 C1
Ocker Hill Rd DY4. . . . . 52 C8
O'Connor Dr DY4 . . . . 41 C1
Oddicombe Croft CV3 . . . . 133 D6
Oddingley Ct B23 . . . . 56 C3
Oddingley Rd B31. . . . . 103 C2
Odell Cres WS3 . . . . 28 C7
Odell Pl B5 . . . . 86 C5
Odell Rd WS3. . . . . 28 B7
Odell Way WS3 . . . . 28 B7
Odensil Gn B92. . . . . 89 B2
Odiham Cl B79. . . . . 21 C7
Odin Cl WS11 . . . . 2 A5
Odnall La DY9 . . . . 99 F3
Odstone Dr LE10. . . . . 74 F8
Offa Dr CV8. . . . . 148 A4
Offadrive B79. . . . . 21 B5
Offa Rd CV31. . . . . 162 B5
Offa's Dr WV6 . . . . 23 E5
Offa St B79. . . . . 21 B5
Offchurch La CV31. . . . . 162 F6
Offchurch Rd CV32. . . . . 157 E4
Offenham Cl B98. . . . . 154 B6
Offenham Covert B38 . . . . 123 E8
Offini Cl B70. . . . . 53 F2
Offlow Mews DY4. . . . . 40 F1
Offmoor Rd B32 . . . . 102 B8
Offmore Cl DY10. . . . . 117 C6
OFFMORE FARM 117 A6
Offmore Farm Cl DY10 . . 117 C6
Offmore La DY10. . . . . 117 B6
Offmore Prim Sch DY10 . 117 B6

Offmore Rd DY10 . . . . 116 F6
Offwell Rd B98 . . . . 154 D1
Ogbury Cl B14. . . . . 104 C2
Ogley Cres WS8. . . . . 16 A7
Ogley Dr B75. . . . . 47 A5
Ogley Hay Rd
Burntwood, Gorstey Ley
WS7 . . . . 7 B8
Burntwood, Triangle WS7,
WS8 . . . . 7 A3
Ogley Rd WS8 . . . . 16 A7
Ogley Vale WS7. . . . . 7 B8
O'Hare Ho WS4 . . . . 28 E3
O'Keeffe Cl B11. . . . . 87 B6
Okeford Way CV10 . . . . 73 A1
Okehampton Dr B71. . . . . . . 53 C6
Okehampton Rd CV3 . . . . . 133 E5
Okement Dr WV11. . . . . 26 C5
Oken Ct CV34. . . . . 160 D7
Oken Rd CV34. . . . . 160 D8
Olaf Pl CV2. . . . . 115 A7
Old Abbey Gdns B17 . . . . . 85 D4
Oldacre Cl B76 . . . . 57 D6
Oldacre Rd B68. . . . . 84 A7
Oldany Way CV10 . . . . 72 F2
Old Bakery Ct DY9 . . . . 99 A5
Old Bank Pl B72. . . . . 46 C5
Old Bank Top B31. . . . . 103 B2
Old Barn Rd
Birmingham B30 . . . . 103 D6
Stourbridge DY8 . . . . 61 A1
Old Beeches B23. . . . . 56 C8
Old Bell Rd B23 . . . . 57 A6
Oldberrow Cl 🖪 B90. . . . . . 127 A6
Old Birchills WS2 . . . . 28 C3
Old Birmingham Rd
Alvechurch B48 . . . . 139 B8
Catshill B60 . . . . 137 C8
Lower Marlbrook B60, B45 121 E1
Old Bridge St B19. . . . . 66 C6
Old Bridge Wlk B65. . . . . . . 62 F5
Old Bromford La B8. . . . . . . 68 C6
Old Brookside B33. . . . . 68 E2
Old Budbrooke Rd CV35. 160 A8
Old Burcot La B60 . . . . 137 C4
OLDBURY 63 F6
Oldbury Bsns Ctr B68. . . . 64 A2
Oldbury Cl B98 . . . . 154 B6
Oldbury Coll of Sport
Oldbury B68. . . . . 64 A2
Oldbury B68. . . . . 64 C4
Oldbury Ct B79 . . . . 21 B5
Oldbury Green Ret Pk
B69. . . . . 63 F8
Oldbury L Ctr B69. . . . . . . 63 D7
Oldbury Rd
Hartshill CV10 . . . . 72 A8
Rowley Regis B65 . . . . 63 D2
Smethwick B66 . . . . 64 D7
West Bromwich B70 . . . . 52 F2
Oldbury Ringway B69 . . . . 63 F8
Oldbury Road Ind Est
Smethwick B66. . . . . 64 D7
West Bromwich B70 . . . . 52 F2
Oldbury St WS10. . . . . 42 B3
Old Bush St DY5. . . . . 61 E3
Old Bush Trad Est DY5. . . 61 E3
Old Camp Hill B12 . . . . 87 A8
Old Canal Wlk 🖪 DY4 . . . . 52 B5
Old Castle Gr WS8 . . . . 6 F2
Old Chapel Rd B67. . . . . 64 F3
Old Chapel Wlk B68. . . . . . . 64 A4
Old Chester Road S
DY10. . . . . 116 E2
Old Church CE Prim Sch 🖪
WS10 . . . . 41 C6
Old Church Ct 🖪 B17 . . . . . . 85 B5
Old Church Gn B33. . . . . 68 E2
Old Church Rd
Birmingham B17 . . . . 85 B4
Coventry CV6. . . . . 96 A1
Water Orton B46. . . . . 59 B3
Old Coll Dr WS10 . . . . 42 A1
Old Crescent Ct 🖪 B68. . . . 84 B8
Old Crest Ave B98. . . . . 153 E2
Old Croft La
Birmingham B34 . . . . 69 C7
Birmingham, Castle Bromwich
B36. . . . . 69 B7
Old Cross St DY4. . . . . 51 E5
Old Crown Cl B32. . . . . 84 B1
Old Crown Mews CV2. . . . . . 96 D5
Old Damson La B92. . . . . 90 A2
Old Dickens Heath Rd
B90. . . . . 126 A5
OLD DOCK 62 B8
Old Dominion Wks WV1. . 40 A7
Olde Hall La WS6. . . . . 4 F3
Olde Hall Rd WV10. . . . . 12 C7
Old End La WV14. . . . . 51 C7
OLD FALLINGS 25 F8
Old Fallings Cres WS11. . . 25 F6
Old Fallings La WV10. . . . . . 25 F8
OLDFALLOW 1 D3
Old Fallow Ave WS11. . . . . . . 1 E3
Old Fallow Rd WS11. . . . . 1 E3
Old Falls Cl WS6 . . . . 4 D3
Old Farm Dr WV8 . . . . 10 A4
Old Farm Rd B14. . . . . 105 D5
Old Farm Mdw WV3. . . . . 38 C8
Old Farm Rd B33. . . . . 68 E4
Oldfield Dr DY8. . . . . 81 A3
Oldfield Rd
Birmingham B12 . . . . 87 A6
Coventry CV5. . . . . 112 C3
Dudley WV14. . . . . 51 A8

Oldfields
Cradley Heath B64. . . . . 82 D8
West Hagley DY9. . . . . 99 B6
Oldfield Trad Est B64. . . . 82 D8
Old Fire Sta The B17 . . . . . . 85 D6
Old Flour Mills 🖪 B70. . . . . 53 C2
Old Foxdrove B76. . . . . 46 B5
Old Forest Way B34 . . . . 69 B6
Old Forge Bsns Ctr B98. 159 C8
Old Forge Cl WS11. . . . . 42 F8
Old Forge Dr B98. . . . . 159 C8
Old Forge Trad Est DY9. . 81 E6
Old Grange Rd B11. . . . . 87 C4
Old Green La CV8 . . . . 129 C1
Old Grove Gdns DY9 . . . . . . 81 D3
Old Hall Cl DY8 . . . . 81 A8
Old Hall Ct WS9. . . . . 44 A5
Old Hall Gdns B90 . . . . 126 F7
Old Hall Ind Est WS3 . . . 28 A6
Old Hall La
Norton Canes WS11, WS12. . 5 B7
Walsall WS9. . . . . 44 B5
Old Hall Specl Sch WS3 . 27 E5
Old Ham La DY9. . . . . 81 D2
Old Hampton La WV11 . . . . 12 B2
Old Hawne La B63. . . . . 83 A5
Old Heath Cres WV1 . . . . . . 26 A1
Old Heath Rd WV1 . . . . 26 A2
Old Hedging La B77. . . . . . . 35 D5
Old Hednesford Rd WS11. . 2 A3
Old High St DY5. . . . . 61 F1
OLD HILL 62 F1
Old Hill WV6. . . . . 24 D5
Old Hill Prim Sch 🖪 B64 . 62 F1
Old Hill Sta B64. . . . . 83 A8
Old Hinckley Rd CV10 . . . . . 73 D5
Old Hobicus La B68. . . . . . . 64 B5
Old Horns Cres B43, B44. . 44 C2
Oldhouse Farm Cl B28 . . 105 F6
Old House La
Hawkes End CV7 . . . . 94 A7
Romsley B62 . . . . 101 B1
Oldington Gr B91. . . . . 127 B8
Oldington Trad Est DY11. 116 B1
Old Kingsbury Rd B76. . . 58 C5
Old Know Ct B10. . . . . 87 E7
Oldknow Jun Sch B10. . . 87 E7
Oldknow Rd B10. . . . . 87 E7
Old La
Featherstone WV10. . . . . 12 C7
Rowney Green B48. . . . . 140 D4
Walsall WS3. . . . . 28 C8
Wolverhampton WV6. . . . . . . 24 A5
Old Landywood La WS6. . . . 13 D7
Old Langley Hall B75. . . . . . 47 C4
Old Level Way DY2. . . . . 62 D4
Old Lime Gdns B38. . . . . . . 123 E8
Old Lindens Cl B74. . . . . 44 E7
Old Lode La B92. . . . . 89 C3
Old London Rd WS14. . . . . . . 9 D1
Old Manor Cl B78. . . . . 34 E5
Old Manor Flats WV6. . . . . . 24 D5
Old Masters Cl WS1. . . . . . . 29 A1
Old Meadow Rd B31. . . . . . 123 C7
Old Meadow La WV11. . . . . . 51 C8
Old Meeting St B70. . . . . 53 B5
Old Meeting Yd 🖪 CV12. . . 78 B3
Old Mill Ave CV4. . . . . 132 D5
Old Mill Cl B90 . . . . 105 D2
Old Mill Gdns
Birmingham B33 . . . . 68 E2
Walsall WS4. . . . . 15 C2
Old Mill Gr B20. . . . . 55 C2
Old Mill House Cl WS4 . . . . 15 B1
Old Mill Rd B46. . . . . 70 F7
OLD MILVERTON 156 B3
Old Milverton Ct CV32. . 156 E5
Old Milverton La CV32. . 156 C5
Old Milverton Rd CV32. . 156 C2
Old Moat Dr B31. . . . . 103 B3
Old Moat Way B8. . . . . 68 B6
Oldnall Cl DY9 . . . . 81 F4
Oldnall Rd
Kidderminster DY10. . . . . . . 117 A4
Stourbridge B63, DY9 . . . . . 82 A4
Old Oak Cl WS9. . . . . 30 B8
Old Oak Rd B38. . . . . 104 A2
OLD OSCOTT 44 F2
Old Oscott Hill B44. . . . . . . 44 F2
Old Oscott La B44. . . . . 55 E8
Old Park Cl B6. . . . . 66 F3
Old Park La B69 . . . . 64 A5
Old Park Prim Sch W10 . 41 E5
Old Park Rd
Darlaston WS10. . . . . 41 E5
Dudley DY1. . . . . 51 A5
Old Park Special Sch DY1 61 F8
Old Park Trad Est WS10 . 41 E6
Old Park Wlk B6. . . . . 66 E7
Old Penkridge Mews WS11 1 D1
Old Penkridge Rd WS11. . . . 1 C2
Old Penns La B46. . . . . 70 F7
Old Penn's Yd 🖪 CV12. . . . . 78 A2
OLD PERTON 23 B2
Old Pk B29 . . . . 103 A6
Old Pl WS3 . . . . 28 C8
Old Pleck Rd WS2. . . . . 42 C7
Old Port Cl DY4. . . . . 52 B2
Old Portway B38 . . . . 123 E7
Old Postway B19. . . . . 66 D7
Old Quarry Cl B45. . . . . 121 F8
Old Quarry Dr DY3 . . . . 50 D5
Old Rd CV7. . . . . 92 F8
Old Rectory Gdns WS9 . . . 30 C6
Old Rectory La B48 . . . . 139 B7
Old School Cl WV13. . . . . . . 27 A2

Old School Dr 🖪 B65. . . . . . 63 C3
Old School Mews CV32. . 157 B3
Old School Wlk B79. . . . . . . 21 B6
Old School Yd The B77. . . . 22 A5
Old Scott Cl B33 . . . . 69 C2
Old Smithy Pl B18 . . . . 66 A5
Old Snow Hill B3 . . . . 164 B4
Old Sq
Birmingham B4 . . . . 164 C3
Warwick CV34 . . . . 160 E6
Old Square Sh Ctr 🖪
WS1. . . . . 28 E1
Old Stables Wlk 🖪 B7. . . . . 67 C7
Old Stafford Rd WV10. . . . . 11 C8
Old Station Rd
Birmingham B33 . . . . 68 D4
Bromsgrove B60 . . . . 137 A1
Hampton-in-A B92. . . . . 109 A8
Old Stone Cl B45. . . . . 101 F1
Old Stone Yd CV32 . . . . 156 E1
Old Stowheath La WV1. . . . 26 C1
Old Stratford Rd B60. . . . . 137 C2
OLD SWINFORD 81 A2
Oldswinford CE Prim Sch 🖪
DY8. . . . . 81 A3
Old Swinford Hospital Sch
DY8. . . . . 81 A4
Old Tokengate 🖪 B17. . . . . . 85 D6
Old Town Cl B38. . . . . 103 F2
Old Town La WS3 . . . . 14 F3
Old Union Mill B16. . . . . 66 B2
Old Vicarage Cl
Walsall WS3. . . . . 15 A2
Wolverhampton WV5. . . . . . . 49 B7
Old Vicarage Gdns B80. . . 159 E4
Old Walsall Rd B42. . . . . 54 F7
Old Warstone La WV11. . . . 13 B8
Old Warwick Ct 🖪 B92. . . . 88 E1
Old Warwick Rd
Solihull B91 . . . . 106 E3
Royal Leamington Spa
CV31. . . . . 161 E7
Solihull B92 . . . . 88 E1
Old Waste La CV7 . . . . 130 E6
Oldway Dr B91. . . . . 107 E2
Old Well Cl WV4 . . . . 29 B7
Old Wharf Rd DY8. . . . . 80 F6
OLDWICH LANE 129 C1
Oldwich Lane E
Balsall Common CV8 . . . . . 129 D1
Honiley CV8. . . . . 145 E8
Oldwich Lane W B93. . . . . . 145 C8
Old Winnings Rd CV7 . . . . . 94 F6
Old Woodyard The DY9. . . . 99 D6
Old Yd The CV2 . . . . 114 F7
Olga Dr DY4 . . . . 41 B1
Olinthus Ave WV11. . . . . 26 E7
Olive Ave
Coventry CV2. . . . . 114 D5
Wolverhampton WV4 . . . . . . 39 E5
Olive Dr B62. . . . . 83 C8
Olive Hill Prim Sch B62 . 83 D7
Olive Hill Rd B62. . . . . 83 D8
Olive La B62. . . . . 83 D8
Olive Mount B69 . . . . 63 D8
Olive Pl B14. . . . . 104 E7
Oliver Cl 🖪 DY2 . . . . 62 E8
Oliver Cres WV14 . . . . 40 F2
Oliver Ct B65 . . . . 63 B2
Oliver Rd
Birmingham, Erdington
B23. . . . . 56 F6
Birmingham, Ladywood B16 65 F2
Smethwick B66 . . . . 65 C3
Oliver St
Birmingham B7 . . . . 67 B5
Coventry CV6. . . . . 113 F6
Olivier Way CV2 . . . . 115 B8
Ollerton Rd B26. . . . . 88 F7
Ollison Dr B74. . . . . 30 F2
Olliver Cl B62. . . . . 84 A3
Olorenshaw Rd B26. . . . . 89 D5
OLTON 88 F1
Olton Ave CV5 . . . . 111 E4
Olton Boulevard E B27. . . . 88 C2
Olton Boulevard W B11 . . . 87 F3
Olton Bridge B92. . . . . 106 F8
Olton Croft B27. . . . . 88 D2
Olton Mere B92. . . . . 88 E1
Olton Pl CV11. . . . . 72 F4
Olton Rd B90. . . . . 106 B5
Olton Sta B92. . . . . 88 E1
Olympus Ave CV34 . . . . 161 D5
Olympus Cl CV5. . . . . 111 B8
Olympus Dr DY4 . . . . 52 D6
Omar Rd CV2 . . . . 114 D2
Ombersley Cl
Oldbury B69. . . . . 63 D5
Redditch B98 . . . . 159 C7
Ombersley Rd
Birmingham B12 . . . . 87 A6
Halesowen B63 . . . . 82 F2
Ombersley Way 🖪 B31. . . . 103 D2
One Stop Sh Ctr B42. . . . 55 D3
Onibury Rd B21. . . . . 54 D1
Onley Terr CV4. . . . . 132 C7
Onslow Cres B92. . . . . 89 A1
Onslow Croft CV32. . . . . . . 156 F2
Onslow Rd B11. . . . . 88 A4
Ontario Cl B38. . . . . 124 A8
Oozells Sq B1 . . . . 66 B2
Oozells St B1. . . . . 66 C2
Oozells Street N B1. . . . . . . 66 B2
Open Field B33. . . . . 103 C2
Openfield Croft B46. . . . . . . 59 C2
Open Univ B7. . . . . 85 D6
Ophelia Dr CV34. . . . . 161 E3
Ophelia Gdns WV10 . . . . 25 E6

Orangery The DY9 . . . . 99 D7
Oratory Dr CV3 . . . . 134 C6
Oratory Rd CV3 Prim Sch B16 65 F2
Orbital Ret Ctr WS11 . . . . . . 4 F6
Orbital Way WS11 . . . . 4 F6

Orion Cl
  Birmingham B8 . . . . 68 B4
  Great Wyrley WS6 . . . . 4 F1
Orion Cres CV2 . . . . 96 E2
Orion Way WS11 . . . . 1 F5
Orkney Ave B34 . . . . 68 F7
Orkney Cl
  Hinckley LE10 . . . . 71 C1
  Nuneaton CV10 . . . . 73 A2
Orkney Croft B36 . . . . 70 B7
Orkney Dr B77 . . . . 35 F7
Orlando Cl WS1 . . . . 42 E8
Orlando Ho ⁴ WS1 . . . . 42 E8
Orlescote Rd CV4 . . . . . 132 E6
Ormande Cl B63 . . . . 82 B7
Orme Cl DY5 . . . . 81 B8
Ormes La WV6 . . . . 24 C3
Ormiston Sandwell Com
  Acad B69 . . . . 52 C1
Ormond Pl WV14 . . . . 40 F6
Ormond Rd B45 . . . . . 101 F1
Ormonds Cl WS13 . . . . 8 E6
Ormsby Gr B27 . . . . . 106 B7
Ormscliffe Rd B45 . . . . . 122 B6
Orphanage Rd B24 . . . . 57 B6
Orpington Dr CV6 . . . . 95 D4
Orpington Rd B44 . . . . 44 E3
Orpwood Rd B33 . . . . 69 B2
Orsino Cl CV34 . . . . . 161 E2
Orslow Wlk WV10 . . . . 26 A5
ORTON 37 F3
Orton Ave B76 . . . . 58 A6
Orton Cl B46 . . . . 59 A3
Orton Gr WV4 . . . . 38 C4
Orton La WV4, WV5 . . . . 38 A2
Orton Rd CV6 . . . . 95 D4
Orton Way B35 . . . . 58 A1

Orwell Cl
  Nuneaton CV10 . . . . 72 A5
  Stourbridge DY8 . . . . 80 D4
  Wednesfield WV11 . . . . 26 F5
Orwell Ct CV1 . . . . . 165 C4
Orwell Dr
  Birmingham B38 . . . . . 123 C8
  West Bromwich B71 . . . . 53 D6
Orwell Pas B5 . . . . . 164 C2
Orwell Rd
  Coventry CV1 . . . . . 113 F1
  Walsall WS1 . . . . 43 B8
Osbaston Cl
  Coventry CV5 . . . . . 111 E4
  Hinckley LE10 . . . . 71 F3
Osberton Dr DY1 . . . . 50 F2
Osborne B19 . . . . 20 D7
Osborne Cl
  Birmingham B6 . . . . 67 A7
  Brierley Hill DY5 . . . . 81 F8
  Kidderminster DY10 . . . . . 117 B6
Osborne Ct ⁷ CV31 . . . . . 162 A7
Osborne Dr WS10 . . . . 41 D8
Osborne Gr B19 . . . . 66 C7
Osborne Prim Sch B23 . . . . 57 A5
Osborne Rd
  Birmingham, Erdington
    B23 . . . . 56 F5
  Birmingham, Handsworth
    B21 . . . . 65 F8
  Bromsgrove B60 . . . . . 137 C1
  Coventry CV5 . . . . . 133 A8
  West Bromwich B70 . . . . 53 C3
  Wolverhampton WV4 . . . . 38 F5
Osborne Road S ⁵ B23 . . . . . 56 F4
Osborne Twr B6 . . . . 67 A8
Osborn Rd B11 . . . . 87 C6
Osbourne Croft B90 . . . . . 126 D5
Osbourne Ho CV1 . . . . . 165 D4
Oscott Coll B73 . . . . 45 D1
Oscott Gdns B42 . . . . 55 E3
Oscott Manor Sen Sch B44 . . . . 44 E2
Oscott Rd B6, B42 . . . . 55 E3
Oscott School La B44 . . . . 44 E2
Osier Cl B23 . . . . 56 B6
Osier Pl WV1 . . . . 25 F2
Osier St WV1 . . . . 25 F2
Osler St B16 . . . . 65 F2
Osmaston Rd
  Birmingham B17 . . . . 85 B3
  Stourbridge DY8 . . . . 80 F2
Osmington Gr B63 . . . . 82 D6
Osnor Ct B60 . . . . . 151 B7
Osprey B77 . . . . 36 A6
Osprey Cl
  Coventry CV2 . . . . . 115 B6
  Nuneaton CV11 . . . . 79 B8
Osprey Ct WS7 . . . . 7 F8
Osprey Dr DY1 . . . . 50 F1
Osprey Gr WS12 . . . . 2 C1
Osprey Ho B80 . . . . . 159 D4
Osprey Park Dr DY10 . . . . . 117 B3
Osprey Rd
  Birmingham, Acock's Green
    B27 . . . . 88 D2
  Birmingham, Perry Common
    B23 . . . . 56 C6
Ostler Cl DY6 . . . . 60 B7
Oswald Rd CV32 . . . . . 161 D8
Oswald St B98 . . . . . 153 E3
Oswestry Cl B97 . . . . . 158 C7
Oswestry Ct B11 . . . . 87 B6
Oswin Gr CV2 . . . . . 114 C4
Oswin Pl WS3 . . . . 28 F5
Oswin Rd WS3 . . . . 28 F5
Othello Ave CV34 . . . . . 161 F3
Othello Cl WV10 . . . . 25 E6
Other Rd B98 . . . . . 153 E4
Otley Gr B9 . . . . 68 C3

Ottawa Twr ② B5 . . . . 86 D7
Otterburn Cl CV6 . . . . . 113 B6
Otterburn Cl WS12 . . . . 2 E2
Otter Cl B98 . . . . . 154 F3
Otter Croft B34 . . . . 69 D5
Otters Rest CV31 . . . . . 162 C5
Otterstone Cl DY3 . . . . 39 C2
Ottery B77 . . . . 36 B5
Oughton Rd B12 . . . . 87 A7
Oulsnam Ct ⁸ B13 . . . . 87 B2
Oulton Cl DY11 . . . . . 116 D8
Oundle Ct ⁷ B74 . . . . 31 F2
Oundle Rd B44 . . . . 55 F7
Ounsdale Cres WV5 . . . . 49 A7
Ounsdale Dr DY2 . . . . 62 C4
Ounty John La LY8 . . . . 81 A1
Our Lady & Kenelm's RC
  Prim Sch B63 . . . . 83 A4
Our Lady of Compassion RC
  Prim Sch B92 . . . . . 106 D7
Our Lady of Fatima RC Prim
  Sch 84 F7
Our Lady of Lourdes RC Prim
  Sch B13 . . . . . 105 D5
Our Lady of Mount Carmel
  RC Fst Sch B97 . . . . . 153 A2
Our Lady of the Angels RC
  Inf Sch CV11 . . . . 73 C3
Our Lady of the Assumption
  RC Prim Sch CV4 . . . . . 111 E1
Our Lady of the Wayside RC
  Prim Sch B90 . . . . . 126 C8
Our Lady & St Chad's RC
  Sports Coll WV10 . . . . 25 F7
Our Lady & St Rose of Lima
  RC Prim Sch B29 . . . . 85 B1
Our Lady & St Teresa's RC
  Comb Sch CV32 . . . . . 157 D5
Our Lady's RC Prim Sch
  B33 . . . . 69 D2
Outermarch Rd CV6 . . . . . 113 C7
Outfields B13 . . . . . 104 E6
Outlands Dr LE10 . . . . 71 B2
Outmore Rd B33 . . . . 69 B1
Outwood Cl B98 . . . . . 158 E7
Out Wood Dr B31 . . . . . 102 D1
OUTWOODS 92 C5
Outwoods The LE10 . . . . 75 F8
Oval Prim Sch The B33 . . . . 68 F2
Oval Rd
  Birmingham B24 . . . . 56 E1
  Tipton DY4 . . . . 51 F6
Oval The
  Dudley DY1 . . . . 61 E8
  Smethwick B67 . . . . 64 D2
  Wednesbury WS10 . . . . 41 F4
Overbare Cl B94 . . . . . 142 A1
Overberry Cl CV2 . . . . 96 D2
Overbrook CV3 . . . . 50 C2
Over Brunton Cl B31 . . . . . 103 B2
Overbury Cl
  Birmingham B31 . . . . . 103 C3
  Halesowen B63 . . . . 83 B2
Overbury Rd B31 . . . . . 103 C3
Overdale B96 . . . . . 158 E1
Overdale Ave B76 . . . . 57 F5
Overdale Cl WS2 . . . . 27 D3
Overdale Ct B13 . . . . 86 F4
Overdale Dr WS2 . . . . 27 D3
Overdale Rd
  Birmingham B32 . . . . 84 E5
  Coventry CV5 . . . . . 112 C3
Overend Rd B63, B64 . . . . 82 D7
Overend St B70 . . . . 53 D2
Overfield Dr WV14 . . . . 40 A3
Overfield Rd
  Birmingham B32 . . . . 84 F1
  Dudley DY1 . . . . 61 E8
OVER GREEN 47 D2
Over Green Dr B37 . . . . 69 F5
Overhill Rd WS7 . . . . 7 B5
Overlea Ave B27 . . . . 88 B3
Overlord Dr LE10 . . . . 71 A2
Overman Cl CV3 . . . . 81 D5
Over Mill Dr B29 . . . . 86 B2
Over Pool Rd B8 . . . . 68 A6
Overseal Rd WV11 . . . . 26 E8
Overslade Cres CV6 . . . . . 112 E8
Overslade Rd B91 . . . . . 106 F2
Oversley Cl B97 . . . . . 153 C5
Oversley Rd B76 . . . . 58 A6
Over St CV6 . . . . . 114 A8
Overstrand WV9 . . . . 10 F3
Overton Cl B28 . . . . . 106 A6
Overton Dr B46 . . . . 59 C3
Overton Gr B27 . . . . . 106 C8
Overton La WS7 . . . . 7 C4
Overton Pl
  Birmingham B7 . . . . 67 A3
  West Bromwich B71 . . . . 53 D6
Overton Rd B27 . . . . . 106 C8
Overtons Cl CV31 . . . . . 162 F5
Overton Wlk WV4 . . . . 38 C6
Overwood Croft B8 . . . . 67 F3
Overwoods Rd B77 . . . . 36 A4
Owenford Rd CV6 . . . . . 113 C7
Owen Pl WV14 . . . . 40 D6
Owen Rd
  Bilston WV14 . . . . 40 D6
  Darlaston WV13 . . . . 41 C8
  Wolverhampton WV3 . . . . 39 A8
Owen Road Ind Est WV13 . . . . 27 C1
Owens Croft B38 . . . . . 104 A1
Owen St
  Darlaston WS10 . . . . 41 D7

Owen St continued
  Dudley DY2 . . . . 62 E8
  Tipton DY4 . . . . 51 E5
Owens Way B64 . . . . 63 A1
Ownall Rd B34 . . . . 69 C6
OXBARN 38 E7
Oxbarn Ave WV3 . . . . 38 E7
Ox Bow Way DY10 . . . . . 116 E8
Oxbridge Way B79 . . . . 20 E6
Ox Cl CV2 . . . . . 114 A6
Oxendon Way CV3 . . . . . 134 E8
Oxenton Croft B63 . . . . 82 D2
Oxford Cl
  Birmingham B8 . . . . 68 B5
  Great Wyrley WS6 . . . . 4 F3
Oxford Dr
  Birmingham B27 . . . . 88 D4
  Stourbridge DY8 . . . . 80 F4
Oxford Gn WS11 . . . . 4 F8
Oxford Gr B37 . . . . 70 A1
Oxford Pl ⁸ CV32 . . . . . 156 F1
Oxford Rd
  Birmingham, Acock's Green
    B27 . . . . 88 C3
  Birmingham, Erdington B23 . . . . 56 F4
  Birmingham, Moseley B13 . . . . 87 A2
  Cannock WS11 . . . . 1 F2
  Ryton-on-D CV8 . . . . . 134 F1
  Smethwick B66 . . . . 65 A7
  West Bromwich B70 . . . . 53 B3
Oxford Row ⁶ CV32 . . . . . 156 F1
Oxford St
  Bilston WV14 . . . . 40 F5
  Birmingham, Digbeth B5 . . . . . 164 D2
  Birmingham, Stirchley B30 104 A7
  Coventry CV1 . . . . . 113 E3
  Dudley DY1 . . . . 51 B1
  Kidderminster DY10 . . . . . 116 E5
  Royal Leamington Spa
    CV32 . . . . . 156 F1
  Walsall WS2 . . . . 42 C7
  Wednesbury WS10 . . . . 42 B3
  Wolverhampton WV1 . . . . . 163 D2
Oxford Street Ind Pk
  WV14 . . . . 40 F5
Oxford Street Island
  WV14 . . . . 40 E5
Oxford Terr WS10 . . . . 42 B2
Oxford Trad Est B5 . . . . . 164 D1
Oxford Way DY4 . . . . 51 D5
Oxhayes Cl CV7 . . . . . 130 C6
Oxhill Cl B98 . . . . . 154 E1
Oxhill Rd
  Birmingham B21 . . . . 54 E2
  Solihull B90 . . . . . 105 C2
Ox Leasow B32 . . . . 84 C2
Oxleasow Rd B98 . . . . . 154 E4
OXLEY 25 B8
Oxley Ave WV10 . . . . 25 C6
Oxley Cl
  Dudley DY2 . . . . 62 B2
  Great Wyrley WS6 . . . . 4 F1
Oxley Dr CV3 . . . . . 133 C3
Oxley Gr B29 . . . . . 103 A8
Oxley La WV1 . . . . . 163 B4
Oxley Links Rd WV10 . . . . 25 B8
Oxley Moor Rd WV9, WV10 25 A8
Oxley Prim Sch WV10 . . . . 25 C7
Ox Leys Rd B75, B76 . . . . 47 D3
Oxleys Rd WV11 . . . . 25 C4
Oxpiece Dr B36 . . . . 68 D8
Ox St DY3 . . . . 50 D5
Oxstall Cl B76 . . . . 58 D5
Oxted Cl WV11 . . . . 26 F5
Oxted Croft B23 . . . . 56 E3
Oxwood La B32 . . . . . 101 C4

P

Pace Cres WV14 . . . . 41 A2
Pacific Ave WS10 . . . . 41 D1
Packenham Dr B76 . . . . 57 F8
Packhorse La B38, B47 . . . . . 124 E6
Packington Ave
  Allesley CV5 . . . . . 112 B6
  Birmingham B34 . . . . 69 D5
Packington Ct B74 . . . . 31 E4
Packington La
  Little Packington CV7 . . . . 91 C6
  Outwoods B46, CV7 . . . . 92 B8
  Weeford B78 . . . . 19 F7
Packington Pl ⁶ CV31 . . . . . 162 A7
PACKMORES 160 E8
Packmores B90 . . . . . 126 A5
Packmore St CV34 . . . . . 160 F8
PACKWOOD 144 A8
Packwood Cl
  ⁷ Birmingham B29 . . . . 84 F1
  Solihull B91 . . . . . 107 C5
Packwood Dr B43 . . . . 43 D1
Packwood Gn CV5 . . . . . 112 A3
PACKWOOD GULLET 144 A6
Packwood Ho
  Birmingham B15 . . . . 86 C8
  Sutton Coldfield B73 . . . . 46 A3

Packwood House ★ B94 . 144 A5
Packwood La B94 . . . . . 144 A4
Packwood Mews ⁵
  CV34 . . . . . 161 B8
Packwood Rd
  Birmingham B26 . . . . 89 B8
  Lapworth B94 . . . . . 144 A7
  Oldbury B69 . . . . 52 A1
Padarn Cl DY3 . . . . 39 C1
Padbury WV9 . . . . 11 B3
Padbury Ho B31 . . . . . 102 D5
Paddiford Pl CV10 . . . . 72 C1
Paddington Cl WV6 . . . . 54 C1
Paddington Rd WS2 . . . . 27 F4
Paddock Cl B77 . . . . 35 F7
Paddock Dr
  Birmingham B26 . . . . 89 A7
  Dorridge B93 . . . . . 128 A2
Paddock Gdns WS5 . . . . 43 B6
Paddock La
  Aldridge WS9 . . . . 30 A5
  Great Wyrley WS6 . . . . 5 A3
  Redditch B98 . . . . . 158 E7
  Walsall WS1 . . . . 28 F1
Paddocks Cl B78 . . . . 22 F1
Paddocks Gn B18 . . . . 66 A5
Paddocks Rd B47 . . . . . 124 F6
Paddocks The
  Bulkington CV12 . . . . 79 B3
  Coventry CV7 . . . . . 130 B8
  Kenilworth CV8 . . . . . 148 B5
  Warwick CV34 . . . . . 160 F7
Paddock The
  Bilston WV14 . . . . 40 D1
  Birmingham B31 . . . . . 103 C4
  Dudley DY3 . . . . 50 E5
  Lichfield WS14 . . . . 9 C5
  Stoke Heath B60 . . . . . 150 D6
  Stourbridge DY9 . . . . 99 C8
  Sutton Coldfield B76 . . . . 47 A4
  Sutton Coldfield B76 . . . . 59 C6
Paddock View WV6 . . . . 25 B5
Paddock Way LE10 . . . . 74 E6
Paddys Wide Water Ind Est
  DY5 . . . . 61 C5
Padgate Cl B35 . . . . 58 B3
Padgets La B98 . . . . . 154 D4
Padmore Ct ⁶ CV31 . . . . . 162 B6
Padstow B77 . . . . 21 F5
Padstow Cl CV11 . . . . 73 F5
Padstow Rd
  Birmingham B24 . . . . 57 D4
  Coventry CV4 . . . . . 131 E8
Padua Rd B60 . . . . . 137 C1
Paganal Dr B70 . . . . 53 E1
Paganel Dr DY1 . . . . 51 C3
Paganel Prim Sch B29 . . . . 85 A2
Paganel Rd B29 . . . . 85 A2
Pageant Ct B12 . . . . 86 E5
Page Rd CV4 . . . . . 131 E7
Pages Cl B75 . . . . 46 C5
Pages Croft B43 . . . . 51 E3
Pages La B43 . . . . 43 E1
Pages La B43 . . . . 43 E1
Paget Cl
  Bromsgrove B61 . . . . . 136 E2
  Dudley WV14 . . . . 51 B8
  Lichfield WS13 . . . . 3 B2
Paget Ct CV2 . . . . 96 B3
Paget Ho ⁹ WV4 . . . . 52 B3
Paget Mews B76 . . . . 46 F1
Paget Prim Sch B24 . . . . 57 C4
Paget Rd
  Birmingham B24 . . . . 57 D4
  Wolverhampton WV3, WV6 . 24 F3
Paget St WV1 . . . . . 163 A4
Pagham Cl WV9 . . . . 10 F2
Pagnell Gr B13 . . . . . 105 C6
Pagoda Cl B74 . . . . 44 F6
Paignton Rd B16 . . . . 65 D3
Pailton Cl CV2 . . . . 96 C2
Pailton Gr B29 . . . . 85 B1
Pailton Rd B90 . . . . . 106 B5
Painswick Cl
  Redditch B98 . . . . . 158 E6
  Walsall WS5 . . . . 43 B3
Painswick Rd B28 . . . . . 105 F7
Paint Cup Row CV2 . . . . 62 C2
Painters Cnr ⁷ B66 . . . . 65 C5
Painters Croft WV14 . . . . 40 E1
Pakefield Rd B30 . . . . . 104 C3
Pakenham Cl B76 . . . . 57 F8
Pakenham Ho B76 . . . . 57 F8
Pakenham Rd B15 . . . . 86 C7
Pakenham Village B15 . . . . 86 C7
Pake's Croft ③ CV6 . . . . . 113 A5
Pakfield Wlk B6 . . . . 66 F8
Palace Cl B65 . . . . 63 D4
Palace Dr B66 . . . . 64 D8
Palace Rd B9 . . . . 67 E1
Paladine Way CV3 . . . . . 134 A4
Palefield Rd B90 . . . . . 126 F6
Pale La B17 . . . . 84 F8
Palermo Ave CV3 . . . . . 133 E6
Pale St DY3 . . . . 50 E5
Palethorpe Rd DY4 . . . . 52 A8
PALFREY 42 E7
Palfrey Girls Sch WS1 . . . . 42 E6
Palfrey Inf Sch WS1 . . . . 42 D7
Palfrey Jun Sch WS1 . . . . 42 D7
Palfrey Rd DY8 . . . . 80 D5
Palisades Sh Ctr The
  B2 . . . . . 164 B2
Pallett Dr CV11 . . . . 73 F7

Palmcourt Ave B28 ...... 105 E7
Palm Croft DY5 .... 81 C8
Palmer Cl WV11 .... 12 F1
Palmer La CV1 .... 165 B3
Palmer Rd
Hinckley LE10 .... 71 B2
Whitnash CV31 .... 162 B4
Palmers Cl
Codsall WV8 .... 10 C1
Solihull B90 .... 106 B5
PALMERS CROSS 24 D8
Palmers Cross Prim Sch
WV6 .... 24 D8
Palmers Gr B36 .... 68 E8
Palmers Rd B98 .... 154 F5
Palmers Rough Nature
Reserve * B90 .... 106 C5
Palmer St B9 .... 67 A2
Palmerston Ave B77 .... 35 E6
Palmerston Ct B77 ..... 35 F6
Palmerston Dr B69 ..... 52 D2
Palmerston Rd
Birmingham B11 .... 87 B6
Coventry CV5 .... 132 F8
Palmers Way WV8 ...... 10 C1
Palm Tree Ave CV2 .... 96 C2
Palmvale Croft B26 .... 89 A6
Palmyra Rd B60 .... 137 C2
Palomino Pl B16 .... 65 F2
Pamela Rd B31 .... 103 A3
Pancras Cl CV2 .... 96 E1
Pan Croft B36 .... 68 C7
Pandora Rd CV2 ...... 114 E7
Pangbourne Cl CV11 ... 73 F8
Pangbourne Rd CV2 ... 114 C8
Pangfield Pk CV5 ..... 112 C4
Panjab Gdns B67 ..... 64 F6
Pannel Croft B19 ..... 66 D6
Panther Croft B34 .... 69 D5
Papenham Gn CV4 ... 132 A8
Paper Mill Cotts B97 . 152 E5
Paper Mill Dr B98 .... 154 B5
Paper Mill End B44 ... 55 D6
Paper Mill End Ind Est
B42 .... 55 D6
Papworth Dr B61 ..... 136 F5
Papyrus Way B36 .... 57 F1
Parade
Birmingham B1 ...... 164 A3
Royal Leamington Spa
CV32 .... 161 F8
Sutton Coldfield B72 .. 46 C5
Parade The
Birmingham B37 ..... 70 A5
Brownhills WS8 ...... 6 E1
Cradley Heath B64 ... 82 E8
Dudley DY1 .... 51 B2
6 Hinckley LE10 .... 75 D8
Kingswinford DY6 .... 60 B7
Nuneaton CV11 ..... 73 C3
Parade View WS8 .... 15 E8
PARADISE 113 F6
Paradise DY2 .... 62 D8
Paradise Circus Queensway
B1, B3 .... 164 A2
Paradise Ct B28 .... 105 D6
Paradise Forum Sh Ctr 1
B2 .... 164 C2
Paradise Gr WS3 .... 14 F3
Paradise Ho 4 CV6 .. 113 F7
Paradise La
Birmingham B28 .... 105 E6
Walsall WS3 .... 14 F3
Wolverhampton WV10 . 11 E8
Paradise Row B60 .. 136 F2
Paradise St
Birmingham B3 ..... 164 B2
Coventry CV1 ...... 165 C1
Warwick CV34 ..... 160 F8
Paradise Way CV2 .. 97 B1
Paradise Works CV6 . 113 F7
Paragon Pk CV1 ... 113 D6
Paragon Way CV7 .. 96 B8
Parbrook Cl CV4 ... 131 E8
Parbury B77 .... 35 D5
Parchments The WS13 . 3 B1
Pardington Cl B92 .. 107 E8
Pargeter Ct 1 B92 .. 28 C2
Pargeter Rd B67 ... 64 F2
Pargeter St
Stourbridge DY8 ... 80 F4
Walsall WS2 .... 28 C3
Par Gn B38 .... 103 D1
Parish End CV31 ... 162 C4
Parish Gdns DY9 ... 81 C1
Parish Hill B61 .... 120 D1
Parisienne Ho CV5 . 112 E2
Park App B23 ...... 56 C2
Park Ave
1 Birmingham, Balsall Heath
B12 .... 86 F5
Birmingham, Hockley B18 . 66 A6
Birmingham, King's Norton
B30 .... 104 A5
Burntwood WS7 .... 7 B5
Coleshill B46 ...... 70 F6
Coventry CV6 ...... 95 C3
Norton Canes WS11 . 6 A5
Nuneaton CV11 .... 73 E3
Oldbury B68 .... 64 B3
Rowley Regis B65 .. 63 C3
Smethwick B67 .... 64 F4
Solihull B91 .... 107 D3
Studley B80 .... 159 E3
Tipton DY4 .... 51 E5

Park Ave continued
Willenhall WV13 ...... 26 F2
Wolverhampton, Goldthorn Park
WV4 .... 39 C5
Wolverhampton WV1 .. 163 A4
Wombourne WV5 ..... 49 A5
Park Bldgs DY3 .... 50 C4
Parkbrook Ind Est 5 DY9 81 F5
Park Butts Ringway
DY11 .... 116 D6
Park Cir B6 .... 66 F7
Park Cl
Brownhills WS8 ..... 15 F8
Cheslyn Hay WS6 .... 4 E3
Dudley DY1 .... 51 B7
Kenilworth CV8 ..... 148 B5
Oldbury B69 .... 63 C7
Solihull B92 .... 89 D2
Sutton Coldfield B24 .. 57 D5
Park Cres
West Bromwich B71 ... 53 D4
Wolverhampton WV1 .. 163 A3
Park Croft
Burntwood WS7 ...... 6 C8
Hollywood B47 ...... 125 A5
Park Ct
Allesley CV5 .... 112 B6
Kidderminster DY11 .. 116 D5
Redditch B98 .... 154 A3
Rowley Regis B65 ... 63 C3
Sutton Coldfield B73 . 45 F1
Parkdale DY3 .... 50 D8
Parkdale Ave WS10 ... 42 A4
Parkdale Cl B24 ...... 56 F2
Parkdale Ct WS10 .... 42 A4
Park Dale Ct WV1 .... 25 A3
Parkdale Dr B31 ..... 123 A7
Park Dale E WV1 .... 25 A3
Parkdale Rd B26 .... 89 D6
Park Dale W WV1 ... 25 A3
Park Dr
Royal Leamington Spa
CV31 .... 161 E7
17 Sutton Coldfield, Four Oaks
B74 .... 31 F2
Sutton Coldfield, Streetly
B74 .... 31 C4
Wolverhampton WV4 . 39 C5
Park Edge B17 ...... 85 C7
Park End WS14 ..... 9 E7
Park End Dr B32 ... 84 D1
Parker Ho B14 ..... 104 F3
Parker Paul Ind Est WV2 . 39 C7
Parker Rd WV11 ... 12 F1
Parker St
Birmingham B16 ... 65 F1
Walsall WS3 ...... 14 A1
Parkes Ave WV8 ... 10 B2
Parkes Ct CV34 ... 160 D7
Parkes Fold DY4 ... 51 F8
PARKES HALL 51 A6
Parkes Hall Rd DY1 .. 51 A6
Parkes Ho 8 B69 ... 64 A7
Parkes La
Dudley DY3 ...... 51 A7
Tipton DY4 .... 51 F8
Parkes St
Brierley Hill DY5 .. 61 D3
Smethwick B67 ... 64 F4
Warwick CV34 .... 160 D7
Willenhall WV13 ... 27 B1
Parkeston Cres WS11 . 45 C1
PARK FARM 159 C8
Park Farm Ind Est B98 . 159 C7
Park Farm Rd
Birmingham B43 ... 44 B3
Tamworth B77 ..... 21 C1
PARKFIELD 39 E5
Parkfield
Birmingham B32 ... 84 A2
Dorridge B93 ..... 128 A1
Parkfield Ave B77 ... 21 C1
Parkfield Chalet Pk WV2 . 39 D6
Parkfield Cl
Birmingham, Lee Bank
B15 .... 86 C7
Birmingham, Quinton B62 . 84 A5
Redditch B98 ..... 154 B6
Parkfield Colliery WV4 . 39 F5
Parkfield Com Sch B88 . 67 E3
Parkfield Cres
Tamworth B77 .... 21 C1
Wolverhampton WV2 . 39 E6
Parkfield Ct
1 Coleshill B46 ... 70 F7
Tamworth B77 .... 35 C8
Parkfield Dr
Birmingham B36 ... 58 C1
Kenilworth CV8 ... 148 B5
Parkfield Gr WV2 ... 39 E6
Parkfield Prim Sch WV4 . 39 E5
Parkfield Rd
Birmingham B8 .... 67 E4
Coleshill B46 ..... 70 F6
Dudley DY2 ...... 62 E6
Keresley CV7 ..... 95 A6
Oldbury B68 ...... 64 A3
Stourbridge DY8 ... 81 B5
Wolverhampton WV2, WV4 . 39 E6
Parkgate Prim Sch CV6 . 95 E3
Parkgate Rd CV6 .... 95 C3
Park Gr
Birmingham B10 ... 87 D8
Water Orton B46 ... 59 C2
Park Hall Acad B36 .. 58 E1
Park Hall Cl WS5 .... 43 C6
Park Hall Cres B36 .. 69 C8

Parkhall Croft B34 ..... 69 C7
Park Hall Inf Sch WS5 .. 43 C7
Park Hall Jun Sch WS5 . 43 C7
Park Hall Rd
Walsall WS5 .... 43 D6
Wolverhampton WV4 .. 39 D5
Park Head Cres DY2 ... 62 B8
Park Head Rd DY2 .... 62 B8
PARK HILL 148 C6
Park Hill
Birmingham B13 ..... 86 E4
Kenilworth CV8 ..... 148 B5
Rowley Regis B65 .. 63 B1
Wednesbury WS10 .. 42 C4
Parkhill Dr CV5 ...... 112 A5
Park Hill Dr B20 ..... 54 F4
Park Hill Jun Sch CV8 . 148 C5
Park Hill La
Allesley CV5 .... 112 A6
Coventry CV5 ...... 112 A5
Park Hill Prim Sch
Birmingham B13 .... 86 F4
Coventry CV5 ...... 112 A4
Wednesbury WS10 .. 42 C4
Parkhill Rd
Burntwood WS7 .... 7 A8
Sutton Coldfield B76 . 57 F6
Park Hill Rd
Birmingham B17 .... 85 C6
Smethwick B67 .... 64 F2
Sutton Coldfield B72 . 62 E8
Park Ho
Essington WV11 .... 13 A3
Kidderminster DY11 . 116 C3
1 Smethwick B66 .. 65 C5
Parkhouse Ave WV11 . 26 E2
Parkhouse Dr B23 ... 56 B5
Parkhouse Gdns DY3 . 50 C4
Park Inn DY4 .... 52 A4
Park La
Berkswell CV7 ..... 110 B2
Birmingham, Aston B6 . 66 F7
Birmingham, Castle Vale
B35 .... 58 C4
Birmingham, Handsworth
B21 .... 54 B3
Fazeley B78 ...... 20 E2
Great Wyrley WS6 .. 5 A3
Kidderminster DY11 . 116 D6
Kingswinford DY6 .. 60 E7
Nuneaton CV10 ... 72 A3
Oldbury B69 ...... 64 A6
Shenstone WS14 ... 18 B4
Wednesbury WS10 .. 42 A5
Wolverhampton WV10 . 25 E6
Parkland Ave DY11 .. 116 B5
Parkland Cl CV6 .... 95 C3
Parklands B91 ...... 107 A3
Parklands Ave
Birmingham B20 ... 66 A8
Royal Leamington Spa
CV32 .... 157 C4
Parklands Cl B97 ... 153 A5
Parklands Ct B37 ... 85 A6
Parklands Dr B74 ... 45 F8
Parklands Gdns WS1 . 43 A8
Parklands Rd
Bilston WV14 ..... 40 D3
Darlaston WS10 .. 41 E5
Wolverhampton WV1 . 26 A1
Parklands The
Birmingham B23 ... 56 D6
Kingswinford DY6 . 60 B8
Stourbridge DY9 .. 81 D3
Wolverhampton WV3 . 24 D1
Park Lane E DY4 ... 52 B4
Park Lane Ind Est
Kidderminster DY11 . 116 D4
West Bromwich B21 . 54 B1
Wolverhampton WV10 . 25 E5
Park Lane Prim Sch CV10 72 A2
Park Lane Trad Est B69 . 64 A6
Park Lane W DY4 ... 51 F4
Parktree Wlk B24 .. 57 D4
Park Lime Dr WS4 .. 29 B4
Park Lime Pits Nature
Reserve * WS4 .... 29 C4
Park Mall WS1 .... 28 E2
Park Meadow Ave WV14 . 40 C8
Park Mews B29 .... 85 B1
Park Moor Gdns DY1 . 51 E3
Park Paling The CV3 . 133 E7
Park Pl B7 .... 67 C7
Park Place Sh Ctr 2 WS1 . 28 E2
Park Rd
Bedworth CV12 ... 78 B2
Bilston WV14 .... 40 C5
Birmingham, Aston B6 . 67 A7
Birmingham, Hockley B18 . 66 A6
Birmingham, Moseley B13 . 86 F4
Birmingham, Sparkhill B11 . 87 C3
Birmingham, Stockland Green
B23 .... 56 C2
Brierley Hill DY5 .. 81 F8
Burntwood, Chase Terrace
WS7 .... 6 F8
Burntwood, Triangle WS7 . 7 B5
Cannock WS11 .... 1 D1
Coleshill B46 .... 70 F6
Coventry CV1 .... 165 B1
Darlaston WS10 .. 41 C6
Dudley, Lower Gornal DY3 . 50 C4
Dudley, West Coseley DY1 . 51 B7
Featherstone WV10 . 12 D8
Halesowen B63 ... 83 A3
Hinckley LE10 .... 75 E8

Park Rd continued
Kenilworth CV8 ...... 148 A6
Norton Canes WS11 .. 6 A5
Oldbury B69 .... 63 C8
Royal Leamington Spa
CV32 .... 157 A4
Smethwick B67 ..... 64 F1
Solihull B91 .... 107 D3
Stourbridge DY8 ... 80 D5
Sutton Coldfield B73 . 46 B5
Tamworth B77 ..... 35 C5
Walsall, Daw End WS4 . 29 C5
Walsall, The Chuckery WS5 . 43 D5
Walsall, Wallington Heath
WS3 .... 14 B1
West Hagley DY9 .. 99 B6
Willenhall WV13 ... 26 F3
Park Retreat B66 ... 65 B5
Park Ridge B74 .... 46 A7
Park Ridge Dr B63 . 82 B6
Park Rise
Kidderminster DY11 . 116 D5
Wolverhampton WV3 . 24 E2
Park Road E WV1 .. 163 A4
Park Road N B6 .... 66 F7
Park Road S B18 ... 66 B5
Park Road W
Stourbridge DY8 ... 80 D5
Wolverhampton WV1 . 25 A3
Parkrose Ind Est B66 . 65 B7
Parks Cres WV11 ... 13 A3
Park Side
Birmingham B32 ... 84 C2
Coventry CV1 ..... 165 C2
Tamworth B77 .... 21 E1
Parkside Ave WV13 . 26 E2
Parkside Bsns Pk CV1 . 165 C1
Parkside Cl WS10 .. 42 B3
Parkside Ct LE10 .. 75 E8
Parkside La WV1 ... 25 F1
Parkside Mid Sch B61 . 137 A3
Parkside Rd B71 ... 53 A8
Parkside Rd
Birmingham B20 ... 54 E6
Halesowen B63 ... 82 D5
Parkside Way
Birmingham B31 .. 102 C1
Sutton Coldfield B74 . 31 A1
Park St
Birmingham, Aston B6 . 67 A7
Birmingham, Digbeth B5 . 164 D2
Cannock WS11 .... 4 E6
Cheslyn Hay WS6 .. 4 E3
Coventry CV6 .... 113 E7
Cradley Heath B64 . 62 E2
Darlaston WS10 .. 41 C5
Kidderminster DY11 . 116 D5
Kingswinford DY6 . 60 D6
Nuneaton CV11 ... 73 D3
Oldbury B69 ..... 63 F6
Rowley Regis B65 . 63 D1
Royal Leamington Spa
CV32 .... 156 F1
Stourbridge DY8 .. 80 F8
Stourbridge, Lye DY9 . 81 F5
Stourbridge, Stambermill
DY8 .... 81 A5
Tamworth B79 .... 21 A5
Tipton DY4 ...... 52 A5
Walsall WS1 ..... 28 E2
Wednesbury WS10 . 41 F3
West Bromwich B70 . 53 D3
Parkstone Ave B61 . 150 D8
Parkstone Cl WS14 . 15 C1
Parkstone Rd CV6 . 95 F2
Park Street Arc 4 WS1 . 28 E2
Park Street Gdns DY11 . 116 D6
Park Street S WV2 . 39 C6
Park Terr
Birmingham B21 .. 65 E8
Darlaston WS10 .. 41 B6
Park The B97 ..... 152 C2
Park Trad Est B18 . 66 A6
Parktree Wlk B26 . 57 D4
Park Venture Ctr WS11 . 4 E6
Parkview CV5 ..... 165 A1
Park View
Birmingham, Rotton Park
B18 .... 65 E4
Birmingham, Small Heath
B10 .... 87 D7
Burntwood WS7 .. 6 E8
Coventry CV3 .... 114 A2
Darlaston WS10 .. 41 C6
Halesowen B94 .. 143 C6
Sutton Coldfield B73 . 46 A6
Park View Bsns & Ent Sch
B8 .... 67 F5
Park View Cl CV7 . 96 A8
Park View Com L Ctr B8 . 67 F5
Parkview Cres WS2 . 28 A4
Park View Ct CV6 . 60 B8
Park View Ct WS11 . 1 D1
Parkview Dr
Birmingham B8 ... 68 A6
Brownhills WS8 .. 6 F2
Park View Rd
Birmingham B31 . 102 F3
Sutton Coldfield B74 . 31 D3
Parkview Trad Est B38 . 103 F3
PARK VILLAGE 25 F5
Park Villas 10 B9 . 67 B2
Parkville B17 .... 85 B3
Parkville Cl CV6 .. 95 B3
Parkville Highway CV6 . 95 B3

Parkway
Birmingham B8 ...... 68 A5
Coventry CV2 .... 115 B8
Park Way
Birmingham B45 .... 122 B8
Redditch B98 ...... 154 A5
Wolverhampton WV11 . 13 A1
Parkway Hospl Spire
(Private) B91 ...... 107 E5
Parkway Ind Ctr B7 . 67 A4
Parkway Rd DY1 .... 51 A2
Parkway Rdbt WS10 . 41 E1
Parkway The
Perton WV6 .... 23 F4
Walsall WS4 ...... 29 C8
Park Wlk
Brierley Hill DY5 .. 81 F8
4 Redditch B97 ... 153 E3
Parkwood Cl WS8 ... 16 A5
Parkwood Croft B43 . 44 B1
Parkwood Ct CV8 ... 148 B5
Park Wood Ct 11 B74 . 31 F2
Parkwood Dr B73 ... 45 C2
Park Wood La CV4 .. 131 D7
Park Wood Nature Reserve *
CV4 .... 131 E7
Parkwood Rd B61 .. 136 E3
Parkyn St WV2 ..... 163 D1
Parliament Piece Nature
Reserve * CV8 .... 147 F6
Parliament St
Birmingham, Aston B6 . 66 F6
Birmingham, Small Heath
B10 .... 87 C8
West Bromwich B70 . 53 D1
Parlows End B38 .. 123 D7
Parmington Cl B97 . 158 B6
Parmiter Ho CV32 . 156 F2
Parnell Ave WS13 .. 9 A6
Parolles Cl CV34 ... 161 E3
Parr Cl CV34 ...... 161 D6
Parrotts Gr CV2 ... 96 D5
Parry Rd
Coventry CV2 ..... 114 C7
Kidderminster DY11 . 116 B3
Wednesfield WV11 . 27 A8
Parsonage Dr
Birmingham B45 ... 122 D4
Halesowen B63 ... 82 A7
Parsonage St
Oldbury B69 ...... 64 B7
West Bromwich B71 . 53 D6
Parsons Hill B68 ... 64 B2
Parson's Hill B30 .. 104 B2
Parsons Hollow B77 . 35 E7
Parson's La LE10 .. 75 F8
Parson's Nook CV2 . 114 A5
Parsons Rd B98 ... 153 E2
Parsons St DY1 ... 51 C1
Parson St B77 ..... 35 E7
Parsons Way WS2 .. 27 F6
Partons Rd B14 ... 104 D6
Partridge Ave WS10 . 41 B6
Partridge Cl
Birmingham B37 .. 70 D3
Cannock WS11 .... 2 A1
Huntington WS12 . 1 D7
Partridge Croft
Coventry CV6 .... 96 A1
Lichfield WS13 ... 9 C8
Partridge Ct
Birmingham B4 ... 164 C2
4 Wednesbury WS10 . 41 F3
Partridge Gr DY10 . 117 A2
Partridge Ho B97 . 153 D2
Partridge La B97 .. 158 A7
Partridge Mill WS3 . 14 E3
Partridge Rd
Birmingham B26 .. 69 A1
Stourbridge DY8 . 80 C4
Passey Rd B13 .... 87 D2
Passfield Ave WS12 . 2 C7
Passfield Rd B33 .. 69 A3
Pastorale Rd B60 . 137 C1
Pasture Gate WS11 . 1 C2
Pastures The WV6 . 23 D4
Pastures Wlk B38 . 123 D7
Pasture Way CV34 . 160 B4
Patch La B98 ..... 158 F6
Pat Davis Ct DY10 . 116 E7
Patent Dr WS10 ... 41 D3
Patent Shaft Rdbt WS10 . 41 D3
Paternoster Row
Birmingham B5 ... 164 C2
4 Kidderminster DY11 . 116 D6
Wolverhampton WV1 . 163 B3
Paterson Ct B93 .. 128 C6
Paterson Pl WS8 .. 16 B5
Pathlow Cres B90 . 106 A1
Pathway The B14 . 104 C5
Pathways Gr CV34 . 161 F3
Patina Cl DY5 .... 81 F8
Patios The DY11 .. 116 C7
Patman Gdns B15 . 65 C1
Paton Gr B13 ..... 86 F2
Patricia Ave
Birmingham B14 . 105 C4
Wolverhampton WV4 . 39 D5
Patricia Cl CV4 ... 111 C3
Patricia Cres DY1 . 51 B7
Patricia Dr DY4 ... 52 A2
Patrick Gregory Rd WV11 . 26 F7
Patrick Ho 2 WS11 . 2 A3
Patrick Rd B26 ... 88 E5
Patridge Cl CV12 . 77 D3
Patriot Cl WS1 ... 42 D5
Patshull Ave WV10 . 11 B3

Patshull Cl B43 . . . . 43 D1
Patshull Ct WV10 . . . . . . 11 B3
Patshull Gr WV10 . . . . . . 11 B3
Patshull Ho WV6 . . . . 24 E5
Patshull Pl 7 B19 . . . . . . 66 C3
Pattenham Cl WV12 . . . . 27 D4
Pattens Rd CV34 . . . . . . 156 B1
Patterdale Rd
 Birmingham B23 . . . . . . 56 D4
 Cannock WS11 . . . . 2 A4
Patterdale Way DY5 . . . . 81 B8
Patterton Dr B76 . . . . 58 A7
Pattingham Rd WV6 . . . . 23 C2
Pattison Coll CV3 . . . . . . 114 A2
Pattison Gdns B23 . . . . . 56 D2
Pattison St WS5 . . . . 42 E5
Paul Byrne Ct B20 . . . . . 55 B1
Pauline Ave CV6 . . . . 96 B2
Paul Pursehouse Rd
 WV14 . . . . 40 D3
Pauls Coppice WS8 . . . . 16 A5
Paul St
 Dudley WV14 . . . . 40 A1
 Wednesbury WS10 . . . . . 42 B2
 Wolverhampton WV2 . . . 163 B2
Paul Stacy Ho CV1 . . . . 165 D4
Pauls Wlk WS13 . . . . 3 A3
Pavenham Dr B5 . . . . 86 C4
Pavilion Ave B67 . . . . 64 D3
Pavilion Dr B6 . . . . 55 F3
Pavilion Gdns
 Bromsgrove B61 . . . . . . 136 F5
 Dudley B62 . . . . 62 C2
Pavilions Sh Ctr B4 . . . . 164 C2
Pavilions The B37 . . . . . 90 E8
Pavilion The B77 . . . . 22 B3
Pavilion Way CV5 . . . . . 112 F3
Pavillion Cl WS9 . . . . 30 C7
Pavior's Rd WS7 . . . . 6 E4
Paxford Cl B98 . . . . 154 B6
Paxford Way B31 . . . . . 102 F6
Paxmead Cl CV6 . . . . 95 A2
Paxton Ave WV6 . . . . 23 E3
Paxton Cl B60 . . . . 137 B1
Paxton Rd
 Birmingham B18 . . . . . . 66 A5
 Coventry CV6 . . . . 113 A4
 Stourbridge DY9 . . . . . . 82 A4
Payne Cl CV32 . . . . 157 A2
Paynell Cl CV6 . . . . 95 B2
Payne's La CV1 . . . . 113 F3
Payton Cl B69 . . . . 63 C1
Payton Rd B21 . . . . 65 D8
PDH Ind Est
 Wednesbury WS10 . . . . . 41 C3
 Willenhall WV13 . . . . 26 B3
Peace Cl WS6 . . . . 4 E3
Peace Wlk B37 . . . . 70 B1
Peach Ave WS10 . . . . 41 C6
Peachley Cl 8 B63 . . . . . 83 B3
Peach Ley Rd B29 . . . . . 102 F7
Peach Rd WV12 . . . . 27 A6
Peacock Ave
 Coventry CV6 . . . . 96 F1
 Wednesfield WV11 . . . . . 27 A7
Peacock Cl DY4 . . . . 52 B4
Peacock Mews DY10 . . 116 E8
Peacock Rd
 Birmingham B13 . . . . . . 104 F6
 Darlaston WS10 . . . . 41 B7
Peacocks Est B64 . . . . . . 62 C1
Peacocks The CV34 . . . 160 B2
Peak Croft B36 . . . . 68 D8
Peak Dr DY3 . . . . 50 E3
Peake Ave CV11 . . . . 73 E7
Peake Cres WS8 . . . . 15 F5
Peake Dr DY4 . . . . 52 B4
Peake Rd WS8 . . . . 16 A5
Peak House Rd B43 . . . . 43 E4
Peakman Cl B45 . . . . . . 122 A6
Peakman St B98 . . . . . . 153 E4
Peak Rd DY8 . . . . 81 B6
Peal St WS1 . . . . 28 F1
Pearce Cl DY1 . . . . 61 E8
Pearl Gr
 Birmingham, Acock's Green
  B27 . . . . 88 B3
 3 Birmingham, Rotton Park
  B18 . . . . 65 E4
Pearl Hyde Com Prim Sch
 CV2 . . . . 115 A5
Pearman Rd
 Birmingham B45 . . . . . . 101 D1
 Smethwick B66 . . . . 65 A3
Pearmans Croft B47 . . . 125 A6
Pearsall Dr B69 . . . . 63 E8
Pears Cl CV8 . . . . 147 F5
Pearson Ave CV6 . . . . . . 96 B2
Pearson Ct WV12 . . . . . . 27 D4
Pearson St
 Brierley Hill DY5 . . . . 61 D3
 Cradley Heath B64 . . . . . 62 E1
 Stourbridge DY9 . . . . 81 F4
 West Bromwich B70 . . . . 53 B4
 Wolverhampton WV2 . . . 163 B1
Peart Dr B80 . . . . 159 C4
Peartree Ave WV13 . . . . 27 B1
Pear Tree Ave
 Nuneaton CV10 . . . . 72 E6
 Tipton DY4 . . . . 51 F5
Pear Tree Cl
 Birmingham, Grove Vale
  B43 . . . . 43 B1
 Birmingham, Stechford B33. 68 D2
 4 Coventry WV2 . . . . 96 B2
 Huntington WS12 . . . . 1 C7

Pear Tree Cl continued
 Kidderminster DY10 . . . 117 B7
 Shuttington B79 . . . . 22 E7
 Solihull B90 . . . . 105 C2
Pear Tree Cres B90 . . . 105 C2
Pear Tree Ct
 Birmingham B43 . . . . 54 C8
 Rowley Regis B65 . . . . . . 63 D3
Pear Tree Dr B78 . . . . . . 81 A2
Pear Tree Dr
 Birmingham B43 . . . . 43 C1
 Rowley Regis B65 . . . . . . 63 D3
Pear Tree Gr B90 . . . . . 105 D2
Peartree Ind Est DY2 . . 62 A6
Peartree La
 Cradley Heath B64 . . . . . 62 E1
 Dudley DY2 . . . . 62 A6
Pear Tree La
 Brownhills WS8 . . . . 6 C2
 Dudley WV14 . . . . 51 D8
 Willenhall WV12 . . . . 26 B8
Pear Tree Rd
 Birmingham B34 . . . . 69 C6
 Birmingham, Grove Vale
  B43 . . . . 43 B1
 Smethwick B67 . . . . 64 E4
Peascroft La WV14 . . . . . 40 E6
Peasefield Cl B21 . . . . . . 65 C8
Pebblebrook Way CV12 . 78 C1
Pebble Cl
 Stourbridge DY8 . . . . 81 B5
 Tamworth B77 . . . . 22 B3
Pebble Island Way CV31 . 162 C5
Pebble Mill Cl WS11 . . . . 1 F2
Pebble Mill Dr WS11 . . . . 2 A2
Pebble Mill Rd B5 . . . . . . 86 C4
Pebworth Ave B90 . . . . 127 B6
Pebworth Cl
 Birmingham B29 . . . . 86 B2
 Coventry CV5 . . . . 112 B3
 Redditch B98 . . . . 154 C7
Pebworth Gr
 Birmingham B33 . . . . 89 C8
 Dudley DY1 . . . . 51 B3
Peckham Rd B44 . . . . 45 A2
Peckingham St 2 B63 . . 83 B3
Peckover Cl B65 . . . . 63 C1
Peckstone Cl CV1 . . . . . 165 C1
Peddimore La B76 . . . . . . 58 C7
PEDMORE 81 B1
Pedmore CE Prim Sch
 DY9 . . . . 81 C1
Pedmore Cl B98 . . . . . . 159 B7
Pedmore Court Rd DY8. . 81 B1
Pedmore Gr B44 . . . . 44 F2
Pedmore Hall La DY9 . . . 99 C8
Pedmore La
 Hagley DY9 . . . . 99 F8
 Stourbridge DY9 . . . . 81 C1
Pedmore Rd
 Brierley Hill DY5, DY2 . . . 61 F4
 Stourbridge DY9 . . . . 81 E5
Pedmore Road Ind Est
 DY5 . . . . 61 F4
Pedmore Tech Coll & Com
 Sch DY9 . . . . 81 D4
Pedmore Wlk B69 . . . . . . 63 D5
Peel Cl
 Coventry CV6 . . . . 113 E6
 Darlaston WS10 . . . . 41 D8
 Drayton Bassett B78 . . . . 34 C5
 Hampton-in-A B92 . . . . 109 B6
 Willenhall WV13 . . . . 27 A1
Peel Dr
 Cannock WS12 . . . . 1 F8
 Tamworth B77 . . . . 35 F6
Peelers Way B77 . . . . 21 C1
Peel La B79 . . . . 21 A4
Peel La CV6 . . . . 113 F5
Peel Rd CV34 . . . . 160 E8
Peel St
 Birmingham B18 . . . . 65 E5
 Coventry CV6 . . . . 113 E6
 Dudley DY2 . . . . 62 E8
 Kidderminster DY11 . . . 116 D5
 Tipton DY4 . . . . 52 A4
 West Bromwich B71 . . . . 53 C5
 Willenhall WV13 . . . . 27 A1
 Wolverhampton WV3 . . . 163 B2
Peel Way B69 . . . . 52 D2
Peel Wlk 8 B17 . . . . 84 F7
Pegasus Ct
 Halesowen B62 . . . . 83 F5
 Sutton Coldfield B74 . . . . 32 A3
Pegasus Sch B35 . . . . . . 58 B3
Pegasus Wlk
 Birmingham B29 . . . . 85 D1
 Tamworth B77 . . . . 20 F7
Pegleg Wlk 2 B14 . . . . 104 C2
Pegmill Cl CV3 . . . . 133 F8
Pelham Bend CV4 . . . . . 111 C3
Pelham Dr DY1 . . . . 51 A2
Pelham Lodge DY10 . . . 117 A5
Pelham Rd B8 . . . . 68 B4
Pelham St WV3 . . . . 25 B1
PELSALL 15 B3
Pelsall La
 Walsall, Little Bloxwich
  WS3 . . . . 14 D3
 Walsall, Shelfield WS4 . . 29 B8
 Walsall WS3, WS4 . . . . . 15 A1
Pelsall North Common
 Nature Reserve* WS3. . 14 E6
Pelsall Rd WS8 . . . . 15 D7
Pelsall Village Sch WS3 . 14 F4

PELSALL WOOD 14 F5
Peltland Trad Ctr B98 . . 154 D4
Pemberley Rd B27 . . . . . 88 A2
Pemberton Cl B66 . . . . . . 65 B3
Pemberton Cres WS10 . . 42 D5
Pemberton Rd
 Dudley WV14 . . . . 40 D1
 West Bromwich B70 . . . . 53 A6
 Bilston B18 . . . . 66 B4
Pembridge Cl
 Birmingham B32 . . . . . . 102 A7
 Brierley Hill DY5 . . . . 61 F1
 Redditch B98 . . . . 154 D2
Pembridge Rd B93 . . . . 127 E3
Pembroke Ave WV2 . . . . 40 A7
Pembroke Cl
 Bedworth CV12 . . . . 77 C1
 Tamworth B79 . . . . 20 D6
 1 Warwick CV34 . . . . . . 160 F8
 West Bromwich B71 . . . . 42 B1
 Willenhall WV12 . . . . 27 B6
Pembroke Croft B28 . . . 106 A5
Pembroke Ct 8 CV32 . . 156 F2
Pembroke Gdns DY8 . . . 60 C2
Pembroke Ho 4 B36 . . . 28 C6
Pembroke Rd
 Birmingham B12 . . . . 87 A4
 West Bromwich B71 . . . . 42 B1
Pembroke Way
 Birmingham, Vauxhall B8.. 67 C5
 Birmingham, Yardley Wood
  B28 . . . . 106 A5
 Nuneaton CV11 . . . . 73 D3
 West Bromwich B71 . . . . 53 B7
Pembrook Dr B31 . . . . . 102 E6
Pembrook Rd CV6 . . . . . . 95 C2
Pembury Ave CV6 . . . . . . 96 A3
Pembury Cl B74 . . . . 44 F6
Pembury Croft B44 . . . . . 45 A1
Penarth Gr CV3 . . . . 134 F7
Pencombe Dr WV4 . . . . . 39 B5
Pencraig Cl CV8 . . . . . . 148 C5
Pencroft Rd B34 . . . . 69 C7
Penda Ct B20 . . . . 66 A8
Penda Gr WV6 . . . . 23 F5
Pendeen Rd B14 . . . . . . 105 C4
PENDEFORD 10 F4
Pendeford Ave WV6 . . . . 24 E8
Pendeford Bsns & Ent Coll
 WV10 . . . . 11 B2
Pendeford Bsns Pk WV9 . 10 F3
Pendeford Cl WV6 . . . . . . 24 E8
Pendeford Hall La WV9 . . 10 D5
Pendeford La WV9 . . . . . . 11 A3
Pendeford Mill La WV8 . . 10 C3
Pendeford Mill Reserve*
 WV9 . . . . 10 E4
Pendene Ct WV4 . . . . 39 A5
Pendenis Cl CV6 . . . . . . 114 A8
Pendigo Way B40 . . . . . . 90 E3
Pendinas Dr WV8 . . . . . . 10 B3
Pendle Ct 4 CV32 . . . . . 161 D8
Pendle Hill WS12 . . . . 2 C4
Pendleton Gr B27 . . . . . 106 B8
Pendock Ct B23 . . . . 56 C3
Pendragon Rd B42 . . . . . 55 C4
Pendrel Cl WS6 . . . . 13 F8
Pendrell Cl
 Birmingham B37 . . . . 70 A3
 Codsall WV8 . . . . 10 A3
Pendrill Rd WV10 . . . . . . 11 E3
Penfields Rd DY8 . . . . . . 81 B6
Penge Gr B44 . . . . 44 E3
Penhallow Dr WV4 . . . . . 39 E5
Penhurst Ave B20 . . . . . . 55 D1
Penk Dr WS7 . . . . 7 D6
Penkridge Cl WS2 . . . . . . 28 D3
Penkridge Gr WS11 . . . . . 1 D1
Penkridge Rd B33 . . . . . . 68 F4
Penkridge St WS2 . . . . . . 28 D3
Penk Rise WV6 . . . . 24 B4
Penley Gr B8 . . . . 68 B6
Penmakers St B67 . . . . . . 65 B4
Penmanor Cl B60 . . . . . 151 D8
PENN 38 E5
Pennant Cl
 Rowley Regis B65 . . . . . . 63 B3
 Wolverhampton WV3 . . . 163 A1
Pennant Gr B29 . . . . 85 A2
Pennant Rd
 Cradley Heath B64 . . . . . 62 D1
 Hinckley LE10 . . . . 75 D5
 Rowley Regis B65 . . . . . . 63 B3
Pennard Gr B32 . . . . 84 F4
Penn Cl WS3 . . . . 28 C8
Penn Common Rd WV4 . . 38 F1
Penncricket Ct B68 . . . . . 63 F3
Penncricket La B65, B68 . 63 F3
Penncroft WV4 . . . . 38 E4
Penn Croft La WV4 . . . . . 39 A1
Penndale Cl B24 . . . . 57 C6
Penney La CV34 . . . . . . 160 B3
Penn Gr B29 . . . . 85 B2
Penn Hall Sch WV4 . . . . . 38 E3
Penn Ho CV4 . . . . 111 F1
Penn Hospl WV4 . . . . 38 E4
Pennhouse Ave WV4 . . . 38 F5
Pennine Dr
 Cannock WS11 . . . . 1 E2
 Dudley DY3 . . . . 50 D3

Pennine Rd B61 . . . . . . 137 A5
Pennine Way
 Birmingham B8 . . . . 67 D6
 Nuneaton CV10 . . . . 72 B3
 Stourbridge DY8 . . . . 81 A6
 Tamworth B77 . . . . 36 C8
 Willenhall WV12 . . . . 27 D4
Pennington Cl B70 . . . . . 53 A2
Pennington Way CV6 . . 113 E8
Penn La B94 . . . . 141 C4
Penn Rd
 Gospel End Village DY3 . 49 F8
 Rowley Regis B65 . . . . . . 63 E3
 Wolverhampton WV2, WV3,
  WV4 . . . . 39 A6
Penn Road Island WV2 . 163 B2
Penns Cl CV32 . . . . 157 E5
Penns Ct B76 . . . . 57 F7
Penns La B72, B76 . . . . . 57 D7
Penns Lake Rd B76 . . . . 57 E7
Penns Prim Sch B72 . . . 57 D6
Penn St
 Birmingham B4 . . . . 67 A3
 6 Cradley Heath B64 . . . 82 F8
 Wolverhampton WV3 . . . 163 A1
Penns Wood Cl DY3 . . . . 39 C2
Penns Wood Dr B76 . . . . 57 F7
Pennwood Ct WV4 . . . . . 38 D6
Pennwood La WV4 . . . . . 38 F3
Pennyacre Rd B14 . . . . 104 D2
Pennycress Gdns WV10 . 12 C7
Penny Cress Gn WS11 . . . 5 F4
Pennycroft Ho B33 . . . . . 68 E3
Penny Ct
 Great Wyrley WS6 . . . . . . 13 F8
 Tamworth B79 . . . . 21 B5
Penny Farthing Arc CV3 . 50 D8
Pennyfield Croft B33 . . . . 68 E3
Pennyford Cl B97 . . . . . 153 A5
Pennyhill La B71 . . . . 53 F7
Pennyhill Prim Sch B71 . 53 F8
Pennymoor Rd B77 . . . . . 36 B7
Penny Park La CV6 . . . . . 95 A3
Penny Royal Cl DY3 . . . . 50 D2
Pennys Croft WS13 . . . . . 3 E1
Pennystone Cl CV31 . . . 162 D6
Penrice Dr B69 . . . . 52 A1
Penrith Cl
 Brierley Hill DY5 . . . . 81 B8
 Coventry CV6 . . . . 95 C2
 Royal Leamington Spa
  CV32 . . . . 156 C2
Penrith Croft B32 . . . . . 102 D8
Penrith Gr B37 . . . . 70 C2
Penrose Cl CV4 . . . . 132 A7
Penryhn Cl CV8 . . . . 148 C5
Penryn Cl
 Nuneaton CV11 . . . . 74 A4
 Walsall WS5 . . . . 43 D7
Penryn Rd WS5 . . . . 43 D7
Ponsby Cl B13 . . . . 105 D8
PENSETT 61 C6
Pensett Trad Est The DY6 . 60 E1
Pensford Rd B31 . . . . . . 103 C3
Pensham Croft B90 . . . . 127 A6
Penshaw Cl WV9 . . . . 11 A2
Penshaw Gr B13 . . . . . . 105 E6
Penshurst Rd B44 . . . . . . 44 E3
Penshurst Way CV11 . . . 78 F8
Pensilva Way 2 CV1 . . . 113 E4
Pens Meadow Specl Sch
 DY8 . . . . 60 E3
PENSNETT 61 C6
Pensnett 14-19 Ed Campus
 DY5 . . . . 61 B6
Pensnett Rd
 Brierley Hill DY5 . . . . 61 C4
 Dudley DY1 . . . . 61 F7
Pensnett Trad Est The
 DY6 . . . . 60 F8
Penstock Ct DY10 . . . . . 117 C8
Penstock Dr B69 . . . . 64 A4
Penstone La WV4 . . . . . . 37 E4
Pentalver Way WS11 . . . . 4 F6
Pentire Cl CV11 . . . . 73 F5
Pentire Rd WS14 . . . . 9 D6
Pentland Cl LE10 . . . . . . 71 B1
Pentland Croft B12 . . . . . 87 A5
Pentland Gdns WV6 . . . . 24 E2
Pentos Dr B11 . . . . 87 D3
Pentridge Cl B76 . . . . . . 57 F5
Penwood Gdns WV14 . . . 51 C8
Penzance Cl LE10 . . . . . . 71 E4
Penzance Way CV11 . . . . 74 A5
Penzer Dr B45 . . . . 138 D8
Penzer St B64 . . . . 62 D7
Peolsford Rd WS3 . . . . . . 15 A4
Peony Wlk B23 . . . . 56 B3
Peplins Way B30 . . . . . . 104 B3
Peplow Rd B33 . . . . 69 A4
Pepperbox Dr DY4 . . . . . 52 A5
Peppercorn Pl B70 . . . . . 53 C4
Pepper Hill DY8 . . . . 81 A4
Pepper La CV1 . . . . 165 B2
Pepperwood Cl B61 . . . . 120 C3
Pepper Wood Dr B31 . . . 102 C1
Pepys Cnr CV4 . . . . 111 E3
Pepys Ct B43 . . . . 54 E7
Perch Ave B37 . . . . 70 A3
Perch Cl WV10 . . . . 26 B4
Perchfoot Cl CV1 . . . . . . 165 C1
Perch Rd WS2 . . . . 28 A4
Percival Rd B16 . . . . 65 C1
Percy Cres CV8 . . . . 147 E2
Percy Rd
 Birmingham B11 . . . . 87 D4

Percy Rd continued
 Kenilworth CV8 . . . . 147 E2
 Warwick CV34 . . . . 160 E8
Percy Shurmer Prim Sch
 B12 . . . . 86 E7
Percy St CV1 . . . . 165 A3
Percy Terr 5 CV32 . . . . 156 D1
Peregrine Cl DY1 . . . . 50 F1
Peregrine Dr CV5 . . . . . 112 A5
Peregrine Gr DY10 . . . . 117 A2
Peregrine Way WS11 . . . . 5 A8
Pereira Rd B17 . . . . 85 C7
Pericles Cl CV34 . . . . . . 161 E3
Perimeter Rd B40 . . . . . . 90 D4
Perivale Gr
 Bilston WV14 . . . . 40 D1
 Dudley WV14 . . . . 51 D8
Perivale Way DY8 . . . . . . 81 A8
Periwinkle Cl WS8 . . . . . 15 D6
Perkins Cl DY1 . . . . 51 C6
Perks Rd WV11 . . . . 13 A1
Perott Dr B75 . . . . 32 C2
Perrett Wlk 5 DY11 . . . . 116 D6
Perrin Ave DY11 . . . . . . 116 B4
Perrins Gr B8 . . . . 68 A6
Perrins La DY9 . . . . 81 F4
Perrins Rise DY9 . . . . 81 F4
Perrott Gdns DY5 . . . . . . 61 B1
Perrott St B18 . . . . 65 E6
PERRY 55 E6
Perry Ave
 Birmingham B42 . . . . 55 C5
 Wolverhampton WV10 . . 25 F8
PERRY BARR 55 B5
Perry Barr Sta B20 . . . . . 55 D2
Perry Barr Stad (Greyhound)
 B42 . . . . 55 D3
PERRY BEECHES 55 B8
Perry Beeches Inf Sch
 B42 . . . . 55 C8
Perry Beeches Jun Sch
 B42 . . . . 55 C8
Perry Beeches Sch B42 . 55 C8
Perry Beeches Sports &
 Fitness Ctr B42 . . . . . . 55 C8
Perry Cl
 Dudley DY2 . . . . 62 D8
 Tamworth B79 . . . . 21 B6
PERRY COMMON 56 C7
Perry Common Prim Sch
 B23 . . . . 56 B7
Perry Common Rd B23 . . 56 C6
PERRY CROFTS 21 B7
Perrycrofts Cres B79 . . . 21 C7
Perry Ct B60 . . . . 84 B7
PERRYFIELDS 136 E4
Perryfields Cl B98 . . . . . 158 F6
Perryfields Cres B61 . . . 136 F5
Perryfields High Sch B68. 84 A8
Perryfields Prim Sch B68. 84 A7
Perryfields Rd B61 . . . . 136 D4
Perryford Dr B91 . . . . . . 127 C8
Perry Green Ho B42 . . . . 55 D5
Perry Hall Prim Sch WV11. 26 F6
Perry Hall Rd WV11 . . . . 26 F6
Perry Hill Cres B68 . . . . . 84 B7
Perry Hill Ho B68 . . . . . . 84 C8
Perry Hill La B68 . . . . 84 B7
Perry Hill Rd B68 . . . . . . 84 B7
Perry La B61 . . . . 136 F2
Perrymill La B96 . . . . . . 159 B1
Perry Park Cres B42 . . . . 55 C6
Perry Park Rd B64 . . . . . . 63 A8
Perry St
 Bilston WV14 . . . . 40 E3
 Darlaston WS10 . . . . 41 D8
 Smethwick B66 . . . . 65 A7
 Tipton DY4 . . . . 52 A4
 Wednesbury WS10 . . . . . 41 F2
Perry Street Ind Est WV14 40 E3
Perry Villa Dr B42 . . . . . . 55 D5
Perry Wood Rd B42 . . . . 55 A8
Persehouse St WS1 . . . . 28 F2
Pershore Ave B29 . . . . . . 85 F3
Pershore Cl WS3 . . . . 13 F2
Pershore Ct CV4 . . . . . . 116 D5
Pershore Pl CV4 . . . . . . 132 E6
Pershore Rd
 Birmingham, Balsall Heath
  B5 . . . . 86 C4
 Birmingham, Breedon Cross
  B30 . . . . 104 A5
 Birmingham, Ten Acres
  B30 . . . . 104 B8
 Halesowen B63 . . . . 83 A2
 Kidderminster DY11 . . . 116 A6
 Walsall WS3 . . . . 13 F2
Pershore Road S B30 . . 103 F3
Pershore St B5 . . . . 164 C1
Pershore Way WS3 . . . . . 13 F2
Perth Rd WV12 . . . . 27 A6
Perth Rise CV5 . . . . 112 A4
PERTON 23 C4
Perton Brook Vale WV6 . . 23 F2
Perton Fst Sch WV6 . . . . 23 F2
Perton Gr
 Birmingham B29 . . . . . . 103 A8
 Wolverhampton WV6 . . . 23 F2
Perton Mid Sch WV6 . . . 24 A5
Perton Rd WV6 . . . . 23 F2
Pestilence La
 Alvechurch, Arrowfield Top
  B48 . . . . 139 C8

Pestilence La continued
Alvechurch B48 ....139 D8
Petard Cl B77............35 C8
Petchells Cl DY5.........61 B5
Peter Ave WV14..........40 F2
Peterborough Dr WS12... 2 C1
Peterbrook Cl B98 .....158 F7
Peterbrook Prim Sch
 B90.....................105 D2
Peterbrook Rd B90.......105 D1
Peterbrook Rise B90.....105 D1
Peterdale Dr WV4.........38 F3
Peter Hall La CV7.......115 F6
Peterhead B77...........21 F5
Peterhouse Mews ■ B13. 87 A2
Peterlee Wlk ■ CV2 ....115 A7
Peters Ave B31.........102 F2
Petersbourne Ct B28....105 F8
Petersfield WS11.........1 F4
Petersfield Ct B28 .....105 F8
Petersfield Dr B65 ......63 E3
Petersfield Rd B28......105 E7
Peter's Hill Rd DY5.....136 F1
Petersham Pl B15........85 E6
Petersham Rd B44........45 C1
Peter's Hill Prim Sch DY5 81 C6
Petershouse Dr B74......31 F5
Peters La WS7 ....8 A5
Peters St B70...........53 A7
Peters Wlk
 Coventry CV6...........96 A4
 Lichfield WS13..........3 A2
Petford St B64..........62 E1
Petitor Cres CV2........96 C1
Peto Gr CV34...........161 F2
Pettitt Cl B14.........104 E2
Petton Cl B98..........158 F3
Pettyfield Cl B26.......89 A6
Pettyfields Cl B93.....128 A5
Petunia Cl CV10.........78 A8
Petworth Cl ■ WV13.....40 F8
Petworth Gr B26.........88 E6
Pevensey Cl B69.........62 F8
Pevensey Rd B60.......137 C1
Peverell Dr B28........105 F7
Peveril Dr CV3.........133 B5
Peveril Gr B76..........46 E4
Peveril Rd
 Perton WV6.............23 F4
 Wolverhampton WV4.....39 E3
Peveril Way B41.........43 F2
Pewter Ct B77..........35 E6
Peyto Cl CV6...........95 C2
Pheasant Cl
 Bedworth CV12.........77 D1
 Kidderminster DY10....117 A2
Pheasant Croft B36......70 A8
Pheasant La B98........158 F7
Pheasant Oak CV4......111 C2
Pheasant Rd B67........64 D1
Pheasant St DY5........61 C3
Pheasant Way WS11 ...... 2 A1
PHEASEY................44 C4
Pheasey Park Farm Prim Sch
 B43..................44 C4
Philip Cl
 ■ Royal Leamington Spa
 CV31.................161 F6
 Sutton Coldfield B76...46 F3
Philip Gr WS11 ....1 E6
Philip Rd
 Halesowen B63.........82 F3
 Tipton DY4............52 D5
Philip Sidney Rd B11....87 C3
Philip St WV14..........40 D1
Philip Victor Rd B20....54 F1
Phillimore Rd B8........67 D5
Phillip Docker Ct CV12..79 B2
Phillippes Rd ■ CV34...155 F1
Phillip Rd WS12.........42 C6
Phillips Ave WV11.......12 F1
Phillips St B6..........66 E6
Phillips Street Ind Est B6 66 E6
Phillips Terr B98......153 F4
Phipson Rd B11.........87 B3
Phoebe Cl CV34........161 E3
Phoenix Bsns Pk
 Birmingham B7 ....67 A6
 Hinckley LE10.........74 E8
Phoenix Ct
 Cannock WS11...........2 A2
 Tipton DY4............51 F6
 Willenhall WV11.......26 D3
Phoenix Ctr WS11........4 E6
Phoenix Gn B15.........85 E7
Phoenix Ind Est WV14...40 F4
Phoenix International Ind Est
 B70..................52 F5
Phoenix Park Ind Est CV7 96 B7
Phoenix Pk B62.........63 E2
Phoenix Prim Sch WS3...28 B7
Phoenix Rd
 Cannock WS11...........2 A2
 Tipton DY4............51 F6
 Willenhall WV11.......26 D3
Phoenix Rise
 Birmingham B23........56 B7
 Wednesbury WS10.......41 E4
 Wolverhampton WV2.....39 C6
Phoenix Road Ind Est
 WV11.................26 D3
Phoenix St
 West Bromwich B70.....52 F4
 Wolverhampton WV2.....39 D6

Phoenix Way CV6........95 E3
Phoenix Works Ind Est
 WS10.................41 E7
Picasso Cl WS11.........2 D2
PICCADILLY.............35 F1
Piccadilly B78.........35 F1
Piccadilly Arc ■ B2...164 B2
Piccadilly Cl B37......70 C1
Piccadilly Cres B78....35 F1
Pickard St CV34.......161 A7
Pickenham Rd B14......105 A1
Pickering Croft B32....84 D1
Pickering Pl LE10......76 A6
Pickering Rd WV11......26 D5
Pickersleigh Cl ■ B63..83 A3
PICKFORD..............111 E8
Pickford Cl CV11.......74 A1
Pickford Grange La CV5.111 C7
PICKFORD GREEN........111 C7
Pickford Green La CV5..111 C7
Pickford St B5.........66 F2
Pickford Way CV5......112 B6
Pickrell Rd WV14.......40 B1
Pickwick Cl B13........87 B2
Pickwick Gr B13........87 C2
Pickwick Pl WV14.......40 E4
Picton Croft ■ B37.....70 D2
Picton Gr B13.........105 B6
Picturedrome Way ■
 WS10.................41 D6
Piddock Rd B66.........65 A5
Pierce Ave B92.........88 E3
Piercy St B70..........53 A3
Piers Cl CV34.........160 F8
Piers Rd B21...........66 A7
Pier St WS8............15 F7
Piggots Croft B37......69 F3
Pig Wood Nature Reserve★
 CV4.................111 E1
Pike Cl
 Birmingham B20........54 F1
 Hinckley LE10.........75 D5
Pike Dr B37............70 C3
Pikehelve St B70.......52 E7
Pike Hill B60.........138 A7
Pikehorne Croft B36....58 D2
Pike Rd WS2............28 A4
Pikes La CV7...........94 A3
Pikes Pool La B60.....137 E2
Pikes The B45.........121 F8
Pikewater Rd B9........67 D2
Pilgrims Gate LE10.....76 A6
Pilgrims Wlk CV6, CV7..95 B6
Pilkington Ave B72.....46 C2
Pilkington Rd CV5.....132 D8
Pillaton Dr WS12........1 C6
Pilling Cl CV2........114 F8
Pilson Cl B36..........68 F8
Pimbury Rd WV12.......27 D7
Pimlico Ct DY3.........50 D3
Pimpernel Dr WS5.......43 A3
Pinbury Croft B37......70 B1
Pinchers Cl DY9.......119 E7
Pineapple Cl B14......104 C6
Pineapple Gr B30......104 C8
Pineapple Pl B14......104 D8
Pineapple Rd B30......104 C7
Pine Ave
 Smethwick B66.........64 E7
 Wednesbury WS10.......41 F4
Pine Cl
 Great Wyrley WS6.......4 F4
 Kingswinford DY6......60 D5
 Solihull B91.........106 F2
 Tamworth B79..........21 B8
 Wolverhampton WV3.....25 A1
Pine Ct
 Coventry CV5.........111 C4
 Royal Leamington Spa
 CV32.................157 B3
 Stourbridge DY8.......81 B1
 Wolverhampton WV11....26 C6
Pine Gn DY1............51 A5
Pine Gr
 Birmingham B14.......105 A5
 Burntwood WS7..........6 F5
 Lower Marlbrook B45..121 F2
Pine Ho B36............70 A8
Pinehurst CV32........157 E6
Pinehurst Dr B38......103 F3
Pine Leigh B74.........32 B1
Pineneedle Croft WV12..27 E4
Pine Rd
 Dudley DY1............51 C4
 Oldbury B69...........63 A8
Pineridge Dr DY11.....116 B5
Pines Park Home Est The
 WS12...................1 D5
Pine Sq B37............70 B2
Pines Specl Sch B36....68 F8
Pines The
 Bedworth CV12.........77 E2
 Birmingham B45.......102 A1
 Cheswick Green B90...126 D5
 Coventry CV4.........131 D7
 Lichfield WS14..........9 F7
 Walsall WS1...........42 F8
 Wolverhampton WV3.....24 D1
Pine Tree Ave CV4.....112 A2
Pine Tree Cl B97......152 F3
Pine Tree Ct CV12......78 C4
Pinetree Dr B74........30 D1
Pine Tree Rd CV12......78 D4
Pineview B31..........102 F2
Pinewall Ave B38......104 A1
Pineways
 Stourbridge DY8.......60 C2

Pineways continued
 Sutton Coldfield B74...31 C3
Pineways Dr WV6........24 E4
Pineways The B69.......63 C5
Pine Wlk
 Birmingham B31.......103 B3
 Stourbridge DY9.......81 D3
Pinewood Ave
 Cannock WS11...........1 D4
 Wood End CV9..........36 C1
Pinewood Bsns Pk B37...90 B8
Pinewood Cl
 Birmingham B45.......121 D8
 Birmingham, Great Barr B44 55 E7
 Brownhills WS8.........6 E2
 Walsall WS5...........43 B4
 Willenhall WV12.......27 E7
 Wolverhampton WV3.....38 A8
 Wombourne WV5.........49 A6
Pinewood Dr
 Binley Woods CV3.....135 C7
 Birmingham B32........84 A1
Pinewood Gr CV5.......133 B8
Pinewoods
 Birmingham, Hurst Green
 B62..................84 A7
 Birmingham, Woodcock Hill
 B31..................102 F8
Pine Woods B32.........84 A1
Pinewoods Ave DY9......98 F4
Pinewoods Cl DY9.......98 F4
Pinewoods Ct DY9......98 F4
Pinewood Wlk DY6.......60 E8
Pinfield Dr B45.......122 B1
Pinfold Cl WS3.........28 C8
Pinfold Ct LE10........74 F2
Pinfold Cres WV4.......38 D6
Pinfold Gdns WV11......26 D5
Pinfold Gr WV4.........38 D6
Pinfold Hill WS14......17 F6
Pinfold Ind Est WS3....28 C8
Pinfold La
 Cheslyn Hay WS6........4 C2
 Norton Canes WS11......5 E4
 Walsall WS9...........44 B6
 Wolverhampton WV4.....38 E5
Pinfold Rd B91........107 E5
Pinfold St
 Bilston WV14..........40 D5
 Birmingham B2........164 B2
 Darlaston WS10........41 D5
 Oldbury B69...........64 A8
Pinfold Street Extension
 WS10.................41 C5
Pinfold Street Prim Sch
 WS10.................41 C5
Pingle Cl B71..........42 F1
Pingle Ct CV11.........73 D2
Pingle La WV7..........73 C3
Pingles L Ctr CV11.....73 C3
PINKETT'S BOOTH.......111 C8
Pink Green La B97.....153 C5
Pinkney Pl B68.........64 C3
PINLEY................134 B7
Pinley Fields CV3.....134 B8
Pinley GDNS...........134 A8
Pinley Gr B43..........54 C3
Pinley Way ■ B91......107 A1
Pinnacle Ho B97.......158 E5
Pinner Ct B17..........85 C6
Pinner Gr B32..........84 E4
Pinner's Croft CV2....114 A5
Pinnock Pl CV4........111 F1
Pinson Gdns WV13.......26 F2
Pinson Rd WV13.........26 F2
Pintail Dr B23.........56 C2
Pintail Gr DY10.......117 B3
Pinto Cl B16...........65 F2
Pinvin Ho B97.........153 A3
Pinza Croft B36........68 D8
Pioli Pl WS2...........28 C5
Pioneer Cl B97.......153 D4
Pioneer Ho CV1........165 D4
Pioneer Way B35........58 B2
Pipe Hall Farm Woodland
 Reserve★ WS14.........8 A8
PIPEHILL................8 C5
Piper Cl WV6...........23 F4
Piper Pl DY8...........80 F8
Pipers Cl B61.........150 D7
Pipers Croft WS13.......3 A2
Pipers Ct CV3.........132 F4
Pipers Gn B28.........105 E5
Piper's La CV8........148 A5
Piper's Row WV1.......163 C3
Pipes Mdw WV14.........40 E5
Pipit Cl DY10.........117 A2
Pipkin Ct CV1.........165 D1
Pippin Ave B63.........82 B7
Pirbright Cl WV14......40 E1
Pirrey Cl WV14.........40 E1
Pitcairn Cl B30.......104 B6
Pitcairn Dr B62........83 C5
Pitcairn Ho B67........64 E2
Pitchcombe Cl B98.....154 A2
Pitcheroak Cotts B97..153 A3
Pitcheroak Specl Sch
 B97..................153 B4
Pitcher Oak Wood Nature
 Reserve★ B97.........153 B4
Pitclose Rd B31.......103 B1
Pitfield Rd B33........69 E1
Pitfield Row ■ DY1.....51 B1
Pitfields Cl B68.......84 A8

Pitfields Rd B68.......84 A8
Pitfield St ■ DY1......51 C1
Pithall Rd B34.........69 D5
Pit Leasow Cl B30.....104 B8
Pitman Rd B32..........84 C5
Pitmaston Ct B13.......86 D3
Pitmaston Rd B28.....106 B6
Pitmeadow Ho B14.....104 E2
Pitsford St B18........66 B4
Pitt La B92............90 D2
Pitts Farm Rd B24......57 C6
Pitt St
 Birmingham B4.........67 A3
 Wolverhampton WV3....163 B2
Pixall Dr B15..........58 B3
Pixhall Wlk B35........58 B3
Placid Cl CV4.........111 C3
Plainview Cl WS9.......30 E2
Plaistow Ave B36.......68 C7
Plane Cl CV10..........72 E7
Plane Gr B37...........70 B1
Planetary Ind Est WV13.26 C4
Planetary Rd WV13......26 C3
Planet Rd DY5..........61 D4
Planetree Cl B60......137 B2
Plane Tree Cl DY10....116 F7
Planetree Rd B74.......44 D8
Plane Tree Rd WS5......43 C4
Plank La B46...........59 A2
Planks La WV5..........49 A7
Plantagenet Pk CV34..161 E3
Plantation Dr B75......46 F6
Plantation La
 Himley DY3............49 B3
 Hopwas B78............20 B4
Plantation Rd WS5......43 A4
Plantation The DY5.....61 B7
Plant Ct ■ DY5.........61 D2
Plant La WS7............6 E7
Plant Lane Bsns Pk WS7..6 D7
Plants Brook Cres B24..57 D3
Plants Brook Rd B76....57 F6
Plantsbrook Reservoirs
 Nature Reserve★ B76...58 A5
Plantsbrook Sch B72....46 C4
Plants Cl
 Great Wyrley WS6......14 A8
 Sutton Coldfield B73...45 D1
Plants Gr B24..........57 D5
Plants Hill Cres CV4..111 E1
Plants Hill Wood Nature
 Reserve★ CV4.........111 D1
Plants Hollow DY5......61 D1
Plant St
 Cradley Heath B64.....62 D1
 Stourbridge DY8.......60 E2
Plant Way WS3.........14 F4
Plascom Rd WV1.........26 A1
Plato Cl CV34.........161 E5
Platts Cres DY8........80 E8
Platts Dr DY8..........80 F8
Platts Rd DY8..........80 E8
Platt St
 Cannock WS11...........2 A5
 Darlaston WS10........41 D5
Playdon Gr B14........105 A3
Pleasant Cl DY6........60 C4
Pleasant St
 Kidderminster DY10....116 E7
 West Bromwich, Hill Top
 B70...................53 A8
 West Bromwich, Lambert's End
 B70...................53 C2
Pleasant View DY3......50 E7
Pleasant Way CV32.....157 A2
PLECK.................42 C8
Pleck Bsns Pk WS2......28 C1
Pleck Ho B14.........104 C1
Pleck Ind Est WS2......28 C8
Pleck Rd WS2...........28 C8
Pleck Wlk B38.........104 A1
Plestowes Cl B90......106 B5
Pleydell Cl CV3.......134 C5
Plimsoll Gr B32........84 C5
Plimsoll St DY11......116 B5
Plough and Harrow Rd
 B16...................65 F1
Plough Ave B32.........84 C2
Plough Ct B75..........32 E3
PLOUGH HILL...........72 A6
Plough Hill Rd CV10....72 A6
Ploughmans Pl B75......32 D4
Ploughmans Wlk
 Kingswinford DY6......60 A7
 Lichfield WS13.........3 C3
 Stoke Heath B60......150 D6
 Wolverhampton WV8.....10 F1
Plover Cl WV10.........12 B7
Ploverdale Cres DY6....61 A6
Plover Gr DY10........117 B1
Plowden Rd B33........69 A3
Plume St B6............67 C8
Plumstead Cl B97......153 C6
Plumstead Rd B44......56 B8
Plym Cl WV11...........26 C5
Plymouth Cl
 Birmingham B31.......123 A7
 Coventry CV2.........114 C7
Plymouth Dr B45.......122 A1
Plymouth Pl CV31......157 C1
Plymouth Rd
 Barnt Green B45......138 A8
 Birmingham B30.......104 B7
 Redditch B97.........153 D2
Plympton Mews ■ B71...53 C6

Pochard Cl DY10.......116 F1
Poets Cnr B10..........87 D7
Poins Cl CV34.........161 F3
Pointon Cl WV14........40 A2
Poitiers Rd CV3.......133 D6
Polden Cl B63..........82 C1
POLESWORTH............36 F8
Polesworth Cl B98.....154 D1
Polesworth Dr B36......69 B6
Polesworth Sch The B78.36 F7
Pollard Rd B27.........88 C1
Pollards The B23.......56 E8
Polly Brooks Yd DY9....81 E5
Polo Fields DY9........81 B1
Polperro Dr CV5.......112 A5
Pomeroy Cl CV4........131 D7
Pomeroy Rd
 Birmingham B32........84 C1
 Birmingham, Pheasey B43..44 D4
Pommel Cl WS5..........42 F4
Pond Cres WV2..........39 F7
Pond Farm Mews CV5....111 E5
Pond Gr WV2............39 F7
Pond La WV2............39 D7
Pondthorpe CV3.......134 E6
Ponesfield Rd WS13......3 B2
Ponesgreen WS13........3 B2
Pontypool Ave CV3.....134 F6
Pool Ave WS11..........6 B5
Pool Bank B98.........153 E2
Pool Bank St CV11......73 B4
Poole Cres
 Birmingham B17........85 C3
 Brownhills WS8.........6 D2
Poole Ho Rd B43........40 D2
Poolehouse Rd B43......43 E3
Pool End Cl B93.......127 F6
Poole Rd CV6..........113 A6
Pooles Cl DY10........116 E7
Pooles La WV12.........27 D8
Poole St
 Stourbridge DY8.......80 E4
 Wolverhampton WV10....25 E4
Poole's Way CV7.........7 C7
Pooley La B78..........22 F2
Pool Farm Rd B27.......88 C1
Pool Field Ave B31....102 E7
Poolfield Dr B91......106 F3
Poolfield Rd WS13.......8 E6
Pool Furlong DY9.......99 E1
Pool Gn WS9............30 A5
Pool Green Terr WS9....30 A5
Pool Hall Cres WV3.....38 A8
Pool Hall Rd WV3.......38 A8
Pool Hayes Com Sch
 WV12.................27 B5
Pool Hayes La WV12.....27 B5
Pool Hayes Prim Sch
 WV12.................27 B6
Poolhead La
 Earlswood B94........141 C7
 Tanworth-In-A B94....141 E5
Pool La B69............63 F3
Pool Mdw
 Cheslyn Hay WS6........4 D1
 Sutton Coldfield B76...58 A8
Pool Meadow Cl
 Birmingham B13........87 C1
 Solihull B91.........107 F2
Pool Rd
 Brownhills WS7.........6 E3
 Burntwood WS7.........6 E4
 Halesowen B63........83 A2
 Nuneaton CV10.........72 F5
 Smethwick B66.........65 B5
 Studley B80..........159 E4
 Wednesfield WV11......27 A6
Pool Road Bsns Ctr CV10.72 F5
Pool Road Ind Est CV10..72 F5
Poolside Gdns CV3.....133 A5
Pool St
 Birmingham B6.........66 F6
 Dudley DY1............51 A6
 Walsall WS1...........28 F1
 Wolverhampton WV2....163 B1
Pooltail Wlk B31......102 D1
Pool View
 Great Wyrley WS6.......5 A4
 Walsall WS4...........29 D7
Pool Way B33...........69 A1
Pope Gr WS12...........1 F6
Pope Rd WV10...........12 B1
Popes La
 Astwood Bank B96.....158 E2
 Birmingham B30, B31, B38 103 D3
 Wolverhampton WV6.....24 A6
Pope's La B69..........64 B7
Pope St
 Birmingham B1.........66 B3
 Smethwick B66.........65 B7
Poplar Ave
 Bedworth CV12.........78 D2
 Birmingham B30........55 C1
 Birmingham, Balsall Heath
 B12..................87 A5
 Birmingham, Coleshill Heath
 B37..................90 C8
 Birmingham, Edgbaston B17 65 B2
 ■ Birmingham, Erdington
 B23..................56 F4
 Birmingham, King's Heath
 B14..................104 F8
 Birmingham, Lozells B19 66 C8
 Brownhills WS8........16 A8
 Burntwood WS7.........6 F6
 Cannock WS11..........1 F4

Poplar Ave continued
Oldbury, Grace Mary Estate
B69 . . . . 63 C8
Oldbury, Langley B69 . . . . . 64 A4
Sutton Coldfield B75 . . . . . 46 F7
Tipton DY4 . . . . 51 D5
Walsall, Yew Tree WS5 . . . 43 A4
West Bromwich B70 . . . . . 53 E2
Willenhall WS2 . . . . 27 E4
Wolverhampton WV11 . . . . 26 B7
Poplar Cl
Catshill B61 . . . . 136 F8
Oldbury B69 . . . . 52 C1
Wombourne WV5 . . . . 49 B6
Poplar Cres
Dudley DY1 . . . . 51 B3
Stourbridge DY8 . . . . 80 D3
Poplar Dr
Barnt Green B45 . . . . 138 D8
Birmingham, Washwood Heath
B8 . . . . 67 D6
Birmingham, Witton B6 . . . . 55 F5
Poplar Gn DY1 . . . . 51 A6
Poplar Gr
4 Birmingham B19 . . . . . . 66 C8
Ryton-on-D CV8 . . . . 135 B1
Smethwick B66 . . . . 65 B3
West Bromwich B70 . . . . . 53 E2
Poplar Ho CV2 . . . . 78 D2
Poplar La
Cannock WS11 . . . . 1 B1
Romsley B62 . . . . 101 A4
Poplar Rd
Bilston WV14 . . . . 40 F7
Birmingham, Moseley B11 . . 86 E1
Birmingham, Sparkhill B11 . 87 C5
Brownhills WS8 . . . . 16 A8
Coventry CV5 . . . . 112 F1
Dorridge B93 . . . . 127 F3
Great Wyrley WS6 . . . . 5 A1
Kidderminster DY11 . . . . 116 C4
Kingswinford DY6 . . . . . . 60 E5
Oldbury B69 . . . . 64 A8
Redditch B97 . . . . 153 A3
Smethwick B66 . . . . 65 C4
Solihull B91 . . . . 107 C4
Stourbridge DY8 . . . . 80 E3
Wednesbury WS10 . . . . . . 42 A5
Wolverhampton WV3 . . . . . 39 A6
Poplar Rise
Birmingham B42 . . . . 55 B7
Oldbury B69 . . . . 63 A8
Sutton Coldfield B74 . . . . . 31 D6
Poplar Row DY11 . . . . . 116 C4
Poplars Dr B36 . . . . 69 B8
Poplars La B96 . . . . 158 A1
Poplar St
Norton Canes WS11 . . . . . . 6 A6
Smethwick B66 . . . . 65 C5
Wolverhampton WV2 . . . . . 39 D6
Poplars The
Birmingham, Rotton Park
B16 . . . . 66 A7
Birmingham, Sparkhill B11 . 87 C6
Brierley Hill DY5 . . . . 61 B7
Cannock WS11 . . . . 1 E4
Nuneaton CV10 . . . . 72 D3
Smethwick B66 . . . . 65 C4
Stourbridge DY8 . . . . 60 F2
Poplars Trad Est B80 . . . 159 D6
Poplars Trad Est B6 . . . . 55 F5
Poplar Trees B47 . . . . . 125 A6
Poplar Way
Nuneaton CV10 . . . . 72 A7
Solihull B91 . . . . 107 C4
Poplarwoods B32 . . . . . . 84 B2
Poppy Cl CV10 . . . . 78 A8
Poppy Dr 3 WS3 . . . . . . 43 A3
Poppyfield Ct CV4 . . . . . 132 D3
Poppy Gn B8 . . . . 67 F4
Poppy La B24 . . . . 57 C5
Poppymead B23 . . . . 56 B8
Porchester Cl
Brownhills WS9 . . . . 16 A2
Coventry CV5 . . . . 115 A2
Porchester Dr B19 . . . . . . 66 D6
Porchester St B19 . . . . . . 66 D6
Porlock Cl CV3 . . . . 133 E5
Porlock Cres B31 . . . . . . 102 D3
Porlock Rd DY8 . . . . 81 A6
Portal Rd WS2 . . . . 27 F2
Porthcester Dr DY11 . . . . 26 D5
Porter Cl
Coventry CV4 . . . . 131 E4
Sutton Coldfield B72 . . . . . 57 B7
Porters Croft B17 . . . . . . 85 A8
Porters Field 6 DY2 . . . . 51 D1
Portersfield Ind Est B64 . . 82 D8
Portersfield Rd B64 . . . . . 82 C8
Portershill Dr B90 . . . . . 106 C1
Porter St DY2 . . . . 51 D1
Porter Street S 9 DY2 . . . 51 D1
Porters Way B9 . . . . 67 E2
Portfield Dr DY4 . . . . 52 A3
Portfield Gr B23 . . . . 57 B7
Porthkerry Gr DY3 . . . . . 50 B7
Port Hope Rd B11 . . . . . . 87 A7
Porthouse Gr WV14 . . . . . 40 B3
Portia Ave B90 . . . . 106 B1
Portia Cl CV11 . . . . 74 A1
Portia Way CV34 . . . . . . 161 E3
Portland Ave
Aldridge WS9 . . . . 30 B5
Tamworth B79 . . . . 20 F8
Portland Cres DY9 . . . . . . 81 B1

Portland Ct
Aldridge WS9 . . . . 30 B6
9 Royal Leamington Spa
CV32 . . . . 161 F8
Portland Dr
Hinckley LE10 . . . . 71 E4
Nuneaton CV10 . . . . 72 C4
Oldbury B69 . . . . 52 D3
Stourbridge DY8 . . . . 80 E3
Portland Mews 10 CV32 . 161 F8
Portland Pl
Cannock WS11 . . . . 4 C7
Dudley WV14 . . . . 51 B7
Portland Place E CV32 . . 161 F8
Portland Place W 5
CV32 . . . . 161 F8
Portland Rd
Aldridge WS9 . . . . 30 B6
Birmingham B16 . . . . 65 D1
Portland St
Birmingham B6 . . . . 67 A7
Royal Leamington Spa
CV32 . . . . 161 F8
Walsall WS2 . . . . 28 E3
Portland Terr 6 B18 . . . . 66 A5
Portleys La B78 . . . . 34 D4
Portman Rd B13 . . . . . . 104 F7
Portmanteau Mews B94 . 143 C6
PORTOBELLO 26 E1
Portobello Cl WV13 . . . . . 26 D1
Portobello Rd B70 . . . . . . 53 A8
Portobello Way CV34 . . . 161 C8
Portreath Dr CV11 . . . . . 74 A5
Portree Ave CV3 . . . . . . 114 A4
Portrush Ave B38 . . . . . 103 D1
Portrush Rd WV6 . . . . . . 23 D4
Portsdown Cl WV10 . . . . . 25 F7
Portsdown Rd B63 . . . . . . 82 D2
Portsea Cl CV3 . . . . 133 D6
Portsea St WS3 . . . . 28 C6
Portswood Cl WV9 . . . . . 10 F1
PORTWAY
Olbury 63 C6
Redditch 141 A5
Portway Cl
Coventry CV4 . . . . 131 E8
Kingswinford DY6 . . . . . . 60 E5
Royal Leamington Spa
CV31 . . . . 162 D6
Solihull B91 . . . . 106 C1
Portway Hill B65 . . . . 63 C6
Portway Rd
Bilston WV14 . . . . 40 F7
Oldbury B69 . . . . 63 F7
Rowley Regis B65 . . . . . . 63 B5
Wednesbury WS10 . . . . . . 41 E2
Portway The DY6 . . . . . . 60 E5
Portway Wlk B65 . . . . 63 C6
Portwrinkle Ave CV6 . . . 114 A6
Poseidon Way CV34 . . . . 161 F4
Posey Cl B21 . . . . 54 C3
Post Box B1 . . . . 164 B1
Postbridge Rd CV3 . . . . 133 D5
Post Office Wlk B96 . . . . 158 E1
Poston Croft B14 . . . . . . 104 D3
Potter Cl B23 . . . . 56 E8
Potter Ct 8 DY5 . . . . 61 D2
Potters Brook 8 WV14 . . 52 E5
POTTER'S GREEN 96 E1
Potters Green Prim Sch
CV2 . . . . 96 E2
Potters Green Rd CV2 . . . 96 E1
Potters La
Birmingham B6 . . . . 66 E7
Wednesbury WS10 . . . . . . 41 F2
Potters Rd CV12 . . . . 77 E1
Potterton Way B66 . . . . . 64 F8
Pottery Rd B68 . . . . 64 D1
Potton Cl CV3 . . . . 134 E6
Potts Cl CV8 . . . . 148 C4
POUK HILL 28 A3
Pouk Hill Cl WS2 . . . . . . 28 A3
Pouk La WS14 . . . . 16 F7
Poultney Rd CV6 . . . . . . 113 A6
Poultney St B70 . . . . 52 F7
Poulton Cl B13 . . . . 87 A2
Pound Cl
Berkswell CV7 . . . . 110 D3
Lapworth B94 . . . . 144 B3
Oldbury B68 . . . . 63 F3
Poundgate La CV4 . . . . . 131 D7
Pound Gn B8 . . . . 67 F6
Pound House La
Nuthurst B94 . . . . 143 A4
Tanworth-in-A B94 . . . . . . 142 F4
Pound La
Birmingham B32 . . . . 101 F3
Royal Leamington Spa
CV32 . . . . 157 A3
Pound Rd
Birmingham B14 . . . . 104 E2
Oldbury B68 . . . . 64 A2
Wednesbury WS10 . . . . . . 42 A3
Pountney St WV2 . . . . . . 163 B1
Pourbaix Ho WS13 . . . . 9 B6
Povey Rd B98 . . . . 158 E2
Powell Ave B32 . . . . 84 A6
Powell Pl
Bilston WV14 . . . . 40 E3
Tipton DY4 . . . . 52 C5
Powell Rd CV2 . . . . 114 A4
Powells Cl B72 . . . . 46 C2
Powells Rd B13 . . . . 45 C2
Powell St
Birmingham B1 . . . . 66 B3
7 Halesowen B63 . . . . . . 83 B3

Powell St continued
Wolverhampton WV10 . . . . 25 F4
Powell Way CV11 . . . . . . 73 C4
Power Cres B16 . . . . 66 A2
Powers Ct 4 CV32 . . . . . 156 F1
Powers Rd LE9 . . . . 71 F5
Power Way DY4 . . . . 52 D8
Powick Rd B23 . . . . 56 D1
Powis Ave DY4 . . . . 52 B7
Powis Gr CV8 . . . . 148 C5
Powke La B65 . . . . 63 A2
Powke Lane Ind Est B65 . 63 A2
Powlers Cl DY9 . . . . 81 A2
Powlett St WV2 . . . . 163 C2
Poxon Rd WS9 . . . . 16 A3
Poynings The WV6 . . . . . 24 C5
Poyser Rd CV10 . . . . 78 C8
Praetor Ho 8 LE10 . . . . . 71 D1
Pratts La B80 . . . . 159 F7
Precinct Sh Ctr CV1 . . . . 165 B2
Precinct The
Tamworth B79 . . . . 21 B5
Willenhall WV12 . . . . 27 B5
Premier Bsns Ctr 3 DY9 . 81 F5
Premier Bsns Pk WS2 . . . 28 D1
Premier Ct B30 . . . . 104 C5
Premier Partnership Ind Est
DY5 . . . . 61 A3
Premier St B7 . . . . 67 D8
Premier Trad Est B7 . . . . 66 F5
Prescelly Cl CV10 . . . . . . 72 B3
Prescelly Ct CV8 . . . . . . 147 F5
Prescot Rd DY9 . . . . 81 C3
President Kennedy Comp
Sch & Com Coll CV6 . . . 95 B4
Prestbury Rd B6 . . . . 66 E8
Presthope Rd B29 . . . . . 103 B7
Prestley Smith Sch B42 . . . 55 C8
Preston Ave B76 . . . . 46 E3
Preston Cl
Coventry CV4 . . . . 131 F7
Redditch B98 . . . . 154 B6
Preston Ho 4 WS1 . . . . . 28 F1
Preston Rd
Birmingham, Hockley B18 . . 65 F6
Birmingham, South Yardley
B26 . . . . 88 D7
Hinckley LE10 . . . . 71 B2
Prestons Row WV14 . . . . 40 A3
Prestwick Cl B75 . . . . . . 46 C7
Prestwick Rd
Birmingham B35 . . . . 58 B4
Kingswinford DY6 . . . . . . 60 C6
Prestwood Ave WV11 . . . 26 D7
Prestwood Dr DY7 . . . . . 80 B7
Prestwood Rd
Birmingham B29 . . . . 103 B8
Wolverhampton WV11 . . . . 26 A5
Prestwood Road W WV11 . 26 B7
Pretoria Rd B9 . . . . 67 E3
Priam Cir CV34 . . . . 161 F3
Priam Gr WS3 . . . . 15 B5
Price Ave B78 . . . . 20 D1
Price Close E CV34 . . . . 160 B4
Price Close W CV34 . . . . 160 B4
Price Cres WV14 . . . . . . 40 D7
Price Rd
Cubbington CV32 . . . . . . 157 E5
Stourbridge DY9 . . . . 82 A6
Wednesbury WS10 . . . . . . 42 C3
Prices Rd DY3 . . . . 50 C3
Price St
Bilston WV14 . . . . 40 F5
Birmingham B4 . . . . 164 C4
Cannock WS11 . . . . 1 E1
Dudley DY2 . . . . 51 E1
Smethwick B66 . . . . 65 B5
West Bromwich B70 . . . . . 53 C3
Pridmore Rd CV6 . . . . . . 113 D7
Priest Meadow Cl B96 . . 158 D1
Priest St B64 . . . . 62 F1
Primley Ave
Birmingham B36 . . . . 68 D7
Tamworth B77 . . . . 35 F5
Walsall WS2 . . . . 28 B2
Primley Cl WS2 . . . . 28 B2
Primrose Ave
Birmingham B11 . . . . 87 C5
Tipton DY4 . . . . 52 C8
Wolverhampton WV10 . . . . 11 D3
Primrose Bank B68 . . . . . 64 B4
Primrose Cl
Cradley Heath B64 . . . . . . 82 B8
Lickey End B60 . . . . 137 C6
Walsall WS3 . . . . 15 A5
Primrose Cres DY1 . . . . . 51 C4
Primrose Croft
Birmingham, Perry Common
B23 . . . . 56 C7
Birmingham, Yardley Wood
B28 . . . . 105 F5
Primrose Dr
Bedworth CV12 . . . . 77 E1
Hinckley LE10 . . . . 75 E5

Primrose Gdns
Birmingham B38 . . . . 123 F8
Codsall WV8 . . . . 10 A3
Featherstone WV10 . . . . . . 12 B7
Primrose Hill
Birmingham B38 . . . . 124 A8
Smethwick B67 . . . . 64 D4
Stourbridge DY8 . . . . 60 E1
Warwick CV34 . . . . 155 E2
Primrose Hill Com Sch
B38 . . . . 123 F8
Primrose Hill St CV1 . . . . 165 C4
Primrose Hill Trad Est
DY2 . . . . 62 D4
Primrose La
Birmingham B28 . . . . 105 F5
Wolverhampton WV10 . . . . 26 A8
Primrose Mdw 1 WS11 . . . 2 C2
Primrose Pk DY5 . . . . 61 C7
Primrose Rd DY2 . . . . 62 C4
Primroses The WS5 . . . . . 43 B4
Primrose Way WV10 . . . . 116 F4
Primrose Woods B32 . . . . 84 B2
Primsland Cl B90 . . . . . . 127 C7

Prince Albert Prim Sch
B6 . . . . 66 E8
Prince Albert St B9 . . . . . 67 D1
Prince Andrew Cres B45 . 101 E2
Prince Charles Cl B45 . . 101 E2
Prince Charles Rd 2
WV14 . . . . 40 F3
Prince Edward Dr B45 . . 101 E2
Prince George Rd WV10 . 42 A5
Prince of Wales La B14 . 105 D3
Prince of Wales Rd CV5 . 112 E3
Prince of Wales Wlk 3
B66 . . . . 65 C5
Princep Cl B43 . . . . 44 D4
Prince Philip Cl B45 . . . 101 E2
Prince Rd B30 . . . . 104 A3
Prince Regent Ct 3
CV31 . . . . 161 F6
Prince Rupert Mews WS13 . 9 A8
Prince Rupert's Way WS13 . 9 A8
Princes Ave WS1 . . . . . . 43 A8
Prince's Ave
Nuneaton CV11 . . . . 73 B3
Walsall WS1 . . . . 29 B1
Princes Cl CV3 . . . . 134 B8
Princes Dr
Codsall WV8 . . . . 10 A2
Coventry CV6 . . . . 96 B1
Kenilworth CV8 . . . . 148 B7
Prince's Dr CV31 . . . . . . 161 E8
Princes Drive Ind Est
CV8 . . . . 148 A8
PRINCES END 51 E8
Princes End Ind Pk DY4 . 40 E1
Princes Gate
Solihull B91 . . . . 107 A4
West Bromwich B70 . . . . . 53 E2
Princes Gdns WV8 . . . . . 10 A2
Prince's Rd DY8 . . . . 80 D3
Prince's Rd B69 . . . . 52 B2
Princess Alice Dr B73 . . . 45 D2
Princess Alley WV1 . . . . 163 C3
Princess Anne Dr B45 . . 101 E2
Princess Anne Rd
Bilston WV14 . . . . 40 F3
Willenhall WS2 . . . . 27 F3
Princess Cl WS7 . . . . 6 E7
Princess Cres B63 . . . . . . 82 E6
Princess Ct WV10 . . . . . . 26 A6
Princess Gr B71 . . . . 53 D8
Princess of Wales Com Hospl
B61 . . . . 137 A4
Princess Rd
Birmingham B5 . . . . 86 E7
Hinckley LE10 . . . . 75 E8
Oldbury B68 . . . . 64 D2
Princess Sq 1 WV14 . . . . 40 F3
Princess St
Burntwood WS7 . . . . 6 E8
Cannock WS11 . . . . 1 F5
Coventry CV6 . . . . 113 F7
Wolverhampton WV1 . . . . 163 C3
Prince's St
Nuneaton CV11 . . . . 73 C3
Royal Leamington Spa
CV32 . . . . 157 B1
Princess Way WS10 . . . . 41 C8
Prince St
Brownhills WS9 . . . . 15 F2
Cannock WS12 . . . . 1 E6
Cradley Heath B64 . . . . . . 82 D8
Dudley DY2 . . . . 62 C6
Walsall WS2 . . . . 42 C8
Prince's St
Nuneaton CV11 . . . . 73 C3
Royal Leamington Spa
CV32 . . . . 157 A3
Princess Way WS10 . . . . 41 C8
Prince St
Brownhills WS9 . . . . 15 F2
Cannock WS12 . . . . 1 E6
Cradley Heath B64 . . . . . . 82 D8
Walsall WS1 . . . . 42 E3
Prince's Way B91 . . . . . 107 D4
Princethorpe Cl
Birmingham B34 . . . . 69 D7
Solihull B90 . . . . 106 A2
Princethorpe Inf Sch B29 . 85 A1
Princethorpe Jun Sch
B29 . . . . 85 A1
Princethorpe Rd B29 . . . . 85 A1
Prince Thorpe Rd WV14 . 41 B8
Princethorpe Way CV3 . . 134 E8
Princeton Gdns WV9 . . . . 10 F2
Prince William Cl
Birmingham B23 . . . . 56 C2
Coventry CV6 . . . . 112 E6
Walsall WS4 . . . . 28 F4
Princip St B4 . . . . 164 C4
Printing House St B4 . . . 164 C3
Prior Ave B60 . . . . 150 C3

Prior Cl DY10 . . . . 117 C5
Prior Deram Wlk CV4 . . . 132 C7
Priors Cl CV7 . . . . 130 B6
Priors Field Prim Sch
CV8 . . . . 147 D7
Priorsfield Rd
4 Coventry CV6 . . . . . . 113 A4
Coventry CV6 . . . . 147 D6
Priorsfield Road N 3
CV6 . . . . 113 A4
Priorsfield Road S CV6 . . 113 A4
Priors Gr CV34 . . . . 160 B3
Priors Harnall CV1 . . . . 165 D4
Priors Mill DY3 . . . . 50 E5
Priors Oak B97 . . . . 153 B4
Priors The CV12 . . . . 78 C2
Priors Way B23 . . . . 56 C8
PRIORY 51 C3
Priory Ave B29 . . . . 86 B2
Priory Cl
Dudley DY1 . . . . 51 B2
Kingswinford B94 . . . . . . 144 D5
Smethwick B66 . . . . 65 C4
Stourbridge DY8 . . . . 81 B3
Tamworth B79 . . . . 20 F7
West Bromwich B70 . . . . . 53 F2
Priory Croft CV8 . . . . . . 148 A4
Priory Ct
Brownhills WS9 . . . . 16 A4
Coventry CV5 . . . . 113 A1
3 Dudley DY1 . . . . 51 C1
Solihull B90 . . . . 127 B7
Stourbridge DY8 . . . . 81 B3
Studley B80 . . . . 159 E5
Wolverhampton WV1 . . . . 163 B4
Priory Cts The B2 . . . . . 164 C3
Priory Dr B68 . . . . 64 B3
Priory Field Cl WV14 . . . . 39 F1
Priorygate Way B9 . . . . . 67 E3
Priory Gdns B28 . . . . . . 105 D4
Priory Green Prim Sch
WV9 . . . . 11 A2
Priory Ho
Halesowen B63 . . . . 82 F5
Kenilworth CV8 . . . . 147 F4
Priory La DY3 . . . . 50 D7
Priory Mews CV34 . . . . . 160 E7
Priory New Way Ind Est
B6 . . . . 66 F5
Priory Place Entertainment
Ctr CV1 . . . . 165 C3
Priory Prim Sch DY1 . . . . . 51 B3
Priory Prim Sch The
WS10 . . . . 42 D2
Priory Queensway The
B4 . . . . 164 C3
Priory Rd
Birmingham, Aston B6 . . . . 67 B8
Birmingham, Edgbaston B5,
B15 . . . . 86 B5
Birmingham, Stirchley B14 . 104 C7
Birmingham, Warstock
B28 . . . . 105 D3
Cannock WS12 . . . . 2 D4
Dodford B61 . . . . 136 A6
Dudley DY1 . . . . 51 C3
Halesowen B63 . . . . 83 F4
Kenilworth CV8 . . . . 148 A4
Stourbridge DY8 . . . . 81 B3
Warwick CV34 . . . . 160 E7
Priory Row CV1 . . . . 165 C3
Priory Sch B15 . . . . 86 B6
Priory Sq
Birmingham B4 . . . . 164 C3
Studley B80 . . . . 159 E5
Priory St
Coventry CV1 . . . . 165 C3
Dudley DY1 . . . . 51 C1
Nuneaton CV10 . . . . 72 D3
Royal Leamington Spa
CV31 . . . . 161 F6
Priory Terr CV31 . . . . . . 162 A7
Priory The DY3 . . . . 50 D8
Priory Visitors Ctr★ CV1 . 165 C3
Priory Wlk
Birmingham B4 . . . . 164 C3
Hinckley LE10 . . . . 71 E1
Sutton Coldfield B72 . . . . . 57 C7
10 Warwick CV34 . . . . . . 160 E7
Priory Woods Nature
Reserve★ B71 . . . . 54 A3
Pritchard Ave WV11 . . . . 26 E6
Pritchard Cl B66 . . . . 65 B5
Pritchard St
Brierley Hill DY5 . . . . 61 B3
Wednesbury WS10 . . . . . . 42 A3
Pritchatts Rd B15 . . . . . . 86 A4
Pritchett Ave WV4 . . . . . 39 F3
Pritchett Rd B31 . . . . . . 123 B7
Pritchett St B6 . . . . 66 E5
Pritchett Twr 4 B10 . . . . 67 B1
Private Way B45 . . . . . . 122 C4
Privet Cl B44 . . . . 44 E3
Privet Rd CV2 . . . . 96 B2
Probert Rd WV10 . . . . . . 11 B1
Proctors Barn La B98 . . . 154 B4
Proctor's Barn Meadows
Nature Reserve★ B98 . . 154 B4
Proctor St B7 . . . . 67 A5
Proffitt Ave CV6 . . . . 96 A1
Proffitt Cl
Brownhills WS8 . . . . 16 A5
Walsall WS2 . . . . 28 E4
Proffitt St WS2 . . . . 28 E4

Progress Cl CV3 . . . . 135 A7
Progress Dr WS11 . . . . 4 F6
Progress Ind Ctr WS11 . 4 F7
Progress Way CV3 . . . . . . 135 A8
Prole St WV10 . . . . 25 E4
Prologis Pk CV6 . . . . 95 B5
Promenade The DY5 . . . . 61 D2
Prophets Cl B97 . . . . . . 153 D3
Prospect Dr WS13 . . . . . . 9 F8
Prospect Gdns DY8 . . . . 81 A4
Prospect Hill
  Kidderminster DY10 . . . 116 E6
  Redditch B97 . . . . 153 E4
  Stourbridge DY8 . . . . . . 81 A4
Prospect La
  Kidderminster DY10 . . . 116 E6
  Solihull B91 . . . . 106 D4
Prospect Manor Ct WS12 . . 2 C3
Prospect Pk WS11 . . . . . . 4 D7
Prospect Pl B12 . . . . 86 F5
Prospect Rd
  Birmingham B13 . . . . . . 86 F1
  Burntwood WS7 . . . . 7 B6
  Dudley DY3 . . . . 50 C2
  Halesowen B62 . . . . 83 C5
  Whitnash CV31 . . . . . . 162 B5
Prospect Road N B98 . . . 154 A4
Prospect Road S B98 . . . 154 A4
Prospect Row
  Dudley DY2 . . . . 62 D8
  Stourbridge DY8 . . . . . . 81 A3
Prospect St
  Bilston WV14 . . . . 40 E6
  Tamworth B79 . . . . 21 A5
  Wednesbury DY4 . . . . . . 41 C1
Prosper Mdw DY6 . . . . . . 60 F7
Prospero Cl B45 . . . . . . 102 A2
Prospero Dr CV34 . . . . . 161 E3
Prosser St
  Bilston WV14 . . . . 40 D5
  Wolverhampton WV10 . . 25 E5
Prossers Wlk B46 . . . . . 70 F7
Proud Cross Ringway
  DY11 . . . . 116 C6
Proud's La WV14 . . . . . . 40 D7
Provence Cl WV10 . . . . . . 25 F4
Providence Cl WS3 . . . . 28 C7
Providence Ct B64 . . . . 82 C8
Providence Dr DY9 . . . . . 81 E6
Providence Ind Est DY9 . 81 E6
Providence La WS3 . . . . 28 C6
Providence Rd B61 . . . 136 F3
Providence Row WV14 . . 51 B8
Providence St
  Coventry CV5 . . . . 132 F8
  Cradley Heath B64 . . . . 62 D1
  Stourbridge DY9 . . . . . . 81 F6
  Tipton DY4 . . . . 52 C5
Providence Terr WS10 . . 41 E6
Provost Williams CE Prim
  Sch CV8 . . . . 135 A1
Prudden Cl B97 . . . . . . 158 C6
Pruden Ave WV14 . . . . . 39 F3
Pryor Rd B68 . . . . 64 C4
Ptarmigan Pl CV11 . . . . 73 F3
Public The B70 . . . . 53 D3
Puckering's La 11 CV34 . 160 E6
Puddlers Dr DY4 . . . . . . 51 E7
Pudsey Dr B75 . . . . 32 C3
Pugh Cres WS2 . . . . 27 E2
Pughe's Cl LE10 . . . . . . 76 A6
Pugh Rd
  Bilston WV14 . . . . 40 E3
  Birmingham B6 . . . . 67 A8
  Wolverhampton WV4, WV14 39 F2
Pugin Cl WV6 . . . . 23 D3
Pugin Gdns B23 . . . . . . 56 D8
Pullman Cl B77 . . . . . . 22 A2
Pulman Cl B97 . . . . . . 153 C4
Puma Way CV1 . . . . 165 C1
Pumphouse Cl CV6 . . . . 96 B6
Pumphouse La
  Blackwell B45, B60 . . 137 F7
  Redditch B97 . . . . 152 D1
Pumphouse Way 2 B69 . 63 F4
Pump St
  Kidderminster DY10 . . . 116 E4
  Wolverhampton WV2 . . . 40 A7
Puppy Gn DY4 . . . . 52 B5
Purbeck Cl B63 . . . . . . 82 D1
Purbeck Croft B32 . . . . 84 F4
Purbrook B77 . . . . 35 E8
Purbrook Rd WV1 . . . . . . 40 A8
Purcell Ave
  Lichfield WS13 . . . . 3 C2
  Nuneaton CV11 . . . . . . 79 A7
Purcell Cl
  Cannock WS11 . . . . 2 C2
  Royal Leamington Spa
  CV32 . . . . 162 A8
Purcell Rd
  Coventry CV6 . . . . 114 B8
  Wolverhampton WV10 . . 25 D8
Purdy Rd WV14 . . . . . . 40 E2
Purefoy Rd
  Birmingham B13 . . . . . 105 C5
  Coventry CV3 . . . . 133 D8
Purley Gr B23 . . . . 56 A5
Purlieu La CV8 . . . . . . 147 D5
Purlin Wharf DY2 . . . . . 62 E4
Purnells Way B93 . . . . 128 A5
Purser Dr CV34 . . . . . . 160 B4
Purshall Cl B97 . . . . . 153 C3
Purslet Rd WV1 . . . . . . 26 A2
Purslow Gr B31 . . . . . . 103 A1

Purton Mews CV31 . . . . . 162 C6
Putney Ave B20 . . . . 55 C1
Putney La B62 . . . . 101 B1
Putney Rd B20 . . . . 55 C1
Putney Wlk B37 . . . . 70 B3
Puxton Dr DY11 . . . . 116 D8
Puxton La CV11 . . . . 116 C7
Pye Green Rd WS11 . . . . . 1 E4
Pye Green Valley Prim Sch
  WS12 . . . . 2 A7
Pyeharps Rd LE10 . . . . . . 75 E5
PYPE HAYES 57 D5
Pype Hayes Cl B24 . . . . . 57 D4
Pype Hayes Rd B24 . . . . . 57 D4
Pyrec Sq CV34 . . . . 160 A8
Pytchley Ho 6 B20 . . . . 54 F3
Pytman Dr B76 . . . . 58 A7
Pyt Pk CV5 . . . . 112 C4

Q

Q3 Acad B43 . . . . 43 D3
Quadrangle The B90 . . . 126 E8
Quadrant Ho B32 . . . . . 84 E7
Quadrant The CV1 . . . . 165 B2
Quadrant The CV11 . . . . 73 E3
Quadrant The DY3 . . . . 39 D1
Quadrille Lawns WV9 . . 10 F2
Quail Cl WS11 . . . . 2 A1
Quail Gn WV6 . . . . 23 F2
Quail Park Dr DY10 . . . 117 A2
Qualcast Rd WV1, WV10 . 25 F2
Qualcast Road Ind Est
  WV1 . . . . 25 F2
Quantock Cl
  Birmingham B45 . . . . . 102 B2
  Brownhills WS8 . . . . . . 16 A4
  Halesowen B63 . . . . . . 82 D2
Quantock Dr
  Kidderminster DY10 . . . 117 A6
  Nuneaton CV10 . . . . . . 72 B3
Quantock Rd DY8 . . . . . 81 B6
Quantry La DY9 . . . . . . 120 F8
Quarrington Gr B14 . . 105 A3
QUARRY BANK 82 A8
Quarry Bank Prim Sch
  DY5 . . . . 62 A1
Quarry Brow DY3 . . . . . 50 E6
Quarry Cl
  Cheslyn Hay WS6 . . . . . 4 E3
  Leek Wootton CV35 . . . 155 F7
Quarryfield La CV1 . . . 165 D1
Quarry Fields CV35 . . . 155 F7
QUARRY HILL 36 A7
Quarry Hill B63 . . . . . . 82 F2
Quarry Hills La WV4 . . 39 A5
Quarry House Cl B45 . . 101 F1
Quarry La
  Birmingham B31 . . . . . 103 A2
  Bromsgrove B61 . . . . . 150 D8
  Halesowen B63 . . . . . . 83 A2
  Walsall WS5 . . . . 43 B6
Quarry Park Rd DY8 . . . 99 A8
Quarry Rd
  Birmingham B29 . . . . . 103 A8
  Dudley DY2 . . . . 62 B1
  Kenilworth CV8 . . . . . 147 E6
Quarry Rise B69 . . . . . 63 B8
Quarry St CV32 . . . . . . 161 C8
Quarry The DY10 . . . . 116 F8
Quarry Wlk B45 . . . . . 122 A7
Quarrywood Gr CV2 . . . 114 A4
Quarry Yd CV10 . . . . . . 72 C4
Quatford Gdns WV10 . . 25 E5
Quayle Gr 2 DY8 . . . . . 60 D3
Quayside B18 . . . . 66 A5
Quayside Cl B69 . . . . . 63 D8
Quayside Dr WS2 . . . . . 42 C8
Queen Alexandra Coll
  B17 . . . . 85 A6
Queen Eleanors Dr B93 . 128 B8
Queen Elizabeth Ave WS2 27 F2
Queen Elizabeth Ct B19 . 66 B6
Queen Elizabeth Hospl
  B15 . . . . 85 E4
Queen Elizabeth Rd
  Birmingham B45 . . . . . 101 E2
  Kidderminster DY10 . . . 117 B5
  Nuneaton CV10 . . . . . . 73 D4
Queen Elizabeth's Mercian
  CV32 . . . . 157 A1
Queen Isabel's Ave CV3 . 133 D8
Queen Margaret's Rd
  CV4 . . . . 132 C8
Queen Mary's Gram Sch
  WS1 . . . . 43 A8
Queen Mary's High Sch
  WS4 . . . . 28 F3
Queen Mary's Rd
  Bedworth CV12 . . . . . . 78 C5
  Coventry CV6 . . . . 113 E8
Queen Mary St WS1 . . . 42 D6
Queen Philippa St CV3 . 133 D6
Queens Arc CV11 . . . . . 73 C4
Queen's Arc WV1 . . . . 163 B3
Queens Ave
  Birmingham B14 . . . . . 104 E8
  Solihull B90 . . . . 106 B1
Queen's Ave B69 . . . . . 52 A1
Queensbridge Rd B13 . . 86 E2
Queensbridge Sch B13 . 86 E2
Queensbury Sped Sch
  B24 . . . . 56 F2
Queens CE Jun Sch CV11 . 73 A4

Queens Cl
  Birmingham B24 . . . . . . 56 F2
  Smethwick B67 . . . . . . 65 A5
Queen's Cl CV8 . . . . . . 147 F3
Queen's Cotts B67 . . . . 65 A5
Queens Court Trad Est
  B70 . . . . 52 F3
Queens Cres WV14 . . . . 40 A1
Queen's Cres DY8 . . . . . 81 A7
Queen's Croft Sch WS13 . 9 B7
Queen's Cross DY1 . . . . 62 B8
Queens Ct
  Birmingham B3 . . . . . . 164 B4
  Birmingham B32 . . . . . 85 A5
  Brierley Hill DY5 . . . . 61 C6
  Nuneaton CV11 . . . . . . 73 A4
Queen's Ct WV10 . . . . . 26 A6
Queens Dr
  Birmingham B5 . . . . . . 164 C2
  Birmingham, Lifford B30 . 104 A4
  Burntwood WS7 . . . . . . 6 F5
  Rowley Regis B65 . . . . 63 D4
Queen's Dr CV35 . . . . . 145 A1
Queen's Dr The B62 . . . 83 C5
Queen's Foundation The
  B15 . . . . 85 F5
Queens Gdns
  Bilston WV14 . . . . 40 D7
  4 Birmingham B23 . . . . 56 B7
  Dudley DY2 . . . . 62 C4
Queens Head Rd B21 . . . 65 E7
Queens Hill DY9 . . . . 119 D7
Queens Hospital Cl B15 . 66 C1
Queensland Ave CV5 . . 112 F2
Queensland Gdns 8 CV12 . 77 F2
Queen's Lea WV13 . . . . 27 C5
Queen's Own Hussars Mus
  The ✱ CV34 . . . . 160 E6
Queens Par 5 B1 . . . . . 14 B1
Queen's Park Ct 3 LE10 . 75 E8
Queen's Park Flats 2
  LE10 . . . . 75 E8
Queen's Park Rd B32 . . 84 F6
Queen's Park Terr 4
  LE10 . . . . 75 E8
Queen Sq WV1 . . . . 163 B3
Queen's Rd
  Birmingham, Aston B6 . . 67 A8
  Birmingham, Yardley B26 . 68 F1
  Sedgley DY3 . . . . 50 E8
  Walsall WS4 . . . . 29 C7
Queen's Rd
  Birmingham B23 . . . . . . 56 C3
  Coventry CV1 . . . . 165 A2
  Hinckley LE10 . . . . . . 75 E8
  Kenilworth CV8 . . . . . 147 F3
  Nuneaton CV11 . . . . . . 73 B4
  Oldbury B68 . . . . 64 D5
  Smethwick B67 . . . . . . 64 D4
  Stourbridge DY8 . . . . . 80 F8
  Tipton DY4 . . . . 51 F5
  Walsall WS5 . . . . 43 B6
Queen's Ride B15 . . . . 86 D4
Queen's Sq CV34 . . . . . . 1 E1
Queen's Sq 3 CV34 . . . 160 D5
Queens Square Sh Ctr
  B70 . . . . 53 D3
Queen St
  Astwood Bank B96 . . . 158 E1
  Bedworth CV12 . . . . . . 78 C2
  Bilston, Bunker's Hill WV14 . 40 E5
  Birmingham B12 . . . . . . 87 B5
  Brierley Hill, Pensnett DY5 . 61 E3
  Brierley Hill, Quarry Bank
  DY5 . . . . 82 A8
  Brownhills WS9 . . . . . . 15 F2
  Burntwood WS7 . . . . . . 6 F5
  Cannock, Blackfords WS11 . 1 D1
  Cannock WS11 . . . . 2 A5
  Cheslyn Hay WS6 . . . . . 4 B3
  Cradley Heath B64 . . . 62 D1
  Cubbington CV32 . . . . 157 E5
  Darlaston, Darlaston Green
  WS10 . . . . 41 D8
  Darlaston, Moxley WS10 . 41 B4
  Halesowen B63 . . . . . . 83 A4
  Kingswinford DY6 . . . 116 E7
  Lichfield WS13 . . . . 9 A7
  Oldbury B68 . . . . 64 A8
  Redditch B98 . . . . . . 153 E4
  Royal Leamington Spa
  CV31 . . . . 161 E6
  Stourbridge DY8 . . . . . 80 F6
  Stourbridge, Wordsley DY8 . 60 E3
  Sutton Coldfield B72 . . 46 C4
  Tipton DY4 . . . . 51 F8
  Walsall WS2 . . . . 28 D1
  Wednesbury WS10 . . . . 41 E3
  West Bromwich B70 . . . 53 D3
  Queen Street Ind Est WS7 . 6 F5
Queen Street Pas 1 DY5 . 82 A8
Queensway
  Birmingham B6 . . . . . . 55 F3
  Halesowen B63 . . . . . . 83 B3
  Nuneaton CV10 . . . . . . 73 E6
  Oldbury B68 . . . . 64 A8
  Royal Leamington Spa
  CV31 . . . . 161 E6
  Stourbridge DY9 . . . . . 81 E2
  Sutton Coldfield B74 . . 45 A8
  Tamworth B79 . . . . 21 A8
Queens Way B78 . . . . . 36 F6
Queensway B68 . . . . . . 64 B1
Queensway Sped Sch
  B24 . . . . 56 F2
Queensway Trad Est
  Birmingham B5 . . . . . . 164 D3

Queensway Trad Est continued
  Royal Leamington Spa
  CV31 . . . . 161 E6
Queensway (Tunnel) B3 . 164 B3
Queenswood Ct CV7 . . . 94 D4
Queens Wood Ho B14 . . 104 D4
Queenswood Rd
  Birmingham B13 . . . . . . 87 A4
  Sutton Coldfield B75 . . 32 B1
Queen Victoria Ct 4
  LE10 . . . . 71 D1
Queen Victoria Prim Sch
  DY3 . . . . 50 E8
Queen Victoria Rd CV1 . 165 B2
Quenby Dr DY1 . . . . . . 51 A3
Quentin Dr DY1 . . . . . . 61 F8
Queslade Cl B43 . . . . . 44 A1
QUESLETT 44 C2
Queslett Rd B43 . . . . . 44 C1
Queslett Road E B74, B43 . 44 F5
Quibury Cl B98 . . . . . . 154 F3
Quicksand La WS9 . . . . 29 F4
Quigley Ave B9 . . . . . . 67 B2
Quillets Rd DY9 . . . . . 60 C3
Quilletts Cl CV6 . . . . . 96 A1
Quilter Cl
  Dudley WV14 . . . . 51 A8
  Willenhall WS2 . . . . . . 27 F3
Quilter Rd B24 . . . . . . 57 B2
Quince B77 . . . . 22 B3
Quincey Dr B24 . . . . . . 57 C3
Quince Rd DY5 . . . . . . 81 C7
Quinn Cl CV3 . . . . 134 B7
Quinneys La B98 . . . . . 159 B6
Quinton Ave WS6 . . . . . 4 F3
Quinton Bsns Pk B32 . . 84 A4
Quinton Church Prim Sch
  B32 . . . . 84 A6
Quinton Cl
  Redditch B98 . . . . . . 154 D1
  Solihull B92 . . . . 89 D3
Quintondale 5 B90 . . . 126 C8
Quinton Expressway B32 . 84 B4
Quinton Fitness Ctr B32 . 84 E6
Quinton Flats CV3 . . . 133 D7
Quinton La B32 . . . . . 84 B4
Quinton Par CV3 . . . . . 133 D7
Quinton Pk CV3 . . . . . 133 D7
Quinton Pl WS11 . . . . . 6 A4
Quinton Rd
  Birmingham B17 . . . . . 85 C3
  Coventry CV1 . . . . 165 C1
  Quinton Road W B32 . . 84 D4
Quonians La WS13 . . . . 9 B8
Quorn Cres DY8 . . . . . 60 C3
Quorn Gr B24 . . . . 57 B2
Quorn Ho 3 B20 . . . . . 54 F3
Quorn Way CV3 . . . . . . 134 E7

R

Rabbit La WV10 . . . . . . 12 A8
Rabone La B66 . . . . . . 65 C6
Raby Cl B69 . . . . 62 F8
Raby St WV2 . . . . 163 C2
Racecourse La DY8 . . . 80 F1
Racecourse Rd WV6 . . . 25 A5
Racecourse Road Ind Est
  WV6 . . . . 25 A5
Race Leys Inf Sch CV12 . 78 B3
Race Leys Jun Sch CV12 . 78 B3
Racemeadow Cres B64 . . 62 C1
Rachael Gdns WS10 . . . 42 C4
Rachel Cl DY4 . . . . . . 41 C1
Rachel Gdns B29 . . . . . 85 D2
Radbourn Dr B74 . . . . . 46 C6
Radbourne Dr B63 . . . . 82 A7
Radbourne La B48 . . . . 69 A4
Radbrook Way CV31 . . . 162 D6
Radcliffe Dr B62 . . . . . 83 E6
Radcliffe Gdns 6 CV31 . 162 A6
Radcliffe Rd CV5 . . . . . 132 F8
Radcliffe Twr 3 B12 . . 86 F8
Radclyffe Ho B16 . . . . 86 A8
Radd Cl B9 . . . . 68 A2
Raddens Rd B62 . . . . . 83 E6
Raddington Dr B92 . . . 106 E8
Raddlebarn Ct B29 . . . . 86 A1
Raddlebarn Farm Dr
  B29 . . . . 103 F8
Raddlebarn Prim Sch B29 85 F1
Raddlebarn Rd B29 . . . 103 F8
RADFORD 116 F7
Radford Ave DY10 . . . 116 E7
Radford Circ 5 CV6 . . . 113 A4
Radford Cl WS5 . . . . . . 43 A3
Radford Dr WV14 . . . . 15 C2
Radford Hall CV31 . . . 162 E6
Radford Ho
  Coventry CV6 . . . . 113 A7
  2 Redditch B97 . . . . . 153 A4
Radford La WV3, WV4 . . 37 F7
Radford Prim Sch CV6 . 113 B5
Radford Rd
  Alvechurch B48 . . . . . 139 D7
  Birmingham B29 . . . . . 103 A6
  Coventry CV1, CV6 . . . 113 B5
  Royal Leamington Spa
  CV31 . . . . 162 C2
Radford Rise B91 . . . . 107 E5
RADFORD SEMELE 162 E5
Radford Semele CE Prim Sch
  CV31 . . . . 162 E5
Radley Ct B26 . . . . . . 89 C7
Radley Dr CV10 . . . . . . 73 A1
Radley Gr B29 . . . . . . 85 A2

Radley Rd
  Stourbridge DY9 . . . . . 81 F4
  Walsall WS4 . . . . 29 C7
Radleys Prim Sch The
  WS4 . . . . 29 D7
Radleys The B33 . . . . . 89 D8
Radley Rise B33 . . . . . 89 D8
Radlow Cres B37 . . . . . 90 B8
Radmore Cl WS7 . . . . . . 6 D8
Radmore Rd LE10 . . . . . 71 D3
Radnor Cl B45 . . . . . . 102 B2
Radnor Croft WS5 . . . . 43 C3
Radnor Ct WS9 . . . . . . 15 F4
Radnor Dr CV10 . . . . . . 72 E2
Radnor Gn B71 . . . . . . 53 C7
Radnor Rd
  Birmingham, Brandhall
  B68 . . . . 84 B7
  Birmingham, Lozells B20 . 66 B8
  Sedgley DY3 . . . . 50 C8
Radnor Rise WS12 . . . . 2 B4
Radnor St B18 . . . . . . 66 A6
Radnor Wlk CV2 . . . . . 114 F8
Radstock Ave B36 . . . . 68 C7
Radstock Rd WV12 . . . . 13 C1
Radway Cl B98 . . . . . . 154 B6
Radway Ind Est B90 . . 126 E7
Radway Rd B90 . . . . . 126 E8
Raeburn Rd B43 . . . . . 44 C4
RAF Cotts B35 . . . . . . 57 F2
Raford Rd B23 . . . . . . 56 D6
Ragdene Rd B33 . . . . . 89 D8
Ragees Rd DY6 . . . . . . 60 F4
Raglan Ave
  Perton WV6 . . . . 23 F3
  Smethwick B66 . . . . . . 65 C4
Raglan Cl
  Nuneaton CV11 . . . . . . 73 D4
  Sedgley DY3 . . . . 50 B7
  Sutton Coldfield WS9 . . 30 F3
Raglan Ct
  Bromsgrove B60 . . . . . 137 A1
  7 Coventry CV1 . . . . . 113 E3
Raglan Gr CV8 . . . . . . 148 B5
Raglan Ho B33 . . . . . . 69 A2
Raglan Rd
  Birmingham, Balsall Heath
  B5 . . . . 86 D5
  Birmingham, Handsworth
  B21 . . . . 65 C8
  Smethwick B66 . . . . . . 65 C4
Raglan St
  Brierley Hill DY5 . . . . 61 C4
  Coventry CV1 . . . . 165 D3
  Wolverhampton WV3 . . . 163 A2
Raglan Way B37 . . . . . 70 D1
Ragley Cl
  Knowle B93 . . . . 128 B7
  Walsall WS3 . . . . 14 A1
Ragley Cres B60 . . . . . 151 A8
Ragley Dr
  Birmingham, Grove Vale
  B43 . . . . 43 D2
  Birmingham, Sheldon B26 . 89 C6
  2 Willenhall WV13 . . . 40 F8
Ragley Ho B87 . . . . . 153 A4
Ragley Wlk 8 B65 . . . . 63 C3
Raglis Cl B97 . . . . . . 153 A1
Ragnall Ave B33 . . . . . 89 D7
Ragstone Cl WS2 . . . . . 28 A3
Raikes La WS14 . . . . . 17 C7
Rail Bridge Est B70 . . 53 A1
Railswood Dr WS3 . . . 15 B3
Railway Cl B80 . . . . . 159 D4
Railway Dr
  Bilston WV14 . . . . 40 E5
  Wolverhampton WV1 . . . 163 C3
Railway La WV13 . . . . . 27 A1
Railway Rd
  Birmingham B20 . . . . . . 55 F2
  Sutton Coldfield B73 . . 46 B5
Railwayside Cl B66 . . . 64 E7
Railway St
  Bilston WV14 . . . . 40 E5
  Cannock WS11 . . . . . . 4 E8
  Norton Canes WS11 . . . . 6 A5
  Tipton DY4 . . . . 52 C5
  West Bromwich B70 . . . 53 B4
  Wolverhampton WV1 . . . 163 C3
Railway Terr
  Bedworth CV12 . . . . . . 78 C2
  Birmingham, Aston B7 . . 67 B6
  Birmingham, Hamstead B42 54 F6
  4 Wednesbury WS10 . . 41 F2
Railway View
  Birmingham B10 . . . . . . 87 C7
  Cannock WS11 . . . . . . 2 B5
Railway Wlk B60 . . . . 151 A6
Railwharf Sidings DY2 . 62 D4
Rainbow Bsns Pk WV13 . 27 C3
Rainbow St
  Dudley WV14 . . . . 40 D2
  Wolverhampton WV2 . . . 163 C1
Rainford Way B38 . . . 123 C8
Rainham Cl DY4 . . . . . 51 D5
Rainsbrook Dr
  Nuneaton CV11 . . . . . . 74 A1
  Solihull B90 . . . . 126 F6
Rainscar B77 . . . . . . 36 B7
Raison Ave CV11 . . . . . 73 F8
Rakegate Cl WV10 . . . 11 B1
Rake Hill WS7 . . . . . . 7 B8
Rake Way B15 . . . . . . 66 B1
Raleigh Cl
  Birmingham B21 . . . . . . 54 B1
  Hinckley LE10 . . . . . . 71 D4

Raleigh Croft B43 43 E3
Raleigh Ind Est B21 54 B1
Raleigh Rd
Bilston WV14 41 A3
Birmingham B9 67 D2
Coventry CV2 114 B2
Raleigh St
Walsall WS2 28 C2
West Bromwich B71 53 C4
Ralph Barlow Gdns B44 56 B8
Ralph Rd
Birmingham B8 67 D4
Coventry CV6 112 F5
Solihull B90 106 C4
Ralphs Mdw B32 84 D2
Ralston Cl WS3 14 A4
Rambures Cl CV34 161 F3
Ramillies Cres WS6 4 F1
Ramp Rd B26 90 C5
Ramsay Cl B71 53 F8
Ramsay Cres CV5 112 B7
Ramsay Rd
Oldbury B68 64 C1
Tipton DY4 51 E7
Walsall WS2 28 A5
Ramsden Ave CV10 72 D6
Ramsden Cl B29 103 B7
Ramsden Ct CV10 72 C7
Ramsey Cl
Birmingham B45 101 F1
Hinckley LE10 71 B1
Ramsey Rd
1 Birmingham B7 67 C7
Royal Leamington Spa CV31 162 B7
Ranby Rd CV2 113 F4
Randall Ave B48 139 A6
Randall Cl DY6 60 F4
Randall Rd CV8 147 F3
Randle Dr
Sutton Coldfield B75 32 C3
Sutton Coldfield B75 32 E2
Randle Rd
Nuneaton CV10 72 D4
Stourbridge DY9 81 C4
Randle St CV6 113 B5
Randolph Cl 11 CV31 162 C6
Randwick Gr B44 44 E1
Ranelagh Ho WV2 39 D7
Ranelagh Rd WV2 39 D6
Ranelagh St CV31 162 A6
Ranelagh Terr CV31 161 F6
Range Meadow Cl CV32 156 C3
Rangemoor CV3 134 D6
Range The B74 44 E7
Rangeview Cl B74 44 F6
Rangeways Rd
Kidderminster DY11 116 A8
Kingswinford DY6 60 F4
Rangeworthy Cl B97 158 C7
Rangifer Rd B78 20 F1
Rangoon Rd B92 89 E4
Ranleigh Ave DY6 60 F4
Rann Cl B16 66 A1
Rannoch Cl
Brierley Hill DY5 81 B8
Hinckley LE10 75 B8
Rannoch Dr CV10 72 C5
Rannock Cl CV3 114 F2
Ranscombe Dr DY3 50 D2
Ransom Rd
Birmingham B23 56 C4
Coventry CV6 113 E8
Ran-tan The B97 158 E5
Ranton Park Area 3 WS11 2 A2
Ranulf Croft CV3 133 C7
Ranulf St CV3 133 C7
Ranworth Rise WV4 39 D4
Raphael Cl CV5 112 C3
Rashwood Cl B94 143 B6
Ratcliffe Ave B30 104 D3
Ratcliffe Cl DY3 50 F6
Ratcliffe Ct CV10 72 C4
Ratcliffe Dr WV13 41 B8
Ratcliffe Rd
Hinckley LE10 75 F6
Solihull B91 107 C7
Wednesfield WV11 27 A6
Ratcliff Way DY4 52 D6
Ratcliff Wlk 3 B69 64 A7
Rathbone Cl
Bilston WV14 40 D5
Birmingham B5 86 E7
Keresley CV7 95 A6
Rathbone Rd B67 64 F2
Rathlin Cl WV9 11 A3
Rathlin Croft B36 70 B6
Rathmore Cl DY8 80 E2
Rathwell Cl WV9 11 A1
Rattle Croft B33 68 E3
Raveloe Dr CV11 73 D1
Ravenall Cl B34 69 B7
Raven Cl
Cannock WS12 2 E4
Cheslyn Hay WS6 4 D2
Huntington WS12 1 C7
Raven Cragg Rd CV5 132 E8
Raven Cres WV11 26 F8
Raven Ct
21 Brierley Hill DY5 61 D2
Wolverhampton WV10 11 B3
Ravenfield Cl B8 68 A5
Ravenhayes La B32 102 A6
Raven Hays Rd B31 102 C2
Ravenhill Dr WV8 10 A4
Ravenhurst Dr B43 43 E3
Ravenhurst Mews B23 56 E3
Ravenhurst Rd B17 85 C6
Ravenhurst St B12 87 A8
Raven Rd WS5 43 B6
Ravens Bank Dr B98 154 E7
Ravensbourne Gr WV13 27 C2
Ravenscroft DY8 80 C6
Ravenscroft Rd
Solihull B92 107 A8
Willenhall WV12 27 B5
Ravens Ct WS8 15 F7
Ravensdale Ave CV32 156 C2
Ravensdale Cl WS5 43 B7
Ravensdale Gdns WS5 43 B7
Ravensdale Prim Sch CV2 114 D4
Ravensdale Rd
Birmingham B10 87 F7
Coventry CV2 114 D3
Ravenshaw La B91 108 A4
Ravenshaw Rd B16 65 C2
Ravenshaw Way B91 108 A3
Ravenshill Rd B14 105 D4
Ravensholme WV6 23 F2
Ravensholt CV4 132 D6
Ravensitch Wlk DY5 61 E1
Ravensmere Rd B98 154 B1
Ravensthorpe Cl CV3 134 E8
Ravenstone B77 36 B8
Ravenswood B15 85 E8
Ravenswood Cl B74 46 B8
Ravenswood Dr B91 106 F1
Ravenswood Drive S B91 106 E1
Ravenswood Hill B46 70 F7
Raven Way CV11 73 F2
Raven Wlk 4 B15 86 C7
Rawdon Gr B44 56 B8
Rawlett Com Sports Coll B79 21 A8
Rawlings Rd B67 65 A2
Rawlins Croft B35 58 C3
Rawlinson Rd CV32 157 B2
Rawlins St B16 66 A1
Rawnsley Dr CV8 148 C6
Rawnsley Rd WS12 2 E6
Raybolds Bridge Rd WS2 28 C4
Raybon Croft B45 122 A6
Raybould's Fold DY2 62 C5
Rayford Dr B71 43 A2
Raygill B77 36 B8
Ray Hall La
Birmingham B43 54 B8
West Bromwich B43, B71 43 A1
Rayleigh Ho B27 88 D3
Rayleigh Rd WV3 39 A8
Ray Mercer Way DY10 116 F5
Raymond Ave B42 55 B6
Raymond Cl
Coventry CV6 95 F5
Walsall WS2 28 D5
Raymond Gdns WV11 26 E6
Raymont Gr B43 44 B4
Rayners Croft B26 68 F2
Raynor Cres CV12 77 D1
Raynor Rd WV10 25 F6
Raynsford Wlk CV34 155 D1
Raywoods The CV10 72 F3
Rea Ave B45 121 E8
Reabrook Rd B31 122 F8
Rea Bsns Pk B7 67 C4
Rea Cl B31 123 A7
Readers Wlk B43 43 F1
Reading Ave CV11 73 F7
Reading Cl CV2 96 B3
Read St CV1 113 E3
Rea Fordway B45 101 F1
Reansway Sq WV6 25 A4
Reapers Cl WV12 27 D5
Reapers Wlk WV8 10 F1
Rear Cotts B48 138 F6
Rea Rd B31 102 F1
Reardon Ct CV34 155 E1
Reaside Cres B14 104 B5
Reaside Croft B12 86 E6
Reaside Dr B45 102 B1
Reaside Jun Sch B45 101 E1
Rea St B5 164 D1
Rea Street S B5 86 F8
Rea Terr B5 66 F2
Rea Twr B19 66 C5
Rea Valley Dr B31 103 B2
Reaview Dr B29 86 B2
Reaymer Cl WS2 28 B6
Reay Nadin Dr B73 45 B4
Rebecca Dr B29 85 E2
Rebecca Gdns WV4 38 F4
Recreation Rd
Bromsgrove B61 136 F3
Coventry CV6 96 A3
Recreation St DY2 62 D5
Rectory Ave WS10 41 D6
Rectory Cl
Allesley CV5 112 C6
Bedworth CV7 78 A1
Drayton Bassett B78 34 E5
Stourbridge DY8 81 B3
Whitnash CV31 162 B4
Rectory Ct B97 153 D1
Rectory Dr CV7 78 A1
Rectory Fields DY8 60 E2
Rectory Gdns
Birmingham B36 69 A8
Oldbury B68 64 C5
Solihull B91 107 D3
Stourbridge DY8 81 B3
Rectory Gr B18 65 E6
Rectory La
Allesley CV5 112 C6
Birmingham B36 69 A8
Rectory La *continued*
Upton Warren B61 150 A4
Rectory Park Ave B75 46 E4
Rectory Park Cl B75 46 E4
Rectory Park Ct 7 B75 46 F6
Rectory Park Rd B26 89 C5
Rectory Rd
Birmingham B31 103 B3
Redditch B97 153 D1
Solihull B91 107 C3
Stourbridge DY8 81 B3
Sutton Coldfield B75 46 E6
Rectory St DY8 60 E3
Redacre Rd B73 45 F2
Redacres WV6 24 E6
Redbank Ave B23 56 C3
Redbourn Rd WS3 14 A4
Red Brick Cl B64 82 D7
Redbrook Cl WS12 2 D2
Redbrook Covert 7 B38 123 E8
Red Brook Rd WS2 28 A5
Redbrooks Cl B91 107 A1
Redburn Dr B14 104 D2
Redcap Croft CV6 95 D4
Redcar Cl
Lower Marlbrook B61 121 B1
Royal Leamington Spa CV32 157 C4
Redcar Croft B36 68 C8
Redcar Rd
Coventry CV1 113 E5
Wolverhampton WV10 11 D4
Redcliff B77 21 F5
Redcliffe Dr WV5 49 B6
Redcotts Cl WV10 26 A8
Redcroft Dr B24 57 C5
Redcroft Rd DY2 62 E6
Reddal Hill Prim Sch 6 B64 62 E1
Reddal Hill Rd B64 62 E2
Red Deeps CV11 78 D8
REDDICAP HEATH 46 F4
Reddicap Heath Rd B75 46 F4
Reddicap Hill B75 46 E4
Reddicap Trad Est B76 46 D4
Reddicroft B73 46 C5
Reddings Ct B13 86 D3
Reddings La B11, B28 87 E3
Reddings Rd B13 86 E2
Reddings The B47 125 A5
REDDITCH 153 C2
Redditch Ho B33 69 E2
Redditch Rd
Alvechurch, Arrowfield Top B48 139 B8
Alvechurch, Rowney Green B48 139 C3
Birmingham B31, B38 123 C8
Hopwood B48 123 B1
Stoke Heath B60 150 D5
Studley B80 159 D5
Redditch Ringway B97, B98 153 D4
Redditch Sta B97 153 D4
Redditch Wlk 4 CV2 115 A7
Redesdale Ave CV6 112 F5
Redfern Ave CV8 148 A6
Redfern Cl B92 89 B1
Redfern Dr WS7 7 B5
Redfern Park Way B11 88 A5
Redfern Rd B11 88 A5
Redfly La DY5 61 C6
Redford Cl B13 87 B2
Redgate Cl B38 103 D2
Redgrave Cl CV2 115 B8
Red Hall Prim Sch DY3 50 C3
Redhall Rd
Birmingham B32 84 E7
Dudley DY3 50 C2
Red Hill
Redditch B98 153 F2
Stourbridge DY8 81 B4
Redhill Ave WV5 49 A6
Redhill Cl
Stourbridge DY8 81 B4
Tamworth B79 21 A7
Red Hill Cl B80 159 E6
Redhill Ct DY8 81 B4
Redhill Furrows CV31 162 C5
Redhill Gdns B38 123 C8
Red Hill Gr B38 123 F7
Redhill Jun & Inf Sch B25 88 A6
Redhill La B45, B61 121 C5
Red Hill Pl B62 101 A7
Redhill Prim Sch WS11 1 F4
Redhill Rd
Birmingham, King's Norton B38 123 D7
Birmingham, Tyseley B25 88 A6
Cannock WS11 1 F4
Redhill Sch DY8 81 B4
Red Hill St WV1 163 B4
Red House Ave WS10 42 B3
Redhouse Cl B93 127 E4
Red House Glass Cone (Mus)* DY8 60 E1
Redhouse Ind Est WS9 29 F6
Red House La WS9 29 F5
Red House Park Rd B43 43 E2
Redhouse Rd WV6 24 B5
Red House Rd B33 69 C8
Redhouse St WS1 42 E7
Redhurst Dr WV10 11 B3
Red La
Burton Green CV8 131 C2
Coventry CV6 113 F5
Essington WV11 13 C3
Gospel End Village DY3 50 B8
Red La *continued*
Kenilworth CV8 147 D8
Redlake B77 35 E8
Redlake Dr DY9 99 B8
Redlake Rd DY9 81 B1
Redland Cl
Coventry CV2 96 E2
Lower Marlbrook B60 121 C1
Redland La CV8 135 A2
Redland Rd CV31 162 B5
Redlands Cl B91 107 D5
Redlands Rd B91 107 D5
Redlands Way B74 31 A1
Red Leasowes Rd B63 83 A3
Redliff Ave B36 58 D1
Red Lion Ave WS11 6 A4
Red Lion Cl B69 52 A1
Red Lion Cres WS11 6 A4
Red Lion La WS11 6 B4
Red Lion St
Alvechurch B48 139 B6
Redditch B98 153 E4
Wolverhampton WV1 163 B3
Redlock Field WS14 9 A5
Redmead Cl B30 103 C4
Redmoor Gdns WV4 39 A5
Redmoor High Sch LE10 71 B3
Redmoor Way B76 58 D6
REDNAL 122 C6
Rednal Hill Jun & Inf Schs B45 122 C7
Rednal Hill La B45 122 A6
Rednal Dr B75 32 C3
Rednal Mill Dr B45 122 C7
Rednal Park Ct B38 103 F2
Rednal Rd B38 103 E1
Rednell Ho B69 63 D6
Redoak Ho WV10 25 F3
Redpine Crest WV12 27 D5
Red River Rd WS2 28 A5
Red Rose Sh Ctr B72 46 C5
Redruth Cl
Coventry CV6 114 A8
Kingswinford DY6 60 D8
Nuneaton CV11 74 A4
Walsall WS5 43 D7
Redruth Rd WS5 43 D7
Red Sands Rd DY10 116 E8
Redstart Ave DY10 117 B2
Redstone Cl B98 154 C6
Redstone Dr WV11 26 F5
Redstone Educational Acad B10 87 D8
Redstone Farm Rd B28 106 B6
Redstone Way DY3 50 D4
Redthorne Gr CV8 148 B8
Redthorn Gr B33 68 D3
Redvers Rd B9 67 E1
Redway Ct B75 46 E4
Redwell Cl B77 21 D5
Redwing B77 36 A6
Redwing Cl WS7 7 D5
Redwing Ct DY10 117 A1
Redwing Dr WS12 1 C7
Redwing Gr B23 56 B7
Red Wing Wlk B36 70 A8
Redwood Ave DY1 50 F5
Redwood Bsns Pk B66 64 C7
Redwood Cl
Birmingham B30 103 E4
Sutton Coldfield B74 30 F2
Redwood Croft
Birmingham B14 104 E7
Nuneaton CV10 73 A1
Redwood Dr
Burntwood WS7 6 F8
Cannock WS11 2 A3
Tipton B69 52 B2
Redwood Gdns B27 88 B5
Redwood Ho B37 69 F5
Redwood Rd
Birmingham B30 103 E4
Dudley WV14 40 D2
Walsall WS5 43 B4
Redwood Way WV12 27 B8
Reedham Gdns WV4 38 D5
Reedly Rd WV12 13 C1
Reedmace B77 21 C2
Reedmace Cl B38 123 F8
Reed Mace Dr B61 137 A5
Reedswood Cl WS2 28 C3
Reedswood Gdns WS2 28 C3
Reedswood La WS2 28 C3
Reedswood Ret Pk WS2 28 B4
Reedswood Way WS2 28 B4
Rees Dr
Coventry CV3 133 D4
Wombourne WV5 49 B7
Reeve Ct DY10 117 A1
Reeve Dr CV8 148 A4
Reeve La WS13 9 B8
Reeves Cl DY4 52 B2
Reeves Gdns WV8 10 A4
REEVES GREEN 131 A8
Reeves Rd
Birmingham B14 104 C6
Hinckley LE10 75 F6
Reeves St WS3 28 B8
Reflex Ind Pk WV13 27 A3
Reform St B70 53 D3
Regal Cl B77 35 C8
Regal Croft B36 68 B8
Regal Dr WS2 42 C8
Regal Ho CV11 73 D3
Regan Ave B90 106 A1
Regan Cres B23 56 E6
Regan Ct B75 47 C5
Regan Dr B69 63 D8
Regan Ho B13 105 D7
Regency Cl
6 Birmingham B9 67 D1
Nuneaton CV10 73 D6
Regency Ct
Coventry CV5 132 F8
Hinckley LE10 76 A7
Walsall WS1 43 A7
Wolverhampton WV1 163 B4
Regency Dr
Birmingham B38 103 F2
Coventry CV3 132 F5
Kenilworth CV8 147 F3
Regency Gdns B14 105 C3
Regency Ho
Birmingham B16 66 A1
Royal Leamington Spa CV32 162 A8
Regency Mews CV32 162 A8
Regency Wlk B74 31 D5
Regent Ave B69 52 A1
Regent Cl
Birmingham B5 86 D6
Halesowen B63 83 A4
Kingswinford DY6 60 C6
Oldbury B69 63 A8
Regent Court Sh Ctr 6 CV32 161 F8
Regent Ct
4 Birmingham B62 84 A7
6 Darlaston WS10 41 D6
5 Hinckley LE10 75 D8
3 Smethwick B66 65 A5
Regent Dr B69 52 A1
Regent Gr CV32 161 F8
Regent Ho
Oldbury B68 64 B2
6 Walsall WS2 28 D3
Regent Mews B61 150 E8
Regent Par B1 66 C4
Regent Park Rd B10 67 C1
Regent Pl
Birmingham B1 66 C4
4 Royal Leamington Spa CV31 162 A7
Tipton B69 52 B2
Regent Rd
Birmingham B17 85 D6
Birmingham, Handsworth B21 65 D8
Oldbury B69 63 A8
Wolverhampton WV4 38 E5
Regents Park Prim Sch B10 87 B8
Regents Park Rd B60 137 C2
Regent St
Bedworth CV12 78 C4
Bilston WV14 40 D6
Birmingham, Hockley B1 66 C4
Birmingham, Stirchley B30 104 A7
Coventry CV1 165 A2
Cradley Heath B64 62 F2
Dudley DY1 51 C6
Hinckley LE10 75 D8
Nuneaton CV11 73 D5
Royal Leamington Spa CV32 161 F8
Smethwick B66 65 A6
Tipton DY4 51 E8
Willenhall WV13 27 A3
Regents The B15 85 D8
Regents Way B75 46 F6
Regent Wlk B8 68 B7
Reg Hadden Ct CV10 73 D6
Regiment Ct CV6 95 A1
Regina Ave B44 55 E8
Regina Cl B45 101 E2
Regina Cres
Coventry CV2 115 A7
Wolverhampton WV6 24 B4
Regina Dr
Birmingham B42 55 D3
Walsall WS4 29 B4
Reginald Rd
Birmingham B8 67 D4
Smethwick B67 64 F2
Regis Beeches WV6 24 C5
Regis Gdns B65 63 C2
Regis Heath Rd B65 63 E2
Regis Rd
Rowley Regis B65 63 C2
Wolverhampton WV6 24 C5
Regis Wlk CV2 114 F7
Reid Ave WV12 27 D6
Reid Cl WS7 7 F7
Reid Rd B68 64 D1
Reigate Ave B8 68 B4
Reignier Pl CV34 161 F2
Reindeer Rd B78 20 E1
Relay Bsns Pk B77 36 C7
Relay Dr B77 36 C7
Reliance Trad Est WV14 40 B5
Relko Dr B36 68 C7
Relton Mews CV6 113 F6
Rembrandt Cl
Cannock WS11 2 D2
Coventry CV5 112 C3
Remburn Gdns CV34 160 F8
Remembrance Rd
Coventry CV3 134 D6
Wednesbury WS10 42 C3
Remington Dr WS11 4 F8
Remington Pl WS2 28 C5
Remington Rd WS2 28 B5
Renaissance Ct 1 B12 67 A1

Rene Rd B77................ 21 E5
Renfrew Cl DY8............. 60 C3
Renfrew Gdns DY11...... 116 C5
Renfrew Sq B35........... 58 B4
Renfrew Wlk CV4........ 132 A8
Renison Rd CV12.......... 77 E1
Rennie Gr B32............. 84 D5
Rennison Dr WV5.......... 49 A6
Renolds Cl CV4........... 112 C2
Renown Cl DY5............ 81 B7
Renshaw Ind Est B80... 159 B4
Renton Gr WV10........... 11 A1
Renton Rd WV10........... 11 A1
Repington Road N B77 ... 22 A5
Repington Road S B77 ... 22 A5
Repington Way B75....... 47 B5
Repton Ave WV6.......... 23 E3
Repton Cl WS11............ 4 B8
Repton Dr CV6............. 96 B2
Repton Gr B9............. 68 B3
Repton Ho B23........... 56 F6
Repton Rd B9............. 68 B3
Reservoir Cl
  Birmingham B31....... 102 D5
  Walsall WS2............ 42 B8
Reservoir Pas WS10...... 41 F3
Reservoir Pl WS2........ 42 B8
Reservoir Rd
  Birmingham B29........ 85 C3
  Birmingham, Edgbaston B16 65 F2
  Birmingham, Rednal B45.. 122 C3
  Birmingham, Stockland Green
    B23.................. 56 E4
  Cannock WS12............. 2 D4
  Kidderminster DY11.... 116 C3
  Oldbury B68............. 64 C4
  Rowley Regis B65....... 63 D3
  Solihull B92........... 106 F8
Reservoir Retreat B16... 65 F1
Reservoir St WS2......... 42 B8
Reswood Cl 3 B24........ 56 F3
Retallack Cl B66.......... 65 B8
Retford Dr B76............ 46 E4
Retford Gr B25........... 88 C6
Retreat Gdns DY5......... 50 E7
Retreat St
  Astwood Bank B96..... 158 E1
  Wolverhampton WV3.... 163 A1
Retreat The B64.......... 82 E7
Reuben Ave CV10......... 72 B6
Revesby Wlk 4 B7........ 67 A4
Revival St WS3........... 14 B1
Rex Cl CV4............... 131 D8
Reyde Cl B97.............. 153 B2
Reynards Cross Sch B92 106 D7
Reynard Cl B97........... 152 F3
Reynards Cl DY3.......... 51 A7
Reynolds Cl
  Hinckley LE10.......... 71 A3
  Lichfield WS13............ 3 B2
Reynolds Gr WV6......... 23 F5
Reynolds Ho B19.......... 66 E7
Reynolds Rd
  Bedworth CV12.......... 78 A4
  Birmingham B21......... 65 B4
Reynoldstown Rd B36.... 68 C8
Reynolds Wlk WV11...... 27 B8
Rhayader Rd B31........ 102 E5
Rhodes Alms Houses The
  B21................... 65 F7
Rhodes Cl DY3........... 50 A4
Rhone Cl B11............ 87 C3
Rhoose Croft B35........ 58 A3
Rhuddlan Way DY10..... 116 E1
Rhyl Rd CV11............ 79 F6
Rhys Thomas Cl WV12.. 27 D4
Rian Ct B64............. 82 D8
Ribbesford Ave WV10 ... 25 B8
Ribbesford Cl B63....... 82 D6
Ribbesford Cres WV14 .. 40 D1
Ribble Cl CV12.......... 79 B2
Ribble Ct 3 B73......... 46 B5
Ribble Rd CV3........... 113 F2
Ribblesdale B77......... 36 B7
Ribblesdale Ave LE10 ... 71 E3
Ribblesdale Rd B29, B30 104 A8
Ribble Wlk B36.......... 69 F8
Ribbonbrook CV11....... 73 D3
Ribbonfields CV11...... 73 D3
Richard Bradley Way DY4 51 E7
Richard Cooper Rd WS14. 17 F5
Richard Joy Cl CV6...... 95 C2
Richard Lee Prim Sch
  CV2................... 114 C3
Richard Lighton Ho 5 B1 66 C3
Richard Pl WS5.......... 43 C8
Richard Rd WS5......... 43 C8
Richards Cl
  Birmingham B31....... 122 F6
  Kenilworth CV8........ 147 F5
  Rowley Regis B65....... 63 E4
Richards Ct WS11......... 5 F6
Richards Gr CV31....... 162 A5
Richards Ho
  3 Oldbury B69......... 63 E4
  2 Walsall WS2.......... 28 D3
Richardson Cl CV34..... 155 F1
Richardson Ct WS7........ 6 E8
Richardson Dr DY8....... 80 E8
Richardson Ho DY4...... 52 C8
Richardson Way CV2.... 115 B8
Richards Rd DY4......... 40 F1
Richards St WS10........ 41 D7

Richard St
  Birmingham B7.......... 66 F5
  West Bromwich B70...... 53 B3
Richard Street S B70.... 53 C2
Richard Street W 1 B70. 53 C2
Richard Watts Dr WS10 .. 41 F5
Richard Williams Rd
  WS10................... 42 B2
Richborough Dr DY1..... 50 F4
Rich Cl CV34............ 161 B7
Riches St WV6........... 24 F3
Richford Gr B33......... 69 D2
Richmere Ct WV6......... 24 B3
Richmond Ash Dr DY4... 52 A5
Richmond Ave
  Birmingham B12......... 86 F5
  Wolverhampton WV3.... 24 F1
Richmond Cl
  Birmingham B20......... 55 A3
  Cannock WS11............ 2 A5
  Hollywood B47......... 125 C7
  Tamworth B79........... 21 A5
Richmond Croft B42..... 54 F6
Richmond Ct
  Birmingham, Calthorpe Fields
    B15.................. 86 B8
  9 Birmingham, Weoley Castle
    B29.................. 103 C7
  Halesowen B63......... 82 E3
  Oldbury B68............. 64 C5
  6 Royal Leamington Spa
    CV31................ 162 B7
  Stourbridge DY9........ 81 B1
  2 Sutton Coldfield B72. 57 B7
Richmond Dr
  Lichfield WS14........... 9 D7
  Perton WV6............. 23 F3
  Sutton Coldfield B75... 46 F6
  Wolverhampton WV3.... 24 E1
Richmond Gdns
  Stourbridge DY9........ 80 F7
  Wombourne WV5........ 49 A5
Richmond Gr DY8........ 80 E8
Richmond Hill B68....... 64 C5
Richmond Hill Gdns B15. 85 E7
Richmond Hill Rd B15... 85 F6
Richmond Ho 2 B37..... 70 D2
Richmond Mews WV3.... 25 A1
Richmond Pk CV6........ 60 C8
Richmond Pl B14....... 104 F8
Richmond Prim Sch The
  LE10.................. 71 C3
Richmond Rd
  Birmingham B45....... 121 E7
  Birmingham, Hockley Hill B18 66 B6
  Birmingham, Yardley B33.. 68 D2
  Dudley DY2............. 62 C8
  Hinckley LE10.......... 71 C3
  Nuneaton CV11.......... 73 A4
  Sedgley DY3............ 50 F7
  Smethwick B66......... 65 A2
  Solihull B92........... 88 F2
  Sutton Coldfield B73... 46 B6
  Wolverhampton WV3.... 24 E1
Richmond St
  Coventry CV2.......... 114 A3
  Halesowen B63......... 83 A4
  Walsall WS1............ 29 A1
  West Bromwich B70...... 52 F6
Richmond Street S B70 .. 52 E5
Richmond Way 2 B37.... 70 C3
Rickyard Cl B33........ 127 E6
Rickman Dr B15......... 86 D8
Rickyard Cl
  Birmingham, Northfield
    B29.................. 103 A6
  Birmingham, Yardley B25.. 68 D1
Rickyard La B94........ 154 D5
Rickyard Piece B32..... 84 C6
Ridgacre Rd
  Birmingham B32........ 84 C6
  West Bromwich B71..... 53 B6
Ridgacre Road W B32... 84 A6
Ridge Cl
  Birmingham B13....... 105 C6
  Willenhall WS2.......... 27 D3
Ridge Ct CV5.......... 112 A6
Ridgefield Rd B62....... 83 C7
Ridge La DY9............ 81 C5
Ridge La WV11.......... 26 D7
Ridgeley Cl CV34....... 155 E2
Ridgemount Dr B38..... 123 D8
Ridge Prim Sch The DY8. 80 C5
Ridge Rd DY6............ 60 C5
Ridge St DY8............ 80 D5
Ridgethorpe CV3....... 134 E6
Ridgewater Cl B45..... 122 B6
Ridgeway
  Birmingham B17........ 65 B2

Ridgeway continued
  Birmingham, Quinton B32.. 84 A4
  Sedgley DY3............ 50 D7
Ridge Way WS9.......... 30 B4
Ridgeway Ave
  Birmingham B62........ 84 A6
  Coventry CV3.......... 133 C6
Ridgeway Cl B80........ 159 E2
Ridgeway Ct WS2........ 27 F2
Ridgeway Dr WV4........ 38 F3
Ridgeway Prim Sch WS7. 7 A5
Ridgeway Rd
  Stourbridge DY8........ 60 F2
  1 Tipton DY4.......... 52 A8
Ridgeway Sch CV34..... 156 A1
Ridgeway The
  Birmingham, Upper Witton
    B23.................. 56 A5
  Burntwood WS7.......... 7 A4
  Hinckley LE10.......... 75 D6
  Warwick CV34.......... 156 A1
Ridgeway Trad Est B96 . 158 E1
Ridgewood B34.......... 69 B6
Ridgewood Ave DY8..... 80 C7
Ridgewood Cl
  Royal Leamington Spa
    CV32................ 156 C1
  7 Walsall WS1......... 42 F8
Ridgewood Dr B75....... 32 B1
Ridgewood Gdns B44.... 55 F7
Ridgewood High Sch DY8 80 C5
Ridgewood Rise B77.... 22 A5
Ridgley Rd CV4........ 131 E8
Ridgmont Croft B32.... 84 E5
Riding Cl B71........... 53 F7
Ridings Brook Dr 3 WS11. 2 A2
Ridings La B98......... 154 B6
Ridings Park Trad Est
  WS11.................. 2 A3
Ridings The WS11........ 4 F8
Riding Way WV12........ 27 D6
Ridley St B1........... 164 A1
Ridpool Prim Sch B33... 69 B3
Ridpool Rd B33.......... 69 B3
Ridware Ho WS13......... 3 E1
Rifle Range Rd DY11.. 116 B3
Rifle St WV14........... 51 A8
Rigby Cl CV34.......... 161 D4
Rigby Dr WS11............ 1 F4
Rigby Hall Specl Sch
  B60.................. 151 C8
Rigby La B60.......... 151 C8
Rigby St WS10........... 42 A1
Rigdale Cl CV2........ 114 E2
Righton Ho B77......... 21 D1
Riland Ave B75.......... 46 D5
Riland Ct B72........... 57 C7
Riland Gr B75.......... 46 C5
Riland Ind Est B75..... 46 D5
Riley B77............... 21 E3
Riley Cl CV8........... 148 D4
Riley Cres WV4......... 39 A6
Riley Dr B36............ 59 A1
Riley Ho CV1.......... 165 B2
Riley Rd B14.......... 105 D3
Riley Sq CV2............ 96 B1
Riley St WV13........... 27 B2
Rills The LE10.......... 71 E2
Rilstone Rd B32........ 84 F5
Rindleford Ave WV4.... 38 C6
Ringhills Rd WV8........ 10 B2
Ringinglow Rd B44..... 44 D2
Ringmere Ave B36...... 69 B7
Ring Rd WS7............. 6 E7
Ring Road N B15........ 85 F4
Ring Road S B15........ 85 F3
Ring Road St Andrews
  WV1.................. 163 A3
Ring Road St Davids
  WV1.................. 163 C3
Ring Road St Georges
  WV2.................. 163 C2
Ring Road St Johns
  WV1.................. 163 B2
Ring Road St Marks
  WV3.................. 163 B2
Ring Road St Patricks
  WV1.................. 163 C4
Ring Road St Peters
  WV1.................. 163 B3
Ringswood Rd B92...... 88 E4
Ring The B25........... 88 C8
Ringway WS11............ 1 E1
Ringway Hill Cross CV1.. 165 A3
Ringway Ind Est WS13.... 3 C2
Ringway Queens CV1.... 165 A2
Ringway Rudge CV1..... 165 A2
Ringway St Johns CV1 . 165 C2
Ringway St Nicholas
  CV1.................. 165 A2
Ringway St Patricks CV1 165 B1
Ringway Swanswell CV1. 165 C3
Ringway The DY10....... 116 F5
Ringway Whitefriars
  CV1.................. 165 C3
Ringwood Ave WS9...... 30 B5
Ringwood Dr B45....... 102 A1
Ringwood Highway CV2.. 96 E2
Ringwood Rd WV10..... 11 D1
Rinhill Gr CV31........ 162 D6
Ripley Cl B69........... 62 F8
Ripley Gr B23........... 56 B5
Riplingham 3 CV32..... 156 F2
Ripon Cl CV5.......... 112 B8
Ripon Dr B71........... 42 D1

Ripon Rd
  Birmingham B14....... 105 C4
  Walsall WS2............ 28 B2
  Wolverhampton WV10.... 25 C7
Rippingille Rd B43..... 44 C4
Ripple Cl B77........... 35 E6
Ripple Rd B30......... 104 B7
Risborough Cl CV5..... 112 C3
Rischale Way WS4....... 29 D8
Risdale Cl CV32....... 156 D2
Rise Ave B45.......... 122 A7
Riseley Cres B5......... 86 D7
Rise The
  Birmingham, Great Barr
    B42.................. 55 A8
  Birmingham, Marston Green
    B37.................. 90 A7
  Hopwood B48.......... 123 B4
  Kingswinford DY6....... 60 E5
  Lichfield WS13.......... 8 F7
Rising Brook WV6....... 24 B4
Rising La
  Chadwick End B93..... 145 B5
  Kingswood B94........ 144 F5
  Solihull B94.......... 144 C4
Rising Rd B94.......... 144 C5
Rissington Ave B29.... 104 A8
Ritchie Cl B13.......... 87 A1
Rivendell Ct B28........ 87 E1
Rivendell Gdns WV6.... 24 B5
Riverbank Rd WV13..... 27 D2
River Brook Dr B30.... 104 B8
River Cl
  Bedworth CV12.......... 77 F1
  Royal Leamington Spa
    CV32................ 161 D8
River Ct 3 CV1........ 113 B3
Riverdrive B78, B79..... 21 B3
Riverfield Gr B77....... 21 D5
Riverford Croft CV4... 132 D4
River Lee Rd B11........ 87 E5
Rivermead CV11......... 73 A4
Rivermead Pk B34...... 69 A6
Riversdale 6 CV32.... 161 E8
Riversdale Rd B14..... 105 D3
RIVERSIDE........... 153 F6
Riverside
  Royal Leamington Spa
    CV32................ 161 E8
  Studley B80.......... 159 F5
Riverside Cl
  Coventry CV3.......... 134 A7
  Lickey End B60........ 137 C6
Riverside Cres B28.... 105 D4
Riverside Dr
  Birmingham B38....... 103 D3
  Cannock WS11............ 4 F8
  1 Coleshill B46........ 70 F7
Riverside Dr
  Birmingham, Cannon Hill
    B29.................. 86 C3
  Birmingham, Stechford B33. 68 F4
  Solihull B91.......... 107 E2
Riverside Ind Est
  Redditch B98.......... 159 C8
  Tamworth B78.......... 21 B1
Riverslea Rd CV3....... 114 C1
Riversleigh Dr DY8..... 80 E8
Riversleigh Rd CV32... 156 C1
Riverslea St B5......... 67 A2
Riverway WS10.......... 42 B2
River Wlk
  Coventry CV2.......... 96 C2
  Wednesbury WS10...... 42 A1
Rivington Cl DY8........ 80 E4
Rivington Cres B44..... 45 C1
Rivulet Cl B77........... 35 E6
RNIB Rushton Hall Sch
  CV7................... 95 D5
Roach B77............... 35 D6
Roach Cl
  Birmingham B37......... 70 C3
  Brierley Hill DY5...... 61 D5
Roach Cres WV11........ 26 F8
Roach Pool Croft B16... 65 C2
Road No 1 DY10........ 116 E2
Road No 2 DY10........ 116 E2
Road No 3 DY10........ 116 E2
Roadway Cl CV12........ 78 B2
Roanne Ringway CV11 .. 73 B4
Robert Ave B23.......... 56 E6
Robert Cl
  Coventry CV34......... 134 C4
  Tamworth B79.......... 20 F7
Robert Cramb Ave CV4.. 131 F8
Robert Ct
  Birmingham, Pheasey Est.. 44 D4
  5 Birmingham, Wake Green
    B13.................. 87 B2
Robert Mountford Way
  CV4.................. 131 F8
Robert Rd
  Bedworth CV7........... 95 F8
  Birmingham B20......... 55 B1
  Tipton DY4............. 51 F6
Roberts Cl
  Brownhills WS9......... 15 F2
  Darlaston WS10.......... 41 B4
Roberts Ct B24.......... 57 C6
Roberts La DY9......... 99 B8
Roberts Green Rd B69.. 50 E4
Robertson Knoll B36.... 68 F6
Robertsons Gdns 5 B7 .. 67 C7
Roberts Prim Sch DY3 .. 50 D4
Roberts Rd
  Birmingham B27......... 88 D3

Roberts Rd continued
  Walsall WS3............ 28 F5
  Wednesbury WS10...... 42 E2
Robert St DY3.......... 50 D4
Robert Wynd WV14..... 40 A1
Robeson Cl DY4......... 51 D5
Robey's La B78.......... 22 D3
Robin Cl
  Birmingham B36......... 70 A8
  Huntington WS12......... 1 C7
  Kingswinford DY6...... 61 A6
  Tamworth B77.......... 35 C8
Robin Ct DY10.......... 117 A2
Robin Gr WV11.......... 26 C7
Robin Hood Cres B28.. 105 E7
Robin Hood Croft B28. 105 F6
Robin Hood La B28.... 105 E7
Robin Hood Prim Sch
  B28.................. 106 B6
Robin Hood Rd
  Brierley Hill DY5...... 61 F2
  Coventry CV3.......... 134 C6
Robinia B77............ 22 A4
Robinia Cl CV32....... 157 B2
Robin Rd B23........... 56 E5
Robins Bsns Pk B70.... 52 E7
Robins Cl WS6.......... 4 D1
Robin's Cl DY8......... 81 A3
Robins Croft WS11....... 2 A1
Robins Gr CV34......... 86 F1
Robinsfield Dr B31.... 123 A7
Robins Gr CV34....... 160 C4
Robins Hill Dr B48.... 139 A5
Robins La B97......... 153 C6
Robinson Cl B79........ 20 E7
Robinson Rd
  Bedworth CV12.......... 95 D8
  Burntwood WS7.......... 6 F8
Robinson's Way B76.... 58 D5
Robinson Way LE10..... 75 F4
Robins Rd WS7........... 6 E7
Robin Wlk WS2.......... 42 A3
Robin Way CV10......... 72 A3
Robin Wlk WS2.......... 27 F3
Robottom Cl WS10...... 28 B6
Robson Cl WS8.......... 15 F5
Rocester Ave WV10.... 26 E7
Rochdale Wlk B10...... 87 C7
Roche Rd WS3........... 13 F1
Rochester Ave WS7...... 7 A7
Rochester Cl
  Nuneaton CV11......... 73 B3
  Redditch B97.......... 158 C8
Rochester Croft WS2... 28 A4
Rochester Rd
  Birmingham B31....... 103 A4
  Coventry CV5.......... 132 E8
Rochester Way WS12..... 2 C1
Rochester Wlk DY10 .. 117 C5
Roche The WS13.......... 8 A8
Roche Way WS3.......... 13 F1
Rochford Cl
  Birmingham B45....... 121 E7
  Halesowen B63......... 82 F2
  Sutton Coldfield B76... 58 A8
  6 Walsall WS2.......... 42 C7
Rochford Ct
  Royal Leamington Spa
    CV31................ 161 E7
  Solihull B90.......... 127 A6
Rochford Gr WV4....... 38 D5
Rock Ave B45.......... 122 C7
Rock Cl CV6............ 96 B1
Rock Cotts 3 DY11.. 116 D6
Rocken End CV6........ 113 D8
Rocket Pool Dr WV14 .. 41 A2
Rockford Cl B98....... 158 F5
Rockford Rd B42........ 55 A7
Rock Gr B92............ 88 E3
Rock Hill
  Bromsgrove B61....... 150 D7
  Weeford B78, WS14 .... 19 C4
Rockingham Cl
  Dorridge B93.......... 127 D2
  Dudley DY3............. 50 B3
  Walsall WS3............ 14 B1
Rockingham Dr
  Nuneaton CV11......... 78 F7
  Perton WV6............. 23 F3
Rockingham Gdns B74.. 46 B6
Rockingham Hall Gdns
  DY9................... 99 D7
Rockingham Rd B25.... 88 D8
Rock La CV7............ 94 C2
Rockland Dr B33........ 68 E4
Rocklands Gdns WV13 .. 40 F8
Rocklands Dr B74....... 46 B8
Rocklands Dr B75....... 46 B8
Rocklands Specl Sch WS13 3 C2
Rockley Gr B45........ 122 B7
Rockley Rd B65......... 63 A8
Rockmead Ave B44..... 44 F2
Rock Mill CV32....... 156 C1
Rock Mill La CV32..... 161 C8
Rockmoor Cl B37....... 69 C3
Rock Rd
  Sedgley WV14.......... 50 F8
  Solihull B92........... 88 E3
Rockrose Gdns WV10 ... 12 A7
Rock St DY3............. 50 E5
Rock The WV6........... 24 D5
Rockville Rd B8......... 68 A4
Rockwell La B48....... 139 E4
Rockwood Rd B77....... 88 B4
Rocky La
  Birmingham, Aston B6... 67 A6
  Birmingham, Great Barr B42 55 B5
  Birmingham, Nechells Green
    B7................... 67 B6

Rocky La *continued*
Catshill B61 136 E7
Kenilworth CV8 148 D2
Rodborough Rd
Birmingham B26 89 B7
Dorridge B93 127 E3
Rodbourne Rd B17 85 C3
Roddis Cl B23 56 D8
Roden Ave DY10 117 A7
Roderick Dr WV11 26 D7
Roderick Rd B11 87 C5
Rodhouse Cl CV4 111 D1
Rodlington Ave B44 44 F1
Rodman Cl B15 85 D8
Rodney Cl
Birmingham B16 66 A2
Hinckley LE10 71 D4
Solihull B92 89 B1
Rodney Rd B92 89 B1
Rodway Cl
Birmingham B19 66 E7
Brierley Hill DY5 81 D7
Wolverhampton WV4 39 D3
Rodway Dr CV5 111 D4
Rodwell Gr B44 56 A8
Rodyard Way CV1 165 C1
Roebuck Cl B34 69 E5
Roebuck Glade WV12 27 E4
Roebuck La
Birmingham B21 54 C2
Smethwick B66 64 F8
West Bromwich B70 53 E1
Roebuck Pl WS3 28 E6
Roebuck Rd
Birmingham B16 65 C2
Walsall WS3 28 E6
Roebuck St B70 53 F1
Roe Cl CV34 160 F8
Roedean Cl B44 56 B7
Roford Ct DY3 50 E5
Rogerfield Rd B23 57 A6
Rogers Cl WV11 13 A2
Rogers Rd B8 68 B5
Rogers Way CV34 160 B4
Rogue's La LE9, LE10 71 C6
Roisin's Vineyard CV12 77 D2
Rokeby Cl B76 46 E4
Rokeby Rd B43 43 F2
Rokeby Wlk B34 69 A6
Rokewood Cl DY6 49 D1
Rokholt Cres WS11 1 C1
Roland Ave CV6 95 C3
Roland Mount CV6 95 C3
Rolan Dr B90 125 E8
Roland Rd B19 66 C8
Roland Vernon Way DY4 52 C7
Rolfe St B66 65 A6
Rollason Cl CV6 113 C8
Rollason Rd
Birmingham B24 57 A3
Coventry CV6 113 B8
5 Dudley DY2 62 D8
Rollason's Yd CV6 96 A3
Rollesby Dr WV13 40 F8
Rollingmill Bsns Pk WS2 28 D1
Rolling Mill Cl B5 86 E7
Rolling Mill Rd WS11 5 F4
Rollingmill St WS2 28 C1
Rollswood Dr B91 107 A4
Rolvenden Ct WV13 27 C2
Roman Cl WS8 6 E2
Roman Ct
Birmingham B38 124 B8
Cannock WS11 4 E5
Tamworth B77 35 E7
Romani Cl CV34 160 D7
Roman La B74 31 B4
Roman Pk B46 59 F1
Roman Pk B74 31 B4
Roman Pl B74 31 B2
Roman Rd
Coventry CV2 114 B3
Sutton Coldfield B74 31 C4
Roman Rd (Sandy La) DY8 80 C3
Romans Grange B74 31 C5
Roman View WS11 4 F5
Roman Way
Birmingham B15 85 D3
Bromsgrove B61 137 B4
Coleshill B46 59 F2
Coventry CV3 133 D3
Lichfield WS14 9 D7
Rowley Regis B65 63 C3
Tamworth B79 20 E7
Roman Way Fst Sch B98 154 E3
Roman Wlk WS14 8 D2
Romany Rd B45 101 D1
Romany Way DY8 80 C3
Roma Rd B11 87 E5
Romeo Arbour CV34 161 E3
Romford Cl B26 89 B6
Romford Rd CV6 95 B2
Romilly Ave B20 55 B3
Romilly Cl
Lichfield WS14 9 E7
Stourbridge DY8 80 E6
Sutton Coldfield B76 47 A4
Romney B77 35 F8
Romney Cl
Birmingham B28 105 F7
Hinckley LE10 71 A3
Romney House Ind Est WS10 41 B7
Romney Way B43 44 D4
Romsey Ave CV10 73 D8
Romsey Gr WV10 11 C3
Romsey Ho WS2 42 C7
Romsey Rd WV10 11 C3
Romsey Way WS3 13 F3
ROMSLEY 101 A4
Romsley Cl
Birmingham B45 121 E8
Halesowen B63 83 B2
Redditch B98 154 F3
Walsall WS4 15 C2
ROMSLEY HILL 101 A2
Romsley Hill Grange B62 100 F1
Romsley Rd
Birmingham B32 102 B8
Coventry CV6 113 C6
Oldbury B68 64 B2
Stourbridge DY9 81 C5
Romulus Cl B20 55 B3
Ronald Gr B36 58 D1
Ronald Pl B9 67 E2
Ronald Rd B9 67 D2
Ron Davis Cl B66 65 B5
Ro-Oak Rd CV6 112 F5
ROOD END 64 C6
Rood End Prim Sch B68 64 C6
Rood End Rd B69 64 C7
Rooker Ave WV2 39 F6
Rooker Cres WV2 39 F6
Rookery Ave
Brierley Hill DY5 61 A2
Wolverhampton WV4 40 A3
Rookery Cl B97 153 D1
Rookery Ct WS13 8 E7
Rookery La
Aldridge WS9 30 B6
Coventry CV6 95 B4
Weeford B75, B78 19 C2
Wolverhampton WV2 39 B6
Rookery Par WS9 30 B6
Rookery Pk DY5 61 B5
Rookery Prim Sch B21 54 E1
Rookery Rd
Birmingham B29 85 F2
Birmingham, Handsworth B21 54 E1
Wolverhampton WV14, WV4 40 A3
Wombourne WV5 49 B6
Rookery Rise WV5 49 B6
Rookery St WV11 26 C5
Rookery The B62 84 A2
Rooks Mdw DY9 99 B6
Rookwood Dr WV6 23 F2
Roosevelt Dr CV4 111 E2
Rooth St WS10 42 B4
Roper Way DY3 50 F6
Roper Wlk DY3 50 F6
Ropewalk (Sh Ctr) CV11 73 C4
Rosafield Ave B62 83 F6
Rosalind Ave DY1 51 B6
Rosalind Gr WV11 27 A5
Rosamond St WS1 42 D7
Rosary RC Prim Sch B8 67 E3
Rosary Rd B23 56 D3
Rosary Villas 1 B11 87 C5
Rosaville Cres CV5 112 A6
Rose Ave
Alvechurch B48 139 A5
Birmingham B68 84 C7
Coventry CV6 112 F5
Kingswinford DY6 60 F5
Rosebank Dr WS3 28 E4
Rosebay Ave B38 123 F8
Rose Bay Mdw 2 WS11 2 C2
Roseberry Ave CV2 96 C1
Rosebery Rd
Smethwick B66 65 C4
Tamworth B77 35 D4
Rosebery St
Birmingham B18 66 A4
Wolverhampton WV3 25 B1
Rosebriars B90 125 E7
Rose Cl B66 65 C5
Rose Cottage Dr 3 DY8 60 D3
Rose Cottage Flats CV5 111 D5
Rose Cotts
6 Birmingham B29 85 F2
Birmingham, Stirchley B30 104 A6
Rose Croft CV8 147 E6
Rosecroft Rd B26 89 C6
Rose Ct
Balsall Common CV7 130 B8
Dudley DY2 51 F1
Rosedale Ave
Birmingham B23 56 E3
Smethwick B66 65 C5
Rosedale CE Inf Sch WV12 27 D5
Rosedale Cl B97 153 A4
Rosedale Gr B25 88 C8
Rosedale Pl WV13 41 A8
Rosedale Rd B25 88 C8
Rosedale Wlk DY6 60 E8
Rosedene Dr B20 54 F2
Rose Dr WS8 15 E5
Rosefield Croft B6 66 F7
Rosefield Ct B67 65 A4
Rosefield Pl 4 CV32 161 F8
Rosefield Rd B67 65 A4
Rosefield St CV32 162 A8
Rosefield Wlk 3 CV32 161 F8
Rosegardens The B63 82 E2
Rosegreen Cl CV3 133 E6
Rosehall Cl
Redditch B98 158 E6
Solihull B91 106 F1
Rosehill WS12 1 F8
Rose Hill
Barnt Green B45 122 B4
Rose Hill *continued*
Brierley Hill DY5 62 A1
Darlaston WV13 41 A8
Rose Hill Cl B36 69 B8
Rose Hill Gdns WV13 27 B1
Rose Hill Rd B21 66 A7
Rosehip Cl WS5 43 A3
Rosehip Dr CV2 114 B6
Rose La
Burntwood WS7 7 C7
Dodford B61 136 A6
Nuneaton CV11 73 C3
Oldbury B69 52 C2
Roseland Ave DY2 51 F1
Roseland Rd CV8 147 F3
Roselands Ave CV2 114 D8
Roseland Way 7 B15 66 B1
Roseleigh Rd B45 122 B6
Rosemary Ave
Bilston WV14 40 F6
Cheslyn Hay WS6 4 D3
Wolverhampton WV4 39 C6
Rosemary Cl
Brownhills WS8 15 D6
Coventry CV4 111 E3
Rosemary Cres
Dudley DY1 51 A6
Wolverhampton WV4 39 C5
Rosemary Crescent W WV4 39 B5
Rosemary Ct
Sutton Coldfield B74 31 D4
Wolverhampton WV11 26 F7
Rosemary Dr
Huntington WS12 1 D5
Stoke Prior B60 150 C1
Sutton Coldfield B74 31 C3
Rosemary Hill CV8 147 F5
Rosemary Hill Rd B74 31 D4
Rosemary La DY8 80 D3
Rosemary Mews CV8 147 F5
Rosemary Nook B74 31 D5
Rosemary Rd
Birmingham B33 68 F2
Cheslyn Hay WS6 4 D3
Halesowen B63 82 E2
Kidderminster DY10 117 B7
Tamworth B77 21 F4
Tipton DY4 52 A6
Rosemary Way
Hinckley LE10 75 B7
Nuneaton CV10 78 A8
Rosemont Ho B93 127 F3
Rosemoor Dr DY5 81 B7
Rosemount
Birmingham B32 84 E5
Wolverhampton WV6 24 D5
Rosemount Cl CV2 114 E7
Rosemullion Cl CV7 96 B8
Rose Rd
Birmingham B17 85 D6
Coleshill B46 70 F8
Rose St WV14 40 F2
Rose Terr B45 138 D8
Rosetti Cl DY10 117 C6
ROSEVILLE 51 B8
Roseville Ct 4 WV14 51 C8
Roseville Gdns WV8 10 A4
Roseville Prec 5 WV14 51 C8
Rosewood CV11 73 F1
Rosewood Cl
Hinckley LE10 75 F6
Tamworth B77 21 D4
Rosewood Cres CV32 157 B2
Rosewood Ct B77 21 D4
Rosewood Dr
Barnt Green B45 138 C7
Birmingham B23 56 D2
Willenhall WV12 27 B8
Rosewood Gdns WV11 13 B3
Rosewood Pk WS6 4 D2
Rosewood Rd DY1 51 B5
Rosewood Specl Sch WV14 40 C2
Roshven Rd B12 87 A4
Roslin Cl B60 137 B1
Roslin Gr B19 66 C6
Roslyn Cl B66 65 A6
Rosneath Cl WV4 39 F5
Ross B65 63 B2
Ross Cl
Coventry CV5 112 A5
Wolverhampton WV6 24 E2
Ross Dr DY6 60 C7
Rosse Ct B92 107 F8
Rossendale Cl B63 82 D6
Rossendale Way CV10 72 E2
Ross Hts B65 63 B3
Rosslyn Ave CV6 112 E6
Rosslyn Rd B76 57 F6
Ross Rd WS3 28 F6
Ross Way CV11 79 B7
Roston Dr LE10 71 A1
Rostrevor Rd B10 67 F1
Rosy Cross B79 21 B5
Rotary Ct 2 WV3 25 B2
Rotary Ho DY1 50 F1
Rothay B77 35 F8
Rothbury Gn WS12 2 E2
Rotherby Gr B37 90 B7
Rotherfield Cl CV31 162 B7
Rotherfield Rd B26 89 B8
Rotherham Rd CV6 95 C2
Rotherhams Oak La B94 142 F7
Rothesay Ave CV4 112 B2
Rothesay Cl CV10 73 A2
Rothesay Croft B32 102 B7
Rothesay Dr DY8 60 C3
Rothesay Gdns WV4 39 E5
Rothesay Way WV12 27 B6
Rothley Wlk B38 123 C8
Rothwell Dr B91 106 D4
Rothwell Rd CV34 155 C1
ROTTEN ROW 128 C3
Rotten Row WS14 9 C7
Rotten Row Barns B93 128 C4
ROTTON PARK 65 E3
Rotton Park Rd B16 65 D2
Rotton Park St B16 65 F3
Rough Coppice Wlk B35 58 A2
ROUGH HAY 41 C7
Rough Hay Pl WS10 41 C7
Rough Hay Prim Sch WS10 41 C7
Rough Hay Rd WS10 41 C7
Rough Hill Dr
Redditch B98 158 F6
Rowley Regis B65 62 F6
ROUGH HILLS 39 F6
Rough Hills Cl WV2 39 F6
Rough Hills Rd WV2 39 F6
Roughknowles Rd CV4 131 D6
Roughlea Ave B36 68 F7
ROUGHLEY 32 D3
Roughley Dr B75 32 C2
Roughley Farm Rd B75 32 E3
Rough Rd B44 45 A3
Rough The B97 158 D8
Rough Wood Chase Nature Reserve★ WS2 27 F8
Rough Wood Ctry Pk★ WV12 27 E6
Rouncil Cl B92 107 D7
Rouncil La CV8 155 C8
Roundabout The B31 102 D1
Round Cl B90 126 A6
Round Croft WV13 27 A2
Round Hill DY3 39 D2
Round Hill Ave DY9 81 C1
Roundhill Cl B76 46 E4
Roundhills Rd B62 83 F8
Roundhill Terr B62 63 E1
Roundhill Way WS8 7 A2
Round Hill Wharf DY11 116 D5
Round House Rd
Coventry CV3 134 B8
Dudley DY3 50 E4
Roundlea Cl WV12 27 B7
Roundlea Rd B31 102 E7
Round Moor Wlk B35 58 A3
Round Oak Sch CV34 161 C6
Round Rd B24 57 B2
Round Saw Croft B45 121 F8
ROUND'S GREEN 63 E8
Rounds Green Prim Sch B69 63 E7
Rounds Green Rd B69 63 F7
Rounds Hill CV8 147 E2
Rounds Hill Rd WV14 51 D8
Rounds Rd WV14 40 D3
Round St DY2 62 C6
Roundway Down WV6 23 F3
Rounton Cl B74 31 D4
Rousay Cl B45 101 F1
Rousdon Gr B43 54 D8
Rover Dr
Birmingham, Acock's Green B27 88 D4
Birmingham, Castle Bromwich B36 58 F1
Rover Rd CV1 165 B2
Rovex Bsns Pk B11 87 F5
Rowallan Rd B75 32 D2
Rowan Cl
Binley Woods CV3 135 D7
Bromsgrove B61 136 E2
Hollywood B47 125 B5
Lichfield WS14 9 D8
Sutton Coldfield B76 46 F2
Rowan Cres
Dudley WV14 40 B1
Redditch B97 153 A4
Wolverhampton WV3 38 E7
Rowan Ct
Birmingham B30 104 A2
2 Oldbury B66 64 D8
Rowan Dr
Birmingham B28 106 A5
Essington WV11 13 B3
6 Warwick CV34 160 F8
Rowan Gr
Burntwood WS7 6 F7
Coventry CV2 96 E2
Rowan Rd
Cannock WS11 1 C2
Nuneaton CV10 72 C6
Redditch B97 153 A4
Sedgley DY3 39 F1
Sutton Coldfield B72 46 C3
Walsall WS5 42 F4
Rowan Rise DY6 60 E6
Rowans The CV12 77 E2
Rowantrees B45 122 B5
Rowan Way
Birmingham, Chelmsley Wood B37 70 C1
Birmingham, Longbridge B31 122 F8
Hartshill CV10 72 A8
Roway La B69 52 F1
Rowberrie Cl B45 122 C7
Rowborough Cl B96 158 E2
Rowbrook Cl B90 125 E8
Rowcroft Covert B14 104 C2
Rowcroft Rd CV2 115 A6
Rowdale Rd B42 55 C6
Rowden Dr
Birmingham B23 57 A6
Solihull B91 106 E2
Rowena Gdns DY3 39 C2
Rowheath Ho B30 103 E5
Rowheath Rd B30 103 F4
Rowington Ave B65 63 D3
Rowington Cl CV6 112 D5
Rowington Gn CV35 144 F1
ROWINGTON GREEN 145 A1
Rowington Rd B34 69 E6
Rowington Terr B25 88 B7
Rowland Ave B80 159 E3
Rowland Gdns WS2 28 C3
Rowland Hill Ave DY11 116 B5
Rowland Hill Dr DY4 52 C5
Rowland Hill Sh Ctr 9 DY10 116 E6
Rowlands Ave
Walsall WS2 27 E3
Wolverhampton WV1 26 B2
Rowlands Cl WS2 27 E4
Rowlands Cres B91 107 B8
Rowlands Rd B26 88 E7
Rowland St WS2 28 C3
Rowland Way (Road 1a) DY11 116 E1
Rowley Cl WS12 2 B8
Rowley Dr CV3 134 B4
Rowley Gr B33 69 D3
Rowley Hall Ave B65 63 C4
Rowley Hall Prim Sch B65 63 C4
Rowley Hill View B64 82 F8
Rowley Pl WS4 29 B7
Rowley Rd
Coventry CV3, CV8 134 B3
Whitnash CV31 162 A2
ROWLEY REGIS 63 B3
Rowley Regis Hospl B65 63 B2
Rowley Regis Sta B65 63 E2
ROWLEY'S GREEN 95 E3
Rowley's Green La CV6 95 E4
Rowleys Green Lane Ind Est CV6 95 E4
Rowley St WS1 29 A2
Rowley View
Bilston WV14 41 A3
Darlaston WS10 41 C4
West Bromwich B70 53 B3
Rowley Village B65 63 C3
Rowney Croft B28 105 E4
ROWNEY GREEN 139 E3
Rowney Green La B48 139 F5
Rowood Dr B91, B92 107 D7
Row The CV7 97 D3
Rowthorn Cl B74 45 A7
Rowthorn Dr B90 127 A6
Rowton Ave WV6 23 E3
Rowton Dr B74 44 F5
Roxall Cl DY10 98 C2
Roxboro Ho B97 153 D2
Roxburgh Croft CV32 157 C6
Roxburgh Gr B43 44 C4
Roxburgh Rd
Nuneaton CV11 73 E1
Sutton Coldfield B73 46 A3
Roxby Gdns WV6 25 A5
Royal Cl
Brierley Hill DY5 81 C8
Rowley Regis B65 63 C5
Royal Cres CV3 134 C5
Royal Ct
Hinckley LE10 75 D7
Sutton Coldfield B73 46 B2
Royal Gr 3 B23 56 B7
ROYAL LEAMINGTON SPA 156 D3
Royal Leamington Spa Rehabilitation Hospl CV34 161 E4
Royal London Bldgs WV1 163 C3
Royal Mail St B1 164 B2
Royal Mdw Way B74 44 E7
Royal Oak La CV7, CV12 95 C7
Royal Oak Rd
Halesowen B62 83 F5
Rowley Regis B65 62 F5
Royal Oak Yd CV12 78 B4
Royal Orthopaedic Hospl The B31 103 B5
Royal Priors Sh Ctr 18 CV32 156 F1
Royal Pump Room & Baths CV32 46 F8
Royal Rd B72 46 C4
Royal Scot Gr WS1 42 D5
Royal Star Cl B33 69 C2
Royal Stop The WV1 163 D2
Royal Way DY4 52 A2
Royal Wolverhampton Sch The WV3 39 B7
Royal Worcester Cres B60 137 C1
Roydon Rd B27 106 C8
Roylesden Cres B73 45 C2
Royston Chase B74 31 A3
Royston Cl CV3 115 A3
Royston Croft B12 86 F6
Royston Ct 7 B13 87 B2
Royston Way DY3 50 C8
RSA Acad DY4 41 B2
RSPCA Birmingham Animal Hospl★ B32 84 E2

Rubens Cl
Coventry CV5 . . . . **112** C3
Dudley DY3 . . . . **50** D5
RUBERY **122** B7
Rubery Ct WS10 . . . . **41** C7
Rubery Farm Gr B45 . . . **121** F7
Rubery Field Cl B45 . . . . **102** A1
Rubery La B45 . . . . **102** A1
Rubery La S B45 . . . . **121** F8
Rubery WS10 . . . . **41** D8
Ruckleigh Sch B91 . . . . . **107** C4
Ruckley Ave 4 B19 . . . . . **66** C7
Ruckley Rd B29 . . . . **103** B8
Rudd Gdns WV10 . . . . . . **26** B4
Rudgard Rd CV6 . . . . **96** A4
Rudge Ave WV1 . . . . **26** B3
Rudge Cl WV12 . . . . **27** C4
Rudge Croft B33 . . . . **69** A4
Rudgewick Croft 1 B6 . . **66** F6
Rudge Wlk B18 . . . . **66** A3
Rudyard Cl WV10 . . . . **11** E2
Rudyard Gr B33. . . . . **69** B3
Rudyngleigh Dr B33 . . . . **68** F4
Rufford Cl
Birmingham B23 . . . . **56** D8
Hinckley LE10 . . . . **75** D3
Rufford Prim Sch DY9. . . **81** C5
Rufford Rd DY9 . . . . **81** C4
Rufford St DY9 . . . . **81** D5
Rufford Way WS9 . . . . **29** E7
Rugby Rd
Binley Woods CV3 . . . . . . **135** D8
Bulkington CV12 . . . . **79** D2
Cubbington CV32 . . . . . . **157** E6
Hinckley LE10 . . . . **75** D5
Royal Leamington Spa
CV32. . . . . **156** D1
Stourbridge DY8 . . . . **80** D7
Rugby St WV1 . . . . **25** B4
Rugeley Ave WV12 . . . . . . **27** D8
Rugeley Cl DY4 . . . . **51** E5
Rugeley Rd
Burntwood, Gorstey Ley
WS7 . . . . **7** C7
Cannock, Hednesford WS12 . . **2** F6
Cannock, West Hill WS12 . . **2** D7
Ruislip Cl B35 . . . . **58** A4
RUITON **50** D5
Ruiton St DY3. . . . . **50** D4
Rumbow B63 . . . . **83** B4
Rumbow La B62 . . . . **100** D3
RUMBUSH **125** E3
Rumbush La
Earlswood B90, B94 . . . . . **125** F3
Solihull B90 . . . . **126** A5
RUMER HILL **4** F7
Rumer Hill Bsns Est WS11 . **4** E7
Rumer Hill Ind Est WS11 . . **4** F7
Rumer Hill Rd WS11. . . . . . **4** B8
Runcorn Cl
Birmingham B37 . . . . **70** C4
Redditch B98 . . . . **158** F8
Runcorn Rd B12 . . . . **87** A5
Runcorn Wlk 10 CV2 . . . **115** A7
Runnemede Gdns CV10. . . **72** F3
Runnymede Dr CV7 . . . . . **130** C5
Runnymede Rd B11 . . . . . **87** E3
Rupert Rd CV6 . . . . **113** B8
Rupert St
Birmingham B7 . . . . **67** A4
Wolverhampton WV3. . . . . **25** A2
RUSHALL **29** C6
Rushall Cl
Stourbridge DY8 . . . . **80** E6
Walsall WS4. . . . . **29** B4
Rushall Ct 1 B43 . . . . . . **54** E7
Rushall JMI Sch WS4 . . . . **15** B1
Rushall Manor Cl WS4 . . . **29** B4
Rushall Manor Rd WS4 . . . **29** B4
Rushall Rd WV10. . . . . **11** E2
RUSHBROOK **141** D3
Rushbrook Cl
Bilston WV14 . . . . **40** B5
Solihull B90 . . . . **106** D4
Rushden Croft B44. . . . . . **44** F1
Rushes Mill WS3 . . . . **14** E3
Rushey La B11. . . . . **88** A4
Rushleigh Rd B90. . . . . . **125** E8
Rushmead Gr B45. . . . . . **122** A7
Rushmere Rd DY4 . . . . . . **52** A8
Rushmoor Cl B74 . . . . **46** B6
Rushmoor Dr CV5 . . . . . **112** F3
Rushmore St CV31. . . . . **162** B7
Rushock Cl B98 . . . . **159** C7
Rushton Cl CV7 . . . . **130** C7
Rushwick Croft B34. . . . . **69** D6
Rushwick Ct B23. . . . . . . **56** B5
Rushwick Gr B90 . . . . . . **127** A6
Rushwood Cl WS4 . . . . . . **29** A3

Rushy Piece B32 . . . . **84** D3
Rusina Ct CV31 . . . . **161** F6
Ruskin Ave
Dudley DY3 . . . . **50** A5
Kidderminster DY10. . . . . **117** C6
Rowley Regis B65 . . . . **63** D2
Wolverhampton WV4. . . . . **39** F7
Ruskin Cl
Birmingham B6 . . . . **66** F7
Coventry CV6. . . . . **112** D6
Nuneaton CV10 . . . . **72** A5
Ruskin Ct 5 B68. . . . . . . **84** B8
Ruskin Glass Ctr ★ DY8 . . **80** F7
Ruskin Gr B27 . . . . **88** B2
Ruskin Hall Gr B6. . . . . . . **66** F7
Ruskin Rd WV10 . . . . **12** A1
Ruskin St B71 . . . . **53** C5
Russel Croft B60 . . . . . . **151** A7
Russell Bank Rd B74 . . . . **31** E4
Russell Ct
7 Royal Leamington Spa
CV31. . . . . **162** A7
Sutton Coldfield B74 . . . . . **31** D3
Wolverhampton WV3. . . . **163** A2
Russell Ho
Tamworth B77 . . . . **21** F2
Wednesbury WS10 . . . . . . **41** F2
Russell Rd
Bilston WV14. . . . . **40** F7
Birmingham, Hall Green B28 **87** E1
Birmingham, Moseley B13. . **86** D3
Kidderminster DY10. . . . . **116** F4
RUSSELL'S HALL **61** E8
Russell's Hall Hospl DY5. . **61** E7
Russells Hall Prim Sch
DY1. . . . . **50** E1
Russell's Hall Rd DY1 . . . . **50** F1
Russell St
Coventry CV1 . . . . **165** C4
Dudley DY1 . . . . **51** B1
Royal Leamington Spa
CV32. . . . . **156** F1
Wednesbury WS10 . . . . . . **41** F2
Willenhall WV13 . . . . **27** B2
Wolverhampton WV3. . . . **163** A2
Russells The B13 . . . . **86** D3
Russell Street N 2 CV1 . **165** C4
Russell Terr CV31. . . . . . **162** A7
Russet Gr CV4. . . . . **132** D3
Russett Cl
Burntwood WS7. . . . . **7** A6
Walsall WS5 . . . . **43** D8
Russett Way DY5. . . . . . . **61** B7
Russet Way B31 . . . . **102** E6
Russet Wlk WV8 . . . . **10** E1
Ruston St B16. . . . . **66** B1
Ruthall Cl B29 . . . . **103** C7
Ruth Chamberlain Ct 3
DY11 . . . . **116** D6
Ruth Cl DY4 . . . . **41** C2
Rutherford Glen CV11. . . . **73** F1
Rutherford Rd
Birmingham B23 . . . . **56** E7
Bromsgrove B60 . . . . **151** B7
Walsall WS2. . . . . **28** A5
Rutherglen Ave CV3. . . . **134** A6
Rutland Ave
Hinckley LE10 . . . . **75** C7
Nuneaton CV10 . . . . **72** F4
Wolverhampton WV4. . . . . **38** D4
Rutland Cres
Aldridge WS9. . . . . **16** B1
Bilston WV14. . . . . **40** E7
Rutland Croft 3 CV3 . . **134** E8
Rutland Ct 2 B29. . . . . . **103** C7
Rutland Dr
Birmingham B26 . . . . **88** E7
Bromsgrove B60 . . . . **151** A8
Tamworth B78 . . . . **21** A1
Rutland Pas 8 DY1 . . . . . **51** C1
Rutland Pl DY8 . . . . **80** D8
Rutland Rd
Cannock WS11. . . . . **2** E1
Smethwick B66 . . . . **65** A1
Wednesbury WS10 . . . . . . **42** D4
West Bromwich B71 . . . . . **53** C7
Rutland St WS3. . . . . **28** E5
Rutland Terr 5 B18. . . . . **66** A5
Rutley Gr B32. . . . . **84** F4
Rutters Mdw B32. . . . . . . **84** B4
Rutter St WS1 . . . . **42** E8
Ryan Ave WV11 . . . . **27** A7
Ryan Pl DY2 . . . . **62** C6
Rycroft Gr B33. . . . . **69** C2
Rydal B77 . . . . **36** A7
Rydal Ave CV11 . . . . **74** A6
Rydal Cl
Allesley CV5. . . . . **112** B8
Cannock WS12. . . . . **2** A8
Hinckley LE10 . . . . **74** F7
Sutton Coldfield B74 . . . . . **30** F2
Wolverhampton WV11. . . . **26** C7
Rydal Dr WV6. . . . . **23** F4
Rydal Ho B69 . . . . **63** D5
Rydal Way B28. . . . . **105** F7
Rydding La B71. . . . . **53** B8
Rydding Sq B71. . . . . **53** B8
Ryde Ave CV10. . . . . **73** D7
Ryde Gr B27 . . . . **88** A1
Ryde Park Rd B45. . . . . . **122** C7
Ryders Green Prim Sch
B70 . . . . **53** A4

Ryders Green Rd B70 . . . . **52** F4
Ryders Hayes Com Prim Sch
WS3 . . . . **15** A5
Ryders Hayes La WS3 . . . . **15** A4
Ryders Hill Cres CV10 . . . **72** C7
Ryder St
Birmingham B4 . . . . **164** C3
Stourbridge DY8 . . . . **60** D2
West Bromwich B70 . . . . . **52** F5
Ryebank Cl B30. . . . . **103** C5
Ryeclose Croft B37 . . . . . **70** D3
RYECROFT **28** E4
Rye Croft
7 Birmingham B27. . . . . . **88** C5
Hollywood B47. . . . . **125** A5
Stourbridge DY9 . . . . **81** E2
Ryecroft Ave WV4. . . . . . . **39** B5
Ryecroft Cl DY3. . . . . **50** C8
Ryecroft Cotts WV4 . . . . . **39** B5
Ryecroft Dr 3 WS7 . . . . . . **7** A8
Ryecroft Pk 4 WS2 . . . . . **28** E3
Ryecroft Pl WS3. . . . . **28** F6
Ryecroft St 2 WS2 . . . . . . **28** E3
Ryefield WV8 . . . . **10** E1
Ryefield Cl
Solihull B91 . . . . **106** E5
West Hagley DY9. . . . . **99** A4
Ryefield La B76. . . . . **48** B2
Ryefields Rd B60. . . . . . . **150** C3
Ryefield Way DY6. . . . . . . **60** C6
Rye Gr B11. . . . . **87** F4
Ryegrass La B97 . . . . **158** C6
Rye Grass Wlk B35 . . . . . . **58** B3
Rye Hill CV5 . . . . **112** A6
Rye Hill Office Pk CV5. . . **112** A7
Ryemarket Sh Ctr 17 DY8 . **81** A5
Rye Piece Ringway CV12 . **78** C3
Ryhope Cl CV12. . . . . **77** C1
Ryhope Wlk WV9 . . . . **11** A3
Ryknild Cl B74 . . . . **31** F6
Ryknild St WS14 . . . . **9** E6

Ryland Cl
Halesowen B63 . . . . **82** E2
Royal Leamington Spa
CV31. . . . . **162** C6
Ryland Ho B19. . . . . **66** D5
Ryland Rd
Birmingham, Edgbaston
B15. . . . . **86** C8
Birmingham, Gravelly Hill
B24 . . . . **56** F1
Rylands Dr WV4 . . . . **39** A4
Rylstone B77. . . . . **36** B1
Rylcroft 7 WV4 . . . . **39** F4
Ryle St WS3 . . . . **14** D1
Ryley St CV1 . . . . **165** A3
Rylston Ave CV6. . . . . **95** A1
Rylstone Way 4 CV34. . . **155** E1
Rymond Rd B34. . . . . **68** E6
RYTON. **79** D2
Ryton B77 . . . . **35** F8
Ryton Cl
Coventry CV4. . . . . **132** B8
Redditch B98 . . . . **154** D1
Sutton Coldfield B73 . . . . . **46** B5
Wolverhampton WV10 . . . . **26** A5
Ryton Gr B34 . . . . **69** D7
RYTON-ON-DUNSMORE **132** B8
Ryton Organic Gdns ★
CV8. . . . . **135** E1

S

Sabell Rd B67 . . . . **64** F6
Sabrina Rd WV6 . . . . **23** E1
Sackville Ho 1 CV1 . . . . **165** D4
Sadler Rd CV6 . . . . **95** E3
Sacred Heart RC Prim Sch
Birmingham B20 . . . . **55** D1
1 Coventry CV2 . . . . **114** A3
Tipton DY4 . . . . **52** A4
Saddington Rd CV3 . . . . . **134** E8
Sadlers Cl
Halesowen B63 . . . . **82** B5
Hinckley LE10 . . . . **75** F6
Lichfield WS14 . . . . **9** E8
Saddlers Court Ind Est
WS2 . . . . **28** A7
Saddlers Ctr WS1. . . . . . . **28** E1
Sadlers Mews B91. . . . . . **107** C1
Saddlestones The WV6. . . **23** D4
Saddleworth Rd WS3. . . . . **14** A4
Sadler Cres B11 . . . . **87** D4
Sadler Gdns CV12. . . . . . . **78** C2
Sadler Ho B19 . . . . **66** C6
Sadler Rd
Brownhills WS8 . . . . **16** A8
Coventry CV6. . . . . **113** A8
Sutton Coldfield B75 . . . . . **46** F7
Sadlers Cl WS2 . . . . **42** B7
Sadlers Mill WS8 . . . . **16** A7
Sadlerswell La B94. . . . . . **143** B6
Sadlers Wlk B16 . . . . **66** A1
Saffron B77 . . . . **22** B4
Saffron Gdns WV4 . . . . . . **39** A4
Saffron Ho 3 B38 . . . . . . **123** E8
Saffron Rd B60. . . . . **150** C1
Sage Croft B31 . . . . **102** F5
St Agatha's Rd
Birmingham B8 . . . . **68** B5
Coventry CV2. . . . . **114** A3
St Agnes Cl
Birmingham B13 . . . . **87** B2
Studley B80 . . . . **159** C4

St Agnes Rd B13 . . . . **87** B1
St Agnes Way CV11 . . . . . . **73** F4
St Aidan's Ct WV4 . . . . **39** A5
St Aidan's Rd WS11 . . . . **1** E5
St Aidans Wlk 3 B10. . . . . **87** C8
St Alban's Acad B12 . . . . . **86** F7
St Alban's Ave DY11. . . . . **116** A7
St Alban's CE Prim Sch
WV11. . . . . **27** B8
St Albans Cl
Royal Leamington Spa
CV32. . . . . **156** C2
Smethwick B67 . . . . **64** E6
Wednesfield WV11 . . . . . . **27** A8
Wolverhampton WV13 . . . . **13** A1
St Albans Ct WV13 . . . . . . **26** E1
St Albans Ho B32 . . . . **84** F5
St Alban's RC Prim Sch
B14. . . . . **104** F4
St Albans Rd
Birmingham B13 . . . . **87** A4
Smethwick B67 . . . . **64** E6
Brownhills WS8 . . . . **15** F1
St Alphege CE Inf Sch
B91. . . . . **107** C3
St Alphege CE Jun Sch
B91. . . . . **107** C2
St Alphege Cl B91. . . . . . **107** C3
St Ambrose Barlow RC Prim
Sch B28. . . . . **106** A6
St Ambrose Cl B62, B65. . . **83** C8
St Ambrose's RC Prim Sch
DY10. . . . . **116** F6
St Andrews B77. . . . . **22** B4
St Andrews Ave WS3 . . . . . **15** B4
St Andrew's CE Fst Sch
B45. . . . . **138** D8
St Andrew's CE Inf Sch
CV5. . . . . **111** C5
St Andrews CE Prim Sch
WV6 . . . . **24** F4
St Andrew's Cl
Birmingham B32 . . . . **85** A3
Stourbridge DY8 . . . . **80** F2
Wolverhampton WV6 . . . . . **25** A4
St Andrew's Cl DY3 . . . . . . **50** B1
St Andrews Cl 2 B10 . . . . **87** B1
St Andrews Dr
Nuneaton CV11 . . . . **74** B1
Oldbury B69. . . . . **63** B7
Perton WV6. . . . . **23** D5
St Andrews Gn DY10 . . . . **116** E4
St Andrews Ho WV6. . . . . . **25** B4
St Andrews Ind Est B9 . . . **67** C2
St Andrew's RC Prim Sch
B92. . . . . **89** A2
St Andrews Rd B75 . . . . . . **46** D7
St Andrew's Rd
Birmingham B9 . . . . **67** B2
Coventry CV5. . . . . **132** F8
Royal Leamington Spa
CV32. . . . . **157** B5
St Andrew's St
Birmingham B9 . . . . **67** B2
Dudley DY2 . . . . **62** C5
**St Andrew's Stadium
(Birmingham City FC)**
B9 . . . . **67** C1
St Andrews Way B61 . . . . **150** D8
St Annes Cl WS7 . . . . **6** E4
St Annes Ct B44 . . . . **56** A7
St Anne's Cl
Birmingham B13 . . . . **86** E4
Willenhall WV13 . . . . **27** B1
St Annes Gr B93 . . . . **128** A6
St Annes Ind Est WV13 . . . **27** B3
St Anne's RC Prim Sch
Birmingham B37 . . . . **70** A2
Coventry CV2. . . . . **134** C6
Nuneaton CV10 . . . . **72** D7
Sutton Coldfield B74 . . . . . **44** E8
St Annes Rd WS13 . . . . **3** B3
St Anne's Rd
Cradley Heath B64. . . . . . . **62** C1
Wednesfield WV13 . . . . . . **27** B3
Wolverhampton WV11. . . . **11** B1
St Annes Way B44 . . . . **56** A7
St Ann's Cl CV31. . . . . . . **162** C7
St Ann's Rd CV2 . . . . **114** A3
St Anthonys Dr WS3. . . . . **15** B5
St Anthony's RC Prim Sch
CV31. . . . . **162** C7
Wolverhampton WV10. . . . **11** D3
St Antony's RC Prim Sch
B37. . . . . **70** A5
St Asaphs Ave B80 . . . . . **159** D4
St Athan Croft B35. . . . . . **58** B3
St Audries Cl B91. . . . . . . **106** F2
St Augustine's RC High Sch
B97 . . . . **158** D5
St Augustine's RC Prim Sch
Birmingham B21 . . . . **54** D2
Coventry CV6. . . . . **113** A7
Kenilworth CV8 . . . . **147** E2
Solihull B91 . . . . **107** A2
St Augustine's Rd B16. . . . **65** D1
St Augustine's Wlk CV6 . . **113** A7
St Augustus Cl B70. . . . . . **53** F2
St Austell Cl
Nuneaton CV11 . . . . **74** A5
Tamworth B79 . . . . **21** A6
St Austell Rd
Coventry CV2. . . . . **114** C3
Walsall WS5. . . . . **43** E7

St Barnabas CE Prim Sch
B24. . . . . **57** A8
St Bartholomew's CE Prim
Sch
9 Coventry CV3 . . . . **134** F1
Wolverhampton WV4. . . . . **38** E1
St Bartholomew Terr 3
WS10 . . . . **41** F
St Bede's RC Mid Sch
B98. . . . . **153** A
St Benedict Bishop CE Prim
Sch WV5 . . . . **49** B
St Benedict's Cl B70 . . . . **53** F
St Benedict's Inf Sch B10 . **87** F
St Benedicts Rd
Birmingham B10 . . . . **87** F
Wombourne WV5. . . . . **49** A
St Benedict's Rd WS7 . . . . **7** B
St Bernadette's RC Prim Sch
Birmingham B25 . . . . **88** B
Brownhills WS8 . . . . **15** F
St Bernard's RC Prim Sch
B13. . . . . **87** C
St Bernards Rd B72. . . . . . **46** C
St Bernard's Rd B92 . . . . **106** E
St Bernard's Wlk CV3 . . . **134** D
St Blaise Ave B46 . . . . **59** C
St Blaise Rd B75. . . . . **32** D
St Brades Cl B69. . . . . **63** C
St Brides Cl DY3 . . . . **50** C
St Bride's Cl CV31. . . . . . **162** C
St Brigid's RC Prim Sch
B31. . . . . **102** F
St Buryan Cl CV11. . . . . . . **74** A
Saintbury Dr B91 . . . . . . **127** C
St Caroline Cl B70 . . . . . . **53** F
St Catharines Cl WS1 . . . . **43** A
St Catherine CE Prim Sch
DY11. . . . . **116** C
St Catherine of Siena RC
Prim Sch 8 B1. . . . . **66** D
St Catherines Cl
Birmingham B15 . . . . **66** D
Blackwell B60 . . . . **138** A
Oldbury DY2. . . . . **52** A
Sutton Coldfield B75 . . . . . **46** F
St Catherine's Cl
Coventry CV3. . . . . **134** B
Hinckley LE10 . . . . **75** F
St Catherine's Cres
Whitnash CV34 . . . . **161** F
Wolverhampton WV4. . . . . **38** F
St Catherine's St B91 . . . **107** B
St Catherine's Lodge 7
CV6 . . . . **113** A
St Catherines Rd WS13. . . . **3** B
St Catherine's Rd B60. . . **138** A
St Cecilia Cl DY10. . . . . . . **116** E
St Cecilia's WV11 . . . . **26** C
St Chad Ct B77 . . . . **21** F
ST CHADS . . . . **40** F
St Chad's Cath ★ B4. . . . **164** B
St Chad's CE (VC) Prim Sch
WS13 . . . . **9** C
St Chad's Circus Queensway
B3 . . . . **164** B
St Chads Cl WS13 . . . . **3** B
St Chad's Cl
Cannock WS11. . . . . **2** A
Dudley DY3 . . . . **50** B
St Chads Ct 3 B19. . . . . . . **66** E
St Chads Ind Est B19. . . . . **66** E
St Chads Mews B94 . . . . . **144** D
St Chads Queensway B4. **164** C
St Chad's RC Prim Sch
DY3. . . . . **50** D
St Chad's RC Prim Sch
B19. . . . . **66** D
St Chads Rd B80 . . . . **159** C
St Chad's Rd
Bilston WV14. . . . . **40** F
Birmingham B45 . . . . **121** F
Lichfield WS13 . . . . **3** C
Sutton Coldfield B75 . . . . . **46** F
Wolverhampton WV10. . . . **25** F
St Christopher Cl
Birmingham B20 . . . . **54** F
1 West Bromwich B70 . . . . **53** D
St Christopher's Croft CV3 **133** E
St Christian's Rd CV3 . . . . **133** E
St Christopher Dr WS10 . . **42** E
St Christopher Prim Sch
CV5. . . . . **112** D
St Christophers B20. . . . . **54** F
St Christopher's Cl CV34 **160** D
St Christopher's Dr B77 . . **21** C
St Christophers RC Prim Sch
WV8 . . . . **10** A
St Clare's Prim Sch B20. . **55** B
St Clement's Ave WS3. . . . **28** D
St Clement's Ct
B7. . . . . **67** C
St Clements Ct CV2 . . . . . **114** D
St Clements Ho 3 B1. . . . . **53** D
St Clement's La B71. . . . . . **53** C
St Clements Rd B7 . . . . . . **67** C
St Columba's Cl CV1. . . . . **165** B
St Columbas Dr B45. . . . . **122** D
St Cuthbert's Cl B70 . . . . . **53** F
St Cuthberts RC Prim Sch
B8. . . . . **68** C
St David Dr WS10 . . . . **42** E
St Davids Cl WS3 . . . . **15** B
St David's Cl
Royal Leamington Spa
CV31. . . . . **162** C
West Bromwich B70 . . . . . **53** F

St Davids Dr B32 . . . . 84 B5
St Davids Gr B20 . . . . 54 F4
St Davids Orch CV3 . . . . 134 F7
St Denis Rd B29 . . . . 103 B7
St Denis Ho B4 B15 . . . . . 65 D7
St Dominic's Rd B24 . . . . . 56 E1
St Dunstan's RC Prim Sch
B14 . . . . 104 F8
St Edburghs Rd B25 . . . . . 68 E1
St Editha's CI B 21 B5
St Editha's Dr B34 . . . . . . 21 B7
St Edith's Gn B3 CV34 . . . 161 B8
St Edith's Ho B2 CV34 . . . 161 B8
St Edmund Campion RC Sch
B23 . . . . 57 B5
St Edmund & John CE Prim
Sch B1 DY2 . . . . 51 E1
St Edmund's CI
West Bromwich B70 . . . . . . 53 F2
Wolverhampton WV6 . . . . 24 F3
St Edmund's RC Prim Sch
B18 . . . . 66 A4
St Edmunds RC Sch WV3 . 24 E3
St Edward's Rd B29 . . . . . 85 F2
St Edward's Rd B29 . . . . . 85 F2
Sainte Foy Ave WS13 . . . . 9 A6
SS John & Monica RC Prim
Sch B13 . . . . 86 E4
St Eleanor CI B70 . . . . 53 F3
St Elizabeth's RC Prim Sch
Coventry CV6 . . . . 113 E7
Tamworth B79 . . . . 20 F8
St Elizabeth's Rd CV6 . . . 113 E7
St Foy CI WS13 . . . . 8 F5
St Francis Ave B91 . . . . . 106 E6
St Francis CE Prim Sch
B30 . . . . 103 D6
St Francis CI
Hinckley LE10 . . . . 71 C3
Walsall WS13 . . . . 15 B5
St Francis Dr B30 . . . . . . 104 D3
St Francis Factory Est
B70 . . . . 53 E2
St Francis of Assisi Tech Coll
WS9 . . . . 30 C5
St Francis RC Comb Sch
CV12 . . . . 78 C3
St Francis RC Prim Sch
Birmingham B19 . . . . 66 B6
Walsall WS4 . . . . 15 C1
St Francis Xavier RC Prim
Sch B69 . . . . 64 A8
St Fremund Way CV31 . . . 162 C5
St Gabriel's RC Prim Sch
B77 . . . . 21 E1
St George CI WS10 . . . . . . 42 E3
St George Dr B66 . . . . 65 A7
ST GEORGE'S 153 F4
St George & St Teresa RC
Prim Sch B93 . . . . 128 A4
St Georges Ave B 57 A5
St George's Ave LE10 . . . . 71 C1
St George's CE Fst Sch
B98 . . . . 153 F3
St George's CE Prim Sch
Birmingham B19 . . . . . . 164 B5
B7 Birmingham, Ladywood
B16 . . . . 65 F1
Kidderminster DY10 . . . . 116 F7
St George's Ct B15 . . . . . . 86 A7
St Georges CI
B5 Darlaston WS10 . . . . . . 41 D7
Sutton Coldfield B75 . . . . 46 F6
St Georges Ct
B10 Kidderminster DY10 . . 116 E6
Sutton Coldfield B74 . . . . 31 E5
B2 Walsall WS1 . . . . 28 F2
St George's Ct
Birmingham B30 . . . . 103 E7
B6 Birmingham B18 . . . . . 66 A4
St George's Gdns B3 B98 153 F4
St George's PI WV1 . . . . . 163 C2
St Georges Rd B70 . . . . . . 53 C4
St George's PI
Kidderminster DY10 . . . . 116 E7
B4 Walsall WS1 . . . . 28 F2
St Georges Rd
Dudley DY2 . . . . 62 E6
Redditch B98 . . . . 153 F4
St George's Rd
Coventry CV1 . . . . 113 F2
Royal Leamington Spa
CV31 . . . . 161 F6
Solihull B90 . . . . 126 D8
Stourbridge DY8 . . . . 80 D2
St Georges Sch Edgbaston
B15 . . . . 86 B8
St George's St
Birmingham B19 . . . . . . 164 B4
B4 Darlaston WS10 . . . . . . 41 D7
St George's Stop WV1 . . . 163 C2
St George's Terr DY10 . . . 116 F6
St George's Way CV10 . . . . 78 B8
St George's Way B7 . . . . . . 21 F4
St George's PI
B4 Walsall WS1 . . . . 28 F2
St Gerards Ct B91 . . . . . . 106 E2
St Gerards RC Prim Sch
B35 . . . . 58 B4
St Gerards RC Prim Sch
B35 . . . . 58 B4
St Giles Ave B65 . . . . 63 B4
St Giles' CE Prim Sch B3
WV13 . . . . 27 B2
St Giles CI B65 . . . . 63 C4
St Giles Cres WV1 . . . . . . 26 A2
St Giles Ct B65 . . . . 63 D3
St Gile's Cr WV13 . . . . 27 B1

St Giles Jun Sch CV7 . . . . 95 F8
St Giles Rd
Birmingham B33 . . . . 69 D2
Burntwood WS7 . . . . 7 B6
Coventry CV7 . . . . 95 D6
Willenhall WV13 . . . . 26 A2
Wolverhampton WV1 . . . . . 26 A2
St Giles Row B2 DY8 . . . . . 81 A6
St Giles St DY2 . . . . 62 C5
St Godwald's Cres B60 . . 151 B8
St Godwald's Rd B60 . . . . 151 C7
St Govan's CI B2 CV31 . . . 162 C6
St Gregory's RC Prim Sch
Coventry CV2 . . . . 114 E3
Smethwick B67 . . . . 64 F2
St Helens Ave DY4 . . . . . . 52 C5
St Helens Pas B1 . . . . 66 C3
St Helens Rd WS13 . . . . 3 B3
St Helen's Rd
Birmingham B91 . . . . 107 A6
Whitnash CV31 . . . . 162 A5
St Helen's Way CV5 . . . . . 112 B8
St Heliers Rd B31 . . . . . . 102 F4
St Hellier Ho B4 B15 . . . . 65 D1
St Hubert's RC Prim Sch
B68 . . . . 84 C8
St Ives CI B79 . . . . 21 B6
St Ives Rd
Coventry CV2 . . . . 114 E3
Walsall WS5 . . . . 43 D7
St Ives Way CV11 . . . . 73 F5
St James Ave B65 . . . . 63 B4
St James CE Jun Sch
Bulkington CV12 . . . . 79 C2
Solihull B90 . . . . 106 B2
St James CE Prim Sch
Birmingham B21 . . . . 54 D1
Oldbury B69 . . . . 63 D5
St James' CE Prim Sch
CV32 . . . . 80 D7
St James CI
Walsall WS3 . . . . 15 B5
West Bromwich B70 . . . . . 53 F2
St James Ct
Bromsgrove B60 . . . . 137 A3
Coventry CV5 . . . . 134 E6
St James Gdns
Brownhills WS8 . . . . 15 F7
Bulkington CV12 . . . . 79 C2
St James' La CV3 . . . . . . 134 D6
St James Meadow Rd
CV32 . . . . 156 C2
St James PI
Birmingham, Edgbaston
B15 . . . . 86 B8
Solihull B90 . . . . 106 B2
St James' PI B7 . . . . 67 A3
St James Prim Sch WS8 . . 15 F8
St James Rd
Birmingham, Edgbaston
B15 . . . . 86 B8
Cannock WS11 . . . . 1 C1
Norton Canes WS11 . . . . . . 6 B5
Oldbury B69 . . . . 63 E8
Sutton Coldfield B75 . . . . 32 C2
St James' Rd B21 . . . . 65 D8
St James's CI LE10 . . . . . . 75 D5
St James's Rd DY1 . . . . . . 51 B2
St James St
Wednesbury WS10 . . . . . . 41 E2
Wolverhampton WV1 . . . . 163 D3
St James' St DY3 . . . . 50 D3
St James's Terr DY1 . . . . . 51 A2
St James Wlk WS8 . . . . . . 15 F7
St John Bosco RC Prim Sch
B71 . . . . 53 D4
St John Fisher RC Prim Sch
Birmingham B31 . . . . 123 B7
Coventry CV2 . . . . 114 D5
St Johns LE10 . . . . 71 E1
St John's CV34 . . . . 160 F7
St John's Arc WV1 . . . . . . 163 B2
St John's Ave B65 . . . . 63 B4
St John's Ave
Kenilworth CV8 . . . . 148 A3
St John's CE JMI Sch
WS9 . . . . 16 A3
St John's CE Mid Sch
B61 . . . . 136 F1
St John's CE Prim Sch
Birmingham B11 . . . . 87 C4
Coventry CV5 . . . . 112 C4
Essington WV11 . . . . 13 A4
Kidderminster DY11 . . . . 116 B6
Wednesbury WS10 . . . . . . 41 F2
St Johns CE B93 . . . . 128 B6
St John's CE
Brownhills WS9 . . . . 15 F3
Cannock WS11 . . . . 4 D8
B6 Kidderminster DY11 . . 116 C6
Lichfield WS13 . . . . 9 B6
West Bromwich B70 . . . . . 53 F3
St Johns CE
B2 Birmingham, Harborne
B17 . . . . 85 B6
Birmingham, Turves Green
B31 . . . . 103 B1
B20 Brierley Hill DY5 . . . . . 61 D2
Bromsgrove B61 . . . . 136 F2
B5 Wednesbury WS10 . . . . 41 F2
St John's Ct
Cannock WS12 . . . . 2 E1
Walsall WS3 . . . . 14 B1
B4 Warwick CV34 . . . . . . 160 F7

St John's Dr WS14 . . . . . . 17 F5
St John's Flats CV8 . . . . . 148 A3
St Johns Gr B37 . . . . 69 F3
St John's Hill WS14 . . . . . 17 F5
St Johns Ho B2 B74 . . . . . 31 E3
St John's House & The Royal
Regiment of Fusiliers
Mus * B4 CV34 . . . . 160 F7
St John's Ladywood CE Prim
Sch B16 . . . . 66 A2
St John's Prim Sch CV8 . . 147 F2
St Johns Rd
Birmingham B11 . . . . 87 C5
Brownhills WS8 . . . . 16 A5
Essington WV11 . . . . 13 A3
Oldbury B68 . . . . 64 C5
Walsall, Pleck WS2 . . . . . . 42 B8
Walsall WS3 . . . . 15 B5
St John's Rd
Birmingham B17 . . . . 85 D6
Cannock WS11 . . . . 4 E7
Darlaston WS10 . . . . 41 C5
Dudley DY2 . . . . 51 E1
Halesowen B63 . . . . 82 E4
Royal Leamington Spa
CV31 . . . . 162 A6
Stourbridge DY8 . . . . 81 A5
Tipton DY4 . . . . 51 F8
St Johns Ret Pk WV2 . . . . 163 B1
St John's Sq WV2 . . . . . . 163 B2
St John's St
Coventry CV1 . . . . 165 C2
Dudley DY2 . . . . 62 C5
Kenilworth CV8 . . . . 148 A3
B5 Kidderminster DY11 . . 116 C6
Tamworth B79 . . . . 21 B5
Wolverhampton WV1 . . . . 163 B2
St John St
Bromsgrove B61 . . . . 136 F2
Lichfield WS13 . . . . 9 B7
St John's Terr B13 CV31 . . 162 A6
St Johns Wlk B42 . . . . 55 D4
St Johns Wood
Birmingham B45 . . . . 122 B5
Shenstone WS14 . . . . 18 A5
St John the Baptist RC Prim
Sch B36 . . . . 70 B7
St John Vianney RC Prim Sch
CV5 . . . . 112 B3
St John Wall RC Sch B21 . 54 C2
St Joseph & St Theresa RC
Prim Sch WV7 . . . . 6 E6
St Josephs Ave B31 . . . . . 103 B5
St Josephs CI WS4 . . . . . . 15 A4
St Joseph's CI WV4 . . . . . 38 D6
St Joseph's RC Jun Sch
CV11 . . . . 73 C3
St Josephs RC Prim Sch
DY8 . . . . 80 F2
St Joseph's RC Prim Sch
Birmingham B7 . . . . 67 B6
Birmingham B30 . . . . 103 F5
Cannock WS12 . . . . 2 C4
B10 Darlaston WS10 . . . . . 41 D7
Dudley DY2 . . . . 51 E1
Lichfield WS14 . . . . 9 C7
Sutton Coldfield B75 . . . . 46 C7
Whitnash CV31 . . . . 162 A3
St Josephs Rd B8 . . . . 68 C5
St Joseph St B7 DY2 . . . . . 51 D1
St Judes Ave B80 . . . . . . 159 D4
St Jude's CE Prim Sch
WV3 . . . . 24 F3
St Judes CI
Birmingham B14 . . . . 104 F2
B4 Sutton Coldfield B75 . . 46 F6
St Jude's Cres CV3 . . . . . 134 D7
St Jude's Ct B14 . . . . 104 F7
St Jude's Ct B4 CV6 . . . . . 24 F3
St Jude's Pas B5 . . . . 164 B1
St Judes RC Prim Sch
B14 . . . . 104 F2
St Jude's Rd WV6 . . . . 24 F3
St Jude's Road W WV6 . . . 24 F3
St Katherine's Rd B68 . . . 64 B2
St Kenelms Ave B63 . . . . . 82 E1
St Kenelm's CE Prim Sch
B62 . . . . 101 A4
St Kenelm's CI B70 . . . . . . 53 F2
St Kenelm's Rd B62 . . . . 100 E5
St Kilda's Rd B8 . . . . 67 E5
St Laurence Ave CV34 . . . 160 D5
St Laurence CE Inf Sch
B31 . . . . 103 B4
St Laurence CE Jun Sch
B31 . . . . 103 B4
St Laurence CI B48 . . . . . 139 B6
St Laurence Mews B31 . . 103 B4
St Laurence Rd B31 . . . . . 103 B5
St Laurence CI
B1 Birmingham B5 . . . . . . 86 D7
Knowle B93 . . . . 128 B5
St Lawrence Dr WS11 . . . . 2 B2
St Lawrence Ho B15 . . . . . 65 D1
St Lawrence Mews B31 . . 103 B4
St Lawrence's Rd CV6 . . . . 95 F1
St Lawrence Way WS10 . . 41 D6
St Leonards CI B37 . . . . . . 90 A7
St Leonards View B78 . . . . 36 F8
St Leonard's Wlk CV8 . . . 135 A1
St Loye's CI B62 . . . . 83 D8
St Luke's CE Fst Sch
B97 . . . . 153 D1
St Lukes CE Prim Sch B1
WV2 . . . . 39 C7
St Lukes CI WS11 . . . . 63 B4
St Luke's CI WS11 . . . . 4 D8
St Luke's Cotts B97 . . . . . 153 D1

St Lukes Prim Sch WS11 . . 1 C1
St Luke's Rd
Birmingham B5 . . . . 86 E7
Burntwood WS7 . . . . 7 C6
Coventry CV6 . . . . 95 D3
Wednesbury WS10 . . . . . . 42 A3
St Lukes Sch B64 . . . . 62 D1
St Luke's Terr CV1 . . . . . . 62 A8
St Lukes Way CV10 . . . . . 72 C4
St Margaret Mary RC Jun &
Inf Sch B23 . . . . 56 C6
St Margaret Rd CV1 . . . . 113 F2
St Margaret's B74 . . . . 31 C3
St Margarets Ave B8 . . . . . 68 B6
St Margaret's CE Jun Sch
CV31 . . . . 162 B3
St Margaret's CE Prim Sch
Birmingham B43 . . . . 43 E4
Solihull B92 . . . . 88 F1
St Margaret's Ct B2 B92 . . 88 E1
St Margarets Dr B63 . . . . . 82 F2
St Margaret's RC Prim Sch
CV31 . . . . 162 B4
St Margarets Rd
Birmingham B88 . . . . 68 B6
Lichfield WS13 . . . . 3 B3
Walsall WS3 . . . . 15 A4
St Margaret's Rd
Birmingham B43 . . . . 43 F2
B2 Solihull B92 . . . . 88 E1
Tamworth B79 . . . . 21 B7
Whitnash CV31 . . . . 162 B3
St Mark's CE Prim Sch
Birmingham B5 . . . . 61 C7
St Marks CI
Great Wyrley WS6 . . . . 4 F4
Nuneaton CV10 . . . . 72 C4
St Mark's Cres B1 . . . . 66 B3
St Mark's Dr DY5 . . . . 61 D7
St Mark's Mews CV32 . . . 156 E1
St Mark's RC Prim Sch
B42 . . . . 54 F6
St Marks Rd
Brownhills WS8 . . . . 16 A5
Walsall WS3 . . . . 15 A4
Burntwood WS7 . . . . 7 C6
Dudley DY2 . . . . 51 F1
Royal Leamington Spa
CV32 . . . . 156 D1
Smethwick B67 . . . . 64 D3
Stourbridge DY9 . . . . 81 D5
Tipton DY4 . . . . 52 A8
Wolverhampton WV3 . . . . 25 B1
St Marks St B1 . . . . 66 B3
St Mark's St WV1 . . . . . . 163 A2
St Martin De Porres RC Prim
Sch B33 . . . . 87 A3
St Martins Ave B80 . . . . . 159 D4
St Martin's CE Prim Sch
Bilston WV14 . . . . 41 A2
Tipton DY4 . . . . 52 B5
St Martin's CI
West Bromwich B70 . . . . . 53 F2
Wolverhampton WV6 . . . . 39 E6
St Martin's Dr DY4 . . . . . . 52 A5
St Martins Ind Est B69 . . . 64 A6
St Martin's Queensway
(Below) B2, B4, B5 . . . . . 164 C2
St Martins Rd B75 . . . . . . 46 F5
St Martin's Sch for Girls
B91 . . . . 107 D3
St Martin's St B8 B15 . . . . 66 B1
St Martin's Terr WV14 . . . 40 E4
St Mary Magdalene CE Prim
Sch B71 . . . . 53 D6
St Mary of the Angels RC
Prim Sch WV9 . . . . 30 B5
St Mary & St Benedict RC
Prim Sch B10 CV1 . . . . . 113 E4
St Mary & St John RC Prim
Sch B23 . . . . 56 E2
St Mary & St Margaret's CE
Prim Sch B36 . . . . 69 B8
St Mary's Ave LE9 . . . . . . 71 F5
St Mary's CE Prim Sch
Birmingham B29 . . . . 85 D1
Birmingham, Handsworth
B20 . . . . 55 B1
B1 Hinckley LE10 . . . . 75 D8
Kidderminster DY10 . . . . 116 E8
Kingswinford DY6 . . . . . . 60 D7
St Mary's CE VA Jun Sch
B80 . . . . 159 E3
St Marys CI B27 . . . . 88 B3
St Mary's CI
Sedgley DY3 . . . . 50 F8
Sutton Coldfield B24 . . . . 57 D4
Warwick CV34 . . . . 160 D8
St Mary's Cres B31 . . . . . 162 B7
St Marys Ct B12 DY5 . . . . . 61 D2
St Mary's Ct
Kenilworth CV8 . . . . 147 F2
Nuneaton CV11 . . . . 73 B5
B3 Willenhall WV13 . . . . . 27 A2
St Mary's Hall WV1 . . . . . 163 C2
St Mary's Ho B71 . . . . 53 D4
St Mary's La DY9 . . . . 81 E4
St Mary's RC Prim Sch
Birmingham B17 . . . . 85 C5
Brierley Hill DY5 . . . . 61 E2
Cannock WS11 . . . . 4 E8
Studley B80 . . . . 159 E4
B1 Warwick CV34 . . . . . . 160 E8
B1 Wednesbury WS10 . . . . 41 F4

St Mary's RC Prim Sch
continued
Wolverhampton WV10 . . . 26 A7
St Marys Rd B17 . . . . 85 C5
St Mary's Rd
Hinckley LE10 . . . . 75 D8
Lichfield WS13 . . . . 3 B3
Nuneaton CV11 . . . . 73 B5
Royal Leamington Spa
CV32 . . . . 162 A1
Smethwick B67 . . . . 64 F1
Wednesbury WS10 . . . . . . 41 F3
St Marys Ringway DY10 . . 116 E6
St Mary's Row
Birmingham, Moseley B13 . 86 F3
Birmingham, New Town Row
B4 . . . . 164 C3
St Mary's St WV1 . . . . . . 163 C3
St Mary St CV1 . . . . 165 C2
St Mary's Terr CV31 . . . . 162 B1
St Mary's The Mount RC Prim
Sch WS1 . . . . 42 F8
St Marys View B23 . . . . . . 56 D8
St Mary's Way
Aldridge WS9 . . . . 30 B5
Tamworth B77 . . . . 21 E4
St Matthew's Ave WS7 . . . . 7 F7
St Matthews CE Prim Sch
B7 . . . . 67 A4
St Matthew's Dr CV34 . . . 65 C5
St Matthews CI
Nuneaton CV10 . . . . 72 C4
Walsall WS3 . . . . 15 B5
St Matthew's CI WS1 . . . . 28 F1
St Matthews Rd
Oldbury B68 . . . . 64 A2
Smethwick B66 . . . . 65 C5
St Matthew's Rd WS7 . . . . 7 F7
St Matthew St WV1 . . . . . 25 F1
St Mawes Rd WV6 . . . . . . 24 A3
St Mawgan CI B35 . . . . . . 58 C4
St Michael Ho B1 B15 . . . . 65 D1
St Michael Rd WS13 . . . . . . 9 C8
St Michael's CE High Sch
B65 . . . . 63 C5
St Michaels CE Jun & Inf Sch
B21 . . . . 66 A7
St Michael's CE Prim Sch
Bedworth CV12 . . . . 78 D3
Birmingham B32 . . . . 102 C8
Lichfield WS13 . . . . 9 C7
Wolverhampton WV6 . . . . 24 E5
St Michaels CI CV9 . . . . . . 36 C1
St Michael's CI WS13 . . . . 15 A2
St Michael's Cres B69 . . . 64 A4
St Michaels Ct
Birmingham B18 . . . . 66 B4
West Bromwich B70 . . . . . 53 C3
St Michael's Ct
Oldbury B68 . . . . 64 A4
B5 Smethwick B66 . . . . . . 65 A5
Wolverhampton WV6 . . . . 24 E5
St Michaels Dr WS12 . . . . . 2 F5
St Michael's Hill B18 . . . . 66 A4
St Michael's Hospl CV34 160 D8
St Michael's Mews B69 . . . 52 A2
St Michael's RC Prim Sch
WV3 . . . . 38 D7
St Michaels Rd DY3 . . . . . 49 F5
St Michael's Rd
Birmingham B18 . . . . 66 A4
Coventry CV1 . . . . 114 A3
Sutton Coldfield B73 . . . . 56 F8
Warwick CV34 . . . . 160 D8
St Michael St
Walsall WS1 . . . . 42 E8
West Bromwich B70 . . . . . 53 C3
St Michaels Way CV10 . . . 72 C4
St Michael's Way CV10 . . . 72 C4
St Nicholas Ave CV8 . . . . . 147 F3
St Nicholas CE Prim Sch
CV8 . . . . 147 F5
St Nicholas Church St
CV34 . . . . 160 F6
St Nicholas CI
Coventry CV1 . . . . 113 C5
Walsall WS3 . . . . 15 A4
B3 Coventry, Edgwick
CV6 . . . . 113 F7
Coventry, Radford CV6 . . . 113 B6
St Nicholas Park L Ctr
CV34 . . . . 160 F6
St Nicholas Rd CV31 . . . . 162 F5
St Nicholas St CV1 . . . . . 165 B4
St Nicholas Terr CV31 . . . 162 E4
St Nicholas Wlk B76 . . . . . 59 B6
St Nicolas CE Prim Sch
CV11 . . . . 73 F6
St Nicolas Gdns B38 . . . . 103 F2
St NICOLAS PARK 74 A7
St Nicolas Park Dr CV11 . . 73 F7
St Nicolas Rd CV11 . . . . . 73 D5
St Osburg's RC Prim Sch
CV1 . . . . 165 A3
St Osburg's Rd CV2 . . . . . 114 A3
St Oswalds CI DY10 . . . . . 116 F8
St Oswald's Ct B7 . . . . 87 E8
St Oswald's Rd B10 . . . . . . 87 E8

St Patricks CE Prim Sch B94 126 C2
St Patricks Cl B14 104 E5
St Patrick's Ct DY11 116 B1
St Patricks RC Prim Sch
Birmingham B18 65 F4
Royal Leamington Spa CV31 161 F6
St Patrick's RC Prim Sch
Coventry CV2 96 D1
9 Walsall WS2 28 D3
Wolverhampton WV11 26 C5
St Patrick's Rd CV1 165 B2
St Paul's Ave
Birmingham B12 87 A5
Kidderminster DY11 116 A6
St Pauls CE Prim Sch WV9 11 A2
St Paul's CE Prim Sch
Nuneaton CV10 72 C3
Royal Leamington Spa CV32 157 B1
Tipton DY4 51 F6
St Paul's Cl
Cannock WS11 2 B1
5 Walsall WS1 28 E2
Warwick CV34 160 D6
St Pauls Cres WS3 15 B5
St Paul's Cres
5 Coleshill B46 70 F7
West Bromwich B70 52 E7
St Pauls Ct
Halesowen B62 63 D1
Water Orton B46 59 B3
St Paul's Ct B77 35 C4
St Pauls Dr B62 63 D1
St Paul's Dr DY4 52 B4
St Pauls Gdns LE10 71 E1
St Paul's RC Prim Sch B38 104 A1
St Paul's Rd
Birmingham B12 87 A5
Burntwood WS7 7 C6
Cannock WS12 2 F3
Coventry CV6 113 E6
Dudley DY2 62 D5
Nuneaton CV10 72 D3
Smethwick B66 64 E7
Wednesbury WS10 42 C5
St Pauls Sch B12 87 A5
St Paul's Sch for Girls B16 65 E1
St Paul's Sq
Birmingham B3 164 A4
4 Royal Leamington Spa CV32 157 A1
St Paul's St WS1 28 E2
St Paul's Sta B19 164 B4
St Pauls Terr B3 164 A4
St Paul's Terr CV34 160 D6
St Peter & St Paul RC Prim Sch
Birmingham B24 57 C3
Coventry CV2 114 F7
Lichfield WS13 3 B1
St Peter's CE Prim Sch
Birmingham B17 85 B4
Cannock WS12 2 D4
Stonnall WS9 16 E4
St Peters Cl
Birmingham B28 105 D6
Bromsgrove B61 136 E1
Sutton Coldfield B72 46 B3
St Peter's Cl
Redditch B97 158 E5
Stonnall WS9 16 E4
Tamworth B77 21 D1
Water Orton B46 59 B2
West Bromwich DY4 52 D4
St Peter's Collegiate CE Sch WV3 24 E3
St Peter's Croft B73 46 B3
St Peters Ct
2 Hinckley LE10 71 E1
Lichfield WS13 3 B2
Walsall WS3 14 B1
St Peter's Ct CV1 165 D4
St Peters Dr WS3 15 A4
St Peters La B92 90 D1
St Peter's RC Fst Sch B61 150 E8
St Peters RC Prim Sch B32 84 C1
St Peter's RC Prim Sch
4 Hinckley LE10 71 E1
Walsall WS3 14 B2
St Peter's RC Sch B91 107 B2
St Peters Rd B17 85 B5
St Peter's Rd
Birmingham B20 66 C8
Burntwood WS7 7 C6
Cannock WS12 2 D4
Dudley DY2 62 D5
7 Royal Leamington Spa CV32 161 F8
Stourbridge DY9 81 C1
St Peters Terr WS2 28 E4
St Philip's Pl B2 164 C3
St Philip's RC Prim Sch 1 B66 65 B6
St Phillips Ave WV3 38 F8
St Phillip's Ave WV3 38 F7
St Phillip's Gr WV3 38 F7
St Quentin St WS2 42 C7
St Saviour's CE Prim Sch B8 67 D5
St Saviour's Cl WV2 39 F6
St Saviour's Ct DY9 99 A6
St Saviour's Rd B8 67 D4
St Silas' Sq B19 66 B7
St Simons Cl 3 B75 46 F6
St Stephen's Ho B97 153 E4
St Stephen's Ave WV13 26 F2
St Stephen's CE Fst Sch B98 153 F5
St Stephen's CE Prim Sch WV10 25 F4
St Stephens Ct WS12 2 C4
St Stephens Gdns B98 153 F5
St Stephen's Gdns 1 WV13 27 A1
St Stephens Rd
Birmingham B29 104 B8
West Bromwich B71 65 B8
St Stephen's Rd WS7 7 C6
St Stephens St B6 66 E6
Saints Way CV10 73 D5
St Teresa's RC Prim Sch
Birmingham B20 55 A3
Wolverhampton WV4 39 E5
St Thomas Aquinas RC Sch B38 103 D3
St Thomas CE Prim Sch WV11 26 D7
St Thomas' CE Prim Sch 6 B15 86 D8
St Thomas Cl
Sutton Coldfield B75 46 F5
Walsall WS3 28 E6
St Thomas' Cl WS9 16 B1
St Thomas More RC Fst Sch B98 159 B7
St Thomas More RC Prim Sch
Coventry CV3 133 D5
Great Wyrley WS6 5 A4
St Thomas More RC Sch
Bilston WV14 41 A7
Nuneaton CV10 73 A3
St Thomas More's RC Prim Sch B26 89 B5
St Thomas of Canterbury RC Prim Sch WS3 28 F6
St Thomas' Rd
Birmingham B23 56 D3
Coventry CV6 96 A3
St Thomas's Cl CV10 72 C3
St Thomas's Ct 13 CV1 113 B2
St Thomas's Ho 12 CV1 113 B2
St Thomas St DY2 62 C5
St Valentines Cl B70 53 F2
St Vincent Cres B70 52 F6
St Vincent's RC Prim Sch B7 67 B3
St Vincent St B16 66 B2
St Vincent Street W B16 66 A2
St Wilfrid's RC Prim Sch B36 68 F8
Saladin Ave B69 63 E5
Salafi Ind Sch B10 87 D8
Salcombe Ave B26 89 C5
Salcombe Cl
Cannock WS11 4 C7
Coventry CV3 134 D6
Nuneaton CV11 73 F5
Salcombe Dr DY5 81 C7
Salcombe Gr WV14 40 D1
Salcombe Rd 3 B66 65 B5
Saldavian Ct WS2 42 B6
Salem Rd LE10 75 F5
Salem St DY4 52 D5
Salford Cir B23 56 D1
Salford Cl
Coventry CV2 114 A5
Redditch B98 159 B6
Salford St B6 67 C8
Salford Trad Est B6 67 C8
Salisbury Ave CV3 133 C6
Salisbury Cl
Birmingham B13 86 E3
Dudley DY1 50 F3
Lichfield WS13 3 C3
Wolston CV8 135 F3
Salisbury Dr
Cannock WS12 2 B1
Kidderminster DY11 116 A6
Nuneaton CV10 72 B7
Water Orton B46 59 C3
Salisbury Gr B72 57 C7
Salisbury Ho
3 Birmingham B24 56 F4
Hinckley LE10 71 C4
Salisbury Pl WV3 25 B1
Salisbury Place Ind Est 1 WV3 25 B1
Salisbury Prim Sch WS10 41 F7
Salisbury Rd
Birmingham, Lozells B19 66 D8
Birmingham, Moseley B13 86 E3
Birmingham, Saltley B8 67 E5
Hinckley LE10 76 B7
Smethwick B66 65 B4
West Bromwich B70 53 E1
Salisbury St
Darlaston WS10 41 E7
Wolverhampton WV3 25 B1
Salisbury Twr B18 66 A3
Sallow Gr WS8 7 A1
Sally Ward Dr WS9 16 A4
Salop Cl B71 53 B6
Salop Dr
Cannock WS11 4 F8
Salop Dr *continued*
Oldbury B68 64 C2
Salop Rd
Oldbury B68 64 C2
Redditch B97 153 D3
Salop St
Bilston WV14 40 E4
Birmingham B12 86 F8
Dudley DY1 51 B2
Oldbury B69 52 E1
Wolverhampton WV3 163 B2
Salstar Cl B6 66 E6
Saltash Gr B25 68 C1
Saltbrook Rd B63 82 A7
Saltbrook Trad Est B63 82 A7
Salter Rd DY4 51 F7
Salters La B79 21 B6
Salter's La
Redditch B97 153 B5
West Bromwich B71 53 E4
Salter's Rd WS9 16 A3
Salter St B94 126 C2
SALTER STREET 126 D2
Salters Vale B70 53 E1
Saltisford CV34 160 D7
Saltisford Canal Ctr★ CV34 160 C8
Saltisford Gdns CV34 160 C8
Salt La CV1 165 B2
SALTLEY 67 E4
Saltley Com L Ctr B9 68 A3
Saltley Ind Ctr B8 67 C3
Saltley Rd B7 67 C5
Saltley Sch & Specialist Science Coll B9 68 A3
Saltley Trad Est B8 67 D6
Saltley Viaduct B8 67 C5
Saltney Cl B24 57 D5
Salts La B78 34 E5
Saltwells La DY2 62 B2
Saltwells Nature Reserve★ DY5, DY2 62 A3
Saltwells Rd DY2 62 C2
Salvia Way 4 CV12 77 D2
Salwarpe Gr B29 84 F2
Salwarpe Rd B60 150 F8
Sam Barber Ct WS12 2 E1
Sambar Rd B78 20 F1
Sambourn Cl B91 107 E6
SAMBOURNE 159 B1
Sambourne Dr B34 69 D7
Sambourne La
Astwood Bank B96 158 F1
Sambourne B96 159 A1
Sambourne Park La B96 159 A1
Sambrook Rd WV10 26 A6
Sam Gault Cl CV3 134 E7
Sammons Way CV4 111 D1
Sampson Cl
Birmingham B21 54 C1
Coventry CV2 114 C8
Oldbury B69 63 C7
Sampson Ho B11 87 B8
Sampson Rd B11 87 B7
Sampson Road N B11 87 B8
Sampson St WS10 42 B3
Samsara Rd B60 137 C1
Sams La B70 53 C1
Sam Spencer Ct DY10 118 A2
Samuel Cl WS13 3 C2
Samuel Hayward Ho 5 CV2 96 B1
Samuel Ho WS3 14 B1
Samuel Johnson Birthplace Mus★ WS13 9 B8
Samuel Johnson Hospl WS13 9 D8
Samuels Rd B32 84 A5
Samuel St WS3 14 B1
Samuel Vale Ho CV1 165 B4
Sanby Cl CV12 78 A4
Sanda Croft B36 70 B6
Sandalls Cl B31 102 D1
Sandal Rise B91 107 E3
Sandals Rise B62 83 D3
Sandalwood Cl WV12 27 B8
Sand Bank WS3 14 A1
Sandbarn Cl B90 126 F6
Sandbeds Rd WV12 27 C4
Sandbourne Rd B8 68 A4
Sanderling Cl WV10 12 B7
Sanderling Ct DY10 117 A1
Sanderling Rise
Burntwood WS7 7 B8
Kingswinford DY6 61 A6
Sanders Cl
Dudley DY2 62 E7
Redditch B97 153 B4
Sanders Ct CV34 161 C8
Sanders Ind Est 1 B61 136 E1
Sanderson Ct DY11 116 C5
Sanders Rd
Bedworth CV6 96 B6
Bromsgrove B61 136 E1
Sanders Way WS14 9 B5
Sandfield Bridge DY5 50 B1
Sandfield Cl B90 126 B8
Sandfield Gr DY3 50 B2
Sandfield Mdw WS13 9 A6
Sandfield Rd
Stourbridge DY8 60 F2
West Bromwich B71 42 E2
SANDFIELDS 9 A5
Sandfields Ave B10 87 B8
Sandfields Rd B68 64 C2
Sandford Ave B65 63 C3
Sandford Cl
Coventry CV2 96 E3
Sandford Cl *continued*
Hinckley LE10 71 F1
Sandford Ho WS13 9 A7
Sandford Rd
Birmingham B13 87 A3
Dudley DY1 50 E1
Sandford Rise WV6 24 E6
Sandford St WS13 9 B7
Sandgate Cres CV2 114 E2
Sandgate Rd
Birmingham B28 106 A4
Tipton DY4 52 A8
Sandhill Farm Cl 1 B19 66 D7
Sandhills Cres B91 127 B8
Sandhills Gn B48 138 E7
Sandhills La B45 138 D7
Sandhills Rd B45 138 D8
Sandhill St WS3 14 A1
Sandhurst Ave
Birmingham B36 68 D6
Stourbridge DY9 81 D2
Sandhurst Cl B98 154 C6
Sandhurst Dr WV4 39 A4
Sandhurst Gr
Coventry CV6 113 B5
Stourbridge DY8 60 E3
Sandhurst Ho B38 104 B1
Sandhurst Rd
Birmingham B13 86 F2
Kingswinford DY6 61 A4
Sutton Coldfield B74 31 F5
Sandicliffe Cl DY11 116 C8
Sandilands Cl CV2 114 E4
Sandland Cl WV14 40 F6
Sandland Rd WV12 27 D8
Sandmartin Cl DY2 62 D2
Sandmartin Way DY10 117 A2
Sandmeadow Pl DY6 60 C5
Sandmere Gr B14 105 D3
Sandmere Rd B14 105 D3
Sandmere Rise WV10 11 E1
Sandon Cl B98 154 A3
Sandon Gr B24 57 B4
Sandon Ho WV6 24 E5
Sandon Rd
Birmingham B17 65 B1
Nuneaton CV11 73 B5
Stourbridge DY9 81 F4
Wolverhampton WV10 11 B2
Sandown B77 21 F5
Sandown Ave CV6 95 F2
Sandown Cl CV32 157 C4
Sandown Ct 18 B29 103 C7
Sandown Dr
Lower Marlbrook B61 121 B1
Perton WV6 23 F4
Sandown Fst Sch WV6 23 F4
Sandown Rd B36 68 D8
Sandown Tower 3 B31 103 A1
Sandpiper B77 36 A5
Sandpiper Cl
Cannock WS12 2 C7
Kidderminster DY10 117 B2
Stourbridge DY9 81 F5
Sandpiper Gdns B38 123 F7
Sandpiper Rd CV2 96 B3
Sandpiper Way B23 56 C6
Sandpit Cl WS10 42 E2
Sand Pits B1 66 B3
Sandpits Cl B76 59 C6
Sandpits Ind Est 4 B1 66 B3
Sandpits La CV6 94 F2
Sandpits The
Birmingham B30 103 E8
Bulkington CV12 79 C2
Sandra Cl WS9 30 B5
Sandringham Ave WV12 27 B6
Sandringham Cl CV4 131 F5
Sandringham Ct
3 Birmingham B43 43 F1
Nuneaton CV10 72 F6
Sandringham Dr
Aldridge WS9 16 B1
Rowley Regis B65 63 C4
Sandringham Ho WV3 163 A1
Sandringham Pl DY8 60 D1
Sandringham Rd
Birmingham B14 105 C3
Birmingham B42 55 B6
Halesowen B62 83 B7
Stourbridge DY8 60 D1
Wolverhampton WV4 39 A4
Sandringham Way DY5 81 C8
Sand St B70 52 E4
Sandstone Ave B45 122 A8
Sandstone Cl DY3 50 D4
Sandstone Ct B77 36 A7
Sandway Gdns B8 67 D6
Sandway Gr B13 105 C7
SANDWELL 65 A7
Sandwell Ave WS10 41 B5
Sandwell Bsns Development Ctr B66 64 C7
Sandwell Bsns Pk B66 64 C8
Sandwell Coll (Oldbury Campus) B68 64 A3
Sandwell Coll (Smethwick Campus) B66 65 A5
Sandwell Coll (West Bromwich Campus) B70 53 C3
Sandwell Ct B21 65 D8
Sandwell & Dudley Sta B70 53 A1
Sandwell General Hospl B71 53 D5
Sandwell Ho 1 WS1 42 F8
Sandwell Park Farm★ B71 53 F3
Sandwell Pl WV12 27 D7
Sandwell Rd
Birmingham B21 54 D1
West Bromwich B70 53 C4
Wolverhampton WV10 11 B1
Sandwell Road N B71 53 D4
Sandwell Road Pas B70 53 C4
Sandwell St WS1 42 F8
Sandwell Valley Ctry Pk★ B70, B71 53 F5
Sandwell Wlk 8 WS1 42 F8
Sandwick Cl CV3 134 F8
Sandwood Dr B44 55 F8
Sandyacre Way DY8 81 B5
Sandy Cres
Hinckley LE10 71 C1
Wednesfield WV11 27 A8
Wolverhampton WV11 13 A1
Sandy Croft
Birmingham B13 105 C7
Sutton Coldfield B72 46 C3
SANDYFIELDS 50 B6
Sandyfields Rd DY3 50 B6
Sandygate Cl B97 152 F2
Sandy Gr WS8 6 F1
Sandy Hill Rd B90 106 A4
Sandy Hill Rise B90 106 A4
Sandy Hollow WV6 24 C2
Sandy La
Birmingham, Aston B6 67 B7
Birmingham, Great Barr B42 55 D8
Blackdown CV32 156 F6
Blakedown DY10 118 C7
Cannock WS11 1 B1
Codsall WV8 10 A4
Coventry CV1 113 C5
Madeley Heath B61, B62 120 E5
Royal Leamington Spa CV32 156 D4
Wednesbury WS10 42 F3
Wolverhampton, Bushbury WV10 11 E1
Wolverhampton WV6 24 E6
Sandy Lane Bsns Pk CV1 113 C5
Sandy Mount WV5 49 B7
Sandy Mount Rd WS1 42 F8
Sandy Rd DY8 80 D1
Sandys Gr DY4 51 E5
Sandythorpe CV3 134 E6
Sandy Way
Birmingham B15 66 B1
Tamworth B77 22 B3
Sandy Wlk LE10 71 B2
Sangwin Rd WV14 51 C7
Sankey Rd WS11 1 F3
Sankey's Cnr WS7 6 F7
Sannders Cres DY4 52 B5
Sansome Rd B90 105 F2
Sansome Rise B90 105 F2
Sanstone Cl WS3 14 C3
Sanstone Rd WS3 14 C3
Santolina Dr WS5 43 A3
Santos Cl CV3 134 F8
Sant Rd B31 123 B7
Santridge Ct B61 137 A4
Santridge La B61 137 A4
Sapcote Bsns Ctr B10 87 E6
Sapcote Gr CV2 96 B4
Sapcote Ind Est B64 62 F3
Sapcote Rd LE10 76 B7
Sapcote Trad Ctr B6 56 D2
Saplings The B76 58 A8
Sapphire Ct
Birmingham B3 164 A4
3 Solihull B92 88 F1
Sapphire Dr
Cannock WS11 2 C3
Royal Leamington Spa CV31 161 F5
Sapphire Gate CV2 114 C2
Sapphire Hts B1 66 B4
Sapphire Twr 2 B6 66 F6
Saracen Dr
Balsall Common CV7 129 E6
Sutton Coldfield B75 47 A6
Sara Cl B74 32 A3
Sarah Cl WV14 40 E1
Sarah Ct B73 45 D1
Sarah Gdns WS5 42 F4
Sarah Siddons Ho 2 WS13 9 B7
Sarah St B9 67 B2
Saredon Cl WS3 15 A1
Saredon Rd
Wedges Mills WS6, WS11, WV10 4 B3
Wolverhampton WV10 4 A4
Sarehole Mill Gdns 9 B13 86 F4
Sarehole Mill (Mus)★ B13 105 D8
Sarehole Rd B28 87 E1
Sargeaunt St CV31 161 F7
Sargent Cl B43 44 D4
Sargent Turner Trad Est DY9 81 F6
Sark Dr B36 70 B6
Satchwell Ct 15 CV32 161 F8
Satchwell Wlk 16 CV32 161 F8
Satellite Ind Pk WV11 26 D4
Saturday Bridge 7 B1 66 C1
Saturn Rd WS11 2 A5
Saumur Way CV34 161 C6
Saunders Ave CV12 78 B2
Saunders Ho 11 CV32 156 F2
Saunton Cl CV5 112 B8
Saunton Rd WS3 14 A3
Saunton Way B29 85 C2

Savannah Cl CV4. . . . . 111 C3
Saveker Dr B76 . . . . 46 E4
Savernake Cl B45 . . . . 102 A2
Saville Cl
  Birmingham B45 . . . . 122 B7
  Hinckley LE10 . . . . 71 E2
Saville Gr CV8 . . . . 148 C5
Savoy Cl B32 . . . . 85 A5
Saw Mill Cl WS4 . . . . 28 E3
Saxelby Cl B14 . . . . 104 E2
Saxelby Ho B14 . . . . 104 E2
Saxifrage Pl DY10 . . . . . . 116 F4
Saxon Bsns Pk B60 . . . . . . 150 E2
Saxon Cl
  Binley Woods CV3 . . . . . . 135 D7
  Great Wyrley WS6 . . . . 5 A2
  Polesworth B78 . . . . 22 F1
  Studley B80 . . . . 159 E5
  Tamworth B77 . . . . 35 F6
Saxon Court WV6. . . . . 24 C5
Saxon Ct WS13 . . . . 3 E7
Saxondale Ave B26. . . . . . . 88 F6
Saxon Dr B65 . . . . 63 C4
Saxondrive B79 . . . . 21 C5
Saxonfields WV6. . . . . 24 C5
Saxon Hill Specl Sch WS14 . 9 C6
Saxon Mdws CV32 . . . . . . 156 C2
Saxon Mill La B79 . . . . 21 C4
Saxon Rd CV2. . . . . 114 B4
Saxons Way B14 . . . . 105 A2
Saxon Way B37 . . . . 69 F3
Saxon Wlk WS13 . . . . 3 E7
Saxon Wood Cl B31 . . . . . 103 A4
Saxon Wood Rd B90 . . . . . 126 D5
Saxton Dr B74 . . . . 31 F6
Scafell Cl CV5 . . . . 112 A4
Scafell Dr
  Bilston WV14 . . . . 40 F7
  Birmingham B23 . . . . 56 D5
Scafell Rd DY8. . . . . 81 B6
Scafell Way B71 . . . . 53 C6
Scaife Rd B60 . . . . 151 B7
Scammerton B77 . . . . 36 B7
Scampton Cl WV6. . . . . 23 E5
Scampton Way B27 . . . . . . 21 C8
Scar Bank CV34 . . . . 155 E1
Scarborough Cl WS2 . . . . . 42 B8
Scarborough Rd WS2 . . . . . 42 B8
Scarborough Way CV4 . . . . 131 F7
Scarecrow La B75 . . . . 32 E4
Scarfield Hill B48 . . . . 138 C5
Scarman Rd CV4 . . . . 132 B5
Scarsdale Rd B42 . . . . 55 D8
Schofield Ave B71 . . . . 53 B8
Schofield Bsns Pk B60 . . . 151 A7
Schofield Rd B37 . . . . 70 A5
Scholars Cl B21 . . . . 66 A7
Scholars Ct DY10 . . . . 116 E4
Scholars Gate
  Birmingham B33 . . . . 69 B2
  Burntwood WS7 . . . . 7 D7
Scholars Wlk WS4 . . . . 29 B7
Scholefield Twr B19 . . . . . . 66 D5
Scholfield Rd CV7. . . . . 95 A6
Schoolacre Rise B74 . . . . . 30 E1
School Ave WS8 . . . . 15 F8
School Bell Mews CV8 . . . 149 B6
School Cl
  Birmingham B31 . . . . 102 C2
  Birmingham, Castle Vale
    B35. . . . . 58 B3
  Birmingham, Kingshurst
    B37 . . . . 70 A6
  Burntwood WS7 . . . . 6 D8
  Codsall WV8 . . . . 10 A4
  Coventry CV3 . . . . 113 F2
  Hinckley LE10 . . . . 76 A6
  Norton Canes WS11 . . . . . . 6 B6
  Oldbury B69 . . . . 63 C7
  Wolverhampton WV8 . . . . . 38 B7
School Cotts CV35 . . . . . . 145 F3
School Cres WS11 . . . . 6 A6
School Croft CV35 . . . . . . 146 C2
School Ct WS12. . . . . 2 C6
School Dr
  Bilston WV14 . . . . 40 C1
  Bilston WV14 . . . . 41 A2
  Bromsgrove B60 . . . . 137 A3
  Stourbridge DY8 . . . . 80 F8
  Wythall B47 . . . . 125 A3
School Dr The DY2. . . . . . . 62 D7
Schoolfields Rd WS14 . . . . 18 A5
Schoolgate Cl
  Birmingham B8 . . . . 68 A6
  Walsall WS4. . . . . 15 D1
School Gn WV14 . . . . 40 C8
School Hill CV10 . . . . 72 A8
School Ho The WS7. . . . . . . 7 D7
Schoolhouse Cl B38. . . . . . 104 B2
School House La CV2 . . . . 115 A6
School La
  Alvechurch B48 . . . . 139 B5
  Bedworth CV7 . . . . 95 F7
  Birmingham, Buckland End
    B34 . . . . 69 B7
  Birmingham, Kitt's Green
    B33 . . . . 68 F1
  Burntwood WS7. . . . . 6 D8
  Hagley DY9 . . . . 99 D6
  Halesowen B63 . . . . 82 F2
  Hopwas B78 . . . . 20 B7
  Kenilworth CV8 . . . . 147 F5
  Lickey End B60. . . . . 137 B6
  Little Packington CV7. . . . . 91 D7
  Norton Canes WS11 . . . . . . 5 E2
  Radford Semele CV31 . . . . 162 E5
  Shuttington B79. . . . . 22 F7

School La continued
  Solihull B91 . . . . 107 D4
  Tamworth B77 . . . . 35 D5
  Walsall WS3. . . . . 14 F4
  Weeford B78 . . . . 19 D2
  Wolverhampton WV10 . . . . 11 E2
  Wroxall CV35. . . . . 145 E4
School Rd
  Birmingham B45 . . . . 121 E6
  Birmingham, Hall Green
    B28. . . . . 106 A8
  Birmingham, Moseley B13. . 86 F1
  Birmingham, Yardley Wood
    B14. . . . . 105 C4
  Brierley Hill DY5 . . . . 62 A2
  Bulkington CV12 . . . . 79 C2
  Himley DY3 . . . . 49 B3
  Hockley Heath B94 . . . . . . 143 B7
  Norton Canes WS11 . . . . . . 6 A6
  Solihull B90 . . . . 106 B2
  Wednesbury WS10 . . . . . . 37 C1
  Wednesbury, Nordley Hill
    WV11 . . . . 26 C6
  Wolverhampton, Tettenhall Wood
    WV6 . . . . 24 B3
  Wombourne WV5. . . . . 49 B7
School St
  Brierley Hill DY5 . . . . 61 D7
  Cradley Heath B64. . . . . . . 62 D1
  Darlaston WS10. . . . . 41 E5
  Dudley, Eve Hill DY1. . . . . . 51 B1
  Dudley DY3. . . . . 50 E8
  Stourbridge DY8 . . . . 80 F6
  Tamworth B77 . . . . 21 E4
  Tipton WV14 . . . . 51 C8
  Walsall WS4. . . . . 15 D1
  Wednesbury WS10 . . . . . . 41 E5
  Wolverhampton WV3 . . . . 163 B2
School Street W WV14 . . . . 51 C8
School Terr B29. . . . . 85 F2
School Wlk
  Bilston WV14 . . . . 40 C8
  Burntwood WS7. . . . . 6 D8
  Nuneaton CV11 . . . . 73 E2
  Tamworth B79 . . . . 21 B6
Scimitar Cl B79 . . . . 20 E7
Scorers Cl B90. . . . . 106 B6
Scotchill The CV6 . . . . 95 A1
Scotchings The B36. . . . . . . 68 E8
Scotch Orch WS13 . . . . 3 D1
Scotch Orchard Prim Sch
  WS13 . . . . 3 D1
Scotland La B32 . . . . 102 C7
SCOTLANDS 26 A7
Scotland St B1 . . . . 66 C3
Scots Cnr B14 . . . . 104 E8
Scots La CV6. . . . . 112 F6
Scott Arms Sh Ctr B43 . . . 43 F1
Scott Ave
  Nuneaton CV10 . . . . 73 D8
  Wednesbury WS10 . . . . . . 42 B2
  Wolverhampton WV4 . . . . . 38 E4
Scott Cl
  Lichfield WS14. . . . . 9 B6
  West Bromwich B71 . . . . . 53 D5
Scott Gr B92. . . . . 88 E3
Scott Ho B43 . . . . 54 F7
Scott Rd
  Birmingham B43 . . . . 43 F2
  Kenilworth CV8 . . . . 147 E2
  Redditch B97. . . . . 158 C8
  Royal Leamington Spa
    CV31. . . . . 162 B6
  Solihull B92 . . . . 88 E2
  Tamworth B77 . . . . 21 E4
  Walsall WS5. . . . . 43 D6
SCOTT'S GREEN 62 A7
Scott's Green Cl DY1. . . . . . 62 A8
Scotts Green Island DY1 . . 61 F7
Scott's Rd DY8. . . . . 80 F6
Scott St WS12 . . . . 2 F3
Scotwell Cl B65. . . . . 63 B3
Scout Cl B33 . . . . 69 C2
Scribban Cl B66. . . . . 65 B4
Scribers La B28. . . . . 105 E4
Scribers Mdw B28 . . . . . . 105 E4
Scrimshaw Ho B1 . . . . 52 A2
Sculthorpe Rd DY10. . . . . . 98 B2
Seacole Rd B97. . . . . 153 B2
Seacroft Ave B25 . . . . 68 E1
Seafield B77 . . . . 21 F5
Seafield Cl CV10 . . . . 60 E4
Seafield La
  Beoley B98. . . . . 141 A2
  Portway B48, B98 . . . . . . 140 E4
Seaford Cl CV6 . . . . 96 B4
Seaforth Dr LE10. . . . . 71 A1
Seaforth Gr WV11. . . . . 13 B1
Seagar St B71 . . . . 53 E4
Seager's La DY5 . . . . 61 D2
Seagrave Rd CV1 . . . . 165 D1
Seagull Bay Dr WV14. . . . . 40 D1
Sealand Dr CV12 . . . . 78 A3
Seal Cl B76. . . . . 46 E3
Seals Gn B38 . . . . 123 D7
Seamless Dr WV11 . . . . 26 D4
Sear Hills Cl CV7. . . . . 130 B6
Seashell Cl CV5. . . . . 112 B8
Seaton B77 . . . . 35 F8
Seaton Cl
  Hinckley LE10 . . . . 76 B7
  Nuneaton CV11 . . . . 73 F7
  Wednesfield WV11 . . . . . . 26 F5
Seaton Gr B13 . . . . 86 D1
Seaton Pl DY8 . . . . 60 C2
Seaton Rd B66. . . . . 65 B5

Sebastian Cl CV3. . . . . . . 134 B5
Seckham Rd B3 WS13 . . . . . 9 A8
Second Ave
  Birmingham B29 . . . . 86 B3
  Birmingham, Bordesley Green
    B9. . . . . 67 F1
  Birmingham, Witton B6. . . . 55 F3
  Brownhills WS8 . . . . 7 A1
  Coventry CV3. . . . . 114 C1
  Kingswinford, Barrow Hill
    DY6. . . . . 61 A7
  Kingswinford, Wall Heath
    DY6. . . . . 60 F8
  Wolverhampton WV10. . . . 25 E7
Second Exhibition Ave
  B40 . . . . 90 D4
Securehold Bsns Ctr
  B98. . . . . 154 B2
Sedge Ave B38 . . . . 123 E8
Sedgeberrow Covert 4
  B38 . . . . 123 B8
Sedgeberrow Rd B63 . . . . . 83 A2
Sedgebourne Way B31. . . . 102 C1
Sedge Dr B61. . . . . 137 A6
Sedgefield Cl DY1. . . . . 50 E3
Sedgefield Gr WV6 . . . . 23 F4
Sedgefield Wlk B61. . . . . . 121 B1
Sedgeford Cl DY5 . . . . 81 D8
Sedgehill Ave B17 . . . . 85 B4
Sedgemere Gr
  Balsall Common CV7 . . . . . 130 C5
  Walsall WS4. . . . . 29 C8
Sedgemere Rd B26 . . . . . . 68 F1
Sedgemoor Ave WS7. . . . . . 7 B5
Sedgemoor Rd CV3 . . . . . . 134 B5
Sedgley Way WS11 . . . . 6 B4
SEDGLEY 50 F7
Sedgley Cl B98 . . . . 153 F4
Sedgley Gr B20. . . . . 54 E4
Sedgley Hall Ave DY3 . . . . 50 C8
Sedgley Rd
  Dudley DY1. . . . . 51 B6
  Gospel End Village WV4 . . . 38 F2
Sedgley Road E DY4. . . . . . 52 A3
Sedgley Road W DY4. . . . . . 51 D5
Sedgley St WV2. . . . . 39 C7
Seed Field Croft CV3 . . . . 133 E7
Seedhouse Cl B64 . . . . 83 B8
Seeds La WS8 . . . . 15 F8
Seekings Dr CV8 . . . . 148 B4
Seekings The CV31. . . . . . . 162 B3
Seeleys Rd B11 . . . . 87 E5
Seeney La B76. . . . . 48 F3
Seeswood Cl CV10 . . . . 72 C2
Sefton Dr B65 . . . . 62 F6
Sefton Gr DY4 . . . . 41 C2
Sefton Rd
  Birmingham B16 . . . . 65 F2
  Coventry CV4. . . . . 132 E6
  Tamworth B77 . . . . 22 B2
Segbourne Rd B45. . . . . . . 121 F8
Segundo Cl WS5 . . . . 42 F4
Segundo Rd WS5 . . . . 42 F4
SEISDON 37 A2
Seisdon Rd WV5 . . . . 37 A1
Selba Dr DY11 . . . . 116 A6
Selborne Cl WS1. . . . . 29 A1
Selborne Gr B13 . . . . 105 C5
Selborne Rd
  Birmingham B20 . . . . 55 A2
  Dudley DY2 . . . . 62 D7
Selborne St WS1. . . . . 29 A1
Selbourne Cres WV1 . . . . . 26 B1
Selby Cl B26. . . . . 68 F1
Selby Gr B13 . . . . 105 C6
Selby Ho B69 . . . . 63 D6
Selby Way
  Nuneaton CV10 . . . . 72 B5
  Walsall WS3 . . . . 13 E2
Selcombe Way B38 . . . . . . 123 F7
Selco Way B76. . . . . 58 A6
Selcroft Ave B32. . . . . 84 F5
Selecta Ave B44 . . . . 44 D2
Selina Dix Ho CV1. . . . . . . 165 C4
Selker Dr B77 . . . . 21 F5
Selkirk Cl B71 . . . . 53 C6
Selly Ave B29. . . . . 86 B2
Selly Cl B29 . . . . 86 B2
Selly Hall Croft B30 . . . . . 104 A6
SELLY HILL 86 A2
Selly Hill Rd B29 . . . . 85 F2
Selly Manor Mus* B30. . . 103 F7
SELLY OAK 85 D1
Selly Oak Hospl B29. . . . . . 85 E5
Selly Oak Ind Est B29 . . . . 85 E1
Selly Oak New Rd B29. . . . 85 E3
Selly Oak Rd B30 . . . . 103 E5
Selly Oak Sch B29 . . . . . . 103 E8
Selly Oak Sta B29. . . . . 85 E2
SELLY PARK 86 A1
Selly Park Rd B29 . . . . 86 A2
Selly Park Tech Coll for Girls
  B29. . . . . 86 B1
Selly Wharf B29 . . . . 85 E2
Selly Wick Dr B29 . . . . 86 B2
Selly Wick Rd B29 . . . . 86 B2
Sellywood Rd B29, B30 . . . 103 E8
Selma Gr B14. . . . . 105 D5
Selmans Hill WS3 . . . . 14 C2
Selman's Par WS3 . . . . 14 C2
Selsdon Cl
  Kidderminster DY11. . . . . . 116 B5
  Wythall B47 . . . . 125 C5
Selsdon Rd WS3 . . . . 13 E3
Selsey Ave B66 . . . . 65 B3
Selsey Cl CV3 . . . . 134 C4
Selsey Rd B17. . . . . 65 B3
Selston Rd B6 . . . . 66 E7

Selvey Ave B43 . . . . 44 C4
Selworthy Rd
  Birmingham B36 . . . . 69 F8
  Coventry CV6. . . . . 95 E3
Selwyn Cl WV2 . . . . 39 C7
Selwyn Ho B37 . . . . 70 D3
Selwyn Rd
  Bilston WV14 . . . . 40 F7
  Birmingham B16 . . . . 65 D2
Semele Cl CV31. . . . . 162 E5
Seneschal Rd CV3. . . . . . . 133 E7
Senior Cl WV11 . . . . 13 A3
Senneleys Park Rd B31. . . . 84 E1
Sennen Cl
  Nuneaton CV11 . . . . 74 A5
  Willenhall WV13 . . . . 26 F1
Sensall Rd DY9 . . . . 81 F3
Sentry Way B75. . . . . 46 F6
Sephton Dr CV6. . . . . 96 C6
Serin Cl DY10. . . . . 117 A1
Serpentine Rd
  Birmingham, Aston B6. . . . . 56 A1
  Birmingham B17 . . . . 85 C6
  Birmingham, Selly Oak B29. 86 A2
Serpentine The DY11. . . . . 116 C4
Servite Ct B14 . . . . 105 A2
Servite Ho
  2 Coleshill B46. . . . . 70 F7
  Kenilworth CV8 . . . . 147 F3
Seton Ho B74. . . . . 31 E2
Settle Ave B34 . . . . 68 F6
Settle Croft B37 . . . . 69 F1
Setton Dr DY3 . . . . 50 E2
Seven Acres WS9 . . . . 30 B5
Seven Acres La B98 . . . . . 154 C5
Seven Acres Rd
  Birmingham, Quinton B62 . . 84 A5
  Birmingham, Turves Green
    B31. . . . . 103 C1
Sevendwellings View DY5 . 61 C1
Seven Star Rd B91 . . . . . . 107 B5
Seven Stars Ind Est CV3 . 134 A7
Seven Stars Rd B69 . . . . . . 64 A7
Severn Ave LE10 . . . . 75 A8
Severn Cl
  Birmingham B36 . . . . 69 F7
  Catshill B61 . . . . 137 A8
  Royal Leamington Spa
    CV32. . . . . 157 C3
  Tipton DY4 . . . . 51 F5
  Wednesfield WV12 . . . . . . 27 A7
Severn Ct
  Birmingham B23 . . . . 56 B3
  6 Sutton Coldfield B73 . . . 46 B5
Severn Dr
  Brierley Hill DY5 . . . . 61 B7
  Burntwood WS7 . . . . 7 D6
  Perton WV6. . . . . 23 E5
Severne Gr B27 . . . . 88 C1
Severne Prim Sch B27 . . . 106 C8
Severne Rd B27. . . . . 106 C8
Severn Gr
  5 Birmingham B19. . . . . . . 66 C7
  Kidderminster DY11. . . . . . 116 B3
Severn Ho
  1 Birmingham B68. . . . . . . 84 B8
  Dudley DY3 . . . . 50 D3
Severn Rd
  Brownhills WS8 . . . . 6 C2
  Bulkington CV12 . . . . 79 A3
  Coventry CV1. . . . . 113 F1
  Halesowen B63 . . . . 82 B5
  Stourbridge DY8 . . . . 80 F2
  Walsall WS3. . . . . 14 E1
Severn Rise B65 . . . . 63 B2
Severn St B1 . . . . 164 B1
Severn Twr B7. . . . . 67 B5
Severn Valley Steam
  Railway* 4 WV16 . . . . . 116 F5
Severn Way B47 . . . . 124 E2
Sevilla Cl CV3. . . . . 115 A2
Sevington Cl B91. . . . . 127 C8
Sewall Ct CV6 . . . . 114 A8
Sewall Highway CV2 . . . . . 114 B6
Seward Cl WS14 . . . . 9 D6
Seymour Cl
  Birmingham B29 . . . . 86 A2
  Cheslyn Hay WS6. . . . . 4 D1
  Coventry CV3. . . . . 134 C5
Seymour Gdns B74. . . . . . . 31 E3
Seymour Gr CV34 . . . . 161 D6
Seymour Ho CV3 . . . . 133 C8
Seymour Rd
  Kidderminster DY11. . . . . . 116 B8
  Nuneaton CV11 . . . . 73 D3
  Oldbury B69. . . . . 64 A5
  Stourbridge DY9 . . . . 82 A4
  Wednesbury DY4 . . . . 41 C8
Seymour St B5 . . . . 164 D2
Shackleton Dr
  Hinckley LE10 . . . . 75 E4
  Perton WV6. . . . . 23 E5
Shackleton Rd WS3 . . . . . . 14 D2
Shadowbrook La B92 . . . . 108 E7
Shadowbrook Rd CV6 . . . . 113 A5
Shadwell Dr DY3 . . . . 50 D3
Shadwell St B4 . . . . 164 C4
Shady La B44. . . . . 44 E2
Shadymoor Dr DY5. . . . . . . 81 C8
Shaftesbury Ave
  Kerseley CV7 . . . . 95 A7
  Stourbridge DY9 . . . . 81 C2
Shaftesbury Cl B60 . . . . . 137 B2
Shaftesbury Dr WS12. . . . . . 2 C7

Shaftesbury Rd
  Coventry CV5. . . . . 132 F8
  Wednesbury WS10 . . . . . . 42 B2
Shaftesbury Sq B71. . . . . . 53 C5
Shaftesbury St B70, B71 . . 53 C4
Shaft La CV7 . . . . 93 A4
Shaftmoor Ind Est B28 . . . 87 F2
Shaftmoor La B27, B28. . . . 87 F2
Shaftsbury Ave B63 . . . . . . 82 B7
Shaftsbury Cl WV14 . . . . . . 40 F7
Shaftsbury Dr WS7. . . . . . . 7 F7
Shaftsbury Rd B26 . . . . 89 C5
Shahjalal Rd B8 . . . . 67 D5
Shakels Cl B97 . . . . 158 E4
Shakespeare Ave
  Bedworth CV12 . . . . 78 D2
  Lichfield WS14. . . . . 9 B6
  Redditch B98. . . . . 154 A2
  Warwick CV34 . . . . 160 C4
Shakespeare Ct
  Dudley WV14 . . . . 40 C2
  Tamworth B79 . . . . 21 A6
Shakespeare Cres WS3. . . . 28 F7
Shakespeare Dr
  Hinckley LE10 . . . . 71 C1
  Kidderminster DY10. . . . . . 117 B6
  Nuneaton CV11 . . . . 74 A1
  Solihull B90 . . . . 106 B1
Shakespeare Gr WS11. . . . . 1 D4
Shakespeare Ho B31 . . . . . 123 A8
Shakespeare Pl WS3 . . . . . 28 F7
Shakespeare Rd
  Birmingham B23 . . . . 56 B3
  Burntwood WS7. . . . . 6 F8
  Dudley DY3. . . . . 50 A4
  Smethwick B67 . . . . 64 E4
  Solihull B90 . . . . 126 D8
  Tipton DY4 . . . . 52 A8
Shakespeare St
  Birmingham B11 . . . . 87 C5
  Coventry CV2. . . . . 114 B4
  Wolverhampton WV1 . . . . 163 D2
Shakleton Rd CV5. . . . . . . 113 A2
Shaldon Wlk 4 B66. . . . . . 65 B5
Shale St WV14. . . . . 40 D5
Shalford Rd B92 . . . . 88 E4
Shallcross La DY3 . . . . 50 D3
Shalnecote Gr B14. . . . . . . 104 C5
Shambles 2 WS10. . . . . . . 41 F2
Shandon Cl B32. . . . . 84 F3
Shanklin Dr CV10. . . . . 5 A3
Shanklin Dr CV10 . . . . 73 D6
Shanklin Rd CV3 . . . . 134 B4
Shannon B77 . . . . 35 F8
Shannon Dr WS8. . . . . 6 C2
Shannon Rd B38 . . . . 123 E7
Shannon's Mill B79 . . . . . . 21 A5
Shannon Wlk WS8 . . . . 6 C2
Shanti Niketan WV2. . . . . . 39 D7
Shapinsay Dr B45. . . . . . . 101 F1
SHARD END 69 D6
Shard End Com Ctr & Sports
  Hall B34. . . . . 69 D6
Shard End Cres B34. . . . . . 69 C6
Shardlow Rd WV11 . . . . . . 26 E8
Shardway The B34. . . . . . . 69 C5
Sharesacre St WV13 . . . . . 27 B3
Sharington Cl 3 DY2 . . . . . 62 E8
Sharman Rd WV10 . . . . . . 25 E6
SHARMANS CROSS 106 E4
Sharmans Cross Jun Sch
  B91. . . . . 106 E4
Sharmans Cross Rd B91. . 106 F4
Sharnford Rd LE10 . . . . . . 76 F6
Sharon Cl WV4 . . . . 39 E5
Sharon St B27 . . . . 88 C3
Sharon Way WS12 . . . . 2 D3
Sharp Cl CV6 . . . . 95 C2
Sharpe Cl CV34 . . . . 160 E8
Sharpe St B77 . . . . 22 A5
Sharpless Rd LE10 . . . . . . 75 F7
Sharpley Ct CV2 . . . . 115 A8
Sharps Cl B45. . . . . 122 A7
Sharrat Field B75 . . . . 32 D2
Sharratt Rd CV12 . . . . 78 A2
Sharrocks St WV1. . . . . . . 163 D2
Shaw Ave DY10 . . . . 117 B6
Shawbank Rd B98. . . . . . . 154 B3
Shawberry Ave B35 . . . . . . 58 B4
Shawberry Rd B37 . . . . 69 F5
Shawbrook Gr 4 B14 . . . . 105 A3
Shawbury Gr B98 . . . . 154 E3
Shawbury Gr
  Birmingham B12 . . . . 86 F8
  Perton WV6. . . . . 23 E5
Shawbury Rd WV10 . . . . . . 25 F5
Shaw Ct WS11 . . . . 6 A5
Shaw Dr B33 . . . . 68 E2
Shawe Ave CV10 . . . . 73 C7
Shawfield B47 . . . . 125 A5
Shaw Hall La WV9 . . . . 11 C7
Shaw Hill Gr B8. . . . . 68 A4
Shaw Hill Prim Sch B8. . . . 67 F4
Shaw Hill Rd B8 . . . . 68 A4
Shawhurst Croft B47. . . . . 125 A7
Shawhurst Gdns B47. . . . . 125 B7
Shawhurst La B47. . . . . . . 125 A6
Shaw La
  Lichfield WS13. . . . . 9 A8
  Stoke Prior B60. . . . . 150 C3
  Wolverhampton WV6 . . . . . 24 B3
Shaw Lane Ind Est B60 . . . 150 C2
Shawley Croft B27 . . . . 88 E4

Shaw Park Bsns Village
WV10 . . . . 25 C6
Shaw Rd
Dudley, Netherton DY2 . . . . . 62 C7
Hurst Hill WV14 . . . . 40 B1
Tipton DY4 . . . . 52 C4
Wolverhampton WV4 . . . . . . 39 C6
Shaws Cl B97 . . . . 152 F2
Shawsdale Rd B36 . . . . 68 F7
Shaw's La WS6 . . . . 5 A2
Shaw's Pas B5 . . . . 164 D2
Shaw St
1 Walsall WS1 . . . . 28 E2
West Bromwich B70 . . . . . . 52 E7
Shayler Gr WV2 . . . . 39 D7
Sheaf La B26 . . . . 89 B4
Sheapecote Ho **1** B71 . . 42 F1
Shearers Pl **4** B75. . . . . . 32 E3
Shearwater Cl
Birmingham B45 . . . . 121 F6
Kidderminster DY10 . . . . . . 117 B1
Shearwater Ct WV10 . . . . . 11 B3
Shearwater Wlk B23 . . . . . 56 B7
Sheaves CV WV14 . . . . 40 B3
Shedden St **3** DY2 . . . . . 62 D8
Sheddington Rd B23 . . . . . 56 D7
Sheen Ho CV2 . . . . 114 D8
Sheen Rd B44 . . . . 44 E4
Sheepclose Dr B37 . . . . . . 70 A3
Sheepcote Cl CV32 . . . . . . 157 A1
Sheepcote Grange B61. . 136 F5
Sheepcote La B77 . . . . 21 F4
Sheepcote St B16 . . . . 66 B2
Sheepcroft Cl B97 . . . . . . 152 F2
Sheepfold Cl B65 . . . . 63 A4
Sheepmoor Cl B17. . . . . . . 84 F8
Sheepwash La DY4 . . . . . . 52 D5
Sheepwash Nature Reserve ★
DY4. . . . . 52 D4
Sheepy Cl LE10 . . . . 71 F1
Sheerwater Dr DY5 . . . . . . 81 D7
Sheffield Rd B73 . . . . 57 A7
Sheffield St DY5 . . . . 62 A1
Shefford Rd B6 . . . . 66 F5
Sheila Ave WV11 . . . . 26 E7
Shelah Rd B63 . . . . 83 A6
Shelbourne Cl B69 . . . . . . 52 D2
SHELDON 89 C5
Sheldon Ave WS10 . . . . . . 42 A4
Sheldon Cl WV14 . . . . 40 D4
Sheldon Ctry Pk★ B26 . . 89 E5
Sheldon Dr B31. . . . . 102 D2
Sheldonfield Rd B26 . . . . . 89 D5
Sheldon Gr
Birmingham B26 . . . . 89 B5
Warwick CV34 . . . . 155 F2
Sheldon Hall Ave B33 . . . . 69 D3
Sheldon Heath Com Arts Coll
B26. . . . . 89 C8
Sheldon Heath Rd B26 . . . 89 B8
Sheldon Rd
Redditch B98 . . . . 159 A8
West Bromwich B71 . . . . . . 53 E8
Wolverhampton WV10 . . . . 11 A1
Sheldon Wlk B33 . . . . 69 C1
Sheldrake Cl CV3 . . . . 115 A1
Shelduck Cl DY10 . . . . . . 117 B3
SHELFIELD 15 C1
Shelfield Cl
Coventry CV5 . . . . 112 B3
Hockley Heath B94 . . . . . 143 C6
Shelfield Com Acad WS4 . 15 C2
Shelfield Rd B14 . . . . 104 C3
Shell Corner Trad Est
B62 . . . . 83 D8
Shelley Ave
Kidderminster DY10 . . . . . 116 E7
Tipton DY4 . . . . 52 B8
Warwick CV34 . . . . 160 C4
Shelley Cl
Bedworth CV12 . . . . 78 D1
Catshill B61 . . . . 137 A8
Dudley DY3 . . . . 50 A5
Redditch B97 . . . . 158 C8
Stourbridge DY8 . . . . 81 A8
Shelley Dr
Birmingham B23 . . . . 56 B5
Sutton Coldfield B74 . . . . . 31 F6
Shelley Gdns LE10 . . . . . . 71 E3
Shelley Ho
Halesowen B63 . . . . 82 B5
1 Oldbury B68 . . . . 64 C4
Shelley Rd
2 Burntwood WS7 . . . . . 7 A8
Cannock WS11 . . . . 1 E5
Coventry CV2 . . . . 114 C3
Tamworth B79 . . . . 21 A7
Wolverhampton WV10 . . . . 11 D2
Shellon Cl CV3 . . . . 134 F8
Shelly Cl B37 . . . . 69 F2
Shelly Cres B90 . . . . 127 B6
Shelly Croft B33 . . . . 69 A3
Shelly La B90. . . . . 127 B6
Shelly Twr B31 . . . . 103 C3
Shelsley Ave B69 . . . . 63 D5
Shelsley Dr B13. . . . . 87 B2
Shelsley Way B91 . . . . . . 107 B1
Shelton Cl WS10 . . . . 42 C5
Shelton La B63 . . . . 82 E5
Shelton Sq CV1 . . . . 165 B2
Shelton St B77 . . . . 35 F7
Sheltwood Cl B97 . . . . . . 153 A2
Sheltwood La B60, B97 . . 152 A3
Shelwick Gr B93 . . . . 127 F4

Shenley Acad B29 . . . . . . 102 F7
Shenley Ave DY1 . . . . 51 C6
Shenley Court Com L Ctr
B29 . . . . 102 F7
SHENLEY FIELDS 102 F7
Shenley Fields Dr B31. . . 102 F8
Shenley Fields Rd B29 . . 103 B8
Shenley Gdns B29 . . . . . 103 A7
Shenley Gn B29 . . . . 102 F6
Shenley Hill B31 . . . . 102 F6
Shenley La B29 . . . . 102 F7
SHENSTONE 18 A5
Shenstone Ave
Halesowen B62 . . . . 82 E5
Stourbridge DY8 . . . . 80 D3
Shenstone Bsns Pk WS14. 17 F6
Shenstone Cl
Bromsgrove B60 . . . . 137 B3
Sutton Coldfield B74 . . . . . 31 E6
Shenstone Ct
Bromsgrove B60 . . . . 137 B3
Solihull B90 . . . . 105 D2
Wolverhampton WV3 . . . . . 39 A6
Shenstone Dr
Aldridge WS9 . . . . 30 A8
Balsall Common CV7 . . . . 130 A6
Shenstone Flats B62 . . . . 83 F5
Shenstone Ho WS13. . . . . . 3 E1
Shenstone Lodge Sch
WS14 . . . . 18 A3
Shenstone Lodge Specl Sch
B69. . . . . 52 D1
Shenstone Rd
Birmingham, Edgbaston
B16 . . . . 65 C3
Birmingham, Great Barr B43 54 E8
Birmingham, Highter's Heath
B14 . . . . 105 A1
Shenstone StaWS14 . . . . . 17 F6
Shenstone Trad Est B63 . 83 C4
Shenstone Valley Rd B62. 83 F6
SHENSTONE WOODEND . . 18 A1
Shenton Wlk B37 . . . . 69 F5
Shepheard Rd B26 . . . . . . 89 D5
Shephards La CV7 . . . . 92 A3
Shepherd Cl
Coventry CV4 . . . . 111 F3
Lichfield WS13 . . . . 3 C3
Shepherd Dr WV12 . . . . . . 27 C5
Shepherds Brook Rd DY9. 81 D5
Shepherds Fold B65 . . . . . 63 B2
Shepherds Gn B15 . . . . . . 86 B1
Shepherds Green Rd B24 . 56 F1
Shepherds Pool Rd B75 . . 32 E2
Shepherds Standing B34 . 69 B6
Shepherds Way B21. . . . . . 56 C8
Shepherds Wlk
Bromsgrove B60 . . . . 150 E7
Wolverhampton WV8. . . . . 10 F2
Shepley Mdw B45. . . . . . . 138 B8
Shepley Rd
Barnt Green B45 . . . . 138 A7
Birmingham B45 . . . . 122 B6
Shepperton Bsns Pk CV11 73 C1
Shepperton Ct CV11. . . . . 73 C1
Shepperton St CV11. . . . . 73 C2
Sheppey Dr B36 . . . . 70 C6
Shepwell Gdns WV10. . . . . 12 C7
Shepwell Gn WV13. . . . . . . 27 C1
SHEPWELL GREEN. 27 C1
Sherard Croft B36 . . . . . . 70 B6
Sheraton Cl
Aldridge WS9 . . . . 30 B6
Cannock WS12. . . . . 2 A7
Sheraton Dr DY10 . . . . . . 117 B6
Sheraton Grange DY8 . . . 80 F2
Sheraton Rd B60. . . . . . . 137 C1
Sherborne Cl WS3 . . . . . . 28 C7
Sherborne Ct WV10 . . . . . 11 E1
Sherborne Gdns WV8 . . . 10 A3
Sherborne Gr B1 . . . . 66 A3
Sherborne Rd
Hinckley LE10 . . . . 76 B7
Wolverhampton WV10 . . . . 11 D1
Sherborne St B16. . . . . . . 66 B2
Sherborne Arc CV1. . . . . 165 B2
Sherborne Ave
Cannock WS12 . . . . 2 E4
Nuneaton CV10 . . . . 72 B4
Sherbourne Cl B98. . . . . 154 D2
Sherbourne Cres CV5 . . 112 E4
Sherbourne Ct CV1 . . . . . 165 B1
Sherbourne Dr B27 . . . . . 88 C4
Sherbourne Fields Sch
CV6. . . . . 112 D5
Sherbourne Rd
Birmingham, Acock's Green
B27. . . . . 88 C4
Birmingham, Balsall Heath
B12. . . . . 86 F7
Cradley Heath B64. . . . . . . 83 B8
Stourbridge DY8 . . . . 81 B4
Sherbourne Road E B12. . 86 F6
Sherbourne St CV1. . . . . 113 A2
Sherbrooke Ave B77 . . . . 35 E6
Sherbrook Prim SchWS11 1 C2
Sherbrook Rd WS11. . . . . . 1 C1
Sherdmore Croft B90 . . 126 F6
Sheridan Cl **3** WS2 . . . . 42 B7
Sheridan Gdns DY3 . . . . . 49 F5
Sheridan St
Walsall WS2 . . . . 42 B7
West Bromwich B71 . . . . . 53 D4
Sheridan Wlk B35. . . . . . . 58 A3
Sheriff Ave CV4 . . . . 132 B7
Sheriff Dr DY5 . . . . 61 F2
Sheriffs CI WS14 . . . . 9 E6
Sheriffs Orch CV1. . . . . . 165 B2

Sherifoot La B75. . . . . 32 B4
Sheringham B15. . . . . 85 E8
Sheringham Cl CV11 . . . . . 73 F2
Sheringham Rd B30. . . . . 104 B3
Sherington Ave CV5. . . . . 112 C4
Sherington Dr WV4 . . . . . . 39 D5
Sherlock Cl WV12. . . . . . . 27 D5
Sherlock Rd CV5. . . . . . . 112 D3
Sherlock St B5 . . . . 86 E8
Sherrans Dell WV4. . . . . . . 39 D4
Sherratt Cl B76. . . . . 57 F8
Sherringham Dr WV11 . . . 13 C1
Sherron Gdns B12 . . . . . . 86 F5
Sherston Covert **1** B30 104 C2
Shervale CI WV4 . . . . 39 A6
Sherwin Ave WV14 . . . . . . 40 A2
Sherwood Ave DY4. . . . . . . 51 F4
Sherwood Cl
Birmingham B28 . . . . 105 F5
Solihull B92 . . . . 106 F7
Wood End CV9 . . . . 36 C1
Sherwood Dr
Brierley Hill DY5 . . . . 61 F2
Cannock WS11 . . . . 2 A3
Sherwood Ho **1** B64. . . 82 F8
Sherwood Jones Cl CV6. 113 B6
Sherwood Mews B28. . . . 105 E6
Sherwood Rd
Birmingham B28 . . . . 105 E7
Bromsgrove B60 . . . . 151 A6
Smethwick B67 . . . . 65 A1
Stourbridge DY8 . . . . 80 E7
Sherwood St WV1. . . . . . 163 B4
Sherwood Wlk
Birmingham B45 . . . . 102 B2
Royal Leamington Spa
CV32 . . . . 157 C4
Walsall WS9. . . . . 29 E7
Shetland Ave B77. . . . . . . 35 F7
Shetland Cl
Birmingham B16 . . . . 65 F2
Coventry CV5 . . . . 112 A4
Wolverhampton WV6. . . . . 25 B5
Shetland Dr
Nuneaton CV10 . . . . 73 A2
Smethwick B66 . . . . 65 A4
Shetland Wlk B36. . . . . . . 70 B6
Shevlock Way CV6 . . . . . 114 A6
Shidas La B69 . . . . 63 E7
Shifnal Wlk B31 . . . . 122 F8
Shifrall Way B75. . . . . 46 F7
Shillcock Gr B19. . . . . 66 E5
Shillingstone Cl CV2 . . . 115 A4
Shillingstone Dr CV10 . . . 73 A1
SHILTON 97 F5
Shilton Cl B90 . . . . 126 F6
Shilton Dr B29. . . . . 102 F8
Shilton Ind Est CV7 . . . . . 97 E7
Shilton La
Barnacle CV2, CV7. . . . . . . 97 B4
Bulkington CV12 . . . . 79 D1
Coventry CV2 . . . . 96 F3
Shilton CV7, CV12. . . . . . . 97 D8
Shinehill La CV9 . . . . 51 E7
Shinwell Cres B69 . . . . . . 52 D2
Shipbourne Cl B32 . . . . . . 84 F5
Shipley Fields B24 . . . . . . 57 A3
Shipley Rd B29. . . . . 103 A8
Shipston Rd
Birmingham B31 . . . . 103 B1
Sutton Coldfield B76 . . . . . 46 F1
Shipton Cl
Dudley DY1. . . . . 50 F3
Redditch B97 . . . . 153 A5
Shipton Rd B72 . . . . 46 C3
Shipway Rd B25 . . . . 88 A7
Shirebrook Cl CV2 . . . . . . 96 D2
Shire Brook Cl B6. . . . . . . 66 E8
Shire Brook Ct **2** B19. . 66 D7
Shire Cl
Birmingham B16 . . . . 65 F2
Coventry CV6. . . . . 96 B1
Oldbury B68. . . . . 64 B2
Shirehall Pl WS11. . . . . 2 B2
Shirehampton Cl B97 . . . 152 F2
Shireland Brook Gdns **1**
B18 . . . . 65 D4
Shireland Cl B20. . . . . 54 F3
Shireland Collegiate Acad
B66. . . . . 65 B3
Shireland Hall Prim Sch
B66. . . . . 65 B3
Shireland La B97 . . . . 153 A4
Shireland Rd B66. . . . . 65 B3
Shire Lea WS8 . . . . 16 B6
Shirelea CI WS7 . . . . 7 B8
Shireview Gdns WS3 . . . . 15 B4
Shireview Rd WS3 . . . . 15 B4
Shirewood WS11. . . . . 1 B2
Shirland Rd B37. . . . . 70 A1
Shirlett Cl CV2. . . . . 96 B4
SHIRLEY 106 C3
Shirleydale **2** B90. . . . . 126 C8
Shirley Dr B72. . . . . 46 C4
SHIRLEY HEATH. 126 C7

Shirley Heath Jun Sch
B90. . . . . 106 C1
Shirley La CV7 . . . . 111 A5
Shirley Park Rd B90. . . . 106 B2
Shirley Rd
Birmingham, Hall Green B27,
B28. . . . . 106 A7
Birmingham, King's Norton
B30. . . . . 104 A5
Coventry CV2. . . . . 115 A7
Dudley DY2 . . . . 62 E8
Oldbury B68. . . . . 64 C6
Shirley Stop B90 . . . . 105 F1
SHIRLEY STREET 106 C2
Shirley Wlk B79 . . . . 20 F7
Shirral Gr B37 . . . . 69 F5
Shirrall Dr B78 . . . . 33 E4
Shoal Hill Cl WS11. . . . . . . 1 B2
Shoal Hill Common Nature
Reserve★ WS11. . . . . 1 B3
Sholing Cl WV8 . . . . 10 F1
Shooters Cl B5. . . . . 86 D6
Shooters Hill B72 . . . . 46 D2
Shop La WV6 . . . . 37 B7
Shopton Rd B34 . . . . 69 A7
Shoreham Cl WV13 . . . . . . 26 D1
Shorncliffe Rd CV6. . . . . 112 E6
Short Acre St WS2. . . . . . . 28 D3
Shortbutts La WS14 . . . . . . 9 B5
Shorters Ave B14 . . . . . . 105 B4
Shortfield CI CV7 . . . . 130 B7
SHORT HEATH
Birmingham 56 E7
Willenhall 27 D6
Short Heath Ct B23 . . . . . 56 F5
Short Heath Jun Sch
WV12 . . . . 27 D5
Short Heath Prim Sch
B23. . . . . 56 D6
Short Heath Rd B23 . . . . . 56 E6
Short La WS6. . . . . 4 E3
Shortland Cl B93. . . . . . . 128 A7
Shortlands Cl B30. . . . . . 104 A2
Shortlands La WS3. . . . . . 14 F3
Shortley Rd CV3 . . . . 133 F8
Short Rd
Smethwick B67 . . . . 64 D3
Wolverhampton WV10 . . . . 11 E1
Short St
Bilston WV14 . . . . 40 D6
Brownhills WS8 . . . . 15 F7
Cannock WS11. . . . . 1 E2
Coventry CV1 . . . . 165 C2
Darlaston WS10. . . . . 41 F7
Dudley DY1 . . . . 51 A2
Halesowen B63 . . . . 82 F5
Nuneaton CV10 . . . . 72 D4
Rowley Regis B65 . . . . 63 C2
Sedgley DY3 . . . . 50 F5
Stourbridge DY8 . . . . 80 F5
Tipton DY4 . . . . 51 E8
Walsall WS2. . . . . 28 D1
Wednesbury WS10 . . . . . . 41 E3
Willenhall WV12 . . . . 27 C5
Wolverhampton WV1. . . . 163 C3
Short Street Ind Est
WV10 . . . . 25 D6
Shortwoods B78. . . . . 22 C1
Shorwell PI DY5. . . . . 61 B1
Shottery Cl
Coventry CV5. . . . . 112 B3
Redditch B98 . . . . 154 C2
Sutton Coldfield B76 . . . . . 46 F1
Shottery Gr B76 . . . . 46 F1
Shotteswell Rd B90 . . . . 126 B8
Showell Cir WV10 . . . . 25 E7
SHOWELL GREEN. 87 B4
Showell Green La B11. . . . 87 C3
Showell Ho **10** B69 . . . . . 64 A7
Showell La
Eaves Green CV7. . . . . 93 A1
Wombourne WV4. . . . . 38 B3
Showell Rd WV10 . . . . 25 D6
Showell Road Ind Est
WV10 . . . . 25 D6
Showells Gdns B7 . . . . . . 67 C7
Shrawley Ave
Birmingham B45 . . . . 121 F7
Halesowen B63 . . . . 83 A2
Shrawley Cl
Birmingham B45 . . . . 121 F7
Kidderminster DY11. . . . . 116 B3
Shrawley Rd
Birmingham B31 . . . . 103 C2
Halesowen B63 . . . . 83 A2
Shrewley Cres B33 . . . . . . 69 E1
Shrewsbury Cl WS3 . . . . . 13 F1
Shrewsbury Rd DY11. . . . 116 A6
Shrewton Ave B14 . . . . . 104 D2
Shropshire Way B71 . . . . 53 C7
Shrubberies The CV4. . . 132 E4
Shrubbery Ave DY4 . . . . . 51 D5
Shrubbery Cl
Sutton Coldfield B76 . . . . . 57 D6
Walsall WS1 . . . . 29 B1
Shrubbery Ct DY10. . . . . 116 F7
Shrubbery Sch The B76. . 57 F7
Shrubbery St DY10 . . . . . 116 F7
Shrubbery The
Birmingham B16 . . . . 65 F3
4 Dudley DY5. . . . . 61 B2
Shrub La B24 . . . . 57 B4
Shrublands Ave B68. . . . . 84 B7
Shrubland St CV31. . . . . 162 A6
Shrubland Street Com Prim
Sch CV31. . . . . 162 A6
Shuckburgh Gr **5** CV32 . 157 A2
Shugborough Cl WS3 . . . . 14 B1
Shugborough Dr DY1 . . . . 50 E2
Shugborough Way WS11 . . 2 C1

Shulman's Wlk CV2 . . . . . 114 D7
Shultern La CV4 . . . . 132 D6
Shuna Croft CV2 . . . . 115 B7
Shustoke La WS5 . . . . 43 B4
Shustoke Rd
Birmingham B34 . . . . 69 C6
Solihull B91. . . . . 107 D5
Shutlock La B13 . . . . 86 D1
Shut Mill La B62 . . . . 100 D3
SHUTTINGTON 22 F7
Shuttington Rd B77, B79. . 22 B6
Shutt La B94. . . . . 126 B1
Shuttle St CV6 . . . . 114 B8
Shylock Gr CV34 . . . . 161 E2
Sibdon Gr B31 . . . . 123 A8
Sibree Rd CV3. . . . . 134 B4
Sibton Cl CV2 . . . . 96 C1
Sidaway Cl B65 . . . . 63 C6
Sidaway St B64 . . . . 62 E1
Sidbury Gr B93 . . . . 127 E3
Sidbury Rd CV6. . . . . 113 C6
Sidcup Cl WV14. . . . . 40 B3
Sidcup Rd B44. . . . . 45 A1
Siddeley Ave
Coventry CV3. . . . . 114 B1
Kenilworth CV8. . . . . 147 E3
Siddons Factory Est B70 . 52 F8
Siddons Rd WV14 . . . . 40 D2
Siddons Way B70 . . . . 53 A7
SIDEMOOR 136 F4
Sidemoor Fst Sch B61 . . 136 D4
Sidenhill Cl B90 . . . . 126 B8
Sidestrand WV9 . . . . 10 F3
Sidford Gdns B24 . . . . . . 57 C3
Sidford Gr B23. . . . . 56 E7
Sidings The
Birmingham, Gravelly Hill
B23. . . . . 56 E3
Birmingham, Lozells B20. . 66 C8
Cannock WS12 . . . . 2 C7
Stourbridge DY8 . . . . 99 A6
5 West Bromwich B70. . . 53 C2
Sidlaw Cl
Halesowen B63 . . . . 82 D2
Wolverhampton WV10 . . . . 25 C6
Sidmouth Cl
Coventry CV2. . . . . 114 C7
Nuneaton CV11 . . . . 73 F5
Sidney St WV2 . . . . 163 B1
Sidney Stringer Acad
CV1. . . . . 165 C3
Sidon Hill Way WS11. . . . . 2 C2
Sidwick Cres WV2. . . . . . . 40 B6
Sigmund Cl WV1 . . . . 26 B3
Signal Gr WS3 . . . . 14 A1
Signal Hayes Rd B76. . . . 47 A2
Signal Wlk B77 . . . . 22 A2
Signet Sq CV2 . . . . 113 F4
Silesbourne Cl B36 . . . . . 69 C8
Silhill Hall Rd B91 . . . . . . 107 A5
Silica Rd B77. . . . . 22 B2
Silken Ct CV11. . . . . 73 B4
Silksby St CV3 . . . . 133 D8
Sillins Ave B98. . . . . 154 A3
Silva Ave DY6. . . . . 60 F4
Silver Birch Ave CV12 . . . 77 E2
Silverbirch Cl CV10 . . . . . 72 A7
Silver Birch Cl
Binley Woods CV3 . . . . . . 135 D7
Birmingham B8 . . . . 67 D6
Silver Birch Coppice B74 . 31 D5
Silverbirch Ct B24 . . . . . . 57 B6
Silver Birch Ct DY10. . . . . 117 A4
Silver Birch Dr
Hollywood B47. . . . . 125 D6
Kidderminster DY10 . . . . . 117 C5
Silver Birches Bsns Pk **3**
B60. . . . . 150 F6
Silver Birch Gr **5** CV31. . 161 F5
Silverbirch Rd B91. . . . . . 107 E3
Silver Birch Rd
Birmingham, Erdington
B24. . . . . 57 B6
Birmingham, Kingshurst B37 69 F6
Huntington WS12. . . . . 1 D8
Norton Canes WS11. . . . . . 6 B5
Sutton Coldfield B74 . . . . . 30 F1
Wolverhampton WV2 . . . . . 39 E7
Silver Court Gdns WS8 . . 15 F7
Silvercroft Ave B21 . . . . . 54 D3
Silver Ct WS8. . . . . 15 F7
Silverdale B61 . . . . 136 F4
Silverdale Cl CV2 . . . . 96 B4
Silverdale Dr
Burntwood WS7. . . . . 6 D7
Wolverhampton WV10 . . . . 25 E5
Silverdale Gdns DY8 . . . . 60 C3
Silverdale Rd B24. . . . . . . 57 D5
SILVER END 61 C2
Silver End Ind Est & Bsns Pk
DY5. . . . . 61 C1
Silverfield Cl B14 . . . . . . 104 E8
Silver Fir Cl WS12. . . . . 2 A8
Silver Innage B63. . . . . . . 82 C7
Silverlands Ave B68. . . . . 64 B3
Silverlands Cl B28 . . . . . . 87 F4
Silver Link Rd B77 . . . . . . 21 F1
Silvermead Ct B47. . . . . . 124 F5
Silvermead Rd B73. . . . . . 46 A1
Silvermere Rd B26 . . . . . . 89 D6
Silver's Cl WS3 . . . . 14 F4
Silver St
Birmingham B14 . . . . 104 E8
Brierley Hill DY5 . . . . 61 C1
Brownhills WS8 . . . . 15 F7
Coventry CV1. . . . . 165 B3
Hollywood B47. . . . . 124 E5
Kidderminster DY10 . . . . . 116 E7

Silver St continued
Redditch B97, B98 . . . . . . 153 E4
Tamworth B79 . . . . 21 B5
Silverstone Ave DY11 . . 116 D8
Silverstone Cl WS2 . . . . . 27 D3
Silverstone Ct B30 . . . . 104 B8
Silverstone Dr
  Coventry CV6 . . . . 95 E5
  Sutton Coldfield B74 . . . 44 F6
SILVER STREET 124 F5
Silverthorne Ave DY4 . . 51 D5
Silverthorne La B64 . . . . 82 B8
Silverton Cres B13 . . . . . 87 D1
Silverton Hts B67 . . . . . . 64 F6
Silverton Rd
  Coventry CV6 . . . . 113 F7
  Smethwick B67 . . . . 64 E6
Silverton Way WV11 . . . 26 F5
Silver Trees Dr CV12 . . . 79 B4
Silvertrees Rd DY4 . . . . . 51 D5
Silver Wlk CV10 . . . . 72 F3
Silvester Cl B70 . . . . 53 E3
Silvester Rd WV14 . . . . . 40 F7
Silvester Way DY5 . . . . . 81 B8
Silvington Cl B29 . . . . . 103 C7
Simcox B32 . . . . 84 D2
Simcox Gdns B32 . . . . . 84 D2
Simcox Rd WS10 . . . . . . 41 F5
Simcox St WS12 . . . . 2 D4
Simeon Bissell Cl DY4 . 52 A5
Simeon's Wlk DY5 . . . . . 81 F7
Simmonds Cl WS3 . . . . . 14 D3
Simmonds Pl WS10 . . . . 41 F7
Simmonds Rd WS3 . . . . . 14 D3
Simmonds Way WS8 . . . 16 A6
Simmons Cl B78 . . . . 34 B1
Simmons Dr B32 . . . . 84 D4
Simmons Leasow B32 . . 84 E2
Simmons Rd WV11 . . . . . 13 B1
Simms La
  Dudley DY2 . . . . 62 C5
  Hollywood B47 . . . . 125 A5
Simon Cl
  Nuneaton CV11 . . . . 73 D2
  West Bromwich B71 . . . 42 E1
Simon Ct CV7 . . . . 96 A8
Simon Rd B47 . . . . 125 A7
Simon Stone St CV6 . . 113 F8
Simpkins Cl WS9 . . . . . . 16 A3
Simpson Gr
  Coventry CV3 . . . . 134 C6
  Wolverhampton WV10 . . 25 E6
Simpson Rd
  Lichfield WS13 . . . . 3 B2
  Sutton Coldfield B72 . . 46 C1
  Walsall WS2 . . . . 28 B5
  Wolverhampton WV10 . . 25 E6
Simpson St B69 . . . . 64 A8
Sinclair Ct B13 . . . . 86 E4
Sinclair Dr CV6 . . . . 96 C6
Singer Cl CV6 . . . . 114 B8
Singer Croft B36 . . . . . . 58 F1
Singh Cl B21 . . . . 54 D2
Sion Cl DY5 . . . . 61 D3
Sir Alfreds Way B76 . . . 46 E3
Sir Anthony Eden Way
  CV34 . . . . 161 C8
Sir Frank Whittle Prim Sch
  B CV7 . . . . 96 A8
Sir George's Mall B
  DY10 . . . . 116 E6
Sir Harrys Rd B5 . . . . . . 86 C6
Sir Henry Parkes Rd
  CV5 . . . . 132 D7
Sir Hilton's Rd B31 . . . 123 C7
Sir John's Rd B29 . . . . . 86 C2
Sir Richards Dr B17 . . . 84 F7
Sir Robert Peel Hospl
  B78 . . . . 20 D2
Sir Thomas White Cl B
  CV34 . . . . 160 D8
Sir Thomas White's Rd
  CV5 . . . . 112 F2
Sir Toby Belch Dr CV34 . 161 F3
Sir Walter's Mall B
  DY10 . . . . 116 E6
Sir William Lyons Rd
  CV4 . . . . 132 C6
Sir Winston Churchill Pl
  CV3 . . . . 135 C7
Sisefield Rd B38 . . . . . . 104 A1
Siskin Cl
  Hammerwich WS7 . . . . . . 7 D5
  Oldbury B68 . . . . 64 C2
Siskin Dr
  Birmingham B12 . . . . . . 86 E6
  Coventry CV3 . . . . 134 C4
Siskin Parkway E CV3 . 134 C2
Siskin Parkway W CV3 . 134 C2
Siskin Rd DY9 . . . . 81 C3
Siskin Way DY10 . . . . . . 117 B1
Sisley Way LE10 . . . . 71 A3
Sister Dora Bldgs 2 WS1. 28 E1
Sister Dora Gdns 1 WS1. 42 B8
Siviter's Cl B65 . . . . 63 B3
Siviter's La B65 . . . . 63 B3
Siviter St B63 . . . . 83 B4
Six Acres B32 . . . . 84 B2
Sixes Indoor Sp & L Ctr
  DY6. . . . . 49 E1
Sixpence Cl CV4 . . . . . . 131 D6
Sixth Form Coll Solihull The
  B91. . . . . 107 D2
Six Towers Rd WS2 . . . . 28 C4
Six Ways B23 . . . . 56 F4
Six Ways Rdbt B23 . . . . 56 F4
Skelcher Rd B90 . . . . . . 106 A3
Skelwith Rise CV11 . . . . 74 A6

Skemp Cl WV14 . . . . 40 D4
SKETCHLEY 75 C6
Sketchley Cl B66 . . . . . . 65 A6
Sketchley Hall Gdns LE10. 75 C5
SKETCHLEY HILL 75 E7
Sketchley Hill Prim Sch
  LE10 . . . . 75 E5
Sketchley La LE10. . . . . . 75 C5
Sketchley Lane Ind Est
  LE10 . . . . 75 B5
Sketchley Manor La LE10. 75 D5
Sketchley Mdws LE10 . . 75 C5
Sketchley Meadows Bsns Pk
  LE10 . . . . 75 C4
Sketchley Old Village
  LE10 . . . . 75 C5
Sketchley Rd LE10 . . . . . 75 E5
Skey Dr CV10 . . . . 72 B6
Skiddaw Cl B B71 . . . . . . 53 F8
Skidmore Ave
  Tamworth B77 . . . . 35 C5
  Wolverhampton WV3 . . . 38 F8
Skidmore Dr B70 . . . . . . 53 A3
Skidmore Rd WV14 . . . . 40 D2
Skilts Ave B98 . . . . 153 F1
Skinner La B5 . . . . 66 E1
Skinner St WV1 . . . . . . 163 B3
Skip La WS9 . . . . 43 E6
Skipness B77 . . . . 21 C5
Skipton Gdns CV2 . . . . 114 B6
Skipton Gn WV6 . . . . . . 25 A5
Skipton Lodge CV2. . . . 114 B6
Skipton Pl WS11 . . . . 4 B7
Skipton Rd B16 . . . . 66 A1
Skipworth Rd CV3 . . . . 115 A1
Skomer Cl B45. . . . . 101 C1
Sky Blue Way CV1 . . . . 113 E3
Skydome The CV1. . . . . 165 A2
Skye Cl
  Birmingham B36 . . . . . . 70 B6
  Nuneaton CV10 . . . . 72 F2
  Tamworth B77 . . . . 35 F7
Skye Wlk B B64 . . . . 62 E1
Skylark Cl
  Birmingham B23 . . . . . . 56 C7
  Dudley DY5 . . . . 50 C1
Skylark Way DY10. . . . . 117 A2
Slack La B19 . . . . 54 E2
Slacky La WS3 . . . . 14 F1
Slade Ave WS7 . . . . 7 A8
Slade Cl
  Nuneaton CV11 . . . . 79 C8
  West Bromwich B71 . . . 42 F2
Sladefield Inf Sch B8 . . 68 A5
Sladefield Rd B8 . . . . . . 68 A5
Slade Gdns WV8 . . . . . . 10 A4
Slade Gr B93 . . . . 127 F6
Slade Hill B WV6 . . . . . . 24 F3
Slade La
  Birmingham B28 . . . . . . 105 E3
  Solihull B75 . . . . 33 A3
  Tamworth B77 . . . . 35 C4
Slade Lanker B34 . . . . . . 69 A5
Slade Mdw WS11 . . . . . 162 E5
Sladepool Farm Rd B14. 105 A2
Slade Prim Sch B23. . . . 56 D2
Slade Rd
  Birmingham B23 . . . . . . 56 D3
  Halesowen B63 . . . . 82 C6
  Sutton Coldfield B75 . . 32 E3
  Wolverhampton WV10 . . 11 C3
Slaithwaite Rd B71. . . . . 53 E4
Slaney Cl WS2 . . . . 42 C7
Slaney Rd WS2 . . . . 42 B6
Slatch House Rd B67 . . 64 E2
Slateley Cres B90 . . . . . 126 F6
Slater Cl B64 . . . . 62 F1
Slater Rd B93 . . . . 127 F4
Slaters La WS2 . . . . 42 B7
Slaters Pl WS2 . . . . 42 B7
Slater St
  Bilston WV14 . . . . 40 E3
  Darlaston WS10 . . . . 41 D6
  Tipton, Dudley Port DY4 . 52 A6
  Tipton, Great Bridge DY4 . 52 D5
  Willenhall WV13 . . . . 27 C3
Sleaford Gr B28 . . . . . . 106 A7
Sleaford Rd B28 . . . . . . 106 B7
Sleath's Yd CV12 . . . . . . 78 B3
Sledmere Cl CV2 . . . . . . 96 B3
Sledmere Prim Sch DY2 . 62 D6
Sledmore Rd DY2 . . . . . . 62 E7
Sleets Yd CV12 . . . . 78 A2
Slideslow Ave B60 . . . . 137 B2
Slideslow Dr B60 . . . . . 137 B3
Slieve The B20. . . . . 55 A3
Slim Ave WV14 . . . . 40 E3
Slimbridge Cl
  Redditch B97 . . . . 158 E5
  2 Solihull B90 . . . . 127 A6
Slims Gate B63 . . . . 83 A4
Slingfield Rd B31 . . . . . 103 C1
Slingsby B77 . . . . 35 C7
Slingsby Cl CV11 . . . . . . 73 F2
Sling The
  Dudley DY2 . . . . 62 C6
  Kidderminster DY10 . . . 116 E6
Slitting Mill Cl B21 . . . . 65 C8
Sloane Ho B B1 . . . . 66 C3
Sloane St B1 . . . . 66 C3
Slough The B97, B80. . . 159 B4
Smallbrook La WV5 . . . . 49 B7
Smallbrook Queensway
  B 164 C1
Small Cl B67. . . . . 64 D5
Smalldale Rd B42 . . . . . 55 D7

Smalley Cl WS11 . . . . 2 A5
Smalley Pl CV8 . . . . 147 F4
SMALL HEATH 87 D7
Small Heath Bridge B10,
  B11 . . . . 87 B8
Small Heath Bsns Pk B10 . 87 F7
Small Heath Highway B10,
  B11 . . . . 87 D6
Small Heath L Ctr B10 . . 87 D8
Small Heath Lower Sch
  B10 . . . . 87 D7
Small Heath Sch & Sixth
  Form Ctr B10. . . . . 87 D8
Small Heath Sta B10 . . . 87 D7
Small Heath Trad Est B11. 87 D6
Small La B94 . . . . 141 E6
Smallman Rd CV10 . . . . 72 A7
Smallshire Cl WV11 . . . . 26 F5
Smallshire Way DY8 . . . 80 E8
Small St
  Walsall WS1 . . . . 42 E8
  West Bromwich B71 . . . 53 B5
SMALLWOOD 153 E2
Smallwood Almshouses
  B98 . . . . 153 E3
Smallwood Arch B B98 . 153 E4
Smallwood Cl
  Birmingham B24 . . . . . . 57 D3
  Sutton Coldfield B76 . . 46 E3
Smallwood Rd B98 . . . . 10 E2
Smallwood St B98 . . . . 153 E3
Smalman Cl DY6. . . . . . . 60 E4
Smarts Ave WS14 . . . . . 32 A7
Smarts Rd CV12. . . . . . . 77 F1
Smeaton Gdns B18. . . . . 65 E4
Smedley Crooke Pl B48 . 123 C2
Smeed Gr B24 . . . . 57 B3
Smercote Cl CV10 . . . . . 77 D1
Smestow Ho B68. . . . . . 64 B1
Smestow Sports Coll
  WV3 . . . . 24 B1
Smestow St WV10. . . . . 25 D4
Smestow Valley Nature
  Reserve★ WV6 . . . . 24 D3
SMETHWICK 65 A4
Smethwick Galton Bridge Sta
  B66. . . . . 64 F2
Smethwick Rolfe Street Sta
  B66. . . . . 65 B4
Smethwick Swimming Ctr
  B67 . . . . 64 F2
Smillie Pl WS11 . . . . 1 F3
Smirrells Rd B28. . . . . . 105 E5
Smith Ave WS10 . . . . . . 41 D4
Smith Cl
  Smethwick B67 . . . . 64 D3
  Wolverhampton WV14 . . 40 A1
Smithfield Rd WS3. . . . . 14 D1
Smithfield Rise B13 . . . . 9 C8
Smithfields B DY8. . . . . 81 A5
Smith Ho WS3 . . . . 14 C3
Smithmoor Cres B71. . . 53 F8
Smith Pl DY4 . . . . 52 B4
Smith Rd
  Walsall WS2. . . . . 42 C6
  Wednesbury WS10 . . . . 41 F1
Smiths Cl B32 . . . . 84 B1
Smith's Cl WS7 . . . . 6 D6
Smith's La B93 . . . . 127 E7
Smith St
  Bedworth CV12 . . . . 77 E1
  Bilston WV14 . . . . 40 D5
  Birmingham B19 . . . . . . 66 C5
  Coventry CV6 . . . . 113 F5
  Dudley DY2 . . . . 62 D7
  2 Royal Leamington Spa
    CV31. . . . . 161 F7
  Warwick CV34 . . . . 160 F7
  Wood End CV9 . . . . 36 C1
Smiths Way
  Bromsgrove B60 . . . . . 150 D2
  Water Orton B46. . . . . . 59 A3
Smiths Wood Com Prim Sch
  B36. . . . . 70 A8
Smiths Wood Nature
  Reserve★ B36 . . . . 70 A7
Smiths Wood Sports Coll
  B36. . . . . 70 A6
Smithy Dr WS3 . . . . 15 A4
Smithy La
  Aston Flamville LE9 . . . . 76 C8
  Dudley DY5 . . . . 50 B1
  Lichfield WS13 . . . . 3 A1
  Tamworth B77 . . . . 35 F7
Smithy The B26. . . . . . . 89 C6
Smout Cres WV14 . . . . . 39 F2
Smythe Gr CV34 . . . . . . 155 E1
Snake La B48 . . . . 139 A6
Snakes Lake La B61. . . . 136 D6
Snake Terr B48 . . . . 139 A6
Snapdragon Dr WS5 . . . 43 A3
Snape Rd
  Coventry CV2. . . . . 114 F5
  Wolverhampton WV11 . . 13 B1
Sneyd Com Sch WS3 . . 13 E2
Sneyd Hall Cl WS3 . . . . 28 A8
Sneyd Hall Rd WS3. . . . 14 A1
Sneyd Ho WS3 . . . . 13 F1
Sneyd La
  Walsall WS3. . . . . 13 F1
  Willenhall WV11 . . . . 13 C1
Snipe Cl WV10 . . . . 12 B7
Snitterfield Cl B B90 . . 106 C1
Snitterfield Dr B B90. . . 106 C1
Snowberry Dr DY5 . . . . . 61 B8
Snowberry Gdns B B25 . 88 C5
Snowdome B79 . . . . 21 B3

Snowdon Cl CV10 . . . . . . 72 B3
Snowdon Gr B63. . . . . . . 82 D1
Snowdon Rd
  Cannock WS11. . . . . 1 E6
  Stourbridge DY8 . . . . . . 81 B6
Snowdon Rise DY3 . . . . 50 D6
Snowdon Way
  Willenhall WV12 . . . . 13 B1
  Wolverhampton WV10 . . 25 B6
Snowdrop Cl
  Bedworth CV12 . . . . 77 E1
  Brownhills WS8 . . . . 15 D6
Snowford Cl B90. . . . . . 105 F1
Snow Hill WV2. . . . . 163 C2
Snow Hill Queensway
  B4 . . . . 164 C3
Snow Hill Stop B3 . . . . 164 B3
Snowshill Cl
  Nuneaton CV11 . . . . 78 F8
  Redditch B98 . . . . 154 B6
Snows Hill Dr B90 . . . . 126 D5
Snowshill Gdns DY1. . . . 50 F4
SNUFF HILL 120 D1
Soar Way LE10 . . . . 75 A8
Soberton Cl WV11 . . . . . 26 F7
Soden Cl CV3 . . . . 134 D6
Soden's Ave CV8 . . . . . 135 A1
SOHO 65 C7
Soho Ave B18. . . . . 66 A7
Soho, Benson Road Stop
  B18 . . . . 65 F6
Soho Cl B66 . . . . 65 C6
Soho Hill B19. . . . . 66 B7
Soho House Mus★ B18. . 66 A7
Soho Pool Way B18 . . . . 66 A6
Soho Rd B21. . . . . 65 D8
Soho St B66 . . . . 65 C6
Soho Way B66 . . . . 65 B6
Solari Cl DY4 . . . . 52 C8
Solent Cl B B73 . . . . 46 B5
Solent Dr CV2 . . . . 96 F1
SOLIHULL 107 D3
Solihull By-Pass B91. . . 107 E4
Solihull Coll (Blossomfield
  Campus) B91. . . . . 107 A3
Solihull Coll (Woodlands
  Campus) B37. . . . . 70 B6
Solihull Gate Ret Pk
  B90. . . . . 126 C8
Solihull Hospl B91 . . . . 107 C4
Solihull La B28 . . . . 106 A6
SOLIHULL LODGE 105 E2
Solihull Parkway B37 . . . 90 E8
Solihull Rd
  Birmingham B11 . . . . . . 87 D3
  Hampton-in-A B92 . . . . 108 E6
  Solihull B90 . . . . 106 D3
Solihull Sch B91. . . . . . 107 D4
Solihull Sta B91 . . . . . . 107 A4
Solly Gr DY4 . . . . 52 D7
Solva Cl WV1 . . . . 26 B1
Solway Cl
  Royal Leamington Spa
    CV31. . . . . 162 C6
  Tamworth B79 . . . . 21 A7
  Wednesbury WS10 . . . . 42 C4
Somerby Dr B91 . . . . . . 127 A8
Somercotes Rd B42 . . . . 55 D8
Somerdale Rd B31 . . . . 103 C4
Somerfield Cl WS4 . . . . 15 C1
Somerfield Rd WS3 . . . . 28 C7
Somerford Cl WS6 . . . . . 4 E1
Somerford Gdns WV10 . 11 E2
Somerford Pl WV13 . . . . 26 F1
Somerford Rd B29 . . . . 102 F8
Somerford Way WV14 . . 51 B8
Somerland Rd B26 . . . . . 69 A1
Somerleyton Ave DY10 . 117 A5
Somerleyton Ct B DY10 . 117 A5
Somerly Cl CV3 . . . . 134 F8
Somerset Cl B78 . . . . . . 21 A1
Somerset Cres WS10 . . . 42 C4
Somerset Dr
  Birmingham B31 . . . . . . 122 F7
  Nuneaton CV10 . . . . 72 E4
  Stourbridge DY8 . . . . . . 80 D7
Somerset Pl WS11 . . . . . . 1 F3
Somerset Rd
  Birmingham B15 . . . . . . 85 F5
  Birmingham, Erdington B23. 56 F6
  Birmingham, Handsworth
    B20. . . . . 54 F2
  Coventry CV1. . . . . 113 C5
  Walsall WS4. . . . . 15 C1
  West Bromwich B71 . . . 53 D6
  Willenhall WV13 . . . . 27 C2
Somers Pl B CV32 . . . . 161 E8
Somers Rd
  Halesowen B62 . . . . 83 C5
  Keresley CV7 . . . . 95 A6
  Meriden CV7 . . . . 91 F1
  Walsall WS2. . . . . 42 A7
Somers Sq B B63. . . . . . 83 B3
Somerton Dr
  Birmingham, Erdington
    B23. . . . . 57 A6
  Birmingham, Marston Green
    B37. . . . . 90 B7
Somerville Ct
  B Sutton Coldfield B73 . . 46 A2
  Tamworth B79 . . . . 20 D6
Somerville Ho B37 . . . . . 70 D3
Somerville Prim Sch B37. 70 D8
Somerville Rd
  Birmingham B10 . . . . . . 87 E8

Somerville Rd continued
  Sutton Coldfield B73 . . . 46 A3
Somery Rd
  Birmingham B29 . . . . . . 85 A2
  Dudley DY1 . . . . 51 C3
Sommerfield Rd B32. . . . 84 D3
Sommerville Ave B24 . . . 56 F4
Sommerville Rd CV2 . . . 114 C4
Sonata Rd B60 . . . . 137 C1
Sonning Dr WV9 . . . . 10 F2
Sopwith Croft B35 . . . . . 58 A2
Sorbus B77. . . . . 22 B4
Soredale Croft CV3 . . . . 115 A1
Sorrel B77. . . . . 22 B5
Sorrel Cl
  Coventry CV4. . . . . 131 E8
  Featherstone WV10. . . . . 12 B7
  Lichfield WS13 . . . . 8 E6
  Tipton B69 . . . . 52 B2
Sorrel Dr
  Birmingham B27 . . . . . . 88 B2
  Walsall WS5. . . . . 43 A3
Sorrel Gr B24 . . . . 57 D3
Sorrel Ho B24 . . . . 57 D3
Sorrell Pl CV10 . . . . 78 D8
Sorrell Rd CV10 . . . . 78 D8
Sorrell Wlk DY5. . . . . 81 B6
Sorrento Ct B13 . . . . 87 A3
Sot's Hole with Bluebell
  Wood Nature Reserve★
  B71. . . . . 53 E5
Soudan B97 . . . . 153 D2
Souters Ho B32 . . . . . . 102 D8
Southacre Ave B5 . . . . . . 66 E8
Southall Cres WV14 . . . 40 C1
Southall Rd WV11. . . . . . 27 A8
Southall's La DY1 . . . . . . 51 B1
Southam Cl
  Birmingham B28 . . . . . . 105 E8
  Coventry CV4. . . . . 131 E7
Southam Dr B73 . . . . 46 B1
Southampton St WV1 . . 163 C4
Southam Rd
  Birmingham B28 . . . . . . 105 E8
  Radford Semele CV31. . . 162 E6
South Ave
  Coventry CV2. . . . . 114 A2
  Stourbridge DY8 . . . . . . 80 F4
  Wolverhampton WV10 . . 26 C5
Southbank Ct CV8 . . . . 147 F4
Southbank Ho B CV34 . 161 D8
Southbank Rd
  Coventry CV6. . . . . 112 E5
  Cradley Heath B64. . . . . 82 F8
  Kenilworth CV8 . . . . . . 147 F4
South Bank Rd B64 . . . . 82 E8
Southbank View B70. . . . 60 E4
South Birmingham Coll
  (Bordesley Green Campus)
  B9 . . . . 67 E2
South Birmingham Coll
  (Digbeth Campus) B
  B5. . . . . 66 F1
Southborough Terr B
  CV31. . . . . 162 A6
Southbourne Ave
  Birmingham B34 . . . . . . 68 D6
  Walsall WS1. . . . . 28 B1
Southbourne Cl B29 . . . 86 A2
Southbourne Pl WS11 . . 1 D2
Southbourne Rd WV10 . 11 C3
South Bromsgrove High
  Tech & Lang Coll B60. . 150 F8
Southbrook Rd B Sutton
  Coldfield DY5 . . . . 46 C6
Southcote Gr B38. . . . . 103 D1
Southcott Ave DY5 . . . . 81 D8
Southcott Way CV2 . . . . 96 F1
South Cres
  Bromsgrove B60 . . . . . 137 A1
  Featherstone WV10. . . . . 12 C6
SOUTHCREST 153 E1
Southcrest Gdns B97. . . 153 D1
Southcrest Rd B98 . . . . 154 A2
Southcrest Wood Nature
  Reserve★ B98 . . . . 153 E1
Southcroft Rd B23 . . . . . 56 E3
South Dene B67 . . . . 64 F5
Southdown Ave B18. . . . 66 A6
Southdown Ct DY6 . . . . . 60 D6
South Dr
  Birmingham B5 . . . . 86 C4
  Coleshill B46 . . . . 70 E6
  Sutton Coldfield B75 . . . 46 C6
Southern Cl DY6 . . . . 60 F3
Southern Cross WS14 . . 9 C7
Southerndown Rd DY3 . 50 B7
Southern Dr B30 . . . . . . 104 D3
Southern Ho B13 . . . . . 105 A7
Southern Rd B8 . . . . 68 C6
Southern Way WS10 . . . 41 C3
Southey Cl
  B Solihull B91 . . . . 127 B8
  Willenhall WV12 . . . . 27 E8
Southfield Ave
  Birmingham, Castle Bromwich
    B36. . . . . 69 B8
  Birmingham, Edgbaston B16. 65 D3
Southfield Cl
  Aldridge WS9. . . . . 30 A6
  Nuneaton CV10 . . . . 73 D5

Southfield Dr
Birmingham B28 . . . . . . 106 A5
Kenilworth CV8 . . . . 148 A6
Southfield Gr WV3. . . . . 38 C7
Southfield Rd
Birmingham B16 . . . . 65 D3
Hinckley LE10 . . . . 75 E7
Wednesfield WV11 . . . . . 26 F5
Southfields CV32. . . . . . 157 A3
Southfields Prim Sch
CV1. . . . . 113 E3
Southfields Rd B91 . . . . 106 F1
Southfield Way WS6 . . . . 4 F7
Southgate
Cannock WS11. . . . . 4 B7
Cradley Heath B64. . . . . . 82 D8
Wolverhampton WV1. . . . 163 A3
Southgate Cl DY11. . . . . 116 A4
Southgate End WS11. . . . . 4 B7
Southgate Rd B44. . . . . . . 44 E2
Southgate Way 8 DY1 . . 51 B2
South Gdns WV4 . . . . 38 D5
South Gn WV4 . . . . 38 D5
South Gr
Birmingham, Aston B6. . . . 66 D8
Birmingham, Erdington B23. 56 F5
South Holme B9 . . . . 67 C2
Southlands CV31. . . . . . . 162 B7
Southlands Ct B97 . . . . . 153 C1
Southlands Rd B13. . . . . . 87 A1
Southlea Ave CV31. . . . . 161 E6
Southlea Cl CV31 . . . . . . 161 E6
Southleigh Ave CV5. . . . 132 F7
Southmead Cres B98. . . . 153 F3
Southmead Dr B60. . . . . 137 B6
Southmead Gdns B80. . . 159 E3
Southmead Way WS2. . . . 28 D4
Southminster Dr B14. . . 104 E6
South Moons Moat Ind Est
B98. . . . . 154 D4
South Oval DY3 . . . . 50 E5
South Par B72. . . . . 46 C4
South Park Mews DY5. . . 61 C2
Southport Cl CV3 . . . . . . 134 B5
South Range 4 B11. . . . . 87 B6
South Rd
Birmingham, Erdington
  B23. . . . . 56 F4
Birmingham, Hockley B18 . 66 A6
Birmingham, King's Heath
  B14. . . . . 104 E8
Birmingham, Northfield
  B31. . . . . 102 F2
Birmingham, Sparkbrook
  B11. . . . . 87 B7
Bromsgrove B60 . . . . 151 B7
Smethwick B67 . . . . 64 F5
Stourbridge DY8 . . . . 80 E4
Tipton DY4. . . . . 52 B8
West Hagley DY9 . . . . 99 A4
Wolverhampton WV4. . . . 39 F4
South Ridge CV5. . . . . . . 112 B4
South Road Ave B18 . . . . 66 A6
South Roundhay B33. . . . 69 A3
Southside Bsns Ctr B12 . 87 A5
South St
Birmingham B17 . . . . 85 D5
Brierley Hill DY5 . . . . 61 C2
Coventry CV1. . . . . 113 E3
3 Kidderminster DY10. . . 116 F6
Redditch B98 . . . . 153 E3
Walsall WS1. . . . . 42 D8
Willenhall WV13 . . . . 26 F1
Wolverhampton WV10 . . . 25 C6
South Staffordshire Coll
(Cannock Campus) WS11. 1 D1
South Staffordshire Coll
(Lichfield Campus) 10
WS13 . . . . 9 B7
South Staffordshire Coll
(Tamworth Campus)
B79. . . . . 21 B6
South Staffordshire Rly Wlk
Nature Reserve* WV4 . . 37 F2
South Street Gdns WS1 . . 42 D8
South Terr CV31. . . . . . . 162 B3
South View
Birmingham B43 . . . . 54 E7
Hampton Magna CV35. . . 160 A6
South View Cl
Codsall WV8. . . . . 10 B2
Featherstone WV10. . . . . 12 B6
South View Rd
Royal Leamington Spa
  CV32. . . . . 157 C5
Sedgley DY3. . . . . 50 C8
Southview Ridge DY5 . . . 81 D7
Southville Bglws for Old
People B14. . . . . 105 B4
Southwark Cl WS13 . . . . . 3 C3
Southway CV31. . . . . 162 A5
South Way B40 . . . . 90 F3
Southway Ct DY6 . . . . 60 F4
Southwell Wlk B70. . . . . . 53 C2
Southwick Dr B77. . . . . . . 21 C3
Southwick Pl WV14 . . . . . 40 D7
Southwick Rd B62 . . . . . . 83 D8
South Wlk B31. . . . . 103 C1
Southwold Ave B30 . . . . 104 C3
South Wolverhampton &
Bilston Acad
Bilston WV14 . . . . 40 D5
Wolverhampton WV4. . . . 39 E5
Southwood Ave B34. . . . . 69 B7

Southwood Cl DY6 . . . . . . 60 E5
Southwood Covert B14. . 104 C2
SOUTH YARDLEY 88 D6
Sovereign Cl CV8 . . . . . . 147 F1
Sovereign Ct 7 B1 . . . . . 66 C3
Sovereign Dr DY1. . . . . . . 50 E2
Sovereign Hts B31 . . . . . 102 C1
Sovereign Rd
Birmingham B30 . . . . 104 A4
Coventry CV5. . . . . 113 A4
Sovereign Row CV5. . . . 113 A2
Sovereign Way B13 . . . . . 86 F4
Sovereign Wlk 7 WS1 . . 28 F2
Sovereign Works DY1 . . . 50 E4
Sowerby March B24. . . . . 57 D4
Sowers Cl WV12 . . . . 27 D5
Sowers Ct B75. . . . . 32 D4
Sowers Gdns WV12 . . . . . 27 D5
Sowe Valley Prim Sch
  CV3. . . . . 134 D7
Spa Cl LE10. . . . . 71 E1
SPADE GREEN 8 A8
Spadesbourne Rd B60. . 137 C6
Spa Gr B30 . . . . 104 C8
Spa La LE10 . . . . 71 E1
SPARKBROOK. 87 B7
Sparkbrook St CV1. . . . . 113 F3
Sparkbrook Workshops
  CV1. . . . . 113 F3
SPARKHILL 87 D4
Spark St B11. . . . . 87 A7
Sparrey Dr B30 . . . . 104 A8
Sparrow Cl WS10 . . . . 42 B5
Sparrow Cock La B93 . . 129 C1
Sparrowhawk Way WS11 . 5 A8
Spartan Cl CV34 . . . . . . 161 C4
Spartan Ind Est B70. . . . . 52 E6
Spa View CV31. . . . . 162 B4
Speakers Cl B69 . . . . 63 B7
Spearhill WS14 . . . . 9 E8
Speed Rd DY4 . . . . 51 E7
Speedway La CV8 . . . . . . 135 F7
Speedwell Cl
Aldridge WS9. . . . . 30 A5
6 Bedworth CV12 . . . . . . 77 D2
Birmingham B25. . . . . 88 A6
Wednesfield WV11 . . . . . 26 E5
Speedwell Dr CV7. . . . . . 130 A6
Speedwell Gdns
Brierley Hill DY5. . . . . 81 B6
Featherstone WV10. . . . . 12 B8
Speedwell Ho B30 . . . . . 104 A1
Speedwell Rd
Birmingham, Balsall Heath
  B5. . . . . 86 D6
Birmingham, Tyseley B25. . 88 A6
Speedwell Trad Est B11 . 88 A6
Speedy Cl WS11 . . . . 1 E5
Spencer Ave
Coventry CV5. . . . . 113 A1
Tipton WV14 . . . . 51 C8
Spencer Cl
Birmingham B24 . . . . 57 D4
Dudley DY3 . . . . 50 A4
Oldbury B69. . . . . 63 B8
5 West Bromwich B71. . . 53 F8
Spencer Dr WS7 . . . . 6 E8
SPENCER PARK. 165 A1
Spencer Rd
Coventry CV5. . . . . 165 A1
Lichfield WS14. . . . . 9 B6
Spencer's La CV7 . . . . . . 110 E1
Spencer St
Birmingham B18 . . . . 66 C4
Hinckley LE10 . . . . 71 D1
2 Kidderminster DY11. . 116 C4
Royal Leamington Spa
  CV31. . . . . 161 F7
Spencer Yd CV31. . . . . . . 161 F7
SPENNELLS. 117 A2
Spennells Valley Nature
Reserve* DY10 . . . . 117 A3
Spennells Valley Rd
  DY10 . . . . 117 A3
Spenser Ave WV6. . . . . . . 23 F4
Spenser Cl B79. . . . . 21 A6
Spenser Wlk B61 . . . . . . 137 A8
SPERNAL ASH. 159 F1
Spernal Ash B80 . . . . . . 159 F1
Spernal La B80 . . . . 159 F1
Spernall Gr B29. . . . . 85 A1
Spetchley Cl B97. . . . . . 158 C6
Spey Cl B5 . . . . 86 D6
Sphinx Dr CV3 . . . . 114 B1
Spiceland Rd B31. . . . . . 102 F6
Spiers Cl B93. . . . . 128 A6
Spies Cl B62. . . . . 83 B6
Spies La B62. . . . . 83 F5
Spills Mdw DY3 . . . . 50 E5
Spilsbury Cl CV32. . . . . . 156 E2
Spilsbury Croft B91. . . . 127 A8
Spindle La B90 . . . . 126 A6
Spindles The CV8. . . . . . 113 D6
Spindles The
Hinckley LE10 . . . . 75 F5
Walsall WS6. . . . . 4 F1
Spindle Tree Rise WV12. . 27 D4
Spindlewood Cl WV12. . 2 D1
Spinners End Dr B64. . . . 62 D1
Spinners End Ind Est B64 82 D8
Spinney Cl
Binley Woods CV3 . . . . . 135 E7
Birmingham B31 . . . . 103 B3
Kidderminster DY11. . . . 116 A7
Norton Canes WS11 . . . . . 5 F7
Polesworth B78. . . . . 36 F8
Stourbridge DY8 . . . . 60 C3
Walsall WS3. . . . . 15 A2

Spinney Dr B90 . . . . 126 D4
Spinney Farm Rd WS11. . . 4 B7
Spinney Hill CV34 . . . . . 156 A1
Spinney La CV10 . . . . 72 C4
Spinney Mews B97. . . . . 153 C1
Spinney Rd LE10 . . . . 75 C6
Spinney The
Birmingham B15 . . . . 85 E5
Birmingham, Brown's Green
  B20 . . . . 54 F3
Coventry CV4. . . . . 132 D3
Dudley DY3 . . . . 50 C2
Royal Leamington Spa
  CV32. . . . . 156 D1
Solihull B91. . . . . 127 C8
Sutton Coldfield B74. . . . 31 B6
Wolverhampton WV3. . . . 24 D1
Wythall B47. . . . . 125 B4
Spinning School La B79. . 21 B5
Spiral Cl B62 . . . . 83 E8
Spiral Ct
Birmingham B24 . . . . 56 E2
Dudley DY3 . . . . 50 D3
Stourbridge DY8 . . . . 81 A4
Sutton Coldfield B76. . . . 46 F3
Wednesfield WV11 . . . . . 26 E7
Spiral Gn B24. . . . . 57 C4
Spirehouse La B60. . . . . 137 E5
Spires The
Lichfield WS14. . . . . 9 E6
Nuneaton CV10 . . . . 72 C4
Spires View B61 . . . . 136 F3
Spitfire Cl CV5. . . . . 112 C1
Spitfire Pk B24 . . . . 57 C2
Spitfire Rd B24 . . . . 57 D2
Spitfire Way B35. . . . . 58 A2
Splash La WS12. . . . . 2 F2
Spode Pl WS11 . . . . 2 B2
Spondon Gr B34 . . . . 69 C5
Spondon Rd WV11 . . . . . 26 E8
SPON END 113 A3
Spon End CV1, CV5 . . . . 113 A3
Spon Gate Ho CV1. . . . . 113 A2
Spon Gate Prim Sch
  CV1. . . . . 113 A3
Spon La B70. . . . . 53 D1
Spon Lane Ind Est B66 . . 64 D8
Spon Lane S B70. . . . . . . 53 D1
Spon Lane Trad Est B70 . 53 D2
Spon St CV1. . . . . 165 A3
Spoon Dr B38. . . . . 103 D2
Spooner Croft B5 . . . . . . 86 E8
Spooners B92. . . . . 107 F7
Sporting Edge Ind Sch
  B19 . . . . 66 D5
Spouthouse La B43 . . . . . 54 F7
Spout La WS1 . . . . 42 E7
Spreadbury Cl B17. . . . . . 84 F8
Sprig Croft B36 . . . . 68 C8
Spring Ave B65 . . . . 63 D2
Springavon Croft B17. . . 85 B6
SPRING BANK. 27 B8
Springbank B9. . . . . 68 A3
Springbank Rd B15 . . . . . 86 D7
Springbrook Cl B36 . . . . . 58 D1
Springbrook La B94. . . . 142 A7
Spring Cl
6 Coventry CV5 . . . . 113 E3
Solihull B91. . . . . 106 F3
Walsall WS4. . . . . 15 C2
West Hagley DY9 . . . . 99 A6
Spring Coppice Dr B93 . 128 A3
Spring Cres B64 . . . . 82 F7
Springcroft Rd B11 . . . . . 87 F2
Spring Ct
Walsall WS1. . . . . 43 A8
West Bromwich B70 . . . . . 53 D2
Springdale Ct CV11 . . . . . 73 D3
Springdale Jun & Inf Scns
  WV4 . . . . 38 D5
SPRINGFIELD
Bedworth. 78 C2
Birmingham 105 E8
Rowley Regis. 62 F5
Wolverhampton 25 E3
Springfield B23. . . . . 56 E3
Springfield Ave
6 Birmingham B12. . . . . . 87 A6
Bromsgrove B60 . . . . 151 A8
Sedgley DY3. . . . . 39 E1
Stourbridge DY9 . . . . 81 E4
Springfield Cl B65 . . . . . . 63 A5
Springfield Cres
Bedworth CV12 . . . . 78 B2
Dudley DY2 . . . . 62 F8
Solihull B92 . . . . 89 C3
Sutton Coldfield B76. . . . 47 A4
West Bromwich B70 . . . . . 53 E1
Springfield Ct
Birmingham B28 . . . . 105 F8
Sutton Coldfield B75. . . . 47 C5
Wolverhampton WV10 . . . 11 D4
Springfield Dr
Birmingham B14. . . . . 86 E1
Halesowen B62. . . . . 83 D7
Springfield Gn DY3 . . . . . 39 E1
Springfield Ho DY10 . . . . 116 F6
Springfield House Sch
  B93 . . . . 129 A5
Springfield Ind Est B69. . 64 B7
Springfield La
Kidderminster DY10 . . . . 116 F8
Rowley Regis B65, DY2. . 62 F5
Wolverhampton WV10 . . . 11 D4
Springfield Mill CV31. . . 161 E6
Springfield Pk LE10 . . . . . 71 A3
Springfield Pl CV1 . . . . . 165 C4

Springfield Prim Sch
Birmingham B13 . . . . 87 D2
Rowley Regis B65 . . . . . . 63 A4
Springfield Rd
Bilston WV14 . . . . 40 E7
Birmingham, Castle Bromwich
  B36 . . . . 69 D8
Birmingham, King's Heath
  B14 . . . . 104 F8
Birmingham, Moseley B13. . 87 D2
Coventry CV1. . . . . 165 C4
Halesowen B62 . . . . 83 D7
Hinckley LE10 . . . . 75 D7
Nuneaton CV11 . . . . 73 E2
Oldbury B68. . . . . 64 C4
Sutton Coldfield B75, B76 . 47 A4
Tamworth B77 . . . . 35 D8
Wolverhampton WV10. . . 25 E3
Springfield Rise WS12. . . 2 C6
Springfields
Coleshill B46. . . . . 70 F5
Walsall WS4. . . . . 29 C6
Springfields Rd DY5. . . . . 61 B2
Springfield St B18 . . . . . . 66 A3
Springfield Terr B65 . . . . 62 F5
Spring Gdns
Birmingham B21 . . . . 65 F7
4 Dudley DY2 . . . . 62 D8
Smethwick B66 . . . . 64 E6
Spring Gr B19. . . . . 66 B6
Spring Grove Cres DY11 . 116 A3
Spring Grove Gdns B18 . . 65 F6
Spring Grove Rd DY11. . 116 B3
Spring Head WV10 . . . . . 41 F2
SPRINGHILL. 16 E8
SPRING HILL 38 C4
Springhill CV10. . . . . 72 A8
Spring Hill
Birmingham, Erdington
  B24 . . . . 56 F3
Birmingham, Hockley B18 . 66 A4
Springhill Ave WV4 . . . . . 38 C4
Springhill Cl
Walsall WS4. . . . . 15 D1
Willenhall WV12 . . . . 27 D7
Springhill Gdns B97. . . . 152 F2
Springhill Gr WV4. . . . . . 38 C4
Spring Hill Ind Est B18. . . 66 A4
Springhill La WV4. . . . . . . 38 B4
Springhill Pas B18 . . . . . . 66 A3
Springhill Pk WV4 . . . . . . 38 B4
Springhill Prim Sch WS7 . 7 B6
Springhill Rd
Brownhills WS8 . . . . 16 A7
Burntwood WS7. . . . . 7 A6
Walsall WS1. . . . . 28 F1
Wednesfield WV11 . . . . . 26 E7
Spring Hill Rd CV10 . . . . . 72 C6
Spring La
Birmingham B24 . . . . 57 A3
Hockley Heath B94 . . . . . 143 B5
Kenilworth CV8 . . . . 148 A5
Lapworth B94 . . . . 143 D3
Radford Semele CV31 . . 162 E5
Romsley B62 . . . . 100 D4
Walsall WS4. . . . . 15 C2
Willenhall WV12 . . . . 27 C4
Spring Mdw
Cheslyn Hay WS6. . . . . 4 D1
3 Cradley Heath B64 . . . . 62 F1
Halesowen B63 . . . . 82 F2
Tipton DY4 . . . . 52 A8
Springmeadow Gr B19 . . . 66 D6
Springmeadow Rd B15. . . 86 D7
Spring Meadow Rd DY2 . . 62 B6
Spring Meadows Cl WV8 . 10 B4
Spring Parklands DY1. . . . 62 A8
Spring Pool CV34 . . . . . . 160 E7
Spring Rd
Barnacle CV7 . . . . 97 B6
Birmingham, Balsall Heath
  B15 . . . . 86 D8
Birmingham, Tyseley B11. . 87 F3
Coventry CV6. . . . . 95 F1
Dudley DY2 . . . . 62 D6
Lichfield WS13. . . . . 3 D2
Smethwick B66 . . . . 64 D8
Walsall WS4. . . . . 15 D1
Wolverhampton WV4. . . . 38 D6
Spring Road Ind Est WV4 . 40 A4
Spring Road Sta B11. . . . . 88 A2
Springs Ave B61. . . . . . . 121 A1
Springside B98. . . . . 159 C8
Springsdale Dr B24. . . . . 57 D3
SPRINGS MIRE 62 A8
Spring St
Birmingham B15 . . . . 86 D8
Cannock WS11. . . . . 4 E8
Halesowen B63 . . . . 82 D6
Stourbridge DY9 . . . . 81 E4
Tipton DY4 . . . . 52 C8
Springs The B61 . . . . 63 A1
Spring Terr WS7 . . . . 6 E5
Springthorpe Gn B24. . . . 57 C4
Springthorpe Rd
Birmingham, Pype Hayes
  B24 . . . . 57 C4
Birmingham, Tyburn B24. . 57 D3
SPRING VALE
Bilston. 40 B4
Birmingham 67 B1
Springvale Ave
Bilston WV14 . . . . 40 B4
Walsall WS5. . . . . 43 C7
Springvale Bsns Pk WV14 . 40 B4
Spring Vale Cl WV14 . . . . 40 A1

Springvale Dr B97 . . . . . 152 F3
Spring Vale Ind Pk WV14 . 40 C5
Spring Vale Island WV14 . 40 C4
Spring Vale Prim Sch
  WV4 . . . . 39 E4
Springvale Rd B97 . . . . . 152 F2
Spring Vale Rd B65 . . . . . 63 A5
Springvale St WV13 . . . . . 27 B3
Springvale Way WV14 . . . 40 C4
Springwell Rd CV31. . . . 162 D6
Spring Wlk
Halesowen B63 . . . . 82 D1
Oldbury B69. . . . . 64 A5
Walsall WS2. . . . . 28 B3
Sproat Ave WS10 . . . . . . 41 C5
Spruce B77. . . . . 22 B4
Spruce Gr
Birmingham B24 . . . . 57 B2
4 Royal Leamington Spa
  CV31. . . . . 161 F5
Spruce Rd
3 Coventry CV2 . . . . 96 B2
Nuneaton CV10 . . . . 72 E7
Walsall WS5. . . . . 43 B3
Spruces The DY9 . . . . 98 F4
Spruce Way WV3 . . . . 24 D1
Spur Tree Ave WV3 . . . . . 24 A1
Squadron Cl B35. . . . . . . 58 C4
Square Cl B32 . . . . 84 C3
Square The
Aldridge WS9. . . . . 30 B6
Alvechurch B48 . . . . 139 B6
Birmingham B17 . . . . 85 B7
3 Birmingham B17. . . . . . 85 C5
Birmingham, Ladywood
  B15 . . . . 66 B1
Brierley Hill DY2 . . . . 61 F6
Coventry CV2. . . . . 115 A7
Fazeley B78. . . . . 35 A8
Kenilworth CV8 . . . . 147 F4
Nuneaton CV11 . . . . 73 E2
Solihull B91. . . . . 107 C3
Tipton DY4 . . . . 52 D7
Willenhall WV12 . . . . 27 D8
Wolverhampton WV2. . . . 163 C1
Squires Croft
Coventry CV2. . . . . 96 F1
Sutton Coldfield B76. . . . 47 A2
Squires Ct DY5 . . . . 81 C8
Squires Gate WV13 . . . 7 B8
Squires Gate Wlk B35. . . 58 A3
Squires Gn LE10 . . . . 75 F6
Squires Way CV4. . . . . . 132 D6
Squires Wlk 7 WS10. . . 41 F3
Squirhill Pl 1 CV31 . . . . 162 B7
Squirrel Cl
Cannock WS12. . . . . 1 C6
Huntington WS12. . . . . 1 D6
Squirrel Hollow B76. . . . . 47 A2
Squirrels Hollow B68 . . . . 84 D7
Squirrels The WS14 . . . . . 9 C7
Squirrel Wlk
Sutton Coldfield B74 . . . . 31 C5
Wolverhampton WV4. . . . 39 A5
Stable Croft B71. . . . . 53 F7
Stable Ct DY3 . . . . 50 E6
Stableford Cl
Birmingham B32 . . . . 84 F3
Redditch B97 . . . . 158 D7
Stables The
Berkswell CV7 . . . . 110 C4
Birmingham B29 . . . . 86 A2
Hinckley LE10 . . . . 75 D5
Royal Leamington Spa
  CV32. . . . . 156 C1
Stable Way B60. . . . . 150 E6
Stable Wlk CV11 . . . . 73 F2
Stablewood Gr WS1. . . . . 43 A7
Stacey Cl B64. . . . . 62 E1
Stacey Dr B13 . . . . 105 A5
Stacey Grange Gdns
  B45. . . . . 122 A6
Stackhouse Cl WS9 . . . . . 16 A4
Stackhouse Dr WS3 . . . . . 15 A4
Stadium Cl
Coventry CV6. . . . . 95 D2
Kidderminster DY10. . . . 116 F4
Willenhall WV13 . . . . 27 B3
Stadium Dr B64. . . . . 62 C1
Stafford Cl
Bulkington CV12 . . . . 79 C2
Walsall WS3. . . . . 14 B2
Stafford Ct B43 . . . . 54 E7
Stafford Ct WV10 . . . . 11 C5
Stafford Dr B71. . . . . 53 B6
Stafford Ho B33 . . . . 69 E2
Stafford La WS12 . . . . 2 B5
Stafford Rd
Birmingham B21 . . . . 65 F6
Cannock WS11. . . . . 1 D1
Coven Heath WV10 . . . . . 11 D4
Darlaston WS10. . . . . 41 C6
Huntington WS11, WV11 . . 1 C5
Walsall WS3. . . . . 14 B4
Staffordshire Pool Cl 2
  B6 . . . . 55 F1
Stafford St
Birmingham WV14 . . . . . . 40 D5
Birmingham B5. . . . . 164 D3
Cannock WS12. . . . . 2 E3
Dudley DY1. . . . . 51 B3
Walsall WS2. . . . . 28 E2
Wednesfield WV11 . . . . . 26 A5
Willenhall WV13 . . . . 27 A1
Wolverhampton WV1. . . . 163 C4
Stafford Way B43 . . . . 54 E7

Staff Way B23 . . . . 56 E4
Stagborough Way WS12 . . . 2 B4
Stag Cres
　Norton Canes WS11 . . . . . . 6 A6
　Walsall WS3 . . . . 28 E6
Stag Dr WS12 . . . . 1 C6
Stag Hill Rd WS3 . . . . 28 E7
Stag Ind Est
　Bilston WV14 . . . . 40 F4
　Coventry CV6 . . . . 113 D8
Stag Rd B B16 . . . . 65 C3
Stag Wlk B76 . . . . 57 D7
Staines Cl CV11 . . . . 73 F7
Stainforth Cl CV11 . . . . . . 74 A2
Stainsby Ave B19 . . . . 66 C5
Stainsby Croft B90 . . . . . 127 B5
Staircase La CV5 . . . . 112 C7
STAKENBRIDGE 98 E3
Stakenbridge La DY10 . . . 98 D4
Staley Croft WS12 . . . . 1 C4
Stallard Cl B97 . . . . 153 C5
Stalling's La DY6 . . . . 60 D8
STAMBERMILL 81 C6
Stambermill Cl DY9 . . . . . 81 D6
Stambermill Ho DY9 . . . . . 81 E5
Stambermill Ind Est DY9 . 81 D6
Stamford Ave CV4 . . . . . . 133 C6
Stamford Cres WS7 . . . . 7 A8
Stamford Croft B91 . . . . . 107 B2
Stamford Gdns CV32 . . . . 156 E1
Stamford Rd B20 . . . . 55 C1
Stamford Rd
　Birmingham B20 . . . . 55 C1
　Brierley Hill DY5 . . . . 81 C6
　Stourbridge DY8 . . . . 80 F7
Stamford Way WS9 . . . . . . 16 C1
Stampings The CV6 . . . . . 113 F8
Stanbrook Rd B90 . . . . . . 127 A5
Stanbury Ave WS10 . . . . . 41 B6
Stanbury Rd B14 . . . . 105 B4
Stancroft Ct CV4 . . . . 89 A8
Standard Ave CV4 . . . . . . 112 B1
Standard Way B24 . . . . . . 67 F8
Standbridge Way DY4 . . . . 52 A5
Standedge B77 . . . . 36 B7
Standhills Rd DY6 . . . . 60 E6
Standish Cl CV2 . . . . 114 E2
Standlake Ave B36 . . . . . . 68 D7
Standlake Mews [14]
　CV31 . . . . 162 C6
Standleys Twr B23 . . . . . . 57 A6
Stand St CV34 . . . . 160 D5
Stanford Rd
　Birmingham B32 . . . . 84 E6
　Birmingham, Pheasey B43. . 44 D5
Stanford Ave B42 . . . . 55 A7
Stanford Cl B97 . . . . 158 D6
Stanford Dr B65 . . . . 63 B4
Stanford Gr B63 . . . . 82 C1
Stanford Rd WV2 . . . . 163 B1
Stanford Way B B69 . . . . . 63 E4
Stanhope Cl DY5 . . . . 81 D8
Stanhope Ho B79 . . . . 21 A4
Stanhope Rd B67 . . . . 64 F3
Stanhope St
　Birmingham B12 . . . . 86 F7
　Dudley DY2 . . . . 62 E4
　Wolverhampton WV3 . . . . 163 A2
Stanhope Way
　Birmingham B43 . . . . 44 E4
　Birmingham B46 . . . . 59 F1
Stanhurst Way B71 . . . . . . 43 A2
Stanier Ave CV1 . . . . 113 B4
Stanier Cl WS4 . . . . 29 B7
Stanier Gr B20 . . . . 55 B2
Staniforth St B4 . . . . 164 C4
STANKLYN 117 D2
Stanklyn La DY10 . . . . . . 117 C1
Stanley Ave
　Birmingham B32 . . . . 84 C7
　Solihull B90 . . . . 106 B4
　Sutton Coldfield B75 . . . . 46 F4
Stanley Bsns Pk WS7 . . . . . 7 B6
Stanley Cl
　Birmingham B28 . . . . 106 A5
　Redditch B98 . . . . 154 A5
　Wednesfield WV11 . . . . . 26 F8
Stanley Ct
　[9] Birmingham B13 . . . . . 87 B2
　Perton WV6 . . . . 23 E4
　Royal Leamington Spa
　　CV31 . . . . 162 C2
Stanley Gr [2] B11 . . . . . . 87 B6
Stanley Pl
　Bilston WV14 . . . . 40 B5
　Birmingham B13 . . . . 86 F3
　Walsall WS4 . . . . 29 B6
Stanley Rd
　Birmingham B68 . . . . 84 C7
　Birmingham, King's Heath
　　B14 . . . . 104 C1
　Birmingham, Nechells B7 . . 67 C7
　Cannock WS12 . . . . 2 B6
　Coventry CV5 . . . . 132 E8
　Darlaston WS10 . . . . 41 D5
　Hinckley LE10 . . . . 71 C2
　Nuneaton CV11 . . . . 73 A5
　Stourbridge DY8 . . . . 80 F3
　Walsall WS4 . . . . 29 B6
　West Bromwich B71 . . . . . 53 E7
　Wolverhampton WV10 . . . 11 D1
Stanley St WS3 . . . . 14 D1
Stanmore Gr B62 . . . . 84 A3
Stanmore Rd B16 . . . . 65 C1
Stansbury Ho [3] WS2 . . . . 42 C8
Stansfield Gr CV8 . . . . . . 148 D4
Stanton Ave DY1 . . . . 51 A6

Stanton Bridge Prim Sch
　CV6 . . . . 113 F6
Stanton Gr
　Birmingham B26 . . . . 88 F8
　Solihull B90 . . . . 106 A4
　Tipton DY4 . . . . 52 A5
Stanton Ho [2] B71 . . . . . 42 F1
Stanton Rd
　Birmingham B43 . . . . 54 D8
　Royal Leamington Spa
　　CV31 . . . . 162 C6
　Solihull B90 . . . . 106 A4
　Wolverhampton WV1 . . . . 25 F2
Stanton Wlk CV34 . . . . . . 155 D1
Stanville Prim Sch B26. . . 89 C6
Stanville Rd B26 . . . . 89 C6
Stanway Gdns B71 . . . . . . 53 D6
Stanway Gr B44. . . . . 44 F3
Stanway Rd
　Coventry CV5 . . . . 133 A8
　Solihull B90 . . . . 106 C4
　West Bromwich B71 . . . . . 53 D6
Stanwell Gr B23 . . . . 56 E6
Stanwick Ave B33. . . . . . . 69 E3
Stan Williams Ct CV11. . . 73 D4
Stapenhall Rd B90 . . . . . 127 A5
Staple Flat B60 . . . . 137 C8
Staplehurst Croft B14. . . 104 C2
Stapleford Gdns WS7 . . . . . 7 D6
Stapleford Gr DY8 . . . . . . 60 E2
Staple Hall Rd B31 . . . . . 103 B2
STAPLE HILL 137 C8
Staplehurst Rd B28 . . . . . 105 F8
Staple Lodge Rd B31 . . . . 103 C2
Staples Cl CV12 . . . . 79 C3
Stapleton Cl
　Redditch B98 . . . . 154 D3
　Studley B80 . . . . 159 D3
　Sutton Coldfield B76 . . . . 58 B6
Stapleton Dr B37 . . . . 70 A4
Stapleton La
　Barwell LE9 . . . . 71 F8
　Hinckley CV13 . . . . 71 A8
Stapleton Rd
　Aldridge WS9 . . . . 29 F5
　Studley B80 . . . . 159 D4
Stapylton Ave B17 . . . . . . 85 B5
Stapylton Ct [5] B17 . . . . . 85 B5
Starbank Prim Sch B10 . . 88 A8
Starbank Rd B10 . . . . 88 A8
Starbold Cres B93 . . . . . 128 B5
Starbold Ct B93 . . . . 128 A6
Star City B7 . . . . 67 D8
Star Cl
　Tipton DY4 . . . . 52 C5
　Willenhall WS2 . . . . 27 F4
Starcrest Ind Est DY5 . . . 61 F1
Starcross Cl CV2 . . . . 114 C7
Starcross Rd B27 . . . . 88 C2
Star Ct B91 . . . . 107 D6
Stare Gn CV4 . . . . 132 D5
Stareton Cl CV4 . . . . 132 E6
Star Hill B15 . . . . 86 B8
Star Ind Pk CV2 . . . . 114 F5
Starkey Croft B37 . . . . . . 70 D2
Starkie Dr B68 . . . . 64 C4
Starley Ct CV3 . . . . 135 A7
Starley Pk CV7 . . . . 96 B8
Starley Rd CV1 . . . . 165 B2
Starley Way B37 . . . . 90 C6
Starling Cl WV10 . . . . 11 B3
Starling Gr B36 . . . . 70 A7
Star St
　Stourbridge DY9 . . . . 81 F5
　Wolverhampton WV3 . . . . 38 E8
Startin Cl CV7 . . . . 95 F7
Startpoint Trad Est B11. . . 87 D4
Statham Dr B16 . . . . 65 C2
Station App
　Barnt Green B45 . . . . 138 D8
　Dorridge B93 . . . . 127 F2
　Kidderminster DY10. . . . . 116 F5
　Lichfield WS13 . . . . 9 F8
　Royal Leamington Spa
　　CV31 . . . . 161 F7
　Solihull B91 . . . . 107 A4
　Sutton Coldfield B74 . . . . 31 F6
Station Ave
　Birmingham B16 . . . . 65 C1
　Coventry CV4 . . . . 131 D8
　Warwick CV34 . . . . 160 F8
Station Bldgs B46. . . . . . . 59 B3
Station Cl WS10 . . . . 33 B8
Station Cotts
　Blackwell B60 . . . . 138 A4
　Shenstone WS14 . . . . 17 F6
Station Ct WS11. . . . . 4 F8
Station Dr
　Blakedown DY10 . . . . 98 C2
　Brierley Hill, Quarry Bank
　　DY5 . . . . 61 E2
　Brierley Hill, Silver End DY5 . 61 D3
　Earlswood B94 . . . . 125 D1
　Solihull B92 . . . . 88 E1
　Sutton Coldfield B74 . . . . 46 B8
　Tipton DY4 . . . . 52 B4
　West Hagley DY9. . . . . . . 99 A6
Stationfields Park Homes
　B79 . . . . 21 C5
Station La B94. . . . . 144 D3
Station Link Rd B26. . . . . 90 D4
Station Pl WS3 . . . . 28 B8
Station Rd
　Aldridge WS9 . . . . 30 A5
　Alvechurch B48 . . . . 139 A5
　Balsall Common CV7 . . . . 130 B7

Station Rd continued
　Bilston WV14 . . . . 40 E5
Birmingham, Acock's Green
　B27 . . . . 88 C3
Birmingham, Aston B6 . . . . 55 F1
Birmingham, B17 . . . . 85 C6
Birmingham, Erdington B23 . 56 C5
Birmingham, Handsworth
　B21. . . . . 65 C8
Birmingham, King's Heath
　B14 . . . . 86 E1
Birmingham, King's Norton
　B30 . . . . 103 E4
Birmingham, Marston Green
　B37 . . . . 90 A8
Birmingham, Northfield
　B31 . . . . 103 A2
Birmingham, Stechford B33 . 68 E3
　Blackwell B60 . . . . 138 A5
　Brierley Hill DY5 . . . . 61 C3
　Cannock WS12 . . . . 2 C6
　Coleshill B46 . . . . 59 F1
Cradley Heath, Haden Cross
　B64 . . . . 82 E8
　Dorridge B93 . . . . 128 B4
　Great Wyrley WS6. . . . . . . 4 F4
　Hammerwich WS7 . . . . 7 E3
　Hampton-in-A B92 . . . . . 109 B7
　Hinckley LE10 . . . . 75 D8
　Kenilworth CV8 . . . . 147 F4
　Lichfield WS13 . . . . 9 C7
　Oldbury B69 . . . . 64 A5
　Rowley Regis B65 . . . . . . 63 D2
　Shenstone WS14 . . . . 17 F6
　Solihull B91 . . . . 107 B4
　Stourbridge DY9 . . . . 81 B4
　Studley B80 . . . . 159 D4
　Sutton Coldfield B73 . . . . 46 A1
　Walsall, Rushall WS4. . . . 29 A7
　Walsall WS3 . . . . 15 A3
　Warwick CV34 . . . . 160 F7
　West Hagley DY9 . . . . 99 A6
　Wombourne WV5. . . . . . . 49 A8
　Wythall B47 . . . . 125 B3
Station Road Ind Est
　Birmingham B46 . . . . 59 F2
　Rowley Regis B65 . . . . . . 63 D2
Station Sq CV1. . . . . 165 B1
Station St
　Birmingham B5 . . . . 164 B2
　Bromsgrove B60 . . . . 136 F1
　Cheslyn Hay WS6. . . . . 4 E3
　Cradley Heath B64. . . . . . 82 C8
　Darlaston WS10 . . . . 41 F7
　Sutton Coldfield B73 . . . . 46 C5
　Tipton DY4 . . . . 52 B5
　Walsall, Blakenall Heath
　　WS3 . . . . 28 B8
　Walsall WS2. . . . . 28 E1
Station Street E CV6. . . . 113 E7
Station Street W CV6. . . . 113 F7
Station Street West Bsns Pk
　CV6 . . . . 113 D7
Station Villas WS10 . . . . . 41 F6
Station Way B47 . . . . 153 D3
Staulton Gn [5] B69 . . . . . 63 E4
Staunton Rd CV31. . . . . . 162 A5
Staveley Rd
　Birmingham B14 . . . . . . 104 D6
　Wolverhampton WV1 . . . . 25 C4
Staverton Cl CV5. . . . . . . 112 A3
Stead Cl
　Walsall WS2. . . . . 28 C5
　Wednesbury DY4 . . . . 41 B1
Steadman Croft DY4 . . . . 52 D8
STECHFORD 68 E3
Stechford Cascades B33 . 68 E3
Stechford La B8 . . . . 68 D5
Stechford Prim Sch B33. . 68 D2
Stechford Rd B34 . . . . 68 E5
Stechford Ret Pk B33 . . . . 68 E4
Stechford Sta B33 . . . . . . 68 D3
Stechford Trad Est B33 . . 68 E3
Steel Bright Rd B66 . . . . . 65 C6
Steel Cl B60 . . . . 151 A6
Steel Dr WV10 . . . . 25 D8
Steel Gr B25. . . . . 88 C7
Steelhouse La
　Birmingham B4 . . . . 164 C3
　Wolverhampton WV2 . . . . 39 E8
Steelmans Rd WS10. . . . . 41 F7
Steelpark Rd B62 . . . . 83 C7
Steelpark Way WV11 . . . . 26 E4
Steel Rdbt WS10 . . . . 41 E2
Steene Gr B31. . . . . 102 D3
Steeplefield Rd CV6. . . . . 113 A5
Steeple Gn DY8 . . . . 81 A3
Steepwood Croft B30 . . . 103 D4
Steere Ave B77 . . . . 21 C7
Steetley Ind Est WS14 . . . 51 C7
Stella Croft B37 . . . . 70 C2
Stella Gr B43 . . . . 54 C8
Stella Rd DY4 . . . . 52 A6
Stencils Dr WS4 . . . . 29 B3
Stencils Rd WS4 . . . . 29 B4
Stennels Ave B62 . . . . 83 E4
Stennels Cl CV6. . . . . 112 F8
Stennels Cres B62 . . . . . . 83 E4
Stephanie Gr B77 . . . . . . 22 B5
Stephens Cl WV11 . . . . . . 26 F8
Stephens Ct DY4 . . . . 52 A6
Stephens Ind Est B11 . . . 87 F4
Stephenson Ave WS2 . . . . 28 B5
Stephenson Cl
　Royal Leamington Spa
　　CV32 . . . . 156 C1

Stephenson Cl continued
　Tamworth B77. . . . . 22 A2
Stephenson Dr
　Birmingham B37 . . . . 70 B2
　Perton WV6 . . . . 23 E5
Stephenson Pl B2. . . . . . . 164 C2
Stephenson Rd
　Bedworth CV7 . . . . 96 C7
　Hinckley LE10 . . . . 74 E7
Stephenson Sq WS2 . . . . . 28 B5
Stephenson St
　Birmingham B2 . . . . 164 B2
　Wolverhampton WV3 . . . . 163 A2
Stephenson Way WS12 . . . . 2 B5
Stephens Rd B76 . . . . 47 A4
Stephens Wlk WS13. . . . . . 3 A2
Stepney Rd CV2. . . . . 114 A4
Stepping Stone Cl WS2. . . 27 F4
Stepping Stones B91. . . . . 31 B5
Stepping Stones Rd CV5. 112 F4
Steppingstone St DY1 . . . 51 B1
Sterling Pk
　Brierley Hill DY5 . . . . 61 F4
　Hinckley LE10 . . . . 74 D8
Sterling Way CV11. . . . . . 78 E8
Sterndale Rd B42 . . . . 55 C6
Stevenage Wlk [2] CV2 . . 115 A7
Steven Dr WV14 . . . . 40 E1
Stevens Ave B32 . . . . 84 D2
Stevens Dr WS12 . . . . 2 D6
Stevens Gate WV2 . . . . . 163 B1
Stevens Ho CV1. . . . . 165 C4
Stevenson Ave B98. . . . . . 153 F3
Stevenson Rd
　Coventry CV6. . . . . 113 A8
　Tamworth B79 . . . . 21 A6
Stevenson Wlk WS14. . . . . 9 B6
Stevens Rd DY9 . . . . 81 D2
Steve Roberts Ct DY11 . . 116 A6
Steward St B18 . . . . 66 A3
Stewart Cl CV4 . . . . 112 D2
Stewart Ct DY10 . . . . 116 F5
Stewart Rd
　Brownhills WS9 . . . . 16 A3
　Kingswinford DY6 . . . . . . 60 D4
Stewarts Rd B62 . . . . 83 D7
Stewart St
　Nuneaton CV11 . . . . 73 C3
　Wolverhampton WV2. . . . 163 B3
Stewkins DY8. . . . . 80 E8
Stewkins Ct [4] DY8 . . . . . 80 E8
Steyning Rd B26 . . . . 88 F5
Stickley La DY3 . . . . 50 C4
Stidfall Gr CV31. . . . . 162 D6
Stilehouse Cres B65 . . . . . 63 C2
Stilthouse Gr B45 . . . . . . 122 A7
STIRCHLEY 104 B7
Stirchley Com Sch B30. . 104 A6
Stirchley Trad Est B30 . . 104 B6
Stirling Ave
　Hinckley LE10 . . . . 71 A1
　Royal Leamington Spa
　　CV32 . . . . 157 B6
Stirling Cl CV3 . . . . 134 F8
Stirling Cres WV12 . . . . . . 27 B6
Stirling Ct B16 . . . . 65 E1
Stirling Ho B75 . . . . 46 C5
Stirling Pk WV9 . . . . 10 E3
Stirling Pl WS11 . . . . 4 B8
Stirling Rd
　Bilston WV14 . . . . 40 F2
　Birmingham B16 . . . . 65 F1
　Dudley DY2 . . . . 62 E6
　Solihull B90 . . . . 126 E8
　Sutton Coldfield B73 . . . . 45 E2
Stirrup Cl WS5. . . . . 42 F4
Stivichall Croft CV3 . . . . 133 D5
Stivichall Prim Sch CV3. 133 A6
Stockbridge Cl WV6. . . . . 23 F2
Stockdale Pl B15 . . . . 85 D8
STOCKFIELD 88 C5
Stockfield Rd B25, B27. . . 88 B5
Stockhay La WS7 . . . . 7 D5
Stockhill Dr B45 . . . . 121 F6
STOCKINGFORD 72 C3
Stockingford Com Inf Sch
　CV10. . . . . 72 D3
Stockingford Cty Jun Sch
　CV10. . . . . 72 D3
Stocking Leys LE10 . . . . . 76 A7
Stocking St DY9 . . . . 81 F5
Stockland Ct B74 . . . . 44 F8
STOCKLAND GREEN 56 C4
Stockland Green Com L Ctr
　B23. . . . . 56 C4
Stockland Green Tech Coll
　B23. . . . . 56 C4
Stockland Rd B23 . . . . 56 D4
Stockley Cres B90 . . . . . . 106 D3
Stockley Rd CV6 . . . . 96 C6
Stockmans Cl B38 . . . . . . 123 E8
Stockton Cl
　Birmingham B76 . . . . 58 B5
　Walsall, Wood B30 . . . . . 103 F8
Stockton Cl
　Dorridge B93 . . . . 128 B4
　Sutton Coldfield B76 . . . . 58 C5
Stockton Ct WV14. . . . . . . 50 A8
Stockton Gr
　Birmingham B33 . . . . 69 D1
　[2] Royal Leamington Spa
　　CV32. . . . . 157 A2
Stockton Rd CV1. . . . . . . 165 D4
Stockwell Ave DY5. . . . . . 81 D8
STOCKWELL END 24 C6
Stockwell End WV6 . . . . . 24 D6
Stockwell Head LE10 . . . . 71 D1

Stephenson Cl
　Royal Leamington Spa
　　CV32 . . . . 156 C1

Stephenson Dr
　Birmingham B37 . . . . 70 B2
　Perton WV6 . . . . 23 E5

Sta–Sto 241

Stockwell Rd
　Birmingham B21 . . . . 54 E2
　Wolverhampton WV6 . . . . 24 D5
Stockwell Rise B92 . . . . . 107 D7
STOKE 114 C2
STOKE ALDERMOOR . . . 134 B8
Stoke Cross B60 . . . . 151 E7
STOKE END 47 F7
Stoke Floods Nature
　Reserve★ CV2 . . . . 114 E3
Stoke Gn CV3 . . . . 114 A2
Stoke Green Cres CV3. . . 114 B1
STOKE HEATH
　Bromsgrove. 150 D5
　Coventry 114 A6
Stoke Heath Prim Sch
　CV2. . . . . 114 A7
Stoke La B98 . . . . 154 B7
STOKE PARK. 114 B3
Stoke Park Mews CV2. . . . 114 A3
Stoke Park Sch & Com Tech
　Coll CV2 . . . . 114 B4
STOKE POUND 151 A4
Stoke Pound La
　Stoke Pound B60 . . . . . . 151 A4
　Stoke Prior B60 . . . . 150 F3
STOKE PRIOR 150 C4
Stoke Prior Fst Sch B60 . 150 C3
Stoke Rd
　Bromsgrove, Aston Fields
　　B60 . . . . 151 A7
　Bromsgrove, Charford B60 150 F7
　Hinckley LE10 . . . . 71 B4
　Stoke Row CV2 . . . . 114 A4
Stokes Ave
　[7] Tipton DY4 . . . . 52 A8
　Willenhall WV13 . . . . 40 F8
Stokesay Ave WV6 . . . . . . 23 F3
Stokesay Cl
　Kidderminster DY10. . . . . 116 E2
　Nuneaton CV11 . . . . 73 A3
　Oldbury B69 . . . . 63 A8
Stokesay Gr B31 . . . . 122 F8
Stokesay Ho B23. . . . . 56 F6
Stokesay Rise DY1 . . . . . . 50 E3
Stoke's La WS11 . . . . 5 F7
Stokes St WS3 . . . . 28 B8
Stoke Turn Ct B61 . . . . . 150 D6
Stoke Way B15 . . . . 66 C1
STOKE WORKS 150 C1
Stom Rd WV14. . . . . 40 B5
STONE 117 E2
Stoneacre Cl WV3 . . . . . . 24 A1
Stone Ave B75. . . . . 47 A5
Stonebow Ave B91 . . . . . 127 B8
STONEBRIDGE 91 D3
Stonebridge Cres B37. . . . 69 F4
Stonebridge Highway
　CV3 . . . . 133 E4
Stonebridge Meadows
　Nature Reserve★ CV3. . 133 C4
Stonebridge Rd
　Birmingham B46 . . . . 91 A7
　Coleshill B46 . . . . 70 F5
Stonebridge Trad Est
　CV3. . . . . 134 B4
Stonebrook Way
　Birmingham B29 . . . . 84 F2
　Coventry CV6. . . . . 95 F3
Stonebury B15. . . . . 85 D8
Stonebury Ave CV5. . . . . . 111 E4
Stonechat Cl DY10 . . . . . 117 B2
Stonechat Dr B23. . . . . . . 56 C2
Stone Cl B38 . . . . 103 F2
Stone Cotts B31 . . . . 103 A3
Stonecroft Ave B45 . . . . . 122 A7
Stonecrop Cl
　Birmingham B38 . . . . 123 F8
　Brownhills WS8 . . . . 15 D6
STONE CROSS 42 D1
Stone Cross B46 . . . . 59 B3
Stonedown Cl WV14 . . . . . 40 A3
Stonefield Cl CV2 . . . . . . 115 A8
Stonefield Dr DY5 . . . . 61 A7
Stonefield Rd WV14. . . . . 40 D5
Stoneford Rd B90. . . . . . 106 A4
Stonehall Rd B97 . . . . . . 153 C3
Stonehaven B77 . . . . 21 F5
Stonehaven Dr CV3 . . . . . 133 C3
Stonehaven Gr B28 . . . . . 106 B8
Stonehenge Croft B14. . . 104 D1
Stone Hill DY10 . . . . 117 E2
Stonehill Croft B90 . . . . . 126 F6
Stonehill Wlk [5] B77 . . . . 35 F6
Stonehouse Ave WV13 . . . 26 F1
Stonehouse Cl
　Cubbington CV32. . . . . . . 157 D5
　Redditch B97 . . . . 153 D1
Stonehouse Cres WS10. . . 42 B2
Stonehouse Dr B74 . . . . . . 31 C4
Stonehouse Gr B32. . . . . . 84 C1
Stonehouse Hill B29 . . . . 85 A3
Stonehouse La
　Birmingham B32 . . . . 84 E2
　Birmingham B32 . . . . 84 F3
　Coventry CV3 . . . . 134 C4
　Hopwood B48. . . . . 123 E2
Stone House La CV7 . . . . 93 F6
Stonehouse Rd
　Bromsgrove B60 . . . . 137 A1
　Sutton Coldfield B73 . . . . 45 F3
Stonehurst Rd B43. . . . . . 44 C3
Stone La B11 . . . . 87 B6
Stonelea WS9 . . . . 30 B5
Stonelea Cl B71. . . . . 53 E8

STONELEIGH 149 B6
Stoneleigh Abbey★ CV8 . 148 F3
Stoneleigh Ave
Coventry CV5 . . . . 132 F7
Kenilworth CV8 . . . . 148 A6
Stoneleigh Cl
Redditch B98 . . . . 158 F6
Stoneleigh CV8 . . . . 149 B6
Sutton Coldfield B74 . . . . 45 F8
Stoneleigh Ct **6** CV11 . . 73 C3
Stoneleigh Deer Park Bsns
Village CV8 . . . . 149 D4
Stoneleigh Gdns **6** CV11. 73 C3
Stoneleigh Ho B32 . . . . . 84 F5
Stoneleigh Pk★ CV8 . . . 149 A4
Stoneleigh Rd
Baginton CV8 . . . . 133 F1
Birmingham B20 . . . . 55 E2
Blackdown CV32 . . . . 157 A7
Coventry CV4 . . . . 132 E2
Kenilworth CV8 . . . . 148 A6
Solihull B91 . . . . 106 E6
Stoneleigh CV8 . . . . 149 B3
Stoneleigh Way DY3 . . . . 50 D6
Stone Pine CV7 . . . . 95 A6
Stone Pine Cl WS12 . . . . . 1 F8
Stonepine Pl DY3 . . . . . . 50 E6
Stonepit B77 . . . . 21 C1
Stonepits La B97 . . . . . . 158 D4
Stone Rd B15 . . . . 86 D7
Stonerwood Ave B28 . . . 105 E8
Stones Gn B23 . . . . 56 F6
Stone St
Dudley DY1 . . . . 51 C1
Oldbury B69 . . . . 64 A7
Stoneton Cres CV7 . . . . . 130 A6
Stoneton Gr B29 . . . . 103 A8
Stoneway Gr CV31 . . . . . 162 D6
Stonewell Cres CV11 . . . . 79 B8
Stoney Cl B92 . . . . 107 E7
Stoney Croft WS11 . . . . 1 F1
Stoneycroft Tower 4
B36 . . . . 68 E8
Stoney Ct CV3 . . . . 135 A7
Stone Yd
Birmingham B12 . . . . 66 F1
Cradley Heath B64 . . . . . . 82 C8
Stoneydelph Prim Sch
B77 . . . . 22 A1
Stoneyfields Cl **3** WS11 . . 1 F2
Stoneyford Gr B14 . . . . . 105 B4
Stoneygate Dr LE10 . . . . 71 F3
STONEY HILL 137 A2
Stoney Hill Cl B60 . . . . . 137 A1
Stoneyhurst Rd B24 . . . . 56 F1
Stoney La
Birmingham B32 . . . . 84 B6
Birmingham, Balsall Heath
B12 . . . . 87 B5
Birmingham, Stechford B25. 68 E1
Blackwell B60 . . . . 138 C2
Dudley DY2 . . . . 62 C3
Kidderminster DY10 . . . . 116 E8
Stakenbridge DY10 . . . . . 98 E3
Walsall WS3 . . . . 14 D3
West Bromwich B71 . . . . 53 D4
Wolverhampton WV4 . . . 39 B5
Stoney Lane Ind Est
DY10 . . . . 116 E8
Stoney Lea Rd WS11 . . . . . 1 F1
Stoneymoor Dr B36 . . . . . 58 D1
Stoney Rd
Coventry CV1, CV3 . . . . . 165 B1
Nuneaton CV10, CV11 . . . 73 B6
Stoney Stanton Rd CV1,
CV6 . . . . 113 E5
Stoneythorpe Cl B91 . . . 107 B1
Stoneywood Rd CV2 . . . 114 F8
Stonnal Gr B23 . . . . 57 A6
STONNALL 16 E4
Stonnall Gate WS9 . . . . . 30 C8
Stonnall Rd WS9 . . . . 30 C8
Stonneyland Dr WS13 . . . 8 F6
Stonor Park Rd B91 . . . . 106 F5
Stonor Rd B28 . . . . 106 A5
Stonydelph La B77 . . . . . 36 A7
Stony La B67 . . . . 64 F5
Stonypre Pr WS13 . . . . 9 A6
Stony St B67 . . . . 64 F6
Stoop The CV3 . . . . 115 B1
Stornoway Rd B35 . . . . . . 58 B4
Storrage La B48 . . . . 139 E3
Storrs Cl B9 . . . . 67 D1
Storrs Pl B10 . . . . 67 D1
Storrs Way The B32 . . . . 102 B7
Stotfold Rd B14 . . . . 104 F2
Stour B77 . . . . 36 A5
STOURBRIDGE 80 D4
Stourbridge Coll DY8 . . . 81 A4
Stourbridge Coll (Longlands)
DY8 . . . . 80 E5
Stourbridge Juntion Sta
DY8 . . . . 81 B3
Stourbridge Rd
Brierley Hill DY1, DY2,
DY5 . . . . 61 E6
Catshill B61 . . . . 136 F7
Churchill DY10 . . . . 98 A6
Clent DY9 . . . . 99 E3
Dudley DY1 . . . . 62 A8
Fairfield B61 . . . . 120 D2
Hackman's Gate DY9 . . . 98 F1
Hagley DY9 . . . . 99 C7
Halesowen B63 . . . . 82 F5
Kidderminster DY10 . . . . 116 F8

Stourbridge Rd *continued*
Madeley Heath DY9 . . . 120 B7
Stourbridge DY9 . . . . 81 D5
Wombourne WV5, DY3. . . 49 B5
Stourbridge Town Sta
DY8 . . . . 81 A5
Stourbridge Trad Est DY8. 81 A6
Stour Cl
Burntwood WS7 . . . . 7 D6
Halesowen B63 . . . . 82 E6
Stour Ct B63 . . . . 83 B5
Stourdale Rd B64 . . . . . . 82 C8
Stourdell Rd B63 . . . . 82 E6
Stour Hill DY5 . . . . 82 A8
Stour Ho **2** B68 . . . . 84 B8
Stourminster Specl Sch
DY10 . . . . 117 B4
Stourmore Cl WV12 . . . . . 27 D6
Stourport Rd DY11 . . . . 116 C2
Stour St
Birmingham B18 . . . . 66 A3
West Bromwich B70 . . . . 52 E3
Stourton Cl
Knowle B93 . . . . 128 B7
Sutton Coldfield B76 . . . . 46 F4
Stourton Dr WV4 . . . . 38 C5
Stourton Rd B32 . . . . 84 B5
Stourvale Ind Est DY9 . . 81 F6
Stourvale Rd DY9 . . . . . . 81 F6
Stourvale Trad Est B63 . . 82 D6
Stour Valley Cl DY5 . . . . 81 F7
Stow Dr DY5 . . . . 81 B6
STOWE 3 C1
Stowecroft WS13 . . . . 3 C2
Stowe Hill Gdns WS13 . . . 3 C1
Stowell Rd B44 . . . . 55 F8
Stowe Pl CV4 . . . . 111 C1
Stowe Rd WS13 . . . . 9 C8
Stowe St
Lichfield WS13 . . . . 9 C8
Walsall WS3 . . . . 28 C7
Stow Gr B36 . . . . 68 E7
STOW HEATH 40 A8
Stowheath Ind Est & New Ent
Ctr WV1 . . . . 40 A8
Stow Heath Jun & Inf Schs
WV13 . . . . 26 D1
Stow Heath La
Bilston WV1 . . . . 40 B8
Wolverhampton WV1 . . . 26 C1
Stow Heath Pl WV1 . . . . . 40 B8
STOW LAWN 40 C8
Stowlawn Prim Sch WV14 40 C8
Stowmans Cl WV14 . . . . . 40 B3
Strachey Ave CV32 . . . . 156 E2
Stradey Cl CV3 . . . . 115 B1
Straight Rd WV12 . . . . . . 27 D6
Straits Gn DY3 . . . . 50 B4
Straits Prim Sch DY3 . . . 50 B5
Straits Rd DY3 . . . . 50 B4
STRAITS THE 50 A5
Straits The DY3 . . . . 50 A4
Strand The B61 . . . . 137 A3
Stratford Cl DY1 . . . . 50 E2
Stratford Ct B72 . . . . 46 B3
Stratford Dr WS9 . . . . . . 30 C8
Stratford Gdns B60 . . . . 137 A2
Stratford Pl B12 . . . . 87 A8
Stratford Rd
Birmingham,
Sparkbrook B11 . . . . 87 B6
Birmingham, Sparkhill B11 . 87 D3
Bromsgrove B94 . . . . 137 A2
Dorridge B94 . . . . 127 B3
Longbridge CV34 . . . . . . 160 C3
Nuthurst B94 . . . . 143 C5
Solihull B90 . . . . 126 D7
Stratford St
Birmingham B11 . . . . 87 C5
Coventry CV2 . . . . 114 A4
Nuneaton CV10 . . . . 73 C4
Stratford Street N B11 . . 87 A8
Stratford Way WS11 . . . . . 1 F5
Strathdene Gdns B29 . . . 85 C1
Strathdene Rd B29 . . . . . 85 C1
Strathearn Rd CV32 . . . 156 E1
Strathern Dr WV14 . . . . . 40 A1
Strathfield Wlk WV3, WV4. 38 C6
Strathmore Ave CV1 . . . 113 E1
Strathmore Cres WV5 . . . 18 A1
Strathmore Pl **6** WS11 . . 1 F2
Strathmore Rd
Hinckley LE10 . . . . 75 A7
Tipton DY4 . . . . 52 A8
Stratton St WV10 . . . . . . 25 E4
Strauss Dr WS11 . . . . 2 C2
Strawberry Cl B69 . . . . . . 63 C7
Strawberry Fields CV7 . . 92 B1
Strawberry La
Great Wyrley WS6 . . . . . . 13 E8
Willenhall WV13 . . . . 26 D3
Strawberry Lane Ind Est
WV13 . . . . 26 C2
Strawberry Wlk CV2. . . . 96 D2
Stray The DY5 . . . . 61 C6
Stream Mdw WS4 . . . . . . 15 D1
Stream Pk DY6 . . . . 60 E4
Stream Rd DY6, DY8 . . . . 60 F4
Streamside Cl CV5 . . . . 112 A8
Streamside Way
Solihull B92 . . . . 89 D4
Walsall WS4 . . . . 29 D8
Streatham Gr B44 . . . . . . 45 A2
Streather Rd B75 . . . . 32 C2
STREETLY 44 F8
Streetly Cres B74 . . . . . . 31 D3
Streetly Dr B74 . . . . 31 D3

Streetly La B74 . . . . 31 D3
Streetly Rd B23 . . . . 56 D5
Streetly Sch The B74 . . . 45 A6
Streetly Wood B74 . . . . . 31 A2
Streetsbrook Inf Sch
B90 . . . . 106 C4
Streetsbrook Rd B90,
B91 . . . . 106 C4
Streets Corner Gdns WS9 16 A4
Streets La WS6 . . . . 4 F1
Streetway Rd WS14 . . . . 18 B7
Strensham Ct B13 . . . . . . 86 E4
Strensham Hill B13 . . . . . 86 F4
Strensham Rd B12 . . . . . 86 E5
Stretton Ave CV3 . . . . . . 134 C6
Stretton CE Sch CV3 . . . 134 C5
Stretton Cl LE10 . . . . 75 D6
Stretton Cres CV31. . . . . 162 B5
Stretton Croft LE10 . . . . 75 E3
Stretton Ct
Birmingham B23 . . . . 56 E2
Hinckley LE10 . . . . 75 D3
Stretton Dr B45. . . . . 122 A2
Stretton Gr
2 Birmingham, Lozells
B19 . . . . 66 C7
Birmingham, Sparkbrook
B11. . . . . 87 C6
Birmingham, Stechford B8 . 68 C6
Stretton Ho **7** B97. . . . . 153 A4
Stretton Pl
Dudley DY2 . . . . 62 D5
Wolverhampton WV14 . . 40 A1
Stretton Rd
Kidderminster DY11. . . . . 116 B4
Nuneaton CV10 . . . . 73 A3
Solihull B90 . . . . 126 B8
Willenhall WV12 . . . . 13 D1
Stretton St B77 . . . . 21 E3
Stringer Cl B75 . . . . 32 A4
Stringers Hill WS12 . . . . . 2 D7
Stringes Cl WV13 . . . . . . 27 C3
Stringes La WV13 . . . . . . 27 B3
Strode Ho B79 . . . . 21 A4
Strode Rd WV2 . . . . 39 C6
Stroma Way CV10 . . . . . . 72 F2
Stronsay Cl B45. . . . . 101 F1
Stroud Ave WV12 . . . . . . 27 D5
Stroud Cl WV12 . . . . 27 C4
Stroud Rd B90 . . . . 105 F2
Strutt Cl B15 . . . . 85 D8
Strutt Rd LE10 . . . . 76 A5
Stuart Bathurst RC High Sch
WS10 . . . . 42 B5
Stuart Cl CV34 . . . . 160 D5
Stuart Cres DY2. . . . . 51 E1
Stuart Ct
Coventry CV6. . . . . 114 A8
7 Royal Leamington Spa
CV32 . . . . 156 F1
Stuart Micheal Way WV10 11 F8
Stuart Rd
Halesowen B62 . . . . 83 F5
Rowley Regis B65 . . . . . . 63 C4
Stuarts Ct DY9 . . . . 99 A5
Stuart's Dr B33 . . . . 68 D1
Stuarts Gn DY9 . . . . 99 B8
Stuarts Rd B33 . . . . 68 D2
Stuart St
Birmingham B7 . . . . 67 C7
Walsall WS3. . . . . 28 B8
Stuarts Way B32 . . . . . . 102 B7
STUBBER'S GREEN 29 E8
Stubbers Green Rd
Aldridge WS9 . . . . 30 A7
Walsall WS9. . . . . 29 E8
Stubbington Cl WV13 . . . 26 D1
Stubbs Cl CV12 . . . . 78 A4
Stubbs Gr CV2 . . . . 114 B5
Stubbs Rd WV3 . . . . 39 A6
Stubby La B33 . . . . 69 E2
Stubley Dr WV10. . . . . . . 25 E6
Stud Farm Cotts B78 . . . 20 E2
Stud La B33 . . . . 68 F4
Studland Gn CV2 . . . . . . 115 A4
Studland Rd B28 . . . . . . 106 A8
STUDLEY 159 F4
Studley Com Inf Sch
B80 . . . . 159 E4
STUDLEY COMMON. 159 C4
Studley Croft B92 . . . . . . 89 D3
Studley Dr DY5 . . . . 81 C8
Studley Gate DY8 . . . . . . 80 D5
Studley High Sch B80 . . 159 E3
Studley Rd
Redditch B98 . . . . 154 A2
Wolverhampton WV3 . . . 38 C8
Studley Twr B12 . . . . 87 B5
Sturgeon's Hill WS14. . . . 9 C7
Sturley Cl CV8 . . . . 148 B6
Sturman Dr B65 . . . . 63 C1
Sturminster Cl CV2 . . . . 115 A4
Stychbrook Gdns WS13. . . 3 B2
Styles Cl CV31. . . . . 162 A7
Styvechale Ave CV5 . . . 133 A8
Suckling Green La WV8 . 10 A2
Sudbury Cl
Royal Leamington Spa
CV32 . . . . 157 C3
Wednesfield WV11 . . . . . 26 C7
Sudbury Gr B44. . . . . 45 B2
Sudeley B77 . . . . 35 C8
Sudeley Cl B36 . . . . 58 B1
Sudeley Gdns DY1 . . . . . 50 D2
Sudeley Rd CV10 . . . . . . 78 C8
Suffield Gr B23 . . . . 56 B5

Suffolk Cl
Bedworth CV12 . . . . 78 A3
Coventry CV5. . . . . 112 B3
Nuneaton CV10 . . . . 72 E3
Oldbury B68 . . . . 64 A4
Wolverhampton WV11. . . 26 C6
Suffolk Dr DY5. . . . . 81 C7
Suffolk Gr WS9 . . . . 30 B8
Suffolk Ho B23 . . . . 56 F5
Suffolk Pl
Birmingham B5 . . . . 164 B1
Walsall WS2. . . . . 28 D5
Suffolk Rd DY2 . . . . 62 A7
Wednesbury WS10 . . . . . 42 C3
Suffolk St CV32 . . . . 157 A1
Suffolk Street Queensway
B1 . . . . 164 B2
Suffolk Way B78 . . . . 21 A1
Suffrage St B66 . . . . 65 B5
Sugarbrook Ct **1** B60 . . 150 F6
Sugarbrook La B60 . . . . 151 A5
Sugarbrook Rd B60 . . . . 151 A7
Sugar Loaf La DY10 . . . . 98 B7
Sugden Gr B5 . . . . 86 E8
Sulgrave Cl
Coventry CV2. . . . . 114 E7
Dudley DY1 . . . . 51 A3
Sullivan Ct CV6 . . . . 114 B7
Sullivan Rd CV6. . . . . . . 114 B7
Sullivan Way WS13 . . . . . 3 C2
Sullivan Wlk WS13 . . . . . 3 C2
Sumburgh Croft B35 . . . 58 A3
Summercourt Dr DY6 . . . 60 C5
Summercourt Sq DY6 . . 60 C5
Summer Croft B19 . . . . . 66 D6
Summer Dr DY3 . . . . 50 C3
Summerfield Ave
Kingswinford DY6 . . . . . . 60 C7
West Bromwich B70 . . . . 53 C4
Summerfield Cl **1** B77 . . 21 D4
Summerfield Com L Ctr
B18. . . . . 65 E5
Summerfield Cres B16 . . 65 E3
Summerfield Ct B15 . . . . 65 C1
Summerfield Dr **2** B29 . 103 A7
Summerfield Dr **3** B18 . . 65 E4
Summerfield Prim Sch
B18. . . . . 65 E4
Summerfield Rd
Birmingham B16 . . . . 65 E3
Burntwood WS7 . . . . 7 A5
Dudley DY2 . . . . 62 D7
Holy Cross DY9 . . . . 99 E2
Solihull B92 . . . . 89 A1
Tamworth B77 . . . . 21 D4
Summerfields Ave B62 . . 83 F7
SUMMERFORD PLACE. . . 26 F2
Summergate DY3 . . . . . . 50 C4
Summer Gr WS13 . . . . . . 3 D2
SUMMERHILL 116 B5
SUMMER HILL 52 A8
Summerhill Ave WS14 . . . 16 E8
Summer Hill
6 Halesowen B63 . . . . . 83 B3
Kingswinford DY6 . . . . . . 60 D6
Summerhill Ave DY11 . . 116 A5
Summer Hill Ind Pk Pk **2** B1 66 B3
Summerhill Prim Sch
DY4. . . . . 52 A6
Summerhill Rd
Dudley WV14 . . . . 40 D1
Tipton DY4 . . . . 51 F7
Summer Hill Rd B1 . . . . . 66 B3
Summerhill Sec Sch The
DY6 . . . . 60 D6
Summer Hill St B1 . . . . . 66 B3
Summer Hill Terr B1 . . . . 66 B3
Summerhouse Cl B97 . . 158 A6
Summerhouse Rd WV14 . 40 A1
Summer La
Birmingham B19 . . . . 66 D5
3 Dudley DY3 . . . . 50 C3
Minworth B76 . . . . 58 D6
Walsall WS4. . . . . 15 C2
Summerlee Rd B24 . . . . . 57 B2
Summer Pl DY11 . . . . 116 C5
Summer Rd
Birmingham, Acock's Green
B27 . . . . 88 A2
Birmingham, Edgbaston B15 86 C7
Birmingham, Erdington B23. 56 F5
Dudley DY1 . . . . 51 A4
Kidderminster DY11. . . . . 116 C3
Rowley Regis B65 . . . . . . 63 D3
Summer Row
Birmingham B3 . . . . 164 A3
Wolverhampton WV2 . . . 163 B2
Summer St
Kingswinford DY6 . . . . . . 60 D6
Redditch B98 . . . . 153 E3
Stourbridge DY8 . . . . 80 F5
Stourbridge, Lye DY9 . . . 81 E5
West Bromwich B71 . . . . 53 D4
Willenhall WV13 . . . . 26 F2
Summerton Rd B69 . . . . . 52 D1
Summit Cres B66 . . . . . . 64 E8
Summit Gdns B63 . . . . . . 82 F3
Summit Pl DY3 . . . . 50 B2
Summit The DY9 . . . . 81 D4
Sumner Rd B46 . . . . 70 F6
Sunart Way CV10 . . . . . . 72 C5

Sunbeam B77. . . . . 21 E3
Sunbeam Cl B36 . . . . 58 F7
Sunbeam Dr WS6 . . . . 4 F1
Sunbeam St WV2 . . . . . . 39 C7
Sunbeam Way B33 . . . . . 69 C1
Sunbury Ave WS14 . . . . . 9 E6
Sunbury Cl WV14 . . . . . . 40 E8
Sunbury Cotts B31 . . . . 103 A4
Sunbury Rd
Birmingham B31 . . . . . . 122 E6
Coventry CV3. . . . . 134 C2
Halesowen B63 . . . . 82 F7
Suncliffe Dr CV8 . . . . 148 A6
Suncroft B32 . . . . 84 C2
Sundbury Rise B31. . . . . 103 B8
Sunderland Dr DY8 . . . . . 81 A4
Sunderton Rd B14 . . . . . 104 E5
Sundew Croft B36 . . . . . . 68 D7
Sundew St CV2 . . . . 96 D3
Sundial La B43 . . . . 43 F7
Sundorne Cl CV5. . . . . . . 112 A4
Sundour Cres WV11. . . . . 12 B8
Sundridge Prim Sch B44 . 44 E1
Sundridge Rd B44 . . . . . . 44 E1
Sundridge Wlk WV4. . . . . 38 C1
Sunfield Gr B11. . . . . 1 E
Sunfield Rd WS11. . . . . 1 E
Sunningdale B77 . . . . 99 E
Sunningdale Cl CV10 . . . 78 A
Sunleigh Gr B27 . . . . 88 E
Sunley Dr WS12. . . . . 2 D
Sunmeam Way CV3 . . . . . 134 A
Sunningdale
Bromsgrove B60 . . . . . . 137 A
Halesowen B62 . . . . 83 E
Sutton Coldfield B73 . . . . 46 B
Tamworth B77 . . . . 22 C
Sunningdale Ave
Coventry CV6. . . . . 95 C
Kenilworth CV8 . . . . 148 B
Perton WV6 . . . . 23 D
Sunningdale Cl
Birmingham B20 . . . . 54 E
Nuneaton CV11 . . . . 74 A
Redditch B98 . . . . 153 F
Stourbridge DY8 . . . . 80 F
Sutton Coldfield B73 . . . . 46 A
Sunningdale Rd
Birmingham B11 . . . . 88 A
Bromsgrove B61 . . . . 150 C
Sedgley DY3 . . . . 39 B
Sunningdale Way WS3 . . 14 A
Sunny Ave B12. . . . . 87 A
Sunny Bank CV1 . . . . . . 165 A
Sunnybank Ave
Birmingham B44 . . . . 56 B
Coventry CV3. . . . . 134 B
Sunnybank Cl WS9 . . . . . 30 E
Sunnybank Rd
Dudley DY3 . . . . 50 F
Sutton Coldfield B73 . . . . 57 A
Sunny Bank Rd B68 . . . . 84 C
Sunnydale Cres LE10. . . . 75 B
Sunnydale Rd LE10 . . . . . 74 F
Sunnydale Wlk B71 . . . . . 53 C
Sunnydene B8 . . . . 68 A
Sunnyhill LE10. . . . . 75 F
Sunnyhill S LE10 . . . . 75 F
Sunnymead B60 . . . . 137 A
Sunnymead Rd
Birmingham B26 . . . . 88 F
1 Burntwood WS7 . . . . . . 7 A
Sunnymead Way B74 . . . 44 F
Sunnymede Rd DY6 . . . . 61 A
Sunnyside
Brownhills WS9 . . . . 16 A
Hinckley LE10 . . . . 71 D
Oldbury B69 . . . . 63 B
Sunnyside Ave B23. . . . . 56 E
Sunnyside Cl
Balsall Common CV7 . . . 130 C
Coventry CV5. . . . . 112 F
Sunnyside Ct CV10 . . . . . 72 D
Sunnyside Ind Est LE10. . 71 D
Sunnyside La CV7 . . . . . 130 C
Sunridge Ave
Birmingham B19 . . . . 66 D
Wombourne WV5. . . . . . . 49 A
Sunrise Bsns Pk DY8 . . . 80 E
Sunrise Bsns Ctr B15 . . . 86 D
Sunrise Hill WS12 . . . . 2 B
Sunrise Wlk B68 . . . . 64 C
Sunset Cl
Great Wyrley WS6 . . . . . . 4 F
Tamworth B79 . . . . 21 A
Sunset Pl WV4. . . . . 39 F
Sunshine Cl CV8 . . . . 148 A
Sunshine Inf Sch WS3 . . 28 C
Sun St
Brierley Hill DY5 . . . . 61 F
Walsall WS1. . . . . 42 E
Wolverhampton WV10. . . 163 D
Sunway Gr CV3 . . . . 133 B
Surfeit Hill Rd B64 . . . . . 82 D
Surrey Cl
Cannock WS11. . . . . 4 F
Hinckley LE10 . . . . 75 E
Nuneaton CV10 . . . . 72 E
Surrey Cres B71 . . . . 53 A
Surrey Ct CV34 . . . . 160 E
Surrey Dr
Kingswinford DY6 . . . . . . 60 F
Tamworth B79 . . . . 21 A
Wolverhampton WV3 . . . 24 E
Surrey Ho **2** DY8 . . . . . . 80 F
Surrey Rd
Birmingham B44 . . . . A

Surrey Rd *continued*
Dudley DY2 62 A7
Surrey Wlk WS9 16 A1
Sussex Ave
Aldridge WS9 30 A8
Wednesbury WS10 42 D4
West Bromwich B71 53 C6
Sussex Cl CV10 72 E3
Sussex Ct
7 Birmingham B29 103 C7
Warwick CV34 160 E8
Sussex Dr
Cannock WS12 2 B5
Wolverhampton WV3 24 E1
Sussex Rd CV5 112 F4
Sutherland Ave
Coventry CV5 112 A4
Solihull B90 106 C3
Wolverhampton WV2 40 A8
Sutherland Cl
Birmingham B43 44 D4
Warwick CV34 155 E1
Sutherland Dr
Bedworth CV12 78 A4
Birmingham B13 86 F4
Wombourne WV5 38 A1
Sutherland Gr WV6 23 F4
Sutherland Ho WV1 25 A3
Sutherland Pl WV2 163 C2
Sutherland Rd
Cheslyn Hay WS6 4 E2
Cradley Heath B64 82 E8
Wolverhampton WV4 39 B5
Sutherland St B6 67 B8
Sutton App B8 68 A4
Sutton Ave
Coventry CV5 111 D4
Tamworth B78 21 A2
Sutton Cl
Hinckley LE10 71 F3
Redditch B98 154 D2
SUTTON COLDFIELD 46 D5
Sutton Coldfield Gram Sch For Girls B73 46 B3
Sutton Coldfield Sta B73 46 B5
Sutton Cottage Hospl B72 46 B4
Sutton Cres B70 53 A3
Sutton Ct
Bedworth CV6 96 C6
3 Birmingham, Erdington B24 57 B6
Birmingham, Hamstead B43 54 E7
Sutton Coldfield B75 46 B7
Wolverhampton WV4 39 E2
SUTTON FARM 116 B4
Sutton Lodge B91 107 A3
Sutton New Rd B23 56 F4
Sutton Oak Cnr B73 45 A5
Sutton Oak Rd B73 45 A5
Sutton Park Com Prim Sch DY11 116 B4
Sutton Park Ct B73 46 B2
Sutton Park Gr DY11 116 C3
Sutton Park National Nature Reserve★ B74 31 D2
Sutton Park Rd DY11 116 B3
Sutton Park Rise DY11 116 B3
Sutton Park Visitor Ctr★ B74 46 A5
Sutton Pk CV10 72 B7
Sutton Pk★ B74 45 D6
Sutton Rd
Aldridge WS9 30 A1
Birmingham B23 57 B6
Darlaston WS10 41 A4
Kidderminster DY11 116 C4
Mile Oak B78 34 A8
Tamworth B78 20 C1
Walsall WS5 43 C8
Sutton's Dr
Birmingham B43 44 A4
Walsall B43 43 F4
Sutton Specl Sch The DY1 61 F8
Sutton Sq B76 58 E6
Sutton St
Birmingham, Aston B6 66 F6
Birmingham B1 66 D1
Stourbridge DY8 60 F1
Sutton Stop CV6 96 B5
Swadling St CV31 161 F6
Swaffield Pk WS11 2 B2
Swain Crofts CV31 162 B6
Swains Gn LE10 75 F6
Swains Gr B44 44 F4
Swaledale CV4 132 D6
Swaledale Cl B60 150 E6
Swale Gr
Birmingham B38 103 F1
Willenhall WV13 27 D2
Swale Rd B76 47 A1
Swallow Ave B36 70 A8
Swallow Cl
Birmingham B12 87 B5
Dudley DY2 62 D2
Huntington WS12 1 C7
Wednesbury WS10 42 B4
Swallow Croft WS13 3 A1
Swallow Ct
Bedworth CV12 95 C8
Wolverhampton, Fordhouses WV10 11 B3
Wolverhampton, Low Hill WV10 25 D7
Swallowdale
Brownhills WS9 16 B4
Wolverhampton WV6 23 F2
Swallowdean Rd CV6 112 E8
Swallow Dr DY10 117 A2
Swallowfall Ave DY8 80 C4
Swallowfield B79 20 E6
Swallowfields Dr WS12 2 B3
Swallowfields Rd DY3 39 C2
Swallowgate Bsns Pk CV6 95 D1
Swallow Rd CV6 95 C1
Swallows Cl WS3 15 A5
Swallows Ind Est The B90 126 D8
Swallows' Mdw B90 126 D8
Swallows Rise Bsns Pk DY5 61 E3
Swallow St
Birmingham B2 164 B2
West Bromwich B70 53 A4
Swanage Gn CV2 115 A4
Swanage Rd B10 87 D8
Swan Ave B66 64 E7
Swan Bank WV4 38 F4
Swan Cl
Birmingham B8 67 F6
Blakedown DY10 98 B1
Cheslyn Hay WS6 4 D2
Swan Copse B25 88 C5
Swancote Dr WV4 38 C6
Swancote Rd
Birmingham B33 68 F5
Dudley DY1 62 A8
Swan Cres B69 63 F4
Swancroft Ho 11 DY4 52 A8
Swancroft Rd
Coventry CV2 114 A5
Tipton DY4 51 F8
Swan Ctyd B25 88 D6
Swan Dr WS8 15 E7
Swanfield Rd DY8 61 A2
Swanfields WS7 7 C6
Swan Gdns B23 56 F4
Swan La
Coventry CV2 113 F4
Fairfield B61 120 E3
Stourbridge DY5, DY8 61 A2
Upton Warren B61 150 A3
West Bromwich B70 53 A5
Swan Lane Ind Est B70 53 A5
Swan Lane Ind Pk B70 53 A5
Swanley Cl B62 84 A3
Swan Lodge B26 89 B4
Swan Mdw CV34 160 B3
Swan Mews WS13 9 A8
Swanmore Cl WV3 38 E8
Swanmote B79 20 F5
Swann Rd WV14 40 A2
Swann Wlk 10 DY4 52 A8
Swan Pk B77 21 C3
Swan Pool Gr WS4 15 D1
Swan Rd WS13 9 A7
Swan Rdbt B70 52 F5
Swansbrook Gdns 4 B38 104 C2
Swan Sh Ctr
Birmingham B25 88 D7
7 Kidderminster DY10 116 E6
Swanshurst Com L Ctr B13 105 B7
Swanshurst Girls Sch B13 105 B7
Swanshurst La B13 105 C8
Swans Length B48 139 A7
Swan St
Alvechurch B48 139 B5
Brierley Hill DY5 61 C6
Dudley DY2 62 C6
Royal Leamington Spa CV32 157 A1
Stourbridge DY8 80 E5
Warwick CV34 160 E6
Wolverhampton WV1 25 F2
Swanswell Rd B92 106 D7
Swanswell St CV1 165 C4
Swans Wlk B48 139 A6
Swanswood Gr 3 B37 70 C3
SWAN VILLAGE
Dudley 51 B6
West Bromwich 52 F4
Swarthmore Rd B29 103 B7
Sweetbriar La WV12 27 D5
Sweetbriar Rd WV2 40 A7
Sweetbriar Way WS12 2 D2
Sweetbrier Dr 4 DY8 60 E1
Sweetman Pl WV6 25 A3
Sweetman St WV6 24 F4
Sweetmoor Cl B36 69 C8
Sweetpool La DY8 98 F5
Swift B77 21 E3
Swift Cl
Birmingham B36 70 A8
Bromsgrove B61 150 E8
Kenilworth CV8 148 A2
Swift Park Gr DY10 117 B2
Swift Rd CV1 165 C1
Swift's Cnr CV3 133 E8
Swillington Rd CV6 113 B5
Swinbrook Gr B44 44 E1
Swinbrook Way B90 106 D4
Swinburne Ave CV2 114 D2
Swinburne Cl CV10 72 A5
Swinburne Rd
Hinckley LE10 71 C1
Redditch B97 158 C7
Swincross Rd DY8 81 B3
Swindale B77 36 B7
Swindale Croft CV3 134 F8
Swindell Rd DY9 81 C1
Swindon Rd
Birmingham B17 65 B2
Swindon Rd *continued*
Kingswinford DY6 60 B6
Swinfen Broun Rd WS13 9 A8
Swinford Gr B93 127 E3
Swinford Old Hall DY8 81 B3
Swinford Rd
Birmingham B29 85 B3
Stourbridge DY8 81 A3
Wolverhampton WV10 25 E5
Swinnerton Heritage CV10 73 C8
Swiss Dr DY8 60 F2
Swiss Lodge Dr B78 34 F8
Sword Dr LE10 71 B3
Swynnerton Dr WV11 12 F4
Sycamore B77 35 E7
Sycamore Ave
Birmingham B12 87 A5
Redditch B98 153 E2
Sycamore Cl
Birmingham B24 56 F3
Dudley DY2 62 B8
Hinckley LE10 75 E5
Kidderminster DY10 116 F7
Stourbridge DY8 80 D2
Sutton Coldfield B76 46 F2
Walsall WS4 29 B8
Sycamore Cres
Birmingham, Erdington B24 56 F3
Birmingham, Marston Green B37 90 A8
Sycamore Ct
Allesley CV5 111 F7
Birmingham, Cotteridge B30 103 E4
Birmingham, Perry Common B23 56 C7
Sycamore Ctr DY1 50 F5
Sycamore Dr
Hollywood B47 125 B6
Wolverhampton WV3 24 D1
Sycamore Gn
Cannock WS11 1 E6
Dudley DY1 50 F5
Sycamore Gr CV34 156 A1
Sycamore Ho
Birmingham B13 87 A3
Redditch B98 158 F8
Sycamore Ind & Trad Est B21 65 D7
Sycamore Paddock 1 DY8 61 A1
Sycamore Pl
Bilston WV14 41 A3
Burntwood WS7 6 F7
Smethwick B67 64 F4
Sycamore Rd
Birmingham, Aston B6 67 A8
Birmingham, Bournville B30 103 F7
Birmingham, Erdington B23 56 F7
Birmingham, Great Barr B43 43 E3
Birmingham, Handsworth B21 65 D7
Burntwood WS7 6 F7
Cannock WS12 2 F4
Coventry CV2 96 B2
Kingswinford DY6 60 E6
Nuneaton CV10 72 D6
Oldbury B69 64 A4
Smethwick B66 65 B3
Tipton DY4 51 F7
Walsall, Shelfield WS4 29 B8
Walsall, The Delves WS5 42 F5
Wednesbury WS10 42 A2
Sycamores The
Bedworth CV12 77 E2
Lichfield WS14 9 B5
2 Sutton Coldfield B74 31 F2
West Hagley DY9 98 F5
Wolverhampton, Elston Hall WV10 25 F8
Wolverhampton WV11 26 B5
Sycamore Terr B14 104 C7
Sycamore Way
1 Birmingham B27 88 C5
Huntington WS12 1 D8
SYDENHAM 162 D5
Sydenham Dr CV31 162 B6
Sydenham Ind Est 3 CV31 162 B6
Sydenham Prim Sch CV31 162 C6
Sydenham Rd
Birmingham B11 87 C6
Smethwick B66 65 A7
Wolverhampton WV1 26 B2
Sydenham Sports Ctr CV31 162 C5
Sydnall Cl B97 152 F2
Sydnall Fields CV6 95 F4
Sydnall Rd CV6 95 F4
Sydney Cl B70 53 A7
Sydney Ct 1 CV12 77 F2
Sydney Rd
Birmingham B9 67 C2
Bromsgrove B61 136 E3
Cradley Heath B64 82 C8
Smethwick B67 64 E2
Sydney Way B34 69 E6
Sykesmoor B77 36 B7
Sylvan Ave B31 102 F3
Sylvan Dr CV3 132 F6
Sylvan Gn B62 83 D5
Sylvan Gr B90 106 B5
Sylvia Ave B31 123 B8
Symphony Ct B16 66 B2
Synkere Cl CV7 95 A6
Sytch La WV5 49 A5

T

Tabbs Gdns DY10 117 A6
Table Oak La CV8 130 B1
Tachbrook Cl CV2 96 C2
Tachbrook Link CV34 161 E4
Tachbrook Park Dr CV34 161 E5
Tachbrook Park Ind Est CV34 161 D5
Tachbrook Rd CV31 161 F4
Tachbrook St CV31 162 A6
Tack Farm Rd DY8 60 D1
Tackford Cl B36 58 D1
Tackford Rd CV6 114 A8
Tackley Cl B90 126 B8
Tadmore Cl WV14 40 D5
Tadworth Cl WV1 26 A2
Tainters Hill CV8 148 A6
Tait Croft B92 107 F8
Talaton Cl WV9 11 A2
Talbot B77 21 E3
Talbot Ave B74 31 B3
Talbot Cl
Birmingham B23 56 D8
Walsall WS2 28 C6
Talbot Ct CV32 157 A1
Talbot Ho
5 Birmingham B24 56 F4
6 Wednesbury WS10 41 F2
Talbot Pass 6 DY8 81 A5
Talbot Pl WV14 40 C6
Talbot Rd
Bromsgrove B60 150 E7
Dudley DY2 62 B4
Smethwick B66 65 A3
Wolverhampton WV2 39 C6
Talbots La DY5 61 F1
Talbots Lane Trad Est DY5 61 F1
Talbot St
Birmingham B18 65 F6
Brierley Hill DY5 61 D3
Halesowen B63 82 C6
Kidderminster DY11 116 C4
Stourbridge, Lye DY9 81 F5
Stourbridge, Stambermill DY8 81 A5
Talbot Way B10 87 F7
Talfourd St B9 67 D1
Talgarth Covert B38 123 E7
Talisman Cl CV8 147 F3
Talisman Sq CV8 147 F4
Talke Rd WS5 42 F5
Talladale B32 102 B7
Talland Ave
Coventry CV6 114 A6
Tamworth B77 21 E5
Tallants Cl CV6 114 A8
Tallants Rd CV6 114 A8
Tallington Rd B33 89 D7
Tall Trees Cl
Catshill B61 136 F8
Sutton Coldfield B74 31 D4
Willenhall WV12 27 D6
Tall Trees Dr DY9 81 D2
Talton Cl B90 127 A5
Tamar Cl WS8 6 C2
Tamar Dr
Birmingham B36 69 F8
Dudley DY3 50 F6
Sutton Coldfield B76 58 B7
Tamar Gr
Perton WV6 23 E4
Willenhall WV13 27 C2
Tamarisk Cl B29 103 B8
Tamar Rd
Bulkington CV12 79 B2
Tamworth B77 36 A5
Tamar Rise DY8 81 A8
Tame Ave
Birmingham B36 70 A8
Burntwood WS7 7 D6
Wednesbury WS10 42 C4
Tamebridge Ind Est B42 55 E4
Tame Bridge Parkway Sta WS10 42 F2
Tame Cl
Tamworth B77 35 E5
Walsall WS1 42 E6
Tame Cres 1 B71 53 C6
Tame Crossing WS10 42 A1
Tame Ct
Fazeley B78 35 B8
Tamworth B79 21 A5
Tame Dr WS3 15 A1
Tamedrive B78, B79 21 A4
Tame Gr WS11 4 D8
Tame Rd
Birmingham, Brandhall B68 84 B8
Birmingham, Witton B6 56 A1
Tipton DY4 52 C5
Tame Rise B68 84 B8
Tame Road Ind Est B6 56 B1
Tamerton Rd B32 84 D1
Tameside Cl WV13 26 F1
Tameside Dr
Birmingham, Castle Bromwich B35 58 A1
Birmingham, Erdington B6 56 A3
Tameside Prim Sch WS10 42 C2
Tameside Way B42 55 E5
Tame St
Bilston WV14 40 F5
Tame St *continued*
Tamworth B77 21 C3
Walsall WS1 42 E6
West Bromwich B70 52 F8
Tame Street E WS1 42 F6
Tame Valley Bsns Pk B77 35 E6
Tame Valley Com Sch B36 68 D8
Tame Valley Ind Est B77 35 E6
Tame Way LE10 75 A8
Tamora Cl CV34 161 D3
TAMWORTH 21 B3
Tamworth Bsns Ctr B77 22 B3
Tamworth Bsns Pk B77 22 B3
Tamworth Castle★ B79 21 B4
Tamworth Cl WS8 6 F2
Tamworth Rd
Cliff B78 35 C2
Keresley CV6, CV7 94 D5
Lichfield WS14 9 E5
Polesworth B78 22 E1
Sutton Coldfield B75 33 A2
Tamworth B77 35 C6
Tamworth, Mount Pleasant B77 21 C1
Tamworth, Two Gates B77 35 D8
Wood End CV9 36 C1
Tamworth Rd (Amington) B77 21 F5
Tamworth St WS13 9 B8
Tamworth Sta B79 21 C5
Tanacetum Dr WS5 43 B3
Tancred Cl CV31 161 F5
Tandy Ct B14 104 F3
Tandy Dr B14 104 F3
Tandy's La DY10 118 E4
Tanfield Cl WV6 24 B3
Tanfield Rd
Birmingham B33 68 F3
Dudley DY2 62 B7
Tanford Rd B92 89 C3
Tanglewood Cl
Birmingham B32 84 B4
Birmingham, Castle Bromwich B34 69 C5
Blackwell B60 138 A5
Tanglewood Gr DY3 39 C2
Tangmere Cl WV6 23 E5
Tangmere Dr B35 58 A3
Tanhill B77 36 B7
Tanhouse Ave B43 54 C7
Tanhouse Farm Rd B92 89 C2
Tanhouse La
Halesowen B63 82 C5
Redditch B98 154 C6
Tanners Cl B75 46 F7
Tanners Ct WS1 42 E8
Tanners Ctyd CV34 160 D5
Tanners Gr CV6 95 D4
TANNER'S GREEN 125 B1
Tanners Green La B47, B94 125 B2
Tanners' La CV4, CV7 111 B1
Tannery Cl WS2 28 D3
Tannery Ct CV8 147 F4
Tansey Ct DY5 61 B7
Tansey Green Rd
Brierley Hill DY5, DY6 61 B8
Kingswinford DY6 50 A1
Tansley Cl B93 127 F4
Tansley Gr B44 44 F1
TANSLEY HILL 62 F7
Tansley Hill Ave DY2 62 F8
Tansley Hill Rd DY2 62 E8
Tansley Rd B44 55 F8
Tansley View WV2 39 D7
Tansy
Sutton Coldfield B74 31 F4
Tamworth B77 21 C3
Tantallon Dr B32 84 D1
Tantany La B71 53 C4
Tantarra St
Walsall, The Chuckery WS1 29 A1
Walsall WS1 28 F1
TANWOOD 119 B2
Tanwood Barns DY10 119 B2
Tanwood Cl
Redditch B97 158 A6
Solihull B91 127 B8
Tanwood Cross DY10 119 B2
Tanwood La DY10 119 A2
Tanworth Gr B12 86 F6
TANWORTH-IN-ARDEN 142 B2
Tanworth-in-Arden CE Prim Sch B94 142 A2
Tanworth La B90 126 C5
Tanyard WS13 9 C8
Tanyard Cl
Alvechurch B48 139 B6
Coventry CV4 111 D1
Tanyard La B48 139 B6
Tanyards B27 88 D3
Tapcon Way CV2 114 F5
Tapestries Ave B70 53 A4
Taplow Pl WS11 1 F4
Tappinger Gr CV8 148 C5
Tapster La B94 143 F2
Tapton Cl WS3 14 C3
Tara Ct CV2 114 B4
Tara La B21 65 F7
TARDEBIGGE 152 B7
Tardebigge CE Fst Sch B60 152 B7
Tardebigge Ct B97 152 C6

Tardebigge Ho B60 . . . . 137 B3
Tarlington Rd CV6 . . . . 112 E6
Tarmac Rd WV14 . . . . 40 B5
Tarn Cl CV12. . . . . 78 A2
Tarquin Cl CV3 . . . . 134 D7
Tarragon Cl CV2 . . . . 96 D1
Tarragon Gdns B31 . . . 102 C6
Tarrant B77 . . . . 35 F8
Tarrant Gr B32. . . . . . 84 F5
Tarrant Wlk CV2 . . . . 115 A5
Tarrington Covert 6
B38 . . . . 123 E8
Tarry Hollow Rd DY5. . . 61 B7
Tarry Rd B8 . . . . 67 B7
Tarvin Mews DY5 . . . . 61 D1
Taryn Dr WS10 . . . . . 41 D7
Tasker St
Walsall WS1. . . . . . . 42 D8
West Bromwich B70 . . 52 E4
Tasman Gr WV6 . . . . 23 E5
TAT BANK 64 B6
Tat Bank Rd B69 . . . . 64 B6
Tatchbrook Ct 5 CV31 . 161 F6
TATCHBROOK
MALLORY 162 A1
Tatnall Gr CV34 . . . . 160 E8
Taunton Ave WV11 . . . 11 D4
Taunton Cl B31 . . . . 102 C2
Taunton Rd B12. . . . . 87 B4
Taunton Way CV6 . . . . 95 A2
Taverners Cl WV12 . . . 13 C1
Taverner's Gn B20 . . . 54 F3
Tavistock Cl B77 . . . . 21 C7
Tavistock Rd B27 . . . 106 C8
Tavistock St CV32. . . 156 F1
Tavistock Way CV11. . . 73 E5
Tavistock Wlk CV2 . . . 114 C7
Tay Cl B36 . . . . 69 F7
Tay Croft B37. . . . . . . 70 C4
Tay Gr
Birmingham B38 . . . . 123 F8
Halesowen B62 . . . . . 83 E8
Taylor Ave CV32 . . . . 157 B2
Taylor Cl CV8. . . . . . 148 B6
Taylor Cl CV34. . . . . 160 D7
Taylor Ho 4 WS2. . . . 42 C7
Taylor Rd
Birmingham B13 . . . . 104 F5
Dudley DY2 . . . . 62 E2
Wolverhampton WV4 . . 39 F5
Taylors La B65 . . . . . 63 E7
Taylor's La
Smethwick B67 . . . . . 64 F5
West Bromwich B71 . . 53 D4
Taylors Orch B23 . . . . 56 B4
Taylor St WV11 . . . . . 26 D5
Taylor Way B69 . . . . . 63 B8
Taynton Covert 4 B30 . 104 C3
Tay Rd
Birmingham B45 . . . . 102 B1
Coventry CV6. . . . . . 113 B6
Taysfield Rd B31. . . . 102 E6
Taywood Dr B10 . . . . 87 C7
Teachers Cl CV6 . . . . 113 A5
Tea Gdn The CV12 . . . . 95 E8
Teal Bsns Ctr LE10 . . . 74 D7
Tealby Gr B29 . . . . . . 86 A1
Teal Cres DY10 . . . . 117 B3
Teal Dr
Birmingham B23 . . . . 56 B3
Hinckley LE10 . . . . . 75 A6
Teal Gr WV14 . . . . . 41 B3
Teall Ct B27 . . . . 88 C3
Teall Rd B8. . . . . 67 E5
Teal Rd B80 . . . . 159 F4
Tean Cl
Birmingham B11 . . . . 88 A3
Burntwood WS7 . . . . . 7 D6
Teasdale Way DY9 . . . . 81 D4
Teasel Gr WV10. . . . . 12 B7
Teasel Rd WV11 . . . . 26 B7
Teazel Ave B30 . . . . 103 D6
Tebworth Cl WV9 . . . . 10 F2
Tedbury Cres B23. . . . 56 E6
Tedder Rd WS2 . . . . . 27 F2
Teddesley Ct WS11. . . . 1 E3
Teddesley Gr B33 . . . . 69 C4
Teddesley St WS4. . . . 28 F3
Teddesley Way WS12. . . 1 C6
Teddington Cl 4 B73 . . 46 A2
Teddington Gr B42 . . . 55 D3
Ted Pitts La CV5 . . . . 94 B2
Tedstone Rd B32 . . . . 84 E5
Teesdale Ave B34. . . . 68 F6
Teesdale Cl WV1. . . . . 26 A2
Tees Gr B38 . . . . 123 F8
Teeswater Cl B60 . . . 150 E6
Teign B77 . . . . 36 A5
Teign Bank Cl LE10 . . . 71 D2
Teign Bank Rd LE10. . . 71 D2
Teignmouth Rd B29. . . 86 A1
Telephone Rd CV3 . . . 114 C2
Telfer Rd CV6. . . . . . 113 B7
Telford Ave
Great Wyrley WS6 . . . . 4 F3
Royal Leamington Spa
CV32. . . . . 157 B5
Telford Cl
Burntwood WS7. . . . . 7 C8
Smethwick B67 . . . . . 64 D3
Walsall WS2. . . . . . . 28 A5
West Bromwich B71 . . 53 A8
Telford Gdns WV3 . . . . 38 D7
Telford Gr WS12 . . . . . 2 B1

Telford Jun & Inf Schs
CV32. . . . . 157 C5
Telford Rd
Bedworth CV7 . . . . . 96 C8
Tamworth B79 . . . . . 20 F8
Walsall WS2. . . . . . . 28 A5
Telford Way B66 . . . . 64 F8
Teme Ave DY11 . . . . 116 E3
Teme Ct B23. . . . . . . 56 B3
Teme Gr WV13. . . . . . 27 D2
Teme Rd
Halesowen B63 . . . . . 82 B5
Stourbridge DY8 . . . . 80 F3
Tempest St
Tamworth B79 . . . . . 21 A5
Wolverhampton WV2 . 163 C2
Templar Ave CV4 . . . 112 A1
Templar Cl 1 CV11 . . . 73 C3
Templar Ct CV3 . . . . 133 D7
Templars' Fields CV4 . 132 B7
Templars Prim Sch CV4 . 112 A1
Templars The
Oldbury B69. . . . . . . 63 E5
Warwick CV34 . . . . 160 F5
Temple Ave
Balsall Common CV7 . . 129 F6
Birmingham B28 . . . 106 A6
TEMPLE BALSALL . . . 129 C4
Temple Bar WV13. . . . 27 A2
Temple Cl B98. . . . . 153 F4
Temple Ct B46. . . . . . 59 F1
Templefield Gdns 2 B9. . 67 C1
Templefield Sq B15. . . 86 B7
Templefield St B9 . . . . 67 C1
Temple Gr CV34 . . . . 160 D5
Temple La B93. . . . . 129 A4
Temple Meadow Prim Sch
B64. . . . . 82 D8
Temple Meadows Rd B71. 53 E6
Templemore Dr B43 . . . 54 E7
Temple Pas B2 . . . . 164 B2
Temple Rd
Dorridge B93. . . . . . 128 A3
Willenhall WV13 . . . . 27 B3
Temple Row B2. . . . 164 C3
Temple Row W B2 . . . 164 B3
Temple Sq 2 WV13 . . . 27 A3
Temple St
Bilston WV14. . . . . . 40 E5
Birmingham B2 . . . . 164 B2
West Bromwich B70 . . 53 C4
Dudley DY3 . . . . 50 D3
Wolverhampton WV2 . 163 C2
Templeton Cl B93. . . . 128 A3
Templeton Rd B44. . . . 44 F2
Temple Way
Coleshill B46. . . . . . 59 F1
Oldbury B69. . . . . . . 52 D2
Temple Wlk WV13 . . . . 27 A2
Tenacre La DY3. . . . . 50 E6
TEN ACRES 104 B8
Ten Acres End B30. . . 104 B8
Tenacres La B98 . . . . 154 F3
Ten Ashes La B45. . . . 122 C4
Tenbury Cl
Aldridge WS9 . . . . . . 30 C8
Redditch B98. . . . . . 154 C6
Willenhall WV13 . . . . 27 D3
Tenbury Ct WV4 . . . . . 38 D5
Tenbury Gdns WV4. . . . 38 D5
Tenbury Ho 1 B63. . . . 83 A3
Tenbury Rd B14. . . . 104 E6
Tenby Cl CV12 . . . . . 77 C1
Tenby Ct CV32 . . . . . 161 E8
Tenby Rd B13. . . . . . 87 D2
Tenby St B1 . . . . 66 B4
Tenby St N B1 . . . . . 66 B4
Tenby Tower 2 B31 . . 103 A1
Teneriffe Rd CV6 . . . . 95 B3
Tenlands Rd B63. . . . . 82 F3
Tenlons Rd CV10. . . . . 72 F2
Tennal Dr B32 . . . . . 84 F6
Tennal La B32 . . . . . 84 F6
Tennal Rd B32 . . . . . 84 F6
Tennant St
Birmingham B15 . . . . 66 B1
Nuneaton CV11 . . . . . 73 E3
Tennessee B13 . . . . . 86 E2
Tennis Ct B38 . . . . . 103 D4
Tennis Ct The B15 . . . 86 A5
Tennscore Ave WS6. . . . 4 E3
Tennyson Ave
Sutton Coldfield B74 . . 31 F6
Tamworth B79 . . . . . 21 A6
Warwick CV34 . . . . 160 C4
Tennyson Ho
Birmingham B31 . . . 123 A8
3 Oldbury B68. . . . . 64 C4
Tennyson Rd
Birmingham B10 . . . . 87 E7
Coventry CV2. . . . . 114 C3
Dudley DY3 . . . . 50 A4
Hinckley LE10 . . . . . 71 C1
Redditch B97. . . . . . 158 C8
Walsall WS3. . . . . . . 28 E8
Willenhall WV12 . . . . 27 E8
Tennyson Way DY10. . . 117 C6
Ten Shilling Dr CV4 . . 131 E6
Ten Shilling Wood Nature
Reserve* CV4 . . . . 132 A2
Tenter Ct B63. . . . . . 83 B4

Tenter Dr B63 . . . . . . 83 C4
Tenterfields B63. . . . . 83 B4
Tenterfields Prim Sch
B63. . . . . 83 C4
Terminal Rd B26. . . . . 89 F3
Tern Cl WV4 . . . . . . 39 D3
Tern Gr B38 . . . . . . 103 E1
Terrace Rd
Birmingham B15 . . . . 85 F3
Birmingham, Lozells B19. . 66 B7
Terrace St
Brierley Hill DY5 . . . . 61 E5
Rowley Regis B65 . . . 63 B1
Wednesbury WS10. . . . 42 A3
Terrace The
Cradley Heath B64. . . . 82 E8
Wolverhampton WV3 . . 24 C1
Terret Cl WS1 . . . . . . 28 F2
Terry Ave CV32 . . . . 156 C1
Terry Dr B76. . . . . . . 46 F2
Terry Rd CV1. . . . . . 113 F1
Terrys Cl B98 . . . . . . 153 F5
TERRY'S GREEN . . . 141 F7
Terrys La B27 . . . . . . 57 C3
Terry St DY2. . . . . . . 51 E1
Tessall La B31 . . . . . 102 D2
Tetbury Gr B31. . . . . 102 D3
Tetley Ave WS4 . . . . . 29 B4
Tetley Rd B11. . . . . . 87 E3
Tetnall St DY2 . . . . . 62 D8
TETTENHALL 24 D5
Tettenhall Arc WV6 . . . 24 D5
Tettenhall Coll WV6. . . 24 D4
Tettenhall Rd B21 3 WV3, . 25 A2
Tettenhall Rd WV1, WV3,
WV6. . . . . 24 F4
TETTENHALL WOOD . 24 C3
Tettenhall Wood Specl Sch
WV6 . . . . 24 B3
Teviot Gdns
Brierley Hill DY5 . . . . 61 B6
Wolverhampton WV8. . . 10 A5
Teviot Gr B38. . . . . . 123 F8
Teviot Twr B19 . . . . . 66 C5
Tewe Pl WS13 . . . . . . 9 A6
Tewkesbury Dr
Bedworth CV12 . . . . . 78 C3
Dudley DY2 . . . . 62 D3
Tewkesbury Rd
Birmingham B20 . . . . 55 E2
Walsall WS3. . . . . . . 13 E2
Tew Park Rd B21. . . . . 65 E7
Thackeray Cl CV10. . . . 72 A4
Thackeray Dr B79 . . . . 21 A7
Thackeray Rd B30 . . . 103 D5
Thacker Dr WS13 . . . . . 9 A6
Thackhall St CV2. . . . 113 F4
Thame Ct B47 . . . . . 124 E2
Thames Cl
Brierley Hill DY5 . . . . 61 B7
Bulkington CV12 . . . . 79 A3
Thames Coll & London
College of Bsns B5 . . 164 C1
Thames Ct 18 B73. . . . 46 B5
Thames Ho DY3 . . . . . 50 B3
Thames Rd WS3 . . . . 14 E1
Thames Twr B7 . . . . . 67 B5
Thamley Rd CV6 . . . . 113 A4
Thanet Cl DY6 . . . . . 60 C7
Thanet Gr B42 . . . . . 55 C4
Thatchers Ct WV5 . . . . 37 C1
Thatchers The B62. . . . 83 E8
Thatchway Gdns B38. . 123 E7
Thaxted Rd B33. . . . . 69 E3
Theatre App B5. . . . . 164 C1
Theatre Ct CV34 . . . . 160 D6
Theatre St CV34 . . . . 160 D7
Thebes Cl CV5 . . . . . 111 A8
Theddingworth Cl CV3 . 134 E8
Thelbridge Rd B31. . . 122 E6
Thelma Rd DY4 . . . . . 51 E5
Thelma St 1 WS1 . . . . 42 D7
Thelsford Way B92 . . . 107 D8
Theodore Cl
4 Birmingham B17. . . 85 D4
Oldbury B69. . . . . . . 52 E1
Theresa Rd B11. . . . . 87 B7
Thetford Cl DY4 . . . . . 51 D5
Thetford Gdns WV11 . . 26 B6
Thetford Rd B42 . . . . 55 B7
Thetford Way WS5 . . . 43 C3
Thickett Cl WS2 . . . . . 42 B8
Thicknall Dr DY9 . . . . 81 C2
Thicknall La DY9 . . . . 99 B3
Thicknall Rise DY9 . . . 99 B4
Thickthorn Cl CV8 . . . 148 B2
Thickthorn Mews CV8 . 148 B2
Thickthorn Orchs CV8 . 148 B2
Thimble Dr B76 . . . . . 46 F4
THIMBLE END 47 A1
Thimble End Rd B76 . . 47 A2
Thimble Mill La B6, B7 . 67 B7
Thimblemill Rd B67 . . 64 E3
Thimbler Rd CV4. . . . 132 C7
Thinktank Science Mus*
B4 . . . . 66 F3
Third Ave
Birmingham, Bordesley Green
B9 . . . . 67 F2
Birmingham, Selly Oak B29 . 86 C3
Birmingham, Witton B6 . 55 F3
Brownhills WS8 . . . . . 7 A1
Kingswinford DY6 . . . . 60 F8
Wolverhampton WV10 . . 25 F7
Third Exhibition Ave B40 . 90 D4
Third Rd B61 . . . . . . 120 F4
Thirlestane Cl CV8 . . . 148 C6

Thirlmere Ave CV11 . . . 73 F6
Thirlmere Cl
Cannock WS11. . . . . . 1 E1
Coventry CV4. . . . . . 111 E3
Wolverhampton WV6. . . 24 D8
Thirlmere Dr
Birmingham B13 . . . . 105 D8
Essington WV11 . . . . 13 A2
Thirlmere Gr WV6 . . . . 23 F4
Thirlmere Ho 3 B15 . . 85 D3
Thirlmere Rd
Bedworth CV12 . . . . . 78 A2
Hinckley LE10 . . . . . 75 A7
Wolverhampton WV6. . . 24 D8
Thirlmere Wlk DY5 . . . 81 B7
Thirsk Croft B36 . . . . 68 C8
Thirsk Rd CV3 . . . . . 133 C5
Thirsk Way B61 . . . . 121 B1
Thirston Cl WV11 . . . . 27 A5
Thistle Cl DY3 . . . . . 50 F6
Thistle Croft WV11. . . . 26 D5
Thistledown Ave WV7 . . 7 A5
Thistle Down Cl B74 . . 31 A2
Thistledown Dr
3 Cannock WS12. . . . . 2 D1
Featherstone WV10 . . . 12 A7
Thistledown Rd B34. . . 69 C7
Thistledown Wlk DY3 . . 50 E2
Thistle Gn B38 . . . . . 123 E7
Thistlegreen Cl B65. . . 63 F5
Thistlegreen Rd DY2 . . 62 E4
Thistle Ho B36. . . . . . 68 D8
Thistle La B32 . . . . . 102 B7
Thistlewood Gr B93. . . 145 B6
Thistley Field E CV6. . . 113 A7
Thistley Field N CV6. . . 113 A7
Thistley Field S CV6. . . 112 F6
Thistley Field W CV6. . . 112 F7
Thistley Nook WS13. . . . 3 A1
Thomas Barnes Prim Sch
B78. . . . . 20 B7
Thomas Benson Pl 8 B12 . 86 F1
Thomas Cres 2 B66 . . . 65 C5
Thomas Greenway WS13 . 3 A2
Thomas Guy Rd B70. . . 52 F6
Thomas Hardy Ct B79. . 21 A7
Thomas Ho WS3 . . . . 14 D3
Thomas King Ho 6 CV1 . 113 E4
Thomas Landsdail St
CV3 . . . . 133 D8
Thomas Lane St CV6 . . 95 F2
Thomas Mason Cl WV11. . 26 D7
Thomas Naul Croft CV4 . 111 F3
Thomas Sharp St CV4 . . 132 A7
Thomas St
Bedworth CV12 . . . . . 78 A2
Birmingham B6 . . . . . 66 F6
Royal Leamington Spa
CV32 . . . . 157 A1
Smethwick B66 . . . . . 65 B5
Tamworth B77 . . . . . 21 D4
Walsall WS2. . . . . . . 28 D2
West Bromwich B70 . . 53 D2
Wolverhampton WV2 . 163 B1
THOMAS TOWN 159 E3
Thomas Wlk B35. . . . . 58 B3
Thompson Ave
Birmingham B25 . . . . 88 B5
Wolverhampton WV2 . . 39 E6
Thompson Cl
Dudley DY2 . . . . 62 B2
Willenhall WV13 . . . . 27 A3
Thompson Dr B24. . . . 67 F8
Thompson Gdns B67 . . 64 F4
Thompson Ho DY4 . . . 52 C8
Thompson Rd
Oldbury B68. . . . . . . 64 B5
Smethwick B67 . . . . . 64 F4
Thompson's La CV7 . . . 94 E6
Thompson's Rd CV7. . . 94 E6
Thompson St
Bilston WV14. . . . . . 40 D5
Willenhall WV13 . . . . 27 A3
Thomson Ave B38. . . . 103 D1
Thor Cl WS11 . . . . . . 2 A5
Thoresby B79. . . . . . 20 D6
Thoresby Croft DY1 . . . 50 F3
Thornberry Dr DY1 . . . 61 E8
Thornberry Wlk B7 . . . 67 C6
Thornbridge Ave B42 . . 55 D7
Thornbridge Gr WV9 . . 15 F3
Thornbury Cl 1 B30 . . 103 F8
Thornbury Ct WV6. . . . 24 A3
Thornbury Ho B98. . . . 148 A3
Thornbury La B98. . . . 154 C7
Thornbury Rd
Birmingham B20 . . . . 55 D2
Walsall WS5. . . . . . . 28 D4
Thornby Ave
Kenilworth CV8 . . . . 148 B3
Solihull B91 . . . . . . 107 B5
Tamworth B77 . . . . . 35 E8
Thornby Rd B23 . . . . 56 C8
Thorn Cl WS10. . . . . . 41 F4
Thorncliffe Cl B97 . . . 158 A6
Thorncliffe Rd B44. . . . 44 E2
Thorncroft Way WS5 . . 43 B4
Thorne Ave WV10 . . . . 25 E7
Thorne Pl B65 . . . . . 63 C2
Thorne Rd WV13 . . . . 27 A4
THORNES 16 E3
Thorne St WV2 . . . . . 40 A7
Thorneycroft La WV10. . 26 A6
Thorneycroft Pl WV14 . 41 B3
Thorneycroft Rd WV14 . 41 B4

Thorney Rd
Coventry CV2. . . . . . 114 E3
Sutton Coldfield B74 . . 30 E6
Thornfield Cres WS7 . . . 7 A6
Thornfield Croft DY3 . . 50 E5
Thornfield Rd B27 . . . . 88 C2
Thornfield Way LE10 . . 75 F7
Thorngrove Ave 8 B91 . 127 C8
Thornham Way B14 . . 104 C1
Thornhill Dr CV11 . . . 79 C5
Thornhill Gr B21 . . . . 65 E8
Thornhill Pk B74. . . . . 45 A6
Thornhill Rd
Birmingham, Handsworth
B21 . . . . 65 E8
Birmingham, Sparkhill B11 . 87 C5
Brierley Hill DY5 . . . . 81 D4
Cannock WS12. . . . . . 1 D5
Coventry CV1. . . . . . 113 C3
Dudley DY1 . . . . 51 C6
Halesowen B63 . . . . . 82 E5
Redditch B98. . . . . . 154 E2
Solihull B91 . . . . . . 107 C5
Sutton Coldfield B74 . . 31 E3
Thornhurst Ave B32. . . 84 E4
Thornleigh DY3. . . . . . 50 C3
Thornleigh Trad Est DY2 . 62 A7
Thornley Cl
Birmingham B13 . . . . 87 A2
Radford Semele CV31 . 162 F6
Wolverhampton WV11. . 12 B6
Thornley Croft WS6 . . . 4 C2
Thornley Gr B76 . . . . 58 C5
Thornley Rd WV11 . . . 12 B7
Thornley St WV1. . . . 163 C3
Thorn Rd B30. . . . . . 103 E8
Thorns Ave DY5. . . . . 61 E3
Thorns Com Coll DY5 . . 81 F4
Thorns Com Inf Sch CV8 . 148 B6
Thornset Gr B90. . . . . 106 B5
Thorns Prim Sch DY5. . . 81 F4
Thorns Rd DY5. . . . . . 81 E3
Thorn Stile Cl CV32 . . 157 C2
Thornthwaite Cl B45. . 102 B7
Thornton Cl
Coventry CV5. . . . . . 111 C1
Oldbury B69. . . . . . . 52 C6
Warwick CV34 . . . . . 155 F1
Thornton Dr DY5. . . . . 61 E6
Thornton Ho B19 . . . . 66 B6
Thornton Prim Sch B8 . . 68 B4
Thornton Rd
Birmingham B8 . . . . . 68 B4
Solihull B90 . . . . . . 126 E4
Wolverhampton WV1 . . 26 B1
Thorntons Way CV10. . . 72 A3
Thornton Way B77 . . . 35 C6
Thornwood Cl B68. . . . 64 C2
Thornyfield Cl B90 . . . 106 D2
Thornyfield Rd B90. . . 106 D2
Thornyhurst La WS14 . . 17 A8
Thorpe Ave WS7 . . . . . 6 E5
Thorpe Cl
Burntwood WS7. . . . . . 6 E5
Sutton Coldfield B75 . . 46 C6
Thorpe Ct B91 . . . . . 106 F4
Thorpe Rd WS1. . . . . . 42 E6
Thorpe St B5 . . . . . . 164 B1
Thorp St B5. . . . . . . 164 B1
Threadneedle St CV1. . 113 C5
Three Acres La B90 . . 125 F7
Three Corner Cl B90 . . 125 E8
Three Cornered Cl CV32 . 157 E8
Three Oaks Rd B47. . . 125 E8
Three Peaks Prim Sch
B77. . . . . 36 B1
Three Pots Rd LE10 . . . 75 E5
Three Shires Oak Rd B67 . 64 F3
Three Spires Ave CV6 . . 113 A4
Three Spires Ind Est CV6 . 96 A3
Three Spires Jct CV6. . . 95 E4
Three Spires Sh Ctr 11
WS13 . . . . 9 B7
Three Spires Specl Sch
CV6. . . . . 112 D7
Three Tuns La WV10 . . 11 D8
Three Tuns Par WV10 . . 11 C8
Threshers Dr WV12 . . . 27 D7
Threshers Way WV12. . . 27 D7
Throckmorton Rd B98. . 159 A4
Throne Cl B65 . . . . . 63 C4
Throne Cres B65. . . . . 63 D4
Throne Rd B65. . . . . . 63 C4
Throstles Cl B43 . . . . 54 E6
Thruppence Cl CV4 . . 131 F6
Thrushel Wlk WV11 . . . 26 B6
Thrush Rd B68. . . . . . 63 F3
Thruxton Cl
Birmingham B14 . . . . 104 F2
Redditch B98. . . . . . 154 F4
Thunderbolt Way DY4. . 51 E4
Thurcroft Cl B8. . . . . . 67 E4
Thuree Rd B67. . . . . . 64 E4
Thurlby Ct WV1. . . . . 25 C5
Thurleigh Cl DY9 . . . . 81 C2
Thurloe Cres B45. . . . 101 E1
Thurlston Ave B92 . . . 89 B3
Thurlstone Dr WV4 . . . 38 F5
Thurlstone Rd WS3 . . . 14 B4
Thurne B77. . . . . 35 E8
Thursfield Rd
Royal Leamington Spa
CV32. . . . . 157 B2

Thursfield Rd continued
Tipton DY4 . . . . 52 A6
West Bromwich B71 . . . . 53 E7
Thurso B77 . . . . 21 E5
Thurston Ave B69 . . . . 63 F6
Thynne St B70 . . . . 53 E2
Tibbats Cl B32 . . . . 84 C3
Tibberton Cl
Halesowen B63 . . . . 83 C4
Solihull B91 . . . . 127 A8
Wolverhampton WV3 . . . . 38 D7
Tibberton Ct B60 . . . . 150 E7
Tibbets La B17 . . . . 85 B4
TIBBINGTON 51 F7
Tibbington Rd DY4 . . . . 51 F7
Tibbington Terr DY4 . . . . . 51 F7
Tibbits Ct 3 CV34 . . . . . 160 E6
Tibbits Ho 1 WS2 . . . . . . 28 D3
Tibblestone B90 . . . . 126 A5
Tiber Cl CV5 . . . . 111 F4
Tiberius CB46 . . . . 59 F1
Tibland Rd B27 . . . . 88 D2
Ticknall Cl B97 . . . . 153 A4
Tidbury Cl B97 . . . . 158 C6
TIDBURY GREEN 125 E4
Tidbury Green Sch B90 . . 125 E4
Tiddington Cl B36 . . . . 58 B1
Tideswell Cl CV3 . . . . 115 A1
Tideswell Rd B42 . . . . 55 C7
Tidmarsh Cl CV7 . . . . 130 A6
Tidmarsh Rd CV34 . . . . . . 156 A1
Tidworth Croft 2 B14 . . 105 A3
Tierney Dr DY4 . . . . 52 C6
Tiffany La WV9 . . . . 10 F2
Tiffield Rd B25 . . . . 88 C5
Tigley Ave B32 . . . . 84 D1
Tilbury Cl WV3 . . . . 38 A8
Tilbury Gr B13 . . . . 86 D1
Tildasley St B70 . . . . 53 B5
Tildesley Dr WV12 . . . . . . 27 B5
Tile Croft DY9 . . . . 81 E5
TILE CROSS 69 E2
Tile Cross Rd B33 . . . . . . 69 E1
Tile Cross Trad Est B33 . . 69 E1
Tiled House La DY5 . . . . . 61 B6
Tile Gr B37 . . . . 70 A5
TILE HILL 111 E1
Tile Hill La
Coventry, Allesley CV4,
CV5 . . . . 112 C2
Coventry, Tile Hill CV4 . . 112 B1
Tile Hill Sta CV4 . . . . 111 E1
Tile Hill Wood Sch &
Language Coll CV4 . . . . 111 D2
Tilehouse B97 . . . . 153 D2
TILEHOUSE GREEN 127 F6
Tilehouse Green La B93 . 127 F6
Tilehouse La B90 . . . . . . 125 E6
Tilehurst Dr CV4 . . . . 111 D1
Tilesford Cl B90 . . . . 127 A6
Tilewood Ave CV5 . . . . . . 111 F4
**Tile Wood Nature Reserve*
CV4 . . . . 111 D3
Tilia Rd B77 . . . . 22 B5
Tiller Gr B75 . . . . 32 D4
Tilley St WS10 . . . . 41 E6
Tillington Cl B98 . . . . 154 E3
Tillyard Croft B29 . . . . . . 85 C1
Tilshead Cl B14 . . . . 104 E3
Tilsley Gr B23 . . . . 56 B5
Tilston Dr DY5 . . . . 61 D1
Tilton Rd
Birmingham B9 . . . . 67 C1
Hinckley LE10 . . . . 75 E6
Timberdine Cl B63 . . . . . . 82 D6
Timberhonger La B61 . . 136 B2
Timberlake Cl B90 . . . . . 127 B6
Timberley Croft B34 . . . . 69 D7
Timberley La B34 . . . . . . 69 C6
Timber Mill Ct 4 B17 . . 85 B6
Timbers Way
Birmingham B11 . . . . 87 A6
Sutton Coldfield B24 . . . . 57 F4
Timbertree Cres B64 . . . . 82 E7
Timbertree Prim Sch B64 82 E7
Timbertree Rd B64 . . . . . . 82 E7
Times Square Ave DY5 . . 61 F2
Timmins Cl B91 . . . . 107 E6
Timmis Cl WV14 . . . . 40 B3
Timmis Rd DY9 . . . . 81 C6
Timon View CV34 . . . . . . 161 E3
Timothy Gr CV4 . . . . 112 B1
Timothy Rd B69 . . . . 63 D7
Tinacre Hill WV6 . . . . 23 B2
Tinchbourne St 1 DY1 . . 51 C1
Tindal Prim Sch B12 . . . . 86 F5
Tindal St B12 . . . . 86 F5
Tink-A-Tank CV34 . . . . . 160 E6
Tinkers Farm Gr B31 . . . 102 E3
Tinkers Farm Rd B31 . . . 102 E3
Tinkers Green Rd B77 . . . 35 F6
Tinkers La
Earlswood B94 . . . . 142 E7
Lapworth B94 . . . . 143 E1
Tinmeadow Cres B45 . . 122 C7
Tinsley Ave B64 . . . . 62 E2
Tinsley St DY4 . . . . 52 E5
Tintagel Cl
Coventry CV3 . . . . 134 D5
Perton WV6 . . . . 23 F3
Tintagel Dr DY1 . . . . 50 E2
Tintagel Gr CV8 . . . . 148 B4
Tintagel Way
Nuneaton CV11 . . . . 74 A5
Walsall WS9 . . . . 29 E7
Tintern Cl
Bromsgrove B61 . . . . . . 136 E1

Tintern Cl continued
Sutton Coldfield B74 . . . . 45 A7
Tintern Cres WS3 . . . . . . 13 F2
Tintern Ct WV6 . . . . 23 E4
Tintern Ho B32 . . . . 84 F5
Tintern Rd B20 . . . . 55 E1
Tintern Villas 4 B12 . . . 87 B5
Tintern Way
Bedworth CV12 . . . . 78 C3
Walsall WS3 . . . . 13 F2
Tipperary Cl B36 . . . . 68 E8
Tipperary Wlk 2 B69 . . . 63 F7
Tipper Trad Est DY9 . . . . 82 A5
Tippett Cl CV11 . . . . 79 A7
Tipping's Hill B97 . . . . . 158 C5
Tippity Gn B65 . . . . 63 A4
TIPPITY GREEN 63 B4
Tipps Stone Cl DY4 . . . . . 51 E4
TIPTON 51 F6
TIPTON GREEN 51 D5
Tipton Green Jun Sch
DY4 . . . . 51 F4
Tipton Rd
Dudley, Tipton Green DY1 . 51 A3
Dudley, Woodsetton DY3 . 50 F7
Oldbury B69 . . . . 52 C2
Tipton Sta DY3 . . . . 50 E7
Tipton Swimming Ctr DY4 51 F5
Tirley Rd B33 . . . . 69 A4
Tisdale Rise CV8 . . . . . . 148 B6
Titan Bsns Ctr CV34 . . . 161 E4
Titania Cl B45 . . . . 102 A3
Titan Way WS13 . . . . 9 F8
Titchfield Cl WV10 . . . . . . 11 E4
TITFORD 63 F4
Titford Cl B69 . . . . 63 F4
Titford La B65 . . . . 63 E4
Titford Rd B69 . . . . 63 F4
Tithe Barn La B44 . . . . . 142 C6
Tithe Croft WV10 . . . . . . 25 F3
Tithe Rd WV11 . . . . 26 D6
Titterstone Rd B31 . . . . 123 A8
Tiverton Cl DY6 . . . . 61 A3
Tiverton Dr
Nuneaton CV11 . . . . 73 F5
West Bromwich B71 . . . . 53 C6
Tiverton Gr
Coventry CV2 . . . . 114 D5
Smethwick B67 . . . . 64 F6
Tiverton Jun & Inf Sch
B29 . . . . 85 F2
Tiverton Pool & Fitness Ctr
B29 . . . . 85 F1
Tiverton Rd
Birmingham B29 . . . . 85 F2
Coventry CV2 . . . . 114 D5
Smethwick B66 . . . . 65 B5
Tiverton Specl Sch CV2 . 112 D5
Tiveycourt Rd CV6 . . . . . . 96 A3
TIVIDALE 52 B2
Tividale Com Sch B69 . . . 52 B2
Tividale Hall Prim Sch
B69 . . . . 63 A8
Tividale Rd B69 . . . . 52 A2
Tividale St DY4 . . . . 52 A2
Tivoli The B26 . . . . 88 D6
Tixall Rd B28 . . . . 105 E5
TLC Coll WV1 . . . . 25 C4
Tobruk Wlk
Brierley Hill DY5 . . . . 61 D3
Willenhall WV13 . . . . 40 E8
Tocil Croft CV4 . . . . 132 D4
Toledo Gr CV5 . . . . 112 E3
Toler Rd CV11 . . . . 73 B5
Tollard Cl CV2 . . . . 114 F5
TOLLBAR END 134 C4
TOLL END 52 C6
Toll End Rd DY4 . . . . 52 C7
Tolley Rd DY11 . . . . 116 B1
Tollgate Cl B31 . . . . 122 F8
Tollgate Dr B20 . . . . 66 B7
Tollgate Prec B67 . . . . . . 64 F6
Tollhouse Rd B60 . . . . . . 150 E6
Toll House Rd B45 . . . . . 122 C7
Tollhouse Way B66 . . . . . 64 F6
Tolman Dr B77 . . . . 21 D3
Tolson Ave B78 . . . . 35 B8
Tolson Cl B77 . . . . 35 B8
Tolworth Gdns WV2 . . . . . 39 E7
Tolworth Hall Rd B24 . . . 57 B3
Tom Ellis Ct CV7 . . . . 96 A8
Tomey Rd B11 . . . . 87 D5
Tom Henderson Cl CV3 . 134 F7
Tom Hill B94 . . . . 142 B2
Tomkinson Rd CV11 . . . . 116 B4
Tomkinson Rd CV10 . . . . . 72 F4
Tomlan Rd B31 . . . . 123 C7
Tomlinson Rd B36 . . . . . . 58 D1
Tompstone Rd B71 . . . . . . 53 F8
Tomson Ave CV6 . . . . . . 113 A4
Toms Town La B80 . . . . . 159 E3
Tom Ward Cl CV3 . . . . . . 134 E7
Tom Williams Way B37 . . 35 C8
Tonadine Cl WV11 . . . . . . 13 A1
Tonbridge Rd
Birmingham B24 . . . . 57 A1
Coventry CV3 . . . . 134 A6
Tong St 3 WS3 . . . . 29 C4
Tong St WS1 . . . . 29 A1
Tongue Ave B78 . . . . 34 E3
Topcliffe Prim Sch B35 . . 58 A3
Topfield Ho B14 . . . . 104 E1
Top Field Wlk B14 . . . . . 104 D2
Topland Gr B31 . . . . 102 C2
Topp's Dr CV12 . . . . 77 E1
Topp's Heath CV12 . . . . . 77 E1

Top Rd
Barnacle CV7, CV12 . . . . . 97 B7
Upper Catshill B61 . . . . 121 A4
Topsham Croft B14 . . . . 104 D5
Topsham Rd B67 . . . . 64 E6
Torbay B77 . . . . 21 E5
Torbay Rd CV5 . . . . 112 C4
Torcastle Cl CV6 . . . . . . 113 F7
Torc Ave B77 . . . . 21 E4
Torcross Ave CV2 . . . . . 114 C6
Torfield WV8 . . . . 10 E2
Toronto Gdns B32 . . . . . . 84 E6
Torpoint Cl CV2 . . . . 114 C7
Torre Ave B31 . . . . 102 E2
Torrent Cl B77 . . . . 35 E6
Torrence CV34 . . . . 160 B4
Torrey Gr B8 . . . . 68 C4
Torridge B77 . . . . 36 A5
Torridge Dr WV11 . . . . . . 26 C5
Torridon Croft B13 . . . . . 86 D3
Torridon Rd WV11 . . . . . . 13 B1
Torridon Way LE10 . . . . . 71 B1
Torrington Ave CV4 . . . . 131 B8
Torrs Cl B97 . . . . 153 D2
Torside B77 . . . . 36 B7
Torvale Rd WV6 . . . . 24 A2
Tor Way WS3 . . . . 14 F3
Torwood Cl CV4 . . . . 131 F6
Tosheath Cl DY4 . . . . 51 A4
Totnes Cl CV2 . . . . 114 C7
Totnes Gr 8 B29 . . . . 85 F2
Totnes Rd B67 . . . . 64 F6
Tottenham Cres B44 . . . . 45 B2
Touchstone Rd CV34 . . . 155 A1
Touchwood Hall Cl B91 . 107 C4
Touchwood Sh Ctr 1
B91 . . . . 107 C3
Tournament Court Bsns Pk
CV34 . . . . 160 B3
TOURNAMENT FIELDS . . 160 B3
Towbury Cl B98 . . . . 158 F5
Towcester Croft B36 . . . . 68 D8
Tower Croft B37 . . . . 70 A4
Tower Dr B61 . . . . 137 A6
TOWER HILL 55 C6
Tower Hill B42 . . . . 55 A6
Tower Rd
Bedworth CV12 . . . . 78 B2
Birmingham, Aston B6 . . . 67 A7
Birmingham, Aston New Town
B6 . . . . 66 F7
Birmingham B23 . . . . 56 E4
Oldbury B69 . . . . 63 C7
Sutton Coldfield B75 . . . . 32 B3
Tower St
Birmingham B19 . . . . . . 164 B5
Coventry CV1 . . . . 165 B3
Dudley DY1 . . . . 51 C1
Royal Leamington Spa
CV31 . . . . 162 A7
Sedgley DY3 . . . . 39 D1
Walsall WS1 . . . . 28 E2
Wolverhampton WV1 . . . 163 C3
Tower View Cres CV10 . . . 72 B3
Tower View Rd WS6 . . . . 13 F8
Tower Works Ind Est
WV3 . . . . 25 A1
Townend WS2 . . . . 28 E2
Townesend Cl CV34 . . . . 155 F1
Town Feilds Cl CV5 . . . . 112 B7
Townfields WS13 . . . . 9 A7
Townfold WS3 . . . . 15 A4
Town Gate Retail Pk DY1 . 51 F2
Town Hill B WS1 . . . . . . 28 E1
Town Jun Sch B72 . . . . . 46 C4
Townley Gdns B6 . . . . 55 E1
Townsend Ave
Bromsgrove B61 . . . . . . 137 B4
Sedgley DY3 . . . . 50 D8
Townsend Croft CV3 . . . 133 C7
Townsend Dr
Nuneaton CV11 . . . . 73 F3
Sutton Coldfield B76 . . . . 57 F7
Townsend Ho B79 . . . . . . 21 A4
Townsend Pl DY6 . . . . 60 D6
Townsend Rd CV3 . . . . . 133 C8
Townsends Cl CV11 . . . . . 75 A1
Townsend Way 5 B1 . . . . 66 B3
Townshend Gr B37 . . . . . . 69 F4
Townson Rd WV11 . . . . . . 27 A8
Town Wall B77 . . . . 35 F6
Townwell Fold WV1 . . . . 163 B3
Town Wharf Bsns Pk
WS2 . . . . 28 D2
Towpath Cl
Bedworth CV6 . . . . 96 B6
Birmingham B9 . . . . 67 B2
Towyn Rd B13 . . . . 87 D2
Toys La B63 . . . . 83 B6
Tozer St DY4 . . . . 51 F7
Traceys Mdw B45 . . . . . 122 A7
Tractor Spares Ind Est
WV13 . . . . 26 D2
Trafalgar Cl WS12 . . . . 2 E4
Trafalgar Ct B69 . . . . 52 B1
Trafalgar Gr B25 . . . . 88 A6
Trafalgar Ho
Birmingham B1 . . . . 87 B8
Cannock WS12 . . . . 2 E4
3 Coventry CV1 . . . . 113 B2
Trafalgar Rd
Birmingham, Erdington
B24 . . . . 56 F3
Birmingham, Handsworth
B21 . . . . 65 E8

Trafalgar Rd continued
Birmingham, Moseley B13 . . 86 F4
Oldbury B69 . . . . 52 B1
Smethwick B66 . . . . 65 C4
Trafalgar Way WS14 . . . . . 9 B5
Trafford Cl CV10 . . . . 72 C6
Trafford Dr CV10 . . . . 72 C6
Trafford Lodge 4 CV31 162 B7
Trafford Pk The B98 . . . 153 F3
Trafford Rd LE10 . . . . 71 F2
Trainor Cl 3 CV6 . . . . . . 95 F1
Trajan Hill B46 . . . . 59 F1
Tram St DY10 . . . . 116 E5
Tram Way B66 . . . . 64 C7
Tramway Cl
1 Bilston WV14 . . . . 41 A7
Darlaston WS10 . . . . 41 A7
**Transport Mus Wythall The*
B47 . . . . 124 E3
Tranter Ave B48 . . . . 139 A5
Tranter Cres WS11 . . . . . . 2 B3
Tranter Rd B8 . . . . 68 A5
Tranwell CV WV9 . . . . 10 F2
Traquain Dr DY1 . . . . 51 A3
Travellers Cl WS7 . . . . 7 A5
Travellers Way B37 . . . . . 70 D3
Treaford La B8 . . . . 68 C4
Treasure B77 . . . . 21 E4
Treddles La B70 . . . . 53 D3
Tredington Cl
8 Birmingham B29 . . . . 103 A7
Redditch B98 . . . . 159 B7
Tredington Rd CV5 . . . . . 111 F4
Tree Acre Gr B63 . . . . 82 C4
Treedale Cl CV4 . . . . 131 D8
Treeford Cl B91 . . . . 106 F1
Treeside Way WS9 . . . . . 30 A6
Trees Rd WS1 . . . . 42 F6
Treeton Croft B33 . . . . . . 69 A2
Treetops Dr WV12 . . . . . . 27 E4
Trefoil B77 . . . . 22 B5
Trefoil Cl B29 . . . . 103 A7
Trefoil Gdns DY8 . . . . 81 A6
Treford Ct DY9 . . . . 81 B1
Treforest Rd CV3 . . . . . . 134 C8
Tregarron Rd B63 . . . . . . 82 C5
Tregea Rise B43 . . . . 54 C7
Tregony Rise WS14 . . . . . . 9 D6
Tregorrick Rd CV7 . . . . . . 96 B8
Tregullan Rd CV7 . . . . 96 B8
Treharne Cl B93 . . . . 128 A5
Treherne Rd CV6 . . . . . . 113 B8
Trehernes Dr DY9 . . . . . . 81 B1
Trehurst Ave B42 . . . . 55 C7
Trelawney Rd CV7 . . . . . . 96 A7
Tremaine Gdns WV10 . . . 25 E4
Tremont Ho WV10 . . . . . . 25 E3
Tremont St WV10 . . . . 25 E3
Trenance Cl B97 . . . . 9 D7
Trenance Rd CV7 . . . . 96 A8
Trenchard Cl B75 . . . . 46 F5
Treneere Rd CV7 . . . . 96 B8
Trensale Ave CV6 . . . . . . 112 F4
Trent Cl
Burntwood WS7 . . . . 7 D6
Perton WV6 . . . . 23 E4
Stourbridge DY8 . . . . 81 A4
Trent Cres B47 . . . . 124 E2
Trent Ct 11 B73 . . . . 46 B5
Trent Dr B36 . . . . 69 F8
Trentham Ave WV12 . . . . 27 B5
Trentham Cl
Cannock WS11 . . . . 2 B1
Nuneaton CV11 . . . . 78 F8
Trentham Gdns CV8 . . . . 148 C5
Trentham Gr B26 . . . . 88 E5
Trentham Rd CV1 . . . . . . 113 F4
Trentham Rise WV2 . . . . . 39 F7
Trent Ho
Cannock WS12 . . . . 2 C5
Dudley DY3 . . . . 50 E3
Trent Pl WS3 . . . . 28 D8
Trent Rd
Bulkington CV12 . . . . 79 A2
Cannock WS11 . . . . 1 E5
Hinckley LE10 . . . . 75 A8
Nuneaton CV11 . . . . 73 D5
Walsall WS3 . . . . 15 A1
Trent St B5 . . . . 66 F2
Trent Twr 3 B7 . . . . 67 A4
Trent Valley Cotts WS13 . . 3 F1
Trent Valley Rd WS13,
WS14 . . . . 9 F8
Trenville Ave B11 . . . . 87 B5
Tresco Cl B45 . . . . 101 E1
TRESCOTT 37 B7
Trescott Prim Sch B31 . . 102 D3
Trescott Rd
Birmingham B31 . . . . . . 102 D4
Redditch B98 . . . . 153 F3
Tresham Rd
Birmingham B44 . . . . 44 F1
2 Kingswinford DY6 . . . . 60 D8
Tresillian Rd CV7 . . . . 96 B8
Tressel Croft CV34 . . . . . 161 E4
Trevanie Ave B32 . . . . 84 C6
Trevan Ho 1 B37 . . . . 70 B1
Treville Cl B98 . . . . 154 E3
Treviscoe Cl CV7 . . . . 96 A7
Trevithick Cl WS7 . . . . 7 C8
Trevor Ave WS6 . . . . 5 A3
Trevor Cl CV4 . . . . 131 C6
Trevorne Cl B12 . . . . 86 F6
Trevor Rd
Hinckley LE10 . . . . 71 F1
Walsall WS3 . . . . 14 F5
Trevor St B7 . . . . 67 C6

Trevor Street Ind Est B7 . . 67 C6
Trevor Street W B7 . . . . . 67 C6
Trevose Ave CV7 . . . . 96 B8
Trevose Cl WS3 . . . . 13 F3
Trevose Retreat B12 . . . . 86 F5
Trewint Cl CV7 . . . . 96 A8
Trewman Cl B76 . . . . 57 F8
Treyamon Rd WS5 . . . . . . 43 D7
Treynham Cl WV1 . . . . . . 26 C1
TRIANGLE 7 B4
Triangle The
Birmingham B18 . . . . 65 F6
Coventry CV5 . . . . 112 B4
Trianon Rd B60 . . . . 137 C1
Tribune Ho 4 LE10 . . . . . 71 D1
Trickley Dr 2 B75 . . . . . . 46 B1
Trident Bsns Pk CV11 . . . 73 D3
Trident Bvd B35 . . . . 58 B2
Trident Cl
Sutton Coldfield, Walmley
B76 . . . . 57 F7
Sutton Coldfield, Wylde Green
B23 . . . . 57 A7
Trident Ct
Birmingham, Coleshill Heath
B37 . . . . 90 E8
Birmingham, Handsworth Wood
B20 . . . . 55 A3
Trident Ctr The DY1 . . . . . 51 C1
Trident Dr
Oldbury B68 . . . . 64 B5
Wednesbury WS10 . . . . . 41 D3
Trident Ho 1 B15 . . . . . . 66 C1
Trident Rd B26 . . . . 90 C4
Trident Ret Pk B9 . . . . . . 67 A2
Trigo Croft B36 . . . . 68 E8
Trimpley Cl B93 . . . . 127 E3
Trimpley Dr
Coventry 113 C6
Kidderminster DY11 . . . . 116 A7
Trimpley Gdns WV4 . . . . . 38 E3
Trimpley Rd B32 . . . . 84 B1
Trinculo Gr CV34 . . . . . . 161 F2
Trinder Rd B67 . . . . 64 D2
Trindle Rd DY2 . . . . 51 D1
Trine CV WV6 . . . . 24 F4
Trinity CE Prim Sch WS3 25 F4
Trinity Cl
1 Birmingham B19 . . . . . 66 D8
Cannock WS11 . . . . 4 E8
Shenstone WS14 . . . . . . 17 F6
Solihull B92 . . . . 89 B1
Stourbridge DY8 . . . . 60 D2
Trinity Ct
Birmingham B6 . . . . 55 D1
Bromsgrove B60 . . . . . . 151 B7
4 Cradley Heath B64 . . 62 E1
Hinckley LE10 . . . . 75 C8
6 Kidderminster DY10 . 116 F6
Wolverhampton WV3 . . . 25 A2
Trinity Ctr 1 B64 . . . . . . 62 E1
Trinity Dr B79 . . . . 20 D6
Trinity Fields DY10 . . . . . 116 F6
Trinity Gr WS10 . . . . 42 A3
Trinity Grange DY10 . . . . 116 F7
Trinity High Sch & Sixth
Form Ctr B98 . . . . 153 F4
Trinity Hill B72 . . . . 46 C5
Trinity Ho B70 . . . . 53 E1
Trinity La
Coventry CV1 . . . . 165 B3
Hinckley LE10 . . . . 71 C1
Trinity Pk B40 . . . . 90 D3
Trinity RC Sch CV32 . . . 156 D2
Trinity Rd
Bilston WV14 . . . . 40 F5
Birmingham B6 . . . . 55 E1
Dudley DY1 . . . . 51 C1
Freasley B78, CV9 . . . . . 36 B3
Stourbridge DY8 . . . . 81 A8
Sutton Coldfield B75 . . . . 32 C1
Willenhall WV12 . . . . 27 D1
Trinity Road N B70 . . . . . 53 D2
Trinity Road S B70 . . . . . 53 D1
Trinity St
Brierley Hill DY5 . . . . 61 D3
Coventry CV1 . . . . 165 B3
Cradley Heath B64 . . . . . 62 E1
Oldbury B69 . . . . 64 A6
Royal Leamington Spa
CV32 . . . . 156 F1
Trinity St B66 . . . . 65 A6
West Bromwich B70 . . . . 53 D1
Trinity Terr 2 B11 . . . . . . 87 A8
Trinity Vicarage Rd LE10 . 75 C8
Trinity Way
Birmingham B20 . . . . 53 D2
West Bromwich B70 . . . . 53 D1
Trinity Way Stop B70 . . . 53 D1
Trinity Wlk CV11 . . . . 73 E3
Trippleton Ave B32 . . . . 102 B8
Tristram Ave B31 . . . . . . 103 B1
Triton Cl WS6 . . . . 4 F1
Triton Rd CV10 . . . . 73 C1
Trittiford Rd B13 . . . . 105 C6
Triumph B77 . . . . 21 E3
Triumph Cl CV2 . . . . 114 E3
Triumph Ho CV1 . . . . 165 B2
Triumph Wlk B36 . . . . 59 A1
Troilus Cl CV34 . . . . 161 F3
Trojan B77 . . . . 21 E3
Trojans Cl B64 . . . . 82 E7
Tromans Ind Est DY2 . . . . 62 E3
Troon B77 . . . . 22 C4

Troon Cl
Sutton Coldfield B75 .... 46 D8
Walsall WS3 .... 14 A3
Troon Ct WV6 .... 23 D5
Troon Pl DY8 .... 60 C3
Troon Way LE10 .... 75 D4
Trossachs Rd CV5 ..... 111 F3
Trostrey Rd B30 .... 104 E3
Trotter's La B71 .... 53 A7
Troughton Cres CV6 .... 113 A5
Trouse La WS10 .... 41 F3
Troutbeck Ave CV32 ... 156 C2
Troutbeck Dr DY5 ..... 81 B8
Troutbeck Rd CV5 ..... 111 F4
Troyes Cl CV3 .... 133 E7
Troy Gr B14 .... 104 D4
Troy Ind Est B96 ...... 159 A3
Truck Stop Bsns Pk B11 .. 88 B5
Truda St **2** WS1 .... 42 D7
Trueman Cl CV34 ...... 160 E8
TRUEMAN'S HEATH 125 C7
Truemans Heath La B47,
B90 .... 125 C7
Truggist La CV7 .... 130 E8
Trundalls La B90 .... 126 A5
Trunkfield Mdw WS13 .... 8 F6
Truro Cl
Hinckley LE10 .... 71 E4
Lichfield WS13 .... 3 B3
Nuneaton CV11 .... 73 F5
Rowley Regis B65 ..... 63 E4
Truro Dr DY11 .... 116 A5
Truro Pl WS12 .... 5 C8
Truro Rd WS5 .... 43 D7
Truro Twr **8** B16 ...... 66 A2
Truro Wlk B37 .... 70 B2
Trustin Cres B92 ...... 107 E8
Tryan Rd CV10 .... 72 E4
Tryon Pl WV14 .... 40 E6
Tryst The B61 .... 137 B5
TRYSULL 37 C1
Trysull Ave B26 .... 89 C4
Trysull Gdns WV3 ..... 38 D7
Trysull Holloway WV5 .. 37 C3
Trysull Rd
Orton WV5 .... 37 E1
Wolverhampton WV3 ... 38 D7
Trysull Way DY2 ...... 62 C4
Tudbury Rd B31 .... 102 E4
Tudman Cl B76 .... 58 A7
Tudor Ave CV5 .... 111 E4
Tudor Bsns Ctr **8** B98 .. 153 E1
Tudor Cl
Balsall Common CV7 .... 130 A6
Birmingham, Highter's Heath
B14 .... 105 A1
Birmingham, King's Heath
B13 .... 104 F6
Cheslyn Hay WS6 ...... 4 E3
Lichfield WS14 .... 9 F6
Sutton Coldfield B73 ... 45 D2
Tudor Coppice B91 .... 107 B2
Tudor Cres
Tamworth B77 .... 21 F4
Wolverhampton WV2 ... 39 B6
Tudor Croft B37 ...... 69 F1
Tudor Ct
Bedworth CV7 .... 95 E7
Coventry CV3 .... 133 C8
Essington WV11 .... 12 F4
Sutton Coldfield B74 ... 32 A2
Tipton DY4 .... 52 A4
Warwick CV34 .... 160 D5
Tudor Eaves **2** B17 .... 85 C5
Tudor Gdns
Birmingham B23 ...... 56 E3
Stourbridge DY8 ...... 80 E5
Tudor Gr B44 .... 45 A8
Tudor Grange L Ctr B91 107 A3
Tudor Grange Sch B91 .. 107 A2
TUDOR HILL 46 B6
Tudor Hill B73 .... 46 B6
Tudor Ho
Dudley DY2 .... 61 F6
Walsall WS1 .... 28 E2
Tudor Ind Est B11 ..... 88 B5
Tudor Park Ct **2** B74 .. 31 F3
Tudor Park Gdns WS7 ... 7 C6
Tudor Pl DY3 .... 50 E6
Tudor Rd
Birmingham B13 ...... 86 F3
Burntwood WS7 .... 7 C6
Cannock WS12 .... 1 F8
Darlaston WV14 .... 41 B4
Dudley DY3 .... 50 E6
Hinckley LE10 .... 71 C3
Nuneaton CV10 .... 72 C6
Oldbury B68 .... 64 C4
Rowley Regis B65 ..... 63 C3
Sutton Coldfield B73 ... 46 B5
Wolverhampton WV10 .. 26 A4
Tudor Row **8** WS13 ..... 9 B7
Tudors Cl **8** B10 .... 87 C8
Tudor St
Birmingham B18 ...... 65 E4
Tipton DY4 .... 52 A4
Tudor Terr
Birmingham B17 ...... 85 C6
Dudley DY2 .... 51 F1
Tudor Vale DY3 .... 50 E6
Tudor Way
Cheslyn Hay WS6 ...... 4 D1
Sutton Coldfield B72 .... 46 B2
Tufnell Gr B8 .... 68 B7

Tugford Rd B29 .... 103 C7
Tulip Gdns B29 .... 102 F7
Tulip Gr B74 .... 44 F7
Tulip Tree Ave CV8. .... 148 B5
Tulip Tree Ct CV8 ..... 148 B4
Tulip Wlk B37 .... 90 C8
Tulliver Cl CV12 .... 78 B3
Tulliver Rd CV10 ...... 73 C1
Tulliver St CV6 .... 113 B5
Tulsi Ctr B19 .... 164 A4
Tulyar Cl B36 .... 68 C8
Tumbler Gr WV10 ..... 25 F3
Tunnel Dr B98 .... 153 E2
Tunnel La
Birmingham, Brandwood End
B14 .... 104 C4
Birmingham, Lifford B30 .. 104 B4
Tunnel Rd B70 .... 53 A7
Tunnel St WV14 .... 51 C8
Tunstall Rd DY6 .... 61 A5
Tunstall Dr B76 .... 58 B8
Turf Cl WS11 .... 6 A4
Turf Cotts WV4 .... 38 F2
Turfpits La B23 .... 56 D6
Turfs Hill B65 .... 32 F4
Turks Head Way B70 .. 53 C2
Turlands Cl CV2 ...... 115 A7
Turley St DY1 .... 51 A6
Turls Hill Rd DY3 ...... 50 E8
Turls St DY3 .... 50 E8
Turnberry B77 .... 22 C5
Turnberry Dr CV11 .... 79 C8
Turnberry Gr WV6 .... 23 D5
Turnberry Rd
Birmingham B42 ...... 55 B8
Walsall WS3 .... 14 A4
Turner Ave WV4, WV14 .. 39 F7
Turner Cl
Bedworth CV12 .... 78 A4
Cannock WS11 .... 2 D2
Warwick CV34 .... 160 B4
Turner Dr
Brierley Hill DY5 ...... 81 D7
Hinckley LE10 .... 71 A3
Turner Gr WV6 .... 24 A4
Turner Rd CV5 .... 112 D3
Turners Croft B71 ..... 54 A8
Turner's Gr DY3 ...... 50 C4
Turner's Hill B65 ...... 63 B6
Turner's Hill Rd DY3 .. 50 C4
Turner's La DY5 ...... 61 D1
Turner St
Birmingham B11 ...... 87 A6
Dudley, Gornalwood DY3 .. 50 D3
2 Dudley, Old Dock DY1 .. 62 B8
Tipton DY4 .... 51 F7
West Bromwich B70 ... 53 A4
Turney Rd DY8 .... 80 F6
Turnham Gn WV6 ..... 23 E3
Turnhouse Rd B35 .... 58 B4
Turnley Rd B34 .... 69 C6
Turnpike Cl
Balsall Common CV7 ... 130 B7
Birmingham B11 ...... 87 A6
Turnpike Dr B46 ...... 59 C2
Turnpike La B97 ...... 153 A4
Turnstone Dr WV10 ... 12 B7
Turnstone Rd DY10 ... 117 A1
Turpin Ct CV31 .... 161 F6
Turquoise Gr WS11 ... 2 C3
Turton Cl WS3 .... 14 A4
Turton Rd
Tipton DY4 .... 40 F1
West Bromwich B70 ... 53 B2
Turtons Croft WV14 ... 40 B3
Turton St DY10 .... 117 A8
Turton Way CV8 ...... 148 C4
Turves Grn
Birmingham, Turves Green
B31 .... 103 B2
Birmingham, West Heath
B31 .... 122 F8
TURVES GREEN 103 A3
Turves Green Boys' Sch **4**
B31 .... 123 A8
Turves Green Com L Ctr
B31 .... 103 A1
Turves Green Girls Sch &
Tech Coll B31 .... 103 A1
Turves Green Prim Sch **5**
B31 .... 103 A1
Turville Cl LE10 .... 75 F5
Turville Rd B20 .... 55 C1
Tustin Gr B27 .... 106 C8
Tutbury B77 .... 35 C7
Tutbury Ave
Coventry CV4 .... 132 E6
Perton WV6 .... 24 A3
Tutbury Cl WS11 ...... 2 C3
Tutehill B77 .... 36 B7
Tutnall Cl B60 .... 137 F1
Tutnall Dr B94 .... 143 B6
Tutnall Grange B60 ... 138 A1
Tutnall La
Blackwell B60 .... 138 A1
Finstall B60 .... 137 F1
Tutors Way DY10 ...... 116 E4
Tuttle Hill CV10 .... 72 F6
Tuxford Cl WV10 .... 25 E4
Twatling Rd B45 ...... 122 A2
Tweedside Cl LE10 ..... 71 F3
Tweeds Well B32 ...... 102 B7
Tweed Twr B20 .... 55 D2
Twickenham Ct CV8 ... 80 C7
Twickenham Dr B13 ... 86 E2
Twickenham Prim Sch
B44 .... 45 C1
Twickenham Rd B44 ... 45 C1

Twickenham Way CV3... 115 B1
Twiners Rd B98 .... 153 F1
TWO GATES 35 D8
Two Gates B63 .... 82 C5
Two Gates Com Prim Sch
B77 .... 35 C8
Two Gates Ind Est B77 .. 35 D7
Two Gates La B63 ...... 82 C5
Two Locks DY5 .... 62 A4
Two Oaks Ave WS7 .... 6 D8
Two Rivers High Sch B77. 21 F1
Two Rivers Sch B77 ... 22 A3
Two Trees Cl B78 ..... 20 B6
Two Woods La DY5 .... 61 E1
Twycross Gr B36 .... 68 D7
Twycross Rd LE10 ..... 75 F6
Twycross Wlk CV34 ... 155 D1
Twydale Ave B69 ...... 52 C2
Twyford Cl WS9 .... 30 B5
Twyford Gr WV11 ..... 26 F7
Twyford Rd B8 .... 68 C5
Twyning Rd
Birmingham, Edgbaston
B16 .... 65 D3
Birmingham, Stirchley B30 104 B7
Tybalt Cl
Coventry CV3 .... 134 C5
Royal Leamington Spa
CV34 .... 161 D4
Tyber Dr B20 .... 55 B3
Tyberry Cl B90 .... 106 A1
TYBURN 57 E3
Tyburn Dr B24 .... 57 D3
Tyburn Gr B24 .... 57 D3
Tyburn Trad Est B24 ... 57 D2
Tyebeams B34 .... 69 C5
Tye Gdns DY9 .... 81 B1
Tyler Ct B24 .... 56 F3
Tyler Gdns WV13 ...... 27 B1
Tyler Gr B43 .... 44 A1
Tyler Rd WV13 .... 27 B1
Tylers Gn B38 .... 104 B1
Tylers Gr B90 .... 126 F6
Tylney Cl
Birmingham B5 .... 86 D7
Coventry CV3 .... 115 B2
Tyndale Cres B43 ..... 44 C3
Tyndall Wlk B32 ...... 84 A2
Tyne Cl
Birmingham B37 ...... 70 C4
Brownhills WS8 .... 6 C2
Tyne Ct **2** B73 .... 46 B5
Tynedale Cres WV4 ... 39 E3
Tynedale Rd B11 ...... 87 F3
Tyne Gr B25 .... 88 D8
Tynemouth Cl CV2 .... 96 D5
Tyne Pl DY5 .... 61 F2
Tynes The B60 .... 150 E7
Tyning Cl WV9 .... 11 A2
Tyninghame Ave WV6 .. 24 D7
Tynings La WS9 .... 30 A5
Tynsall Ave B97 ...... 152 F2
Tynward Cl CV3 .... 133 B5
Tyrley Cl WV6 .... 24 B2
Tyrol Cl DY8 .... 80 D6
TYSELEY 88 A4
Tyseley Hill Rd B11 .... 88 A4
Tyseley Ind Est B11 ... 87 E5
Tyseley La B11 .... 88 A4
Tyseley Locomotive Wks
Visitor Ctr * B11 ..... 87 F5
Tyseley Sta B11 .... 88 A5
Tysoe Cl
Hockley Heath B94 .... 143 C6
Redditch B98 .... 154 D2
Tysoe Croft CV3 ...... 134 F8
Tysoe Dr B76 .... 46 F4
Tysoe Rd B44 .... 55 F7
Tythe Barn Cl B60 .... 150 D6
Tythebarn Dr DY6 .... 60 A7
Tythe Barn La B90 .... 126 A6
Tyzack Cl DY5 .... 61 C2

U

Udall Rd WV14 .... 40 D3
Uffculme Rd B30 ...... 104 D8
Uffculme Specl Sch B13. 86 E1
UFFMOOR 82 E1
Uffmoor Est B63 ...... 82 E2
Uffmoor La B62 .... 100 D7
Ufton Cl B90 .... 106 D3
Ufton Cres B90 .... 106 D3
Ufton Croft CV5 ...... 112 A3
Ullapool Cl B97 .... 158 D5
Ullenhall Rd
Dorridge B93 .... 128 A6
Sutton Coldfield B76 ... 57 F8
Ullenwood B21 .... 65 D7
Ulleries Rd B92 .... 89 A2
Ullrik Gn B24 .... 56 F2
Ullswater B77 .... 36 B7
Ullswater Ave
Nuneaton CV11 .... 73 F6
Royal Leamington Spa
CV32 .... 156 C2
Ullswater Cl B32 ...... 84 F2
Ullswater Gdns DY6 ... 60 D6
Ullswater Ho **4** B69 ... 63 D5
Ullswater Rd
Bedworth CV12 .... 78 A2
Coventry CV3 .... 114 E1

Ullswater Rd continued
Willenhall WV11 ...... 13 B1
Ullswater Rise DY5 .... 61 E5
Ulster Cl WV11 .... 2 A3
Ulster Dr DY6 .... 60 E4
Ulverley Cres B92 ..... 106 F8
ULVERLEY GREEN 89 A1
Ulverley Green Rd B92. 88 F1
Ulverley Sch B92 ..... 89 B1
Ulverscroft Rd CV3 .... 133 D7
Ulwine Dr B31 .... 102 F8
Umberslade Farm Pk*
B94 .... 142 C2
Umberslade Rd
Birmingham B29 ...... 104 A8
Earlswood B94 .... 142 C7
Tanworth-In-A B94 .... 142 E3
Uncle Ben's Cl **1** B69 .. 63 F4
UNDERHILL 12 B2
Underhill Cl
Coventry CV3 .... 133 D3
Redditch B98 .... 158 F6
Underhill La WV10 .... 12 A2
Underhill Rd
Birmingham B8 .... 67 F3
Tipton DY4 .... 52 C6
Underhill St B69 ...... 64 A5
Underhill Wlk B69 .... 64 A5
Underley Cl DY6 ...... 60 B7
Underpass The B40 ... 90 E4
Underwood Cl
Birmingham B15 ...... 85 D4
Birmingham, Stockland Green
B23 .... 56 C4
Redditch B97 .... 158 A7
Underwood Rd B20 ... 54 E5
Unett Cl **8** B66 .... 65 C5
Unett St
Birmingham B19 ...... 66 C5
Smethwick B66 .... 65 C4
Unett Wlk B19 .... 66 C5
Unicorn Ave CV5 ...... 111 E4
Unicorn Hill B97 ...... 153 D4
Unicorn La CV5 .... 111 F4
Union Bldgs CV1 ...... 165 B2
Union Dr B73 .... 45 F2
Union Ho B73 .... 45 F2
Union La WV5 .... 37 D2
Union Mill St WV1 .... 163 D3
Union Pas B2 .... 164 C2
Union Pl
Birmingham B29 ...... 86 B2
Coventry CV6 .... 95 F4
Union Rd
Birmingham B6 .... 67 B8
Oldbury B69 .... 52 E2
Royal Leamington Spa
CV32 .... 156 E1
Solihull, Lode Heath B91. 107 C4
Solihull, Shirley B90 ... 106 C2
West Bromwich B70 ... 52 F2
Union Row B21 .... 65 F7
Union St
Bilston WV14 .... 40 C5
Birmingham B2 .... 164 C2
Burntwood WS7 .... 6 E5
Cannock WS11 .... 4 E6
6 Dudley DY1 .... 51 C1
Kidderminster DY10 ... 116 E7
Redditch B98 .... 153 F3
Rowley Regis B65 ..... 63 C1
Stourbridge, Lye DY9 ... 81 E5
Stourbridge, Stambermill
DY8 .... 81 A4
Tipton, Princes End DY1 . 51 F8
Tipton, Tipton Green DY4. 51 F5
Walsall WS1 .... 28 F1
Wednesbury WS10 .... 41 F2
West Bromwich B70 ... 64 D8
Willenhall WV13 ...... 27 A2
Wolverhampton WV1 ... 163 C3
Unisant Trad Est B64 .. 62 F2
Unitt Dr B64 .... 62 E8
Unity Cl WS10 .... 41 C4
Unity Ho CV1 .... 165 C4
Unity Pl
8 Birmingham B29 .... 85 F2
Oldbury B69 .... 64 A8
Unity Wlk DY4 .... 51 F5
Univ Coll Birmingham
B3 .... 164 A3
University Hospital Coventry
CV2 .... 115 A5
University Rd CV4 ..... 132 C5
University Road W B15.. 85 F4
University Sta B15 .... 85 G4
Univ of Birmingham
(Edgbaston Campus)
B15 .... 85 F4
Univ of Birmingham (School
of Dentistry) B4 ..... 164 C3
Univ of Birmingham (Selly
Oak Campus) B29 .... 103 D8
Univ of Warwick (Central
Campus) CV4 .... 132 C4
Univ of Warwick (Gibbet Hill)
CV4 .... 132 D3
Univ of Warwick Science Pk
CV4 .... 132 C5
Univ of Warwick (Westwood
Campus) CV4 .... 132 B6
Univ of Wolverhampton (City
Campus North) WV1 .. 163 B4
Univ of Wolverhampton (City
Campus South) WV1 .. 163 B3
Univ of Wolverhampton
(Compton Park Campus)
WV6 .... 24 E2

Univ of Wolverhampton
(Walsall Campus) WS1.. 43 A7
Univ of Wolverhampton
(Wolverhampton Science
Pk) **1** WV10 .... 25 C6
Unketts Rd B67 .... 64 E8
Unwin Cres DY8 ...... 80 E5
Upavon Cl B35 .... 58 A4
Upfield Cotts WS7 .... 7 E7
Upland Gr B61 .... 137 A4
Upland Rd
Birmingham B29 ...... 86 B3
Bromsgrove B61 ...... 137 B4
Uplands
Coventry CV2 .... 114 A5
Halesowen B63 .... 82 E2
Uplands Ave
Rowley Regis B65 ..... 63 D3
Willenhall WV13 ...... 26 D1
Wolverhampton WV3 ... 38 D8
Uplands Cl DY2 .... 62 E7
Uplands Dr
Sedgley DY3 .... 50 D8
Wombourne WV5 ...... 38 E8
Wombourne WV5 ..... 49 A6
Uplands Gr WV13 ..... 26 C1
Uplands Jun Sch WV3.. 38 D8
Uplands Manor Prim Sch
B67 .... 64 F3
Uplands Rd
Birmingham B21 ...... 54 D2
Dudley DY2 .... 62 F7
Wolverhampton WV13.. 26 C1
Uplands The B67 ...... 64 F4
Upleadon Cl B97 ...... 158 A6
Upper Ashby St CV11 .. 73 B5
Upper Ashley St B62 .. 63 C1
Upper Balsall Heath Rd
B12 .... 86 F6
UPPER BENTLEY 152 A1
Upper Bond St LE10 ... 71 D1
Upper Brook St WS2 .. 28 D1
Upper Cape CV34 ..... 160 D8
UPPER CATSHILL 121 B2
Upper Chapel St B69 .. 52 B2
Upper Church La DY4 .. 52 A6
Upper Cl B32 .... 84 D3
Upper Clifton Rd B73 .. 46 B6
Upper Conybere St **6**
B12 .... 86 F7
Upper Crossgate Rd B98 159 C8
Upper Dean St B5 ..... 164 C1
UPPER EASTERN
GREEN 111 D4
Upper Eastern Green La
CV5 .... 111 E5
Upper Ettingshall Rd
WV14 .... 51 B8
Upper Field Cl B98 .... 154 C6
Upperfield Way CV3 ... 115 A1
Upper Forster St WS4.. 28 F3
Upper Gambolds La B60. 151 C5
Upper Gn WV6 .... 24 D5
UPPER GORNAL 50 F6
Upper Gough St B1 ... 164 B1
Upper Green La WS2 ... 28 C4
Upper Grosvenor Rd B20. 55 B2
Upper Grove St **8** CV32 156 E1
Upper Gungate B79 ... 21 B6
Upper Hall Cl B98 .... 154 D2
Upper Hall La **6** WS1 .. 28 E2
Upper Hattons Cotts WV9 10 D5
Upper Highgate St B12. 86 F7
Upper High St
Cradley Heath B64 .... 62 D1
Wednesbury WS10 .... 41 F3
Upper Hill St
Coventry CV1 .... 165 A3
Royal Leamington Spa
CV32 .... 157 A1
Upper Holland Rd B72.. 46 C4
Upper Kent St WV13 ... 27 A1
Upper Keys Bsns Pk WS12. 2 E3
Upper Ladies Hills CV8. 148 A6
UPPER LANDYWOOD ... 13 E8
Upper Landywood La
Cheslyn Hay WS6 ...... 4 D1
Great Wyrley WS6 .... 13 D8
Upper Lichfield St WV13 27 A2
UPPER MARLBROOK ... 121 D2
Upper Marshall St B1.. 164 B1
Upper Meadow Rd B32. 84 C5
Upper Mill La B5 ...... 164 C1
Upper Norgrove Ho B97. 152 F1
Upper Pk CV3 .... 134 D6
Upper Portland St B6.. 67 A7
Upper Prescot St CV34. 134 D5
Upper Rushall St WS1.. 28 F1
Upper Russell St **1** WS10 41 F2
Upper St John St WS1.. 9 B6
Upper St Mary's Rd B67. 64 F4
Upper Short St WS2 ... 28 D1
Upper Sneyd Rd WV11. 13 B2
Upper Spon St CV1 .... 113 A3
Upper Spring La CV8 .. 147 F7
Upper St WV6 .... 24 D5
UPPER STOKE 114 A1
Upper Stone Cl B76 ... 46 E4
Upper Sutton St B6 .... 66 F7
Upper Thomas St B6 .. 66 F7
Upper Trinity St B9 ... 67 A1
Upper Vauxhall WV1 ... 25 A2
Upper Villiers St WV2.. 39 C6
Upper Well St CV1 .... 165 B3
Upper William St B15.. 66 C1
UPPER WITTON 56 B5

Upper York St CV1 . . . . . . 113 B2
Upper Zoar St WV3 . . . . . 163 A1
Upton Cl B98 . . . . 154 F3
Upton Ct B23 . . . . 56 B3
Upton Dr CV11 . . . . 78 F8
Upton Gdns WV14 . . . . . . 40 C5
Upton Gn WV10 . . . . 11 B3
Upton Gr B33 . . . . 68 C1
Upton Rd B33 . . . . 68 C2
Upton St DY4 . . . . 62 C5
UPTON WARREN 150 A3
Upwey Ave B91 . . . . 107 A4
USAM Trad Est WV10 . . . . 11 D2
Usk Cl WS3 . . . . 28 D8
Usk Way B36 . . . . 69 F8
Usmere Rd DY10 . . . . 116 F8
Utrillo Cl CV5 . . . . 112 C3
Uttoxeter Cl WV6 . . . . . . 25 B5
Uxbridge Ave CV3 . . . . . . 114 C2
Uxbridge Cl DY3 . . . . 50 D2
Uxbridge Ct
　Burntwood WS7 . . . . . . .6 F5
　Cannock WS12 . . . . 2 C5
　Kidderminster DY11 . . . 116 D5
Uxbridge St
　Birmingham B19 . . . . . . 66 D5
　Cannock WS12 . . . . 2 C4

V

Valbourne Rd B14 . . . . . . 104 C4
Vale
　Aldridge WS9 . . . . 30 D3
　Dudley DY3 . . . . 50 D6
Vale Cl
　Birmingham B32 . . . . . . 84 F3
　Lichfield WS13 . . . . 3 B1
Vale Ct B64 . . . . 82 D7
Vale Gr B60 . . . . 151 A7
Vale Head Dr WV6 . . . . . 24 A2
Vale Ind Est DY11 . . . . . . 116 C1
Valencia Croft B35 . . . . . 58 B4
Valencia Rd
　Bromsgrove B60 . . . . . . 137 D1
　Coventry CV3 . . . . 115 A2
Valentine Cl B14 . . . . 44 F7
Valentine Ct B14 . . . . 86 E1
Valentine Rd
　Birmingham B14 . . . . . . 86 F1
　Oldbury B68 . . . . 64 C2
Valepits Rd B33 . . . . 69 C1
Vale Rd DY2 . . . . 62 E4
Valerian
　Kidderminster DY10 . . . 116 E2
　Sutton Coldfield B43 . . 31 F4
Valerie Gr B43 . . . . 54 C8
Vale Row DY3 . . . . 50 D5
Vale St B76 . . . . 57 E7
Vale St
　Dudley DY3 . . . . 50 D5
　Stourbridge DY8 . . . . . . 81 A8
　West Bromwich B71 . . . . 53 E6
　Wolverhampton WV2 . . . 40 A6
Vale Stadium B35 . . . . 58 C2
Vale Student Village The
　B15 . . . . 86 A6
Vale The
　Birmingham, Moseley B11 . 87 B2
　Coventry CV3 . . . . 134 C8
Vale View
　Aldridge WS9 . . . . 30 B4
　Nuneaton CV10 . . . . 72 E4
Valiant Cl LE10 . . . . 75 E4
Valiant Ho B97 . . . . 158 A6
Valley Dr B77 . . . . 35 E5
Valley Farm Rd B45 . . . . 122 A6
Valley Gn WS6 . . . . .4 E2
Valley Inf Sch B92 . . . . . . 89 D3
Valley La
　Kingswood B94 . . . . 144 E7
　Lichfield WS13 . . . . 9 D8
　Tamworth B77 . . . . 35 E7
Valley Rd
　Birmingham B43 . . . . . . 54 C7
　Bournheath B61 . . . . . . 136 E7
　Cannock, Hednesford WS12 . 2 D6
　Coventry CV2 . . . . 114 A4
　Cradley Heath B64 . . . . 82 F2
　Dudley DY3 . . . . 50 E6
　Earlswood B94 . . . . 126 A1
　Halesowen B62 . . . . 83 F8
　Radford Semele CV31 . 162 E4
　Royal Leamington Spa
　　CV32 . . . . 157 C3
　Smethwick B67 . . . . 64 F3
　Solihull B92 . . . . 89 D4
　Stourbridge DY9 . . . . . . 81 F6
　Sutton Coldfield B74 . . 44 F7
　Walsall WS3 . . . . 14 D1
　Wolverhampton WV10 . . 25 F5
Valley Side WS3 . . . . 14 F2
Valley Stadium (Redditch FC)
　B97 . . . . 153 C4
Valley The
　Burntwood WS7 . . . . 6 D8
　Radford Semele CV31 . 162 E4
Valley View WS8 . . . . 16 A7
Vallian Croft B36 . . . . 68 F7
Vanborough Wlk DY1 . . . 51 A2
Vanbrugh Ct WV6 . . . . . . 23 E3
Van Dyke Cl CV5 . . . . 112 C3
Van Gogh Cl WS11 . . . . . .2 D2
Vanguard B77 . . . . 35 D6
Vanguard Ave CV5 . . . . . 112 C1
Vanguard Cl B36 . . . . 69 B8
Vanguard Ctr CV4 . . . . . . 132 C6
Vanguard Rd B26 . . . . . . 90 C4

Vann Cl ② B10 . . . . 87 C8
Vantage Point ② B70 . . . 53 C2
Vantage Way B24 . . . . . . 71 D2
Varden Croft B5 . . . . 86 D7
Vardon Ct CV3 . . . . 133 D4
Vardon Way B38 . . . . 103 D1
Varley Rd B24 . . . . 57 D4
Varley Vale B24 . . . . 57 D4
Varlins Way B38 . . . . 123 D6
Varney Ave B70 . . . . 53 D2
Vaughan Cl B74 . . . . 31 F6
Vaughan Rd WV13 . . . . . 26 E1
Vaughan Trad Est DY4 . . 52 B3
Vaughton Dr B75 . . . . 46 E6
Vaughton Ho B15 . . . . . . 86 C7
Vaughton St B12 . . . . 86 E8
Vaughton Street S B12 . . 86 E8
VAUXHALL 67 B4
Vauxhall Ave ② B1 . . . . . 25 A2
Vauxhall Cl ④ CV1 . . . . . 113 E3
Vauxhall Cres B36 . . . . . . 58 F1
Vauxhall Gdns DY2 . . . . . 62 E7
Vauxhall Gr B7 . . . . 67 B3
Vauxhall Ho ② WV1 . . . . 25 A2
Vauxhall Pl B7 . . . . 67 A3
Vauxhall Rd
　Birmingham B7 . . . . 67 A3
　Stourbridge DY8 . . . . . . 81 A5
Vauxhall St
　Coventry CV1 . . . . 113 E3
　Dudley DY1 . . . . 62 B8
Vauxhall Trad Est B7 . . . 67 B4
Vaynor Dr B97 . . . . 158 D8
Vaynor Fst Sch The B97 . 158 C7
Veasey Cl CV11 . . . . 73 E3
Vecqueray St CV1 . . . . . 113 E2
Vector Ind Pk B71 . . . . . . 53 C6
Velsheda Rd B90 . . . . . . 106 A2
Venetia Rd B9 . . . . 67 C2
Venice Ct ② B13 . . . . 87 B2
Venning Gr B43 . . . . 54 D7
Ventnor Ave
　Birmingham, Lozells B19 . 66 D7
　Birmingham, Ward End B8 . 68 D7
Ventnor Cl
　Birmingham B68 . . . . . . 84 C7
　Coventry CV2 . . . . 114 E3
Ventnor Rd B92 . . . . 85 A4
Ventnor St CV10 . . . . 73 D6
Ventura Park Rd B78 . . . 20 F3
Ventura Pk Rd B78 . . . . . 21 A3
Ventura Ret Pk B78 . . . . 21 A3
Venture Ct LE10 . . . . 74 E8
Venture Way
　Birmingham B7 . . . . 66 F4
　Brierley Hill DY5 . . . . . . 61 D3
Vera Rd B26 . . . . 88 E2
Vera Roberts Way DY11 . 116 B3
Verbena Cl
　Coventry CV2 . . . . 96 B1
Verbena Gdns B7 . . . . . . 67 A5
Verbena Rd B31 . . . . 102 F6
Vercourt B74 . . . . 31 B3
Verden Ave CV34 . . . . . . 160 B4
Verdi Cl WS13 . . . . 3 C2
Verdun Cl CV31 . . . . 162 B2
Verdun Cres DY2 . . . . 51 F2
Vere St B5 . . . . 86 D8
Verity Wlk DY8 . . . . 60 E1
Vermont Gn ④ WS11 . . . 2 A3
Vermont Gr CV31 . . . . . . 162 D6
Verney Ave B33 . . . . 89 D7
Vernier Ave DY6 . . . . 61 A5
Vernolds Croft B5 . . . . . . 86 E8
Vernon Ave
　Birmingham B20 . . . . . . 54 F4
　Brownhills WS8 . . . . . . 16 A8
　Tipton DY4 . . . . 51 E4
Vernon Cl
　Birmingham B16 . . . . . . 65 E1
　② Coventry CV1 . . . . . . 113 E4
Vernon Ct
　Birmingham B16 . . . . . . 65 E1
　③ Coventry CV1 . . . . . . 113 E4
Vernon Rd
　Bilston WV14 . . . . 40 F6
　Birmingham B16 . . . . . . 65 E1
　Halesowen B62 . . . . 64 C6
　Oldbury B68 . . . . 64 C6
Vernons Ct CV10 . . . . 72 F4
Vernons La CV10, CV11 . 72 F4
Vernons Mews CV10 . . . 72 F4
Vernon St B70 . . . . 52 E3
Vernon Trad Est B62 . . . 83 C8
Vernon Way WS3 . . . . . 14 A1
Verona Cl CV11 . . . . 74 A1
Verona Ct WV10 . . . . 26 A4
Verona Rd B60 . . . . 137 C1
Veronica Ave WV4 . . . . . 39 E5
Veronica Cl B29 . . . . 103 A6
Veronica Rd DY6 . . . . . . 61 A6
Verstone Croft B31 . . . . 103 A5
Verstone Rd B90 . . . . . . 106 C4
Verwood Cl WV13 . . . . . 26 D1
Vesey Cl
　Sutton Coldfield B74 . . 31 F2
　Water Orton B46 . . . . . . 59 B2
Vesey Rd B73 . . . . 46 B1
Vesey St B4 . . . . 164 C4
Vestry Cl B64 . . . . 62 F1
Vestry Ct DY8 . . . . 80 E6

Viaduct Dr WV6 . . . . 25 B6
Viaduct St B7 . . . . 67 A3
Vibart Rd B26 . . . . 88 F8
Vicarage Cl
　Birmingham, Great Barr
　　B42 . . . . 55 D7
　Birmingham, Stirchley B30 . 104 C7
　Brierley Hill DY5 . . . . . . 81 C8
　Bromsgrove B60 . . . . . 151 B8
　Brownhills WS8 . . . . . . 16 A7
　Dordon B78 . . . . 36 F5
　Tipton DY4 . . . . 51 E5
Vicarage Cres
　Kidderminster DY10 . . . 116 F5
　Redditch B97 . . . . 153 C3
Vicarage Ct WS7 . . . . . . 6 F6
Vicarage Field CV34 . . . 161 B8
Vicarage Gdns
　Halesowen B62 . . . . 63 D1
　Sutton Coldfield B76 . . 57 F7
Vicarage Gr B27 . . . . 106 B8
Vicarage Hill
　Middleton B78 . . . . 34 B1
　Tamworth-In-A B94 . . . 141 F3
Vicarage La
　Brierley Hill DY5 . . . . . . 95 D7
　Coventry CV7 . . . . 95 D7
　Longbridge CV35 . . . . . 160 A1
　Water Orton B46 . . . . . . 59 B2
Vicarage Pl WS1 . . . . 28 E1
Vicarage Prospect DY1 . 51 B1
Vicarage Rd
　Birmingham, Aston B6 . . 67 A7
　Birmingham, Chad Valley
　　B15 . . . . 85 F8
　Birmingham, Handsworth
　　B18 . . . . 66 A7
　Birmingham, Harts Green
　　B17 . . . . 85 B5
　Birmingham, King's Heath
　　B14 . . . . 104 D7
　Birmingham, Stechford B33 . 68 D1
　Brierley Hill DY5 . . . . . . 81 C7
　Brownhills WS8 . . . . . . 16 A7
　Cheswick Green B90, B94 . 126 C3
　Dudley, West Coseley WV14 . 51 C7
　Dudley, Woodsetton DY3 . 50 F5
　Halesowen B62 . . . . 63 C1
　Hockley Heath B94 . . . 143 F7
　Oldbury B68 . . . . 64 C5
　Royal Leamington Spa
　　CV32 . . . . 157 B3
　Smethwick B67 . . . . 64 F5
　Stone CV10 . . . . 117 E2
　Stoneleigh CV8 . . . . . . 149 B6
　Stourbridge DY8 . . . . . . 80 D7
　Stourbridge, Lye DY9 . . 81 F5
　Walsall WS3 . . . . 15 B2
　Wednesbury WS10 . . . 42 A4
　West Bromwich B71 . . . 53 D6
　Wolverhampton, Blakenhall
　　WV2 . . . . 163 C1
　Wolverhampton, Penn WV4 . 38 C3
　Wolverhampton, New Cross WV11 . 26 B6
Vicarage Road S DY9 . . . 81 E5
Vicarage Road W DY1 . . . 51 C6
Vicarage St
　Nuneaton CV11 . . . . 73 C4
　Oldbury B68 . . . . 64 B5
Vicarage Terr ① WS2 . . 42 C8
Vicarage View B97 . . . . 153 D3
Vicarage Wlk ⑨ WS1 . . 28 E1
Vicar's Cl WS13 . . . . 9 A8
Vicar St
　Dudley DY2 . . . . 62 C8
　Kidderminster DY10 . . . 116 E6
　Sedgley DY3 . . . . 50 D8
　⑦ Wednesbury WS10 . . 42 A3
Vicars Wlk DY9 . . . . 81 E2
Viceroy Cl
　Birmingham B5 . . . . 86 C6
　Coventry CV6 . . . . 61 A5
Vicroft Ct CV1 . . . . 165 A2
Victor Bsns Ctr B98 . . . 154 B3
Victor Cl WV2 . . . . 40 B6
Victoria Arc WV1 . . . . . . 163 B3
Victoria Ave
　Birmingham B21 . . . . . . 65 F8
　Birmingham, Small Heath
　　B10 . . . . 87 D8
　Halesowen B62 . . . . 83 F6
　Smethwick B66 . . . . 65 A5
　Walsall, Blakenall Heath
　　WS3 . . . . 28 D8
　Walsall, Wallington Heath
　　WS3 . . . . 14 C1
Victoria Bldgs B16 . . . . . 65 E3
Victoria Bsns Ctr ⑪
　CV31 . . . . 162 A7
Victoria Colonnade ⑤
　CV31 . . . . 161 F7
Victoria Ct
　⑥ Birmingham B11 . . . . . 87 C6
　⑥ Birmingham, Hurst Green
　　B62 . . . . 84 A7
　② Birmingham, Showell Green
　　B13 . . . . 86 F4
　Brierley Hill DY5 . . . . . . 81 C7
　Coventry CV5 . . . . 112 D4
　Halesowen B62 . . . . 83 F6
　② Kidderminster DY10 . . 116 F6
　Norton Canes WS11 . . . 6 B5
Victoria Dr B78 . . . . 35 A8
Victoria Fold WV1 . . . . . 163 B2
Victoria Gdns
　Cradley Heath B64 . . . . 62 F2
　Lichfield WS13 . . . . 8 F6

Victoria Gr
　① Birmingham B18 . . . . . 65 E4
　Wombourne WV5 . . . . . . 49 A8
Victoria Ho
　② Birmingham B2 . . . . . 164 C2
　④ Birmingham, Ladywood
　　B16 . . . . 66 B2
　Birmingham, Small Heath
　　② 87 D8
　Darlaston WS10 . . . . . . 41 C6
Victoria Ind Sch DY4 . . . 51 F5
Victoria Law Cts B2 . . . 164 C3
Victoria Mews
　Barnt Green B45 . . . . . . 138 D8
　Coventry CV3 . . . . 114 E2
　Oldbury B69 . . . . 63 F3
　Walsall WS4 . . . . 29 A3
　Warwick CV34 . . . . 160 D7
Victoriana Way B20 . . . . 55 A1
Victoria Park Prim Sch
　B66 . . . . 65 B5
Victoria Park Rd B66 . . . 65 B5
Victoria Pass WV1 . . . . . 163 B3
Victoria Pass ⑤ DY8 . . 81 A5
Victoria Pl WV1 . . . . 116 B2
Victoria Rd
　Birmingham, Acock's Green
　　B27 . . . . 88 C2
　Birmingham, Aston B6 . . 66 F7
　Birmingham, Handsworth
　　B21 . . . . 65 E7
　Birmingham, Stechford B33 . 68 D3
　Birmingham, Stirchley B30 . 104 D3
　Birmingham, Stockland Green
　　B23 . . . . 56 D3
　Brierley Hill DY5 . . . . . . 62 A1
　Bromsgrove B61 . . . . . . 137 A3
　Cradley Heath B64 . . . . 62 F2
　Darlaston WS10 . . . . . . 41 D6
　Dodford B61 . . . . 136 A7
　Halesowen B63 . . . . 83 D6
　Hartshill CV10 . . . . 72 B8
　Hinckley LE10 . . . . 75 F5
　Oldbury B68 . . . . 64 D6
　Royal Leamington Spa
　　CV31 . . . . 161 E8
　Sedgley DY3 . . . . 50 E8
　Sutton Coldfield B72 . . 46 C5
　Tamworth B79 . . . . 21 C5
　Tipton DY4 . . . . 52 A4
　Walsall WS3 . . . . 15 A3
　Wolverhampton, Newbolds
　　WV10 . . . . 25 F5
　Wolverhampton, New Cross
　　WV11 . . . . 26 B6
　Wolverhampton, Oxbarn
　　WV3 . . . . 38 E7
　Wolverhampton, Tettenhall
　　WV6 . . . . 24 E5
Victoria Sq
　Birmingham B 164 B2
　Wolverhampton WV1 . . . 163 C3
Victoria St
　Birmingham B9 . . . . 87 D1
　Brierley Hill, Barrow Hill
　　DY5 . . . . 61 C7
　Brierley Hill, Merry Hill DY5 . 61 D3
　Cannock, Bridgtown WS11 . 4 D8
　Cannock, Broomhill WS11 . 1 E4
　Cannock WS12 . . . . 2 C6
　Coventry CV1 . . . . 165 D4
　Halesowen B63 . . . . 83 A4
　Hinckley LE10 . . . . 71 D1
　Kingswinford DY6 . . . . 49 B1
　Nuneaton CV11 . . . . 73 C4
　⑦ Redditch B98 . . . . . . 153 E4
　Royal Leamington Spa
　　CV31 . . . . 161 E8
　Stourbridge DY8 . . . . . . 81 A5
　Wednesbury WS10 . . . 42 C6
　West Bromwich, Lambert's End
　　B70 . . . . 53 C3
　West Bromwich, Swan Village
　　B70 . . . . 52 F5
　Willenhall WV13 . . . . . 27 B3
　Wolverhampton WV1 . . 163 B3
Victoria Terr
　Royal Leamington Spa
　　CV31 . . . . 161 F7
　④ Walsall WS4 . . . . 28 F3
Victor Rd
　Birmingham B18 . . . . . . 65 E6
　Solihull B92 . . . . 65 E3
Victor St
　Walsall, Caldmore WS1 . 42 E8
　Walsall WS3 . . . . 15 A1
Victor Tower B7 . . . . 67 B6
Victory Ave
　Burntwood WS7 . . . . . . .6 F7
　Darlaston WS10 . . . . . . 41 C6
Victory Cl
　Cannock WS12 . . . . 2 F4
　Lichfield WS13 . . . . 9 B5
Victory Ho ⑥ B13 . . . . . 86 F4
Victory La WS2 . . . . 28 A4
Victory Rd CV6 . . . . 95 E1
Victory Rise B71 . . . . . . 53 D5
Victory Terr B78 . . . . . . 35 B8
Vienna Ho CV5 . . . . 112 C2
View Dr DY2 . . . . 62 E8
Viewfield Ave WS12 . . . . 1 F7
Viewfield Cres DY3 . . . 50 D6
Viewlands Dr WV6 . . . . . 24 A2
View Point B69 . . . . 63 B7
View St WS12 . . . . .1 F6

VIGO 15 F2
Vigo Cl WS9 . . . . 15 F2
Vigo Pl WS9 . . . . 30 A8
Vigo Rd WS9 . . . . 15 F2
Vigo Terr WS9 . . . . 15 F2
Viking B77 . . . . 35 D7
Viking Rise B65 . . . . 63 C4
Villa Cl LE10 . . . . 75 F4
Villa Cl CV12 . . . . 79 C2
Villa Cotts B19 . . . . 66 B7
Villa Cres CV12 . . . . 79 C1
Villa Cross B20 . . . . 66 B7
Village Mews B32 . . . . . . 84 A6
Village Mews The WV6 . . 24 C5
Village Rd B6 . . . . 56 A1
Village The DY6 . . . . 60 E5
Village Way WV14 . . . . . 40 C5
Village Wlk WS10 . . . . . 42 B3
Villa Park (Aston Villa FC)
　B6 . . . . 55 F1
Villa Rd
　Birmingham B19 . . . . . . 66 B7
　Coventry CV6 . . . . 113 B6
Villa St
　Birmingham B19 . . . . . . 66 C6
　Stourbridge DY8 . . . . . . 81 A8
Villa Wlk B19 . . . . 66 C6
Villebon Way CV31 . . . . 162 A2
Villette Gr B14 . . . . 105 C4
Villiers Ave WV14 . . . . . 40 D7
Villiers Ind Est WV2 . . . 39 B7
Villiers Prim Sch WV14 . 40 D7
Villiers Rd
　Bromsgrove B60 . . . . . 150 E1
　Kenilworth CV8 . . . . . . 148 B5
Villiers Sq WV14 . . . . . . 40 D7
Villiers St
　Birmingham B18 . . . . . . 65 E5
　Coventry CV2 . . . . 114 A3
　Kidderminster DY10 . . . 117 A5
　Nuneaton CV11 . . . . 73 B3
　Royal Leamington Spa
　　CV32 . . . . 157 A1
　Willenhall WV13 . . . . . 27 B2
Vimy Rd
　Birmingham B13 . . . . . . 105 B8
　Wednesbury WS10 . . . 42 A4
Vimy Terr WS10 . . . . 42 A4
Vincent Cl B12 . . . . 86 F6
Vincent Dr B15 . . . . 85 E4
Vincent Par B12 . . . . 86 F6
Vincent Rd B75 . . . . 46 E7
Vincent St
　Birmingham B12 . . . . . . 86 F5
　Coventry CV1 . . . . 113 B2
　Royal Leamington Spa
　　CV32 . . . . 157 A1
　Walsall WS1 . . . . 42 F7
Vincent Wyles Ho CV2 . . 114 E3
Vince St B66 . . . . 65 A5
Vinculum Way WV13 . . . 41 B8
Vine Ave B12 . . . . 87 A5
Vine Cl WV10 . . . . 11 D3
Vinecote Rd CV6 . . . . . . 95 F4
Vine Cres B71 . . . . 53 D6
Vine Ct
　Cradley Heath B64 . . . . 82 D8
　Warwick CV34 . . . . 160 F8
Vine Gdns B64 . . . . 62 F2
Vine La
　Birmingham B27 . . . . . . 88 E3
　Cannock WS11 . . . . 4 D5
　Clent DY9 . . . . 99 F3
　Halesowen B63 . . . . 83 B3
　Warwick CV34 . . . . 160 F8
Vineries The B27 . . . . . . 88 E4
Vine St
　Birmingham B6 . . . . 67 B4
　Brierley Hill DY2, DY5 . . 61 E5
　Coventry CV1 . . . . 165 C4
　Kidderminster DY10 . . . 117 A8
　Redditch B97 . . . . 153 D4
　Stourbridge DY8 . . . . . . 60 E1
Vineyard Rd B31 . . . . . . 102 F5
Vineyard Rd B32 . . . . . . 102 B8
Vintage Cl B34 . . . . 69 A5
Vinyard Cl B34 . . . . 65 F7
Violet Cl
　Bedworth CV12 . . . . . . 77 E2
　Cannock WS12 . . . . 1 C6
　Coventry CV2 . . . . 96 C3
Violet Croft DY4 . . . . 41 B1
Violet La DY9 . . . . 99 F4
Virginia Dr WV4 . . . . . . 38 F4
Virginia Pl CV10 . . . . . . 72 E3
Virginia Rd CV1 . . . . 113 E3
Viscount Cl
　Birmingham B35 . . . . . . 58 A2
　Royal Leamington Spa
　　CV31 . . . . 161 F6
Viscount Dr B35 . . . . 58 B2
Vista The DY3 . . . . 39 D2
Vittle Dr CV34 . . . . 160 D7
Vittoria St
　Birmingham B1 . . . . 66 C4
　Smethwick B66 . . . . 66 C3
Vittoria Works B1 . . . . . . 66 C3
Vivaldi Dr WS11 . . . . 2 C2
Vivian Cl B17 . . . . 85 C5
Vivian Gdns 85 C5
Vixen Cl B76 . . . . 57 D7
Vodena Ct ⑤ CV32 . . . . 156 F1
Vogue Cl CV1 . . . . 165 D3

Vowchurch Cl B97 . . . . 153 A5
Vowles Rd B71. . . . . 53 D6
Voyager Dr WS11 . . . . .4 F6
Vulcan Ho B91. . . . . 107 C6
Vulcan House Ind Est
B91. . . . . 107 C6
Vulcan Ind Est WS2 . . . . . 28 C6
Vulcan Rd
Bilston WV14. . . . . 40 F5
Lichfield WS13. . . . . 3 E1
Solihull B91 . . . . 107 C7
Vulcan Road Island WV14 40 F5
Vyrnwy Gr B38. . . . . 123 E8
Vyse St
Birmingham, Aston B6. . . . . 67 B8
Birmingham, Hockley B18. . 66 C4

W

Wackrill Dr CV32. . . . . 157 C3
Wadbarn B90. . . . . 126 A5
Waddam's Pool DY2 . . . . . 51 D1
Waddell Cl WV14 . . . . 39 F2
Waddens Brook La WV11 . 26 E5
Waddens Brook Noose Lane
Nature Reserve ★ WV13 . 26 E3
Waddington Ave B43. . . . . 43 E1
Wade Ave CV3 . . . . 133 B5
Wadebridge Dr CV11. . . . . 73 F5
Wade Gr CV34 . . . . 155 E2
Wades Cl ③ DY4. . . . . 51 E5
Wadesmill Lawns WV10 . . 11 E4
Wade St WS13 . . . . .9 B7
Wadham Cl B65. . . . . 63 C6
Wadham Ho B37. . . . . 70 D3
Wadham's Fold WV1 . . . . 163 B3
Wadhurst Rd B17. . . . . 65 B2
Wadleys Rd B91. . . . . 106 F6
Waen Cl DY4 . . . . 52 B8
Waggestaff Dr CV10. . . . . . 72 A7
Waggoners Cl ① B60 . . . . 150 E6
Waggoner's La B78 . . . . . . 33 E8
Waggon La DY10. . . . . 98 A3
Waggon St B64 . . . . 62 F2
Waggon Wlk B38 . . . . . . 123 C8
Wagoners Cl B8 . . . . 67 F6
Wagon La B26, B92. . . . . . 88 F4
Wagstaff Cl WV14. . . . . . . 51 B8
Wagstaff Way B37 . . . . . . 90 A8
Wainbody Avenue N
CV3 . . . . 133 A6
Wainbody Avenue S CV3 132 F5
Wainbody Wood & Stivichall
Common, Kenilworth Rd
Spinney Nature Reserve ★
CV4. . . . . 132 A2
Wainrigg B77 . . . . 36 B7
Wainwright Cl CV8. . . . . . . 60 A8
Wainwright St B6. . . . . . . 67 A7
Waite Rd WV13 . . . . 40 E8
Wakefield Cl
Coventry CV3. . . . . 134 F7
Sutton Coldfield B73 . . . . . 46 A2
Wakefield Ct B13 . . . . 87 B2
Wakefield Gr B46. . . . . 59 B3
Wakeford Rd B31. . . . . . . 103 C1
Wake Gr CV34 . . . . 160 B5
Wake Green Pk B13. . . . . . 87 B1
Wake Green Rd
Birmingham B13 . . . . 87 A2
Wednesbury DY4 . . . . 41 A1
Wakehurst Cl CV11. . . . . . . 78 F8
Wakelam Gdns B43 . . . . . 43 D1
Wakelams Fold DY3. . . . . . 50 C3
Wakeley Hill WV4 . . . . 38 F4
Wakelin Rd B90. . . . . 126 B7
Wakeman Ct WV11. . . . . . 12 F7
Wakeman Dr B69 . . . . 63 B8
Wakeman Gr B33 . . . . 89 D7
Wakes Cl WV13 . . . . 27 B1
Wakes Rd WS10 . . . . 42 A2
Walcot Cl B75 . . . . 32 B3
Walcot Dr B43. . . . . 54 F6
Walcot Gdns WV14. . . . . . 40 B4
Walcot Gn B93. . . . . 128 A2
Waldale Cl WV11. . . . . 13 C1
Walden Gdns WV4 . . . . . . 38 E6
Walden Rd B11 . . . . 88 A3
Waldeve Gr B92 . . . . 107 F8
Waldley Gr B24 . . . . 57 D3
Waldon Wlk B36. . . . . 69 F8
Waldron Ave DY5 . . . . 61 B2
Waldron Cl WS10 . . . . 41 F6
Waldrons Moor B14. . . . . 104 C5
Walford Ave WV3. . . . . 38 F8
Walford Dr B92. . . . . 89 D3
Walford Gn B32. . . . . 102 B7
Walford Gr CV34 . . . . 155 F1
Walford Rd B11. . . . . 87 C6
Walford St B69. . . . . 52 A5
Walford Wlk ⑥ B97. . . . . 153 E3
Walhouse Cl ⑥ WS1 . . . . 28 F2
Walhouse Rd WS1. . . . . . . 29 A2
Walhouse St WS11. . . . . . . .4 E8
Walker Ave
Brierley Hill DY5 . . . . 81 D7
Oldbury B69. . . . . 63 C7
Stourbridge DY9 . . . . 81 E3
Wolverhampton WV10. . . . 25 E8
Walker Dr B24. . . . . 67 E8
Walker Grange DY4 . . . . . . 51 F5
Walker Pl WS3. . . . . 28 E8

Walker Rd WS3 . . . . 28 E8
Walkers Croft WS13. . . . . . 3 C2
Walkers Fold WV12 . . . . . 27 D6
WALKER'S HEATH. 104 B1
Walkers Heath Rd B38 . . 104 B1
Walkers Orch CV8 . . . . . . 149 B6
Walkers Rd B98. . . . . 154 E6
Walkers Rise WS12 . . . . . . 2 D8
Walker St
Dudley DY2 . . . . 62 C4
Tipton DY4. . . . . 52 C7
Walkers Way
Bedworth CV12 . . . . 77 F1
Kenilworth CV8 . . . . 147 F2
Walk La WV5 . . . . 49 A6
Walkmill Bsns Pk WS11 . . 4 D5
Walkmill La WS11. . . . . . . .4 D5
Walk The DY3 . . . . 39 D1
WALKWOOD. 158 B6
Walkwood CE Mid Sch
B97. . . . . 158 C8
Walkwood Coppice Nature
Reserve ★ B97. . . . . 158 B7
Walkwood Cres B97. . . . . 158 C6
Walkwood Rd B97 . . . . . . 158 C6
WALL 8 D2
Wallace Cl
Norton Canes WS11 . . . . . .5 F5
Oldbury B69. . . . . 63 D6
Walsall WS11 . . . . .4 D1
Wallace Ho
⑥ Oldbury B69. . . . . 63 D5
Warwick CV34 . . . . 160 D7
Wallace Rd
Bilston WV14. . . . . 41 A2
Birmingham B29 . . . . 86 B2
Brownhills WS8 . . . . 15 E8
Coventry CV6. . . . . 113 A8
Oldbury B69. . . . . 63 D6
Wallace Rise B64 . . . . 82 E7
Wall Ave B46 . . . . 70 F5
Wallbank Rd B8 . . . . 68 A6
WALLBROOK. 51 D8
Wallbrook Prim Sch
WV14 . . . . 51 E8
Wallbrook St WV14. . . . . . 51 D8
Wall Cl B67. . . . . 64 D4
Wall Croft WS9 . . . . 30 B7
Wall Dr B74 . . . . 31 F4
Wall End Cl WS2. . . . . 28 A7
Waller Cl CV35. . . . . 155 F7
Waller St CV32. . . . . 157 A2
Wallface B71. . . . . 53 B7
WALL HEATH 60 B8
Wallheath Cres WS14 . . . . 16 E5
Wallheath La CV7 . . . . 58 E6
WALL HILL. 94 A4
Wall Hill Rd CV5, CV7 . . . . 94 B4
Walling Croft WV14 . . . . . 40 B3
Wallingford Ave CV11 . . . . 73 F7
Wallington Cl WS3. . . . . . . 14 B2
WALLINGTON HEATH 14 B2
Wallington Heath WS3 . . . 14 B2
Wallis Ct ① B13 . . . . 87 B2
Wall La WS13, WS14 . . . . . 8 D3
Walnut Wlk WS13 . . . . .8 F6
Wallows Ind Est The DY5 . 61 D5
Wallows La WS1, WS2 . . . . 42 C6
Wallows Pl DY5 . . . . 61 C5
Wallows Rd DY5 . . . . 61 D5
Wallows Wood DY3 . . . . . . 50 A4
Wallsgrove Cl CV32 . . . . . 157 B3
Wall's Rd B60. . . . . 150 C3
Wall St WV1 . . . . 26 B2
Wall Well B63 . . . . 82 F3
Wall Well La B63. . . . . 82 F3
Wallwin Ct CV34 . . . . 160 D6
Walmead Croft ① B17 . . . 84 F7
Walmer Ct B16 . . . . 65 D2
Walmer Gr B23. . . . . 56 B5
Walmers The WS9 . . . . . . 30 B7
Walmers Wlk The B31. . . 102 D1
Walmer Way B37 . . . . 70 C3
Walmesley Way B31 . . . . 102 E3
WALMLEY. 57 F8
Walmley Ash Cl B76 . . . . . 57 F8
Walmley Ash La B76 . . . . . 58 C6
Walmley Ash Rd B76 . . . . 58 A7
Walmley Cl
Halesowen B63 . . . . 82 B7
Sutton Coldfield B76 . . . . . 57 F8
Walmley Jun & Inf Schs
B76. . . . . 58 A7
Walmley Park Ct B76. . . . . 57 F8
Walmley Rd B76 . . . . 46 F2
Walney Cl LE10 . . . . 71 B1
Walnut Ave WV8 . . . . 10 B3
Walnut Cl
Birmingham B37. . . . . 70 B1
Cannock WS11. . . . . 1 F3
Hartshill CV10 . . . . 72 A8
Nuneaton, Camp Hill CV10 . 72 E6
Stourbridge DY9 . . . . 81 B1
Walnut Dr
Cannock WS11. . . . . 1 F3
Royal Leamington Spa
CV32. . . . . 157 B3
⑥ Smethwick B66. . . . . . 65 B5
Wolverhampton WV3 . . . . 24 D1
Walnut Gr WS14 . . . . .9 F7
Walnut La
Finstall B60 . . . . 151 D8
Wednesbury WS10 . . . . . 42 A2
Walnut Rd WS5 . . . . 43 A4
Walnut St CV2 . . . . 96 B2
Walnut Tree Cl CV8 . . . . . 148 A3
Walnut Way B31 . . . . 122 F8

Walpole St WV6 . . . . 25 A3
Walpole Wlk ③ B70. . . . . 53 D1
WALSAL END 109 A3
Walsal End La B92 . . . . . . 108 F3
WALSALL. 28 B3
Walsall Acad WS3. . . . . . . 14 C2
Walsall Arboretum ★ WS1 29 A2
Walsall Bsns Pk WS9. . . . . 29 E4
Walsall Coll (Green Lane
Campus) ① WS2. . . . . 28 D3
Walsall Coll (Wisemore
Campus) WS1. . . . . 28 E2
Walsall Ent Pk WS2 . . . . . 42 C8
Walsall Mus ★ WS1 . . . . . 28 F2
Walsall New Firms Ctr
WS1 . . . . 42 D8
Walsall Rd
Aldridge WS9. . . . . 30 A5
Birmingham B42 . . . . 55 B6
Brownhills WS9 . . . . 15 E2
Cannock WS11. . . . . 4 E7
Darlaston WS10. . . . . 41 E6
Great Wyrley WS6 . . . . . . 5 A2
Leamonsley WS13 . . . . . . 8 E6
Lichfield, Christ Church WS13 9 A7
Lichfield, Pipehill WS13,
WS14 . . . . 8 C5
Norton Canes WS11 . . . . . .5 F4
Stonnall WS14 . . . . 16 E8
Sutton Coldfield B74 . . . . . 31 D4
Walsall, The Delves WS5 . . 42 F4
Walsall WS3. . . . . 15 A1
Wednesbury WS10, B71,
WS5 . . . . 42 F2
West Bromwich B71 . . . . . 53 E8
Willenhall WV13 . . . . 27 C2
Walsall St
Bilston WV14. . . . . 40 D6
Coventry CV4. . . . . 132 B7
Darlaston WS10. . . . . 41 D7
Wednesbury WS10 . . . . . 41 F3
West Bromwich B70 . . . . . 53 D3
Willenhall WV13 . . . . 27 B1
Wolverhampton WV1. . . . 163 D2
Walsall Sta WS2 . . . . 28 E2
WALSALL WOOD 15 F4
Walsall Wood Prim Sch
WS8 . . . . 16 A4
Walsall Wood Rd WS9. . . . 30 B7
Walsgrave CE Prim Sch
CV2 . . . . 115 A6
Walsgrave Cl B92 . . . . 107 D6
Walsgrave Dr B92 . . . . . . 107 D6
Walsgrave Gdns ⑤ CV2 . 115 A7
WALSGRAVE ON SOWE. . 115 B7
Walsgrave Rd CV2 . . . . . . 114 B3
Walsham Croft B34 . . . . . . 69 C5
Walsh Dr B76. . . . . 46 F4
Walsh Gr B23 . . . . 56 D8
Walsh La CV7 . . . . 92 E2
Walsingham Dr CV10. . . . . 78 A7
Walsingham St WS1 . . . . . 29 A1
Walstead Cl WS5 . . . . 43 C5
Walstead Rd WS5. . . . . . . 43 A5
Walstead Road W WS5. . . 42 E5
Waltdene Cl B43. . . . . 43 E3
Walter Burden Ho B66 . . . 65 C3
Walter Cobb Dr B73. . . . . 46 A1
Walter Cl B20. . . . . 55 C2
Walter Nash Road E
DY11 . . . . 116 B2
Walter Nash Road W
DY11 . . . . 116 A1
Walter Rd
Bilston WV14. . . . . 40 F3
Smethwick B67 . . . . 64 E6
Walters Cl B31. . . . . 122 F6
Walter Scott Rd CV12 . . . . 78 F1
Walters Rd B68 . . . . 84 B6
Walters Row DY1 . . . . 51 A1
Walter St
Birmingham B7 . . . . 67 B6
Walsall WS3. . . . . 15 A1
West Bromwich B70 . . . . . 53 E2
Waltham Cl B61 . . . . 136 E1
Waltham Cres CV10 . . . . . 72 B5
Waltham Gr B44 . . . . 45 B2
Waltham Ho
Birmingham B38 . . . . 104 B1
West Bromwich B70 . . . . . 53 D3
Walthamstow Ct DY5. . . . . 61 D1
Walton Ave B65. . . . . 83 B8
Walton Cl
Coventry CV3. . . . . 134 E7
Halesowen B63 . . . . 82 F2
Kidderminster DY11. . . . . 116 B2
Nuneaton CV11 . . . . 79 A7
Redditch B98. . . . . 154 E3
Rowley Regis B65 . . . . . . 63 A4
Walton Cres WV4 . . . . 39 E5
Walton Ct B63 . . . . 82 F3
Walton Dr B90 . . . . 105 C5
Walton Gr B30. . . . . 104 B2
Walton Heath WS3 . . . . . . 13 F3
WALTON POOL. 100 A2
Walton Pool La DY9 . . . . . 99 F2
Walton Rd
Aldridge WS9. . . . . 16 A1
Bromsgrove B61 . . . . 137 B4
Oldbury B68. . . . . 64 C2
Stourbridge DY8 . . . . 81 A6
Wednesbury WS10 . . . . . 42 C2
Wolverhampton WV4. . . . 39 F5
Walton Rise DY9 . . . . 100 A3
Walton St DY4 . . . . 51 F5
Wanderers Ave WV2. . . . . 39 C6
Wanderer Wlk B36. . . . . . 57 E1

Wandle Gr B11. . . . . 88 A3
Wandsbeck B77 . . . . 35 E8
Wandsworth Rd B44. . . . . 44 F3
Wanley Rd CV3 . . . . 133 D6
Wannerton Rd DY10. . . . . 98 B1
Wansbeck Gr B38. . . . . . 123 E8
Wansbeck Wlk DY3 . . . . . 50 F6
Wansfell Cl CV4. . . . . 132 A7
Wanstead Gr B44 . . . . 45 A1
Wantage Rd B46. . . . . 59 E1
Wappenbury Cl CV2. . . . . 96 C2
Wappenbury Rd CV2 . . . . 96 D2
WAPPING 159 E5
Warbage La
Belbroughton DY9 . . . . . 119 F1
Dodford B61 . . . . 136 A7
Warbank Cl B48 . . . . 139 A6
Warbler Pl DY10. . . . . 117 A2
Ward Cl B8. . . . . 68 A5
Warden Ave B73. . . . . 56 F8
WARD END. 68 A5
Ward End Cl B8. . . . . 67 F6
Ward End Com Coll B8. . . 68 C5
Ward End Hall Gr B8. . . . . 68 A6
Ward End Park Rd B8. . . . 67 F5
Ward End Prim Sch B8. . . 68 B6
Wardend Rd B8. . . . . 68 A6
Warden Rd
Coventry CV6. . . . . 113 B6
Sutton Coldfield B73 . . . . . 56 F8
Wardens Ave The CV5. . . 112 B6
Wardens The CV8. . . . . . . 148 C5
Ward Gr
Warwick CV34 . . . . 161 C7
Wolverhampton WV4 . . . . 39 F3
Wardle Cl B75 . . . . 32 A4
Wardle Pl WS11 . . . . 1 E5
Wardles La WS6 . . . . .4 F2
Wardle St B79 . . . . 21 A5
Wardlow Cl WV4. . . . . 39 B6
Wardlow Rd B7. . . . . 67 B4
Wardour Dr B37 . . . . 70 C2
Wardour Gr B44. . . . . 56 C8
Ward Rd WV4. . . . . 39 D5
Ward St
Bilston WV2. . . . . 40 B6
Birmingham B19 . . . . . . 164 C5
Birmingham B23 . . . . 56 E4
Cannock WS12. . . . . 1 E6
Dudley WV14. . . . . 51 B8
Walsall WS1. . . . . 28 F2
Willenhall WV13 . . . . 27 B3
Wolverhampton WV1. . . . 163 D3
Wareham Cl WS3 . . . . 28 F5
Wareham Gn CV2 . . . . . . 115 A5
Wareham Ho B28 . . . . . . 105 E3
Wareham Rd B45 . . . . . . 102 B2
Wareing Dr B23. . . . . 56 D8
Warewell Cl ③ WS1. . . . . 28 F2
Warewell St ⑨ WS1. . . . . 28 F2
Waring Cl DY4 . . . . 51 E8
Waring Rd DY4. . . . . 52 A8
WARING'S GREEN 142 D8
Warings Green Rd B94 . . 126 D1
War La B17. . . . . 85 B5
Warley Croft B68 . . . . 84 E8
Warley Ct B68. . . . . 64 B2
Warley Hall Rd B68 . . . . . 64 D1
Warley Ho B67. . . . . 64 F2
Warley Inf Sch B68. . . . . . 64 C1
Warley Rd B68. . . . . 64 C5
WARLEY WOODS 84 E8
Warmington Cl CV3 . . . . . 134 E8
Warmington Dr B73. . . . . . 46 B4
Warmington Gr CV34. . . . 160 B8
Warmington Rd
Birmingham B26 . . . . 89 C5
Hollywood B47. . . . . 125 A6
Warmley Cl
Solihull B91 . . . . 107 D5
Wolverhampton WV6. . . . 25 B5
Warmley Rd B60. . . . . . . 137 C1
Warmwell Cl CV2 . . . . 114 F4
Warneford Mews ⑨
CV31 . . . . 162 A7
Warner Cl CV34 . . . . 155 D1
Warner Dr DY5 . . . . 61 D1
Warner Pl ① WS3 . . . . . . 28 F6
Warner Rd
Walsall WS3. . . . . 29 A6
Wednesbury WS10 . . . . . 42 C2
Warner Row ② CV6 . . . . . 113 F7
Warner St ① B12. . . . . . . 87 A8
Warners Wlk ① B10 . . . . . 87 C8
Warnford Wlk WV4 . . . . . . 38 C6
Warple Rd B32 . . . . 84 C5
Warren Ave
Birmingham B13 . . . . 86 F2
Wolverhampton WV10. . . 25 F5
Warren Cl
Earlswood B94 . . . . 142 A8
Lichfield WS14. . . . . 9 E7
Royal Leamington Spa
CV32. . . . . 157 A3
Ryton-on-D CV8 . . . . 135 A1
Tipton DY4. . . . . 52 A7
Warren Dr
Dorridge B93 . . . . 128 A3
Rowley Regis B65 . . . . . . 62 F5
Sedgley DY3. . . . . 39 D2
Warren Farm Prim Sch
B44. . . . . 56 A8
Warren Farm Rd B44. . . . . 56 A8
Warren Field CV8. . . . . . . 135 A1
Warren Gdns DY6. . . . . . . 60 C6
Warren Gn CV4 . . . . 131 F7
Warren Gr B8 . . . . 67 F5
Warren Hill Rd B44 . . . . . . 56 A7

Warren House Ct B76 . . . . 46 F3
Warren House Wlk B76. . . 46 F3
Warren La B45. . . . . 122 B3
Warren Pl WS8 . . . . 16 A7
Warren Rd
Birmingham, Perry B44 . . . 56 A7
Birmingham, Stirchley B30 104 A6
Birmingham, Washwood Heath
B8. . . . . 67 E6
Burntwood WS7 . . . . .7 D5
Warrens Croft WS5 . . . . . . 43 D5
Warrens End ① B38 . . . . 103 F1
Warren's Hall Ctry Pk Nature
Reserve ★ DY2. . . . . 62 E6
Warrens Hall Rd DY2. . . . . 62 E7
Warrington Cl B76. . . . . . . 47 A3
Warrington Dr B23. . . . . . . 56 D7
Warsash Cl WV1. . . . . 40 B8
WARSTOCK. 105 C3
Warstock Cl B14. . . . . 105 C3
Warstock La B14. . . . . 105 A4
Warstock Rd B14 . . . . 105 A3
Warston Ave B32 . . . . 84 D5
Warstone Dr B71. . . . . 53 E4
Warstone La B18 . . . . 66 B4
Warstone Mews ② B18 . . 66 C4
Warstone Parade E B18 . . 66 B4
Warstone Rd WS6/WV11 . 13 C7
Warstones Cres WV4. . . . 38 D5
Warstones Dr WV4. . . . . . 38 C6
Warstones Ho WV4 . . . . . 38 C6
Warstones Prim Sch WV4 38 E6
Warstones Rd WV4 . . . . . . 38 D5
Warstone Terr B21. . . . . . . 65 E6
Warstone Tower B36. . . . . 68 C8
Wartell Bank DY6 . . . . 60 D7
Wartell Bank Ind Est DY6 . 60 D7
Warton Cl CV8. . . . . 148 C4
Warwards La B29 . . . . 104 A8
Warwell La B26. . . . . 88 D6
WARWICK. 160 E2
Warwick Ave
Bromsgrove B60 . . . . 151 A8
Coventry CV5. . . . . 133 A6
Perton WV6 . . . . 23 F7
Wednesbury WS10 . . . . . 42 C6
Willenhall WV13 . . . . 27 D2
Warwick By-Pass
Hampton Magna CV34,
CV35. . . . . 160 A5
Warwick CV34 . . . . 161 A3
Warwick Castle ★ CV34 . 160 E6
Warwick Cl
Cannock WS11. . . . . 4 F6
Oldbury B68. . . . . 64 B2
Studley B80 . . . . 159 D1
West Bromwich B70 . . . . . 52 E1
Warwick Crest B15. . . . . . 86 B2
Warwick Ct
① Birmingham, Acock's Green
B27 . . . . 88 C2
⑤ Birmingham, Chelmsley Wood
B37. . . . . 70 D2
Birmingham, Moseley B13. . 87 A2
② Birmingham, Weoley Castle
B29 . . . . 103 C2
Coventry CV3. . . . . 133 D1
Dudley DY3 . . . . 50 D3
⑤ Solihull B91 . . . . 107 C2
Solihull, Lode Heath B91 . 107 B4
⑥ Wolverhampton WV4 . . 39 F4
Warwick Gdns
Hinckley LE10 . . . . 71 E3
Nuneaton CV10 . . . . 72 E4
Oldbury B69. . . . . 52 C2
Willenhall WV13 . . . . 27 D2
Warwick Gn CV12 . . . . 79 C3
Warwick Gr B92 . . . . 88 E1
Warwick Grange B91. . . . 106 F7
Warwick Hall Gdns B60 . . 151 A8
Warwick Highway B98 . . . 154 C2
Warwick Ho
⑥ Birmingham B24. . . . . . 56 F4
Sutton Coldfield B73 . . . . . 46 A3
Warwick Hospl CV34 . . . . 160 EE
Warwick La CV1 . . . . 165 B2
Warwick New Rd CV32 . . 161 C2
Warwick Park Ct B92 . . . . 106 F6
Warwick Parkway Sta
CV35. . . . . 160 A2
Warwick Pas ③ B2 . . . . . 164 C2
Warwick Pl CV32. . . . . . . 156 E1
Warwick Prep Sch CV34 . 160 F6
Warwick Racecourse
CV34. . . . . 160 C6
Warwick Rd
Birmingham, Birchfield
B42. . . . . 55 E2
Birmingham, Sparkhill B11 . 87 A6
Birmingham, Warley Woods
B68. . . . . 84 D1
Chadwick End B93 . . . . . . 145 A4
Coventry CV3. . . . . 165 B3
Dudley DY2 . . . . 62 E3
Kenilworth CV8 . . . . 148 A3
Knowle B93 . . . . 128 D2
Leek Wootton CV35 . . . . . 155 F3
Solihull B27, B92, B90 . . . 106 F6
Stourbridge DY8 . . . . 60 D3
Sutton Coldfield B73 . . . . . 45 C2
Tamworth B77 . . . . 21 E4
Wolston CV8 . . . . 135 F7
Warwick Road Trad Est
B11. . . . . 87 D4
Warwick Sch CV34 . . . . . 161 A6

Warwickshire Coll (Leamington) CV32 161 D8
Warwickshire Coll (Trident Warwick) CV34 161 F4
Warwickshire Nuffield Health Hospl (Private) CV32 156 E5
Warwick St
Bilston WV14 40 E5
Birmingham B12 67 A1
Coventry CV5 112 F1
Royal Leamington Spa CV32 156 F1
Walsall WS4 28 F3
Wolverhampton WV1 163 D2
Warwick Sta CV34 160 F7
Warwick Tech Pk CV34 161 B5
Warwick Terr CV32 156 E1
Warwick Way WS9 16 A1
Wasdale Cl CV32 156 C2
Wasdale Dr DY6 60 E6
Wasdale Rd
Birmingham B31 102 F4
Brownhills WS8 15 D6
Waseley Hills Ctry Pk (Nature Reserve)* B45 121 C8
Waseley Hills High Sch & Sixth Form Ctr B45 121 D7
Waseley Rd B45 121 E8
Washbourne Rd CV31 162 A2
Washbrook La
Hawkes End CV5 94 A1
Norton Canes WS11 5 D5
Washbrook Rd B8 68 A6
WASHFORD 159 E7
Washford Dr B98 159 D7
Washford Gr B25 88 B8
Washford Ind Est The B98 159 E8
Washford La B98 159 D8
Washington Ct
Birmingham B1 164 A1
Wolverhampton WV3 24 D1
Washington Ctr DY2 62 D4
Washington Dr B20 55 B3
Washington St
Birmingham B1 164 A1
Dudley DY2 62 D3
Kidderminster DY11 116 C5
Washington Street Ind Est DY2 62 D3
Washington Wharf B1 164 A1
Wash La B25 88 C8
WASHWOOD HEATH 67 E6
Washwood Heath Rd B8 67 E6
Washwood Heath Tech Coll B8 68 C5
Wasperton Cl
Birmingham B36 69 B8
6 Coventry CV3 134 F8
Wassell Ct B63 82 E2
Wassell Grove Bsns Ctr DY9 82 A2
Wassell Grove Rd
Hagley DY9 99 F8
Halesowen B63 82 A2
Wassell Rd
Bilston WV14 40 D7
Halesowen B63 82 E2
Stourbridge DY9 81 E2
Waste La
Balsall Common CV7 130 F5
Coventry CV6 94 F1
Wast Hill Gr B38 123 F7
Wasthill La B38, B48 123 D5
Wastwater Ct WV6 23 F4
Watchbury Cl B36 58 C1
Watch Cl CV1 165 A3
Watchmakers Ct CV1 165 A2
Watchman Ave DY5 81 F7
Watcombe Rd CV2 114 E8
Waterbrook Way WS11 4 E6
Watercall Ave CV3 133 C6
Waterdale B90 126 D5
Water Dale WV3 24 E2
Waterfall Cl
Meriden CV7 92 C1
Smethwick B66 64 E7
Tamworth B77 35 E6
Waterfall La B64 63 A1
Waterfall Lane Ind Est B64 63 A1
Waterfall Rd DY5 81 D7
Waterfall Way LE9 71 F5
Waterfield Cl DY4 51 D5
Waterfield Gdns CV31 162 C7
Waterfield Way
Birmingham B26 89 C7
Hinckley LE10 75 C5
Waterford Ct B23 56 B4
Waterford Pl B33 69 D3
Waterford Rd DY6 60 D7
Waterford Way CV3 114 C1
Waterfront Bsns Pk DY5 61 E4
Waterfront E DY5 61 E4
Waterfront The CV7 78 B1
Waterfront W DY5 61 E4
Waterfront Way
Brierley Hill DY2, DY5 61 F4
2 Walsall WS2 28 D2
Waterfront Wlk B1 164 A1
Water Gdns The WV4 38 C2
Waterglade La WV13 27 A1
Waterhaynes Cl B45 122 A6
Waterhead Cl WV10 12 A2
Waterhead Dr WV10 12 B2
Water La B71 53 F7
Waterlily Cl WS12 2 E3
Water Lily Gr WS8 15 E7
Water Lily Way CV10 78 A8
Waterlinks Bvd B6 67 A7
Waterloo Ave B37 70 B4
Waterloo Bvd WS12 2 E4
Waterloo Croft WS14 8 F5
Waterloo Ct CV34 161 A8
Waterloo Ind Est B37 70 B5
5 Waterloo Pl CV32 156 F1
Waterloo Rd
Birmingham, King's Heath B14 104 E8
Birmingham, South Yardley B25 88 C6
Hinckley LE10 75 D8
Smethwick B66 65 A3
Wolverhampton WV1 163 B4
Waterloo St
Birmingham B2 164 B2
8 Coventry CV1 113 E4
Dudley DY1 62 B8
Kidderminster DY10 116 E6
Royal Leamington Spa CV31 162 B7
Tipton DY4 51 F5
Waterloo Street E DY4 51 F5
Waterloo Terr WV1 163 A4
Waterman Rd CV6 113 F6
2 Watermarque B16 66 B2
Watermead Grange WS8 15 F7
Watermeadow Dr WS4 15 D1
Watermere WS4 29 D8
Watermill Cl WV10 11 D3
Water Mill Cl B29 85 D3
Water Mill Cres B76 46 F1
Water Mill Prim Sch B29 85 D3
Watermint Cl WS12 2 E4
WATER ORTON 59 C3
Water Orton La B46, B76 58 E4
Water Orton Prim Sch B46 59 B2
Water Orton Rd B36 58 E1
Water Orton Sta B46 59 A3
Water Rd DY3 50 C2
Water Reed Gr WS2 28 B6
Watersbridge Gdns CV10 73 C1
Waters Dr B74 31 D3
Waters Edge The B1 66 C2
Waterside
Bedworth CV6 96 C6
1 Birmingham B15 66 C1
9 Birmingham, Edgbaston B15 86 C8
Birmingham, Hamstead B43 54 E7
Royal Leamington Spa CV31 161 D7
Waterside Ave WS10 42 A1
Waterside Cl
Birmingham, Bordesley B9 67 B2
Birmingham, Pype Hayes B24 58 A5
Wolverhampton WV2 39 D7
Waterside Ct
6 Birmingham B16 66 B2
Hinckley LE10 74 F7
Royal Leamington Spa CV31 162 B6
Tamworth B77 21 F5
Waterside Dr B18 65 F5
Waterside Est DY2 62 C3
Waterside Grange DY10 116 E8
Waterside Ind Est
Rowley Regis B65 62 F4
Wolverhampton WV2 40 A6
Waterside Orch B48 123 B2
Waterside View
Birmingham B18 66 A5
Brierley Hill DY5 81 B8
Waterside Way
Brownhills WS8 6 D2
Wolverhampton WV9 11 A3
Watersmead Cl WS12 2 F4
Watersmeet Gr CV2 114 B6
Watersmeet Ho B78 35 B8
Watersmeet Rd CV2 114 B6
Waterson Croft B37 70 D3
Water St
Birmingham B3 164 B3
Burntwood WS7 6 E8
Kingswinford DY6 60 D7
West Bromwich B70 53 D2
Wolverhampton WV10 163 D4
Waters View WS3 15 B5
Water Tower La CV8 147 F6
Waterward Cl B17 85 C5
Waterway Ct B14 105 C3
Waterways Dr B69 63 E8
Waterways Gdns DY8 60 E1
Waterworks Dr B31 102 D4
Waterworks Rd B16 65 F1
Waterworks St B6 67 B8
Watery La
Alvechurch B48 124 C1
Birmingham B62 84 A3
Blakedown DY9 118 F7
Cheswick Green B90 126 D4
Codsall WV8 10 A5
Corley Moor CV7 93 D5
Coventry CV6 95 A4
Hopwood B48 123 F2
Keresley CV7 94 F4
Knowle B93 128 E4
Lichfield WS13 3 C4
Longbridge CV35 160 A1
Portway B47, B48 140 D7
Redditch B98 154 B2
Smethwick B67 65 A5
Watery La *continued*
Stourbridge DY8 60 E2
Tipton DY4 51 F5
Walsall WS1 42 E8
Willenhall WV13 26 E3
Watery Lane Ind Est WV13 26 E3
Watery Lane Middleway B9 67 B2
Watford Gap WS14 32 A7
Watford Gap Rd WS14 32 A7
Watford Rd B30 103 F5
Wathan Ave WV14 39 F1
3 Wathecroft The B17 85 B6
8 Wathen Grange Sch CV32 157 A2
Wathen Rd
Royal Leamington Spa CV32 157 A2
Warwick CV34 160 E8
Watkins Gdns B31 103 C4
Watkins Rd WV12 27 C5
Watland Gn B34 69 B5
Watling Cl LE10 75 C4
Watling Ct CV11 73 F3
Watling Dr LE10 75 C4
Watling Rd CV8 148 B6
Watling St
Brownhills WS8 6 D1
Cannock WS11 4 D6
Dordon B77, B78 36 D6
Hinckley CV11, LE10 74 C8
Hints B78 19 D3
Norton Canes WS11 5 D3
Tamworth, Bonehill B78 20 E1
Tamworth, Wilnecote B77 35 E7
Watling Street Bsns Pk WS11 6 A2
Watling Street JMI Sch WS8 6 E1
Watney Gr B44 56 C8
Watson Cl
Sutton Coldfield B72 46 C2
3 Warwick CV34 155 E1
Watson Rd
Birmingham B7 67 D7
Birmingham, Nechells B24 67 D8
Birmingham, Saltley B8 67 F5
Coventry CV5 112 D2
Darlaston WS10 41 A5
Wolverhampton, Pendeford WV10 11 B2
Wolverhampton WV14 39 F2
Watson Road E B7 67 D7
Watsons Cl DY2 62 E8
Watson's Green Fields DY2 62 F8
Watson's Green Rd DY2 51 E1
Watson Way CV7 130 C8
Watt Cl B60 136 F1
Watt Ho DY6 60 F7
Wattisham Sq B35 58 A4
Wattis Rd B67 65 A2
Wattle Gn B70 53 A3
Wattle Rd B70 53 A4
Watton Cl WV14 40 A1
Watton Ct B6 66 E8
Watton Gn B35 58 A2
Watton La B46 59 D2
Watton St B70 53 D2
Watt Rd
Birmingham B23 56 E4
Tipton DY4 52 B8
Watts Cl DY4 51 D5
Watts Rd B80 159 E2
Watt's Rd B10 87 D8
Watt St
Birmingham B21 65 D7
Smethwick B66 65 B6
Wattville Ave B21 65 C8
Wattville Prim Sch B21 65 B8
Wattville Rd B21 65 C8
Wattville Road Ind Est B66 65 B7
Watwood Rd B28, B90 105 F3
Waugh Cl B37 70 B2
Waugh Dr B63 100 D8
Waveley Rd CV1 113 A3
Wavell Rd
Birmingham B8 67 E5
Brierley Hill DY5 81 F7
Walsall WS2 27 E2
Wavendon Cl CV2 96 F1
Waveney B77 35 E8
Waveney Ave WV6 23 E4
Waveney Cl LE10 75 A8
Waveney Croft B36 69 F8
Waveney Gr WS11 1 B1
Wavenham Cl B74 31 E5
Waverhill Rd B21 65 F7
Waverley Ave
Birmingham B43 44 B4
Nuneaton CV11 73 F1
Waverley Cl DY10 117 A8
Waverley Cres
Romsley B62 100 F4
Wolverhampton, Goldthorn Hill WV4 39 B6
Wolverhampton, Lanesfield WV4 39 F3
Waverley Gdns WV5 49 B7
Waverley Gr B91 106 F3
Waverley Rd
Birmingham B10 87 D7
Darlaston WS10 41 D6
Kenilworth CV8 148 A4
Royal Leamington Spa CV31 162 B6
Waverley Rd *continued*
Walsall WS3 13 F2
Waverley Sch B10 88 A8
Waverley Sq CV11 73 F1
Waverley St DY2 62 A8
Waverley Wlk WS14 9 B6
Wavers Marston B37 90 A8
15 Waverton Mews CV31 162 C6
Wavytree Cl CV34 160 D7
Waxland Rd B63 83 B2
Wayfield Cl B90 106 C3
Wayfield Rd B90 106 C3
Wayford Dr B72 57 D7
Wayford Glade WV13 40 F8
Wayford Gr B8 68 B4
Waynecroft Rd B43 43 E2
Wayside
Birmingham B37 90 A8
Wolverhampton WV8 10 F2
Wayside Dr B74 31 C3
Wayside Gdns WV12 27 E5
Wayside Wlk WS2 28 A3
Waystone La DY9 119 D4
Wealden Hatch WV10 11 E4
Wealdstone Dr DY3 50 D2
Weale Gr CV34 155 F2
Weaman St B4 164 C3
Weates Yd B27 88 C4
Weatheroak Cl B97 153 A1
WEATHEROAK HILL 124 B1
Weatheroak Hill B48 124 B1
Weatheroak Rd B11 87 C5
Weatheroaks
Birmingham B62 84 A7
Brownhills WS9 16 B4
Weather Oaks B17 85 B6
Weaver Ave
Birmingham B26 89 B6
Sutton Coldfield B76 47 A1
Weaver Cl DY5 61 B6
8 Weaver Ct B75 32 E3
Weaver Gr WV13 27 D2
Weavers Cl
Bedworth CV12 79 A2
Redditch B97 158 D4
WEAVERS HILL 158 C4
Weavers Hill B97 158 D4
Weavers Rise DY2 62 D3
Weavers Wharf Sh Ctr DY10 116 D6
Weavers Wlk CV6 114 B8
Weaves Cl WS6 4 F1
1 Weaving Gdns WS11 1 E1
Webb Ave WV6 23 E5
Webbcroft Rd B33 68 F4
Webb La B28 105 E6
Webb Rd DY4 52 C7
Webb St
Dudley WV14 40 C1
Nuneaton CV10 72 D3
Willenhall WV13 26 F2
WEBHEATH 153 A2
Webheath Fst Sch B97 153 A2
Webley Rise WV10 11 F4
Webner Ind Est WV2 40 A6
Webster Ave CV8 148 B5
Webster Cl
Birmingham B11 87 B6
Sutton Coldfield B72 57 B7
Webster Rd
Walsall WS2 28 E5
Willenhall WV13 27 A3
Webster St CV6 113 E7
Webster Way B76 58 B8
Webster Wlk WS11 2 A4
Weddell Wynd WV14 40 F1
WEDDINGTON 73 D7
Weddington Ctry Wlk* CV10 73 B8
Weddington Ind Est CV10 73 C5
Weddington Prim Sch CV10 73 D7
Weddington Rd CV10 73 C7
Weddington Terr CV10 73 D5
Wedgbury Cl WS10 42 A1
Wedgbury Way DY5 61 B1
WEDGES MILLS 4 B6
10 Wedge St WS1 28 F2
Wedgewood Ave B70 52 F7
Wedgewood Cl
Burntwood WS7 7 C7
Coventry CV2 114 E8
Wedgewood Ct WS4 15 C1
Wedgewood Dr B20 55 B2
Wedgewood Ho B37 70 B4
Wedgewood Pl B70 52 F7
Wedgewood Rd B32 84 D5
Wedge-Woods CV5 132 F8
Wedgnock Gn CV34 160 D8
Wedgnock Ind Est CV34 160 C8
Wedgnock La CV34 155 C1
Wedgwood Cl WV1 26 A1
Wedmore Rd B73 45 F1
WEDNESBURY 41 D3
Wednesbury, Great Western Street Stop WS10 41 E2
Wednesbury L Ctr WS10 41 E3
Wednesbury Mus & Art Gall* WS10 41 F2
WEDNESBURY OAK 41 B1
Wednesbury Oak Prim Sch DY4 41 A1
Wednesbury Oak Rd DY4 41 A1
Wednesbury Parkway Stop WS10 41 D2
Wednesbury Rd WS1 42 D7
Wednesbury Trad Est WS10 41 E4
WEDNESFIELD 26 E6
Wednesfield High Sch Engineering Sch WV11 26 E5
Wednesfield Rd
Willenhall WV13 27 A3
Wolverhampton WV1, WV10 163 D4
Wednesfield Village Prim Sch WV11 26 D5
Wednesfield Way WV11 26 D4
Wedon Cl CV4 131 E7
WEEFORD 19 A4
2 Weeford Dell B75 32 E3
Weeford Dr B20 54 F4
Weeford Rd B75 32 F3
6 Weethley Ho B97 153 A4
Weights Farm B97 153 C7
Weights La B97 153 C7
Weights Lane Bsns Pk B97 153 C7
Weilerswist Dr CV31 161 F4
Weirbrook Cl B29 103 C7
Weland Cl B46 59 B2
Weland Ct B46 59 B2
Welbeck Ave
Hinckley LE10 75 D4
Wolverhampton WV10 25 D7
Welbeck Cl B62 83 E6
Welbeck Dr
Kidderminster DY11 116 B5
Walsall WS4 29 D7
Welbeck Gr B23 56 B5
Welbury Gdns WV6 24 F5
Welby Gate CV7 130 B5
Welby Rd B28 87 F1
Welch Cl DY4 52 B7
Welches Cl B31 103 B5
Welches Meadow Nature Reserve* CV31 162 B8
Welcombe Dr B76 57 F7
Welcombe Gr B91 106 F4
Welcome Dr B61 121 A1
Welford Ave B26 88 F8
Welford Cl B98 158 F5
Welford Gr B74 31 F3
Welford Pl CV6 113 D7
Welford Prim Sch B20 66 A8
Welford Rd
Birmingham B20 66 A8
Solihull B90 106 C4
Sutton Coldfield B73 45 E1
Tamworth B77 35 C5
Welgarth Ave CV6 112 F6
Welham Croft B90 127 A6
Welland Dr DY8 81 A8
Welland Gr
Birmingham B24 57 D3
Willenhall WV13 27 C2
Welland Rd
Coventry CV1 113 F1
Halesowen B63 83 A2
Welland Way B76 58 A7
Well Cl
Birmingham B36 68 E8
Redditch B97 158 E5
Wellcroft Rd B34 69 A7
Wellcroft St WS10 41 F3
Weller Ct WV3 24 D1
Wellesbourne B79 21 C8
Wellesbourne Cl
Redditch B98 153 E4
Wolverhampton WV3 38 B8
Wellesbourne Dr WV14 51 B7
Wellesbourne Rd
Birmingham B20 55 B1
Coventry CV5 112 A3
3 Wellesbourne Twr B5 86 E8
Wellesley Dr DY4 51 F5
Wellesley Gdns B13 87 D1
Wellesley Rd B68 64 B6
Wellfield Cl
Balsall Common CV7 130 D5
Cannock WS11 4 B7
Wellfield Gdns DY2 62 E6
Wellfield Rd
Aldridge WS9 30 B8
Birmingham B28 106 B6
Wellhead La B42 55 E3
Wellhead Way B42 55 F2
Wellington Ave WV3 38 F7
Wellington Cl
Hinckley LE10 75 E4
Kingswinford DY6 60 E4
Wellington Cres B20 55 B2
Wellington Ct
Birmingham B32 84 F5
Birmingham, Handsworth Wood B20 55 C2
Cradley Heath B64 62 F2
Kidderminster DY11 116 C5
Willenhall WV13 26 F3
Wellington Dr WS11 4 B8
1 Wellington Gdns CV1 113 B2
Wellington Gr B91 106 F6
Wellington Ho B32 84 F4
Wellington Ind Est WV14 51 C7
Wellington Pl WV13 26 F3
WELLINGTON PLACE 27 A4
Wellington Rd
Bilston WV14 40 D6
Birmingham B20 55 C2
Birmingham, Edgbaston B15 86 C7
Bromsgrove B60 151 A8
Dudley DY1 51 B1

Wellington Rd continued
Royal Leamington Spa
CV32. . . . . .157 C2
Smethwick B67 . . . . 65 A3
Tipton DY4. . . . . 52 A4
Walsall WS5. . . . . 43 C6
Wellington St
Birmingham B18 . . . . 65 D5
Coventry CV1. . . . . .165 D4
Cradley Heath B64. . . . . 62 F2
Oldbury B69. . . . . 64 B6
🔟 Redditch B98 . . . . .153 E4
Walsall WS2. . . . . 42 B7
West Bromwich B71 . . . . . . 53 C4
Wellington Street S B70. . 53 C4
Wellington Terr 🔟 B19. . . 66 B7
Wellington Tower 🔟
B31 . . . . .103 A1
Wellington Way B35 . . . . 58 B2
Well La
Birmingham B5 . . . . .164 D2
Great Wyrley WS6 . . . . 5 A1
Hinckley LE10 . . . . 71 D1
Tanworth-In-A B94 . . . . . . .142 A1
Walsall, Harden WS3. . . . . . 28 D7
Walsall WS3. . . . . 28 D7
Wolverhampton WV11. . . . . 26 C4
Wellman Croft B29. . . . . . 85 D1
Wellman's Rd WV13. . . . . 27 C1
Well Mdw B45. . . . . .122 A6
Wellmeadow Gr B92 . . . .109 A7
Wellmead Wlk B45. . . . . .121 F8
Well Pl WS3 . . . . 28 E8
Wells Ave WS10. . . . . 41 B6
Wells Cl
Coventry CV3. . . . . .133 F7
Kidderminster DY11. . . . . .116 A6
Perton WV6 . . . . 23 D4
Wednesbury DY4. . . . . 41 A1
West Bromwich B71 . . . . . . 53 D8
Wells Ct
Coventry CV3. . . . . .133 F7
Dudley DY2 . . . . 62 C5
Wellsford Ave B92 . . . . . . 89 B4
WELLS GREEN 89 B4
Wells Green Rd B92 . . . . . 89 A4
Wells Rd
Bilston WV14. . . . . 40 E3
Brierley Hill DY5 . . . . 61 B3
Rowley Regis B65 . . . . 63 E4
Solihull B92 . . . . 89 C4
Wolverhampton WV4. . . . . . 38 F5
Well St
Birmingham B19 . . . . 66 C5
Coventry CV1. . . . . .165 B3
Darlaston WS10. . . . . 41 E6
Wells Twr B16. . . . . 66 A2
Wells Wlk B37 . . . . 70 A1
Welney Gdns WV9 . . . . . . 11 A3
Welsby Ave B43. . . . . 54 E7
Welsh Cl CV34 . . . . .155 E2
Welsh House Farm Com Sch
B32. 84 F4
Welsh House Farm Rd
B32 . . . . 84 F4
Welshmans Hill B73. . . . . 45 C3
Welsh Rd
Coventry CV2. . . . . .114 B4
Cubbington CV32, CV33. . .157 A7
Welton Cl B76 . . . . 47 A2
Welton Rd CV34 . . . . .155 D1
Welwyndale Rd B72. . . . . 57 C6
Welwyn Rd LE10 . . . . 71 F1
Wembley Gr B25. . . . . 88 C8
Wembley La WV7 . . . . 6 D8
Wembrook Cl CV11 . . . . . 73 D2
Wembrook Ho CV11. . . . . 73 D2
Wembrook Prim Sch
CV11. . . . . 73 C2
Wembury B77 . . . . 21 E5
Wem Gdns WV11. . . . . . . 26 D6
Wendell Crest WV10 . . . . 11 F4
Wendiburgh St CV4 . . . . .132 B7
Wendover Dr LE10 . . . . . . 71 E4
Wendover Rd
Birmingham B23 . . . . 56 C7
Rowley Regis B65 . . . . 63 A5
Wolverhampton WV4. . . . . . 39 F2
Wendover Rise CV5 . . . . .112 C4
Wendron Cl B60 . . . . .137 B2
Wendron Gr B14. . . . . . . .104 D4
Wenlock B77 . . . . 21 E8
Wenlock Ave WV3 . . . . . . 38 E3
Wenlock Cl
Halesowen B63 . . . . 82 D2
Sedgley DY3. . . . . 50 C7
Wenlock Dr B61 . . . . .137 A5
Wenlock Gdns WS3 . . . . . 28 E5
Wenlock Rd
Birmingham B20. . . . . 55 F1
Stourbridge DY8 . . . . 81 B6
Wenlock Way CV10 . . . . . 72 B3
Wenman St B12 . . . . 86 F6
Wensley Croft B90 . . . . . .106 B6
Wensleydale Rd B42 . . . . 55 B6
Wensley Rd B26. . . . . 88 F6
Wensum Cl LE10. . . . . 75 B8
Wentbridge Rd WV1 . . . . 26 C1
Wentworth Ave B36. . . . . . 69 B8
Wentworth Cl
Burntwood WS7. . . . . 7 C7
Hinckley LE10 . . . . 71 E3
Wentworth Ct
Birmingham B24 . . . . 56 F2
Sutton Coldfield B75 . . . . . . 32 B1

Wentworth Dr
Blackwell B60 . . . . .138 A5
Coventry CV6. . . . . 95 B4
Lichfield WS14. . . . . 9 D5
Nuneaton CV11 . . . . 74 A1
Oldbury B69. . . . . 63 A7
Wentworth Gate B17. . . . 85 B6
Wentworth Gr WV6 . . . . . 23 D5
Wentworth Park Ave B17. 85 B6
Wentworth Rd
Birmingham B17 . . . . 85 B6
Royal Leamington Spa
CV31. . . . . .162 D6
Solihull B92 . . . . 88 F3
Stourbridge DY8 . . . . 80 E7
Sutton Coldfield B74 . . . . . . 46 A8
Walsall WS3. . . . . 13 F3
Wolverhampton WV10. . . . . 11 F3
Wentworth Rise B62 . . . . 83 D3
Wentworth Way B32 . . . . 84 F3
Wenyon Cl DY4 . . . . 52 B4
Weoley Ave B29 . . . . 85 C2
WEOLEY CASTLE 85 A1
Weoley Castle 🟊 B29 . . . 85 A2
Weoley Castle Rd B29. . . 84 F1
Weoley Hill B29. . . . . . . .103 C8
Weoley Park Rd B29 . . . . 85 C1
WERGS 24 A6
Wergs Dr WV6. . . . . 24 A7
Wergs Hall WV8 . . . . 23 F7
Wergs Hall Rd WV6, WV8 . 24 A7
Wergs Rd
Codsall WV6. . . . . 23 F7
Wolverhampton WV6. . . . . . 24 B6
Werneth Gr WS3. . . . . 14 A4
Wesleyan St WS4 . . . . 29 A4
Wesley Ave
Cheslyn Hay WS6. . . . . 4 D3
Codsall WV8. . . . . 10 B2
Halesowen B63 . . . . 82 B8
Wesley Cl B64 . . . . 62 F1
Wesley Ct
Birmingham B16 . . . . 65 C2
Cannock WS11. . . . . 1 E1
🔟 Cradley Heath B64. . . . . 82 F8
🔟 Wolverhampton WV4 . . . 39 F4
Wesley Gr WS10. . . . . 41 E3
Wesley Ho 🟠 WS2 . . . . . . 42 C7
Wesley Pl
Cannock WS12. . . . . 2 C7
Tipton DY4. . . . . 52 C7
Wesley Rd
Birmingham B23 . . . . 56 F5
Brierley Hill DY5 . . . . 61 B5
Codsall WV8. . . . . 10 B2
Willenhall WV12 . . . . 27 C6
Wesley's Fold WS10. . . . . 41 D6
Wesley St
Bilston WV14. . . . . 40 E2
Oldbury B69. . . . . 64 A8
Wolverhampton WV2. . . . . . 40 A6
Wesley Way B77 . . . . 21 F4
Wesley Wlk B60 . . . . .150 E7
Wessenden B77 . . . . 36 B7
Wessex Cl
Bedworth CV12 . . . . 78 A4
Brownhills WS8. . . . . 15 F7
Wessex Ct B79. . . . . 22 F7
Wessex Dr WS11. . . . . 1 F2
Wessex Rd WV2 . . . . 39 F6
Wesson Gdns B63. . . . . . . 83 A3
Wesson Rd WS10 . . . . 41 C8
West Acre WV13 . . . . 26 F1
Westacre Cres WV3 . . . . . 24 C1
Westacre Dr DY5 . . . . 81 F8
Westacre Gdns B33 . . . . . 68 F3
Westacre Inf Sch WV3. . . 24 C1
West Ave
Bedworth CV12 . . . . 78 D2
Birmingham, Castle Bromwich
B36. 69 D8
Birmingham, Handsworth
B20. 55 A4
Coventry CV6, CV7. . . . . . . 95 A5
Coventry, Middle Stoke
CV2. . . . . .114 A2
Oldbury B69. . . . . 63 B7
Redditch B98 . . . . .153 E3
Wolverhampton WV11. . . . . 26 C6
Westbourne Ave
Birmingham B34 . . . . 68 E6
Cannock WS11. . . . . 1 D3
Cheslyn Hay WS6. . . . . 4 E3
Westbourne Cl 🟠 B61. . .136 E1
Westbourne Cres
Birmingham B15 . . . . 86 A8
Burntwood WS7. . . . . 7 B7
Westbourne Ct
Darlaston WS10. . . . . 41 F7
Walsall WS4. . . . . 29 A3
Westbourne Gdns B15 . . . 86 A7
Westbourne Gr B21. . . . . . 65 F7
Westbourne Rd
Birmingham, Edgbaston
B15. 86 A8
Birmingham, Handsworth
B21. 54 D1
Darlaston WS10. . . . . 41 F7
Halesowen B62 . . . . 83 E7
Solihull B92 . . . . .106 F8
Walsall, Ryecroft WS4. . . . . 28 F4
Walsall WS4. . . . . 29 A4
West Bromwich B70 . . . . . . 53 B2
Wolverhampton WV3. . . . . . 39 A3
Westbourne St WS4. . . . . 28 F3
Westbourne Terr 🟠 B61 .136 E1
WEST BROMWICH 53 E3

West Bromwich Central Stop
B70. 53 C2
West Bromwich Rd WS5. . 42 F5
West Bromwich Ringway
B70. 53 D2
West Bromwich St
Oldbury B69. . . . . 52 F1
Walsall WS1. . . . . 42 E7
Westbrook Ave
Aldridge WS9 . . . . 29 F5
Aldridge WS9 . . . . 30 A5
Westbrook Ct CV5 . . . . . .112 A4
Westbury Ave WS10. . . . . 41 F6
Westbury Ct
🟢 Brierley Hill DY5. . . . . . . 61 D2
Coventry CV2. . . . . .114 A3
Warwick CV34 . . . . .161 A7
Westbury Ho B97 . . . . . . .153 B2
Westbury Rd
Coventry CV5. . . . . .112 D5
Nuneaton CV10 . . . . 72 D3
Smethwick B17 . . . . 65 B3
Wednesbury WS10 . . . . 41 F6
Wolverhampton WV1 . . . . .163 C3
West Bvd B32. . . . . 84 F4
Westcliff Dr CV34 . . . . . .155 E2
Westcliffe Dr CV3, CV8. . .133 B5
Westcliff Pl B31 . . . . .102 F4
Westcombe Gr B32 . . . . . . 84 A1
West Coppice Rd WS8. . . 15 C8
WEST COSELEY 51 B7
Westcote Ave B31 . . . . . .102 C2
Westcote Cl B92. . . . . 89 A8
Westcotes CV4 . . . . .112 B1
Westcott Cl DY6 . . . . 60 F3
Westcott Rd B26. . . . . 89 A8
WESTCROFT 12 B3
Westcroft Ave WV10 . . . . 12 A1
Westcroft Gr B38 . . . . . . .103 D3
Westcroft Rd
Sedgley DY3. . . . . 39 B2
Wolverhampton WV6. . . . . . 23 F6
**Westcroft Specl Sch &
Sports Coll** WV10 . . . . . . 12 B2
Westcroft Way B14 . . . . .105 B1
West Cl B60. . . . . .150 F6
Westdean Cl B62 . . . . 83 C4
West Dr
Birmingham, Edgbaston
B5. . . . . 86 C5
Birmingham, Handsworth
B20. 66 B8
Fazeley B78. . . . . 20 E2
West End Ave B66 . . . . . . 64 D7
West End Ct CV34. . . . . . .160 D6
West End Villas B38. . . . .103 F2
Westerdale Cl DY3. . . . . . . 51 A7
Westerham CV3 B93 . . . . .127 A6
Westerhope Gr B19 . . . . . 66 C5
Westeria Cl B36 . . . . 69 C8
Westeria Ho B36. . . . . 69 C8
Westering Parkway WV10 11 F4
Westerings B20. . . . . 55 C2
Western Ave
Brierley Hill DY5 . . . . 61 B2
Halesowen B62 . . . . 83 E4
Sedgley DY3. . . . . 50 B8
Willenhall WS2. . . . . 27 D3
Western Bsns Pk B62 . . . 83 E4
Western By-Pass WS13 . . . 8 F8
Western Cl WS2 . . . . 27 D3
Western Hill Cl B96 . . . . .158 E1
Western Rd
Birmingham, Edgbaston
B18. 65 F4
Birmingham, Erdington B24. 57 A3
Cannock WS12. . . . . 2 B6
Cradley Heath B64. . . . . 82 E8
Oldbury B69. . . . . 64 A8
Stourbridge DY8 . . . . 80 F4
Sutton Coldfield B73 . . . . . . 46 A1
West Hagley DY9 . . . . 99 B4
Western Way
Darlaston WS10. . . . . 41 C3
Kidderminster DY11. . . . . .116 A5
Willenhall B14 . . . . .105 B1
Westfield Cl
Dorridge B93 . . . . .127 F2
Nuneaton CV10 . . . . 73 D5
Westfield Ct LE10 . . . . 75 C7
Westfield Dr WS9. . . . . . . 30 A6
Westfield Gr WV3. . . . . . . 38 C8
Westfield Grange B14. . . 86 E1
Westfield Hall 🟠 B16 . . . . 65 D1
Westfield Ho B36. . . . . 70 A7
Westfield Inf Sch LE10 . . 75 B7
Westfield Jun Sch LE10 . . 75 B7
Westfield Manor B75. . . . . 32 A4
Westfield Prim Sch 🟠
WV5 . . . . 49 A7
Westfield Rd
Bilston WV14. . . . . 40 E4
Birmingham, Acock's Green
B27. 88 B3
Birmingham B15 . . . . 85 D7
Birmingham, Moseley B14. . 86 E1
Brierley Hill DY5 . . . . 81 F8
Dudley DY2 . . . . 62 D7
Halesowen B62 . . . . 63 E1
Hinckley LE10 . . . . 75 B7
Sedgley DY3. . . . . 39 E1
Smethwick B67 . . . . 64 F5
Willenhall WV13 . . . . 40 E8
Westfields
Birchmoor B78. . . . . 36 D8
Catshill B61. . . . . .136 F8

Westford Gr B28. . . . . . . .105 E3
Westgate
Aldridge WS9. . . . . 29 E6
Birmingham B15 . . . . 85 E4
Cannock WS12. . . . . 2 F6
Oldbury B65. . . . . 63 E4
West Gate B16. . . . . 65 E3
Westgate Cl
Sedgley DY3. . . . . 50 E7
Warwick CV34 . . . . .160 D6
Westgate Ho 🔟 CV34 . . .160 E6
Westgate Park Ind Est
WS9 . . . . 29 E6
Westgate Prim Sch
CV34. . . . . .160 D6
Westgate Trad Est WS9 . . 29 E6
West Gn WV4. . . . . 38 C5
West Green Cl B15. . . . . . . 86 B8
Westgrove Ave 🟢 B90 . .127 A6
Westgrove Terr 🟠 CV32 .161 D8
WEST HAGLEY 99 A5
Westhall Gate WS3 . . . . . 14 B2
Westham Ho B37 . . . . 70 B4
Westhaven Dr B31. . . . . . .102 E7
Westhaven Rd B72. . . . . . . 46 C5
Westhay Rd B28 . . . . .106 B7
WEST HEATH 123 B7
West Heath Prim Sch
B38. . . . . .123 C8
West Heath Rd
🟢 Birmingham, Edgbaston
B18. 65 D4
Birmingham, Northfield
B31. . . . . .103 B1
WEST HILL. 2 B6
Westhill WV3 . . . . 24 C2
West Hill Ave WS12 . . . . . . 2 B6
Westhill Cl
Birmingham B29 . . . . 85 D1
Solihull B92 . . . . .106 E8
West Hill Ct B14 . . . . .104 C4
West Hill Prim Sch WS12. . 2 B6
Westhill Rd
Birmingham B38 . . . . .103 F3
Blackdown CV32 . . . . .157 A6
Coventry CV6. . . . . .112 F6
West Holme B9 . . . . 67 C2
Westholme Croft B30 . . .103 E8
Westhouse Ct B14. . . . . . .104 D4
Westhouse Gr B14 . . . . . .104 D4
West House Sch B15. . . . . 86 C8
West Hyde LE10. . . . . 74 F7
Westland Ave WV3 . . . . . . 24 F2
Westland Cl B23. . . . . 56 F5
Westland Gdns
Stourbridge DY8 . . . . 80 F7
🟢 Wolverhampton WV3 . . . 25 A2
Westland Rd WV6. . . . . . . 24 F2
Westlands Rd
Birmingham B13 . . . . 87 A1
Sutton Coldfield B76 . . . . . . 57 F6
Westland Wlk B35 . . . . . . 57 F2
Westlea Rd CV31. . . . . . . .161 E6
Westleigh Ave CV5. . . . . .132 F7
Westley Brook Cl B26 . . . 89 B5
Westley Cl B28 . . . . .106 B6
Westley Ct B71 . . . . 53 D6
Westley Rd B27. . . . . 88 B3
Westley St
Birmingham B9 . . . . 67 A2
🟢 Dudley DY1. . . . . 62 B8
West Lodge WV1. . . . . 25 A3
Westmead Ave B80 . . . . .159 E4
Westmead Cres B24 . . . . . 57 C4
Westmead Dr B68. . . . . . . 64 B4
West Mead Dr B14 . . . . . .104 E6
Westmede Ctr CV5. . . . . .112 C4
West Mews B44. . . . . 44 D2
**West Midlands Hospl
(Private)** B63. . . . . 82 D5
West Midlands Police Mus🟊
B21 . . . . 87 C4
West Mill Croft B38 . . . . .123 E7
Westminster B37 . . . . 69 F5
Westminster Ave WV4. . . 39 B5
Westminster Cl
Bromsgrove B61 . . . . .136 D1
Dudley DY1. . . . . 51 A2
Westminster Cres B20 . . . 55 C1
Westminster Ct
Birmingham B20 . . . . 55 C2
🟢 Bromsgrove B60. . . . . . .137 A2
Westminster Dr
Birmingham B14 . . . . .104 E6
Hinckley LE10 . . . . 75 F4
Nuneaton CV10 . . . . 72 B7
Westminster Ind Est DY2 . 62 D2
Westminster Pl B31. . . . . .123 B8
Westminster Prim Sch
B20. 55 C1
Westminster Rd
Birmingham, Handsworth
B20. 55 C1
Birmingham, Stirchley B29 .104 A8
Cannock WS11. . . . . 1 E6
Coventry CV1. . . . . .165 A1
Kidderminster DY11. . . . . .116 A6
Stourbridge DY8 . . . . 60 D2
Walsall WS4. . . . . 29 B7
West Bromwich B71 . . . . . . 53 D8
Westminster Sch The
B71. 53 D8
Westmoreland Ave CV10 . 72 E4
Westmore Way WS10 . . . . 42 D5
Westmorland Cl B78 . . . . . 21 A1
Westmorland Ct B71. . . . . 53 D7
Westmorland Rd
Coventry CV2. . . . . .114 F4

Westmorland Rd continued
West Bromwich B71 . . . . . . 53 D7
Weston Ave
🔟 Birmingham, Lozells
B19 . . . . 66 C7
Birmingham, Sparkbrook
B11. 87 C6
Oldbury B69. . . . . 52 B1
Westonbirt Cl CV8 . . . . . .148 C6
Weston Cl
Cannock WS11. . . . . 2 C1
Dorridge B93 . . . . .128 A2
Hinckley LE10 . . . . 71 A1
🟢 Royal Leamington Spa
CV31. . . . . .162 C6
Walsall WS1. . . . . 42 E6
Warwick CV34 . . . . .160 F7
Weston Cres WS9 . . . . 30 B4
Weston Ct B16 WV3 . . . . . 25 C4
Weston Dr
Bilston WV14. . . . . 40 B5
Great Wyrley WS6 . . . . 4 F1
Wednesbury DY4 . . . . 41 C2
Westonhall Rd B60. . . . . .150 D1
Weston Hall Stables CV12 79 A3
Weston Ho
Birmingham B19 . . . . 66 C6
Wolverhampton WV6. . . . . . 24 E5
WESTON IN ARDEN 79 A3
Weston Ind Est B11 . . . . . 87 C4
Weston La
Birmingham B11 . . . . 87 E4
Bulkington CV12 . . . . 79 B3
Weston Rd
Birmingham B19 . . . . 66 B7
Lichfield WS13. . . . . 3 A2
Smethwick B67 . . . . 64 F2
Weston St WS1 . . . . 42 E7
Weston Terr 🟠 B19. . . . . . 66 D8
West Orchards Sh Ctr
CV1 . . . . .165 B3
Westover Rd B20 . . . . 54 E4
West Park Ave B31. . . . . .102 E2
West Park Cl WS9. . . . . . . 29 E5
West Park Ct WV1 . . . . 25 A2
West Park Prim Sch
WV1 . . . . .163 A4
West Park Rd B67. . . . . . . 64 D6
**West Park Rehabilitation
Hospl** WV1 . . . . 25 A2
West Pathway B17 . . . . . . 85 C6
West Plaza B70. . . . . 53 D2
West Point B17 . . . . 85 B6
Westport Cres WV11 . . . . 26 F5
Westray Cl B45 . . . . .101 F1
Westray Dr LE10 . . . . 71 C1
West Rd
Birmingham, Hamstead
B43. 54 E7
Birmingham, Handsworth
B6. . . . . 55 E2
Bromsgrove B60 . . . . .137 A2
Halesowen B63 . . . . 82 B6
Tipton DY4. . . . . 52 B3
Wolverhampton WV4. . . . . . 39 F5
West Rise B75. . . . . 46 C6
West Road S B63 . . . . 82 B6
West Rock CV34 . . . . .160 D7
West Side Bsns Ctr CV4 . .131 F8
Westside Dr B32. . . . . 84 D1
WEST SMETHWICK 64 C7
West St
Brierley Hill DY5 . . . . 81 F8
Cannock WS11. . . . . 4 E6
Coventry CV1. . . . . .113 E3
Redditch B98 . . . . .153 E3
Rowley Regis B65 . . . . 63 C1
🔟 Royal Leamington Spa
CV31. . . . . .162 A2
Stourbridge DY8 . . . . 80 F5
Tamworth B79 . . . . 21 C5
Tamworth, Kettlebrook B77. 21 C3
Walsall WS3. . . . . 28 C7
Warwick CV34 . . . . .160 D5
Wolverhampton WV6. . . . . . 25 C5
West View B8 . . . . 68 C4
West View B75. . . . . 46 E6
West View Dr DY6. . . . . . . 60 E5
West View Rd
Royal Leamington Spa
CV32. . . . . .157 C5
Sutton Coldfield B75 . . . . . . 46 E6
Westville Ave DY11. . . . . .116 A5
Westville Rd WS2. . . . . . . 28 A3
Westward Cl B44 . . . . 55 F8
West Way
Birmingham B31 . . . . .123 B7
Walsall WS4. . . . . 15 B2
Westway Ho WS4 . . . . 15 B1
Westwick Cl WS9 . . . . 16 E4
West Winds WV10. . . . . . . 12 C7
Westwood Ave
Birmingham B11 . . . . 87 D4
Stourbridge DY8 . . . . 80 D3
Westwood Bsns Pk
Birmingham B6. . . . . 56 B1
Coventry CV4. . . . . .131 F6
Westwood Cl CV10. . . . . . . 72 E3
Westwood Dr B45. . . . . . . 85 B4
Westwood Rd B6 . . . . . . .102 B1
WESTWOOD GARDENS . .132 D8
Westwood Gr B91. . . . . . .106 D2
WESTWOOD HEATH 131 E6
Westwood Heath Rd
CV4 . . . . .131 E6

Westwood Holdings WS12 . .1 B6
Westwood Rd
 Birmingham, Aston B6.... 56 A2
 Coventry CV5............113 A1
 Sutton Coldfield B73 ... 45 A4
Westwood Sch The CV4 .132 A6
Westwood St DY5........64 A3
Westwood View B24.....57 C3
Westwood Way CV4... 132 A6
Wetherby Cl
 Birmingham B36 ....68 D8
 Wolverhampton WV10 ...11 D5
Wetherby Rd
 Birmingham B27 ....88 C2
 Walsall WS3............14 A4
Wetherfield Rd B11 .... 88 A3
Wexford Cl DY1.........50 F2
Wexford Rd CV2 ....96 D1
Weybourne Rd B44 .....44 E2
Weycroft Rd B23........56 B7
Weyhill Cl WV9 ....10 F2
Weymoor Rd B17........85 B3
Weymouth Cl CV3.....134 D5
Weymouth Dr B74 ......31 F4
Weymouth Rd B19 ......21 B5
Whaley's Croft CV6 ...113 B8
Wharf App WS9.........29 F7
Wharf Cl WS14..........9 C7
Wharfdale Rd B11 ......88 A5
Wharfedale Cl DY6......60 B7
Wharfedale St WS10 ....42 A2
Wharf La
 Birmingham B18 ....66 A6
 Burntwood WS8..........6 F3
 Nuthurst B94...........143 D4
 Solihull B91 ....107 D6
 Tardebigge B60 ....138 B1
Wharf Lodge CV31......161 D7
Wharf Rd
 Birmingham, King's Norton
 B30 ....104 A2
 Birmingham, Tyseley B11...88 B5
 Coventry CV6...........113 F5
Wharfside B69..........63 F7
Wharf St
 Birmingham, Aston B6....67 A7
 Birmingham, Hockley B18...66 A6
 Walsall WS2............28 C1
 Warwick CV34..........161 A8
 Wolverhampton WV1....163 D2
Wharf Yd LE10.........75 A7
War Hall Rd B92........107 E8
Warrington Cl B98.....159 A8
Warrington Hill B98...159 A8
Wharton Ave B92.......107 E7
Wharton St B7..........67 D8
Wharton Street Ind Est
 B7.-...................92 D8
Wharwell La WS6........5 A1
Whatcote Grn B92......107 E8
WHATELEY.............35 F3
Whateley Ave WS3......35 E3
Whateley Cres B36.....69 D8
Whateley Ct CV11......73 B4
Whateley Gn B74.......46 A8
Whateley Hall Cl B93...128 C7
Whateley Hall Rd B93...128 B7
Whateley La B77, B78...35 F4
Whateley Lodge Dr B36...69 C8
Whateley Pl WS3 ....28 F6
Whateley Rd
 Birmingham B21 ....65 E8
 Walsall WS3............28 F6
Whateley's Dr CV8....148 A5
Whateley Villas CV9 ...36 A2
Wheatcroft Cl
 Burntwood WS7..........7 A5
 Halesowen B62 ....83 F8
 Redditch B97...........153 A5
 3 Sutton Coldfield B75 ...32 E3
Wheatcroft Dr B37.....70 C1
Wheatcroft Gr DY2.....51 F1
Wheatcroft Rd B33.....68 F2
Wheate Croft CV4......111 F2
Wheaten Cl B37........70 D3
Wheatfield Cl B36......70 A7
Wheatfield View B31...102 D6
Wheatfield Way LE10...71 C4
Wheat Hill WS5........43 E8
Wheathill Cl
 Royal Leamington Spa
 CV32..................156 E2
 Wolverhampton WV4....38 E3
Wheatland Gr WS9......30 B4
Wheatlands Cl **1** B1 ......2 C1
Wheatlands Croft B33...69 E3
Wheatlands The WV6 ...23 D3
Wheatley Cl
 Birmingham B68 ....84 C8
 Solihull B92 ....107 E8
 Sutton Coldfield B75 ...32 C3
Wheatley Gr WS6.......5 A2
Wheatley Grange B46...70 F6
Wheatley Rd B68.......84 D8
Wheatley St
 West Bromwich B70 .....53 A3
 Wolverhampton WV2....39 F6
Wheatmill Cl DY10......98 B2
Wheatmoor Rd B74.....46 A6
Wheatmoor Rise B75...46 E6
Wheaton Cl WV10......25 C7
Wheaton Vale B20......54 E3
Wheatridge Cl DY6.....60 A8
Wheatridge Rd B60.....150 E6
Wheats Ave B17........85 B3
Wheatsheaf Cl B75.....32 E4

Wheatsheaf Rd
 Birmingham B16 ....65 D2
 Oldbury B69............63 A8
 Wolverhampton WV8....10 E1
Wheat St CV11.........73 D4
Wheatstone Cl DY3.....50 E6
Wheatstone Gr B33.....68 F5
Wheaton Ho B26........88 E4
Wheeler Cl B93.........14 B7
Wheeler Ho **12** B69.....64 A7
Wheeler Rd WV11.......26 C8
Wheeler's Fold WV1...163 C3
Wheelers La
 Birmingham B13 ....104 F7
 Redditch B97...........153 C6
Wheeler's La B13.......105 A7
Wheelers Lane Prim Sch
 B13....................104 F7
Wheelers Lane Tech Coll
 B13....................104 F7
Wheeler St
 Birmingham B19 ....66 D7
 Stourbridge DY8........80 F5
Wheeley Moor Rd B37...70 A5
Wheeley Rd
 Alvechurch B48 ....138 D5
 Solihull B92 ....107 E8
Wheeley's La B15......66 C1
Wheeleys Rd B15.......86 B8
Wheelock Cl B74.......44 F7
Wheels Pk* B9.........67 C2
Wheelwright Cl
 Bromsgrove B60 ....150 E6
 2 Darlaston WS10 ......41 C6
Wheelwright Ct **5** B24...56 E2
Wheelwright La CV6, CV7 .95 C4
Wheelwright Lane Prim Sch
 CV7....................95 D5
Wheelwright Rd B24...56 F1
Wheldrake Ave B34....69 C6
Wheler Rd CV3 ....134 A7
Whernside Dr WV6.....25 A5
Wherretts Well La B91 .107 E6
Whetstone Cl B15......85 F5
Whetstone Field Prim Sch
 WS9 ....30 B4
Whetstone Gn WV10 ...1 D1
Whetstone La WS9.....30 B4
Whetstone Rd WV10 ...25 D8
Whettybridge Rd B45...121 E6
Whichbury Ct B65......65 C5
Whichcote Ave CV7....92 C1
Whichford Cl B76......57 D6
Whichford Gr B9.......68 C2
While Rd B72...........46 B4
Whilmot Cl WV10......12 B6
Whimbrel Gr DY10 ....117 A1
Whinberry Rise DY5....50 C1
Whinchat Gr DY10.....117 A2
Whinfield Rd B61......136 B6
Whinyates Rise WV9...30 B4
Whisley Brook La B28...87 F2
Whistler Gr WV10......26 A8
Whiston Ave WV11.....27 A7
Whiston Gr B29........103 B8
Whiston Ho **9** WS1.....28 F1
Whitacre La WS14......16 E7
Whitacre Rd
 Birmingham B9 ....67 F3
 Knowle B93 ....128 B7
 Nuneaton CV11........73 E4
 3 Royal Leamington Spa
 CV32..................157 A2
Whitacre Road Ind Est
 CV11..................73 E4
Whitaker Rd CV5.......112 C3
Whitbourne Cl B12.....87 B5
Whitburn Ave B42......55 A5
Whitburn Cl
 Kidderminster DY11....116 B5
 Wolverhampton WV9...11 A2
Whitby Cl WS3.........13 F3
Whitby Rd B12.........87 A4
Whitby Way WS11......4 D8
Whitchurch Cl B98....158 F6
Whitchurch Way CV4...131 F8
Whitcot Gr B31........122 F8
White Bark Cl WS12....2 A8
White Beam Cl
 Brownhills WS8........15 E6
 Coventry CV4..........111 D1
Whitebeam Croft **3** B38 .103 E1
White Beam Rd B37....90 D8
Whitebeam Way CV10...72 D7
White City Rd DY5.....62 A1
White Cl DY9..........81 D6
Whitecrest B43........44 A2
Whitecrest Prim Sch B43..44 A2
Whitecroft Rd B26.....89 D5
White Falcon Ct B91...106 F2
White Farm Rd B74....31 E4
White Field Ave B17...85 A6
Whitefield Cl
 Codsall WV8...........10 B2
 Coventry CV4..........131 D6
Whitefields Cres B91...107 B2
Whitefields Gate B91...107 A1
Whitefields Rd B91....107 A2
Whites Wood WV5.....49 A5
Whitethorn Cl WS12....2 A8
White Friars La CV1...165 C2
White Friars St CV1...165 C2
Whitegate Dr DY1.....116 A3
Whitegates Rd WV14...40 D2
Whitehall Ct WV3......38 F6

Whitehall Dr
 Dudley DY1.............51 A2
 Halesowen B63.........83 B4
Whitehall Ind Pk DY4...52 E5
Whitehall Inf Sch WS1 ...42 E7
Whitehall Jun Sch WS1 ...42 F6
Whitehall Rd
 Birmingham, Bordesley Green
 B9.....................67 E1
 Birmingham, Handsworth
 B21....................66 A8
 Cradley Heath B64......82 C8
 Halesowen B63 ....83 B4
 Kingswinford DY6......60 C6
 Stourbridge DY8.......81 B2
 Tipton DY4, B70........52 E4
 2 Walsall WS1 ....42 E7
 Wolverhampton WV4....39 B4
White Hart The **6** WS1 ...42 E8
Whitehead Dr
 Kenilworth CV8........148 C7
 Minworth B76..........58 D6
Whitehead Gr CV7.....130 B7
Whitehead Rd B6.......66 A8
Whiteheads Cl **17** CV32 .156 F1
Whiteheath Ct **6** B65...63 E4
WHITEHEATH GATE.....63 D4
Whiteheath PRU B65...63 D4
White Hill B31.........103 B6
Whitehill La B29, B31...103 A5
Whitehill Rd DY11......116 A4
White Hollies WS3......14 F4
Whitehorse Cl CV6.....96 B6
White Horse Rd WS8...6 E2
Whitehouse Ave
 Darlaston WS10........41 B7
 Wednesbury WS10.....41 F3
 Wolverhampton WV3...38 D8
White House Ave WV11...26 F7
White House Cl B91....106 F3
Whitehouse Common Prim
 Sch B75................46 D7
Whitehouse Common Rd
 B75....................46 E7
Whitehouse Cres
 Burntwood WS7..........7 B7
 Nuneaton CV10........72 D3
 Sutton Coldfield B75 ...46 E7
 Wolverhampton WV11...12 F1
Whitehouse Ct **8** B75...46 F6
Whitehouse Dr
 Lichfield WS13..........8 F6
 Smethwick B66.........65 A7
White House Gn B91...106 F3
Whitehouse La
 Codsall WV8...........10 A6
 Redditch B98..........154 E4
Whitehouse Pl B45....121 F6
Whitehouse Rd
 Kidderminster DY10....116 D4
 Polesworth B78........36 F7
White Houses La WV10 ...12 B5
Whitehouse St
 Birmingham B6 ....66 F6
 Tipton, Burnt Tree DY4...52 A2
 Tipton, Wallbrook WV14 ...51 C8
 Walsall WS2............28 D3
Whitehouse Way WS9...29 F4
White House Way B91...107 A3
Whitelaw Cres CV5.....112 C6
WHITEMOOR............148 B5
Whitemoor Dr B90.....127 A7
Whitemoor Rd CV8....148 B5
WHITEMORE PARK......95 C1
Whitemore Reans Children's
 Ctr WV1...............163 A4
White Oak Dr
 Kingswinford DY6......60 C6
 Wolverhampton WV3...24 C1
Whitepits La B48......140 F4
Whitepoplars Cl DY5...61 C4
White Rd
 Birmingham B32 ....84 D6
 Birmingham, Sparkbrook
 B11....................87 C7
 Smethwick B67.........64 F6
White Rose Ho **4** B67...156 F2
White Row WV5........37 C1
Whitesands Cl B77.....21 E5
White's Dr DY3.........50 E8
Whiteside Cl CV3......133 E8
Whiteslade Cl B93......128 A7
Whitesmith Croft B14...104 E8
Whitesmiths Cl DY3....50 D8
White's Rd B71.........53 C6
Whites Row CV8.......148 A3
White St
 Birmingham B12 ....87 A5
 Coventry CV1..........165 C3
 Walsall WS1............42 E8
WHITE STITCH.........92 C3
Whitestitch La CV7....92 C3
WHITESTONE...........79 B7
Whitestone Cty Inf Sch
 CV11..................79 A8
Whitestone Rd
 Halesowen B63 ....83 A4
 Nuneaton CV11........79 B7
Whitethorn Cres B74...31 C7
Whitethorn Dr CV32...157 B2
Whitethorn Rd DY8....81 A1
Whitewood Glade WV12...27 A4
Whitfield Gr B15.......86 D8
Whitfield Rd WS12.....2 C7

Whitford Bridge Rd B60.151 A2
Whitford Cl B61........150 D8
Whitford Dr B90.......127 C7
Whitford Gdns B61....136 D2
Whitford Rd B61......136 D2
Whitgreave Ave
 Featherstone WV10....12 B7
 Wolverhampton WV10...25 F8
Whitgreave Ct
 Featherstone WV10....12 B6
 West Bromwich B70 ....52 E3
Whitgreave Inf Sch WV10.25 E8
Whitgreave Jun Sch
 WV10..................25 E8
Whitgreave Prim Sch
 WV10..................12 B7
Whitgreave St B70.....52 E3
Whiting B77............35 D7
Whitland Cl B45.......122 B6
Whitland Dr B14.......104 F3
Whitley Abbey Bsns & Ent
 Coll CV3..............133 F6
Whitley Abbey Prim Sch
 CV3....................134 A6
Whitley Ave B77.......21 E5
Whitley Cl WV6........24 B2
Whitley Court Rd B32...84 C6
Whitley Ct
 Birmingham B20 ....54 E3
 Coventry CV3..........133 F7
Whitley St B74.........45 A8
Whitley St WS10.......41 E3
Whitley Village CV3...133 F7
Whitlock Gr B14.......105 A3
WHITLOCK'S END.......125 E6
Whitlocks End Sta B90...125 E7
Whitminster Ave B24...57 B3
Whitminster Cl WV12 ...27 C4
Whitmore Hill WV1....163 B3
Whitmore Ho WV6.....25 A4
Whitmore Park Prim Sch
 CV6....................95 A1
Whitmore Park Rd CV6...95 D3
Whitmore Rd
 Birmingham B10 ....87 C8
 Stourbridge DY8.......80 D5
Whitmore St
 Birmingham B18 ....66 B6
 Walsall WS1............42 D7
 Wolverhampton WV1....163 C3
WHITNASH.............162 C3
Whitnash Bsns Nature
 Reserve* CV31........162 D6
Whitnash Cl CV7......130 A6
Whitnash Gr CV2......114 D5
Whitnash Prim Sch
 CV31..................162 A4
Whitney Ave DY8......80 D6
Whittaker St WV2......39 E6
Whittall Drive E DY11...116 B1
Whittall Drive W DY11...116 A1
Whittall St B4.........164 C3
Whittimere St WS1 ....28 F2
Whittingham Gr WV11...26 F6
Whittingham Rd B63...83 A5
Whittington Cl
 Birmingham B14 ....104 E5
 West Bromwich B71 ....53 F8
Whittington Gr B33....68 F2
Whittington Hall La DY7...92 D8
Whittington Oval B33...69 A2
Whittington Rd DY8....80 E3
Whittle Cl CV3.........134 F8
Whittle Croft B35......57 F2
Whittle Ct **9** CV32.....157 A1
WHITTLEFORD..........72 C5
Whittleford Gr B36....58 C1
Whittleford Rd CV10...72 C4
Whittle Rd LE10.......74 E7
Whittles Ct DY11......116 B8
Whitton St WS10.......41 E6
Whitville Cl DY11......116 C7
Whitville Cl B90.......126 F6
Whitworth Ave
 Coventry CV3..........114 B1
 Hinckley LE10.........74 F7
Whitworth Cl WS10....41 E7
Whitworth Dr B71.....42 E1
Whitworth Ind Pk B9...67 C2
WHOBERLEY............112 D2
Whoberley Ave CV5....112 D2
Whoberley Hall Prim Sch
 CV5....................112 C3
Whyley St B70.........53 A4
Whyley Wlk B69.......64 A5
Whynot St B60........150 C2
Whynot St B63.........82 B5
Whytmore The WS13...8 F5
Wibert Cl B29.........86 A1
Wichnor Rd B92.......88 F5
Wickets Twr B5........86 C5
Wickham Cl CV6.......94 F2
Wickham Gdns WV11...26 A6
Wickham Rd B80......159 F4
Wickham Sq B70.......53 B2
Wicklow Cl B63........82 D1
Wickmans Dr CV4......111 C2
Wiclif Way CV10.......72 D5
Widdecombe Cl CV2...114 D7
Widdrington Rd CV1...113 C5
Wideacre Dr B44.......55 F7
Wide Acres B45........101 F1
Widgeon Gr WV10.....12 B7

Widney Ave
 Aldridge WS9..........16 B1
 Birmingham B29 ....85 C1
Widney Cl B93.........127 F5
Widney Ho B97.........153 C4
Widney Jun Sch B91...106 F1
Widney La B91.........127 B8
Widney Manor Rd B91,
 B93...................127 D7
Widney Manor Sta B91...127 C8
Widney Rd B93.........127 C8
Wigford Rd B77........35 C5
Wiggin Cotts **8** B17...85 C5
Wiggin Ho WS3........14 C3
Wiggins Croft B76.....46 F3
Wiggins Hill Rd B76...58 F7
Wigginsmill Rd WS10 ...41 D1
Wiggin St B16.........65 F3
Wigginton Rd B79.....21 B7
Wight Croft B36.......70 B6
Wightman Cl WS14.....9 E6
WIGHTWICK...........23 E1
Wightwick Bank WV6...24 A2
Wightwick Cl WS3.....14 B1
Wightwick Gr WV6.....24 A2
Wightwick Gr WV6.....24 A2
Wightwick Hall Rd WV6...23 E1
Wightwick Hall Specl Sch
 WV6...................23 E2
Wightwick Manor* WV6 .23 F1
Wigland Way B38......104 A1
Wigmore Gr B44.......56 B8
Wigmore La B71.......54 A8
Wigorn Ho B67........84 F8
Wigorn La DY9........99 B8
Wigorn Rd B67........54 F1
Wigston Rd CV2.......96 F8
Wilberforce Way B92...107 F7
Wilbraham Rd WS2....28 C1
Wilcote Gr B27........106 C8
Wilcox Ave WS12......2 B7
Wildacres DY8.........80 C6
Wilday Cl DY4.........52 A5
Wildcroft Rd CV5......112 C3
Wilde Cl B14..........104 D4
Wilden Cl B31.........102 C3
Wilden La DY10.......116 E5
Wilderness La B43.....43 D3
Wildfell Rd CV2.......114 D7
Wildfell Rd B27........88 D2
Wild Goose La B98....159 D8
WILDMOOR............106 B5
Wildmoor Cl CV2......96 B4
Wildmoor La B61......121 A3
Wildmoor Rd B90.....106 B5
Wild Rose Ave WV10...12 A2
Wiley Ave WS10.......41 C5
Wiley Avenue S WS10 ...41 C5
Wilford Gr
 Solihull B91 ....107 B2
 Sutton Coldfield B76 ...58 B6
Wilford Rd B71........53 D6
Wilhelmina Cl CV32...161 E8
Wilkes Ave WS2.......27 F2
Wilkes Cl WS3.........14 E3
Wilkes Croft DY2......50 D7
Wilkes Green Jun & Inf Sch
 B21....................54 E1
Wilkes St
 West Bromwich B71 ....53 E7
 Willenhall WV13.......27 A1
Wilkin Rd WS8.........6 C2
Wilkins Ho WS3........14 A1
Wilkinson Ave WV14...40 E3
Wilkinson Cl
 Burntwood WS7..........7 B8
 Sutton Coldfield B73 ...46 A2
Wilkinson Croft B8....68 C6
Wilkinson Prim Sch WV14.40 F3
Wilkinson Rd WS10....41 A4
Wilkins Rd WV14......40 A7
Wilks Gn B21..........54 D4
Willard Rd B25........88 C6
Willaston Rd B33......89 D7
Willclare Rd B26.......89 A6
Willcock Rd WV2......39 E7
WILLENHALL
 Coventry..............134 D6
 Wolverhampton........27 B4
Willenhall Com Prim Sch
 CV3...................134 D6
Willenhall La
 Coventry CV3..........134 F7
 Walsall WS3...........28 A3
Willenhall Lane Ind Est
 WS3...................28 A8
Willenhall L Ctr WV13...27 B3
Willenhall Rd
 Bilston WV14..........40 F7
 Darlaston WS10........41 D8
 Wolverhampton WV1,
 WV13..................26 C1
Willenhall Sch Sports Coll
 WV12..................27 E5
Willenhall St WS10....41 C7
Willenhall Trad Est WV13.27 A1
Willenhall Wood Nature
 Reserve* CV3.........134 E5
Willersey Rd B13......105 D8
Willes Ct
 2 Birmingham B62.....84 A7
 2 Royal Leamington Spa
 CV31..................162 B7

Willes Rd
Birmingham B18 . . . . 65 E6
Royal Leamington Spa CV31,
CV32 . . . . 162 A8
Willes Terr CV31 . . . . 162 B8
Willett Ave WS7 . . . . 6 E5
Willett Rd B71 . . . . 53 E8
Willetts Dr B63 . . . . 82 B4
Willetts Rd B31 . . . . 103 A1
Willetts Way B64 . . . . 62 F2
Willey Gr B24 . . . . 57 B2
William Arnold Cl CV2 . . . 114 A4
William Barrows Way
DY4 . . . . 51 E7
William Batchelor Ho
CV1 . . . . 165 B4
William Beesley Cres
CV11 . . . . 79 E6
William Bentley Ct WV11 . 26 C5
William Booth La B4 . . . . 164 B4
William Bree Rd CV5 . . . . 111 C5
William Bristow Rd CV3 . 133 C7
William Cook Rd B8 . . . . . 68 B5
William Cowper Prim Sch
B19 . . . . 66 E6
William Cree Cl CV8 . . . . 135 F3
William Ct
Birmingham, Rotton Park
B16 . . . . 65 E1
7 Birmingham, Showell Green
B13 . . . . 86 F4
William Edward St 1 B12 86 F7
William Green Rd WS10 . . 42 C3
William Groubb Cl CV3 . . 134 D7
William Hanie Ind Est
DY5 . . . . 61 E1
William Harper Rd WV13 . 27 B1
William Henry St B7 . . . . . 67 A6
William Ker Rd DY4 . . . . . . 52 C5
William Kirby Cl CV4 . . . 112 A1
William Lunn's Homes 2
WS14 . . . . 9 C8
William McCool Cl CV3 . . 134 F7
William MacGregor Prim Sch
B77 . . . . 21 D4
William McKee Cl CV3 . . 134 E7
William Malcolm Ho
CV2 . . . . 114 E3
William Morris Gr WS11 . . 1 E4
William Rd
Birmingham B31 . . . . 102 F1
Smethwick B67 . . . . 64 D3
Williams Cl WV12 . . . . 27 C5
William Sheriden Ho
CV2 . . . . 114 E3
Williamson St WV3 . . . . . 163 A2
Williams Rd CV31 . . . . 162 E4
William St
Bedworth CV12 . . . . 78 D2
Birmingham B15 . . . . 66 C1
Brierley Hill DY5 . . . . 61 C3
Nuneaton CV11 . . . . 73 E3
Redditch B97 . . . . 153 E4
Royal Leamington Spa
CV32 . . . . 162 A8
Walsall WS4 . . . . 28 F3
West Bromwich B70 . . . . . . 52 E5
William Street N B19 . . . 164 B4
William Street W B66 . . . . 65 B7
William Tarver Cl CV34 . 161 A7
William Thomas Ho 7
CV32 . . . . 157 A1
William Thomson Ho 2
CV1 . . . . 165 D4
William Tolson's Ind Est
B78 . . . . 35 A8
William Wiggin Ave WS3 . 14 B2
Willingsworth Rd WS10 . . 41 D1
Willington Rd B79 . . . . 21 A7
Willington St CV11 . . . . . . 73 B5
Willingworth Cl WV14 . . . . 40 A3
Willis Gr CV12 . . . . 78 C3
Willis Ho CV11 . . . . 73 B2
Willis Pearson Ave WV14 . 41 A3
Willis St DY11 . . . . 116 C5
Willmore Gr 4 B38 . . . . . 123 F8
Willmore Rd B20 . . . . 55 D2
Willmott Cl B75 . . . . 32 D3
Willmott Rd B75 . . . . 32 D3
Willoughby Ave CV8 . . . . 147 E3
Willoughby Cl CV3 . . . . . 134 E8
Willoughby Ct B76 . . . . . . 46 F2
Willoughby Dr B91 . . . . . . 107 B1
Willoughby Rd B29 . . . . . . 85 A1
Willoughby Rd B79 . . . . . . 20 E7
Willow Ave
Birmingham B17 . . . . 65 A2
Burntwood WS7 . . . . 7 C6
Wednesbury WS10 . . . . 41 F4
Wolverhampton WV11 . . . . . 26 B8
Willowbank B78 . . . . 21 B1
Willow Bank WV3 . . . . 24 C1
Willowbank Rd LE10 . . . . . 75 C7
Willow Bank Rd B93 . . . . 127 F6
Willow Brook Rd B48 . . . 139 A7
Willowbud Ho B98 . . . . . . 158 F8
Willow Cl
Bedworth CV12 . . . . 78 A5
Bromsgrove B61 . . . . 136 E2
Cradley Heath B64 . . . . 62 E1
Hinckley LE10 . . . . 75 E5
Nuneaton CV10 . . . . 72 A7
West Hagley DY9 . . . . 99 F5
Whitnash CV31 . . . . 162 B2

Willow Coppice B32 . . . . . 84 C1
Willow Ct
Birmingham B13 . . . . 87 A3
Bromsgrove B61 . . . . 136 E3
Lichfield WS14 . . . . 9 C5
Oldbury B66 . . . . 64 D8
Smethwick B17 . . . . 65 A2
Walsall CV34 . . . . 161 E2
Willow Ctyd CV2 . . . . 114 D7
Willowdale LE10 . . . . 75 A7
Willowdale Grange WV6 . . 24 E5
Willow Dr
Birmingham B21 . . . . 54 C1
Cheswick Green B90 . . . . . 126 D4
Codsall WV8 . . . . 10 B3
Oldbury B69 . . . . 63 C7
Willow End DY9 . . . . 81 D3
Willowfield Dr DY11 . . . . . 116 C8
Willowfields Rd CV11 . . . . 74 A1
Willow Gdns
Birmingham B16 . . . . 65 F4
Bromsgrove B61 . . . . 136 E3
Willow Gr
Coventry CV4 . . . . 112 B2
Essington WV11 . . . . 13 B3
Willenhall WV13 . . . . 27 B1
Willowherb Cl
Cannock WS11 . . . . 2 C2
5 Coventry CV3 . . . . 134 F8
Walsall WS5 . . . . 43 A3
Willowherb Way B90 . . . . 126 A5
Willow Ho
Birmingham B7 . . . . 67 B4
Walsall WS4 . . . . 15 D1
11 Warwick CV34 . . . . . . 161 D8
Willow Hts B64 . . . . 83 A8
Willow Meer V8 . . . . 148 B5
Willow Mews B29 . . . . 85 B1
Willow Park Dr DY8 . . . . . . 81 B2
Willow Rd
Birmingham, Bournville B29,
B30 . . . . 103 F8
Birmingham, Great Barr
B43 . . . . 44 A2
Bromsgrove B61 . . . . 136 E3
Dudley DY1 . . . . 51 A4
Nuneaton CV10 . . . . 72 F5
Solihull B91 . . . . 106 E2
Wolverhampton WV3 . . . . . . 38 D8
Willow Rise DY5 . . . . 81 C1
Willowsbrook Rd B62 . . . . 83 F8
Willows Cres B12 . . . . 86 E5
Willows Croft WS12 . . . . . . 2 D4
Willow Sheets Mdw
CV32 . . . . 157 E6
Willowside WS4 . . . . 29 C8
Willowsmere Dr WS14 . . . . 9 F7
Willows Prim Sch WS13 . . 3 B2
Willows Rd
Birmingham B12 . . . . 86 E5
Walsall, Sheffield WS4 . . . . . 29 C8
Walsall, The Chuckery WS1 . 29 A1
Willows The
Bedworth CV12 . . . . 77 E2
Birmingham B27 . . . . 88 B2
Cannock WS11 . . . . 1 C1
Dudley DY2 . . . . 62 E5
Hollywood B47 . . . . 125 A6
Portway B47 . . . . 140 F7
10 Sutton Coldfield B74 . . 31 F2
Sutton Coldfield, Walmley
B76 . . . . 46 F2
Wolverhampton WV11 . . . . . 26 B5
Willowtree Cl WS13 . . . . . . 3 B2
Willow Tree Dr B45 . . . . . 138 D8
Willow Way
Birmingham B37 . . . . 70 B1
Redditch B97 . . . . 153 B4
Studley B80 . . . . 159 E2
Willow Wlk WS12 . . . . 1 D8
Wills Ave B71 . . . . 53 B7
Wills Ho B70 . . . . 53 C2
Willson Croft B28 . . . . . . 105 D3
Wills St B19 . . . . 66 C7
Wills Way B66 . . . . 65 C4
Wilmcote Cl B12 . . . . 86 E6
Wilmcote Ct B61 . . . . 150 D8
Wilmcote Dr B75 . . . . 32 B3
Wilmcote Gn CV5 . . . . 112 A3
Wilmcote Ho B97 . . . . 153 B4
Wilmcote Rd B91 . . . . 106 F6
Wilmcote Twr 5 B12 . . . . 86 F7
Wilmhurst Rd CV34 . . . . . 160 C8
Wilmington Rd B32 . . . . . . 84 B6
Wilmore Ho B20 . . . . 55 D1
Wilmore La B47 . . . . 124 F4
Wilmot Ave B46 . . . . 70 F6
Wilmot Cl CV7 . . . . 130 B8
Wilmot Dr
Birmingham B23 . . . . 57 A6
Tipton DY4 . . . . 51 E6
Wilmot Gdns DY1 . . . . 51 A2
Wilmott Cl WS13 . . . . 9 A7
WILNCOTE 35 F8
WILNECOTE 35 F8
Wilnecote Gr
Birmingham B42 . . . . 55 D4
Whitnash CV31 . . . . 162 B5
Wilnecote High Sch B77 . 35 F6
Wilnecote House Dr 1
B77 . . . . 35 F7
Wilnecote Jun Sch B77 . . 35 F7
Wilnecote La B77 . . . . 21 D2
Wilnecote Sta B77 . . . . . . 35 D7
Wilner's View WS3 . . . . . . 14 F5

Wilsford Cl
Birmingham B14 . . . . 104 D1
Walsall WS4 . . . . 29 C8
Wilsford Gn B15 . . . . 85 E7
Wilson Cl B97 . . . . 153 C1
Wilson Dr
Oldbury B69 . . . . 52 C3
Sutton Coldfield B75 . . . . . . 47 A5
Wilson Gn CV3 . . . . 114 F1
Wilson Gr
Cannock WS11 . . . . 2 C2
Kenilworth CV8 . . . . 148 C4
Wilson Rd
Birmingham B19 . . . . 66 D8
Brierley Hill DY5 . . . . 61 C4
Oldbury B68 . . . . 51 C7
Oldbury B68 . . . . 64 B2
Smethwick B66 . . . . 65 B3
Wilsons La CV7 . . . . 96 A6
Wilson's La CV6 . . . . 95 F6
Wilsons Rd B93 . . . . 128 C6
Wilson St
Tipton DY4 . . . . 52 A5
Wolverhampton WV1 . . . . . 163 C4
Wilson Stuart Sch & Sports
Coll B23 . . . . 56 C6
Wiltell Rd WS14 . . . . 9 B6
Wiltell Road Ind Est 12
WS3 . . . . 9 B7
Wilton Ave DY11 . . . . 116 B8
Wilton Cl DY3 . . . . 50 E7
Wilton Rd
Balsall Common CV7 . . . . . 130 B5
Birmingham, Balsall Heath
B11 . . . . 87 B5
Birmingham, Erdington B23 . 57 A5
Birmingham, Handsworth
B20 . . . . 55 B1
Wilton St B19 . . . . 66 D8
Wiltshire Cl
Bedworth CV12 . . . . 78 A3
Coventry CV5 . . . . 112 B3
Walsall WS2 . . . . 28 D4
Wiltshire Cl 10 B29 . . . . . 103 C7
Wiltshire Dr B63 . . . . 82 B7
Wiltshire Rd 3 DY8 . . . . . 80 F8
Wiltshire Way B71 . . . . 53 C7
Wimberger Ho 2 B7 . . . . . 53 D4
WIMBLEBURY 2 F3
Wimblebury Rd WS12 . . . . . 2 F2
Wimbledon Dr DY8 . . . . . . 81 B2
Wimborne Dr CV2 . . . . . . 115 A4
Wimborne Rd WV10 . . . . . . 26 A6
Wimbourne Cl CV10 . . . . . 72 B5
Wimbourne Rd
Birmingham B16 . . . . 65 D3
Sutton Coldfield B76 . . . . . . 47 A4
Wimperis Way B43 . . . . . . 44 C4
Wimpole Gr B44 . . . . 56 B7
Wimshurst Mdw WV10 . . . 11 F4
Wincanton Croft B36 . . . . . 68 C8
Winceby Pl CV4 . . . . 111 D1
Winceby Rd WV6 . . . . 23 F3
Winchat Cl CV3 . . . . 114 F1
Winchat Dr WS11 . . . . 5 B8
Winchcombe Cl
Dudley DY1 . . . . 50 E3
Solihull B92 . . . . 89 B2
Winchcombe Rd B92 . . . . . 89 B2
Winchester Ave
Kidderminster DY11 . . . . . 116 A6
Nuneaton CV10 . . . . 73 C7
Winchester Cl
Lichfield WS13 . . . . 3 C3
8 Rowley Regis B65 . . . . . 63 E4
West Hagley DY9 . . . . 99 A6
Winchester Ct 4 B74 . . . . 31 F2
Winchester Dr
Birmingham B37 . . . . 70 A2
Hinckley LE10 . . . . 76 B7
Stourbridge DY8 . . . . 81 A3
Winchester Gdns B31 . . . 103 A3
Winchester Gr B21 . . . . . . 65 C8
Winchester Mews WS9 . . . 30 B4
Winchester Rd
Birmingham B20 . . . . 55 D1
Cannock WS11 . . . . 2 A3
Tamworth B78 . . . . 20 F3
West Bromwich B71 . . . . . . 53 B8
Wolverhampton WV10 . . . . . 11 C3
Winchester Rise DY1 . . . . . 51 A2
Winchester St CV1 . . . . . . 113 E3
Winchfield Dr B17 . . . . 84 F7
Wincote Dr WV6 . . . . 24 C4
Wincrest Way B34 . . . . 69 C5
Windermere B77 . . . . 36 A7
Windermere Ave
Coventry, Binley CV3 . . . . . 114 C1
Coventry, Upper Eastern Green
CV5 . . . . 111 A4
Nuneaton CV11 . . . . 73 F6
Windermere Dr
Kingswinford DY6 . . . . 60 D6
Royal Leamington Spa
CV32 . . . . 156 D2
Sutton Coldfield B74 . . . . . . 30 F3
Windermere Ho
Kidderminster DY10 . . . . . 116 E7
10 Oldbury B69 . . . . 63 D5
Windermere Pl WS11 . . . . . 1 E1
Windermere Rd
Birmingham, Handsworth
B21 . . . . 54 E2
Birmingham, Moseley B13 . . 87 B1
Wolverhampton WV6 . . . . . . 24 D8
Windermere Ho 2 B15 . . . 85 D3
Windfall Ct B24 . . . . 57 D4

Winding House La CV6,
CV7 . . . . 95 C4
Winding Mill N DY5 . . . . . . 81 E7
Winding Mill S DY5 . . . . . . 81 E7
Windings The WS13 . . . . . . 3 A1
Windlass Croft B31 . . . . . 102 F4
Windleaves Rd B36 . . . . . . 69 E8
Windley Ho B73 . . . . 45 C2
Windmill Ave
Birmingham B45 . . . . 121 E8
4 Coleshill B46 . . . . 70 F7
Windmill Bank WV5 . . . . . . 49 A7
Windmill Cl
Birmingham B31 . . . . 103 C5
Kenilworth CV8 . . . . 148 A6
Lichfield WS13 . . . . 3 A2
Tamworth B79 . . . . 21 A8
Windmill Cres
Smethwick B66 . . . . 65 C5
Wolverhampton WV3 . . . . . . 24 A1
Windmill Croft CV32 . . . . 157 D5
Windmill Cl CV6 . . . . 96 A3
Windmill Dr B97 . . . . 158 C6
Windmill End DY2 . . . . 62 E5
Windmill Gdns B97 . . . . . 158 B6
Windmill Gr DY6 . . . . 60 B8
Windmill Hill
Birmingham B31 . . . . 103 B5
Cubbington CV32 . . . . 157 D5
Halesowen B63 . . . . 82 D5
Windmill Hill The CV5 . . . 112 A7
Windmill Ind Est CV5 . . . . 111 F7
Windmill La
Balsall Common CV7 . . . . . 130 D4
Corley Moor CV7 . . . . 93 D6
Dorridge B93 . . . . 127 F1
Lichfield WS13 . . . . 3 A2
Smethwick B66 . . . . 65 B5
Tamworth-in-A B94 . . . . . . 144 A8
Wolverhampton WV3 . . . . . . 24 A1
Windmill Prec B66 . . . . 65 C5
Windmill Rd
Bedworth CV7 . . . . 96 A8
Coventry CV6 . . . . 96 A3
Nuneaton CV10 . . . . 72 D7
Solihull B90 . . . . 105 E2
Whitnash CV31 . . . . 161 F5
Windmills Sh Ctr B67 . . . . 65 B4
Windmill St
Birmingham B1 . . . . 164 B1
Dudley DY1 . . . . 51 A2
Dudley, Gornalwood DY3 . . 50 D5
Walsall WS1 . . . . 42 F8
Wednesbury WS10 . . . . 42 A3
Windmill Terr WS10 . . . . . . 42 A3
Windmill View DY1 . . . . 51 B7
Windmill Works Ind Pk
DY2 . . . . 62 B6
Windridge Cl CV3 . . . . 134 C6
Windridge Cres B92 . . . . 107 F8
Windrow The WV6 . . . . 23 D4
Windrush Cl
Redditch B97 . . . . 158 D6
Solihull B92 . . . . 89 A2
Walsall WS3 . . . . 15 A1
Windrush Dr LE10 . . . . 75 A8
Windrush Gr B29 . . . . 104 A8
Windrush Rd
Cannock WS11 . . . . 1 E6
Hollywood B47 . . . . 125 B7
Windsor Arc B2 . . . . 164 C3
Windsor Ave
Cannock WS12 . . . . 2 B6
Oldbury B68 . . . . 64 A3
Wolverhampton WV4 . . . . . . 38 E6
Windsor Cl
Birmingham, Coft Common
B31 . . . . 123 A6
Birmingham, Frankley B45 102 A2
Dudley DY3 . . . . 50 B2
Halesowen B63 . . . . 82 F4
Rowley Regis B65 . . . . 63 C4
Tamworth B79 . . . . 21 C7
Windsor Cres DY2 . . . . 62 D6
Windsor Ct
Birmingham B38 . . . . 103 F1
Cannock WS12 . . . . 2 B6
Coventry CV4 . . . . 112 B2
Hinckley LE10 . . . . 76 A5
Lichfield WS14 . . . . 9 B6
Nuneaton CV10 . . . . 72 E6
Windsor Dr
Birmingham B24 . . . . 57 C5
Kidderminster DY10 . . . . . 116 E7
Solihull B92 . . . . 89 B2
Windsor Gate WV12 . . . . . . 27 C4
Windsor Gdns
Bromsgrove B60 . . . . 137 A2
Nuneaton CV10 . . . . 72 E4
Wolverhampton WV3 . . . . . . 38 A8
Windsor Gr
Stourbridge DY8 . . . . 60 E1
Walsall WS4 . . . . 15 C2
Windsor High Sch B63 . . . 82 F4
Windsor Ho
Birmingham B23 . . . . 56 F6
Dudley DY2 . . . . 61 F7
Wolverhampton WV3 . . . . . 163 A1
Windsor Ind Est B7 . . . . . . 67 A5
Windsor Lodge B92 . . . . . 106 D8
Windsor Pl
Birmingham B7 . . . . 67 A3
Birmingham, Erdington B23 . 56 E3
10 Royal Leamington Spa
CV32 . . . . 156 F1

Windsor Rd
Birmingham, Castle Bromwich
B36 . . . . 69 F7
Birmingham, New Oscott
B73 . . . . 45 D1
Birmingham, Stirchley B30 104 B5
Cheslyn Hay WS6 . . . . 4 E4
Halesowen B63 . . . . 82 F4
Oldbury B68 . . . . 64 A3
Redditch B97 . . . . 153 D5
Rowley Regis B65 . . . . 63 C5
Stourbridge DY8 . . . . 80 E3
Tipton DY4 . . . . 52 A8
West Bromwich B71 . . . . . . 42 B1
Wolverhampton WV4 . . . . . . 39 F5
Windsor St
Bilston WV14 . . . . 40 C6
Birmingham B7 . . . . 67 A4
Bromsgrove B60 . . . . 137 A2
Coventry CV1 . . . . 113 B2
Hinckley LE10 . . . . 76 A5
Nuneaton CV11 . . . . 73 B4
Royal Leamington Spa
CV32 . . . . 161 F8
Walsall WS1 . . . . 42 E7
Windsor Street S B7 . . . . . 67 A4
Windsor Terr 5 B16 . . . . . 65 F1
Windsor View B32 . . . . . . 102 B7
Windsor Way WS4 . . . . 29 D7
Windsor Wlk WS10 . . . . . . 41 D8
Winds Point DY9 . . . . 99 A6
Windward Way B36 . . . . . . 70 B6
Windward Way Ind Est
B36 . . . . 69 F8
Windy Arbor Prim Sch
B37 . . . . 70 D2
WINDY ARBOUR 148 B3
Windy Arbour CV8 . . . . . . 148 B4
Windyridge Rd B76 . . . . . . 58 A6
Winfield Rd CV11 . . . . 73 B5
Winford Ave DY6 . . . . 60 E4
Winforton Cl B98 . . . . 154 E3
Wingate Cl B30 . . . . 103 F4
Wingate Rd B74 . . . . 31 E4
Wingate Rd WS2 . . . . 27 E2
Wing Cl WS2 . . . . 27 F4
Wingfield Cl B37 . . . . 69 F3
Wingfield Ho B37 . . . . 69 F5
Wingfield Rd
Birmingham B42 . . . . 55 C7
Coleshill B46 . . . . 70 F5
Wingfield Way CV6 . . . . . . 95 A2
Wingfoot Ave WV10 . . . . . . 25 E8
Wingfoot Cl B24 . . . . 57 C1
Wingfoot Way B24 . . . . 57 C2
Wingrave Cl CV5 . . . . 112 A6
Winifred Ave CV5 . . . . 113 A1
Winifride Ct B17 . . . . 85 B5
Winkle St B70 . . . . 53 B4
Winleigh Rd B20 . . . . 54 F2
Winnall Cl WV14 . . . . 40 D2
Winnallthorpe CV3 . . . . . 134 E6
Winn Cl CV8 . . . . 148 C6
Winn Ho 3 WS2 . . . . 28 D3
Winnie Rd B29 . . . . 85 E1
Winnington Rd B8 . . . . 68 A7
Winnipeg Rd B38 . . . . 124 A8
Winrush Cl DY3 . . . . 50 D3
Winscar Croft DY3 . . . . . . 50 D3
Winsford Ave CV5 . . . . 112 B4
Winsford Cl
Balsall Common CV7 . . . . . 130 A6
Halesowen B63 . . . . 83 A6
Sutton Coldfield B76 . . . . . . 46 E3
Winsham Gr B21 . . . . 65 E8
Winsham Wlk CV3 . . . . . . 133 C3
Winslow Ave B8 . . . . 68 B4
Winslow Cl
Coventry CV5 . . . . 112 B3
Redditch B98 . . . . 154 F3
Royal Leamington Spa
CV32 . . . . 156 C1
Winslow Dr WV6 . . . . 24 E4
Winslow Ho 11 CV1 . . . . . 113 B2
WINSON GREEN 65 F5
Winson Green, Outer Circle
Stop B21 . . . . 65 E7
Winson Green Rd B18 . . . . 65 E5
Winson St B18 . . . . 65 D4
Winsor Ave WS12 . . . . 2 B6
Winspear Cl CV7 . . . . 92 B1
Winstanley Rd B33 . . . . . . 68 D2
Winster Ave B93 . . . . 127 E4
Winster Cl CV7 . . . . 95 A7
Winster Gr B44 . . . . 44 D2
Winster Grove Ind Ctr
B44 . . . . 44 D2
Winster Rd
Birmingham B43 . . . . 54 D8
Wolverhampton WV1 . . . . . . 26 B1
Winston Ave CV2 . . . . 114 D8
Winston Churchill Ct
WV14 . . . . 40 C8
Winston Cl CV2 . . . . 114 D8
Winston Dr
Birmingham B20 . . . . 55 B1
Romsley B62 . . . . 100 F8
Winston Rd DY3 . . . . 50 C7
Winterborne Cl B98 . . . . . 153 F3
Winterborne Gdns CV10 . 73 A2
Winterbourne Botanic Gdn*
B15 . . . . 86 A5
Winterbourne Croft B14 . 104 C1
Winterbourne Rd B91 . . . 106 F4
Winter Cl WS13 . . . . 3 A2
Winterdene CV7 . . . . 130 B7
Winterfold Cl DY10 . . . . . 117 B6

Winterley Gdns DY3...... 50 E6
Winterley La WS4....... 29 C6
Winterton Rd
  Birmingham B44 .... 45 A3
  Bulkington CV12 .... 79 C2
Winthorpe Dr B91 ...... 127 C8
Wintney CI B17 .... 85 A7
Winton Gr B76 .... 58 A6
Wintour Wlk B60 .... 150 E7
Winward Rd B48 .... 154 F1
Winwood Ct DY8........ 80 F4
Winwood Heath Rd B62 . 100 E2
Winwood Rd B65 .... 63 E3
Winwoods Gr B32 ..... 102 A8
Winyate Hill B98....... 154 A2
WINYATES............... 154 E2
Winyates Crafts Ctr B98. 154 E3
Winyates Ctr B98 ..... 154 E3
Winyates Way B98 .... 154 F4
WIREHILL............... 159 B5
Wirehill Dr B98 .... 153 F1
Wiremill CI B44........ 55 E6
Wirral Rd B31 .... 102 F6
Wise Gr CV34 .... 155 E2
Wiseman Gr B23....... 45 D1
Wisemeadow B90...... 105 E2
Wisemore WS2 .... 28 E2
Wise St CV31 .... 161 F7
Wise Terr CV31 .... 161 F7
Wishaw CI 48 B2
Wishaw La
  Redditch B98.......... 159 A8
  Solihull B90 .... 105 E2
Wishaw Gr B37 .... 69 F5
Wishaw La
  Curdworth B76 .... 59 A7
  Middleton B76, B78..... 48 C6
  Minworth B76 .... 58 E7
Wisley Gr CV8 .... 148 C5
Wisley Way B32........ 84 F5
Wissage Ct WS13 ...... 9 D8
Wissage La WS13 ...... 3 D1
Wissage Rd WS13...... 9 D8
Wistaria
  Birmingham B31 ...... 103 A6
  2 Coventry CV2 ...... 96 B2
Wisteria Dr
  Brownhills WS8 .... 6 C2
  2 Walsall WS5 .... 42 F4
Wisteria Gr B44 .... 44 E2
Wisteria Way CV10..... 78 A8
Wistmans CI DY1 ...... 50 E2
Wistwood Hayes WV10 . 11 F4
Witham CI B76......... 47 A1
Witham Croft B91...... 107 C1
Withdean CI B11....... 87 D6
Witherford CI B29 .... 103 C8
Witherford Croft B91. 106 E2
Witherford Way B29 .. 103 C8
Withern Way DY3 ...... 50 D3
Withers Rd WV8 .... 10 B3
Withers Way B71 ...... 53 D4
Withington Covert B14 . 104 D2
Withington Gr B93 .... 127 E2
Withy Bank CV31 ..... 162 C4
Withybed CI B48 ..... 139 A6
WITHYBED GREEN 138 F6
Withybed La B48....... 139 A6
Withybrook CI CV2..... 96 D2
Withybrook La CV7..... 97 F5
Withybrook Rd
  Bulkington CV12 .... 79 D2
  Solihull B90 .... 126 B8
Withy Gr B37 .... 69 F5
Withy Hill Rd B75 ..... 47 B8
Withymere La WV5..... 49 C8
Withymoor Prim Sch DY5 61 D1
Withymoor Rd
  Dudley DY2 .... 62 E4
  Stourbridge DY8 ...... 81 A7
WITHYMOOR VILLAGE... 81 C8
Withymore Ct WV3..... 25 A1
Withy Rd WV14 .... 40 C3
Withy Road Ind EstWV14. 40 C3
Withywood CI WV12.... 13 C1
Witley Ave
  Halesowen B63 .... 82 E4
  Solihull B91 .... 107 C2
Witley CI DY11........ 116 B2
Witley Cres B69....... 63 E5
Witley Dr 1 WS13 ..... 9 E8
Witley Farm CI B91 ... 107 C2
Witley Rd 1 B31 ..... 103 D2
Witnell Rd CV6 .... 113 C6
Witney CI B79 .... 20 F7
Witney Dr B37 .... 69 F2
Witney Gr WV10 ...... 11 B3
Wittersham Ct 5 WV13 . 27 B2
WITTON............... 66 A3
Witton Bank B62....... 83 F7
Witton La
  Birmingham B6 .... 55 F1
  West Bromwich B71 ... 53 B8
Witton Lodge Rd B23 .. 56 C7
Witton Rd
  Birmingham B6 .... 66 E8
  Wolverhampton WV4 ... 39 A6
Witton St
  Birmingham B9 .... 67 B2
  Stourbridge DY8 ...... 80 F4
Witton Sta 66 C6
Wixford Gr B90 .... 106 D2
Wobaston Ct WV10..... 11 B3
Wobaston Rd
  Codsall WV9.......... 10 D4
  Wolverhampton WV9, WV10 11 B3
Woburn B77 .... 21 D3

Woburn Ave WV12 ..... 27 B6
Woburn CI
  Bromsgrove B61 ..... 136 D1
  Hinckley LE10 .... 71 E3
  Royal Leamington Spa
    CV31............... 162 C6
Woburn Cres B43 ..... 43 D1
Woburn Dr
  Brierley Hill DY5 ..... 81 B8
  Cradley Heath B62..... 83 B7
  Nuneaton CV10 .... 73 A2
Woburn Gr B27 .... 88 C1
Woburn Ho B15........ 86 C7
Woodhouse Cotts WV5 . 49 D8
Woodhouse La WV5, DY3. 49 E8
Woden Ave WV11 ...... 26 C6
Woden Cres WV11 ..... 26 C6
Woden Prim Sch WV10.. 25 E4
Woden Rd WS10 .... 41 F4
Woden Road E WS10 ... 42 A4
Woden Road N WS10... 41 F5
Woden Road S WS10 ... 42 A1
Woden Road W WS10 .. 41 D4
Wodensborough Com Tech
  Coll WS10 .... 42 B2
Wodensfield Prim Sch
  WV11 .... 26 A6
Wodensfield Twr WV11.. 26 C5
Woden Way WV11 ..... 26 C6
Wold Wlk B13 .... 105 C6
Wolfe Rd CV4.......... 131 F8
Wolfsbane Dr WS5..... 43 A3
Wollaston 80 D6
Wollaston Cres WV11 .. 26 D6
Wollaston Ct
  Stourbridge DY8 ..... 80 C6
  1 Walsall WS1 .... 28 F2
Wollaston Rd
  Stourbridge DY7 ..... 80 C7
  Stourbridge DY8 ..... 80 E8
Wollerton Gr 9 B75 ... 46 F6
WOLLESCOTE.......... 81 E4
Wollescote Bsns Pk 6
  DY9................. 81 F5
Wollescote Dr B91 ... 107 B2
Wollescote Prim Sch DY9 81 F4
Wollescote Rd DY9..... 81 D3
Wolmer Rd WV11 ...... 13 A2
Wolseley B77 .... 21 F3
Wolseley Ave B27 ..... 88 D4
Wolseley Bank WV10... 25 F7
Wolseley CI
  Birmingham B36 ...... 59 A1
  Wolverhampton WV10 .. 25 F7
Wolseley Dr B8 .... 68 A7
Wolseley Gate WV10... 25 F7
Wolseley Rd
  Bilston WV14.......... 40 C7
  West Bromwich B70 ... 52 F6
Wolseley St B9 .... 67 B2
WOLSTON............. 135 F3
Wolston CI B90 ...... 106 B5
Wolston La
  Kenilworth CV8 ..... 135 D1
  Wolston CV8 .... 135 E2
Wolston Way CV3 ..... 134 C6
WOLVERHAMPTON 163 D1
Wolverhampton Arts Gall★
  WV1................. 163 B3
Wolverhampton & Bilston
  Acad WV4 .... 39 E5
Wolverhampton Civic Hall★
  WV1................. 163 B3
Wolverhampton Coll
  WV1................. 163 B4
Wolverhampton (Dunstall
  Park) Racecourse WV6.. 25 A4
Wolverhampton Girls' High
  Sch WV6 .... 24 F3
Wolverhampton Gram Sch
  WV3 .... 24 F2
Wolverhampton Nuffield
  Health Hospl (Private)
  WV6 .... 24 C4
Wolverhampton Rd
  Cannock WS11......... 4 B4
  Cheslyn Hay WV10, WS6.. 4 B2
  Codsall WV8.......... 10 A3
  Essington WV11 ...... 13 A3
  Kingswinford DY6 ..... 49 C1
  Nurton WV6 .... 23 A3
  Oldbury B69 .... 63 F4
  Sedgley DY3 .... 39 D2
  Walsall, Birchills WS2 . 28 B2
  Walsall, Pelsall WS3 ... 14 F3
  Walsall, Wallington Heath
    WS3................ 14 B1
  Wedges Mills WS11..... 4 B6
  Wolverhampton WV10,
    WV11............... 26 A4
Wolverhampton Road E
  WV4................. 39 E4
Wolverhampton Road S
  B32................. 84 E7
Wolverhampton Road W
  WV13, WV12 .... 27 D2
Wolverhampton St
  Bilston WV14......... 40 C6
  Darlaston WS10....... 41 C6
  Dudley DY1 .... 51 B1
  Walsall WS2.......... 28 D2
  Willenhall WV13 ...... 27 A1
Wolverhampton Sta
  WV1................. 163 C3
Wolverhampton Swimming &
  Fitness Ctr WV13 ..... 26 B4
Wolverley Ave
  Stourbridge DY8 ..... 80 C6

Wolverley Ave continued
  Wolverhampton WV4..... 38 D5
Wolverley Cres B69..... 63 E5
Wolverley Rd
  Birmingham B32 ..... 102 B8
  Halesowen B63 .... 82 F2
  Solihull B92 .... 89 C2
Wolverson CI WV12 .... 27 C4
Wolverson Rd WS9..... 16 A4
Wolverton CI B98 ..... 154 E2
Wolverton Rd
  Birmingham, Marston Green
    B37 .... 90 B7
  Birmingham, Rednal B45.. 122 C6
  Coventry CV5......... 112 A3
  Dudley DY2 .... 51 E1
Wolvey Rd
  Bulkington CV12 ...... 79 E2
  Hinckley LE10 .... 75 E4
WOMBOURNE 49 B6
Wombourne CI DY3 .... 50 C8
Wombourne Rd B24.... 57 C4
Woodall Ho WS3....... 28 C8
Woodall Rd B6 .... 55 F1
Woodall St
  Cradley Heath B64..... 62 C1
  Walsall WS3.......... 28 C8
Woodard Rd DY4 ...... 52 C7
Wood Ave
  Dudley DY3 .... 50 C4
  Wednesfield WV11 .... 26 D6
Woodbank LE10 .... 76 A7
Woodbank Rd DY3 .... 50 C4
Woodbank Rd WV3 ... 38 A8
Woodberrow La B97 ... 158 D6
Woodberry Dr B76..... 47 A2
Woodberry Wlk B27... 88 D3
Woodbine Ave B10..... 87 D8
Woodbine Cotts
  Kingswood CV35 ..... 144 D3
  2 Royal Leamington Spa
    CV32............... 161 E8
Woodbine Croft B26 ... 89 A6
Woodbine Wlk B37 .... 70 D2
Woodbourne B15...... 85 D8
Woodbourne Priory Hospl
  the (Private) B17 ..... 85 C8
Woodbourne Rd
  Birmingham B15, B16... 85 C8
  Smethwick B67 ...... 64 E2
Woodbridge CI
  Walsall, Wallington Heath
    WS3................ 14 A3
  Walsall WS4.......... 15 D1
Woodbridge Rd B13.... 86 F3
Woodbrooke Gr B31 .. 103 C6
Woodbrooke Rd B30... 103 E7
Woodbrook Ho B38 ... 103 F2
Woodburn CI CV5...... 112 B4
Woodburn Rd B66 ..... 65 D7
Woodbury CI
  Birmingham B34 ...... 69 A6
  Brierley Hill DY5 ..... 61 E2
  Halesowen B62 .... 83 F8
  Redditch B97 .... 158 A6
Woodbury Gr B91..... 107 B1
Woodbury Rd
  Birmingham B62 ...... 84 A8
  Kidderminster DY11... 116 B2
Woodchester B93..... 127 E2
Woodchester Rd B93.. 127 E2
Woodchurch Grange B73. 56 F8
Wood CI B46 .... 70 F7
Woodclose Ave CV6.... 112 F6
Woodclose Rd B37..... 69 F3
Woodcock CI
  Birmingham B31 ..... 102 C1
  Tanworth-In-A B94 ... 141 E3
Woodcock Gdns WV10 . 12 B7
WOODCOCK HILL...... 102 E8
Woodcock Hill Prim Sch
  B31................. 102 E7
Woodcock La
  Birmingham, Acock's Green
    B27 .... 88 D3
  Birmingham, Northfield
    B31 .... 102 C1
Woodcock Lane N B27 .. 88 D4
Woodcock Sports Ctr B4. 66 F4
Woodcock St B7 ...... 66 F4
Woodcombe CI DY5.... 81 B7
Wood Common Grange
  WS3 .... 14 F4
Woodcote Ave
  Kenilworth CV8 ..... 147 D6
  Nuneaton CV11 .... 73 F8
Woodcote CI B98 .... 154 E3
Woodcote Dr
  Birmingham B8 .... 67 F5
  Dorridge B93......... 128 B2
  Leek Wootton CV35 .. 155 F7
Woodcote La
  Belbroughton DY9 ... 119 E1
  Leek Wootton CV8, CV35 .. 155 F7
Woodcote Rd
  Birmingham B24 ...... 57 D5
  Royal Leamington Spa
    CV32............... 156 F3
  Warwick CV34 .... 160 F8
  Wolverhampton WV6... 24 C4
Woodcote Way
  Birmingham B18 ...... 66 A4
  Sutton Coldfield B74... 44 F6
Woodcraft CI CV4..... 112 A2
Wood Croft B47 ..... 125 B6

Woodcroft Ave
  Birmingham B20 ...... 54 E3
  Dudley DY4 .... 51 C4
  Tamworth B79 .... 21 B6
Woodcroft CI
  Blackwell B60 .... 137 F5
  Cradley Heath B64..... 62 D7
  Walsall WS3.......... 15 A4
WOODCROSS 40 A2
Woodcross La WV14 ... 40 A2
Woodcross St WV14.... 39 F2
Wood Ct
  Birmingham B20 ...... 55 A2
  Coventry CV2......... 114 D7
  Redditch B97 .... 153 C1
Woodcutter CI WS1 ... 28 D1
WOOD END
  Coventry 96 C1
  Tamworth............ 36 C1
  Tanworth-in-Arden.... 141 F3
  Wednesfield.......... 26 D7
Woodend B20 .... 54 E6
Woodend CI B97...... 153 B2
Woodend Croft CV4 .. 131 E8
Wood End Dr B45...... 138 A8
Wood End La
  Birmingham B24 ...... 56 F3
  Lichfield WS13 .... 3 B7
  Solihull B94 .... 141 F8
  Tanworth-In-A B94 .. 141 F5
Woodend PI WV6 ..... 24 B4
Wood End Prim Sch
  Wolverhampton WV11.. 26 C7
  Wood End CV9........ 36 C1
Wood End Rd
  Birmingham B24 ...... 56 F3
  Walsall WS5.......... 43 D8
  Wednesfield WV11 .... 26 D7
  Wolverhampton WV11.. 12 C1
  Wood End Sta B94.... 141 F4
Wood End Way WS9.... 16 B1
Woodfall Ave B30..... 103 F5
Woodfield DY9 .... 119 E7
Woodfield Ave
  Brierley Hill DY5 ..... 61 B7
  Cradley Heath B64..... 82 D8
  Oldbury B69 .... 64 A4
  Stourbridge DY9 ..... 81 F2
  Wolverhampton WV4... 38 F6
Woodfield CI
  Norton Canes WS11.... 5 F7
  Redditch B98 .... 154 A5
  Sutton Coldfield B74... 46 B8
  Walsall WS5.......... 43 E5
Woodfield Cres
  Birmingham B12 ...... 87 A6
  Kidderminster DY11... 116 D5
Woodfield Ct B14..... 104 F8
Woodfield Dr WS14 .... 9 E5
Woodfield Ho B90 ... 107 B5
Woodfield Hts WV6 ... 24 D4
Woodfield Jun & Inf Schs
  WV4 .... 38 F6
Woodfield La B62..... 120 D8
Woodfield Mid Sch B98 . 154 A2
Woodfield Rd
  Birmingham, Balsall Heath
    B12 .... 87 A6
  Birmingham, King's Heath
    B13 .... 104 F8
  Coventry CV5........ 132 E8
  Dudley DY3 .... 50 C4
  Hinckley LE10 .... 75 C6
  Solihull B91 .... 107 B6
Woodfield Sch
  Coventry CV4........ 111 E3
  Coventry CV4........ 132 D2
Woodfields Dr WS14 ... 9 E5
Woodford CI 5 DY11.. 116 C6
Woodford Gr WV9 .... 10 F2
Woodford Green Rd B28 106 B8
Woodford Way WS12.... 2 D1
Woodford Rd B43 ..... 54 E7
WOODGATE
  Birmingham.......... 84 A1
  Bromsgrove......... 151 B2
Woodgate Bsns Pk B32 . 84 B2
Woodgate Dr B32..... 84 A1
Woodgate Gdns B32 .. 84 A2
Woodgate Ho B97 .... 153 B4
Woodgate La B32..... 84 A2
Woodgate Prim Sch B32 . 84 B1
Woodgate Rd
  Hinckley LE10 .... 76 A8
  Stoke Prior B60...... 151 B1
WOODGATE VALLEY.... 84 C3
Woodgate Valley Ctry Pk★
  B32................. 84 D3
Woodgate Valley CI B32 . 84 A1
Woodgate Croft B38 .. 103 E2
WOOD GREEN......... 42 A5
Woodgreen WS6........ 4 E5
Woodgreen CI B97.... 158 B7
Woodgreen Croft B68 . 84 C7
Wood Green High Sch Coll of
  Sport WS10.......... 42 A4
Wood Green Jun Sch
  WS10............... 42 A4
Woodgreen Rd B68 ... 84 C7
Wood Green Rd
  Birmingham B18 ...... 65 D4

Wood Green Rd continued
  Wednesbury WS10 .... 42 B4
Woodhall CI
  Nuneaton CV11 .... 74 A2
  Tipton DY4 .... 52 A8
Woodhall Croft B92.... 88 F3
Woodhall Rd WV4..... 38 E5
Woodham CI B45 ..... 101 E1
Woodhams Rd CV3.... 134 C3
Woodhaven
  Walsall WS4.......... 15 D1
  Walsall WS5.......... 4 B5
Wood Hayes Croft WV10. 12 C2
Wood Hayes Rd WV11 . 12 C1
Wood Hill Rise CV6 .... 95 D2
Wood Ho 1 WS1 ...... 42 A4
Woodhouse Bsns & Ent Coll
  B77................. 21 F4
Woodhouse CI CV3 ... 134 E8
Woodhouse Fold WV11 . 26 D5
Woodhouse La B77 .... 22 A5
Woodhouse Orch DY9.. 119 E7
Woodhouse Prim Sch
  B32................. 84 E6
Woodhouse Rd
  Birmingham B32 ...... 84 E5
  Wolverhampton WV6... 24 B4
Woodhouse Road N WV6. 24 B4
Woodhouses La WS7..... 7 F6
Woodhouses Rd WS7 ... 7 E5
Woodhouse St CV34... 160 D6
Woodhouse Way B64 .. 62 C1
Woodhurst CI B77 .... 21 F5
Woodhurst Rd B13..... 87 A4
Wooding Cres DY4..... 41 B1
Woodington Rd B75.... 47 B5
Wood La
  Birmingham, Erdington
    B24 .... 57 C1
  Birmingham, Handsworth
    B20 .... 55 B2
  Birmingham, Marston Green
    B37 .... 90 A8
  Birmingham, Queen's Park
    B17 .... 85 A6
  Cannock WS12......... 2 C4
  Earlswood B94....... 125 E1
  Eastcote B92 .... 108 F2
  Fairfield B61 .... 120 C3
  Hartshill CV10 .... 72 A8
  Shenstone WS14 ..... 17 B2
  Shilton CV7 .... 97 D5
  Sutton Coldfield B74... 30 E2
  Walsall WS3.......... 14 F4
  Wedges Mills WS11..... 4 B6
  West Bromwich B71 ... 53 A3
  Willenhall WV12 ...... 27 E7
  Wolverhampton WV10.. 11 D2
Woodland Ave
  Brierley Hill DY5 ..... 62 A1
  Coventry CV5........ 132 F7
  Dudley DY1 .... 51 C3
  Hinckley LE10 .... 76 A7
  Kidderminster DY11... 116 C7
  West Hagley DY8...... 98 F5
  Wolverhampton WV6... 24 B3
Woodland CI
  Cannock WS12......... 2 B8
  Stourbridge DY9 ..... 81 D2
  Willenhall WV12 ...... 27 D6
Woodland Cres WV3 .. 38 D7
Woodland Ct
  Cannock WS12......... 1 C4
  Shenstone WS14 ..... 32 A7
Woodland Dr
  Barnt Green B45 .... 122 A2
  Cheslyn Hay WS6...... 4 E4
  Smethwick B66 ...... 64 E7
Woodland Gr
  Birmingham B43 ...... 43 E3
  Dudley DY3 .... 50 B3
Woodland Rd
  Birmingham, Handsworth
    B21 .... 65 C8
  Birmingham, Northfield
    B31 .... 103 B3
  Dodford B61 .... 136 A7
  Halesowen B62 ...... 83 D8
  Hinckley LE10 .... 71 F1
  Kenilworth CV8 ..... 148 B7
  Redditch B97 .... 153 B3
  Tamworth B77 .... 22 A4
  Wolverhampton WV3... 38 D7
Woodland Rise
  Cradley Heath B64.... 82 F8
  Sutton Coldfield B73 .. 46 B4
Woodlands Ave
  Walsall WS5.......... 43 E5
  Water Orton B46..... 59 B2
Woodlands CI B78 ..... 20 A6
Woodlands Com Prim Sch
  B29................. 21 E4
Woodlands Cotts WV4 . 38 F4
Woodlands Cres WS3 .. 14 F5
Woodlands Ct
  Binley Woods CV3 ... 135 D7
  Coventry CV5........ 133 A8
Woodlands Farm Rd B24 . 57 F4
Woodlands La B90 ... 126 B8
Woodlands La
  Bedworth CV12 .... 77 E4
  Solihull B90 .... 126 B8
Woodlands Paddock WV4 38 E4
Woodlands Park Rd B30. 103 C5

Woodlands Prim Sch
WV12 . . . . 27 D6
Woodlands Rd
Bedworth CV12 . . . . 77 F3
Binley Woods CV3 . . . . . 135 D7
Birmingham B45 . . . . 121 D7
Birmingham, Moseley B11. . 87 C2
Birmingham, Saltley B8 . . . 67 F3
Wombourne WV5 . . . . 49 A5
Woodlands Sch & Sports Coll
The CV5 . . . . 111 D3
Woodlands Sports Complex
CV5 . . . . 111 D3
Woodlands St B66 . . . . . 65 C5
Woodlands The
Cradley Heath B64 . . . . . . 83 A7
Hartshill CV10 . . . . 72 A8
Lichfield WS13 . . . . 9 D8
Stourbridge DY8 . . . . 81 A2
Sutton Coldfield B75 . . . . 47 A6
Wood End CV9 . . . . 36 C1
Woodlands Way B37 . . . 70 D3
Woodland Way
Burntwood WS7 . . . . 7 A6
Polesworth B78 . . . . 36 F8
Wood Lane CI WV12 . . . . 27 E7
Woodlawn B91 . . . . 107 E4
Woodlawn Gr DY6 . . . . . 60 D5
Woodlea Dr
Birmingham B24 . . . . 56 F2
Solihull B91 . . . . 106 E4
Wood Leasow B32 . . . . . 84 D2
Woodleaves B47 . . . . . 124 F8
Woodleigh Ave B17 . . . . 85 D4
Woodleigh CI B63. . . . . . 83 A6
Woodleigh Ct B38 . . . . 103 F1
Woodleigh Rd
Coventry CV4 . . . . 131 F5
Sutton Coldfield B72 . . . . 46 C1
Woodleys The B14 . . . . 105 B4
Woodloes Avenue N
CV34 . . . . 155 F1
Woodloes Avenue S
CV34 . . . . 155 F1
Woodloes La CV34, CV35 . 155 F2
WOODLOES PARK 155 D2
Woodloes Prim Sch
CV34 . . . . 155 E1
Woodloes Rd B90 . . . . . 126 B7
Woodman CI
Halesowen B63 . . . . 83 C3
Wednesbury WS10 . . . . . . 42 B4
Woodman Gr 5 B75 . . . . 32 E3
Woodman La
Cheslyn Hay WS6. . . . . 4 E4
Clent DY9 . . . . 99 E4
Woodman Rd
Birmingham B14 . . . . 105 A1
Halesowen B63 . . . . 83 C3
Woodman Wlk B23. . . . . 56 A5
Woodmeadow Rd B30. . 104 B3
Woodmill Mdw CV8 . . . 148 B6
Woodnorton Dr B13. . . . 86 E2
Woodnorton Rd B65 . . . . 63 F2
Woodpecker Gr
Birmingham B36 . . . . 70 A7
Kidderminster DY10. . . . . 117 B2
Woodpecker Rd B33 . . . . 68 F4
Woodpecker Way WS11. . . 2 C3
Woodperry Ave B91. . . . 107 C1
Wood Piece La B98 . . . . 154 D7
Woodpigeon Dr WS11. . . . 2 A1
Wood Rd
Dudley DY3 . . . . 50 C4
Wolverhampton WV6. . . . . 24 C3
Wombourne WV5 . . . . 49 B7
Woodridge B6. . . . . 55 E1
Woodridge Ave
Birmingham B32 . . . . 84 B4
Coventry CV5 . . . . 112 A6
Woodridge Rd B63. . . . . 83 A5
Woodriffe Wlk CV6. . . . . 96 A4
Woodrough Dr B13 . . . . . 86 F2
WOODROW
Kidderminster 118 D3
Redditch. 159 B7
Woodrow CI B61. . . . . . 120 F1
Woodrow Cres B93 . . . . 128 A5
Woodrow Dr B98 . . . . . . 159 B8
Woodrow Dr B98 . . . . . . 159 B6
Woodrow Fst Sch B98. . . 159 B7
Woodrow La
Bluntington DY10. . . . . . . 118 E3
Lower Marlbrook B61 . . . . 121 B2
Woodrow N B98 . . . . . . 159 A7
Woodrow S B98 . . . . . . 159 B7
Woodrow Wlk B98. . . . . 159 A7
Woodruff Way WS5 . . . . 43 A3
Woodrush Com High Sch The
B47. . . . . 125 A6
Woodrush Dr B47. . . . . . 125 A5
WOODS BANK 41 B5
Woodsbank Ind Est The
WS10 . . . . 41 D4
Woods Bank Terr WS10 . 41 C5
Woods Cres DY5. . . . . . . 62 A1
Woods Croft WS13 . . . . . 3 A1
WOODSETTON 50 E6
Woodsetton CI DY1 . . . . 51 B6
Woodsetton Spec! Sch The
DY3. . . . . 50 F7
Woodshill Ave B45. . . . . 122 A2
WOODSHIRES GREEN . . . 95 E5

Woodshires Rd
Coventry CV6. . . . . 95 F5
Solihull B92. . . . . 106 E7
WOODSIDE 61 E6
Woodside
Birmingham B37 . . . . 69 E4
Sutton Coldfield B74 . . . . 31 E2
Wood Side WV11 . . . . . . 27 A8
Woodside Ave B97 . . . . 153 B2
Woodside Avenue N CV3 132 F6
Woodside Avenue S CV3 132 F5
Woodside CI
Walsall WS5. . . . . 43 D6
Wood End CV9 . . . . 36 C1
Woodside Com Sch &
Childrens Ctr DY2. . . . . . . 61 F6
Woodside Cres B93 . . . 128 E4
Woodside Dr
Barnt Green B45 . . . . 138 B8
Sutton Coldfield B74 . . . . 31 C5
Woodside Gr WV8 . . . . . . 10 B2
Woodside Ind Est DY2. . . 61 F5
Woodside Park Mobile
Homes Pk B94 . . . . 141 B7
Woodside PI WS11. . . . . . 1 E5
Woodside Rd
Birmingham B29 . . . . 86 A1
Dudley DY2 . . . . 61 F7
Walsall WS5. . . . . 43 E6
Woodside Way
Aldridge WS9. . . . . 30 B5
Birmingham B32 . . . . 102 A8
Solihull B91. . . . . 106 E5
Willenhall WV12 . . . . 27 E7
Woods La
Brierley Hill DY5 . . . . 81 D7
Cradley Heath B64. . . . . . 82 C8
Woodsome Gr B23 . . . . . 56 C7
Woodsorrel Rd DY1. . . . . 50 F4
Woods Piece CV7 . . . . . . 94 F6
Wood St
Bedworth CV12 . . . . 78 B5
Bilston WV14. . . . . 40 D5
Birmingham B16 . . . . 66 A2
Darlaston WS10. . . . . 41 F6
Dudley DY2 . . . . 61 F6
Hinckley LE10 . . . . 71 D1
Kidderminster DY11. . . . . 116 D5
Nuneaton CV10 . . . . 72 F4
Royal Leamington Spa
CV32 . . . . 162 A8
Stourbridge DY8 . . . . 80 D6
Stourbridge, Lye DY9. . . . 81 F5
Tipton DY4. . . . . 51 E5
Willenhall WV13 . . . . 27 B2
Wolverhampton, Park Village
WV10 . . . . 25 F5
Woodcross WV4 . . . . 40 A3
Wood End CV9 . . . . 36 C1
WOODS THE 42 C4
Woods The B14. . . . . 86 F1
Woodstile B34 . . . . 69 B6
Woodstile CI B75 . . . . . . 32 D3
Woodstock CI
Dudley DY1 . . . . 62 A8
Hinckley LE10 . . . . 76 A5
Stourbridge DY8 . . . . 60 C1
2 Walsall WS5 . . . . 43 A3
Woodstock Cres B93 . . . 127 F3
Woodstock Ct B13 . . . . . 87 B4
Woodstock La B13
Huntington WS12. . . . . 1 C7
Stourbridge DY8 . . . . 60 C2
Sutton Coldfield B74 . . . . 31 D4
Woodstock Girls Sch B13 87 A4
Woodstock Ho B13. . . . . 105 A7
Woodstock Rd
Birmingham, Handsworth
B21. . . . . 65 F8
Birmingham, Moseley B13. . 87 B3
Coventry CV3. . . . . 133 D7
Nuneaton CV11 . . . . 73 E1
Wolverhampton WV1. . . . . 26 B1
Woodston Gr B91. . . . . . 127 C8
Wood Street CI LE10 . . . . 71 E1
Wood Terr B96 . . . . 159 B1
Woodthorne CI DY1. . . . . 50 D2
Woodthorne Prim Sch
WV6. . . . . 24 A4
Woodthorne Rd WV6. . . . 24 A6
Woodthorne Road S WV6. 24 A5
Woodthorne Wlk DY6. . . . 60 E8
Woodthorpe Dr DY8. . . . . 81 D3
Woodthorpe Gdns B14 . . 104 E5
Woodthorpe Prim Sch
B14. . . . . 104 E5
Woodthorpe Rd B14 . . . 104 E5
Woodvale Rd B13. . . . . . 87 A4
Woodvale Dr B28 . . . . . 105 E4
Woodvale Rd
Birmingham B32 . . . . 84 A1
Birmingham, Yardley Wood
B28. . . . . 105 E4
Woodview Dr B15. . . . . . 86 C7
Woodview Primary Sch
B15. . . . . 86 C7
Woodville Ct
3 Birmingham B23. . . . . 56 E2
Warwick CV34 . . . . 160 F1
Woodville Gdns DY3 . . . . 39 F1
Woodville Rd
Birmingham B17 . . . . 85 A6
Birmingham, King's Heath
B14. . . . . 104 E8
Warwick CV34 . . . . 160 E8
Woodward CI CV31. . . . . 162 A2
Woodward PI DY9 . . . . . . 81 C4
Woodward Rd DY11. . . . . 116 C4

Woodwards CI WS2 . . . . . 42 B8
Woodwards PI WS2 . . . . . 42 B8
Woodwards Rd WS2 . . . . 42 B8
Woodward St B71. . . . . . 53 E4
Woodway B24 . . . . 57 B5
Woodway CI CV2. . . . . . 114 F8
Woodway La CV2 . . . . . . 96 F1
WOODWAY PARK. 114 E8
Woodway Wlk CV2. . . . . 114 E8
Woodwells Rd B8. . . . . . . 68 B5
Woody Bank WS6. . . . . . . 4 E2
Woolacombe Lodge Rd
B29 . . . . 85 C2
Woolaston Rd B98 . . . . . 159 C8
Woolgrove St CV6 . . . . . . 96 A3
Woolhope CI B98 . . . . . . 154 F3
Woolmore Rd B23 . . . . . . 56 C5
Woolpack CI B65 . . . . 63 A4
Woolpack St WV1. . . . . . 163 B3
Woolpack The 2 CV34. . 160 E6
Woolwich Rd CV11. . . . . . 79 F6
Wooton CI B97 . . . . 153 A4
Wootton Ave WV11 . . . . . 26 D7
Wootton CI WS11 . . . . 2 B3
Wootton Ct
Coventry CV2. . . . . 114 D7
8 Royal Leamington Spa
CV32. . . . . 156 F2
WOOTTON GREEN 110 A1
Wootton Green La CV7 . . 130 A8
Wootton La CV7 . . . . . . 109 E1
Wootton Rd
Birmingham B31. . . . . . . 123 A6
Wolverhampton WV3 . . . . 38 D8
Woottons CI WV11 . . . . . . 1 F1
Wootton's Sq WV14 . . . . 40 E2
Wootton St CV12. . . . . . . 78 D3
Worcester Cl
Allesley CV5. . . . . 112 B7
Cannock WS11 . . . . 4 F8
Lichfield WS13 . . . . 3 C3
Sutton Coldfield B75 . . . . 32 D3
West Hagley DY9. . . . . . . 99 A5
Worcester Cross 3
DY10 . . . . 116 E5
Worcester Ct
Coventry CV6. . . . . 96 B4
Wolverhampton WV3 . . . . 39 A6
Worcester Gn B71. . . . . . 53 C7
Worcester Gr WV6 . . . . . 23 D4
Worcester Ho
Birmingham B36 . . . . 70 A8
4 Halesowen B63 . . . . . 83 A3
Worcester La
Stourbridge DY9 . . . . 99 B7
Sutton Coldfield B75 . . . . 32 D3
Worcester Lane Nature
Reserve* DY9 . . . . 99 A8
Worcester Rd
Birmingham, Brandhall
B68. . . . . 84 A8
Bromsgrove B61 . . . . 136 F1
Dudley DY2 . . . . 62 E3
Harvington DY9, DY10. . . 118 C4
Kenilworth CV8 . . . . 148 B3
Kidderminster DY10. . . . . 116 E2
Mustow Green DY10 . . . . 117 F1
Stoke Heath B61 . . . . 150 B4
West Hagley DY9. . . . . . . 99 A5
Willenhall WV13 . . . . 27 D2
Worcester Rise B29 . . . . . 86 B1
Worcester Sq 1 B97. . . . 153 E4
Worcester St
Birmingham B2 . . . . 164 C2
Kidderminster DY10. . . . . 116 E6
Stourbridge DY8 . . . . 81 A4
Wolverhampton WV10 . . . 25 D4
Worcester St CV3 . . . . . 133 D8
Worcester Wlk B37 . . . . . 70 A1
Word Hill B17 . . . . 84 F7
WORDSLEY 60 E3
Wordsley CI B98 . . . . . . 154 B7
Wordsley Ct DY8. . . . . . . 60 E3
Wordsley Sch The DY8 . . 60 F3
Wordsworth Ave
Redditch B97 . . . . 158 C8
Tamworth B79 . . . . 21 A6
Warwick CV34 . . . . 160 D5
Wolverhampton WV4 . . . . 39 F4
Wordsworth CI
Cannock WS11 . . . . 1 D4
Lichfield WS14 . . . . 9 B5
Tipton DY4. . . . . 52 A8
Wordsworth Cres DY10. . 117 B6
Wordsworth Ct WV6 . . . . 23 E4
Wordsworth Dr CV8. . . . 148 C4
Wordsworth Ho
Birmingham B31. . . . . . . 123 A8
Halesowen B63. . . . . 82 B5
4 Oldbury B68 . . . . 64 C4
Wordsworth Rd
Bedworth CV12 . . . . 78 D1
Birmingham B10 . . . . 87 D7
Burntwood WS7 . . . . 7 A8
Coventry CV2. . . . . 114 C4
Dudley DY3 . . . . 50 B5
Walsall WS3. . . . . 28 E8
Willenhall WV12 . . . . 27 E7
Wolverhampton WV10. . . . 26 A5
Wordsworth St B71. . . . . 53 C5
Worfield CI WS4 . . . . 29 A4
Worfield Gdns WV3 . . . . . 38 F6
Workhouse La LE10. . . . . 76 A4
Works Rd B26 . . . . 90 A3
WORLDS END 107 A6
WORLD'S END 84 D5
World's End Ave B32. . . . 84 D6

World's End Jun & Inf Sch
B32. . . . . 84 D5
World's End La B32 . . . . . 84 D5
Worlds End Rd B20 . . . . . 55 A3
Worleys Wharf Ave WS10. 42 E2
WORMS ASH. 136 C6
Worsdell CI CV1. . . . . . . 113 B4
Worsey Dr DY4 . . . . 52 D6
Worsfold CI CV5 . . . . . . 112 A7
Worthen Gr B31 . . . . 123 A8
Worthings The B30 . . . . 104 B6
Worthy Down WV11. . . . . 26 F5
Worthy Down Wlk B35 . . 58 B3
Wortley Ave WV10 . . . . . 25 E6
Worton Rd DY9 . . . . 81 F2
Wragby CI WV9 . . . . 11 B3
Wrekin CI
Halesowen B63. . . . . 82 C1
Kidderminster DY11. . . . . 116 B2
Wrekin Ct 8 B74 . . . . . . 31 F2
Wrekin Dr
Bromsgrove B61 . . . . 137 A5
Stourbridge DY9 . . . . 81 D4
Wolverhampton, Bradmore
WV3 . . . . 38 E8
Wolverhampton, Wergs
WV6 . . . . 24 A5
Wrekin Gr WV11 . . . . 13 B1
Wrekin La WV6 . . . . 24 A5
Wrekin Rd
Birmingham B44 . . . . 56 A6
Sutton Coldfield B73 . . . . 46 A1
Wrekin View
Brownhills WS8 . . . . 16 A5
Huntington WS12. . . . . 1 C7
Wolverhampton WV1. . . . 163 B3
Wrekin View Rd DY3 . . . . 50 C8
Wren Ave WV6. . . . . 23 D3
Wrenbury Dr
Bilston WV14. . . . . 41 A7
Coventry CV6. . . . . 96 A4
Wrens Ave
Kingswinford DY6 . . . . . . 61 A4
Tipton DY4. . . . . 51 D4
Wrens Croft WS11 . . . . . . 2 B1
Wrens Hill Rd DY1 . . . . . . 51 B5
WREN'S NEST. 51 A4
Wren's Nest CI B90 . . . . 126 A5
Wren's Nest National Nature
Reserve* DY1. . . . . 51 B4
Wrens Nest PI DY1. . . . . . 51 A5
Wren's Nest Rd DY1. . . . . 51 A5
Wrens Park Ave B76 . . . . 57 E7
Wren St
Coventry CV2. . . . . 113 F3
Dudley DY1 . . . . 51 C6
Dudley, Netherton DY2 . . . 62 B5
Wrentham St B5. . . . . . . 86 E8
Wretham Ct B19 . . . . 66 B7
Wretham Rd B19. . . . . . . 66 B6
Wrexham Ave WS2. . . . . 27 F1
Wright Ave WV11 . . . . . . 26 E7
Wrighton CI WV12 . . . . . 27 C8
Wrighton Dr DY5 . . . . . . 50 C1
Wrighton Gr B78. . . . . . . 35 A8
Wright Rd B8. . . . . 67 E5
Wright's Ave WS11. . . . . . 1 F5
Wright's La B64. . . . . 63 A1
Wright St
Bilston WV14. . . . . 40 E4
Birmingham B10 . . . . 87 D8
Halesowen B63. . . . . 83 B4
Wolverhampton WV10. . . . 25 D4
Wrigsham St CV3 . . . . . . 133 D8
Wrottesley Ct WV8 . . . . . 10 B3
Wrottesley Park Rd WV6,
WV8. . . . . 23 D5
Wrottesley Rd
Birmingham B43 . . . . 43 D1
Wolverhampton WV6. . . . . 24 B5
Wrottesley Road W
Perton WV6. . . . . 23 F6
Wolverhampton WV6. . . . . 24 A6
Wrottesley St B5. . . . . . 164 C1
WROXALL 145 E3
Wroxall CI DY5 . . . . 81 C8
Wroxall Dr CV3 . . . . 134 D5
Wroxall Gr B13 . . . . 105 A6
Wroxall Rd B91 . . . . 106 E6
Wroxham Glen WV13. . . . 40 F8
Wroxton Rd B26 . . . . 88 E8
Wryley & Essington Canal
Nature Reserve* WV11 . . 13 E7
Wulfruna Ct WV3 . . . . . . 163 A2
Wulfruna Gdns WV3 . . . . 24 F1
Wulfruna St WV1 . . . . . . 163 B3
Wulfrun Hall* WV1. . . . . 163 B3
Wulfrun Sh Ctr WV1. . . . 163 C2
Wulfrun Sq WV1 . . . . . . 163 C2
Wulfrun Trad Est WV6. . . 25 C5
Wulfrun Way WV1 . . . . . 163 B2
Wyatt CI B5 . . . . 86 C5
Wyatt Ho CV2. . . . . 114 D7
Wyatt Rd B75. . . . . 47 B5
Wyatts Ct CV12 . . . . 78 B3
Wychall Dr WV10 . . . . . . 11 E4
Wychall La B38. . . . . 103 E2
Wychall Park Gr B38 . . . 103 D2
Wychall Prim Sch B31 . . 103 C3
Wychall Rd B31 . . . . 103 C3
Wychbold CI
Redditch B97 . . . . 158 A6
Willenhall WV12 . . . . 13 D1
Wychbold Cres B33 . . . . 69 C3

Wychbold Ct DY9 . . . . . . 99 C8
Wychbold Way WV12. . . . 13 D1
Wychbury B76 . . . . 47 A3
Wychbury Ct B63 . . . . . . 83 A3
Wychbury Dr DY9 . . . . . . 99 C7
Wychbury Grange DY9 . . 81 C1
Wychbury Rd
Birmingham B32 . . . . 102 B7
Brierley Hill DY5 . . . . 81 E8
Stourbridge DY9 . . . . 81 E2
Wolverhampton WV3. . . . . 38 C7
Wyche Ave B14 . . . . 104 D4
Wych Elm CI B66 . . . . . . 150 C3
Wych Elm Dr 6 CV31. . . 161 F5
Wychelm Farm Rd B14 . . 105 A1
Wych Elm Rd WS8 . . . . . . 15 E5
Wycherley Way B64. . . . . 82 E6
Wychnor Gr B71. . . . . . . 42 E2
Wychwood Ave
Coventry CV3. . . . . 133 C3
Knowle B93. . . . . 128 B8
Wychwood Cres B26 . . . . 89 A6
Wychwood Dr B97. . . . . 158 D6
Wyckham CI B17. . . . . . . 85 A4
Wyckham Rd B36 . . . . . . 69 F8
Wycliffe Gr
Coventry CV2. . . . . 114 B5
5 Walsall WS2 . . . . 42 C8
Wycliffe Road W CV2. . . 114 C5
Wycome Rd B28 . . . . . . 106 A7
Wye CI
Bulkington CV12 . . . . 79 B2
Hinckley LE10 . . . . 75 A8
Perton WV6 . . . . 23 F4
Royal Leamington Spa
CV32. . . . . 157 C2
Sutton Coldfield B76 . . . . 58 B7
Wye Cliff Rd B20. . . . . . . 66 B8
Wyegate CI B36. . . . . 69 F8
Wye Ho DY3 . . . . 50 D3
Wyemanton CI B43. . . . . 43 C1
Wye Rd WS3. . . . . 14 E1
Wykeham Gr WV6. . . . . . 23 D3
Wykeley Rd CV2 . . . . 114 C4
Wyken Ave CV2 . . . . 114 C4
Wyken CI B93 . . . . 127 E2
Wyken Croft CV2. . . . . . 114 D6
Wyken Croft Nature Pk*
CV2. . . . . 114 D6
Wyken Croft Prim Sch
CV2. . . . . 114 E5
Wyken Grange Rd CV2 . . 114 C5
WYKEN GREEN. 114 C6
Wyken Slough Nature
Reserve* CV2 . . . . 96 C3
Wyken Way CV2 . . . . . . 114 B5
Wykin Rd CV2 . . . . 114 C6
Wykin Rd LE10 . . . . 71 A3
Wyld CI B71. . . . . 53 A6
Wyld Ct CV5 . . . . 112 B5
Wylde Cres B65 . . . . 63 C4
WYLDE GREEN. 46 C7
Wylde Green Prim Sch
B73 . . . . 57 B2
Wylde Green Rd B72, B76. 46 D3
Wylde Green Sta B73 . . . 46 B3
Wyley Rd CV6. . . . . 113 B5
Wymering Ave WV11. . . . 26 F2
Wynall La DY9 . . . . 81 F2
Wynall Lane S DY9 . . . . . 82 A2
Wynbrook Gr B90. . . . . . 127 A6
Wynchcombe Ave WV4. . 38 D4
Wyncote CI CV8. . . . . . . 148 A6
Wyndcliffe Prim Sch B9. . 67 C3
Wyndcliff Rd B9 . . . . 67 D1
Wyndham Gdns B30. . . . 103 D6
Wyndham Rd B16. . . . . . 65 F1
Wyndhurst Rd B33 . . . . . 68 E5
Wyndley CI B74. . . . . 31 F6
Wyndley Dr B73 . . . . 46 B6
Wyndley Gr B72. . . . . 46 C2
Wyndley La B73 . . . . 46 A4
Wyndley L Ctr B73 . . . . . 46 A5
Wyndley Manor B74. . . . 32 A4
Wynds Covert B14 . . . . . 104 D2
Wynds Point B31 . . . . . . 103 B5
Wynd The DY3 . . . . 39 D1
Wynfield Gdns B14. . . . . 104 F5
Wynford Ind Trad Est B27. 88 C5
Wynford Rd B27. . . . . . . 88 C5
Wyn-Griffith Dr DY4 . . . . 52 A1
Wynne Cres WV4 . . . . . . 38 C1
Wynn Rd WV4 . . . . 38 F4
Wynn St B15. . . . . 86 D8
Wynstead Covert 6 B14. 104 C2
Wyntor La B71. . . . . 53 B6
Wynyates B79 . . . . 20 E3
Wyre CI
Birmingham B45 . . . . 102 B8
Brownhills WS9 . . . . 15 F4
Wyre Rd DY8 . . . . 80 E1
Wyrley Brook Pk WS11 . . 4 D6
Wyrley Brook Ret Pk WS11. 4 D8
Wyrley CI
Burntwood WS8. . . . . 6 F1
Lichfield WS14. . . . . 9 A1
Willenhall WV12 . . . . 27 D7
Wyrley Ho
Birmingham B23 . . . . 56 C1
Tipton DY4. . . . . 52 B4
Wyrley La WS3. . . . . 14 E1
Wyrley Rd
Birmingham B6 . . . . 56 A4
Sutton Coldfield B75 . . . . 32 D2
Wednesfield WV11 . . . . . . 27 A4
Wyrley St WV10. . . . . 25 F7

Wyrley Way B23 . . . . 56 A6
WYTHALL 125 B3
WYTHALL GREEN 124 E3
Wythall Green Way B47 . 124 E3
Wythall Rd B63 . . . . 83 A2
Wythall Sta B47 . . . . 125 C4
Wythwood Cl DY9 . . . . 81 D1
Wythwood Gr
  Hollywood B47 . . . . 125 C6
  Tipton DY4 . . . . 52 A8
Wythwood Rd B47 . . . . . . 125 C6
Wyton Ave B68 . . . . 64 C2
Wyver Cres CV2 . . . . 114 C3
Wyvern B77 . . . . 21 F3
Wyvern Cl
  Hinckley LE10 . . . . 75 E4
  Oldbury B68 . . . . 64 B4
  Sutton Coldfield B74 . . . . . 46 B7
  Wednesfield WV12 . . . . . . 27 A7
Wyvern Gr
  Birmingham B29 . . . . 85 C2
  Cannock WS12 . . . . 2 A5
Wyvern Rd B74 . . . . 46 B7
Wyvis Cl WV6 . . . . 24 E2

Y

Yale Dr WV11 . . . . 26 E5
Yale Rd WV13 . . . . 41 A7
YARDLEY 88 D8
Yardley Cl
  Oldbury B68 . . . . 64 B1
  Redditch B98 . . . . 154 E3
  Warwick CV34 . . . . 155 F2
YARDLEY FIELDS 68 D1
Yardley Fields Rd B33 . . . . 68 E2
Yardley Green Rd B9, B25,
  B33 . . . . 68 A2
Yardley Prim Sch B26 . . . . 88 D7
Yardley Rd B27 . . . . 88 C5
Yardleys Sch B11 . . . . 87 F4
Yardley St
  Coventry CV1 . . . . 113 E4
  Darlaston WS10 . . . . 41 C7
  Stourbridge DY9 . . . . 81 C6
YARDLEY WOOD 105 E5
Yardley Wood Prim Sch
  B14 . . . . 105 D4
Yardley Wood Rd B13,
  B14 . . . . 105 B5
Yardley Wood Sta B28 . . 105 D5
Yardley Works DY9 . . . . . . 81 C5
Yare Gr WV13 . . . . 27 D1
Yarmouth Gn CV4 . . . . . . 131 E8
Yarnborough Hill DY8 . . . 81 A2
Yarnbury Cl B14 . . . . 104 E1
Yarn Cl B47 . . . . 125 A5

Yarner Cl DY1 . . . . 50 E2
Yarnfield Prim Sch B11 . . 88 A3
Yarnfield Rd B11 . . . . 88 A3
Yarningale Cl B98 . . . . 158 F6
Yarningale Rd
  Birmingham B14 . . . . 104 D5
  Coventry CV3 . . . . 134 D5
Yarningdale 7 B90 . . . . . 126 C8
Yarn La B90 . . . . 126 A6
Yarnold La
  Bournheath B61 . . . . 136 C8
  Fairfield B61 . . . . 120 C1
Yarr Mill Cl B98 . . . . 158 F5
Yarrow Cl
  Walsall WS3 . . . . 15 A5
  Wednesfield WV11 . . . . . . 26 F5
Yarrow Dr B38 . . . . 123 F8
Yarrow Wlk CV6 . . . . 95 E3
Yarwell Cl WV10 . . . . 163 C4
Yateley Ave B42 . . . . 55 A7
Yateley Cres B42 . . . . 55 A7
Yateley Rd B15 . . . . 85 E7
Yatesbury Ave B35 . . . . 58 A3
Yates Croft B74 . . . . 31 F6
Yates Ind Est WS3 . . . . 5 F2
Yates La B65 . . . . 63 F2
Yeadon Cl B97 . . . . 153 A1
Yeadon Gdns WV3 . . . . 38 D8
Yeames Cl B43 . . . . 44 C4
Yelverton Cl WS3 . . . . 14 B4
Yelverton Dr B15 . . . . 85 E8
Yelverton Rd CV6 . . . . 113 D8
Yeman Rd B68 . . . . 64 D3
Yemscroft WS6 . . . . 14 A8
Yenns Croft WS4 . . . . 29 A6
Yenton Cl B78 . . . . 21 A1
Yenton Gr B24 . . . . 57 C6
Yenton Prim Sch B24 . . . . 57 C6
Yeomanry Cl
  Sutton Coldfield B75 . . . . 47 A6
  12 Warwick CV34 . . . . . . 160 F7
Yeomans Cl B96 . . . . 158 E2
Yeomans Grange 8 B75 . 46 F6
Yeomans Way B75 . . . . 46 F6
Yeomans Wlk B60 . . . . . . 150 E8
Yeovil Ct 15 DY5 . . . . 61 D2
Yeovilton B79 . . . . 21 C8
Yerbury Gr B23 . . . . 56 B4
Yew Cl CV3 . . . . 114 C1
Yew Croft Ave B17 . . . . 85 B6
Yewdale B17 . . . . 85 C4
Yewdale Cres CV2 . . . . 96 E1
Yewdale Gn CV2 . . . . 96 F1
Yewhurst Rd B91 . . . . 106 E4
Yew St WV3 . . . . 25 A1
Yews The CV12 . . . . 77 E2

YEW TREE
  Balsall Common 130 A6
  Wednesbury 43 B4
Yew Tree Ave
  Belbroughton DY9 . . . . . . 119 E8
  Birmingham B26 . . . . 88 E7
  Lichfield WS14 . . . . 9 E8
Yew Tree Cl
  Kingswood B94 . . . . 144 D3
  Norton Canes WS11 . . . . . . 6 A5
  Redditch B97 . . . . 153 A4
Yew Tree Com Prim Sch
  B6 . . . . 56 A1
Yew Tree Ct 1 CV31 . . . . 161 F5
Yewtree Dr B60 . . . . 137 B2
Yew Tree Gdns WV8 . . . . . . 10 A4
YEW TREE HILL 62 B4
Yew Tree Hills DY2 . . . . . . 62 C4
Yewtree La B65 . . . . 63 B2
Yew Tree La
  Birmingham, Frankley
    B32 . . . . 101 E3
  Birmingham, Yardley B26 . . 88 E7
  Dudley WV14 . . . . 40 D1
  Fairfield B61 . . . . 120 D2
  Lapworth B94 . . . . 144 B1
  Solihull B91 . . . . 107 E5
  Wednesbury WS10 . . . . . . 42 A2
  Wolverhampton WV6 . . . . 24 A5
Yew Tree Pl
  Romsley B62 . . . . 101 A5
  Walsall WS3 . . . . 14 D3
Yew Tree Prim Sch
  Solihull B91 . . . . 107 E6
  Walsall WS5 . . . . 43 C4
Yewtree Rd
  Sutton Coldfield, Boldmere
    B73 . . . . 57 A7
  Sutton Coldfield, Streetly
    B74 . . . . 44 D8
Yew Tree Rd
  Birmingham, Castle Bromwich
    B36 . . . . 69 E8
  Birmingham, Edgbaston B15 86 C8
  Birmingham, Handsworth
    B6 . . . . 56 A1
  Birmingham, Moseley B13 . 86 D2
  Dudley DY2 . . . . 62 C4
  Halesowen B63 . . . . 82 F3
  Kidderminster DY10 . . . . 116 F5
  Smethwick B67 . . . . 64 E4
  Walsall, The Delves WS5 . . 43 A5
  Walsall WS4 . . . . 15 B1
Yew Tree Ret Pk B25 . . . . . 88 D8
Yew Tree Rise B76 . . . . 46 F3
Yew Tree Villas B73 . . . . . . 57 A7
Yew Wlk B37 . . . . 70 B2
YIELDINGTREE 118 F8

Yockleton Rd B33 . . . . 69 C3
York Ave
  Bedworth CV12 . . . . 78 D2
  Bromsgrove B61 . . . . 136 E4
  Walsall WS2 . . . . 28 B2
  Willenhall WV13 . . . . 27 D2
  Wolverhampton WV3 . . . . 24 E1
Yorkbrooke Dr B26 . . . . . . 89 B5
York Cl
  Birmingham B30 . . . . 104 A6
  Bromsgrove B61 . . . . 136 E4
  Coventry CV3 . . . . 134 C5
  Lichfield WS13 . . . . 3 C3
  Studley B80 . . . . 159 C4
  Tipton DY4 . . . . 51 D4
York Cres
  Birmingham B34 . . . . 69 E6
  Darlaston WS10 . . . . 41 D6
  Stourbridge DY8 . . . . 80 D7
  West Bromwich B70 . . . . . 53 A6
  Wolverhampton WV3 . . . . 24 E1
York Ct DY10 . . . . 116 E7
York Dr B36 . . . . 68 B8
Yorke Ave DY5 . . . . 61 A1
York Gdns WV3 . . . . 24 E1
Yorklea Croft B37 . . . . 69 F2
Yorkmead Prim Sch B28 . . 87 F2
York Mews B17 . . . . 85 D6
York Rd
  Birmingham B23 . . . . 56 F4
  Birmingham, Edgbaston B16 65 E1
  Birmingham, Handsworth
    B21 . . . . 65 F8
  Birmingham, King's Heath
    B14 . . . . 104 E8
  Birmingham, Tyseley B28 . . 87 F2
  Bromsgrove B61 . . . . 136 F4
  Cannock WS11 . . . . 4 F7
  Dudley DY2 . . . . 62 E3
  Hinckley LE10 . . . . 71 D3
  Rowley Regis B65 . . . . 63 E3
  Royal Leamington Spa
    CV31 . . . . 161 F8
  Walsall WS4 . . . . 29 D7
  Wolverhampton WV3 . . . . 38 B8
Yorksand Rd B78 . . . . 34 F8
Yorkshire Way WS7 . . . . 7 F8
York St
  Birmingham B17 . . . . 85 D6
  Coventry CV1 . . . . 113 B2
  Kidderminster DY10 . . . . 116 E7
  Nuneaton CV11 . . . . 73 A4
  Wolverhampton WV1 . . . . 163 D2
Yorks Wood Dr B37 . . . . . . 69 E5
York's Wood Nature
  Reserve★ B34 . . . . 69 E5

Yorkswood Prim Sch B37 69 F5
York Terr B18 . . . . 66 C5
Young Cl CV34 . . . . 160 B5
Young St B70 . . . . 53 A3
Yoxall Gr B33 . . . . 69 A3
Yoxall Rd B90 . . . . 106 D2
Yule Rd CV2 . . . . 114 D5
Yvonne Rd B97 . . . . 158 D7

Z

Zealand Cl LE10 . . . . 71 F3
Zion Cl WS6 . . . . 4 D3
Zions Cl B64 . . . . 62 F1
Zion St DY4 . . . . 51 F8
Zoar St
  Dudley DY3 . . . . 50 C3
  Wolverhampton WV3 . . . . 25 B1
Zorrina Cl CV10 . . . . 72 B5
Zouche Cl DY8 . . . . 80 E8

PHILIP'S MAPS
the Gold Standard for drivers

◆ **Philip's street atlases cover all of England, Wales, Northern Ireland and much of Scotland**

◆ Every named street is shown, including alleys, lanes and walkways

◆ Thousands of additional features marked: stations, public buildings, car parks, places of interest

◆ Route-planning maps to get you close to your destination

◆ Postcodes on the maps and in the index

◆ Widely used by the emergency services, transport companies and local authorities

For national mapping, choose
Philip's Navigator Britain
the most detailed road atlas available of England, Wales and Scotland. Hailed by Auto Express as 'the ultimate road atlas', Navigator shows every road and lane in Britain.

Street atlases currently available

England
Bedfordshire and Luton
Berkshire
Birmingham and West Midlands
Bristol and Bath
Buckinghamshire and Milton Keynes
Cambridgeshire and Peterborough
Cheshire
Cornwall
Cumbria
Derbyshire
Devon
Dorset
County Durham and Teesside
Essex
North Essex
South Essex
Gloucestershire and Bristol
Hampshire
North Hampshire
South Hampshire
Herefordshire Monmouthshire
Hertfordshire
Isle of Wight
Kent
East Kent
West Kent
Lancashire
Leicestershire and Rutland
Lincolnshire
Liverpool and Merseyside
London
Greater Manchester
Norfolk
Northamptonshire
Northumberland
Nottinghamshire
Oxfordshire
Shropshire
Somerset
Staffordshire
Suffolk

Surrey
East Sussex
West Sussex
Tyne and Wear
Warwickshire and Coventry
Wiltshire and Swindon
Worcestershire
East Yorkshire
Northern Lincolnshire
North Yorkshire
South Yorkshire
West Yorkshire

Wales
Anglesey, Conwy and Gwynedd
Cardiff, Swansea and The Valleys
Carmarthenshire, Pembrokeshire and Swansea
Ceredigion and South Gwynedd
Denbighshire, Flintshire, Wrexham
Herefordshire Monmouthshire
Powys

Scotland
Aberdeenshire
Ayrshire
Dumfries and Galloway
Edinburgh and East Central Scotland
Fife and Tayside
Glasgow and West Central Scotland
Inverness and Moray
Lanarkshire
Scottish Borders

Northern Ireland
County Antrim and County Londonderry
County Armagh and County Down
Belfast
County Tyrone and County Fermanagh

Philip's maps and atlases are available from bookshops, motorway services and petrol static

For further details visit
www.philips-maps.co.uk